Lecture Notes in Computer Science

Commenced Publication in 1973
Founding and Former Series Editors:
Gerhard Goos, Juris Hartmanis, and Jan van Leeuwen

Editorial Board

David Hutchison
  Lancaster University, UK
Takeo Kanade
  Carnegie Mellon University, Pittsburgh, PA, USA
Josef Kittler
  University of Surrey, Guildford, UK
Jon M. Kleinberg
  Cornell University, Ithaca, NY, USA
Friedemann Mattern
  ETH Zurich, Switzerland
John C. Mitchell
  Stanford University, CA, USA
Moni Naor
  Weizmann Institute of Science, Rehovot, Israel
Oscar Nierstrasz
  University of Bern, Switzerland
C. Pandu Rangan
  Indian Institute of Technology, Madras, India
Bernhard Steffen
  University of Dortmund, Germany
Madhu Sudan
  Massachusetts Institute of Technology, MA, USA
Demetri Terzopoulos
  University of California, Los Angeles, CA, USA
Doug Tygar
  University of California, Berkeley, CA, USA
Moshe Y. Vardi
  Rice University, Houston, TX, USA
Gerhard Weikum
  Max-Planck Institute of Computer Science, Saarbruecken, Germany

Isabel Cruz   Stefan Decker
Dean Allemang   Chris Preist
Daniel Schwabe   Peter Mika
Mike Uschold   Lora Aroyo (Eds.)

The Semantic Web – ISWC 2006

5th International Semantic Web Conference, ISWC 2006
Athens, GA, USA, November 5-9, 2006
Proceedings

Volume Editors

Isabel Cruz
University of Illinois at Chicago, USA, E-mail: ifc@cs.uic.edu

Stefan Decker
DERI Galway, Ireland, E-mail: stefan.decker@deri.org

Dean Allemang
TopQuadrant, Inc., Alexandria, VA,USA, E-mail: dallemang@topquadrant.com

Chris Preist
HP Laboratories, Bristol, UK, E-mail: chris.preist@hp.com

Daniel Schwabe
Pontifical Catholic University, Rio de Janeiro, Brazil (PUC-Rio)
E-mail: dschwabe@inf.puc-rio.br

Peter Mika
Vrije Universiteit Amsterdam, The Netherlands, E-mail: pmika@cs.vu.nl

Mike Uschold
The Boeing Company, Seattle, WA, USA, E-mail: michael.f.uschold@boeing.com

Lora Aroyo
Eindhoven University of Technology, The Netherlands, E-mail: l.m.aroyo@tue.nl

Library of Congress Control Number: 2006935688

CR Subject Classification (1998): H.4, H.3, C.2, H.5, F.3, I.2, K.4

LNCS Sublibrary: SL 3 – Information Systems and Application, incl. Internet/Web and HCI

ISSN   0302-9743
ISBN-10   3-540-49029-9 Springer Berlin Heidelberg New York
ISBN-13   978-3-540-49029-6 Springer Berlin Heidelberg New York

This work is subject to copyright. All rights are reserved, whether the whole or part of the material is concerned, specifically the rights of translation, reprinting, re-use of illustrations, recitation, broadcasting, reproduction on microfilms or in any other way, and storage in data banks. Duplication of this publication or parts thereof is permitted only under the provisions of the German Copyright Law of September 9, 1965, in its current version, and permission for use must always be obtained from Springer. Violations are liable to prosecution under the German Copyright Law.

Springer is a part of Springer Science+Business Media

springer.com

© Springer-Verlag Berlin Heidelberg 2006
Printed in Germany

Typesetting: Camera-ready by author, data conversion by Scientific Publishing Services, Chennai, India
Printed on acid-free paper   SPIN: 11926078   06/3142   5 4 3 2 1 0

Preface

"Evolve or perish" – this is the motto for living systems. Judging by this saying, the Web is alive and well: new sites and business ideas are coming online almost daily and are able to attract millions of users often. The more recently coined term "Web 2.0" summarizes many of the new developments, capturing efforts making the Web more interactive (like Ajax), more collaborative (like Wikis), or more relationship oriented (like online social networks), aiming to partially fulfill the original promise of the Web.

These new Web developments offer an opportunity and challenge for the Semantic Web: what previously manifested itself mostly in "dry" specifications is now becoming the foundation for information exchange on the Web, creating a shared semantic information space. These and other challenges have been picked up by several hundred computer scientists, developers, vendors, government workers, venture capitalists, students, and users, gathered in Athens, Atlanta, USA, November 5–9, 2006, for the Fifth International Semantic Web Conference (ISWC 2006). Building on previous successful meetings in Sardinia, Sanibel Island, Hiroshima, and Galway, this sixth annual conference demonstrates new research results, technology, and applications that show current incarnations of the Semantic Web. Especially encouraging is the shift towards more applications—whereas the Research Track attracted roughly as many papers as in the previous year, the contributions submitted to the In-Use Track doubled.

This volume contains the main proceedings of ISWC 2006, which we are excited to offer to the growing community of researchers and practitioners of the Semantic Web. The tremendous response to our call for papers from a truly international community of researchers and practitioners from 33 countries, the careful nature of the review process, and the breadth and scope of the papers finally selected for inclusion in this volume all speak to the quality of the conference and to the contributions made by the papers in these proceedings. Through an unprecedented agreement with Springer, the papers in these proceedings will also be freely available online to all interested parties. In addition, several online applications will provide access to semantically annotated information about the papers and the conference itself.

The Research Track attracted 215 submissions, comparable to the number of papers submitted to ISWC 2005, which shows the robustness of the research base in this area. The review process included three distinct phases. First, all papers were evaluated by three members of the Research Track Program Committee. Then, each paper and associated reviews provided the basis for the meta-review phase, led by an experienced member of the Program Committee who had not participated in the first phase. This strategy produced a joint recommendation from reviewers and the meta-reviewer to the Research Track Program Co-chairs, who, in a final review phase, analyzed each recommendation in detail, in some cases commissioning additional reviews and initiating further discussions. The Program Chairs then made a definitive decision regarding each paper. Such a structured process, which required a great deal of effort from the members of the Program Committee, ensured a thorough review while attesting to the health of our community. In total, 52 papers were accepted, out of 215 submissions, a 24% acceptance rate.

The In-Use Track replaces the Industrial Track of former years. This change was prompted by the observation that many deployed applications of the Semantic Web come from diverse sectors including government, public health, and academia, in addition to industry. Since the goal of this track is to provide exposure to Semantic Web deployments, the ISWC 2006 Organizing Committee felt that a change of name was in order. The In-Use Track received 42 submissions. As part of the process in which each paper received three reviews from the In-Use Track Program Committee, three papers were determined to be more appropriate to the Research Track. Of the remaining papers, 14 were selected for acceptance, exactly one third of the submissions. Three themes dominated both the submissions and the accepted papers: Knowledge Management, Semantic Integration, and Semantic Search. The decision process was particularly difficult this year, as there were many fine papers. Consequently, the chairs had to make a number of difficult decisions for the final cut.

A unique aspect of the International Semantic Web Conferences is the Semantic Web Challenge. This is a competition in which participants from both academia and industry are encouraged to show how Semantic Web techniques can provide useful or interesting applications to end-users. In the four years since this competition was first organized, we have seen more than 30 integrated applications built around distributed data sources, which use some kind of semantic descriptions to handle the data. This year we had 18 submissions, double the number of the previous year, making the selection process harder. The topics range from multimedia retrieval to music recommendation, from emergency management to traditional Chinese medicine. Keeping with the broad international appeal, there were submissions from Europe US, China, Singapore, Japan and New Zealand, from both industry and academia. The winners of the challenge were announced at the ISWC Conference and received €1.000 travel support plus a €250 voucher to purchase books from Springer.

This was the second year offering a Doctoral Consortium, which also showed an increase in submissions, 23, of which 6 full presentations and 8 poster presentations were accepted. Each paper was reviewed by senior members of the ISWC community, providing detailed feedback on how to structure, justify and present their work. The topics of the submissions cover a broad range from ontology engineering, reasoning, security, trust, multi-agent systems, and bioinformatics to cultural heritage. Submissions came in from the US, Austria, China, UK, the Czech Republic, Brazil, Italy, Turkey, the Netherlands, Portugal, Germany and Switzerland. Hoppers@KWeb, which is part of the Knowledge Web Network of Excellence, provided grants to support participation of PhD students in this event.

Keynote Talks from prominent scientists further enriched IWSC 2006: Tom Gruber presented his vision of the Semantic Web as a substrate for collective intelligence, and in particular for the Social Web; Jane Fountain, discussed the mutual influences of the Semantic Web and Digital Government, and, more generally, between information technologies and society; finally, Rudi Studer examined the extent to which interdisciplinary work has played and can play a role in Semantic Web research.

A Panel provided the setting for discussions about the relationship between the Semantic Web and Web 2.0. In addition, the conference was enlivened by a large Poster and Demo Session, and a Tutorial Program. Another sign of vitality was the large number, 20, of high quality proposals to the Workshop Program, of which 13 were selected. Some workshops are almost as old as the conference itself, with topics ranging from Semantic Desktop, User Interaction, Trust and Policies to Geospatial Data and Uncertainty Reasoning. We are grateful to Mark Greaves (Web 2.0 Panel Moderator), Max Wilson, Daniel A. Smith, m.c. schraefel, and Libby Miller (Poster and Demo Co-chairs), Wolfgang Nejdl (Tutorial Chair), and Vipul Kashyap (Workshop Chair) for ensuring the success of these events.

We are indebted to Jen Golbeck, Proceedings Chair, who provided invaluable support in compiling both the printed proceedings and the CD-ROM with additional material. We also offer many thanks to Eric Miller, Meta Data Chair, for his expert coordination of the production of the semantic mark-up associated with each contribution to the conference.

The meeting would not have been possible without the tireless work of the Local Organizer Chair, Budak Arpinar. We thank him and his team for providing excellent local arrangements. We would also like to thank the generous contribution from our sponsors and the fine work of the Sponsorship Chairs, Amit Sheth and Steffen Staab. We are thankful to Manos Papagelis, for providing timely support for the Confious Conference Management System, which was used to manage the review process.

Finally, we would like to acknowledge the Semantic Web Science Association for providing the organizational oversight for ISWC 2006.

In conclusion, ISWC 2006 was an exciting event, reflecting the high level of energy, creativity, and productivity that permeates the Semantic Web community. This is a great time to be involved in all sorts of booming and stimulating activities associated with the Semantic Web.

November 2006

Isabel Cruz
Stefan Decker
Program Committee Co-chairs, Research/Academic Track
Dean Allemang
Chris Preist
Program Committee Co-chairs, Semantic Web In-Use Track
Peter Mika
Mike Uschold
Co-chairs, Semantic Web Challenge
Lora Aroyo
Chair, Doctoral Consortium
Daniel Schwabe
Conference Chair

Organizing Committee

General Chair	Daniel Schwabe (Catholic University of Rio de Janeiro, PUC-Rio, Brazil)
Research Track Co-chairs	Isabel Cruz (University of Illinois at Chicago, USA)
	Stefan Decker (DERI Galway, Ireland)
Semantic Web In-Use Track Co-chairs	Dean Allemang (TopQuadrant, USA)
	Chris Preist (HP Labs, UK)
Tutorials Chair	Wolfgang Nejdl (L3S and University of Hannover, Germany)
Workshops Chair	Vipul Kashyap (Partners HealthCare System, USA)
Meta-data Chair	Eric Miller (W3C, USA)
Sponsorship Chairs	Amit Sheth, for the Americas (University of Georgia and Semagix Inc., USA)
	Steffen Staab, for Europe (University of Koblenz, Germany)
Local Organization Chair	Budak Arpinar (University of Georgia, USA)
Proceedings Chair	Jennifer Golbeck (University of Maryland, College Park, USA)
Doctoral Symposium	Lora Aroyo (Eindhoven University of Technology, Netherlands)
Poster and Demo Chairs	Max Wilson (University of Southampton, UK)
	Daniel A. Smith (University of Southampton, UK)
	M.C. Schraefel (University of Southampton, UK)
	Libby Miller (Asemantics, UK)
Semantic Web Challenge Chairs	Peter Mika (Vrije Universiteit Amsterdam, Netherlands)
	Mike Uschold (Boeing Corporation, USA)

Local Organization Committee

Chair: I. Budak Arpinar (LSDIS Lab., Department of Computer Science, University of Georgia, USA)

Holly Blanchard (Georgia Center, University of Georgia, USA)

Boanerges Aleman-Meza (LSDIS Lab., Department of Computer Science, University of Georgia, USA)

William Weems (Franking College of Arts and Sciences, University of Georgia, USA)

Matt Perry (LSDIS Lab., Department of Computer Science, University of Georgia, USA)

Meenakshi Nagarajan (LSDIS Lab., Department of Computer Science, University of Georgia, USA)

Maciej Janik (LSDIS Lab., Department of Computer Science, University of Georgia, USA)
Samir Tartir (LSDIS Lab., Department of Computer Science, University of Georgia, USA)
Cartic Ramakrishnan (LSDIS Lab., Department of Computer Science, University of Georgia, USA)

Program Committee

José Luis Ambite (USC-ISI, USA)
Troels Andreasen (Roskilde University, Denmark)
Anupriya Ankolekar (University of Karlsruhe, Germany)
Wolf-Tilo Balke (University of Hannover, Germany)
Sean Bechhofer (University of Manchester, UK)
Zohra Bellahsène (Université Montpellier II, France)
Richard Benjamins (ISOCO S.A., Spain)
Abraham Bernstein (University of Zurich, Switzerland)
Walter Binder (EPFL, Switzerland)
Kalina Bontcheva (University of Sheffield, UK)
Paolo Bouquet (University of Trento, Italy)
François Bry (University of Munich, Germany)
Paul Buitelaar (DFKI, Germany)
Liliana Cabral (The Open University, UK)
Andrea Calì (Free University of Bolzano, Italy)
Diego Calvanese (Free University of Bolzano, Italy)
Mario Cannataro (University "Magna Græcia" of Catanzaro, Italy)
Silvana Castano (Università degli Studi di Milano, Italy)
Vinay Chaudhri (SRI International, USA)
Weiqin Chen (University of Bergen, Norway)
Philipp Cimiano (University of Karlsruhe, Germany)
Kendall Clark (Mindlab, University of Maryland, USA)
Nigel Collier (National Institute of Informatics, NII, Japan)
Ion Constantinescu (EPFL, Switzerland)
Óscar Corcho (University of Manchester, UK)
Philippe Cudré-Mauroux (EPFL, Switzerland)
Hamish Cunningham (University of Sheffield, UK)
Jos de Bruijn (University of Innsbruck, Austria)
David De Roure (University of Southampton, UK)
Olga De Troyer (Vrije Universiteit Brussel, Belgium)
Mike Dean (BBN Technologies, USA)
Keith Decker (University of Delaware)
Thierry Declerck (DFKI GmbH, Germany)
Grit Denker (SRI International, USA)
Ian Dickinson (Hewlett Packard, UK)
John Domingue (Knowledge Media Institute, The Open University, UK)
Jin Song Dong (National University of Singapore, Singapore)
Erik Duval (Katholieke Universiteit Leuven, Belgium)

Martin Dzbor (Knowledge Media Institute, Open University, UK)
Lim Ee-Peng (Nanyang Technical University, Singapore)
Max Egenhofer (University of Maine, USA)
Vadim Ermolayev (Zaporozhye National University, Ukraine)
Jérôme Euzenat (INRIA, France)
Boi Faltings (EPFL, Switzerland)
Dieter Fensel (University of Innsbruck, Austria)
Tim Finin (University of Maryland, Baltimore County, USA)
Fred Fonseca (Penn State, USA)
Gerhard Friedrich (University Klagenfurt, Austria)
Aldo Gangemi (CNR-ISTC, Italy)
Vladimir Geroimenko (University of Plymouth, UK)
Nick Gibbins (University of Southampton, UK)
Maria Gini (University of Minnesota, USA)
Fausto Giunchiglia (University of Trento, Italy)
Carole Goble (University of Manchester, UK)
Christine Golbreich (Université de Rennes 1, France)
Asunción Gómez-Pérez (UPM, Spain)
Marko Grobelnik (Jožef Stefan Institute, Slovenia)
William Grosky (University of Michigan-Dearborn, USA)
Volker Haarslev (Concordia University, Canada)
Mohand-Said Hacid (Université Lyon 1, France)
Sung-Kuk Han (Wonkwang University, Korea)
Siegfried Handschuh (National University of Ireland in Galway, Ireland)
Jeff Heflin (Lehigh University, USA)
Kaoru Hiramatsu (NTT CS Lab, Japan)
Masahiro Hori (Kansai University, Japan)
Ian Horrocks (University of Manchester, UK)
Jane Hunter (DSTC, Australia)
Nancy Ide (Vassar College, USA)
Toru Ishida (Kyoto University, Japan)
Anupam Joshi (University of Maryland, Baltimore County, USA)
Takahiro Kawamura (Toshiba Corporation, Japan)
Rich Keller (NASA Ames, USA)
Hong-Gee Kim (Seoul National University, Korea)
Roger King (University of Colorado, USA)
Yasuhiko Kitamura (Kwansei Gakuin University, Japan)
Michel Klein (Vrije Universiteit Amsterdam, Netherlands)
Matthias Klusch (DFKI, Germany)
Yiannis Kompatsiaris (ITI, Thessaloniki, Greece)
Manolis Koubarakis (National and Kapodistrian University of Athens, Greece)
Thibaud Latour (CRP Henri Tudor, Luxembourg)
Georg Lausen (Albert-Ludwigs Universität Freiburg, Germany)
David Leake (Indiana University, USA)
Domenico Lembo (Università di Roma "La Sapienza," Italy)
Maurizio Lenzerini (Università di Roma "La Sapienza," Italy)
Fernanda Lima (Universidade Católica de Brasília, Brazil)

Ling Liu (Georgia Tech, USA)
Joanne Luciano (Harvard Medical School, USA)
Bob MacGregor (Siderean Software, USA)
David Maluf (NASA Ames, USA)
David Martin (SRI, USA)
Mihhail Matskin (KTH, Sweden)
Diana Maynard (University of Sheffield, UK)
Brian McBride (Hewlett Packard, Bristol, UK)
Luke McDowell (United States Naval Academy, USA)
Deborah McGuinness (KSL, Stanford University, USA)
Simon Miles (University of Southampton, UK)
Prasenjit Mitra (Pennsylvania State University, USA)
Riichiro Mizoguchi (Osaka University, Japan)
Marina Mongiello (Politecnico di Bari, Italy)
Pavlos Moraitis (Ren Descartes University, France)
Boris Motik (University of Manchester, UK)
Enrico Motta (Knowledge Media Institute, Open University, UK)
John Mylopoulos (University of Toronto, Canada)
Natasha Noy (Stanford University, USA)
Tim Oates (University of Maryland Baltimore County, USA)
Sam Gyun Oh (SungKyunKwan University, Korea)
Jeff Pan (University of Aberdeen, UK)
Yue Pan (IBM China Research Laboratory, China)
Massimo Paolucci (DoCoMo Euro-labs, Germany)
Bijan Parsia (University of Manchester, UK)
Peter Patel-Schneider (Bell Labs, USA)
Terry Payne (University of Southampton, UK)
Paulo Pinheiro da Silva (The University of Texas at El Paso, USA)
Dimitris Plexousakis (FORTH, University of Crete, Greece)
Line Pouchard (Oak Ridge National Laboratory, USA)
Wolfgang Prinz (Fraunhofer Institute for Applied Information Technology FIT, Germany)
Yuzhong Qu (Southeast University, China)
Zbigniew Ras (University of North Carolina, USA)
Chantal Reynaud (Université Paris-Sud, Orsay - LRI, France)
Mark Roantree (Dublin City University, Ireland)
Andrea Rodríguez (Universidad de Concepción, Chile)
Alan Ruttenberg (Millennium Pharmaceuticals, USA)
Henryk Rybinski (Warsaw University of Technology, Poland)
Marta Sabou (The Open University, UK)
Norman Sadeh (CMU, USA)
Fereidoon Sadri (University of North Carolina, USA)
Ulrike Sattler (University of Manchester, UK)
Michel Scholl (CNAM, France)
mc schraefel (University of Southampton, UK)
Guus Schreiber (Vrije Universiteit Amsterdam, Netherlands)
Michael Schumacher (EPFL, Switzerland)

Amit Sheth (University of Georgia, USA)
Wolf Siberski (University of Hannover, Germany)
Carles Sierra (IIIA/CSIC, Spain)
Nuno Silva (ISEP, Portugal)
Munindar Singh (North Carolina State University, USA)
Michael Sintek (DFKI, Germany)
Andrzej Skowron (Institute of Mathematics, Warsaw University, Poland)
Derek Sleeman (University of Aberdeen, UK)
Steffen Staab (Univerity of Koblenz, Germany)
Giorgos Stamou (University of Athens, Greece)
Lynn Andrea Stein (Franklin W. Olin College of Engineering, USA)
Umberto Straccia (ISTI-NCR, Italy)
Heiner Stuckenschmidt (Universität Mannheim, Germany)
Rudi Studer (Institute AIFB, University of Karlsruhe, Germany)
Gerd Stumme (University of Kassel, Germany)
York Sure (University of Karlsruhe, Germany)
Katia Sycara (Carnegie Mellon University, USA)
Said Tabet (Inferware Corp., USA)
Hideaki Takeda (National Institute for Informatics, Japan)
Valentina Tamma (University of Liverpool, UK)
Val Tannen (University of Pennsylvania, USA)
Herman ter Horst (Philips Research, The Netherlands)
Sergio Tessaris (Free University of Bolzano, Italy)
Bhavani Thuraisingham (University of Texas at Dallas, USA)
Robert Tolksdorf (Freie Universität Berlin, Germany)
Raphal Troncy (CWI, The Netherlands)
Yannis Tzitzikas (University of Crete, Greece)
Andrzej Uszok (Institute for Human and Machine Cognition, USA)
Frank van Harmelen (Vrije Universiteit Amsterdam, Netherlands)
Ubbo Visser (University of Bremen, Germany)
Dan Vodislav (CNAM, France)
Christopher Welty (IBM T. J. Watson Research Center, USA)
Graham Wilcock (University of Helsinki, Finland)
Steve Willmott (Universitat Politècnica de Catalunya, Spain)
Michael Wooldridge (University of Liverpool, UK)
Takahira Yamaguchi (Keio University, Japan)
Guizhen Yang (SRI International, USA)
Yiyu Yao (University of Regina, Canada)
Yong Yu (Shanghai Jiao Tong University, China)
Hai Zhuge (Chinese Academy of Sciences, China)
Djamel A. Zighed (University of Lyon, France)

Program Committee - Semantic Web In-Use Track

Ama Akkiraju (IBM T. J. Watson Research Center, New York, USA)
Richard Benjamins (iSOCO, Spain)

Dan Brickley (W3C, UK)
David Karger (MIT, USA)
Steve Cayzer (HPLabs, UK)
Andy Crapo (GE, USA)
Mike Dean (BBN Technologies, USA)
Michael Denny (Consultant, USA)
John Domingue (Open University, UK)
Garry Edwards (ISX, USA)
Lars M. Garshol (Ontopia, Norway)
Ivan Herman (W3C, Netherlands)
Atanas Kiryakov (Ontotext, Bulgaria)
Ruediger Klein (DaimlerChrysler, Germany)
Joanne Luciano (Harvard Medical School, USA)
Libby Miller (Asemantics, UK)
Mark Musen (Stanford University, USA)
Andreas Presidis (Biovista, Greece)
Paul Shabajee (Bristol University, UK)
Christian de Sainte Marie (ILOG, France)
Susan Thomas (SAP, Germany)
Ralph Traphoener (Empolis, Germany)
Chris van Aart (Acklin, Netherlands)

Additional Reviewers

Ahmed Alasoud (Concordia University, Canada)
Padmapriya Ayyagari (Pennsylvania State University, USA)
Salima Benbernou (LIRIS, France)
Janez Brank (Jožef Stefan Institute, Slovenia)
John Breslin (DERI, NUI Galway, Ireland)
Christopher Brewster (University of Sheffield, UK)
Jean-Sébastien Brunner (Centre de Recherche Public Henri Tudor, Luxembourg)
Henrik Bulskov (Roskilde University, Denmark)
Kenta Cho (Toshiba Corporation, Japan)
Bernardo Cuenca Grau (University of Manchester, UK)
Alexandre Delteil (France Telecom R&D, France)
Xi Deng (Concordia University, Canada)
Marin Dimitrov (Sirma AI Ltd., Bulgaria)
Yannis Dimopoulos (University of Cyprus, Cyprus)
Nikhil Dinesh (University of Pennsylvania, USA)
Paolo Dongilli (Free University of Bozen-Bolzano, Italy)
Cedric du Mouza (LAMSADE, Université Paris-Dauphine, France)
Alistair Duke (British Telecom, UK)
Cristina Feier (DERI, University of Innsbruck, Austria)
Miriam Fernandez (Universidad Autónoma de Madrid, Spain)
Blaz Fortuna (Jožef Stefan Institute, Slovenia)
Enrico Franconi (Free University of Bozen-Bolzano, Italy)

Stefania Galizia (KMi, Open University, UK)
Daniel Giacomuzzi (University of Trento, Italy)
Antoon Goderis (University of Manchester, UK)
Rafael González-Cabero (Universidad Politécnica de Madrid, Spain)
Gunnar Grimnes (DFKI, Germany)
Tudor Groza (DERI, NUI Galway, Ireland)
Christian Halaschek-Wiener (University of Maryland, USA)
Sung-Kook Han (Won Kwang University, Korea)
Siegfried Handschuh (DERI, NUI Galway, Ireland)
Andreas Harth (DERI, NUI Galway, Ireland)
Masumi Inaba (University of Utsunomiya, Japan)
Anuj R. Jaiswal (Pennsylvania State University, USA)
Zoi Kaoudi (National and Kapodistrian University of Athens, Greece)
Grigoris Karvounarakis (University of Pennsylvania, USA)
Esther Kaufmann (University of Zurich, Switzerland)
Peihong Ke (University of Manchester, UK)
Malte Kiesel (DFKI, Germany)
Joey Lam (University of Aberdeen, UK)
Yang Liu (National University of Singapore, Singapore)
Yaoyong Li (University of Sheffield, UK)
Davide Martinenghi (Free University of Bozen-Bolzano, Italy)
Iris Miliaraki (University of Athens, Greece)
Yumiko Mizoguchi (Toshiba Corporation, Japan)
Shinichi Nagano (Toshiba Corporation, Japan)
Barry Norton (KMi, Open University, UK)
Guillermo Nudelman Hess (Universidade Federal do Rio Grande do Sul, Brazil)
Hsueh-Ieng Pai (Concordia University, Canada)
Adrián Perreau de Pinninck (IIIA-CSIC, Spain)
Axel Polleres (Universidad Rey Juan Carlos, Spain)
Josep M. Pujol (Universitat Politècnica de Catalunya, Spain)
Jinghai Rao (Carnegie Mellon University, USA)
Marco Ruzzi (Università di Roma "La Sapienza," Italy)
Jordi Sabater-Mir (IIIA-CSIC, Spain)
Leonardo Salayandia (University of Texas at El Paso, USA)
Arash Shaban-Nejad (Concordia University, Canada)
Heiko Stoermer (University of Trento, Italy)
Giorgos Stoilos (National and Technical University of Athens, Greece)
Edward Thomas (University of Aberdeen, UK)
Farouk Toumani (LIMOS, France)
Goce Trajcevski (Northwestern University, USA)
Ludger van Elst (DFKI, Germany)
Thomas Vestskov Terney (Roskilde University, Denmark)
Max Wilson (University of Southampton, UK)
Chris Wroe (British Telecom, UK)
Yeliz Yesilada (University of Manchester, UK)
Qiankun Zhao (Pennsylvania State University, USA)
Ziming Zhuang (Pennsylvania State University, USA)

Sponsors

Gold Sponsors
DIP- Data, Information, and Process Integration with Semantic Web Services
SUPER - Semantics Utilised for Process Management within and between Enterprises
Ontotext
Vulcan

Silver Sponsors
Aduna
Elsevier
Microsoft Live Labs
NeOn
Nepomuk
Nokia
Journal of Web Semantics
Ontoprise
SEKT (Semantically-Enabled Knowledge Technologies)
TopQuadrant

Table of Contents

1 Research Track

Ranking Ontologies with AKTiveRank 1
   Harith Alani, Christopher Brewster, Nigel Shadbolt

Three Semantics for Distributed Systems and Their Relations
with Alignment Composition 16
   Antoine Zimmermann, Jérôme Euzenat

Semantics and Complexity of SPARQL 30
   Jorge A. Pérez, Marcelo Arenas, Claudio Gutierrez

Ontology-Driven Automatic Entity Disambiguation in Unstructured
Text 44
   Joseph Hassell, Boanerges Aleman-Meza, I. Budak Arpinar

Augmenting Navigation for Collaborative Tagging with Emergent
Semantics 58
   Melanie Aurnhammer, Peter Hanappe, Luc Steels

On the Semantics of Linking and Importing in Modular Ontologies 72
   Jie Bao, Doina Caragea, Vasant G. Honavar

RS2D: Fast Adaptive Search for Semantic Web Services in Unstructured
P2P Networks 87
   Ulrich Basters, Matthias Klusch

SADIe: Semantic Annotation for Accessibility 101
   Sean Bechhofer, Simon Harper, Darren Lunn

Automatic Annotation of Web Services Based on Workflow Definitions... 116
   *Khalid Belhajjame, Suzanne M. Embury, Norman W. Paton,
   Robert Stevens, Carole A. Goble*

A Constraint-Based Approach to Horizontal Web Service Composition ... 130
   Ahlem Hassine Ben, Shigeo Matsubara, Toru Ishida

GINO - A Guided Input Natural Language Ontology Editor 144
   Abraham Bernstein, Esther Kaufmann

Fresnel: A Browser-Independent Presentation Vocabulary for RDF 158
   Emmanuel Pietriga, Christian Bizer, David Karger, Ryan Lee

A Software Engineering Approach to Design and Development
of Semantic Web Service Applications 172
  Marco Brambilla, Irene Celino, Stefano Ceri, Dario Cerizza,
  Emanuele Della Valle, Federico Michele Facca

A Model Driven Approach for Building OWL DL and OWL Full
Ontologies 187
  Saartje Brockmans, Robert M. Colomb, Peter Haase,
  Elisa F. Kendall, Evan K. Wallace, Chris Welty, Guo Tong Xie

IRS-III: A Broker for Semantic Web Services Based Applications 201
  Liliana Cabral, John Domingue, Stefania Galizia, Alessio Gugliotta,
  Vlad Tanasescu, Carlos Pedrinaci, Barry Norton

Provenance Explorer – Customized Provenance Views Using Semantic
Inferencing 215
  Kwok Cheung, Jane Hunter

On How to Perform a Gold Standard Based Evaluation of Ontology
Learning 228
  Klaas Dellschaft, Steffen Staab

Characterizing the Semantic Web on the Web 242
  Li Ding, Tim Finin

MultiCrawler: A Pipelined Architecture for Crawling and Indexing
Semantic Web Data 258
  Andreas Harth, Jürgen Umbrich, Stefan Decker

/facet: A Browser for Heterogeneous Semantic Web Repositories 272
  Michiel Hildebrand, Jacco van Ossenbruggen, Lynda Hardman

Using Ontologies for Extracting Product Features from Web Pages 286
  Wolfgang Holzinger, Bernhard Krüpl, Marcus Herzog

Block Matching for Ontologies 300
  Wei Hu, Yuzhong Qu

A Relaxed Approach to RDF Querying 314
  Carlos A. Hurtado, Alexandra Poulovassilis, Peter T. Wood

Mining Information for Instance Unification 329
  Niraj Aswani, Bontcheva Kalina, Hamish Cunningham

The Summary Abox: Cutting Ontologies Down to Size 343
  Achille Fokoue, Aaron Kershenbaum, Li Ma, Edith Schonberg,
  Kavitha Srinivas

Semantic Metadata Generation for Large Scientific Workflows 357
  Jihie Kim, Yolanda Gil, Varun Ratnakar

Reaching Agreement over Ontology Alignments 371
  Loredana Laera, Valentina Tamma, Jérôme Euzenat,
  Trevor Bench-Capon, Terry Payne

A Formal Model for Semantic Web Service Composition 385
  Freddy Lécué, Alain Léger

Evaluating Conjunctive Triple Pattern Queries over Large Structured
Overlay Networks 399
  Erietta Liarou, Stratos Idreos, Manolis Koubarakis

PowerMap: Mapping the Real Semantic Web on the Fly 414
  Vanessa Lopez, Marta Sabou, Enrico Motta

Ontology-Driven Information Extraction with OntoSyphon 428
  Luke K. McDowell, Michael Cafarella

Ontology Query Answering on Databases 445
  Jing Mei, Li Ma, Yue Pan

Formal Model for Ontology Mapping Creation 459
  Adrian Mocan, Emilia Cimpian, Mick Kerrigan

A Semantic Context-Aware Access Control Framework for Secure
Collaborations in Pervasive Computing Environments 473
  Alessandra Toninelli, Rebecca Montanari, Lalana Kagal, Ora Lassila

Extracting Relations in Social Networks from the Web Using
Similarity Between Collective Contexts 487
  Junichiro Mori, Takumi Tsujishita, Yutaka Matsuo, Mitsuru Ishizuka

Can OWL and Logic Programming Live Together Happily
Ever After? 501
  Boris Motik, Ian Horrocks, Riccardo Rosati, Ulrike Sattler

Innovation Detection Based on User-Interest Ontology
of Blog Community 515
  Makoto Nakatsuji, Yu Miyoshi, Yoshihiro Otsuka

Modeling Social Attitudes on the Web 529
  Matthias Nickles

A Framework for Ontology Evolution in Collaborative Environments 544
  Natalya F. Noy, Abhita Chugh, William Liu, Mark A. Musen

Extending Faceted Navigation for RDF Data 559
  Eyal Oren, Renaud Delbru, Stefan Decker

Reducing the Inferred Type Statements with Individual Grouping
Constructs 573
  Övünç Öztürk, Tuğba Özacar, Murat Osman Ünalır

A Framework for Schema-Driven Relationship Discovery from
Unstructured Text 583
  Cartic Ramakrishnan, Krys J. Kochut, Amit P. Sheth

Web Service Composition Via Generic Procedures and Customizing
User Preferences 597
  Shirin Sohrabi, Nataliya Prokoshyna, Sheila A. McIlraith

Querying the Semantic Web with Preferences 612
  Wolf Siberski, Jeff Z. Pan, Uwe Thaden

ONTOCOM: A Cost Estimation Model for Ontology Engineering 625
  Elena Paslaru Bontas Simperl, Christoph Tempich, York Sure

Tree-Structured Conditional Random Fields for Semantic Annotation.... 640
  Jie Tang, Mingcai Hong, Juanzi Li, Bangyong Liang

Framework for an Automated Comparison of Description Logic
Reasoners 654
  Tom Gardiner, Dmitry Tsarkov, Ian Horrocks

Integrating and Querying Parallel Leaf Shape Descriptions 668
  Shenghui Wang, Jeff Z. Pan

A Survey of the Web Ontology Landscape 682
  Taowei David Wang, Bijan Parsia, James Hendler

CropCircles: Topology Sensitive Visualization of OWL
Class Hierarchies 695
  Taowei David Wang, Bijan Parsia

Towards Knowledge Acquisition from Information Extraction 709
  Chris Welty, J. William Murdock

A Method for Learning Part-Whole Relations 723
    Willem Robert van Hage, Hap Kolb, Guus Schreiber

2 Semantic Web in Use

OntoWiki – A Tool for Social, Semantic Collaboration 736
    Sören Auer, Sebastian Dietzold, Thomas Riechert

Towards a Semantic Web of Relational Databases: A Practical
Semantic Toolkit and an In-Use Case from Traditional Chinese
Medicine.. 750
    Huajun Chen, Yimin Wang, Heng Wang, Yuxin Mao,
    Jinmin Tang, Cunyin Zhou, Ainin Yin, Zhaohui Wu

Information Integration Via an End-to-End Distributed Semantic
Web System.. 764
    Dimitre A. Dimitrov, Jeff Heflin, Abir Qasem, Nanbor Wang

NEWS: Bringing Semantic Web Technologies into News Agencies 778
    Norberto Fernández, José M. Blázquez, Jesús A. Fisteus,
    Luis Sánchez, Michael Sintek, Ansgar Bernardi, Manuel Fuentes,
    Angelo Marrara, Zohar Ben-Asher

Semantically-Enabled Large-Scale Science Data Repositories............ 792
    Peter Fox, Deborah McGuinness, Don Middleton, Luca Cinquini,
    J. Anthony Darnell, Jose Garcia, Patrick West, James Benedict,
    Stan Solomon

Construction and Use of Role-Ontology for Task-Based Service
Navigation System 806
    Yusuke Fukazawa, Takefumi Naganuma, Kunihiro Fujii,
    Shoji Kurakake

Enabling an Online Community for Sharing Oral Medicine Cases
Using Semantic Web Technologies................................ 820
    Marie Gustafsson, Göran Falkman, Fredrik Lindahl,
    Olof Torgersson

EKOSS: A Knowledge-User Centered Approach to Knowledge
Sharing, Discovery, and Integration on the Semantic Web 833
    Steven Kraines, Weisen Guo, Brian Kemper, Yutaka Nakamura

Ontogator — A Semantic View-Based Search Engine Service
for Web Applications 847
    Eetu Mäkelä, Eero Hyvönen, Samppa Saarela

Explaining Conclusions from Diverse Knowledge Sources 861
  J. William Murdock, Deborah L. McGuinness,
  Paulo Pinheiro da Silva, Chris Welty, David Ferrucci

A Mixed Initiative Semantic Web Framework for Process Composition ... 873
  Jinghai Rao, Dimitar Dimitrov, Paul Hofmann, Norman Sadeh

Semantic Desktop 2.0: The Gnowsis Experience 887
  Leo Sauermann, Gunnar Aastrand Grimnes, Malte Kiesel,
  Christiaan Fluit, Heiko Maus, Dominik Heim, Danish Nadeem,
  Benjamin Horak, Andreas Dengel

Towards Semantic Interoperability in a Clinical Trials Management
System 901
  Ravi D. Shankar, Susana B. Martins, Martin J. O'Connor,
  David B. Parrish, Amar K. Das

Active Semantic Electronic Medical Record 913
  A. Sheth, S. Agrawal, J. Lathem, N. Oldham, H. Wingate,
  P. Yadav, K. Gallagher

3 Semantic Web Challenge

Foafing the Music: Bridging the Semantic Gap in Music
Recommendation 927
  Òscar Celma

Semantic MediaWiki 935
  Markus Krötzsch, Denny Vrandečić, Max Völkel

Enabling Semantic Web Communities with DBin: An Overview 943
  Giovanni Tummarello, Christian Morbidoni, Michele Nucci

MultimediaN E-Culture Demonstrator 951
  Guus Schreiber, Alia Amin, Mark van Assem, Victor de Boer,
  Lynda Hardman, Michiel Hildebrand, Laura Hollink,
  Zhisheng Huang, Janneke van Kersen, Marco de Niet,
  Borys Omelayenko, Jacco van Ossenbruggen, Ronny Siebes,
  Jos Taekema, Jan Wielemaker, Bob Wielinga

A Semantic Web Services GIS Based Emergency Management
Application 959
  Vlad Tanasescu, Alessio Gugliotta, John Domingue, Rob Davies,
  Leticia Gutiérrez-Villarías, Mary Rowlatt, Marc Richardson,
  Sandra Stinčić

4 Doctoral Consortium

Package-Based Description Logics - Preliminary Results 967
   Jie Bao, Doina Caragea, Vasant G. Honavar

Distributed Policy Management in Semantic Web 970
   Özgü Can, Murat Osman Ünalır

Evaluation of SPARQL Queries Using Relational Databases 972
   Jiří Dokulil

Dynamic Contextual Regulations in Open Multi-agent Systems 974
   Carolina Howard Felicíssimo

From Typed-Functional Semantic Web Services to Proofs 976
   Harry Halpin

Towards a Usable Group Editor for Ontologies........................ 978
   Jan Henke

Talking to the Semantic Web - Query Interfaces to Ontologies
for the Casual User 980
   Esther Kaufmann

Changing Ontology Breaks Queries................................... 982
   Yaozhong Liang, Harith Alani, Nigel Shadbolt

Towards a Global Scale Semantic Web 986
   Zhengxiang Pan

Schema Mappings for the Web...................................... 988
   François Scharffe

Triple Space Computing for Semantic Web Services – A PhD
Roadmap 989
   M. Omair Shafiq

Toward Making Online Biological Data Machine Understandable 992
   Cui Tao

5 Keynote Abstracts

Where the Social Web Meets the Semantic Web 994
   Tom Gruber

The Semantic Web: Suppliers and Customers 995
  Rudi Studer

The Semantic Web and Networked Governance: Promise
and Challenges 997
  Jane E. Fountain

Author Index 999

Ranking Ontologies with AKTiveRank

Harith Alani[1], Christopher Brewster[2], and Nigel Shadbolt[1]

[1] Intelligence, Agents, Multimedia
School of Electronics and Computer Science
University of Southampton, Southampton, UK
{h.alani, nrs}@ecs.soton.ac.uk
[2] Dept. of Computer Science
University of Sheffield, Sheffield, UK
C.Brewster@dcs.shef.ac.uk

Abstract. Ontology search and reuse is becoming increasingly important as the quest for methods to reduce the cost of constructing such knowledge structures continues. A number of ontology libraries and search engines are coming to existence to facilitate locating and retrieving potentially relevant ontologies. The number of ontologies available for reuse is steadily growing, and so is the need for methods to evaluate and rank existing ontologies in terms of their relevance to the needs of the knowledge engineer. This paper presents AKTiveRank, a prototype system for ranking ontologies based on a number of structural metrics.

1 Introduction

Knowledge representation in the Semantic Web will be largely based on ontologies. However, ontology construction remains challenging, mainly due to the skill, time, effort, and domain specific knowledge required. In order to minimise this, one of the major advantages claimed of ontologies is the potential of "reuse". Publicly available ontologies are to be reused, modified, extended, and pruned as required, thereby avoiding the huge effort of starting from scratch [1].

Search engines to help finding relevant ontologies have started to appear in recent years. Swoogle[1] [5] is currently dominating this area of development, indexing an increasing number of ontologies covering a wide range of domains.

As the number of ontologies that such search engines can find increases, so will the need increase for a proper ranking method to order the returned lists of ontologies in terms of their relevancy to the query. This could save a lot of time and effort by reducing the need to examine in detail each and every ontology returned to find out how well it suits the needs of the agent or knowledge engineer.

Evaluating and ranking ontologies can be based on many different criteria [8]. This paper presents AKTiveRank, a prototype of an ontology ranking system which applies a number of analytic methods to rate each ontology based on an estimation of how well it represents the given search terms. AKTiveRank could be integrated with other, different, ranking systems to include additional ranking criteria, such as user ratings or content coverage.

---
[1] http://swoogle.umbc.edu/

Related work concerning ontology evaluation and ranking is reviewed in the following section. A full description of the architecture and ranking method is given in section 3. An experiment is detailed in section 4 and evaluated in section 5. Future work and Conclusions are discussed in the final sections of the paper.

2 Ontology Evaluation and Ranking

Lack of automatic, well grounded, methodologies to evaluate ontologies may seriously hinder their adoption by the industry and the wider web community [8]. Ontologies may be assessed from different angles, such as how the ontologies have been rated and reviewed by users (e.g. [21]), how well they meet the requirements of certain evaluation tests (e.g. [10]) or general ontological properties (e.g. [13]).

Gangemi and colleagues [8] define three main types of evaluation; functional, usability-based, and structural evaluation. Functional evaluation focuses on measuring how well an ontology is serving its purpose (e.g. [3]). Usability evaluations is concerned with metadata and annotations (e.g. [9]). Structural evaluation focuses on the structural properties of the ontology as a graph (e.g. [2]).

Other criteria for evaluating an ontology can be based on its content coverage. Jones and Alani are experimenting with ranking ontologies based on a tf/idf comparison of each potentially relevant ontology with an automatically gathered corpus that describes the domain of interest [11].

Some ontology search engines adopted a PageRank-like method to rank ontologies by analysing links and referrals between the ontologies in the hope of identifying the most popular ones (e.g. Swoogle [5,6] and OntoKhoj [16]). However, this method of ranking will not work for a large number of existing ontologies because of their poor connectivity and lack of referrals from other ontologies [5]. Such 'self contained' or 'isolated' ontologies would certainly receive poor PageRank results, thus highlighting the need for additional ranking methods. Furthermore, the *popularity* of an ontology could be a good overall assessment of the ontology, but it does not necessarily correlate with 'good' or appropriate representations of specific pieces of knowledge (e.g. certain classes) [2].

Based on the various evaluation and ranking methods mentioned above, it is clear that there is a need to assess all important features of an ontology. This can provide a multi-dimensional ranking approach that users can control as required.

AKTiveRank is an experimental system for ranking ontologies based on a number of measures that assess the ontology in terms of how well it represents the concepts of interest. Users are assumed to be using an ontology search engine (e.g. Swoogle) to do the search. The query submitted to the search engine is used by AKTiveRank to identify the concepts that match the user's request. The ranking measures applied by AKTiveRank will be based on the representation of those concepts and their neighbourhoods.

This paper experiments with a modified set of ranking measures to those we previously used and described in [2]. The measures and an experiment are presented in the following sections.

3 AKTiveRank

Figure 1 shows the current architecture of AKTiveRank. The main component (number 2 in the figure) is a Java Servlet that receives an HTTP query from a user or an agent (no. 1). The query contains the terms to search for. Currently it is only possible to search for concepts. In other words, search terms will only be matched with ontology classes, and not with properties or comments. This is simply to focus AKTiveRank on assessing the representation of the concepts of interest to the user.

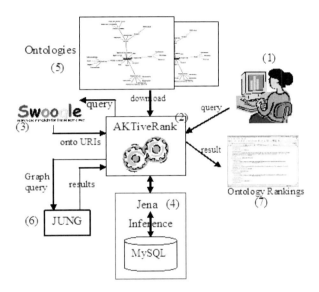

Fig. 1. AKTiveRank Architecture

When a search query is received, AKTiveRank forwards the query to Swoogle (no. 3) and retrieves the returned ontology URIs. Even though AKTiveRank currently relies on Swoogle to get the list of potentially relevant ontologies to be ranked, it is in no way restricted to it. Other sources and methods for searching for ontologies can also be used to feed AKTiveRank with lists of ontologies.

Once a list of ontology candidates is gathered, AKTiveRank starts to check whether those ontologies are already stored in a Jena MySQL database back-end (no. 4), and if not, downloads them from the web (no. 5) and add them to the database. The Jena API is used here to read the ontologies and handle the database storage.

Existing RDF query languages are not well suited for graph queries. To this end, the current version of AKTiveRank is connected to a purpose-built JUNG servlet (no. 6), which receives an ontology URI and sends back results of JUNG queries in RDF. JUNG (Java Universal Network/Graph framework) is a software library for analysing and visualising network graphs.

AKTiveRank then analyses each of the ontology candidates to determine which is most relevant to the given search terms. This analysis will produce a ranking of the retrieved ontologies, and the results are returned to the user as an OWL file containing the ontology URIs and their total ranks.

3.1 The Ranking Measures

AKTiveRank applies four measures to evaluate different representational aspects of the ontology and calculate its ranking. Each ontology is examined separately. Once those measures are all calculated for an ontology, the resulting values will be merged to produce the total rank for the ontology.

The measures used in AKTiveRank are experimental and subject to change. In a previous version of AKTiveRank which was reported in [2], one of the measures applied was the Centrality Measure (CEM). That measure aimed to assess how representative a class is of an ontology based on the observation that the closer a class is to the middle level of the hierarchy, the more likely it is that the representation of the class is well detailed [19]. However, in some experiments we found a few ontologies that placed our concept of interest near the top of the hierarchy. Those few ontologies were entirely focused around the concept we were searching for. This meant that even though such ontologies can be highly relevant to our search, they scored very low in CEM. Furthermore, we also found that CEM values corresponded in most cases to the values of the Density measure, and rendered CEM somewhat redundant.

The new implementation of AKTiveRank also introduces a new measure; the Betweenness measure, and extends the Class Match measure as described in the following sections. An example on calculating the values for an ontology will be given for each of the four measures currently used by AKTiveRank.

Class Match Measure. The Class Match Measure (CMM) is meant to evaluate the coverage of an ontology for the given search terms. Similar metrics have been used in the past as part of measures to estimate similarity of software descriptions [20].

AKTiveRank looks for classes in each ontology that have labels matching a search term either exactly (class label "identical to" search term) or partially (class label "contains" the search term). An ontology that covers all search terms will obviously score higher than others, and exact matches are regarded as better than partial matches. For example if searching for "Student" and "University", then an ontology with two classes labelled exactly as the search terms will score higher in this measure than another ontology which contains partially matching classes, e.g. "UniversityBuilding" and "PhD-Student" (see example below).

This measure has been extended from its previous version used in [2] by allowing it to take into account the total number of partially matching classes. In other words, if we are interested in the concept "student", then the CMM value for this ontology will be higher the more classes it has with the given word appearing in their labels or URIs. In another study we found that taking partial matches into account can sometimes be problematic and may reduce the search quality [11] (e.g. "gene" and "generator"). Therefore, the use of partially matching class labels has been limited to CMM only for the time being. Only if an exact match is unavailable that a partial match is considered in the other three measures.

Definition 1. *Let C[o] be a set of classes in ontology o, and T is the set of search terms.*

$$E(o,T) = \sum_{c \in C[o]} \sum_{t \in T} I(c,t) \qquad (1)$$

$$I(c,t) = \begin{cases} 1 & : \; if \; label(c) = t \\ 0 & : \; if \; label(c) \neq t \end{cases} \qquad (2)$$

$$P(o,T) = \sum_{c \in C[o]} \sum_{t \in T} J(c,t) \qquad (3)$$

$$J(c,t) = \begin{cases} 1 & : \; if \; label(c) \; contains \; t \\ 0 & : \; if \; label(c) \; not \; contain \; t \end{cases} \qquad (4)$$

where $E(o,T)$ and $P(o,T)$ are the number of classes of ontology o that have labels that match any of the search terms t exactly or partially, respectively.

$$CMM(o,\tau) = \alpha E(o,T) + \beta P(o,T) \qquad (5)$$

where $CMM(o,\tau)$ is the Class Match Measure for ontology o with respect to search terms τ. α and β are the exact matching and partial matching weight factors respectively. Exact matching is favoured over partial matching if $\alpha > \beta$. In the experiments described in this paper, $\alpha = 0.6$ & $\beta = 0.4$, thus putting more emphasis on exact matching.

Example: When searching the ontology o (aktive-portal-ontology-latest.owl[2]) for class labels that equals, or contains, the terms "student" or "university", the following classes can be found: *Student, PhD-Student, University, Distance-teaching-university* and *University-faculty*. So the results is two classes with identical labels to our search terms, and three classes with labels containing the search terms. CMM can therefore be calculated as follows:

$cmm(student) = 1 * 0.6 + 1 * 0.4 = 1$
$cmm(university) = 1 * 0.6 + 2 * 0.4 = 1.4$
$CMM(o, \{student, university\}) = 1 + 1.4 = 2.4$

Density Measure. When searching for a specific concept, one would expect to find a certain degree of detail in the representation of the knowledge concerning that concept (i.e. a rich conceptual neighbourhood). This may include how well the concept is further specified (the number of subclasses), the number of properties associated with that concept, number of siblings, etc. All this is taken into account in the Density Measure (DEM). DEM is intended to approximate the representational-density or information-content of classes and consequently the level of knowledge detail.

Density calculations are currently limited to the numbers of *direct* relations, subclasses, superclasses, and siblings. We dropped the number of instances from this measure as this might skew the results unfairly towards populated ontologies which may not necessarily reflect the quality of the schema itself.

---
[2] http://www.mindswap.org/2004/SSSW04/aktive-portal-ontology-latest.owl

Definition 2. Let $S = \{S_1, S_2, S_3, S_4\} = \{subclasses[c], superclasses[c], relations[c], siblings[c]\}$

$$dem(c) = \sum_{i=1}^{4} w_i |S_i| \qquad (6)$$

$$DEM(o) = \frac{1}{n} \sum_{i=1}^{n} dem(c) \qquad (7)$$

where $dem(c)$ is the Density Measure for class c. w_i is a weight factor set to a default value of 1, and $n = E(o,T) + P(o,T)$ which is the number of matched classes in ontology o.

Example: The neighbourhoods of the classes *Student* and *University* in the ontology ita.owl[3] are shown in figure 2. When using the weights 1, 0.25, 0.5 and 0.5, for subclasses, superclasses, relationships and siblings respectively, we get the following:

$dem(student) = 1 * 2 + 0.25 * 1 + 0.5 * 0 + 0.5 * 1 = 2.75$
$dem(university) = 1 * 0 + 0.25 * 1 + 0.5 * 0 + 0.5 * 5 = 2.75$
$DEM(ita.owl) = \frac{2.75 + 2.75}{2} = 2.75$

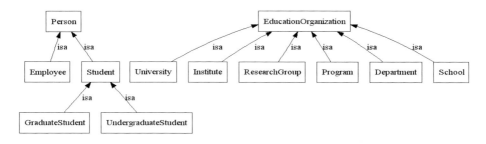

Fig. 2. Neighbourhood of *Student* and *University* in ita.owl ontology

Semantic Similarity Measure. Similarity measures have often been frequently explored in information retrieval systems to provide better ranking for query results (e.g. [4,17]). Ontologies can be viewed as semantic graphs of concepts and relations, and hence similarity measures can be applied to explore these conceptual graphs. Resnik applied a similarity measure to WordNet to resolve ambiguities [18]. The measure he used is based on the comparison of shared features, which was first proposed in [22]. Another common-feature based similarity is the shortest-path measure, introduced by Rada [17]. He argues that the more relationships objects have in common, the closer they will be in an ontology. Variations of these techniques have been used to measure similarity between whole ontology structures [14,23].

The Semantic Similarity Measure (SSM) calculates how close are the concepts of interest laid out in the ontology structure. If the concepts are positioned relatively far from each others, then it becomes unlikely for those concepts to be represented in a

---
[3] http://www.mondeca.com/owl/moses/ita.owl

compact manner, rendering their extraction and reuse more difficult. Further studies are required to find whether or not this assumption is dependent on certain ontological properties, such as size or level of detail.

The SSM formula used here is based on the simple shortest path measure defined in [17]. SSM is measured from the minimum number of links that connects a pair of concepts. These links can be isA relationships or other object properties.

Definition 3. *Let $c_i, c_j \in \{classes[o]\}$, and $c_i \overset{p}{\leadsto} c_j$ is a path $p \in P$ of paths between classes c_i and c_j*

$$ssm(c_i, c_j) = \begin{cases} \frac{1}{length(min_{p \in P}\{c_i \overset{p}{\leadsto} c_j\})} & : \quad if\ i \neq j \\ 1 & : \quad if\ i = j \end{cases} \quad (8)$$

$$SSM(o) = \frac{1}{k} \sum_{i=1}^{n-1} \sum_{j=i+1}^{n} ssm(c_i, c_j) \quad (9)$$

where n is the number of matched classes, and k = $\sum_{k=1}^{n-1} k$. Note that even though $ssm(c_i, c_i) = 1$, the system never actually needs to compare a class with itself.

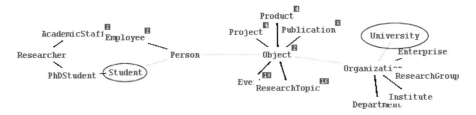

Fig. 3. Shortest path between *Student* and *University* in ka.owl ontology

Example: Figure 3 shows the shortest path between the classes *Student* and *University* in the ka.owl[4] ontology. Applying SSM to these two classes will produce:

$ssm(student, university) = \frac{1}{4}$
$SSM(ka.owl) = \frac{1}{1} ssm(student, university) = 0.25$

Betweenness Measure. One of the algorithms that JUNG provides is Betweenness [7]. This algorithm calculates the number of shortest paths that pass through each node in the graph. Nodes that occur on many shortest paths between other nodes have higher betweenness value than others. The assumption for using this measure in AKTiveRank is that if a class has a high betweenness value in an ontology then this class is *graphically central* to that ontology.

The BEtweenness Measure (BEM) calculates the betweenness value of each queried concept in the given ontologies. The ontologies where those classes are more central will receive a higher BEM value.

Definition 4. *Let $c_i, c_j \in \{classes[o]\}$, c_i and c_j are any two classes in ontology o, $C[o]$ is the set of class in ontology o, $bem(c)$ is the BEtweenness Measure for class c.*

---
[4] http://protege.stanford.edu/plugins/owl/owl-library/ka.owl

$$bem(c) = \sum_{c_i \neq c_j \neq c \in C[o]} \frac{\sigma_{c_i c_j}(c)}{\sigma_{c_i c_j}} \qquad (10)$$

where $\sigma_{c_i c_j}$ is the shortest path from c_i to c_j, and $\sigma_{c_i c_j}(c)$ is the number of shortest paths from c_i to c_j that passes through c.

$$BEM(o) = \frac{1}{n} \sum_{k=1}^{n} bem(c_k) \qquad (11)$$

where n is the number of matched classes in ontology o, and BEM(o) is the average Betweenness value for ontology o.

Example: When BEM is applied to the classes *Student* and *University* of the univ.owl[5] ontology, the class *Student* received a value of 0.00468, while *University* got a 0 betweenness value (using the Betweenness Centrality measure of Jung). This means that the former class is more central in the ontology graph than the later class. Final BEM value can then be calculated as follows:

$BEM(univ.owl) = \frac{1}{2}(0.00468 + 0.0) = 0.00234$.

3.2 Total AKTiveRank Score

The total score of an ontology can be calculated once the four measures are applied to all the ontologies that the search engine returned. Total score is calculated by aggregating all the measures' values, taking into account the *weight* of each measure, which can be used to determine the relative importance of each measure for ranking.

The first rank will be given to the ontology with the highest overall score, the second rank to the second highest score, and so on.

Definition 5. Let $M = \{M[1], .., M[i], M[4]\} = \{CMM, DEM, SSM, BEM\}$, w_i is a weight factor, and O is the set of ontologies to rank.

$$Score(o \in O) = \sum_{i=1}^{4} w_i \frac{M[i]}{\max_{1 \leq j \leq |O|} M[j]} \qquad (12)$$

Values of each measure are normalised to be in the range (0–1) by dividing by the maximum measure value for all ontologies. For example, if the maximum DEM value calculated for a set of ontologies is 4.75, then the normalised DEM value for the ontology ita.owl (example in sec. 3.1) will be $\frac{2.75}{4.75} = 0.579$ (table 2).

4 Experiment

In this section we report the results of running AKTiveRank over an example query submitted to Swoogle[6].

---

[5] http://www.mondeca.com/owl/moses/univ.owl
[6] Using Swoogle 2005

The weights for calculating total score (equation 12) for our experiment are set to 0.4,0.3,0.2,0.1 for the CMM, BEM, SSM, DEM measures respectively. The relative weighs for these measures are selected based on how well each measure performed in our evaluation (section 5). Further tests are required to identify the best weights to use, and whether the chosen mix of weights applies equally well to other queries and ontologies.

Table 1. Order of search result for "student university" as returned by Swoogle. Duplicates were removed.

	Ontology URL
a	http://www.csd.abdn.ac.uk/∼cmckenzi/playpen/rdf/akt_ontology_LITE.owl
b	http://protege.stanford.edu/plugins/owl/owl-library/koala.owl
c	http://protege.stanford.edu/plugins/owl/owl-library/ka.owl
d	http://reliant.teknowledge.com/DAML/Mid-level-ontology.owl
–	http://www.csee.umbc.edu/∼shashi1/Ontologies/Student.owl
e	http://www.mindswap.org/2004/SSSW04/aktive-portal-ontology-latest.owl
f	http://www.mondeca.com/owl/moses/univ2.owl
g	http://www.mondeca.com/owl/moses/univ.owl
–	http://www.lehigh.edu/∼yug2/Research/SemanticWeb/LUBM/University0_0.owl
h	http://www.lri.jur.uva.nl/∼rinke/aargh.owl
–	http://www.srdc.metu.edu.tr/∼yildiray/HW3.OWL
i	http://www.mondeca.com/owl/moses/ita.owl
j	http://triplestore.aktors.org/data/portal.owl
k	http://annotation.semanticweb.org/ontologies/iswc.owl
–	http://www.csd.abdn.ac.uk/ cmckenzi/playpen/rdf/abdn_ontology_LITE.owl
l	http://ontoware.org/frs/download.php/18/semiport.owl

Now lets assume that we need to find an OWL ontology that represents the concepts of "University" and "Student". The domain of academia is good for such experiments due to the relatively large number of relevant ontologies about this domain. The list of ontologies returned by Swoogle at the time of the experiment as a result of the query "university student type:owl" is shown in table 1. Some of those ontologies were duplicates (i.e. the same ontology was available under two slightly different URLs). As expected, the same rank was produced by AKTiveRank for all duplicated ontologies, and therefore were removed from the table to reduce complexity.

Some ontologies were no longer online and hence were dropped from the ranking experiment (they are given index "–" in the table).

When AKTiveRank was applied to the results list in table 1, it produced the values given in table 2. Figure 4 shows the sum of results per ontology, without applying any measure weightings. These values are obtained by calculating the values for each of AKTiveRank's measure, then normalising each value by dividing it by the maximum value calculated for that measure when applied to all identified ontologies.

4.1 Results Analysis

From the results of this experiment, it can be seen that ontology *a* scored the highest value in AKTiveRank. The ontologies *c* and *h* where given the second and third rank respectively. The *koala* ontology, which was placed second in Swoogle's results list, got the least AKTiveRank score, and thus was places last in the ranked list. Even though this ontology contains classes labelled "Student" and "University", those classes are not

Table 2. Normalised AKTiveRank results. Results for each ontology are weighted and aggregating to produce a final score, which is compared with the other scores to set the rank.

Onto	CMM	DEM	SSM	BEM	Score	Rank
a	0.833	0.632	0.250	0.806	0.688	1
b	0.5	0.197	0	0	0.220	12
c	0.667	0.5	0.25	1	0.667	2
d	0.417	1	0	0	0.267	11
e	1	0.632	0.111	0.452	0.621	3
f	0.833	0.579	0	0	0.391	7.5
g	0.833	0.579	0.167	0.065	0.444	6
h	0.5	0.553	1	0.323	0.552	4
i	0.5	0.579	0.167	0	0.291	10
j	0.5	0.579	0.125	0.839	0.535	5
k	0.667	0.579	0	0.097	0.354	9
l	0.667	0.685	0	0.194	0.391	7.5

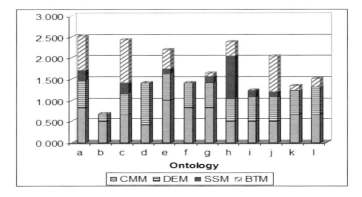

Fig. 4. Aggregated AKTiveRank scores using equal weights

closely associated (i.e. zero SSM[7]) and not graphically central to the ontology structure (i.e. zero BEM). The *koala* ontology is not exactly about students or universities, and therefore deserves the last rank in this context.

Note that 5 of our ontologies received a SSM of 0.0. This indicates that AKTiveRank did not manage to find any paths connecting the two given queried classes. Semantic paths that cross via *owl:Thing* class are ignored.

The ontology that scored the highest in the Class Match measure (CMM, section 3.1) was ontology *e*. This ontology had 2 classes with labels exactly matching our search terms, and 3 partially matching ones; *Phd-Student, University-Faculty* and *Distance-Teaching-University*.

The highest DEM value was calculated for ontology *d*. This ontology had a total of 5 subclasses and 10 siblings for the two classes matching our search terms. This added to its DEM value and made this ontology score best on this measure.

Ontology *h* received the maximum SSM value because it has the relation *enrolled_at* which directly connects the classes "Student" and "University".

---

[7] Jena disagrees with Proègè OWL on its rendering of a restriction in the Koala ontology between the classes Student and University.

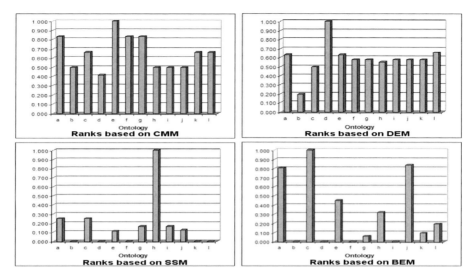

Fig. 5. Ontology rankings based on each measure separately

And finally, ontology c was found to have the highest average betweenness value for the two classes in question, which indicates that these classes are more structurally central in this ontology than in the other ontologies.

Ranking based on each measure separately is displayed in figure 5. When considered separately, none of the measures seemed to provide the same ranking list as when the measures were combined as will be discussed in the following section.

5 Evaluation

In order to evaluate the utility of the output of AKTiveRank, it is important to compare the results with those produced by some expert users. We have already conducted a small user-based experiment and used it to evaluate earlier versions of AKTiveRank [2]. Due to time constraints, we will use the results of that experiment again to evaluate our current results.

The users in our user-based experiment were presented with a general scenario, a set of screen shots of the relevant ontologies and a set of simple questions. Users were asked to rank the ontologies from the set presented, and were also given the opportunity to give comments and feedback. The total population sample was only four participants so we cannot make claims of any statistical accuracy or significance. Further and wider user-based experiments are planned for the very near future. The ranking as given by the users are listed in table 3:

When comparing the ranks produced by AKTiveRank in our experiments with the ranks generated from our user-based evaluation using the Pearson Correlation Coefficient (PCC), we get the value of 0.952. This value shows that the ranks produced by AKTiveRank are very close to the ranks produced by our users (a value of 0 indicates no relation, and 1 indicates an exact linear relationship between the two datasets). Note

Table 3. Ranks given by users

Ontology	Rank	Ontology	Rank	Ontology	Rank
a	2.5	b	12	c	11
d	9	e	2.5	f	5.5
g	5.5	h	1	i	10
j	7.5	k	4	l	7.5

Table 4. Pearson Correlation Coefficient for each measures separately against rankings provided by users

Measure	Value
CMM	0.499
DEM	0.270
SSM	0.292
BEM	0.298
AktiveRank	0.952
Swoogle	-0.144

that PCC value for Swoogle ranks against our user based results is -0.144, which indicates a very low and inversed correlation. Table 4 provides the PCC results above, as well as the PCC values when comparing each of our measure with the user results separately. It shows that the performance of each measure on its own was less than when they where combined (much higher PCC value when combined).

As can be seen in table 4, the measure that performed best when compared to the user results in table 3 was CMM, followed by BEM, SSM, then DEM. Based on this observation, the weights given to each measure when calculating the total score in our experiment were 0.4, 0.3, 0.2, and 0.1 respectively, to reflect the performance of each individual measures. These results are only representative of this experiment, and can not be generalised without further studies.

6 Conclusions and Future Work

In this paper we presented an extension to our previous work on ontology ranking based on an internal analysis of the concepts in the ontologies. The evaluation was based on four measures, but of course others may be added in the future if necessary. Even though our initial results are promising, a great deal of research and a much wider experiment are required before making any conclusive remarks about AKTiveRank's measures.

The work presented here on the ranking of ontologies has been partly motivated by an awareness that ontologies are not artefacts like any other document on the web. They are crafted usually with considerable care where (for example) the importation of other ontologies usually has a certain significance. On the other hand, it is usual when constructing a domain specific ontology to import general ontologies like *foaf* which contain relatively little domain specific content. It is important to distinguish the function of an ontology from that of a web page. A web page is read by a human being and any links it may have may or may not be followed by the reader. In contrast, an ontology is designed to be read by a machine and any links it may have are by definition imports pointing to other ontologies which must be included. This poses a dilemma in ranking an ontology as to whether to include all imports or not. Because the imports tend to be high level general ontologies, they are relatively vacuous if the user is seeking a domain specific ontology. Further more if ontology O_1 is dependent on ontology O_2 to represent class c, then O_2 will be evaluated separately anyway assuming it is included in the set retrieved.

It is very difficult to pinpoint the right selection of parameters or structural properties to investigate when ranking ontologies. The selection can be dependent on personal preference as well as use requirements (i.e. the purpose for which the ontology is intended). One focus of our future research will be to extend the user evaluation to include a larger number of human participants and a significant number of queries. Queries need to be posed to the system over a sufficient range of topics so as to allow confidence in the ranking methods we have used. Previous experience has shown it is difficult to present ontologies effectively to evaluators. Screen shots often show only a partial picture of the whole ontology, and some individuals prefer to examine the native OWL in understanding the ontology and making judgements. This is highly dependent on the background and skills of the user. Users must be given the freedom to browse the ontologies in an ontology editing tool such as Protégé[15] or Swoop [12], rather than given screen dumps or schema descriptions. For this reason, extensive user-based experiments are required to at least find out what are the properties that users tend to look at when judging the general quality or suitability of an ontology. Unlike ordinary search engines, where the user can be safely assumed to be relatively naive, with ontologies the typical user is either a knowledge engineer or software developer who has preconceptions of a technical nature.

Another area of future research lies in understanding further how these non-naive users set about finding an ontology so as to better model the user behaviour and tailor the system to that behaviour. In this regard, we have observed how users ask for ontologies in the Protégé mailing list and found that they tend to ask for topics (e.g. Transport, Algebra), which may not necessarily map to specific class names, but should rather be regarded as a general description of the domain. As consequence, we are currently investigating evaluating ontologies on their content coverage of a corpus [3], which is collected using the given general topic name (e.g. Cancer, Education)[11].

Other parameters can be taken into account, such as whether a class is defined or primitive (currently indirectly covered by the Density measure), of if the classes of interest are hubs or authoritative in a graph-network sense, which might increase their ontology's ranking.

The most appropriate criteria for searching for ontologies are still unclear. Swoogle is mainly based on keyword search, but other searching techniques can be imagined, based for example on the structure of ontologies or based on whether the ontologies meet certain requirements [13]. However, whatever the search mechanism is, there will always be a need for ranking. The ranking criteria will obviously have to be designed to fit the chosen search technique.

Acknowledgments

This work is supported under the Advanced Knowledge Technologies (AKT) Interdisciplinary Research Collaboration (IRC), which is sponsored by the UK Engineering and Physical Sciences Research Council under grant number GR/N15764/01. The AKT

IRC comprises the Universities of Aberdeen, Edinburgh, Sheffield, Southampton and the Open University. Christopher Brewster has also been supported by the UK EPSRC under grant number GR/T22902/01.

References

1. H. Alani. Ontology construction from online ontologies. In *Proc. 15th International World Wide Web Conference*, Edinburgh, 2006.
2. H. Alani and C. Brewster. Ontology ranking based on the analysis of concept sructures. In *3rd Int. Conf. Knowledge Capture (K-Cap)*, pages 51–58, Banff, Canada, 2005.
3. C. Brewster, H. Alani, S. Dasmahapatra, and Y. Wilks. Data driven ontology evaluation. In *Int. Conf. on Language Resources and Evaluation*, Lisbon, Portugal, 2004.
4. P. R. Cohen and R. Kjeldsen. Information retrieval by constrained spreading activation in semantic networks. *Information Processing & Management*, 23(4):255–268, 1987.
5. L. Ding, T. Finin, A. Joshi, R. Pan, R. S. Cost, Y. Peng, P. Reddivari, V. C. Doshi, and J. Sachs. Swoogle: A semantic web search and metadata engine. In *Proc. 13th ACM Conf. on Information and Knowledge Management*, Nov. 2004.
6. L. Ding, R. Pan, T. Finin, A. Joshi, Y. Peng, and P. Kolari. Finding and ranking knowledge on the semantic web. In *Proc. 4th Int. Semantic Web Conf. (ISWC)*, pages 156–170, Galway, Ireland, 2005.
7. L. Freeman. A set of measures of centrality based on betweenness. *Sociometry*, 40:35–41, 1977.
8. A. Gangemi, C. Catenacci, M. Ciaramita, and J. Lehmann. A theoretical framework for ontology evaluation and validation. In *Semantic Web Applications and Perspectives (SWAP) – 2nd Italian Semantic Web Workshop*, Trento, Italy, 2005.
9. A. Gomez-Perez. Some ideas and examples to evaluate ontologies. In *11th Conference on Artificial Intelligence for Applications*. IEEE Computer Society, 1995.
10. N. Guarino and C. Welty. Evaluating ontological decisions with ontoclean. *Communications of the ACM*, 45(2):61–65, 2002.
11. M. Jones and H. Alani. Content-based ontology ranking. In *Proceedings of the 9th Int. Protege Conf.*, Stanford, CA, 2006.
12. A. Kalyanpur, B. Parsia, E. Sirin, B. Cuenca-Grau, and J. Hendler. Swoop: A 'web' ontology editing browser. *Journal of Web Semantics*, 4(2), 2005.
13. A. Lozano-Tello and A. Gomez-Perez. Ontometric: A method to choose the appropriate ontology. *Journal of Database Management*, 15(2), 2005.
14. A. Maedche and S. Staab. Measuring similarity between ontologies. In *Proc. European Conf. on Knowledge Acquisition and Management (EKAW)*, pages 251–263, Madrid, 2002.
15. N. F. Noy, M. Sintek, S. Decker, M. Crubezy, R. W. Fergerson, and M. A. Musen. Creating semantic web contents with protege-2000. *IEEE Intelligent Systems*, pages 60–71, 2001.
16. C. Patel, K. Supekar, Y. Lee, and E. Park. Ontokhoj: A semantic web portal for ontology searching, ranking, and classification. In *Proc. 5th ACM Int. Workshop on Web Information and Data Management*, pages 58–61, New Orleans, Louisiana, USA, 2003.
17. R. Rada, H. Mili, E. Bicknell, and M. Blettner. Development and application of a metric on semantic nets. *IEEE Trans. on Systems Management and Cybernetics*, 19(1):17–30, 1989.
18. P. Resnik. Semantic similarity in a taxonomy: An information-based measure and its application to problems of ambiguity in natural language. *Journal of Artificial Intelligence Research*, 11:95–130, 1999.

19. E. Rosch. *Principles of Categorization.* in E. Rosch and B. B. Lloyd editors. Cognition and Categorization, Lawrence Erlbaum, Hillsdale, New Jersey, 1978.
20. G. Spanoudakis and P. Constantopoulos. Similarity for analogical software reuse: A computational model. In *Proc. 11th European Conf. on AI, ECAI'94*, pages 18–22, 1994.
21. K. Supekar. A peer-review approach for ontology evaluation. In *8th Int. Protege Conf.*, pages 77–79, Madrid, Spain, July 2005.
22. A. Tversky. Features of similarity. *Psychological Review*, 84(4), 1977.
23. P. C. Weinstein and W. P. Birmingham. Comparing concepts in differentiated ontologies. In *Proc. 12th Workshop on Knowledge Acquisition, Modeling and Management (KAW'99)*, Banff, Alberta, Canada, 1999.

Three Semantics for Distributed Systems and Their Relations with Alignment Composition*

Antoine Zimmermann and Jérôme Euzenat

INRIA Rhône-Alpes
Montbonnot Saint-Martin, France
{Antoine.Zimmermann, Jerome.Euzenat}@inrialpes.fr

Abstract. An ontology alignment explicitly describes the relations holding between two ontologies. A system composed of ontologies and alignments interconnecting them is herein called a distributed system. We give three different semantics of a distributed system, that do not interfere with the semantics of ontologies. Their advantages are compared with respect to allowing consistent merge of ontologies, managing heterogeneity and complying with an alignment composition operation. We show that only the first two variants, which differ from other proposed semantics, can offer a sound composition operation.

1 Introduction

In a general sense, ontology alignment is an explicit description of the semantic relationship that exists between different ontologies. However, in several practical applications, it is restricted to a set of syntactical correspondences or mapping. For instance, the Alignment API [1] defines a correspondence as a pair of entities (one from each ontology), together with the type of relation, and the confidence in its correctness. The API output format has been used in several ontology matching tools but has intentionally no associated formal semantics. Our goal is to consider alternative semantics for this generic type of alignments.

We define three different semantics that have advantages and drawbacks. The first one, *simple distributed semantics*, considers the whole distributed system as a coherent knowledge base which can be interpreted in a single domain. It is appropriate for consistently merging ontologies, based on correspondences. However, it is not tolerant to inconsistency, be it local or global. In very heterogeneous systems, like the semantic web or semantic P2P systems, this feature is not desirable. So we extend the first semantics to *integrated distributed semantics* where each local knowledge representation is interpreted in its own domain but these interpretation are then correlated in a global domain. Finally, we define a *contextualized distributed semantics*, inspired by DFOL/DDL/C-OWL [2,3,4], where there is no global domain of interpretation: each local ontologies "imports" knowledge from other ontologies in its own context.

---

* This work is partly supported by the Knowledge Web NoE (IST-2004-507482).

Additionally, the semantics is parameterized by the set of expressible relations between ontology entities. It means that this semantics is usable to reason about class relations (*e.g.*, equivalence, subsumption, disjunction), as well as temporal or spatial relations, *etc.*

Finally, we study the semantics of an alignment composition operator and prove that only the first two semantics comply with it.

This paper is articulated as follows: Sect. 2 gives an overview of previously proposed semantics for schema mappings, ontology alignments and matching, or distributed knowledge representation. Sect. 3 describes the syntax of distributed systems. Sect. 4 gives the simple distributed semantics. Sect. 5.1 extends the semantics to integrated distributed semantics, through the use of an *equalizing function* to a global domain. Sect. 5.2 presents the contextualized variant of the semantics. Sect. 6 discusses the composition of alignments within each of the proposed semantics.

2 Related Work

Ontology matching is strongly related to database schema matching. However, as noted in [5], there are foundational differences between schema matching and ontology matching. The most prominent being the weakness of schemata semantics. As a result, the schema mapping community is concerned about *query answering*, while ontology alignment must offer more general *reasoning* capabilities in distributed systems. Of particular interest is [6], which develops a notion of satisfied mappings that is very generic and the approach in this paper is very similar to theirs. The difference resides in their using of "helper models", and they do not provide a composition operator. Such operator is provided by [7] for relational databases, and cannot be exploited as it is for more general ontology alignment composition. Other database-related work about composition comprises [8,9,10].

Another different approach to the semantics of schema mapping and alignments is found in [11] and generalized in [12] where the authors use the theory of institutions [13] to characterize the relation between models of related ontologies or schemata. The approach is seducing for our ontology alignment purpose: it allows a language independent definition of ontology relation, elegant constructions of merging, composing and it is grounded on model theory. Nonetheless, it has a major problem: the "ontology morphisms" can only account for the most basic relations between ontological entities, namely equivalence. So we consider such an abstraction to be inappropriate for more general types of relations [14].

Other semantics for distributed knowledge based systems have been proposed. Various distributed logics are found in [2] (DFOL), [3] (DDL), [4] (C-OWL). They all assume that each ontology is interpreted within a context that has to be related to others in order to interpret the whole system. This approach effectively solves the problem of mutual inconsistencies in heterogeneous knowledge representations, but we show here that contextualizing the semantics forbids a sound composition operation.

3 Syntax

We want to design a model-theoretic semantics for distributed systems, which are composed of (1) ontologies and (2) alignments. The present section discusses the syntax of those components.

One of the key features of our alignment semantics is its independence from the ontology language. Sometimes, we will use the term "element of an ontology" to refer to any syntactical entity mentioned in the ontology, *e.g.*, class, property, individual. The only restriction upon the choice of the ontology language is the existence of a model-theoretic semantics. Among such languages, we can cite FOL, RDF [15], OWL [16], Conceptual Graphs [17], *etc.*

We follow the definition of alignment found in [18], but we intentionally discard the confidence value.[1]

Definition 1 (Ontology element). *An* ontology element *is either a term of the ontology (e.g., class, property, individual) or a compound entity built out of other ontology elements and constructors from the ontological language.*

Definition 2 (Ontology element relation). *An* ontology element relation R *is a symbol denoting a binary relation or predicate $\widetilde{R}$. Given a specific alignment language, the set of usable relation symbols is written $\mathfrak{R}$.*

The relations an alignment language can capture may be: equivalence, subsumption, disjunction of classes; temporal/spatial relations; fuzzy relations; *etc.*

These definitions makes the components of a correspondence.

Definition 3 (Correspondence). *A* correspondence *is a triple* $\langle e_1, e_2, R \rangle$ *where:*

- e_1 *and* e_2 *are ontology elements from the two ontologies to align;*
- R *is an ontology element relation that is asserted to hold between* e_1 *and* e_2.

Example 1. $\langle \texttt{Man1} \sqcup \texttt{Woman1}, \texttt{Human2}, \equiv \rangle$ or $\langle \texttt{Girl1}, \texttt{Human2} \sqcap \texttt{Female2}, \sqsubseteq \rangle$ are examples of correspondences.

Definition 4 (Ontology alignment). *An* ontology alignment *between ontologies O_1 and O_2 is a set of correspondences with ontology elements belonging to O_1 and O_2.*

Our semantics interprets distributed systems: a structure composed of multiple ontologies and alignments between them.

Definition 5 (Distributed system). *A* distributed system *(DS for short) is a pair $\langle (O_i), (A_{ij}) \rangle$ consisting of a family of ontologies $(O_i)_{i \in I}$ over a set of indexes I interconnected by a family of alignments $(A_{ij})_{i,j \in I}$.*[2]

Although there can be pairs of ontologies that are not connected by an alignment, we will then consider the missing alignment as an empty set of correspondences. Moreover, several alignments between two ontologies are considered here as a single alignment equals to the union of all their correspondences. So A_{ij} is always defined.

---
[1] How to treat uncertainty in this semantics is still a subject of investigations.
[2] When there is no ambiguity, we will write (X_i) to represent the family $(X_i)_{i \in I}$.

4 Simple Distributed Semantics

The simple distributed semantics considers a distributed system (DS) as a coherent knowledge base. This means that all ontologies are interpreted within the same domain. We first give the definitions for local semantics (given by the ontological language), then our proposed DS semantics follows.

4.1 Local Semantics

The semantics of a DS depends on the semantics of the ontology language. In fact, given a set of ontologies and a set of alignments between them, we can evaluate the semantics of the whole system in function of the semantics of each individual ontology.

Definition 6 (Interpretation of an ontology). *Given an ontology O, an interpretation of O is a function m from elements of O to elements of a domain of interpretation D.*

This is a very general notion of interpretation. In practice, ontologies are composed of axioms that constrain valid interpretations. Among interpretations, there are particular ones that are said to *satisfy* axioms, and if all axioms are satisfied, then the ontology is itself satisfied. So, the local semantics of ontologies determine the satisfaction relation $\models$ that relates interpretations to satisfied ontologies, i.e., $m \models O$ iff m satisfies O. For instance, $A \mathtt{subclassof} B$ would be satisfied iff A is interpreted as a subset of the interpretation of B. The collection of interpretations that satisfy O (the models of O) is written $\mathrm{Mod}(O)$.

4.2 Satisfaction of an Alignment

In order to determine the semantics of a DS, we first define when a pair of local interpretations satisfies a correspondence and an alignment.

Definition 7 (Satisfied correspondence). *Let O_1, O_2 be two ontologies and $c = \langle e_1, e_2, R \rangle$ be a correspondence between O_1 and O_2. c is satisfied by interpretations m_1, m_2 of O_1, O_2 iff $m_1(e_1) \widetilde{R} m_2(e_2)$. This is written $m_1, m_2 \models c$.*

The relation symbol R is out of the ontology languages. So it does not have to be interpreted in the local semantics. For instance, a temporal relation can be expressed between two OWL classes. The associated relation $\widetilde{R}$ is fixed, given a set of relation $\mathfrak{R}$. For instance, relation symbol $\equiv$ could be associated to the relation "=" (equality) over sets.

If all correspondences are satisfied, then it is said that the pair of interpretations is a model of the alignment.

Definition 8 (Model of an alignment). *A model of an alignment A between ontologies O_1 and O_2 is a pair m_1, m_2 of interpretations of O_1, O_2 such that for all $c \in A, m_1, m_2 \models c$. It is noted $m_1, m_2 \models A$.*

The models of an alignment do not take the semantics of the ontologies into account. They just consider the internal consistency of the correspondences. This is interesting because we can reason with and about alignments without actually accessing the aligned ontologies. The collection of all models of an alignment A is written $\text{Mod}(A)$.

Correspondences play the role of axioms that constrain the satisfying interpretations of the aligned ontologies. They therefore act as interpretation constraints of the distributed system.

4.3 Models of a DS

Informally, interpretations of a DS are tuples of local interpretations.[3]

Definition 9 (Interpretation of a DS). *An interpretation of a DS $\langle(O_i),(A_{ij})\rangle$ is a family (m_i) of local interpretations over a common domain D such that for all $i \in I$, m_i is an interpretation of O_i.*

Among interpretations, some are said to *satisfy* the DS. In order to satisfy a DS, interpretations must satisfy constraints given by (1) the ontologies axioms and (2) the alignments correspondences.

Definition 10 (Model of a DS). *A model of a DS $\mathcal{S} = \langle(O_i),(A_{ij})\rangle$ is an interpretation (m_i) of $\mathcal{S}$ such that:*

- $\forall i \in I$, $m_i \in \text{Mod}(O_i)$ *(i.e., m_i is a (local) model of O_i);*
- $\forall i, j \in I, m_i, m_j \models A_{ij}$.

This is written $(m_i) \models \mathcal{S}$. If a model exists for $\mathcal{S}$, we say that $\mathcal{S}$ is satisfiable.

We can see that this definition employs a very global view of the models. All ontologies and alignments are taken into account at the same time, and there are strong interdependencies. This is because the DS is seen as a single theory, with ontologies being but mere modules.

However, it is often the case when we only want to reason about local data, while taking advantage of external knowledge. So we define local models modulo a DS:

Definition 11 (Local models modulo a DS). *Local models of an ontology O_i modulo $\mathcal{S}$ are the local models $\text{Mod}_{\mathcal{S}}(O_i) = \{m_i \in \text{Mod}(O_i); \exists (m_j)_{j \neq i} \in \text{Mod}(O_j), (m_i)_{i \in I} \models \mathcal{S}\}$. It corresponds to the projection of the models of a DS on the ith component.*

With this definition, the models of the full system must be known to compute the local models. In order to build more efficient reasoners, we define another notion of models that do not require total integration of all ontologies and alignments at once. It is based on an iterative process of gradually reducing the local models.

---

[3] As in Sect. 3, I denotes a set of indexes and is omitted in expressions like (A_{ij}), when there is no ambiguity.

Definition 12 (Models of an ontology modulo alignment). *Given an ontology O_1 aligned with O_2 according to alignment A, the models of O_1 modulo A are those models of O_1 that can satisfy A:*

$$\mathrm{Mod}_A(O_1) = \{m_1 \in \mathrm{Mod}(O_1); \exists m_2 \in \mathrm{Mod}(O_2); m_1, m_2 \models A\}$$

Models modulo alignment is the first step of the following iterative definition.

Definition 13 (Iterated local models modulo a DS). *Given a DS $\mathcal{S} = \langle (O_i), (A_{ij}) \rangle$, consider $\mathrm{Mod}_{\mathcal{S}}^0(O_i) = \mathrm{Mod}(O_i)$, and the following iterative definition:*

$$\mathrm{Mod}_{\mathcal{S}}^k(O_i) = \{m_i \in \mathrm{Mod}_{\mathcal{S}}^{k-1}(O_i); \forall j \in I \setminus \{i\}, \exists m_j \in \mathrm{Mod}_{\mathcal{S}}^{k-1}(O_j); m_i, m_j \models A_{ij}\}$$

$\overline{\mathrm{Mod}}_{\mathcal{S}}(O)$ denotes the limit of the sequence $(\mathrm{Mod}_{\mathcal{S}}^n(O))$ when $n \to \infty$, i.e., $\overline{\mathrm{Mod}}_{\mathcal{S}}(O) = \mathrm{Mod}_{\mathcal{S}}^{\infty}(O)$.

Definition 14 (Local satisfiability). *A DS $\mathcal{S}$ is locally satisfiable iff for each ontology O, $\overline{\mathrm{Mod}}_{\mathcal{S}}(O) \neq \emptyset$.*

So, the iterated models only give a local view of what happens in the DS. Moreover, the stepwise restriction of the models allows for a faster but approximate reasoning while trying to find new ontologies and alignments.

Proposition 1. *Let $\mathcal{S}$ be a DS and O an ontology of $\mathcal{S}$. For all $n \in \mathbb{N}$, $\mathrm{Mod}_{\mathcal{S}}(O) \subseteq \overline{\mathrm{Mod}}_{\mathcal{S}}(O) \subseteq \mathrm{Mod}_{\mathcal{S}}^{n+1}(O) \subseteq \mathrm{Mod}_{\mathcal{S}}^n(O)$.*

Proposition 2. *There exists a DS S such that $\mathrm{Mod}_S(O) \neq \overline{\mathrm{Mod}}_S(O)$.*

Proof. We give a sketch of the proof[4] with a diagram representing the DS.

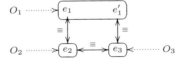

In this DS, we have $\mathrm{Mod}_S^n(O_i) = \mathrm{Mod}(O_i)$ for all $n \in \mathbb{N}$ and $i \in \{1,2,3\}$. But $\mathrm{Mod}_S(O_1)$ is restricted to the models of O_1 where e_1 and e_1' are interpreted as the same entity. □

In spite of this unfavorable property, $\mathrm{Mod}_{\mathcal{S}}(O)$ and $\overline{\mathrm{Mod}}_{\mathcal{S}}(O)$ are two solutions to the fixed-point equation $\widetilde{\mathrm{Mod}}_{\mathcal{S}}(O_i) = \{m \in \mathrm{Mod}(O_i); \forall j \in I \setminus \{i\}, \exists m_j \in \widetilde{\mathrm{Mod}}_{\mathcal{S}}(O_j); m_i, m_j \models A_{ij}\}$. This means that locally reasoning with iterated models will not contradict neighborhood reasoning.

The proposed semantics is somewhat strict, with regard to heterogeneous systems, because it only allows to assert a correspondence when it is fully compatible with both ontologies. While it may be desirable in a few applications, this semantics is not adapted to every ontology alignment use cases. For instance, in the semantic web, ontologies will vary tremendously in size, scope, scale, point of view and quality. We consider two semantics that address this problem.

---

[4] For a detailed proof of this proposition, please refer to the following url: http://www.inrialpes.fr/exmo/people/zimmer/ISWC2006proof.pdf.

5 Dealing with Heterogeneous Domains

In very heterogeneous applications, having a unified interpretation of a distributed system is not feasible. To address this issue, we propose two variants of the primary semantics: (1) in the *integrated distributed semantics*, local interpretation domains are separated, and they are reconciled in a global domain, thanks to the use of *equalizing functions* (Def. 15) that act as filters; (2) in the *contextualized distributed semantics*, no global domain exists, but interpretation domains are interrelated by as many translation function as there are pairs of domains.

5.1 Integrated Distributed Semantics

The choice of the interpretation domain is not only guided by the interpreter, but also partly decided by the local language semantics. So we will use the concept of an equalizing function to help making the domain commensurate.

Definition 15 (Equalizing function). *Given an interpretation (m_i) of a DS, an equalizing function (γ_i) over (m_i) is a family of functions from the local domains of interpretation of (m_i) to a global domain $\mathcal{U}$.*

So equalizing functions not only define a global domain for the interpretation of the DS, but also define how local domains are correlated in the global interpretation.

Definition 16 (Integrated interpretation of a DS). *An integrated interpretation of a DS $\mathcal{S}$ is a pair $\langle (m_i), \gamma \rangle$ where (m_i) is a simple interpretation of $\mathcal{S}$ and γ is an equalizing functions over (m_i).*

The integrated interpretations that satisfy the DS are given by the following definition.

Definition 17 (Integrated model of a DS). *An integrated interpretation $\langle (m_i), \gamma \rangle$ of a DS $\mathcal{S}$ is an integrated model iff $\forall i, j \in I, \gamma_i m_i, \gamma_j m_j \models A_{ij}$ and m_i is a local model of O_i.*[5]

We can define the iterated models of a DS in the following way:

Definition 18 (Integrated iterated local models modulo a DS). *Given a DS $\mathcal{S} = \langle (O_i), (A_{ij}) \rangle$, consider $\text{Mod}^0_\mathcal{S}(O_i) = \text{Mod}(O_i)$, and the following iterative definition:*

$$\text{Mod}^k_\mathcal{S}(O_i) =$$
$$\{m_i \in \text{Mod}^{k-1}_\mathcal{S}(O_i); \forall j \in I \setminus \{i\}, \exists m_j \in \text{Mod}^{k-1}_\mathcal{S}(O_j), \exists \gamma; \gamma_i m_i, \gamma_j m_j \models A_{ij}\}$$

---
[5] The notation $\gamma_i m_i$ is used to denote the composition of functions γ_i and m_i. In fact, $\gamma_i m_i$ is an interpretation of O_i in the global domain.

As with simple distributed semantics, there is a notion of local and global satisfiability (see Def. 14). The integrated iterated models have the same property as the simple iterated models (Prop. 1 and Prop. 2).

Proof (of Prop. 2). We give a sketch of the proof[6] with a diagram representing the DS.

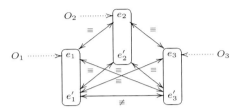

This system is locally satisfiable but not globally satisfiable. □

For particular applications, it may prove useful to give restrictions on equalizing functions. For instance, it might be needed to have injective functions, or to have inclusion-preserving functions. Although we do not describe the treatment of such restrictions, they should be compared to domain relation constraints in DFOL [2]. However, the approach in DFOL differs, because no global domain exists. They rather relates the local domains to each others, allowing to contextualize import of knowledge from and to each DS node. We extend our semantics in order to match this approach.

5.2 Contextualized Distributed Semantics

The contextualized semantics uses domain relation instead of equalizing functions. Domain relations differ from equalizing function because there exists one function for each pair of ontologies and they relate two local interpretation domains.

Definition 19 (Domain relation). *Given two domains of interpretation D_1 and D_2, a domain relation is a mapping $r_{12} : D_1 \to D_2$.*

These domain relations form a part of a contextualized interpretation.

Definition 20 (Contextualized interpretation of a DS). *A contextualized interpretation of a DS $\mathcal{S}$ is a pair $\langle (m_i), (r_{ij}) \rangle$ where (m_i) is a simple interpretation of $\mathcal{S}$ and $(r_{ij})_{i \neq j}$ is a family of domain relations such that r_{ij} relates the domain of m_i to the domain of m_j.*

The models in the contextualized semantics are defined as follows.

Definition 21 (Contextualized model of a DS). *A contextualized interpretation $\langle (m_i), (r_{ij}) \rangle$ of a DS $\mathcal{S}$ is a contextualized model iff $\forall i, j \in I, m_i, r_{ji} m_j \models A_{ij}$ and each m_i is a local model of O_i.*

---

[6] For a detailed proof of this proposition, please refer to the following url: http://www.inrialpes.fr/exmo/people/zimmer/ISWC2006proof.pdf.

We again define the iterative models of a DS in the following way:

Definition 22 (Contextualized iterated local models modulo a DS).
Given a DS $\mathcal{S} = \langle (O_i), (A_{ij}) \rangle$, consider $\mathrm{Mod}_{\mathcal{S}}^0(O_i) = \mathrm{Mod}(O_i)$, and the following iterative definition:

$\mathrm{Mod}_{\mathcal{S}}^k(O_i) =$
$\{m_i \in \mathrm{Mod}_{\mathcal{S}}^{k-1}(O_i); \forall j \in I \setminus \{i\}, \exists m_j \in \mathrm{Mod}_{\mathcal{S}}^{k-1}(O_j), \exists r_{ji}; m_i, r_{ji} m_j \models A_{ij}\}$

Again, there is a notion of local and global satisfiability (see Def. 14). The contextualized iterated models have the same property as the simple iterated models.

Proof (of Prop. 2). We give a sketch of the proof[7] with a diagram representing the DS.

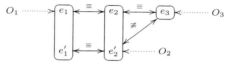

Among the local models of O_1 modulo this DS, there are interpretations where e_1 and e_1' are interpreted identically, while the global models necessitate that they are interpreted differently. □

The three approaches are compared in Sect. 7.

6 Composing Alignments

Building alignments is a difficult task that can hardly be done fully automatically. So existing alignments shall be reused to offer faster interoperable applications. Alignment composition is one of the key operations permitting this. Given three ontologies O_1, O_2 and O_3, with alignments A of O_1 and O_2, and B of O_2 and O_3, it must be possible to deduce a third alignment of O_1 and O_3, which we call the composition of A and B.

We propose here two notions of composition: the first is the syntactic composition of alignments, which can straightforwardly be implemented; the second is "semantic composition". Semantic composition is informally defined as follows: given a DS of 3 ontologies and 2 alignments $\mathcal{S} = \langle \langle O_1, O_2, O_3 \rangle, \langle A_{12}, A_{23} \rangle \rangle$, the semantic composition is the submodels of $\mathrm{Mod}(\mathcal{S})$ that are models of the subsystem $\langle \langle O_1, O_3 \rangle, \emptyset \rangle$ (see below for a more formal definition in each of the three semantics).

Definition 23 (Syntactic composition). *Let A_{12} be an alignment of O_1 and O_2, and A_{23} an alignment of O_2 and O_3. The composition of A_{12} and A_{23}, noted $A_{23} \circ A_{12}$ is the set of triples $\langle e_1, e_3, R \rangle$ such that there exist e_2, R_1, R_2 s.t. $\langle e_1, e_2, R_1 \rangle \in A_{12}, \langle e_2, e_3, R_2 \rangle \in A_{23}$ and $R = R_1; R_2$ with ";": $\mathfrak{R} \times \mathfrak{R} \to \mathfrak{R}$ being an associative operator.*

---
[7] For a detailed proof of this proposition, please refer to the following url: http://www.inrialpes.fr/exmo/people/zimmer/ISWC2006proof.pdf.

Remark 1. ";" may also be given by a table of composition. In that case, relations $R \in \mathfrak{R}$ are sets of primitive relations. Moreover, composition is associative iff ";" is associative.

In our first semantic approach, the models of A are pairs of interpretations of O_1 and O_2, so $\mathrm{Mod}(A_{12})$ is a set-theoretic relation. Relations are composable, and ideally the composition of A_{12} and A_{23} should have equal models as the composition of $\mathrm{Mod}(A_{12})$ and $\mathrm{Mod}(A_{23})$.

Let $\mathcal{S}$ be a DS having 3 ontologies O_1, O_2, O_3 and 2 alignments A_{12}, A_{23}.

Definition 24 (Simple semantic composition). *The* simple semantic composition *of the simple models of A_{12} and A_{23}, noted* $\mathrm{Mod}(A_{23}) \circ_s \mathrm{Mod}(A_{12})$ *is the set:*

$$\{\langle m_1, m_3\rangle \in \mathrm{Mod}(O_1) \times \mathrm{Mod}(O_3); \exists m_2 \in \mathrm{Mod}(O_2), \langle m_1, m_2, m_3\rangle \in \mathrm{Mod}(\mathcal{S})\}$$

In the case of the integrated semantics, the definition should include the equalizing function.

Definition 25 (Integrated semantic composition). *The* integrated semantic composition *of the integrated models of A_{12} and A_{23}, noted* $\mathrm{Mod}(A_{23}) \circ_i \mathrm{Mod}(A_{12})$ *is the set:*

$$\{\langle\langle m_1, m_3\rangle, \langle \gamma_1, \gamma_3\rangle\rangle; \exists m_2, \gamma_2, \langle\langle m_1, m_2, m_3\rangle, \langle \gamma_1, \gamma_2, \gamma_3\rangle\rangle \in \mathrm{Mod}(\mathcal{S})\}$$

Similarly, the contextualized semantics define a composition with domain relations.

Definition 26 (Contextualized semantic composition). *The* contextualized semantic composition *of the contextualized models of A_{12} and A_{23}, noted* $\mathrm{Mod}(A_{23}) \circ_c \mathrm{Mod}(A_{12})$ *is the set:*

$$\{\langle\langle m_1, m_3\rangle, \langle r_{13}, r_{31}\rangle\rangle; \exists m_2, r_{12}, r_{21}, r_{23}, r_{32}, \langle(m_i)_{i\in\{1,2,3\}}, (r_{ij})_{i\neq j}\rangle \in \mathrm{Mod}(\mathcal{S})\}$$

These definitions are rather intuitive and correspond to what is found in constraint reasoning literature, with slight variants due to the presence of equalizing functions and domain relations. The following section compares the three ontologies, and shows that composition is semantically sound in the first two semantics, but not in the contextualized one.

7 Comparing Semantics

Our three semantics do not only differ by their conceptual design. They also imply technical differences.

7.1 Simple Semantics

The following diagram helps visualizing the idea behind the simple semantics. Each ontology is treated as a module of a bigger ontology, interpreted in a single domain.

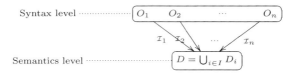

This semantics offer several advantages. It may be used as a general semantics for modules composition in ontology engineering. In practical cases, modules are generally related to each others with an import directive, and sometimes additional bridge axioms are added in the ontological language. With this semantics, modules can be written in different languages and aligned with yet another alignment language. Besides, the decision procedure is easier than in the other distributed semantics. Consider the case of OWL[8] ontologies with possible relations being `subclassOf`, `equivalentClass`, `disjointClass`, `subPropertyOf`, `equivalentProperty`, then reasoning will not differ from reasoning with a single OWL ontology.

Additionally, composition has the following property:

Property 1. If for all $R_1, R_2 \in \mathfrak{R}$, for all appropriate X, Y, Z, $X\widetilde{R_1}Y \wedge Y\widetilde{R_2}Z \Rightarrow X\widetilde{R_1; R_2}Z$, then the simple semantic composition of the models of the alignments is included in the models of the syntactic composition of alignments, *i.e.*, :

$$\mathrm{Mod}(B) \circ \mathrm{Mod}(A) \subseteq \mathrm{Mod}(B \circ A).$$

Proof. Let $m_1, m_3 \in \mathrm{Mod}(B) \circ \mathrm{Mod}(A)$. There exists $m_2 \in \mathrm{Mod}(O_2)$ such that $m_1, m_2 \models A$ and $m_2, m_3 \models B$. Let $c = (e_1, e_3, R)$ be a correspondence of $B \circ A$. There exists $R_1, R_2 \in \mathfrak{R}$ and e_2 in O_2 such that $R = R_1; R_2$, $(e_1, e_2, R_1) \in A$ and $(e_2, e_3, R_2) \in B$. We have $m_1(e_1)\widetilde{R_1}m_2(e_2)$ and $m_2(e_2)\widetilde{R_2}m_3(e_3)$. The assumption made ensures that $m_1(e_1)\widetilde{R_1; R_2}m_3(e_3)$. So for all $c \in B \circ A, m_1, m_3 \models c$. As a result, all m_1, m_3 in $\mathrm{Mod}(B) \circ \mathrm{Mod}(A)$ are also in $\mathrm{Mod}(B \circ A)$. □

The property required ($\forall R_1, R_2 \in \mathfrak{R}, \forall X, Y, Z, X\widetilde{R_1}Y \wedge Y\widetilde{R_2}Z \Rightarrow X\widetilde{R_1; R_2}Z$) fits with the common sense meaning of what must be a composition operation. This property is mentioned in work on composition tables (*e.g.*, [19]) as a basic property for a sound composition operation. This property encourage reuse of alignments by combining them.

Nonetheless, as explained in [2], interpreting a distributed system in a unique domain is only feasible in the least heterogeneous systems.

7.2 Integrated Semantics

In the integrated semantics, ontologies are interpreted at the local level, and the equalizing function γ serves to coordinate local interpretations in a global domain.

---

[8] http://www.w3.org/TR/owl-guide/

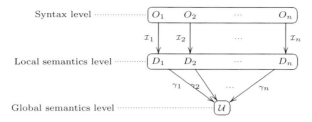

This approach is much more tolerant to inconsistencies, because the equalizing functions act as a filter between local and global interpretations. Having two levels of interpretations allows one to maintain local specificities while integrating knowledge into one consistent interpretation. And, obviously, if a simple distributed model exists, then an integrated model exists.

The following example demonstrates the interest of equalizing function.

Example 2. Consider two instances of class `Child` that have different ages and different heights, but truly represent the same person at different moments. In some ontology languages, it may not be possible to interpret these different instances as only one unique individual because age and height may be restricted in cardinality. However, an equalizing function can map two different instances of child with different ages in the local domain, to one instance of a person having no attribute `age` in the global domain.

Moreover, Prop. 1 holds too in this semantics. Therefore, it is also appropriate to manipulate and reuse several alignments in a consistent way. So, this semantics consistently extends the previous one.

However, the reasoning procedure is rendered more difficult because of the presence of equalizing functions. This is quite inevitable since dealing with inconsistencies has always been a time-consuming and complex task.

7.3 Contextualized Semantics

In the contextualized semantics, we drop the global domain, but the domain relations enables each ontology to integrate the whole distributed system in its own context.

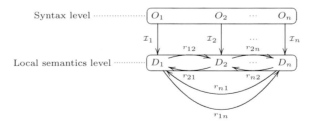

This approach is very similar to context-based logics approach and the interest of contextualizing inferences is explained in *e.g.*, [2].

However, the following result tend to disqualify this semantics when composing alignments becomes a necessity:

Proposition 3. *Prop. 1 does not hold in contextualized semantics.*

Proof. Consider the following DS[9]:

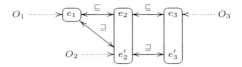

Additionally, we show the generality of our integrated semantics with the following proposition:

Proposition 4. *If a contextualized model exists for a DS, then there exists an integrated model.*

Proof. Let $\langle (m_i), (r_{ij}) \rangle$ be a model of a DS. Let $k \in I$ be an indice then $\langle (m_i), (r_{ik})_{i \in I} \rangle$, with $r_{kk} = \mathrm{id}_{D_k}$ is an integrated model of the DS with global domain D_k. □

This property was in fact predictable. The contextualized semantics has a different purpose: it interprets semantic relations from one ontology's point of view. Composing alignments in this way is not sound because two consecutive alignments are interpreted according to two different points of view. However, it has a strong advantage with regard to the integration of external knowledge into a specific ontology.

8 Conclusion and Future Work

We presented three variant semantics (*simple*, *integrated* and *contextualized*) for ontology alignments and distributed systems. Our characterization of an alignment allows the definition of an alignment composition operator, which is sound in the first two proposed semantics. We gave the advantages and drawbacks of each approach, and highlighted the benefits of using the first two semantics in comparison to using a contextualized semantics. We also make our approach distinct from others by using a set of relations as a parameter. It enables one to use the same meta-semantics for different types of relations (*e.g.*, temporal/spatial relations, class relations or even data types relations).

We will extend this semantics to include operations such as inverse alignment, union/intersection, and data transformations induced by them (along the line of the schema mapping algebra in [7]). Finally, our semantics and composition operator shall be extended to correspondences with confidence value.

---

[9] For a detailed proof of this proposition, please refer to the following url: http://www.inrialpes.fr/exmo/people/zimmer/ISWC2006proof.pdf.

References

1. Euzenat, J.: An API for ontology alignment. In: Proc. Third International Semantic Web Conference (ISWC'04). (2004) 698–712
2. Ghidini, C., Serafini, L.: Distributed First Order Logics. In: Frontiers of Combining Systems 2. (2000) 121–139
3. Borgida, A., Serafini, L.: Distributed Description Logics: Assimilating information from peer sources. J. Data Semantics (2003) 153–184
4. Bouquet, P., Giunchiglia, F., van Harmelen, F., Serafini, L., Stuckenschmidt, H.: C-OWL: Contextualizing ontologies. In: Proc. 2nd ISWC. (2003)
5. Kalfoglou, Y., Schorlemmer, M.: Ontology mapping: The state of the art. In: Semantic Interoperability and Integration. Dagstuhl Seminar Proceedings (2005)
6. Madhavan, J., Bernstein, P.A., Domingos, P., Halevy, A.Y.: Representing and reasoning about mappings between domain models. In: Proc. 18th AAAI'02. (2002) 80–86
7. Bernstein, P.A., Halevy, A.Y., Pottinger, R.A.: A vision for management of complex models. SIGMOD Record (2000) 55–63
8. Madhavan, J., Halevy, A.Y.: Composing mappings among data sources. In: Proc. 29th VLDB. (2003) 572–583
9. Fagin, R., Kolaitis, P.G., Popa, L., Tan, W.C.: Composing schema mappings: Second-order dependencies to the rescue. In: Proc. 23rd ACM SIGMOD-SIGACT-SIGART symposium on Principles of Database Systems (PODS'04). (2004) 83–94
10. Dragut, E., Lawrence, R.: Composing mappings between schemas using a reference ontology. In: Proc. ODBASE. (2004) 783–800
11. Alagić, S., Bernstein, P.A.: A model theory for generic schema management. In: Proc. 8th DBPL. (2001) 228–246
12. Goguen, J.A.: Data, schema and ontology integration. In: CombLog workshop. (2004)
13. Goguen, J.A., Burstall, R.M.: Institutions: abstract model theory for specification and programming. Journal of the ACM (1992) 95–146
14. Zimmermann, A., Krötzsch, M., Euzenat, J., Hitzler, P.: Formalizing ontology alignment and its operations with category theory. In: Proc. of 4th FOIS. (2006) To appear.
15. Hayes, P.: RDF Semantics. Technical report, W3C (2004)
16. Patel-Schneider, P.F., Hayes, P., Horrocks, I.: OWL Web Ontology Language Semantics and Abstract Syntax. Technical report, W3C (2004)
17. Sowa, J.F.: Conceptual graphs for a data base interface. IBM Journal of Research and Development **20** (1976) 336–357
18. Bouquet, P., Euzenat, J., Franconi, E., Serafini, L., Stamou, G., Tessaris, S.: Specification of a common framework for characterizing alignment. Deliverable 2.2.1, Knowledge Web NoE (2004)
19. Eschenbach, C.: Viewing composition tables as axiomatic systems. In: Proc. 2nd FOIS. (2001) 93–104

Semantics and Complexity of SPARQL

Jorge Pérez[1], Marcelo Arenas[2], and Claudio Gutierrez[3]

[1] Universidad de Talca, Chile
[2] Pontificia Universidad Católica de Chile
[3] Universidad de Chile

Abstract. SPARQL is the W3C candidate recommendation query language for RDF. In this paper we address systematically the formal study of SPARQL, concentrating in its graph pattern facility. We consider for this study simple RDF graphs without special semantics for literals and a simplified version of filters which encompasses all the main issues. We provide a compositional semantics, prove there are normal forms, prove complexity bounds, among others that the evaluation of SPARQL patterns is PSPACE-complete, compare our semantics to an alternative operational semantics, give simple and natural conditions when both semantics coincide and discuss optimization procedures.

1 Introduction

The Resource Description Framework (RDF) [12] is a data model for representing information about World Wide Web resources. Jointly with its release in 1998 as Recommendation of the W3C, the natural problem of querying RDF data was raised. Since then, several designs and implementations of RDF query languages have been proposed (see [9] for a recent survey). In 2004 the RDF Data Access Working Group (part of the Semantic Web Activity) released a first public working draft of a query language for RDF, called SPARQL [15]. Currently (August 2006) SPARQL is a W3C Candidate Recommendation.

Essentially, SPARQL is a graph-matching query language. Given a data source D, a query consists of a pattern which is matched against D, and the values obtained from this matching are processed to give the answer. The data source D to be queried can be composed of multiple sources. A SPARQL query consists of three parts. The *pattern matching part*, which includes several interesting features of pattern matching of graphs, like optional parts, union of patterns, nesting, filtering (or restricting) values of possible matchings, and the possibility of choosing the data source to be matched by a pattern. The *solution modifiers*, which once the output of the pattern has been computed (in the form of a table of values of variables), allows to modify these values applying classical operators like projection, distinct, order, limit, and offset. Finally, the *output* of a SPARQL query can be of different types: yes/no queries, selections of values of the variables which match the patterns, construction of new triples from these values, and descriptions of resources.

Although taken one by one the features of SPARQL are simple to describe and understand, it turns out that the combination of them makes SPARQL into a complex language, whose semantics is far from being understood. In fact, the semantics of SPARQL currently given in the document [15], as we show in this paper, does not cover all the complexities brought by the constructs involved in SPARQL, and includes ambiguities, gaps and features difficult to understand. The interpretations of the examples and the semantics of cases not covered in [15] are currently matter of long discussions in the W3C mailing lists.

The natural conclusion is that work on formalization of the semantics of SPARQL is needed. A formal approach to this subject is beneficial for several reasons, including to serve as a tool to identify and derive relations among the constructors, identify redundant and contradicting notions, and to study the complexity, expressiveness, and further natural database questions like rewriting and optimization. To the best of our knowledge, there is no work today addressing this formalization systematically. There are proposals addressing partial aspects of the semantics of some fragments of SPARQL. There is also some work addressing formal issues of the semantics of query languages for RDF which can be of use for SPARQL. In fact, SPARQL shares several constructs with other proposals of query languages for RDF. In the related work section, we discuss these developments in more detail. None of these works, nevertheless, covers the problems posed by the core constructors of SPARQL from the syntactic, semantic, algorithmic and computational complexity point of view, which is the subject of this paper.

Contributions. An in depth analysis of the semantics benefits from abstracting some features, which although relevant, in a first stage tend to obscure the interplay of the basic constructors used in the language. One of our main goals was to isolate a core fragment of SPARQL simple enough to be the subject matter of a formal analysis, but which is expressive enough to capture the core complexities of the language. In this direction, we chose the graph pattern matching facility, which is additionally one of the most complex parts of the language. The fragment isolated consists of the grammar of patterns restricted to queries on one dataset (i.e. not considering the dataset graph pattern) over simple RDF graphs, not considering RDF/S vocabulary and without special semantics for literals. There are other two sources of abstractions which do not alter in essential ways SPARQL: we use set semantics as opposed to the bag semantics implied in the document of the W3C, and we avoid blanks in the syntax of patterns, because in our fragment can be replaced by variables [8,4].

The contributions of this paper are:

- A streamlined version of the core fragment of SPARQL with precise syntax and semantics. A formal version of SPARQL helps clarifying cases where the current English-wording semantics gives little information, identify areas of problems and permits to propose solutions.
- We present a compositional semantics for patterns in SPARQL, prove that there is a notion of normal form for graph patterns, and indicate optimization procedures and rules for the operators based on them.
- We give thorough analysis of the computational complexity of the fragment. Among other bounds, we prove that the complexity of evaluation of SPARQL general graph patterns is PSPACE-complete even without filter conditions.

- We formalize a natural procedural semantics which is implicitly used by developers. We compare these two semantics, the operational and the compositional mentioned above. We show that putting some slight and reasonable syntactic restrictions on the scope of variables, they coincide, thus isolating a natural fragment having a clear semantics and an efficient evaluation procedure.

Organization of the paper. Section 2 presents a formalized algebraic syntax and a compositional semantics for SPARQL. Section 3 presents the complexity study of the fragment considered. Section 4 presents and in depth discussion of graph patterns not including the UNION operator. Finally, Section 5 discusses related work and gives some concluding remarks.

2 Syntax and Semantics of SPARQL

In this section, we give an algebraic formalization of the core fragment of SPARQL over simple RDF, that is, RDF without RDFS vocabulary and literal rules. This allows us to take a close look at the core components of the language and identify some of its fundamental properties (for details on RDF formalization see [8], or [13] for a complete reference including RDFS vocabulary).

Assume there are pairwise disjoint infinite sets I, B, and L (IRIs, Blank nodes, and literals). A triple $(s, p, o) \in (I \cup B) \times I \times (I \cup B \cup L)$ is called an *RDF triple*. In this tuple, s is the *subject*, p the *predicate* and o the *object*. We denote by IL the union $I \cup L$, and by T the union $I \cup B \cup L$. Assume additionally the existence of an infinite set V of variables disjoint from the above sets.

Definition 1. *An* RDF *graph [11] is a set of RDF triples. In our context, we refer to an* RDF *graph as an* RDF *dataset, or simply a dataset.*

2.1 Syntax of SPARQL Graph Pattern Expressions

In order to avoid ambiguities in the parsing, we present the syntax of SPARQL graph patterns in a more traditional algebraic way, using the binary operators UNION, AND and OPT, and FILTER. We fully parenthesize expressions and make explicit the left associativity of OPT (OPTIONAL) and the precedence of AND over OPT implicit in [15].

A SPARQL graph pattern expression is defined recursively as follows:

(1) A tuple from $(IL \cup V) \times (I \cup V) \times (IL \cup V)$ is a graph pattern (a *triple pattern*).
(2) If P_1 and P_2 are graph patterns, then expressions $(P_1$ AND $P_2)$, $(P_1$ OPT $P_2)$, and $(P_1$ UNION $P_2)$ are graph patterns.
(3) If P is a graph pattern and R is a SPARQL *built-in* condition, then the expression $(P$ FILTER $R)$ is a graph pattern.

A SPARQL *built-in* condition is constructed using elements of the set $V \cup IL$ and constants, logical connectives ($\neg$, $\wedge$, $\vee$), inequality symbols ($<, \leq, \geq, >$), the equality symbol ($=$), unary predicates like bound, isBlank, and isIRI, plus other features (see [15] for a complete list).

In this paper, we restrict to the fragment of filters where the built-in condition is a Boolean combination of terms constructed by using = and bound, that is:

(1) If $?X, ?Y \in V$ and $c \in I \cup L$, then bound($?X$), $?X = c$ and $?X = ?Y$ are built-in conditions.
(2) If R_1 and R_2 are built-in conditions, then $(\neg R_1)$, $(R_1 \vee R_2)$ and $(R_1 \wedge R_2)$ are built-in conditions.

Additionally, we assume that for $(P\text{ FILTER }R)$ the condition var$(R) \subseteq$ var(P) holds, where var(R) and var(P) are the sets of variables occurring in R and P, respectively. Variables in R not occurring in P bring issues that are not computationally desirable. Consider the example of a built in condition R defined as $?X = ?Y$ for two variables not occurring in P. What should be the result of evaluating $(P\text{ FILTER }R)$? We decide not to address this discussion here.

2.2 Semantics of SPARQL Graph Pattern Expressions

To define the semantics of SPARQL graph pattern expressions, we need to introduce some terminology. A *mapping* μ from V to T is a partial function $\mu : V \to T$. Abusing notation, for a triple pattern t we denote by $\mu(t)$ the triple obtained by replacing the variables in t according to μ. The domain of μ, dom(μ), is the subset of V where μ is defined. Two mappings μ_1 and μ_2 are *compatible* when for all $x \in$ dom$(\mu_1) \cap$ dom(μ_2), it is the case that $\mu_1(x) = \mu_2(x)$, i.e. when $\mu_1 \cup \mu_2$ is also a mapping. Note that two mappings with disjoint domains are always compatible, and that the empty mapping (i.e. the mapping with empty domain) $\mu_\emptyset$ is compatible with any other mapping. Let Ω_1 and Ω_2 be sets of mappings. We define the join of, the union of and the difference between Ω_1 and Ω_2 as:

$$\Omega_1 \bowtie \Omega_2 = \{\mu_1 \cup \mu_2 \mid \mu_1 \in \Omega_1, \mu_2 \in \Omega_2 \text{ are compatible mappings}\},$$
$$\Omega_1 \cup \Omega_2 = \{\mu \mid \mu \in \Omega_1 \text{ or } \mu \in \Omega_2\},$$
$$\Omega_1 \smallsetminus \Omega_2 = \{\mu \in \Omega_1 \mid \text{ for all } \mu' \in \Omega_2, \mu \text{ and } \mu' \text{ are not compatible}\}.$$

Based on the previous operators, we define the left outer-join as:

$$\Omega_1 ⟕ \Omega_2 = (\Omega_1 \bowtie \Omega_2) \cup (\Omega_1 \smallsetminus \Omega_2).$$

We are ready to define the semantics of graph pattern expressions as a function $[\![\,\cdot\,]\!]_D$ which takes a pattern expression and returns a set of mappings. We follow the approach in [8] defining the semantics as the set of mappings that matches the dataset D.

Definition 2. *Let D be an RDF dataset over T, t a triple pattern and P_1, P_2 graph patterns. Then the evaluation of a graph pattern over D, denoted by $[\![\,\cdot\,]\!]_D$, is defined recursively as follows:*

(1) $[\![t]\!]_D = \{\mu \mid$ dom$(\mu) =$ var(t) and $\mu(t) \in D\}$, where var(t) is the set of variables occurring in t.

(2) $[\![(P_1 \text{ AND } P_2)]\!]_D = [\![P_1]\!]_D \bowtie [\![P_2]\!]_D$.
(3) $[\![(P_1 \text{ OPT } P_2)]\!]_D = [\![P_1]\!]_D \mathbin{⟕} [\![P_2]\!]_D$.
(4) $[\![(P_1 \text{ UNION } P_2)]\!]_D = [\![P_1]\!]_D \cup [\![P_2]\!]_D$.

Consider pattern expression $(P_1 \text{ OPT } P_2)$ and let μ_1 be a mapping in $[\![P_1]\!]_D$. If there exists a mapping $\mu_2 \in [\![P_2]\!]_D$ such that μ_1 and μ_2 are compatible, then $\mu_1 \cup \mu_2$ belongs to $[\![(P_1 \text{ OPT } P_2)]\!]_D$. But if no such a mapping μ_2 exists, then μ_1 belongs to $[\![(P_1 \text{ OPT } P_2)]\!]_D$. Thus, operator OPT (optional) allows information to be added to a mapping μ if the information is available, instead of just rejecting μ whenever some part of the pattern does not match.

The semantics of FILTER expressions goes as follows. Given a mapping μ and a built-in condition R, we say that μ satisfies R, denoted by $\mu \models R$, if:

(1) R is bound($?X$) and $?X \in \text{dom}(\mu)$;
(2) R is $?X = c$, $?X \in \text{dom}(\mu)$ and $\mu(?X) = c$;
(3) R is $?X = ?Y$, $?X \in \text{dom}(\mu)$, $?Y \in \text{dom}(\mu)$ and $\mu(?X) = \mu(?Y)$;
(4) R is $(\neg R_1)$, R_1 is a built-in condition, and it is not the case that $\mu \models R_1$;
(5) R is $(R_1 \vee R_2)$, R_1 and R_2 are built-in conditions, and $\mu \models R_1$ or $\mu \models R_2$;
(6) R is $(R_1 \wedge R_2)$, R_1 and R_2 are built-in conditions, and $\mu \models R_1$ and $\mu \models R_2$.

Definition 3. *Given an RDF dataset D and a FILTER expression $(P \text{ FILTER } R)$,*

$$[\![(P \text{ FILTER } R)]\!]_D = \{\mu \in [\![P]\!]_D \mid \mu \models R\}.$$

Example 1. Consider the RDF dataset D:

$D = \{$ (B_1, name, paul), (B_1, phone, 777-3426),
(B_2, name, john), (B_2, email, john@acd.edu),
(B_3, name, george), (B_3, webPage, www.george.edu),
(B_4, name, ringo), (B_4, email, ringo@acd.edu),
(B_4, webPage, www.starr.edu), (B_4, phone, 888-4537), $\}$

The following are graph pattern expressions and their evaluations over D according to the above semantics:

(1) $P_1 = ((?A, \text{email}, ?E) \text{ OPT } (?A, \text{webPage}, ?W))$. Then

$[\![P_1]\!]_D = $

	?A	?E	?W
$\mu_1:$	B_2	john@acd.edu	
$\mu_2:$	B_4	ringo@acd.edu	www.starr.edu

(2) $P_2 = (((?A, \text{name}, ?N) \text{ OPT } (?A, \text{email}, ?E)) \text{ OPT } (?A, \text{webPage}, ?W))$. Then

$[\![P_2]\!]_D = $

	?A	?N	?E	?W
$\mu_1:$	B_1	paul		
$\mu_2:$	B_2	john	john@acd.edu	
$\mu_3:$	B_3	george		www.george.edu
$\mu_4:$	B_4	ringo	ringo@acd.edu	www.starr.edu

(3) $P_3 = ((?A, \text{name}, ?N) \text{ OPT } ((?A, \text{email}, ?E) \text{ OPT } (?A, \text{webPage}, ?W)))$. Then

$$[\![P_3]\!]_D = \begin{array}{c|c|c|c|c|} \cline{2-5} & ?A & ?N & ?E & ?W \\ \cline{2-5} \mu_1: & B_1 & \text{paul} & & \\ \mu_2: & B_2 & \text{john} & \text{john@acd.edu} & \\ \mu_3: & B_3 & \text{george} & & \\ \mu_4: & B_4 & \text{ringo} & \text{ringo@acd.edu} & \text{www.starr.edu} \\ \cline{2-5} \end{array}$$

Note the difference between $[\![P_2]\!]_D$ and $[\![P_3]\!]_D$. These two examples show that $[\![((A \text{ OPT } B) \text{ OPT } C)]\!]_D \neq [\![(A \text{ OPT } (B \text{ OPT } C))]\!]_D$ in general.

(4) $P_4 = ((?A, \text{name}, ?N) \text{ AND } ((?A, \text{email}, ?E) \text{ UNION } (?A, \text{webPage}, ?W)))$. Then

$$[\![P_4]\!]_D = \begin{array}{c|c|c|c|c|} \cline{2-5} & ?A & ?N & ?E & ?W \\ \cline{2-5} \mu_1: & B_2 & \text{john} & \text{john@acd.edu} & \\ \mu_2: & B_3 & \text{george} & & \text{www.george.edu} \\ \mu_3: & B_4 & \text{ringo} & \text{ringo@acd.edu} & \\ \mu_4: & B_4 & \text{ringo} & & \text{www.starr.edu} \\ \cline{2-5} \end{array}$$

(5) $P_5 = (((?A, \text{name}, ?N) \text{ OPT } (?A, \text{phone}, ?P)) \text{ FILTER } \neg\text{bound}(?P))$. Then

$$[\![P_5]\!]_D = \begin{array}{c|c|c|c|} \cline{2-4} & ?A & ?N & ?P \\ \cline{2-4} \mu_1: & B_2 & \text{john} & \\ \mu_2: & B_3 & \text{george} & \\ \cline{2-4} \end{array}$$

2.3 A Simple Normal Form for Graph Patterns

We say that two graph pattern expressions P_1 and P_2 are *equivalent*, denoted by $P_1 \equiv P_2$, if $[\![P_1]\!]_D = [\![P_2]\!]_D$ for every RDF dataset D.

Proposition 1. *Let P_1, P_2 and P_3 be graph pattern expressions and R a built-in condition. Then:*

(1) AND and UNION are associative and commutative.
(2) $(P_1 \text{ AND } (P_2 \text{ UNION } P_3)) \equiv ((P_1 \text{ AND } P_2) \text{ UNION } (P_1 \text{ AND } P_3))$.
(3) $(P_1 \text{ OPT } (P_2 \text{ UNION } P_3)) \equiv ((P_1 \text{ OPT } P_2) \text{ UNION } (P_1 \text{ OPT } P_3))$.
(4) $((P_1 \text{ UNION } P_2) \text{ OPT } P_3) \equiv ((P_1 \text{ OPT } P_3) \text{ UNION } (P_2 \text{ OPT } P_3))$.
(5) $((P_1 \text{ UNION } P_2) \text{ FILTER } R) \equiv ((P_1 \text{ FILTER } R) \text{ UNION } (P_2 \text{ FILTER } R))$.

The application of the above equivalences permits to translate any graph pattern into an equivalent one of the form:

$$P_1 \text{ UNION } P_2 \text{ UNION } P_3 \text{ UNION } \cdots \text{ UNION } P_n, \quad (1)$$

where each P_i $(1 \leq i \leq n)$ is a UNION-free expression. In Section 4, we study UNION-free graph pattern expressions.

3 Complexity of Evaluating Graph Pattern Expressions

A fundamental issue in every query language is the complexity of query evaluation and, in particular, what is the influence of each component of the language in this complexity. In this section, we address these issues for graph pattern expressions.

As it is customary when studying the complexity of the evaluation problem for a query language, we consider its associated decision problem. We denote this problem by EVALUATION and we define it as follows:

INPUT   : An RDF dataset D, a graph pattern P and a mapping μ.
QUESTION : Is $\mu \in [\![P]\!]_D$?

We start this study by considering the fragment consisting of graph pattern expressions constructed by using only AND and FILTER operators. This simple fragment is interesting as it does not use the two most complicated operators in SPARQL, namely UNION and OPT. Given an RDF dataset D, a graph pattern P in this fragment and a mapping μ, it is possible to efficiently check whether $\mu \in [\![P]\!]_D$ by using the following algorithm. First, for each triple t in P, verify whether $\mu(t) \in D$. If this is not the case, then return *false*. Otherwise, by using a bottom-up approach, verify whether the expression generated by instantiating the variables in P according to μ satisfies the FILTER conditions in P. If this is the case, then return *true*, else return *false*. Thus, we conclude that:

Theorem 1. EVALUATION *can be solved in time* $O(|P| \cdot |D|)$ *for graph pattern expressions constructed by using only* AND *and* FILTER *operators.*

We continue this study by adding to the above fragment the UNION operator. It is important to notice that the inclusion of UNION in SPARQL is one of the most controversial issues in the definition of this language. In fact, in the W3C candidate recommendation for SPARQL [15], one can read the following: *"The working group decided on this design and closed the disjunction issue without reaching consensus. The objection was that adding UNION would complicate implementation and discourage adoption"*. In the following theorem, we show that indeed the inclusion of UNION operator makes the evaluation problem for SPARQL considerably harder:

Theorem 2. EVALUATION *is NP-complete for graph pattern expressions constructed by using only* AND, FILTER *and* UNION *operators.*

We conclude this study by adding to the above fragments the OPT operator. This operator is probably the most complicated in graph pattern expressions and, definitively, the most difficult to define. The following theorem shows that the evaluation problem becomes even harder if we include the OPT operator:

Theorem 3. EVALUATION *is PSPACE-complete for graph pattern expressions.*

It is worth mentioning that in the proof of Theorem 3, we actually show that EVALUATION remains PSPACE-complete if we consider expressions without FILTER conditions, showing that the main source of complexity in SPARQL comes from the combination of UNION and OPT operators.

When verifying whether $\mu \in [\![P]\!]_D$, it is natural to assume that the size of P is considerably smaller that the size of D. This assumption is very common when studying the complexity of a query language. In fact, it is named data-complexity in the database literature [19] and it is defined as the complexity of the evaluation problem for a fixed query. More precisely, for the case of SPARQL, given a graph pattern expression P, the evaluation problem for P, denoted by EVALUATION(P), has as input an RDF dataset D and a mapping μ, and the problem is to verify whether $\mu \in [\![P]\!]_D$. From known results for the data-complexity of first-order logic [19], it is easy to deduce that:

Theorem 4. EVALUATION(P) *is in LOGSPACE for every graph pattern expression P.*

4 On the Semantics of UNION-Free Pattern Expressions

The exact semantics of graph pattern expressions has been largely discussed on the mailing list of the W3C. There seems to be two main approaches proposed to compute answers to a graph pattern expression P. The first uses an operational semantics and consists essentially in the execution of a depth-first traversal of the parse tree of P and the use of the intermediate results to avoid some computations. This approach is the one followed by ARQ [1] (a language developed by HPLabs) in the cases we test, and by the W3C when evaluating graph pattern expressions containing nested optionals [17]. For instance, the computation of the mappings satisfying (A OPT (B OPT C)) is done by first computing the mappings that match A, then checking which of these mappings match B, and for those who match B checking whether they also match C [17]. The second approach, compositional in spirit and the one we advocate here, extends classical conjunctive query evaluation [8] and is based on a bottom up evaluation of the parse tree, borrowing notions of relational algebra evaluation [3,10] plus some additional features.

As expected, there are queries for which both approaches do not coincide (see Section 4.1 for examples). However, both semantics coincide in most of the "real-life" examples. For instance, for all the queries in the W3C candidate recommendation for SPARQL, both semantics coincide [15]. Thus, a natural question is what is the exact relationship between the two approaches mentioned above and, in particular, whether there is a "natural" condition under which both approaches coincide. In this section, we address these questions: Section 4.1 formally introduces the depth-first approach, discusses some issues concerning it, and presents queries for which the two semantics do not coincide; Section 4.2 identifies a natural and simple condition under which these two semantics are equivalent; Section 4.3 defines a normal form and simple optimization procedures for patterns satisfying the condition of Section 4.2

Based on the results of Section 2.3, we concentrate in the critical fragment of UNION-free graph pattern expressions.

4.1 A Depth-First Approach to Evaluate Graph Pattern Expressions

As we mentioned earlier, one alternative to evaluate graph pattern expressions is based on a "greedy" approach that computes the mappings satisfying a graph pattern expression P by traversing the parse tree of P in a depth-first manner and using the intermediate results to avoid some computations. This evaluation includes at each stage three parameters: the dataset, the subtree pattern of P to be evaluated, and a set of mappings already collected. Formally, given an RDF dataset D, the evaluation of pattern P with the set of mappings Ω, denoted by $Eval_D(P, \Omega)$, is a recursive function defined as follows:

$Eval_D(P$: graph pattern expression, Ω: set of mappings)
    if $\Omega = \emptyset$ then return($\emptyset$)
    if P is a triple pattern t then return($\Omega \bowtie [\![t]\!]_D$)
    if $P = (P_1$ AND $P_2)$ then return $Eval_D(P_2, Eval_D(P_1, \Omega))$
    if $P = (P_1$ OPT $P_2)$ then return $Eval_D(P_1, \Omega) \boxtimes Eval_D(P_2, Eval_D(P_1, \Omega))$
    if $P = (P_1$ FILTER $R)$ then return $\{\mu \in Eval_D(P_1, \Omega) \mid \mu \models R\}$

Then, the evaluation of P against a dataset D, which we denote simply by $Eval_D(P)$, is $Eval_D(P, \{\mu_\emptyset\})$, where $\mu_\emptyset$ is the mapping with empty domain.

Example 2. Assume that $P = (t_1$ OPT $(t_2$ OPT $t_3))$, where t_1, t_2 and t_3 are triple patterns. To compute $Eval_D(P)$, we invoke function $Eval_D(P, \{\mu_\emptyset\})$. This function in turn invokes function $Eval_D(t_1, \{\mu_\emptyset\})$, which returns $[\![t_1]\!]_D$ since t_1 is a triple pattern and $[\![t_1]\!]_D \bowtie \{\mu_\emptyset\} = [\![t_1]\!]_D$, and then it invokes $Eval_D((t_2$ OPT $t_3), [\![t_1]\!]_D)$. As in the previous case, $Eval_D((t_2$ OPT $t_3), [\![t_1]\!]_D)$ first invokes $Eval_D(t_2, [\![t_1]\!]_D)$, which returns $[\![t_1]\!]_D \bowtie [\![t_2]\!]_D$ since t_2 is a triple pattern, and then it invokes $Eval_D(t_3, [\![t_1]\!]_D \bowtie [\![t_2]\!]_D)$. Since t_3 is a triple pattern, the latter invocation returns $[\![t_1]\!]_D \bowtie [\![t_2]\!]_D \bowtie [\![t_3]\!]_D$. Thus, by the definition of $Eval_D$ we have that $Eval_D((t_2$ OPT $t_3), [\![t_1]\!]_D)$ returns $([\![t_1]\!]_D \bowtie [\![t_2]\!]_D) \boxtimes ([\![t_1]\!]_D \bowtie [\![t_2]\!]_D \bowtie [\![t_3]\!]_D)$. Therefore, $Eval_D(P)$ returns

$$[\![t_1]\!]_D \boxtimes \bigl(([\![t_1]\!]_D \bowtie [\![t_2]\!]_D) \boxtimes ([\![t_1]\!]_D \bowtie [\![t_2]\!]_D \bowtie [\![t_3]\!]_D)\bigr).$$

Note that the previous result coincides with the evaluation algorithm proposed by the W3C for graph pattern $(t_1$ OPT $(t_2$ OPT $t_3))$ [17], as we first compute the mappings that match t_1, then we check which of these mappings match t_2, and for those who match t_2 we check whether they also match t_3. Also note that the result of $Eval_D(P)$ is not necessarily the same as $[\![P]\!]_D$ since $[\![(t_1$ OPT $(t_2$ OPT $t_3))]\!]_D = [\![t_1]\!]_D \boxtimes ([\![t_2]\!]_D \boxtimes [\![t_3]\!]_D)$. In Example 3 we actually show a case where the two semantics do not coincide.

Some issues in the depth-first approach. There are two relevant issues to consider when using the depth-first approach to evaluate SPARQL queries. First, this approach is not compositional. For instance, the result of $Eval_D(P)$ cannot in general be used to obtain the result of $Eval_D((P'$ OPT $P))$, or even the result of $Eval_D((P'$ AND $P))$, as $Eval_D(P)$ results from the computation of $Eval_D(P, \{\mu_\emptyset\})$ while $Eval_D((P'$ OPT $P))$ results from the computation of $\Omega = Eval_D(P', \{\mu_\emptyset\})$ and $Eval_D(P, \Omega)$. This can become a problem in cases of data integration where global answers are obtained by combining the results from several data sources; or when storing some pre–answered queries in order to obtain the results of more complex queries by composition. Second, under the depth-first approach some natural properties of widely used operators do not hold, which may confuse some users. For example, it is not always the case that $Eval_D((P_1$ AND $P_2)) = Eval_D((P_2$ AND $P_1))$, violating the commutativity of the conjunction and making the result to depend on the order of the query.

Example 3. Let D be the RDF dataset shown in Example 1 and consider the pattern $P = ((?X, $ name, paul$)$ OPT $((?Y, $ name, george$)$ OPT $(?X, $ email, $?Z)))$.

Then $[\![P]\!]_D = \{\,\{?X \to B_1\}\,\}$, that is, $[\![P]\!]_D$ contains only one mapping. On the other hand, following the recursive definition of $Eval_D$ we obtain that $Eval_D(P) = \{\,\{?X \to B_1, ?Y \to B_3\}\,\}$, which is different from $[\![P]\!]_D$.

Example 4 (Not commutativity of AND*).* Let D be the RDF dataset in Example 1, $P_1 = ((?X, \text{name}, \text{paul})$ AND $((?Y, \text{name}, \text{george})$ OPT $(?X, \text{email}, ?Z)))$ and $P_2 = (((?Y, \text{name}, \text{george})$ OPT $(?X, \text{email}, ?Z))$ AND $(?X, \text{name}, \text{paul}))$. Then $Eval_D(P_1) = \{\,\{?X \to B_1, ?Y \to B_3\}\,\}$ while $Eval_D(P_2) = \emptyset$. Using the compositional semantics, we obtain $[\![P_1]\!]_D = [\![P_2]\!]_D = \emptyset$.

Let us mention that ARQ [1] gives the same non-commutative evaluation.

4.2 A Natural Condition Ensuring $[\![P]\!]_D = Eval_D(P)$

If for a pattern P we have that $[\![P]\!]_D = Eval_D(P)$ for every RDF dataset D, then we have the best of both worlds for P as the compositional approach gives a formal semantics to P while the depth-first approach gives an efficient way of evaluating it. Thus, it is desirable to identify natural syntactic conditions on P ensuring $[\![P]\!]_D = Eval_D(P)$. In this section, we introduce one such condition.

One of the most delicate issues in the definition of a semantics for graph pattern expressions is the semantics of OPT operator. A careful examination of the conflicting examples reveals a common pattern: A graph pattern P mentions an expression $P' = (P_1$ OPT $P_2)$ and a variable $?X$ occurring both inside P_2 and outside P' but not occurring in P_1. For instance, in the graph pattern expression shown in Example 3:

$$P = ((?X, \text{name}, \text{paul}) \text{ OPT } ((?Y, \text{name}, \text{george}) \text{ OPT } (?X, \text{email}, ?Z))),$$

variable $?X$ occurs both inside the optional part of the sub-pattern $P' = ((?Y, \text{name}, \text{george})$ OPT $(?X, \text{email}, ?Z))$ and outside P' in the triple $(?X, \text{name}, \text{paul})$, but it is not mentioned in $(?Y, \text{name}, \text{george})$.

What is unnatural about graph pattern P is the fact that $(?X, \text{email}, ?Z)$ is giving optional information for $(?X, \text{name}, \text{paul})$ but in P appears as giving optional information for $(?Y, \text{name}, \text{george})$. In general, graph pattern expressions having the condition mentioned above are not natural. In fact, no queries in the W3C candidate recommendation for SPARQL [15] exhibit this condition. This motivates the following definition:

Definition 4. *A graph pattern P is* well designed *if for every occurrence of a sub-pattern $P' = (P_1$ OPT $P_2)$ of P and for every variable $?X$ occurring in P, the following condition holds:*

if $?X$ occurs both inside P_2 and outside P', then it also occurs in P_1.

Graph pattern expressions that are not well designed are shown in Examples 3 and 4. For all these patterns, the two semantics differ. The next result shows a fundamental property of well-designed graph pattern expressions, and is a welcome surprise as a very simple restriction on graph patterns allows the users of SPARQL to alternatively use any of the two semantics shown in this section:

Theorem 5. *Let D be an RDF dataset and P a well-designed graph pattern expression. Then $Eval_D(P) = [\![P]\!]_D$.*

4.3 Well-Designed Patterns and Normalization

Due to the evident similarity between certain operators of SPARQL and relational algebra, a natural question is whether the classical results of normal forms and optimization in relational algebra are applicable in the SPARQL context. The answer is not straightforward, at least for the case of optional patterns and its relational counterpoint, the left outer join. The classical results about outer join query reordering and optimization by Galindo-Legaria and Rosenthal [7] are not directly applicable in the SPARQL context because they assume constraints on the relational queries that are rarely found in SPARQL. The first and more problematic issue, is the assumption on predicates used for joining (outer joining) relations to be *null-rejecting* [7]. In SPARQL, those predicates are implicit in the variables that the graph patterns share and by the definition of compatible mappings they are never *null-rejecting*. In [7] the queries are also enforced not to contain Cartesian products, situation that occurs often in SPARQL when joining graph patterns that do not share variables. Thus, specific techniques must be developed in the SPARQL context.

In what follows we show that the property of a pattern being well designed has important consequences for the study of normalization and optimization for a fragment of SPARQL queries. We will restrict in this section to graph patterns without FILTER.

Proposition 2. *Given a well-designed graph pattern P, if the left hand sides of the following equations are sub-patterns of P, then:*

$$(P_1 \text{ AND } (P_2 \text{ OPT } P_3)) \equiv ((P_1 \text{ AND } P_2) \text{ OPT } P_3), \qquad (2)$$

$$((P_1 \text{ OPT } P_2) \text{ OPT } P_3) \equiv ((P_1 \text{ OPT } P_3) \text{ OPT } P_2). \qquad (3)$$

Moreover, in both equivalences, if one replaces in P the left hand side by the right hand side, then the resulting pattern is still well designed.

From this proposition plus associativity and commutativity of AND, it follows:

Theorem 6. *Every well-designed graph pattern P is equivalent to a pattern in the following normal form:*

$$(\cdots (t_1 \text{ AND } \cdots \text{ AND } t_k) \text{ OPT } O_1) \text{ OPT } O_2) \cdots) \text{ OPT } O_n), \qquad (4)$$

where each t_i is a triple pattern, $n \geq 0$ and each O_j has the same form (4).

The proof of the theorem is based on term rewriting techniques. The next example shows the benefits of using the above normal form.

Example 5. Consider dataset D of Example 1 and well-designed pattern $P = ((((?X, \text{name}, ?Y) \text{ OPT } (?X, \text{email}, ?E)) \text{ AND } (?X, \text{phone}, 888\text{-}4537))$. The normalized form of P is $P' = ((((?X, \text{name}, ?Y) \text{ AND } (?X, \text{phone}, 888\text{-}4537)) \text{ OPT } (?X, \text{email}, ?E))$. The advantage of evaluating P' over P follows from a simple counting of maps.

Two examples of implicit use of the normal form. There are implementations (not ARQ[1]) that do not permit nested optionals, and when evaluating a pattern they first evaluate all patterns that are outside optionals and then *extend* the results with the matchings of patterns inside optionals. That is, they are implicitly using the normal form mentioned above. In [3], when evaluating a graph pattern with relational algebra, a similar assumption is made. First the join of all triple patterns is evaluated, and then the optional patterns are taken into account. Again, this is an implicit use of the normal form.

5 Related Work and Conclusions

Related Work. A rich source on the intended semantics of the constructors of SPARQL are the discussions around W3C document [15], which is still in the stage of Candidate Recommendation. Nevertheless, systematic and comprehensive approaches to define the semantics are not present, and most of the discussion is based on use cases.

In [15], in defining the semantics of SPARQL a notion of entailment is introduced with the idea of making the definition generic enough to support notions more general than simple entailment (e.g. OWL entailment [14], etc.). Current developments of the W3C (August 2006) have not settled yet this issue. What is clear consensus is that in the case of simple RDF any definition should coincide with subgraph matching, which is the approach followed in this paper.

Cyganiak [3] presents a relational model of SPARQL. The author uses relational algebra operators (join, left outer join, projection, selection, etc.) to model SPARQL SELECT clauses. The central idea in [3] is to make a correspondence between SPARQL queries and relational algebra queries over a single relation $T(S, P, O)$. Indeed a translation system between SPARQL and SQL is outlined. The system needs extensive use of COALESCE and IS NULL operations to resemble SPARQL features. The relational algebra operators and their semantics in [3] are similar to our operators and have similar syntactic and semantic issues. With different motivations, but similar philosophy, Harris [10] presents an implementation of SPARQL queries in a relational database engine. He uses relational algebra operators similar to [3]. This line of work, which models the semantics of SPARQL based on the semantics of some relational operators, seems to be very influent in the decisions on the W3C semantics of SPARQL.

De Bruin et al. [4] address the definition of mapping for SPARQL from a logical point of view. It slightly differs from the definition in [15] on the issue of blank nodes. Although De Bruin et al.'s definition allows blank nodes in graph patterns, it is similar to our definition which does not allow blanks in patterns. In their approach, these blanks play the role of "non-distinguished" variables, that is, variables which are not presented in the answer.

Franconi and Tessaris [5], in an ongoing work on the semantics of SPARQL, formally define the solution for a basic graph pattern (an RDF graph with variables) as a set of partial functions. They also consider RDF datasets and several forms of RDF–entailment. Finally, they propose high level operators (*Join*,

Optional, etc.) that take set of mappings and give set of mappings, but currently they do not have formal definitions for them, stating only their types.

There are several works on the semantics of RDF query languages which tangentially touch the issues addressed by SPARQL. Gutierrez et al. [8] discuss the basic issues of the semantics and complexity of a conjunctive query language for RDF with basic patterns which underlies the basic evaluation approach of SPARQL. Haase et al. [9] present a comparison of functionalities of pre-SPARQL query languages, many of which served as inspiration for the constructs of SPARQL. Nevertheless, there is no formal semantics involved.

The idea of having an algebraic query language for RDF is not new. In fact, there are several proposals. Chen et al. [2] present a set of operators for manipulating RDF graphs, Frasincar et al. [6] study algebraic operators on the lines of the RQL query language, and Robertson [16] introduces an algebra of triadic relations for RDF. Although they evidence the power of having an algebraic approach to query RDF, the frameworks presented in each of these works makes not evident how to model with them the constructors of SPARQL.

Finally Serfiotis et al. [18] study RDFS query fragments using a logical framework, presenting results on the classical database problems of containment and minimization of queries for a model of RDF/S. They concentrate on patterns using the RDF/S vocabulary of classes and properties in conjunctive queries, making the overlap with our fragment and approach almost empty.

Concluding remarks. The query language SPARQL is in the process of standardization, and in this process the semantics of the language plays a key role. A formalization of a semantics will be beneficial on several grounds: help identify relationships among the constructors that stay hidden in the use cases, identify redundant and contradicting notions, study the expressiveness and complexity of the language, help in optimization, etc.

In this paper, we provided such a formal semantics for the graph pattern matching facility, which is the core of SPARQL. We isolated a fragment which is rich enough to present the main issues and favor a good formalization. We presented a formal semantics, made observations to the current syntax based on it, and proved several properties of it. We did a complexity analysis showing that unlimited used of OPT could lead to high complexity, namely PSPACE. We presented an alternative formal procedural semantics which closely resembles the one used by most developers. We proved that under simple syntactic restrictions both semantics are equivalent, thus having the advantages of a formal compositional semantics and the efficiency of a procedural semantics. Finally, we discussed optimization based on relational algebra and show limitations based on features of SPARQL. On these lines, we presented optimizations based on normal forms.

The approach followed in this paper for simple RDF can be extended to RDFS using the method proposed in [8], which introduces the notion of normal form for RDF graphs. This notion can be used to extend to RDFS the graph-theoretic characterization of simple RDF entailment. Then by replacing an RDF graph by its unique normal form, all the semantic results of this paper are preserved. Further work should include the extension of this approach to typed literals.

Acknowledgments. Pérez is supported by Dirección de Investigación, Universidad de Talca, Arenas by FONDECYT 1050701, and Arenas and Gutierrez by Millennium Nucleus Center for Web Research, P04-067-F, Mideplan, Chile.

References

1. *ARQ - A SPARQL Processor for Jena*, version 1.3 March 2006, Hewlett-Packard Development Company. http://jena.sourceforge.net/ARQ.
2. L. Chen, A. Gupta and M. E. Kurul. *A Semantic-aware RDF Query Algebra*. In *COMAD* 2005.
3. R. Cyganiak. *A Relational Algebra for Sparql*. HP-Labs Technical Report, HPL-2005-170. http://www.hpl.hp.com/techreports/2005/HPL-2005-170.html.
4. J. de Bruijn, E. Franconi, S. Tessaris. *Logical Reconstruction of normative RDF*. In *OWLED 2005*, Galway, Ireland, November 2005
5. E. Franconi and S. Tessaris. *The Sematics of SPARQL*. Working Draft 2 November 2005. http://www.inf.unibz.it/krdb/w3c/sparql/.
6. F. Frasincar, C. Houben, R. Vdovjak and P. Barna. *RAL: An algebra for querying RDF*. In *WISE 2002*.
7. C. A. Galindo-Legaria and A. Rosenthal. *Outerjoin Simplification and Reordering for Query Optimization*. In *TODS* 22(1): 43–73, 1997.
8. C. Gutierrez, C. Hurtado and A. Mendelzon. *Foundations of Semantic Web Databases*. In *PODS 2004*, pages 95–106.
9. P. Haase, J. Broekstra, A. Eberhart and R. Volz. *A Comparison of RDF Query Languages*. In *ISWC 2004*, pages 502–517.
10. S. Harris. *Sparql query processing with conventional relational database systems*. In *SSWS 2005*.
11. G. Klyne, J. J. Carroll and B. McBride. *Resource Description Framework (RDF): Concepts and Abstract Syntax*. W3C Rec. 10 February 2004. http://www.w3.org/TR/rdf-concepts/.
12. F. Manola, E. Miller, B. McBride. *RDF Primer*, W3C Rec. 10 February 2004.
13. D. Marin. *RDF Formalization*, Santiago de Chile, 2004. Tech. Report Univ. Chile, TR/DCC-2006-8. http://www.dcc.uchile.cl/~cgutierr/ftp/draltan.pdf
14. Peter Patel-Schneider, Patrick Hayes and Ian Horrocks. *OWL Web Ontology Language Semantics and Abstract Syntax*. W3C Recommendation 10 February 2004, http://www.w3.org/TR/owl-semantics/.
15. E. Prud'hommeaux and A. Seaborne. *SPARQL Query Language for RDF*. W3C Candidate Rec. 6 April 2006. http://www.w3.org/TR/rdf-sparql-query/.
16. E. L. Robertson. *Triadic Relations: An Algebra for the Semantic Web*. In *SWDB 2004*, pages 91–108
17. A. Seaborne. *Personal Communication*. April 13, 2006.
18. G. Serfiotis, I. Koffina, V. Christophides and V. Tannen. *Containment and Minimization of RDF/S Query Patterns*. In *ISWC 2005*, pages 607–623.
19. M. Vardi. *The Complexity of Relational Query Languages (Extended Abstract)*. In *STOC 1982*, pages 137–146.

Ontology-Driven Automatic Entity Disambiguation in Unstructured Text

Joseph Hassell, Boanerges Aleman-Meza, and I. Budak Arpinar

Large Scale Distributed Information Systems (LSDIS) Lab
Computer Science Department, University of Georgia
Athens, GA 30602-7404, USA
{hassell, boanerg, budak}@cs.uga.edu

Abstract. Precisely identifying entities in web documents is essential for document indexing, web search and data integration. Entity disambiguation is the challenge of determining the correct entity out of various candidate entities. Our novel method utilizes background knowledge in the form of a populated ontology. Additionally, it does not rely on the existence of any structure in a document or the appearance of data items that can provide strong evidence, such as email addresses, for disambiguating person names. Originality of our method is demonstrated in the way it uses different relationships in a document as well as from the ontology to provide clues in determining the correct entity. We demonstrate the applicability of our method by disambiguating names of researchers appearing in a collection of DBWorld posts using a large scale, real-world ontology extracted from the DBLP bibliography website. The precision and recall measurements provide encouraging results.

Keywords: Entity disambiguation, ontology, semantic web, DBLP, DBWorld.

1 Introduction

A significant problem with the World Wide Web today is that there is no explicit semantic information about the data and objects being presented in the web pages. Most of the content encoded in HTML format serves its purpose of describing the presentation of the information to be displayed to human users. HTML lacks the ability to semantically express or indicate that specific pieces of content refer to real-world named entities or concepts. For instance, if "George Bush" is mentioned on a web page, there is no way for a computer to identify which "George Bush" the document is referring to or even if "George Bush" is the name of a person.

The Semantic Web aims at solving this problem by providing an underlying mechanism to add semantic metadata on any content, such as web pages. However, an issue that the Semantic Web currently faces is that there is not enough semantically annotated web content available. The addition of semantic metadata can be in the form of an explicit relationship from each appearance of named entities within a document to some identifier or reference to the entity itself. The architecture of the Semantic Web relies upon URIs [4] for this purpose. Examples of this would be the entity "UGA" pointing to http://www.uga.edu and "George Bush" pointing to a URL of his official web page at the White House. However, more benefit can be obtained by referring to actual entities of an ontology where such entities would be related to concepts and/or other entities. The problem that arises is that of entity disambiguation, which is concerned with determining the right entity within a document out of various possibilities due to same syntactical name match. For example, "A. Joshi" is ambiguous due to various real-world entities (i.e. computer scientists) having the same name.

Entity disambiguation is an important research area within Computer Science. The more information that is gathered and merged, the more important it is for this information to accurately reflect the objects they are referring to. It is a challenge in part due to the difficulty of exploiting, or lack of background knowledge about the entities involved. If a human is asked to determine the correct entities mentioned within a document, s/he would have to rely upon some background knowledge accumulated over time from other documents, experiences, etc. The research problem that we are addressing is how to exploit background knowledge for entity disambiguation, which is quite complicated particularly when the only available information is an initial and last name of a person. In fact, this type of information is already available on the World Wide Web in databases, ontologies or other forms of knowledge bases. Our method utilizes background knowledge stored in the form of an ontology to pinpoint, with high accuracy, the correct object in the ontology that a document refers to. Consider a web page with a "Call for Papers" announcement where various researchers are listed as part of the Program Committee. The name of each of them can be linked to their respective homepage or other known identifiers maintained elsewhere, such as the DBLP bibliography server. Our approach for entity disambiguation is targeted at solving this type of problem, as opposed to entity disambiguation in databases which aims at determining similarity of attributes from different database schemas to be merged and identifying which record instances refer to the same entity (e.g., [7]).

The contributions of our work are two-fold: (1) a novel method to disambiguate entities within unstructured text by using clues in the text and exploiting metadata from an ontology; (2) an implementation of our method that uses a very large, real-world ontology to demonstrate effective entity disambiguation in the domain of Computer Science researchers. According to our knowledge, our method is the first work of its type to exploit an ontology and use relations within this ontology to recognize entities without relying on structure of the document. We show that our method can determine the correct entities mentioned in a document with high accuracy by comparing to a manually created and disambiguated dataset.

2 Dataset

Our dataset consists of two parts. First, an ontology created from the DBLP bibliography [14] and a corpus of DBWorld documents [6] that we use to evaluate our system. We chose the DBLP dataset because it is a rich source of information in the Computer Science domain and DBWorld because it contains documents which include names of people that typically exist in DBLP.

2.1 DBLP

Our goal is to demonstrate real-world applicability of our approach. Therefore, we chose to use data from the DBLP bibliography site (which has been around since the

1980's). This is a web site that contains bibliographic information for computer science researchers, journals and proceedings. Currently, it indexes more than 725,000 articles and contains a few thousand links to home pages of computer scientists. Conveniently, the site provides two XML files that contain most of the information stored in its servers. One of the files contains objects such as authors, proceedings and journals. The other file contains lists of papers usually organized by tracks or sessions of the conference or workshop where they were presented. We have taken the former and converted it into RDF. The resulting RDF is very large, approximately one and a half gigabytes. It contains 3,079,414 entities and 447,121 of these are authors from around the world. Table 1 lists the classes with the most instances.

Table 1. Instances of classes in DBLP ontology

Authors	447,121
Journal Articles	262,562
Articles in Proceedings	445,530

The conversion to RDF was designed to create entities out of peoples' names, instead of treating the names as literal values being part of the metadata of a publication. For this reason, we did not make use of other available RDF-converted data of DBLP (e.g., http://www.semanticweb.org/library/#dblp). Additionally, the data in RDF is enriched by adding relationships to affiliations (i.e., universities) and research topics for researchers. For further details see http://lsdis.cs.uga.edu/projects/semdis/swetodblp/.

2.2 DBWorld

DBWorld is a mailing list of information for upcoming conferences related to the databases field. Although it does contain some random post about open positions, etc., we are only interested in postings about conferences, workshops, and symposiums.

We created an HTML scraper that visits the DBWorld site and downloads only the posts that contain "Call for Papers", "Call for Participation" or "CFP" in the subject. Our system disambiguates the people listed in these postings and provides a URI to the corresponding entity in the ontology.

A DBWorld post typically contains an introduction, topics of interest, important dates and a list of committee members. The general layout of the DBWorld post is rarely consistent in terms of its structure. For example, sometimes the participants of a conference are listed with their school or company affiliation and sometimes they are listed along with the name of a country.

3 Approach

In our approach, different relationships in the ontology provide clues for determining the correct entity out of various possible matches. Figure 1 provides an overview of the main modules in our approach. We argue that rich semantic metadata representations allow a variety of ways to describe a resource. We characterize several relationship types that we identified and explain how they contribute towards the disambiguation process. As mentioned, we use the scenario of disambiguating researchers by their names appearing in DBWorld postings. However, we believe that the following relationship types are applicable to other scenarios (such as disambiguating actor names in movie reviews).

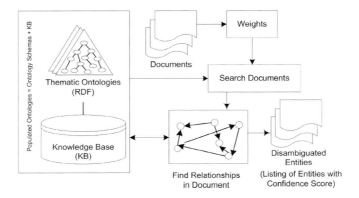

Fig. 1. Overview of the Main Modules for Entity Disambiguation

3.1 Entity Names

An ontology contains a variety of concepts and instance data. The first step of our approach is specifying which entities from a populated ontology are to be spotted in text and later disambiguated. To do this, it is necessary to indicate which literal property is the one that contains the 'name' of entities to be spotted. In most cases, such a literal property would be 'rdfs:label.' However, in some cases, additional 'name' properties may need to be listed, such as aliases and alternate names. Additionally, a different ontology may have its own way of representing the name for each entity.

3.2 Text-Proximity Relationships

Various relationships contain metadata that can be expected to be in 'text-proximity' of the entity to be disambiguated. For example, affiliation data commonly appears near names of researchers in DBWorld posts. Hence, when the known affiliation (from the ontology) appears near an entity, there is an increased likelihood that this entity is the correct entity that the text refers to. This 'nearness' is measured by the number of space characters between two objects. Figure 2 illustrates an example where the affiliation "Stanford University" appears next to the entity of interest, "Michael Kassoff", whose known affiliation is "Stanford University" according to the populated DBLP ontology. We acknowledge the fact that the *up to date* status of an ontology can have an impact on the quality of disambiguation results yet measuring the degree of such impact is outside the scope of this paper.

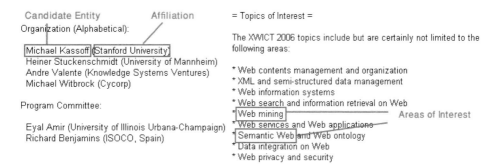

Fig. 2. Snippet from a DBWorld post   **Fig. 3.** Snippet from the same post in Figure 2

3.3 Text Co-occurrence Relationships

Text co-occurrence relationships are similar to text-proximity relationships with the exception that 'proximity' is not relevant. For example, the intuition of using affiliation data is applicable as long as it appears 'near' a person entity, but it would not be relevant if it appears somewhere else in the text because it could be the affiliation of a different person (or referring to something else). Text co-occurrence relationships are intended to specify data items that, when appearing in the same document, provide clues about the correct entity being referred in the text. For example, in DBWorld posts, the listed 'topics' fit the idea of text co-occurrence relationships. Figure 3 shows a portion of the same document in Figure 2, where "Web mining" and "Semantic Web" are spotted and are both areas of interest that match research topics related to "Michael Kassoff." Thus, by specifying the text co-occurrence relationship, specific metadata contained in the ontology helps disambiguate the correct person, depending on the topics mentioned in the text.

It is important to mention that this co-occurrence relationship is applicable only on well focused content. That is, if a document contains multiple DBWorld postings then its content could bring 'noise' and negatively impact the results of the disambiguation process. In such cases, it may be necessary to perform a text-segmentation process [9] to separate and deal with specific subparts of a document.

3.4 Popular Entities

The intuition behind using popular entities is to bias the right entity to be the one having more occurrences of 'popular' relationships (specified in advance). For example, researchers listed in Program Committees of DBWorld posts typically have a high number of publications. An 'author' relationship specified as popular can bias the candidate entities with many publications to be the right entity. For example, the abbreviated name "A. Joshi" matches up to 20 entities in DBLP but only a couple of such researchers have more than 70 papers published. The usage of this type of relationship for entity-disambiguation would depend on whether it is applicable for a given domain.

3.5 Semantic Relationships

Semantic relationships are intended to consider relationships that go beyond metadata which consists of literal values, such as syntactical matching of peoples' names [5]. For example, researchers are related to other researchers by means of their collaboration network. Researchers are also closely related to their co-authors and other authors through complex relationships. In DBWorld posts, it is common that the persons listed have relationships among themselves within a list of accepted papers and/or program committee members of a conference. Thus, the semantic relationship helps with determining the correct entity being referred in the text.

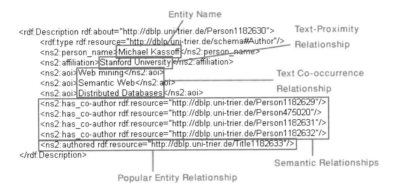

Fig. 4. Sample RDF object

In Figure 4, we present a part of our DBLP RDF file, which is an input to the system for entity disambiguation. In this example, the entity's name is "Michael Kassoff" who is affiliated with "Stanford University" and has authored one paper. The author has three areas of interest and is related to four other authors via semantic relationships described above (e.g., has_co-author).

4 Algorithm

In this section, we describe our method for disambiguating entities in unstructured text. Figure 5 explains the steps of our method using pseudocode. The general idea is to spot entity names in text and then assign each potential match a confidence score. The confidence score for each ambiguous entity is adjusted based on whether existing information of the entity from the ontology matches accordingly to the relationship types found in the ontology as explained in the previous section. Throughout this paper, we will use *cf* to represent the initial confidence score, *acf* to represent the initial, abbreviated confidence score, *pr* to represent proximity score, *co* to represent text co-occurrence score, *sr* to represent the semantic relationship score and *pe* to represent the popular entity score. These variables are adjustable to capture the relative importance of each factor in the disambiguation process.

```
Algorithm. Disambiguation( ) {
  for (each entity in ontology) {
    if (entity found in document) {
      create 'candidate entity'
        $c_s$ for 'candidate entity' ← cf / (entities in ontology)
    }
  }
  for (each 'candidate entity') {
    search for 'candidate entity's text proximity relationship
    if (text proximity relationship found near 'candidate entity'){
      $c_s$ for 'candidate entity' ← $c_s$ for 'candidate entity' + pr
    }
    search for 'candidate entity's text co-occurrence relationship
    if (text co-occurrence relationship found) {
      $c_s$ for 'candidate entity' ← $c_s$ for 'candidate entity' + co
    }
    if (ten or more popular entity relationships exist){
    {
      $c_s$ for 'candidate entity' ← $c_s$ for 'candidate entity' + pe
    }
  }
  iterate ← false
  while (iterate == true) {
    iterate ← true
    for (each 'candidate entity') {
      search for semantic relationships in the ontology to other 'candidate entities'
      for (each relation found that has not been seen AND
          target entity $c_s$ is above 'threshold') {
        $c_s$ for 'candidate entity' ← $c_s$ for 'candidate entity' + sr
        mark relation as seen
        if ('candidate entity' score has risen above 'threshold') {
          iterate ← false
}}}}}
```

Fig. 5. Algorithm pseudocode

4.1 Spotting Entity Names

The first step in our algorithm consists of spotting (within a document) the *names* of the entities to be disambiguated (see Section 3.1). The system only looks for entity-names of the ontology. Each entity name found in the document is a potential match for one or more entities in the populated ontology. Each of the entities of the ontology that matches a name becomes a *candidate entity*. A confidence score is initially assigned to each candidate entity depending on how many of them match the same name. The formula for assigning this confidence score (c_s) is as follows.

$$e_s = \frac{cf}{\text{Number of entities with the same label}} \qquad (1)$$

Techniques for spotting person names can be as simple as regular expressions that find anything that looks like a person name (e.g., two words having their first letter capitalized). We did not choose this type of techniques to avoid spotting irrelevant information, which would have had to be filtered out later. Our technique for spotting simply uses the known names of entities from the ontology and looks for them in the text (we were not very concerned with time-efficiency of this step in our prototype implementation). In addition to spotting based on name, this step also looks for abbreviated names, such as "A. Joshi". This type of entities gets a e_s that is initialized differently to reflect the fact that many more entities from the ontology can syntactically match to the same name. The formula for assigning this confidence score in this case is as follows.

$$e_s = \frac{acf}{\text{Number of related entities in the ontology}} \qquad (2)$$

The consideration for abbreviated names is a feature that can be turned on or off. We found that it is suitable for use with peoples' names yet we did not explore further considerations such as canonical names (i.e., Tim and Timothy) and other techniques for name matching [5, 13, 19].

4.2 Spotting Literal Values of Text-Proximity Relationships

The second step of our algorithm consists of spotting literal values based on *text-proximity* relationships (see Section 3.2). In order to narrow down the search for such literals, only the candidate entities found in the previous step are considered when determining literal values of text-proximity relationships to be spotted. By checking the ontology, it is then possible to determine whether a candidate entity appears near one of the spotted literal values based on text-proximity relationships, such as a known affiliation of a person appearing within a predefined window of the person name. We argue that this type of evidence is a strong indication that it might be the right entity. Hence, the confidence-score of an entity is increased substantially. Figure 2 shows an example where the affiliation is a highly relevant hint for the disambiguation of the candidate entity "Michael Kassoff."

4.3 Spotting Literal Values of Text Co-occurrence Relationships

This step consists of spotting literal values based on *text co-occurrence* relationships (see Section 3.3). For every candidate entity, if one of its literal values considering text co-occurrence relationships is found within the document, its confidence score is increased. In our DBLP dataset, this step finds literal values appearing in the document based on the relationship 'aoi' which contains areas of interest of a researcher. For example, in Figure 3 "Web mining" and "Semantic Web" are spotted as *areas of interest* that match those of candidate entities. Thus, any candidate entity having such areas of interest receives an increase on its disambiguation e_s.

4.4 Using Popular Entities

The degree of popularity among the candidate entities is considered to adjust the c_s of candidate entities (see Section 3.4). The intention is to slightly increase the c_s for those entities that, according to the ontology, have many relationships that were predefined as popular (e.g. authored). In the scenario of DBWorld posts, this step slightly increases the score of candidate entities that have many publications as indicated in the ontology (as it is more likely that they would be listed in Program Committees). We acknowledge that this step may not be applicable in all domains. However, we found that it is a useful tie-breaker for candidate entities that have the same c_s.

4.5 Using Semantic Relationships

This step goes beyond just using literal values as evidence for disambiguating entities. The intuition is to use relationships to create a propagation or network effect that can increase the c_s of candidate entities based on *semantic* relationships (see Section 3.5). In the scenario of disambiguating researchers in DBWorld posts, this step considers whether the candidate entities have co-authorship relationships and increases the c_s for the ones that do. Such c_s adjustments can only be done fairly by starting with the candidate entities having the highest score so far. Each candidate entity with a high score is analyzed through its semantic relationships in the ontology to increase the score of other candidate entities whenever they are connected through the ontology. On the other hand, it may not be necessary to perform this analysis on candidate entities with very low c_s. To deal with this issue, our algorithm uses a *threshold* c_s, which can be customized. Additionally, the process of adjusting c_s is repeated if at least one candidate entity gets its c_s increased over such threshold. Any such entity could then help boost the c_s of remaining candidate entities with low scores until no more adjustments to c_s take place. Thus, this step is iterative and always converges.

```
<entity>
    <uri>http://www.informatik.uni-trier.de/~ley/db/indices/a-tree/k/Kassoff:Michael.html</uri>
    <entityName>Michael Kassoff</entityName>
    <confidence>90</confidence>
    <charOffset>5688, 5703</charOffset>
</entity>

<entity>
    <uri>http://www.informatik.uni-trier.de/~ley/db/indices/a-tree/s/Schroeder:Michael.html</uri>
    <entityName>Michael Schroeder</entityName>
    <confidence>100</confidence>
    <charOffset>16241, 16259</charOffset>
</entity>

<entity>
    <uri>http://www.informatik.uni-trier.de/~ley/db/indices/a-tree/s/Schroeder_0002:Michael.html</uri>
    <entityName>Michael Schroeder</entityName>
    <confidence>45</confidence>
    <charOffset>16241, 16259</charOffset>
</entity>
```

Fig. 6. Sample Output of Spotted Entities with their Disambiguation Score

4.6 Output

As shown in Figure 6, we have chosen to output our results in XML format because of its universally accepted syntax. For each entity found in the document and the ontology, we output its URI, name, confidence score and character offset. The URI of each entity represents the DBLP web page containing information regarding it. The name is the literal found in the documents and the character offset is the location of the entity within the document.

5 Evaluation

We chose to evaluate our method for entity disambiguation using a golden standard, which we created manually and we will refer to as *disambiguated dataset*. This dataset consists of 20 documents from DBWorld. For the purpose of having a representative dataset, the documents were chosen by first picking a random DBWorld announcement and the 19 next documents, as they were posted in chronological order. Each document was processed manually by inspecting peoples' names. For each person's name, we added a link to its corresponding DBLP web page, which we use in the ontology as the URI that uniquely identifies a researcher. Ideally, every DBWorld post would have a golden standard representation but this does not exist because it is extremely time consuming to create. By creating this disambiguated dataset, it is possible to evaluate our method's results and measure precision and recall.

We use a set A as the set of unique names identified using the disambiguated dataset and a set B as the set of entities found by our method. The intersection of these sets represents the set of entities correctly identified by our method. We measured precision as the proportion of correctly identified entities with regard to B. We measured recall as the proportion of correctly disambiguated entities with regard to A.

$$Precision = \frac{sizeof(A \cap B)}{sizeof(B)} \quad (3)$$

$$Recall = \frac{sizeof(A \cap B)}{sizeof(A)} \quad (4)$$

Our method computes the c_s of candidate entities using weights for the different disambiguation aspects in Section 4. These weights are part of input settings that allow fine tuning depending on the domain and importance of available relationships in a given ontology. We adjusted the settings so that an entity's affiliation and relations (co-authorship) to other researchers is considered far more valuable than the areas of interest of the researcher. Table 2 lists the assignments that produced the most accurate results when running our test data.

Within our golden standard set of documents, we were able to find 758 entities that have representations in our ontology. In the 20 documents of our disambiguated-set, only 17 person names were not represented in the DBLP ontology. These mainly consisted of local organizers and researchers listed in cross-disciplinary conferences.

Table 2. Values of Input Settings used in the Evaluation

Description	Variable	Value
charOffset		50
Text proximity relationships	*pr*	50
Text co-occurrence relationships	*co*	10
Popular entity score	*pe*	10
Semantic relationship	*sr*	20
Initial confidence score	*cf*	90
Initial abbreviated confidence score	*acf*	70
Threshold	*threshold*	90

When comparing the results of our method with the disambiguated-set, our method was able to find 620 entities. Only 18 of these were incorrectly disambiguated. We calculated the precision to be 97.1 percent and recall to be 79.6 percent. Table 3 is a summary of our results.

Table 3. Precision and Recall

Correct Disambiguation	Found Entities	Total Entities	Precision	Recall
602	620	758	97.1%	79.4%

Figure 7 illustrates the precision and recall evaluation on a per document basis. The document numbers coincide with our golden standard set available at http://lsdis.cs.uga.edu/~aleman/research/dbworlddis/. The precision is quite accurate in most cases and the recall varies from document to document.

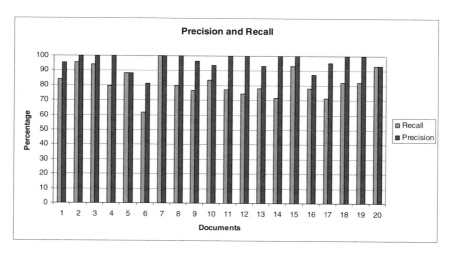

Fig. 7. Measures of Precision and Recall in a per-document basis

There are several situations where our method did not disambiguate the correct entity. This was mostly due to the ontology which, although largely populated, does not have complete coverage. For example, some of the authors within the ontology have only one relationship to a paper while some authors have a variety of relationships to papers, other authors, affiliation, etc. Because of this, it was not possible to precisely disambiguate some entities. Another error that is common is the situation where we find an entity's name that matches a portion of the name of another entity. We provide some safeguards against this as long as both of the candidate entities exist in the ontology, but the algorithm still misses in a few cases.

6 Related Work

Research on the problem of entity disambiguation has taken place using a variety of techniques. Some techniques only work on structured parts of a document. The applicability of disambiguating peoples' names is evident when finding citations within documents. Han et al [13] provides an assessment of several techniques used to disambiguate citations within a document. These methods use string similarity techniques and do not consider various candidate entities that may have the same name.

Our method differs from other approaches by a few important features. First, our method performs well on unstructured text. Second, by exploiting background knowledge in the form of a populated ontology, the process of spotting entities within the text is more focused and reduces the need for string similarity computations. Third, our method does not require any training data, as all of the data that is necessary for disambiguation is straightforward and provided in the ontology. Last but not least, our method exploits the capability provided by relationships among entities in the ontology to go beyond techniques traditionally based on syntactical matches.

The iterative step in our work is similar in spirit to a recent work on entity reconciliation [8]. In such an approach, the results of disambiguated entities are propagated to other ambiguous entities, which could then be reconciled based on recently reconciled entities. That method is part of a Personal Information Management system that works with a user's desktop environment to facilitate access and querying of a user's email address book, personal word documents, spreadsheets, etc. Thus, it makes use of predictable structures such as fields that contain known types of data (i.e., emails, dates and person names) whereas in our method we do not make any assumptions about the structure of the text. This is a key difference as the characteristics of the data to be disambiguated pose different challenges. Our method uses an ontology and runs on un-structured text, an approach that theirs does not consider.

Citation matching is a related problem aiming at deciding the right citation referring to a publication [11]. In our work, we do not assume the existence of citation information such as publication venue and date. However, we believe that our method is a significant step to the Identity Uncertainty problem [16] by automatically determining unique identifiers for person names with respect to a populated ontology.

KIM is an application that aims to be an automatic ontology population system that runs over text documents to provide content for the Semantic Web [17]. The KIM platform has many components that are unrelated to our work but within these components, there is an entity recognition portion. KIM disambiguates entities within a document by using a natural language processor and then attempts to index these entities. The evaluation of the KIM system is done by comparing the results to human-annotated corpora, much like our method of evaluation.

The SCORE system for management of semantic metadata (and data extraction) also contains a component for resolving ambiguities [18]. SCORE uses associations from a knowledgebase to determine the best match from candidate entities but detailed implementation is not available from this commercial system.

In ESpotter, named entities are recognized using a lexicon and/or atterns [20]. Ambiguities are resolved by using the URI of the webpage to determine the most likely domain of the term (probabilities are computed using hit count of search-engine results). The main difference with our work is our method uses only named entities within the domain of a specific populated ontology.

Finally, our approach is different to that of disambiguating word senses [2, 12, 15]. Instead, our focus is to disambiguate named entities such as peoples' names, which has recently gained attention for its applicability in Social Networks [3, 1]. Thus, instead of exploiting homonymy, synonymy, etc., our method works on relationships that real-world entities have such as affiliation of a researcher and his/her topics.

7 Conclusions

We proposed a new ontology-driven solution to the entity disambiguation problem in unstructured text. In particular, our method uses relationships between entities in the ontology to go beyond traditional syntactic-based disambiguation techniques. The output of our method consists of a list of spotted entity names, each with an entity disambiguation score e_s. We demonstrated the effectiveness of our approach through evaluations against a manually disambiguated document set containing over 700 entities. This evaluation was performed over DBWorld announcements using an ontology created from DBLP (consisting of over one million entities). The results of this evaluation lead us to claim that our method has successfully demonstrated its applicability to scenarios involving real-world data. To the best of our knowledge, this work is among the first which successfully uses a large, populated ontology for identifying entities in text without relying on the structure of the text.

In future work, we plan to integrate the results of entity disambiguation into a more robust platform such as UIMA [10]. The work we presented can be combined with other existing work so that the results may be more useful in certain scenarios. For example, the results of entity-disambiguation can be included within a document using initiatives such as Microformats (microformats.org) and RDFa (w3.org/TR/xhtml-rdfa-primer/).

Acknowledgments. This work is funded by NSF-ITR-IDM Award#0325464 (SemDIS: Discovering Complex Relationships in the Semantic Web).

References

1. Aleman-Meza, B., Nagarajan, M., Ramakrishnan, C., Ding, L., Kolari, P., Sheth, A., Arpinar, I. B., Joshi, A., Finin, T.: Semantic Analytics on Social Networks: Experiences in Addressing the Problem of Conflict of Interest Detection. *15th International World Wide Web Conference,* Edinburgh, Scotland (May 23-26, 2006)

2. Basili, R., Rocca, M. D., Pazienza, M. T.: Contextual Word Sense Tuning and Disambiguation. *Applied Artificial Intelligence*, 11(3) (1997) 235-262
3. Bekkerman, R., McCallum, A.: Disambiguating Web Appearances of People in a Social Network. *14th International World Wide Web Conference*, Chiba, Japan, (2005) 463-470
4. Berners-Lee, T., Fielding R., Masinter, L.: Uniform Resource Identifier (URI): Generic Syntax. *RFC 3986, IETF,* (2005)
5. Bilenko, M., Mooney, R., Cohen, W., Ravikumar, P., Fienberg, S.: Adaptive Name Matching in Information Integration. *IEEE Intelligent Systems*, 18(5). (2003) 16-23
6. DBWorld. http://www.cs.wisc.edu/dbworld/ April 9, 2006
7. Dey, D., Sarkar, S., De, P.: A Distance-Based Approach to Entity Reconciliation in Heterogeneous Databases. *IEEE Transactions on Knowledge and Data Engineering*, 14(3) (May 2002) 567-582
8. Dong, X. L., Halevy, A., Madhaven, J.: Reference Reconciliation in Complex Information Spaces. *Proc. of SIGMOD*, Baltimore, MD. (2005)
9. Embley, D. W., Jiang, Y. S., Ng, Y.: Record-Boundary Discovery in Web Documents. *Proc. of SIGMOD*, Philadelphia, Pennsylvania (1999) 467-478
10. Ferrucci, D., Lally, A.: UIMA: An Architectural Approach to Unstructured Information Processing in the Corporate Research Environment. *Natural Language Engineering*, 10(3-4) (2004) 327-348
11. Giles, C.L., Bollacker, K.D., Lawrence, S.: CiteSeer: An Automatic Citation Indexing System. *Proc. of the 3rd ACM International Conference on Digital Libraries*, Pittsburgh, PA, (June 23-26, 1998) 89-98
12. Gomes, P., Pereira, F. C., Paiva, P., Seco, N., Carreiro, P., Ferreira, J. L., Bento, C.: Noun Sense Disambiguation with WordNet for Software Design Retrieval. *Proc. of the 16th Conference of the Canadian Society for Computational Studies of Intelligence (AI 2003)*, Halifax, Canada (June 11-13, 2003) 537-543
13. Han, H., Giles, L., Zha, H., Li, C., Tsioutsiouliklis, K.: Two Supervised Learning Approaches for Name Disambiguation in Author Citations. *Proc. ACM/IEEE Joint Conf on Digital Libraries,* Tucson, Arizona (2004)
14. Ley, M.: The DBLP Computer Science Bibliography: Evolution, Research Issues, Perspectives. *Proc. of the 9th International Symposium on String Processing and Information Retrieval,* Lisbon, Portugal (Sept. 2002) 1-10
15. Navigli, R., Velardi, P.: Structural Semantic Interconnections: A Knowledge-Based Approach to Word Sense Disambiguation. *IEEE Transactions on Pattern Analysis and Machine Intelligence,* 27(7) (2005) 1075-1086
16. Pasula, H., Marthi, B., Milch, B., Russell, S. J., Shpitser, I.: Identity Uncertainty and Citation Matching, Neural Information Processing Systems. Vancouver, British Columbia (2002) 1401-1408
17. Popov, B., Kiryakov, A., Kirilov, A., Manov, D., Ognyanoff, D., Goranov, M.: KIM - Semantic Annotation Platform. *Proc. of the 2nd International Semantic Web Conference,* Sanibel Island, Florida (2003)
18. Sheth, A., Bertram, C., Avant, D., Hammond, B., Kochut, K., Warke, Y.: Managing Semantic Content for the Web, *IEEE Internet Computing*, 6(4), (2002) 80-87
19. Torvik, V. I., Weeber, M., Swanson, D. R., Smalheiser, N. R.: A Probabilistic Similarity Metric for Medline Records: A Model for Author Name Disambiguation. *Journal of the American Society for Information Science and Technology*, 56(2) (2005) 40-158
20. Zhu, J., Uren, V., Motta, E.: ESpotter: Adaptive Named Entity Recognition for Web Browsing, *Proc. of the 3rd Professional Knowledge Management Conference (WM2005)*, Kaiserslautern, Germany (2005)

Augmenting Navigation for Collaborative Tagging with Emergent Semantics

Melanie Aurnhammer[1], Peter Hanappe[1], and Luc Steels[1,2]

[1] Sony Computer Science Laboratory, Paris, France
[2] Vrije Universiteit Brussel, Brussels, Belgium
{melanie, hanappe}@csl.sony.fr, steels@arti.vub.ac.be

Abstract. We propose an approach that unifies browsing by tags and visual features for intuitive exploration of image databases. In contrast to traditional image retrieval approaches, we utilise tags provided by users on collaborative tagging sites, complemented by simple image analysis and classification. This allows us to find new relations between data elements. We introduce the concept of a navigation map, that describes links between users, tags, and data elements for the example of the collaborative tagging site Flickr. We show that introducing similarity search based on image features yields additional links on this map. These theoretical considerations are supported by examples provided by our system, using data and tags from real Flickr users.

1 Introduction

Collaborative tagging is a form of social software that has recently attracted a huge number of users. Web sites like Flickr, del.icio.us, Technorati, CiteULike, Buzznet, and Last.fm, to name but a few, encourage users to share photos, URLs, blogs, article references, and music titles. These data objects are associated with tags, common words freely chosen by the user. They describe a data item in a subjective and often associative way. It is an intuitive and effective method to organise and retrieve data. Tags are used to organise personal data, and are made public so that other users can access and browse them.

Tagging addresses the problem of providing meta-data for Web resources very differently from the method proposed by the Semantic Web initiative [1]. In the latter approach, Web content creators annotate their work using an ontology that was defined a priori by a group of experts. With tagging, Internet users describe resources using their own labels. This bottom-up approach is an instance of Semiotic Dynamics[2,3], in which the uncoordinated actions of many users lead to the emergence of partially shared taxonomies. It resonates with earlier studies that used computational models to investigate the emergence of a shared lexicon by a population of autonomous agents [4,5].

The effect of public exposure of tags is twofold. First, it creates an incentive for people to tag their data items in order to make them accessible to others. Second, the motivation of a high exposure of their data encourages people to align their tags with those of other users. Indeed, it has been observed that over time, the relative frequency of tags used to annotate a data element stabilises [2]. Thus, collaborative or social tags are not completely arbitrary and hence provide an interesting means to search databases. Especially domains like images or music, where semantic retrieval is an extremely hard problem, benefit from the tagging approach.

However, using tags alone for searching and browsing databases clearly has its limitations. First, people make mistakes while tagging, such as spelling mistakes, or accidental tagging with the wrong tag. Second, there is no solution to cope with homonymy, i.e. to distinguish different meanings of a word. Third, synonymy or different languages can only be handled by tagging data explicitly with all terms. One possible approach to solve the synonymy problem is to translate the local taxonomies into a global taxonomy which is used for querying and information exchange. The translation could be aided by mediators [6] and achieved through automated schema matching [7,8]. However, this approach requires a one-to-one mapping of taxonomies, which is not always possible.

Our approach to tackle the shortcomings of collaborative tagging is to employ content-based image retrieval techniques. The combination of social tagging and data analysis provides the user with an intuitive way to browse databases, and allows him to experience and explore interesting new relationships between data, tags, and users, which we summarise in an augmented navigation map. It is a way to achieve emergent semantics because it can potentially ground the meaning of tags into the data [9,10,11,12]. To allow seemless integration bewmeen tagging and data analysis, an adequate interface is obviously a crucial factor for user acceptance. Although there has recently been some effort to design tools that apply simple image analysis algorithms to Flickr images [13,14], these tools work separately and are not employed for integrated navigation. Previous approaches for combining textual and image information such as [15] have been concentrating on recognising objects, which is an extremely hard problem. Using social tags has the advantage that semantic information is already provided by the user. Instead of attempting automatic semantic interpretation, we thus restrict ourselves on extracting global, low-level features.

In the following section, we describe first the user interface, including navigation possibilities and the tag visualisation. In Section 3 we present our method and give technical details of our implementation. Our concept of a navigation map is explained in Section 4. An example in Section 5 illustrates the improvement of the navigation map by introducing data analysis. We then conclude our work and present plans for future work.

2   The Interface

The interface of our system provides an intuitive way to combine collaborative tagging and content-based image retrieval. Data can be explored in different ways, either according to tags or using visual features. The application follows the user actions without enforcing a particular interaction pattern on him. The visualisation of tags is easy to understand and intuitive to use. The interface can be used to assemble a collection that can e.g. be shown as a slide show, or printed as photo album.

2.1 Tag Search

The entry point to assemble a collection is to search with a tag. When the user enters a tag, images annotated by this tag are shown in the *suggestion display area* at the lower right part of the screen (see Figure 1). The user has the possibility to perform a search on tags at any time in the process.

2.2 Suggestion Display

The images displayed in the suggestion display can be considered propositions from the archive. These images are either selected according to a common tag (see above), or by using similarity search. If images have been proposed according to a tag, the user can select one or more of these images and add them to his collection (*user collection area*, see Figure 1).

As soon as an image has been added to the user collection, two more functionalities are available: the *tag visualisation* (see section 2.4) and the search engine. The search can be started by choosing one or more examples of the collection in order to find visually similar images (see Section 3.2). The images proposed by the system are again shown at the lower right part of the screen. The user has the possibility to refine his search by simply selecting more images as positive examples, or others as negative examples, from the results.

2.3 User Collection Area

This area can be found in the top right part of the screen. The images selected by the user are displayed here and form his collection. Within this area, the user can start a search for visually similar images, or move images forward or backward inside his collection to change the order. In addition, he can display his images in a slide show.

2.4 Tag Visualisation

The visualisation of sets is shown in the upper left part of the screen (see Figure 1 and 2). The white circle in the centre of this area represents the collection of the user. The related tags – and their corresponding sets of photos – are shown as circles arranged around this centre. The visualisation feature has two modes. The first mode shows only the visualisation of tags related to the user collection. Before a search has been performed, the displayed circles are filled with a single colour. For clarity reasons, the number of displayed sets is restricted to the 32 largest sets. The size of each circle indicates the number of the photos contained in the set. The distance of the sets from the inner circle denotes the overlap of

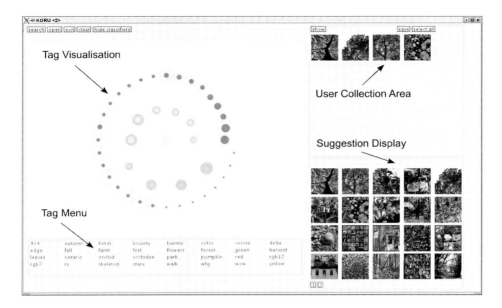

Fig. 1. Screenshot of the Interface. User Collection: images selected by the user to the theme "fall". Suggestion Display: Search results returned for first image of User Collection.

the images in the collection with the set, estimated by the number of common photos. When the user click on any of the circles, the corresponding images are shown in the suggestion area. We call the visualisation of these sets the *tag-sphere*.

The second mode is shown when the user applies a similarity search. The tag-sphere gets in the background and a second sphere of sets is drawn in a different colour. Each circle represents a tag that is related to the search results. The newly-added circles consist of two different colours. The inner, darker colour represents those images, which have been suggested by the classifier-engine. The outer, lighter circle represents images possessing the same tag, i.e. belonging to the same set, but those were not found by the classifier. A higher proportion of the inner circle indicates a relation between visual features and the tag related to the images in the set. The number of displayed sets is again restricted to the 32 largest sets. We will call the visualisation of these sets the *classifier-sphere*.

When images are added from the search results to the collection, the tag-sphere changes as well. Lighter circles inside some of the displayed circles get visible. These inner circles denote images found by similarity search that belong to the displayed set (i.e. they possess the same tag). The higher the proportion of the inner circle, the more likely is a relation between the visual similarity of the search image(s) and the tag. Every time an image is added to the user collection, the tag-sphere is updated. New sets are appended at the end of the sphere and thus a kind of tag history is represented. When an image is selected, the sets in which it is represented are highlighted and the corresponding tags displayed.

Below the tag visualisation is the *tag menu* (see Figure 5), where the tags of the current sphere are shown in alphabetic order. This gives the user the additional possibility to access the sets by going through the tags menu.

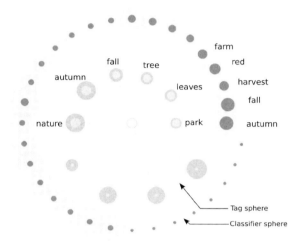

Fig. 2. Visualisation of Tags

Figure 2 shows an example visualisation, where a search has been performed on an image found by the tag "fall" (see first image User Collection, Figure 1). The two spheres show that there is indeed some correspondence between the tags of the search results and the visual features. In the classifier-sphere, there are at least five sets, where the inner circle takes a large part. The tags corresponding to these sets are "autumn", "fall", "harvest", "red", "farm". This shows, that there is a high percentage of images among the search results, which are labelled with these tags. A similar behaviour can be observed in the tag-sphere after the user added some images from the results to his collection. Here, the sets with a large inner part are "park", "leaves", "tree", "autumn", and "nature". These results are very interesting, since all these tags can be seen as reflecting the "fall-theme" of the user.

3 Technical Details

We tested our system with photographs downloaded from Flickr. Currently, we use about 3000 photographs from 12 randomly chosen users. In the following, we describe the visual features and the implementation of our retrieval process. Most of the techniques we used reflect either the state-of-the-art in image retrieval or are well-established standards in image analysis and pattern recognition. The idea of our system is to advance neither of these fields but to use the available tools in a new, intuitive, and creative way.

3.1 Features

We intentionally employ simple global features in our system. Rather than trying to recognise objects or even explain the meaning of an image, we seek to measure a certain "atmosphere", or a vague visual pattern, which we believe is possible to capture by low-level image features.

The visual features we used are colour and texture, i.e.

$$F = \{f_i\} = \{\text{colour,texture}\}$$

Colour Features. Comparison of colour histograms is known to be sensitive to small colour variations caused e.g. by lighting conditions. In order to obtain a more robust and simpler measure of the colour distribution, we calculate the first two moments (mean and standard deviation) in RGB colour space. In addition, we use the standard deviation between the means of the three colour channels. Intuitively, this yields a measure for the "colourfulness" of an image. The feature has a value of zero for grey-scale images and increases for images with stronger colours. We map the values to a logarithmic scale in order to distribute them more equally. In total, the colour feature vector has thus seven dimensions.

Texture Features. Texture refers to the properties that represent the surface or structure of an object. In our work, we seek to employ texture features that give a rough measure of the structural properties, such as linearity, periodicity, or directivity of an image. In experiments, we found *oriented gaussian derivatives* (OGD) to be well-suited for our purposes [16]. This feature descriptor uses the steerable property of the OGD to generate rotation invariant feature vectors. It is based on the idea of computing the "energy" of an image as a steerable function.

The features are extracted by a 2nd order dyadic pyramid of OGDs with four levels and a kernel size of 13x13. The generated feature vector has 24 dimensions. The first order OGD can be seen as a measure of "edge energy", and the second order OGD as a measure of the "line energy" of an image.

Feature Integration. The distance between a query image and an image in the database is calculated according to the $l2$ norm (Euclidean distance). We use a linear combination of the distances in the colour and texture spaces to combine both features. In order to give the same initial weight to all features, the values are normalised linearly before calculating the distance. The joint distance d between a database image x_l and a query image s_k over all features spaces f_i is thus

$$d(x_l, s_k) = \sum_{i=1}^{N} w_i d_i, \quad \text{with} \quad \sum_{i=1}^{N} w_i = 1$$

where N is the number of features in the set F and w is a weighting factor. In our implementation, w was set to $\frac{1}{N}$.

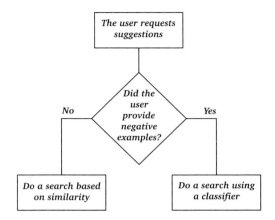

Fig. 3. Based on the user selection, KORU either performs a similarity search, or a classification

3.2 Search Process

The search for visually similar images starts with one or more images selected by the user. These initial images can be found through tags. In our implementation, we focussed on a totally user defined process: Not only is the number of selected images left to the user, he is also free in all further actions to take. When the results of the similarity search are displayed, the user can either (1) exclude images, (2) select images for refinement, (3) combine (1) and (2), or (4) simply not take any action. This distinguishes our approach from methods suggested for *relevance feedback* in image retrieval (see e.g. [17]), where the user is forced to take certain actions, such as giving feedback to every retrieved image, or where he has to follow a strict order of interaction.

Image Selection. In case the user selects several images for his query (multi-image query), we think of these images as representing different classes. Thus, we accept images for retrieval that are similar to one of the query images. An alternative approach would be to average over the selected images which is, however, rarely relevant because the user might select visually distinct images. To give a simple example, a user selection of a yellow and a blue image should not yield green images as a result, but images that are either yellow or blue. Selection of the retrieved images is performed according to the following equation. Let X denote the archive and let x_l denote the l-th image in the archive. Let S denote

a set of query images selected by the user. The distance D of x_l to S is then defined by
$$D(x_l, S) = \min_k d(x_l, s_k) \qquad (1)$$
where d represents the distance of x_l to an image s_k contained in S, and k denotes the number of query images in S.

Refinement of Results. If the user is not entirely satisfied with the retrieved images, he has the possibility to refine the results. He can choose (1) one or more images as positive examples, or (2) one or more images as negative examples, or (3) combine (1) and (2). In case only positive examples are chosen, these are added to the initial query images and the query is started anew by evaluating Equation 1 and selecting the n closest images. If the user chooses to provide the system with one or more negative examples, the retrieval process becomes a classification problem. (see Figure 3). The set of all user-selected images can then be seen as prototypes labelled either "positive" or "negative".

It is important to note that the user might choose very different examples for the same label, i.e. he might choose for example, a red image with a very smooth texture, and a green image showing high contrast leaves both as positive examples. Therefore, a parametric classification method is not suited since it assumes the distribution of the underlying density function to be unimodal. In our case, it is a much better choice to employ a non-parametric approach that can be applied for arbitrary distributions and without the assumption that the forms of the underlying densities are known. Furthermore, it is important to ensure a smooth transition between retrieval and classification in order to avoid a drastic change of the results as soon as negative examples are selected.

A method that fulfils these requirements is a simple nearest neighbour classifier. Equation 1 basically defines the distance of an image in the database to a set of query images to be the distance between the test image and its nearest neighbour in the query set. For this reason, nearest neighbour classification is the natural choice to follow similarity retrieval. Let $P^n = \{x_1, \ldots, x_n\}$ denote a set of n labelled prototypes and let $x' \in P^n$ be the prototype nearest to a test point x. Then the nearest neighbour rule for classifying x is to assign it the label associated with x'.

4 Navigation Map

In this section, we introduce our concept of a navigation map to analyse the relationships between users, tags, and data in tagging systems. We compare the navigation possibilities between a simple tagging system, a system exploiting co-occurrence relationships between tags, and our proposed system. We show that we are able to introduce new links into the navigation map by combining tagging and data analysis.

4.1 Notation

We will refer to the set of all photos available on the server as the set P. The set of users of the tagging site will be denoted by U. The relation $\pi \subset U \times P$ defines which photos belong to which users. We define the set T to be the set of all the tags of all users. The relation $\tau \subset U \times T \times P$ represents which tags are used by which user to label a photo.

In addition to the entities presented above, users can create groups, in some form or another, and they can organise their photos in *sets*. For the sake of simplicity, we will focus here only on users, tags, and photos as the main entities.

Given the above mentioned relations, it is possible to define the navigation map that allows users to navigate from one entity (a user u, a photo p, or a tag t) to any other one. In general, any entity can provide an entry point for a navigation, based on its name (user name, tag, file name, photo title).

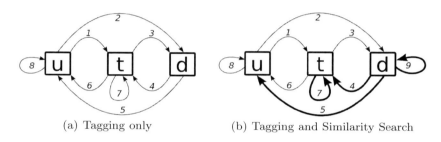

(a) Tagging only   (b) Tagging and Similarity Search

Fig. 4. The navigation map with links between users (u), tags (t), and data (d)

4.2 Navigation Using Tags

In the following, we describe the navigation possibilities on a typical tagging site like Flickr, without taking into account co-occurrence relations. In such a system, a user can view all available tags (link 1, see Figure 4(a)). He can also directly access the photo collection of himself or another user (link 2). Through selection of a tag, the user can view all photos annotated by this tag (link 3). For a given photo, its associated tags can be displayed (link 4). There is a direct navigation possibility from a given photo to its owner (link 5). Most tagging sites allow users to establish *contacts*, which are direct links to other users (link 8).

4.3 Navigation by Co-occurrence of Tags

One way to improve navigation is to exploit the co-occurrence relations between tags. This feature is already provided by Flickr, where it is referred to as "clusters". Navigation between related tags is represented in the navigation map by link 7 (see Fig. 4(a)). Clustering allows to solve the problem of synonymy to some extent. For instance, the tags "fall" and "autumn" appear in one cluster. However, this approach relies on a large number of people tagging their images explicitly with both "fall" and "autumn". For example, establishing links between tags in different languages using co-occurrence does not work very well because most users tag in their native language only.

4.4 Augmenting the Navigation Map by Visual Features

The navigation map can be augmented further by introducing links that are not represented directly in the relations $\pi \subset U \times P$ and $\tau \subset U \times T \times P$ but can be found through analysis of the image data (see Figure 4(b)).

As mentioned in the introduction, tagging has some inherent shortcomings. Among them, the most problematic are the use of synonyms or different languages by different users, as well as incomplete tagging or the lack of any tags at all. To overcome these problems, we propose an approach that extends the navigation map by introducing an important link that is not represented directly in the relations π and τ. This link is based on visual similarity, which gives a direct relation between data (link 9, Fig. 4(b))). This new relation augments the possible navigation paths through the photo archive even further. By retrieving visually similar images, their associated tags are accessible as well, which yields additional links of type 4. Since the retrieved images link also to users, we get supplementary links of type 5. Furthermore, the relationship between the tags of the query image(s) and the retrieved images provides additional links of type 7.

In summary, visual features can introduce a link between photos that might be very remote in the existing structure provided by the relations π and τ. This way, it is possible to discover new photos that were previously difficult or even impossible to find.

5 Finding New Relations – An Example

The following example shows a possible navigation path of a user through a data collection. We illustrate, how these new links that connect data elements based on visual features can be found in our implemented system.

5.1 Initial Query

The user might want to start his search by a certain tag, e.g. "rust" in our example. Looking at the set of images labelled by this tag, he might select two interesting photos showing old, rusty windows (see Figure 5).

5.2 Similarity Search

Inspired by his initial selection, the user might want to find more images related to the "window" theme. He has two possibilities to continue his search: either

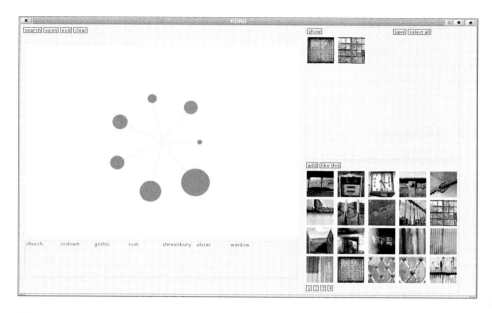

Fig. 5. Screenshot of the Interface. Suggestion Display: shows first 20 images tagged "rust", User Collection: images selected from this set.

going directly to the tag "window" and view other images labelled with this tag, or he can start a similarity search. Let us assume that the "window" set does not provide any images that suit the user's taste. Instead, he wants to do a similarity search based on the two photos he selected (see Figure 4, link 9). In Figure 6, three examples of the images retrieved by this search are shown. Among the tags attached to the image shown in Figure 6(c) is "fenêtre" (french for "window") but not "window" itself. The image shown in Figure 6(a) is tagged only "downtown" and "oakland", while no tags at all are provided for the photo shown in Figure 6(b). It can clearly be seen that none of these images could have been found with "window" as tag.

The results of the search can be further refined by the user as described in Section 3.

5.3 Further Exploration Possibilities

The new links the user has found by similarity search give starting points for further data exploration. He can, for example, follow the link for "fenêtre", leading him to a whole new set of images of windows (see Figure 4(b), link 4). Another possibility is to start by the tags related to the set of retrieved images (shown in the *Tag Menu*, see Figure 1 and 5) and continue navigating through these tags and their co-occurrence relations (see Figure 4(b), link 7). For example, the results also include an image showing a photo of a high-rise building tagged with "tokyo". The user might find this relation interesting and might want to

(a) Tags: downtown, oakland (b) No Tags (c) Tags: fenêtre, façade, france, paris, rivegauche, ...

Fig. 6. Examples of photos retrieved by similarity search, and corresponding tags

look at more images tagged with "tokyo". And indeed, this data set contains several photos of high-rise buildings with many windows. Other, perhaps interesting new links are provided by tags such as "façade", "reflection", "grid", or "downtown". A further possibility is to navigate from an interesting photo to its owner (see Figure 4(b), link 5).

6 Conclusions

We introduced an approach that combines social tags and visual features in order to extend the navigation possibilities in image archives. Our user interface including an intuitive visualisation of tags was presented as well as the implementation details described. Furthermore, we explained our concept of a navigation map and showed how the initial map based on tags can be augmented by using visual features. A simple example illustrated how such additional links can be found in our implemented system.

We showed an example of our tag visualisation for a similarity search on an image tagged "fall". The results indicate that there is some correspondence between the visual features of the search results, and the tags that are attached to the result images. Although we cannot expect a simple one-to-one mapping from a tag to a visual category, there is indication that visual features can support the suggestion of new tags.

The work presented in this paper concentrated on establishing a framework for analysing our concept as well as a first implementation. An important next step will be to develop a quantitative measure of the improvement in navigation using formal methods and through user studies.

7 Future Work

Future work will also concentrate on exploiting the new relationships between data objects in order to propose tags for unannotated images. Moreover, we will investigate possibilities to add new user-to-user links based on profile matching according not only to the users' tags, but also to visual similarity of the users' data sets. Furthermore, we plan to show the generality of our approach by extending it to the music domain as well as to video clips.

Acknowlegements

This research was carried out and funded by the Sony Computer Science Laboratory in Paris with additional funding from the EU IST project TAGora (FP6-2005-IST-5).

References

1. Berners-Lee, T., Hendler, J., Lassila, O.: The semantic web. Scientific American (2001)
2. Cattuto, C.: Collaborative tagging as a complex system. Talk given at International School on Semiotic Dynamics, Language and Complexity, Erice (2005)
3. Steels, L.: Semiotic dynamics for embodied agents. IEEE Intelligent Systems (2006) 32–38
4. Steels, L., Kaplan, F.: Collective learning and semiotic dynamics. In Floreano, D., Nicoud, J.D., Mondada, F., eds.: Advances in Artificial Life: 5th European Conference (ECAL 99). Lecture Notes in Artificial Intelligence 1674, Springer-Verlag (1999) 679–688
5. Steels, L., Hanappe, P.: Interoperability through emergent semantics: A semiotic dynamics approach. Journal of Data Semantics (2006) To appear.
6. Wiederhold, G.: Mediators in the architecture of future information systems. IEEE Computer (1992) 38–49
7. Rahm, E., Bernstein, A.P.: A survey of approaches to automatic schema matching. VLDB Journal: Very Large Data Bases (10) (2001) 334–350 http://citeseer.ist.psu.edu/rahm01survey.html.
8. Tzitzikas, Y., Meghini, C.: Ostensive automatic schema mapping for taxonomy-based peer-to-peer systems. In: Proc. of CIA–2003, 7th International Workshop on Cooperative Information Agents - Intelligent Agents for the Internet and Web. Number 2782 in Lecture Notes in Artificial Intelligence (2003) 78–92
9. Santini, S., Gupta, A., Jain, R.: Emergent semantics through interaction in image databases. IEEE Transactions on Knowledge and Data Engineering **13** (2001) 337–351
10. Aberer, K., Cudré-Mauroux, P., Ouksel, A.M., Catarci, T., Hacid, M.S., Illarramendi, A., Kashyap, V., Mecella, M., Mena, E., Neuhold, E.J., Troyer, O.D., Risse, T., Scannapieco, M., Saltor, F., Santis, L.D., Spaccapietra, S., Staab, S., Studer, R.: Emergent semantics principles and issues. In: DASFAA. (2004) 25–38 http://www.ipsi.fraunhofer.de/~risse/pub/P2004-01.pdf.
11. Staab, S.: Emergent semantics. IEEE Intelligent Systems (2002) 78–86 http://www.cwi.nl/media/publications/nack-ieee-intsys-2002.pdf.
12. Steels, L.: Emergent semantics. IEEE Intelligent Systems (2002) 83–85
13. Bumgardner, J.: Experimental colr pickr. http://www.krazydad.com/colrpickr/ (2006)
14. Langreiter, C.: Retrievr. http://labs.systemone.at/retrievr/ (2006)

15. Grosky, W.I., Fotouhi, F., Sethi, I.K., Capatina, B.: Using metadata for the intelligent browsing of structured media objects. ACM SIGMOD Record **23**(4) (1994) 49–56
16. Alvarado, P., Doerfler, P., Wickel, J.: Axon2 – a visual object recognition system for non-rigid objects. In: Proceedings International Conference on Signal Processing, Pattern Recognition and Applications (SPPRA). (2001)
17. Rui, Y., Huang, T.S., Ortega, M., Mehrotra, S.: Relevance feedback: A power tool for interactive content–based image retrieval. IEEE Transactions on Circuits and Systems for Video Technology **8**(5) (1998) 644–655

On the Semantics of Linking and Importing in Modular Ontologies

Jie Bao[1], Doina Caragea[2], and Vasant G Honavar[1]

[1] Artificial Intelligence Research Laboratory,
Department of Computer Science,
Iowa State University, Ames, IA 50011-1040, USA
{baojie, honavar}@cs.iastate.edu
[2] Department of Computing and Information Sciences
Kansas State University, Manhattan, KS 66506, USA
dcaragea@ksu.edu

Abstract. Modular ontology languages, such as Distributed Description Logics (DDL), $\mathcal{E}$-connections and Package-based Description Logics (P-DL) offer two broad classes of approaches to connect multiple ontology modules: the use of *mappings* or *linkings* between ontology modules e.g., DDL and $\mathcal{E}$-connections; and the use of *importing* e.g., P-DL. The major difference between the two approaches is on the usage of "foreign terms" at the syntactic level, and on the local model disjointness at the semantic level. We compare the semantics of linking in DDL and $\mathcal{E}$-connections, and importing in P-DL within the Distributed First Order Logics (DFOL) framework. Our investigation shows that the domain disjointness assumption adopted by the linking approach leads to several semantic difficulties. We explore the possibility of avoiding some of these difficulties using the importing approach to linking ontology modules.

1 Introduction

Because the web is a network of loosely coupled, distributed, autonomous entities, it is inevitable that the ontologies on the web to be modular, collaboratively built and partially connected. Hence, there is significant interest on modular ontology languages, such as, Distributed Description Logics (DDL) [4], $\mathcal{E}$-connections [12,9] and Package-based Description Logics (P-DL) [3].

These proposals adopt two broad classes of approaches to asserting semantic relations between multiple ontology modules: the use of *mappings* or *linkings* between ontology modules e.g., DDL and $\mathcal{E}$-connections; and the use of *importing* e.g., P-DL. The major difference between the two approaches has to do with the use of "foreign terms" in ontology modules. In a linked ontology, different modules have *disjoint terminologies* and *disjoint interpretation* domains, and semantic relations between ontology modules are only enabled by a set of *mapping axioms*, such as bridge rules in DDL or $\mathcal{E}$-connections. Therefore, the direct usage of terms defined in one module is forbidden in another module. In contrast, *importing* allows an ontology module to make direct reference to terms defined in other ontology modules, i.e., *importing of foreign terms*.

Serafini *et.al.* (2005) [15] compare mapping or linking based approaches to the "integration" of multiple ontology modules such as DDL and $\mathcal{E}$-connections by reducing them to the Distributed First Order Logics (DFOL) [6] framework. However, there is little work on the formal investigation of the importing approach to integrating ontology modules. Against this background, we compare the semantics of the two approaches within the DFOL framework, with the study of their strengths and limitations. Such an investigation reveals that the importing approach, with the removing of the module disjointness assumption adopted by the linking approach, can provide stronger expressivity and avoid many of the semantic difficulties in current modular ontology language proposals.

2 Desiderata for Modular Ontology Languages

We first list a set of minimal requirements for modular ontology languages [2] on the semantic web as the basis for our comparison of the semantics of DDL, $\mathcal{E}$-connections and P-DL within the DFOL framework:

1. **Localized Semantics.** A modular ontology should not only be *syntactically modular* (e.g. stored in separated XML name spaces), but also *semantically modular*. That is, the existence of a *global model* should not be a requirement for integration of ontology modules.
2. **Exact Reasoning.** The answer to a reasoning problem over a collection of ontology modules should be *semantically equivalent* to that obtained by reasoning over an ontology resulting from an *integration* of the relevant ontology modules. Thus, if an ontology O contains $A \sqsubseteq B, B \sqsubseteq C, C \sqsubseteq D$, and a modularized version of O has two modules $M_1 = \{A \sqsubseteq B\}, M_2 = \{C \sqsubseteq D\}$ and a semantic connection $r(B,C)$, which represents the modularized version of $B \sqsubseteq C$, the answer to any reasoning problem obtained by integration of M_1, M_2 and $r(B,C)$ should be the same as that obtained by using a sound and complete reasoner on O.
3. **Directed Semantic Relations.** The framework must support *directional semantic relations* from a *source* module to a *target* module. A directional semantic relation affects only the reasoning within the target module and not the source module.
4. **Transitive Reusability.** Knowledge contained in ontology modules should be directly or indirectly reusable. That is, if a module A reuses module B, and module B reuses module C, then effectively, module A reuses module C.

Other desiderata that have been considered in the literature include: the ability to cope with local inconsistency or global inconsistency, and local logic completeness. We believe that the desiderata listed above are among the most critical ones for a modular ontology to be semantically sound and practically usable.

3 Distributed First Order Logics

A DFOL knowledge base (KB) [6] (and hence, a DFOL ontology) includes a family of first order languages $\{L_i\}_{i \in I}$, defined over a finite set of indices I. We will use L_i to refer to the ith module of the ontology. An (i-)variable x or (i-)formula ϕ occurring in module L_i is denoted as $i : x$ or $i : \phi$ (we drop the prefix when there is no confusion).

The semantics of DFOL includes a set of local models and domain relations. For each L_i, there is an interpretation domain Δ_i. Let M_i be the set of all first order models of L_i on Δ_i. We call each $m \in M_i$ a *local model* of L_i. A *domain relation* r_{ij}, where $i \neq j$, is a subset of $\Delta_i \times \Delta_j$. The domain relation r_{ij} represents the capability of the module j to map the objects of Δ_i in Δ_j, or, the j's *subjective view* of the relation between Δ_i and Δ_j. In general, $r_{ij} \neq r_{ji}^-$.

We use $\langle d, d' \rangle$ in r_{ij} to denote that from the point of view of j, the object d in Δ_i is *mapped* to the object d' in Δ_j; d is called a *pre-image* of d', and d' is called an *image* of d. In general, domain relations can be injective, surjective, bijective, or arbitrary. For an object $d \in \Delta_i$, $r_{ij}(d)$ denotes the set $\{d' \in \Delta_j | \langle d, d' \rangle \in r_{ij}\}$. For a subset $D \subseteq \Delta_i$, $r_{ij}(D)$ denotes $\cup_{d \in D} r_{ij}(d)$, is the image set of D.

4 Semantics of Linking in DDL

One influential family of modular ontology formalisms is the linking approach. The linking approach is aimed at preserving the autonomy of loosely coupled modules, while allowing restricted "mappings" between formulae of linked modules. Formally, a linking approach holds the follow assumptions:

– For any L_i and $L_j, i \neq j$, i-terms and j-terms are disjoint.
– The semantic connection between L_i and L_j is enabled only by mapping rules between i-terms and j-terms, which are interpreted as domain relations $r_{ij} \subseteq \Delta_i \times \Delta_j$.
– Local interpretation domains and domain relations are disjoint. For any $i \neq j$, $\Delta_i \times \Delta_i$ (or $\Delta_j \times \Delta_j$) has intersection neither with r_{ij} nor with r_{ji}.

Based on DFOL, Distributed Description Logics (DDL) [4] is one of the first linking-based modular ontology formalisms. In DDL, the semantic mappings between disjoint modules L_i and L_j are established by a set of inter-module axioms called "Bridge Rules"(B_{ij}) of the form:

– INTO rule: $i : \phi \stackrel{\sqsubseteq}{\longrightarrow} j : \psi$, semantics: $r_{ij}(\phi^{m_i}) \subseteq \psi^{m_j}$
– ONTO rule: $i : \phi \stackrel{\sqsupseteq}{\longrightarrow} j : \psi$, semantics: $r_{ij}(\phi^{m_i}) \supseteq \psi^{m_j}$

where $m_i(m_j)$ is a model of $L_i(L_j)$, ϕ, ψ are formulae, r_{ij} is a domain relation which serves as the interpretation of B_{ij}. Note that B_{ij} is directional. We will only consider bridge rules between concepts, not roles [5], since there is still no reasoning support for role bridge rules [14].

Distributed concept correspondence between two modules in DDL covers some important scenarios that require mapping between ontology modules. However, the expressivity of DDL is limited in some settings that arise in practical applications: For example, DDL cannot be used to express "a person x works in a region y". In general, it can not construct new concepts using terms across modules, such as restrictions $\forall 1 : R.2 : D$ and $\exists 1 : R.2 : D$, where C, D are concepts and R is role.

In addition to the expressivity limitations, DDL may present semantic difficulties in some situations. While DDL bridge rules are intended to simulate *concept inclusions* [4,5], arbitrary modelling with bridge rules may lead to undesired semantics, such as in the *Subsumption Propagation problem* and *Inter-module Unsatisfiability problem*, as noted in [9,7]:

Example 1 (Subsumption Propagation). *A KB Σ_d includes modules $L_{\{1,2,3\}}$, each with an empty TBox; bridge rules $B_{12} = \{1 : Bird \xrightarrow{\exists} 2 : Fowl\}$, $B_{23} = \{2 : Fowl \xrightarrow{\exists} 3 : Chicken\}$. The entailment problem $1 : Bird \xrightarrow{\exists} 3 : Chicken$ cannot be answered since bridge rules B_{13} are not given, nor can be inferred.*

Note that bridge rules may be inferred between the *same* pair of modules. For example, if $1 : A \xrightarrow{\sqsubseteq} 2 : B$ and $2 : B \sqsubseteq 2 : C$, it can be inferred that $1 : A \xrightarrow{\sqsubseteq} 2 : C$. Intra-module subsumption may also be reused in some particular cases. For example, if $1 : A \sqsubseteq 1 : B$, $1 : A \xrightarrow{\exists} 2 : C$ and $1 : B \xrightarrow{\sqsubseteq} 2 : D$, it can be inferred that $2 : C \sqsubseteq 2 : D$ [16]. However, Example 1 shows that in general bridge rules in DDLs are not transitively reusable, thereby are restricted for many application scenarios.

Example 2 (Inter-module Unsatisfiability[9,7]). *DDLs may not detect unsatisfiability across ontology modules. A KB Σ_d includes modules $L_{\{1,2\}}$, $L_1 = \{1 : Bird \sqsubseteq 1 : Fly\}$, $L_2 = \{2 : Penguin \sqsubseteq \top\}$, $B_{12} = \{1 : Bird \xrightarrow{\exists} 2 : Penguin, 1 : \neg Fly \xrightarrow{\exists} 2 : Penguin\}$. Penguin is still satisfiable in Σ_d.*

Such difficulties are rooted in the implicit local domain disjointness assumption of DDL: individuals in each local domain are private to that domain, and DDL semantics does not take into account if individuals in different local domains may represent the same physical world object. Therefore, a bridge rule, while intended to simulate concept inclusion, cannot be read directly as concept inclusion, such as $i : A \sqsubseteq j : B$. Instead, it must be read as a classic DL axiom in the following way [4]:

- $i : A \xrightarrow{\sqsubseteq} j : B \Rightarrow (i : A) \sqsubseteq \forall R_{ij}.(j : B)$
- $i : A \xrightarrow{\exists} j : B \Rightarrow (j : B) \sqsubseteq \exists R_{ij}^-.(i : A)$

where R_{ij} is a new role representing correspondences B_{ij} between L_i and L_j. Such translations are best understood as shown in Figure 1.

Therefore, for the given subsumption propagation example, if $B_{13} = \emptyset$, entailment $Chicken \sqsubseteq \exists R_{13}^-.Bird$ is not always true. For the inter-module unsatisfiability problem, concept $Penguin$ ($\sqsubseteq \exists R_{12}^-.(Fly) \sqcap \exists R_{12}^-.(\neg Fly)$) is satisfiable.

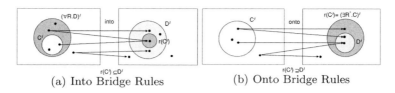

(a) Into Bridge Rules (b) Onto Bridge Rules

Fig. 1. Semantics of DDL Bridge Rules

Thus, the semantics of DDL are designed to simulate concept inclusion with a special type of roles, i.e., bridge rules. However, in the absence of a principled approach to avoid arbitrary domain relation interpretations for bridge rules, all semantic relations (bridge rules) between DDL modules are *localized* to pairs of modules that are bridged by the rules in question. Consequently, semantic relations between a pair of DDL modules cannot be safely reused by other modules, thereby precluding general subsumption propagation, and more generally, module transitive reusability. Note further that in order to enable distributed (not necessarily exact) reasoning in general, a DDL KB needs explicit declaration of domain relations between *each* pair of modules, leading to an exponential blowup in the number of bridge rules, with the attendant inefficiency and increased risk of inconsistencies.

Serafini et al. [14] has asserted that the inter-module unsatisfiability difficulty is the result of incomplete modelling. They have argued that it can be eliminated if extra information, for example, $1 : \neg Bird \xrightarrow{\sqsubseteq} 2 : \neg Penguin$ and $1 : Fly \xrightarrow{\sqsubseteq} \neg 2 : Penguin$, is added to guarantee one-to-one domain relations. Our investigation reveals a more general result: one-to-one domain relations can guarantee that reasoning over DDL always yields the same result as that obtained from an integrated ontology when bridge rules are replaced with general concept inclusions (GCI). First, we have the definition:

Definition 1. *A domain relation r_{ij} for bridge rules B_{ij} is said to be* **one-to-one** *if for any bridge rule $C \xrightarrow{\sqsubseteq} D$ or $C \xrightarrow{\sqsupseteq} D$, for any $x \in C^{\mathcal{I}_i}$, there is one and only one unique $y \in \Delta_j$ such that $\langle x, y \rangle \in r_{ij}$.*

The integration process from a DDL ontology to a ordinary (global) DL ontology is given in [4]. For a DDL ontology $\{L_i\}$, the global DL (GDL) ontology is defined as follows:

- There is a new top concept $\top_g$ and a new bottom concept $\bot_g$ in GDL.
- The primitive concepts of GDL consist of $i : A$ obtained from primitive concepts or constant concepts A (such as $\top_i$ and $\bot_i$) of L_i
- The primitive roles of GDL include $i : p$ obtained from primitive or constant roles p of L_i

The mapping $\#()$ from concepts/roles in L_i to concepts/roles in GDL is defined as follows: for atomic concepts, roles, and individuals $i : M$, $\#(i : M) = i : M$;

for a complex concept constructor ρ with k arguments, $\#(i : \rho(X_1, ..., X_k)) = \top_i \sqcap \rho(\#(X_1), ..., \#(X_k))$. For example, $\#i : (\forall p.C) = \top_i \sqcap \forall(i : p).(\top_i \sqcap i : C)$.

Applying $\#()$ to a DDL knowledge base $\Sigma = \langle\{L_i\}, \{B_{ij}\}\rangle$, we get an integrated GDL [4] $\#(\Sigma)$ that contains:

- $\#(i : A) \sqsubseteq \#(i : B)$ for all $i : A \sqsubseteq B \in L_i$
- $\bot_i \sqsubseteq \bot_g$
- $\#(i : A) \sqsubseteq \top_i$ for each atomic concept A of L_i
- Axioms that ensure the domain and range of any i-role to be $\top_i$: $\top_i \sqsubseteq \forall(i : s).\top_i$, $\neg \top_i \sqsubseteq \forall(i : s).\bot_g$

However, in contrast to the approach taken in [4], we will translate bridge rules in DDL as GCIs in GDL. Hence, $\#(\Sigma)$ will include in addition to the above:

- $\#(i : C) \sqsubseteq \#(j : D)$ for all $i : C \xrightarrow{\sqsubseteq} j : D \in B_{ij}$
- $\#(i : C) \sqsupseteq \#(j : D)$ for all $i : C \xrightarrow{\sqsupseteq} j : D \in B_{ij}$

Since the motivation of DDL bridge rules is to simulate concept subsumption as mentioned in DDL proposals [4,5,14], we believe that GCIs offer a more appropriate translation for bridge rules in comparing the result of reasoning in the distributed setting with that of the centralized setting. Note that the semantic difficulties of DDL under incomplete modelling is actually due to the semantic differences between concept subsumptions (i.e., GCIs) and bridge rules (as shown in the Examples 1 and 2). The following theorem reveals that the domain relations being one-to-one is a sufficient condition for exact reasoning in DDL if bridge rules are intended to represent inter-module concept inclusions (proof can be found in the longer version of the paper [1]).

Theorem 1. *Suppose* $\Sigma = \langle\{L_i\}, \{B_{ij}\}\rangle$ *is a DDL KB, where none of L_i uses role constants or role constructors, and all domain relations in all models of Σ are one-to-one, then*

- $\#(\Sigma) \models \#(i : X) \sqsubseteq \#(i : Y)$ if and only if $\Sigma \models_d i : X \sqsubseteq i : Y$
- $\#(\Sigma) \models \#(i : X) \sqsubseteq \#(j : Y)$ if and only if $\Sigma \models_d (i : X \xrightarrow{\sqsubseteq} j : Y$ or $(j : Y \xrightarrow{\sqsupseteq} i : X)$

At present, there is no principled approach in DDL to specify such domain relations. Adding $\neg C \xrightarrow{\sqsubseteq} \neg D$ for each $C \xrightarrow{\sqsupseteq} D$, as suggested in [14], does not necessarily result in injective (and hence, also not one-to-one) domain relations for any inter-module concept relations.

Example 3. *A KB Σ_d includes modules $L_{\{1,2\}}$, TBox of L_1 is $\{Woman \equiv \neg Man\}$, TBox of L_2 is $\{Girl \equiv \neg Boy\}$; bridge rules $B_{12} = \{1 : Man \xrightarrow{\sqsupseteq} 2 : Boy\}$. According to [14], we should also add $\neg 1 : Man \xrightarrow{\sqsubseteq} \neg 2 : Boy$ i.e.*

---

[1] http://archives.cs.iastate.edu/documents/disk0/00/00/04/08/index.html

$1 : Woman \stackrel{\sqsubseteq}{\Longrightarrow} 2 : Girl$ to B_{12}. However, that doesn't rule out the possibility of a $Girl$ object being both an image of a Man object and a $Woman$ object, neither ensure one-to-one correspondence between Man objects and Boy objects.

Example 4. (adopted from [17]) Module L_1 entails $\top \sqsubseteq 1 : Car$, module L_2 entails $UsefulThing \sqsubseteq \neg UselessThing$, and there are bridge rules $1 : Car \stackrel{\sqsubseteq}{\Longrightarrow} 2 : UsefulThing$ and $1 : Car \stackrel{\sqsubseteq}{\Longrightarrow} 2 : UselessThing$. There is no required new bridge rules to be added according to [14]. However, $1 : Car$ is not unsatisfiable, since DDL semantics allows empty domain relations.

DDL, as presented in [4], meets the *localized semantics* and *directional semantic relations* requirements, but *not* the *exact reasoning* and *transitive reusability* requirements. In general, DDL in its present form does not provide a satisfactory formalism for inter-module or inter-ontology subsumption. In the following text, we will show it can be improved by restricting domain relations to be one-to-one, by P-DL or a combination of DDL and $\mathcal{E}$-connections.

5 Semantics of Linking in $\mathcal{E}$-Connections

While DDL allows only one type of domain relations, $\mathcal{E}$-connections allow multiple "link" relations between two domains, such as *worksIn* and *bornIn* between $2 : Person$ and $1 : Region$. $\mathcal{E}$-connections between ADSs [12], and in particular, between DLs [11,9], restrict the local domains of the $\mathcal{E}$-connected ontology modules to be disjoint. Roles are divided into disjoint sets of *local roles* (connecting concepts in one module) and *links* (connecting inter-module concepts).

Formally, given ontology modules $\{L_i\}$, an (one-way binary) link (more expressive $\mathcal{E}$-connections are beyond the scope of this paper) $E \in \mathcal{E}_{ij}$, where $\mathcal{E}_{ij}, i \neq j$ is the set of all links from the module i to the module j, can be used to construct a concept in module i, with the syntax and semantics specified as follows:

- $\langle E \rangle (j : C)$ or $\exists E.(j : C) : \{x \in \Delta_i | \exists y \in \Delta_j, (x, y) \in E^M, y \in C^M\}$
- $\forall E.(j : C) : \{x \in \Delta_i | \forall y \in \Delta_j, (x, y) \in E^M \to y \in C^M\}\}$

where $M = \langle \{m_i\}, \{E^M\}_{E \in \mathcal{E}_{ij}} \rangle$ is a model of the $\mathcal{E}$-connected ontology, m_i is the local model of L_i; C is a concept in L_j, with interpretation $C^M = C^{m_j}$; $E^M \subseteq \Delta_i \times \Delta_j$ is the interpretation of an $\mathcal{E}$-connection E. $\mathcal{E}$-connections also permit number restrictions on links [12].

An $\mathcal{E}$-connection model M can be mapped to a DFOL model $M_d = \langle \{m_i\}, \{r_{ij}\} \rangle$ with each E^M ($E \in \mathcal{E}_{ij}$) acting as a domain relation r_{ij} [15]. Extending the semantics of $\mathcal{E}$-connection axioms ((1) and (3) below) given in [15] so as to allow the use of constructed concepts ($\exists E.D$ and $\forall E.D$) on either side of the subsumption, we have (also see Figure 2):

1) $C \sqsubseteq \forall E.D : E^M(C^{m_i}) \subseteq D^{m_j}$
2) $C \sqsupseteq \forall E.D : (\neg C)^{m_i} \subseteq (E^M)^-((\neg D)^{m_j})$, i.e., $\forall x \in \Delta_i, E^M(x) \subseteq D^{m_j} \to x \in C^{m_i}$

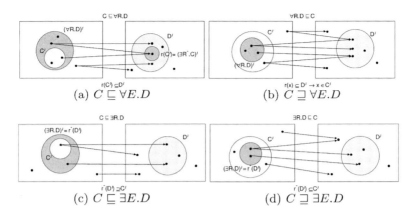

r is the interpretation of link E, also acting as the domain relation between the two local domain.

Fig. 2. Semantics of $\mathcal{E}$-Connections

3) $C \sqsubseteq \exists E.D : C^{m_i} \subseteq (E^M)^-(D^{m_j})$
4) $C \sqsupseteq \exists E.D : E^M((\neg C)^{m_i}) \subseteq (\neg D)^{m_j}$, i.e., $C^{m_i} \supseteq (E^M)^-(D^{m_j})$

where $(E^M)^-$ is the inverse of E^M, C is an i-concept and D is a j-concept, C can be an atomic or complex concept. Note that case (2)(similarly also for (4)) can not be reduce to defining $C' \equiv \forall E.D$ and $C' \sqsubseteq C$ in i, since $\equiv$ is the short for $\sqsubseteq$ and $\sqsupseteq$.

It has been argued that $\mathcal{E}$-connections are more expressive than DDL [12,7] because DDL can be reduced to $\mathcal{E}$-connections. However, the reliance of the reduction on the equivalence of $C \xrightarrow{\sqsubseteq} D$ to $\langle E \rangle.C \sqsubseteq D$ and $C \xrightarrow{\sqsupseteq} D$ to $\langle E \rangle.C \sqsupseteq D$ [12,7], presents semantic difficulties with regard to DDL and $\mathcal{E}$-connections semantics in the DFOL framework [15]: ONTO($\xrightarrow{\sqsupseteq}$) rules in DDL is actually mapped to type d interpretation constraints in DFOL while $\langle E \rangle.C \sqsupseteq D$ is mapped to type b interpretation constraints in DFOL.

We show that *inverse links* being allowed is a necessary condition for $\mathcal{E}$-connections to be more expressive than DDL bridge rules:

Theorem 2. *$\mathcal{E}$-connections, as presented in [12,7] is strictly more expressive than DDL as presented in [4], only if inverse links are allowed.*

Proof Sketch: Comparison of the semantics of DDL and $\mathcal{E}$-connections, if we treat the only domain relation in DDL as a $\mathcal{E}$-connection E, as shown in [15,4], $C \sqsubseteq \forall E.D$ has the same semantics as the "into" rule $C \xrightarrow{\sqsubseteq} D$ ($r_{ij}(C^{m_i}) \subseteq D^{m_j}$). However, onto rules, such as $C \xrightarrow{\sqsupseteq} D$ ($r_{ij}(C^{m_i}) \supseteq D^{m_j}$), can be translated into $D \sqsubseteq \exists E^-.C$ only if the inversion of $\mathcal{E}$-connections is allowed. □

Thus, the language $\mathcal{C}^{\mathcal{E}}_{\mathcal{HI}}(\mathcal{SHIQ}, \mathcal{SHOQ}, \mathcal{SHIO})$ is more expressive than DDL but $\mathcal{C}^{\mathcal{E}}_{\mathcal{HQ}}(\mathcal{SHIQ}, \mathcal{SHOQ}, \mathcal{SHIO})$ (allowing no inverse link) [7] is *not*.

Note that for $i : C \xrightarrow{\exists} j : D$, defining an $\mathcal{E}$-connection F from j to i, the onto rule still cannot be translated into $D \sqsubseteq \exists F.C$, since DDL semantics doesn't assume $r_{ij} = r_{ji}^-$, therefore $F \neq E^-$. To assert the inverse relation, we still need inverse link constructors in $\mathcal{E}$-connections.

$\mathcal{E}$-connections allow multiple links between modules and the construction of new concepts e.g. $WorkForce \equiv \langle worksIn \rangle Region$, while DDL does not. Module transitive useability can be realized in a limited form by transitive links [13]. $\mathcal{E}$-connections are also directional. Reasoning in $\mathcal{E}$-connections without generalized links is exact w.r.t a combined TBox of the $\mathcal{E}$-connected ontology, since a concept is satisfiable in the $\mathcal{E}$-connected ontology if and only if there is a combined model for the combined TBox and the concept [9,8].

However, the applicability of $\mathcal{E}$-connections in practice is also limited by the need to ensure that the local domains are disjoint:

– To enforce local domain disjointness, a concept cannot be declared as subclass of another concept in a foreign module thereby ruling out the possibility of asserting inter-module subsumption and the general support for transitive useability; a property cannot be declared as sub-relation of a foreign property; neither foreign classes nor foreign properties can be instantiated; cross-module concept conjunction or disjunction are also illegal.
– $\mathcal{E}$-connected ontologies have difficulties to be used with OWL importing mechanism, since importing may actually "decouple" the combination and result in inconsistency [7].

6 Semantics of Importing – P-DL

Our investigation of the semantics of DDL and $\mathcal{E}$-connections suggests that many of the semantic difficulties of linking approaches might be the result of a fundamental assumption that the local language and local models are disjoint. Thus, it is interesting to consider formalisms that relax this assumption.

OWL does not make such module disjointness assumption. Instead, it adopts an *importing* mechanism to support integration of ontology modules. However, the importing mechanism in OWL, in its current form, suffers from several serious drawbacks: (a) It directly introduces both terms and axioms of the imported ontologies into the importing ontology, and thus fails to support *local semantics* (b) It provides no support for *partial reuse* of an ontology module.

Package-based Description Logics (P-DL)[3] offer a tradeoff between the strong module disjointness assumption of DDL and $\mathcal{E}$-connections, and the OWL importing mechanics, which forces *complete overlapping* of modules.

6.1 Syntax and Semantics of P-DL

In P-DL, an ontology is composed of a collection of modules called *packages*. Each term (name of a concept, a property or an individual) and each axiom is associated with a *home package*. A package can use terms defined in other packages i.e., *foreign terms*. If a package L_j uses a term $i : t$ with home package

L_i ($i \neq j$), then we say t is *imported* into L_j, and the importing relation is denoted as r_{ij}^t. L_i may contain the usual TBox and ABox of DL. For simplicity, we do not present advanced features of P-DL, such as package hierarchy and scope limitation modifiers [3].

We denote the package extension to DL as $\mathcal{P}$. For example, $\mathcal{ALCP}$ is the package-based version of DL $\mathcal{ALC}$. In what follows, we will examine a restricted type of package extension which only allows import of concept names, denoted as $\mathcal{P_C}$. We will show that even this restricted form of package extension is not trivial and is more expressive than DDL and $\mathcal{E}$-connection.

The semantics of P-DL is expressed in DFOL as follows: For a package-based ontology $\langle \{L_i\}, \{r_{ij}^t\}_{i \neq j} \rangle$, a distributed model is $M = \langle \{m_i\}, \{(r_{ij}^t)^M\}_{i \neq j} \rangle$, where m_i is the local model of module i, $(r_{ij}^t)^M \subseteq \Delta_i \times \Delta_j$ is the interpretation for the importing relation r_{ij}^t, which meets the following requirements:

– Every importing relation is one-to-one, and for every object in t^{m_j} there is a single unique object in t^{m_i} as its pre-image (therefore $r_{ij}(t^{m_i}) = t^{m_j}$).
– Term Consistency: importing relations are consistent for different terms. Each object in the model of a source package corresponds uniquely to an object in the model of any target package for interpretations of importing relations of all terms, i.e., for any $i : t_1 \neq i : t_2$ and any $x, x_1, x_2 \in \Delta_i$, $(r_{ij}^{t_1})^M(x) = (r_{ij}^{t_2})^M(x)$ and $(r_{ij}^{t_1})^M(x_1) = (r_{ij}^{t_2})^M(x_2) \neq \emptyset \rightarrow x_1 = x_2$.
– Compositional Consistency: if $(r_{ik}^{i:t_1})^M(x) = y_1$, $(r_{ij}^{i:t_2})^M(x) = y_2$, $(r_{jk}^{j:t_3})^M(y_2) = y_3$, , (where t_1 and t_2 may or may not be same), and y_1, y_2, y_3 are not null, then $y_1 = y_3$. Compositional consistency helps ensure that the transitive reusability property holds for P-DL.

The domain relation between m_i and m_j is $r_{ij} = \cup_t (r_{ij}^t)^M$.

Lemma 1. *Domain relations in a P-DL model are one-to-one.*

Lemma 1 states that a domain relation r_{ij} in a P-DL model isomorphically maps, or copies, the relevant partial domain from m_i to m_j. For any concept $i : C$, $r_{ij}(C^{m_i})$, if not empty, contains the copy of a subset of objects in C^{m_i}. Such domain relations allow us to relax the domain disjointness assumption adopted in DDL and $\mathcal{E}$-connections, since the construction of a local model is partially dependent on the structure of local models of imported modules, with the benefits of preserving exact semantics of terms shared by different modules.

Immediately from the one-to-one domain relation property, we have:

Lemma 2. *In a P-DL model m, for any domain relation r_{ij} and concept $i : C$, we have $r_{ij}(C^{m_i}) \cap r_{ij}((\neg C)^{m_i}) = \emptyset$.*

If a term is indirectly used in a non-home package, compositional consistency property of domain relations makes the domain relation inferrable. For example, if some terms defined in L_1 are imported into L_2, and some terms in L_2 are imported into L_3, then the importing relation r_{13} can be inferred from the composition $r_{12} \circ r_{23}$.

Lemma 3. *For domain relations in a model of P-DL, $r_{ik} = r_{ij} \circ r_{jk}, i \neq j, j \neq k$.*

In the following text, r_{ij} refers to either an explicitly given domain relation or an inferred domain relation, or their union, between package i and j.

If $i : C$ is imported into j, we define inter-module subsumption $i : C \sqsubseteq_P j : D$ as $r_{ij}(C^{m_i}) = C^{m_j} \subseteq D^{m_j}$ and $i : C \sqsupseteq_P j : D$ as $r_{ij}(C^{m_i}) = C^{m_j} \supseteq D^{m_j}$ (see Figure 3). Note that inter-module subsumption is substantially different from bridge rules in DDL. DDL bridge rules bridge semantic gaps between *different* concepts, and there is no principled way to ensure subjective domain relations to be semantically consistent (in the sense of one-to-one mappings and compositional consistency). In contrast, P-DL importing mechanism bridges the semantic gaps between multiple references of the *same* concept in different modules. Importing of C from i to j cannot be reduced to a DDL equivalency bridge rule $C \xrightarrow{\equiv} C'$, since in DDL $r_{ij}(C^{m_i}) = C'^{m_j}$ does not guarantee C^{m_i} and C'^{m_j} are interpretations for the same concept.

We show below that such a relaxation of module disjointness does not sacrifice localized semantics and can help us to solve many semantic difficulties presented in other approaches and provide stronger expressivity.

6.2 Features of P-DL Semantics

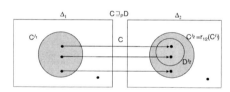

Fig. 3. Semantics of P-DL

The loss of local model disjointness in P-DL does not sacrifice *localized semantics* property of modules, since the local models (unlike in OWL which requires *completely* overlapping of local models) are, only *partially* overlapping. The semantics of the part of a module that is not exported to any other module remains local to that module. Consequently, there is no required global model. The example below demonstrates that P-DL also satisfies *directional semantic relation* and module *transitive reusability* properties.

Example 5. *Consider four modules $L_{\{1,2,3,4\}}$ as shown in Figure 4.*

1. Transitivity of inter-module subsumption holds: $r_{14}(A^{m_1}) = r_{24}(r_{12}(A^{m_1})) \subseteq r_{24}(r_{12}(B^{m_1})) = r_{24}(B^{m_2}) \subseteq r_{24}(C^{m_2}) \subseteq r_{24}(P^{m_2}) = P^{m_4} \subseteq Q^{m_4}$, i.e., $A \sqsubseteq_P Q$. Although no term in L_1 is directly imported into L_4, we can infer the domain relation r_{14} from $r_{12j} \circ r_{24}$ utilizing their compositional consistency property.
2. The importing relation is directional. Thus, $r_{12}(A^{m_1}) \subseteq r_{12}(D^{m_1})$ is enforced only in L_2, while $A^{m_1} \subseteq D^{m_1}$ is not required in L_1. There is no information "backflow" in importing. Therefore, while L_2 and L_3 are inconsistent, they are all consistent to L_1, and the consistency of L_1 is still guaranteed.
3. The model overlapping is only partial, e.g., E and F in 1 are semantically separated from L_2 and have no correspondence in the local model m_2.

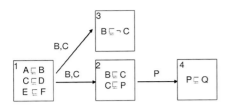

Fig. 4. P-DL Ontology Example

An integrated KB can be obtained from a P-DL KB by combining axioms in all packages. Because of the isomorphic nature of importing relations, we have the theorem (proof is in the longer version of the paper):

Theorem 3. *Reasoning in a P-DL KB is exact w.r.t. its integrated KB.*

The intuition behind this proof is as follows: since the only type of semantic relations between modules are importing relations, and shared terms are always interpreted consistently in different modules, we can transform a distributed P-DL model into a classic DL model by merging all "copied" objects in each of the local models.

However, a limitation of the importing approach adopted by P-DL is that the general decidability transfer property does not always hold in P-DL since the union of two decidable fragments of DL may not in general be decidable [1]. This presents semantic difficulties in the general setting of connecting ADSs [1,12]. Fortunately, in the case of a web ontology language where different ontology modules are specified using subsets of the *same* decidable DL language such as $\mathcal{SHOIQ}(D)$ (OWL-DL), the union of such modules is decidable. With the availability of the decision procedure [10] and highly optimized reasoners for $\mathcal{SHOIQ}(D)$, we can ensure the decidability of P-DL ontology within the modular web ontology setting. Therefore we have:

Theorem 4. $\mathcal{SHOIQP}_\mathcal{C}(D)$ *is decidable*

P-DL also has some expressivity limitations. $\mathcal{P}_\mathcal{C}$ does not allow role inclusions across different modules, using foreign role to construct local concept, declaring a local role as the inverse of a foreign role, nor the importing of nominals defined in other modules. Due to the one-to-one domain relation requirement, P-DL can support only one-to-one ABox mappings, and not many-to-one, one-to-many, or many-to-many ABox mappings. The semantics of more expressive P-DL that allows importing of role and individual names still needs further investigation.

6.3 Relation Between P-DL, DDL and $\mathcal{E}$-Connections

P-DL, despite its stronger domain relation restrictions, can be used to model DDLs and $\mathcal{E}$-Connections.

The reduction from DDL to P-DL is straightforward. An into rule $i : C \xrightarrow{\sqsubseteq} j : D$ in DDL can be reduced to a P-DL axiom $C \sqsubseteq_P D$ in module j and C is an imported concept; similarly, an onto rule $i : C \xrightarrow{\sqsupseteq} j : D$ in DDL is translated as $C \sqsupseteq_P D$ in module j and C is an imported concept. The semantic interpretation of such a reduction is clear since $r_{ij}(C^{m_i}) = C^{m_j}$, therefore $r_{ij}(C^{m_i}) \subseteq D^{m_j}$ iff $C^{m_j} \subseteq D^{m_j}$ and $r_{ij}(C^{m_i}) \supseteq D^{m_j}$ iff $C^{m_j} \supseteq D^{m_j}$.

P-DL may avoid the semantic difficulties presented in DDL.

Example 6 (Subsumption Propagation). *A P-DL KB includes three modules* $L_{\{1,2,3\}}$, L_1 *has empty TBox,* $L_2 = \{1 : Bird \sqsupseteq 2 : Fowl\}$, $L_3 = \{2 : Fowl \sqsupseteq 3 : Chicken\}$, *importing relations are* $r_{12}^{Bird}, r_{23}^{Fowl}$. *The inter-module subsumption problem* $1 : Bird \sqsupseteq 3 : Chicken$ *can be answered, since in any model of the KB,* $Chicken^{m_3} \subseteq r_{23}(Fowl^{m_2}) \subseteq r_{23}(r_{12}(Bird^{m_1})) = r_{13}(Bird^{m_1})$, *therefore* $Bird \sqsupseteq_P Chicken$ *is always true.*

Example 7 (Inter-module Unsatisfiability). *A P-DL ontology contains two modules* $L_{\{1,2\}}$, $L_1 = \{1 : Bird \sqsubseteq 1 : Fly\}$, $L_2 = \{1 : Bird \sqsupseteq 2 : Penguin, \neg 1 : Fly \sqsupseteq 2 : Penguin\}$, *importing relations are* $r_{12}^{Bird}, r_{12}^{Fly}$. *For any model m of the ontology,* $Penguin^{m_2} \subseteq r_{12}((\neg Fly)^{m_1}) \cap r_{12}(Bird^{m_1})$, *and* $r_{12}(Bird^{m_1}) \subseteq r_{12}(Fly^{m_1})$. *Therefore* $Penguin^{m_2} \subseteq r_{12}((\neg Fly)^{m_1}) \cap r_{12}(Fly^{m_1}) \subseteq \emptyset$ *is not satisfiable.*

An $\mathcal{E}$-connection-like constructed concept such as $\exists (i : E).(j : D)$ can be defined in the module i, where $j : D$ is imported into i, with semantics: $\{x \in \Delta_i | \exists y \in \Delta_j, y' = r_{ji}(y) \in \Delta_i, (x, y') \in E^{m_i}, y \in D^{m_j}\}\}$. $\forall (i : E).(j : D)$ can be constructed similarly. It is easy to see a combined model (Tableau) of $\mathcal{E}$-connections [7] can be reduced to a P-DL model by transforming every $\mathcal{E}$-connection instance $e(i : x, j : y)$ to a role instance $e(i : x, i : y')$ and adding (y, y') to the domain relation r_{ji} if it has not already been added.

Since "links" in $\mathcal{E}$-connections can be specified as local roles in P-DL with foreign concepts as ranges, link inclusion, link inverse, and link number restriction can also be reduced into normal role axioms in P-DL. Therefore, we have:

Theorem 5. *P-DL* $\mathcal{SHOIQP}_\mathcal{C}(D)$ *is strictly more expressive than the DDL extension to* $\mathcal{SHOIQ}$ *with bridge rules between concepts, and $\mathcal{E}$-Connections* $\mathcal{C}_{\mathcal{HQ}}^{\mathcal{E}}$ ($\mathcal{SHIQ}, \mathcal{SHOQ}, \mathcal{SHIO}$) *and* $\mathcal{C}_{\mathcal{HI}}^{\mathcal{E}}$($\mathcal{SHIQ}, \mathcal{SHOQ}, \mathcal{SHIO}$).

Some types of DDL and $\mathcal{E}$-Connections can not be reduced to the P-DL extension $\mathcal{P}_\mathcal{C}$, e.g., DDL bridge rules between roles and individuals or generalized links [13] in $\mathcal{E}$-connections. However, we believe future extension of P-DL may cover some of these scenarios.

Another observation is that it is possible to simulate the one-to-one domain relations that are required in P-DL by the combination of DDL and E-connections[2]. If we use bridge rules as a special type of $\mathcal{E}$-connections with "≤ 1" cardinality restriction in $\mathcal{E}$-connections, it effectively encodes the one-to-one domain relations. More precisely, for any pair of module i, j, if we denote E as the $\mathcal{E}$-connection for bridge rules from i to j, F as the $\mathcal{E}$-connection for bridge rules from j to i,, the following axioms can be added:

- In module i: $\top_i \sqsubseteq\ \leq 1E.\top_j$
- In module j: $\top_j \sqsubseteq\ \leq 1F.\top_i$
- $F = E^-$.

---

[2] We thank the anonymous reviewers of the Description Logics Workshop for pointing this out.

However, such a simulation does not always meet the compositional consistency requirement of P-DL. Therefore, such a combination of DDL and $\mathcal{E}$-connections, while it can solve the inter-module unsatisfiability problem, may fail on some problems that require module transitive reusability, such as the general subsumption propagation problem as outlined in Example 1.

7 Summary

In this paper, we have investigated the semantics of DDL, $\mathcal{E}$-connections and P-DL. We have shown that (a) one-to-one domain relation is a sufficient condition for exact DDL reasoning; (b) $\mathcal{E}$-connections, in general, are more expressive than DDL only with inverse links; c) an importing approach in P-DL can be used to ensure transitivity of inter-module subsumption without sacrificing the exactness of inference in P-DL with only a compromise of local semantics. Our results raise the possibility of avoiding many of the semantic difficulties in current modular ontology language proposals by removing the strong assumption of module disjointness.

Acknowledgements. This research was supported in part by grants from the US NSF (0219699, 0639230) and NIH (GM 066387).

References

1. F. Baader, C. Lutz, H. Sturm, and F. Wolter. Fusions of description logics. In *Description Logics*, pages 21–30, 2000.
2. J. Bao, D. Caragea, and V. Honavar. Modular ontologies - a formal investigation of semantics and expressivity. In *R. Mizoguchi, Z. Shi, and F. Giunchiglia (Eds.): Asian Semantic Web Conference 2006, LNCS 4185*, pages 616–631, 2006.
3. J. Bao, D. Caragea, and V. Honavar. Towards collaborative environments for ontology construction and sharing. In *International Symposium on Collaborative Technologies and Systems (CTS 2006)*, pages 99–108. IEEE Press, 2006.
4. A. Borgida and L. Serafini. Distributed description logics: Directed domain correspondences in federated information sources. In *CoopIS*, pages 36–53, 2002.
5. P. Bouquet, F. Giunchiglia, and F. van Harmelen. C-OWL: Contextualizing ontologies. In *Second International Semantic Web Conference*, volume 2870 of *Lecture Notes in Computer Science*, pages 164–179. Springer Verlag, 2003.
6. C. Ghidini and L. Serafini. *Frontiers Of Combining Systems 2, Studies in Logic and Computation*, chapter Distributed First Order Logics, pages 121–140. Research Studies Press, 1998.
7. B. C. Grau. *Combination and Integration of Ontologies on the Semantic Web*. PhD thesis, Dpto. de Informatica, Universitat de Valencia, Spain, 2005.
8. B. C. Grau, B. Parsia, and E. Sirin. Tableau algorithms for e-connections of description logics. Technical report, University of Maryland Institute for Advanced Computer Studies (UMIACS), TR 2004-72, 2004.
9. B. C. Grau, B. Parsia, and E. Sirin. Working with multiple ontologies on the semantic web. In *International Semantic Web Conference*, pages 620–634, 2004.

10. I. Horrocks and U. Sattler. A Tableaux Decision Procedure for SHOIQ. In *IJCAI*, pages 448–453, 2005.
11. O. Kutz, C. Lutz, F. Wolter, and M. Zakharyaschev. E-connections of description logics. In *Description Logics Workshop, CEUR-WS Vol 81*, 2003.
12. O. Kutz, C. Lutz, F. Wolter, and M. Zakharyaschev. E-connections of abstract description systems. *Artif. Intell.*, 156(1):1–73, 2004.
13. B. Parsia and B. C. Grau. Generalized link properties for expressive epsilon-connections of description logics. In *AAAI*, pages 657–662, 2005.
14. L. Serafini, A. Borgida, and A. Tamilin. Aspects of distributed and modular ontology reasoning. In *IJCAI*, pages 570–575, 2005.
15. L. Serafini, H. Stuckenschmidt, and H. Wache. A formal investigation of mapping language for terminological knowledge. In *IJCAI*, pages 576–581, 2005.
16. L. Serafini and A. Tamilin. Drago: Distributed reasoning architecture for the semantic web. In *ESWC*, pages 361–376, 2005.
17. H. Stuckenschmidt, L. Serafini, and H. Wache. Reasoning about ontology mappings. Technical report, Department for Mathematics and Computer Science, University of Mannheim ; TR-2005-011, 2005.

RS2D: Fast Adaptive Search for Semantic Web Services in Unstructured P2P Networks

Ulrich Basters and Matthias Klusch

German Research Center for Artificial Intelligence
Stuhlsatzenhausweg 3, 66121 Saarbruecken, Germany
uli@basters.de, klusch@dfki.de

Abstract. In this paper, we present an approach, called RS2D v1, to adaptive probabilistic search for semantic web services in unstructured P2P networks. Each service agent dynamically learns the averaged query-answer behavior of its neighbor peers, and forwards service requests to those with minimal mixed Bayesian risk of doing so in terms of estimated semantic gain and commmunication cost. Experimental evaluation shows that the RS2D search mechanism is robust against changes in the network, and fast with reasonably high precision compared to other existing relevant approaches[1].

1 Introduction

Agent based service provision in the future open semantic Web in one extreme would ad hoc connected autonomous agents require to efficiently search for relevant services without any central coordination means and prior knowledge about their environment. This corresponds to the known challenge of searching unstructured peer-to-peer (P2P) networks with reasonably high performance and low communication efforts, but no prior knowledge about service distribution, ontologies, or network topology. Different solutions to this problem have been proposed in the P2P research literature; an accessible survey is provided in [1]. In contrast to structured P2P networks, unstructured approaches lack of global routing guarantees provided by the overlay, that is, they offer arbitrary network topology, file placement and search. Though blind flooding based search, or variants of it, in such networks like Gnutella [9], performs very robustly with high precision but suffers from insufficient scalability due to high communication overhead. Randomized routing usually keeps the communication effort low, but exhibits low performance due to its random nature and inability to adapt to different query loads. Approaches to informed probabilistic adaptive P2P search in unstructured P2P networks like in [15] improve on such random walks but do not exploit the qualitative results of semantic matching of services to drive the search. In fact, as of today, there exist only few approaches that explicitly perform semantic service retrieval in unstructured P2P networks, that are

---

[1] This work has been supported by the German ministry of education and research (BMB+F 01-IW-D02-SCALLOPS), and the European Commission (FP6 IST-511632-CASCOM).

Bibster[10] and GSD[5]. Both approaches are still limited in the sense that they require prior knowledge on the semantic overlay, and a fixed (static) global ontology to be used by each peer, respectively.

This motivated us to develop the first risk-driven and behavior based approach, named RS2D, to combine adaptive probabilistic with semantic search for OWL-S services in unstructured P2P networks. RS2D enables each autonomous peer to dynamically build up and manage its own local ontology in OWL based on a minimal shared vocabulary only. Furthermore, and more importantly, RS2D peers do not perform object-specific but average peer behavior based semantic search, that is each of them quickly learns which of its direct neighbours in the network will most probably return relevant semantic web services for a given query with minimal mixed Bayesian risk of both semantic loss and high communication in average. Although the implemented RS2D routing decision scheme works for OWL-S services only, its core decision routing mechanism is independent from the service description language, hence can be, in principle, used to search for any other kind of web services as well, such as WSDL, WSDL-S, and WSMO, by means of replacing our OWLS-MX matchmaker at each peer with an adequate one for local semantic service selection.

The remainder of this paper is organized as follows. Section 2 presents the original version of our RS2D approach (RS2D v1) for risk driven probabilistic search of OWL-S services in unstructured P2P service networks in detail. Sections 3 and 4 provide the results of the comparative experimental evaluation of RS2D v1 and related work, respectively, and we conclude in section 5. Complementary work on RS2D v2 with alternate semantic loss function is in [4].

2 Adaptive Search for OWL-S Services

How does the adaptive probabilistic search for OWL-S services in unstructured P2P networks according to the RS2D routing decision scheme? Each peer first determines the set of OWL-S services that are semantically relevant to a given service request (query) by use of its local OWL-S matchmaker, and then forwards the same query only to those of its direct neighbor peers from which it expects to most probably receive semantically relevant services in reasonable time. For this purpose, it continuously observes the individual average query answering behavior of these peers, caching not only the number but semantic qualities of their replies, and requests in its local training set and updates. These data are then used to estimate the mixed conditional probabilistic risk of semantic query routing for each of its neighbor peers. We present the details of this adaptive mixed risk-driven search in subsequent sections.

2.1 Local Observations

What does an RS2D enabled peer v in an unstructured network observe in concrete terms? From each reply to a given query q it receives from some of its direct neighbour v_k, it extracts data into a training record

$$t = (q, S_q, S'_q, L(S_q), L(S'_q), fid, tid, c_j, a)$$

and stores it in its local training set TS. These observation data are as follows:

q: Request in terms of the description of a desired service written in a semantic web service description language such as OWL-S.
S_q: Set of top-k relevant services retrieved *before* forwarding the request.
S'_q: Set of top-k relevant services retrieved *after* forwarding the request.
$L(S_q), L(S'_q)$: Semantic score of S_q, S''_q. This score measures the semantic quality of the set of retrieved services with respect to q by summarizing the numeric results of their semantic matching performed by an appropriate matchmaker, that is $L(S_q) := \sum_{s \in S_q} \sigma(s, q)$. For example, searching for OWL-S services in RS2D enabled P2P networks may be achieved by using the OWLS-MX matchmaker (cf. section 2.2), as we did for evaluating the RS2D performance (cf. section 4).
fid, tid: Identifier of the peer from/to which the request was received/forwarded.
c_j: Query answer result class, that is c_0 meaning that the query got rejected because it was processed by v_k already, or c_1 meaning that v_k answers to the query with a semantic gain, i.e. with $L(S'_q) - L(S_q) > 0$. That is, the reply is considered of real benefit for v, only if it contains services previously unknown to v with higher degree of semantic relevance.
a: Communication effort entailed by the decision to route the request to v_k, i.e. the number of message hops in the routing subtree of the request.

The observation vector $x \in \mathbb{N}^2$ used for risk estimations is defined as $x = (fid, tid)$. Our experiments showed, that already the use of these two parameters yield an reasonably well prediction. To be able to predict the values of $\lambda, E(y), E(a)$ and $P(c_j|x)$, we filter the training set TS in different ways.

2.2 Local Semantic Service Selection

In order to compute the numeric semantic scores $LS(S_q)$, each RS2D peer maps the oputput of its local OWL-S service matchmaker OWLS-MX [12] to the interval $[0, 1]$ (cf. figure 1). The mapping is defined by $\sigma_{mx} : (S^* \times S^*) \mapsto [0, 1] \subset \mathbb{R}$; $\sigma_{mx}(s, q) := (5 - dom + sim)/6$ with $dom = \{0, 1, 2, 3, 4, 5\}$ coding the degrees of match (exact = 0, plug-in = 1, subsumes = 2, subsumed-by = 3, nearest-neighbour = 4, fail = 5), and $sim \in [0, 1]$ the syntactic similarity value, as returned by the matchmaker OWLS-MX.

OWLS-MX takes any OWL-S service description as a query, and returns an ordered set of relevant services that match the query in terms of both crisp logic based and syntactic similarity. For this purpose, it applies five different hybrid matching filters with one selected IR similarity metric each. Logical subsumption failures produced by the integrated OWL-DL reasoner Pellet are tolerated, if the computed syntactic similarity value is sufficient. It turned out that this is beneficial in terms of both recall and precision. For more details on OWLS-MX, we refer the interested reader to [12]; the sources are available at [13].

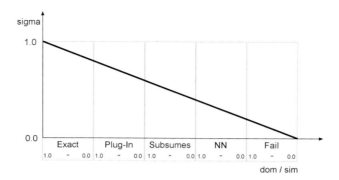

Fig. 1. Mapping of the degrees of semantic service matching returned by the OWLS-MX matchmaker to [0,1] used by RS2D peers to determine the numeric semantic gain of received replies from their neighbour peers

What makes OWLS-MX particularly suitable to semantic service selection in unstructured P2P service networks is its ability to dynamically maintain a local (matchmaker) ontology on the basis of a shared minimal vocabulary of primitive components only. This renders RS2D peers independent from the exclusive use of a fixed global ontology. Instead the minimal set of shared primitive components from which each peer may canonically define local concept semantics constitutes the weakest form of a shared ontology. Further, we assume that RS2D peers do exchange not only the names but terminologic expansions of service I/O concepts. This enables peers to gradually learn about the expertise of other peers through appropriate classification of the concepts of their queries and replies into its local ontology. The same holds in case service descriptions change. Hence, RS2D peers do not have to adopt a static global ontology like in GSD[5].

2.3 Individual Semantic Loss

The estimated semantic loss of routing some query q to a peer v_k (alternatives α_0, α_1) for possible query answer classes (c_0, c_1) based on its average Q/A behavior according to the actual training set is essentially driving the risk based decision making of each RS2D peer. In the original version of the RS2D system v1, the semantic loss $\lambda(\alpha_i, c_j)$ is computed as follows:

$$\begin{array}{c|c|c} & \lambda(\alpha_0|\cdot) & \lambda(\alpha_1|\cdot) \\ \hline c_0 & 0 & 2\kappa \\ c_1 & E(y) - E(a)\kappa & -E(y) + E(a)\kappa \end{array} \quad (1)$$

The average message transmission costs are denoted by κ, and assumed to be constant. In addition, the average expected semantic gain $E(y)$ and average number of messages $E(a)$ are defined as follows:

$$E(y) := \frac{1}{|TS_{fid,tid}|} \sum_{t \in TS_{fid,tid}} [L(S''_q)]_t - [L(S'_q)]_t \qquad (2)$$

$$E(a) := \frac{1}{|TS_{fid,tid}|} \sum_{t \in TS_{fid,tid}} [a]_t \qquad (3)$$

with $[x]_t$ extracting the parameter x from observation record t in the training set TS. An alternative definition of the semantic loss function we used in the second version of the RS2D system is presented in [4] together with the results of its experimental evaluation. As expected, both RS2D versions significantly differ in the quality of their results. In particular, the second version improved the retrieval performance of the original one in terms of precision but at the cost of increased communication efforts.

2.4 Learning of Individual Q/A Behavior

Each peer learns the most probable query answering (Q/A) behavior of each of its direct neighbours individually in order to be able to decide on whether it is beneficial to forward queries to theses peers, or not. In particular, the conditional probability $P(c_j|x)$ of possible answering result classes of the considered peer v_k based on its observed Q/A behavior in the past is computed based on the prior probability $P(x|c_j)$, the likelihood $P(c_j)$, and the normalizing evidence factor $P(x)$ from the training set TS, with

$$P(c_j) = \frac{|TS_{c_j}|}{|TS|}; P(x|c_j) = \prod_{l=1}^{n} P(x_l|c_j); P(x) = \sum_{j=1}^{|C|} P(x|c_j) \cdot P(c_j) \qquad (4)$$

and the feature probability $P(x_l|c_j) = \frac{|TS_{x_l,c_j}|}{|TS_{c_j}|}$ of the occurence of the observation feature component x_l for given class c_j.

The decision making process heavily relies on the training set TS that each peer maintains individually. Initially, when a peer joins the network, its training set TS is empty; in this case, it sends its queries to all its direct neighbours until the size $(\theta(TS))$ of its training set, more specifically $TS_{fid,tid}$ is sufficiently large for continuing with risk assessment driven routing decisions from this point. Our experiments provide evidence in favor of $\theta(TS_{fid,tid}) = 8$.

2.5 Mixed Risk Based Query Routing Decision

The risk assessment driven routing decision of each peer v whether to route a given query q to a given neighbour v_k, or not, is then based on the mixed conditional Bayesian risk of doing so in terms of both semantic gain and communication costs. It is computed as follows

$$R(\alpha_i|x) = \sum_{j=1}^{|C|} \lambda(\alpha_i, c_j) \cdot P(c_j|x) \qquad (5)$$

It sends the request $r = (q, S_q, S'_q, a)$ based on its actual training set TS to v_k, if the risk of forwarding r to v_k is minimal. Otherwise, it rejects a received request r, if it has been already processed locally, or a fixed number of forwarding steps (hops) is reached, or the risk of further forwarding is maximal for each of its neighbours. As a consequence of routing r only to those peers for which the corresponding alternative with minimal risk

$$\alpha^* = argmin\{R(\alpha_0|x), R(\alpha_1|x)\} \qquad (6)$$

is α_1, the overall risk $R = \int R(\alpha(x)|x)P(x)dx$ is also minimal.

For each request r, each peer collects the replies it receives from its neighbours for r, that is the set of top-k semantically matching services, and merges them together with its local answer set. The top-k services of the merged set with semantic gain is then recursively returned on the unique return path to the one who did forward the request. That is, the complete answer set for a query is created while being propagated back to its origin. At the same time, each peer involved in this process continuously learns about the query answering behaviour of each of its neighbours in general. It caches the individual observations in its local training set each time it receives a reply. This, in turn, enables each peer to estimate the corresponding risk of forwarding a query to individual peers.

The computational complexity of RS2D is $O(nm \cdot T_\sigma + nm \cdot \log k + nt)$ with n and m of peers, respectively, services in the network, and t and k maximal size of the training, respectively, answer sets. That is, the adaptive RS2D search is linear with respect to the routing decision but subject to the computational complexity $O(T_\sigma)$ of the used matchmaker in total; the proof is given in [2].

2.6 Join/Leave Operations

RS2D requires minimal message exchange on dynamic operations such as node arrivals or departures. The join-operation of a peer in RS2D enabled P2P networks is implemented as a simple handshake-advertisement: Each peer that wants to join the network, broadcasts a one-hop advertisement (TTL = 1) to all peers in its neighbourhood, and then waits for acknowledgement-messages. If at least one peer answers, the requesting peer considers itself to be on line and part of the network, and both peers mutually take themselves into account for future routing decisions. The leave-operation is completely passive: A peer just drops out and stops answering to messages. Its neighbouring peers will detect its absence as soon as they attempt to send a new message to it, and consequently remove those training records from their local training sets that relate to it.

In its current version, the RS2D protocol does not explicitly enforce the propagation of changes in the expertise of each peer through the network. Such changes are caused by the insertion, deletion, or modification service descriptions. Rather, each RS2D peer gradually adapts to such changes each time it receives a response to a query from the owner of the changed service by observing possibly implied changes of the answering behaviour including, in particular, the semantic gain.

3 Comparative Evaluation of RS2D

We have implemented the P2P service retrieval mechanism RS2D v1, and evaluated it by means of simulation. In the following, we present the results of the evaluation of the original RS2D protocol compared to the classic broadcast based routing (BCST), random selection of two neighbor peers (RND2), and Bibster like routing (BIBL) [10] based on peers that have prior knowledge on the semantic overlay network.

For testing purposes, we randomly generated unstructured, sparsely connected P2P networks of different size with 50, 100, 200, and 576 peers, and used the OWLS-TC2 service retrieval test collection [14] which contains 576 OWL-S services, 36 queries with relevance sets, and the OWLS-MX matchmaker [13] for semantic matching by each peer. In each simulation run, the queries are sequentially processed by each peer to generate the training set, and the top 20 services are returned by each peer only. The P2P service retrieval performance is measured in terms of micro-averaged precision and recall against communication overhead with respect to the maximum hop count for query propagation.

Testing of RS2D in large scale networks with thousands of peers requires, in particular, a correspondingly large and meaningful semantic web service retrieval test collection, which is not available yet. For details on the implementation of the RS2D simulator, as well as the improved RS2D v2, and the results of its experimental evaluation, we refer the interested reader to [4,2]. We were not able to run the GSD

3.1 Service Retrieval Performance

In our experiments, we evaluated two essential aspects of P2P service retrieval performance measurement:

1. Service distribution to peers: Uniformly at random Vs. Single peer hosts all relevant services per query
2. Query distribution to peers by the user: Random querying of peers Vs. One central Q/A peer, considered as exclusive querying interface to the system for the user

For reasons of space limitation, we present only the representative experimental results, and refer the interested reader for complete set of our RS2D performance and robustness experiments to the RS2D project web page [3].

Experiment 1: As figure 2 shows, in a network of 576 peers with evenly distributed 576 services, and random querying of peers, RS2D outperforms BIBL as well as RND2 in terms of precision with lesser number of hops which yields a

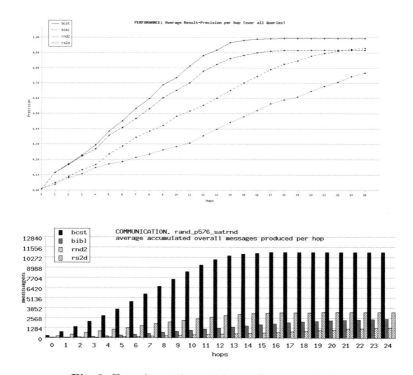

Fig. 2. Experiment 1, precision and communication

faster response time. However, after around 22 hops it gets slightly overtaken by BIBL due to its query-specific routing with prior knowledge on the peer expertises. The second version of RS2D ([4], fig. 2) performs totally different in that it could not be outperformed by BIBL at all while being almost close to optimal from the beginning. Each of both results were confirmed by the respective version of RS2D also for smaller P2P networks (50, 100, 200 peers).

When it comes to communication overhead, RS2D performs as bad as broadcast based routing in the initial training phase. In fact, RS2D does a multicast in the initial training phase, though this phase may be very short (eight recorded replies in average were sufficient to initialize successful risk driven query routing), so BIBL outruns RS2D because it exploits its prior semantic overlay knowledge for routing. However, the situation changes when processing the last query of the test collection: RS2D is faster than the initially more savvy BIBL (see fig.3). The same holds for RS2D v2 ([4], fig. 4), though RS2D v1 turned out to be much more efficient in this respect, hence faster in its response time.

Experiment 2: We also simulated the case of single query authorities, i.e., one peer hosts all the relevant services to a query, with random querying of the peers.

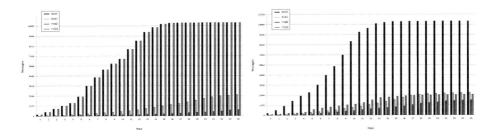

Fig. 3. Experiment 1, communication, first/last query

For each query a different but distinguished peer was chosen at random to host the relevance set. The results (fig. 4) show that BIBL eventually outperforms RS2D, because it can exploit its knowledge on the semantic overlay for optimal query-specific routing. RS2D v1 gets outperformed even by RND2 in the end. Main reason for that is that relying only on the *average* query answer behaviour renders it very difficult to find the single authority for each individual query. In any case, this clear deficiency of RS2D v1 motivated us to let each peer adapt according to a differently designed semantic loss function in the second version of RS2D ([4], fig. 5) which then performed almost optimal from the beginning, strongly outperforming both BIBL and RND2, but at the cost of (reasonably) higher communication efforts.

Experiment 3: We also tested RS2D in a setting with one distinguished (central querying) peer executing all queries on behalf of a user with 576 services distributed uniformly at random in a 576 peer network, and initial size of training set $\theta_{TS} = 8$.

According to the experimental results (cf. fig. 5), RS2D performs optimal (curve is on that of BCST) in terms of precision but drastically reduced communication overhead. The same was experimentally shown to hold for the performance of RS2D v2 ([4], fig. 7) with comparably minor reduction of communication only. Main reason for the good performance in this case is that the central RS2D peer is able to directly search the minimal spanning tree for all queries after its initial multicast.

In fact, further evaluation revealed that for the same reason the observed deficiency of RS2D in case of authorities in an unstructured network with uniform at random query and service distribution (cf. fig. 4) can be largely mitigated by the introduction of a central query-answering peer (cf. fig. 6). In this case, RS2D remains to perform optimal whereas both savvy BIBL and random walk RND2 are able to eventually close up, though BIBL gets partially outperformed by RND2. Interestingly, RS2D gets even faster than its competitors in terms of communication cost. This setting also turned out to be the best for RS2D in terms of achieved performance and communication according to our simulations.

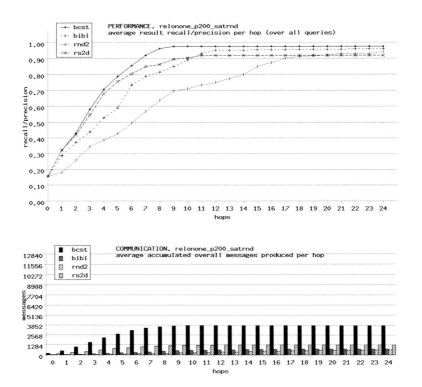

Fig. 4. Experiment 2, precision and communication (query authorities, n = 200)

3.2 Robustness

We tested the robustness of RS2D against dynamic changes of the topology of a network of 576 peers.

Experiment 4: During simulation peers may randomly join or leave the network with a rate of about one such operation for each five simulation steps, with around 80% of all peers (= 460) being on line in average.

If a RS2D peer is not able to route a return message to relevant peers according to the return path because they are not reachable for some reason, it tries to contact the subsequent peers in the path to establish a detour for this case. If this strategy fails, it issues a limited 2-hop broadcast to all of its neighbours. Only if the peer turns out to be isolated, or none of the contacted peers is able to forward the return message to any of the subsequent ones in the respective return path, the return message is discarded yielding a total loss of all related intermediate results of the query. The experimental results show that albeit the implied communication effort of RS2D is higher than that of BIBL compared to the static cases, it remains to be more efficient in terms of performance except the optimal BCST. Not surprisingly, the performance of all systems went down

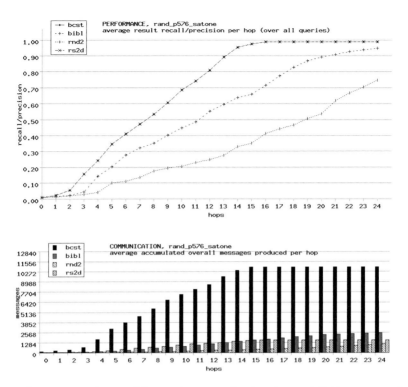

Fig. 5. Experiment 3a, precision and communication (central Q/A peer, random)

compared to those in the static cases; the second version of RS2D performed slightly better than the original one also in the dynamic case.

4 Related work

Relevant work includes approaches to probabilistic adaptive object retrieval in unstructured P2P networks such as in [15,11,8] as well as systems that do exploit semantic web technologies for this task such as Bibster[10] and GSD[5].

In APS [15], each peer forwards a query to k of its N neighbors. If a hit (match) occurs, the request terminates successfully, otherwise it gets forwarded to only one of this peers neighbors. This procedure continues until all k requests (with the same query) have terminated, either with success, or failure. Each APS peer keeps a local index with one value for each object (service) it requested, or forwarded a request for, per neighbor. Along the paths of all k queries, indices are updated as follows. In the pessimistic learning approach, each peer on a querys path decreases the respective object index value by a fixed amount reflecting the relative probability of its being the next hop choice in a subsequent search for the same object concurrently with the actual search. If the query succeeds by

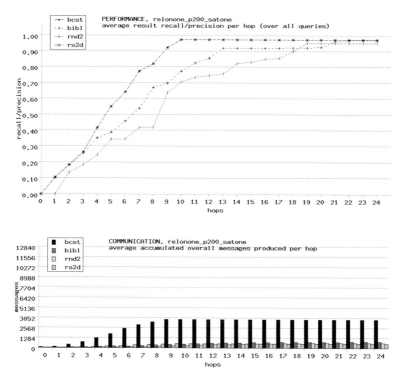

Fig. 6. Experiment 3b, precision and communication (central Q/A peer, authorities, n = 200)

eventually locating (an exact copy of) the object at some peer, the respective index values of all peers in the return path get updated by a fixed amount larger than the previously subtracted amount (positive feedback). The optimistic search operates in an opposite fashion (negative feedback) after a query fails. Hence, the initial probability of a peer for a certain object increases if the object was discovered through (or at) that node, and decreases otherwise. In contrast to RS2D, APS peers perform an informed exact object search only with index update by same amount of values for each peer. Hence, APS does not exploit different qualities of semantic matching at individual peers, nor the combined use of semantic gain and estimated communication efforts to drive the search like in RS2D. Finally, RS2D's minimal risk driven routing scheme is based on the average but not object specific Q/A behavior of peers.

The GSD routing scheme [5], in contrast to RS2D, relies on an acyclic ontology to be used by each peer to categorize its services by associating their identifiers with appropriate concepts. The degree of semantic relevance of any service to a given query is assumed to be inverse proportional to the computed distance between their concepts in the ontology.

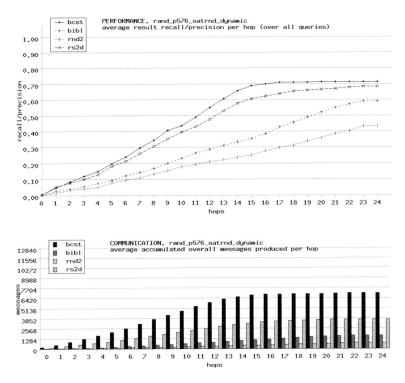

Fig. 7. Experiment 4, precision and communication

Bibster's object specific search [10], in contrast to RS2D, exploits prior knowledge about the expertise of peers. In an initial advertisement round, each peer caches the advertised services of its neighbours only if they are semantically close to at least one of its own. Any query is then forwarded only to two neighbours with maximum matching expertise. The additional communication overhead induced by the initial expertise building is not included in the comparative evaluation results shown in section 4.

5 Conclusion

This paper presents RS2D v1, an approach to adaptive and mixed probabilistic risk driven search for OWL-S services in unstructured P2P networks in the semantic web. Experimental results showed that RS2D is fast and robust with comparatively high precision. It is, however, weak in finding single query authority peers, and its scalability to large scale networks with more than 576 service peers remains to be investigated due to lack of a sufficiently large OWL-S service retrieval test collection. In [4], we showed that the performance of RS2D v1 can be significantly improved by means of a different semantic loss function but at the cost of communication efforts. RS2D will be made available to the semantic web community under LGPL-like license at semwebcentral.org.

References

1. S. Androutsellis-Theotokis and D. Spinellis. *A survey of peer-to-peer content distribution technologies.* ACM Computing Surveys, 36(4):335371, 2004
2. U. Basters. *RS2D - Risikobasierte semantische Suche nach OWL-S Diensten in unstrukturierten P2P Netzen.* Diploma thesis, University of the Saarland, Computer Science Department (in German).
3. U. Basters. RS2D v1.0 and RS2D v2.0 online: http://www.basters.de/rs2d/.
4. U. Basters and M. Klusch *Risk Driven Semantic P2P Service Retrieval.* Proc. 6th Int. IEEE Conference on P2P Computing, Cambridge, UK, 2006.
5. D. Chakraborty, A. Joshi, T. Finin, and Y. Yesha. *GSD: A novel groupbased service discovery protocol for MANETS.* Proc. 4th IEEE Conference on Mobile and Wireless Communications Networks (MWCN), 2002.
6. Y. Chawathe, S. Ratnasamy, L. Breslau, N. Lanham, and S. Shenker. *Making Gnutella-like p2p systems scalable.* Proc. Int. Conference on Applications, Technologies, Architectures, and Protocols for Computer Communications, Karlsruhe, Germany, 2003.
7. C. Elkan. *Boosting and Naive Bayesian learning.* Technical report, Department of Computer Science and Engineering, University of California, San Diego, 1997.
8. R. Ferreira, M. Ramanathan, A. Awan, A. Grama, S. Jagannathan. *Search with Probabilistic Guarantees in Unstructured Peer-to-Peer Networks.* Proc. Int. IEEE Conference on P2P Computing, Konstanz, Germany, 2005.
9. Gnutella. http://gnutella.wego.com/.
10. P. Haase, R. Siebes, and F. van Harmelen. *Expertise-based Peer selection in Peer-to-Peer Networks.* Knowledge and Information Systems, Springer, 2006.
11. V. Kalogeraki, D. Gunopulos, and D. Zeinalipour-Yazti. *A local search mechanism for peer-to-peer networks.* Proc. 11th Int. Conference on Information and Knowledge management (CIKM), ACM Press, 2002.
12. M. Klusch, B. Fries, and K. Sycara. *Automated Semantic Web Service Discovery with OWLS-MX.* Proc. 5th Intl. Conference on Autonomous Agents and Multiagent Systems (AAMAS), Hakodate, Japan, 2006
13. OWLS-MX: http://projects.semwebcentral.org/projects/owls-mx/.
14. OWLS-TC: http://projects.semwebcentral.org/projects/owls-tc/.
15. D. Tsoumakos and N. Roussopoulos. *Adaptive Probabilistic Search (APS) for Peer-to-Peer Networks.* Proc. Int. IEEE Conference on P2P Computing, 2003.

SADIe: Semantic Annotation for Accessibility

Sean Bechhofer, Simon Harper, and Darren Lunn

School of Computer Science, University of Manchester,
Kilburn Building, Oxford Road, Manchester, M13 9PL, UK
{sean.bechhofer, simon.harper, darren.lunn}@manchester.ac.uk

Abstract. Visually impaired users are hindered in their efforts to access the largest repository of electronic information in the world – the World Wide Web (Web). The web is visually-centric with regard to presentation and information order / layout, this can (and does) hinder users who need presentation-agnostic access to information. Transcoding can help to make information more accessible via a restructuring of pages. We describe an approach based on annotation of web pages, encoding semantic information that can then be used by tools in order to manipulate and present web pages in a form that provides easier access to content. Annotations are made directly to style sheet information, allowing the annotation of large numbers of similar pages with little effort.

1 Introduction

Access to, and movement around, complex hypermedia environments, of which the web is the most obvious example, has long been considered an important and major issue in the Web design and usability field [9,13]. The commonly used slang phrase 'surfing the web' implies rapid and free access, pointing to its importance among designers and users alike. It has also been long established [7,10] that this potentially complex and difficult access is further complicated, and becomes neither rapid nor free, if the user is visually impaired[1].

Annotation of web pages provides a mechanism to enhance visually impaired peoples' access to information on web-pages through an encoding of the meaning of that information. Annotations can then be consumed by tools that restructure or reorganise pages in order to pull out salient information. However, when working in the real world, there are issues we must face. Empirical evidence suggests that authors and designers will **not** create separate semantic mark up to sit with standard XHTML[2] because they see it as an unnecessary overhead. In addition, designers will not compromise their desire to produce "beautiful and effective" web sites.

Recent moves towards a separation of presentation, metadata and information such as Cascading Style Sheets (CSS) [6], can help to alleviate some of the

---
[1] Here used as a general term encompassing the WHO definition of both profoundly blind and partially sighted individuals [23].
[2] Extensible Hypertext Markup Language.

problems, but there are still many issues to be addressed. Sites such as CSSZen-Garden[3] are models of the state of the art, but still remain relatively inaccessible to visually impaired people, however, as the information is rendered in an order defined by the *designer* and not in the order required by the *user*.

Visually impaired users interact with these systems in a 'serial' (audio) manner as opposed to a 'parallel' (visual) manner. Content is read from top left to bottom right, there is no scanning and progress through information is slow. Visually impaired users are at a disadvantage because they have no idea which items are menus, what the page layout is, what the extent is, and where the focus of the information is. Even when CSS concepts *do* look as though they have a meaning with regard to the information there is no way of relating this due to the lack of machine interpretable semantics. At this point, we can turn our attention to advances and developments in the Semantic Web.

Before doing so, we must stress that a key consideration for us is the support of designers. We wish to support the designer because in doing this we make sure our target user group are supported by the designers' creation. In our conversations with designers [26,16] the message we hear given is:

> *"If there is any kind of overhead above the normal concept creation then we are less likely to implement it. If our design is compromised in any way we will not implement. We create beautiful and effective sites, we're not information architects."*

We suggest that designers need a lightweight no-frills [20] approach to include semantic information relating to the role of document elements within XHTML documents; thus we need to ensure that any technical solutions proposed should incur a minimal costs in design overhead. We consider this to be "semantics" as it exposes additional information about page elements that would otherwise be implicit – for example a `menu` is an element that should be treated in a particular way by a client browser. CSS information may describe how to render the element in an appropriate way, but tells us nothing about the intended interpretation (and thus semantics) of the element.

The Semantic Web vision [4] is of a Web in which the underlying semantics of resources are made explicit using representations that are amenable to machine processing. The consideration of the problem outlined above leads us to the question:

> *Can semantic information be exposed in general purpose web-pages such that the information within the page can be transformed into a version as accessible to visually impaired users as it is to sighted users, without compromising the page's design vision?*

Our proposed approach, known as SADIe, can be summarised as follows. We provide an ontology that describes the meaning of elements found within XHTML meta tags and associate this with the data found in pages through an annotation of CSS style sheets. In this way, CSS presentation will be unaffected

---
[3] `http://www.csszengarden.com/`

but semantics will be an explicit part of the data. We can then provide tools that consume this information, manipulating the documents and providing appropriate presentations to the user. A characteristic of our approach which is worth highlighting is that – in contrast to the majority of Semantic Web work concerning semantic annotation – we are *not* here concerned directly with annotation of domain content, but rather in exposing semantics relating to the presentation of material and the document structure. In addition, there is novelty in the attempt to annotate the CSS style sheet rather than the individual documents. Although this may not allow us to provide detailed annotations of individual document elements in particular documents, the broad-brush approach results in a low-pain, high-gain situation. As we see in our example discussed throughout the paper, annotation of a single CSS style sheet can result in the ability to transcode large numbers of pages that share the CSS presentation. Annotation via the CSS also allows us to deal with legacy sites.

The needs of visually impaired users accessing pages via audio are similar in a number of ways to those using mobile or small-screen devices – for example, only a small portion of the page is viewable at any point. Thus, although our primary motivation for this work is in supporting the needs of visually impaired users, we see potential benefit in the support of small-screen and mobile devices.

Earlier work[4] puts forward the basic ideas behind our approach [15]. Here, we expand on those ideas, providing a more detailed description of our prototype implementation along with an evaluation. The remaining sections of the paper are structured as follows. We provide a brief overview of background and context. This is followed by a description of the technical approach being taken by SADIe, along with examples. We present results from a preliminary *technical* evaluation, showing the viability of our approach, and conclude with discussion and pointers to future directions.

2 Background and Context

An overview of related work and technology is given in [15]. A brief summary is given here. Our work draws on a number of strands, including the Semantic Web, encoding semantics in documents, transcoding, and annotation.

A variety of techniques have been proposed for embedding XML/RDF information in HTML documents. This includes work from the TAG project [5,19], the use of the XHTML `link` element [22], the HyperRDF system [12], Augmented Metadata for XHTML [1] and the W3C Web Co-ordination Group's work on GRDDL [17].

None of these methods prove ideal for our purposes, some due to problems with validation (TAG, XHTML `link`, and HyperRDF). GRDDL is about embedding extra information through *modification* of that document. We are interested in associating additional information with documents, but not through an embedding – rather we aim to make use of existing information already present and *expose* it in a more explicit fashion. This is similar to the Deep Annotation [28]

---

[4] Going under the name of LLIS.

approach proposed by Volz et. al., where annotation of a logical schema can lead to annotation of resources or web pages that are dynamically generated from a database.

Transcoding is a technology used to adapt Web content so that it can be viewed on any of the increasingly diverse devices found on today's market. Transcoding normally involves: (1) Syntactic changes like shrinking or removing images [18]; (2) Semantic rearrangements and fragmentation of pages based on the meaning of a section [21,11]; (3) Annotation of the page created by a reader [8]; and (4) Generated annotations created by the content management system [8]. In **Semantic Transcoding**, the semantics provide the machine understand-ability and knowledge reasoning and the transcoding provides the transformation technique. Current systems are at present however limited to page analysis [24] where a page built after a set template can be analysed and transformed by semantic or semantic like technologies.

The goal of **annotations** for Web content transcoding is to provide better support either for audio rendering, and thus for visually impaired users, or for visual rendering in small screen devices. Various proxy-based systems to transcode Web pages based on external annotations for visually impaired users have been proposed [27,3]. The main focus is on extracting visually fragmented groupings, their roles and importance. They do not support deep understanding and analysis of pages, and in consequence the supported transcoding is somewhat constrained. DANTE [30] uses an ontology known as WAfA, providing a representation of knowledge about mobility of visually impaired people. Annotations made on pages then drive a page transformation process. The DANTE approach annotates individual page fragments using XPointer which results in a rather brittle solution. Annotation at the level of the stylesheet (as proposed here) should, provide a solution which is more resilient to change. Other work centres on small-screen devices and proposes a system to transcode an HTML document by fragmenting it into several documents [18]. The transcoding is based on an external annotation framework. Annotation in the **Semantic Web** context [14] has tended to focus on providing annotations on documents in order to improve search/retrieval or integration. The focus is thus on identifying particular concept instances that are described by web pages. Here though, as introduced in Section 1 we are providing an explicit description of the meaning or intended interpretation of the structure of the document, rather than the objects in the world that the document is talking about.

Each of the transformations described above are fraught with problems with regard to the acceptability of the resulting generation. This is especially the case when sighted users as well as visually impaired users wish to use the same page. Automatic transcoding based on removing parts of the page results in too much information loss and manual transcoding is near impossible when applied to dynamic web sites. Most systems use their own bespoke proxy-servers or client side interfaces and these systems require a greater setup cost in-terms of user time. Finally, some systems require bespoke automatic annotation by a content generator and so are not usable by every user and all systems.

3 System Description

From the preceding discussion, we can identify the following requirements for our system.

- Semantic descriptions of element roles
- Non-destructive, unobtrusive annotation of pages
- Transcoding based on descriptions

The approach taken in our prototype system can be loosely described as follows. An upper level ontology provides basic notions that encapsulate the role of document elements. In the current implementatino, this is largely a taxonomy consisting of elements such as menu or header. In addition, an element can be characterised as a removableCSSComponent – one which can be removed without significantly impacting on the information carried within the document or given a priority that express how important the element is considered to be. This upper level ontology is defined in isolation from a particular site, providing an abstraction over the document structure. For a particular CSS stylesheet, we provide an extension of the ontology giving the particular characteristics of the elements appearing in that stylesheet. We can consider this extension to be an annotation of the stylesheet elements – it provides information telling us, for example, whether particular elements in the stylesheet can be considered to be removable or important. Figure 1 shows an example of a site-specific ontology extension.

Fig. 1. blogger.com ontology fragment

Annotation of the CSS elements allows us to make our assertions about the meaning of the document structure at an appropriate level. A CSS stylesheet often contains inherent "semantic" information about the implicit intended function of the elements, but which is not necessarily presented in a manner which is amenable to machine processing. For example, blogger.com (see below) provides elements such as comment and profile. This is, we feel, a clear example of a problem that Semantic Web technology and approaches are intended to represent – there is (currently) no explicit characterisation of the semantics of these tags, and they are thus opaque to understanding by machine. By providing a mapping from these elements to a shared upper level ontology of document elements, we can provide the opportunity for applications to manipulate documents in appropriate ways. The SADIe application then uses the ontology to determine appropriate transformations to be made to a source document.

Our prototype is delivered as a Mozilla toolbar extension called SADIe (see Fig. 2) which has three types of functionality; *De-Fluff*, *ReOrder*, and *Toggle Menu*. *De-fluff* removes all the information that is removable based on its location in the ontology not in the CSS or XHTML. *ReOrder* rearranges the page so that the most important pieces of information are moved to the top of the document based on the values assigned to the elements in the ontology. Finally, *Toggle Menu* moves menu items from their current location to the top of the DOM (as a child of the DOM body). In the current prototype, requests and operations are pre-configured and anchored to checkboxes on the toolbar (see Fig 2), with checkboxes for the functionalities described above and a button to execute the SADIe transformations. When transformation is selected, appropriate requests are sent to the Ontology Service. In de-fluffing, for example, all of the removable items are requested. The Service complies and the SADIe parses the Document Object Model (DOM) looking for removable components and discarding them.

As an illustrative example, we consider a blogging site blogger.com, a legacy site for which we have created a sample ontology, and show how our application can transform pages into more accessible forms. Blogs are fast becoming ubiquitous on the web, with sites such as blogger.com providing easy mechanisms allowing users to publish their thoughts or opinions on a wide range of subjects. As many users are neither interested nor competent in issues surrounding web design or the use of markup languages, blogger.com provides standard mechanisms for marking up and structuring pages. CSS stylesheets are used to control the presentation. In this way, a large number of pages can be delivered with almost identical underlying structure, but with widely differing "look and feel" in terms of the colour, fonts, layout etc. It is this similarity in structure that we exploit – by providing a mechanism that allows us to annotate at the CSS level. A single annotation is then applicable to a large number of pages. One key feature is that because we do not annotate or modify the actual XHTML document our system does not force developers into costly and time consuming re-engineering to achieve backward compatibility. We extended our SADIe Ontology with web logging terms and from these created a specific ontology for blogger.com (see earlier Fig. 1). The ontology was created in OWL using the Protégé tool; it comprises a small set of concepts and sub-concepts derived from the blogger.com CSS Template. Some of these concepts were described as being removable, and a measure of importance assigned using integer values. A fragment of the ontology is shown in Fig. 1. The hierarchical (subclass) relationships for the class removableCSSComponents have been inferred using a reasoner and show that deleted-comment, description, footer, profile-container, and sidebar can all be removed.

Interestingly our ontology contains two concepts (recently and archive-list) which have no CSS entry but which *are* used as CSS-class identifiers in blogger. Thus there is no extra presentational information associated with elements using these identifiers. These two concepts enclose the recent posts list and the archive month lists and so, in fact, act like menus into previous postings. Axioms asserting that the concepts recently and archive-list are subclasses of menu are added

SADIe: Semantic Annotation for Accessibility   107

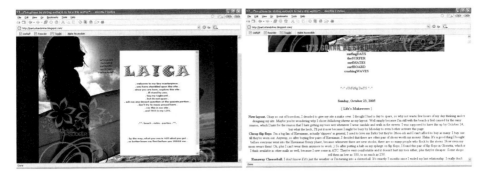

Fig. 2. Transcoding a Blog (see `http://partystands4me.blogspot.com/` for the original)

to the ontology. As we will see below our application can then treat **recently** and **archive-list** as kinds of menus and perform appropriate operations up on them. Again, this is an example of the explicit specification of the information content of the document.

Figure 2 illustrates the tool in action. To the left we see the original page before transcoding. In this case, the blog contents are relatively inaccessible, even to sighted users. After transcoding (on the right), the blog entries are exposed.

When an XHTML document arrives in the Mozilla browser with a SADIe toolbar the application first determines whether there is an ontology associated with the document (see Section 3). If such an ontology is present it is retrieved much like Mozilla retrieves the CSS document. The ontology is then passed to an Ontology Service which is used to provide functionality relating to the ontology such as classification (e.g. what are all the **removable** elements?).

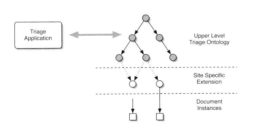

Fig. 3. Ontology and Site-specific extensions

In this way all pages created using `blogger.com` (close to a million blogs) can be modified by using this one simple ontology and tool. The particular ontology is specific to the site. However, the upper level definitions which are used by the tool in order to determine which elements to be removed are generic – integrating an additional site into the system simply requires the definition of a mapping from the CSS elements of the site into the base SADIe ontology. Any site's pages can be de-fluffed as long as the elements that are removable are identified. We do not need to hard-wire the information about the CSS elements into the application – this is encoded in the ontology which is then used by the application (see Figure 3). The upper level ontology describes concepts that are relevant to the process – for example **menu** – and the application's behaviour is specified in terms of these concepts. Site specific extensions describe their CSS elements in terms of these upper level concepts (e.g. recently as discussed in the example).

The approach is non-intrusive and works hand-in-hand with existing technologies used to control presentation. Users view the document in a web browser as normal. Browsers that are 'semantic-aware', however, can use the extra information to provide more intelligent access to the information than before.

In additoin, as we do not annotate or modify the actual XHTML document our system does not force developers into costly and time consuming re-engineering to achieve backward compatibility.

We are suggesting a simple and flexible system without a significant semantic overhead. To achieve this we use a group of techniques to encode semantics directly into a page:

Class and ID Attributes. XHTML class or id attributes are used to encode a piece of semantic information in the form of a concept-class or property into a defined piece of XHTML delimited by the closing element identifier. This is normally achieved by using the div and span elements to conjoin both the presentation style (CSS) and the semantic meaning (ontology) to the user.

Ontology. Our approach involves an annotation on CSS elements in order to describe their properties. The identification of the ontology to use may be done in a number of ways. These follow the methods laid down by the originators of CSS in order to link stylesheets to XHTML pages, e.g. through an explicit XHTML <link> element, a direct encoding of the ontology in the page or by searching for an ontology in the root directory of the web site;

The SADIe application parses the XHTML DOM and the document is then viewed as a knowledge base – instances are elements from the document such as <span> or <div> elements with their associated classes being taken from CSS id or class attributes (see Fig. 2 - 'ID / CLASS Results'). Information about the classes in the ontology is then used to determine the actions to take. For instance, if we wanted to remove all the concepts (and therefore CSS-blocks) that are removable, then this involves a query for those elements classified as removable in the ontology. We can here make use of the concept hierarchy, potentially providing descriptions of the document elements that are organised and classified using inference. Inference may be brought into play here – for example, it may be that we use a number of characteristics to determine whether an element should be considered as removable.

Similarly, as discussed above, concepts such as recently and archive-list are classified as kinds of menu. As SADIe knows how to process menu concepts (from the SADIe Ontology), when it encounters an archive-list, this can be handled using appropriate mechanisms – say moving it to the top of the document or back to its original position. A key point to note here is that the reordering of the DOM in general does *not* change the visual appearance as the CSS takes care of the layout. It does however move the information in the XHTML document and changes are noticeable if the style information is removed. This is exactly the

Table 1. SADIe Evaluation Results

Category	Name	URL	CSS	Failure	Entry Point
Corporate Sites	Microsoft Corporation	http://www.microsoft.com/	Mixed	2	Success
	Digital Designs	http://www.digitaldesign.us	Pure	0	Success
	Stagecoach Buses	http://www.stagecoachbus.com/	Pure	0	Success
	British Nuclear Fuels	http://www.bnfl.com/	Pure	0	Success
	Epson Corporation	http://www.epson.co.jp/e/	Mixed	1	Success
Content & Media	Blogger	http://www.blogger.com/	Pure	0	Success
	The Mac Observer	http://www.macobserver.com/	Pure	0	Success
	New Musical Express	http://www.nme.com/	Mixed	5	Failure
	BBC News	http://news.bbc.co.uk/	Mixed	2	Failure
	CNN International	http://edition.cnn.com/	Mixed	1	Failure
Search Engines	Google	http://www.google.co.uk/	None	5	Failure
	Yahoo	http://uk.yahoo.com/	Mixed	0	Success
	Ask Jeeves	http://www.askjeeves.co.uk/	Mixed	0	Success
	MSN Search	http://search.msn.com/	Pure	0	Success
	HotBot	http://www.hotbot.co.uk/	Pure	0	Success
Directories	Google Directory	http://directory.google.co.uk/	None	5	Failure
	Yahoo Directory	http://uk.dir.yahoo.com/	None	5	Failure
	This Is Our Year	http://www.thisisouryear.com/	Mixed	2	Success
	HotSheet	http://www.hotsheet.com/	Pure	0	Success
	HaaBaa Web Directory	http://www.haabaa.com/	Mixed	0	Success
Portals	AOL UK	http://www.aol.co.uk/	Mixed	0	Success
	MSN UK	http://www.msn.co.uk/	Mixed	2	Success
	Wanadoo	http://www.wanadoo.co.uk/	Mixed	4	Success
	Virgin Net	http://www.virgin.net/	Mixed	4	Success
	Tiscali UK	http://www.tiscali.co.uk/	Pure	0	Success
E-stores	Play	http://www.play.com/	Mixed	0	Success
	Amazon UK	http://www.amazon.co.uk/	None	5	Failure
	Tiny	http://www.tiny.com/	Mixed	1	Success
	Tesco	http://www.tesco.com/	Mixed	1	Success
	Red Letter Days	http://www.redletterdays.co.uk/	Mixed	1	Success
Virtual Hosting	Bravenet	http://www.bravenet.com/	Mixed	1	Success
	InMotion Hosting	http://www.inmotionhosting.com/	None	5	Failure
	Path Host	http://www.pathhost.net/	Mixed	0	Success
	Honest Web Host	http://www.honestwebhost.com/	Mixed	5	Failure
	Netwalker Internet Services	http://www.netwalker.biz/	Mixed	0	Success
Universities	University of Manchester	http://www.manchester.ac.uk/	Mixed	0	Success
	University of York	http://www.york.ac.uk/	Mixed	0	Success
	University of Sheffield	http://www.shef.ac.uk/	Mixed	1	Success
	University of Oxford	http://www.ox.ac.uk/	Mixed	0	Success
	University of Southampton	http://www.soton.ac.uk/	Mixed	1	Success

outcome we hoped for because access technologies access the XHTML DOM as presented and often exclude the style and placement information.

Building a transformable web site is now a relatively straightforward activity. XHTML pages and the CSS are already built as part of the standard site creation. The addition required is the identification of the ontology that assists in the transformation task. As discussed above, this could be either via a `<link>`, a direct encoding, or the inclusion of the ontology in a standard location.

4 Evaluation

In order to explore the viability of our proposed approach, we conducted a small *technical* evaluation. We are chiefly interested here in evaluating the first part of our objective: *Can semantic information be exposed in general purpose web-pages such that the information within the page can be transformed?* Thus for the purposes of this evaluation, we make an assumption that the proposed transformations such as removal of unnecessary items of reordering of menus *are* useful operations in improving accessibility[5].

The W3C's Web Accessibility Initiative (WAI) provides strategies and guidelines that web designers can use to make the Web accessible to people with

---

[5] Of course, such a claim is open to challenge, and we intend to pursue further User Evaluations in order to investigate this.

disabilities. These guidelines are targeted at designers using current technology and techniques, such CSS and XHTML. The main focus of our approach is not web site design, but some of the principles in the guidelines can be applied when evaluating SADIe. The W3C guidelines [29] include steps such as:

1. Select a sample of different kinds of pages from the Web site to be reviewed. This must include all the pages that people are likely to use to enter the site.
2. Use a graphical user interface browser and examine a selection of pages while adjusting the browser settings.
3. Use a voice browser or a text browser and examine the Web site while checking if equivalent information available through the voice or text browser is available through the GUI browser and that the information presented is in a meaningful order if read serially.

Choose Sample Web Pages. Amitay et. al. [2] propose that while web sites are different visually, if a web site's role is taken into account, then there are some similarities. By using web site roles, they produced eight categories that can be used for classifying web sites. These categories are Corporate Sites, Content and Media, Search Engines, Web Hierarchies and Directories, Portals, E-Stores, Virtual Hosting and Universities. By using these eight categories, we can gain some confidence that our evaluation uses a reasonable sample of the kinds of web sites that potential users of SADIe may access.

Five web sites from each category were selected, giving a total of 40 sites in the sample. The W3C guidelines specify that when evaluating a web site the entry point should be tested, as this is the first page the users will access. Therefore, the samples include the site entry point (usually index.html) of the web site, plus 4 other randomly chosen pages on the web site. This gave us a total of 5 pages per web site. With 40 web sites, we examined 200 web pages in total.

Apply SADIe to Each Page. We applied De-fluff, Reorder and Toggle to the page and observed the results.

Evaluate Results of SADIe for Each Page. Success of the transcoding was determined by observation of the resulting page. Taking into account what SADIe was designed to do, we asked the following questions of a transcoded page:

1. Have all obstacles marked removable been removed?
2. Are there multiple columns on the page?
3. Has all formatting that uses tables been removed?
4. Is there anything that breaks up the flow of text?
5. Are all blocks of text aligned vertically as opposed to horizontally?
6. Are all navigation links at the top of the page?

A positive answer to all these questions, was considered to indicate a successful transcoding by SADIe. A negative answer to any question was considered a failure. This assessment was performed by one of the authors.

Determine Web Site Success. In determining a web site's success or failure, we used the entry point to determine if the site succeeded or failed, following the

Table 2. SADIe Web Site Evaluation Summary

CSS Type	Site Sample	Site Failures	Sample Error (%)	True Error Range (%)
Pure	9	0	0	0 - 0
Mixed	26	4	15	2 - 28
None	5	5	100	100 - 100
All	40	9	23	11 - 35
Pure/Mixed	35	4	11	1 - 21

WAI philosophy. If we can make a page that most people use accessible, then that is more important for the site than providing access to a page that few people will ever read.

Having established a framework for the evaluation, it was then applied to a sample of web pages. The sample sites were obtained by taking the first five web sites from each of the eight IBM categories were used.

Table 1 shows the results of the SADIe evaluation. The 40 web sites and their categories are noted as well as how many of the web pages on the site failed the SADIe evaluation and if the entry point was a success or not. We also note how the presentation of the site was achieved. Pages using only CSS are designated Pure. None indicates no CSS usage. Mixed was for those sites that use CSS for formatting fonts and colours and headings etc, but use tables for layout purposes.

Table 2 shows a summary of results. The results are broken down to show the success rate of the various classes of CSS usage. These three categories are then further summarised. The Pure/Mixed CSS Type is the combined results of only those web sites that used Pure CSS for presentation and those that used a mixture of CSS and tables for presentation. We factor out the web sites that used no CSS as our design rationale is to make use of document structure as encapsulated through the use of CSS and XHTML. If there is no CSS then by design, we are unlikely to be able to transcode the page[6].

The column "Site Failure" indicates how many entry points in the sample failed to be correctly transcoded. The sample error is the proportion of web sites from the sample that failed. The True Error Range provides a range in which the true error lies for that class of web site (using a 95% confidence interval). From Table 2, we can see that all the sites that used no CSS for presentation failed. This was expected – SADIe relies upon the CSS to capture the structure of the web page. If there is no CSS, there is nothing for SADIe to use for transcoding.

Discounting the sites that used no CSS, we consider that SADIe obtained reasonable results. All sites that used pure CSS were successfully transcoded. When the sites that used mixed presentation are included, the error rate increases. This is partly due to problems in separating columns of text. We observed that a common approach adopted by these mixed sites was to give the entire table a CSS class value, which SADIe could use, but not give the elements within the cells of the table a Class or ID value. So while SADIe could remove or reorder the table as a whole, the contents within the table were inaccessible to SADIe and so remained in columns. This in turn meant the screen reader would be unable to read the text properly and the page was deemed a failure. However, there

---

[6] Clearly this is a limitation here, but we surmise that both the number and relative proportion of sites that use CSS and XHTML is likely to continue to increase.

were still a large number of web pages that were successful that mixed CSS and tables for presentation. Table 2 shows that the error rate for this category was 11%, with the true error lying in the range of 1% and 21%.

While these results are encouraging, they must be taken with a pinch of salt as we are making several assumptions. The first is that our confidence values assume that web site design follows a Normal Distribution. Secondly, we are assuming that our sample is an accurate reflection of the web pages that are available on the Web. Amitay et. al's proposal of categories based roles provides a good guidance for selection. However, it is difficult to say that choosing only 5 web sites for each category, which we did, could accurately reflect that category when the number is so small and the selection was not purely random. Recall that we are basing success and failure on the structure and content of page after transcoding. While we can make a value judgement that the transcoded page will be more accessible, based on research in the field, a true user evaluation will be needed before we can be sure of SADIe's success.

While these assumptions need to be addressed, the initial results are promising. As Table 2 shows, the combined error rate when we tested web pages that used pure and mixed presentation was only 11%. While we are not claiming that SADIe can successfully transcode 89% of all web sites and make them accessible, this initial result does provide a good basis for continued investigation of the SADIe approach.

5 Conclusions and Further Work

We have described the first stage in a more elaborate system that will increase free access to information for all users. By knowing more about the intended meaning of the information that is being encountered visually impaired users can perform their own transformations on that information.

Transcoding can help to make information more accessible via a restructuring of pages. Unnecessary items that introduce clutter can be removed, while important items can be promoted to a position on the page where they are encountered earlier by assistive technologies such as screen readers. Doing this in a principled manner, however, requires that the implicit semantics of the document be made explicit. We have described an approach based on annotation of web pages, encoding semantic information that can then be used by tools in order to manipulate and present web pages in a form that provides easier access to content. The annotations use an ontology describing the basic semantic units found in the pages as described in style sheets. Annotations are made directly to style sheet information, allowing the annotation of large numbers of similar pages with little effort.

The approach is minimal in the overhead presented to the site designer. No constraints are made on the ways in which the layout and presentation of the site can be produced. This is one of our key requirements – as discussed, designers will ignore, or at the very least fight against, initiatives that compromise their work.

Rather we make use of the fact that CSS elements are identified in the document – in a large number of cases, these elements do, in fact, already correspond to "meaningful" units of information. In addition, the approach makes no impact on the validation of XHTML documents.

An alternative approach might have been to use the underlying XML structure of the XHTML documents and then apply basic XSL technology to transcode. We see at least two problems with this. First, the current number of resources that are actually marked up using valid XHTML is small [25]. While browsers continue to be successful in handling badly formatted HTML, there is little incentive for authors to rectify this. Of course, our approach requires HTML+CSS, but our investigations (see Section 4) suggest that the proportion of sites using CSS is significant enough to merit this requirement – CSS does not necessarily require valid HTML in order to allow the production of good-looking web pages. The second problem is that even if the documents are valid, the underlying XML structure is not sufficient to carry the required information. The XML document will have structure in the form of h1 or p or possibly even div and span elements, but these alone are not sufficient to represent the various roles played by elements in a page – this richer detail is usually encoded in the style sheet.

The current prototype is still very much at the level of a proof-of-concept demonstrator and will benefit from further refinement. We plan to extend the upper level ontology to include more concepts covering document constructs along with the specification of further transcoding operations. Site-specific extensions of the ontology are currently produced manually – investigations of the automation or semi-automation of this process are also planned. Finally, we need further user evaluations of the tool to determine how effective it really is in increasing accessibility.

In summary, we propose that the inclusion of semantic information directly into XHTML is an effective way to assist visually impaired users in accessing web pages while not increasing or compromising the creation activity of authors and designers. By knowing the meaning of the information that is being encountered visually impaired users can perform their own transformations on that information.

References

1. M. Altheim and S. B. Palmer. Augmented Metadata in XHTML, 2002. http://infomesh.net/2002/augmeta/.
2. E. Amitay, D. Carmel, A. Darlow, R. Lempel, and A. Soffer. The connectivity sonar: Detecting site functionality by structural patterns. ACM Press, 2003.
3. C. Asakawa and H. Takagi. Annotation-based transcoding for nonvisual web access. In *Proceedings of the Fourth International ACM Conference on Assistive Technologies*, pages 172–179. ACM Press, 2000.
4. T. Berners-Lee. *Weaving the Web*. Orion Business Books, 1999.
5. T. Berners-Lee. RDF in HTML, 2002. http://www.w3.org/2002/04/htmlrdf.

6. B. Bos, T. Çelik, I. Hickson, and H. W. Lie. Cascading Style Sheets, level 2 revision 1 CSS 2.1 Specification. Candidate recommendation, W3C, February 2004. http://www.w3.org/TR/CSS21/.
7. M. Brambring. Mobility and orientation processes of the blind. In D. H. Warren and E. R. Strelow, editors, *Electronic Spatial Sensing for the Blind*, pages 493–508, USA, 1984. Dordrecht, Lancaster, Nijhoff.
8. O. Buyukkokten, H. G. Molina, A. Paepcke, and T. Winograd. Power browser: Efficient web browsing for PDAs. In *Proceedings of the SIGCHI conference on Human factors in computing systems*, pages 430–437. ACM Press, 2000.
9. C. Chen. Structuring and visualising the www by generalised similarity analysis. In *Proceedings of the 8th ACM Conference on Hypertext and Hypermedia*, New York, USA, 1997. ACM Press.
10. A. Chieko and C. Lewis. Home page reader: IBM's talking web browser. In *Closing the Gap Conference Proceedings*, 1998.
11. Codix.net;. *Textualize*;.http://codix.net/solutions/products/textualise/index.html.
12. D. Connolly. HyperRDF: Using XHTML Authoring Tools with XSLT to produce RDF Schemas, 2000. http://www.w3.org/2000/07/hs78/.
13. R. Furuta. Hypertext paths and the www: Experiences with walden's paths. In *Proceedings of the 8th ACM Conference on Hypertext and Hypermedia*, New York, USA, 1997. ACM Press.
14. S. Handschuh and S. Staab, editors. *Annotation for the Semantic Web*, volume 96 of *Frontiers in Artifical Intelligence and Applications*. IOS Press, 2003.
15. S. Harper and S. Bechhofer. Semantic Triage for Accessibility. *IBM Systems Journal*, 44(3):637–648, 2005.
16. S. Harper, Y. Yesilada, and C. Goble. Proceedings of the International Cross-Disciplinary Workshop on Web Accessibility. W4A, ACM Press, May 2004.
17. D. Hazaël-Massieux and D. Connolly. Gleaning Resource Descriptions from Dialects of Languages (GRDDL). W3c team submission, World Wide Web Consortium, May 2005. http://www.w3.org/TeamSubmission/grddl/.
18. M. Hori, G. Kondoh, K. Ono, S. ichi Hirose, and S. Singhal. Annotation-based web content transcoding. In *In Proceedings of 9th International World Wide Web Conference*, 2000.
19. N. Kew. Why Validate?, 2002. http://lists.w3.org/Archives/Public/www-validator/2001Sep/0126.html.
20. V. Mirabella, S. Kimani, and T. Catarci. A no-frills approach for accessible web-based learning material. In *Proceedings of W4A 2004*, pages 19–27. ACM Press, 2004.
21. W. Myers. *BETSIE:BBC Education Text to Speech Internet Enhancer*. British Broadcasting Corporation (BBC) Education. http://www.bbc.co.uk/education/betsie/.
22. Palmer, Sean B. RDF in HTML: Approaches, 2002. http://infomesh.net/2002/rdfinhtml/.
23. V. RNIB. A short guide to blindness. Booklet, Feb 1996. http://www.rnib.org.uk.
24. L. Seeman. The semantic web, web accessibility, and device independence. In Harper et al. [16], pages 67–73.
25. V. Y. S. Shan Chen, Dan Hong. An experimental study on validation problems with existing html webpages. In *International Conference on Internet Computing ICOMP 2005*, pages 373–379, 2005.
26. Simon Harper and Yeliz Yesilada and Carole Goble. Workshop Report: W4A - International Cross Disciplinary Workshop on Web Accessibility 2004. In *SIGCAPH Comput. Phys. Handicap.*, number 76, pages 2–20. ACM Press, November 2004.

27. H. Takagi and C. Asakawa. Transcoding proxy for nonvisual web access. In *Proceedings of the Fourth International ACM Conference on Assistive Technologies*, pages 164–171. ACM Press, 2000.
28. R. Volz, S. Handschuh, S. Staab, L. Stojanovic, and N. Stojanovic:. Unveiling the hidden bride: deep annotation for mapping and migrating legacy data to the Semantic Web. *Journal of Web Semantics*, 1(2):187–206, February 2004.
29. World Wide Web Consortium, http://www.w3.org/WAI/eval/Overview.html. *Web Accessibility Initiative*.
30. Y. Yesilada, S. Harper, C. Goble, and R. Stevens. Dante annotation and transformation of web pages for visually impaired users. In *The Thirteenth International World Wide Web Conference*, 2004.

Automatic Annotation of Web Services Based on Workflow Definitions

Khalid Belhajjame, Suzanne M. Embury, Norman W. Paton, Robert Stevens, and Carole A. Goble

School of Computer Science
University of Manchester
Oxford Road, Manchester, UK
{khalidb, sembury, norm, rds, carole}@cs.man.ac.uk

Abstract. Semantic annotations of web services can facilitate the discovery of services, as well as their composition into workflows. At present, however, the practical utility of such annotations is limited by the small number of service annotations available for general use. Resources for manual annotation are scarce, and therefore some means is required by which services can be automatically (or semi-automatically) annotated. In this paper, we show how information can be inferred about the semantics of operation parameters based on their connections to other (annotated) operation parameters within tried-and-tested workflows. In an open-world context, we can infer only constraints on the semantics of parameters, but these so-called *loose annotations* are still of value in detecting errors within workflows, annotations and ontologies, as well as in simplifying the manual annotation task.

1 Introduction

Semantic annotations of web services have several applications in the construction and management of service-oriented applications. As well as assisting in the discovery of services relevant to a particular task [7], such annotations can be used to support the user in composing workflows, both by suggesting operations that can meaningfully extend an incomplete workflow [3] and by highlighting inappropriate operation selections [1,9]. As yet, however, few usable semantic annotations exist. Manual annotation is a time-consuming process that demands deep domain knowledge from individual annotators, as well as consistency of interpretation within annotation teams. Because of this, the rate at which existing services are annotated lags well behind the rate of development of new services. Moreover, stable shared ontologies are still comparatively rare, with the result that the annotations produced by one community may be of limited value to those outside it.

Since resources for manual annotation are so scarce and expensive, some means by which annotations can be generated automatically (or semi-automatically) is urgently required. This has been recognised by a handful of researchers, who have proposed mechanisms by which annotations can be learnt or inferred. Heß *et al.*

have designed a tool called ASSAM [4], which uses text classification techniques to learn new semantic annotations for individual web services from existing annotations [5]. The tool extracts a set of candidate concepts, from which the user selects the correct annotation. Patil *et al.*, taking inspiration from the classic schema matching problem [10], have constructed a framework for automatically matching WSDL elements to ontology concepts based on their linguistic and structural similarity [12]. The framework was then adapted to make use of machine learning classification techniques in order to select an appropriate domain ontology to be used for annotation [11]. More recently, Bowers *et al.* have proposed a technique by which the semantics of the output of a service operation can be computed from information describing the semantics of the operation's inputs and a query expression specifying the transformation it performs [2].

All the above proposals attempt to derive new annotations based on the information present in existing annotations. In this paper, we explore the potential uses of an additional source of information about semantic annotations: namely, repositories of trusted data-driven workflows. A workflow is a network of service operations, connected together by data links describing how the outputs of the operations are to be fed into the inputs of others. If a workflow is known to generate sensible results, then it must be the case that the operation parameters that are connected within the workflow are compatible with one another (to some degree). In this case, if one side of a data link is annotated, we can use that information to derive annotation information for the parameter on the other side of the link. Or, if both sides are annotated, we can compare their annotations for compatibility and thus detect errors and inconsistencies in their manually-asserted semantics.

The remainder of the paper is organised as follows. We begin (in Section 2) by formally defining the concept of a data-driven workflow, and the notion of *compatibility* between connected parameters in such workflows. We then discuss how far we can use the information contained within a set of tested workflows in order to automatically derive annotations, and present the derivation algorithm (Section 3). As we shall show, we cannot derive exact annotations using this approach, but it is possible to derive a looser form of annotation which indicates a superset of the concepts that describe the parameters' semantics. We go on to demonstrate that these *loose annotations* have utility, despite their imprecise nature, by showing how they can be used to determine the compatibility of connected service parameters during workflow composition, as well as cutting down the search-space for manual annotators (Section 4). We present a prototype annotation tool that derives loose annotations from workflows (Section 5), and present the results of applying the tool to a collection of real biological workflows and annotations, which show the practical applicability of our approach (Section 6). Finally, we close by discussing our ongoing work (Section 7).

2 Parameter Compatibility in Data-Driven Workflows

A data-driven workflow is a set of operations connected together using data links. Thus, for our purposes, we regard a data-driven workflow as a triple *swf*

$= \langle nameWf, OP, DL \rangle$, where $nameWf$ is a unique identifier for the workflow, OP is the set of operations from which the workflow is composed, and DL is the set of data links connecting the operations in OP.

Operations: an operation $op \in OP$ is a quadruple $\langle nameOp, loc, in, out \rangle$, where $nameOP$ is the unique identifier for the operation, loc is the URL of the web service that implements the operation, and in and out are sets representing the input and output parameters of the operation, respectively.

Parameters: an operation parameter specifies the data type of an input or output, and is a pair $\langle nameP, type \rangle$, where $nameP$ is the parameter's identifier (unique within the operation) and $type$ is the parameter's data type. For web services, parameters are commonly typed using the XML Schema type system, which supports both simple types (such as *xs:string* and *xs:int*) and complex types constructed from other simpler ones.

Data links: a data link describes a data flow between the output of one operation and the input of another. Let IN be the set of all input parameters of all operations present in the workflow swf, i.e. $IN \equiv \{ i \mid i \in in \land \langle \_, \_, in, \_ \rangle \in OP \}$. Similarly, let OUT be the set of output parameters present in swf, i.e. $OUT \equiv \{ o \mid o \in out \land \langle \_, \_, \_, out \rangle \in OP \}$. The set of data links connecting the operations in swf must then satisfy:

$$DL \subseteq (OP \times OUT) \times (OP \times IN)$$

Notation: in the remainder of this paper, we will use the following notation:

- SWF is the set of trusted workflows given as input to the annotation process.
- OPS is the set of all operations used in SWF, i.e. $OPS = \{ op \mid op \in OP \land \langle \_, OP, \_ \rangle \in SWF \}$
- DLS is the set of all data link connections in SWF, i.e. $DLS = \{ dl \mid dl \in DL \land \langle \_, \_, DL \rangle \in SWF \}$.
- INS is the set of all input parameters appearing in SWF, i.e. $INS = \{ i \mid i \in in \land \langle \_, \_, in, \_ \rangle \in OPS \}$.
- $OUTS$ is the set of all output parameters appearing in SWF, i.e. $OUTS = \{ o \mid o \in out \land \langle \_, \_, \_, out \rangle \in OPS \}$.

2.1 Parameter Compatibility

If a workflow is well-formed then we can expect that the data links within it will link only those parameters that are compatible with one another. In its simplest form, this means that the two parameters must have compatible data types (as described within the WSDL description file for web service operations). However, when services are semantically annotated, it is also necessary to consider the semantic compatibility of connected parameters. Exactly what this means will depend on the form of annotation used to characterise parameter semantics, although the basic principles should be the same in most cases.

For the purposes of this paper, we will consider a particular form of semantic annotation that was developed within the ISPIDER project[1], to facilitate the identification and correction of parameter mismatches in scientific workflows [1]. In ISPIDER, semantic annotations are based upon three distinct ontologies, each of which describes a different aspect of parameter semantics and each of which is defined using the Web Ontology Language (OWL) [8]. These are the *Domain Ontology*, the *Representation Ontology* and the *Extent Ontology*.

The Domain Ontology describes the concepts of interest in the application domain covered by the operation. This is the commonest form of semantic annotation for services, and several domain ontologies have been developed for different application domains. An example is the ontology that was created with the ^{my}Grid project, that describes the domain of bioinformatics [13]. Typical concepts in this ontology are *ProteinSequence* and *ProteinRecord*.

Although useful for service discovery, the Domain Ontology is not sufficient by itself to describe parameter compatibility within workflows, hence the need for the two additional ontologies. The first of these, the Representation Ontology, describes the particular representation format expected by the parameter. In an ideal world, the data type of the parameter would give us all the information required about its internal structuring. Unfortunately, however, it is extremely common for the parameters of real web services to be typed as simple strings, on the assumption that the operations themselves will parse and interpret their internal components. This is partly a legacy issue (for older services) but it is also partly caused by the weak type systems offered by many current workflow management systems, which do not encourage web service authors to type operation parameters accurately. Because of this, to determine parameter compatibility, it is necessary to augment the information present in the WSDL data types with more detailed descriptions of the representation formats expected, using concepts from the Representation Ontology. An ontology of this kind for molecular biology formats has already been developed under the aegis of the ^{my}Grid project [13], containing concepts such as *UniprotRecord*, which refers to a well known format for representing protein sequences, and *UniprotAC*, which refers to the accession number format dictated by the *Uniprot* database.

The final annotation ontology that we use is the *Extents Ontology*, which contains concepts describing the scope of values that can be taken by some parameter. Although in general it is not possible to accurately describe the extents of all parameters, in some cases this information is known. For example, the TrEMBL database[2] is known to contain information about a superset of the proteins recorded in the SwissProt database[3], and there are several species-specific gene databases that are known not to overlap. Information about the intended extents of parameters can help us to detect incompatibilities of scope in

---

[1] http://www.ispider.man.ac.uk/
[2] http://www.ebi.ac.uk/trembl/
[3] http://www.ebi.ac.uk/swissprot

workflows that would otherwise appear to be well-formed. An example concept from the Extent Ontology is *UniprotDatastore*, which denotes the set of protein entries stored within the *Uniprot* database.

In order to state the conditions for parameter compatibility in terms of these three ontologies, we assume the existence of the following functions for returning annotation details for a given parameter

$$domain: OPS \times (INS \cup OUTS) \rightarrow \theta_{domain}$$
$$represent: OPS \times (INS \cup OUTS) \rightarrow \theta_{represent}$$
$$extent: OPS \times (INS \cup OUTS) \rightarrow \theta_{extent}$$

where θ_{domain} is the set of concepts in the Domain Ontology, $\theta_{represent}$ the set of concepts in the Representation Ontology and θ_{extent} the set of concepts in the Extent Ontology. We also assume the existence of the function *coveredBy()* for comparing extents (since the standard set of OWL operators are not sufficient for reasoning with Extent Ontology concepts). Given two extents *e1* and *e2*, the expression *coveredBy(e1, e2)* has the value *true* if the space of values designated by *e1* is a subset of the space of values designated by *e2* and the value *false* otherwise.

Parameter compatibility: Let *(op1,o,op2,i)* be a data link connecting the output parameter *o* of the operation *op1* to the input parameter *i* of the operation *op2*. The parameters *op1.o* and *op2.i* are compatible iff[4]:

(i) $o.type \preceq i.type$: the data type of the output *op1.o* is a subtype of the data type of the input *op2.i*; and
(ii) $domain(op1,o) \subseteq domain(op2,i)$: the semantic domain of *op1.o* is a subconcept of *op2.i*'s domain; and
(iii) *represent(op1,o) = represent(op2,i)*: the output and input parameters adopt the same representation; and
(iv) *coveredBy(extent(op1,o),extent(op2,i))*: the extent of *op1.o* is contained within the extent of *op2.i*.

3 Deriving Parameter Annotations

In addition to using the rules for parameter compatibility to test a workflow for errors, we can also use them in a generative way to infer information about the semantics of linked parameters in workflows that the user believes to be error-free. We will use a simple example to illustrate this idea. Consider the pair of workflows shown in Figure 1. Both these workflows are intended to perform simple similarity searches over biological sequences. The first finds the most similar protein to the one specified in the input parameter. To do this, it retrieves the specified protein entry from the *Uniprot* database, runs the *Blast* algorithm to find similar proteins, and then extracts the protein with the highest similarity score from the resulting *Blast* report. The second workflow finds similar

---

[4] The symbol $\preceq$ stands for a subtype of, and the symbol $\subseteq$ for a subconcept of.

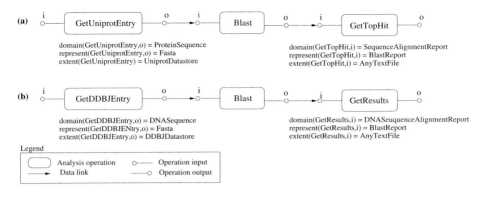

Fig. 1. Example workflows

sequences to a given DNA sequence. It retrieves the DNA sequence from the DDBJ database[5], searches for similar sequences using Blast and finally extracts the sequences of all matches from the *Blast* report.

Notice that, in this simple example, the parameters of the *Blast* operation have not been annotated, while the parameters of the other operations have. However, since these are thoroughly tested workflows, their data links must all be compatible and we can therefore infer some information about the annotations that the *Blast* operation ought to have. For example, if we focus on just the domain annotations, we can see that the input *Blast* parameter must be compatible with both *ProteinSequence* and *DNASequence*, since parameters conforming to both these concepts are connected to it. In fact, by the rules of parameter compatibility, just given, we can infer that:

$$(ProteinSequence \cup DNASequence) \subseteq domain(Blast, i)$$

Unfortunately, we cannot infer the exact annotation, as we may not have been given a complete set of workflows (by which we mean a set of workflows that contains every possible connection of compatible parameters). All we can safely do is infer a lower bound on the annotation of the input parameters and an upper bound on the annotation of the output parameters. Thus, in the case of the *Blast* input parameter, we can use the derived lower bound just given to indicate the fragment of the ontology that must contain its true domain annotation (shown in Figure 2)—in this case, all the super-concepts of the union of *ProteinSequence* and *DNASequence*[6].

---

[5] http://www.ddbj.nig.ac.jp
[6] The ontology fragment shown in Figure 2 does not contain the lower bound concept *ProteinSequence* ∪ *DNASequence*, since it is not a (named) concept within the ontology. However, since OWL language allows the formation of new concepts using, amongst others, the union and intersection operators, the true annotation may in fact be the lower bound itself (i.e. *ProteinSequence* ∪ *DNASequence*). Other, less expressive, ontology languages such as RDFS, do not allow this possibility.

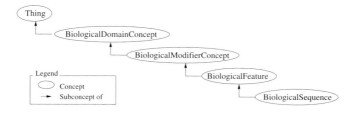

Fig. 2. Fragment of the domain ontology

We call these lower and upper bounds *loose annotations*, to distinguish them from the more usual (*tight*) form of annotation in which the exact concept corresponding to the semantics of the parameter is given. All manually asserted annotations at present are tight annotations (though in the future users may prefer to assert loose annotations for difficult cases where they are unsure of the correct semantics).

Based on this reasoning, we can derive a method for inferring loose annotations for operation parameters, given a set of tested workflows SWF and a set of (tight) annotations for some subset of the operations that appear in SWF. Since the compatibility relationship between input and output parameters is not symmetrical, we must use a different method for deriving input parameter semantics from that used for deriving output semantics.

3.1 Derivation of Input Parameter Annotations

Given an input parameter of some operation, we can compute three sets of loose annotations, based on the compatibility rules for each of the three annotation ontologies, as follows.
− *getInputDomains*: $OPS \times INS \rightarrow \mathcal{P}(\theta_{domain})$
This function computes a loose domain annotation, by locating the subset of the ontology that must contain the correct annotation. It first finds all operation outputs that are connected to the given input in SWF. It then retrieves the domain annotations for these outputs, unions them and returns all super-concepts of the resulting new concept.
− *getInputRepresentation*: $OPS \times INS \rightarrow \theta_{represent}$
This function computes a representation annotation. Since we assume that each parameter can support only one representation format, we can infer a tight representation annotation for the input parameter, rather than a loose one. To do this, we first find all output parameters that are connected to the given input, and retrieve their representations from the annotation repository. If all the output parameters have the same representation, then this can be returned as the derived annotation for the input parameter. Otherwise, a null result should be returned and the conflict should be flagged to the user. In our example (Figure 1), the representation that is inferred for the *Blast* input parameter is *Fasta*.

– *getInputExtents*: $OPS \times INS \rightarrow \mathcal{P}(\theta_{extent})$

This function computes a loose extent annotation, by locating the fragment of the extent ontology that must contain the correct annotation. It first finds all output parameters that are connected to the input by workflows in SWF, and then retrieves their extent annotations. Finally, it searches the Extent Ontology for all extents known to cover the union of the retrieved extents, and returns the resulting set of concepts. In our example, the extent of the *Blast* input parameter is an extent which covers the union of *UniprotDatastore* and *DDBJDatastore*.

3.2 Derivation of Output Parameter Annotations

Derivation of annotations for output parameters follows much the same pattern as for input parameters, except that we infer upper bounds on their semantics rather than lower bounds.

– *getOutputDomains*: $OPS \times OUTS \rightarrow \mathcal{P}(\theta_{domain})$

This function computes a loose domain annotation for the given output parameter. It first finds all input parameters that are connected to it in the workflows in SWF, and retrieves their domain annotations. It then returns all domain concepts that are subconcepts of the intersection of the retrieved concepts. In our example, the output parameter of the *Blast* operation must be a subconcept of (*SequenceAlignmentReport* ∩ *ProteinSequenceAlignmentReport*). Since, according to the domain ontology, the second of these two concepts is a subconcept of the first, this can be simplified to:

$$domain(Blast, o) \subseteq ProteinSequenceAlignmentReport.$$

– *getOutputRepresentation*: $OPS \times INS \rightarrow \theta_{represent}$

As with the inference of input representation annotations, the representation of an output parameter should be the same as that given for all connected inputs, provided there is no conflict. In our example, the annotation inferred for the *Blast* operation output parameter is *BlastReport*.

– *getOutputExtents*: $OPS \times OUTS \rightarrow \mathcal{P}(\theta_{extent})$

This function computes a loose extent annotation by locating the subset of the Extent Ontology that must contain the correct extent. It first finds all input parameters that are connected to the given output and retrieves their extent annotations. It then searches the Extent Ontology for all extents that are covered by the intersection of the retrieved extents, and returns the result. In our example, we can infer that the extent of the *Blast* operation output must be contained within the *AnyTextFile* extent.

3.3 Annotation Algorithm

Given the functions for deriving annotations for individual parameters just described, we can construct an algorithm (shown in Figure 3) that will derive all annotations automatically from a set of tested workflows and an incomplete repository of semantic annotations. This algorithm iterates over the parameters present in the workflows, deriving new annotations for each of them using the

```
Algorithm DeriveAnnotations
inputs OPS
outputs OPS
begin
1      for each op ∈ OPS do
2         for each i ∈ op.in do
3            C_domain    := getInputDomains(op,i)
4            c_represent := getInputRepresentation(op,i)
5            C_extent    := getInputExtents(op,i)
6            ActOnDerivedAnnotations(op,i,C_domain,c_represent,C_extent)
7         for each o ∈ op.out do
8            C_domain    := getOutputDomains(op,o)
9            c_represent := getOutputRepresentation(op,o)
10           C_extent    := getOutputExtents(op,o)
11           ActOnDerivedAnnotations(op,o,C_domain,c_represent,C_extent)
end
```

Fig. 3. Annotation algorithm

functions given above. The resulting annotations are then examined by the subroutine presented in Figure 4. If there is no existing annotation for a parameter, then the derived annotation is asserted (i.e. entered into the annotation repository). If a manual annotation is already present, then this is compared with the derived annotation to check for any conflicts. If the two are compatible, then no further action need be taken. If not then the discrepancy should be flagged to the user. Conflicts are detected in the following cases:

- **Domain conflict:** there exists a conflict in the domain semantics when a tight domain annotation does not belong to the subset of the domain ontology indicated by the derived (loose) annotation for the same parameter (*line 5*).
- **Representation conflict:** there exists a conflict in representation if the derived representation concept is different from the asserted representation concept for that parameter (*line 11*).
- **Extent conflict:** there exists a conflict in extent if the tight extent annotation does not belong to the subset of the extent ontology specified by the derived annotation for the same parameter (*line 17*).

There are several situations that can lead to conflicts, each of which requires a different corrective action.

− In the case of domain and extent conflicts, it may be that manual and derived annotations are in reality compatible, but that an error in the ontology means that this compatibility cannot be detected by our algorithm. In this case, the problem may be corrected by adding new relationships to the ontology, until the annotations become compatible.
− One or more of the previously asserted annotations for the parameters involved in the conflict may be incorrect. Once the user is confident that the incorrect annotations have been identified, they can be deleted or refined to remove the conflict. However, since the problem parameter may be linked to many services in the

```
Algorithm ActOnDerivedAnnotations
inputs (op,p) ∈ (OPS × (INS ∪ OUTS)),
        C_domain ⊆ θ_domain, c_represent ∈ θ_represent, C_extent ⊆ θ_extent
outputs op ∈ OPS
begin
1       if (C_domain ≠ φ) then
2           if (domain(op,p) = null) then
3               assertDomain(op,p,C_domain)
4           else
5               if (domain(op,p) ∉ C_domain) then
6                   domainConflict(op,p,C_domain)
7       if (c_represent ≠ null) then
8           if (represent(op,p) = null) then
9               assertRepresentation(op,p,c_represent)
10          else
11              if (represent(op,p) ≠ c_represent) then
12                  representationConflict(op,p,c_represent)
13      if (C_extent ≠ φ) then
14          if (extent(op,p) = null) then
15              assertExtent(op,p,C_extent)
16          else
17              if (extent(op,p) ∉ C_extent) then
18                  extentConflict(op,p,C_extent)
end
```

Fig. 4. Algorithm for Acting on Derived Annotations

workflow repository, determining exactly where the problem lies (i.e. with which parameter annotation) may require some detective work on the part of the user. If workflow provenance logs exist, then they can help in this process, since they would allow the user to examine the data values produced by or for the offending parameter during workflow execution. This may reveal the source of the error.
– One of the workflows involved in the conflict may not in fact have been thoroughly tested and may contain some connected parameters that are incompatible. It should be deleted from the workflow repository and the process of annotation derivation begun again from scratch.

4 Uses of Loose Annotations

The loose annotations derived by the method described in the preceding section contain considerably less information than conventional tight annotations, and they are therefore correspondingly less useful. This raises the question of whether the effort in collecting loose annotations is worthwhile. In this section, we demonstrate that loose annotations do have utility, despite their imprecise nature, by considering two potential applications: the inspection of parameter compatibility in workflows and speeding up the process of manual annotation for unannotated service parameters.

4.1 Inspecting Parameter Compatibility in Workflows

One of the original aims of the three annotation ontologies made use of in this paper was to allow mismatched data links (i.e. data links connecting incompatible parameters) to be detected and flagged to the user for correction. However, this assumes that all annotations are tight. When we have the possibility of loose annotations also being present in the annotation repository, can we still detect parameter compatibility in workflows?

In fact, even with loose annotations, it is still possible to determine compatibility of parameters in the following cases. Let $op1$ and $op2$ be two linked operations, and o and i their respective output and input parameters. Suppose that loose annotations for both parameters $op1.o$ and $op2.i$ have been derived by the algorithm presented in the previous section. In this case, the parameters $op1.o$ and $op2.i$ are definitely compatible if:

(i) $o.type \preceq i.type$, and
(ii) $\forall\ c_i \in getOutputDomains(op1,o),\ \forall\ c_j \in getInputDomains(op2,i),\ c_i \subseteq c_j$, and
(iii) $represent(op1,o) = represent(op2,i)$, and
(iv) $\forall\ c_i \in getOutputExtents(op1,o),\ \forall\ c_j \in getInputExtents(op2,i),\ coveredBy(c_i,c_j)$.

If we compare these conditions with those for full parameter compatibility (based on tight annotations), we can see that conditions (i) and (iii) are unchanged. Conditions (ii) and (iv) have both been altered to take into account the presence of loose annotations. In the case of domain compatibility, for example, we require that all the concepts returned by $getOutputDomains(op1,o)$ must be subconcepts of all the concepts returned by $getInputDomains(op2,i)$. This may well be a stronger condition for compatibility than is actually required, but it is conservatively true, given the information we have available in the loose annotations.

If the conditions given above are not satisfied, however, then we cannot say whether the parameters are compatible or not. We can still flag these connections to the user for their attention, but must allow the user to accept them as correct (i.e. compatible) based on their better knowledge of the real semantics of the parameters involved.

4.2 Supporting the Manual Annotator

Another application for loose annotations is in supporting human annotators in extending the repository of service annotations. If the user starts to annotate an operation parameter that has a loose annotation derived for it, then he or she only has to choose from the (hopefully small) subset of the ontology indicated by the loose annotation, rather than from the full set of ontology concepts. Where the ontology is large and/or complex, this can result in a significant time saving for the human annotator. For example, when specifying the domain semantics of the input parameter belonging to the *Blast* operation given in our earlier example, the user has only to choose from a collection of 5 concepts specified by the loose annotation, rather than all the concepts in the ^{my}Grid ontology. This also helps to avoid errors and inconsistencies in manual annotation.

5 Implementation

In order to assess the value of this method of deriving annotations, we have developed a prototype annotation tool that infers loose annotations and presents the results to the user through the GUI illustrated in Figure 5. The Annotation Editor, labelled A, shows the contents of the workflow repository being used for annotation derivation, and any existing (tight) annotations presently stored for the operation parameters in the annotation repository. This panel also contains the controls that launch the annotation derivation process.

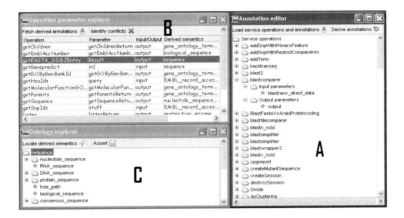

Fig. 5. Annotation system (GUI)

The resulting annotations are shown in the Operation Parameter Explorer panel (labelled B). Tight and loose annotations are distinguished here, and any conflicts will be highlighted. The final panel (labelled C) is the Ontology Explorer, which allows the user to view the fragments of the ontology indicated by a loose annotation, and to make a selection of a specific concept, to convert the loose annotation into a tight one.

6 Application to Bioinformatics Web Services

In order to further assess the value of the annotation derivation mechanism described here, we applied the algorithm and tool to a repository of workflows and annotations taken from the domain of bioinformatics. A large number of public web services are available in bioinformatics. For example, the ^{my}Grid toolkit provides access to over 3000 third party bioinformatics web services. The Taverna repository also contains 131 workflow specifications, and the ^{my}Grid web service registry, Feta [6] provides parameter annotations for 33 services[7].

---

[7] Note how the number of annotations lags far behind the number of available services.

We used these as inputs to our algorithm, and were able to derive 35 domain annotations for operation parameters, a selection of which are shown in Table 1. The concept given in the final column indicates either the upper bound (in the case of an output parameter) or the lower bound (in the case of an input parameter) derived by our algorithm. Upon analysis with the help of a domain expert, 18 of the derived annotations were found to be correct and 11 were found to be incorrect. A further 6 annotations could not be checked as the parameters in question belonged to services that have either moved or no longer exist, and thus could not be examined to determine the semantics of their parameters.

Table 1. Examples of derived parameter annotations

	Service operation	Provider[a]	Parameter	I/O	Derived concept
1	addTerm	EBI	geneOntologyID	I	GeneOntologyTermID
2	blastFileComparer	^{my}Grid	blastResult	I	BlastAlignmentReport
3	getFastaDDBJEntry	DDBJ	result	O	Sequence
4	getGenePredict	VBI	in0	I	Sequence
5	getHsaIds	^{my}Grid	query	I	EMBLAccessionNumber
6	blastx_ncbi	^{my}Grid	query_sequence	I	Sequence
7	lister	^{my}Grid	listerReturn	O	EnzRestReport ∩ DNASeq

[a] EBI stands for European Bioinformatics Institute, DDBJ for DNA Data Bank of Japan, and VBI for Virginia Bioinformatics Institute.

Of the 11 incorrect annotations, 3 were identified thanks to the conflicts automatically detected between the asserted and derived annotations. For example, the annotation manually asserted for the input parameter *query_sequence* of the *blastx_ncbi* operation states that it is a *NucleotideSequence*, while the derived annotation specified that it must be a superconcept of *Sequence* (row 6). According to the ^{my}Grid ontology, *NucleotideSequence* is not a super-concept of *Sequence*, hence the conflict. After diagnosis, the derived annotation was found to be incorrect due to a data link that connect the parameter *query_sequence* to an incompatible parameter. 2 further errors were discovered when the derived loose annotation specifies an empty subset of the ontology, it is the case for the output *listerReturn* (row 7).

The remaining 6 incorrect derived annotations were not detected automatically by our tool, but were diagnosed when we investigated the derived annotations for correctness. They were all found to be due to either incorrect manual annotation or incompatibilities in the input workflows. In summary, of the 11 errors, 4 were found to be due to errors in the original annotations and 7 due to incompatibilities between connected parameters in the workflows.

This experiment showed that it is possible to derive a significant number of new annotations from even a small annotation repository. We were also able to detect 5 incorrect parameter annotations—quite a high number given the small scale of the inputs. However, the results also show that errors in workflows can lead to errors in derived annotations, and hence highlight the importance of using only tried and tested workflows. This is not a problem where derived annotations can be examined for correctness by a user, but more care must be taken if they are to be created in a wholly automatic manner.

7 Conclusions

In this paper, we have presented an approach for automatically deriving semantic annotations for web service parameters. Our method improves over existing work in this area in that, in addition to facilitating the manual annotation task, it can also be used for examining the compatibility of parameters in workflows.

Our preliminary experiment has provided evidence in support of our annotation mechanism and shown its effectiveness and ability to discover a significant number of new annotations and to help detecting mistakes in existing annotations, based on a relatively small set of annotations. The next step is to evaluate the proposed techniques on a larger scale, and to explore their applications in supporting the annotation task more generally. For example, it may be possible to use collections of loose annotations to diagnose problems in ontology design, as well as in semantic annotations and workflows. There are also potential applications in guiding the work of teams of human annotators, to ensure that the most useful services are given priority during annotation.

References

1. K. Belhajjame, S. M. Embury, and N. W. Paton. On characterising and identifying mismatches in scientific workflows. In *International Workshop on Data Integration in the Life Sciences (DILS 06)*. Springer, 2006.
2. S. Bowers and B. Ludäscher. Towards automatic generation of semantic types in scientific workflows. In *WISE Workshops*, 2005.
3. J. Cardoso and A. P. Sheth. Semantic e-workflow composition. *J. Intell. Inf. Syst.*, 21(3), 2003.
4. A. Heß, E. Johnston, and N. Kushmerick. Assam: A tool for semi-automatically annotating semantic web services. In *ISWC*, 2004.
5. A. Heß and N. Kushmerick. Learning to attach semantic metadata to web services. In *ISWC*, pages 258–273, 2003.
6. P. W. Lord, P. Alper, Ch. Wroe, and C. A. Goble. Feta: A light-weight architecture for user oriented semantic service discovery. In *ESWC*, 2005.
7. E. M. Maximilien and M. P. Singh. A framework and ontology for dynamic web services selection. *IEEE Internet Computing*, 8(5), 2004.
8. D. L. McGuinness and F. v. Harmelen. Owl web ontology language overview. In *W3C Recommendation*, 2004.
9. B. Medjahed, A. Bouguettaya, and A. K. Elmagarmid. Composing web services on the semantic web. *VLDB J.*, 12(4), 2003.
10. P. Mitra, G. Wiederhold, and M. L. Kersten. A graph-oriented model for articulation of ontology interdependencies. In *EDBT*, 2000.
11. N. Oldham, Ch. Thomas, A. P. Sheth, and K. Verma. METEOR-S web service annotation framework with machine learning classification. In *SWSWPC*, 2004.
12. A. A. Patil, S. A. Oundhakar, A. P. Sheth, and K. Verma. METEOR-S web service annotation framework. In *WWW*, 2004.
13. Ch. Wroe, R. Stevens, C. A. Goble, A. Roberts, and R. M. Greenwood. A suite of daml+oil ontologies to describe bioinformatics web services and data. *Int. J. Cooperative Inf. Syst.*, 12(2), 2003.

A Constraint-Based Approach to Horizontal Web Service Composition

Ahlem Ben Hassine[1], Shigeo Matsubara[1,2], and Toru Ishida[1,3]

[1] Language Grid Project, National Institute of Information and Communications Technology
ahlem@nict.go.jp
[2] NTT Communication Science Laboratories, NTT Corporation
matsubara@cslab.kecl.ntt.co.jp
[3] Department of Social Informatics, Kyoto University
ishida@i.kyoto-u.ac.jp

Abstract. The task of automatically composing Web services involves two main composition processes, vertical and horizontal composition. Vertical composition consists of defining an appropriate combination of simple processes to perform a composition task. Horizontal composition process consists of determining the most appropriate Web service, from among a set of functionally equivalent ones for each component process. Several recent research efforts have dealt with the Web service composition problem. Nevertheless, most of them tackled only the vertical composition of Web services despite the growing trend towards functionally equivalent Web services. In an attempt to facilitate and streamline the process of horizontal composition of Web services while taking the above limitation into consideration, this work includes two main contributions. The first is a generic formalization of any Web service composition problem based on a constraint optimization problem (COP); this formalization is compatible to any Web service description language. The second contribution is an incremental user-intervention-based protocol to find the optimal composite Web service according to some predefined criteria at run-time. Our goal is *i*) to deal with many crucial natural features of Web services such as dynamic and distributed environment, uncertain and incomplete Web service information, etc; and *ii*) to allow human user intervention to enhance the solving process. Three approaches are described in this work, a centralized approach, a distributed approach and a multi-agent approach to deal with realistic domains.

1 Introduction

The great success of Web services, due especially to their richness of application made possible by open common standards, has led to their wide proliferation and a tremendous variety of Web services are now available. However, this proliferation has rendered the discovery, search and use of an appropriate Web services arduous. These tasks are increasingly complicated, especially while dealing with composite Web service to responde to an ostensible long-term complex user's goal. The automatic Web service composition task consists of finding an appropriate combination of existing Web services to achieve a global goal. Solving this problem involves mixing and matching component Web services according to certain features. These features can be divided into two main groups:

- Features related to the user, including the user's constraints and preferences.
- Features related to Web services and which can be divided into two subgroups, *internal* and *external* features. *Internal* features include quality of service (QoS) attributes, and *external* features include existing restrictions on the connection of Web services, (e.g., a hotel room should be reserved for the ISWC2006 conference usually after booking the flight). *External* features are specified in the Web service ontology language, OWL-S [12], through a set of control constructs such as, *Sequence*, *Unordered*, *Choice*, etc.

However, there is usually a choice of many Web services for each subtask that has to be done to fulfill the main goal. We refer to these Web services as functionally equivalent Web services. In the sequel of this paper, as is generally done in the literature, we refer to each of subtasks making up the main goal as an *abstract* Web service and to each Web service able to perform a subtask as a *concrete* Web service. Solving a Web service composition problem means going through two types of composition process:

- *Vertical* composition, is aimed at finding the "best" combination of the *abstract* Web services, i.e., abstract workflow, for achieving the main goal while satisfying all existing interdependent restrictions.
- *Horizontal* composition, is aimed at finding the "best" *concrete* Web service, from among a set of available functionally equivalent Web services, i.e., executable workflow, to perform each *abstract* Web service. The quality of the response to the user's query (the composition task) considerably depends on the selected *concrete* Web services. The choice of a *concrete* Web service is dictated to functional (i.e., related to the inputs) and/or non-functional attributes (i.e., related to the quality of service attributes).

The main benefits from distinguishing between these two composition processes are: *i*) simplifying Web service composition problem to reduce it computational complexity, *ii*) avoiding any *horizontal* composition redundancy that may appear while searching for the "best" orchestration of *abstract* Web services, and mainly *iii*) ensuring more flexibility to the user intervention, i.e., user is able to modify/adjust the *abstract* workflow when needed.

The combination of Web services has attracted the interest of many researchers, amongst [9], [13], [8], [14], and several approaches have been reported. Most of these deal only with vertical composition, where only single concrete Web service is available for each abstract one. However, the tremendous growing number of functionally equivalent concrete Web services makes the search for an appropriate one, i.e., *horizontal* composition of concrete Web services, an NP-hard task [5]. This composition process has the following characteristics.

- Information is often incomplete and uncertain.
- The environment is naturally distributed and dynamic.
- Many (non)-functional features, inter-related restrictions and especially the preferences of the user may affect the quality of the response to a user's query.

Existing research efforts have tackled only some parts of the natural features of the Web service composition problem [1], [7], none have tried to deal with all of them. Also, some complex real-world problems require some level of abstract interactions with the user to better search for a valid composite Web service. Finally, very few studies have considered the validity of the information concerning a concrete Web service during the composition process and none have dealt with this question of validity during the execution process. We have learned from all these works and we have focused our research on the requirements of the Web service composition problem that are derived from the natural features of the problem, search-based user interventions and the information validity during the composition and execution processes. Our main goal is to provide a means by which an optimal composite executable workflow can be created for a given set of sub-tasks with their inter-relation restrictions, i.e., an abstract workflow.

This paper consists of two main parts. The first is a generic formalization of any Web service composition problem as a constraint optimization problem (COP) in which we try to express most of the Web service composition problem features in a simple and natural way. Our main purpose is to develop a common and robust means of expressing any Web service composition problem that ideally reflects realistic domains. The second contribution is a real-time interactive protocol to solve any Web service composition problem by overcoming most of the above encountered limitations. Although, there are various techniques for solving a COP, none of these integrate any user interaction issues. The constraint optimization problem formalism is especially promising for ideally describing any realistic Web service composition problem, because this problem is a combinatorial problem that can be represented by a set of variables connected by constraints. Three approaches are proposed in this paper, a centralized approach, a distributed approach and finally a multi-agent approach to reflect ideally realistic domains.

This paper is organized as follows. In Section 2, we give an overview of existing researches. In Section 3, we present the proposed formalization. In Section 4, we describe a real-world scenario. In Section 5, we describe the proposed algorithm. In Section 6, we discuss possibilities of extensions of the previous algorithm. In Section 7, we conclude the paper.

2 Related Work

Several solutions to the Web service composition problem have been reported including, integer programming (IP)-based techniques [2], [16], non-classical planning-based techniques and logic-based techniques [9], [11]. Recently, some researchers have suggested applying existing artificial intelligence (AI) optimization techniques, such as genetic algorithms (GA), mainly to include some Quality of Service attributes in the search process. Regarding IP-based proposed solutions [2], [16], authors assume linearity of the constraints and of the objective function. As for non-classical planning techniques, Sirin et al. proposed an HTN-planning based approach [13] to solve this problem. Their efforts were directed toward encoding the OWL-S Web service description as a SHOP2 planning problem, so that SHOP2 can be used to automatically generate a composite web service. McIlraith and Son [9] proposed an approach to building agent technology based on the notion of generic procedures and customizing user constraints. The authors claim that an augmented version of the logic programming language Golog provides a natural formalism for automatically composing services on the semantic web. They suggested not to consider this problem as a simple planning, but as a customizations of reusable, high level generic procedures. Canfora et al. in [5] proposed to tackle QoS-aware composition problem using Genetic Algorithm (GA). This work deals with both vertical and horizontal compositions. However, to accomplish the Web service composition task, the Web service composition procedure may need to retrieve information from Web services while operating. Most studies have assumed that such information is static [9], [13], [5]. Other studies have required an interactive process with the user to get all the necessary information as inputs. Nevertheless, the static information assumption is not always valid, the information of various Web services may change (i.e., it may be "volatile information" [1]) either while the Web service composition procedure is operating or during execution of the composition process. Kuter et al. [7] present an extension of earlier non-classical planning-based research efforts to better cope with *volatile* information. This arises when the information-providing Web services do not return the needed information immediately after it is requested (or not at all). In addition, Au et al. [1] proposed two different approaches for translating static information into volatile information. They propose assigning a validity duration for each item of information received from information-providing services.

3 Constraint-Based Formalization of Horizontal Web Service Composition

The constraint satisfaction problem (CSP) framework is a key formalism for many combinatorial problems. The great success of this paradigm is due to its simplicity, its natural expressiveness of several real-world applications and especially the efficiency of existing underlying solvers. We therefore believe that CSP formalism allows a better and more generic representation of any Web service composition problem. Hence, we formalize the Web service composition problem as a *constraint optimization problem* (COP) in which we have two kinds of constraints: *hard* and *soft* constraints.

A *static* CSP is a triplet (X, D, C) composed of a finite set X of n variables, each of which takes a value in an associated finite domain D and a set C of e constraints between these n variables [10]. Solving a CSP consists of finding one or all complete assignments of values to variables that satisfy all the constraints. This formalism was extended to the COP to deal with applications where we need to optimize an objective function. A constraint optimization problem is a CSP that includes an objective function. The goal is to choose values for variables such that the given objective function is minimized or maximized.

We define a Web service composition problem as a COP by (X, D, C, $f(sl)$) where:

- X={X_1, ..., X_n} is the set of *abstract* Web services, each X_i being a complex variable represented by a pair ($X_i.in$, $X_i.out$) where
  - $X_i.in$={in_{i1}, in_{i2}, ..., in_{ip}} represents the set of p inputs of the *concrete* Web service, and
  - $X_i.out$={out_{i1}, out_{i2}, ..., out_{iq}} represents the set of q outputs of the *concrete* Web service.

- D={$D_1, \ldots, D_n$} is the set of domains, each D_i representing possible *concrete* Web services that fulfill the task of the corresponding *abstract* Web service.
  D_i={$s_{ij}(s_{ij}.in, s_{ij}.out) \mid s_{ij}.in \subseteq X_i.in$ AND $X_i.out \subseteq s_{ij}.out$}
- C=$C_S \cup C_H$
  - C_S represents the soft constraints related to the preferences of the user and to some Quality of Service attributes. For each soft constraint $C_{Si} \in C_S$ we assign a penalty $\rho_{C_{Si}} \in [0, 1]$. This penalty reflects the degree of unsatisfiability of the soft constraint C_{Si}.
  - C_H represents the hard constraints related to the inter-*abstract* Web services relations, the OWL-S defined control constructs[1], and the preconditions of each *concrete* Web service. For each hard constraint $C_{Hi} \in C_H$ we assign a weight $\perp$ (i.e. it should be imperatively satisfied). It is noteworthy that C_H may include also some *hard* constraints specified by the user, these hard constraints can be *relaxed* upon request whenever no solution is found for the problem.
- For each *concrete* Web service we assign a weight to express the degree of user preference, $w_{s_{ij}} \in [0,1]$. Weights are automatically accorded to the values of variables in a dynamic way with respect to the goal.
- $f(sl)$ is the objective function to optimize, $f(sl)= \otimes_{s_{ij} \in sl}(user's\ preferences, penalty\ over\ soft\ constraints, Quality\ of\ Service\ attributes, probability\ of\ information\ expiration$), and *sl* is a solution of the problem defined by the instantiation of all the variables of the problem. In this work, we focus on optimizing both *i*) the user's preferences toward selected *concrete* Web services denoted by φ (*sl*) and *ii*) the penalty over soft constraints denoted by $\psi(sl)$. The Quality of Service attributes and the probability of information expiration will be tackled in our future work.

Solving a Web service composition problem consists of finding a "good" assignment $sl^* \in Sol$:=$D_1 \times \ldots \times D_n$ of the variables in X such that all the hard constraints are satisfied while the objective function $f(sl)$ is optimized according to Eq. 1.

$$f(sl^*) = arg \max_{sl \in Sol} \otimes(\varphi(sl), \psi(sl)) \qquad (1)$$

In this paper, we maximize the summation of the user preferences for all *concrete* Web services involved in the solution *sl* and minimize the summation of the penalties associated to all soft constraints[2] according to Eq. 2.

$$f(sl^*) = arg \max_{sl \in Sol}(\sum_{s_{ij} \in sl} w_{s_{ij}} - \sum_{C_{Si} \in C_S} \rho_{C_{Si}}) \qquad (2)$$

Since the solution might not be only a sequence of *concrete* Web services, i.e., it may include concurrent *concrete* Web services, we use "," to indicate the sequential execution and "||" to indicate concurrent execution. This information is useful in the execution process. The obtained solution will have a structure such as, sl={$s_{1i}, \{s_{2j} \| s_{3k}\}, s_{4h},\ldots, s_{nm}$}. This problem is considered to be a dynamic problem since the set of *abstract*

---

[1] Our formalization for the OWL-S control constructs will be described below in more detail.
[2] To allow more flexible and wider expression, we do not restrict the objective function to any kind of function.

Web services (the set of variables) is not fixed; i.e., an *abstract* Web service can be divided into other *abstract* Web services if there is no available *concrete* Web services to perform the required task. In addition, the set of values in the domain of each variable (the set of possible *concrete* Web services) is not fixed. *Concrete* Web services can be added/removed to/from the system.

In the Web services composition problem, several control constructs connecting Web services can be used. The main ones, defined in the OWL-S description, can be divided into four groups and we describe our formalization for these four groups below.

- Ordered, which involves the SEQUENCE control construct, can be expressed using a hard constraint. Each pair of *abstract* Web services linked by a sequence control construct are involved in the same $C_{Sequence}$ constraint.
- Concurrency involves the SPLIT, SPLIT+JOIN, and UNORDERED control constructs. The natural aspect of the following proposed agent-based approach (Section 5) allows the formalization of this control construct in a natural way. Note that only "JOIN" will be associated with a C_{Join} constraint. SPLIT and UNORDERED will be modeled using an "empty" constraint C_{empty}, that represents a universal constraint. This constraint will be used to propagate information about parallel execution to concerned variables in the following proposed protocol.
- Choice involves IF-THEN-ELSE and CHOICE control constructs. For each set of *abstract* Web services (two or more) related by the IF-THEN-ELSE or CHOICE control construct, the corresponding variables are merged into the same global variable (X_j for example), and their domains are combined and ranked according to the preference of the user. For example a set of *m abstract* Web services ($\{t_1, t_2, \ldots, t_m\}$) related by the "CHOICE" control construct, we combine them into a global variable (X_k for example) and *rank* their domains. For their preconditions, we assign a sub-constraint to each condition $\{C_{cond1}, C_{cond2}, \ldots, C_{condm}\}$ and create a global constraint $C_{Choice} = \cup_i C_{condi}$. At any time we are sure that only one condition will be satisfied since $\cap_i C_{condi} = \emptyset$.
- LOOP, neither the CSP formalism nor any of its extensions can handle iterative processing. It will be considered in our future work.

4 Real-World Scenario

Consider a situation where a person living in France wants to organize a trip to Japan to have laser eye-surgery. After the surgery, he will have to make appointments with his ophthalmologist in France for post-operative examinations. This task involves several interrelated subtasks as shown in Figure 1(a):

- t_1 = Withdraw money from the bank to pay for the plane fare, surgery, accommodation, and treatment,
- t_2 = Make an appointment with the doctor, get the address of the clinic and determine the price of the surgery,
- t_3 = Reserve a flight,
- t_4 = Reserve accommodation, which involves,

- t_{4-1} = Reserve accommodation in a nearby hotel if the price is less than or equal to US$100 per night,
- t_{4-2} = Reserve accommodation at a hostel if the cost of a hotel exceeds US$100 per night,

- t_5 = Make an appointment with his ophthalmologist for an examination one week after returning to France.

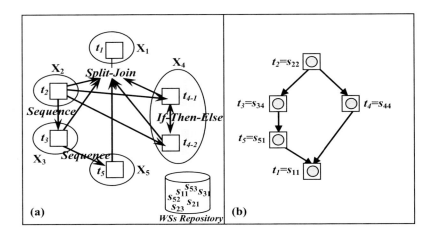

Fig. 1. (a) The set of tasks for the example with their pairwise control constructs, (b) The corresponding executable workflow solution for the problem

This problem can be formalized as follow:

- $X=\{X_1, X_2, X_3, X_4, X_5\}$, where each $X_i=(X_i.in; X_i.out)$ corresponds to one of the above tasks (Figure 1(a)).
  - X_1 corresponds to the task of withdrawing the required amount of money; $X_1.in$={Id, Password, Amount}; $X_1.out$={RemainAmount};
  - X_2 corresponds to the task of making appointment for the surgery; $X_2.in$= {Disease, Date}; $X_2.out$={ClinicName, Place, Confirmation, Price};
  - X_3 corresponds to the task of booking a flight; $X_3.in$={Destination, Date, PatientName}; $X_3.out$={FlightNumber, Price};
  - X_4 corresponds to the two tasks to reserve accommodation in either a hotel or a hostel depending to the cost. Recall that in our formalization we combine into the same variable the tasks implied in the same CHOICE relation. In this example t_{4-1} and t_{4-2} are involved in the same IF-THEN-ELSE control construct, so we combine them into X_4; $X_4.in$={Name, Place, Date, NightsNumber, MaxPrice}; $X_4.out$={Hotel/hostelName, Address, Price};
  - $X_5.in$={DoctorName, PatientName, Date, TreatmentType}; $X_5.out$= {Confirmation, Price};

- D={D_1, D_2, D_3, D_4, D_5}, where:
  D_1={s_{11}}, D_2={s_{21}, s_{22}, s_{23}}, D_3={$s_{31}, s_{32}, s_{33}, s_{34}, s_{35}$}[3], D_4={$s_{41}, s_{42}, s_{43}, s_{44}$},
  D_5={$s_{51}, s_{52}, s_{53}, s_{54}$},
- C=$C_S \cup C_H$, where
  - C_H including
    * X_1.Id $\neq$ nil;
    * X_1.Amount $\geq X_2$.Price + X_3.Price + X_4.Price + X_5.Price
    * X_2.Date < X_3.Date;
    * X_3.Date < X_4.Date;
    * X_4.Price $\leq$ US$100;
    * X_4.Date + X_4.NightsNumber+7 < X_5.Date;
  - C_S including
    * Distance(X_4.Place, X_2.Place)$\leq$10km[4].
- For each $s_{ij} \in D_i$, we assign a weight $w_{s_{ij}}$ to express the degree of preferences of the user *PrefUser*(D_j),
  PrefUser(D_1)={1}, *PrefUser*(D_2)={0.26, 0.73, 0.58}, *PrefUser*(D_3)={0.53, 0.61, 0.35, 0.82, 0.12}, *PrefUser*(D_4)={0.33, 0.71, 0.63, 0.84}, *PrefUser*(D_5)={0.87, 0.25, 0.59, 0.66}.
  These degrees of preferences are subjective values and depend on the user.
- The main objective is to find the best combination *sl* of the above *abstract* Web services and assign the most appropriate *concrete* Web services such that *sl* maximizes the objective function $f(sl)$ defined in Section 3 Eq. 2. Note that for simplicity, we assume inter-independence between the values of the different domains. We will consider dependence issues in future work.

Assume that *Distance*(s_{21}, s_{44})= 13km, *Distance*(s_{22}, s_{44})= 11km and *Distance*(s_{23}, s_{44})=20km, and the penalty over this soft constraint, *Distance*(X_4.Place, X_2.Place)$\leq$10km decreases as the *distance* converges to 10km, then $\rho_{Distance(s_{22},s_{44})} < \rho_{Distance(s_{21},s_{44})} < \rho_{Distance(s_{23},s_{44})}$. The most preferred solution for this problem is, *sl*={s_{22}, {{s_{34}, s_{51}} ∥ s_{44}}, s_{11}} (Figure 1(b)) with $\varphi(sl)$= 0.73+0.82+0.84+0.87+1=4.26.

5 Constraint Optimization Problem Interactive Algorithm for Solving the Web Service Composition Problem

The overall objective of our approach is to generate the *best* executable workflow (according to the aforementioned criteria) within a feasible time. Several constraint optimization problem algorithms can be applied to solve this problem, but none allows the intervention of the human user during the search process. In the following, we propose an algorithm (Algorithm 1) that allows human interaction with the system to enhance the solving process.

For each variable X_j[5] we first determine a set of candidate *concrete* Web services, $Cand_{X_j}$ for its *abstract* Web service that satisfies all the hard constraints $C_{Hl} \in C_H$ (Algorithm 1 line 4), and then we *rank* $Cand_{X_j}$ according to the objective function defined

---
[3] For example, Air France Web service, Lufthansa Web service, etc.
[4] *Distance*(x, y) is a function that returns the distance between two places.
[5] The variables are ordered according to the input *abstract* workflow.

in Section 3. This ranked set is used to guide the selection of the next variable X_{j+1} in the search process. For X_{j+1} we proceed first by applying *join* operation to the received list $Cand_{X_j}$ and the current one $Cand_{X_{j+1}}$, i.e., $Cand_{X_j} \bowtie Cand_{X_{j+1}}$ (Algorithm 1 line 12). The obtained sub-solutions are then *filtered* (Algorithm 1 line 12) according to the set of existing hard constraints. Finally, the resulting set of sub-solutions is ranked according to the objective function for optimization. If the set of candidates $Cand_{X_j}$ is large, to avoid explosion in the join operation, we select a fixed number of the most preferred *concrete* Web services for each variable, (i.e., a subset of candidates), and try to propagate these to the next variable. Whenever this subset does not lead to a complete solution, we backtrack and then seek a solution using the remaining candidates. The order of the values in the candidate set is established to avoid missing any solution. The obtained sets of sub-solutions are propagated to the next variable (Algorithm 1 line 16) and the same dynamic resumes until the instantiation of all the *abstract* Web services. If the set of candidate Web services becomes empty (i.e., none of the available Web services satisfies the hard constraints), or the set of sub-solutions resulting from the join and filter operations becomes empty and no more *backtrack* can be performed, the user is asked to relax some of his/her constraints (Algorithm 1 line 23). However, if the relaxed user's constraints involve the first instantiated variable in the search tree then the search process is performed from scratch. It is noteworthy that three issues are possible in this algorithm, *i*) Ask user intervention whenever a local failure is detected, which may reduce the number of backtracks, *ii*) Ask user intervention only when a global failure is detected, no more backtracks can be performed, *iii*) keep trace of the explored search tree to be able to point directly to the concerned variable by user relaxation and pursue the solving process and avoid some computational redundancy.

In addition, whenever we need any information concerning any *concrete* Web services, a request-message is sent to an information-providing Web service to get the necessary information along with both its validity duration and the maximum time required to execute the underlying Web service. The agent should maintain this time so that it can detect the information expiration and perform right decision (Algorithm 1 line 20). To deal with the main characteristic of this real-world problem, the dynamic environment, we maintain the validity of necessary information during the solving and execution processes, *totalTime*. *totalTime* should be less than the minimum validity time required for any Web service information. We use the following denotation:

– $T_{plan}(sl)$: necessary time needed to provide a plan *sl*,
– $t_{exe}(s_i)$: needed time to execute one *concrete* Web service,
– $t_{val}(inf_j)$: estimated time before the expiration of solicited information inf_j.

Naturally, the validity of information is usually considered as uncertain. Hence, for each validity time a *probability of information alteration* $p_{alt}(inf_i)$ can be associated with to the underlying information inf_i. We will consider this probability of information alteration in our future work. The maximal time T_{plan} required to provide a solution is defined by Eq. 3.

$$T_{plan}(sl) < \min_{\forall\ s_i\ \in\ sl;} t_{val}(inf_j) - \sum_{s_j \in sl} t_{exe}(s_j); \qquad (3)$$

Algorithm 1. User-intervenstion-based algorithm for Web service composition

WSCSolver(i, setSubSol, totalTime, checkedValues)
1:. **if** $i > \|X\|$ **then**
2:.   return *setSubSol*;
3:. **end if**
4:. $Cand_X[i] \leftarrow \{s_{ik} \in D_i \mid s_{ik} \text{ satisfies all the } C_H\} \setminus checkedValues[i]$;
5:. **if** *information required for any* $s_{ij} \in Cand_X[i]$ **then**
6:.   Collect necessary information; Update t_{val}, t_{exe} and *totalTime*;
7:. **end if**
8:. Rank $Cand_X[i]$ according to $w_{s_{ij}}$ and $\rho_{C_{Sj}}$ and while checking t_{val}, t_{exe} and *totalTime*;
9:. $subSol \leftarrow \emptyset$;
10:. **while** $subSol = \emptyset$ **do**
11:. $subCand \leftarrow$ subset of the $Cand_X[i]$; add(*checkedValues*[i], *subCand*);
12:. $subSol \leftarrow setSubSol \bowtie subCand$; Filter and Rank *subSol* according to $f(subSol)$;
13:. **end while**
14:. **if** $subSol \neq \emptyset$ **then**
15:.   add(*setSubSol*, *subSol*);
16:.   return **WSCSolver**(*i*+1, *setSubSol*, *totalTime*, *checkedValues*);
17:. **else**
18:.   **if** $i > 1$ **then**
19:.   reset to $\emptyset$ all *checkedValues*[j] for $j > i$;
20:.   Update *totalTime*; Update *setSubSol*;
21:.   return **WSCSolver**(*i*-1, *setSubSol*, *totalTime*, *checkedValues*);
22:.   **else**
23:.   *RelaxedConst* $\leftarrow$ ask User to relax constraints involving X_k where $k < i$;
24:.   Update(C_H, C_S, *RelaxedConst*);
25:. $i \leftarrow j$ such that $\forall\, X_k$ involved in C_l and $C_l \in RelaxedConst$, $X_j \prec_{lo} X_k$;
26:.   Update *setSubSol*;
27:.   return **WSCSolver**(*i*+1, *setSubSol*, *totalTime*, *checkedValues*);
28:.   **end if**
29:. **end if**

Each sub-solution based on expired information will be temporarily discarded but kept for use in case the agent cannot find any possible solution. This measurement is an efficient way to cope with Web services with effects characterized mainly by their volatile information because it allows a forward estimation of the validity of information during both the composition process and the execution process.

6 Extended Algorithms

6.1 Web Service Composition Problem Distributed Algorithm

The main limitation of the previous algorithm is that it cannot be easily adapted to any alteration in the environment. Whenever a user decides to relax some of his/her constraints, and these constraints involve already invoked variable, especially the first one in the search tree, the search for a solution will be performed from scratch. However, distributed approaches can be easily adapted to the user intervention. In this solution the same algorithm will be split on among set of homogeneous entities. Each entity will be responsible of one variable and the same algorithm will be performed in parallel by this set of entities. In case of conflicts, i.e., no solution can be generated and no *backtrack* can be performed, the system will ask the user to relax some constraints. The concerned entity will update its view, generate new candidates and exchange them with other concerned entities. The process resumes until either a solution for the problem is generated or its insolubility, even with all possible relaxations, is proven. Nevertheless, this distributed solution might be inefficient for some real-world scenarios where we need to access a specialized Web service. A specialized Web service maintains information about a set of Web services; for example, HotelsByCity.com maintains information about several hotels' Web services. The information concerning involved Web services is considered private, which makes it difficult to gather Web services needed information on same site and process them. Hence, we believe that extending the above algorithm to a multi-agent system is more effective for realistic domains.

6.2 Multi-agent System for Web Service Composition Problem

The underlying multi-agent architecture consists of three kinds of agents, *abstract* Web service agents, one or more Information-providing agents and an Interface agent. The Interface agent is added to the system to inform the user of the result. Each agent A_i maintains total validity time for all selected Web services, $valTime^{A_i}$. This information is locally maintained by each agent and updated each time a requested information is received. All the agents will cooperate together via sending point-to-point messages to accomplish their global goal. We assume that messages are received in the order in which they are sent. The delivery time for each message is finite. The agents are ordered, according to the input *abstract* workflow, from higher priority agents to lower priority ones so that each constraint will be checked by only one agent. For each successive two subtasks t_i and t_j such that $t_i < t_j$, their corresponding agents will be ordered as follows: $A_i \prec_{lo} A_j$, and the agent A_i (*resp.* A_j) is called *Parent* (*resp. Children*) for A_j (*resp.* A_i). The ordered links between agents, from the *Parents* to their *Children*, represent the inter-agent hard constraints between the corresponding *abstract* Web service; i.e., these relations represent OWL-S control constructs (sequence, choice, ordered, etc.) and/or hard/soft user constraints.

Each agent A_i first reduces the set of candidate *concrete* Web services, $Cand_{X_j}$ for its *abstract* Web service by keeping only those that satisfy all the hard constraints (Algorithm 2, line 1), *ranks* it according to the user preferences (i.e., $w_{s_{j_k}}$), and to the degree to which the soft intra-constraints are satisfied (Algorithm 2, line 15), selects subset of "best" candidates then sends it to its $Children^{A_i}$ (Algorithm 2, line 17). If the set of candidate Web services is empty, then the user is asked to relax some of his/her constraints. In addition, whenever the agent needs information concerning any *concrete* Web service, it sends a message (*RequestInformationFor:*) to the information-providing agent to get the necessary information along with its validity and the maximum time needed to execute the underlying Web service (Algorithm 2, line 10). The agent should retain this time so that it can detect information expiration and perform right decision, i.e., update the current solution when necessary. Each agent receiving needed infor-

Algorithm 2. *Start* message executed by each agent A_j.

Start
1:. Select $Cand_{X_j} \subseteq D_j$ / all intra-$C_H^{A_j}$ are satisfied;
2:. $listRequest \leftarrow \emptyset$;
3:. **while** $Cand_{X_j} = \emptyset$ **do**
4:.   Ask user to relax some of his hard constraints;
5:. **end while**
6:. **for all** $s_k \in Cand_{X_j}$ **do**
7:.   **if** inf_k required for s_k **then**
8:. $listRequest \leftarrow listRequest \cup s_k$;
9:.   **end if**
10:. $send(Information\text{-}providing, self, RequestInformationFor:listRequest)$;
11:. **end for**
12:. **while** $listRequest \neq \emptyset$ **do**
13:.   Wait; /*Information required for Web services*/
14:. **end while**
15:. Rank $Cand_{X_j}$ according to $w_{s_{jk}}$ and $\rho_{C_{Sl}}$;
16:. **for all** $A_i \in Children^{A_j}$ **do**
17:. $send(A_i, self, process:CandX_j \text{ within}:valTime^{A_j})$;
18:. **end for**

mation from the Information-providing agent first updates its dynamic knowledge, and then checks whether any of the information may expire before executing the workflow. If this is the case for any of the received information, the affected Web service, s_{jk} will be discarded from the set of possible candidates. Finally, the agent ranks the remaining candidates and sends them to its *Children* for further processing. Each agent A_i receiving a message to process candidate *concrete* Web services from its Parents or to process a set of sub-solutions proceeds by first performing a *join* operation on all received lists (Algorithm 3 line 1). The obtained sub-solutions are then filtered according to the set of existing hard constraints and then ranked according to the soft constraints and user preferences (Algorithm 3 line 3). If the set of sub-solutions is empty for the agent A_i, then a request is sent to parents to ask for more possible candidates in a predefined order to ensure the completeness of the proposed protocol (Algorithm 3, line 7). In case, all the possible candidates are processed and the set of possible solution is still empty, the concerned agent asks the user to relax some of his/her constraints related directly or indirectly to the variable X_i maintained by A_i. Thus, the appropriate agent will be invoked to first update its set of hard constraints and then define new candidates and send them again to the *Children* (Algorithm 3, line 14). The same process resumes until stable state is detected.

In real-world scenarios, the Web service composition problem is subject to many changes, defined on one side by the arrival of new Web services and on the other side by the inaccessibility of one or more Web services. For each new Web service, the appropriate agent will check whether this Web service can be included in the set of candidates. If this new Web service satisfies the hard constraints and increases $f(sl)$, it will be communicated to the *Children* to upgrade their set of sub-solutions, if possible.

Algorithm 3. *Process-within* message executed by each agent A_i.

Process:*list*^{A_h} **within:***t*
1:. *PossibleTuple*^{A_i} ← *Cand*$_{X_i}$; *PossibleTuple*^{A_i} ← *PossibleTuple*^{A_i} ⋈ *list*^{A_h};
2:. **if** All *list*^{A_h} are received from *Parents*^{A_i} **then**
3:.   Filter *PossibleTuple*^{A_i} such that $\forall$ *tuple*^{X_i} ∈ *PossibleTuple*^{A_i}, *tuple*^{X_i} satisfies the inter-agent constraints ($C_H^{A_i}$) and optimize the predefined criteria (Section 3);
4:.   update *totalTime*^{A_i};
5:.   **if** *PossibleTuple*^{A_i} = ∅ **then**
6:.   **if** Possible *backtrack* **then**
7:.   send *Backtrack* message to *Parents*^{A_i} to ask for more candidates;
8:.   **else**
9:.   Ask user to relax some of his hard constraints related in/directly to X_i;
10:.   **end if**
11:.   **else**
12:.   Rank *PossibleTuple*^{A_i} according to the criteria defined in Section 3;
13:.   **for all** $A_j \in$ *Children*^{A_i} **do**
14:.   send(A_j, *self*, *process*:*PossibleTuple*^{A_i} within:*valTime*^{A_j});
15:.   **end for**
16:.   **end if**
17:. **end if**

Otherwise, the new candidate will be ignored. As for each Web service that becomes inaccessible during the composition process, the appropriate agent should first check whether this Web service is included in the set of sent candidates. If this is not the case, the agent will only update its dynamic knowledge; if the inaccessible Web service has already been communicated to the *Children*, the agent should ask its *Children* temporarily not consider this Web service in case it is involved in their sub-solutions.

The stable state is progressively detected by all the *abstract* Web service agents [4]. The main idea is to define an *internal state* for each agent A_i. This state is set to *true* if and only if the internal states of all the children are *true* and agent A_i succeeds in finding an appropriate *concrete* Web service for its *abstract* one. The stable state will be detected by the children and progressively propagated to the parents. Each agent that has no parents, *Parents*^{A_i} = ∅, informs the Interface agent regarding the final state. The Interface agent communicates the result to the user.

7 Conclusion

The Web service composition problem is a challenging research issue because of the tremendous growth in the number of Web services available, the dynamic environment and changing user needs. In this paper, we have proposed a real-time interactive solution for the Web service composition problem. This problem consists of two main composition processes, vertical composition and horizontal composition and we have focused on the horizontal composition process. This work complements existing techniques dealing with vertical composition in that it exploits their abstract workflow to determine the *best* executable one according to predefined optimality criteria. We have developed a protocol that overcomes the most ascertained limitations of the existing works and comply with most natural features of a realistic Web service composition problem such as the dynamism of the environment and the need to deal with volatile information during the composition and execution processes, etc. Three main approaches were proposed in this paper, the first is a user-intervention based-centralized approach, the second is a distributed version of the previous one that can be easily adapted to any environment's alterations and the third is a multi-agent approach to cope better with realistic domains where problem required information is maintained by specialized Web services. The multi-agent approach is currently under implementation and testing.

References

1. Au, T-C., Kuter, U. and Nau, D., Web Services Composition with Volatile Information. *In proc. ISWC'05*, pp. 52-66, 2005.
2. Aggarwal, R., Verma, K., Miller, J., and Milnor, W. Constraint Driven Web Service Composition in METEOR-S. *In proc. IEEE Int. Conf. on Services Computing*, pp.23-30, 2004.
3. Aversano, L., Canfora, G. Ciampi, A., An algorithm for web service discovery through their composition. *In proc. IEEE ICWS'04*, 2004.
4. Ben Hassine, A., and T.B. Ho, Asynchronous Constraint-based Approach - New Solution for any Constraint Problem. *In proc. AAMAS RSS'2006*, 2006.
5. Canfora, G., Penta, M.D., Esposito, R. and Villani, M.L., An Approach for QoS-aware Service Composition bsed on Genetic Algorithms. *In proc. ACM GECCO'05*, pp. 25-29, 2005.
6. Dechter, R. and Dechter, A., Belief Maintenance in Dynamic Constraint Networks. *In proc. 7th National Conf. on Artificial Intelligence, AAAI-88*, pp. 37-42, 1988.
7. Kuter, U., Sirin, E., Parsia, B., Nau, D. and Hendler, J., Information Gathering During Planning for Web Service Composition. *In proc. ISWC'04*, 2004.
8. Lin, M., Xie, J., Guo, H. and Wang, H., Solving Qos-driven Web Service Dynamic Composition as Fuzzy Constraint Satisfaction. *In proc. IEEE Int. Conf. on e-Technology, e-Commerce and e-service, EEE'05*, pp. 9-14, 2005.
9. McIlraith, S. and Son, T.C., Adapting Golog for Composition of Semantic Web Services. *KR-2002, France*, 2002.
10. Montanari, U., NetWorks of Constraints: Fundamental Properties and Applications to Picture Processing. *In Information Sciences*, Vol. 7, pp. 95-132, 1974.
11. Narayanan, S. and McIlraith, S., Simulation, Verification and automated Composition of Web Services. *In Proceeding 11th Int. Conf. WWW*, 2002.
12. OWL Services Coalition, OWL-S: Semantic markup for web services, *OWL-S White Paper http://www.daml.org/services/owl-s/1.0/owl-s.pdf*, 2003.
13. Sirin, E., Parsia, B., Wu, D., Hendler, J. and Nau, D., HTN Planning for Web Service Composition Using SHOP2. *In Journal of Web Semantic Vol. 1*, pp. 377-396, 2004.
14. Ishida, T., Language Grid: An Infrastructure for Intercultural Collaboration. Valued Constraint Satisfaction Problems: Hard and Easy Problems. *In IEEE/IPSJ Symposium on Applications and the Internet (SAINT-06)*, pp. 96-100, 2006.
15. Yokoo, M. Ishida. T, and Kuwabara, K. Distributed Constraints Satisfaction for DAI Problems. *In 10th Int. Workshop in Distributed Artificial Intelligence (DAI-90)*, 1990.
16. Zeng, L., Benatallah, B., Ngu, A.H.H., Dumas, M., Kalagnanam, J., and Chang, H. QoS-aware middleware for web services composition. *IEEE Trans. Software Engineering, 30(5)*, 2004.

GINO - A Guided Input Natural Language Ontology Editor

Abraham Bernstein and Esther Kaufmann

University of Zurich, Dynamic and Distributed Information Systems, Switzerland
{bernstein, kaufmann}@ifi.unizh.ch

Abstract. The casual user is typically overwhelmed by the formal logic of the Semantic Web. The gap between the end user and the logic-based scaffolding has to be bridged if the Semantic Web's capabilities are to be utilized by the general public. This paper proposes that controlled natural languages offer one way to bridge the gap. We introduce GINO, a *guided input natural language ontology editor* that allows users to edit and query ontologies in a language akin to English. It uses a small static grammar, which it dynamically extends with elements from the loaded ontologies. The usability evaluation shows that GINO is well-suited for novice users when editing ontologies. We believe that the use of guided entry overcomes the *habitability problem*, which adversely affects most natural language systems. Additionally, the approach's dynamic grammar generation allows for easy adaptation to new ontologies.

1 Introduction

The Semantic Web's logical underpinning provides a stable scaffolding for machine-based processing. The common or occasional user, however, is typically overwhelmed with formal logic. The resulting gap between the logical underpinning of the Semantic Web and the average users' ability to command formal logic manifests itself in at least two situations. First, the gap manifests itself when the untrained user tries to use an existing, usually graph-based, ontology editing tool [14,12] – the *editing disconnection*. Second, it can be found in the disconnection between a user's information needs and the query (language) with which the user tries to find the required information in an ontology [28,27,9] – the *querying disconnection*. Since editing and querying are two of the major interaction modes with the Semantic Web, bridging them is central to its practical use by end users. Consequently, the question how to bridge the gap is pivotal for the success of the Semantic Web for end users. This paper proposes to address these two manifestations of the gap using natural language interfaces (NLIs).

NLI systems have the potential to bridge the editing disconnection between the untrained user and the triple- and graph-based ontology editing/creating tools. Although there are good ontology building tools [10,17,22,3,29,30] editing and building ontologies is hard for experts but close to impossible for common and occasional users [26]. NLIs can help to overcome this gap by allowing users to formulate their knowledge domain and information needs in familiar natural language (NL), rather than having to learn unfamiliar formal and complex data manipulation and query languages. The major drawback of NLIs, however, is their adaptivity to new domains. Even though natural language processing (NLP) has made good progress in recent years, much current NLI research relies on techniques that remind users more of information retrieval than NLP [19]. The systems that can perform complex semantic interpretation and inference tend to require large amounts of domain-specific knowledge- and engineering-intensive algorithms making the systems hardly (if any) adaptable to other domains and applications. Hence, they have a substantial *adaptivity barrier*.

Even if we could provide domain-independent NLI a second problem would arise from the users' side. Typically, users do not know what capabilities a NL system has. Therefore, many of their assertions/questions will not be understood correctly or might even be rejected because the statements exceed or fall short of the capability of the system. The mismatch between the users' expectations and the capabilities of a NL system is called the *habitability problem* [32]. Thus, for the successful use of NLI, users need to know what is possible to say/ask [2]. Analogously, NLI can help addressing the querying disconnection assuming that the adaptivity barrier and the habitability problem can be overcome. As a consequence, the domain-dependency of intelligent NLI and the habitability problem account for the fact that we are still far away from the successful use of full NL to command and query the Semantic Web (and arbitrary information systems). In this paper, we argue that we can address the before-mentioned problems by using a *guided and controlled NLI* that supports the user in both the tasks of ontology building and query formulation. We present GINO, the **g**uided **i**nput **n**atural language **o**ntology editor for the Semantic Web. GINO, an extension of the purely querying focused Ginseng [5], essentially provides quasi-NL querying and editing access to any OWL knowledge base [18]. It relies on a simple static sentence structure grammar which is dynamically extended based on the structure and vocabulary of the loaded ontologies. The extended grammar can be used to parse sentences, which strongly resemble plain English. When the user enters a sentence, an incremental parser relies on the grammar to constantly check the user's entries to (1) propose possible continuations of the sentence similar to completion suggestions in Unix shells or "code assist" (or intellisense) in integrated development environments and (2) prevent entries that would not be grammatical and, hence, not executable/interpretable. Once a sentence is fully entered, GINO uses some additional statement construction information in the grammar to translate the quasi English sentence into new triple sets (to add/change the ontology) or SPARQL statements [25] and pass them on to the Semantic Web framework Jena for execution.

The main difference between GINO and full NLIs [2] is that GINO does not use any predefined lexicon beyond the vocabulary that is defined in the static sentence structure grammar and provided by the loaded ontologies. Furthermore, it does not try to semantically understand the entries. Instead, GINO "only knows" the vocabulary that is being defined by the grammar and by the currently loaded ontologies. It relies directly on the semantic relationships of the loaded ontology. Hence, the vocabulary is closed and the user has to follow it limiting the user but ensuring that all queries and sentences "make sense" in the context of the loaded ontologies and can be interpreted by simple transformations.

The remainder of the paper is structured as follows. First, we will introduce GINO by describing how the user experiences GINO as an ontology building and editing tool. Next, we will provide an overview of its technical setup and functionality. We will then describe the empirical evaluation of the approach and discuss the results, which leads to a discussion of GINO's limitations. The paper closes with a section on related work and some conclusions.

2 GINO - The User Experience

GINO allows users to query any OWL knowledge base using a guided input NL akin to English. The user enters the query or sentence in English into a free form entry field (as shown in Fig. 1). Based on the grammar, the system's incremental parser offers the possible completions of the user's entry by presenting the user with choice pop-up boxes. These pop-up menus offer suggestions on how to complete a current word or what the next word might be. Obviously, the possible choices get reduced as the user continues typing. Fig. 1 shows that typing the letter "c" within the middle of a query or sentence causes the interface to propose all the possible completions of the words that begin with "c."

Fig. 1. The GINO user interface

Users can navigate the pop-up with the arrow keys or with the mouse and choose a highlighted proposed option with the space key. Entries that are not in the pop-up list are ungrammatical and not accepted by the system. In this way, GINO guides the user through the set of possible sentences preventing statements unacceptable by the grammar. Once a sentence is completed, GINO translates the entry to triple-sets or SPARQL statements. Users who are familiar with the common graph representations or with other ontology editors basing on graph structures (e.g., Protégé [22]) can also edit elements of an ontology by using the graph structure on the right side of the interface window (in Fig. 1).

Consider a user who wants to construct a class *lake*, a datatype property *lakeDepth*, and an instance *tahoe* to which the value of the before specified property is added. To create a new class *lake* and add it to an ontology that contains geographical information the user starts typing a sentence beginning with "there is" or "there exits." The pop-up shows possible completions of the sentence and the user can continue the sentence with "a" and "class." Choosing "class" (as we want to create a class) leads to the alternatives "named" and "called." Either choice then prompts the user to enter the class's label (i.e., "lake"). Finishing the sentence with a full stop prompts GINO to translate the completed sentence "There is a class named lake" into corresponding OWL triples that are loaded into the Jena ontology model, thereby enabling that the class can be queried or offered in a pop-up. To ensure consistency all entries are then checked by the JENA Eyeball RDF/OWL model checker (http://jena.sourceforge.net/Eyeball/). The newly produced class is immediately displayed in the graph representation on the right side of the user interface.

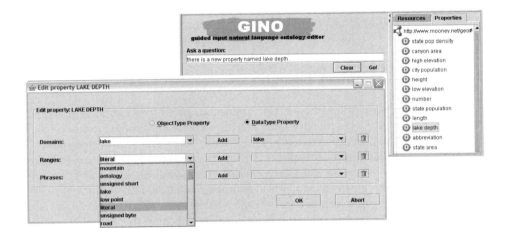

Fig. 2. The GINO user interface and property editing window

In order to specify a datatype property *lakeDepth* to the class *lake*, the user again starts a sentence with "there is." After entering "a" or "a new", the user is offered "property" to choose. Next, the label of the property has to be defined. When finishing the entry "There is a new property named lake depth" with a full stop, a window opens where the user can now specify whether the new property is a datatype or an object property (Fig. 2). Furthermore, domain and range can be specified. GINO offers the possible choices for the domain/range specification by showing the existing classes and datatypes in a pop-up. The user can, for example, choose the previously created class *lake* as domain of the property and click on "add" to actually add the chosen class. If the property has been declared as datatype property, GINO offers "literal" as possible entry for the range of the property. Again, the user adds the range to the property *lakeDepth*. Clicking on "ok" closes the property editing window and adds the specified information to the Jena ontology model. The new property appears in the graph representation as datatype property (Fig. 2). Object properties are created analogously.

An instance of the class *lake* can now be added by entering a simple sentence beginning with "there is an instance." After continuing the sentence with "of" and "class" GINO's popup offers the list of currently defined classes. Having chosen "lake" the user can then add a label (e.g., *tahoe*) to the new instance analogously to when entering a new class resulting in "there is an instance of class lake named tahoe." Alternatively, the user could have entered a sentence "there is a lake named tahoe" where GINO would have listed the possible classes at the position of "lake' in the sentence. Values of instance attributes can also be entered using a NL input sentence, e.g. "the depth of lake tahoe is 1645 feet."

The graph representation on the right side of the GINO user interface offers an overview of the classes, properties, and instances as well as an easy editing function. By double-clicking on an element, an edit window is opened where the user can add, change, or delete elements, values, etc. Double-clicking on the instance "tahoe" in the instance tree, for example, opens an edit window showing the possible properties of the class to which the instance belongs. The value "1645" can be entered as literal of the property *lakeDepth*.

3 GINO's Technical Design

From an architectural point of view, GINO has four parts (see Fig. 3): a grammar compiler, a partially dynamically generated multi-level grammar, an incremental parser, and an ontology-access layer (i.e., Jena; http://jena.sourceforge.net/). When starting GINO, all ontologies in a predefined search path are loaded. For each ontology, the *grammar compiler* generates the necessary dynamic grammar rules to extend the static part of the grammar, which contains the ontology-independent rules specifying general sentence structures. The *grammar* is used by the incremental parser in two ways: First, it specifies the complete set of parsable questions/sentences, which is used to provide the user with alternatives during entry and prevent incorrect entries as described above. Second, the grammar also contains information on how to construct the SPARQL statements from entered sentences. Thus, a complete parse tree of an entered question can be used to generate the resulting SPARQL statements to be executed with Jena's SPARQL engine ARQ. As SPARQL does not offer any data manipulation statements (e.g., CREATE, INSERT, DELETE) we have to specify and execute the generation and insertion of the corresponding triples separately by using the Jena API in GINO's source-code.

The *incremental parser* maintains an in-memory structure representing all possible parse paths of the currently entered sequence of characters. This has various benefits. First, it allows the parser to generate a set of possible continuations (i.e., possible next character sequences by expanding all existing parse paths, which are displayed by GINO's popup). One parse path might generate multiple options when the parser expands a non-terminal being specified in more

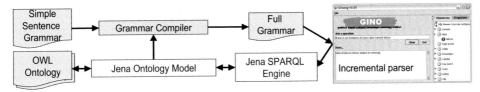

Fig. 3. The GINO architecture

than one place in the grammar. Second, the parser can compare every character entered against the possible entries providing immediate feedback when the user attempts to enter an non-interpretable (i.e., non-parsable) sentence/character to mitigate the habitability problem. Third, when the user has finished entering the sentence, the parser can immediately provide the set of acceptable parse paths. When querying a simple transformation relying on the query construction grammar elements can translate the parse paths to SPARQL queries avoiding lengthy semantic interpretation (and possible delays in answering the query) of the sentence as usual in NLIs. The fact that there might be multiple parse paths possibly being ambiguous is simply handled by returning the union of answers back to the user. When making assertions, GINO could use the parse paths to alleviate possible ambiguities by asking the user. Currently, however, we assured that the assertions grammar is unambiguous not requiring this interaction.

Since both the use of an ontology access layer and the construction of an incremental parser are well documented in the literature [5], the rest of the section will focus on the functionality of the grammar and the grammar compiler.

3.1 The Functionality of the Grammar

The grammar describes the parse rules for the sentences that are entered by the user. Consider the following grammar excerpt as an example:

(1) <START> ::= there is a <NS_S> .
(2) <NS_S> ::= class named <ENTER_NEW_CLASS_NAME> .
(3) <NS_S> ::= <CLASS> named <ENTER_NEW_INSTANCE_NAME> .
(4) <CLASS> ::= <NCc>|<http://www.w3.org/1999/02/22-rdf-syntax-ns#type><NCc>
(5) <NCc> ::= water area|<http://www.mooney.net/geo#state>
(6) <ENTER_NEW_CLASS_NAME> ::= enter_new_class_name
(7) <ENTER_NEW_INSTANCE_NAME> ::= enter_new_instance_name

The grammar's representation mostly follows the Backus-Naur-Form notation: Non-terminal symbols use uppercase characters (e.g., <CLASS>), whereas terminal symbols such as named that can be displayed to the user in a pop-up use lowercase characters. Grammar elements after the "|" symbol denote type restrictions. Note that we have radically simplified the example rules to keep things understandable.

While parsing, the incremental parser recursively searches for possible matches for the symbols on the left side of the rules and replaces them by the symbols on the right side of a conformable rule. The parse is completed when no non-terminal symbols are left. By keeping every replacement step during the parsing process, a parse tree of an entered sentence is successively built. Every sentence starts with the <START> symbol. To replace the <START> symbol, this simple grammar offers the terminal symbols there is a followed by the non-terminal symbol <NS_S> and a full stop (rule 1). The terminal symbol is displayed to the user in a pop-up menu as possible beginning of an entry. If the user enters "there is a", then the parser can bind <START> to rule 1. Next, the parser tries to match the non-terminal <NS_S>, for which this grammar offers two rules (2 and 3). If the user enters "class named", the parser binds rule 2 to <NS_S> and discards rule 3. To replace the symbol <ENTER_NEW_CLASS_NAME> in rule 2, only rule 6 can be applied. The application of rule 6 replaces the non-terminal symbol by the terminal symbol enter_new_class_name. This special terminal symbol additionally causes the interface to provide the user with a text entry field. If the user enters a string as label of the class (e.g., *lake*) and finishes the sentence with a full stop, GINO uses the complete parse tree to generate the appropriate OWL triples and loads them into the Jena ontology model. The new class is shown in the graph representation of the ontology. After entering "there is a" according to rule 1, rules 3 and 4 provide the list of all possible class-labels. In our limited grammar, only rule 5 binds to the terminal <CLASS>. As an alternative to entering "class named" as described above the user can, thus, also choose (one of) the class labels that are shown to the user (e.g.,*water area*).

3.2 The Grammar Compiler

When loading an ontology, GINO generates a dynamic grammar rule for every class, property, and instance. These dynamic rules enable the display of the labels used in the ontology in the pop-up boxes. While the *static grammar rules* (all rules above except rule 5) provide the basic sentence structures, the *dynamic rules* (rule 5) allow that certain non-terminal symbols of the static rules can be "filled" with terminal symbols (i.e., the labels) that are extracted from the ontology model or provide the structure to specify relationships between elements in the ontology.

The *static grammar rules* provide the basic syntactic structures and phrases for questions and declarative sentences. Its rules supply a small set of declarative sentence structures such as "There is a subclass of class water area named lake." (static grammar terminals in courier) in order to ensure the correct translation into OWL syntax. The same grammar also handles general question structures as "Which state borders Georgia?" as well as other types of queries such as closed questions ("Is there a city that is the highest point of a state?", typically resulting in an answer of "yes" or "no") or questions resulting in numbers (e.g., "How many rivers run through Georgia?"). Furthermore, it provides sentence construction rules for the conjunction or disjunction of two phrases (or sentence parts). The static grammar consists of about 120 mostly empirically constructed domain-independent rules. We are currently working on specifying these rules in an OWL-relying syntax such as SWRL (http://www.daml.org/2003/11/swrl/) to be able to use consistency checking and other features from standard Semantic Web APIs.

The *dynamic grammar rules* get generated from the loaded OWL ontologies (rule 5 in the above grammar example). The grammar compiler essentially parses an ontology and generates a rule for each class, instance, object property, and data type property. To illustrate the dynamic rule generation, we will show the translation of an OWL class into its corresponding generated rules. Consider the OWL class definition (in the file specifying the URIs at http://www-mooney.net/geo):

```
<owl:Class rdf:ID="waterArea">
    <gino:phrase rdf:value="water areas"/>
</owl:Class>
```

Its transcription generates two GINO rules for noun clauses; one for the actual class definition and one for the `gino` tag facilitating that plurals of nouns can be used in GINO. Since both labels start with a consonant, the resulting rules are describing the non-terminal <NCc> for **n**oun **c**lause **c**onsonants as follows (rather than <NCv> for **v**owels[1]):

```
<NCc> ::= water area|<http://www.mooney.net/geo#waterArea>
<NCc> ::= water areas|<http://www.mooney.net/geo#waterArea>
```

GINO also allows that synonyms of the labels used in the ontology model can be included by annotating the ontology with additional tags from the `gino` name space. As such, GINO generates a dynamic grammar rule for each synonym.

```
<owl:Class rdf:ID="waterArea">
    <gino:phrase rdf:value="water areas"/>
    <gino:phrase rdf:value="body of water"/>
    <gino:phrase rdf:value="bodies of water"/>
</owl:Class>
```

While such annotations are not necessary for GINO to run correctly, they do extend its vocabulary and increase its usability. Additionally, they reduce the limitation that the approach, to some extent, depends on the choice of vocabulary, when the ontology was built. The more meaningful the labels of an ontology are chosen, the wider and more useful the vocabulary provided by GINO is.

4 Usability Evaluation

To get a first feedback on the usability of GINO, we confronted six users who had no experience in ontology building and editing whatsoever with our prototype written in Java. We intended to find out how the controlled NLI of GINO can support untrained and casual users in an ontology creating and editing task and help overcome the editing disconnection. Note that we did not test GINO's ability to overcome the querying disconnection, as it has already been addressed in the literature (see the related work section for more details [5,13,23,6,32]).

---

[1] Thus, we handle determiner-noun (e.g., *a class* vs. *an instance*) and also subject-predicate (e.g., *Which class is...* vs. *Which classes are...*) agreement.

4.1 Setup of the Experiment

The experiment was based on the *Mooney Natural Language Learning Data* [31]. Its geography database consists of a knowledge base that contains geographical information about the US and their logical representations. To make the knowledge base accessible to GINO we translated it to OWL and designed a simple class structure as meta model. We removed the class *lake* and the class *river* including their instances in order to make the experiment realistic. We recruited six subjects who were not familiar with Semantic Web technologies and ontologies; they did not even know what an ontology was in the sense of the Semantic Web. We purposely recruited people with no computer science background as GINO is intended for casual or occasional users. Each subject was given a two-page introduction on what the idea of the Semantic Web is and how contents of ontologies are basically specified (i.e., subject - predicate - object). The subjects were first asked to enter a query into GINO in order to get used to the tool. We then gave the subjects the following tasks with respect to the adapted geography ontology. The subjects were first asked to create a class *waterArea*. Second, they had to specify a new class *lake* as a subclass of *waterArea*. Next, the subjects had to define a datatype property *lakeDepth* as well as an object property *isLocatedIn* with the domain *lake*. They were then requested to add an instance *tahoe* to the class *lake* and to enter values for the two properties' ranges that they had defined before. Finally, the subjects had to change the value for the depth of Lake Tahoe (*lakeDepth*) from metric to the English units.

Using a key-logger, we logged and timed each key entry. At the end of the experiment, we performed the SUS standardized usability test [7] – a standardized collection of questions (e.g., "I think that the interface was easy to use.") each answered on the Likert scale providing a global view of subjective assessments of usability. The test covers a variety of usability aspects such as the need for support, training, and complexity. To collect more specific details on how the subjects experienced GINO we followed up on each SUS question with either "If you disagreed, what did you find difficult?" or "If you agreed, what did you find especially easy?"

4.2 Results of the Experiment

To our surprise all subjects successfully performed the given tasks having only minor difficulties with the user interface (such as clicking on the wrong button). Each subject managed to correctly add the two classes, two properties of different type, and an instance including the specification of the values for its properties. As only "mistake" three of the subjects mixed up the definition of domain and range when entering the object property, but immediately corrected their error after reconsulting the instructions. One subject even wrote down that the domain corresponded to *subject* and the range to *object* of the subject-predicate-object triple structure. This questions the suitability of these mathematics-rooted terms for casual users. Examining the entry logs we found that the subjects corrected very few of their entries (e.g., using the backspace button) indicating that they had quickly learned the capabilities of GINO's NL parser. Even though we can only hypothesize that this was due to GINO's popup-based guidance, we know that other NLIs without that feature suffer from the habitability problem.

The users gave GINO an average SUS score of 70.83 ($\sigma = 11.15$, median = 73.75), which ranges from 0 to 100. As usability is not an absolute criterion the resulting score can only be understood relatively to others [21,24]. A similar SUS evaluation of two NLI-based query systems, for example, resulted in average SUS scores of 49.29 for GINO's predecessor Ginseng [5] and 52.14 for a controlled English based NLI SWAT [6]. As the SUS score shows, users found GINO significantly better suited to the task. This is a very good result considering that our subjects were *unfamiliar* with ontology issues before the experiment and that "they were thrown in the deep end of ontology building/editing tasks" after a very general and brief introduction.

To the questions "Why would you like to use GINO frequently?" and "Why would most people learn to use GINO quickly?" the answer "easy and intuitive" was given four out of six times. Two subjects thought that the interface had a clear and logic design. Nevertheless, four subjects reported that they would prefer the support of a person for the first time, but after that they would be able to use GINO on their own. One person specifically stated that the most convenient feature of GINO was that one can enter elements using NL. Five subjects found the Semantic Web fundamentals were the most difficult and time-consuming part of the experiment. The subjects did not use the right-hand graph view to do any editing apart from the task where they were explicitly asked to do so.

4.3 Discussion and Summary of Experimental Results

Obviously, our test does not provide (final) quantitative proof of GINO's suitability for ontology editing by casual users. As we will discuss in the limitations section below, we need a full user evaluation with many subjects from a variety of backgrounds to provide such evidence. Nevertheless, our experiment strongly indicates that novice users (1) can edit ontologies with a NL-based ontology editor without being overwhelmed by formal logic, (2) can do so with virtually flawless results, (3) preferred using the NL entry to a direct manipulation graph-based view, and (4) provided some interesting insight into the confusion behind the semantics of the terms the Semantic Web uses for the general public. Consequently, we can conclude that the GINO NLI has great potential to overcome the gap between the average user's ability to command formal logic and the Semantic Web's logic-based scaffolding. It also seemed to successfully circumvent the habitability problem.

5 Limitations and Future Work

Although the preliminary usability evaluation showed promising results, the approach has its limitations. First, the evaluation is limited with regard to the number and choice of the subject pool as well as the extent of the task. Furthermore, our subjects had never used any other ontology tool before the experiment, therefore making a comparison with these tools impossible. To address this issue we intend to undertake more intensive user testing in the future to determine whether NLIs are capable of bridging the logic gap. Such experimentation would include an extended editing task, a larger subject pool, and the use of additional tools as a benchmark. Specifically, we need to compare GINO with a simplified version of an ontology editor (such as Protégé [22]) to establish whether the users' ability to edit the ontology came from the *deliberate simplification* of GINO or from its *langauge capabilities*. Nonetheless, we think that our results are extremely encouraging and provide a strong indication that GINO enabled the casual/novice users to correctly accomplish a simple ontology editing task. Users who intend to embark on large ontology editing/design tasks, however, might prefer to invest the time to learn a full-fledged ontology editor.

Second, GINO is not a full-fledged ontology building and editing tool. It deliberately has a simple design to allow its use by novices (who might be overwhelmed by advanced logic features such as quantified restrictions). However, the simple approach can also be regarded as a strength, since the casual user is able to handle the tool and is not confused by many complex functions.

Furthermore, the controlled language limits the expressiveness of the user, but this restriction is not overly severe as shown in the evaluation. We think that the limitation is justified by two benefits. First, by using a controlled NL, we can avoid one of the biggest problems of NL: ambiguity. Handling ambiguity, in turn, is still regarded as a prerequisite for the successful usage of NLIs [20]. Second, the use of a controlled language (together with a guidance feature) addresses the habitability problem.

One question which we left unanswered was GINO's scalability. As the grammar compiler generates at least one rule for every class/instance/property in the ontology, the grammar is likely to grow very fast for large ontologies. We believe that this issue could be easily ddressed by using standard knowledge-base optimization techniques such as storing instances related rules on disk and retrieving them only when needed.

In the future, we intend to specifically address the adaptivity barrier. To adapt a new ontology of the size of the geography ontology to GINO took us about one hour. The task mainly consisted of adding synonyms of words and word phrases as `gino` tags to the ontology. Given a graphical user interface this task could be accomplished by a novice. M-PIRO [1], a tool for multi-lingual ontology-based language generation, for example, found that users could do so easily. Note that such a tool could be extended with user support functions based on WordNet (http://wordnet.princeton.edu/).

6 Related Work

The idea of NLIs is not new. NLIs to databases have repeatedly been developed since the seventies, but oftentimes with moderate success [2,9,19,32]. Considering the difficulties with full NL, the side step to restricted NL or menu-guided interfaces, which has often been proposed, seems obvious [8,4,11,32]. Even though there exist good and sophisticated ontology construction and editing tools (e.g.,

Ontolingua [10], Chimaera [17], OilED [3], Protégé [22], OntoEdit [29]), they all follow the menu/graph-based user interface paradigm. Swoop [12] tries to make use of people's familiarity with standard web browsers and offers a user interface that reflects the "webiness" with which people are used to interact.

There are some NLI-based projects that closely relate to GINO. [26] show how (OWL) ontologies can be constructed using a controlled NL to express the specifications. Their approach relies on a bidirectional grammar that translates entered facts, axioms, and restrictions into OWL abstract syntax. The controlled language does not have to be learned as a text editor guides the user through the writing process by offering look-ahead information (i.e., word categories). Unfortunately, no user evaluation is reported on. One major difference between their approach and GINO is that their lookahead feature does not show the actual words but displays the acceptable word-categories. This enhances the cognitive load on the user, as he/she has to map the grammatical word-category to possible words. Also, their project is aimed at finding an alternative notation to OWL resulting in logic-alike statements such as "Iff X is a pizza then X is a dish." While this might be grammatically correct English, it is clearly not aimed at the casual user but at someone who understands the general principles of first-order logic. In contrast, [30] offers a simple controlled language for specifying ontologies. However, it does not provide direct guidance or look-ahead support.

LingoLogic [32] is a user interface technology that combats the habitability problem by using menus to specify NL queries and commands that can be executed on relational databases. A parser checks a user's entries, displays possible completions of the words/phrases to the user, and translates the entries to the target query language SQL. In contrast to GINO LingoLogic seems to be limited to querying databases. We did not find any data manipulation capabilities. Hence, LingoLogic seems to belong to the category of NLI-based ontology/database querying tools such as PRECISE [23], AquaLog/PowerAqua [16,15], START [13], SWAT [6], or Ginseng [5] – the GINO predecessor. PRECISE, Ginseng, and SWAT were evaluated with the Mooney databases [31], which also have associated NL queries collected from users. Ginseng and SWAT were additionally tested with end users in a task setting. All evaluations show that NLIs can be successfully used to overcome the querying disconnection. As such, they complement our findings, which focused on bridging the editing disconnection.

7 Conclusions

In order to be usable to the casual or novice user, the logic-based scaffolding of the Semantic Web needs to be made accessible for editing and querying. We propose that NLIs offer one way to achieve that goal. To that end, we introduced GINO, the guided input natural language ontology editor that allows users to edit and query ontologies in a quasi-English guided language. Our evaluation with six end users provides some evidence that novice users are capable of virtually flawlessly add new elements to an ontology. It also showed that end users were confused by the terms for the major Semantic Web elements that the research community currently uses. Additionally, we found that the use of guided entry seemed to overcome the habitability problem that hampers users' ability to use most full NLIs. We believe that this paper shows the potential of NLIs for end user access to the Semantic Web, providing a chance to offer the Semantic Web's capabilities to the general public.[2]

References

1. I. Androutsopoulos, S. Kallonis, and V. Karkaletsis. Exploiting owl ontologies in the multilingual generation of object. In *10th European Workshop on Natural Language Generation (ENLG 2005)*, pages 150–155, Aberdeen, UK, 2005.
2. I. Androutsopoulos, G. D. Ritchie, and P. Thanisch. Natural language interfaces to databases - an introduction. *Natural Language Engineering*, 1(1):29–81, 1995.
3. S. Bechhofer, I. Horrocks, C. Goble, and R. Stevens. Oiled: A reason-able ontology editor for the semantic web. In *Intl. Description Logics Workshop*, Stanford, CA, 2001.
4. S. Bechhofer, R. Stevens, G. Ng, A. Jacoby, and C. Goble. Guiding the user: An ontology driven interface. In *1999 User Interfaces to Data Intensive Systems (UIDIS 1999)*, pages 158–161, Edinburgh, Scotland, 1999.
5. A. Bernstein and E. Kaufmann. Making the semantic web accessible to the casual user: Empirical evidence on the usefulness of semiformal query languages. *IEEE Transactions on Knowlwdge and Data Engineering*, under review.
6. A. Bernstein, E. Kaufmann, A. Göhring, and C. Kiefer. Querying ontologies: A controlled english interface for end-users. In *4th Intl. Semantic Web Conf. (ISWC 2005)*, pages 112–126, 2005.
7. J. Brooke. Sus - a "quick and dirty usability scale. In P. Jordan, B. Thomas, B. Weerdmeester, and A. McClelland, editors, *Usability Evaluation in Industry*. Taylor Francis, London, 1996.
8. S. K. Cha. Kaleidoscope: A cooperative menu-guided query interface (sql version). *IEEE Transactions on Knowledge and Data Engineering*, 3(1):42–47, 1991.
9. S. Chakrabarti. Breaking through the syntax barrier: Searching with entities and relations. In *15th European Conf. on Machine Learning (ECML 2004)*, pages 9–16, Pisa, Italy, 2004.
10. R. Fikes, A. Farquhar, and J. Rice. Tools for assembling modular ontologies in ontolingua. In *AAAI/IAAI*, pages 436–441, 1997.
11. C. Hallett, R. Power, and D. Scott. Intuitive querying of e-health data repositories. In *UK E-Science All-hands Meeting*, Nottingham, UK, 2005.
12. A. Kalyanpur, B. Parsia, and J. Hendler. A tool for working with web ontologies. *Intl. Journal on Semantic Web and Information Systems*, 1(1):36–49, 2005.
13. B. Katz, J. Lin, and D. Quan. Natural language annotations for the semantic web. In *Intl. Conf. on Ontologies, Databases, and Applications of Semantics (ODBASE 2002)*, Irvine, CA, 2002.
14. P. Lambrix, M. Habbouche, and M. Prez. Evaluation of ontology development tools for bioinformatics. *Bioinformatics*, 19(12):1564–1571, 2003.

---

[2] The authors would like to thank R. Mooney's team for having generously supplied the dataset, Gian Marco Laube for his support in implementing the prototype, and the anonymous reviewers for their insightful comments. This work was partially supported by the Swiss National Science Foundation (200021-100149/1).

15. V. Lopez, E. Motta, and V. Uren. Poweraqua: Fisching the semantic web. In *3rd European Semantic Web Conference (ESWC 2006)*, pages 393–410, Budva, Montenegro, 2006.
16. V. Lopez, M. Pasin, and E. Motta. Aqualog: An ontology-portable question answering system for the semantic web. In *2nd European Semantic Web Conference (ESWC 2005)*, pages 546–562, Heraklion, Greece, 2005.
17. D. L. McGuinness, R. Fikes, J. Rice, and S. Wilder. An environment for merging and testing large ontologies. In *Seventh Intl. Conf. on Principles of Knowledge Representation and Reasoning (KR2000)*, pages 483–493, Breckenridge, CO, 2000.
18. D. L. McGuinness and F. van Harmelen. Owl web ontology language overview. W3c recommendation, 2004.
19. R. J. Mooney. Learning semantic parsers: An important but under-studied problem. In *AAAI 2004 Spring Symposium on Language Learning: An Interdisciplinary Perspective*, pages 39–44, Stanford, CA, 2004.
20. H. A. Napier, D. M. Lane, R. R. Batsell, and N. S. Guadango. Impact of a restricted natural language interface on ease of learnng and productivity. *Communications of the ACM*, 32(10):1190–1198, 1989.
21. J. Nielsen. *Usability Engineering*. Academic Press, San Diego/New York, 1993.
22. N. F. Noy, M. Sintek, S. Decker, M. Crubzy, R. W. Fergerson, and M. A. Musen. Creating semantic web contents with protege-2000. *IEEE Intelligent Systems*, 16(2):60–71, 2001.
23. A.-M. Popescu, O. Etzioni, and H. Kautz. Towards a theory of natural language interfaces to databases. In *8th Intl. Conf. on Intelligent User Interfaces*, pages 149–157, Miami, FL, 2003.
24. J. Preece, Y. Rogers, and H. Sharp. *Interaction Design: Beyond Human-Computer Interaction*. John Wiley and Sons, New York, 2002.
25. E. Prud'hommeaux and A. Seaborne. Sparql query language for rdf. Technical report, W3C Candidate Recommendation, 2006.
26. R. Schwitter and M. Tilbrook. Let's talk in description logic via controlled natural language. In *Logic and Engineering of Natural Language Semantics (LENLS2006)*, Tokyo, Japan, 2006.
27. A. Spink, W. Dietmar, B. J. Jansen, and T. Saracevic. Searching the web: The public and their queries. *Journal of the American Society for Information Science and Technology*, 52(3):226–234, 2001.
28. A. Spoerri. Infocrystal: A visual tool for information retrieval management. In *Second Intl. Conf. on Information and Knowledge Management*, pages 11–20, Washington, D.C., 1993. ACM Press.
29. Y. Sure, E. Michael, J. Angele, S. Staab, R. Studer, and D. Wenke. Ontoedit: Collaborative ontology development for the semantic web. In *First Intl. Semantic Web Conf. 2002 (ISWC 2002)*, pages 221–235, Sardinia, Italy, 2002.
30. V. Tablan, T. Polajnar, H. Cunningham, and K. Bontcheva. User-friendly ontology authoring using a controlled language. Research Memorandum CS-05-10, Department of Computer Science, University of Sheffield, 2005.
31. L. R. Tang and R. J. Mooney. Using multiple clause constructors in inductive logic programming for semantic parsing. In *12th European Conf. on Machine Learning (ECML-2001)*, pages 466–477, Freiburg, Germany, 2001.
32. C. W. Thompson, P. Pazandak, and H. R. Tennant. Talk to your semantic web. *IEEE Internet Computing*, 9(6):75–78, 2005.

Fresnel: A Browser-Independent Presentation Vocabulary for RDF

Emmanuel Pietriga[1], Christian Bizer[2], David Karger[3], and Ryan Lee[3,4]

[1] INRIA & Laboratoire de Recherche en Informatique (LRI), Orsay, France
emmanuel.pietriga@inria.fr
[2] Freie Universität Berlin, Germany
chris@bizer.de
[3] MIT CSAIL, Cambridge, MA, USA
karger@mit.edu
[4] W3C (World Wide Web Consortium), Cambridge, MA, USA
ryanlee@w3.org

Abstract. Semantic Web browsers and other tools aimed at displaying RDF data to end users are all concerned with the same problem: presenting content primarily intended for machine consumption in a human-readable way. Their solutions differ but in the end address the same two high-level issues, no matter the underlying representation paradigm: specifying (i) *what* information contained in RDF models should be presented (content selection) and (ii) *how* this information should be presented (content formatting and styling). However, each tool currently relies on its own *ad hoc* mechanisms and vocabulary for specifying RDF presentation knowledge, making it difficult to share and reuse such knowledge across applications. Recognizing the general need for presenting RDF content to users and wanting to promote the exchange of presentation knowledge, we designed Fresnel as a browser-independent vocabulary of core RDF display concepts. In this paper we describe Fresnel's main concepts and present several RDF browsers and visualization tools that have adopted the vocabulary so far.

1 Introduction

RDF (Resource Description Framework) is designed to facilitate machine interpretability of information and does not define a visual presentation model since human readability is not one of its stated goals. Displaying RDF data in a user-friendly manner is a problem addressed by various types of applications using different representation paradigms. Web-based tools such as Longwell [1] (see Figure 1-a) and Piggy-Bank [2] use nested box layouts, or table-like layouts (e.g. Brownsauce [3], Noadster [4], Swoop [5]) for displaying properties of RDF resources with varying levels of details. Other tools like IsaViz [6] (see Figure 1-b) and Welkin [7] represent RDF models as node-link diagrams, explicitly showing their graph structure. A third approach combines these paradigms and extends them with specialized user interface widgets designed for specific information items like calendar data, tree structures, or even DNA sequences, providing advanced navigation tools and other interaction capabilities: Haystack [8] (see Figure 1-c), mSpace [9] and Tabulator [10].

Fresnel: A Browser-Independent Presentation Vocabulary for RDF 159

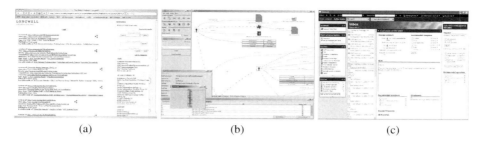

Fig. 1. Various types of RDF browsers: Longwell, IsaViz and Haystack

Such applications are confronted with the same two issues, independently of the underlying representation paradigm and interface capabilities: selecting what content to show and specifying how to format and style this content. Each application takes its own approach and defines its own vocabulary to specify how to present data to users. As with other kinds of knowledge, we believe that being able to share what we consider *presentation knowledge* makes sense in the context of the Semantic Web and that being able to exchange and reuse presentation knowledge between browsers and other visualization tools will benefit both programmers and end users. However, the current diversity of approaches and vocabularies for representing this knowledge makes such exchange and reuse difficult at best, if not impossible.

1.1 Related Work

Early RDF visualization tools rendered RDF models in a predefined, non-customizable way [3]. Recent tools provide more flexible visualizations that can be customized by writing style sheets, transformations, or templates, following either a declarative or a procedural approach.

Procedural approaches consider the presentation process as a series of transformation steps. One such approach consists in using XSLT to transform RDF graphs encoded as RDF/XML trees in an environment such as Cocoon [11]. Authoring XSLT templates and XPath expressions to handle arbitrary RDF/XML is complex, if not impossible, considering the many potential serializations of a given RDF graph and the present lack of a commonly accepted RDF canonicalization in XML [12]. This problem has been partly addressed by Xenon [13], an RDF style sheet ontology that builds on the ideas of XSLT but combines a recursive template mechanism with SPARQL as an RDF-specific selector language. Xenon succeeds in addressing XSLT's RDF canonicalization problem but still has a drawback common to all procedural approaches, that transformation rules are tied to a specific display paradigm and output format, thus preventing the reuse of presentation knowledge across applications.

Declarative approaches are based on formatting and styling rules applied to a generic representation of the content. They can be compared to XHTML+CSS, which has been successful for the classic Web. The Haystack Slide ontology [14], used to describe how Haystack display widgets are laid out, is one example. Another is IsaViz's Graph Style Sheets [15], which modifies the formatting, styling, and visibility of RDF graph elements represented as node-link diagrams. The main drawback of the declarative approaches developed so far is that they make strong assumptions about, and are thus tied to, the specific display paradigm for which they have been developed and are therefore unlikely to be meaningful across different representation paradigms.

1.2 Toward the Specification of Presentation Knowledge

Providing a single global view of all the information contained in an RDF model is often not useful. The mass of data makes it difficult to extract information relevant to the current task and represents a significant cognitive overload for the user. From an abstract perspective, the first step of the presentation process thus consists in restricting the visualization to small but cohesive parts of the RDF graph, similarly to views in the database world. But identifying what content to show is not sufficient for making a human-friendly presentation from the information. To achieve this goal, the selected content items must be laid out properly and rendered with graphical attributes that favor legibility in order to facilitate general understanding of the displayed information. Relying solely on the content's structure and exploiting knowledge contained in the schema associated with the data is insufficient for producing sophisticated presentations and visualizations. The second step thus consists in formatting and styling selected content items.

Fresnel's goal is to provide an RDF vocabulary to encode information about how to present Semantic Web content to users (i.e., *what* content to show, and *how* to show it) as presentation knowledge that can be exchanged and reused between browsers and other visualization tools. However, we do not expect all applications, which do not necessarily rely on the same representation paradigms and formats, to exchange and reuse all formatting and styling instructions as some might not be appropriate for all paradigms. We therefore identified a set of core presentation concepts that are applicable across applications and which form the core modules of Fresnel. One of the design goals of these modules was to make them easy to learn and use, but also easy to implement in order to promote their adoption by many applications. On top of these modules, we have also begun to define additional Fresnel vocabulary items which are grouped in extension modules. The remainder of this article mainly focuses on the core selection and formatting modules. More information about extension modules can be found in the Fresnel User Manual [16].

2 Core Vocabulary Overview

Fresnel is an RDF vocabulary, described by an OWL ontology [16]. Fresnel presentation knowledge is thus expressed declaratively in RDF and relies on two foundational concepts: *lenses* and *formats* (see Figure 2). Lenses specify which properties of RDF resources are shown and how these properties are ordered while formats indicate how to format content selected by lenses and optionally generate additional static content and hooks in the form of CSS class names that can be used to style the output through external CSS style sheets. The following sections introduce the main vocabulary elements using the examples in Figures 3 and 4.

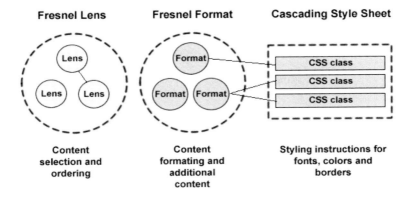

Fig. 2. Fresnel foundational concepts

Figure 3 shows a simple lens and associated formats used to present information about a person described with the FOAF vocabulary [17]. This figure also shows a possible rendering of such a resource, that a browser like Horus [18] or Longwell [1] could produce. Examples use the Notation 3 syntax [19].

2.1 Content Selection

The domain of a lens indicates the set of resources to which a lens applies (line 301: the lens applies to instances of class `foaf:Person`). Property `fresnel:showProperties` is used to specify what properties of these resources to show and in what order (lines 302-308). In this example, the values of both `fresnel:classLensDomain` and `fresnel:showProperties` are basic selectors, which take the form of plain URIs (represented here as qualified names), respectively identifying the class of resources and property types to select. More advanced selection expressions can be written using either FSL or SPARQL. They make it possible to associate lenses with untyped RDF resources, which do occur in real-world models since `rdf:type` properties are not mandatory. They can also be used to specify that a lens should display all properties of a given namespace, or any other complex selection condition(s) that can be represented by an FSL or SPARQL expression (see Section 3).

Fresnel Core provides additional constructs for specifying what properties of resources to display. The special value `fresnel:allProperties` is used when the list of properties that can potentially be associated with resources handled by a lens is unknown to the lens' author but should nevertheless be displayed. When it appears as a member of the list of properties to be shown by a lens, `fresnel:allProperties` designates the set of properties that are not explicitly designated by other property URI references in the list, except for properties that appear in the list of properties to hide (`fresnel:hideProperties`). Two other constructs are used to handle the potential irregularity of RDF data stemming from the fact that different authors might use similar terms coming from different vocabularies to make equivalent statements. Sets of such similar properties can be said to be `fresnel:alternateProperties`. For instance, `foaf:depiction`, `foaf:img` and `p3p:image` could be considered as providing

```
(300)  :PersonLens a fresnel:Lens ;
(301)    fresnel:classLensDomain foaf:Person ;
(302)    fresnel:showProperties (
(303)      foaf:name
(304)      foaf:mbox
(305)      [rdf:type fresnel:PropertyDescription;
(306)       fresnel:alternateProperties (
(307)         foaf:depiction foaf:img p3p:image )
(308)      ] ) .

(309)  :nameFormat a fresnel:Format ;
(310)      fresnel:propertyFormatDomain foaf:name ;
(311)      fresnel:label "Name" .

(312)  :mboxFormat a fresnel:Format ;
(313)      fresnel:propertyFormatDomain foaf:mbox ;
(314)      fresnel:label "Mailbox" ;
(315)      fresnel:value fresnel:externalLink ;
(316)      fresnel:valueFormat [ fresnel:contentAfter "," ] .

(317)  :depictFormat a fresnel:Format ;
(318)      fresnel:propertyFormatDomain foaf:depiction ;
(319)      fresnel:label fresnel:none ;
(320)      fresnel:value fresnel:image .
```

Fig. 3. A lens and some formats for presenting instances of class `foaf:Person`

the same information about resources displayed by a given lens. A browser using this lens would try to display the resource's `foaf:depiction`. If the latter did not exist, the browser would then look for `foaf:img` or `p3p:image` (see lines 305-307). Such knowledge can also be represented through ontology mapping mechanisms, but Fresnel provides this alternative as the ontology layer should not be made a requirement of the Fresnel presentation process. The other construct, `fresnel:mergeProperties`, is used to merge the values of related properties (e.g. `foaf:homepage` and `foaf:work-Homepage`) into one single set of values that can later be formatted as a whole.

The presentation of property values is not limited to a single level, and (possibly recursive) calls to lenses can be made to display details about the value of a property. Lenses used in this context are referred to as *sublenses*. Modifying the example of Figure 3, we specify in Figure 4 that the browser should render values of the property `foaf:knows` (lines 405-407) using another lens (`PersonLabelLens`, lines 410-413). The FSL expression (see Section 3) on line 406 specifies in an XPath-like manner that only values of `foaf:knows` that are instances of `foaf:Person` should be selected.

The sublens mechanism implies that a lens can recursively call itself as a sublens for displaying property values. In order to prevent infinite loops caused by such recursive calls, Fresnel defines a closure mechanism that allows Fresnel presentation designers to specify the maximum depth of the recursion.

2.2 Content Formatting

The default layout of selected information items is highly dependent on the browser's representation paradigm (e.g. nested box layout, node-link diagrams, etc.), but the final rendering can be customized by associating formatting and styling instructions with elements of the representation.

```
(400) :PersonLens a fresnel:Lens ;
(401)    fresnel:classLensDomain foaf:Person ;
(402)    fresnel:showProperties (
(403)       foaf:name
(404)       foaf:mbox
(405)       [rdf:type fresnel:PropertyDescription ;
(406)        fresnel:property "foaf:knows[foaf:Person]"^^fresnel:fslSelector;
(407)        fresnel:sublens :PersonLabelLens]
(408)    ) ;
(409)    fresnel:group :FOAFmainGroup .

(410) :PersonLabelLens a fresnel:Lens ;
(411)    fresnel:classLensDomain foaf:Person ;
(412)    fresnel:showProperties ( foaf:name ) ;
(413)    fresnel:group :FOAFsubGroup .

(414) :nameFormat a fresnel:Format ;
(415)    fresnel:propertyFormatDomain foaf:name ;
(416)    fresnel:label "Name" ;
(417)    fresnel:group :FOAFmainGroup .

(418) :mboxFormat a fresnel:Format ;
(419)    fresnel:propertyFormatDomain foaf:mbox ;
(420)    fresnel:label "Mailbox" ;
(421)    fresnel:value fresnel:externalLink ;
(422)    fresnel:valueFormat [ fresnel:contentAfter "," ] ;
(423)    fresnel:group :FOAFmainGroup .

(424) :friendsFormat a fresnel:Format ;
(425)    fresnel:propertyFormatDomain foaf:name ;
(426)    fresnel:label "Friends" ;
(427)    fresnel:group :FOAFsubGroup .

(428) :FOAFmainGroup a fresnel:Group .
(429) :FOAFsubGroup a fresnel:Group .
```

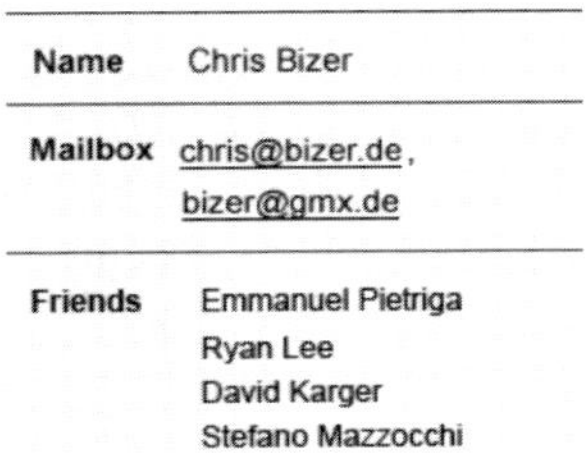

Name	Chris Bizer
Mailbox	chris@bizer.de, bizer@gmx.de
Friends	Emmanuel Pietriga, Ryan Lee, David Karger, Stefano Mazzocchi

Fig. 4. An example of a lens using another lens to display some property values

Formats apply to resources, or to properties and their values, depending on the specified domain. The three example formats of Figure 3 apply respectively to the properties `foaf:name`, `foaf:mbox` and `foaf:depiction` (lines 310, 313, 318). Formats can be used to set properties' labels (lines 311, 314, 319). Property `fresnel:label` does not specify a particular layout but simply gives a text string that can be used to identify the property. Labels might already be defined for many properties (e.g., in the associated vocabulary description using `rdfs:label`), but such labels are not guaranteed to exist. Moreover, a given label might not always be the most appropriate depending on the context in which the property is displayed. For instance, the default label associated with property `foaf:name` in the FOAF schema is *name*. When displaying the persons known by the current person in Figure 4, this default label is replaced by *Friends* (line 426) so as to indicate the appropriate interpretation of the corresponding `foaf:name` property values in this context. The customization of labels also proves useful when displaying property values that are not direct properties of the current resource, as is made possible by the use of SPARQL or FSL expressions such as:

```
foaf:knows/*[airport:iataCode/text() = 'CDG']/foaf:name
```

which would require an explanatory label such as *Friends that leave near Paris*.

Formats can also give instructions regarding how to render values. For instance, line 315 indicates that `foaf:mbox` values should be rendered as clickable links (email addresses). Values of `foaf:depiction` should be fetched from the Web and rendered as bitmap images (line 320).

Property values can be grouped, and additional content such as commas and an ending period can be specified to present multi-valued properties (line 316: inserting a comma in-between each email address). CSS class names can also be associated with the various elements being formatted. These names appear in the output document and can be used to style the output by authoring and referencing CSS style sheets that use rules with the same class names as selectors.

2.3 Lens and Format Grouping

Lenses and formats can be associated through `fresnel:Groups` so that browsers can determine which lenses and formats work together. Fresnel groups are taken into account by browsers when selecting what format(s) to apply to the data selected by a given lens, as several formats might be applicable to the same property values.

Figure 4 illustrates the use of Fresnel groups to display different labels for the `foaf:name` property depending on the context in which the property is shown: the property is labeled *Name* when displayed in the context of the `PersonLens` lens, but is labeled *Friends* when displayed in the context of the `PersonLabelLens` lens. This is achieved by associating the `PersonLens` (lines 400-409) and the `nameFormat` (lines 414-417) to one group: `FOAFmainGroup`, and by associating the `PersonLabelLens` (lines 410-413) and the `friendsFormat` (lines 424-427) to a second group: `FOAFsubGroup`.

A Fresnel group can also serve as a placeholder for formatting instructions that apply to all formats associated with that group, thus making it possible to factorize the declarations. It is also typically used to declare group-wide data, relevant to both lenses and formats, such as namespace prefix bindings.

3 Fresnel Selectors

Selection in Fresnel occurs when specifying the domain of a lens or format and when specifying what properties of a resource a lens should show. Such selection expressions identify elements of the RDF model to be presented; in other words, specific nodes and arcs in the graph. As we expect selection conditions to be of varying complexity, we allow them to be expressed using different languages in an attempt to balance expressive power against ease of use.

3.1 Basic Selectors

The simplest selectors, called basic selectors, take the form of plain URI references as shown in section 2. Depending on whether they are used as values of `fresnel:instanceLensDomain` or `fresnel:classLensDomain`, these URI references are interpreted respectively either as:

- URI equality constraints (the resource to be selected should be identified by this URI),
- or type constraints (the resources to be selected should be instances of the class identified by this URI).

Basic selectors are also used to identify properties, which are used for instance as values of `fresnel:showProperties` or `fresnel:alternateProperties`.

Basic selectors are easy to use but have very limited expressive power. For instance, they cannot be used to specify that a lens should apply to all instances of class `foaf:Person` that are the subject of at least five `foaf:knows` statements. More powerful languages are required to express such selection constraints.

3.2 Languages for Complex Selection Expressions

Fresnel presentation designers can use two different languages for expressing complex selection expressions. The first option is the SPARQL query language for RDF [20]. In the context of Fresnel, SPARQL queries must always return exactly one result set, meaning that only one variable is allowed in the query's SELECT clause. Figure 5-a gives an example of a lens whose domain is defined by a SPARQL expression. Alternatively, designers who prefer a more XPath-like approach, which proved to be a well-adapted selector language for XSLT, can use the Fresnel Selector Language (FSL). FSL is a language for modeling traversal paths in RDF graphs, designed to address the specific requirements of a selector language for Fresnel. It does not pretend to be a full so-called RDFPath language (contrary to XPR [21], an extension of FSL) but tries to be as simple as possible, both from usability and implementation perspectives. FSL is strongly inspired by XPath [22], reusing many of its concepts and syntactic constructs while adapting them to RDF's graph-based data model. RDF models are considered directed labeled graphs according to RDF Concepts and Abstract Syntax [23]. FSL is therefore fully independent from any serialization. A lens definition using two FSL expressions is shown in Figure 5-b. More information about FSL, including its grammar, data model and semantics is available in the FSL specification [24].

Applications implementing Fresnel are required to support basic selectors, and we expect a reasonable share of them to support the two other languages: SPARQL is gaining

```
# (a) Lens for John Doe's mailboxes      (SPARQL)
:PersonLens a fresnel:Lens ;
            fresnel:instanceLensDomain
                "SELECT ?mbox WHERE ( ?x foaf:name 'John Doe' )
                                    ( ?x foaf:mbox ?mbox )"^^fresnel:sparqlSelector .
# (b) Lens for foaf:Person instances that know at least five other resources   (FSL)
:PersonLens a fresnel:Lens ;
            fresnel:instanceLensDomain
                        "foaf:Person[count(foaf:knows) >= 5]"^^fresnel:fslSelector ;
# and which shows the foaf:name property of all foaf:Person
# instances known by the current resource.
            fresnel:showProperties (
                    "foaf:knows/foaf:Person/foaf:name"^^fresnel:fslSelector) .
```

Fig. 5. Examples of SPARQL and FSL expressions used in Fresnel lens definitions

momentum as a W3C recommendation, and four open-source Java implementations of FSL are already available[1] for HP's Jena Semantic Web Toolkit[2], for IsaViz (providing a visual FSL debugger) and for different versions of the Sesame RDF database[3].

4 Implementations

Fresnel has been designed as an application- and output format-independent RDF presentation vocabulary. In this section we give an overview of various applications implementing Fresnel: Longwell [1] and Horus [18] which both render RDF data as HTML Web pages using nested box layouts, IsaViz [6] which represents RDF graphs as node-link diagrams, and Cardovan, a browser and lens editor based on the SWT GUI toolkit.

Longwell is a Web-based RDF browser whose foundational navigation paradigm is faceted browsing. Faceted browsing displays only the properties that are configured to be 'facets' (i.e., to be important for the user browsing data in one or more specific domains) using values for those fields as a means for zooming into a collection by selecting those items with a particular field-value pair.

The latest version of Longwell relies on the SIMILE Fresnel rendering engine, a Java library built on the Sesame triple store. The engine implements all of the Fresnel core vocabulary and the portion of the extended vocabulary relating to linking groups to CSS stylesheets as well as the option of using FSL as a selector language. The Fresnel engine output consists solely of an XML representation of the Fresnel lenses and formats as they apply to one resource. Longwell then applies an XSLT transformation to the XML to generate XHTML. The default XSLT stylesheet shipped with Longwell will generate a traditional nested box layout, as Horus does, but the stylesheet can be modified by XSLT developers to change the model as they see fit.

The left side of Figure 6 shows the rendering of a `foaf:Organization` resource using a lens that gives some details about the organization and lists its constituent members, all `foaf:Persons`, each listed with their corresponding nickname information to assist in identification.

---
[1] http://dev.w3.org/cvsweb/java/classes/org/w3c/IsaViz/fresnel/
[2] http://jena.sourceforge.net
[3] http://openrdf.org

Fresnel: A Browser-Independent Presentation Vocabulary for RDF   167

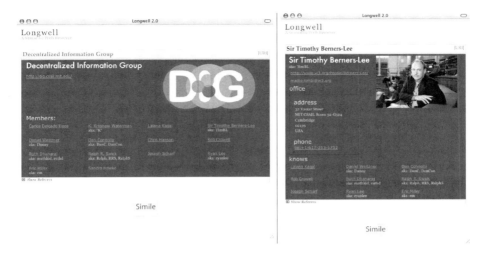

Fig. 6. Displaying a view of an organization (left) and a constituent member (right) in Longwell

The nickname list for each person is preceded by the string 'aka: ', added to the display by using the `fresnel:contentFirst` directive. The list is also comma separated, accomplished by setting `fresnel:contentAfter` to a comma. Clicking on a URI in the display brings the user to that URI; clicking on a textual label changes Longwell's focus to the resource represented by that label.

On the right side of Figure 6, the focus is on one specific member of the organization featured in the left side. A sublens is used to generate office contact details, and the same sublens used in the organization focus (left image) to describe an organization's members is used in the person focus (right image) to describe who this person claims to know.

Horus is an RDF browser that displays RDF information using a nested box layout. The browser provides a simple navigation paradigm for selecting RDF resources and allows users to switch between different lenses for rendering the resources. Horus supports Fresnel lenses and formats, which can be associated together using Fresnel groups. Groups can refer to external CSS style sheets which are used to define fonts, colors and borders. Horus supports basic selectors, but does not offer SPARQL and FSL as selector languages. Horus is implemented using PHP and is backed by a MySQL database. Applying a lens to an RDF resource results in an intermediate tree, which is formatted afterwards using the formats that are associated to the group of the selected lens. The ordered and formatted intermediate tree is then serialized into XHTML.

Figure 7 shows two different views on the same person in Horus. The view on the left uses a lens that displays many details about persons. The sentence "*This person knows the following people*" is a custom label for property `foaf:knows`. The disclaimer "*That a person knows somebody does...*" is static content added using property `fresnel:contentLast`. Some of the links are formatted as external links (`fresnel:value` formatting instruction set to `fresnel:externalLink`), while others refer to RDF resources in the knowledge base, and thus have a different rendering.

Fig. 7. Two different views on the same person in Horus: detailed view (left), friends view (right)

On the right side of Figure 7, the same person is shown using a different lens. This lens displays less details about the person itself, but refers to a second lens (used as a sublens) for displaying details about other persons known by this person. As the sublens belongs to a different group, another CSS class is used to style the names of the person's friends.

IsaViz is an RDF authoring environment representing RDF models as node-link diagrams. The interpretation of Fresnel in IsaViz is inspired by both Generalized Fisheye Views [25] and Magic Lenses [26]. Fresnel lenses, in conjunction with the formats associated with them through groups, are considered as "genuine" lenses that modify the visual appearance of objects below them.

Figure 8 (left) shows the default rendering of a region of an RDF model containing a foaf:Person resource. At this level of magnification, only a few of the many property values associated with the resource are visible. Users need to navigate in the graph in order to get to the values of properties, which can be cumbersome. Alternatively, users can select a Fresnel lens from the list of available lenses loaded in IsaViz through the graphical user interface. The selected lens is then tied to the mouse cursor, and when the lens hovers over a resource that matches its domain, the resource's visual appearance gets modified according to the lens and associated format(s). Resources that match the selected lens' domain are made visually prominent by rendering all other nodes and all arcs using shades of gray with minimum contrast. When the lens hovers over a resource, properties selected by the lens are temporarily rendered with highly-contrasted vivid colors and brought within the current view, closer to the main resource and reordered clockwise according to the ordering of properties in the lens definition, as illustrated in Figure 8 (right). Property values revert back to their original state when the lens moves away from the resource. All these visual modifications, including color and position changes, are smoothly animated thanks to the underlying graphical toolkit's animation capabilities [27], thus keeping the user's cognitive load low following the principles of perceptual continuity.

Fresnel core formatting instructions are interpreted as customizations of the original layout and rendering of nodes and links in the diagram. For instance, nodes representing foaf:image property values can be rendered by fetching the actual image from the

Web, as illustrated in Figure 8 (right). The default labels of nodes and arcs can be customized using fresnel:label instructions. In case a resource is the subject of multiple statements involving the same property or properties defined as fresnel:mergeProperties, the arcs and nodes representing these statements can be merged as a single arc and node with all values within that node, optionally separated by text as specified in fresnel:contentBefore, fresnel:contentAfter and related formatting instructions.

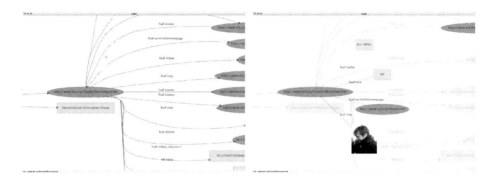

Fig. 8. Zoomed-in view of a foaf:Person resource in IsaViz: default presentation (left) and rendered with a Fresnel lens (right)

Fig. 9. Editing a lens (left) and visualizing the result (right) in Cardovan

Cardovan is IBM's implementation of Fresnel lenses (see Figure 9). Written in Java, Cardovan renders lenses with the SWT graphical user interface toolkit. Cardovan is similar to other implementations in that it uses a subset of CSS to specify the layout of lens components on the screen. A remarkable feature of Cardovan is that it allows users to modify a lens in place. Users can add new properties to the lens, modify property values, and rearrange the physical layout of the properties displayed, though it is not a full WYSIWYG Fresnel lens designer. The project is still in its early stages, but is functional and is already being used for internal projects at IBM.

5 Conclusion

We have given an overview of Fresnel, a browser-independent, extensible vocabulary for modeling Semantic Web presentation knowledge. Fresnel has been designed as a modularized, declarative language manipulating selection, formatting, and styling concepts that are applicable across representation paradigms and output formats. We have presented applications implementing Fresnel core modules while based on different representation and navigation paradigms, thus substantiating the claim that Fresnel can be used to model presentation knowledge that is reusable across browsers and other Semantic Web visualization tools.

Although core modules have been frozen for the time being, the Fresnel vocabulary remains a work in progress as new extension modules meeting special needs are being developed (e.g., for describing the *purpose* of lenses and for *editing* information). Extension modules are not necessarily aimed at being application- and paradigm-independent, as they might not be relevant in all cases; but their inclusion in Fresnel provides users with a unified framework for modeling presentation knowledge. Another field for future work is enabling Fresnel formats and lenses to be retrieved transparently from the Web so that RDF browsers could query the Web for display knowledge about previously unknown vocabularies.

The development of Fresnel is an open, community-based effort and new contributors are welcome to participate in it. More information can be found on its Web site http://www.w3.org/2005/04/fresnel-info/.

Acknowledgments

We would like to thank Stefano Mazzocchi, Stephen Garland, David Huynh, Karun Bakshi, Hannes Gassert, Jacco van Ossenbruggen, Dennis Quan, Lloyd Rutledge, Rob Gonzalez and Rouben Meschian for their valuable input to the design of the Fresnel vocabulary, their contributions to the discussions on the Fresnel mailing list, and work on Fresnel implementations.

References

1. SIMILE: Longwell RDF Browser (2003-2005) http://simile.mit.edu/longwell/.
2. Huynh, D., Mazzocchi, S., Karger, D.: Piggy Bank: Experience the Semantic Web Inside Your Web Browser. In: Proceedings of the 4th International Semantic Web Conference (ISWC). (2005) 413–430
3. Steer, D.: BrownSauce: An RDF Browser. http://www.xml.com/pub/a/2003/02/05/brownsauce.html (2003) XML.com.
4. Rutledge, L., van Ossenbruggen, J., Hardman, L.: Making RDF Presentable: Selection, Structure and Surfability for the Semantic Web. In: Proceedings of the 14th international conference on World Wide Web. (2005) 199–206

5. Kalyanpur, A., Parsia, B., Hendler, J.: A Tool for Working with Web Ontologies. In: Proceedings of Extreme Markup Languages. (2004)
6. Pietriga, E.: IsaViz: A Visual Authoring Tool for RDF. http://www.w3.org/2001/11/IsaViz/ (2001-2006)
7. SIMILE: Welkin. http://simile.mit.edu/welkin/ (2004-2005)
8. Quan, D., Huynh, D., Karger, D.R.: Haystack: A Platform for Authoring End User Semantic Web Applications. In: 2nd International Semantic Web Conference (ISWC). (2003) 738–753
9. mc schraefel, Smith, D., Owens, A., Russell, A., Harris, C.: The evolving mSpace platform: leveraging the Semantic Web on the Trail of the Memex. In: 16th ACM Conference on Hypertext and Hypermedia. (2005) 174–183
10. Berners-Lee, T., Chen, Y., Chilton, L., Connolly, D., Dhanaraj, R., Hollenbach, J., Lerer, A., Sheets, D.: Tabulator: Exploring and Analyzing linked data on the Semantic Web. In: Proceedings of the 3rd Int. Semantic Web User Interaction Workshop, Athens, USA (2006)
11. ASF: The Apache Cocoon Project. http://cocoon.apache.org (2005)
12. Carroll, J.J., Stickler, P.: TriX: RDF triples in XML. In: In the International Journal on Semantic Web and Information Systems, Vol.1, No.1, Jan-Mar 2005. (2005)
13. Quan, D., Karger, D.: Xenon: An RDF Stylesheet Ontology. general@simile.mit.edu mailing list attachment (2004)
14. Huynh, D.: Haystack's User Interface Framework: Tutorial and Reference. http://haystack.lcs.mit.edu/documentation/ui.pdf (2003)
15. Pietriga, E.: Semantic Web Data Visualization with Graph Style Sheets. In: Proceedings of the ACM Symposium on Software Visualization (SoftVis'06), Brighton, UK (2006)
16. Bizer, C., Lee, R., Pietriga, E.: Fresnel - Display Vocabulary for RDF. http://www.w3.org/2005/04/fresnel-info/manual-20050726/ (2005)
17. FOAFers: Friend-of-a-Friend (FOAF). http://www.foaf-project.org/ (2001)
18. Erdmann, T.I., Bizer, C.: Horus RDF Browser. http://www.wiwiss.fu-berlin.de/suhl/bizer/rdfapi/tutorial/horus/ (2005)
19. Berners-Lee, T.: Primer: Getting into RDF & Semantic Web using N3. http://www.w3.org/2000/10/swap/Primer.html (2005)
20. Prud'hommeaux, E., Seaborne, A.: SPARQL Query Language for RDF. http://www.w3.org/TR/rdf-sparql-query/ (2005)
21. Cohen-Boulakia, S., Froidevaux, C., Pietriga, E.: Selecting Biological Data Sources and Tools with XPR, a Path Language for RDF. In: Pacific Symposium on Biocomputing (PSB), Maui, Hawaii. (2006) 116–127
22. Clark, J., DeRose, S.: XML Path Language (XPath) version 1.0. http://www.w3.org/TR/xpath (1999)
23. W3C: Resource Description Framework (RDF): Concepts and Abstract Syntax. http://www.w3.org/TR/rdf-concepts/ (2004)
24. Pietriga, E.: Fresnel Selector Language for RDF. http://www.w3.org/2005/04/fresnel-info/fsl-20050726/ (2005)
25. Furnas, G.W.: A fisheye follow-up: further reflections on focus + context. In: CHI '06: Proceedings of the SIGCHI conference on Human Factors in computing systems, ACM Press (2006) 999–1008
26. Bier, E.A., Stone, M.C., Pier, K., Buxton, W., DeRose, T.D.: Toolglass and magic lenses: the see-through interface. In: SIGGRAPH '93: Proc. of the 20th conference on Computer graphics and interactive techniques, ACM Press (1993) 73–80
27. Pietriga, E.: A Toolkit for Addressing HCI Issues in Visual Language Environments. In: IEEE Symposium on Visual Languages and Human-Centric Computing (VL/HCC'05), Dallas, USA (2005) 145–152

A Software Engineering Approach to Design and Development of Semantic Web Service Applications

Marco Brambilla[1], Irene Celino[2], Stefano Ceri[1], Dario Cerizza[2],
Emanuele Della Valle[2], and Federico Michele Facca[1]

[1] Politecnico di Milano, Dipartimento di Elettronica e Informazione, 20133 Milano, Italy
{Marco.Brambilla, Stefano.Ceri, Federico.Facca}@polimi.it
[2] CEFRIEL, 20133 Milano, Italy
{celino, cerizza, dellavalle}@cefriel.it

Abstract. We present a framework for designing and developing Semantic Web Service applications that span over several enterprises by applying techniques, methodologies, and notations offered by Software engineering, Web engineering, and Business Process modeling. In particular, we propose to exploit existing standards for the specification of business processes (e.g., BPMN), for modeling the cross enterprise process, combined with powerful methodologies, tools and notations (e.g., WebML) borrowed from the Web engineering field for designing and developing semantically rich Web applications, with semi-automatic elicitation of semantic descriptions (i.e., WSMO Ontologies, Goals, Web Services and Mediators) from the design of the applications, with huge advantages in terms of efficiency of the design and reduction of the extra work necessary for semantically annotating the information crossing the organization boundaries.

Keywords: Business Process Modeling, Semantic Web Services, Software Engineering, Web Engineering, Model Driven Design, Methodology.

1 Introduction

Taking the e-challenges (e-business, e-government, e-health, etc.) seriously means dealing with business processes that: *(i)* span over several enterprises; *(ii)* involve multiple actors, *(iii)* require asynchronous communication; and *(iv)* are situated in frequently changing scenarios. Current ICT solutions have serious technological and methodological limitations when addressing the abovementioned aspects; the emerging field of Semantic Web Services is offering the most promising approach to overcome such limitations, providing paradigms based on program annotation and self-descriptive implementation, for building cross-enterprise applications which favor flexibility, automatic resource discovery, and dynamic evolution. However, the development of applications based on Semantic Web Services is currently lacking a set of high level software engineering abstractions that may push the spreading of such technology. One of the main problems faced by developers to adopt Semantic Web technologies is the extra cost of semantic annotation of the developed software components. This is mostly because software engineering techniques are seldom used in the context of Semantic Web; hence, no automatic mechanism can be applied for extracting semantic descriptions. Therefore, annotations are still added manually, in a very expensive and subjective manner.

In this work, we propose both a method and a toolset for fostering the adoption of Semantic Web Services (i.e., WSMO) in cross-enterprise applications. We exploit Web engineering methods, including visual declarative modeling (i.e., WebML), automatic code generation (locally and globally executable through Semantic Execution Environments such as WSMX), and automatic elicitation of semantic descriptions (i.e., WSMO Ontologies, Goals, Web Services and Mediators) from the design of the application. Global choreography (in W3C sense), front-end, and services implementations are modeled from Business Process models and WebML models, whereas goals, descriptions of Web services (i.e., capability and choreography interface), and descriptions of mediators are automatically generated. The approach also comprises the importing/ exporting of ontologies. The following techniques and notations shall be used for covering the various design aspects:

- *High-level design of the global choreography of the interaction between services:* we adopt BPMN (Business Process Management Notation) to build process models, involving several actors possibly from different enterprises.
- *Design of the underlying data model of the cross-enterprise application:* we use extended E-R (Entity Relationship) diagrams or equivalent subset of object oriented class diagrams (whose expressive power is equivalent to WSML Flight) to model the local ontology of the application and to import existing ontologies; we expose the resulting set of ontologies to the underling WSMX;
- *Design of web services interfaces, of integration platform, and of application front end:* we use visual diagrams representing Web sites and services according to the WebML models [5], including specific hypertext primitives for Web service invocation and publishing [18], and explicit representation of workflows [6].

In this way, instead of coping with textual semantic descriptions of Semantic Web Services, application developers will obtain them from the use of abstractions that are supported by software engineering tools. The use of description generators, sometimes helped by designer's annotations, guarantees the benefits of Semantic Web Services at nearly zero extra-cost, thus positioning the implemented applications within an infrastructure that allows for flexible and dynamic reconfiguration.

The paper is structured as follows: Section 2 presents a running example; Section 3 reviews the background; Section 4 presents the proposed approach to the elicitation of semantic descriptions; Section 5 briefly outlines our implementation experience; Section 6 offers a view of the related work and finally Section 7 concludes.

2 Running Example

We will consider a running example derived by the *Purchase Order Mediation* and the *Shipment Discovery* scenarios proposed at the SWS Challenge 2006 [8], properly extended to represent a classical B2B application. In this scenario, two companies, Blue and Moon, need to integrate their purchase process. In summary (Fig. 1), the architecture includes the two companies, the mediation service, a general-purpose web service built by Blue for interacting with external services, and a discovery engine.Blue usually handles its purchase orders towards its partners by using a standard RosettaNet PIP 3A4 conversation, while the Moon partner offers a set of legacy Web Services. Blue employees want to use their usual *RosettaNet Purchase Order Interface* to interact with their counterparts in the Moon company, therefore a mediation component is needed. The mediator is in charge of *(i)* transforming the single RosettaNet message (containing all the order details) to the various messages needed by Moon to create and handle a purchase order (data mediation); and *(ii)* of translating the set of confirmation messages by Moon into a whole RosettaNet Purchase Order Confirmation to be sent back to Blue (process mediation). After completing the purchase of a set of products, Blue employees organize the shipment of the products through the *Shipment Organize Interface*. This interface is implemented by a Blue Web Service, whose internal orchestration relies on a WSMX compliant *Discovery Engine* for retrieving available shipment services, and hence needs the shipment goal to be described according to the WSMO standard. The Web Services returned by the Discovery Engine are then invoked to obtain the actual shipment offers. Finally, the system proceeds with the orchestration of the chosen service.

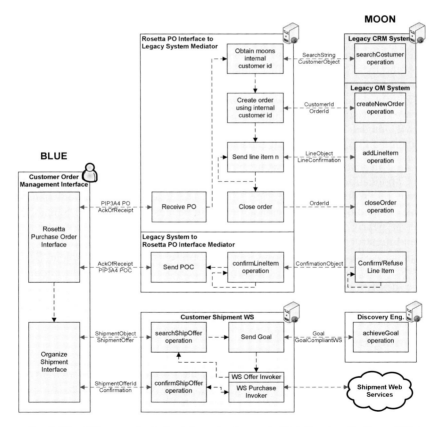

Fig. 1. The B2B scenario derived from the Semantic Web Service Challenge 2006

3 Background

Our approach relies on methodologies, tools and techniques from the fields of Software Engineering, Web Engineering, and Business Process Management.

3.1 Modeling Business Processes Using BPMN

All the B2B Web applications implement a business process, which is represented by using a workflow model. Several notations have been proposed for workflow design. We adopt Business Process Management Notation (http://bpmn.org), which is associated to the BPML standard, issued by the Business Process Management Initiative. The BPMN notation allows one to represent all the basic process concepts defined by the WfMC (http://wfmc.org) model and others, such as data and control flow, activity, actor, conditional/split/join gateways, event and exception management, and others. BPMN activities can be grouped into pools, and one pool contains all activities that are to be enacted by a given process participant. The BPMN formalization of the running case scenario can be seen in Fig. 4.

3.2 Semantic Web Service Modeling Using WSMO

The Web Service Modeling Ontology (WSMO) [23] aims at solving the application integration problem for Web services by defining a coherent technology for Semantic Web services, using four modeling elements: ontologies, Web services, goals, and mediators [13]. *Ontologies* provide the formal semantics to the information used by all other components, by describing concepts, relations, axioms, instances and so on. *Web services* represent the functional and behavioral aspects, which must be semantically described in order to allow semi-automated use. Each Web service represents an atomic piece of functionality that can be reused to build more complex ones. Web services are described in WSMO in terms of non-functional properties, functionality (capabilities), and behavior. The behavior of a Web service is described in its interface from two perspectives: communication and collaboration. A Web service can be described by multiple interfaces, but has one and only one capability. *Goals* specify objectives that a client might have when invoking a Web service. Finally, *mediators* provide interoperability facilities among the other elements, aiming at overcoming structural, semantic or conceptual mismatches between the components of a WSMO description.

3.3 Model-Driven Web Application Design Using WebML

Several Web engineering methodologies provide conceptual models, notations, and tools for the design of Web applications ([20], [14], [12], and others). In this paper, we adopt the WebML methodology [5], envisioning the following steps in the development process: *(i)* design of workflow model of the business process to be implemented; *(ii)* automatic generation of hypertext model and data model skeletons implementing the workflow; *(iii)* refinement of the produced skeletons by designers; *(iv)* automatic generation of the running Web application starting from the specified models.

The specification of a WebML application consists of a set of models: the application *data model* (an extended Entity-Relationship or UML Class Diagram), one or more *hypertext models* (i.e., different site views for different types of users), describing the

Web application structure; the *presentation model*, describing the visual aspects. The hypertext main concept is the site view, which is a graph of pages; pages are composed by units, representing publishing of atomic pieces of information, and operations for modifying data or performing arbitrary business actions. Units are connected by links, to allow navigation, parameter passing, and computation of the hypertext. The WebML service model includes a set of *Web service units* [18], corresponding to the WSDL classes of Web service operations, and components for workflow management and tracking [6].

The Web services units include *request-response* and *one-way* operations, which model services invocation, and *notification* and *solicit-response* operations, which are instead triggered by the reception of a message (thus they represent the publishing of a Web service). The model supports both the *grounding* of Web services to the XML format of Web service messages, and *data-mediation* capabilities.

WebML covers also the development Web applications implementing business processes [6], thereby supporting full-fledged collaborative workflow-based applications, spanning multiple individuals, services, and organizations. The *data model* is extended with the meta-data necessary for tracking the execution of the business process; in particular, *Case* stores information about each instantiation of the process and *Activity* stores the status of each executed activity. The *hypertext model* is extended by specifying activity boundaries and business-dependent navigation links. A*ctivities* are represented by areas tagged with a marker "A"; *workflow links* traverse the boundary of activity areas, starting or ending the activity. *Distributed processes* can be obtained by combining workflow and Web services primitives.

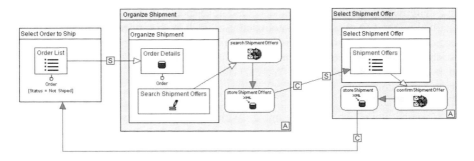

Fig. 2. The Blue Web interface to organize shipments for successful orders

Fig. 2 shows a WebML hypertext model representing a fragment of the Blue Web application: a home page (*Select Order to Ship*) allows the user to choose an *Order* (with *Status* "Not shipped") from the *Order List* index unit. When an order is chosen, the "S" link starts the Organize Shipment activity, showing the Order Details data unit and a form (*Search Shipment Offers*). The data submission triggers the invocation of a remote service (*searchShipmentOffers*), whose results are lifted by *storeShipmentOffer* XML-in. The activity is completed (link "C") and the following one is started. The *Select Shipment Offer* page is shown, containing a list of *Shipment Offers* (the results of the service call). The user chooses an offer and thus triggers the *confirmShipmentOffer*.

4 Design of Semantic Web Service Applications

This section describes our proposal for semi-automatically generating WSMO-compliant semantic specifications of a Web application. Our approach extends the WebML methodology presented in section 3.3 towards the design of semantic Web services and Web applications. Fig. 3 summarizes the envisioned development process. The main design flow, supported on conventional Web technology [6], seamlessly leads the designer from the process modeling to the running Web application, by producing some intermediate artifacts (BPMN models, WebML skeletons, data models, hypertext models) and by delegating part of the execution to a Semantic Execution Environment (e.g. WSMX). Such models are enriched by imported ontological descriptions (on top of the figure) and are exploited for devising the set of WSMO specifications (at the bottom of the figure): the ontology is derived from BP model, data model, and hypertext model; the web services capability description is derived from hypertext model; the choreography information is derived from BP model and hypertext model; the user goals are derived from the BP model.

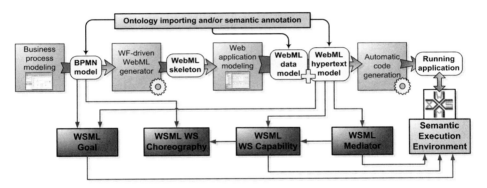

Fig. 3. Overall picture of the approach.

4.1 Design of the Business Process

The business process (BP) design task, focusing on the high-level schematization of the processes underlying the application, results in one or more BP diagrams. The reader may refer to [6] for a methodology for the design of business process-based Web applications. The BP diagram of the running case is represented in Fig. 4, with a well-defined workflow semantics (lacking in Fig. 1): for sake of clarity, the process is split into two sub-processes: part (a) describes the purchase and part (b) describes the shipment management. In the following, we will exemplify the design of the mediator of part (a), and the extraction of ontology, capability and choreography of part (b).

4.2 Design of the Data Model and Extraction of the Ontologies

The elicitation of the ontologies involved in the application is addressed by four steps, each addressing different aspects of the application ontology (see Fig. 3 again):

1. First, existing remote ontologies, possibly provided by third parties, can be imported.
2. Then, the data model is considered as a piece of ontology. This means that an appropriate transformation of the WebML data model transforms it into a WSMO-compliant ontology, which is then registered on the WSMX resource manager [23];
3. Then, the process ontology is extracted from the BPMN specification. The elements of the workflow model (e.g., activity names, lanes) are extracted as semantic concepts and used as additional piece of the ontology that will be useful in defining the state signature of the choreography interfaces of the Web services;
4. Finally, the BPMN model and the WebML data model are annotated with concepts imported from existing ontologies.

This approach is oriented towards T. Berners-Lee vision for Web applications connected by concept annotations [2].

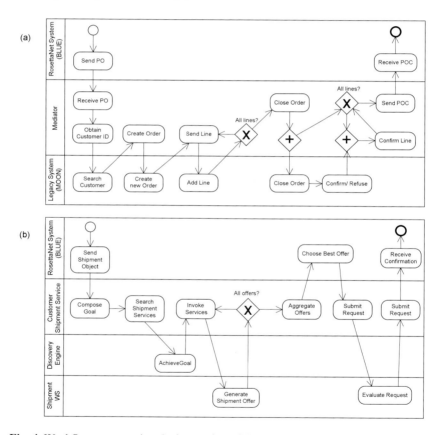

Fig. 4. Workflow representing the interaction of the running example (BPMN notation)

Fig. 5 shows the data model used by the Shipment Web Service. It includes three main domain entities: *Shipment*, *ShipmentService* (shipment partners), and *Location* (geographical places). The diagram includes *Case* and *Activity* entities described in

Section 3.3. Each *Shipment* is related to a *ShipmentService*, to an origin and a destination *Location*, and to an *Activity* indicating its current state. *ShipmentService* is connected to *Location* through the *shipTo* relationship, describing the set of possible shipment locations for each partner; the *hasLocation* relationship specifies the set of valid pick up points for each carrier.

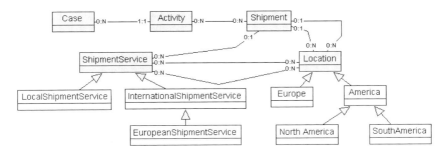

Fig. 5. A portion of the WebML data model used by the Shipment Web Service

WebML data model can be easily converted to a WSML-Flight ontology maintaining all its constraints. E.g., the *EuropeanShipmentService* entity is a sub entity of the *InternationalShipmentService* that is located in *Europe*. This subentity is described in the WebML-OQL syntax as:

```
InternationalShipmentService(as SuperEntity) where
    InternationalShipmentService.hasLocation isa Europe.
```

Its translation to WSML-Flight is:

```
concept EuropeanShipmentService subConceptOf InternationalShipmentService
    nfp dc#relation hasValue { EuShipmentServiceDef } endnfp
axiom EuShipmentServiceDef
    definedBy
?x memberOf InternationlShipmentService
and hasLocation(?x,?nation) and ?nation memberOf Europe
implies ?x memberOf EuropeanShipmentService.
```

The process of WSML ontologies generation starts by importing external ontologies used in the WebML data model to enrich WebML data types definitions. Then, for each entity in the data model, a corresponding WSML concept is generated with its direct super concept, attributes (also relationships are mapped to attributes), and possible axioms.

4.3 Design of the Service and the User Interfaces in WebML

Once the business process has been designed, workflow constraints must be turned into navigation constraints among the pages of the activities of the hypertext and into data queries on the workflow metadata for checking the status of the process. This applies both to the human-consumed pieces of contents (i.e., site interfaces) and to the machine-consumed contents (i.e., Semantic Web Services interactions).

A flexible transformation, depending on several tuning and styling parameters, has been devised for transforming workflow models into skeletons of WebML hypertext diagrams [6]. Since no a-priori semantics is implied by the activity descriptions, the generated skeleton can only implement with the hypertext and queries that are needed for enforcing the workflow constraints. The designer remains in charge of implementing the internals of each activity. Additionally, it is possible to annotate the activities, thus allowing automatic generation of a coarse hypertext that implements the specified behavior, which then needs to be refined by the designer.

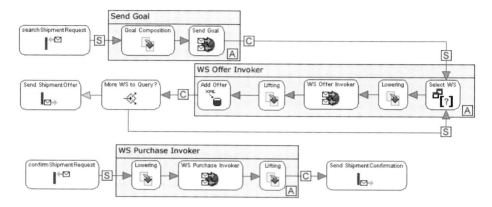

Fig. 6. The Blue Shipment Web Service

For instance, Fig. 6 shows a possible WebML specification of the Blue Shipment service. The upper part in Fig. 6 presents the *searchShipmentRequest* operation: the ShipmentObject, is passed to the *Goal Composition* that transforms it to a Goal description for the WSMX compliant Discovery Engine; the obtained goal description is passed to the *Send Goal*, which sends the goal to Web Service exposed by the Discovery Engine. The Discovery Engine returns a result with a set of Web Services compatible with the original shipment goal. For each Web Service the Lowering and Lifting operations by an appropriate XSLT Stylesheet are applied. Then, for each Web Service returned, a request for a shipment offer is made. The results are combined and converted to the Blue data model and the set of offers is returned the service requester. Once the service requester selects one of the offers and he sends it to the *confirmShipmentRequest* operation (lower part of Fig. 6), the offer is purchased by invoking the appropriate Web Service and the confirmation message is sent back.

4.4 Extraction of the Description of the Web Services

Another important aspect that can be semi-automatically derived from the design specification is the description of Web services. Some information about the services can be directly extracted by the high-level BPMN description of the interactions (in particular, information about possible choreography of the service and basic interface and parameter specification). More details can be elicited from the WebML diagrams, which provide a more refined representation of the specification of the application.

Extraction of Web Services capabilities. The BPMN and WebML models of the Web services provide enough information for describing its behavior. Assuming a BPMN activity as an atomic Web service call, we can exploit the BPMN *data flow* for providing good hints for the extraction of inputs and outputs of the service. Indeed, the data flow specifies the objects that are passed between the various activities. By isolating a single activity, it is possible to automatically extract the WSML pre-conditions (inputs) and post-conditions (outputs). However, designer refinements are then typically required.

WSML pre-conditions are obtained from the first unit of WebML chain describing a Web Service operation (Solicit Unit), while post-conditions are obtained from the last one (Response Unit). These two units contain information about the exact structure of the exchanged message and eventually the mapping of message elements to the domain model and hence to the extracted ontologies (see Section 4.2). Effects are extracted by searching for WebML units that modify or create instances of entities that are related to the activities involved by the process described in WebML Web Service. Shared variables are obtained from the generated conditions by grouping all the variables involved in the operations data flow.

The following WSML description of the Web Service capabilities is automatically generated once the WebML models are fully specified.

```
capability
   sharedVariables (?Req)
   precondition
      definedBy
         (?Req memberOf searchShipmentRequest) or
         (?Req memberOf ConfirmShipmentRequest).
   postcondition
      definedBy
         (?Req[
         pickupdate hasValue ?pkd, deliverydate hasValue ?dd,
         start hasValue ?s, destination hasValue ?dest,
         weight hasValue ?w, maxCost hasValue ?maxc
         ] memberOf searchShipmentRequest)
         implies
         exists ?Res (
            ?Res memberOf ShipmentOfferContainer and
               forall ?offer (
               ?Res [offers hasValue ?offer]
               implies (
                  ?offer [
                     offerID hasValue ?OID, pickupdate hasValue ?pkd,
                     deliverydate hasValue ?dd, start hasValue ?s,
                     destination hasValue ?dest, weight hasValue ?w,
                     cost hasValue ?c] memberOf ShipmentOffer
                     and ?c<=?maxc
         )))) and
         (?Req[ offerID hasValue ?OID] memberOf ConfirmShipmentRequest)
         implies
            exists ?Confirmation (
               ?Confirmation[
                  offerID hasValue ?OID, confirmationID hasValue ?CID
               ] memberOf ShipmentConfirmation
            ))
```

Extraction of the service choreography. The service choreography is a piece of information that typically requires some annotation by the designer, in order to establish all the possible interaction sequences with the service. However, at least one of the choreography sequences can be extracted from the BPMN model, by analyzing the order of invocation of the different operations of the service. Obviously, this does not guarantee that all the possible scenarios are considered, since only one enactment can be analyzed. The extraction of this kind of information is rather simple: provided that a lane describes a single Web service, we can assume that all the control flow links traversing its borders contribute to specifying a possible invocation order of the operations, i.e., a choreography interface of the Web service. The automatically generated WSML description of the Web Service choreography is the following:

```
interface
   choreography
      stateSignature
         in
            searchShipmentRequest withGrounding [...]
            ConfirmShipmentRequest withGrounding [...]
         out
            ShipmentOfferContainer withGrounding [...]
            ShipmentConfirmation withGrounding [...]
         controlled oasm#ControlState
         transitionRules
            forall {?x, ?state} with (
               ?state[oasm#value hasValue oasm#InitialState]
                  memberOf oasm#ControlState and
               ?x memberOf ShipmentRequest
            ) do
               add(?state[oasm#value hasValue ShipmentOfferRequested])
               delete(?state[oasm#value hasValue oasm#InitialState])
               add(_# memberOf ShipmentOfferContainer)
            endForall
            forall {?x, ?state} with (
               ?state[oasm#value hasValue ShipmentOfferRequested] and
               ?x memberOf ConfirmShipmentRequest) do
               add(_# memberOf ShipmentConfirmation)
            endForall
```

4.5 Extraction of User's Goal

Extraction of user's goals can be performed by combining information available at the BPMN level with information available at the WebML level. A first level of goal elicitation can be achieved by extracting the sequence of conditions and objects passed to the Web services by the user's lane in the BPMN diagram.

A deeper level of details requires using the WebML hypertext models and analyzing the semantics embedded in the navigation and composition of the pages. Such refined goal is detailed in terms of the tasks performed by the user and of the data manipulated, thus increasing the significance of the WSMO goals that can be generated. In this case we omit the automatically generated code due to space limitation.

4.6 Design of wwMediators with WebML

One of the main strength points of the approach is the ease of design and implementation of complex wwMediators. If a lane is identified as a wwMediator at

A Software Engineering Approach to Design and Development 183

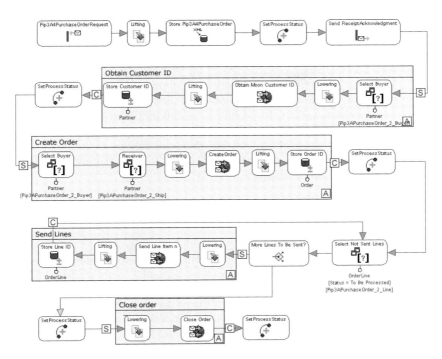

Fig. 7. The WebML model of wwMediator Web Service

the BPMN level, the basic information about the design of the mediation services can be extracted from the high-level BPMN description of the interactions (in particular, information about possible choreography of the service and basic interface and parameter specification). The skeleton model of the mediator is automatically generated and the designer can refine it at a conceptual design level. Then, the WSMO description of the mediator can be derived from the WebML diagrams.

Fig. 7 presents the detailed specification of the wwMediator within WebML. This specification can be used to generate a working Web Service providing mediation between Blue and Moon Web Service. The WebML specification includes some *Lowering* and *Lifting* operations corresponding to WSMO ooMediators and provides mediation between the data model of the source Web Service and the destination one. In WebML this mediation consists in XSLT stylesheets generated by a visual tool.

5 Implementation Experience

The presented approach relies on solid implementation of the background concepts: the WebML methodology is supported by a commercial CASE tool called WebRatio (www.webratio.com), providing visual design interfaces and automatic code generation; the modeling of the business process requirements and their transformation into WebML skeletons are implemented in a prototype tool [3].

A proof of concepts of the integration with the semantic aspects discussed in this paper has been presented at the SWS Challenge 2006 [4, 8]. The first phase of the challenge allowed us to prove the advantages of a Software Engineering approach to Semantic Web Services design. We presented the WebML design and implementation of the wwMediator of the running case addressed in this paper (Fig. 9) and the usage of the CASE tool WebRatio in the context of Semantic Web applications. For validating our approach, we developed several prototypical transformers that generate WSMO-compliant descriptions of Web applications and services starting from WebML models of the applications and BPMN specifications of the processes. The pieces of WSMO specification presented in Sections 4.2 and 4.4 are samples of the generated output of the transformations.

6 Related Work

The Semantic Web is a quite new research area that grew up quickly and in few years produced a great number of publications. However, few of them concern the systematic and methodological development of Semantic Web applications. Some early proposals (e.g., [9]) offered the definition of UML profiles for easily handling ontological definitions; however they haven't been adopted because of the lack of an overall methodology. A number of researches concentrated on the development of tools to support the generation of semantic descriptions for existing Web Services [17, 22, 10]. Most of these tools still require the learning of the annotation language used (e.g., OWL-S or WSMO) and hence do not push enough the adoption of Semantic Web Services towards the standard software development. Furthermore, they do not exploit the advantages of conceptual models of the Web Services to semi-automatically derive any part of the semantic descriptions.

Our research effort is more similar to the recent efforts of the Object Management Group (http://www.omg.org). The OMG proposed the Ontology Definition Metamodel (ODM) [19] to define a suitable language for modeling Semantic Web ontology languages and hence Semantic Web applications in the context of the Model Driven Architecture (http://www.omg.org/mda). In [1] MIDAS, a framework based on MDA to model and develop Semantic Web applications, is introduced. The framework proposed focuses on the creation of Semantic Web Services and associated WSML descriptions using a UML model according to the MDA approach. This proposal inherits the limits of the MDA approach: the use of a UML model is not always fitting the Semantic Web needs, and often the model is too far from the implementation details to provide an effective automatic code generation. Furthermore, MIDAS does not provide a clear overall roadmap to the design of Semantic Web applications.

Other research efforts are converging on the proposal of combining Semantic Web Services (SWS) and Business Process Management (BPM) to create one consolidated technology, which we call Semantic Business Process Management (SBPM) [16]. This is based on the fact that mechanization of BPM can be addressed through machine-accessible semantics, that can be naturally provided by SWS frameworks (e.g., WSMO).

In the last years, realizing the benefits of the Semantic Web platform, some research from the Web Engineering field is spent to design a methodology to develop Semantic Web Information Systems. Traditional Web design methodologies (like OOHDM [20]) and new approaches (like Hera [21]) are now focusing on designing

Semantic Web applications. However, these methodologies are not supported by an effective CASE tool and do not consider the development of Semantic Web Services; instead, they concentrate only on Semantic Web Portals.

7 Conclusions and Future Work

This paper presented an approach for designing Semantic web applications exploiting software engineering techniques. The following results have been shown:

- ontologies can be imported as models of the data necessary for the cross-enterprise application. They can be extended for addressing the specific needs of the application and registered as shared resources in WSMX.
- WSMO Web Services functional capabilities for delegating sub-processes execution from one enterprise to another are automatically provided for each Web Service modelled in WebML. Choreography interfaces can be derived by combining information in the Business Process Model and at application level in the hypertext model of WebML. In particular, service (local) choreography can be derived by taking the point of an external observer of the Web Services that must know the order in which operation can be invoked and the constrains for their successful invocation. In a similar manner we plan to derive an orchestration interface by translating in WSMO the hypertext model of the application.
- WSMO goals can be produced (e.g., goals that triggers the discovery component of WSMX) from gathering data required to perform a given action of the business process, whereas its choreography interface is derived by the explicit representation of workflow primitives within the hypertext.
- mediation services (except for ontology-to-ontology mediation) can be modeled as WebML applications and registered in WSMX according to their roles (e.g., a wwMediator).

At the current stage of development, we propose using existing software engineering abstractions for the semi-automatic extraction of the components of the WSMO architecture. Thus, by means of "conventional design" (although supported by an advanced visual design studio), we build software that can run on conventional Web technology and at the same time is ready to become part of a WSMO execution environment (i.e. WSMX). Our next steps, which we will do in parallel with the widespreading and enhancement of WSMO standards, will concentrate upon empowering our design abstractions so as to further improve and simplify the design of native WSMO components.

References

1. Acuña, C. J., Marcos, E.: *Modeling semantic web services: a case study*. In Proceedings of the 6th International Conference on Web Engineering (ICWE 2006), Palo Alto, California, USA, 32-39.
2. Berners-Lee, T.: Web Services - Semantic Web Talk. http://www.w3.org/2003/Talks/08-mitre-tbl

3. Brambilla, M.: Generation of WebML Web Application Models from Business Process Specifications. 6th International Conference on Web Engineering (ICWE) 2006, Palo Alto, ACM press, p. 85-86, 2006.
4. Brambilla, M., Ceri, S., Cerizza, D., Della Valle, E., Facca, F. M., Fraternali, P., Tziviskou, C.: Web Modeling-based Approach to Automating Web Services Mediation, Choreography and Discovery. In SWS Challenge I , 2006, Palo Alto, CA. (http://sws-challenge.org/wiki/index.php/Workshop_Stanford)
5. Ceri, S., Fraternali, P., Bongio, A., Brambilla, M., Comai, S., Matera, M.: Designing Data-Intensive Web Applications, Morgan-Kaufmann, December 2002.
6. Brambilla, M., Ceri, S., Fraternali, P., Manolescu, I.: Process Modeling in Web Applications. In ACM Transactions on Software Engineering and Methodology (TOSEM), 2006. In print.
7. Della Valle, E. and Cerizza, D.: The mediators centric approach to automatic webservice discovery of Glue. In MEDIATE2005, volume 168 of CEUR. Workshop Proceedings, 35–50.
8. DERI Stanford. Semantic Web Services Challenge 2006. http://sws-challenge.org.
9. Djurić , D., Gašević , D., Devedžić, V. , Damjanović , V.: *UML Profile for OWL*. 4th International Conference on Web Engineering (ICWE 2004), (LNCS 3140, Springer-Verlag), pp. 607-608, 2004.
10. Elenius D., Denker G., Martin D., Gilham F., Khouri J., Sadaati S., Senanayake R.: *The owl-s editor – a development tool for semantic Web services*. In 2nd European Semantic Web Conference, May 2005.
11. Feier, C., Domingue, J.: *WSMO Primer*. http://www.wsmo.org/TR/d3/d3.1/v0.1/
12. Fernandez, M.F., Florescu, D., Levy, A.Y., Suciu, D.: Declarative Specification of Web Sites with Strudel. In VLDB Journal, 9 (1), 38-55.
13. Fensel, D., Bussler, C.: *The Web Service Modeling Framework WSMF*. Electronic Commerce Research and Applications, 1(2), 2002.
14. Fons, J., Pelechano, V., Albert, M. and Pastor, Ó. Development of Web Applications from Web Enhanced Conceptual Schemas. In ER 2003, LNCS, 2813, 232-245.
15. Garrigós, I., Gómez, J. and Cachero, C., Modelling Dynamic Personalization in Web Applications. In ICWE 2003, 472-475.
16. Hepp, M., Leymann, F., Domingue, J., Wahler, A., Fensel, D.: *Semantic Business Process Management: A Vision Towards Using Semantic Web Services for Business Process Management*. In Proceedings of the IEEE ICEBE 2005, October 18-20, Beijing, China, 535-540.
17. Jaeger M., Engel L, Geihs K.: *A methodology for developing owl-s descriptions*. 1st Int. Conf. on Interoperability of Enterprise Software and Applications. Workshop on Web Services and Interoperability. February 2005.
18. Manolescu, I., Brambilla, M., Ceri, S., Comai, S., Fraternali, P.: Model-Driven Design and Deployment of Service-Enabled Web Applications. In ACM TOIT, Vol. 5, number 3 (August 2005).
19. OMG: Ontology Definition Metamodel (ODM). http://www.omg.org/cgi-bin/doc?ad/06-05-01.pdf
20. Schwabe, D. and Rossi, G. The Object-Oriented Hypermedia Design Model. In Communications of the ACM, 38 (8), 45-46.
21. Vdovjak, R., Frasincar, F., Houben, G. J., Barna, P.: *Engineering semantic web information systems in Hera*. Journal of Web Engineering, Rinton Press, 2(1-2), 3 -26, 2003.
22. Web Service Modeling Toolkit. http://sourceforge.net/projects/wsmt
23. WSMO: Web Service Execution Environment (WSMX). http://www.w3.org/Submission/WSMX.

A Model Driven Approach for Building OWL DL and OWL Full Ontologies

Saartje Brockmans[1], Robert M. Colomb[2], Peter Haase[1], Elisa F. Kendall[3],
Evan K. Wallace[4], Chris Welty[5], and Guo Tong Xie[6]

[1] AIFB, Universität Karlsruhe (TH), Germany
[2] School of Information Technology and Electrical Engineering, The University of Queensland, Australia
[3] Sandpiper Software, Inc., Los Altos, California
[4] US National Institute of Standards and Technology, Gaithersburg, Maryland
[5] IBM Watson Research Center, New York
[6] IBM China Research Lab, China

Abstract. This paper presents an approach for visually modeling OWL DL and OWL Full ontologies based on the well-established visual modeling language UML. We discuss a metamodel for OWL based on the Meta-Object Facility, an associated UML profile as visual syntax, and transformations between both. The work we present supports model-driven development of OWL ontologies and is currently undergoing the standardization process of the Object Management Group. After describing our approach, we present the implementation of our approach and an example, showing how the metamodel and UML profile can be used to improve developing Semantic Web applications.

1 Introduction

The standardization of the Web Ontology Language (OWL, [8]) by the World Wide Web Consortium (W3C) contributed heavily to the wide-spread use of ontologies. In 2003, the Object Management Group (OMG), a standardization consortium for various aspects of software engineering including the well-established Unified Modeling Language (UML, [24]), replied to this by issuing a Request for Proposal for an Ontology Definition Metamodel (ODM, [18]). The intention was to provide a Meta-Object Facility (MOF, [23]) based metamodel to support the development of ontologies using UML modeling tools and the two-way transformation between ontologies written in a specific ontology representation language and ontologies modeled using a dedicated UML syntax. Since that time, a submission team has developed a submission (see [7] for a concise overview) which has undergone several revisions, based on comments solicited not only of the OMG but from the W3C, ISO and Semantic Web communities as well.

The ODM submission supports the knowledge representation languages OWL [8], RDF [1], Common Logic [15] and Topic Maps [14]. The modular structure of MOF makes it straightforward for third parties to extend and enhance the metamodel.

This paper focuses on the OWL portions of the ODM submission, which is currently in adoption recommendation vote at OMG. It supports model-driven development of OWL DL as well as OWL Full ontologies using UML and two-way transformations between ontologies modeled in OWL and ontologies modeled using the UML profile. We have not explicitly covered OWL Lite, but all constructs are provided in the base OWL and OWL DL packages. The paper starts with an introduction of the Model Driven Architecture and its Meta-Object Facility, and UML profiles in Section 2. Then, the metamodel for OWL, the associated UML profile and the transformations between the different models are described in Section 3. Section 4 shows the implementation of our approach and an example. Finally, after discussing related work in Section 5, we conclude by summarizing our work and addressing future investigations in Section 6.

2 Background

2.1 Model Driven Architecture and the Meta-object Facility

Before presenting the model-driven approach to ontology engineering in the next sections, we summarize the Object Management Group's Model Driven Architecture (MDA, [5]) and its Meta-Object Facility (MOF, [23]), which is one of the main pillars of our approach.

In the history of software engineering, there has been a notable increase of the use of models and the level of abstraction in the models. The basic idea of MDA is that the system functionality is defined as a platform-independent model, using an appropriate specification language and then translated to one or more platform-specific models for the actual implementation. To accomplish this goal, MDA defines an architecture that provides a set of guidelines for structuring specifications expressed as models. The translation between a platform-independent model and platform-specific models is often performed using automated tools.

MDA comprises of a four-layer metamodel architecture: meta-metamodel (M3) layer, metamodel (M2) layer, model (M1) layer, and instance (M0) layer. At the top of the MDA architecture is the meta-metamodel, i.e., MOF. It defines an abstract language and framework for specifying, constructing and managing technology neutral metamodels. It is the foundation for defining any modeling language such as UML. MOF also defines a framework for implementing repositories that hold metadata (models) described by metamodels. The main objective of having the four layers with a common meta-metamodel is to support multiple metamodels and models and to enable their extensibility, integration and generic model and metamodel management. Note that the meta-metamodel layer is hard wired in the sense that it is fixed, while the layer of the metamodels is flexible and allows expression of various metamodels. All metamodels, standard or custom, defined by MOF are positioned at the M2 layer. One of these is UML, a graphical modeling language for specifying, visualizing and documenting software systems. The models of the real world, represented by concepts defined in the corresponding metamodel at M2 layer (e.g., UML metamodel) are at M1 layer. Finally, at M0 layer, are objects from the real world or information objects representing these in an information system.

A MOF-based metamodel has clear advantages being based on a standard meta-metamodelling system with a well-developed suite of software tools and integrated transformation possibilities with other MOF-based metamodels.[11].

2.2 UML Profiles

UML methodology, tools and technology seem to be a feasible approach for supporting the development and maintenance of ontologies. The UML class diagram is a rich representation system, widely used, and well-supported with software tools. However, an ontology cannot be sufficiently represented in UML [12] and a dedicated visual ontology modeling language is needed. The two representations share a set of core functionalities but despite this overlap, there are many features which can only be expressed in OWL, and others which can only be expressed in UML. Examples for this disjointness are transitive and symmetric properties in OWL or methods in UML.

The UML profile mechanism is an extension mechanism to tailor UML to specific application areas. UML profiles provide specializations, using stereotypes, of existing UML constructs. They are grounded in MOF, in that they are defined in terms of the MOF meta-metamodel. Moreover, they are based on the UML Kernel package and the Profiles section defined in [21].

3 Approach

In this section, we present a MOF-based metamodel for OWL DL and OWL Full. Models based on these metamodels are OWL ontologies. OWL constructs have a direct correspondence with those of the metamodel. Analogously, we define a MOF-based UML profile, which is instantiated by concrete UML models, to enable the use of UML notation and tools for ontology modeling. Within the MOF framework, the UML models are transformed into OWL definitions and vice versa.

3.1 A Metamodel for OWL DL and OWL Full

Overview and Design Considerations. As mentioned in Section 1, although we focus on OWL in this paper, the ODM submission at OMG provides metamodels for several knowledge representation languages. All these are independent of each other, except the OWL metamodel which extends the RDFS metamodel, as the OWL language itself extends the RDF-S language. The metamodel for OWL specifically, contains three packages. First of all, the primary OWLBase package contains the metamodel constructs common to both OWL DL and OWL Full. Two additional subpackages, the OWLDL package and the OWLFull package, contain constraints and extensions required to distinguish the two dialects OWL DL and OWL Full from one another, as explained in more detail later in this section. Users can elect to support the primary package and either or both of the subordinate packages in order to have complete coverage of either or both dialects of OWL. All metamodel packages are provided with constraints in the Object Constraint Language (OCL, [20]). These expressions specify invariant conditions that must hold for the ontologies being modeled. For the constraints on the metamodel, we refer the user to [13].

We now go through the different parts of the OWLBase metamodel package and show some of the diagrams. Subsequently, we introduce the OWLDL and OWLFull packages.

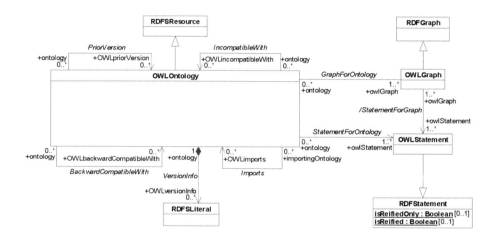

Fig. 1. The Ontology Diagram

OWLBase Package - OWL Ontology. The RDF metamodel represents an RDFStatement as a triple, containing subject, predicate and object whereas an RDFGraph is a set of triples (RDFStatements). As shown in Figure 1, the OWLGraph class specifies the subset of RDF graphs that are valid OWL graphs, consisting of all OWL expressions. Similarly, the subset of RDF statements that are valid OWL statements is reflected by the OWLStatement class. The distinction between OWLStatement and RDFStatement is required, as in OWL DL not every RDFStatement is a valid OWLStatement. An ontology is identified by a URI reference (inherited from RDFSResource), which allows us to make statements about that ontology.

OWLBase Package - Class Descriptions. The metamodel has a class OWLClass for simple OWL class definitions defined as a special type of RDFSClass. Moreover, it has subclasses which represent special types of OWL class descriptions: ComplementClass, EnumeratedClass, IntersectionClass,

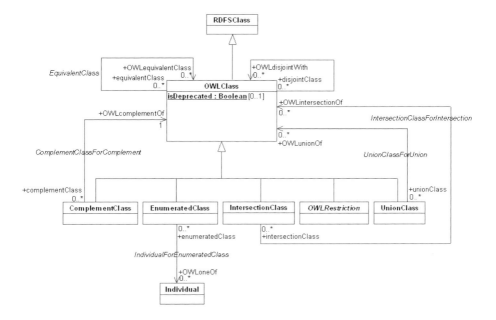

Fig. 2. OWL Class Descriptions

`OWLRestriction` and `UnionClass`. An `EnumeratedClass` is connected to `Individuals` through an association role `OWLoneOf`. Associatons between the classes define the classes in the class descriptions, e.g. the association `IntersectionClassForIntersection` between `IntersectionClass` and `OWLClass` connects the classes of an intersection. Associations `EquivalentClass` and `DisjointClass` represent the OWL class axioms, e.g. `EquivalentClass` connects a class to another class with which it is defined to be equivalent.

The class `OWLRestriction` is defined as a subclass of `OWLClass`. OWL distinguishes two kinds of property restrictions: value constraints and cardinality constraints. All OWL property restriction types are defined as subclasses of the class `OWLRestriction`. A restriction class should have exactly one property `OWLonProperty` linking the restriction to a particular property. The restriction class must also have a property that represents the value or cardinality constraint on the property under consideration.

OWLBase Package - Properties. As shown in Figure 3, the OWL metamodel refines the `RDFProperty` class to support specific OWL properties. Both object properties and datatype properties can be declared as "functional". For this purpose, we define the class `FunctionalProperty` as a special subclass of the class `Property`. `Property` is an abstract class that simplifies representation of property equivalence and deprecation, simplifies constraints for OWL DL and OWL Full, and facilitates mappings with other metamodels.

The class InverseFunctionalProperty is a subclass of OWLObjectProperty, since only object properties can be declared to be inverse functional. A property is defined as symmetric or transitive by making it an instance of the class SymmetricProperty or TransitiveProperty respectively, both defined as subclasses of OWLObjectProperty. Equivalent and inverse properties can be specified with the associations EquivalentProperty and InverseProperty.

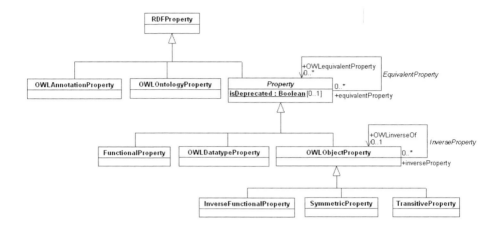

Fig. 3. The OWL Properties Diagram

OWLBase Package - Individuals. Individuals are represented in a subclass Individual of the class RDFSResource. OWL does not make the so-called unique name assumption. For the statements that two individuals are different or the same, the ODM has two associations DifferentIndividual and SameIndividual connected to the class Individual. The OWL construct owl:AllDifferent is represented by a subclass of OWLClass, the class OWLAllDifferent, for which the property DistinctIndividuals is defined to link an instance of OWLAllDifferent to a list of Individuals.

OWLBase Package - Datatypes. OWL makes use of the RDF datatyping scheme and provides an additional construct, OWLDataRange, for defining a range of data values, namely an enumerated datatype. It makes use of the owl:oneOf construct. The subject of OWLoneOf is an anonymous node of class OWLDataRange and the object is a list of RDFSLiterals.

OWLBase Package - OWL Universe. In Figure 4, we provide the part of the metamodel which facilitates ontology traversal for mapping purposes as well as utility in defining constraints for distinguishing OWL DL and OWL

Full. The class `OWLUniverse` specifies the set of ontology elements (i.e. classes, individuals, and properties) that together comprise a particular OWL ontology. It is intended to simplify packaging/mapping requirements for cases where the ability to determine the set of all elements is required.

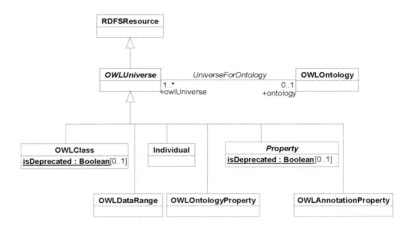

Fig. 4. The OWL Universe Diagram

OWLDL and OWLFull Package. The OWLBase package we just described supports the constructs common to both OWL DL and OWL Full. We provide two additional subpackages to distinguish between the two dialects. Both consist of either extensions or constraints on the OWLBase package. Users can use either or both of the subpackages together with the OWLBase package, depending on whether they want to work with OWL DL or OWL Full. For a complete listing of OWLDL and the OWLFull package, we refer the reader to Sections 11.8 and 11.9 of [13]. An extract of them is given here.

Some of the constraints in the OWLDL package are:

- The set of classes, datatypes, datatype properties, object properties, annotation properties, ontology properties, individuals, data values, and other built-in vocabulary are pairwise disjoint.
- All classes and properties must be explicitly typed as class respectively properties.
- Axioms about individual equality and difference must be about named individuals only (a consequence of category separation).

The OWLFull package contains additional extensions to support the lack of disjointness between classes, properties and individuals. In particular, these extensions provide additional attributes on the OWLBase metamodel classes as well as definitions of new intersection classes required as a workaround to implement OWL Full. The need for this workaround results from a limitation in the MOF2 instances model, which requires that an InstanceSpecification be associated with exactly one classifier. This makes it impossible to have an object as an instance both of Individual and OWLClass, for example. When a future revision of MOF relaxes the instances model to permit multiple classifiers, the OWLFull Package will become superfluous.

3.2 A UML Profile for OWL Ontologies

Our UML profile is designed to support modelers developing ontologies in OWL through reuse of UML notation using tools that support UML2 extension mechanisms. The profile reflects the structure of the OWL metamodel (and the OWL language). We reuse the standard UML2 notation when the constructs have the same intuitive semantics as OWL, or, when this is not possible, stereotyped UML constructs that are consistent and as close as possible to OWL semantics. Stereotypes are leveraged extensively and are represented as the OWL metaclass names enclosed in '<<...>>'. In the following, we introduce our UML2 profile for OWL ontologies. We focus on property representation and refer the reader to Chapter 14 of [13] for a full account. First, we represent the constructs for RDF properties, since the OWL profile package imports the RDF profile package. Then, we show how we refine these RDF property constructs for OWL. We provide considerable flexibility so that property representation is truly intuitive for those familiar with UML.

In UML, a property can be defined as part of an association or on the class that defines the domain of the property. In this case the type of the property is the class that defines its range. When a property is part of an association, the association is binary with unidirectional navigation, from the class that defines the domain of the property to the class that defines its range. In RDF and OWL, properties are defined globally, that is, they are available to all classes in all ontologies. For RDF properties that are defined without specifying a domain or range, the profile uses a global `Thing` class (`Thing` for RDF/S, `owl:Thing` in OWL ontologies) as default for the ŞmissingT end class. Properties that are defined with such a default domain or range may not have multiplicities (other than [0..*]) or other constraints that correspond to OWL restrictions. Figure 5 shows an example of a property without a specified domain. From a UML perspective, properties are semantically equivalent to binary associations with unidirectional navigation (Şone-wayT associations). Figure 6 shows the alternate representation for properties. Just like a UML property, there is efficient navigation from an instance of `Thing` to an instance of `Color` through the `hasColor` end. Moreover, associations can be classes, as shown in Figure 7. An association class can have properties, associations, and participate in generalization as any other class. Notice that the association has a (slightly) different name than the property, by capitalizing the first letter, to distinguish the association class from the property itself. A stereotype `<<rdfProperty>>` is introduced to highlight such binary, unidirectional association classes, as shown in the Figure.

Fig. 5. Property `hasColor` without specified domain

Fig. 6. Property `hasColor` without specified domain - alternate representation

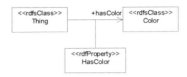

Fig. 7. Property `hasColor` - association class representation

The representation of RDF/S and OWL property subtyping (i.e., rdfs:subPropertyOf) is depending on which of the three notations above is used. In case of the UML property representation (Figure 5), we add a second property entry in the class, and use subsetting by adding {subsets <super-property-name>} at the end of that property entry. For the unidirectional association (Figure 6), we add another association for the subproperty, and add {subsets <super-property-name>} to the association. In case of the association classes (Figure 7), a UML generalization with the stereotype <<rdfsSubPropertyOf>> is preferred. For specific OWL properties, we use stereotypes like <<objectProperty>> instead of <<rdfProperty>>. In these properties, additional characteristics, e.g. a property being functional or a property being symmetric, are represented as UML properties.

If users want to specify a `owl:equivalentProperty` or `owl:inverseOf` relation between two properties, the notation is quite straightforward as well. For instance, Figure 8 shows an `owl:inverseOf` relation being modeled between two association classes using an <<inverseOf>> stereotype. An arrowhead is used opposite from the association class that will have owl:inverseOf in XML syntax.

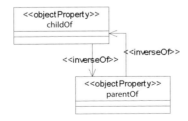

Fig. 8. Using owl:inverseOf Between Association Classes

3.3 Mappings Between UML and OWL

This Section introduces mappings to transform models between OWL and UML, based on the metamodel and the profile described in the previous sections. The ODM Request for Proposals (RFP [19]) called for a normative mapping between the single, unified Ontology Definition Metamodel originally envisioned and UML. If a such a single, normative mapping were provided, for a given implementation to be considered compliant, it would necessarily support that exact mapping. Over the course of development of the ODM, we determined that restricting our potential user community to any specific dialect of OWL (Lite, DL, or Full) would not support the long term vision we outlined in the usage scenarios given in Chapter 7 of the specification. Any single, normative mapping would necessarily force adherence to a specific dialect of OWL.

That said, we claim that the mappings given in the specification can be very informative, and are included in the specification for a number of reasons. First, they demonstrate feasibility of mapping in general and implement one set of design choices, providing a baseline from which a particular implementation can vary. Second, they bring clearly to the fore the detailed relationships among the metamodels. These relationships can help those who understand one of the target languages to come to an understanding of the others. Finally, for many applications, particularly lighter weight vocabularies and ontologies, the mapping provided is sufficient to support transformations between OWL and equivalent UML models, which remains a primary goal of the ODM.

Table 1. Feasible Mappings between UML and OWL

UML Feature	OWL Feature	Comment
class, type	class	
instance	individual	
ownedAttribute, binary association	property, inverseOf	
subclass, generalization	subclass, subproperty	
N-ary association, association class	class, property	Requires decomposition
enumeration	oneOf	
disjoint, cover	disjointWith, unionOf	
multiplicity	minCardinality, maxCardinality, FunctionalProperty, InverseFunctionalProperty	OWL cardinality restrictions declared only for range
package	ontology	

Table 1 provides a very high level summary comparison of some features of UML giving the equivalent OWL feature. UML features are grouped in clusters that translate to a single OWL feature or a cluster of related OWL features. The mapping itself, as described in Chapter 16 of [13], reflects transformation of a model represented in the ODM metamodels for RDF and OWL to the corresponding UML metamodel element(s), and is informed by the profile(s) given in Chapter 14. The representation given in the specification includes both explanatory text and a formal mapping expressed in the recently adopted MOF Query/Views/Transformations (QVT) language [19], which provides a standardized MOF-based platform for mapping instances of MOF metamodels from one metamodel to another. The mapping provided is explicitly between UML 2 and the DL dialect of OWL. For a full account of the informative mappings and their formal expressions in QVT, we refer to [13].

4 Implementation and Examples

This section demonstrates two implementations which have been developed in the context of the ODM submission at OMG: the Visual Ontology Modeler and the Integrated Ontology Development Toolkit[1].

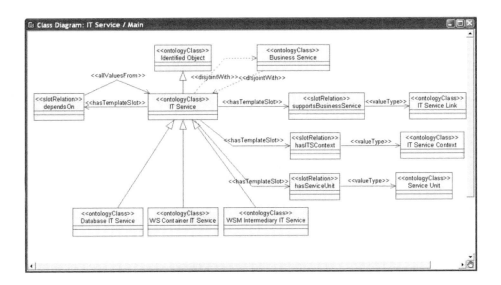

Fig. 9. A diagram modeled with the VOM tool

---

[1] Commercial equipment and materials might be identified to adequately specify certain procedures. In no case does such identification imply recommendation or endorsement by the U.S. National Institute of Standards and Technology, nor does it imply that the materials or equipment identified are necessarily the best available for the purpose.

Visual Ontology Modeler. Visual Ontology Modeler (VOM), developed at the company Sandpiper, is currently implemented as an add-in to IBMŠs Rational Rose product. The current release is compatible with our ODM metamodels and profile for RDFS/OWL. A library of ontology components including ontologies representing several metadata and ISO standards are available for use with the tool. VOM supports forward and reverse engineering of RDFS/OWL ontologies and import/export of ODM/XMI ([22]) (and thus of any MOF metamodel or UML model that can be transformed to ODM/XMI). VOM users have demonstrated measurable productivity gains in ontology development and maintenance as well as increased consistency in RDFS/OWL generation for new and existing ontologies. Figure 9 shows a simple ontology fragment for management application integration ([17]) modeled using VOM (for lack of space we do not show a full screenshot). The second-generation VOM, which is currently in development, will support IBMŠs Eclipse ([9]) and Eclipse Modeling Framework (EMF, [6]) based modeling environment. An open-source version of the software that provides basic functionality will be available for EMF users.

Integrated Ontology Development Toolkit. The EMF-based IBM Integrated Ontology Development Toolkit (IODT) is a toolkit for ontology-driven development, including an EMF Ontology Definition Metamodel ([25]) (EODM[2], based on our ODM), an Eclipse-based ontology-engineering environment, and an OWL ontology repository, which has been evaluated to be highly scalable and perform better than several other well-known systems [16]. The toolkit supports RDFS/OWL parsing and serialization, TBox and ABox reasoning, transformation between RDFS/OWL and other data-modeling languages, and SPARQL[3] query. This toolkit has over 1,800 downloads in alphaWorks and Eclipse.

5 Related Work

In recent years, an increasing range of software systems engage in a variety of ontology management tasks, including the creation, storage, search, query, reuse, maintenance, and integration of ontologies. Recently, there have been efforts to externalize such ontology management burden from individual software systems and put them together in middleware known as an ontology management system. However, as far as we know, other proposals based on the visual UML and MOF ([2], [3], [4], [10]) provide an approach with some similarities and some different design considerations as well, but no full implementation. [2], [3] and [4] are currently being merged with our solution.

6 Conclusion and Future Investigations

We presented a MOF based metamodel and a respective UML profile for OWL DL and OWL Full. Furthermore, we provided feasible mappings which support

---
[2] http://www.eclipse.org/emft/projects/eodm/
[3] http://www.w3.org/TR/rdf-sparql-query/

the transformation between OWL ontologies and UML models and vice versa. This enables ontology engineers to build OWL ontologies based on UML using existing UML tools. Considering the amount of people familiar to UML, our solution will be an good approach to ontology modeling for ordinary developers. With the ODM defined in MOF, we can further utilize MDA's support in modeling tools, model management and interoperability with other MOF-defined metamodels. We expect that the interoperability with existing software tools and applications will ease ontology development and thus contribute to the adoption of semantic technologies and their success in real-life applications.

We have implemented our approach to validate our ideas in the Visual Ontology Modeler and the Integrated Ontology Development Toolkit.

Next to finishing and evaluating the ODM submission in the near future, we plan to extend the ODM to facilitate the development of rules as well. Which rule formalisms we will eventually support, is heavily depending on the outcome of the Rule Interchange Format working group at W3C ([26]). Some initial work on a metamodel and UML Profile for rules is presented in [2].

References

1. D. Brickley and R.V. Guha. RDF Vocabulary Description Language 1.0: RDF Schema. Technical report, W3C, February 2004. W3C Recommendation.
2. S. Brockmans, P. Haase, P. Hitzler, and R. Studer. A Metamodel and UML Profile for Rule-extended OWL DL Ontologies. In *3rd Annual European Semantic Web Conference*, Budva, Montenegro, June 2006. Springer.
3. S. Brockmans, P. Haase, and H. Stuckenschmidt. Formalism-Independent Specification of Ontology Mappings - A Metamodeling Approach. In *5th International Conference on Ontologies, DataBases, and Applications of Semantics (ODBASE 2006*, Montpellier, France, November 2006.
4. S. Brockmans, R. Volz, A. Eberhart, and P. Loeffler. Visual modeling of OWL DL ontologies using UML. In *Proceedings of the Third International Semantic Web Conference*, pages 198–213, Hiroshima, Japan, November 2004. Springer.
5. A. Brown. An introduction to Model Driven Architecture - Part I: MDA and today's systems, February 2004. http://www-106.ibm.com/developerworks/rational/library/3100.html.
6. F. Budinsky, R. Ellersick, T. J. Grose, E. Merks, and D. Steinberg. *Eclipse Modeling Framework*. The Eclipse Series. Addison Wesley Professional, first edition, 2003.
7. R. Colomb, K. Raymond, L. Hart, P. Emery, C. Welty, G. T. Xie, and E. Kendall. The Object Management Group Ontology Definition Metamodel. In F. Ruiz, C. Calero, and M. Piattini, editors, *Ontologies for Software Engineering and Technology*. Springer, 2006. to appear.
8. M. Dean and G. Schreiber. OWL Web Ontology Language Reference. Technical report, World Wide Web Consortium (W3C), Feb 2004. W3C Recommendation.
9. J. des Rivieres and W. Beaton. Eclipse Platform Technical Overview. July 2001. Updated April 2006 for Eclipse 3.1.
10. D. Djuric, D. Gaževic, V. Devedđic, and V. Damjanovic. MDA Development of Ontology Infrastructure. In *Proceedings of the IADIS International Conference Applied Computing*, pages II–23–II–26, Lisbon, Portugal, 2004.

11. D. Frankel, P. Hayes, E. Kendall, and D. McGuinness. The Model Driven Semantic Web. In *The 1st International Workshop on the Model-Driven Semantic Web (MSDW 2004)*, Monterey, California, USA, September 2004. http://www.sandsoft.com/edoc2004/FHKM-MDSWOverview.pdf.
12. L. Hart, P. Emery, R. Colomb, K. Raymond, S. Taraporewalla, D. Chang, Y. Ye, E. Kendall, and M. Dutra. OWL Full and UML 2.0 Compared, March 2004. http:// www.itee.uq.edu.au/~colomb/Papers/UML-OWLont04.03.01.pdf.
13. IBM and Sandpiper Software. Ontology Definition Metamodel. Sixth Revised Submission, Object Management Group, June 2006. http://www.omg.org/cgi-bin/doc?ad/2006-05-01.
14. ISO/IEC. Topic Maps Ũ Data Model. Technical Report 13250-2, December 2005.
15. ISO/IEC. Information technology – Common Logic (CL) - A framework for a family of logic-based languages. Technical Report 24707, April 2006. Official ISO FCD Draft.
16. L. Ma, Y. Yang, Z. Qiu, G. Xie, and Y. Pan. Towards A Complete OWL Ontology Benchmark. In *3rd Annual European Semantic Web Conference*, Budva, Montenegro, June 2006. Springer.
17. T. Nitzsche, J. Mukerji, D. Reynolds, and E. Kendall. Using Semantic Web Technologies for Management Application Integration. In *proceedings of the workshop on Semantic Web Enabled Software Engineering (SWESE)*, Galway, Ireland, November 2005. http://www.mel.nist.gov/msid/conferences/SWESE/accepted_papers.html.
18. Object Management Group. Ontology Definition Metamodel – Request For Proposal, March 2003. http://www.omg.org/docs/ontology/03-03-01.rtf.
19. Object Management Group. Revised submission for MOF 2.0 Query/Views/Transformations RFP. http://www.qvtp.org/downloads/1.1/qvtpartners1.1.pdf, August 2003.
20. Object Management Group. OCL 2.0 Specification. Technical Report Version 2.0, June 2005.
21. Object Management Group. Unified Modeling Language: Superstructure. Technical Report Version 2.0, August 2005.
22. Object Management Group. XMI Mapping Specification. Technical Report Version 2.1, September 2005.
23. Object Management Group. Meta Object Facility (MOF) Core Specification. Technical Report Version 2.0, January 2006. OMG Available Specification.
24. Object Management Group. Unified Modeling Language: Infrastructure. Technical Report Version 2.0, March 2006.
25. Y. Pan, G. Xie, L. Ma, Y. Yang, Z. Qiu, and J. Lee. Model-Driven Ontology Engineering. *In Journal of Data Semantics VII*, 2006. Springer.
26. W3C. Rule interchange format working group charter. http://www.w3.org/2005/rules/wg/charter, 2005.

IRS-III: A Broker for Semantic Web Services Based Applications

Liliana Cabral, John Domingue, Stefania Galizia, Alessio Gugliotta,
Vlad Tanasescu, Carlos Pedrinaci, and Barry Norton

Knowledge Media Institute, The Open University, Milton Keynes, UK
{L.S.Cabral, J.B.Domingue}@open.ac.uk

Abstract. In this paper we describe IRS-III which takes a semantic broker based approach to creating applications from Semantic Web Services by mediating between a service requester and one or more service providers. Business organisations can view Semantic Web Services as the basic mechanism for integrating data and processes across applications on the Web. This paper extends previous publications on IRS by providing an overall description of our framework from the point of view of application development. More specifically, we describe the IRS-III methodology for building applications using Semantic Web Services and illustrate our approach through a use case on e-government.

1 Introduction

The integration of business applications on the Web became a far easier task with the advent of Web Services as part of a trend in XML-based distributed computing. Web Services enable companies to provide services by exposing process functionalities through a standard interface description, keeping intact their legacy implementation of computing systems. Thus, applications in diverse areas such as e-commerce and e-government can interoperate through Web Services implemented in heterogeneous platforms. For example, Google (http://www.google.com) has a Web Service interface to its search engine and Amazon (http://www.amazon.com) allows software developers to access product data through its Web Service platform.

A key problem with the use of standards for Web Service description (e.g. WSDL) and publishing (e.g. UDDI) is that the syntactic definitions used in these descriptions do not completely describe the capability of a service and cannot be understood by software programs. It requires a human to interpret the meaning of inputs, outputs and applicable constraints as well as the context in which services can be used.

Semantic Web Services (SWS) research aims to automate the development of Web Service based applications through Semantic Web technology. By providing formal representations based on ontologies we can facilitate the machine interpretation of Web Service descriptions. Thus, business organisations can view Semantic Web Services as the basic mechanism for integrating data and processes across applications on the Web.

In this paper we describe IRS-III (Internet Reasoning Service), a framework which takes a semantic broker based approach to creating applications from Semantic Web

Services by mediating between a service requester and one or more service providers. This paper extends previous publications on IRS by providing an overall description of our framework from the point of view of application development. More specifically, we describe the IRS-III methodology for building applications using Semantic Web Services and illustrate our approach through a use case on e-government.

The rest of the paper is structured as follows: section 2 describes the overall approach and design principles of IRS-III; section 3 describes the IRS-III service ontology; in section 4 we present the framework including our approach for choreography, orchestration and mediation; section 5 describes how to develop applications using IRS-III followed by an example on e-government; finally, the last sections discuss related work and present our conclusions.

2 IRS-III Approach

The IRS project (http://kmi.open.ac.uk/projects/irs) has the overall aim of supporting the automated or semi-automated construction of semantically enhanced systems over the internet. IRS-I [3] supported the creation of knowledge intensive systems structured according to the UPML framework [10] and IRS-II [9] integrated the UPML framework with Web Service technology. IRS-III [5] has incorporated and extended the WSMO ontology [11] so that the implemented infrastructure allows the description, publication and execution of Semantic Web Services (SWS). The meta-model of WSMO describes four top level elements (in italics hence forth):

- *Ontologies*,
- *Goals*,
- *Web Services*, and
- *Mediator*s.

Ontologies provide the foundation for semantically describing data in order to achieve semantic interoperability and are used by the three other WSMO elements. *Goals* define the tasks that a service requester expects a *web service* to fulfil. In this sense they express the service requester's intent. *Web services* represent the functional behaviour of an existing deployed Web Service. The description also outlines how Web Services communicate (*choreography*) and how they are composed (*orchestration*). *Mediator*s describe the connections between the components above and represent the type of conceptual mismatches that can occur. In particular, WSMO provides four kinds of *mediator*s: *oo-mediators* link and map between heterogeneous ontologies; *ww-mediators* link *web services* to *web services*; *wg-mediators* connect *web services* to *goals*; *gg-mediators* link different *goals*.

IRS-III provides the representational and reasoning mechanisms for implementing the WSMO meta-model mentioned above in order to describe Web Services. Additionally, IRS-III provides a powerful execution environment which enables these descriptions to be associated to a deployed Web Service and instantiated during selection, composition, mediation and invocation activities.

The following describes the main application development activities supported by IRS-III when building Semantic Web Services:

- **Using domain ontologies** – The concepts and relations involved in the application scenario which are used to describe client requests and Web Service capability are provided in domain ontologies.
- **Describing client requests as** *goals* – The request for a service can be expressed from a business viewpoint and represented as a *goal*.
- **Semantically describing deployed Web Services** – The concepts defined in domain ontologies can be used in a *web service* description to represent the types of inputs and outputs of services and in logical expressions for expressing applied restrictions. This description can also include many other aspects such as *orchestration* and *choreography*.
- **Resolving conceptual mismatches** – *Mediator* descriptions can be used to declare which *mediation service* or *mapping rules* will provide conceptual alignment between *goals*, *web services* and domain *ontologies*.
- **Publishing and invoking semantically described Web Services** – Once a semantic description has been created for a deployed Web Service as above, it can be registered into IRS-III for *goal*-based invocation.

The IRS-III tooling consists of a Java API and a browser/editor which support developers in building applications out of Semantic Web Services. The IRS-III browser provides an easy to use graphical interface to support the creation of WSMO descriptions, to publish deployed Web Services against these descriptions and then to invoke the Web Services. The IRS-III Java API provides a data model for our WSMO implementation and remote access to the operations available from the IRS-III server. Recently, we have also developed a plug-in for WSMO Studio [4] for interoperability purposes, by aligning the IRS-III and WSMO4J (http://wsmo4j.sourceforge.net) APIs.

2.1 IRS-III Design Principles

The ever growing popularity of the Semantic Web is largely due to the extensive use of ontologies [7]. By providing an explicit formal model, ontologies facilitate knowledge sharing by machines and humans. The IRS-III approach is based on a set of design principles which use ontological metamodels as the means underlying selection, composition, mediation and invocation of Semantic Web Services as follows.

A) Semantic Descriptions as Knowledge Components – Within IRS-III, semantic descriptions of Web Services are provided as knowledge components representing the WSMO top-level elements. These knowledge components are executable ontological meta-models which are semantically linked and can be represented using our ontology representation language OCML [8].

B) Reasoning is ubiquitous – Reasoning is seen as an essential mechanism of all Semantic Web Service activities. IRS-III execution environment can easily invoke ontological queries over the underlying WSMO conceptual model as well as existing domain ontologies.

C) *Goal*-based invocation – A key feature of IRS-III is that Web Service invocation is capability driven. IRS-III supports this by providing a *goal*-centric invocation mechanism. A client application simply asks for a *goal* to be solved and IRS-III selects an appropriate *web service* invoking the associated Web Service.

D) *Goal*-based decomposition – In IRS-III a *web service* is either executable or composed. A composite *web service* expresses its functionality in terms of *goals*, following on the previous design principle for invocation.

E) Explicit mediation description – IRS-III uses the *mediator* description for two purposes. First, it can represent the role of a specific Web Service as a *mediation service*. Second, the different types of *mediators* can be associated with different mediation activities.

F) One-click Publishing – For supporting users who have an existing system which they would like to be made available for invocation through IRS-III, we provide 'one click' publishing mechanism of standalone code written in Java or Lisp in addition to the publishing of existing Web Services through WSDL descriptions.

G) Complete Descriptions – Within an ontological framework, it is easy to represent distinct aspects of a Web Service for different uses. The next section describes these aspects in more details.

3 The IRS-III Service Ontology

The IRS-III service ontology has originally been based on the UPML framework [10] [9], which forms the epistemological basis for IRS-III. This framework has been extended in order to incorporate the following main aspects specified by the WSMO conceptual model [11]:

- **Non-functional properties** – These properties are associated with every main WSMO element and can range from information about the provider such as organisation, to information about the service such as category, cost or trust, to execution requirements such as scalability, security or robustness.
- **Goal-related information** – a *goal* represents the user perspective of the required functional capabilities. It includes a description of the requested *web service capability*.
- **Web Service functional capabilities** – Represent the provider perspective of what the service does in terms of inputs, output, pre-conditions and post-conditions. Pre-conditions and post-conditions are expressed by logical expressions that constrain the state or the type of inputs and outputs.
- **Choreography** – The *choreography* specifies how to communicate with a Web Service. In WSMO this specification is formalized as Abstract State Machines.
- **Grounding** – The grounding is associated with the *web service choreography* and describes how the semantic declarations are mapped to a syntactic specification such as WSDL.
- **Orchestration** – The *orchestration* of a *web service* specifies the decomposition of its capability in terms of the functionality of other Web Services. In WSMO this specification is also formalized as Abstract State Machines.
- **Mediators** – In WSMO, a *mediator* defines which WSMO top elements are connected and which type of mismatches can be resolved between them.

The IRS-III implementation of the WSMO conceptual model has been extended in the following ways.

- **Explicit input and output role declaration** – IRS-III requires that *goals* and *web services* have input and output roles, which include a name and a semantic type. The declared types are imported from domain ontologies.
- *Web Services* **are linked to** *Goals* **via** *mediators* - If a wg-*mediator* associated with a *web service* has a *goal* as a source, then this *web service* is considered to solve that *goal*. An *assumption* expression can be introduced for further refining the applicability of the *web service*.
- **GG-mediators provide data-flow between sub-***goals* – In IRS-III, *gg-mediators* are used to link sub-*goals* within an *orchestration*, and therefore they can provide dataflow and data mediation between the sub-*goals*.
- **Web Service can inherit from** *Goal*s - *Web services* which are linked to *goals* 'inherit' the *goal's* input and output roles. This means that input role declarations within a *web service* are not mandatory and can be used to either add extra input roles or to change an input role type.
- **Client Choreography** – The provider of a *web service* must describe the *choreography* from the viewpoint of the client. This means IRS-III can interpret the choreography in order to communicate with the deployed Web Service.
- **Mediation services are** *goals* – A *mediator* can declare a *goal* as the *mediation service* which can simply be invoked. The associated *web service* actually performs the necessary data transformation.

4   The IRS-III Framework

IRS-III is based on a distributed architecture composed of the IRS-III server, the publishing platforms and clients which communicate through the SOAP protocol, as shown in figure 1. The server handles ontology management and the execution of knowledge models defined for WSMO. The server also receives SOAP requests (through the API) from client applications for creating and editing WSMO descriptions of *goals*, *web services* and *mediators* as well as goal-based invocation. At the lowest level the IRS-III Server uses an HTTP server written in Lisp, which has been extended with a SOAP handler.

The publishing platforms allow providers of services to attach semantic descriptions to their deployed services and provide handlers to invoke services in a specific language or platform (Web Services WSDL, Lisp code, Java code, and Web applications). When a Web Service is published in IRS-III the information about the publishing platform (URL) is also associated with the *web service* description in order to be invoked. The IRS-III server is written in Lisp and is available as an executable file. The publishing platforms are delivered as Java Web applications; and client applications use the Java API.

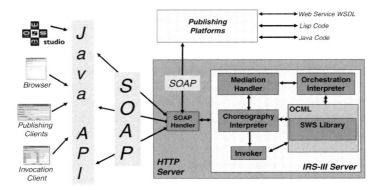

Fig. 1. The IRS-III framework

The main components of IRS-III are explained in the following:

- **SWS Library** – At the core of the IRS-III server is the SWS library where the semantic descriptions are stored using our representation language OCML [8]. The library is structured into knowledge models for *goals*, *web services* and *mediators*. Domain *ontologies* and knowledge bases (instances) are also available from the library.
- **Choreography Interpreter** – This component interprets the *grounding* and *guarded transitions* of the *choreography* description when requested by the mediation handler.
- **Orchestration Interpreter** – This component interprets the workflow of the orchestration description when requested by the mediation handler.
- **Mediation Handler** – The brokering activities of IRS-III including selection, composition and invocation are each supported by a specific mediation component within the mediation handler. These activities may involve executing a mediation service or mapping rules declared in a *mediator* description.
- **Invoker** – The invoker component of the server communicates with the publishing platform, sending the inputs from the client and bringing the result back to the client.

The following sections give more details of how choreography, orchestration and mediation of Semantic Web Services are implemented in IRS-III.

4.1 IRS-III Choreography

In IRS-III the choreography describes how to interact with a single deployed Web Service (client choreography). At the semantic level the choreography is represented by a set of forward-chaining rules and a grounding declaration expressed in OCML (see an example in listing 3). A rule executes actions based on communication primitives when the associated conditions (asserted facts) are satisfied. The *grounding* declares the operations involved in the invocation (communication primitives) and the associated mappings to the implementation level. More specifically, each operation input and output is associated with a lifting or lowering function. The grounding also relates to information about the corresponding publishing platform.

This approach allows the functionality of a Web Service to be realized by calling one or more declared operations. The set of core communication primitives, which enables the exchange of messages between IRS-III and a deployed service, are listed below.

- *init-choreography* – The initial assertion made by IRS-III when the state of the choreography is initialized. IRS-III obtains the input values of operations from the *goal* invocation request.
- *send-message* - Calls a specific operation in the associated Web service.
- *received-message* - Contains the result of a successful *send-message* for a specific operation.
- *received-error* - If an operation generates an error then this primitive is used including the error message and the name of the operation causing it.
- *end-choreography* - Stops the choreography. No other rule will be executed.

More details about the formalization of IRS-III choreography, which is based on Abstract State Machines can be found in [6].

4.2 IRS-III Orchestration

In IRS-III the orchestration is used to describe a composed Web Service. At the semantic level the orchestration is represented by a workflow model expressed in OCML. The distinguishing characteristic of this model is that the basic unit within composition is a *goal*. Thus, the model provides control and data flow constructs over a set of *goals*. Further, dataflow and solving mismatches between *goals* are supported by *mediators*. An example of an orchestration description is given in listing 3. The set of control flow primitives which have been implemented so far in IRS-III are listed below.

- *orch-sequence* – Contains the list of *goals* to be invoked sequentially. A gg-*mediator* can optionally be declared between the *goals*, in which case the output of the source *goal* is transformed by the *mediation service* (if there is one) and used as input of the target *goal*.
- *orch-if* – Contains a condition and a body with one or more workflow primitives. The body part is executed if the declared condition is true.
- *orch-repeat* – Contains a condition and a body with one or more workflow primitives. The body part is repeated until the declared condition is false.
- *orch-get-goal-value* - Returns the result of the last invocation of the declared *goal* (used for example as part of a condition).
- *orch-return* – Returns the result of the current *goal* execution.

Further work is under specification in order to provide a three-layer orchestration model which integrates this semantic representation with a high-level (UML based) workflow representation and a low-level Abstract State Machine representation.

4.3 IRS-III Mediation

At the semantic level, IRS-III represents four basic types of conceptual mismatches that can occur when using Semantic Web Services. These types correspond to the WSMO models of *oo-mediator*, *wg-mediator*, *gg-mediator* and *ww-mediator* as described in section 2. In general there will be mismatches between the *goal* requests and available *web services* and between the *goals* themselves. The IRS-III mediation handler components are responsible for resolving the conceptual mismatches which may occur by reasoning over the given *goal*, *web service* and *mediator* descriptions. The mediation handler interprets each type of mediator accordingly during selection, invocation and orchestration.

Basically, a *mediator* declares a source component, a target component and either a *mediation service* or *mapping rules*. Hence, the *mediator* provides a semantic link between the source component and the target component, which enables *mediation services* or *mapping rules* to solve mismatches between the two. More details of mediation in IRS-III can be found in [1].

In this model, the *mediation service* is just another *goal*. As an example (see listing 3), the *mediation service* of a *wg-mediator* can transform input values coming from the source *goal* into an input value used by the target *web service*.

Mapping rules are used between two *ontologies* (source and target components). These mappings only concern to the concepts used during invocation and consist of three main mapping primitives:

- ***maps-to*** – relation created internally for every mapped instance.
- ***def-concept-mapping*** – generate the mappings (*maps-to* relation) between the instances of two concepts within an ontology.
- ***def-relation-mapping*** – generate a mapping between two relations using a rule definition within an ontology. As OCML represents concept attributes as relations, this primitive can be used to map between *input* and *output* descriptions.

5 Application Development with IRS-III

A Web application can invoke Semantic Web Services by sending "achieve-goal" requests to IRS-III with the input values from the user. IRS-III will then execute the appropriate deployed Web Services (see figure 2). This Semantic Web Service brokering scenario enables data and process integration across many business partners. The SWS provided can be shared or used to send common information to the diverse participating organisations.

In our methodology for developing applications using SWS with IRS-III we devise a customer team for creating *goal* descriptions according to user requests and a development team for creating *web service* descriptions for the available deployed Web Services. The application developer then creates *mediator* descriptions which connect domain *ontologies*, *goals* and *web services* and provide *mediation services* or *mapping rules* for solving mismatches between ontological elements.

Fig. 2. A simple SWS brokering scenario using IRS-III

We created a generic application architecture which reflects our methodology for using IRS-III following on the steps described on section 2 as depicted in figure 3. Briefly, such architecture enables the functionality provided by existing legacy systems from the involved business partners to be exposed as Web Services, which are then semantically annotated and published using the SWS infrastructure. The architecture consists of four layers as explained next.

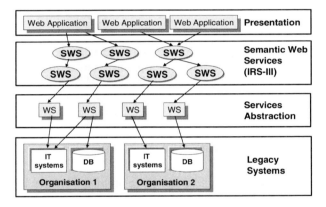

Fig. 3. A generic application architecture using IRS-III

The legacy system layer consists of the existing data sources and information technology systems available from each organisation involved in the integrated application. The service abstraction layer enables the functionality of the legacy systems to be available as Web Services, abstracting from the implementation details. Current Enterprise Application Integration (EAI) software generally enables the easy creation of the necessary Web Services. Note that for the integration of standard databases the necessary functionality of the Web Services can simply be implemented as query (SQL) functions. The SWS layer is based on the Web Services provided by the service abstraction layer. The activities in this layer are mainly supported by the IRS-III infrastructure as outlined in section 2. Given a goal request, IRS-III will: a) discover a candidate set of *web services*; b) select the most appropriate one; c) resolve any mismatches at the ontological level; and d) invoke the relevant set of Web Services satisfying any data, control flow and invocation requirements. To achieve this, IRS-III, utilizes the set of Semantic Web Service descriptions which are composed of *goals*, *mediators*, and *web services*, supported by relevant domain ontologies. Finally, the presentation layer consists of the user interface, which is built on top of the SWS layer as a Web application accessible using a standard Web browser. G*oal* invocation requests are generated with the data provided by the user through the user interface triggering the invocation of applicable SWS and as a result the execution of deployed Web Services in the service abstraction layer

In the next section we will further explain our methodology by mapping each architecture layer to the development activities related to a specific application in e-government. In the following we point out some generic considerations when using SWS as outlined in the architecture described above.

In general, during the requirements phase of application development, the stakeholders involved in the application scenario should provide information to ontology builders in order to create or reuse domain ontologies related to the application context. SWS make this process very simple and efficient because the only knowledge which must be modelled is related to the exposed functionality implemented by the Web Services. Developers do not need to model entire data sources or create class instances corresponding to thousands of database records; we only model the information used by Web Services.

By taking a top-down approach for semantically annotating services, IRS-III facilitates querying and reasoning about the capability of the service before its execution since the semantic relations between the descriptions used (*goal*, *web services*, *mediators* and domain *ontologies*) are well defined in the WSMO metamodel. The reasoning needed during the invocation of one service is efficient because it is limited to the scope of the invocation.

6 Application Example on E-Government

In the following we present relevant details of the prototype created for the case study on e-government within the DIP project (http://dip.semanticweb.org) for illustrating an application based on Semantic Web Services using IRS-III. The main requirement for applications in E-government relates to the interoperability of data and processes between services provided by different government agencies.

Our implemented scenario named "Change of Circumstances" involved two governmental agencies coordinated by Essex County Council (ECC) in UK. In this scenario a disabled mother moves into her daughter's home and both are eligible to receive services and benefits – health and housing equipments – from service providing agencies. A case worker of the Community Care department helps a citizen to report her change of circumstance (e.g. address) to different agencies involved in the process.

Following from the architecture in Figure 3, at the presentation level we created an application user interface for the Change of Circumstances scenario. From the interface a case worker from Essex County Council has access to some functionality such as "update client details" and "create client assessment". Behind each functionality there is one or more associated *goal* requests such as "update citizen address" or "find equipment". A case worker can select a suitable functionality, fill in the required fields and then submit his request which will trigger the execution of the defined *goals*.

At the semantic level, we used IRS-III to provide WSMO descriptions to the deployed Web Services, including mediator descriptions for declaring the mappings between concepts not aligned. We then published the Web Services in IRS-III. The relevant integration aspect was the implementation of a composed *web service*, which accesses information from two different agencies. This composed service named "change-address-ws" will be explained in more details in the illustration of the semantic descriptions in the next section. This service is composed of two basic services. The first changes the address of the citizen within ECC, and the second service changes the address of the citizen within the agency providing services related to housing equipment.

At the service level, we developed a set of Web Services which performed basic operations on top of the databases of the two involved agencies. These Web services were deployed into an application server (SAP Exchange Infrastructure) provided by a partner at SAP in Germany and then published in IRS-III, running at the Open University in England. At the legacy systems level, we recreated anonymous content (due to privacy reasons) of the existing data sources for each agency involved.

6.1 Semantic Descriptions

In the following we present the domain ontologies and Semantic Web Service descriptions used in the application prototype. Each agency involved in the prototype development provided a domain ontology which represents its own information concerning the application scenario. A domain ontology can represent the viewpoint of the user and then be used to define *goals* or it can represent the viewpoint of a service provider and therefore be used for describing deployed Web Services. The ontologies were developed independently but both used a common upper-level ontology describing general concepts from the e-government domain (e.g. government-organisation, county-council, public-service, health-service).

Listing 1. Partial source code for concepts in the domain ontologies

```
(def-class equipment ()
  ((has-product-code :type string)
   (has-description :type string)
   (has-cost :type string)
   (has-max-user-weight :type integer)
   (has-charging-value :type string)
   (has-product-widtht :type string)
   (has-product-height :type string)
   (has-product-seat-height :type string)))

(def-class citizen-address ()
  ((has-address-key :type integer)
   (has-postcode :type post-code-string)
   (has-premise-number :type integer)
   (has-premise-name :type string)
   (has-street :type string)
   (has-locality :type string)
   (has-town :type string)))
```

The two developed ontologies are as follow:
- Citizens ontology - Domain ontology created by Essex County Council describing information related to a citizen assessment for social benefits and services. Contain classes defining for example: address, assessment, health problem, benefit, case worker and others.

- Equipment ontology – Domain ontology created by the Housing Department describing information related to ordering housing equipments. Contain classes defining for example: order, equipment, supplier, delivery descriptor and so on.

Listing 1 shows an excerpt of two concepts defined in the domain ontologies (attributes are self-explanatory). "Equipment" is used as output of the *goal* (listing 2) and "citizen-address" as input of one of the *web service*s. Instances of these classes can be created with the values of attributes provided through the user interface. Otherwise they can be lifted from the results of service invocations.

Listing 2 shows the definition of *goal* "find-equipment-goal". This instance of a *goal* defines 2 inputs ("has-input-role" slot) and one output ("has-output-role" slot). This *goal* takes the client weight and purpose and returns a list of suitable equipments.

Listing 2. Partial source code for the goal FIND-EQUIPMENT-GOAL

```
(DEF-CLASS FIND-EQUIPMENT-GOAL (GOAL)?GOAL
   ((HAS-INPUT-ROLE
        :VALUE HAS-CLIENT-WEIGHT
        :VALUE HAS-CLIENT-PURPOSE)
   (HAS-OUTPUT-ROLE
        :VALUE HAS-SUITABLE-ITEMS-LIST)
   (HAS-CLIENT-WEIGHT :TYPE NUMBER)
   (HAS-CLIENT-PURPOSE :TYPE PURPOSE-DESCRIPTOR)
   (HAS-SUITABLE-ITEM-LIST :TYPE EQUIPMENT)
   (HAS-NON-FUNCTIONAL-PROPERTIES
        :VALUE E-GOV-ASSESS-ITEM-GOAL-NON-FUNCTIONAL-PROPERTIES)))
```

Listing 3 shows a partial definition of the *web service* "change-address-ws". This description declares a *capability* and an *interface* which are described in corresponding classes. The *interface* declares an *orchestration*, which is defined in another class. The "problem solving pattern" slot of the *orchestration* defines the workflow (sequence) for the composition of 2 sub-*goal*s. The choreography of one of the sub-*goal*s is defined by another class ("change-citizen-detatils-ws-choreography") which has a grounding and guarded transitions. The grounding includes information about the WSDL associated with the described service, the lowering of the inputs and lifting of the output; there is one rule in the guarded transitions which uses the operation "change-details-operation" defined.

Listing 3. Partial source code for the web service CHANGE-ADDRESS-WS

```
(DEF-CLASS CHANGE-ADDRESS-WS (WEB-SERVICE) ?WEB-SERVICE
   ((HAS-CAPABILITY :VALUE CHANGE-ADDRESS-WS-WEB-SERVICE-CAPABILITY)
    (HAS-INTERFACE :VALUE CHANGE-ADDRESS-WS-WEB-SERVICE-INTERFACE)
    (HAS-NON-FUNCTIONAL-PROPERTIES
        :VALUE CHANGE-ADDRESS-WS-WEB-SERVICE-NON-FUNCTIONAL-POPERTIES)))

(DEF-CLASS CHANGE-ADDRESS-WS-WEB-SERVICE-INTERFACE (INTERFACE)?INTERFACE
   ((HAS-ORCHESTRATION :VALUE CHANGE-ADDRESS-WS-ORCHESTRATION)
    (HAS-NON-FUNCTIONAL-PROPERTIES
        :VALUE CHANGE-ADDRESS-WS-INTERFACE-NON-FUNCTIONAL-PROPERTIES)))

(DEF-CLASS CHANGE-ADDRESS-WS-ORCHESTRATION (ORCHESTRATION)
   ((HAS-PROBLEM-SOLVING-PATTERN
        :VALUE CHANGE-ADDRESS-WS-ORCHESTRATION-PROBLEM-SOLVING-PATTERN)))
```

```
(DEF-CLASS CHANGE-ADDRESS-WS-ORCHESTRATION-PROBLEM-SOLVING-PATTERN
    (PROBLEM-SOLVING-PATTERN)
        ((HAS-BODY :VALUE
            ((ORCH-SEQUENCE
                CHANGE-CITIZEN-DETAILS-GOAL
                REDIRECT-EQUIPMENT-GOAL)
             (ORCH-RETURN (ORCH-GET-GOAL-VALUE REDIRECT-EQUIPMENT-GOAL))))))

(DEF-CLASS CHANGE-CITIZEN-DETAILS-WS-CHOREOGRAPHY (CHOREOGRAPHY)
    ((HAS-GROUNDING :VALUE
        (GROUNDED-TO-WSDL CHANGE-DETAILS-OPERATION
            ("http://changeDetails.wsdl" "changeDetails" "changeDetailsPort"
             http://sap.com/research/dip/wp9/elmdb "AXIS")
            ((LOWER-TO HAS_CLIENT_ADDRESS "STRING"))
            (LIFT-TO HAS_ACKNOWLEDGMENT "STRING")))
     (HAS-GUARDED-TRANSITIONS :VALUE
        ((RULE1
            (INIT-CHOREOGRAPHY)
            THEN
            (SEND-MESSAGE 'CHANGE-DETAILS-OPERATION))))
```

Listing 4 shows the definition of mediator "address-mediator". This is an instance of a WSMO GG-mediator. It was used to transform "citizen-address" type to a string used by "redirect-equipment-goal".

Listing 4. Partial source code for the ADDRESS-MEDIATOR mediator

```
(DEF-CLASS ADDRESS-MEDIATOR (GG-MEDIATOR) ?MEDIATOR
    ((HAS-SOURCE-COMPONENT :VALUE CHANGE-ADDRESS-GOAL)
     (HAS-TARGET-COMPONENT :VALUE REDIRECT-EQUIPMENT-GOAL)
     (HAS-MEDIATION-SERVICE
        :VALUE ADDRESS-MEDIATION-SERVICE-GOAL)
     (HAS-NON-FUNCTIONAL-PROPERTIES :VALUE
        ADDRESS-MEDIATOR-MEDIATOR-NON-FUNCTIONAL-PROPERTIES)))
```

7 Related Work and Conclusions

In this paper we have presented our approach to developing Semantic Web Services, supporting selection, composition, mediation and invocation of Web Services as well as our methodology for developing Web applications which use the IRS-III infrastructure. We have validated our approach in the context of a case study in e-government, which offers a motivating scenario for the use of Semantic Web Services with requirements and data provided by real users. In addition we use the case study to illustrate the semantic descriptions used by IRS-III.

Although a number of Semantic Web Service approaches now exist in addition to IRS-III and WSMO, including for example, OWL-S (http://www.w3.org/ Submission/OWL-S), SWSF (http://www.w3.org/Submission/SWSF) and WSDL-S (http://www.w3.org/Submission/WSDL-S); there are few frameworks which can comprehensively support the development of Semantic Web Services based applications. A more detailed comparison between approaches can be found in [2].

Overall, the work on IRS-III is more closely related to WSMX (http:// www. wsmx.org/) since both environments are based on WSMO. However, IRS-III is founded on a knowledge-based approach and infrastructure which introduces distinguishing design principles and semantic primitives for executing choreography, orchestration and mediation of Semantic Web Services. The SWS approaches listed above share a number of common features with IRS-III; in particular, there are similarities between the ontological structures used for Web service functional descriptions. Additionally, these approaches enable grounding to WSDL. The main differences concern the behavioral aspects of service description; although a process-oriented abstraction could be constructed for orchestration, a state-based behavior is explicitly represented in our ontology. Moreover, IRS-III focuses on the problems that clients need to solve, providing for this reason a goal-centric invocation mechanism.

Acknowledgements

This work is supported by the DIP project (Data, Information and Process Integration with Semantic Web Services) (EU FP6 - 507483). The authors gratefully acknowledge the members of the DIP project and the WSMO working group for their insightful comments on our work. We also acknowledge the contribution of DIP members Mary Rowlatt, Robert Davies and Leticia Gutierrez from Essex County Council - UK.

References

1. Cabral, L. and Domingue, J.: Mediation of Semantic Web Services in IRS-III. In Workshop on Mediation in Semantic Web Services (MEDIATE 2005) in conjunction with the 3rd International Conference on Service Oriented Computing (ICSOC 2005), Amsterdam (2005)
2. Cabral, L., Domingue, J., Motta, E., Payne, T. and Hakimpour, F. (2004). Approaches to Semantic Web Services: An Overview and Comparisons. In proceedings of the First European Semantic Web Symposium, ESWS 2004, Heraklion, Crete, Greece. LNCS 3053
3. Crubezy, M., Motta, E., Lu, W. and Musen, M.: Configuring Online Problem-Solving Resources with the Internet Reasoning Service. IEEE Intelligent Systems, 2 (2003) 34-42
4. Dimitrov, M., Simov, A., Montchev, V. and Ognanov, D.: WSMO Studio: an Interfaced Service Environment for WSMO. In Workshop on WSMO Implementations (WIW 2005) Frankfurt, Germany. CEUR Workshop Proceedings, Vol. 134 (2005)
5. Domingue, J., Cabral, L., Hakimpour, F., Sell, D. and Motta, E.: IRS-III: A Platform and Infrastructure for Creating WSMO-based Semantic Web Services. In Workshop on WSMO Implementations (WIW 2004) Frankfurt, Germany. CEUR Workshop Proceedings, Vol. 113 (2004)
6. Domingue, J., Galizia, S. and Cabral, L.: The Choreography Model for IRS-III. In proceedings of Hawaii International Conference on System Sciences (HICSS 2006), Hawaii (2006)
7. Gruber, T. R.: A Translation Approach to Portable Ontology Specifications. Knowledge Acquisition, 5(2) (1993)
8. Motta, E.: Reusable Components for Knowledge Modelling. IOSPress, Amsterdam (1999)
9. Motta, E., Domingue, J., Cabral, L. and Gaspari, M.: IRS-II: A Framework and Infrastructure for Semantic Web Services. In proceeding of the 2nd International Semantic Web Conference (ISWC 2003). LNCS 2870 (2003)
10. Omelayenko, B., Crubezy, M., Fensel, D., Benjamins, R., Wielinga, B., Motta, E., Musen, M., Ding, Y.: UPML: The language and Tool Support for Making the Semantic Web Alive. In: Fensel, D. et al. (eds.): Spinning the Semantic Web: Bringing the WWW to its Full Potential. MIT Press (2003) 141–170
11. WSMO Working Group. Deliverable D2v1.2 Web Service Modeling Ontology (WSMO). http://www.wsmo.org/TR/d2/v1.2/ (2005)

Provenance Explorer – Customized Provenance Views Using Semantic Inferencing

Kwok Cheung[1] and Jane Hunter[2]

[1] AIBN, The University of Queensland
St Lucia, Queensland, Australia
kwokc@itee.uq.edu.au
[2] ITEE, The University of Queensland
St Lucia, Queensland, Australia
jane@itee.uq.edu.au

Abstract. This paper presents *Provenance Explorer*, a secure provenance visualization tool, designed to dynamically generate customized views of scientific data provenance that depend on the viewer's requirements and/or access privileges. Using RDF and graph visualizations, it enables scientists to view the data, states and events associated with a scientific workflow in order to understand the scientific methodology and validate the results. Initially the Provenance Explorer presents a simple, coarse-grained view of the scientific process or experiment. However the GUI allows permitted users to expand links between nodes (input states, events and output states) to reveal more fine-grained information about particular sub-events and their inputs and outputs. Access control is implemented using Shibboleth to identify and authenticate users and XACML to define access control policies. The system also provides a platform for publishing scientific results. It enables users to select particular nodes within the visualized workflow and drag-and-drop them into an RDF package for publication or e-learning. The direct relationships between the individual components selected for such packages are inferred by the rule-inference engine.

Keywords: eScience, Provenance, Visualization, Inferencing.

1 Introduction and Objectives

Provenance is essential within science because it provides a history or documentation of the steps taken during the scientific discovery process. Understanding the source of data or how scientific results were arrived at, is essential in order to verify or trust that data and to enable its re-use and comparison. A record of the complete scientific discovery process enables peers to review the method of conducting the science as well as the final conclusions. Precise, authenticated provenance data reduces duplication and insures against data loss because the additional contextual and provenance information ensures the repeatability and verifiability of the results[1]. It also enables precise attribution of individual credit during collaborations involving teams of scientists.

Ideally provenance capture systems are in place that are capable of recording both the domain-specific steps in the physical world (e.g., the laboratories or processing plants) as well as the data derivation steps in the digital domain. Increasingly, e-Laboratory notebooks and workflow systems are being developed specifically to relieve the effort required by scientists to capture the precise provenance metadata required to validate scientific results and enable their duplication. Assuming appropriate metadata is being captured at each stage in the workflow associated with scientific discovery process, then many of the relationships between the individual components are either explicitly captured or can be inferred later, as required. This is particularly true of systems that record the sequence of events, inputs and outputs in machine-processable descriptions represented using RDF graphs and domain-specific OWL ontologies.

We are interested in those workflow and e-Lab notebook systems that are based on RDF. Recentris' Collaborative Electronic Research Framework (CERF)[1]. and the SmartTea [2] and MyTea [3] systems are examples of RDF-based laboratory notebook systems. RDF-based workflow systems that support the capture of provenance information include Kepler [4], Taverna [5] and Triana [6]. Our objective is to take the output from such systems (i.e., the RDF instances that describe the sequence of events and data products recorded during the execution of a scientific workflow) and apply reasoning across these sets of records to infer new relationships between indirectly related data products. These inferred relationships can be used to generate alternative but still correct views of the data provenance. Alternative views of provenance are required for a number of reasons. Simplified views of highly complex workflows may be required for teaching or publication purposes. Restricted views which hide certain information or details are required to protect the intellectual property associated with particular scientific processes. This is particularly important within collaborating teams of scientists to protect individual IP but still enable controlled sharing and validation of the overall process. Hence our objectives are to leverage existing RDF-based workflow tools and the captured provenance data and metadata in order to:

- generate visualizations of the lineage of the data and its products i.e., the relationships between the different derivative products generated during the scientific process;
- dynamically infer customized views of provenance depending on the user's requirements and privileges;
- restrict access to specific data or processing steps (using Shibboleth [7] to authenticate users and XACML [8] to define policies) - in order to protect intellectual property and maintain competitive advantage;
- streamline the construction of publication or e-learning packages (that link the raw data to its derivatives and traditional scholarly publications).

The remainder of this paper is structured as follows: Section 2 describes related work; Section 3 describes the case study we used for evaluation and testing; Section 4 describes the system architecture and components; Section 5 describes the implementation and user interface and Section 6 concludes with an evaluation, discussion and future work plans.

---

[1] http://www.rescentris.com/

2 Related Work

Our aim is to take the output from existing RDF-based provenance capture systems and to develop a visualization tool that dynamically generates customized views of the provenance trail. For example, Kepler [4] is a scientific workflow system designed for multiple disciplines that enables scientists to design and execute workflows. Recently, Kepler embedded a new provenance recording component that collects data and workflow provenance at runtime. Similarly, CERF provides a unified electronic record-keeping environment for scientists, in particular for biologists, to capture, curate, annotate, and archive their data, and to integrate the data into electronic lab notebook-like pages. Either of these two systems could integrate seamlessly into Provenance Explorer because they are both java-based applications. Furthermore, the Protégé-OWL Plugin API can be used as the interface between either system and Provenance Explorer.

The *Prototype Lineage Server* [9] allows users to browse lineage information by navigating through the sets of metadata that provide useful details about the data products and transformations in a workflow invocation. Web server scripts on the lineage server query the lineage database, and provide a Web browser interface that allows navigation via HTML links. Views are restricted to parent and children metadata objects. Clicking on a parent object will move that link to the center of the screen and show that object's parents. Clicking on the metadata object link in the center of the screen will bring up the XML metadata for an object.

Pedigree Graph [10], one of tools in Multi-Scale Chemistry (MCS) portal from the Collaboratory for Multi-Scale Chemical Science (CMCS), is designed to enable users to view multi-scale data provenance. The portlet provides scientists with a two-dimensional visualization of a data object or file and all of its scientific pedigree relationships. The view is static, and rendered straight from GXL (Graphical eXchange Language) files but users are able to traverse the tree by clicking on links.

The MyGrid project renders graph-based views of RDF-coded provenances using Haystack [11]. This is used to visualize networks of semantic relationships among provenance resources associated with experiments. Haystack is a Semantic Web browser that enables developers to provide tailored views over RDF-metadata. The authors point out that Haystack is highly resource-consumptive because its execution is based on Adenine, a high level programming language developed on top of Java Programming Language. Hence the response time to user's instructions could be slow.

The *VisTrails* system [12] was developed by the University of Utah for building, storing, editing and visualizing workflows and interactively tracking workflow execution and evolution. Although it uses graphs to visualize workflows and provenance trails, it differs from the Provenance Explorer in that it is not designed to generate personalized views of provenance – adapted for publication or teaching purposes or to suit a user's interest or access permissions.

So although there are existing systems that enable visualization of RDF-encoded provenance graphs, the unique aspect of our Provenance Explorer system is its ability to generate personalized views of the provenance relationships automatically using a combination of user input, semantic reasoning and access policies.

3 Case Study

Within the University of Queensland, materials scientists within the Australian Institute for Bioengineering and Nanotechnology are investigating the optimization of fuel cells – an alternative environment-friendly energy source to fossil fuels. The efficiency of a fuel cell depends on the internal structure of the fuel cell components and their interfaces. Electrolytes are one of the primary fuel-cell components. Figure 1 illustrates the complex set of steps involved in manufacturing and testing electrolytes. Associated with each step in the workflow is a set of parameters, only some of which are controllable. The challenge for the fuel-cell scientist is to determine the optimum combination of controllable parameters in order to attain the maximum strength, efficiency and longevity of the fuel cell for the minimum cost [13].

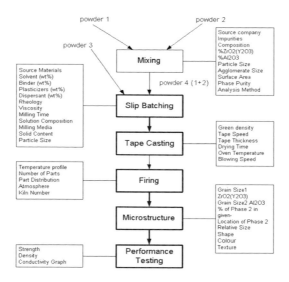

Fig. 1. A logical view of the manufacture and testing process of Fuel-Cell Electrolyte

Through the FUSION project [14] we have been collaborating with a team of fuel cell scientists on the development of an eScience workflow and provenance capture system that records the data associated with each of the steps in the electrolyte manufacturing and testing process and enables its statistical analysis in order to generate new workflows [13]. Through this work we have access to data records from a series of manufacturing and testing experiments. Hence we decided to use this application as a case study for evaluating and attaining user feedback on the Provenance Explorer system. The first step involved modeling the workflow in Figure 1 and representing it in OWL. We decided to use the event-aware ABC ontology [15], developed within the Harmony project, to track the life cycle of digital objects. We first had to extend the ABC ontology to describe processing, simulation and

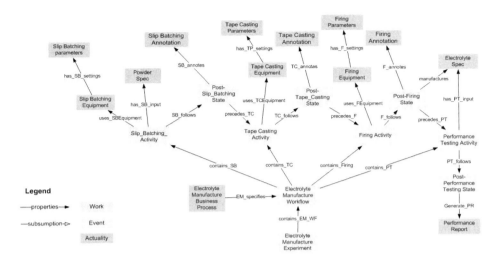

Fig. 2. Provenance Model of the Electrolyte Manufacture and Analysis Process

experimental events. Given this extended ontology, we were able to represent the workflow instances corresponding to Figure 1 in OWL. This is illustrated in Figure 2.

Given the OWL representations of the provenance data associated with the fuel cell manufacturing and testing process, the aim was to generate customized graphical visualizations of the data using the Provenance Explorer system – to satisfy the requirements of the scientists. In addition to the OWL instance data, we also had to develop rules for inferring relationships between entities that were not directly related and represent them in the Semantic Web Rule Language (SWRL)[16]. For example:

> IF (Experiment A includes Workflow B) AND
> (Workflow B contains Slip Batching C) AND
> (Slip Batching C hasInput Powder D)
> THEN (Experiment A hasInput Powder D)

4 System Architecture

Figure 3 illustrates the overall system architecture and its key components. The three key components of the system are:

- The knowledge base which consists of SWRL.OWL files that contain the provenance instance data and metadata and the inference rules.
- the Provenance Visualizer and
- Algernon, a rule-inference engine.

The SWRL.OWL files are input to both the Provenance Visualizer and Algernon. Jena and Protégé-OWL Plugin act as the interface between the Provenance Visualizer and the SWRL.OWL files, and between Algernon and the SWRL.OWL files, respectively. Jena [17], developed by HP Labs, provides the programmatic environment for RDF, RDFS and OWL. Jena supports SPARQL[18] which is used to query the SWRL.OWL files. The Protégé-OWL Plugin was used to generate the SWRL.OWL files and to retrieve the rules from the SWRL.OWL files for Algernon to process at runtime. Algernon [19] is a rule-inference engine that supports both forward and backward chaining rules of inference, and implements Access-Limited Logic. However Algernon does not support the inference of subsumption between properties or comply with the SWRL rule format, the rules retrieved from SWRL.OWL files by Protégé-OWL Plugin APIs had to be transformed to the Algernon-compliant rules before being imported to Algernon at runtime.

The Provenance Visualizer, is the graphical user interface (GUI) powered by JGraph [20] (an extension of Java Swing GUI Component to support directed graphs). The Provenance Visualizer GUI is divided into three panels horizontally:

1) The Provenance View, in the upper panel, presents a graphical view of the provenance process modeled using RDF graphs.
2) The Publishing Interface, in the central panel, enables users to construct packages for publishing scientific results. The users can drag and drop selected components from the upper panel into an RDF package. When two components are linked manually then the direct relationship is inferred automatically using the inferencing rules and Algernon.
3) Finally, the Provenance data, in the bottom panel displays the provenance details (metadata) for the object highlighted in the upper panel.

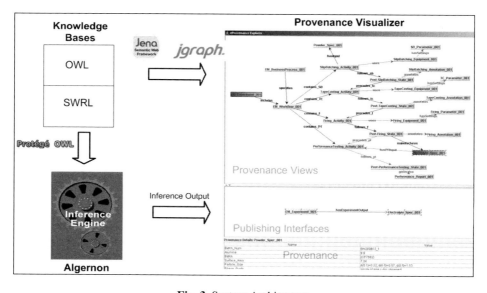

Fig. 3. System Architecture

Access controls are imposed on the upper panel's graphical view. The granularity of the view depends on user privileges and access policies, enforced and defined by Shibboleth and XACML.

To enforce the inter-institutional authentication and access control, Shibboleth , a centralized identity and authorization mechanism developed by the NSF Middleware Initiative, was adopted and incorporated within the Provenance Explorer. Shibboleth is standards-based, open source middleware software which provides Web Single SignOn (SSO) across or within organizational boundaries. Figure 4 demonstrates the two primary components of Shibboleth: the Identity Provider (IdP) and Service Provider (SP). The IdP maintains user credentials and attributes. Upon request the IdP will assert authentication and attribute statements to requesting parties, specifically SPs. The SP then uses predefined-XACML policies to control access to the Provenance Explorer and fine-grained provenance views on the upper panel.

XACML complements Shibboleth to address fine-grained access control on the resources. XACML, the Extensible Access Control Markup Language, provides a vocabulary for expressing the rules needed to define fine-grained and machine-readable policies and make authorization decisions. In this system we use Sun's XACML[2] implementation which includes an XACML engine and an API for easy integration.

Initially, authenticated users of Provenance Explorer are presented with the coarsest view of provenance. When a user attempts to retrieve finer-grained views by clicking on links between entities, a request is generated, the XACML engine compares the request with the policies on these entities and makes the authorization decision.

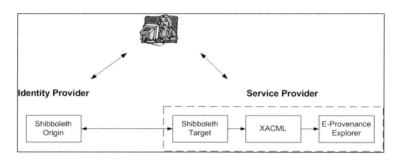

Fig. 4. Authentication and Authorization System Architecture

5 Demonstration and User Interface

Within the FUSION project, members of the "Virtual Organization" (those users collaborating on the project and sharing different aspects of the data) can be classified into three main role types with three different levels of access:

1. the fuel-cell researcher from the AIBN (also the project leader);
2. the technicians from the fuel-cell manufacturing company;
3. post-graduate students from the University of Queensland and Monash University.

The fuel-cell researcher designed the original workflows, over-saw the entire process, developed new hypotheses and models, designed new experiments, and wrote

---

[2] http://sunxacml.sourceforge.net/

publications describing the results and conclusions. The technicians carried out the manufacturing (slip batching, tape casting, firing) and performance testing activities. Finally, the post-graduate students working on specific aspects of fuel cells were entitled to view different components of the process to different levels. The fuel-cell researcher had the highest privileges and was entitled to explore the complete set of provenance records. He/she was also able to select provenance components to incorporate within publication or e-learning packages. The technicians had modest privileges – they were able to access the provenance associated with each of their own activities, whereas the students had the minimum privileges with restricted access to provenance details. In the following section we describe the system from the point of view of each of these user types.

Firstly consider the researcher/project leader. He/she logs onto the Shibboleth Service provider where the Provenance Explorer service is installed. Initially, the user is redirected to Shibboleth's Identity Provider for authentication and authorization. Once authenticated, the user's attributes are returned back to the Service Provider and the user is granted access to the Provenance Explorer. The researcher searches for the provenance of Batch Number 280818. Initially the researcher is presented with the basic view of the experiment provenance. This is the default view for all users with access privileges to the FUSION project's Provenance Explorer service. Figure 5 demonstrates the default expandable view. The pink arrows indicate relationships that can be expanded to reveal further fine-grained information about the sub-activities.

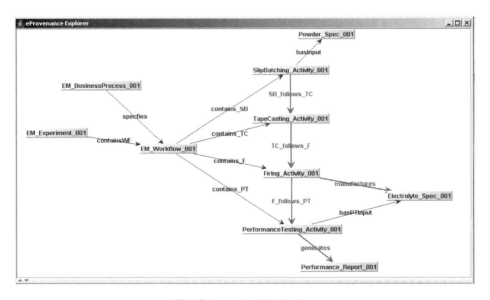

Fig. 5. A standard basic view

When the researcher clicks on a pink arrow, a request for additional information is generated and submitted to the XACML engine. The XACML engine compares the request with the policy and makes an authorization decision accordingly. Figure 6 demonstrates the policy and request.

Provenance Explorer – Customized Provenance Views Using Semantic Inferencing 223

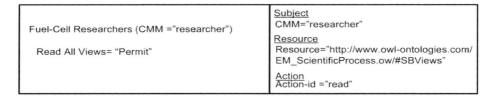

Fig. 6. Example policies and requests

Eventually by interactively drilling down via the links, the researcher is presented with the complete view. Figure 7 illustrates the complete view in the upper panel. The dark green arrows indicate links that can be collapsed manually back to the original view i.e., the pink expandable links. If an individual node on the upper panel is selected, the complete provenance metadata for this node is displayed in the bottom panel. Figure 7 demonstrates this feature. Node *Powder_Spec_001* is highlighted in a red circle on the upper panel, and the associated provenance information is displayed in the bottom panel.

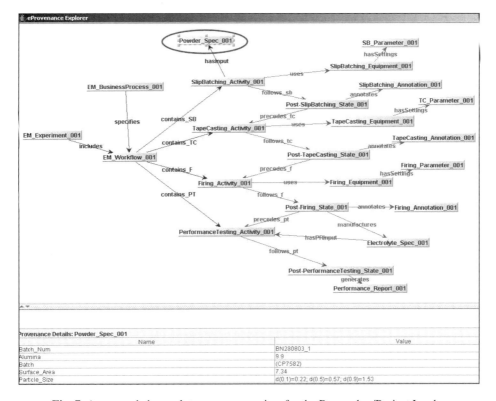

Fig. 7. An expanded complete provenance view for the Researcher/Project Leader

Furthermore, using this interface, the researcher is able to manually construct a package of related components for publication or dissemination. This is performed by selecting nodes in the top panel and dragging and dropping them into the middle panel. By linking them manually, the relationship between the nodes is inferred by the rule-inference engine. For example, Figure 8 demonstrates that the relationship inferred between the two selected nodes, Experiment_001 and Electrolyte_Spec_001 is *hasExperimentOutput*. The path used to infer this relationship is highlighted in blue (with the beginning and end nodes highlighted in red) in the upper panel. Figure 2 illustrates that in the ontology we define an experiment as comprising a sequence of activities with particular post-event states. The inferencing rule states that any product generated by one of the activities in the sequence is an output of the experiment.

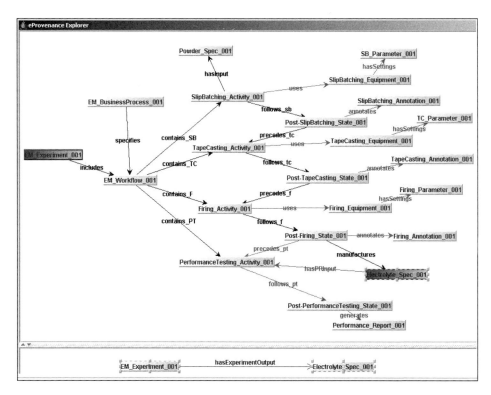

Fig. 8. Demonstration of Provenance Inferencing

Now consider the system from the point of view of the Slip-batching operator. After logging in and being authenticated, the operator/technician is presented with the default view. This is almost identical to Figure 6, except that there is just one expandable pink arrow *SB_follows_TC*, indicating that further expansion is restricted to the slip batching activity. Finally, the Post-graduate students were also entitled to access the default coarse-grained view of the experiment – but with no expandable pink arrows.

6 Discussion and Conclusion

6.1 User Feedback

Initial feedback from the fuel-cell scientists involved in the FUSION project has been very positive. The system enables them to quickly and intuitively understand quite complex workflows and to compare different workflows. They are able to pinpoint problems within a particular workflow and to generate new experimental workflows accordingly. Users can understand the system very quickly because of its close analogy to the web – using hyperlinks for information exploration and navigation. Furthermore, with regard to the data's validity, the scientists can intuitively track the data's provenance with the aid of the complete graphical view of visualized scientific processes and the ability to view detailed metadata associated with any node. The users were also very positive about the security framework – in particular the advantages of the single sign-on capability of Shibboleth and the ability to hide certain steps or the details associated with specific steps in the process.

However, users did raise concerns regarding scalability and searching. At this stage, our demonstration involves multiple instances of a single workflow. In reality, the scientists may need to search, retrieve and compare multiple experiments simultaneously and the experimental workflows may be very different. Moreover, the current methods by which scientists can discover and retrieve experimental workflows is limited. Currently the system only permits search and retrieval of experiments via a unique ID. Scientists would like to be able to search for experiments via particular attributes e.g., particular parameter values. The optimum methods for describing, indexing and discovering workflows require further investigation and direct input from the end-users.

6.2 Limitations and Future Work

The provenance metadata, graphical views and inferencing rules of the Provenance Explorer were all based on the provenance model in Figure 2. This model is an extension of the ABC model developed within the Harmony project - extended to support experiments in laboratories. This model provides the semantic underpinning of the system, and the ontology's robustness may become a significant issue if/when the system is expanded across domains and organizations. Colomb argues that formal ontologies, such as DOLCE [21] and BWW [22], provide a rich meta-vocabulary and abstract data types, and well-understood structural organizational principles, thereby technically enhancing the reliability of material ontologies [23] like our ontology. Thus, it may be worth carrying out further investigation on formal ontologies to determine how they can make the provenance model more reliable and rational in terms of the data structures.

To date the workflows that we have considered have really only focused on the provenance data/metadata and inferencing rules associated with processing events in a laboratory or manufacturing/processing plant. We need to extend the underlying model and the inferencing rules to support the data processing activities in the digital domain e.g., reformatting, segmentation, normalization etc.

Currently the XACML access policies are defined manually and are manually associated with relationships between nodes in the RDF graphs. This is a relatively time-consuming process. We need to determine a more streamlined mechanism for defining access policies and associating them with provenance relationships. For example, the individual or type of participant who is responsible for a particular activity or set of activities should have access to all of the provenance data associated with those activities and all sub-activities.

Another limitation of the current system is that it only supports expansion down one level of detail. Ideally users would be able to incrementally drill down to multiple levels of detail. For example one link can be expanded to two links, each of which can be further expanded. This may prove quite complex to implement because it involves multiple levels of inferencing rules and the specification of access policies associated with provenance information at multiple levels.

Finally the packages of components that are able to be constructed provide a very efficient mechanism: for publishing and sharing scientific results; for teaching complex scientific concepts; and for the selective archival, curation and preservation of scientific data. Although we currently enable these packages to be saved, they are not indexed or able to be searched and retrieved. Tools are required to enable these RDF packages to be described, stored to institutional repositories and searched and retrieved for reuse.

6.3 Conclusions

In this paper, we have described the Provenance Explorer system that we have developed. It is a provenance visualization system that dynamically generates different graphical views of provenance trails depending on the user's requirements and access privileges. It enables users to search and retrieve the data provenance associated with scientific workflows or experiments, without compromising the security of the data. Even within the context of workflows that capture and share data across institutional boundaries, the system is able to authenticate users to enforce fine-grained, role-based access controls. The hypermedia user interface that we have developed enables easy drilling down from simple high-level views to detailed views of complex sub-activities by enabling links to be expanded or collapsed. This feature was easy to implement and can quickly be refined or customized because it is implemented using SWRL rules and the Algernon inferencing engine.

Finally scientists are under increasing pressure from funding organizations to publish their experimental and evidential data together with the related traditional scholarly publication(s). This system makes it easy for scientists to wrap related outputs into a single package for publication, peer-review, e-learning or selective preservation purposes – and to have the provenance trail between the components automatically inferred to enable validation and verification.

References

1. Goble, C. *Position Statement: Musings on Provenance, Workflow and (Semantic Web) Annotations for Bioinformatics*. in *Workshop on Data Derivation and Provenance*. 2002.
2. schraefel, m.c., et al. *Breaking the Book: Translating the Chemistry Lab Book into a Pervasive Computing Lab Environment*. in *CHI*. 2004. Vienna, Austria.

3. Gibson, A., et al. *myTea: Connecting the Web to Digital Science on the Desktop.* in *World Wide Web Conference 2006.* 2006. Edinburgh.
4. Altintas, I., O. Barney, and E. Jaeger-Frank. *Provenance Collection Support in the Kepler Scientific Workflow System.* in *International Provenance and Annotation Workshop (IPAW'06).* 2006. Chicago, Illinois, USA.
5. Oinn, T., et al., *Taverna: A tool for the composition and enactment of bioinformatics workflows.* Bioinformatics Journal, 2004. 20(3045-3054).
6. Majithia, S., et al. *Triana: A Graphical Web Service Composition and Execution Toolkit.* in *IEEE International Conference on Web Services (ICWS'04).* 2004: IEEE Computer Society.
7. Morgan, R.L.B., et al., *Federated Security: The Shibboleth Approach.* EDUCAUSE QUARTERLY, 2004. 4: p. 12 - 17.
8. Lorch, M., et al. *First Experiences Using XACML for Access Control in Distributed Systems.* in *ACM Workshop on XML Security.* 2003. Fairfax, Virginia.
9. Bose, R. and J. Frew. *Composing lineage metadata with XML for custom satellite-derived data products.* in *Scientific and Statistical Database Management, 2004. Proceedings. 16th International Conference on.* 2004.
10. Myers, J.D., Pancerella, C., Lansing, R., Schuchardt, K.L. & Didier, B. *Multi-scale science: supporting emerging practice with semantically derived provenance.* in *ISWC 2003 Workshop: Semantic Web Technologies for Searching and Retrieving Scientific Data,.* 2003. Sanibel Island, Florida, USA.
11. Zhao, J., et al. *Using Semantic Web Technologies for Representing E-science Provenance.* in *Third International Semantic Web Conference.* 2004. Hiroshima, Japan.
12. Freire, J., et al. *Managing Rapidly-Evolving Scientific Workflows.* in *International Provenance and Annotation Workshop (IPAW'06).* 2006. Chicago, Illinois, USA.
13. Hunter, J. and K. Cheung. *Generating eScience Workflows from Statistical Analysis of Prior Data.* in *APAC'05.* 2005. Royal Pines Resort, Gold Coast.
14. Hunter, J., J. Drennan, and S. Little, *Realizing the Hydrogen Economy through Semantic Web Technologies.* IEEE Intelligent Systems Journal - Special Issue on eScience, 2004: p. 40-47.
15. Lagoze, C. and J. Hunter, *The ABC Ontology and Model.* Journal of Digital Information, 2001. 2(2).
16. Horrocks I., P.-S.P., Boley H., Tabet S, Grosof B, Dean M, *SWRL: A Semantic Web Rule Language Combining OWL and RuleML.* 2004.
17. Carroll, J.J., et al., *Jena: implementing the semantic web recommendations*, in *Proceedings of the 13th international World Wide Web conference on Alternate track papers \& posters.* 2004, ACM Press: New York, NY, USA. p. 74-83.
18. McCarthy, P., *Search RDF data with SPARQL: SPARQL and the Jena Toolkit open up the semantic Web*, in *developerWorks.* 2005, IBM.
19. Crawford, J.M. and B.J. Kuipers, *Algernon - a tractable system for knowledge-representation.* SIGART Bull., 1991. 2(3): p. 35-44.
20. Alder, G., *The JGraph Swing Component*, in *Department of Computer Science.* 2002, Federal Institute of Technology ETH: Zurich, Switzerland.
21. Gangemi, A., et al. *Sweetening ontologies with DOLCE.* in *13th International Conference on Knowledge Engineering and Knowledge Management (EKAW02).* 2002. Siguenza, Spain: Springer, Berlin.
22. Weber, R., *Ontological foundations of information systems.* Monograph No. 4. 1997, Melbourne: Coopers & Lybrand Accounting Research Methodology.
23. Colomb, R.M., *Formal versus Material Ontologies for information Systems interoperation in the Semantic Web.* The Computer Journal, 2006. 49(1).

On How to Perform a Gold Standard Based Evaluation of Ontology Learning

Klaas Dellschaft and Steffen Staab

Universität Koblenz-Landau, ISWeb Working Group
Universitätsstr. 1, 56070 Koblenz, Germany
{klaasd, staab}@uni-koblenz.de
http://isweb.uni-koblenz.de

Abstract. In recent years several measures for the gold standard based evaluation of ontology learning were proposed. They can be distinguished by the layers of an ontology (e.g. lexical term layer and concept hierarchy) they evaluate. Judging those measures with a list of criteria we show that there exist some measures sufficient for evaluating the lexical term layer. However, existing measures for the evaluation of concept hierarchies fail to meet basic criteria. This paper presents a new taxonomic measure which overcomes the problems of current approaches.

1 Introduction

The capabilities of ontology learning approaches may be tested by (i) evaluation in a running application, (ii) a posteriori evaluation by experts, or (iii) evaluation by comparison of learned results against a pre-defined "gold standard". Though approaches (i) and (ii) exhibit some considerable advantages over approach (iii), when it comes to frequent and large-scale evaluations and comparisons of multiple ontology learning approaches, only approach (iii) is feasible in practice. Since such – comparably – easily repeatable evaluation schemes contributed heavily to the overwhelming success of disciplines like information retrieval, machine learning or speech recognition, we conjecture that a similar success of ontology learning requires an analogous scheme for evaluation with gold standards, too.

Examples of gold standard-based evaluations of ontology learning can be found in [1], [2] and [3] – to name but a few. However, it is apparent that there does not exist a canonical way of performing gold-standard based evaluations of ontology learning. Moreover, we argue in this paper that existing gold-standard based evaluations are faulty and that a well-founded evaluation model is largely missing. Therefore, we describe here a new framework for gold standard-based evaluation of ontology learning that avoids common mistakes and we show by some analytical considerations and by some experiments that the new framework fulfills crucial evaluation criteria that other frameworks do not meet.

2 Related Work

There exist many measures for the reference-based evaluation of ontologies. One may distinguish between measures which only evaluate the lexical term layer of an ontology, those which also take the concept hierarchy into account and the ones which evaluate the non-taxonomic relations contained in an ontology. In this paper we will concentrate on the measures for evaluating concept hierarchies and the lexical term layer.

On the lexical term layer "binary" measures are often used that compare the terms from the reference and the learned ontology based on an exact match of strings. Examples for this kind of measure are the *Term Precision and Term Recall* as they are presented in [3]. There exist also several other names for these measures like *Lexical Precision and Recall* or simply *precision and recall* (see [4] and [5]). Another example of a term level evaluation measure is the *String Matching* measure presented in [6] and [7]. This measure is based on the edit distance between two strings. It is therefore more robust with regard to slightly different spellings and typing errors (e.g. "center" and "centre").

The comparison of concept hierarchies is more complicated than the comparison of the lexical term layer of ontologies. Such concept hierarchy measures are often divided into kinds of local and global measures. The local measure compares the similarity of the positions of two concepts in the learned and the reference hierarchy. The global measure is then computed by averaging the results of the local measure for concept pairs from the reference and the learned ontology.

One of the first examples of a concept hierarchy evaluation measure is the *Taxonomic Overlap* (TO) presented in [6] and [7]. The local taxonomic overlap compares two concepts based on the set of all their super- and sub concepts. In opposite to the local overlap, which is a symmetric measure, this is not the case for the global taxonomic overlap measures proposed in [6], [7] and [8], i.e. they can be computed into two directions. In [8] this asymmetry is interpreted as a kind of precision and recall. But in section 4.5 we will show that this is a misinterpretation of the asymmetry, as local taxonomic overlap already constitutes a kind of combination of precision and recall.

Another example is the *Augmented Precision and Recall* (AP & AR) presented in [9]. It is also divided into a global and a local part of the measure. For the local part two alternatives may be used: The *Learning Accuracy* (LA) and the *Balanced Distance Metric* (BDM). LA was proposed by [10]. It compares two concepts based on their distance in the tree (e.g. the length of the shortest path between the root and their most specific common abstraction). BDM further develops the idea of LA by taking further types of paths and a branching factor of the concepts into account (see [9]).

The latest measure for comparing concept hierarchies is the *OntoRand* index proposed in [11]. It is a symmetric measure which extends techniques used in the clustering community for comparing two partitions of the same set of instances. A concept hierarchy is seen as a hierarchical partitioning of instances. For OntoRand two alternatives exist to measure the similarity of concepts. The first alternative is based on the set of common ancestors. The second alternative is based on the distance between two concepts in the tree (like LA and BDM). An important constraint imposed on the concept hierarchy is that both compared hierarchies must contain the same set of instances.

3 Criteria for Good Evaluation Measures

Given this variety of evaluation measures for concept hierarchies it is now the question what is a "good" measure and can we give some criteria according to which to evaluate the different measures. Measures fulfilling the following criteria will help to avoid the misinterpretation of evaluation results and ease drawing the right conclusions for the improvement of the evaluated ontology learning procedure.

The most important criterion is that a measure allows to evaluate an ontology along multiple dimensions. This criterion is formulated in several papers like [9] and [12]. Thus a user can weight different kinds of errors based on his own preferences. This enables to better analyze the strengths and weaknesses of a learned ontology.

If a multi dimensional evaluation is performed, each measure should be influenced just by one dimension, i.e. by one type of error only. For example, if one uses measures for evaluating the lexical term layer of an ontology (e.g the lexical precision and recall) and one also wants to evaluate the quality of the learned concept hierarchy (e.g. with the taxonomic overlap), then a dependency between those measures should be avoided.

The second criterion is that the effect of an error onto the measure should be proportional to the distance between the correct and the given result. For example, an error near the root of a concept hierarchy should have a stronger effect on the evaluation measure than an error nearer to the leafs (see also [12]).

The third criterion is closely related to the previous one. For measures with a closed scale interval (e.g. $[0..1]$), a gradual increase in the error rate should also lead to a gradual decrease in the evaluation results. For example, if a measure has the interval $[0..1]$ as its scale but already slight errors lead to a decrease of the returned results from 1 to 0.2 then it is difficult to distinguish between slight and severe errors (see [11]).

In Tab. 1 it is shown in how far the measures described in section 2 meet the criteria listed in this section. The rating is based on the descriptions in [7], [9] and [11]. Additionally, the new findings from section 4.5 were used for rating the taxonomic overlap. A measure can improve its multi dimensionality by two factors: either by removing the influence of the lexical term layer on the evaluation of the concept hierarchy or by separately measuring different aspects of the hierarchy (e.g. precision and recall). None of the measures removes the influence of the lexical term layer and only the augmented precision and recall distinguishes between two aspects of the hierarchy. The Learning Accuracy does not achieve the best score for the proportional error effect because it

Table 1. Rating of concept hierarchy measures

	multi dimensionality	proportional error effect	usage of interval
TO	−	+	?
AP & AR	○	+	?
LA	−	○	?
OntoRand[1]	−	+/−	+/−
TP_{csc} (cf. section 4.3)	+	+	+

considers the distance between the correct and the given answer only to some small extent (see [9]). In the following a truly multi dimensional approach for evaluating an ontology will be presented, thus overcoming the problems of the current measures.

4 Comparing Learned Ontologies with Gold Standards

In this section measures will be presented which can be used for an evaluation of the lexical term layer and the concept hierarchy of an ontology. The measures extend the idea of precision and recall to the gold standard based evaluation of ontologies. The lexical term layer of an ontology will be evaluated with lexical precision and recall (see section 4.2). For the concept hierarchy a framework of building blocks will be defined in section 4.3. This framework defines a family of measures and it will be used for systematically constructing a measure which fulfills the criteria from section 3.

In the following the simplified definition of a core ontology will be used. This definition of an ontology only contains the lexical term layer and the concept hierarchy. Similarly to [8], we define a core ontology as follows:

Definition 1. *The structure $\mathcal{O} := (\mathcal{C}, root, \leq_{\mathcal{C}})$ is called a core ontology. $\mathcal{C}$ is a set of concept identifiers and $root$ is a designated root concept for the partial order $\leq_{\mathcal{C}}$ on $\mathcal{C}$. This partial order is called concept hierarchy or taxonomy. The equation $\forall c \in \mathcal{C} : c \leq_{\mathcal{C}} root$ holds for this concept hierarchy.*

In this definition of a core ontology the relation between lexical terms and their associated concept is a bijection, i.e. each term is associated with exactly one concept and each concept with exactly one term. Thus it is possible to use the a lexical term as the identifier of a concept. This restriction simplifies the following formulas. Nevertheless it would be possible to generalize them to the case where an $n : m$ relation between concepts and lexical terms exists (in analogy to [6] and [7]).

4.1 Precision and Recall

This section gives a short overview of precision, recall and F-measure, as they are known from information retrieval (see [13]). They are used for comparing a reference retrieval (Ref) with a computed retrieval ($Comp$) returned by a system. Precision and recall are defined as follows:

$$P(Ref, Comp) = \frac{|Comp \cap Ref|}{|Comp|} \qquad R(Ref, Comp) = \frac{|Comp \cap Ref|}{|Ref|} \qquad (1)$$

It is interesting that precision and recall are the inverse of each other:

$$P(Ref, Comp) = \frac{|Comp \cap Ref|}{|Comp|} = R(Comp, Ref) \qquad (2)$$

---

[1] It is shown in [11] that the measures based on tree distance in some cases do not show an proportional error effect and that they do not use the complete interval. These problems do not exist for the OntoRand measure based on common ancestors.

The F_1-measure is used for giving a summarizing overview and for balancing the precision and recall values. The F_1-measure is the harmonic mean of P and R.

$$F_1(\textit{Ref}, \textit{Comp}) = \frac{2 \cdot P(\textit{Ref}, \textit{Comp}) \cdot R(\textit{Ref}, \textit{Comp})}{P(\textit{Ref}, \textit{Comp}) + R(\textit{Ref}, \textit{Comp})} \quad (3)$$

4.2 Lexical Precision and Recall

There exist several measures sufficient for evaluating the lexical term layer of an ontology (see section 2). In this subsection the lexical precision and recall measures, as they are described in [4], will be explained in a bit more detail. Later on they will be used in conjunction with the measures for evaluating concept hierarchies, as they are presented in section 4.3. Given a computed core ontology $\mathcal{O}_C$ and a reference ontology $\mathcal{O}_R$, the lexical precision (LP) and lexical recall (LR) are defined as follows:

$$LP(\mathcal{O}_C, \mathcal{O}_R) = \frac{|\mathcal{C}_C \cap \mathcal{C}_R|}{|\mathcal{C}_C|} \qquad LR(\mathcal{O}_C, \mathcal{O}_R) = \frac{|\mathcal{C}_C \cap \mathcal{C}_R|}{|\mathcal{C}_R|} \quad (4)$$

Fig. 1. Example reference ontology ($\mathcal{O}_{R1}$, left) and computed ontology ($\mathcal{O}_{C1}$, right)

The lexical precision and recall reflect how good the learned lexical terms cover the target domain. For example, if one compares $\mathcal{O}_{C1}$ and $\mathcal{O}_{R1}$ in Fig. 1 with each other, one gets $LP(\mathcal{O}_{C1}, \mathcal{O}_{R1}) = \frac{4}{6} = 0.67$ and $LR(\mathcal{O}_{C1}, \mathcal{O}_{R1}) = \frac{4}{5} = 0.8$.

4.3 Taxonomic Precision and Recall

In this subsection a framework of building blocks is described. It defines a family of taxonomic precision and recall measures from which two concrete measures will be selected afterward. Only the equations for the taxonomic precision measures will be presented. The corresponding equations for the taxonomic recall measures can be easily derived from them because of equation (2). This framework extends and improves the framework used for the taxonomic overlap measures in [7]. It especially replaces the previously used equation for comparing the position of two concepts with each other *leading to a completely different behavior of the measure* (see also section 4.5).

Comparing Concepts. As mentioned before, measures for comparing two concept hierarchies with each other are usually divided into a kind of local and a global measure (cf. section 2). The local measure compares the positions of two concepts and the global measure is used for comparing two whole concept hierarchies. We start describing the framework's local measure. It is then used in the definition of the global measure.

For the local taxonomic precision the similarity of two concepts will be computed based on characteristic extracts from the concept hierarchy. Such an extract should characterize the position of a concept in the hierarchy, i.e. two extracts should contain many common objects if the characterized objects are at similar positions in the hierarchy. The proportion of common objects in the extracts should decrease with increasing dissimilarity of the characterized concepts. Given such an characteristic extract ce, the local taxonomic precision tp_{ce} of two concepts $c_1 \in \mathcal{O}_C$ and $c_2 \in \mathcal{O}_R$ is defined as

$$tp_{ce}(c_1, c_2, \mathcal{O}_C, \mathcal{O}_R) := \frac{|ce(c_1, \mathcal{O}_C) \cap ce(c_2, \mathcal{O}_R)|}{|ce(c_1, \mathcal{O}_C)|} \qquad (5)$$

The characteristic extract from the concept hierarchy is an important building block of the local taxonomic measure and several alternative instantiations exist. As we will see below, they have a major influence on the properties of the corresponding global measure. For the taxonomic overlap measure described in [7] it was suggested to characterize a concept by its semantic cotopy, i.e. all its super- and subconcepts. Given the concept $c \in \mathcal{C}$ and the ontology $\mathcal{O}$, the semantic cotopy sc is defined as follows:

$$sc(c, \mathcal{O}) := \{c_i | c_i \in \mathcal{C} \wedge (c_i \leq c \vee c \leq c_i)\} \qquad (6)$$

If one uses the semantic cotopy for defining the local taxonomic precision measure tp_{sc}, the results will be heavily influenced by the lexical precision of $\mathcal{O}_C$ because with decreasing lexical precision more and more concepts of $sc(c, \mathcal{O}_C)$ are not contained in $\mathcal{O}_R$ and $sc(c, \mathcal{O}_R)$. This increases the probability that $sc(c, \mathcal{O}_C)$ contains such concepts, leading to a direct dependency between the lexical and the taxonomic precision. But according to section 3, evaluation measures should be judged by whether the different measures are independent of each other. So taxonomic measures based on the semantic cotopy shouldn't be used in conjunction with the lexical precision and recall.

This influence of lexical precision and recall on the taxonomic measures can be avoided if one uses the common semantic cotopy csc as the characteristic extract. The common semantic cotopy excludes all concepts which are not also available in the other ontology's set of concepts:

$$csc(c, \mathcal{O}_1, \mathcal{O}_2) := \{c_i | c_i \in \mathcal{C}_1 \cap \mathcal{C}_2 \wedge (c_i <_1 c \vee c <_1 c_i)\} \qquad (7)$$

In Tab. 2 and 3 one can see the influence of inserting and replacing concepts in a hierarchy. The tables contain the sets sc and csc for the ontologies $\mathcal{O}_{R1}$ and $\mathcal{O}_{C1}$ which were already used as an example for lexical precision and recall (see Fig. 1). One can see that inserting and replacing concepts without actually changing the hierarchy has no effect on the common semantic cotopy while the semantic cotopy is heavily influenced by these changes on the lexical term layer of an ontology.

Besides the previously described extracts of the concept hierarchy, further extracts are imaginable. For example, the upwards cotopy (see [7]) or the set of all direct subconcepts might be used. In [14] also measures based on the direct subconcepts were evaluated. But [14] shows also that measures based on the semantic cotopy meet more of the criteria from section 3.

Table 2. Semantic cotopies for the ontologies in Fig. 1

c	$sc(c, \mathcal{O}_{R1})$	$sc(c, \mathcal{O}_{C1})$
root	{root, bike, car, van, coupé}	{root, bike, BMX, auto, van, coupé}
car	{root, car, van, coupé}	–
auto	–	{root, auto, van, coupé}
van	{root, car, van}	{root, auto, van}
coupé	{root, car, coupé}	{root, auto, coupé}
bike	{root, bike}	{root, bike, BMX}
BMX	–	{root, bike, BMX}

Table 3. Common semantic cotopies for the ontologies in Fig. 1

c	$csc(c, \mathcal{O}_{R1}, \mathcal{O}_{C1})$	$csc(c, \mathcal{O}_{C1}, \mathcal{O}_{R1})$
root	{bike, van, coupé}	{bike, van, coupé}
car	{root, van, coupé}	–
auto	–	{root, van, coupé}
van	{root}	{root}
coupé	{root}	{root}
bike	{root}	{root}
BMX	–	{root, bike}

Comparing Concept Hierarchies. It is now possible to define a framework for constructing a global taxonomic precision measure. Fig. 2 shows the building blocks used in this framework for a global taxonomic precision measure.

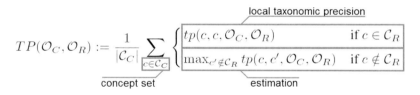

$$TP(\mathcal{O}_C, \mathcal{O}_R) := \frac{1}{|\mathcal{C}_C|} \sum_{c \in \mathcal{C}_C} \begin{cases} tp(c, c, \mathcal{O}_C, \mathcal{O}_R) & \text{if } c \in \mathcal{C}_R \\ \max_{c' \notin \mathcal{C}_R} tp(c, c', \mathcal{O}_C, \mathcal{O}_R) & \text{if } c \notin \mathcal{C}_R \end{cases}$$

Fig. 2. Building blocks of the global taxonomic precision measure

The *set of concepts* whose local taxonomic precision values are summed up is the first building block. Two alternatives may be used. The first alternative is to use the set of concepts $\mathcal{C}_C$ from the learned ontology. If one chooses this alternative, the global taxonomic precision is influenced by the lexical precision. For example, if the lexical precision of a learned ontology is approximately 5% (like in the empirical evaluation in section 5.2) then for 95% of the concepts a local taxonomic precision value has to be estimated because there doesn't exist a corresponding concept in the reference ontology (see below). If such an influence of the lexical precision should be avoided then the set of common concepts $\mathcal{C}_C \cap \mathcal{C}_R$ should be preferred. It especially makes sense if one also uses a local taxonomic precision value based on the common semantic cotopy.

The *local taxonomic precision* is the next building block. It is used for comparing the position of a concept in the learned hierarchy with the position of the same concept in the reference hierarchy. Thus the current concept has to exist in both hierarchies.

An *estimation* of a local taxonomic precision value is the last building block. It is only used if the current concept isn't contained in both ontologies. Its usage is therefore influenced by the chosen set of concepts (see above). In [7] it is suggested to make an optimistic estimation by comparing the current concept with all concepts from the reference ontology and choose the highest local taxonomic precision value. This ensures that concepts which do not match on the lexical term layer (e.g. "auto" and "car" in Fig. 1) will nonetheless match in the concept hierarchy and thus return a high local taxonomic precision value. The optimistic estimation reduces the influence of lexical precision but it may also cause misleading results.

In opposite to that, assuming a local taxonomic precision value of 0% if no match on the lexical term layer can be found maximizes the influence of the lexical precision. But if one wants to completely eliminate the influence of lexical precision one should avoid this estimation building block anyway. This is done by only averaging the local taxonomic precision values of the common concepts.

Concrete Measures. In the following the previously presented building blocks will be combined to concrete measures fulfilling the criteria from section 3. The measures will be evaluated in section 5. In [14] further measures are described and evaluated. This paper only contains the best two pairs of measures.

The first pair of measures consists of TP_{sc} and TR_{sc}. They are based on the semantic cotopy and are thus influenced by the lexical term layer. In the evaluation in section 5 they will be used for demonstrating the disadvantages of mixing the evaluation of lexical term layer and concept hierarchy. The other building blocks are selected so that they further increase this influence. This is achieved by computing the local taxonomic precision for all learned concepts and by estimating the local taxonomic precision as 0 if the current concept isn't also contained in the reference ontology.

$$TP_{sc}(\mathcal{O}_C, \mathcal{O}_R) := \frac{1}{|\mathcal{C}_C|} \sum_{c \in \mathcal{C}_C} \begin{cases} tp_{sc}(c, c, \mathcal{O}_C, \mathcal{O}_R) & \text{if } c \in \mathcal{C}_R \\ 0 & \text{if } c \notin \mathcal{C}_R \end{cases} \qquad (8)$$

$$TR_{sc}(\mathcal{O}_C, \mathcal{O}_R) := TP_{sc}(\mathcal{O}_R, \mathcal{O}_C) \qquad (9)$$

All in all, the measures TP_{sc} and TR_{sc} do not allow a separate evaluation of lexical term layer and concept hierarchy. For evaluation scenarios where a thorough analysis of the learned ontologies is needed the measures TP_{csc} and TR_{csc} are better suited. Here the building blocks will be selected so that the influence of the lexical term layer is minimized. This is achieved by using the common semantic cotopy and by computing the taxonomic precision values only for the common concepts of both ontologies. The latter makes the estimation of local taxonomic precision values unnecessary.

$$TP_{csc}(\mathcal{O}_C, \mathcal{O}_R) := \frac{1}{|\mathcal{C}_C \cap \mathcal{C}_R|} \sum_{c \in \mathcal{C}_C \cap \mathcal{C}_R} tp_{csc}(c, c, \mathcal{O}_C, \mathcal{O}_R) \qquad (10)$$

$$TR_{csc}(\mathcal{O}_C, \mathcal{O}_R) := TP_{csc}(\mathcal{O}_R, \mathcal{O}_C) \qquad (11)$$

4.4 Taxonomic F- and F'-Measure

Like it is the case for precision and recall in information retrieval, also the taxonomic precision and recall have to be balanced if one wants to output a combined measure. Therefore the taxonomic F-measure is introduced, which is the harmonic mean of the global taxonomic precision and recall.

$$TF(\mathcal{O}_C, \mathcal{O}_R) := \frac{2 \cdot TP(\mathcal{O}_C, \mathcal{O}_R) \cdot TR(\mathcal{O}_C, \mathcal{O}_R)}{TP(\mathcal{O}_C, \mathcal{O}_R) + TR(\mathcal{O}_C, \mathcal{O}_R)} \quad (12)$$

A higher taxonomic F-measure corresponds to a better quality of the concept hierarchy. The meaningfulness with regard to the overall quality of the ontology (lexical level + taxxonomy) depends on the chosen building blocks. If TF is not influenced by the lexical level then the taxonomic F'-measure (see [8]) may additionally be computed. It is the harmonic mean of LR and TF:

$$TF'(\mathcal{O}_C, \mathcal{O}_R) := \frac{2 \cdot LR(\mathcal{O}_C, \mathcal{O}_R) \cdot TF(\mathcal{O}_C, \mathcal{O}_R)}{LR(\mathcal{O}_C, \mathcal{O}_R) + TF(\mathcal{O}_C, \mathcal{O}_R)} \quad (13)$$

4.5 Taxonomic Overlap

In [6] and [8] the taxonomic overlap measure is defined. It is also divided into a global and a local part of the measure. The global taxonomic overlap TO has the same building blocks like TP but instead of the local taxonomic precision it uses the local overlap to:

$$to_{sc}(c_1, c_2, \mathcal{O}_1, \mathcal{O}_2) := \frac{|sc(c_1, \mathcal{O}_1) \cap sc(c_2, \mathcal{O}_2)|}{|sc(c_1, \mathcal{O}_1) \cup sc(c_2, \mathcal{O}_2)|} \quad (14)$$

Because to is a symmetric measure, it depends on the other building blocks (concept set and estimation component) whether the global taxonomic overlap is symmetric or asymmetric. We have shown the following lemma (cf. [14] for its proof):

Lemma 1. *Symmetric global taxonomic overlap measures can be solely derived from taxonomic F-measures. The equation $TO = TF/(2 - TF)$ holds.*

This lemma implies that symmetric TO measures behave like TF measures (see [14] for a symmetric TO measure). In [6] and [8] an asymmetric overlap measure is defined. There, this asymmetry is interpreted like a kind of precision and recall. But in [14] it was shown that no strictly monotonic dependency exists between that asymmetric TO measure and corresponding TP and TR measures. Thus the asymmetry can not be interpreted like precision and recall. It should be avoided to use asymmetric TO measures until the unclarity with regard to their interpretation is resolved. Instead corresponding taxonomic precision and recall measures should be used.

5 Evaluation

In this section the measures presented in 4.3 will be analytically and empirically evaluated. In the analytical evaluation it will be checked in how far they fulfill the criteria defined in section 3. Subsequently in the empirical evaluation, it will be shown in how far the choice of the measure influences the outcome of the evaluation of an ontology learning task.

5.1 Analytical Evaluation

First, it will be checked in how far the taxonomic measures are independent of the measures for the lexical term layer. This corresponds to the first criterion that a good set of measures allows an evaluation along multiple dimensions. Closely related to this criterion is the objective that each measure is independent of the other measures. The ontologies in Fig. 3 will be used for this purpose. Compared to $\mathcal{O}_{R2}$ there are three concepts missing in $\mathcal{O}_{C2}$, but the hierarchy of the remaining concepts is not changed. Also in $\mathcal{O}_{C3}$ the hierarchy is not changed but the natural language identifier of two concepts is changed (e.g. "car" is renamed to "auto"). Thus the hierarchy of both ontologies is perfectly learned but there are errors on the lexical term layer. This has to be reflected by taxonomy measures which are not influenced by errors on the lexical term layer.

As one can see in Tab. 4 and 5 only the measures TP_{csc} and TR_{csc} are independent of the lexical precision and recall. But this was already expected from the properties of the single building blocks of the taxonomic measures. It is more surprising to which extent the lexical precision and recall influence TP_{sc} and TR_{sc}. The errors on the lexical term layer of both learned ontologies lead to a higher decrease of the taxonomic measures than of the lexical measures. This can be seen by comparing the values of the taxonomic measures and of the lexical measures in Tab. 4. The values of the taxonomic measures are lower than the corresponding values of the lexical measures although the evaluated ontologies only contain errors on the lexical term layer.

The second criterion of good evaluation measures was that the effect of an error onto the measure should be proportional to the distance between the correct and the given result. This criterion will be checked with the ontologies in Fig. 4. There, in $\mathcal{O}_{C4}$, the

Table 4. Evaluation of the ontologies in Fig. 3 with a semantic cotopy based measure

Compare $\mathcal{O}_{R2}$ with	LP	LR	TP_{sc}	TR_{sc}	TF_{sc}	TF'_{sc}
$\mathcal{O}_{C2}$	100.00%	57.14%	100.00%	51.02%	67.57%	61.92%
$\mathcal{O}_{C3}$	71.43%	71.43%	54.25%	54.25%	54.25%	61.67%

Fig. 3. Reference ontology ($\mathcal{O}_{R2}$, left) and two learned ontologies ($\mathcal{O}_{C2}$, middle; $\mathcal{O}_{C3}$, right)

Table 5. Evaluation of the ontologies in Fig. 3 with a common semantic cotopy based measure

Compare $\mathcal{O}_{R2}$ with	LP	LR	TP_{csc}	TR_{csc}	TF_{csc}	TF'_{csc}
$\mathcal{O}_{C2}$	100.00%	57.14%	100.00%	100.00%	100.00%	72.73%
$\mathcal{O}_{C3}$	71.43%	71.43%	100.00%	100.00%	100.00%	83.33%

two concepts "car" and "bike" are interchanged, corresponding to an error near the root of the hierarchy. In $\mathcal{O}_{C5}$ the two leaf concepts "coupé" and "BMX" are interchanged. Altogether the errors in $\mathcal{O}_{C4}$ are more serious than the errors in $\mathcal{O}_{C5}$. Thus measures which fulfill this second criterion should rate $\mathcal{O}_{C4}$ worse than $\mathcal{O}_{C5}$. In Tab. 6 and 7 one can see that both pairs of measures fulfill this criterion.

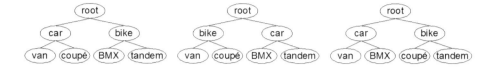

Fig. 4. Reference ontology ($\mathcal{O}_{R3}$, left) and two learned ontologies ($\mathcal{O}_{C4}$, middle; $\mathcal{O}_{C5}$, right)

Table 6. Evaluation of the ontologies in Fig. 4 with a semantic cotopy based measure

Compare $\mathcal{O}_{R3}$ with	LP	LR	TP_{sc}	TR_{sc}	TF_{sc}	TF'_{sc}
$\mathcal{O}_{C4}$	100.00%	100.00%	66.67%	66.67%	66.67%	80.00%
$\mathcal{O}_{C5}$	100.00%	100.00%	83.33%	83.33%	83.33%	90.91%

The third and last criterion of good evaluation measures was that a gradual increase in the error rate should lead to a more or less gradual decrease in the evaluation results. One can see from the previously given examples that TP_{csc} and TR_{csc} fulfill this criterion. Especially for the ontologies in Fig. 3 it returned perfect evaluation results. The opposite is true for TP_{sc} and TR_{sc}: Because these measures are influenced by errors in the lexical term layer as well as by errors in the concept hierarchy they will drop very fast if both kinds of errors occur in an ontology. Additionally it was shown that they are stronger influenced by errors in the lexical term layer than the lexical precision and recall measure itself.

TP_{csc} and TR_{csc} are all in all better suited for evaluating a concept hierarchy and drawing conclusions about the strengths and weaknesses of the used learning procedure.

Table 7. Evaluation of the ontologies in Fig. 4 with a common semantic cotopy based measure

Compare $\mathcal{O}_{R3}$ with	LP	LR	TP_{csc}	TR_{csc}	TF_{csc}	TF'_{csc}
$\mathcal{O}_{C4}$	100.00%	100.00%	52.38%	52.38%	52.38%	68.75%
$\mathcal{O}_{C5}$	100.00%	100.00%	76.19%	76.19%	76.19%	84.49%

5.2 Empirical Evaluation

In this section the previously described measures will be used in a real evaluation of concept hierarchies learned with Hearst patterns (cf. [15], [1]). In this evaluation it will be shown in how far the choice of the measure influences the lessons learned from evaluating an ontology learning task. For this evaluation, several ontologies for the tourism domain were learned from a corpus of 4596 tourism related Wikipedia articles with 6.54 million tokens. The reference ontology was created by an experienced ontology engineer within the GETESS project (see [16] and Tab. 9 for more details about the ontology). A more detailed description of the experiment and further results for ontologies learned with other learning procedures and from other document corpora are available for download [14].

Tab. 8 and 10 contain the evaluation results for the ontologies learned with the Hearst patterns applied on the Wikipedia corpus. The learned ontologies were compared with the GETESS reference ontology. These raw evaluation results should now be used for deciding for which threshold the best results were achieved. Both tables contain the results for the same ontologies but evaluated with the two different measures from section 4.3.

Table 8. Evaluation of learned ontologies with TP_{csc} depending on threshold θ

θ	LP	LR	TP_{csc}	TR_{csc}	TF_{csc}	TF'_{csc}
0.0	1.00%	49.66%	22.26%	83.81%	35.18%	41.18%
0.3	7.27%	22.79%	81.01%	59.60%	68.67%	34.22%
0.6	12.09%	11.22%	83.08%	62.11%	71.08%	19.39%
0.9	17.04%	7.82%	84.06%	73.85%	78.62%	14.23%

Looking at the results in Tab. 8 one can see that there is a major improvement of the taxonomic precision if the threshold is increased from 0.0 to 0.3. But this improvement on the taxonomic layer of the ontology is accompanied by a decrease of the lexical recall. According to the TF'_{csc} one would judge the unfiltered ontology better. But from the low lexical and taxonomic precision of the unfiltered ontology one may also conclude that it more or less "accidentally" contains correct lexical entries and taxonomic relations. So after a deeper analysis of the evaluation results one may come to the conclusion that a moderate filtering based on the confidence value should be applied.

This conclusion based on the results in Tab. 8 are also supported by the ontology's additional statistical values in Tab. 9. The first row of the table contains the values of the reference ontology against which the learned ontologies are compared. The following rows contain the statistical values of the learned ontologies. One can see that the

Table 9. Additional statistical values for the reference and the learned ontologies

θ	concepts	loops	avg. depth	avg. sub	sub. dev.	avg. super	super dev.
ref	294	1	5.14	5.22	4.42	1.03	0.17
0.0	14569	4973	119.29	3.57	53.2	1.52	2.2
0.3	893	97	3.8	2.81	14.89	1.22	0.87
0.6	246	24	3.29	2.68	8.39	1.16	0.78
0.9	116	2	3.17	2.76	6.06	1.08	0.35

unfiltered concept hierarchy contains 4,973 loops (i.e. a concept is also one of its superconcepts) and that a leaf concept has 119 superconcepts in average. Additionally, it is interesting to look at the branching factor of the hierarchy. There one can see that a concept has 3.57 direct subconcepts in average with a very high deviation of 53.2. Also the average number of direct superconcepts is quite high with 1.52 and a deviation of 2.2. All these statistical values show that the unfiltered ontology is more or less degenerated. Compared to these results the statistical values of the filtered ontologies are much better.

This exemplary evaluation with TP_{csc} and TR_{csc} shows that they allow to make conclusions about the real problems of a learned ontology and subsequently to identify the best parameters for optimizing the used learning procedure. It is now the question whether an evaluation with TP_{sc} and TR_{sc} leads to the same conclusions.

Looking at the evaluation results in Tab. 10 one may also draw the conclusion that a moderate filtering of the learned lexical entries and taxonomic relations improves the results because the best TF'_{sc} value is achieved for the ontology filtered with a threshold of 0.3. But it is not clear in how far this improvement is only caused by the changes on the lexical level (especially the improvement of the lexical precision) because the improvement of the taxonomy is superposed by the influence of lexical precision and recall on TP_{sc} and TR_{sc}. Thus, a truly multidimensional evaluation of the learned ontologies is impossible because the used measures are not independent of each other.

Table 10. Evaluation of learned ontologies with TP_{sc} depending on threshold θ

θ	LP	LR	TP_{sc}	TR_{sc}	TF_{sc}	TF'_{sc}
0.0	1.00%	49.66%	0.10%	27.84%	0.21%	0.41%
0.3	7.27%	22.79%	3.23%	8.67%	4.71%	7.80%
0.6	12.09%	11.22%	6.44%	3.61%	4.63%	6.55%
0.9	17.04%	7.82%	10.40%	2.53%	4.07%	5.35%

6 Conclusions

This paper presented a framework useful for gold standard based evaluation of ontologies. It was used for creating a new measure which allows to do a multi dimensional evaluation. Furthermore, it was ensured that errors are weighted differently based on their position in the concept hierarchy and that, compared to existing measures, the scale interval of the measure is used more evenly.

Acknowledgments

This work has been supported by the european projects Lifecycle Support for Networked Ontologies (NeOn, IST-2006-027595) and Semiotic Dynamics in Online Social Communities (Tagora, FP6-2005-34721).

References

1. Cimiano, P., Pivk, A., Schmidt-Thieme, L., Staab, S.: Learning taxonomic relations from heterogenous sources of evidence. In: Ontology Learning from Text: Methods, Applications, Evaluation. IOS Press (2005)
2. Spyns, P., Reinberger, M.L.: Lexically evaluating ontology triples generated automatically from texts. In: Proc. of the second European Conference on the Semantic Web. (2005)
3. Sabou, M., Wroe, C., Goble, C., Stuckenschmidt, H.: Learning domain ontologies for semantic web service descriptions. Journal of Web Semantics **3**(4) (2005)
4. Sabou, M., Wroe, C., Goble, C., Mishne, G.: Learning domain ontologies for web service descriptions: an experiment in bioinformatics. In: Proc. of WWW05. (2005)
5. Reinberger, M.L., Spyns, P.: Unsupervised text mining for the learning of dogma-inspired ontologies. (In: Ontology Learning from Text: Methods, Applications and Evaluation)
6. Maedche, A.: Ontology Learning for the Semantic Web. Kluwer, Boston (2002)
7. Maedche, A., Staab, S.: Measuring similarity between ontologies. In: Proc. of the European Conference on Knowledge Acquisition and Management (EKAW-2002). (2002)
8. Cimiano, P., Hotho, A., Staab, S.: Learning concept hierarchies from text corpora using formal concept analysis. JAIR – Journal of AI Research **24** (2005) 305–339
9. Maynard, D., Peters, W., Li, Y.: Metrics for evaluation of ontology-based information extraction. In: Proc. of the EON 2006 Workshop. (2006)
10. Hahn, U., Schnattinger, K.: Towards text knowledge engineering. In: Proc. of the 15th National Conference on Artificial Intelligence (AAAI-98). (1998)
11. Brank, J., Mladenic, D., Grobelnik, M.: Gold standard based ontology evaluation using instance assignment. In: Proc. of the EON 2006 Workshop. (2006)
12. Hartmann, J., Spyns, P., Maynard, D., Cuel, R., Carmen Suarez de Figueroa, M., Sure, Y.: Methods for ontology evaluation. Deliverable D1.2.3, Knowledge Web (2004)
13. van Rijsbergen, C.: Information Retrieval. Butterworths, London (1979)
14. Dellschaft, K.: Measuring the similiarity of concept hierarchies and its influence on the evaluation of learning procedures. Diploma thesis, Universität Koblenz-Landau (2005) http://www.uni-koblenz.de/FB4/Institutes/IFI/AGStaab/Theses/2005/DADellschaft.pdf.
15. Hearst, M.: Automatic aquisition of hyponyms from large text corpora. In: Proc. of the 14th International Conference on Computational Linguistics. (1992)
16. Staab, S., et al.: Getess - searching the web exploiting german texts. In: Proc. of the 3rd Workshop on Cooperative Information Agents. (1999)

Characterizing the Semantic Web on the Web*

Li Ding[1] and Tim Finin[2]

[1] Knowledge Systems Laboratory
Stanford University, Stanford CA 94305
ding@ksl.stanford.edu
[2] Computer Science and Electrical Engineering
University of Maryland, Baltimore County, Baltimore MD 21250
finin@umbc.edu

Abstract. Semantic Web languages are being used to represent, encode and exchange *semantic* data in many contexts beyond the Web – in databases, multiagent systems, mobile computing, and ad hoc networking environments. The core paradigm, however, remains what we call the *Web aspect* of the Semantic Web – its use by independent and distributed agents who publish and consume data on the World Wide Web. To better understand this central use case, we have harvested and analyzed a collection of Semantic Web documents from an estimated ten million available on the Web. Using a corpus of more than 1.7 million documents comprising over 300 million RDF triples, we describe a number of global metrics, properties and usage patterns. Most of the metrics, such as the size of Semantic Web documents and the use frequency of Semantic Web terms, were found to follow a power law distribution.

1 Introduction

Unpacking the phrase *Semantic Web* immediately produces its two constituent concepts: it is (i) a semantic framework to represent the meaning of data that is (ii) designed for use on the Web. Most current research, both basic and applied, has focused on the first of these and largely ignored the second. An obvious lesson from the last ten years of Web-based developments is we must not underestimate the impact of the (still emerging) Web on technology and society.

Reviewing recent papers in journals and conferences one finds many on all aspects of RDF and OWL as knowledge representation languages – complexity, scalability, completeness, efficient reasoning algorithms, integration with databases, rule extensions, expressing uncertainty, human friendly encodings, etc. Developing systems and tools that use these languages for ontology engineering, visualization, manual markup, etc. is also a popular topic. Finally, application papers typically center on using RDF based representations to express the knowledge and data needed for particular problem domains, such as workflow models, action descriptions, healthcare records, policy enforcement, or user preferences. For the most part, this work touches little on issues that stem for the (initial) intended use of Semantic Web languages for publishing and using ontologies and data on the World Wide Web.

---

* Partial support was provided by NSF awards ITR-IIS-0326460 and ITR-IDM-0219649.

A great deal of practical work has been done, of course, on developing Web appropriate standards for the Semantic Web and harmonizing them with existing Web standards and practices. Many applications and testbeds have also focused on core Web paradigms, such as semantically enhanced Web services and policy-driven negotiation for Web resource access. Our claim is that we need more research on modeling and understanding how Semantic Web concepts and technology is and can be used on the Web. In this respect, we stand on the shoulders of those who call for *"Creating a Science of the Web"* [1].

There are also many useful and important applications of Semantic Web languages and systems that do not involve the Web. RDF and OWL are used in agent communication languages [2], instant messaging [3], and in GIS systems [4], to name just a few. We believe that the *Web aspect* of the Semantic Web remains as the common, unifying vision, one in which millions of people, agents and applications publish and consume knowledge and data using the evolving Web standards and protocols [5].

In this paper, we focus on characterizing the Semantic Web on the Web, i.e., as a collection of loosely federated knowledge bases that are semantically encoded in Semantic Web languages but are physically published and consumed on the Web by independent agents. Our work consists of three parts:

- **designing a conceptual model.** Instead of using the current model of the Semantic Web, i.e., one universal RDF graph, our new model covers both structure (RDF graphs) and provenance (Web documents and associated agents).
- **creating a global catalog.** A global catalog of online Semantic Web data has long been desired but missing; therefore, we have developed effective harvesting methods and have accumulated a significant dataset.
- **measuring data.** Using our conceptual model, we measure the collected dataset to derive interesting global statistics and implications.

Related work. While some research has tried to characterize the reach and patterns of use of the Semantic Web on the Web, they have not attempted to be systematic and have used limited datasets.

Harvesting and simple summary. A number of simple systems have been designed to find and collect RDF documents on the web, including Eberhart's RDF crawler [6], OntoKhoj [7], the DAML Crawler [8]. Several repositories for Semantic Web documents have been created and maintained using a combination of manual and automatic techniques. These include the DAML Ontology Library [9] which collected a modest number of Semantic Web documents (at most 22,000) with a limited summary of document properties such as parse error types, document size, documents per website, and namespace building usage. Additional relevant work can be found in Web characterization literature [10,11] which studies global distributions of document properties such as the average size of web documents.

Characterizing the universal RDF graph. Gil et al. [12] analyzed the structure of a RDF graph that results from merging nearly 200 documents from the DAML Ontology Library. The dataset is too limited to be a representative of the entire Semantic Web and even the subset of ontologies on the Semantic Web.

Rating Semantic Web ontologies. Several studies have tried to measure the quality of Semantic Web ontologies, i.e. Semantic Web documents that define or contribute to the definition of classes and properties. Most [13,14] employ content analysis on ontologies with various foci, such as building a comprehensive evaluation framework [15], qualifying concept consistency [16,17], quantifying the graph structure of class and property taxonomy hierarchy [18,19,20,21], and measuring the structure and the instance space of a given ontology [22]. These studies have been limited in two ways. First, they have only analyzed ontologies, which we estimate account for only about 1% of the RDF documents on the Web. Second, the empirical evaluations are based on very small datasets, typically of fewer than 30 documents.

Characterizing social networks in FOAF. One of the most successful application of RDF is the use of the FOAF ontology to encode social networks. Several studies [23,24,25,26] have analyzed large amounts of FOAF data, typically by collecting FOAF documents via specialized crawlers and then making statistical measurements on vocabulary usage and network structure. Although the evaluation datasets are large, their sources and vocabularies are limited. Most FOAF documents are obtained from a few portal websites such as the *www.livejournal.com* blogging system.

Contributions. Our work is a systematic study of the semantic aspect and the web aspect of the Semantic Web. It is highlighted by contributing a new conceptual model of the Semantic Web on the Web, harvesting a significant dataset that is much larger and more diverse than other existing work, and inheriting and introducing wide spectrum of measurements for global properties on both semantic structure and knowledge provenance of the Semantic Web.

In section two of this paper we explain our conceptualization of the Semantic Web on the Web. Section three briefly illustrates our harvesting methods and evaluates the significance of harvest result. Sections four and five elaborate our metrics and findings about the global properties of the Semantic Web and section six offers some concluding remarks. In this paper, we assume, for simplicity's sake, that the following namespaces are defined: *rdf* for RDF, *rdfs* for RDF schema, *owl* for OWL, *foaf* for FOAF, *dc* for Dublin Core Element and *wn* for WordNet.

2 The Conceptual Model of the Semantic Web on the Web

The foundation for our Semantic Web characterization is the Web Of Belief Ontology which captures not only the semantic structure of RDF graph but also its provenance in terms of the Web and the agent world. This paper only covers the essential notions from the model and readers are invited to see [27] for details.

A **Semantic Web document** (SWD) is an atomic Semantic Web "data transfer packet" on the Web. It is both a Web page addressable by a URL and an RDF graph containing Semantic Web data. It can be a static or dynamic web page, for example one generated by a database query. In particular, SWDs can be divided into *pure SWDs* (PSWDs), which are completely written in Semantic Web languages, and *embedded SWDs* (ESWDs), which embed RDF graphs in their text content, e.g., HTML documents containing Creative Commons license metadata.

The *URI reference* (URIref) of an *rdfs:Resource* conveys dual semantics: (i) a unique identifier for the resource, and (ii) the Web address of the SWD defining the resource. URIrefs are widely used to merge RDF graphs distributed on the Semantic Web.

A resource's semantics depends on its usage in an RDF graph. In particular, we are interested in **Semantic Web terms** (SWTs), i.e., named resources that have **meta-usages** (being used as classes or properties) in SWDs. Six types of use are defined below and illustrated in Figure 1. For a given RDF graph, a resource X is:

- **defined as a class (DEF-C)** if there exists a triple of the form *(X, rdf:type, C)* where C is *rdfs:subClassOf rdfs:Class*. For example, *foaf:Person* is defined as a class in triple *t3*.
- **defined as a property (DEF-P)** if there exists a triple *(X, rdf:type, P)* where P is *rdfs:subClassOf rdf:Property*. For example, *foaf:mbox* is defined as a property in triple *t1*.
- **populated (or instantiated) as a class (POP-C)** if there exists a triple *(_a , rdf:type , X)* where *_a* can be any resource. For example, *rdfs:Class* has been populated as a class in triple *t3*.
- **populated (or instantiated) as a property (POP-P)** if there exists a triple *(_a , X , _b)* where *_a* and *_b* can be any resource (or literal). For example, *rdf:type* has been populated as a property in triple *t3*.
- **referenced as a class (REF-C)** if X is of type *rdfs:Class* according to the ontology constructs from Semantic Web languages except *rdf:type*. For example, *foaf:Person* is referenced as a class in triple *t2*.
- **referenced as a property (REF-P)** if X is of type *rdf:Property* according to ontology constructs from Semantic Web languages except *rdf:type*. For example, *foaf:mbox* is referenced as a property in triple *t2*.

Fig. 1. This RDF graph adapted from the FOAF ontology illustrates some of the relations defined in the *Web of Belief* ontology

Note that we may find multiple types of meta-usage of a URI in different SWDs, including some rare and undesired cases: the SWT *rdfs:subClassOf* is defined as a property by the RDFS ontology and also as a class by another SWD[1].

Two additional concepts are used studying ontologies. **Semantic Web Ontology** (SWO) is a sub-class of Semantic Web document and physically groups definitions of SWTs. An SWO is identified by containing (i) DEF-C, DEF-P, RDF-C, REF-P meta-usages or (ii) instances of *owl:Ontology*[2]. **Semantic Web Namespace** (SWN) is a sub-class of *rdfs:Resource* and logically groups SWTs and enables distributed definition (i.e., users can define the SWTs using the same SWN in different SWOs). An SWN is identified as the namespace part of an SWT.

---

[1] http://ilrt.org/discovery/2001/09/rdf-schema-tests/rdf-schema.rdfs
[2] The Swoogle system has experimented with different heuristics for identifying a SWD as an SWO and is currently using this very liberal one.

3 Creating a Global Catalog

In order to build a global catalog of the Semantic Web on the Web, we need to harvest publicly accessible SWDs. There are two primary difficulties: (i) SWDs are sparsely distributed on the Web and found on sites in varying density, e.g. *www.cnn.com* hosts no SWDs but *www.livejournal.com* has millions; and (ii) Confirming that a document contains RDF content requires RDF parsing which entails high cost when done for millions of documents.

3.1 Estimating the Number of Online SWDs

The scale and complexity of harvesting task is dominated by the number of online SWDs, which we have estimated using the Google search engine[3] Since Google does not index all SWDs and its estimated total result is coarse, we use it to derived an *order of magnitude* estimate of the total number of online SWDs.

In theory, the search query *"rdf"* would suffice because the RDF namespace is declared by virtually all SWDs. In pracice, however, this simple Google query has two problems. First, it does not cover all indexed SWDs. For example, many RSS 1.0 files, which are RDF documents, are not matched by it. Second, it matches many documents that are not SWDs. For example the query "rdf filetype:html" identifies more than 38 million HTML documents. Based on queries run on 12 May 2006, we estimate that there are between 10^7 and 10^9 Semantic Web documents online.

- For a conservative estimate we emphasize precision and use a query where most results will be SWDs. The query *"rdf filetype:rdf"* produced 4.91M estimated matches. The constraint "filetype:rdf" was chosen because it is the most common file extension used among SWDs, and more than 75% web documents using it are SWDs[4]. This yields a conservative estimate of 10^7 SWDs.
- For an optimistic estimate we emphasize recall using a query whose results will include most online SWDs. The query *"rdf OR inurl:rss OR inurl:foaf -filetype:html"* produces about 205M results. This derives an optimistic estimate of 10^9 SWDs.

3.2 A Hybrid Semantic Web Harvesting Framework

Most existing harvesting methods are limited in significance or diversity. Conventional Web crawling approaches [6,7] are inefficient because most hyperlinks in Web documents (including SWDs) point to conventional Web documents. Similarly, brute-force sampling, i.e., testing port 80 of reachable IP addresses [11], introduces prohibitive cost in validating millions of web documents. Meta-search based approaches [28] are limited by the inability to filter out conventional web documents from search engine results and the fact that some search engines intentionally ignore SWDs. Manual submission based approaches, such as that used for the DAML ontology library [9] and SchemaWeb [29] scale poorly and are difficult to maintain. RDF crawlers (also known as scutters[5] or

---

[3] We have found the Google and Yahoo search engines to have the most RDF documents indexed, with Google having more than twice as many as Yahoo.
[4] Other constraints usually returns fewer results, e.g. "owl filetype:owl" returns 55K results.
[5] See the Scutter specification at http://rdfweb.org/topic/ScutterSpec.

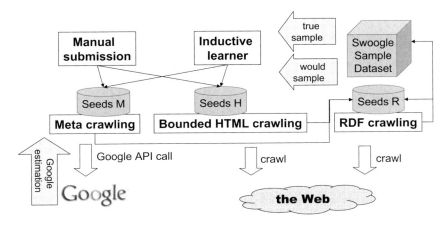

Fig. 2. The Swoogle system uses an adaptive Semantic Web harvesting framework with three different kinds of crawlers

Semantic Web crawlers) [30,31] are limited because the seeding URLs (i.e., the starting points of crawling) are hard to obtain and surfing heuristics (i.e., patterns for selecting hyperlinks to SWDs) are often biased.

In order to effectively harvest as many as possible SWDs on the Web with minimum cost, we developed a automatic, hybrid Semantic Web harvesting framework [27] that integrates several harvesting methods. Figure 2 illustrates its work-flow, which has the following major steps.

1. **Bootstrapping.** Manual submissions are used to bootstrap the harvesting, providing seeds for Google-based meta-crawling and bounded HTML crawling.
2. **Google-based Meta-crawling.** *Meta crawling* [32] involves directly harvesting URLs from search engines without crawling the Web. Google is chosen because it indexes the largest number of Web documents and offers richer query constraints than others. We collect seeds from manual bootstrapping input and the *inductive learner* that selects "good" seeds from the harvested *Swoogle sample dataset*. A "good" seed is a Google query whose results contain high percentage of SWDs, e.g., most URLs returned by the query *rdf filetype:rdf* are indeed SWDs.
3. **Bounded HTML crawling.** *HTML crawling* (i.e., conventional Web crawling) harvests web documents by extracting and following hyperlinks, and is useful in harvesting clusters of SWDs on the Web. Our *bounded HTML crawling* imposes some thresholds (e.g., search depth, maximum number of URLs, and minimum percentage of SWD) to limit search space and ensure efficiency. For example, we have harvested many PML documents[6] by a bounded HTML crawl starting at http://iw.standford.edu/proofs. Again, manual submission and automated inductive learner are involved in collecting seeding URLs.
4. **RDF crawling.** The *RDF crawler* enhances conventional HTML crawling by adding RDF validation and hyperlink extraction components. It visits newly discovered

---
[6] SWDs that populate instances of the Proof Markup Language(PML) ontology (http://inferenceweb.stanford.edu/2004/07/iw.owl).

URLs and periodically revisits pages to keep metadata current. For each URL, it tries to parse an RDF graph from the document using RDF parsers (e.g. Jena). If successful, it generates document level metadata and also enqueues the new discovered URLS that may link to SWDs.

5. **Inductive learner and Swoogle Sample dataset.** The sample dataset covers the metadata of the SWDs confirmed by RDF crawling. Based on the features (e.g. URL, term frequency, the source website) of harvested documents and their labels (e.g. whether they are SWD, embedded SWD or non-SWD), an automated inductive learner is used to generate new seeds for Google-based Meta-crawling and Bounded HTML crawling.

The crawler schedules its methods using the following harvesting strategies: (i) SWO harvesting has the highest priority since they are critical for users to encode and understand Semantic Web data; (ii) PSWDs are harvested with higher priorities than ESWDs because the former usually contain more Semantic Web data than the latter; and (iii) we delay harvesting URLs from websites where more than 10,000 SWDs have already been found (e.g., liveJournal) to avoid having the catalog dominated by SWDs from a few websites.

3.3 Harvesting Result and Performance

The dataset **SW06MAY** resulted from harvesting data between January 2005 and May 2006. It has 3,675,153 URLs, including 1,448,504 (40%) confirmed as SWDs, 13% confirmed as non-SWDs, 9% unreachable URLs, and 38% unpinged (not yet visited) URLs. The confirmed SWDs are from 162,245 websites[7] and contribute 279,461,895 triples. Although *SW06MAY* is much smaller than the Web with its 11.5 billion documents [33], it is much larger than any existing datasets, including:

- (2002) Eberhard [6] reported 1,479 valid SWDs out of nearly 3,000,000 URLs.
- (2003) OntoKhoj [7] reported 418 ontologies out of 2,018,412 URLs after 48-hour crawling.
- (2004) DAML Crawler reported 21,021 DAML files out of 743,017 URLs.

Significance of ontology discovery. SW06MAY contributes 83,007 SWOs including many unintended ones, such as (i) instance data with unnecessary class or property definitions or references, e.g., 55,565 (66.9%) *PML documents* from *onto.stanford.edu*, and 882 (1.1%) *semantic blog documents* from *lojjic.net*, and (ii) instance data that has unnecessary instances of *owl:Ontology*, e.g., 4,437 (5.3%) *publication metadata pages* from *www.aifb.uni-karlsruhe.de* and more *web portal metadata pages* from *ontoware.org*. Therefore, the "true" number of SWOs in SW06MAY is just 22,123 (26.7%) SWOs after removing the "unintended" ones. Moreover, this number can further reduced to 13,012 (15.7%) since there are many duplications[8].

---

[7] A website is uniquely identified by its domain name (host name part of a URL) but not it's IP address. Virtual hosting can result in one IP address hosting many web domains.

[8] We are currently detecting duplicate SWDs by simply comparing the md5sum of two target documents. While crude, the method is efficient and useful. For example, we have found 166 different SWDs having the same md5sum as the SWO *http://purl.org/dc/terms*. Trying to proving semantic equivalence is in general, not an option.

Significance of dataset growth. The significance of *SW06MAY* can be verified by its fast growth trend. Figure 3a shows the numbers of total URLs (*url*), *pinged URLs* (ping), confirmed SWDs (*swd*) *and confirmed pure SWDs* (pswd) discovered before the date on x-axis, and it exhibits a steady growing trend. The "ping" curve touches the "url" curve because our harvesting strategy delays harvesting URLs from websites hosting more than 10,000 URLs until all other URLs have been visited. The increasing gap between "ping" curve and "swd" curve indicates that harvesting recall increases at the expense of the decrease of precision.

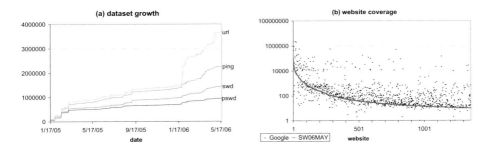

Fig. 3. The SW06MAY dataset has nearly 4M URLs collected from more than 160K sites. An analysis of the dataset demonstrates the growth in Semantic Web documents (left) and also provides evidence that our hybrid harvesting framework is sound (right).

Significance analysis on website coverage. We further evaluate the significance of *SW06MAY* by comparing its *website coverage* (i.e., the number of pure SWDs per website) with Google's estimation. In Figure 3b, each dot on the curve denotes the website coverage of one website that hosts at least ten pure SWDs. For each of the 1,355 websites in the graph, we use "Google" dots to show the optimistic Google estimation of website coverage with an additional "site" constraint, e.g., "(rdf OR inurl:foaf OR inurl:rss) -filetype:html site:www.cs.umbc.edu". The figure shows that Google's estimate, even with high variance, exhibits a trend similar to *SW06MAY*'s estimate. We conclude that the *SW06MAY* provides evidence in the basic soundness of our harvesting approach. Moreover, we suggest three causes of the variance: (i) Google's estimation may be too high since it is optimistic; (ii) The Google query site constraint searches all sub-domains of the site (e.g., site:w3.org also returns results from www4.w3.org), but *SW06MAY*'s results only return results from the specified site; and (iii) our harvesting framework may index fewer SWDs (see Google dots above the curve) because it uses far less harvesting seeds than Google and keeps a long "unpinged" list, or index more SWDs (see Google dots below the curve) because it complements Google's crawling limitation.

4 Measuring Semantic Web Documents

SWD Top-level Domains. Analyzing the top-level domains (TLDs) of SWDs suggests the degree to which Semantic Web data is published by region and type of organization.

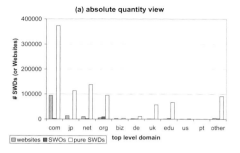
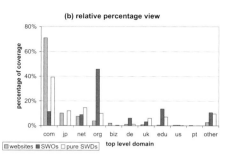

Fig. 4. An analysis of the SW06MAY dataset shows the distribution of SWDs and SWOs (after removing unintended ones) over selected top-level domains. Codes used are jp:Japan, de:Germany, uk:United Kingdom, us:United States, pt:Portugal, and other:remaining TLDs.

Using SW06MAY we calculated the number of websites, SWDs and pure SWDs for the top ten TLDs as shown in Figure 4. The TLDs are ordered by the number of websites. Figure 4a shows that pure SWDs dominate the Semantic Web while SWOs are few in number. Figure 4b reveals several points. First, the ".com" domains have contributed the largest portion of hosts (71%) and pure SWDs (39%). Examining the data indicated two reasons: ".com" sites make heavier use of virtual hosting technology and publish many RSS and FOAF documents. Second, most SWOs are from ".org" domains (46%) and "edu" (14%). This is likely due of the deep interests in developing ontologies from academic and non-profit organizations.

SWD Source Websites. Figure 5 depicts the cumulative distribution of the number of PSWDs per website. The curves do contain skewed parts: (i) the sharp drop at the tail of curve (near 100,000 on x-axis) is caused by our harvesting strategy that delays harvesting websites after finding more than 10K SWDs; and (ii) the drop at the head of curve is due to virtual hosting technology[9]. Interestingly, *livejournal.com* is involved in both. Both curves in Figure 5 show power law distribution and the similar parameters of the two regressed equations support the conclusion that the distribution is invariant.

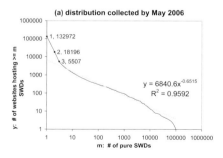
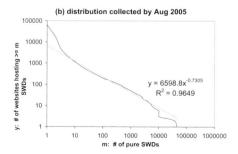

Fig. 5. Data from SW06MAY shows that the distribution of the number of websites hosting more than m pure SWDs follows a power law. The straight lines correspond to regression function with the given equations. The R^2 values close to one indicate good regressions.

---

[9] Many social networking sites offer each user a unique virtual host name.

Table 1. This table lists the ten largest source websites of pure Semantic Web documents (PSWDs) from May 2006. The *unpinged* column gives the number of URLs discovered on the site that are suspected of also being Semantic Web documents but have not yet been processed.

rank	website	# PSWDs	# unpinged	content
1	www.livejournal.com	100,518	88,962	foaf, personal profile
2	www.tribe.net	80,402	25,234	foaf
3	www.greatestjournal.com	62,453	849	foaf
4	onto.stanford.edu	45,278	403	pml, portal proof
5	blog.livedoor.jp	31,741	12,776	foaf
6	r622-1.mpiwg-berlin.mpg.de	25,733	136	vml annotation
7	www.ecademy.com	23,242	3,308	foaf
8	www.hackcraft.net	16,238	0	dc, book annotation
9	open.bbc.co.uk	14,544	350,473	dc, BBC program annotation
10	www.uklug.co.uk	13,263	2	rss

Table 1 lists the ten domains hosting the largest number of pure SWDs. The "content" column shows the topic of website, and the "unpinged" column indicates that we intentionally delay crawling some giant websites. SWDs from these websites are automatically generated and well inter-linked. The 6th and 9th websites are recently promoted to this list.

SWD Age. We measure an SWD's age by its last-modified time extracted from the HTTP response header. Figure 6a shows cumulative distribution of last-modified time, i.e., the number of PSWDs and SWOs with a last-modified before the date on X-axis. SWD's with no reported last-modified time are excluded. Note that the "pswd" curve exhibits an exponential distribution, indicating that many new PSWDs have been added to the Semantic Web or that many old ones are being actively modified. The "swo" curve additionally excludes PML documents and exhibits exponential distribution with a flat tail, which we interpret as indicating a more active ontology development earlier in the time period transitioning to more reuse later.

Figure 6b shows two distributions of last-modified time collected in Aug 2005 and May 2006 respectively. The difference before August 2005 represents a loss of 155,709 PSWDs and is due to documents going offline (25%) and being updated (75%). The difference after that is caused by updated documents and newly discovered PSWDs. The non-trivial at which PSWDs go offline significantly affects the growth of Semantic Web data.

SWD Size. We measure an SWD's size as the number of triples in the SWD's RDF graph. Figure 7a shows the distribution of SWD's size, i.e., the number of SWDs having exactly m triples, and Figure 7b the corresponding cumulative distribution. Figure 7c depicts the distribution of ESWD's size. Most ESWDs are very small with 62% having exactly three triples and 97% having ten or fewer triples. These contribute significantly to the big peak in Figure 7a. Figure 7d shows the distribution of the size of PSWDs, with most (60%) having five to 1000 triples. The peaks in the curve are caused by automatically generated SWDs which publish Semantic Web data in fixed patterns. For example, many PML documents have exactly 28 or 36 triples, and many

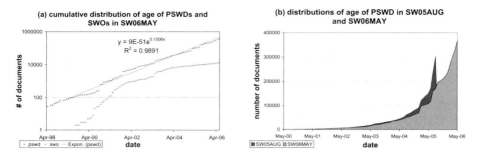

Fig. 6. Distributions of the last-modified time of PSWDs and SWOs

RSS documents have exactly 130 triples[10]. The large number of SWOs with fewer than four triples are mainly RDF and OWL test documents. SW06MAY's largest SWO[11] has 1,013,493 triples and defines 337,831 classes and properties.

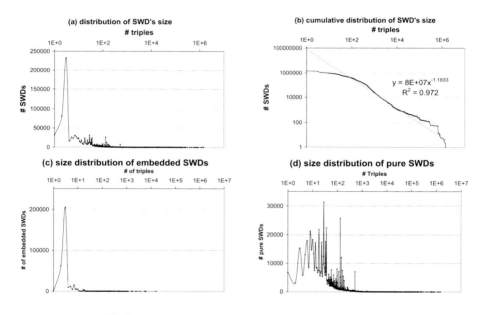

Fig. 7. The distributions of the number of triples per SWD

SWD Size Change. Updating a SWD usually result in in a change in its size. We have investigated this by tracking the size changes for different versions of an SWD. The *SW06MAY* dataset has 183,464 PSWDs that are alive (sill online) and for which we

---

[10] A typical RSS file has one *rss:channel* with eight triples, fifteen *rss:item* instances each with seven triples, and one *rdf:Seq* with seventeen triples connecting the *rss:channel* to the item instances.

[11] http://www.fruitfly.org/~cjm/obo-download/obo-all/ncbi_taxonomy/ncbi_taxonomy.owl

have at least three versions. For these, 37,012 (20%) lost a total of 1,774,161 triples; 73,964 (40%) gained a combination of 6,064,218 triples, and the rest 72,488 (40%) maintained their original size[12]. The statistics also show that the total number of triples keeps increasing; therefore, we hypothesize the volume of Semantic Web data is increasing.

5 Measuring Semantic Web Terms

Semantic Web Terms (SWTs) are classes and properties that are named by non-anonymous URIrefs. The *SW06MAR* dataset has 1,576,927 distinct Semantic Web terms defined with respect to 14,488 Semantic Web namespaces. We derive four SWT-usage patterns by analyzing the combination of six basic types of meta-usages.

- Only a few classes (1.5%) and properties (1.0%) have both explicit definitions and instances.
- Most SWTs (95.1%) have no instances, and some SWTs (2.2%) have no definitions.
- Some SWTs (0.08%) mistakenly have both class and property meta-usage.
- Some SWTs (0.08%) only have REF-C or REF-P meta-usages. While some are *XMLSchma* terms and not RDF, others appear to be due to errors or misuse.

SWT Definition Complexity. A simple way to measure the complexity of a SWT is to count the number of triples used to define it. Figure 8a shows the cumulative distribution of the size of SWT definitions in the curve labeled "all". This follows a power law distribution with the deviations at the head and tail reflecting a preference for defining SWTs using a manageable number of triples, two to ten triples in most cases. Terms that can be defined in just a few triples are not very useful, and the definitional size of complex terms can be reduced by defining and using auxiliary definitions. One observed definition has nearly 1000 triples[13]. We've divided definitional triples into two classes: annotation and relation triples, whose *rdf:object*s are *rdfs:Literal*s and *rdf:object*s, respectively. Note that relation triples are more common. We also noticed that 104,152 SWTs have been defined in more than one SWOs.

SWT Instance Space. Since Semantic Web data include both definitions and instance data, we measure the instance space of the Semantic Web by counting POP-C and POP-P meta-usages of SWTs[14]. Figure 8b shows the cumulative distribution of the number of SWTs populated as a class (or property) by at least m instances (or SWDs). All four curves follow a power law distribution. For both classes and properties, most are defined but never directly used. Only 423 classes have been instantiated by more than 100 SWDs and just 2,115 have more than 100 instances. The number of properties used is somewhat higher, with 1,489 SWTs used to define data in more than 100 SWDs and 5,404 properties used in more than 100 assertions.

---
[12] Most of the PSWDs maintaining their size are RSS documents.
[13] The SWD http://elikonas.ced.tuc.gr/ontologies/DomainOntologies/middle_ontology defines the *MOSemanticRelationType* class using 973 triples.
[14] Since no RDFS or OWL inferencing is done, the statistics reflect immediate class instances.

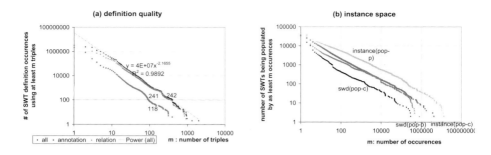

Fig. 8. The cumulative distribution of meta-usages of SWT

Table 2 lists popular classes and properties. The number of an SWT's class-instances is usually proportional to the number of SWDs populating the SWT; however, exceptions exist. For example, while the *wn:Noun* class has significant number of instances, they are mostly in a few huge SWDs. In general, the Semantic Web's instance space is dominated by three categories: (i) instances of meta-ontologies such as OWL, (ii) instances of a small number of very popular ontologies such as DC, FOAF, and RSS; and (iii) instances from giant data files, such as WordNet and National Library of Medicine's Medical Subject Headings (MeSH) ontology.

Table 2. This table shows the most popular Semantic Web classes and properties based on the number of Semantic Web documents (SWDs) that use them and, for classes, also on the number of immediate instances.

resource URI	#swd	#instance
Most instantiated classes ordered by #swd		
http://xmlns.com/foaf/0.1/Person	499,671	11,686,519
http://www.w3.org/1999/02/22-rdf-syntax-ns#Seq	290,321	308,907
http://purl.org/rss/1.0/channel	282,677	289,160
http://purl.org/rss/1.0/item	259,220	4,277,868
http://xmlns.com/foaf/0.1/Document	223,510	247,311
Most instantiated classes ordered by #instance		
http://xmlns.com/foaf/0.1/Person	499,671	11,686,519
http://purl.org/rss/1.0/item	259,220	4,277,868
http://www.cogsci.princeton.edu/~wn/schema/Noun	56	3,697,400
http://www.w3.org/2002/07/owl#Class	68,053	1,795,941
http://www.nlm.nih.gov/mesh/2004#Concept	38	1,551,046
Most instantiated properties ordered by #swd		
http://www.w3.org/1999/02/22-rdf-syntax-ns#type	1,170,975	43,291,848
http://purl.org/dc/elements/1.1/title	801,254	13,448,548
http://xmlns.com/foaf/0.1/mbox_sha1sum	462,198	2,633,739
http://purl.org/dc/elements/1.1/description	453,826	2,874,327
http://www.w3.org/2000/01/rdf-schema#seeAlso	432,288	12,330,223

RDFS and OWL usage. To what degree does the current Semantic Web make use of RDFS and OWL? One simple way of addressing this question is to examine the number of SWDs that use the RDFS and OWL namespaces. The OWL namespace has been declared by 112,870 SWDs (8%) and actually used by 108,059 (7%). The RDFS namespace enjoys more use, being declared by 677,049 (47%) and used by 537,614 (37%) SWDs.

What about their terms? Not surprisingly, *owl:Class* is the most used term from the OWL namespace with 1,795,941 instantiations in 68,053 SWDs. Contrasting this with *rdfs:Class*, which has 327,485 instantiations by 8,572 SWDs, seems to suggest that OWL is being more heavily used than RDFS. However, the relationship is not so simple. When examining properties, rdf:Property has 529,052 immediate instantiations from 58,598 SWDs, considerably more than the OWL property terms owl:ObjectProperty (169,885 assertions in 8,041 SWDs) and owl:DatatypeProperty (48,386 assertions in 4,557 SWDs).

For RDFS and OWL properties, the most used properties is *rdf:type*, followed by some annotation properties such as *rdfs:seeAlso* and *rdfs:label*. Among those properties that are used as ontology constructs, *owl:sameAs* and *rdfs:subClassOf* are the most used. We also noticed significant use of two OWL equality assertions: *owl:sameAs* (279,648 assertions in 17,425 SWDs) and *owl:equivalentClass* (69,681 assertions in 4,341 SWDs). Their common use may be an indication of increased ontology alignment. We have found limited use of properties that require OWL DL or OWL FULL reasoning support. The most common one in our dataset was *owl:unionOf* which is used in only 2,527 SWDs.

Instantiation of *rdfs:domain*. Semantic Web data is published asynchronously by autonomous and distributed agents which may use, and misuse, a variety of ontologies. Given enough data, we can attempt to reverse-engineer the definitions of classes and terms introduced by ontologies. Consider instances of the *rdfs:domain* relation which associates a class with properties that describe its instances. We have observed 111,071 unique instantiations of *rdfs:domain*, and the number of instantiations that have been observed in at least m instances (or SWDs), again, follows a power law distribution.

The highly instantiated *rdfs:domain* relations are mainly from popular instance space such as FOAF and RSS documents. An interesting observation is that *rdfs:seeAlso* property has been frequently used as *instance property* of *foaf:Person*. This corresponding definition cannot be found in the RDFS or FOAF ontologies although it has been informally mentioned in FOAF specification. The popularity of instantiation is usually determined by the number of SWDs that has the instantiation; moreover, we also noticed a popular instantiation – the domain of *wn:wordFrom* is *wn:Noun* which has over 6.5 million occurrences in only 56 SWDs.

We can use data on the instantiations of *rdfs:domain* relation to derive the most used properties of a given class. For example, for immediate *foaf:Person* instances, the most common properties used are *foaf:mbox_sha1sum* (461,922 SWDs), *rdfs:seeAlso* (385,516), and *foaf:nick* (361,901). We can also find strong co-occurrence association among properties of a class. The properties *geo:lat* (85,742) and *geo:long* (85,741) are virtually always used together in modifying a class *geo:Point*. This kind of information can be used to help publishers choose a good set of properties, which may be from different ontologies, for a given class. Moreover, we can use such information in ontology revision, e.g., adding the missing *rdfs:domain* definition or revise incompatible definition.

6 Conclusions

The Semantic Web is not just one universal RDF graph but a federated collection documents distributed on and accessed via the World Wide Web. It must be studied from both the *Web perspective* and the *semantic perspective*. In order to characterize the Semantic Web on the Web and guide Web-scale data access, we estimated the size of the Semantic Web using Google, implemented a hybrid framework for harvesting Semantic Web data, and measured the results to answer questions on the Semantic Web's current deployment status.

The statistics where characterized by power law distributions and "complex system" behavior in many cases and, in general, support several conclusions about the emerging Semantic Web. (i) Semantic Web data is growing steadily on the Web even when many documents are only online for a short-while. (ii) The space of instances is sparsely populated since most classes (>97%) have no instances and the majority of properties (>70%) have never been used to assert data. (iii) Ontologies can be induced or amended by *reverse engineering* the instantiations of ontological definition in instance space [27].

Our work raises question about the current paradigm for ontologies and URIrefs. Is the concept of an "ontology" as a collection or container for Semantic Web terms needed or even useful? An ontology object encourages self consistency but introduces some limitations as well. Recent work on ontology partitions argues against large, monolithic ontologies in favor of having many interconnected components. We might even eliminate namespaces as boundaries. For example, the Dublin Core Element ontology has been widely used together with terms from many other semantic web ontologies. Another debatable item is the URIref. We use triples to annotate an URIref that is an identifier of a resource. Multiple RDF graphs from different documents describing the same URIref can introduce inconsistency. Integrating these definitions may encounter several questions: (i) are URIrefs good enough for grouping the triples describing it; (ii) can we ensure that all of the graphs are accessible to consumers; and (ii) should all be used or should some be rejected as untrustworthy.

References

1. Berners-Lee, T., Hall, W., Hendler, J., Shadbolt, N., Weitzner, D.J.: Creating a science of the web. Science **313** (2006) 769–771
2. Zou, Y., Finin, T., Ding, L., Chen, H., Pan, R.: Using Semantic web technology in Multi-Agent systems: a case study in the TAGA Trading agent environment. In: Proceeding of the 5th International Conference on Electronic Commerce. (2003)
3. Franz, T., Staab, S.: Sam: Semantics aware instant messaging for the networked semantic desktop. In: Proceedings of the ISWC 2005 Workshop on The Semantic Desktop - Next Generation Information Management and Collaboration Infrastructure. (2005)
4. Visser, U., Stuckenschmidt, H., Schuster, G., Vogele, T.: Ontologies for geographic information processing. Computers and Geoscience **28** (2002) 103–117

5. Berners-Lee, T., Hendler, J., Lassila, O.: The semantic web. Scientific American **284** (2001) 35–43
6. Eberhart, A.: Survey of rdf data on the web. Technical report, International University in Germany (2002)
7. Patel, C., Supekar, K., Lee, Y., Park, E.K.: OntoKhoj: a semantic web portal for ontology searching, ranking and classification. In: WIDM'03. (2003)
8. Dean, M., Barber, K.: Daml crawler. http://www.daml.org/crawler/ (August 2006) (2002)
9. DAML: The DAML ontology library. http://www.daml.org/ontologies/ (August 2006) (2004)
10. Pitkow, J.E.: Summary of www characterizations. Computer Networks **30** (1998)
11. Lawrence, S., Giles, C.L.: Accessibility of information on the web. Nature **400** (1999)
12. Gil, R., Garca, R., Delgado, J.: Measuring the semantic web. SIGSEMIS Bulletin **1** (2004)
13. Hartmann, J., Sure, Y., Giboin, A., Maynard, D., del Carmen Surez-Figueroa, M., Cuel, R.: Methods for ontology evaluation. Technical report, University of Karlsruhe (2004)
14. Gangemi, A., Catenacci, C., Ciaramita, M., Lehmann, J.: A theoretical framework for ontology evaluation and validation. In: Proc. of the 2nd Italian Semantic Web Workshop. (2005)
15. Lozano-Tello, A., Gomez-Perez, A.: ONTOMETRIC:a method to choose the appropriate ontology. Journal of Database Management **15** (2003)
16. Welty, C.A., Guarino, N.: Supporting ontological analysis of taxonomic relationships. Data Knowledge Engineering **39** (2001)
17. Parsia, B., Sirin, E., Kalyanpur, A.: Debugging owl ontologies. In: WWW'05. (2005)
18. Magkanaraki, A., Alexaki, S., Christophides, V., Plexousakis, D.: Benchmarking RDF schemas for the semantic web. In: ISWC'02. (2002)
19. Supekar, K., Patel, C., Lee, Y.: Characterizing quality of knowledge on semantic web. In: FLAIRS'02. (2002)
20. Alani, H., Brewster, C.: Ontology ranking based on the analysis of concept structures. In: K-CAP'05. (2005)
21. Yao, H., Orme, A.M., Etzkorn, L.: Cohesion metrics for ontology design and application. Journal of Computer Science **1** (2005)
22. Tartir, S., Arpinar, I.B., Moore, M., Sheth, A.P., Aleman-Meza, B.: Ontoqa: Metric-based ontology quality analysis. In: Proc. of Workshop on Knowledge Acquisition from Distributed, Autonomous, Semantically Heterogeneous Data and Knowledge Sources. (2006)
23. John C. Paolillo and Elijah Wright: The Challenges of FOAF Characterization. In: Proc. of the 1st Workshop on Friend of a Friend, Social Networking and the (Semantic) Web. (2004)
24. Grimnes, G.A., Edwards, P., Preece, A.: Learning meta-descriptions of the foaf network. In: ISWC'04. (2004)
25. Mika, P.: Social Networks and the Semantic Web: An Experiment in Online Social Network Analysis. In: Proc. of International Conference on Web Intelligence. (2004)
26. Ding, L., Zhou, L., Finin, T., Joshi, A.: How the semantic web is being used:an analysis of foaf. In: Proceedings of the 38th International Conference on System Sciences. (2005)
27. Ding, L.: Enhancing Semantic Web Data Access. PhD thesis, UMBC (2006)
28. Zhang, Y., Vasconcelos, W., Sleeman, D.: Ontosearch: An ontology search engine. In: Proc. of 24th Conf. on Innovative Techniques and Applications of Artificial Intelligence. (2004)
29. Lindesay, V.: The schemaweb repository. http://www.schemaweb.info/ (August 2006) (2005)
30. Biddulph, M.: Crawling the semantic web. In: XML Europe. (2004)
31. Apsitis, K., Staab, S., Handschuh, S., Oppermann, H.: Specification of an RDF Crawler. http://ontobroker.semanticweb.org/rdfcrawl/help/specification.html (March 2006) (2005)
32. Sherman, C.: Metacrawlers and metasearch engines. http://searchenginewatch.com/links/-article.php/2156241 (March 2006) (2004)
33. Gulli, A., Signorini, A.: The indexable web is more than 11.5 billion pages. In: WWW'05 (poster). (2005)

MultiCrawler: A Pipelined Architecture for Crawling and Indexing Semantic Web Data

Andreas Harth, Jürgen Umbrich, and Stefan Decker

National University of Ireland, Galway
Digital Enterprise Research Institute
`firstname.lastname@deri.org`

Abstract. The goal of the work presented in this paper is to obtain large amounts of semistructured data from the web. Harvesting semistructured data is a prerequisite to enabling large-scale query answering over web sources. We contrast our approach to conventional web crawlers, and describe and evaluate a five-step pipelined architecture to crawl and index data from both the traditional and the Semantic Web.

1 Introduction

The enormous success of Google and similar search engines for the HTML web has demonstrated the value of both crawling and indexing HTML documents.

However, recently more and more information in structured formats such as XHTML, microformats, DC, RSS, Podcast, Atom, WSDL, FOAF, RDF/A etc. has become available – and we expect this trend to continue. In conjunction with Semantic Web based RDF data, these data formats are poorly handled by current search engines: for instance, query answering based on keywords does not allow to exploit the semantics inherent to structured content. Consequently, current well developed and understood web crawling and indexing techniques are not directly applicable, since they focus almost exclusively on text indexing.

In other words, to be able to answer queries which exploit the semantics of Semantic Web sources, different crawling and indexing techniques compared to conventional search engines are necessary. The differences between conventional crawling/indexing approaches and crawling/indexing heterogeneous semantic data sources can be summarized as follows:

1. *URI extraction.* HTML crawlers extract links from HTML pages in order to find additional sources to crawl. This mechanism usually does not work as straightforwardly for structured sources, since very often there exists no direct concept of a hyperlink. Therefore different methods for extracting URIs must be found.
2. *Indexing.* Conventional text indexes for the HTML web are well understood. However, these text indexes perform poorly at capturing the structure and semantics of heterogeneous sources, e.g., a FOAF file or an RSS source. A different way for indexing and integrating the various data formats is needed.

These two key differences illustrate the need for new approaches compared to traditional web crawling. A pipelined document indexing infrastructure has already been defined and analyzed (see [8]). However, the same approach is not applicable for Semantic Web data due to the variety of stages and different time and space behavior.

The main contributions of this paper are:

- Following the general approach of [8] we define a pipelined approach for the Semantic Web with respect to structured data crawling and indexing. The pipeline can be adapted to arbitrary content.
- We define a general URI extraction method from structured sources that helps to find more sources for indexing.
- We describe a general representation format for heterogeneous data on the web which allows indexing and answering of expressive queries.
- We describe an implementation of our pipelined architecture and determine the optimal configuration of the entire pipeline to maximize parallel processing and crawling.
- We evaluate the pipeline by conducting experiments on a cluster.

The remainder of this paper is organized as follows: In Section 2 we give an overview of the architecture. Section 3 describes the processing pipeline in detail, including complexity analysis and experimental results derived from each individual phase. In Section 4, we analyze the results, discuss tradeoffs for distributing the pipeline to multiple machines and running multiple pipelines in parallel. Section 5 covers related work and Section 6 concludes the paper.

2 Crawler and Indexer Architecture

When designing a crawler and indexer architecture a number of requirements need to be taken into account:

- *Performance and scalability.* The architecture needs to be as performance oriented as possible in order to handle data on a web-scale and keep up with the increase in structured data sources. The system should scale up by adding new hardware – without a fundamental redesign.
- *Utilizing data from different formats and disparate sources.* The system has to syntactically transform and index data from different web sources to arrive at an integrated dataset.

Text indexing software pipelines have been investigated by [8] as a means to optimize and decouple the crawling and indexing process. The pipelined architecture in [8] has lead to considerable performance improvements. We have adopted the pipelined architecture and defined a *software pipeline* for Semantic Web data crawling and indexing. The idea behind a software pipeline is to improve performance by executing different steps concurrently.

Our crawling algorithm is an adaption of the standard breadth-first search algorithm. Najork and Wiener [10] argue that breadth-first crawling yields high-quality pages early on in the crawling process.

Fig. 1. Five phases for crawling and indexing Semantic Web data

The process of crawling and indexing Semantic Web data can be logically split into 5 phases, as illustrated in Figure 1. We refer to these phases as *fetch*, *detect*, *transform*, *index*, and *extract*. During the fetch phase, the information is fetched from the web. The detect phase detects the type of the content, eg. RDF, WSDL, GIF etc. The transform phase is a key difference compared to conventional text indexing and translates the data into the common data format. The index phase builds an index, which is used during the extract phase to query for URIs to more information sources.

We provide a rationale for some of the different phases in more detail.

Detect. A challenge in dealing with multiple data formats is to be able to accurately detect the content type and format of documents. Most of the data formats can be detected by using the file extension or the content-type returned with the header part of an HTTP request. In the case of XML files, the MIME type and the file extension give indication for XML content, but do not give any information about whether the content is well-formed, or which schema is used. Sometimes this information is important, therefore the content itself has to be investigated.

Transform. Since we are aiming at a general indexing and querying infrastructure we need mechanisms to extract information from the files and transform them to a structured representation. Ideally, we would like to use a declarative transformation language so that users can define transformations without the need to write code in a procedural language. However, the system should be also able to use procedural language code to extract data from binary data or natural language text, ultimately arriving at a representation of the metadata.

To describe transformations in a declarative way, we decided to use XSL Transformations (XSLT)[1]. With XSLT we are able to translate arbitrary XML content to RDF. Even though XSLT is Turing complete [5] and therefore might be too expressive, using XSLT has the benefit of permitting the reuse of already available stylesheets. Besides, it is possible to integrate GRDDL[2], a recent effort which aims at standardizing the mechanism of using XSLT to extract information from web pages.

Index. An index over the data can be used to extract links and finally perform searches and answer queries. The index should enable keyword-based searches because that is a good method to explore a dataset with unknown structure. Equally important we require an index on the graph structure for the ability to pose structured queries.

Extract. For extracting URIs, we decided to use an RDF query against the final cleaned and structured dataset. We perform URI extraction at the end of

---

[1] http://www.w3.org/TR/xslt
[2] http://www.w3.org/TeamSubmission/grddl/

the pipeline, since at that stage the indexes over a uniform representation of the data have been built already and we are able to extract URIs cheaply. Depending on the crawling strategy (only crawl one site, perform shallow crawling and only take external links into account, etc), we can adapt queries to extract URIs. We need to extract links also from HTML pages, otherwise we will not discover the URI of structured pages, since files with structured data are currently not well interlinked. URIs to structured sources appear mainly in `a href` links within HTML documents.

To be able to scale, we need to parallelize and distribute the system. Fetching the data takes much less time than processing. Thus, we want to perform steps in parallel, which means we have to use multiple threads that fetch data and multiple threads that process data etc. Communication between the steps is done via queues. If we want to scale up the process even further, we replace threads with multiple computers, queues with remote/persistent queues, and pipes with network data transfer. As a result, we are able to speed-up the entire process even more. Besides, in the distributed setup it is easy to identify bottlenecks – and resolve them by adding new machines to a phase. Another benefit of a distributed architecture is that it facilitates the integration of external components (i.e., web services) into the process.

Our goal is to analyze the complexity of the single tasks and to find the right balance in server ratios to keep the average utilization of the servers as high as possible. In the next section we describe each processing step, investigate the complexity and present experimental measurements.

3 Processing Pipeline

In this section, we describe each step in the processing pipeline in detail. The processing pipeline is composed of five different modules, each of which is capable of running the task in a multi-threaded fashion. First, the fetching module downloads the content and header information of a web page. Second, the detecting module determines the file type of the web page. Third, based on the file type, the transformation module converts the original content into RDF. Fourth, the indexing module constructs an index over the RDF data to enable URI extraction. Fifth, the extracting module poses a query over the index to extract URIs and feeds the resulting URIs back into the pipeline.

To be able to pass parameters between different phases, the system needs to store information associated with the URIs. We put the metadata associated with a URI as RDF triples in a metadata store which runs on a separate machine.

Each phase has an associated queue which contains URIs of pages to be processed. Each phase takes a URI from the queue, retrieves the content from a previous phase if necessary, processes the content, stores the content on disk, and puts the URI into the queue corresponding to the next step in the pipeline. Content is passed to successive steps via an Apache HTTP server.

In the following sections, we include complexity analysis and experimental results for each step. We carried out the experiments using a random sample of 100k URIs obtained from the Open Directory Project[3]. We performed all experiments on nodes with a single Opteron 2.2 GHz CPU, 4 GB of main memory and two SATA 160GB disks. The machines were interconnected via a 1GBbp network adapter on a switched Ethernet network.

3.1 Fetching Data

The functionality of the fetching module includes obtaining a new URI from the queue, checking for a `robots.txt` file to adhere to the Robots Exclusion Protocol[4], and fetching and storing header information and content.

After obtaining the next URI from the queue, we retrieve the `robots.txt` information for the host either from the metadata store or directly from the host. Then we determine if the fetcher is allowed to crawl the page or not. If the URI passes the check, we look at the content length provided by the header information. To avoid downloading very large files we compare the content-length from the header-field with a given file size threshold.

If the URI passes all these checks, we connect to the web server and download the content of the page. Then we store or update the header information on the metadata store. Finally, we send the URI to the next module in the pipeline and return to the beginning, to poll the next URI from the queue.

To provide an estimate of the complexity of the step, let N be the size of the documents fetched, including header information. The fetch step needs to transfer N bytes from the Internet, which takes linear time in the size of the content, $O(N)$.

We verified the complexity analysis experimentally. We chose randomly 100k URIs from ODP's collection of over 5M sites. Figure 2 shows the experimental results for the crawling component resulting in 78038 downloaded pages (1.4 GBytes of data). The fetching component achieved an average download rate of around 600 KBytes/sec.

3.2 Detecting File Types

The detecting module tries to determine the exact content type of the data, which is used in the transformation phase to execute the right transformation module. The type detection is based on the information we are able to derive from the URI, the header fields and the content of the page itself.

In the first step of the file type detection process we try to detect the content type based on the file extension of the URI. The second step retrieves the content-type header field from the metadata store and compares the header field to a list of content types. Table 1 lists all supported content types and the information the system needs to detect them. If one of these checks successfully detects a type, we can stop the process and store the type on the metadata repository. In case of XML content, we perform another check to figure out the schema of this XML file. In this case we must parse the content itself.

---
[3] http://dmoz.org/
[4] http://www.robotstxt.org/wc/exclusion.html

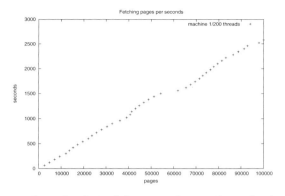

Fig. 2. Experimental results derived from crawling 100k randomly selected URIs

Table 1. File types the system is currently able to handle

TypeID	RFC	MIME media type	File extension	Root element
HTML	2854	text/html	.html .htm	html
XHMTL	3236	application/xhtml+xml	.xhtml	`xhtml:html`
XML	3023	text/xml application/xml	.xml	-
RSS2.0	-	application/rss+xml	.rss	rss
Atom	4287	application/atom+xml	.atom	`atom:feed`
RDF	3870	application/rdf+xml	.rdf	`rdf:RDF`

If we detect XML content, we try to find out the special type of the XML content, that is, we retrieve the content data from the file system and parse it with a SAX XML parser. We try to extract namespaces and root element of the XML file and compare the values to the known content types. If all checks fail, we assume an unknown or unsupported content type. Finally, we store the type on the metadata store and forward the URI to the next pipeline module.

During the complexity analysis, we do not consider the simplest case where we can detect the file type based on file extension or header information. Let N be the size of the XML document which content type we want to detect. Parsing the XML content utilizing SAX to retrieve the root element has a time complexity of $O(N)$.

Figure 3 shows the experimental results for the file type detection phase.

3.3 Transforming to RDF

For transforming the content into the common data format RDF, the system applies different transformation modules depending on the type of the content. The transformation phase can be split into two steps: (i) conversion from non-XML data, such as HTML, into XML by using user specified transformation tools and (ii) transformation of XML data to RDF via XSLTs and xsltproc[5].

---
[5] http://xmlsoft.org/XSLT/

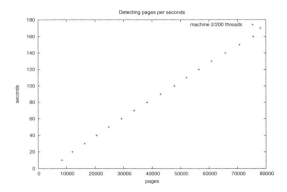

Fig. 3. Experimental results for detecting file types

For a given URI we retrieve the content type, which has been added in the detect phase, from the metadata store. Depending on the result of the query, we execute different transformation modules on the content. Naturally, if the data format is already RDF, we can skip the transforming step.

To transform non-XML data, we can call out to external services which convert the data directly into XML or RDF. At the moment our support for non-XML data consists only of cleaning up HTML using the tool Tidy[6] running as a cgi-bin on a HTTP server, but various external services for extracting metadata from e.g. image or video files can be easily plugged in.

To transform XML data, we use xsltproc with an XSLT from the file system, depending on the type identifier of the page. We use an XSLT that transforms RSS 2.0 and Atom to RDF[7]. We also developed an XSLT[8] which transforms XHTML pages into an RDF representation based on RDFS, DC, and FOAF vocabularies. In this stylesheet we extract from a HTML document the following information: title, email addresses, images, and relative and absolute links and their anchor labels.

After the URI passes successfully all transformation steps, we pass it to next step of the pipeline.

The worst case scenario when performing the transforming step is in dealing with HTML documents, because we must first pass the content to Tidy and then perform the XSLT transformation. Imagine a document of size N and a XSLT stylesheet of size M. We assume Tidy takes time linear to the size of the content $O(N)$. The worst-case complexity for XPATH has shown to be $O(N^4 * M^2)$ [5], however, for a large fragment called Core XPath the complexity is O(N*M). Our XHTML XSLT uses only simple Core XPath queries, therefore the worst-case complexity for the step is O(N*M).

Figure 4 shows the experimental results for the transformation component utilizing the xhtml2rdf.xsl and rss2rdf.xsl stylesheets. Using 200 threads as in all other tests, the transformation performance decreased rapidly after around

---

[6] http://tidy.sourceforge.net/
[7] http://www.guha.com/rss2rdf/
[8] http://sw.deri.org/2006/05/transform/xhtml2rdf.xsl

13k pages because the machine was assigned with too many transformation tasks and had to swap. Therefore we plotted only the first 60 minutes of running time. We repeated the tests with only 50 threads to not overload the machine. In the end, the transformation step yields 907Mbytes of XHTML resulting in 385Mbytes RDF/XML.

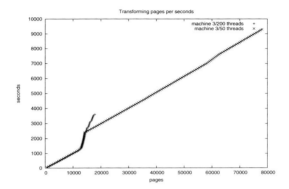

Fig. 4. Experimental transformation performance using 50 and 200 threads

3.4 Building Indexes

We summarize the index organization and building process here. For a more detailed description of the index organization we refer the interested reader to a previous paper [6]. Please observe that we operate on an extension of the RDF data model which includes the notion of context to store the provenance of RDF triples. Tracking provenance is achieved by adding a fourth field and therefore using quadruples.

The goal of the index structure is to support efficient evaluation of *select-project-join* queries. The selection operation enables the retrieval of quads, given any combination of subject, predicate, object, and context. To be able to perform the quad retrieval with just one index lookup, the index organization uses a complete index on quads which covers all 16 possible access patterns on quadruples. Conceptually, we have (key, value) pairs stored in a B+ tree, which allows to perform lookups – especially prefix and range lookups – on keys. We also use an inverted index on string literals to allow to search the index via keyword-based searches.

The index structure contains two sets of indexes: the *Lexicon* covers the string representation of the graph, and the *Quad Index* covers the quads. The Lexicon maps values of resources and literals to objects identifiers (OIDs) using two B+ tree indexes for node/OID mapping. In addition we employ an inverted index for string literals. The quad index covers the triples of the graph plus context. We use concatenated keys on all combinations of subject, predicate, object, and context and therefore are able to retrieve any combination with a single index lookup without performing joins.

When the indexer receives a quad for indexing, it first performs lookups for each element of the quad in the Lexicon to either retrieve its OID or assign a new OID. New OIDs are assigned monotonically for each new quad element. In case the element is a string literal, we include the string literal in the inverted index. Next, the keys for the quad are constructed based on the OIDs of the individual elements of a quad. Given our index organization with concatenated keys and prefix lookups, we only need six indexes to cover all 16 quad patterns [6]. In total, given our index organization, there are 6 keys for insertion into the 6 indexes.

The two indexes mapping from quad element values and back are implemented in Berkeley DB JE[9]. Additionally, we store string literals in Apache Lucene[10] for textual search. The quad indexes are maintained in Berkeley DB as well, with one index acting as the primary index and five secondary indexes, to implement a complete index on quadruples.

Since index construction is technically involved, we will describe the time complexity in more detail. Let N be the size of the input in RDF/NTRIPLES, N_L the number of Lexicon entries, N_K the number of words per Lexicon entry, M_L the order of the Lexicon B trees, N_T the number of quadruples and M_T the order of the B+ tree with respect to the quads. First, the system performs OID lookups/assignments in the Lexicon which is largely determined by the input size of the data $O(N*4*2*log_{M_L}N_L)$, next creates a text index in Lucene over the newly added string literals which takes $O(N_L*N_K)$ time, and finally adds the quads into the respective B+ trees $O(N*6*log_{M_T}N_T)$.

Figure 5 shows the experimental results for constructing the index on the 26906 pages that were transformed without errors resulting in 76.3MBytes of data in RDF/NTRIPLES format (and a total of 571915 triples).

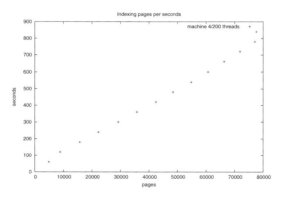

Fig. 5. Performance for indexing the syntactically integrated dataset

3.5 Extracting URIs

To feed the processing pipeline with new URIs we have to extract URIs from the indexed content, which is done in the extracting module. The process can

---
[9] http://www.sleepycat.com/products/bdbje.html
[10] http://lucene.apache.org/

be divided into two steps. The first step is to extract URIs from the data and the second step is to filter the URIs to make sure only URIs matching specified criteria get processed.

To extract new URIs we execute a query on the index for typical link predicates such as `rdfs:seeAlso` and `rss:link`. We are able to perform conjunctive queries, which are evaluated by translating a N3QL[11] query expression to a relational algebra expression to an executable query plan.

If an extracted URI is to be added to the queue, we pass this URI through the installed filter. In this filter we can restrict which URI should be sent to the fetching module. If we want to crawl only a domain or a set of domains, we can filter the addition of URIs using regular expressions. These expressions are stored in memory. It is also possible to add new expressions during the runtime to the filter.

The main functionality for the link extraction phase is the processing of (conjunctive) queries utilizing the index. Let N_L the number of Lexicon entries, M_L the order of the Lexicon B+ trees, N_T the number of quadruples, M_T the order of the B tree with the quads, M the number of conjuncts in the query, and R the result size. We first sort the conjuncts starting with the conjunct which contains the least number of variables taking $O(MlogM)$ time, then detect the join conditions (similar to union-find) $O(MlgM/2)$, translate the elements of the quads to OIDs which can be done in $O(4*M*log_{M_L}N_L)$, perform the selections on the index and index nested loops joins, $O(log_{M_T}N_T{}^M)$, and finally translate the resulting OIDs to element values, which takes $O(R*log_{M_L}N_L)$.

Figure 6 shows the experimental results for the extraction component. We discuss the results of all phases in the next section.

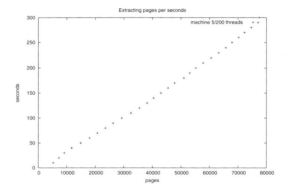

Fig. 6. Experimental link extraction performance

4 Analysis and Tradeoffs

In the following we analyze the performance results for the five phases of the pipeline process and discuss two questions: i) how to distribute the individual

---

[11] http://www.w3.org/DesignIssues/N3QL.html

phases to remove potential bottlenecks and fully utilize the processing power of each machine and ii) how to run multiple pipelines in parallel to achieve a throughput of the total system which can be calculated by: *number of pipelines * pipeline throughput*.

Currently, the transform phase represents the bottleneck in the pipeline and can only process a fraction of the pages delivered by the fetch and detect phase. The random sample of URIs are biased towards HTML data, which means that during the transform phase almost every page has to be processed. If we are able to reduce the amount of HTML and XML sources and increase the amount of RDF sources, the transform phase has to process less pages and as a result the throughput (in terms of time per page) increases. However, given the fact that the majority of content on the web is in HTML format, we have to distribute the transform component to achieve acceptable performance.

Assuming an architecture as described in this paper, we can distribute phases by just adding more machines. Pages are assigned to nodes using a hash function. In initial experiments we observed that we can scale up the fetch step by a constant factor if we add more fetcher machines and all fetcher nodes take URIs concurrently from the queue. The case is a bit different for the transform step; here, we employ one thread pool with individual threads which retrieve a URI from the previous step in the pipeline and invoke Tidy and XSLT operations on cgi-bins running on a web server. In other words, while the other phases employ a pull model, inside the transform component tasks are pushed to external processors. We chose the push model because the ability to include external transformation services was a requirement.

Figure 7 shows the performance results where all steps and external processors run on one node, where one node was used for the steps and two nodes for external processors (1+2), and the case where four external processors (1+4) were used. Why was the scale-up not constant in the number of machines added? The reason is that the hash function assigns the pages equally to the external processors. In case a single page takes a very long time to process, the external

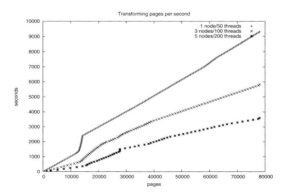

Fig. 7. Performance measurement for the transform phase with 1, 3 (1+2), and 5 (1+4) transform nodes

processor node cannot keep up with the assigned operations and at some point in time needs to swap, which leads to a decrease in performance.

Apart from the issues described for the transform steps, we claim all other steps can be scaled by a constant factor (number of machines added) using a hash function to distribute URIs to nodes since URIs in those phases can be processed independently. Table 2 shows the throughput in pages per second for each phase, and a ratio that determines which fraction of the stream (assuming that the fastest component determines the throughput) one node can process.

Table 2. The number of servers and the achieved performance. Ratio is calculated based on the fasted phase (1 = 460 pages/sec).

Phase	Servers	Pages/sec	Ratio.
fetch	1	38	0.082
detect	1	460	1.0
transform	1	5	0.011
transform	1+2	13	0.028
transform	1+4	21	0.045
index	1	92	0.2
extract	1	260	0.565

To be able to scale up the system even further, we can just employ more pipelines and achieve a total throughput which can be calculated by multiplying the number of pipelines with the throughput achieved on one pipeline. The limit is then only determined by how many resources (Internet bandwidth and number of machines) are available.

5   Related Work

There are two types of related work to our framework: the first consist of large scale web crawling and indexing systems, and the second are systems extracting information from semistructured sources.

Crawler frameworks such as UbiCrawler [2] or Mercator [7] are focused on the performance of the crawling step only. Google [3] handles HTML and some link structure. We focus less on crawling but on detecting Semantic Web data, the transformation of XHTML and XML to RDF and the indexing.

A few efforts have been undertaken to extract structured content from web pages, but these efforts differ considerably in scale. Fetch Technologies' wrapper generation framework[12] and Lixto [1] are examples of commercially available information extraction tools. Lixto defines a full-fledged visual editor for creating transformation programs in their own transformation language, whereas we use XSLT as transformation language and focus on large-scale processing of data.

---

[12] http://www.fetch.com/

Fetch (similarly [9]) combine wrapper generation and a virtual integration approach, whereas we use a data warehousing approach and therefore need scalable index structures.

SemTag (Semantic Annotations with TAP) [4] perform mostly text analysis on documents, albeit on a very large scale. In contrast, we extract structured information from documents and XML sources, and combine the information with RDF files available on the web.

6 Conclusion

We have presented a distributed system for syntactically integrating a large amount of web content. The steps involved are crawling the web pages, transforming the content into a directed labelled graph, constructing an index over the resulting graph, and extracting URIs that are fed back into the pipeline. We have shown both theoretical complexity and experimental performance of the five-step pipeline. We are currently working on performing a long-term continuous crawl and testing the system on larger datasets.

Acknowledgements

We thank Hak Lae Kim for discussing various requirements related to RSS crawling and Brian Davis for commenting on an earlier draft of this paper. This work is supported by Science Foundation Ireland (SFI) under the DERI-Lion project (SFI/02/CE1/l131). We gratefully acknowledge an SFI Equipment Supplement Award.

References

1. R. Baumgartner, S. Flesca, and G. Gottlob. Visual Web Information Extraction with Lixto. In *Proceedings of 27th International Conference on Very Large Data Bases*, pages 119–128, September 2001.
2. P. Boldi, B. Codenotti, M. Santini, and S. Vigna. UbiCrawler: a Scalable Fully Distributed Web Crawler. *Software: Practice and Experience*, 34(8):711–726, 2004.
3. S. Brin and L. Page. The Anatomy of a Large-Scale Hypertextual Web Search Engine. *Computer Networks*, 30(1-7):107–117, 1998.
4. S. Dill, N. Eiron, D. Gibson, D. Gruhl, R. Guha, A. Jhingran, T. Kanungo, S. Rajagopalan, A. Tomkins, J. A. Tomlin, and J. Y. Zien. SemTag and Seeker: Bootstrapping the Semantic Web via Automated Semantic Annotation. In *Proceedings of the Twelfth International World Wide Web Conference*, pages 178–186, May 2003.
5. G. Gottlob, C. Koch, R. Pichler, and L. Segoufin. The Complexity of XPath Query Evaluation and XML Typing. *Journal of the ACM*, 52(2):284–335, 2005.
6. A. Harth and S. Decker. Optimized Index Structures for Querying RDF from the Web. In *Proceedings of the 3rd Latin American Web Congress*, pages 71–80. IEEE, 2005.

7. A. Heydon and M. Najork. Mercator: A Scalable, Extensible Web Crawler. *World Wide Web*, 2(4):219–229, 1999.
8. S. Melnik, S. Raghavan, B. Yang, and H. Garcia-Molina. Building a Distributed Full-Text Index for the Web. In *Proceedings of the 10th International World Wide Web Conference*, pages 396–406, 2001.
9. M. Michalowski, J. L. Ambite, S. Thakkar, R. Tuchinda, C. A. Knoblock, and S. Minton. Retrieving and Semantically Integrating Heterogeneous Data from the Web. *IEEE Intelligent Systems*, 19(3):72–79, 2004.
10. M. Najork and J. L. Wiener. Breadth-First Crawling Yields High-Quality Pages. In *Proceedings of the Tenth International World Wide Web Conference*, pages 114–118, May 2001.

/facet: A Browser for Heterogeneous Semantic Web Repositories

Michiel Hildebrand, Jacco van Ossenbruggen, and Lynda Hardman*

CWI, Amsterdam, The Netherlands
`firstname.lastname@cwi.nl`

Abstract. Facet browsing has become popular as a user friendly interface to data repositories. The Semantic Web raises new challenges due to the heterogeneous character of the data. First, users should be able to select and navigate through facets of resources of any type and to make selections based on properties of other, semantically related, types. Second, where traditional facet browsers require manual configuration of the software, a semantic web browser should be able to handle any RDFS dataset without any additional configuration. Third, hierarchical data on the semantic web is not designed for browsing: complementary techniques, such as search, should be available to overcome this problem. We address these requirements in our browser, /facet. Additionally, the interface allows the inclusion of facet-specific display options that go beyond the hierarchical navigation that characterizes current facet browsing. /facet is a tool for Semantic Web developers as an instant interface to their complete dataset. The automatic facet configuration generated by the system can then be further refined to configure it as a tool for end users. The implementation is based on current Web standards and open source software. The new functionality is motivated using a scenario from the cultural heritage domain.

1 Introduction

Facet browser interfaces provide a convenient and user-friendly way to navigate through a wide range of data collections. Originally demonstrated in the Flamenco system [1], facet browsing has also become popular in the Semantic Web community thanks to MUSEUMFINLAND [2] and other systems [3]. An individual facet highlights one dimension of the underlying data. Often, the values of this dimension are hierarchically structured. By visualizing and navigating this hierarchy in the user interface, the user is able to specify constraints on the items selected from the repository. To use an example from the art domain: by navigating the tree associated with a "location created" facet from the root "World", via "Europe" to "Netherlands", the results set is constrained to contain only paintings that have been painted in the Netherlands. By combining constraints from multiple facets, a user is able to specify relatively complex queries through an intuitive Web navigation interface. All values of a dimension that would lead to an over-constrained query are dynamically removed from the interface, preventing the user from running into frustrating dead ends containing zero results.

---
* Lynda Hardman is also affiliated with the Technical University of Eindhoven.

We are working on repository exploration in the context of a national e-culture project [4]. Our project's goals are similar to those of MUSEUMFINLAND, and aim at providing a syntactic and semantic interoperable portal to on-line collections of national museums. A major difference, however, is that we work with each museum's original metadata as much as possible. This means, for example, that we do not map all metadata relations of the various museums to a common set of ontological properties, nor do we map all metadata values to terms from a common thesaurus or ontology.

Initially, we experimented with traditional facet browsers, which assume a fixed set of facets to select and navigate through relatively homogeneous data. This, however, conflicts with our approach for the following reasons. First, our dataset is too diverse to use a single set of facets: facets that make perfect sense for one type of resource are typically inappropriate for other types. A related problem is that we cannot fix the facets at design time. When new data is added, the system should be able to add new facets at run time. This requires an extension of the facet paradigm to cater for resources of multiple types, to associate a set of appropriate facets to each type dynamically and to navigate and search larger sets of facets. Second, we use a rich and extensive set of art-related background knowledge. As a result, users expect to be able to base their selection not only on facets of museum artifacts, but also on facets from concepts from the background knowledge, such as artists and art styles. This requires two other extensions: one that allows users to switch the topic of interest, for example from artworks to art styles; and another one that allows selection of resources of one type based on the facets of another. For example, a set of artworks can be selected based on the properties (facets) of their creators.

This article discusses these extensions as they are realized in /facet, the browser of the project's demonstrator[1]. The article is structured as follows. The next section introduces a scenario to illustrate the requirements for enhanced facet-browsing across multiple types. Section 3 discusses the requirements in detail and section 4 explains our design solutions in a Web-based interface. Section 5 discusses related work and open issues.

2 Example Scenario

Throughout the paper, we use examples from the art domain. The system itself, however, is domain independent and used on several other domains[2]. The scenario is divided in two parts: the first part illustrates typical usage of facet browsers; the second part illustrates search tasks that go beyond the current state of the art and introduce new requirements for facet browsers.

Our protagonist is Simon, a high school student who recently visited the Dutch Kröller-Müller museum. The museum's collection features several works

---

[1] See [4] for a more detailed description and http://e-culture.multimedian.nl/demo/facet for an on-line demo of /facet.
[2] Demos on various domains are available at the /facet website http://slashfacet.semanticweb.org/

from Vincent van Gogh. Back at home, Simon has to write an essay on post-impressionism. He remembers seeing a particular post-impressionist painting but can no longer remember the name of the painter nor the title of the painting. The only thing he remembers is that the painting depicted a city street at night time. He uses a facet browser to restrict the search space step by step. He selects the current location of the painting (Kröller Müller), the art style of the painting (post-impressionist), its subject type (cityscape), and the subject time (night). He finds the painting he was looking for among the few results matching his constraints (Vincent van Gogh's "Cafe Terrace on the Place du Forum").

He now wants to further explore the work of Van Gogh, and selects this painter from the creator facet, and resets all previous selections. The interface displays the 56 paintings from Van Gogh that are in the repository. The facets now only contain values of the remaining paintings. For example, the create location facet instantly shows Simon that van Gogh made paintings in the Netherlands and in France, and how many in each country. Simon asks the system to group the results on create location and notices the significant difference in the color palette Van Gogh used in each country. By selecting "France" he zooms in further to explore potential differences on the city level.

In addition to the types of browsing possible in typical facet browsers, Simon also wants to explore works from painters born in the area of Arles. Unfortunately, the artworks in the repository have not been annotated with the birthplace of their creator. Simon uses multi type facet browsing and switches from searching on artworks to searching on persons. The interface now shows the facets available for persons, which include place of birth. Searching on Arles, he sees that four painters with unfamiliar names have been born here, but that the repository does not contain any of their works. Expanding his query by navigating up the place name hierarchy, he selects artists from the Provence-Alpes-Côte d'Azur, the region Arles is part of. He quickly discovers that Paul Cézanne, a contemporary of Van Gogh, was born in Aix-en-Provence in the same region.

Simon reaches his original goal by switching back from searching on persons to searching on artworks. Despite this switch, the interface allows him to *keep* his constraint on Provence-Alpes-Côte d'Azur as a place of birth. It thus shows only artworks created by artists that were born in this region.

Backstage area. The experimentation environment in which /facet was developed, contains sufficient data to cover the scenario above. It uses a triple store containing three different collections with artwork metadata: the collection of the Dutch National Museum of Ethnology[3], the ARIA collection from the Rijksmuseum[4], and Mark Harden's Artchive collection[5]. RDF-versions of WordNet[6] and

---

[3] http://www.rmv.nl/
[4] http://www.rijksmuseum.nl/collectie/, thanks to the Dutch CATCH/CHIP project (http://chip-project.org/) for allowing us to use their translation of the dataset to RDF.
[5] http://www.artchive.com/
[6] http://www.w3.org/2001/sw/BestPractices/WNET/wn-conversion.html

the Getty AAT, ULAN and TGN thesauri[7] are also included. For the annotation schema, we use Dublin Core[8] and VRA Core 3[9].

In total, the store contains more than 10.8 million RDF triples. Artwork images are served directly from the websites of the museums involved. All the collection metadata has been converted to RDF, with some minimal alignment to fit the VRA Core 3 schema. In addition, explicit links were created from the art works to the Getty thesauri: literal names of painters and other artists were automatically converted to a URI of the ULAN entry; literal names of art styles and art materials to a URI of the AAT entry; and literal place names to a URI of the TGN entry. For example, in the scenario, some `vra:Works` have a `dc:creator` property referring to the painter `ulan:Person` Paul Cézanne, born in `tgn:Place` Aix-en-Provence in the `tgn:Region` of Provence-Alpes-Côte d'Azur. Additionally, some artworks have been manually annotated using concepts from the Getty thesauri and WordNet. In the remainder of the paper, we will use the following prefixes for the corresponding namespaces: `wn`, `aat`, `tgn`, `ulan`, `vp`, `dc` and `vra`.

3 Requirements for Multi-type Facet Browsing

While the second half of the scenario sketches a seemingly simple means of accessing information, a number of issues have to be addressed before it can become a reality. Most facet browsers provide an interface to a single type of resource. Including multiple types, however, leads to an explosion in the number of corresponding properties and thus the number of available facets. A facet browser still needs to be able to present instances of all the types and allow a user to select a particular type of interest. In addition, the relations between the types also need to be made explicit and selectable by the user. To a large extent, the requirements we discuss are a direct consequence of these two key points.

3.1 Dynamically Selecting Facets

Fortunately, a first way to deal with the increased number of facets lies in the facet paradigm itself. One of the key aspects of all facet browsers is that, while constraining the dataset, all links that would lead to an over-constrained query are automatically removed from the interface, thus protecting the user against dead ends. As a consequence, if no instance in the current result set has a particular property, the facet associated with this property is removed from the interface. In our multiple type scenario, this means that if two types have no properties in common, the entire set of facets displayed is replaced when the user switches from one type to the other.

Facets in context of the `rdfs:subClassOf` hierarchy. For most classes that have no subclasses, just hiding facets of properties that have no corresponding

---
[7] http://www.getty.edu/research/conducting_research/vocabularies/, used with permission
[8] http://dublincore.org/documents/dcq-rdf-xml/
[9] http://www.w3.org/2001/sw/BestPractices/MM/vra-conversion.html

instances will result in an interface with a set of facets that intuitively belong to instances of that class[10]. For the superclasses, however, it is not immediately obvious what this "intuitive" set of facets is.

A first possibility is to associate with a specific class the *union* of the facets of its subclasses. This has the advantage that users can immediately start browsing, even if they have selected a class too high up in the hierarchy. By selecting a facet that only applies to instances of one of the subclasses, the result set is automatically constrained to instances of the intended class. A major drawback is that the number of facets displayed rapidly grows when moving up the class hierarchy, culminating in the complete set of all facets for rdf:Resource.

An alternative is to use the *intersection* of the facets of the rdfs:subClassOf hierarchy. This has the advantage that the user only sees facets that are common to all subclasses, and in practice these are, from the perspective of the superclass, often the most important ones. A drawback is that when moving up the hierarchy, one quickly reaches the point where the intersection becomes empty, leaving no facet to continue the search process. This forces the user to navigate down the class hierarchy to return to a usable facet interface.

A final possibility is to view the association of a set of facets with a certain class as an aspect of the personalization of the system. While personalization is one of the key aspects in our project, it is beyond the scope of this paper.

Facets in context of the rdfs:subPropertyOf hierarchy. As described above, the rdfs:subClassOf hierarchy helps to reduce the number of facets by only showing facets that are relevant to a particular class. A similar argument applies to the rdfs:subPropertyOf hierarchy. On the one hand, the property hierarchy worsens the problem by introducing even more facets: in addition to the facets corresponding to the "leaf node" properties, their superproperties also become facet candidates. On the other hand, the property hierarchy also provides an opportunity for an interface to organize and navigate the property (and thus the facet) hierarchy, allowing the user to select facets as part of the interaction.

3.2 Search in Addition to Navigation

While the beauty of facet browsing lies in the ease of constructing queries by navigation, an often heard critique is that navigating deep tree structures is complex, in particular for users who are not expert in the domain modeled by the hierarchy. A second critique is that facet browsers become complex in applications with many facets and when users do not know what facets to use for their task. Multi-type facet browsing only makes this problem worse, by radically increasing the number of facets in the system. A search interface in addition to the navigation interface is thus required, and the two interaction styles should be well integrated and complement each other.

---

[10] For simplicity, we ignore the question of whether or not to show sparsely populated properties, of which only a few instances have values.

3.3 Creating Multi-type Queries

The example of selecting artworks created by artists born in a particular region requires a facet on a resource of one type (`ulan:Person`) to be applied to find resources of another type (`vra:Work`). This is just one example of how such combinations can be used to exploit background knowledge in the selection process.

Using facets across types only makes sense if the resources involved are semantically related so the browser is required to know which relation to use. For the end user, the power of the facet interface lies in the ease of combining multiple facets to construct a complex query. This should be no different in a multi-type browser. So in addition a transparent interface needs to be available to easily constrain a dataset of one type, based on facets of another type.

3.4 Run-Time Facet Specification

Manual definition of relevant facets and hard-coding them in a facet browser might be feasible for homogeneous datasets. This approach does not scale, however, to heterogeneous datasets, where typically each type of resource has its own set of associated facets. Even for simple applications, the total number of facets might rapidly grow to several hundreds. Instead of hard-coding the facets in the browser software, some means is needed to externalize the facet definitions and make them configurable independently from the software. This simplifies maintenance and, by simply reloading a new configuration, allows adding and changing facets at runtime. The system also needs to be able to derive facet configurations from the dataset automatically. This allows the facet browser to run instantly on any dataset without prior manual configuration, while also allowing later manual refinement of the generated configuration. The latter is important, since it allows developers to tune the interface for specific end users, who might not be best served by a generic tool that gives access to all data.

3.5 Facet-Dependent Interfaces

A typical facet browser visualizes the possible values of the facet either as a hierarchy or as a flat list. Related interfaces, such as those of mSpace [5] and Piggybank [6], have shown that some facets are better shown using a more specialized visualization or interaction technique, such as geographical data displayed in an interactive map. To be able to tune a generic, multi-type facet browser to a tool for end-users that have a specific task in a specific domain, we require a mechanism for supporting visualization and interaction plug-ins.

4 Functional Design for Multi-type Facet Browsing

We have explored the design consequences of these requirements in /facet. This section explains and motivates our design decisions in the prototype.

Fig. 1. Snapshot of the /facet GUI. vra:Work has been selected in the type facet on the left, so only facets applicable to artworks are visible. Simon has restricted the results to have tgn:Arles as the place of creation. The interface shows Simon that the four matching paintings are created by either ulan:Gauguin or ulan:Van Gogh (picked from a flat list of artists), and that all four have aat:post-impressionist as the art style (shown in the context of its place in the AAT hierarchy).

4.1 Browsing Multiple Resource Types

To support facet search for all resource types, the /facet user interface needs a way to search for resources other than artworks[11]. A natural and convenient way to integrate such functionality is by regarding the rdf:type property as "just" another facet. The facet applies to all resources and the values from its range are typically organized by the rdfs:subclassOf hierarchy, allowing navigation just as for any other facet. Since the semantics of this facet is derived directly from that of rdfs:type, by making a selection users indicate the type of resource they are interested in. This constraint automatically selects which other facets are also active.

This is illustrated in Figure 1, which shows the upper half of the /facet interface. On the left is the type facet with a part of the domain's class hierarchy. Simon has already selected artworks (e.g. resources of rdf:type vra:Work) and, as a result, only facets applicable to artworks are available from the facet bar at the top. Simon has expanded three of these from submenus of the facet bar: Creation Site, Creator and Style/Period. He selected "Arles" in the Creation Site facet. Apparently, the dataset contains only four resources of type vra:Work that were painted in Arles, indicated next to the selected type and location tgn:Arles. Simon has made no selections in the Creator and Style/Period facets, indicating that all four paintings are "post-impressionist" and that one painting is by Gauguin and three are by Van Gogh.

4.2 Semantic Keyword Search

In Figure 1, the art style's full path in the AAT concept hierarchy is automatically unfolded because all paintings with "Arles" as the Creation Site share the same style "post-impressionist". Showing the tree structure has the advantage

---
[11] We still use artworks as the default type to give users a familiar interface when starting up the browser.

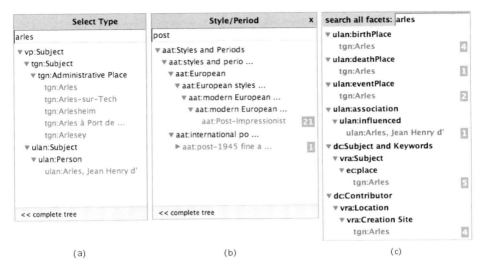

Fig. 2. Three types of keyword suggestion and search. (a) show search on all instances, helping to select the right type. (b) shows search within a single facet, helping to move in complex facet hierarchies. (c) searches across all active facets, showing the user the different uses of the keyword "Arles" in different facets.

that Simon could quickly select related art styles by simply navigating this hierarchy. This illustrates a well-known disadvantage of navigating complex tree structures: if Simon had instead started by selecting the art style, he would need to have known the AAT's art style classification to navigate quickly to the style of his choice, which is hidden six levels deep in the hierarchy.

To overcome this problem, we added a keyword search box to each facet, with a dynamic suggestion facility, (b) in Figure 2. This allows Simon to find the style of his choice based on a simple keyword search. This interface dynamically starts suggesting possible keywords after Simon has typed a few characters. Note that the typical "no dead ends" style of facet browsing is retained: only keywords that produce actual results are suggested. Backstage, this means that in this case the suggested keywords are picked from the (labels of) concepts under the AAT "Style and Periods" subtree that are associated with art works in the current result set. In practice, the intended keyword is typically suggested after only a few keystrokes. This makes the interaction often faster than navigating the tree, even for expert users who know the tree structure by heart.

The keyword search discussed above addresses the problem of navigation difficulties within the hierarchy of a single facet. Another problem could be picking the right facet in the first place. The keyword search box shown in (c) of Figure 2 addresses this problem. It provides the same search as the facet keyword search in (b), only across all facets of the selected type. For the figure, no type was selected and all facets have been searched. Arles is suggested as a TGN concept used in the facet corresponding to the `vra:location.creationSite` property (for paintings created in Arles), but also as the place used in the facet of the

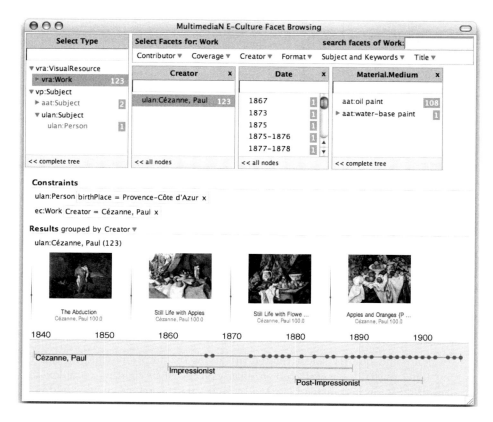

Fig. 3. Facet search on type vra:Work, but with a still active constraint on ulan:Person (birthplace Provence-Alpes-Côte d'Azur). Also note the timeline in the bottom, visualizing multiple time-related facets. Images courtesy of Mark Harden, used with permission.

vra:subject property (for paintings that depict Arles), the birth and death place of Persons, etc. As a result, this search box can be used to find the right facet, but also to disambiguate keywords that have different meanings or are used in different ways.

A final problem can be that the user does not know the type to select to start with. This is addressed by adding also a keyword search box to the type facet, as shown in (a) in Figure 2. This searches over all literal properties of all instances and highlights matching instances and their types in the context of their location in the class hierarchy.

4.3 Specifying Queries over Multiple Resource Types

We strive to support selection of facets from resources with different types in a transparent way, without further complicating the interface. In the example scenario, Simon searched on resources of `ulan:Person`, selecting `ulan:Provence-Alpes-Côte d'Azur` as the place of birth.

After making this selection, Simon can just switch back to searching on artworks by selecting `vra:Work` in the type facet. In /facet, this would yield a page such as the one shown in Figure 3. Note that under the facets, the currently active constraints are shown, including the `ulan:Provence-Alpes-Côte d'Azur` constraint on the `ulan:birthPlace` facet of `ulan:Person`. For comparison, also a facet on `vra:Work` has been selected, in this case `ulan:Paul Cezanne` as the `dc:creator`.

To realize the example above, the facet browser needs to know the relation that can be used to connect a set of `vra:Works` with a set of `ulan:Persons` born in `ulan:Provence-Alpes-Côte d'Azur`. The current prototype searches for such properties at run time, and in this case finds the `dc:creator` property, as intended. To keep the user interface simple, we only support one property (that is, the first suitable candidate found by the system) to connect the different sets. Properties with the same domain and range can be used for normal facet browsing within a single type, but not for relating instances of different types.

4.4 Run-Time Facet Specification

The facets that are shown in the interface can be configured in a separate file. Because a facet is defined in terms of RDF classes and properties, the configuration file itself is also in RDF, using a simple RDF vocabulary.

The vocabulary defines instances of `Facet` by three key properties. For example, the `birthday` facet is modeled by the `hierarchyTopConcept` and `hierarchyRelation` properties defining the hierarchy to be shown in the interface, by specifying the top of the tree (`tgn:World`) and the `rdf:Property` used for the hierarchical relation (in this case `vp:parent`, the universal parent relation that is used across the Getty vocabularies). The `resourceProperty` defines how places are related to the painters, in this case by the `ulan:birthPlace` property.

Some other properties are optional and used to speed up or improve the user interface. The explicit definition of the type of resources the facet applies to, for example, makes it much more efficient to quickly switch to the right set of facets when users move from one type to the other. The `rdfs:label` property can be used to specify the name of the facet, which defaults to the label or name of the corresponding property.

To generate a first configuration file (that can later be hand edited), /facet analyzes the dataset and generates a set of RDF facet definitions similar to the birthPlace facet example given above. For each property, the current algorithm search for a hierarchical relation in the set of related values to find the top concepts. If this relation is not found, or if the values literal are literals, it generates a facet with a flat list of values. For the scenario dataset, 22 hierarchical facets, 84 literal facets and 154 facets with a flat list of resource values were found.

4.5 Facet-Specific Interface Extensions

The values of a facet are typically presented in a list or a tree structure with textual labels. However, some structures are more easy to understand when presented differently. In particular, data which can be ordered linearly can be presented as points on an axis. Time, in particular, is a quantity that is often associated with resources, not only in the cultural heritage domain. It is useful to give a timeline representation of date data where this is appropriate. We have developed a timeline plug-in to visualize time-related facets (such as `dc:date` and it subproperties).

Not only artworks have associated dates, but also related resources such as the lifespan of the artist, Van Gogh, and the period associated with the `aat:post-impressionist` art style. Since the temporal information is related to the set of resources, this can be displayed together on a single timeline, as shown on the bottom of Figure 3.

A timeline interface could also be extended to not only show the temporal information, but also allow it to be used as part of the facet constraint mechanism. A similar facet dependent interface extension would be to relate geographical information together and display it on a two-dimensional spatial-axes interface such as a map.

5 Discussion and Related Work

Initial development of /facet has been heavily inspired by the facet interface of the MUSEUMFINLAND portal [2]. Where MUSEUMFINLAND is built on a strongly aligned dataset, we focus on supporting heterogeneous, loosely coupled collections with multiple thesauri from external sources. They provide mapping rules that hide the peculiarities of the underlying data model from the user interface. We have sacrificed this abstraction level and expose the underlying data model, but with the advantage that the software is independent of the data model and requires no manual configuration or mapping rules.

In comparison with mSpace [5], /facet retains the original facet browsing principle to constrain a set of results. In a visually oriented domain such as ours, this leads to an intuitive interface where, after each step, users can see a set of images that reflect their choices: even users who do not know what "post-impressionist" paintings are, can immediately see from the results whether they like them or not. Also note that a heterogeneous dataset, such as ours, would lead to an m-dimensional space with $m > 250$, which would make the mSpace interface unusable. Alternatively, we could split up the data in multiple smaller mSpaces, but would then have no way of connecting them.

Unlike /facet, the Simile project's Longwell [3] facet browser requires to be configured for a specific dataset and its interface provides no solutions for dealing with large numbers of facets. An advantage of Longwell over /facet is that the display of the results is fully configurable using Fresnel [7].

While Noadster [8] is not specifically a facet browser, it is a generic RDF browser. Noadster applies concept lattices to cluster search results based on common properties. It clusters on any property, but ignores "stop properties" that occur too frequently. The resulting hierarchy forms a Table of Contents, with the original search results typically as leaf nodes, and common properties as branches. An advantage of Noadster is that its clustering prioritizes facets by placing those occurring more frequently in the matches higher in the tree. A disadvantage is the occasional "noisy" excess of properties in the clustering.

While we claim that /facet has some key advantages over the systems discussed above, the current prototype also suffers from some limitations. First, the algorithm for determining the facet configuration automatically needs further refinement. We now treat every RDF property as a potential facet. We then filter out many "schema level" properties from the RDF, RDFS and OWL namespace, and from our own internal namespaces (including the namespace we use for our facet specifications). It is still possible that a certain type of resource will be associated with so many facets that the interface becomes hard to use. The techniques discussed in this paper only partially address this problem, and they are highly dependent on the structure of the `rdfs:subpropertyOf` hierarchy. More research is needed to classify facets into a hierarchy that is optimized for usage in a user interface. In addition, we currently generate facets for all literal properties. On the one hand, this has the disadvantage that facets are generated for properties such as comments in RDFS, gloss entries in WordNet and scope notes in the AAT. The values of such properties are unlikely to become useful for constraining the dataset. On the other hand, other properties with literal values, such as labels in RDFS or titles in Dublin Core, provide useful facets. More research is needed to provide heuristics for determining the type of literal values that are useful in the facet interface. In the type hierarchy, we display all classes from the underlying domain, filtering out only the classes from the RDF(S) and OWL namespaces and the system's internal namespaces. Still, this often leaves classes that are not helpful for most users. Examples include the abstract classes that characterize the top levels of many thesauri, such as the `vp:Subject`, `aat:Subject` and `aat:Concept` classes in our domain. The prototype's current facet-mining algorithm is unable to deal with multiple hierarchies within a single facet. For example, many of our paintings have subject matter annotations referring to concepts from WordNet. There are, however, several different relations that can be used to organize these into a hierarchy, such as hypernym/hyponym and holonym/meronym. For the user interface, it may be appropriate to merge the different hierarchies in a single tree or to keep them separate.

On the implementation side, the current prototype is developed directly on SWI-Prolog. The server side is a Prolog module built on top of the SWI-Prolog Semantic Web Server [9,10]. The client side is a standard Web browser that uses AJAX [11] for the dynamics of the suggestion interface. A drawback of this implementation is that users have to upload their data into /facet's triple store. We are planning to make future versions of the browser using the SPARQL [12] API, so that /facet can be used to browse any RDF repository that is served by a SPARQL compliant triple store. The large amount of RDFS and OWL-based reasoning at run time slowed down the system and gave the impression of an unresponsive interface. To address this, we reduced the amount of run-time reasoning by explicitly deriving the triples needed for calculating the result set when starting up the server so we can quickly traverse the expanded RDF-graph at run time. For example, we compute and add closures of transitive and inverse properties to the triple set at start up or when new data is added.

6 Conclusion and Future Work

We have discussed the requirements for a fully generic RDFS/OWL facet browser interface: automatic facet generation; support for multiple resource types; cross-type selection so resources of one type can be selected using properties of another, semantically related, type; keyword search to complement hierarchical navigation; and supporting visualization plug-ins for selected data types.

We developed the /facet Web interface to experiment with facet browsing in a highly heterogeneous semantic web environment. The current prototype meets the requirements discussed, it fulfills the described scenario in a cultural heritage domain and similar scenarios in other domains. A number of drawbacks remain, which we would like to address in future work. First, determining the facets automatically needs further refinement. Second, we are still fine tuning which classes from the class hierarchy we want to show and which facets we want to associate with the superclasses. Third, the prototype's current facet-mining algorithm is unable to deal with multiple hierarchies within a single facet. Finally, we need to develop a version of /facet that is independent of a particular triple store implementation and runs on any SPARQL compliant triple store.

Acknowledgments. We like to thank our CWI colleagues and members of the MultimediaN E-culture project for their feedback on the /facet prototype and earlier versions of this paper. Jan Wielemaker developed the SWI-Prolog infrastructure and helped solve many problems during development. Alia Amin provided invaluable feedback on the user interface design. Željko Obrenović provided helpful insights on the conceptual architecture of the system.

This research was supported by the MultimediaN project funded through the BSIK programme of the Dutch Government and by the European Commission under contract FP6-027026, Knowledge Space of semantic inference for automatic annotation and retrieval of multimedia content — K-Space.

References

1. Yee, K.P., Swearingen, K., Li, K., Hearst, M.: Faceted Metadata for Image Search and Browsing. In: CHI '03: Proceedings of the SIGCHI conference on Human factors in computing systems, Ft. Lauderdale, Florida, USA, ACM Press (2003) 401–408
2. Hyvönen, E., Junnila, M., Kettula, S., Mäkelä, E., Saarela, S., Salminen, M., Syreeni, A., Valo, A., Viljanen, K.: MuseumFinland — Finnish museums on the semantic web. Journal of Web Semantics **3**(2-3) (2005) 224–241
3. SIMILE: Longwell RDF Browser. http://simile.mit.edu/longwell/ (2003-2005)

4. Schreiber, G., Amin, A., van Assem, M., de Boer, V., Hardman, L., Hildebrand, M., Hollink, L., Huang, Z., van Kersen, J., de Niet, M., Omelayenjko, B., van Ossenbruggen, J., Siebes, R., Taekema, J., Wielemaker, J., Wielinga, B.: MultimediaN E-Culture demonstrator. In: International Semantic Web Conference (ISWC2006). (2006) to be published.
5. m.c. schraefel, Smith, D.A., Owens, A., Russell, A., Harris, C., Wilson, M.L.: The evolving mSpace platform: leveraging the Semantic Web on the Trail of the Memex. In: Proceedings of Hypertext 2005, Salzburg (2005) 174–183
6. Huynh, D., Mazzocchi, S., Karger, D.R.: Piggy Bank: Experience the Semantic Web Inside Your Web Browser. [13] 413–430
7. Bizer, C., Lee, R., Pietriga, E.: Fresnel — A Browser-Independent Presentation Vocabulary for RDF. In: Proceedings of the Second International Workshop on Interaction Design and the Semantic Web, Galway, Ireland (2005)
8. Rutledge, L., van Ossenbruggen, J., Hardman, L.: Making RDF Presentable – Integrated Global and Local Semantic Web Browsing. In: The Fourteenth International World Wide Web Conference, Chiba, Japan, IW3C2, ACM Press (2005) 199–206
9. Wielemaker, J., Schreiber, G., Wielinga, B.: Prolog-Based Infrastructure for RDF: Scalability and Performance. In: The SemanticWeb - ISWC 2003, Sanibel Island, Florida, USA, Springer-Verlag Heidelberg (2003) 644–658
10. Wielemaker, J.: An optimised Semantic Web query language implementation in Prolog. In: ICLP 2005. (2005) 128–142 LNCS 3668.
11. Paulson, L.D.: Building Rich Web Applications with Ajax. IEEE Computer **38**(10) (2005) 14–17
12. W3C: SPARQL Query Language for RDF. W3C Candidate Recommendations are available at http://www.w3.org/TR (2006) Edited by Eric Prud'hommeaux and Andy Seaborne.
13. Gil, Y., Motta, E., Benjamins, V.R., Musen, M.A., eds.: 4th International Semantic Web Conference, ISWC 2005. In Gil, Y., Motta, E., Benjamins, V.R., Musen, M.A., eds.: 4th International Semantic Web Conference, ISWC 2005. Lecture Notes in Computer Science, Galway, Ireland, Springer (2005)

Using Ontologies for Extracting Product Features from Web Pages*

Wolfgang Holzinger, Bernhard Krüpl, and Marcus Herzog

Database and Artificial Intelligence Group, Vienna University of Technology,
Favoritenstraße 9-11, A-1040 Wien, Austria
{holzing, kruepl, herzog}@dbai.tuwien.ac.at

Abstract. In this paper, we show how to use ontologies to bootstrap a knowledge acquisition process that extracts product information from tabular data on Web pages. Furthermore, we use logical rules to reason about product specific properties and to derive higher-order knowledge about product features. We will also explain the knowledge acquisition process, covering both ontological and procedural aspects. Finally, we will give an qualitative and quantitative evaluation of our results.

1 Introduction

The World Wide Web is an excellent source for product information. Product descriptions are posted on numerous Web sites, be it manufacturer Web sites, review portals, or online shops. However, product presentations on the Web are primarily designed for a human audience. Product features are not encoded in a way that they can be automatically processed by machines. In this paper, we investigate the task of extracting product features, i.e., attribute name-value pairs, from Web pages. The extraction process is assumed to work fully autonomous, given some seed knowledge about a product domain of interest. We will use the digital camera domain to illustrate our approach.

Due to the very nature of the World Wide Web, information about the same product is often spread over a large number of Web sites and is presented in quite different formats. However, technical product information tends to be presented in a more structured way, usually in some form of list or table structure. Still, the presentation variety of this semi-structured information is enormous. In the AllRight project, we strive for distilling knowledge about products and their features from the product descriptions found on large numbers of Web sites. This project is also part of a larger research initiative that deals with various aspects of data extraction from Web pages [2].

We assume that the product descriptions are posted on "regular" Web pages that are not semantically annotated in any way. It is therefore part of our task to annotate to these Web data as much relevant semantics as possible. Semantics

---

* This research is supported in part by the Austrian Federal Ministry for Transport, Innovation and Technology under the FIT-IT contract FFG 809261 and by the REWERSE Network of Excellence.

is always a matter of perspective: when examined from different points of view, completely different properties of a subject matter may become important. For most technical products, though, a common understanding about the relevance of features exists. It is exactly this feature set that manufacturers, dealers, and reviewers list when they post product descriptions on the Web. We exploit this common feature set when we retrieve information about products. For each product, we build a feature space and populate it with instance data extracted from Web pages.

Related work. Table extraction from Web documents has been addressed in a number of publications [4,6] and has been used as a basis for the more general notion of knowledge extraction [13,1] from the Web by the way of constructing ontologies from tables [10,11]. In most of these approaches however ontologies are only used for storing the knowledge gathered from the extraction process performed by conventional procedural algorithms.

In [3], the authors describe the use of a domain ontology to create a wrapper for data extraction from Web tables. They use data integration techniques to match the extracted data to the domain description. In the same line, our approach tries to integrate table extraction with table interpretation [6], but uses the classification capabilities of the OWL reasoner Pellet [8] to resolve the gap between tabular presentation and the domain model's semantics, without resorting to external matching algorithms.

The OntoGenie system [9] populates a given ontology with instances using the linguistic WordNet ontology as an interpretative bridge between the unstructured data from the Web and the target ontology. Our system has the same goal of instantiating a domain ontology, but relies on structural information about the data in the form of tabular arrangement and a small domain specific vocabulary.

We believe that migrating parts of the logic to OWL reasoning helps building a modular system with easily exchangeable logical table and domain models. The logic needed to build higher level semantic concepts can be formulated in a natural declarative manner, which helps development and elaboration of these concepts. The procedural components in the process are decoupled from each other, with each component having a clear purpose and responsibility. Usage of OWL as a glue representation between them helps keeping the whole system transparent and eases debugging and evaluation.

Architecture. The overall knowledge acquisition process is outlined in Figure 1. In a first step, the table extraction algorithm analyzes an input HTML page for tabular structures, given a specific table ontology T. The output of this step is an instantiated table ontology $I(T)$ resembling the information found in a tabular structure on the HTML page. Note that the tabular structure on the HTML page is not necessarily encoded in HTML `table` elements, but only needs to look like a table. This will be explained in more detail later.

In the next step, a content spotter algorithm analyzes the instantiated table ontology $I(T)$ for occurrences of specific domain dependent concepts. The content spotter algorithm utilizes keywords and expressions defined in the domain

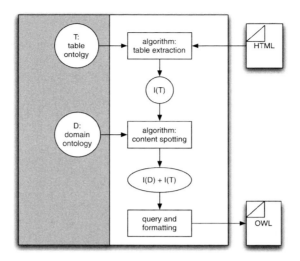

Fig. 1. The knowledge acquisition process, covering both ontological and procedural aspects

ontology D and annotates the content found in the table structure with the respective concepts. The output of this step is the combination of both the instantiated table ontology $I(T)$ and the instantiated domain ontology $I(D)$, containing enough basic facts to allow for derivation of higher level concepts in D.

The final step interprets the instantiated ontologies using a standard OWL reasoner which classifies the instances present in terms of the higher level concepts of the domain ontology. The relevant product information is extracted and stored externally for further processing.

In the following section we will describe how we use OWL ontologies to formalize knowledge about both table structures and product features, as well as how we represent intermediate and final results of the knowledge acquisition process. Section 3 describes in detail the process depicted in Figure 1, covering the table extraction algorithm, the content spotting algorithm, and the derivation of higher-level domain concepts from pure facts extracted from the Web pages. Section 4 presents a quantitative and qualitative evaluation of our process. Finally, in Section 5 we discuss our main findings and discuss further ideas and potential improvements.

2 Ontologies

We use two separate ontologies to represent different aspects in our problem domain: knowledge about table structures, i.e., rows and columns, and knowledge about product features, i.e., product attribute keyword–value pairs. We use OWL to represent the ontologies. Moreover, we use the Pellet [8] OWL reasoner to reason about concepts in our ontologies.

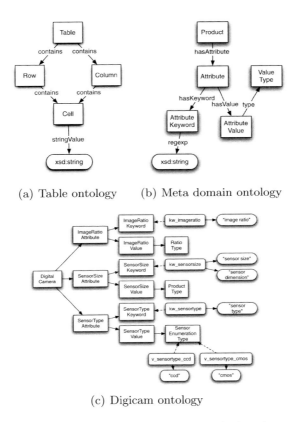

Fig. 2. The two base ontologies and a sample domain ontology

2.1 Modeling

Figure 2a shows our ontological modeling of tables. The most concise concept is the table cell, represented as concept `Cell`, which contains a textual unformatted string value modeled as an OWL datatype property. Cells are grouped into rows and columns, which is reflected by the `contains`–relation and the concepts `Row` and `Column`. This table model can represent the most basic table type, the rectangular grid table [6] and is adequate in modelling the tables found in the digital camera domain.

The meta domain ontology (Figure 2b) is our basic schema for the description of products. This ontology represents a product as a flat list of attributes, where each attribute is associated with a set of keywords and a typed attribute value. For the description of specific products, we subclass the concepts in the meta domain ontology 2b and fill it with domain specific information, i.e., domain specific attributes. Figure 2c shows an extension of the base ontology for digital cameras (only 3 attributes of the 23 modelled are shown.) For each feature of the camera, we provide an appropriately named attribute. Each attribute is associated with a matching keyword and value concept. Keyword concepts are basically singleton concepts with only one instance representing the keyword. However, as seen on the instance kw_sensorsize in Figure 2c, this single instance can have multiple independent string representations, allowing for various syntactic variants of the keyword. In this way, the domain dictionary is integrated in the domain ontology. Attribute values contain a reference to a type concept which denotes the allowed attribute types. Besides simple numerical types like RatioType and ProductType that have no further elaborated description in the domain ontology, enumeration types are described in the ontology in a way similar to keywords. For instance, the SensorTypeValue of a digital camera can be either v_sensortype_ccd or v_sensortype_cmos, which are tagged with the respective strings "ccd" and "cmos".

2.2 Reasoning: The "Containment Forms Context" Assumption

Up to this point, we have two distinct ontologies that are not related to each other. To make a successful interpretation of the content of a table with the semantics defined by the domain model, we have to provide a way to integrate those two ontologies.

Our method is based on the observation that individuals that belong to a certain concept in one ontology, e.g. being a Cell in the table ontology, can *at the same time* belong to another unrelated concept in a different ontology, i.e., being the value of a specific attribute in the product ontology.

The crucial point is what we call the "containment forms context" assumption. We use the hierarchical containment relation between texts and cells and rows and columns that is present in the table model to decide on the context that a cell is in. The fact that a cell c belongs to a row r establishes a common context on all the members c_i of r.

Consider the attribute value SensorSizeValue. We want to classify a cell as a valid sensor size value, iff its text contains both a numerical value and a length unit (like "in" or "cm"). Any cell containing both text fragments binds this two fragments into a common context that we call SensorSizeValue:

$$\texttt{SensorSizeValue} == \exists.\texttt{contains NumericalType} \cap \exists.\texttt{contains LengthUnit}$$

In the same way, we recognize an individual to be an sensor dimension attribute, iff it contains both a sensor dimension attribute keyword and a sensor dimension attribute value. Any individual that contains both a SensorSizeValue and SensorSizeValue should become a SensorSizeAttribute also:

$$\texttt{SensorSizeAttribute} == \exists.\texttt{contains SensorSizeValue}$$
$$\cap\ \exists.\texttt{contains SensorSizeValue}$$

At present all definitions of values and attributes follow this simple schema. However, we perceive it to be one of the strong points of our approach that those simple definitions can easily be replaced by more intricate ones if the need arises.

without having to modify any other part of the system, because the handling of these rules is encapsulated in the ontology reasoner.

3 The Knowledge Acquisition Process

In the following we will give a detailed description of the knowledge acquisition process as introduced in Section 1. Once started, this process works autonomously until a specified number of product descriptions are harvested from the Web.

3.1 Table Extraction

Typical tasks that cannot be handled efficiently by ontological means only are the location and recognition [6] of tabular data regions on Web pages. While table location aims at finding tables in a document, the task of table recognition is to identify the spatial properties of a table. For these tasks we rely on an algorithmic approach that is described in this section. Our approach to table extraction [7] is quite different from previously described ones: we do not operate on the DOM tree or any other incarnation of the HTML source code, but rely on the visual rendition of the Web page. (See [5] for a different variant where they also use positional information of non-text nodes.)

Figure 3 through Figure 5 visualize the process of table extraction, starting from the input HTML page and ending at the output table structure that contains the unlabeled product features. The extraction algorithm detects a product feature table on a Web page, and extracts the spatial features of the table structure along with its content. The result is an explicit representation of the table structure derived from the interpretation of the spatial table features. Note that we do not rely on the structural properties of the HTML source code, e.g. <table> elements, to interpret the table structure, but instead utilize visual features that are also accessible to a typical human reader, i.e., word positions and styles. No matter how a table was realized in the HTML source code, whatever looks like a table, i.e., follows certain alignment conditions, will be interpreted as a table.

The table extraction algorithm first groups adjacent words into larger cells (①), thus working in a bottom-up manner starting from the bounding boxes of individual words in a table. Next, the algorithm tries to identify possible table columns (②). We consider a possible table column a set of vertically neighboring cells that are aligned either on the left-hand side, right-hand side, or at the middle. If any cells are found that interrupt the sequence of directly neighboring cells within an identified column candidate, we check if these cells could be intermediate table headings by also testing against an alignment hypothesis (③). Such headings can be important for the further processing because they can give an important context for the cells below the headings.

Once all possible columns were found, the table extraction algorithm tries to identify the column combinations that actually form tables. The strategy looks for adjacent columns that share a common row structure (④): All gaps between

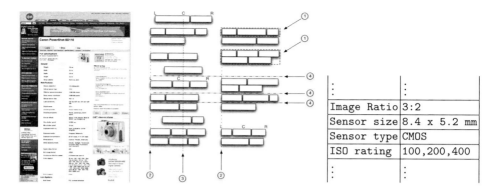

Fig. 3. Sample HTML page

Fig. 4. Schema of table extraction algorithm

Fig. 5. Tabular data structure for product features

the column rows must also be found in the adjacent column. By loosening this requirement to hold only in one direction, we can also allow for rows where a cell in one column corresponds to many cells in another column. We call that procedure *comb alignment* of columns. The strategy also allows for the identification of top, centre, and bottom aligned cells within any table row. Tables that fulfill the comb alignment criterion for columns are returned for further processing.

3.2 Applying the Table Ontology

In the next step, we express the structural relationships of the identified tables by means of our table ontology. To this means we translate the spatial properties from the bounding box model into a qualitative model. Consider Figure 5, showing four rows from a typical table describing the features of some digital camera. Applying the table ontology will derive the shown facts about the table, where r1 refers to the first row, c1 to the left-hand side cell in the first row, and c2 to the right-hand cell in the first row. Furthermore, `Row` and `Cell` are concepts of the table ontology, and `contains` and `stringValue` are relations defined in the table ontology. The result is an instance of the table ontology expressing facts about the structural properties of tables produced by analyzing the Web page by means of the table extraction algorithm.

```
r1 a Row.                    c1 a Cell.                  c2 a Cell.
r1 contains c1.              r1 contains c2.
c1 stringValue "Image Ratio". c2 stringValue "3:2".
```

3.3 Content Spotting

Once the structure of a table is represented in the table domain ontology, we turn to the content within the table cells to derive the meaning of the table, i.e., to interpret the table structure in terms of product features represented as attribute name-value pairs. We utilize *content spotters* for this task. Content spotters are small programs with the purpose to recognize certain semantic concepts in texts. A content spotter is equipped with the necessary knowledge to detect an instance of the concept it represents and, more importantly, to name it and to state the fact in an OWL statement.

Table 1. Type spotters detect values with distinctive formatting

NumberType	2,453
ProductType	8.4 x 5.2 mm
TripleProductType	3.9 x 8.4 x 5.2 in
FractionType	1/400
RatioType	1:2.8

Presently we employ two types of content spotters: *keyword spotters* and *type spotters*. Keyword spotters detect the presence of a particular word or phrase in a number of alternative syntactic representations. Keyword spotters utilize the domain ontology by accessing the regular expressions associated with instances of the various keywords concepts. The keyword spotter remembers the most specific concept for each keyword and will use this concept when it detects the regular expression in a text.

Type spotters contain more intrinsic knowledge than keyword spotters. While keyword spotters are only able to detect a limited number of alternative expressions, type spotters are able to detect a whole class of expressions that follow a common schema. Table 1 shows a number of type spotters and the kind of values they typically detect.

Both kinds of content spotters operate by matching a text to a regular expression. Content spotters fetch their regular expressions from the domain ontology. If a substring of the text matches the regular expression of a content spotter, that substring is extracted and annotated with the reference to the annotating spotter.

3.4 Applying the Domain Ontology

Once the content spotters have annotated the content within the table cells, the domain ontology can be employed to derive additional facts. Given the table ontology instance as described in Subsection 3.2 and the annotated content, the application of the product ontology can derive the following facts:

```
c1 contains kw_imageratio.    c2 contains v1.    v1 a TypeRatio.
c3 contains kw_sensorsize.    c4 contains v2.    v2 a DoubleProduct.
c4 contains u_mm.
```

Since cell $c2$ contains an individual that is of type `RatioType`, the definition given for the concept `ImageRatioValue` is triggered: cell $c2$ is classified accordingly as an attribute value. Moreover, row $r1$ contains $c1$, which in turn contains the keyword `kw_imageratio`. Row $r1$ also contains $c2$, which in turn contains a value of the matching type `TypeRatio`. Therefore it is concluded that $r1$ is an `ImageRatioAttribute` according to the product ontology. The following facts are added to the domain knowledge:

```
c2 a ImageRatioValue.
r1 a ImageRatioAttribute.
```

In this way, table rows are successively identified as instances of product attributes.

To conclude, we started from an HTML page, identified the tabular structure containing text fragments, annotated the text fragments with simple semantic concepts according to the domain ontology, and finally derived from those basic building blocks high–level product attributes. The following section gives an evaluation of the quality of both the intermediate and the final derived concepts.

4 Evaluation

The automatic, unsupervised identification and extraction of product attributes from Web pages is our ultimate goal. We perform the evaluation of our approach in two steps:

- Firstly, we provide an analysis of the performance of the content spotters that we described in Section 3.3.
- Secondly, we analyze the performance of the whole system by comparing the automatically generated results with manually generated ground truth.

4.1 Content Spotter Evaluation

We used the AllRight crawler [2] to automatically locate and retrieve about 6400 Web pages. The crawler searches for pages that, with a high likelihood, contain tables representing the technical specification of digital cameras. The pages originated from manufacturer, dealer and review sites. Due to space constraints, we will not present the AllRight crawler in detail here. It is worth mentioning, though, that the crawling process runs completely unsupervised. The table extraction algorithm we described in Section 3.1 was used to extract 1955 product specification tables from the crawled pages. These 1955 Web pages were then used as candidate pages for the content spotting process.

Figure 6a shows the distribution of the number of rows in the candidate pages along with the distribution of recognized keywords in those tables. The distributions are of similar form, with about 35% of the rows showing an attribute match. The mean value of the identified table rows is 50.4, whereas the mean value for the number of identified attributes is 17.8

Figure 7 shows an overview of how many times each of the keywords matched within the textual content of a table, measuring the ambiguity a of the keyword. There is a clear distinction between keywords appearing with relative high frequency, which also have a tendency to generate outliers — matching extremely

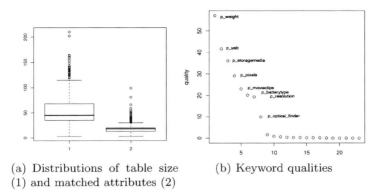

(a) Distributions of table size (1) and matched attributes (2)

(b) Keyword qualities

Fig. 6. Attribute distribution and quality

often in a table —, and low frequency keywords that seldom match and never produce excessive multiple matches.

Closely related to Figure 7 is Table 2, showing the number of candidate tables in which each keyword matched at least once, measuring the coverage c of a keyword. Again, the distinction between frequent and infrequent matchers is clearly visible: most keywords either match on more than 80% of the tables, or they match in less than 5%. The keyword p_weight matched in 94% of all tables, and produced on average 1.5 matches per table. It is our prime example for a perfect attribute: matching in almost every case, and matching with minimum ambiguity. We strive for high coverage of a keyword to be of maximum use in every case, and we need low ambiguity of the keyword to achieve precise classification.

We measured keyword quality using the simple formula $q = \frac{c}{a}$, where quality is proportional to coverage and inversely proportional to ambiguity. Figure 6b, displaying keyword qualities in descending order, shows that keyword quality

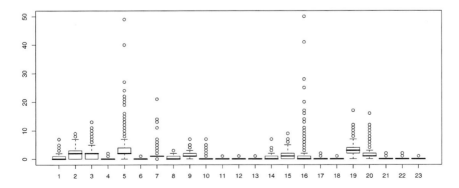

Fig. 7. Keyword ambiguity (see table 2 for keyword names)

decreases exponentially. Therefore, the top 1/3 keywords are responsible for most of the semantic annotation, while the remaining keywords are almost useless. This is a hint that those attributes were either underspecified in the domain knowledge, or that these attributes are really so infrequently mentioned to make them negligible. In any case, they should be used with caution in subsequent evaluations of the generated data.

Table 2. Keyword coverage

1	p_rechargeable	649	2	p_resolution	1380
3	p_batterytype	1465	4	p_denomination	242
5	p_pixels	1669	6	p_display_size	4
7	p_movieclips	1620	8	p_firewire	688
9	p_weight	1850	10	p_guarantee	140
11	p_vendor	11	12	p_internal_memory	11
13	p_lcd_display	3	14	p_brand	895
15	p_optical_finder	1432	16	p_price	866
17	p_productdescription	27	18	p_slrcamera	5
19	p_storagemedia	1805	20	p_usb	1854
21	p_videoout	7	22	p_zoomfactor_digital	7
23	p_zoomfactor_optical	6			

4.2 Evaluation Against Ground Truth

As explained in a previous section, the extraction stage is fed by a retrieval component that automatically retrieves domain relevant pages containing semi-structured data. We randomly selected 30 of these retrieved pages for manual annotation by a human domain expert. To make the annotation process less time consuming and error prone, we devised a ground truth annotation tool that we use to annotate relevant Web pages. We do not try to annotate all of the information on a page, but cover only a fraction of it by selecting a set of 5 attributes. We assume that the extraction quality for the other attributes will be comparable.

We need to provide ground truth to be able to verify results at different stages in our process: the location of tables on a page, the recognition of the table, and the interpretation of the function of table cells. Therefore, ground truth has to provide information about: left top and right bottom corners of the table, which word tokens in the table form a table cell, and the functional relations of table cells.

Several table models have been proposed in the literature [4,6,12]. We restrict our analysis to those table types that only contain a single level of table nesting, i.e., the nesting that is defined by intermediate headings. In addition to reducing the complexity of the problem, we can give more arguments for this restriction: Our system is not an isolated experiment in the table extraction field, but has to link the table interpretation results into our domain ontology. This ontology is centered around the concepts of products and attributes. If there are more complex structural relationships contained in a particular table, it is very likely that these relationships, or the table as a whole, just are not appropriate for our extraction task.

The notion of subjectivity is an important factor in our considerations. When we want to extract product information from tables, we want it to be aligned with our (subjective) domain ontology, therefore we need to find those tables on the Web that share the same conceptualization basics. If an author describes a product from a completely unique perspective, this document cannot be included in our analysis, even when it is semi-structured. This is due to the fact that a common ontological understanding is missing in this case.

The ground truth generation tool we devised lets the user operate on the visual rendition of a Web page. We implemented an extension for the Mozilla Firefox browser that can be invoked for any Web page displayed in the browser. If activated, the user will be able to select any word on the page by pointing the mouse cursor over it; the selected word can then be annotated as a certain attribute keyword or value by performing some key strokes. In addition, there is a mode to indicate which of the word tokens belong together to form a functional unit. The results of the annotation process are stored in instances of an OWL ontology that allows for an easy comparison with the automatically generated results of our system.

Table 3. Results of evaluation against ground truth

Average number of (per document) **ground truth**			Average number (per document) **identified**		
keywords	values	attributes	keywords	values	attributes
5.13	6.78	4.82	3.22	4.02	3.38
Recall			**Precision**		
keywords	values	attributes	keywords	values	attributes
62.8%	59.3%	70.1%	65.8%	41.6%	92.4%
F-measure					
keywords		values		attributes	
64.27%		48.90%		79.72%	

4.3 Results

We asked different users to annotate 30 documents with 5 concepts from our domain ontology. We quickly found out that the annotation heavily depends on qualification of the user in the domain: Identifying CCD sensor sizes in documents is very difficult for users who do not have an appropriate background. On the other hand, even within the group of domain experts, there were differences in what users considered being related to a domain concept or not (e.g. in the case of sensor resolutions). For us, this proves our assumption that subjectivity plays a key role in the extraction process that has been underestimated so far.

Table 3 summarizes the results. The section "average number of ground truth" gives the average numbers for annotated `keywords`, `values` and `attributes` within a document. `Keyword` and `value` denote the respective parts of a keyword-value pair. Together, these elements form an `attribute`, i.e., a product feature. Note that the total number of keywords, values, and attributes is not equal. This is due to the fact that multiple values can exist for a single keyword, and attributes must comprise both a keyword and a value. The "average number identified" section gives the average numbers for the automatically identified attributes over all documents examined. For both recall and precision we get significantly better values for attributes than for keywords and values alone, showing the benefit of the effort to derive higher level domain concepts.

5 Conclusions and Outlook

We presented a system that uses ontology reasoning to integrate table extraction and table interpretation. A first evaluation has shown that the classification work done by the reasoner can significantly increase precision and recall of high level semantic product information.

Presently, the content spotters use regular expressions to match keywords and types. Experience has shown that tables frequently contain phrases that are not easily recognizable by regular expressions. Recognizing only simple phrases and assembling them with complex ontology concepts is computationally expensive. Simple grammars with a limited capability of recognizing natural language phrases could be used in place of the regular expressions.

Our current rectangular table model, while capturing the essential information, does not make use of the additional structural information that is present in more complex layouts. For example, many tables in our testing set used column spanning rows as sub–headers to segment a long table. The information in these sub–headers can give valuable context information to the interpretation of the row–attributes. We are currently working on an extended table model that can represent segmented nested tables. Such a model requires generalizing the containment–context axiom to multiple levels.

References

1. Harith Alani, Sanghee Kim, David E. Millard, Mark J. Weal, Wendy Hall, Paul H. Lewis, and Nigel R. Shadbolt. "Automatic Ontology-Based Knowledge Extraction from Web Documents" In *IEEE Intelligent Systems, Vol. 18, No. 1, pages 14–21*, 2003.
2. Julien Carme, Michal Ceresna, Oliver Frölich, Georg Gottlob, Tamir Hassan, Marcus Herzog, Wolfgang Holzinger, and Bernhard Krüpl. "The Lixto Project: Exploring New Frontiers of Web Data Extraction" In *Proc. of the 23rd British National Conf. on Databases*, 2006.
3. David W. Embley, Cui Tao, Stephen W. Liddle. "Automatically Extracting Ontologically Specified Data from HTML Tables of Unknown Structure" In *Proc. of the 21st Int. Conf. on Conceptual Modeling (ER02), Tampere, Finland*, 2002.

4. David W. Embley, Daniel Lopresti, and George Nagy. "Notes on Contemporary Table Recognition" In *Proc. of the 2nd IEEE Int. Conf. on Document Image Analysis for Libraries*, 2006.
5. Wolfgang Gatterbauer and Paul Bohunsky. Table Extraction Using Spatial Reasoning on the CSS2 Visual Box Model In *Proc. of the 21st National Conf. on Artificial Intelligence*, 2006.
6. Matthew Hurst. "Layout and Language: Challenges for Table Understanding on the Web" In *Proc. of the 1st Int. Workshop on Web Document Analysis*, 2001.
7. Bernhard Krüpl and Marcus Herzog. Visually Guided Bottom-Up Table Detection and Segmentation in Web Documents. In *Proc. of the 15th Int. World Wide Web Conf.*, 2006.
8. Bijan Parsia, Evren Sivrin, Mike Grove, and Ron Alford. Pellet OWL Reasoner, 2003. Maryland Information and Networks Dynamics Lab *http://www.mindswap.org/2003/pellet/* (as of May 2006).
9. Chintan Patel, Kaustubh Supekar, and Yugyung Lee. "Ontogenie: Extracting Ontology Instances from WWW" In *Human Language Technology for the Semantic Web and Web Services*, ISWC'03, Sanibel Island, Florida, 2003.
10. Masahiro Tanaka and Toru Ishida. "Ontology Extraction from Tables on the Web" In *Proc. of the Int. Symposium on Applications on Internet*, 2006.
11. Yuri A. Tijerino, David W. Embley, Deryle W. Lonsdale, and George Nagy. "Ontology Generation from Tables" In *Proc. of the Fourth Int. Conf. on Web Information Systems Engineering*, 2003.
12. Xinxin Wang. "Tabular Abstraction, Editing, and Formatting" *PhD thesis, Univ. of Waterloo*, 1996.
13. Alan Wessman, Stephen W. Liddle, and David W. Embley. "A Generalized Framework for an Ontology-Based Data-Extraction System" In *Proc. of the 4th Int. Conf. on Information Systems Technology and its Applications, pages 239–253*, 2005.

Block Matching for Ontologies

Wei Hu and Yuzhong Qu

School of Computer Science and Engineering, Southeast University,
Nanjing 210096, P.R. China
{whu, yzqu}@seu.edu.cn

Abstract. Ontology matching is a crucial task to enable interoperation between Web applications using different but related ontologies. Today, most of the ontology matching techniques are targeted to find 1:1 mappings. However, block mappings are in fact more pervasive. In this paper, we discuss the block matching problem and suggest that both the mapping quality and the partitioning quality should be considered in block matching. We propose a novel partitioning-based approach to address the block matching issue. It considers both linguistic and structural characteristics of domain entities based on virtual documents, and uses a hierarchical bisection algorithm for partitioning. We set up two kinds of metrics to evaluate of the quality of block matching. The experimental results demonstrate that our approach is feasible.

1 Introduction

Web ontologies written in RDF [12] or OWL [19] play a prominent role in the Semantic Web. Due to the decentralized nature of the Web, there always exist multiple ontologies from overlapped domains or even from the same domain. In order to enable interoperation between Web applications using different but related ontologies, we need to establish mappings between ontologies for capturing the semantic correspondence between them.

The common relationship cardinality of mappings between concepts, relations or instances (we uniformly name them as *domain entities*) of ontologies is 1:1. However, mappings between sets of domain entities are more pervasive. In particular, 1:1 mappings can be viewed as a special case of mappings between sets of domain entities. In this paper, *a block* is a set of domain entities. *A block mapping* is a pair of matched blocks from two ontologies in correspondence. We refer to the process of discovering block mappings as *block matching*.

Block matching is required in many occasions. Two discriminative examples are illustrated as follows.

Example 1. Given two ontologies (denoted by O_1 and O_2), O_1 contains three domain entities: `Month`, `Day` and `Year`; while O_2 contains a single domain entity: `Date`. We can see `Month`, `Day` and `Year` are parts of `Date`. So it is more natural to match the block {`Month`, `Day`, `Year`} in O_1 with the block {`Date`} in O_2.

Example 2. When two ontologies being compared, block matching can provide us a general picture at a higher level to explore macroscopical correspondences between the main topics assigned to these two ontologies, and it may also help to generate some new focused ontologies from the original block mappings.

The blocking matching problem can be transformed to a special kind of partitioning problem. Usually, it is required that blocks in either of the two ontologies should be disjointed with each other. So all the block mappings essentially compose a partitioning of all domain entities from the two ontologies with the requirement that each partition should contain at least one domain entity from each of the two ontologies. From the viewpoint of partitioning, the cohesiveness within each block mapping should be high; while the coupling crossing different block mappings should be low. Therefore, in addition to the inherent difficulties in discovering the high quality mappings, the block matching problem is exacerbated by having to consider the partitioning quality of the block matching.

Nowadays, quite a lot of algorithms have been proposed in literature addressing the ontology matching problem. GLUE [6], QOM [7], OLA [8], S-MATCH [10], HCONE-MERGE [13], PROMPT [14], V-DOC [20] and I-SUB [23] are such works. However, these algorithms cannot solve the block matching problem since they are targeted to find 1:1 mappings. To our knowledge, the block matching problem has only been addressed before in PBM [11]. But it merely partitions two large class hierarchies separately without considering the correspondence between them. Certainly, the mapping quality is not satisfied. In addition, it just copes with mappings between classes, thus it is not a general solution for ontology matching.

In this paper, we propose a new partitioning-based approach to address the block matching problem. Partitioning entails both developing a relatedness measure and choosing an appropriate partitioning algorithm. We consider both linguistic and structural characteristics of domain entities based on virtual documents for the relatedness measure [20]. The novelty of this measure is that both the mapping quality and the partitioning quality can be guaranteed simultaneously. We present a hierarchical bisection algorithm for partitioning, which can provide block mappings at different levels of granularity. We also describe an automatical process to extract the optimal block mappings with a given number of block mappings. Besides, we assume the mappings between blocks is 1:1 in order to avoid the combinatorial explosion of the search space.

The remainder of this paper is organized as follows. Section 2 sketches out our approach. Section 3 introduces the computation of the relatedness among domain entities by virtual documents. Section 4 presents a hierarchical bisection algorithm based on the relatedness, and describes a method to automatically extract the optimal block mappings for a flat partitioning. Section 5 sets up two kinds of metrics to evaluate of the quality of the block matching generated by our approach. Section 6 discusses some related works on ontology matching as well as some related works on ontology partitioning. Finally, Section 7 provides concluding remarks.

2 Overview of the Approach

The overview of the approach is illustrated in Figure 1. Generally speaking, our approach starts with two ontologies to be compared as input, and then after four processing stages, the output returns block mappings between the two ontologies.

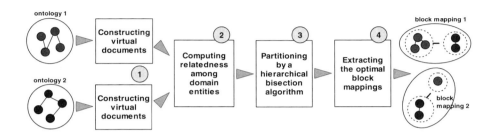

Fig. 1. The overview of the approach

1. *Constructing virtual documents.* The process constructs virtual document for each domain entity of the input ontologies. We make use of the virtual documents as the features of domain entities to be compared. The virtual document of a domain entity consists of a collection of weighted words; these words come from not only the local descriptions (e.g., labels) but also the neighboring information to reflect the intended meaning of the entity.

2. *Computing relatedness among domain entities.* The process sets up the relatedness for any two domain entities by computing the similarity between the virtual documents of them in correspondence. More precisely, it includes the comparison among domain entities within each of the two ontologies as well as those crossing the two ontologies. Therefore, the linguistic and structural characteristics are both revealed simultaneously in a uniform process.

3. *Partitioning by a hierarchical bisection algorithm.* The hierarchical bisection algorithm acts on the set of domain entities from the two ontologies. It recursively partitions the unrelated or dissimilar domain entities into disjoint blocks mappings. As a result, the similar ones are fallen into the same block mapping (containing the domain entities from the two ontologies). The algorithm returns a dendrogram (a typical type of tree structure) consisting of layers of block mappings at different levels of granularity.

4. *Extracting the optimal block mappings.* The process finds the optimal block mappings in the dendrogram derived from the hierarchical bisection algorithm for a flat partitioning with a given number of block mappings.

We will further describe each process in the next two sections.

3 Relatedness Among Domain Entities

In this section, we construct virtual documents for the domain entities declared in OWL/RDF ontologies. Then, we compute the relatedness among the domain entities by calculating the similarity among the virtual documents.

3.1 Construction of Virtual Documents

The RDF graph model is the foundation of the Semantic Web ontologies, and OWL ontologies can also be mapped to RDF graphs [19]. Therefore, we uniformly use the RDF graph model to represent ontologies.

An RDF graph is a set of triples (statements). An RDF triple is conventionally written in the order (subject, predicate, object). A node in an RDF graph may be a literal, a URI with an optional local name (URI reference, or URIref), or a blank node. Please note that a predicate is always a URIref, and a literal cannot be a subject.

In the field of Information Retrieval, the content of a document might be represented as a collection of tokens: words, stems, phrases, or other units derived or inferred from the text of the document. These tokens are usually weighted to indicate their importance within the document which can then be viewed as a vector in a high dimensional space. In this paper, a virtual document represents a collection of weighted tokens, and the weights are rational numbers. To simplify the expression, we use the term *a collection of words* instead of a collection of weighted tokens.

As a collection of words, the virtual document of a domain entity contains not only the local descriptions but also the neighboring information to reflect the intended meaning of the entity.

- *Local descriptions.* For a literal node, the local description is a collection of words derived from the literal itself. For a URIref, it is a collection of words extracted from the local name, rdfs:label(s), rdfs:comment(s) and other possible annotations. For a blank node, it is a collection of words extracted from the information originated from the forward neighbors. A weighting scheme is incorporated in the formation of the description.

- *Neighboring Information.* We capture different kinds of neighbors (subject neighbors, predicate neighbors and object neighbors) by distinguishing the places the nodes occurred in triples. The descriptions of these neighbors are integrated as neighboring information in the virtual document of a domain entity to reflect the structural information of the domain entity.

For formal definitions, please refer to [20].

3.2 Computation of Relatedness

The similarity among virtual documents of domain entities is calculated in the Vector Space Model (VSM) [17]. In this model, the virtual document of a domain entity is considered to be a vector. In particular, we employ the TF/IDF [21] term weighting model, in which each virtual document can be represented as follows:

$$(tf_1 \cdot idf_1, tf_2 \cdot idf_2, ..., tf_n \cdot idf_n), \qquad (1)$$

where tf_i is the frequency of the ith word in a given virtual document and idf_i is the distinguishability of the word in such document w.r.t. the whole. So the TF/IDF term weighting model gives prominence to the words close by related to the given virtual documents, which to some extent exposes the latent features of the virtual documents.

The similarity between virtual documents is measured by the cosine value between the two vectors $\overrightarrow{N_i}$ and $\overrightarrow{N_j}$, corresponding to two virtual documents D_i and D_j in the Vector Space Model. The measure is defined as follows:

$$sim(D_i, D_j) = cos(\overrightarrow{N_i}, \overrightarrow{N_j}) = \frac{\sum_{k=1}^{d} n_{ik} n_{jk}}{\sqrt{(\sum_{k=1}^{d} n_{ik}^2)(\sum_{k=1}^{d} n_{jk}^2)}}, \qquad (2)$$

where d is the dimension of the vector space, and n_{ik} (n_{jk}) is the kth component of the vector $\overrightarrow{N_i}$ ($\overrightarrow{N_j}$). If the two virtual documents do not share any words, the similarity will be 0.0. If all the word scores equal completely, it will be 1.0.

After computing the similarity among virtual documents within each of the two ontologies as well as crossing the two ontologies, we can obtain a relatedness matrix, denoted by W. The matrix has the following block structure:

$$W = \begin{pmatrix} W_{11} & W_{12} \\ W_{12}^T & W_{22} \end{pmatrix}, \qquad (3)$$

where W_{11} is a matrix representing the relatedness among domain entities within the ontology O_1, and W_{22} is similarly defined for the ontology O_2. W_{12} is a matrix representing the relatedness among domain entities between O_1 and O_2. Please note that we assume that the relatedness among domain entities is symmetric in our approach.

The relatedness matrix W has two features. Firstly, both of linguistic and structural relatedness within each of the two ontologies are reflected in W_{11} and W_{22}, respectively. For example, to exhibit structural relatedness within O_1 or O_2, each domain entity collects its neighboring information, i.e., the local descriptions of the subject, predicate or object neighbors, and then the structural affinity between any two entities is revealed through shared words obtained from neighborhood relationship in Vector Space Model. In other words, two entities within O_1 or O_2 are more related if they co-occur in more statements. Secondly, linguistic relatedness crossing ontologies is characterized by W_{12}. This matrix is one of the most important key points in this paper.

4 Partitioning for Block Matching

In this section, we present a hierarchical bisection algorithm based on the relatedness among domain entities. Besides, we describe a method to automatically find the optimal block mappings with a given number of block mappings.

4.1 The Hierarchical Bisection Algorithm

The objective of a partitioning solution is seeking to partition the set of vertices V into disjoint clusters $V_1, V_2, ..., V_n$, where by some measure the cohesiveness among the vertices in a cluster V_i is high; while the coupling crossing different clusters V_i, V_j is low. In the context of this paper, we seek to partition domain entities of two ontologies into block mappings, so that the relatedness among the domain entities in a block mapping is high, and that crossing different block mappings is low.

The partitioning approach we present in this paper is a hierarchical bisection algorithm. In each bisection, it partitions the domain entities into two disjoint block mappings B_1, B_2. We adopt the min-max cut ($Mcut$) function [5] as the criterion function. It minimizes the relatedness between the two block mappings meanwhile maximizes the relatedness within each block mapping. The $Mcut$ function is defined as follows:

$$Mcut(B_1, B_2) = \frac{cut(B_1, B_2)}{W(B_1)} + \frac{cut(B_1, B_2)}{W(B_2)}, \quad (4)$$

where $cut(B_1, B_2)$ is the sum of the relatedness among domain entities across B_1 and B_2. $W(B_1)$ is the sum of the relatedness within B_1 and $W(B_2)$ is similarly defined. The optimal bisection is the one that minimizes the $Mcut$.

The optimal solution of $Mcut$ is NP-complete. However, the relaxed version of this objective function optimization can be well solved in a spectral way. Roughly speaking, spectral partitioning makes use of the eigenvalues and eigenvectors of the relatedness matrix to find a partitioning. The merit of the spectral methods is the easiness in implementation and the reasonable performance. Furthermore, they do not intrinsically suffer from the problem of local optima.

In addition, our approach is a hierarchical approach. The reason is that it is usually difficult to specify the exact partitioning for a given domain, and there may not be a single correct answer. The block mappings in each bisection form a dendrogram. The dendrogram provides a view of the block mappings at different levels of granularity, which allows flat partitions of different granularity to be extracted. In Section 4.2, we make use of the dendrogram to extract the optimal block mappings.

The algorithm is illustrated in Table 1. The input of the algorithm is a relatedness matrix W. During a run, it recursively bisects a matrix into two submatrices by searching the minimum $Mcut$. In the end, it returns a dendrogram consisting of layers of block mappings at different levels of granularity. The eigenvector corresponding to the second smallest eigenvalue in Step 3 is also called the Fielder vector [9]. It provides a linear search order (Fielder order). The discussion on the properties of the Fielder vector is out of the scope of this paper. In Step 4, we set a parameter ϵ to limit the minimum number of domain entities in each block mapping, which can decrease the recursion times. In our experiments, we set the parameter ϵ to 10.

Table 1. The hierarchical bisection algorithm

Algorithm. The hierarchical bisection algorithm.

Input. A relatedness matrix W, and a parameter ϵ.
Output. A dendrogram consisting of layers of block mappings.

1. Initialize a diagonal matrix D with the row sums of W on its diagonal.
2. Solve the eigenvalues and eigenvectors of $(D - W)$.
3. Let v be the eigenvector corresponding to the second smallest eigenvalue.
    3.1 Sort v so that $v_i < v_{i+1}$
    3.2 Find the splitting point t such that
        $(A, B) = (\{1, ..., t\}, \{t + 1, ..., |v|\})$ minimizes the $Mcut$.
4. Let W_A, W_B be the submatrices of W, respectively.
    4.1 Recurse (Steps 1–3) on W_A until
        the number of domain entities within W_A is less than ϵ.
    4.2 Recurse (Steps 1–3) on W_B until
        the number of domain entities within W_B is less than ϵ.

The time complexity of Steps 1–4 is $O(m+n)$, where m denotes the number of nonzero components in W and n denotes the number of domain entities (equals to the row (or column) dimension of W). The most time-consuming step is Step 2. Usually, the time complexity of eigenvalue decomposition is $O(n^3)$. Since we only need a vector with the second smallest eigenvalue, the time complexity can be decreased to $O(m + n)$ via the Lanczos method [16].

4.2 Extraction of the Optimal Block Mappings

So far, we have constructed a dendrogram by the hierarchical bisection algorithm presented above. In some cases, we would like to obtain a flat partitioning with a given number of block mappings k. For this purpose, we need to extract the optimal block mappings from the dendrogram. In this paper, we use the dynamic programming method proposed in [2,5].

Let $opt(B_i, p)$ be the optimal block mappings for B_i using p block mappings. B_l, B_r denotes the left and right children of B_i in the dendrogram, respectively. Then, we have the following recurrence:

$$opt(B_i, p) = \begin{cases} B_i & \text{if } p = 1 \\ \arg\min_{1 \leq j < p} g(opt(B_l, j) \cup opt(B_r, p - j)) & \text{otherwise} \end{cases}, \quad (5)$$

where g is the objective function, which is defined as follows:

$$g(\{B_1, B_2, ..., B_p\}) = \min(\frac{cut(B_1, \overline{B_1})}{W(B_1)} + \frac{cut(B_2, \overline{B_2})}{W(B_2)} + \cdots + \frac{cut(B_p, \overline{B_p})}{W(B_p)}). \quad (6)$$

By computing the optimal block mappings from the leaf nodes in the dendrogram firstly, we can finally gain $opt(B_{root}, k)$, which includes k optimal block mappings for a flat partitioning.

5 Evaluation

We have implemented our approach in Java, called BMO, and then evaluated its performance experimentally. Due to lack of space, we cannot list all the details about our experiments. The test cases and all the experimental results can be downloaded from our website [1]. Please note that in our evaluation, we focus on the domain entities at the schema level, i.e., we just consider the classes and properties in ontologies. However, it is worthy of noting that our approach can easily be extended to the ontologies containing instances.

5.1 Case Study

In our evaluation, we choose two pairs of ontologies: russia12 and tourismAB. They can be downloaded from the website [2]. The reasons for selecting them as test cases are: (i) they are from real world domains and famous in the field of ontology matching, (ii) their sizes are moderate. If the sizes of ontologies are too small, it is unnecessary to partition them into blocks; while if the sizes are too large, they are not appropriate for human observation, and (iii) they have reference files contains aligned domain entity pairs. Short descriptions of the two pairs of ontologies are given below.

- russia12. The two ontologies are created independently by different people from the contents of two travel websites about Russia. russia1 contains 151 classes and 76 properties. russia2 contains 162 classes and 81 properties. The reference alignment file contains 85 aligned domain entity pairs.
- tourismAB. The two ontologies are created separately by different communities describing the tourism domain of Mecklenburg-Vorpommern (a federal state in the northeast of Germany). tourismA contains 340 classes and 97 properties. tourismB contains 474 classes and 100 properties. The reference alignment file contains 226 aligned domain entity pairs.

5.2 Experimental Methodology and Evaluation Metrics

Let us recall that the ideal block mappings should have both high mapping quality and high partitioning quality. In order to measure the two kinds of quality,

---
[1] http://xobjects.seu.edu.cn/project/falcon/
[2] http://www.aifb.uni-karlsruhe.de/WBS/meh/foam/

two experiments are designed to evaluate the effectiveness of BMO. The first experiment is to measure the mapping quality of block mappings. The other one is to assess the partitioning quality of block mappings. Besides, we also make a comparison between BMO and PBM [11].

In the first experiment, we evaluate the mapping quality of the computed block mappings by observing the *correctness* with the variation of the number of the block mappings. The rationale is that the higher the quality of the block matching is, the more aligned domain entity pairs could be found in the block mappings.

Let B be a set of the computed block mappings ($|B| = n$). B_i denotes the ith block mapping in B. Let R be a set of aligned domain entity pairs in a reference alignment file ($|R| = r$). R_p denotes the pth aligned domain entity pair in R. The correctness of B is defined as follows:

$$correctness(B) = \frac{1}{r} \sum_{i=1}^{n} |\{R_p | R_p \subseteq B_i, 1 \leq p \leq r\}|. \tag{7}$$

Intuitively, the correctness of B increases when the number of the block mappings decreases. In particular, when $n = 1$, the correctness of B is 1.0. However, it is clear that merely considering the metric of the correctness is not sound. We need to evaluate the quality of block mappings in other aspects.

In the second experiment, we focus on evaluating the partitioning quality of the block matching. Three volunteers are trained to set up manual block mappings. We assess the partitioning quality of the computed block mappings by comparing with the manual ones. In this experiment, we set n equal to the number of block mappings of the manual ones. This kind of measurement is widely adopted in the field of Data Clustering.

We use two well-known metrics to compare the gained block mappings with the manual ones. The first metric is *f-measure*. The other one is *entropy*. Before introducing the two metrics, we firstly defined two basic operations (*precision* and *recall*), which are used to compare a gained block mapping with a manual one. Let C be the set of the manual block mappings ($|C| = m$). C_j denotes the jth block mapping in C. $|B_i|$ returns the number of domain entities in B_i, and $|C_j|$ is defined analogously. $|B_i \cap C_j|$ calculates the mutual domain entities in both B_i and C_j. The precision and recall of a computed block mapping B_i referring to C_j are defined as follows respectively:

$$prec(B_i, C_j) = \frac{|B_i \cap C_j|}{|B_i|}, \tag{8}$$

$$reca(B_i, C_j) = \frac{|B_i \cap C_j|}{|C_j|}. \tag{9}$$

The f-measure is defined as a combination of the precision and recall. Its score is in the range $[0, 1]$, and a higher f-measure score implies a better partitioning quality. The f-measure of the set of computed block mappings B is defined as follows:

$$f\text{-}measure(B) = \frac{1}{\sum_{i=1}^{n}|B_i|} \cdot \sum_{i=1}^{n} f\text{-}measure(B_i) \cdot |B_i|, \quad (10)$$

$$f\text{-}measure(B_i) = \max_{1 \leq j \leq m} \frac{2 \cdot prec(B_i, C_j) \cdot reca(B_i, C_j)}{prec(B_i, C_j) + reca(B_i, C_j)}. \quad (11)$$

The other metric is the entropy. It considers the distribution of domain entities in block mappings and reflects the overall partitioning quality. A lower entropy score implies a better partitioning quality. The best possible entropy score is 0; while the worst is 1. The entropy of the set of the computed block mappings B is defined as follows:

$$entropy(B) = \frac{1}{\sum_{i=1}^{n}|B_i|} \cdot \sum_{i=1}^{n} entropy(B_i) \cdot |B_i|, \quad (12)$$

$$entropy(B_i) = -\frac{1}{\log m} \cdot \sum_{j=1}^{m} prec(B_i, C_j) \cdot \log(prec(B_i, C_j)). \quad (13)$$

In the last experiment, we compare both the mapping quality and the partitioning quality of BMO with PBM [11]. Because PBM merely copes with mappings between classes, for comparing the mapping quality, we remove the aligned property pairs in the reference alignment files, only retaining 70 aligned class pairs in `russia12` and 190 aligned class pairs in `tourismAB`. In addition, we construct the manual block mappings only between classes to evaluate the partitioning quality of these two approaches.

5.3 Discussion on Experimental Results

Firstly, the correctness with the variation of the number of the block mappings (denoted by n) is depicted in Figure 2. We can see that in the two test cases, when n increases, the correctness of the block mappings decreases. We can also find that in most situations, the correctness of the results is fine. In particular, in `tourismAB`, when $n = 50$, the correctness is still larger than 95%. It demonstrates that the mapping quality of the block mappings computed by BMO is high. In addition, the correctness does not decrease drastically as n increases. It implies that BMO is stable with a pretty good accuracy.

Secondly, by setting the number of the required block mappings (25 block mappings for `russia12`, and 26 block mappings for `tourismAB`), we can compare the results of BMO with the manual ones to evaluate the partitioning quality. The partitioning quality of the computed block mappings are shown in Table 2. Both the f-measure and the entropy are moderate.

Finally, the comparison results of the mapping quality and the partitioning quality between BMO and PBM are presented in Table 3. Both the number of the required block mappings for `russia12` and for `tourismAB` are 13. From the table, we can see that the partitioning quality between the two approach are almost the same. However, the mapping quality of the BMO approach is far beyond the one of PBM. For example, in `russia12`, the correctness of the BMO approach is 0.84; while the one of PBM is merely 0.57.

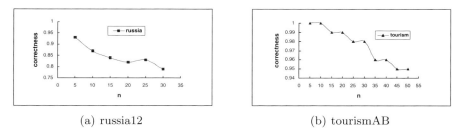

Fig. 2. The correctness with the variation of the number of the block mappings n

Table 2. The partitioning quality of BMO

	number	f-measure	entropy
russia12	25	0.61	0.28
tourismAB	26	0.52	0.22

Table 3. The comparison between BMO and PBM

	approach	number	correctness	f-measure	entropy
russia12	BMO	13	0.84	0.56	0.37
	PBM	13	0.57	0.65	0.33
tourismAB	BMO	13	0.98	0.67	0.31
	PBM	13	0.66	0.57	0.30

Based on the observations above, we can make a preliminary and empirical conclusion that our approach is feasible for achieving a good mapping quality as well as a good partitioning quality.

6 Related Work

In this section, we firstly discuss some related works on ontology matching, and then we present some related works on ontology partitioning.

6.1 Ontology Matching

Despite many works (e.g., [6,7,8,10,11,13,14,20,23]) have addressed the ontology matching (also called ontology mapping or alignment) problem, there exist very few approaches raising the issue of block matching. PBM [11] is the only work we know so far that considers the block matching problem. It exploits block mappings between two class hierarchies by firstly partitioning them into blocks respectively, and then constructing the mappings between blocks via the pre-defined anchors generated by the string comparison techniques. The weakness of that work is that it ignores the correspondence between the two hierarchies when doing partitioning, so the mapping quality is not satisfied. Furthermore, it just copes with mappings between classes, so it might not be applicable to ontology matching in general.

In the field of schema matching (please see [18] for a survey), iMAP [4] is semi-automatically discovers both the 1:1 and complex mappings (e.g., room-price = room-rate $*(1 +$ tax-rate$)$). It embeds two new kinds of domain knowledge (overlapped data and external data) to find complex mappings. However, iMAP may not be a universal solution, because it is not easy to specify the domain knowledge in some cases. ARTEMIS [1] is another work which vaguely presents the idea of block matching. It firstly computes the 1:1 mappings between two ontologies by using WordNet, and then constructs block mappings from the 1:1 mappings via a clustering algorithm. This is similar to the framework of our approach. But it is clear that the method always suffers from the high computational complexity for calculating the 1:1 mappings. More importantly, it discards both the linguistic and structural characteristics in each of the two ontologies, thus the partitioning quality cannot be guaranteed.

6.2 Ontology Partitioning

From another viewpoint, our method partitions two ontologies into blocks throughout the process of searching the block mappings. So it might be broken down into the category of ontology partitioning. [3,15,22,24] are some representative works. However, these works only provide a flat partitioning on a single ontology; while our work supports a hierarchical view with different levels of granularity, and partitions two ontologies at the same time. But, we should note that these ontology partitioning techniques might also be used to find block mappings by partitioning two ontologies separately, and then matching these blocks. This is just the method adopted in PBM. Although this kind of methodology could deal with the block matching problem between large-scale ontologies, as shown in our experiments, the mapping quality is usually not so good as BMO's.

7 Concluding Remarks

In summary, the main contributions of this paper are as follows.

- We discussed the block matching problem and suggested both the mapping quality and the partitioning quality should be considered in block matching.
- We proposed a relatedness measure based on virtual documents that simultaneously importing both linguistic and structural characteristics of domain entities.
- We presented a hierarchical bisection algorithm to provide block mappings at different levels of granularity. Also, we described a method to automatically extract the optimal block mappings for a flat partitioning.
- We set up two kinds of metrics to evaluate of the quality of block matching. The experimental results demonstrated that our approach is feasible.

The work reported here is a first step towards block matching for ontologies, and many issues still need to be addressed. In future work, we plan to find other possible approaches to block matching, and compare them with each other. Furthermore, in order to make steady progress on the block matching problem, it is valuable to set up systematic test cases for block matching. Another issue is block matching for very large-scale ontologies.

Acknowledgements

The work is supported in part by the NSFC under Grant 60573083, and in part by the 973 Program of China under Grant 2003CB317004, and also in part by the JSNSF under Grant BK2003001. We are grateful to Prof. Jianming Deng and Dr. Yanbing Wang for their valuable suggestions. We also thank Gong Cheng, Yuanyuan Zhao and Dongdong Zheng for their work in the experiments related to this paper. In the end, we appreciate anonymous reviewers for their precious comments.

References

1. Castano, S., De Antonellis, V., and De Capitani Di Vimercati, S.: Global viewing of heterogeneous data sources. IEEE Transactions on Knowledge and Data Engineering. **13(2)** (2001) 277–297
2. Cheng, D., Kannan, R., Vempala, S., and Wang, G.: A divide-and-merge methodology for clustering. In Proceedings of the 24th ACM Symposium on Principles of Database Systems (PODS'05). (2005) 196–205
3. Cuenca Grau, B., Parsia, B., and Sirin, E.: Combining OWL ontologies using ε-connections. Journal of Web Semantics. **4(1)** (2005)
4. Dhamankar, R., Lee, Y., Doan, A. H., Halevy, A., and Domingos, P.: iMAP: Discovering complex semantic matches between database schemas. In Proceedings of the 23th ACM International Conference on Management of Data (SIGMOD'04). (2004) 383–394
5. Ding, C. H. Q., He, X., Zha, H., Gu, M., and Simon, H. D.: A min-max cut algorithm for graph partitioning and data clustering. In Proceedings of the 2001 IEEE International Conference on Data Mining (ICDM'01). (2001) 107–114
6. Doan, A., Madhavan, J., Dhamankar, R., Domingos, P., and Halevy, A. Y.: Learning to match ontologies on the semantic web. VLDB Journal. **12(4)** (2003) 303–319
7. Ehrig, M., and Staab, S.: QOM - quick ontology mapping. In Proceedings of the 3rd International Semantic Web Conference (ISWC'04). (2004) 683–697
8. Euzenat, J., and Valtchev, P.: Similarity-based ontology alignment in OWL-Lite. In Proceedings of the 16th European Conference on Artificial Intelligence (ECAI'04). (2004) 333–337
9. Fiedler, M.: A property of eigenvectors of nonnegative symmetric matrices and its application to graph theory. Czechoslovak Mathematical Journal. **25** (1975) 619–633
10. Giunchiglia, F., Shvaiko, P., and Yatskevich, M.: S-Match: An algorithm and an implementation of semantic matching. In Proceedings of the 1st European Semantic Web Symposium (ESWS'04). (2004) 61–75

11. Hu, W., Zhao, Y. Y., and Qu, Y. Z.: Partition-based block matching of large class hierarchies. In Proceedings of the 1st Asian Semantic Web Conference (ASWC'06). (2006) 72–83
12. Klyne, G., and Carroll, J. J. (eds.): Resource description framework (RDF): Concepts and abstract syntax. W3C Recommendation 10 February 2004. Latest version is available at http://www.w3.org/TR/rdf-concepts/
13. Kotis, K., Vouros, G. A., and Stergiou, K.: Towards automatic merging of domain ontologies: The HCONE-merge approach. Journal of Web Semantics. **4(1)** (2005)
14. Noy, N. F., and Musen, M. A.: The PROMPT suite: Interactive tools for ontology merging and mapping. International Journal of Human-Computer Studies. **59** (2003) 983–1024
15. Noy, N. F., and Musen, M. A.: Specifying ontology views by traversal. In Proceedings of the 3rd International Semantic Web Conference (ISWC'04). (2004) 713–725
16. Parlett, B. N.: The symmetric eigenvalue problem. SIAM Press. (1998)
17. Raghavan, V. V., and Wong, S. K. M.: A critical analysis of vector space model for information retrieval. Journal of the American Society for Information Science. **37(5)** (1986) 279–287
18. Rahm, E., and Bernstein, P.: A survey of approaches to automatic schema matching. VLDB Journal. **10** (2001) 334–350
19. Patel-Schneider, P. F., Hayes, P., and Horrocks, I. (eds.): OWL web ontology language semantics and abstract syntax. W3C Recommendation 10 February 2004. Latest version is available at http://www.w3.org/TR/owl-semantics/
20. Qu, Y. Z., Hu, W., and Cheng, G.: Constructing virtual documents for ontology matching. In Proceedings of the 15th International World Wide Web Conference (WWW'06). (2006) 23–31
21. Salton, G., and McGill, M. H.: Introduction to modern information retrieval. McGraw-Hill. (1983)
22. Seidenberg, J., and Rector, A.: Web ontology segmentation: analysis, classification and use. In Proceedings of the 15th International World Wide Web Conference (WWW'06). (2006) 13–22
23. Stoilos, G., Stamou, G., and Kollias, S.: A string metric for ontology alignment. In Proceedings of the 4th International Semantic Web Conference (ISWC'05). (2005) 623–637
24. Stuckenschmidt, H., and Klein, M.: Structure-based partitioning of large concept hierarchies. In Proceedings of the 3rd International Semantic Web Conference (ISWC'04). (2004) 289–303

A Relaxed Approach to RDF Querying

Carlos A. Hurtado[1,*], Alexandra Poulovassilis[2], and Peter T. Wood[2]

[1] Universidad de Chile
churtado@dcc.uchile.cl
[2] Birkbeck, University of London
{ap, ptw}@dcs.bbk.ac.uk

Abstract. We explore flexible querying of RDF data, with the aim of making it possible to return data satisfying query conditions with varying degrees of exactness, and also to rank the results of a query depending on how "closely" they satisfy the query conditions. We make queries more flexible by logical relaxation of their conditions based on RDFS entailment and RDFS ontologies. We develop a notion of ranking of query answers, and present a query processing algorithm for incrementally computing the relaxed answer of a query. Our approach has application in scenarios where there is a lack of understanding of the ontology underlying the data, or where the data objects have heterogeneous sets of properties or irregular structures.

1 Introduction

The conjunctive fragment of most RDF query languages (e.g., see [8,9]) consists of queries of the form $H \leftarrow B$, where the body of the query B is a graph pattern, that is, an RDF graph over IRIs, literals, blanks, and variables. The head of the query H is either a graph pattern or a tuple variable (list of variables). The semantics of these queries is simple. It is based on finding matchings from the body of the query to the data and then applying the matchings to the head of the query to obtain the answers.

Recently, the W3C RDF data access group has emphasized the importance of enhancing RDF query languages to meet the requirements of contexts where RDF can be used to solve real problems. In particular, it has been stated that in RDF querying "it must be possible to express a query that does not fail when some specified part of the query fails to match" [5]. This requirement has motivated the OPTIONAL clause, presented in the emerging SPARQL W3C proposal for querying RDF [13] and previously introduced in SeRQL [3]. The OPTIONAL clause allows the query to find matchings that fail to match some conditions in the body. In contrast to other approaches to flexible querying (e.g., [1,11]), the OPTIONAL construct incorporates flexibility from a "logical" standpoint, via relaxation of the query's conditions. This idea, however, is exploited only to a limited extent, since the conditions of a query could be relaxed in ways

---

[*] Carlos A. Hurtado was supported by Millennium Nucleus, Center for Web Research (P04-067-F), Mideplan, and by project FONDECYT 1030810, Chile.

other than simply dropping optional triple patterns, for example by replacing constants with variables or by using the class and property hierarchies in an ontology associated with the data (such as that shown in Figure 1).

1.1 RDFS Ontologies

It is common that users interact with RDF applications in the context of an ontology. We assume that the ontology is modeled as an RDF graph with interpreted RDFS vocabulary. The RDFS vocabulary defines classes and properties that may be used for describing groups of related resources and relationships between resources. To state that a resource is an instance of a class, the property rdf:type may be used. In this paper we use a fragment of the RDFS vocabulary, which comprises (in brackets is the shorter name we will use) rdfs: range [range], rdfs:domain [dom], rdf:type [type], rdfs: subClassOf [sc] and rdfs:subPropertyOf [sp][1].

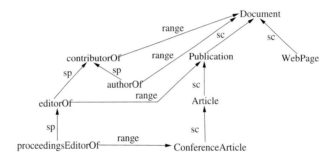

Fig. 1. An RDFS ontology modeling documents and people who contribute to them

As an example, the ontology of Figure 1 is used to model documents along with properties that model different ways people contribute to them (e.g., as authors, editors, or being the editor of the proceedings where an article is published).

1.2 The RELAX Clause

In this paper, we propose the introduction of a RELAX clause as a generalization of the OPTIONAL clause for conjunctive queries. As an example, consider the following SPARQL-like query Q^2:

$$?Z, ?Y \leftarrow \{(?X, name, ?Z), \texttt{OPTIONAL}\{(?X, proceedingsEditorOf, ?Y)\}\}.$$

---

[1] We omit in this paper vocabulary used to refer to basic classes in RDF/S such as rdf: Property, rdfs: Class, rdfs:Resource, rdfs:Literal, rdfs:XMLLiteral, rdfs:Datatype, among others. We also omit vocabulary for lists, collections, and variations on these, as well as vocabulary used to place comments in RDF/S data.

[2] SPARQL has SQL-like syntax; for brevity, in this paper we express queries as rules.

The body of this query is a graph pattern comprising two triple patterns. This query returns names of people along with the IRIs of conference articles whose proceedings they have edited. Because the second triple pattern in the body of the query is within the scope of an OPTIONAL clause, the query also returns names of people for which the second pattern fails to match the data (i.e., people who have not edited proceedings).

Now consider the ontology of Figure 1. Although the user may want to retrieve editors of proceedings at first, she/he might also be interested in knowing about people who have contributed to publications in other roles, along with the publications themselves. In order to save the user the effort of inspecting the ontology and rewriting the query, the system could automatically return more relaxed answers for the same original query. This is achieved by rewriting Q to replace OPTIONAL with RELAX. Now after returning editors of conference proceedings, the system can replace the triple pattern $(?X, proceedingsEditorOf, ?Y)$ with $(?X, editorOf, ?Y)$, yielding a new, relaxed query that returns editors of publications along with their publications. Subsequently, this triple pattern can be rewritten to the triple pattern $(?X, contributorOf, ?Y)$ to obtain more general answers.

Group A (Subproperty) (1) $\frac{(a,\mathrm{sp},b)\ (b,\mathrm{sp},c)}{(a,\mathrm{sp},c)}$ (2) $\frac{(a,\mathrm{sp},b)\ (x,a,y)}{(x,b,y)}$

Group B (Subclass) (3) $\frac{(a,\mathrm{sc},b)\ (b,\mathrm{sc},c)}{(a,\mathrm{sc},c)}$ (4) $\frac{(a,\mathrm{sc},b)\ (x,\mathrm{type},a)}{(x,\mathrm{type},b)}$

Group C (Typing) (5) $\frac{(a,\mathrm{dom},c)\ (x,a,y)}{(x,\mathrm{type},c)}$ (6) $\frac{(a,\mathrm{range},d)\ (x,a,y)}{(y,\mathrm{type},d)}$

(Simple Entailment) (7) For a map $\mu : G' \to G : \frac{G}{G'}$

Fig. 2. RDFS Inference Rules

The idea of making queries more flexible by the logical relaxation of their conditions is not new in database research. Gaasterland et al. [7] established the foundations of such a mechanism in the context of deductive databases and logic programming, and called the technique *query relaxation*.

1.3 Notion of Query Relaxation for RDF

We study the query relaxation problem in the setting of the RDF/S data model and RDF query languages and show that query relaxation can be naturally formalized using RDFS entailment. We use an operational semantics for the notion of RDFS entailment, denoted $\models$, characterized by the derivation rules given in Figure 2 (for details, see [8,10]). Rules in groups (A), (B), and (C) describe the semantics of the RDFS vocabulary we use in this paper (i.e., sp, sc, type, dom, and range), and rule 7 (which is based on the notion of map which we will explain in Section 2), essentially states that blank nodes behave like existentially quantified variables. As an example, from a graph we can entail another graph which replaces constants with blanks or blanks with other blanks.

Intuitively, as RDFS entailment is characterized by the rules of Figure 2, a relaxed triple pattern t' can be obtained from triple t by applying the derivation rules to t and triples from the ontology. As an example, the triple pattern $(?X, proceedingsEditorOf, ?Y)$ can be relaxed to $(?X, editorOf, ?Y)$, by applying rule 3 to the former and the triple $(proceedingsEditorOf, \texttt{sp}, editorOf)$ in the ontology of Figure 1. The different relaxed versions of an original query are obtained by combining relaxations of triple patterns that appear inside a `RELAX` clause.

The notion of query relaxation we propose naturally subsumes two broad classes of relaxations (further types of relaxations within these two classes are listed in Section 3.4). The first class of relaxation, which we call *simple relaxations*, consists of relaxations that can be entailed without an ontology, which include dropping triple patterns, replacing constants with variables, and breaking join dependencies. These are captured by derivation rule 7 (Figure 2). The second class of relaxations, which we call *ontology relaxations*, includes relaxations entailed using information from the ontology and are captured by rule groups (A),(B) and (C); these include relaxing type conditions, relaxing properties using domain or range restrictions and others.

1.4 Summary of Contributions and Outline

In this paper, we develop a framework for query relaxation for RDF. We introduce a notion of query relaxation based on RDFS entailment, which naturally incorporates RDFS ontologies and captures necessary information for relaxation such as the class and property hierarchies.

By formalizing query relaxation in terms of entailment, we obtain a semantic notion which is by no means limited to RDFS and could also be extended to more expressive settings such as OWL entailment and OWL ontologies, to capture further relaxations. Our framework generalizes, for the conjunctive fragment of SPARQL, the idea of dropping query conditions provided by the `OPTIONAL` construct.

An essential aspect of our proposal, which sets it apart from previous work on query relaxation, is to rank the results of a query based on how "closely" they satisfy the query. We present a notion of ranking based on a structure called the *relaxation graph*, in which relaxed versions of the original query are ordered from less to more general from a logical standpoint. Since the relaxation graph is based on logic subsumption, ranking does not depend on any syntactic condition on the knowledge used for relaxation (such as rule ordering in logic-programming approaches [7]). Finally, we sketch a query processing algorithm to compute the relaxed answer of a query, and examine its correctness and complexity.

The rest of the paper is organized as follows. Section 2 introduces preliminary notation. Section 3 formalizes query relaxation and Section 4 studies query processing. In Section 5 we study related work and in Section 6 we present some concluding remarks.

2 Preliminary Definitions

In this section we present the basic notation and definitions that will be used subsequently in this paper. Some of these were introduced in [2,8,10,12].

RDF Graphs. In this paper we work with RDF graphs which may mention the RDFS vocabulary. We assume there are infinite sets I (IRIs), B (blank nodes), and L (RDF literals). The elements in $I \cup B \cup L$ are called RDF *terms*. A triple $(v_1, v_2, v_3) \in (I \cup B) \times I \times (I \cup B \cup L)$ is called an *RDF triple*. In such a triple, v_1 is called the *subject*, v_2 the *predicate* and v_3 the *object*. An *RDF graph* (just graph from now on) is a set of RDF triples. Given two RDF graphs G_1, G_2, a *map* from G_1 to G_2 is a function μ from terms of G_1 to terms of G_2, preserving IRIs and literals, such that for each triple $(a, b, c) \in G_1$ we have $(\mu(a), \mu(b), \mu(c)) \in G_2$.

Entailment. We will decompose RDFS entailment into two notions of entailment. The first is simple entailment [10], which depends only on the basic logical form of RDF graphs and therefore holds for any vocabulary. An RDF graph G_1 *simply entails* G_2, denoted $G_1 \models_{\texttt{simple}} G_2$, if and only if there exists a map from G_2 to G_1. That is, simple entailment is captured by rule 7 of Figure 2.

The second notion of entailment captures the semantics added by the RDFS vocabulary. We write that $G_1 \models_{\texttt{rule}} G_2$ if G_2 can be derived from G_1 by iteratively applying rules in groups (A), (B) and (C) of Figure 2. In this paper, we also use a notion of closure of an RDF graph G [10], denoted $\text{cl}(G)$, which is the closure of G under the rules in groups (A), (B) and (C). We have that $G_1 \models_{\texttt{rule}} G_2$ if and only if $G_2 \in \text{cl}(G_1)$.

Now, by a result from from [10], RDFS entailment (for the fragment of RDFS we use in this paper) can be characterized as follows: G_1 RDFS-entails G_2, denoted $G_1 \models_{\texttt{RDFS}} G_2$, if and only if there is a graph G such that $G_1 \models_{\texttt{rule}} G$ and $G \models_{\texttt{simple}} G_2$. An alternative characterization of RDFS entailment is the following: $G_1 \models_{\texttt{RDFS}} G_2$ if and only if there is a map from G_2 to $\text{cl}(G_1)$. Therefore, in order to test the entailment $G_1 \models_{\texttt{RDFS}} G_2$, we can first apply rules in groups (A), (B), and (C) to compute $\text{cl}(G_1)$, and then check whether there exists a map from G_2 to $\text{cl}(G_1)$.

Graph Patterns. Consider a set of variables V disjoint from the sets I, B, and L. A *triple pattern* is a triple $(v_1, v_2, v_3) \in (I \cup V) \times (I \cup V) \times (I \cup V \cup L)$. A *graph pattern* is a set of triple patterns. Given a graph pattern P, we denote by $\texttt{var}(P)$ the variables mentioned in P. The following notation is needed to define triple pattern relaxation in Section 3. The notion of map is generalized to graph patterns by treating variables as blank nodes. . In addition, t_1 is S-isomorphic to t_2 if there are maps μ_1 from t_1 to t_2 and μ_2 from t_2 to t_1 that both preserve S. In our examples, variables are indicated by a leading question mark, while literals are enclosed in quotes.

Conjunctive Queries for RDF. A *conjunctive query* Q is an expression $T \leftarrow B$, where B is a graph pattern, and $T = \langle T_1, \ldots, T_n \rangle$ is a list of variables which belongs to $\texttt{var}(B)$. (The framework formalized in this paper can be easily extended to queries with graph patterns as query heads.) We denote T by $\texttt{Head}(Q)$, and B by $\text{Body}(Q)$. A query Q may be formulated over an RDFS ontology O, which means that Q may mention vocabulary from O and its answer is obtained taking into account the semantics of O. We assume that the ontology is well designed in the sense that predicates of triples in O cannot be in the set $\{\text{type}, \text{dom}, \text{range}, \text{sp}, \text{sc}\}$. We define a *matching* to be a function from variables in $\text{Body}(Q)$ to blanks, IRIs and literals. Given a matching Θ, we denote by $\Theta(\text{Body}(Q))$ the graph resulting from $\text{Body}(Q)$ by replacing each variable X by $\Theta(X)$. Given an RDF graph G, the *answer* of Q is the set of tuples, denoted $\text{ans}(Q, O, G)$, defined as follows: for each matching Θ such that $\Theta(\text{Body}(Q)) \subseteq \text{cl}(O \cup G)$, return $\Theta(\text{Head}(Q))$. When O is clear from the context, we omit it, and write $\text{ans}(Q, G)$ instead of $\text{ans}(Q, O, G)$.

3 Formalizing Query Relaxation

We will present a relaxed semantics for queries in a stepwise manner. In Section 3.1, we present the notion of relaxation of triple patterns, and in Section 3.2 we introduce the notion of the relaxation graph of a triple pattern. This is used in Section 3.3 to define the relaxation graph of a query. The relaxation graph is the basis for the notion of the relaxed answer and ranking of a query we propose in Section 3.5. In Section 3.4, we explain different types of relaxations.

3.1 Triple Pattern Relaxation

We model relaxation as a combination of two types of relaxations, *ontology relaxation* and *simple relaxation*. Intuitively, the former comprises relaxations that are based on the ontology at hand and do not replace terms of the original triple pattern. In contrast, simple relaxations consist only of replacements of terms of the original triple pattern (e.g., replacing a literal or URI with a variable or a variable with another variable).

Relaxation will be defined in the context of an ontology, denoted by O, and a set of variables, called *fixed variables*, denoted by F. So we fix O and F for the definitions that follow.

Let t_1, t_2 be triple patterns, where $t_1 \notin \text{cl}(O)$, $t_2 \notin \text{cl}(O)$, and $\text{var}(t_2) = \text{var}(t_1) \subseteq F$. Ontology relaxation is defined as follows: $t_1 \prec^*_{\text{onto}} t_2$ if $(\{t_1\} \cup O) \models_{\text{rule}} t_2$. As an example, let O be the ontology of Figure 1 and let $F = \{?X\}$. Then, we have that $(?X, \text{type}, \textit{ConferenceArticle}) \prec^*_{\text{onto}} (?X, \text{type}, \textit{Article})$, and we have that $(\textit{JohnRobert}, \textit{ContributorOf}, ?X) \prec^*_{\text{onto}} (?X, \text{type}, \textit{Document})$, among other ontology relaxations. It is not the case that $(?X, \textit{ContributorOf}, ?Y) \prec^*_{\text{onto}} (?Y, \text{type}, \textit{Document})$, since the set of variables of the triples are different.

Simple relaxation is defined as follows: $t_1 \prec^*_{\text{simple}} t_2$ if $t_1 \models_{\text{simple}} t_2$ via a map μ that preserves F (recall the notion of a map preserving a set of variables from Section 2). As an example, we have $(?X, \text{type}, \textit{Article}) \prec^*_{\text{simple}} (?X, \text{type}, ?Z)$ and $(?X, \text{type}, \textit{Article}) \prec^*_{\text{simple}} (?X, ?W, \textit{Article})$, among other simple relaxations.

We now define relaxation. We say that t_2 *relaxes* t_1, denoted $t_1 \prec^* t_2$, if one of the following hold: (i) $t_1 \prec^*_{\text{onto}} t_2$, (ii) $t_1 \prec^*_{\text{simple}} t_2$, or (iii) there exists a triple pattern t such that $t_1 \prec^* t$ and $t \prec^* t_2$. The following proposition proves that simple relaxations always arise after ontology relaxations.

Proposition 1. *Let t_1, t_2 be triple patterns. Then $t_1 \prec^* t_2$ if and only if there exists t such that $t_1 \prec^*_{\text{onto}} t$ and $t \prec^*_{\text{simple}} t_2$.*

We will end this section by proving some properties of the relaxation relationships introduced. We define an ontology O to be acyclic if the subgraphs defined by sc and sp are acyclic. Acyclicity is considered good practice in modeling ontologies. Recall the notion of graph pattern isomorphism with respect to a set of fixed variables from Section 2.

Proposition 2. *Let $\prec^*_{\text{onto}}$, $\prec^*_{\text{simple}}$ and $\prec^*$ be defined in the context of an ontology O and a set F of fixed variables. (i) $\prec^*_{\text{onto}}$ is a partial order if and only if O is acyclic. (ii) $\prec^*_{\text{simple}}$ is a partial order up to F-isomorphism. (iii) $\prec^*$ is a partial order up to F-isomorphism if and only if O is acyclic.*

In what follows we assume that O is acyclic, and assume triple patterns to be equal if they are F-isomorphic. Therefore, we consider the relaxation relations to be partial orders. In particular, if a variable is not in F, without loss of generality we assume it appears in no more that one triple pattern. We denote by $\prec$ (direct relaxation) the reflexive and transitive reduction of $\prec^*$ (relaxation). We use similar notation for ontology and simple relaxation.

3.2 Relaxation Graph of a Triple Pattern

We are interested in relaxing each of the triple patterns that occurs inside the RELAX clause of a query, so we next adapt the relaxation relationship to use relaxation "above" a given triple pattern. The relaxation relation "above" a triple pattern t, denoted by $\prec^*_t$, is $\prec^*$ restricted to triple patterns t' such that $t \prec^* t'$, and where $F = \text{var}(t)$ (i.e., the variables of t are the fixed variables in the relaxation). The *relaxation graph* of a triple pattern t is the directed acyclic graph induced by $\prec_t$.

As an example, consider the ontology O of Figure 1. Let t be the triple pattern $(?X, \text{type}, \textit{Publication})$. Figure 3 (A) shows the relaxation graph of $(?X, \text{type}, \textit{Publication})$. We have that $?X$ is the unique fixed variable. The non-fixed variables in this graph are $?V1, \ldots, ?V5$. Figure 3 (B) shows the relaxation graph of $(\textit{JohnRobert}, \textit{editorOf}, ?X)$. Now the non-fixed variables are $?U1, \ldots, ?U9$. Notice that this pattern directly relaxes to $(?X, \text{type}, \textit{Publication})$, so this relaxation graph has as a subgraph the relaxation graph of Figure 3 (A).

3.3 Query Relaxation

In this section, we define query relaxation as the direct product of the relaxation relations of its triple patterns. We define the *direct product* of two partial order relations α_1, α_2, denoted $\alpha_1 \otimes \alpha_2$, as the relation α such that $(e_1, e_2) \alpha (e'_1, e'_2)$ if and only if $e_1 \alpha_1 e'_1$ and $e_2 \alpha_2 e'_2$. The generalization of this definition to more than two relations is straightforward.

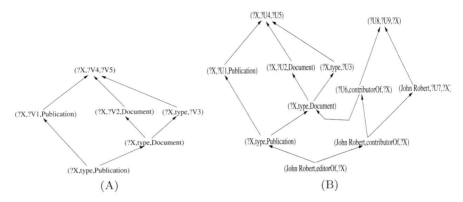

Fig. 3. (A) Relaxation graph of the triple pattern $(?X, \texttt{type}, Publication)$. (B) Relaxation graph of the triple pattern $(JohnRobert, editorOf, ?X)$.

Given a query Q, let $\texttt{Body}(Q) = \{t_1, \ldots, t_n\}$. For any triple t_i not inside a RELAX clause, we overload the notation $\prec^*_{t_i}$ and assume that t_i relaxes only to t_i. The relaxation relation "above" Q, denoted by $\prec^*_Q$, is defined as $\prec^*_{t_1} \otimes \prec^*_{t_2}$ $\ldots \otimes \prec^*_{t_n}$. Direct relaxation, denoted $\prec_Q$, is the reflexive and transitive reduction of $\prec^*_Q$. The *relaxation graph* of Q is the directed acyclic graph induced by $\prec_Q$.

Each node $(t'_1, \ldots, t'_n)$ in the relaxation graph of Q denotes the conjunctive query $\texttt{Head}(Q) \leftarrow t'_1, \ldots, t'_n$. In order to avoid name clashes, we assume that the sets of non-fixed variables introduced in the relaxation relations of the triple pattern are pairwise disjoint.

3.4 Types of Relaxation

The notion of relaxation that we propose in this paper encompasses several different types of relaxation. Those captured by simple relaxation are as follows:

1. Dropping triple patterns. We can model the dropping of triple patterns by introducing an "empty" triple pattern, which can be regarded as a "true" condition to which any triple pattern relaxes. In this form, relaxation generalizes the use of the OPTIONAL clause within the conjunctive fragment of SPARQL.
2. Constant relaxation: replacing a constant with a variable in a triple pattern. This can be further classified according to whether the variable replaces a property or a subject/object constant.
3. Breaking join dependencies: generating new variable names for a variable that appears in multiple triple patterns. In order to model this type of relaxation, we first transform queries by applying variable substitution. If a variable $?X$ appears $n > 1$ times in a query Q we replace each occurrence with a different variable and add triple patterns $(?X_i, \texttt{equal}, ?X_j)$ for each pair of new variables $?X_i, ?X_j$ introduced. The predicate equal represents equality. Each of the equality clauses in a query can now also be subject to relaxation.

The following types of relaxation are captured by our notion of ontology relaxation (the examples given use the ontology of Figure 1):

1. Type relaxation: replacing a triple pattern $(a, \texttt{type}, b)$ with $(a, \texttt{type}, c)$, where $(b, \texttt{sc}, c) \in \text{cl}(O)$. For example, the triple pattern $(?X, \texttt{type}, ConferenceArticle)$ can be relaxed to $(?X, \texttt{type}, Article)$ and then to $(?X, \texttt{type}, Publication)$.
2. Predicate relaxation: replacing a triple pattern (a, p, b) with (a, q, c), where $(p, \texttt{sp}, q) \in \text{cl}(O)$. For example, the triple pattern $(?X, proceedingsEditorOf, ?Y)$ can be relaxed to $(?X, editorOf, ?Y)$ and then to $(?X, contributorOf, ?Y)$.
3. Predicate to domain relaxation: replacing a triple pattern (a, p, b) with $(a, \texttt{type}, c)$, where $(p, \texttt{dom}, c) \in \text{cl}(O)$. There are no domain declarations in Figure 1.
4. Predicate to range relaxation: replacing a triple pattern (a, p, b) with $(b, \texttt{type}, c)$, where $(p, \texttt{range}, c) \in \text{cl}(O)$. For example, the triple pattern $(?X, editorOf, ?Y)$ can be relaxed to $(?Y, \texttt{type}, Publication)$.
5. Additional relaxations induced by additional rules from Figure 2. Combinations of rules yield additional forms of relaxation. For example, the triple pattern $(Article, \texttt{sc}, ?Y)$ can be relaxed to $(ConferenceArticle, \texttt{sc}, ?Y)$.

3.5 Relaxed Answer and Ranking

Any algorithm that computes a relaxed answer to a query should also return the tuples in the relaxed answer according to some ordering. So the output of a query processing algorithm can be viewed as twofold: (a) the relaxed answer (already defined) and (b) a rank function that defines an ordering for the tuples in the relaxed answer. We next define the notions of *relaxed answer*, *rank function* and *consistency* of a rank function. Roughly, consistency means that the tuple ordering defined by the rank function agrees with the ordering of queries imposed by the query relaxation graph.

Let Q be an RDF query and G be an RDF graph. The *level of a query* Q_i in the relaxation graph of Q is the length of the shortest path from Q to Q_i. We denote by $\texttt{relax}(Q, k)$ the set of queries in the relaxation graph whose level is less than or equal to k. The *relaxed answer* of Q over G at level $k \geq 1$, $\texttt{ans}_{\texttt{relax}}(Q, G, k)$, is the set of tuples $\bigcup_{Q' \in \texttt{relax}(Q,k)} \texttt{ans}(Q', G)$. We will frequently mention $\texttt{ans}_{\texttt{relax}}(Q, G, k)$ in a context where k is fixed, and in this context we will write $\texttt{ans}_{\texttt{relax}}(Q, G, k)$ simply as $\texttt{ans}_{\texttt{relax}}(Q, G)$.

For a query Q' in the relaxation graph of Q, and an RDF graph G, we define $\texttt{newAnswer}(Q', G)$ as $\texttt{ans}(Q', G) - (\bigcup_{Q_i : Q_i \prec^*_Q Q'} \texttt{ans}(Q_i, G))$.

Let Q be a query and G be an RDF graph. A *rank function* for the relaxed answer of Q over G is any function $\tau_{Q,G}$ with signature $\tau_{Q,G} : (\texttt{ans}_{\texttt{relax}}(Q, G)) \to N$. A rank function $\tau_{Q,G}$ is *consistent* if and only if for each pair of tuples $t_i, t_j \in \texttt{ans}_{\texttt{relax}}(Q, G)$, if there are queries Q_i, Q_j such that $Q_i \prec^*_Q Q_j$, $t_i \in \texttt{newAnswer}(Q_i, G)$, $t_j \in \texttt{newAnswer}(Q_j, G)$, then $\tau_{Q,G}(t_i) < \tau_{Q,G}(t_j)$.

Notice that in consistent rank functions, tuples in $\texttt{ans}(Q, G)$ are returned first among the tuples in the relaxed answer. The notion of answer ranking sketched here can be improved in several directions. We may impose additional ordering constraints in the relaxation graph. Other extensions may consider distance metrics based on paths in the relaxation graph.

4 Query Processing

In this section, we study the problem of computing the relaxed answer of a query. We propose an algorithm that incrementally generates matchings from a query to an RDF graph and also ranks tuples in the answer. In Section 4.1, we provide a procedure that computes the relaxation graph of a given triple pattern. In Section 4.2 we present an algorithm that efficiently computes the relaxed answer.

4.1 Computing Relaxations of a Triple Pattern

We first describe the computation of the relaxation graph for ontology relaxations. The procedure we propose is based on a variation of the notion of reduction of an RDFS ontology from [8]. The idea is to compute relaxed versions of a triple pattern t by applying the derivation rules (Figure 2) to t and and triples from the reduction. Given an ontology O, we denote by $\text{red}(O)$ the RDF graph resulting as follows (reverse rule means deleting the triple deduced by the rule): (i) compute $\text{cl}(O)$; (ii) apply reverse rules 2 and 4 until no longer applicable; and (iii) apply reverse rules 1 and 3 until no longer applicable. In what follows, we assume that $\text{red}(O)$ has been precomputed.

We denote by $\Gamma(t)$ the set containing triples t' such that (i) there exists a triple $t_o \in \text{red}(O)$ and $\frac{t,t_o}{t'}$ is an instance of a rule from groups (A), (B), or (C) (Figure 2), (ii) $\text{var}(t') = \text{var}(t)$, and (iii) $t' \notin \text{cl}(O)$.

Proposition 3. *Let t be a triple pattern, such that $t \notin \text{cl}(O)$ and $\text{var}(t) \subseteq F$, where F is the set of fix variables. (i) $\{t' \ : \ t \prec_{\text{onto}} t'\} \subseteq \Gamma(t)$. (ii) $\Gamma(t) \subseteq \{t' \ : \ t \prec_{\text{onto}}^* t'\}$.*

Proposition 3 (i) does not longer hold if we reduce the ontology also using reverse rules 5 or 6. Proposition 3 (ii) follows directly from the definition of ontology relaxation. The set $\Gamma(t)$ can be easily computed in time $O(|\text{red}(O)|)$ by searching for triples $t_o \in \text{red}(O)$ such that t, t_o instantiates the antecedent of a rule, and testing the additional conditions given in the definition of Γ for the triple patterns derived. The relaxation graph of a triple t can be computed as follows. We start by computing $\Gamma(t)$, and in iteration i, we compute $\Gamma(t')$ with each new triple pattern t' obtained in iteration $i-1$, and add to the graph an edge (t', t'') for each $t'' \in \Gamma(t')$. In each iteration, we detect and delete transitive edges (an edge is transitive if it connects two nodes that are also connected by a path of length greater than one). In addition, we keep a list with triple patterns for which Γ has been already computed so that we do not repeat computations of Γ for the same triple pattern.

It is straightforward to generalize this procedure to compute direct simple relaxations. We just need to add in each iteration direct relaxations to triples that rename a constant with a variable or a variable (not in the original triple pattern t) with another variable. In each iteration, we also have to delete triple patterns that are isomorphic to some triple pattern already in the graph, and delete transitive edge.

Proposition 4. *Let $t = (a, p, b)$ be a triple pattern and O be an ontology. Let R be the relaxation graph of t. (i) R has $O(m^2)$ triples, where m is the number of triples in* red(O). *(ii) Computing R takes time in $O(r^2 m)$, where r is the number of triples in R.*

From Proposition 4, it follows that the relaxation graph of a query has $O(m^{2n})$ nodes, where n is the number of triple patterns inside RELAX clauses in the query.

4.2 Computing the Relaxed Answer

In this section, we sketch a query processing algorithm which works by adapting the RDQL query processing scheme provided by Jena [15] to the processing of successive relaxations of a query. We assume the simplest storage scheme provided by Jena, in which the RDF triples are stored in a single table, called the *statement table*. The Jena query processing approach is to convert an RDF query into a pipeline of "find patterns" connected by join variables. Each triple pattern (find pattern in Jena's terminology) can be evaluated by a single SQL select query over the statement table. We formalize this with an operator called find that receives a triple pattern t and a statement table G and returns all matchings from t to the table.

In what follows, Q is the query whose relaxed answer we intend to compute, and Q' is an arbitrary query in the relaxation graph of Q. We have that $H =$ Head(Q) = Head(Q'). For the sake of simplicity, we assume that each triple pattern in the body of Q is inside a RELAX clause. We assume that Body(Q) = $\{t_1, \ldots, t_n\}$, and Body(Q') = $\{t'_1, \ldots, \ldots, t'_n\}$. We also fix the statement table G we are querying. The answer of Q' can be computed by processing (in a pipelined fashion) a view, denoted $V_{Q'}$, defined by the following expression:

$$\pi_H(\text{find}(t'_1, G) \bowtie \ldots \bowtie \text{find}(t'_n, G)),$$

where π is the standard projection operator and $\bowtie$ is the natural join on variables shared by triple patterns. The answer of Q can be computed by a naive algorithm that traverses the relaxation graph of Q upwards, and in each step of the traversal, builds a view $V_{Q'}$, computes it, and returns those tuples which were not returned in previous steps.

Next, we propose an algorithm that avoids the redundant processing of tuples that arises with this naive approach. We define deltaFind(t'_i, G) as the set containing triples $p \in G$ such that t'_i matches p, and no triple pattern directly below t'_i in the relaxation graph of t_i, matches p. The set deltaFind(t'_i, G) can be computed similarly to find(t'_i, G) by filtering triples from the statement table. Define a *delta view* for Q', denoted $\Delta_{Q'}$, as the following expression:

$$\pi_H(\text{deltaFind}(t'_1, G) \bowtie \ldots \bowtie \text{deltaFind}(t'_n, G)).$$

The following proposition shows that new answers (Section 3.5) correspond to delta views.

Proposition 5. *Let Q be a query and G be a RDF graph. For each query Q' in the relaxation graph of Q, (i) $\mathtt{ans}(Q', G) = \bigcup_{Q_i : Q_i \prec_Q^* Q'} \Delta_{Q_i}(G)$, and (ii) $\mathtt{newAnswer}(Q', G) = \Delta_{Q'}(G)$.*

The algorithm we propose (Figure 4), called `RelaxEval`, performs a breadth-first traversal of the relaxation graph of Q, building and processing each delta view $\Delta_{Q'}$ in each step of the traversal. The function *level* returns the level of a triple pattern t'_i in the relaxation graph R_i of t_i. Line 3(a) outputs the new answer of each query at level k. In order to find the queries at level k of the relaxation graph, the algorithm applies the following property. The queries Q' (defined by the join expression in Line 3 (a)) that belong to the level k of the relaxation graph of Q are those satisfying $\sum_i level(t'_i, R_i) = k$.

Algorithm `RelaxEval`
Input: a query Q (interpreted over an ontology O), where $\mathtt{Body}(Q) = \{t_1, \ldots, t_n\}$, a statement table G, and an integer *maxLevel*.
Output: the set of tuples $\mathtt{ans_{relax}}(Q, G, maxLevel)$, where new answers are returned successively at each level of the relaxation graph.

1. $k := 0$, *stillMore* := *true*
2. For each triple pattern $t_i \in \mathtt{Body}(Q)$, compute the relaxation graph R_i of t_i up to level *maxLevel* (see Section 4.1).
3. While ($k \leq maxLevel$ and *stillMore*) do
   (a) For each combination $t'_1 \in R_1, \ldots, t'_n \in R_n$ such that $\sum_i level(t'_i, R_i) = k$ do output $\pi_H(\mathtt{deltaFind}(t'_1, G) \bowtie \ldots \bowtie \mathtt{deltaFind}(t'_n, G))$
   (b) $k := k + 1$
   (c) *stillMore* := exist nodes $t'_1 \in R_1, \ldots, t'_n \in R_n$ such that $\sum_i level(t'_i, R_i) = k$

Fig. 4. Algorithm that computes the relaxed answer of a query

The algorithm `RelaxEval` induces a rank function, denoted $\mathtt{rank}_{Q,G}$, which maps each tuple to the position at which `RelaxEval` returns it. The following proposition proves the correctness of `RelaxEval` (recall the notion of a consistent rank function from Section 3.5), where for a level k of the relaxation graph, we denote by $\mathtt{RelaxEval}(Q, G, k)$ the set of tuples returned in Line 3(a) of `RelaxEval`.

Proposition 6. *Let Q be a query and G be a RDF graph. (i) For all k we have $\mathtt{RelaxEval}(Q, G, k) = \mathtt{ans_{relax}}(Q, G, k)$. (ii) The rank function $\mathtt{rank}_{Q,G}$ is consistent.*

Both (i) and (ii) follow from Proposition 5 and the fact that the algorithm `RelaxEval` traverses the relaxation graph of Q in breadth-first fashion.

We end this section by comparing the computation cost of `RelaxEval` with the naive approach. We estimate the cost of computing a view $V_{Q'}$ as the expression $|\texttt{find}(t'_1, G)| \times \ldots \times |\texttt{find}(t'_n, G)|$, which represents the cost of the join operations. Roughly, it can be assumed that the `find` and `deltaFind` operations have the same cost, so we omit this cost in the expression. In the following proposition, we assume that $\delta = \frac{|\texttt{find}(t'_i, G)|}{|\texttt{deltaFind}(t'_i, G)|}$ is constant for every t'_i in the relaxation graph of every triple pattern $t_i \in \texttt{Body}(Q)$.

Proposition 7. *Let Q be a query (assume for simplicity that all its triple pattern are subject to relaxation), O be an ontology and G an RDF graph. (i) The naive approach to compute the relax answer at level k runs in time $O(\delta^n pT)$, where T denotes the time taken by `RelaxEval(Q,G,k)`, $n = |\texttt{Body}(Q)|$, and $p = |\texttt{relax}(Q, k)|$. (ii) `RelaxEval(Q, G, k)` runs in time $O(m^{2n} |G|^n)$, where m is the number of triples in $\texttt{red}(O)$.*

The above proposition shows that the algorithm has exponential complexity, however its complexity is polynomial in the size of the data queried for a fixed query Q (data complexity). In addition, the answer is generated incrementally and hence the processing can be halted at any level in the relaxation graph. The number of triples in $\texttt{red}(O)$ provides an upper bound for k, the number of levels in the evaluation.

An improvement to the algorithm would be to process several delta views at the same time in an integrated pipelined fashion. In practice, we can improve query processing performance by further caching the results of $\texttt{deltaFind}(t, G)$ for all triple patterns t that occur more than once in the query relaxation graph (such duplicate occurrences can be detected as the relaxation graphs of the individual triple patterns in the original query are being constructed).

5 Related Work

Query languages based on regular expressions provide a form of flexible querying. The G+ query language by Cruz et al. [6] proposes graph patterns where edges are annotated with regular expressions over labels. In this form, each graph pattern represents a set of more basic graph patterns, and therefore, a query extracts matchings that relate to its body in a variety of ways. This work considers queries over directed labeled graphs.

Kanza and Sagiv [11] propose a form of flexible querying based on a notion of homeomorphism between the query and the graph. Their data model is a simplified form of the Object Exchange Model (OEM).

Bernstein and Kiefer [1] incorporate similarity joins into the RDQL query language. This is done by allowing sets of variables in an RDQL query to be declared as *imprecise*. Bindings for these variables are then compared based on a specified similarity measure, such as edit distance.

Stuckenschmidt and van Harmelen [14] consider conjunctive queries over a terminological knowledge base that includes class, relation and object definitions. They also use query containment as a way of viewing query approximations, but are concerned about evaluating less complex queries first, so that the original query is evaluated last. They use a query graph to decide which conjuncts from the original query should be successively added to the approximate query. This is analogous to SPARQL queries in which every conjunct is optional.

Bulskov et al. [4] consider the language ONTOLOG which allows compound concepts to be formed from atomic concepts attributed with semantic relations. They define a similarity measure between concepts based on subsumption in a hierarchy of concepts. This gives rise to a fuzzy set of concepts similar to a given concept. They also introduce specialization/generalization operators into a query language that allow specializations or generalizations of concepts to be returned. They admit that combining this with similarity may make answers confusing.

6 Concluding Remarks

Despite being a relatively unexplored technique in the semantic Web, query relaxation may have an important role in improving RDF data access. One motivation for this technique is for querying data where there is a lack of understanding of the ontology that underlies the data. Another application is the extraction of objects with heterogeneous sets of properties because the data is incomplete or has irregular structure. As an example, a relaxed query can retrieve the properties that are applicable to each resource among a set of resources having different properties. Query relaxation can also make it possible to retrieve data that satisfies the query conditions with different degrees of exactitude.

There are several areas for future work. One is the introduction of relaxation into general SPARQL queries, including disjunctions and optionals. This should also involve a generalization of the **RELAX** clause so that it can be applied to entire graph patterns instead of single triple patterns. Another important issue for future work is the design, implementation and empirical evaluation of algorithms for computing relaxed answers. The graph-like nature of RDF provides additional richness for a query relaxation framework, which can be exploited in future work. For example, join dependencies between triple patterns of the query can be relaxed to connectivity relationships in RDF graphs.

References

1. A. Bernstein and C. Kiefer. Imprecise RDQL: Towards generic retrieval in ontologies using similarity joins. In *21th Annual ACM Symposium on Applied Computing (SAC/SIGAPP)*, Dijon, France, 2006.
2. D. Brickley and R. V. Guha, editors. *RDF Vocabulary Description Language 1.0: RDF Schema*, W3C Recommendation, 10 February 2004.
3. J. Broekstra. SeRQL: Sesame RDF query language. In *In M. Ehrig et al., editors, SWAP Deliverable 3.2 Method Design*, pages 55+68, http://swap.semanticweb.org/public/Publications/swap-d3.2.pdf, 2003.

4. H. Bulskov, R. Knappe, and T. Andreasen. On querying ontologies and databases. In *6th International Conference on Flexible Query Answering Systems*, pages 191–202, 2004.
5. K. G. Clark, editor. *RDF Data Access Use Cases and Requirements*, W3C Working Draft, 25 March 2005.
6. I. F. Cruz, A. O. Mendelzon, and P. T. Wood. A graphical query language supporting recursion. In *SIGMOD Conference*, pages 323–330, 1987.
7. T. Gaasterland, P. Godfrey, and J. Minker. Relaxation as a platform for cooperative answering. *J. Intell. Inf. Syst.*, 1(3/4):293–321, 1992.
8. C. Gutierrez, C. Hurtado, and A. O. Mendelzon. Foundations of semantic web databases. In *23rd Symposium on Principles of Database Systems*, pages 95–106, 2004.
9. P. Haase, J. Broekstra, A. Eberhart, and R. Volz. A comparison of RDF query languages. In *International Semantic Web Conference*, 2004.
10. P. Hayes, editor. *RDF Semantics*, W3C Recommendation, 10 February 2004.
11. Y. Kanza and Y. Sagiv. Flexible queries over semistructured data. In *Symposium on Principles of Database Systems*, 2001.
12. F. Manola and E. Miller, editors. *RDF Primer*, W3C Recommendation, 10 February 2004.
13. E. Prud'hommeaux and A. Seaborne, editors. *SPARQL Query Language for RDF*, W3C Candidate Recommendation, 6 April 2006.
14. H. Stuckenschmidt and F. van Harmelen. Approximating terminological queries. In *5th International Conference on Flexible Query Answering Systems*, pages 329–343, 2002.
15. K. Wilkinson, C. Sayers, H. Kuno, and D. Reynolds. Efficient RDF storage and retrieval in Jena. In *Proceedings of VLDB Workshop on Semantic Web and Databases*, 2003.

Mining Information for Instance Unification

Niraj Aswani, Kalina Bontcheva, and Hamish Cunningham[*]

Department of Computer Science, University of Sheffield
Regent Court, 211 Portobello Street, Sheffield, UK
{niraj, kalina, hamish}@dcs.shef.ac.uk

Abstract. Instance unification determines whether two instances in an ontology refer to the same object in the real world. More specifically, this paper addresses the instance unification problem for person names. The approach combines the use of citation information (i.e., abstract, initials, titles and co-authorship information) with web mining, in order to gather additional evidence for the instance unification algorithm. The method is evaluated on two datasets – one from the BT digital library and one used in previous work on name disambiguation. The results show that the information mined from the web contributes substantially towards the successful handling of highly ambiguous cases which lowered the performance of previous methods.

1 Introduction

Many Semantic Web (SW) and knowledge management applications need to populate their ontologies[1] from structured, semi-structured, or unstructured data sources. Frequently the same name (e.g., a person or a company name) would appear in more than one source (e.g. database records) and the system then needs to decide whether these names refer to the same real-world object or not. This problem is known as *instance unification* [2], i.e., given two instances in an ontology one needs to determine whether or not they refer to the same object. A typical example in applications such as Google scholar is the need to determine whether the authors "N.J. Davies" and "J. Davies" of two different papers are actually the same person. Or even, whether there are two different individuals both called J. Davies and therefore it is wrong to assume that two papers whose author is "J. Davies" are authored by the same person.

In this paper we address the instance unification problem for person names. The work is carried out in the context of the British Telecom digital library, as part of the SEKT project[2], which aims to build the next generation of knowledge management technology. The digital library consists of metadata about

---

[*] This work is partially supported by the EU-funded SEKT project (http://www.sekt-project.com)
[1] For the purposes of this paper an ontology is defined as the datamodel that describes classes (a.k.a. concepts), instances (a.k.a. individuals), attributes (a.k.a. properties) and relations (i.e. ways that objects can be related to one another).
[2] For further details see http://www.sekt-project.com

papers, including paper authors (initials and surname), title, place and date of publication, abstract, and, optionally, author affiliation. Some of the records also provide a link to the full text of the paper, however, we decided to not use it in the current experiment as only 30% of all papers have full text available. In addition, we wanted to develop a method that can work using only information from the ontology, without access to the original data sources.

Due to name variations, identical names and spelling mistakes, disambiguating person names is difficult. Researchers have been exploring various ways to address this problem. Perhaps the closest in spirit is work on Ontocopi [1] and name disambiguation in author citations [8]. Ontocopi exploits relations in the ontology in order to calculate the similarity between two instances, based on the overlap between their properties. The overlap is calculated based on string similarity and the approach was deployed in the context of disambiguating authors and project members. Similarly, the work on name disambiguation in author citations [8] exploits overlap in the co-authors, paper titles, and place of publication. The main shortcoming of these approaches is that they have difficulty distinguishing between authors with the same name, who work in the same area, and where the number of citations is not sufficient to build a good co-authorship model as is the case with our data.

This paper presents a fully automatic web-based approach for instance unification in ontologies containing publications, titles, authors, abstracts, etc., where different instances of these are created from bibliography records. In other words, the ontology population algorithm has assumed that all authors of all publications are different and a corresponding instance is created in the ontology for each of them. Then the instance unification task addressed here is to determine how many authors are there in the real world and insert the required "sameIndividualAs" statements in the ontology.

The approach is evaluated on two datasets – one from the BT digital library and one used in previous work on name disambiguation. The results show that the information mined from the web contributes substantially towards the successful handling of highly ambiguous cases which lowered the performance of previous methods.

A major part of the work focused on identifying which features lead to the best performance on the author disambiguation task and, consequently, these features are specific to this problem. Nevertheless, the algorithms discussed here (normalising names, identifying an author's publication page, identifying an author's full name) and the evaluation methodology can be applied to the more generic problem of instance unification.

The paper is structured as follows. Section 2 discussed related work and identifies outstanding problems. Next Section 3 presents the ontology used in these experiments. The web-based instance disambiguation algorithm is presented in Section 4. Several issues, such as normalising names, identifying author's publication page, identifying author's full name, calculating similarities based on the collected features and making the overall decision are discussed in this section. Evaluation results are discussed in Section 5. The paper concludes by outlining future work.

2   Related Work

The author disambiguation problem bears similarities to citation matching, which typically applies machine learning in order to identify whether two citations actually refer to the same publication, by using string similarity and frequency-based features (e.g., [10]). However, citation matching is different from the problem of resolving person name ambiguities, because it is only concerned with paper references and does not disambiguate the authors in them.

The research most relevant to our is on name disambiguation. A survey carried out in the United States showed that names can be very ambiguous as over 90,000 names are being shared by 100 million people in the United States alone [6]. However, name disambiguation is particularly difficult when there is limited contextual data. Such problem arises in the domain of citations, or in bibliographies, where no additional information other than the citation itself is available. Various approaches have been tried, some directly linked to the problem of disambiguating authors in citations (e.g., [6], [8]) and others to disambiguation of person names (e.g., [9]).

One such recent approach for author name disambiguation uses a K-means clustering algorithm based on an extensible Naive Bayes probability model [7]. The algorithm is based on three features collected from citations: co-author names, the title of the paper and the title of the journal or proceedings. The work is based on the assumption that a researcher usually has research areas that are stable over a period and tends to co-author papers with a particular group of people during that period. The disambiguation system, given an author name, clusters the citations of different similar named entities. However, their method uses manually collected publications pages, where the correct publication pages are identified manually among the results returned by Google with a query consisting of the author name and "publication" as a keyword.

The approach is evaluated on two names "J Anderson"(6) and "J Smith"(9) with accuracy of 70.6% and 73.6% respectively. The work was improved further by using information about aliases and name invariants from a database [8]. Co-author names were identified as the most robust attribute for name disambiguation. They also show that using journal titles gives better performance than using words from the paper title. The reported results are more than 90% accurate in disambiguating the two names "J Anderson" and "J Smith". This paper demonstrates how these results can be improved further by mining information from the web.

Another method [6] is semi-automatic and uses user feedback where people are asked to provide some contextual information to help identify the author unambiguously. Examples include *Location*, *Contact* such as email or phone, *Organization*, *Relation to other person(s)*, etc. While the goal of their work is different from ours, they use co-occurrence of the given person name and the contextual information as disambiguation evidence, which bears similarities to the way we identify the person's full name (see Section 4.1).

Fietelson [5] discusses disambiguating first names using lexical means. In his approach, elements of a name, the first name and the last name, are identified using self-citations among other features. Afterwards, the names are normalised into lower-case and foreign accents and special characters are replaced. In our approach we employ part of the described technique in order to normalise author names. In addition, [5] demonstrated that full names lead to better results than initials and surname information. Consequently, given an abbreviated name of an author, we first search the web and try to identify their full name.

As our approach mines the web for people's publication pages as part of the instance unification process, therefore work on finding such pages is also relevant. Perhaps the most similar in spirit is the Armadillo system [3], which discovers who works for a given department and their home pages. The system identifies automatically person names and checks them against DBLP, then relies on HomePageSearch[3] to identify the author's home page. Alternatively, the given department web site is searched for the home page. However, this approach is not applicable in our case for two reasons. Firstly, Armadillo assumes that the homepage is located within a specified website, whereas in the general case (e.g., a digital library) the system does not have such information. Secondly, the algorithm for checking the person name is dependent on the existence of an external domain-specific resource, which means that the system needs to be tailored specifically for each domain.

In the SW context, instance unification in ontologies is important for interoperability among ontologies and for cross ontology reasoning. Two general means of detecting whether two instances refer to the same real-world object have been identified [2]. One of them is the exact case, where the instances are unifiable and the another one is the probabilistic case, where each pair of two instances is assigned some probability (between 0 and 1). A threshold is used to decide if the instances are same. The aim of our work is precisely to identify the features which are important for the instance disambiguation task. Therefore, we experiment with various combinations of features and collect probability measures for each of these combinations of features. Having obtained these measures, one can use machine learning methods to learn a threshold and unify or disambiguate instances automatically.

In the section below we describe our work on instance disambiguation and present different experiments.

3 The Ontology and the Author Instance Disambiguation Problem

The ontology used in these experiments is Proton[4], a basic upper-level ontology developed in the SEKT project which contains about 300 classes and 100 properties, providing coverage of the general concepts necessary for a wide range of tasks, including semantic annotation, indexing, and retrieval of documents.

---

[3] http://hpsearch.uni-trier.de/
[4] http://proton.semanticweb.org/

Table 1. An example dataset for the name "J. Davies"

ID	Author Name	Co-authors	Publication Title
1	Davies, J	Merali, Y	Knowledge capture and utilization in virtual communities
2	Davies, J	Chaomei, C	Integrating spatial, semantic, and social structures for knowledge management
3	Davies, B.J.	Shuliang Li	Key issues in using information systems for strategic marketing decisions
4	Davies, N.J.	Krohn, U Weeks, R.	Concept lattices for knowledge management
5	Davies, J	Mabin, V.J.	Knowledge management and the framing of information: a contribution to OR/MS practice and pedagogy
6	Davies, N. J.	Crossley, M. McGrath, A.J. Rejman-Green, M.A.Z.	The knowledge garden

The metadata from the digital library is automatically inserted as instances in the ontology. The total number of papers in the library is 5 million and our test set contains 4429 instances of papers in the area of knowledge management with 9065 author names.

Table 1 shows an example dataset for the author "J. Davies" giving information on his publications (author name, co-author names, and publication titles)[5].

As discussed in Section 2, previous work has used a number of features to disambiguate author names: compatibility between initials and first names, overlap in paper titles, co-authorship, the name of conference or journal where the paper is published, etc. The disambiguation problem is made harder on our dataset, as the papers were chosen from within the same field (knowledge management), where different authors would publish at the same set of conferences and journals and have similar words in the paper titles. In addition, the data only provides the surname and initials of the authors. In case of "B.J. Davies" and "N.J. Davies", where the first name initials are also available, one can easily distinguish them by simply referring to their names. On the other hand, it is difficult to identify whether the first "J. Davies" is same as any other "Davies" in the table. There is a very little overlap in the names of co-authors of different "J. Davies" (Table 1). Similar to "J. Davies", we could not find any overlap in the names of co-authors of "Smith" (21 instances).

Consequently, it is difficult to disambiguate author names by computing similarities only on the basis of the citation details. However, the information available on the web can be exploited to perform instance disambiguation. An approach specifically tailored to mining computer science department web sites was discussed earlier in Section 2. In the following section, we describe a more general method for web-based instance disambiguation.

---

[5] Abstract details are excluded from the table due to space limitations.

4 Web-Assisted Instance Disambiguation

Given the ontology and a surname, the first step is to retrieve all publications authored by authors with the given surname. For each citation information such as co-authors, title of the paper and abstract is collected.

After collecting all citations of authors with the given surname, the task is to exploit these features and identify which author names refer to the same real persons and how many real persons have authored each of the papers in our dataset. Below we describe an application, which, step-by-step, carries out various operations to disambiguate instances of different authors in the ontology.

It is assumed that each author with the same surname has a different instance ID and therefore the task is to identify which two IDs (i.e., instances) refer to the same author. For each pair of author IDs we calculate a number of similarity measures based on features such as the following:

- whether the authors have the same full names as identified from the web (Section 4.1)
- whether the authors share the same publication page (Section 4.2)
- title similarity (Section 4.3)
- abstract similarity (Section 4.3)
- name initials similarity (Section 4.3)
- co-author similarity (Section 4.4)

Based on the collected individual similarity measures, the overall similarity is calculated for each author pair and a binary equivalence decision is made. Next we explain the method of calculating similarity for each of the features.

4.1 Finding Authors' Full Names

As explained in [5], people write their names in different forms, so as a first step we try to calculate the similarity in authors' names. In our case, however most of the names in citations remain ambiguous due to the use of initials or incomplete names. For example "D. Jones" can refer to either "David Jones" or "Daniel Jones" or maybe to some other author whose first name starts with "D". Consequently if the authors' full names are discovered, then the ambiguity problem can be reduced substantially.

Therefore we implemented a method which from a surname and a publication tries to retrieve the author's full name from the web—based on the assumption that a web page may exist that contains the author's full name and the given publication. The method first tries to locate such a page and, if successful, verifies that the name is indeed a full name according to the following orthographig constraints[6].

1. If the name consists of two words:
    (a) the first letters of both words must be in uppercase
    (b) if one of the words is identical to the surname, and if the length of the other word is two characters, they must not be in upper case. If they are, they are considered to be the initials of the first and second names.

---

[6] The algorithm assumes that the first and the middle names are one token each.

2. If the name consists of three words:
   (a) the first letters of all three words must be in upper case
   (b) if the first word is identical to the surname, the second word must contain at least two letters. In this case the last word is considered to be the middle name and can have a single upper case initial.
   (c) if the last word is identical to the surname, the first word must contain at least two letters. In this case, the middle word is considered to be the middle name.

The top five pages that contain the author surname and the publication are considered as candidates for retrieval of the full name. Using the above heuristics, names are retrieved from each of these pages and the distance between the full name and the publication in terms of number of characters is calculated. The name that is nearest to the publication title is deemed to be the full name of the author under consideration. Having obtained as many full names as possible, for each pair of author IDs we calculate a full-name similarity matrix as follows: a value of 1 is given to authors having identical full names and 0 otherwise (including cases in which full names were not found for either or both of the authors).

4.2 Identifying Authors' Publication Pages

For each pair of author IDs and their associated publications, Google or Yahoo is queried in an attempt to find a page that contains the author surname and the titles of the two publications. This search is based on the assumption that if the author IDs refer to the same real person, the relevant papers will most likely appear together on his publication page.

Digital libraries such as ACM and CiteSeer are the most likely and obvious source of bibliographies. Since they use various approaches to index citations (e.g. conservative or normalizing names), when queried, they are the most likely hits. As a result, they show the entire bibliography page that contains both the titles and the surname specified. Since such bibliography pages are the results of pure text search, they do not help in disambiguating names but add more complexity to the problem, so such digital libraries are excluded from this search. The Google query is prepared with the following elements:

- The keyword "publication" or "papers"
- Author Surname
- Title of the publication of the first author
- Title of the publication of the second author
- -site:<sitesToExclude> digital libraries such as acm.org, sigmond.ord, ist.psu.edu and informatik.uni-trier.de

The query is then sent to a search engine. An empty result set is interpreted as an indication *against* considering the two author IDs as references to the same person. However, the final decision on whether these IDs should be unified is not based on this criterion alone, as there can be other explanations for the lack of matching pages. (For instance, the author's publications page may not be up to date or he may not have one.)

Although we exclude some digital libraries from the engine query, this does not guarantee that the results will not contain any bibliography pages, e.g., a bibliography of knowledge management publications. These need to be filtered out as they are not single-person publication pages (and therefore not evidence that the two papers were written by the same person).

After a careful analysis of several bibliography web pages, we developed a filtering module that removes a whole web page from the search results if it contains the word "bibliography" in any of the following contexts:

- title
- headers (i.e. h1, h2, h3, h4, h5 and h6)
- **boldface** tag
- *italic* tag
- head
- meta
- centered

The top five pages in the result set after filtering out bibliographies are processed further in order to identify the author's publication page (assuming that indeed both publications have been authored by the same person).

The formulation of the query means that all matched pages will contain the publication titles and the author's surname and, if it is indeed a publication page, the author's name would appear in it with a higher frequency than any other person name. Therefore each page is processed with the ANNIE named entity recognition system [4] in order to identify sentence boundaries and locate person names.

The final step is to determine which of several returned pages is actually the given author's publication page. Analysis of the matching pages showed that some would be the author's publication page but others would be more complex (e.g., CVs). The contents of such complex web pages tend to be divided into several sections, such as personal interests, work history, names of supervised students, recommended readings, publications, etc. Consequently, straightforward counting of the frequency of author names cannot reliably distinguish the publication page from other pages. Instead, the algorithm assigns the highest score to the page which contains the highest percentage of author names and references over its total length.

Another assumption is that it is likely to find more of a given author's publications on his own publication page than on any other webpage and therefore the page that contains, for example, 5 publications by that author out of 10 references in total is deemed less relevant than the page that contains 10 publications by the given author out of 20 or 25 references. In other words, preference is given to the page that contains the most publications by the given author.

Each pair of author IDs for which a page is successfully identified is given the score 1 to indicate a possible match. When no page is located, the score 0 is assigned instead. It is possible that the search engine does not respond to some queries and in such case the score of -1 is given to indicate that the results should not be taken into account. The identified page is re-used later to find other titles of other authors under consideration. If the match is located for any other author name, the author name is considered to be the same as the other two names for which originally the page was identified.

4.3 Use of Titles, Abstracts and Initials

Before computing overlap in titles and abstracts, stop words such as articles and prepositions are removed and the remaining content words (e.g. nouns, proper names, adjectives and verbs) are stemmed so that their lemmas can be compared. Word order is not important for comparing titles and abstracts, but it plays a very important role when comparing initials and surnames. For example, given a pair of author IDs and titles (or abstracts), the similarity measure is calculated as follows:

$$S_{(e_1,e_2)} = \frac{2n}{L_1 + L_2} \quad (1)$$

where

S = similarity
e_1 = instance id of the first author
e_2 = instance id of the second author
n = number of identical tokens in the title (or abstract) feature of e_1 and e_2
L_1 = total number of tokens in the title (or abstract) feature of e_1
L_2 = total number of tokens in the title (or abstract) feature of e_2

The same formula is used for titles and abstracts. When there are co-authors, the number of identical co-authors is taken into account. As pointed out before, the order of tokens is very important when comparing initials of two authors: for example the initials "N.D." would mean different from the initials "D.N.". Similarly, the initials "N.D." can have some similarity with the initial "N." but not with the initial "D.". In the former case, it is possible that the first name of both authors is same and hence the initials. One can not exclude a possibility of people using their middle name as first name, but considering it as a first initial is more likely to introduce more errors so this comparison is not used in our algorithm.

4.4 Co-authorship Information

In the case of co-authorship information, the overlap among the co-authors of each pair of publications is calculated. Consider Table 2, which presents co-authorship information for various instances referring to the **same** author.

In this case, co-authors of each instance are compared with co-authors of other instances. The third column shows the similarity figures. In this case, the first two instances do share at least one co-author but none of the rest have any common co-authors. The results show some probability for the first two instances referring to the same author, but it will be unfair to comment anything for the third and the fourth instances. If the instances are identified as referring to different authors, just because they do not share any co-author, the disambiguation would be incorrect—at least for the given example where all instances do refer to the same author. The same is true for the earlier example of "J. Davies" (see Table 1), where actually the first, second, fourth and the sixth instances in the table are referring to the same author and none of them share any co-author. Thus, in our dataset, the co-authorship does not give us much evidence in some cases.

Table 2. Co-authorship information for the name "Y. Wilks"

ID	Author Name	Co-authors	similarities
1	Y. Wilks	N. Webb, H. Hardy, M. Ursu, T. Strzalkowski	id:2=0.33, id:3=0, id:4=0
2	Y. Wilks	N. Webb, M. Hepple	id:1=0.33, id:3=0, id:4=0
3	Y. Wilks	N. Ide	id:1=0, id:2=0, id:4 =0
4	Y. Wilks	-	id:1=0, id:2=0, id:3=0

5 Overall Similarity and Results

After independently obtaining similarity measures for the various features, the overall similarity needs to be calculated for each pair of author IDs. Because the features vary in importance, each feature is assigned a weight and the overall similarity for a given pair of author IDs (e_1 and e_2) is computed as the sum of each individual similarity measure multiplied by its weight. Equation 2 is used for obtaining the overall similarity for the given pair of author IDs (e_1 and e_2). Finally, we specify a minimum similarity threshold for for a pair of author IDs to be deemed torefer to the same author.

Table 3 shows the name disambiguation results for the author "J. Davies". The instance pairs in **bold** refer to the same person and consequently the instance unification algorithm should consider them the same. The overall similarity measures in **bold** indicate a correct result, whereas those in *italics* indicate an incorrect result. The first six columns show the individual similarity measures for the features (shared publication page, identical full name, etc.). Columns C1 to C6 then show the overall similarity measure for the given pair of IDs, when a given set of features is taken into account. C1 corresponds to only using titles, initials, and abstracts for disambiguation; whereas C2 uses the co-authorship information as well. Therefore, C2 uses the features suggested in previous name disambiguation work, as discussed in Section 2.

$$f = \sum_{i=1}^{6} w_i S_{i(e_1,e_2)} \qquad (2)$$

where

$f = overallsimilarity$
$w_i = weightassignedtothe i^{th} feature$
$i = \begin{cases} 1 \ sharingpublication \\ 2 \ identicalfullname \\ 3 \ abstractsimilarity \\ 4 \ initialssimilarity \\ 5 \ titlesimilarity \\ 6 \ co-authorsimilarity \end{cases}$

$S_i = similarity for the i^{th} feature$
where,
$S_1 = \begin{cases} 1 \ authorssharepublicationpage \\ 0 \ authorsdonotshareanypublicationpage \\ -1 \ searchenginedoesnotrespond \end{cases}$
$S_2 = \begin{cases} 1 \ authorshavesamefullname \\ 0 \ authorshavedifferentfullname \\ -1 \ searchenginedoesnotrespond \end{cases}$
$S_{i \in \{3,4,5,6\}} = (see equation 1)$

For the initial experiments, all the features were given equal weight. Table 4 shows the name disambiguation results for the authors "D. Smith", "J. Davies", "Cooper", "Williams", "Brown", and "Jones", using different combinations of

Table 3. Instance unification results for a particular person called "J. Davies" (the author IDs in bold refer to this person)

ID1	ID2	P	F	A	I	T	C	C1	C2	C3	C4	C5	C6
threshold								0.4	0.26	0.4	0.4	0.35	0.385
14Davies,N.J.	65Davies,J.	1	1	0.12	0.67	0.22	0	0.34	0.25	**0.45**	**0.40**	**0.60**	**0.50**
14Davies,N.J.	68Davies,N.J.	0	1	0.28	1	0.33	0	**0.54**	**0.40**	**0.58**	**0.52**	**0.52**	**0.44**
14Davies,N.J.	89Davies,J.	-1	0	0.13	0.67	0.18	0	0.33	0.25	0.20	0.20	0.25	0.20
14Davies,N.J.	30Davies,J.	1	1	0.27	0.67	0.33	0	**0.42**	**0.32**	**0.49**	**0.45**	**0.65**	**0.54**
14Davies,N.J.	98Davies,B.J.	-1	0	0.09	0	0	0	0.03	0.02	0.02	0.02	0.02	0.02
65Davies,J.	**68Davies,N.J.**	0	1	0.18	0.67	0.36	0	**0.40**	**0.30**	**0.47**	**0.44**	**0.44**	0.37
65Davies,J.	89Davies,J.	-1	0	0.08	1	0.25	0	*0.44*	*0.33*	0.28	0.27	0.33	0.27
65Davies,J.	**30Davies,J.**	1	1	0.16	1	0.18	0	**0.45**	**0.33**	**0.54**	**0.47**	**0.67**	**0.56**
65Davies,J.	98Davies,B.J.	-1	0	0.10	0.67	0	0	0.25	0.19	0.19	0.15	0.19	0.15
68Davies,N.J.	89Davies,J.	-1	0	0.18	0.67	0.31	0	0.38	0.29	0.22	0.23	0.29	0.23
68Davies,N.J.	**30Davies,J.**	-1	1	0.20	0.67	0.25	0	*0.37*	*0.28*	**0.47**	**0.42**	**0.53**	**0.42**
68Davies,N.J.	98Davies,B.J.	-1	0	0.12	0	0	0	0.04	0.03	0.03	0.02	0.03	0.02
89Davies,J.	30Davies,J.	-1	0	0.16	1	0.15	0	*0.44*	*0.33*	0.29	0.26	0.33	0.26
89Davies,J.	98Davies,B.J.	-1	0	0.20	0.67	0.12	0	0.33	0.25	0.22	0.20	0.25	0.20
30Davies,J.	98Davies,B.J.	-1	0	0.30	0.67	0	0	0.32	0.24	0.24	0.19	0.24	0.19
Accuracy								73.33	73.33	100	100	100	100

KEY: P=Sharing Publication Page, F=Identical Full Name, A=Abstract Similarity
I=Initials Similarity, T=Title Similarity, C=Co-author Similarity
C1=AIT, C2=AITC, C3=FAIT, C4=FAITC, C5=PFAIT, C6=PFAITC

features. As discussed earlier, the similarity threshold for each different combination of features needs to be determined empirically. Therefore, we chose the values that yielded the maximum accuracy for the given combination of features on the first two authors "D. Smith" and "J. Davies", and used these threshold values to evaluate the algorithm's performance on the remaining authors.

To enable comparison between our approach to name disambiguation and previous work, we re-created the evaluation sets used in [8] by manually collecting the publications of the six authors named J. Anderson and seven named J. Smith. The original evaluation used eleven J. Smith authors, but we had to exclude four of them whose publications we could not find on the web. In comparison to the best score of 90% for the six J. Anderson authors reported in [8], our approach obtained 97.01% accuracy using all features (i.e. including the mined information). In case of J. Smith, [8] obtained accuracy of about 90%, whereas the accuracy obtained by our algorithm (although only for 7 authors in comparison to their 11 J. Smith authors) is 97.78%.

Since the main goal of this work is to identify which features lead to the best performance, we carried out an analysis of the results and the most interesting findings are as follows:

1. In some cases (e.g. D. Smith, J. Anderson), the combination of basic features (such as abstract, initials and title similarities) performed better than any other combinations. There are two reasons: (1) in these cases there were many similar words in the paper titles and abstracts, thus leading to high similarity scores on these features; and (2) some of these authors do not

Table 4. Evaluation of instance disambiguation for various authors

Name	AIT	AITC	FAIT	FAITC	PFAIT	PFAITC
threshold	0.4	0.26	0.4	0.4	0.35	0.385
D. Smith(7)	95.24	95.24	85.71	85.71	80.95	90.48
J. Davies(6)	73.33	73.33	100	100	100	100
Cooper(5)	90	90	90	90	90	90
Brown(10)	100	100	100	100	100	100
Jones(10)	93.28	93.28	99.16	99.16	98.32	99.16
J. Anderson(6)	97.01	97.01	77.61	88.06	85.07	97.01
J. Smith(7)	93.33	93.33	84.44	95.56	93.33	97.78
Mean	94.72	94.72	90.24	94.56	93.34	96.79

maintain their own publication pages or the web mining algorithm was not able to find them.

2. Co-authorship information does not help in most cases in our dataset. Given 100 author IDs, each ID pair referring to the same author, the algorithm was able to find only 23 author IDs where there was some overlap in the co-authors. On the other hand, surprisingly, we could find only 1 overlap in the names of co-authors among 300+ author ID pairs, where the authors were not identical. The first and the second columns in Table 4 show that there is no change in the results after co-authorship information is added.
3. Although though the algorithm for identifying authors' publication pages is very efficient, due to various limitations of the Google API (such as communication problems with the main Google server), results[7] are not guaranteed every time a query is issued. On the other hand, the Yahoo search engine's ranking algorithm has a poorer performance than Google's, so there is often a trade-off in using them.
4. As explained earlier, if the authors' full names are known, the names themselves can be used as the first disambiguation step (e.g. see results for "Jones" in Table 4). But in some cases (e.g. J. Anderson), where all the names in the dataset have the same first name "James", the similarity for each such pair will be equal to 1 (given that the middle name can not be identified or it is the same). Also, the initials similarities will be nearing 1. In such circumstances, the features such as full name similarity and initials similarity do not contribute much and should not be used on their own.
5. Last but not least, it must be noted that the evaluation experiments reported here are somewhat limited by the lack of bigger human-annotated datasets.

6 Conclusion and Future work

This paper addresses the instance unification problem and presents a fully automatic method which, given an ontology and an author name (either surname or

---
[7] A result is a valid response from the Google server (i.e. it may return a set of documents, or no documents). By the term communication problems, we mean that the server encounters some errors and does not respond correctly.

initials and surname), retrieves the author IDs (instances) and relevant publications for the given name. It then tries to unify all instances which refer to the same individual in the real world. Citation information typically used in citation matching and author name disambiguation work is used as a basis (i.e., abstract, initials, titles and co-authorship information). The novel aspect is in the use of web mining in order to retrieve the full name of a given author and to find a publication page which contains the publications corresponding to the author IDs being considered for unification.

The approach is evaluated in a number of experiments carried out over some of the ambiguous author names in our ontology (i.e. "D. Smith", "J. Smith", "J. Davies", "J. Anderson" etc.). Since the aim of this work is to identify a set of relevant features that can be used for the instance disambiguation task, we perform an analysis over the results. In addition, we demonstrate that the information mined from the web leads to a substantial performance improvement on previous name disambiguation work using the J. Anderson and J. Smith dataset.

In our approach the two values weight and threshold are very important in deciding whether the two author IDs refer to the same person. For the experiments shown in this paper, equal weight was assigned to all features and the threshold was determined from the results of two authors "J. Davies" and "D. Smith".

As part of our future work, we will assign different weights to the features based on their importance and contribution in the overall result. Most of the previous work on instance disambiguation is based on Machine Learning (ML) algorithms. Having identified the correct combinations of relevant features, the next task will be to use these features and train some ML model (e.g., SVM or Naive Bayes). The threshold value, which helps in transforming probabilistic results into the exact results, will be derived for different combinations of features. According to the results "sameIndividualAs" statements will be added to the ontology.

References

1. H. Alani, S. Dasmahapatra, N. Gibbins, H. Glaser, S. Harris, Y. Kalfoglou, K. O'Hara, and N. Shadbolt. Managing Reference: Ensuring Referential Integrity of Ontologies for the Semantic Web. In *13th International Conference on Knowledge Engineering and Knowledge Management (EKAW02)*, pages 317–334, Siguenza, Spain, 2002.
2. J. Bruijn and A. Polleres. Towards An Ontology Mapping Specification Language For the Semantic Web. Technical report, Digital Enterprise Research Institute, 2004.
3. F. Ciravegna, S. Chapman, A. Dingli, and Y. Wilks. Learning to Harvest Information for the Semantic Web. In *Proceedings of the 1st European Semantic Web Symposium*, Heraklion, Greece, May 2004.
4. H. Cunningham, D. Maynard, K. Bontcheva, and V. Tablan. GATE: A Framework and Graphical Development Environment for Robust NLP Tools and Applications. In *Proceedings of the 40th Anniversary Meeting of the Association for Computational Linguistics (ACL'02)*, 2002.

5. D. G. Feitelson. On identifying name equivalences in digital libraries. *Information Research*, 9(4), 2004.
6. R. V. Guha and A. Garg. Disambiguating People in Search. In *Proceedings of the 13th World Wide Web Conference (WWW 2004), ACM Press*, 2004.
7. H. Han, C. L. Giles, and H. Zha. A model-based k-means algorithm for name disambiguation. In *Proceedings of the 2nd International Semantic Web Technologies for Searching and Retrieving Scientific Data*, Florida, USA, 2003.
8. H. Han, L. Giles, H. Zha, C. Li, and K. Tsioutsiouliklis. Two supervised learning approaches for name disambiguation in author citations. In *Proceedings of the 4th ACM/IEEE-CS Joint Conference on Digital Libraries (JCDL'04)*, 2004.
9. G. S. Mann and D. Yarowsky. Unsupervised personal name disambiguation. In W. Daelemans and M. Osborne, editors, *Proceedings of the 7th Conference on Natural Language Learning (CoNLL-2003)*, pages 33–40. Edmonton, Canada, May 2003.
10. B. Wellner, A. McCallum, F. Peng, and M. Hay. An integrated, conditional model of information extraction and coreference with application to citation matching. In *Proceedings of the 20th conference on Uncertainty in artificial intelligence*, pages 593 – 601, Banff, Canada, 2004.

The Summary Abox: Cutting Ontologies Down to Size

Achille Fokoue[1], Aaron Kershenbaum[1], Li Ma[2],
Edith Schonberg[1], and Kavitha Srinivas[1]

[1] IBM Watson Research Center, P.O.Box 704, Yorktown Heights, NY 10598, USA
{achille, aaronk, ediths, ksrinivs}@us.ibm.com
[2] IBM China Research Lab, Beijing 100094, China
malli@cn.ibm.com

Abstract. Reasoning on OWL ontologies is known to be intractable in the worst-case, which is a serious problem because in practice, most OWL ontologies have large Aboxes, i.e., numerous assertions about individuals and their relations. We propose a technique that uses a summary of the ontology (*summary Abox*) to reduce reasoning to a small subset of the original Abox, and prove that our techniques are sound and complete. We demonstrate the scalability of this technique for consistency detection in 4 ontologies, the largest of which has 6.5 million role assertions.

1 Introduction

Description Logic (DL) provides the theoretical foundation for semantic web ontologies (OWL). A DL ontology can be divided conceptually into three components: the Tbox, the Rbox and the Abox. The Tbox contains assertions about concepts such as subsumption ($Man \sqsubseteq Person$) and equivalence ($Man \equiv MaleHuman$). The Rbox contains assertions about roles and role hierarchies ($hasSon \sqsubseteq hasChild$). The Abox contains role assertions between individuals ($hasChild(John, Mary)$) and membership assertions ($John : Man$).

All common reasoning tasks in expressive DL ontologies, such as query answering [1], reduce to consistency detection. As an example, a standard approach to testing if *John* is a member of the concept *Man* requires testing if the addition of the assertion ($John : \neg Man$) makes the Abox inconsistent. A challenge is that consistency detection in expressive DL is well known to be intractable in the worst-case [2]. Given that the size of an Abox may be in the order of millions of assertions, this complexity poses a serious problem for the practical use of DL ontologies, which often reside in frequently updated transactional databases. Although highly optimized DL tableau algorithms exist, they cannot be easily adapted to Aboxes in secondary storage, especially for frequently changing Aboxes. One approach that has been applied to reasoning on Aboxes in secondary storage is to convert DL to disjunctive datalog, and use deductive databases to reason over the Abox [3].

We propose an alternative technique that operates on Aboxes stored in traditional relational databases. Our technique exploits a key observation about real world Aboxes, namely, similar individuals are related to other individuals in similar ways (e.g. fathers and mothers are related to their children by the *hasChild* role). Specifically, our technique builds a summary Abox $\mathcal{A}'$ of the original Abox $\mathcal{A}$, by aggregating similar individuals and assertions. The advantages of our summary Abox $\mathcal{A}'$ are: (a) $\mathcal{A}'$ is dramatically smaller than $\mathcal{A}$; (b) Reasoning on $\mathcal{A}'$ isolates a small relevant portion of $\mathcal{A}$ needed to obtain the correct answer; (c) $\mathcal{A}'$ can be computed efficiently using straightforward relational database queries; (d) $\mathcal{A}'$ can be maintained as changes occur to $\mathcal{A}$, and is thus resilient to change; (e) $\mathcal{A}'$ only needs to be computed once, and can be reused for answering subsequent queries.

To isolate relevant portions of $\mathcal{A}$ for a specific reasoning task, we introduce efficient filtering techniques that operate on $\mathcal{A}'$. In this paper, we demonstrate the utility of such filtering techniques for the task of Abox consistency detection, although the approach can be generalized to query answering. Our filtering techniques are based on the conservative assumption that any individual in the Abox may be inferred to be a member of any concept in the closure of the Abox. Informally, the closure is the set of concepts used in the Abox, and their sub-expressions. (To generalize this to query answering, the closure would include the negated concept in the query.) The effect of filtering is to produce multiple partitions in the summary Abox. In practice, most partitions consist of a single individual, which can be checked with a concept satisfiability test. For partitions of $\mathcal{A}'$ with multiple individuals, if the partition is consistent, then the image in $\mathcal{A}$ that corresponds to the partition is also consistent. If a partition is inconsistent, the inconsistency could arise from either the summarization technique, or a real inconsistency in the original Abox. In this case, we perform a consistency check on the image in $\mathcal{A}$ of the inconsistent partition in $\mathcal{A}'$.

Our techniques proved very effective on the 4 large Aboxes that we studied: a vast majority of partitions (95%) had just one individual. Only one of the 4 ontologies we studied required us to check the image of the partition in the original Abox. Even in this case, our consistency check was performed in 6.3 s on 4045 individuals and 2942 role assertions instead of the 1,106,858 individuals and 6,494,950 role assertions in the entire Abox.

Our key contributions in this paper are as follows: (a) We present a technique to summarize an Abox in secondary storage into a dramatically smaller $\mathcal{A}'$. (b) We describe the use of filtering techniques to construct a reduced version of $\mathcal{A}'$. This filtering produces many partitions, which are then exploited in scaling the consistency check. The filtering techniques we describe works for SHIN Aboxes (SHIN is a DL language that is described in the Background). (c) We show the application of these techniques to 4 ontologies, where we show dramatic reductions in space and time requirements for consistency checking.

1.1 Background

The techniques we apply in this paper assume ontologies of SHIN expressiveness. In this section, we briefly introduce the semantics of SHIN, which is equivalent to OWL-DL (http://www.w3.org/2001/sw/WebOnt) minus nominals and datatype reasoning, as shown in Table 1 (We assume the reader is familiar with Description Logics). In the definition of the semantics of SHIN, $\mathcal{I} = (\Delta^{\mathcal{I}}, \cdot^{\mathcal{I}})$ refers to an interpretation where $\Delta^{\mathcal{I}}$ is a non-empty set (the domain of the interpretation), and $\cdot^{\mathcal{I}}$, the interpretation function, maps every atomic concept C to a set $C^{\mathcal{I}} \subseteq \Delta^{\mathcal{I}}$, every atomic role R to a binary relation $R^{\mathcal{I}} \subseteq \Delta^{\mathcal{I}} X \Delta^{\mathcal{I}}$, and every individual a to $a^{\mathcal{I}} \in \Delta^{\mathcal{I}}$. Trans($R$) in the table refers to a transitive role R.

Table 1. SHIN Description Logic

Definitions	Semantics
$C \sqcap D$	$C^{\mathcal{I}} \cap D^{\mathcal{I}}$
$C \sqcup D$	$C^{\mathcal{I}} \cup D^{\mathcal{I}}$
$\neg C$	$\Delta^{\mathcal{I}} \setminus C^{\mathcal{I}}$
$\exists R.C$	$\{x | \exists y. <x,y> \in R^{\mathcal{I}}, y \in C^{\mathcal{I}}\}$
$\forall R.C$	$\{x | \forall y. <x,y> \in R^{\mathcal{I}} \Rightarrow y \in C^{\mathcal{I}}\}$
$\leq nR$	$\{x | |\{<x,y> \in R^{\mathcal{I}}\}| \leq n\}$
$\geq nR$	$\{x | |\{<x,y> \in R^{\mathcal{I}}\}| \geq n\}$
R^{-}	$\{<x,y> | <y,x> \in R^{\mathcal{I}}\}$

(a) Constructors

Axioms	Satisfiability conditions
Trans(R)	$(R^{\mathcal{I}})^{+} = R^{\mathcal{I}}$
$R \sqsubseteq P$	$<x,y> \in R^{\mathcal{I}} \Rightarrow <x,y> \in P^{\mathcal{I}}$
$C \sqsubseteq D$	$C^{\mathcal{I}} \subseteq D^{\mathcal{I}}$
$a : C$	$a^{\mathcal{I}} \in C^{\mathcal{I}}$
$R(a,b)$	$<a^{\mathcal{I}},b^{\mathcal{I}}> \in R^{\mathcal{I}}$
$a \neq b$	$a^{\mathcal{I}} \neq b^{\mathcal{I}}$

(b) Axioms

An RBox $\mathcal{R}$ is a finite set of transitivity axioms of the form Trans(R) and role inclusion axioms of the form $R \sqsubseteq P$ where R and P are roles. $\sqsubseteq^{*}$ denotes the reflexive transitive closure of the $\sqsubseteq$ relation on roles. A Tbox $\mathcal{T}$ is a set of concept inclusion axioms of the form $C \sqsubseteq D$ where C and D are concept expressions. An Abox $\mathcal{A}$ is a set of axioms of the form $a : C$, $R(a,b)$, and $a \neq b$.

An interpretation $\mathcal{I}$ is a model of an Abox $\mathcal{A}$ w.r.t. a Tbox $\mathcal{T}$ and a Rbox $\mathcal{R}$ iff it satisfies all the axioms in $\mathcal{A}$, $\mathcal{R}$, and $\mathcal{T}$ (see Table 1(b)). An Abox $\mathcal{A}$ is said to be consistent w.r.t. a Tbox $\mathcal{T}$ and a Rbox $\mathcal{R}$ iff there is a model of $\mathcal{A}$ w.r.t. $\mathcal{T}$ and $\mathcal{R}$. If there is no ambiguity from the context, we simply say that $\mathcal{A}$ is consistent. A standard technique for checking the consistency of a SHIN Abox is to use a tableau algorithm [4], which executes a set of non-deterministic expansion rules to satisfy constraints in $\mathcal{A}$ until either no rule is applicable or an obvious inconsistency (clash) is detected.

2 Summary Abox

Intuitively, the Abox contains many redundant assertions from the point of view of consistency checking that can be collapsed to create a reduced *summary Abox*. The summary Abox captures this redundancy by collapsing across individuals that are members of the same concept sets as shown in Figures 1 and 2 below. As shown in Figure 2, a single node a represents $a1$ and $a2$ because they are both members of A, and they are not explicitly asserted to be different from each other (similarly for b and d). Any explicit assertions that two individuals are different from each other ($c1$ and $c2$) are maintained in the summary Abox. Reasoning over such a summary corresponds to reasoning over the original Abox, as shown formally below.

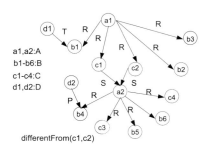
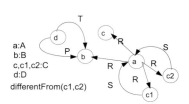

Fig. 1. Original Abox   **Fig. 2.** Canonical Summary Abox

Definition 1. A summary Abox is an Abox $\mathcal{A}'$ that is generated from any SHIN Abox $\mathcal{A}$ using a mapping function $\mathbf{f}$ that satisfies the following constraints:

(1) if $a : C \in \mathcal{A}$ then $\mathbf{f}(a) : C \in \mathcal{A}'$
(2) if $R(a, b) \in \mathcal{A}$ then $R(\mathbf{f}(a), \mathbf{f}(b)) \in \mathcal{A}'$
(3) if $a \dot{\neq} b \in \mathcal{A}$ then $\mathbf{f}(a) \dot{\neq} \mathbf{f}(b) \in \mathcal{A}'$

Theorem 2. If the summary Abox $\mathcal{A}'$ obtained by applying the mapping function $\mathbf{f}$ to $\mathcal{A}$ is consistent w.r.t. a Tbox $\mathcal{T}$ and a Rbox $\mathcal{R}$, then $\mathcal{A}$ is consistent w.r.t. $\mathcal{T}$ and $\mathcal{R}$.
However, the converse of Theorem 2 does not hold.

Proof. Let us assume that $\mathcal{A}'$ is consistent w.r.t. $\mathcal{T}$ and $\mathcal{R}$. Therefore there is a model $\mathcal{I}' = (\Delta^{\mathcal{I}'}, \cdot^{\mathcal{I}'})$ of $\mathcal{A}'$ w.r.t. $\mathcal{T}$ and $\mathcal{R}$. A model of $\mathcal{A}$ can easily be built from $\mathcal{I}'$ by interpreting an individual a in $\mathcal{A}$ in the same way as $\mathbf{f}(a)$ is interpreted by $\mathcal{I}'$. Formally, let $\mathcal{I} = (\Delta^{\mathcal{I}}, \cdot^{\mathcal{I}})$ be the interpretation of the $\mathcal{A}$ w.r.t. $\mathcal{T}$ and $\mathcal{R}$ defined as follows: $\Delta^{\mathcal{I}} = \Delta^{\mathcal{I}'}$; for a concept $C \in \mathcal{T}$, $C^{\mathcal{I}} = C^{\mathcal{I}'}$; for a role R in $\mathcal{R}$, $R^{\mathcal{I}} = R^{\mathcal{I}'}$; for an individual a in $\mathcal{A}$, $a^{\mathcal{I}} = \mathbf{f}(a)^{\mathcal{I}'}$. $\mathcal{I}$ is a model of $\mathcal{A}$ w.r.t. $\mathcal{T}$ and $\mathcal{R}$ as a direct consequence of the fact that $\mathcal{I}'$ is a model of $\mathcal{A}'$ and $\mathcal{A}'$ satisfies the 3 conditions stated in definition 1 (See [5] for more details). □

Let $\mathcal{L}$ be a mapping from each individual in $\mathcal{A}$ to a set of concepts, such that $a : C \in \mathcal{A}$ iff $C \in \mathcal{L}(a)$. We call $\mathcal{L}(a)$ the *concept set* of a. In practice, we use a *canonical function* $\mathbf{f}$ to create a summary Abox, which maps non-distinct individuals that have identical concept sets to the same individual in $\mathcal{A}'$. More precisely, the converse of constraints (1) and (3) hold for the canonical summary, and:

(4) If $R(a', b') \in \mathcal{A}'$ then there are a and b in $\mathcal{A}$ such that $a' = \mathbf{f}(a)$, $b' = \mathbf{f}(b)$ and $R(a, b) \in \mathcal{A}$.
(5) If for all $x \in \mathcal{A}$, $a \dot{\neq} x \notin \mathcal{A}$, $b \dot{\neq} x \notin \mathcal{A}$, and $\mathcal{L}(a) = \mathcal{L}(b)$, then $\mathbf{f}(a) = \mathbf{f}(b)$.
(6) $\mathbf{f}(a) \dot{\neq} \mathbf{f}(b) \in \mathcal{A}'$ implies a is the only individual in $\mathcal{A}$ mapped to $\mathbf{f}(a)$ (same for b).

If a summary Abox $\mathcal{A}'$ is not consistent, either there is a real inconsistency in $\mathcal{A}$ or the process of summarization caused an artificial inconsistency. In section 3.4, we explain how we apply filtering to partition the summary, to provide a scalable consistency check of the original Abox even when the summary is inconsistent. Note that the summary Abox can be computed efficiently from a relational database. Furthermore, it only needs to be computed once, and can be maintained incrementally with changes to the Abox.

3 Abox Filtering

We perform filtering on the canonical summary Abox described in Section 2, but for the purpose of exposition, we describe filtering techniques on the original Abox first. Our filtering technique assumes that the Tbox $\mathcal{T}$ is transformed, through splitting and absorption [6], into two disjoint sets $\mathcal{T}_u$ and $\mathcal{T}_g$ such that $\mathcal{T}_u$, the unfoldable part of $\mathcal{T}$, only contains axioms of the form $A \sqsubseteq D$ and $\neg A \sqsubseteq D$, where A is an atomic concept. $\mathcal{T}_g$ contains general concept inclusions of the form $C \sqsubseteq D$ that could not be absorbed in $\mathcal{T}_u$ (where C is a complex concept).

We assume that for an Abox $\mathcal{A}$, an Rbox $\mathcal{R}$, and a Tbox $\mathcal{T} = \mathcal{T}_u \cup \mathcal{T}_g$, all concepts appearing in $\mathcal{T}$ and $\mathcal{A}$ are in the negation normal form (NNF). For a concept expression C in NNF, $clos(C, \mathcal{T}, \mathcal{R})$ is the smallest set X containing C, closed under concept sub-expression, such that, for an atomic concept A, (1) if $A \in X$ and $A \sqsubseteq D \in \mathcal{T}_u$, then $D \in X$, (2) if $\neg A \in X$ and $\neg A \sqsubseteq D \in \mathcal{T}_u$, then $D \in X$, and (3) if $\forall P.C \in X$ and there is a role R with $R \sqsubseteq^* P$ and $\text{Trans}(R)$, then $\forall R.C \in X$. Formally, we define the closure of $\mathcal{A}$ w.r.t. $\mathcal{T}$ and $\mathcal{R}$, denoted $clos(\mathcal{A}, \mathcal{T}, \mathcal{R})$, as $\bigcup_{a:C \in \mathcal{A}} clos(C, \mathcal{T}, \mathcal{R}) \cup \bigcup_{C \sqsubseteq D \in \mathcal{T}_g} clos(NNF(\neg C) \sqcup D, \mathcal{T}, \mathcal{R})$. When there is no ambiguity, we use $clos(\mathcal{A})$ instead of $clos(\mathcal{A}, \mathcal{T}, \mathcal{R})$.

3.1 Motivation

To provide an intuition for our criteria for filtering role assertions, we first informally describe a subset of tableau expansion rules defined in [4]. We assume that a and b are named individuals in $\mathcal{A}$, x is an unnamed individual, C is a concept in $clos(\mathcal{A})$, and R is a role. Named individuals are in $\mathcal{A}$ before applying any expansion rules, while unnamed individuals are introduced as a result of expansion rules. An individual b is defined to be an R-neighbor of a iff there is an assertion $Q(a,b)$ or $Q^-(b,a)$ in $\mathcal{A}$ where $Q \sqsubseteq^* R$.

$\forall$-rule: $a : (\forall R.C) \in \mathcal{A}$, b is an R-neighbor of a, and $b : C \notin \mathcal{A} \Rightarrow$ add $b : C$ to $\mathcal{A}$.
$\leq$-rule: $a : (\leq nR) \in \mathcal{A}$ and, for $1 \leq i \leq m, m > n$, b_i is an R-neighbor of a, and for two of these b_k and b_j the assertion $b_k \neq b_j$ is not in $\mathcal{A} \Rightarrow$
  (i) Merge (identify) b_j with b_k (the precise rules to determine which of b_j or b_k is selected is detailed in [4].)
  (ii) add the assertions in $\mathcal{L}(b_j)$ to $\mathcal{L}(b_k)$
  (iii) for every role assertion with b_j, replace b_j with b_k. In effect, this step adds new role assertions to the $\mathcal{A}$.
$\exists$-rule: $a : (\exists R.C) \in \mathcal{A}$ and for R-neighbors b of a, $b : C \notin \mathcal{A} \Rightarrow$ add $R(a, x)$ and $x : C$ to $\mathcal{A}$.
$\geq$-rule: $a : (\geq nR) \in \mathcal{A}$ and a does not have n distinct R-neighbors $\Rightarrow$ add $R(a, x_i)$ to $\mathcal{A}$, $1 \leq i \leq n$ where the x_i are new distinct unnamed individuals.
$\forall_+$-rule: $a : \forall R.C \in \mathcal{A}$, $P \sqsubseteq^* R$ is transitive, b is a P-neighbor of a, and $b : (\forall P.C) \notin \mathcal{A} \Rightarrow$ add $b : (\forall P.C)$ to $\mathcal{A}$.

We make the key observation that role assertions of the form $R(a, b)$ may affect the outcome of an execution of the tableau algorithm only if one of the following two conditions holds:

1. They can be used to trigger the application of tableau rules that alter the original Abox. As an example of such alteration, a role assertion can be used to add new membership assertions about named individuals (e.g., a new concept C can be propagated to b's concept set through a role assertion $R(a,b)$ by the application of the $\forall$ rule on a if $a : (\forall R.C) \in \mathcal{A}$, and b is an R-neighbor of a).
2. They can be involved in clash detection due to a violation of a maximum cardinality restriction. As an example, if $a : (\leq nR)$ is in the Abox and b is one of $n + 1$ mutually distinct R-neighbors of a, then $R(a,b)$ is important for clash detection.

These conditions can *only* be brought about by either the application of the $\forall$, $\leq$ or $\forall_+$-rules or the presence of a maximum cardinality constraint. In contrast, the $\exists$-rule and $\geq$-rule do not use existing role assertions $R(a,b)$; instead, they result in the creation of new role assertions and new unnamed individuals for satisfying the $\exists R.C$ and $\geq nR$ constraints.

3.2 Criteria for Filtering Role Assertions

Our filtering criteria guarantee that the absence of a role assertion will not affect the outcome of any execution of the non-deterministic tableau algorithm. Our goal is to define criteria which are efficient to evaluate using simple queries against relational databases, while balancing the tradeoff between filtering precision and cost. For instance, by assuming any concept in the $clos(\mathcal{A})$ can reach the concept set of any individual in the Abox during any execution of the tableau algorithm, we avoid tableau operations which are expensive in relational databases. We will say that a role R is *part of a universal restriction* $\forall P.C$ iff $R \sqsubseteq^* P$. (Similarly for maximum cardinality restriction).

To filter a role assertion $R(a,b)$, it must satisfy either 1) or both 2) and 3):

1) Absence of universal and maximum cardinality restrictions: We make the simple observation that if a role R and its inverse R^- are not part of any universal or maximum cardinality restrictions, then $R(a,b)$ can never be used to alter the original Abox or detect a clash, so it can be ignored.

2) Absence of universal rules triggering: Even if R is part of a universal restriction, it may never trigger the application of the universal rules ($\forall_+, \forall$). We define the conditions under which we can guarantee that the universal rules will never be triggered as follows. If R (resp. R^-) is part of a universal restriction $\forall P.C$ in $clos(\mathcal{A})$, then $R(a,b)$ is *irrelevant with respect to* $\forall P.C$ if $b : C \in \mathcal{A}$ (resp. $a : C \in \mathcal{A}$) and R (resp. R^-) has no transitive superroles.

To satisfy the filtering condition, $R(a,b)$ must be irrelevant with respect to all universal restrictions $\forall P.C$ in $clos(\mathcal{A})$, where R or R^- is part of $\forall P.C$.

3) Absence of maximum cardinality restrictions triggering: For the $\leq$-rule to be triggered, there needs to be a violation of a maximum cardinality constraint $a :\leq nP$, where the individual a has more than n P-neighbors, which then causes a merger between individuals. We introduce a technique to conservatively estimate an upper bound on P-neighbors, such that at any step of any possible execution of tableau algorithm, the number of P-neighbors of a is less than or equal to this upper bound. If R (resp. R^-) is part of a maximum cardinality restriction $\leq nP$ in $clos(\mathcal{A})$, then $R(a,b)$ is *irrelevant with respect to* $\leq nP$ if the upper bound on the number of P-neighbors of a (resp. b) is less than or equal to n. Note that this also guarantees that no clash can occur from the presence of the role assertion.

To satisfy the filtering condition, $R(a,b)$ must be irrelevant with respect to all maximum cardinality restrictions $\leq nP$ in $clos(\mathcal{A})$, where R or R^- is part of $\leq nP$.

Upper bound on the number of P-neighbors. Unfortunately, in expressive logics such as SHIN, computing an upper bound does not simply involve counting the number of explicit P-neighbors of a that are present in $\mathcal{A}$. Figure 3 shows examples of the three ways that an individual a can acquire a new P-neighbor during the execution of the tableau algorithm:

3(A) Individual a acquires a new P-neighbor x, where x is an unnamed individual, to satisfy $\exists P.C$ in a's concept set.

3(B) Individual a is merged with a named individual d and acquires a new P-neighbor in order to satisfy a maximum cardinality restriction $c :\leq nQ$.

3(C) Individual a is merged with an unnamed individual x and acquires a new P-neighbor c, where c is either a named or unnamed individual. This occurs in this example because of two conditions: (i) there is a role S^- that is *attracted* to P^- because a common super role Q is part of a maximum cardinality restriction and (ii) a role generator of the form $\exists T.B$ or $\geq mT$ is in the concept set of c, where $T \sqsubseteq^* P^-$.

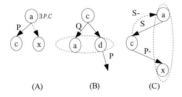

Fig. 3. Acquisition of P-neighbors

Accounting for P-neighbors acquired through situations like 3(B) and 3(C) is not obvious. Therefore we define sufficient conditions under which these situations cannot occur, so that an upper bound of $a's$ P-neighbors can be computed safely and efficiently. If any of these conditions are violated, then a merger of a may result in an increase of its number of P-neighbors, and hence we do not filter $R(a,b)$:

(C1) P is *safe* in $\mathcal{A}$.
Intuitively, the notion of safety ensures that a merger of a named individual a with an unnamed individual x that would increase the number of P-neighbors of a, as illustrated in 3(C), cannot occur. If P is safe, then either

condition (i) or (ii) in 3(C) must be false. More generally, for a given role P, we say that T belongs to the set $attractant(P)$ iff there is a role Q such that $P \sqsubseteq^* Q$, $T \sqsubseteq^* Q$, and $\leq nQ \in clos(\mathcal{A})$. A role P is *safe* if one of the two conditions hold: (a) $attractant(P) \subseteq \{P\}$ and $attractant(P^-) \subseteq \{P^-\}$ (b) For all subroles Q of P or P^- there are no Q-generators (i.e. $\geq mQ$ or $\exists Q.C$) in $clos(\mathcal{A})$.

(C2) For any role Q, if a is a Q-neighbor of some named individual c then there is no concept of the form $(\leq nQ)$ in $clos(\mathcal{A})$.

(C3) For any role S, if some named individual c is a S-neighbor of a and $\leq nS$ is in $clos(\mathcal{A})$, then S is safe in $\mathcal{A}$.

Conditions (C2) and (C3) ensure that a merger of a and a named individual as illustrated in 3(B) is impossible. (C2) by itself is not sufficient because, even if Q is not part of a maximum cardinality restriction, Q^- may have an attractant T^-, where $\exists T^- B$ is in the concept set of a. As described in 3(C), these conditions can cause a merger between c and an unnamed individual x, so that a becomes a T-neighbor of c. If T is part of a maximum cardinality restriction, a itself may become mergable. Condition (C3) prevents mergers between c and unnamed individuals that would make a a T-neighbor of c, thus preventing a from becoming mergable.

If a and P satisfy (C1), (C2) and (C3), an upper bound on the number of P-neighbors can be computed using the following formula:

$$|P(a)| + |Some(P,a)| + \sum_{\geq mP \in Min(P,a)} m$$

where before the application of any tableau rules, $|P(a)|$ denotes the number of P-neighbors of a, $Some(P,a) = \{\exists P.C \in clos(\mathcal{A}) \mid$ there is no P-neighbor d of a such that $d : C \in \mathcal{A}\ \}$, and $Min(P,a) = \{\geq mP \in clos(\mathcal{A}) \mid$ there are no individuals d_i such that, for $1 \leq i \leq m$, d_i is a P-neighbors of a, and if $j \neq k$, then $d_k \dot{\neq} d_j \in \mathcal{A}\ \}$

Intuitively, the upper bound is the sum of the explicit P-neighbors of a before the application of tableau rules, plus the maximum number of unnamed individuals that can be generated by the application of the $\exists$- and $\geq$- rules, excluding any existential or minimum cardinality restrictions that are already satisfied prior to the application of tableau rules.

3.3 Correctness of Filtering Criteria

Since some of the notions introduced in the previous section are defined in the context of the tableau algorithm, we first briefly present some important concepts related to this algorithm. As described in [4], the tableau algorithm operates on completion forest $F = (G, \mathcal{L}, \dot{\neq}, \dot{=})$ where G is graph; $\mathcal{L}$ is a mapping from a node x in F to a set of concepts, $\mathcal{L}(x)$, in $clos(\mathcal{A})$, and from an edge $<x,y>$ in F to a set of roles, $\mathcal{L}(<x,y>)$, in $\mathcal{R}$; $\dot{=}$ is an equivalence relation on nodes of G; and $\dot{\neq}$ is the binary relation *distinct from* on nodes of G. To check the consistency of $\mathcal{A}$, F is initialized as follows. There is a node a in G iff there is an individual a in $\mathcal{A}$. $<x,y>$ is an edge in G with $R \in \mathcal{L}(<x,y>)$ iff $R(x,y) \in \mathcal{A}$.

For x and y in G, $x \dot{\neq} y$ iff $x \dot{\neq} y \in \mathcal{A}$. A *root* node a is a node present in the initial forest, and *unnamed* nodes are created by $\exists$ and $\geq$ rules.

Next, we show that conditions (C1), (C2) and (C3) in Section 3.2 are sufficient to rule out mergers which can increase the number of P-neighbors as shown in Figure 3(B) and (C). Lemma 3 below is an important step towards this goal.

Lemma 3. Let P be a role that is safe in $\mathcal{A}$. At any step of any execution of the tableau algorithm on $\mathcal{A}$, the following holds: if there is an unnamed node x such that P or P^- is in the $\mathcal{L}(<parent(x), x>)$, then $|\mathcal{L}(<parent(x), x>)| = 1$, where $parent(x)$ denotes the parent node of x in the completion forest (Note that in a SHIN completion forest, unnamed nodes are always in a tree rooted at a root node).

Proof. Easily proven by induction on the iterations of the tableau algorithm. See [5] for more details. A direct consequence of this lemma is that a merger between a and an unnamed node cannot increase the number of P-neighbors of a if P is safe (See [5] for more details).

Now, we need to prove that if (C2) and (C3) are satisfied for a named individual a, a cannot be merged with another named individual. First, we formally define the notion of *mergeability with a named individual*.

Definition 4. A named individual a in $\mathcal{A}$ is *mergeable with named individuals* in $\mathcal{A}$ iff there is at least one execution of the tableau algorithm on $\mathcal{A}$ such that, at some step, the root node a is merged with another root node b. When there is no ambiguity, we simply say that a is mergeable.

Theorem 5: If a named individual a in $\mathcal{A}$ satisfies conditions (C2) and (C3), then a is *not mergeable with named individuals* in $\mathcal{A}$.

Proof Sketch. By induction on the iterations of the tableau algorithm using Lemma 3 [5]. □

Finally, the correctness of our filtering criteria relies on the following theorem:

Theorem 6. A role assertion $R(a, b)$ can safely be ignored in an Abox $\mathcal{A}$ if it is irrelevant with respect to universal restrictions and irrelevant with respect to maximum cardinality restrictions, as defined in section 3.2.

Proof. Let $R(a, b)$ be a role assertion irrelevant w.r.t. maximum cardinality and universal restrictions in an Abox $\mathcal{A}$. Let $\mathcal{A}'$ be the Abox defined as $\mathcal{A}' = \mathcal{A} - \{R(a, b), R^-(b, a)\}$. If $\mathcal{A}$ is consistent, $\mathcal{A}'$ is obviously consistent. We show that if $\mathcal{A}'$ is consistent, a model of $\mathcal{A}$ can be constructed by applying the tableau algorithm rules in a particular way. [1]

First, for a root node c in the completion forest F, the root node $\alpha(c)$ is defined as follows (Informally, $\alpha(c)$ corresponds to the node in which c has been directly or indirectly merged): if $\mathcal{L}(c) \neq \emptyset$ then $\alpha(c) = c$; otherwise, $\alpha(c) = d$, where d is the unique root node in F with $\mathcal{L}(d) \neq \emptyset$ and $d \dot{=} c$.

---
[1] A direct model-theoretic proof cannot easily be provided here, see [5] for details.

Since $\mathcal{A}'$ is consistent, we can apply the tableau expansion rules on $\mathcal{A}'$ without creating a clash in such a way that: (1) $\exists$-rule is never triggered to satisfy a constraint $\exists P.C \in \mathcal{L}(\alpha(a))$(resp. $\mathcal{L}(\alpha(b))$) where $\leq nP \in clos(\mathcal{A})$, R (resp. R^-) is part of $\leq nP$, and $b : C \in \mathcal{A}$ (resp. $a : C \in \mathcal{A}$); and (2) $\geq$-rule is never triggered to satisfy a constraint $\geq nP \in \mathcal{L}(\alpha(a))$ (resp. $\mathcal{L}(\alpha(b))$) where $\leq nP \in clos(\mathcal{A})$, R (resp. R^-) is part of $\leq nP$, and, in the Abox $\mathcal{A}$, b (resp. a) is one of n P-neighbors of a (resp. P-neighbors of b) explicitly asserted to be distinct. Such a rule application yields a clash-free completion forest F, and the only nodes on which expansion rules may be applicable are $\alpha(a)$ and $\alpha(b)$ (The only applicable rules are $\exists$-rule and $\geq$-rule).

Next, we modify F to create a completion forest F' by adding to F the edge $<\alpha(a), \alpha(b)>$ if it was not already in F, and by adding R to $\mathcal{L}(<\alpha(a), \alpha(b)>)$, if it was not already there. We show that F' is complete (i.e. no rules are applicable) and clash-free. The fact that, in F', $R \in \mathcal{L}(<\alpha(a), \alpha(b)>)$ ensures that the $\exists$ and $\geq$ rules, which may have been applicable on $\alpha(a)$ or $\alpha(b)$ in F, are not applicable on $\alpha(a)$ and $\alpha(b)$ in F'. However, the same fact may now make the $\forall$, $\forall_+$, $\leq$, and $\leq_r$ rules applicable on $\alpha(a)$ or $\alpha(b)$ in F'. We show that this cannot be the case.

The definition of irrelevance w.r.t. universal restrictions given in section 3.2 obviously ensures that $\forall$ and $\forall_+$ rules are not applicable on $\alpha(a)$ or $\alpha(b)$ in F'. $\leq$, and $\leq_r$ rules are not applicable on $\alpha(a)$ or $\alpha(b)$ in F' as a direct consequence of the following claim: **Claim:** if $R(a, b)$ is irrelevant w.r.t $\leq nP \in clos(\mathcal{A})$ and R (resp. R^-) is part $\leq nP$, then the number of P-neighbors of a (resp. P-neighbors of b) in F is less than or equal to n. Furthermore, if it is equal to n, then, in F, $\alpha(b)$ is a P-neighbor of $\alpha(a)$ (resp. $\alpha(a)$ is a P-neighbor of $\alpha(b)$).

The proof of this claim is a direct consequence of Lemma 3, Theorem 5 and the fact that the upper-bound (defined in section 3.2) of P-neighbors of a is less than or equal to n (See [5] for more details).

The addition of $R \in \mathcal{L}(<\alpha(a), \alpha(b)>)$ to F cannot create a clash of the form $\{C, \neg C\}$ in F', and the previous claim implies that a clash in F' due to a violation of a maximum cardinality constraint on $\alpha(a)$ or $\alpha(b)$ is not possible. Thus, F' is a complete clash-free completion forest such that $R \in \mathcal{L}(<\alpha(a), \alpha(b)>)$. Therefore, a tableau for $\mathcal{A}$ can be built from F' as in [4], so $\mathcal{A}$ has a model. □

3.4 Summary Abox Filtering

We apply the filtering criteria described in Section 3.2 to a canonical summary Abox $\mathcal{A}'$. For correctness with respect to cardinality restrictions, we need to augment the canonical summary Abox with role assertion statistics, since role assertions are merged by the summary Abox transformation. For each role R that is part of a cardinality restriction, we associated with R the maximum number of R-neighbors that any individual a has in $\mathcal{A}$. With this augmentation, it is clear that the proofs in Section 3.3 apply to the canonical summary Abox.

Typically, filtering $\mathcal{A}'$ creates distinct partitions, and we apply the tableau algorithm to each partition separately. If all of the partitions are consistent, then we are done. Otherwise, we need to check $\mathcal{A}$. However, even when $\mathcal{A}'$ itself is inconsistent, some of its partitions may be consistent, and we only have to check portions of $\mathcal{A}$ which correspond to the filtered inconsistent partitions of $\mathcal{A}'$. Thus, partitioning a summary Abox is an effective way of isolating a potential inconsistency in $\mathcal{A}$. Furthermore, filtering $\mathcal{A}'$ is very efficient since $\mathcal{A}'$ is relatively small. For partitions consisting of a single individual, checking consistency is just checking concept satisfiability.

More precisely, let $\mathcal{A}'_p$ be a partition of individuals and assertions in $\mathcal{A}'$. The *image* of $\mathcal{A}'_p$ in $\mathcal{A}$ is defined to be the maximum subset of the individuals and assertions in $\mathcal{A}$ which map to $\mathcal{A}'_p$ via the summary Abox function **f**. If a role assertion $R(a, b)$ is irrelevant in $\mathcal{A}'$, then all role assertions in its image in $\mathcal{A}$ are also irrelevant. By theorem 2, if a partition $\mathcal{A}'_p$ is consistent, then its entire image in $\mathcal{A}$ can be ignored. Finally, retrieving the image in $\mathcal{A}$ of an inconsistent partition $\mathcal{A}'_p$ is a simple database operation.

For example, suppose we filter all R-role assertions from the summary Abox $\mathcal{A}'$ in Figure 2. The resulting summary Abox shown in Figure 4 consists of three partitions: X, Y, and Z. We run the consistency check on each partition. For singleton partition Z, we just need to check concept satisfiability. Assuming only partition X is inconsistent, we need to check only the consistency of its image in $\mathcal{A}$, shown in Figure 5, which is $d1, d2 : D; b1 - b6 : B; T(d1, b1)$ and $P(d2, b4)$. Checking isolated individuals $b2, b3, b5$ and $b6$, involves just concept satisfiability.

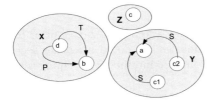 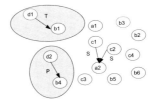

Fig. 4. Filtered summary Abox   **Fig. 5.** Filtered Abox

4 Computational Experience

We tested our approach on the four ontologies shown in Table 2(a). Their expressiveness is given in the first column (Exp) of Table 2(a) . The number of concepts (C) and roles (R) reported in the table reflect concepts and roles actually used in the Abox. In the tables, R.A. stands for role assertions, and I for individuals. In all the experiments reported here, the Aboxes were stored in a relational database on a 64 bit AMD 997 Mhz dual processor 8G RAM machine. We tested our program as a client to the database server both on a 32 bit single 1.8 Ghz processor 1.5 G RAM machine, and on the 64 bit machine described above. Running times reported in the tables are in seconds on the 64 bit machine. On the 32 bit machine the times were 2 times slower, but the program ran on both machines with minimal space requirements (512 M heap).

The Biopax ontology contains biological pathway data for 11 organisms publicly available from Biocyc (http://biocyc.org). LUBM [7] is a benchmark ontology that was scaled to different numbers of universities (5-30) in our experiments. We used an OWL-DL version of LUBM [8], but with nominals removed. The NIMD ontology expresses relationships between persons, places and events (http://ksl.stanford.edu/projects/NIMD/Kani-dl-v1.owl). Its Abox was generated from text analysis of unstructured documents [9]. The semantic traceability (ST) ontology specifies the relationships among software artifacts. Its Abox was generated from a program that extracted relationships between software artifacts of a middleware application. The sizes of the last 4 Aboxes shown in Table 2(a) are beyond the capabilities of in-memory reasoners such as Pellet and KAON2, when tested on the 64-bit machine with a 4G heap size.

Table 2. ABoxes and Summary Aboxes prior to filtering

Ontology	Exp	C	R	I	R.A.
Biopax	ALCHF	31	40	261,149	582,655
LUBM-1	SHIN	91	27	42,585	214,177
LUBM-5	SHIN	91	27	179,871	927,854
LUBM-10	SHIN	91	27	351,422	1,816,153
LUBM-30	SHIN	91	27	1,106,858	6,494,950
NIMD	SHIF	19	27	1,278,540	1,999,787
ST	SHI	16	11	874,319	3,595,132

(a) Experimental Aboxes

Ontology	C	R	I	R.A	Time
Biopax	31	40	81	583	46
LUBM-1	91	27	410	16,233	12
LUBM-5	91	27	598	35,375	60
LUBM-10	91	27	673	49,176	128
LUBM-30	91	27	765	79,845	485
NIMD	19	27	19	55	77
ST	16	11	21	183	197

(b) Summaries

Table 2(b) shows the size of the corresponding summary Aboxes prior to any filtering, and the time to compute the summaries. As noted in earlier sections, the summary Abox can be computed once, and maintained with changes to the Abox.

Table 3(a) shows the effectiveness of filtering the summary ABox for the consistency detection test, and the time to perform filtering. Note that the filtering step is dynamic, i.e., it must be computed on the summary box for each incoming query. The filtering step can create partitions. In Table 3(a), the first number in the first column (Sin.+Mult) indicates the number of partitions with single individuals, and the second number indicates the number of partitions with multiple individuals. The rest of the columns show the size of the Abox that is left after removing all partitions with single individuals.

Table 3(b) shows the size of the Abox on which we had to perform the consistency check. All times for the consistency check were measured using the Pellet OWL reasoner. For those Aboxes where the filtered summary Abox in Table 3(a) was consistent, the size of the ABox was simply that in Table 3(a). For some ontologies, however (e.g., all LUBM ontologies marked with an asterisk), the filtered Abox was inconsistent because of our summarization techniques. For these ontologies, we had to retrieve the image of the inconsistent partition from the original Abox. In these cases, the size shown in Table 3(b) is the image of the partition in the original Abox. Time for consistency check is provided in seconds. This includes the time for the concept satisfiability check for partitions with single individuals, the time for the consistency check on the filtered summary, and

Table 3. Filtering and consistency check

Ontology	Sin.+Mult.	C	R	I	R.A.	Time
Biopax	42+1	13	1	38	98	1.6
LUBM-1	130+2	28	5	280	284	1.4
LUBM-5	172+2	28	5	426	444	2.1
LUBM-10	199+2	28	5	474	492	2.5
LUBM-30	220+2	28	5	545	574	2.8
NIMD	17+1	2	1	2	1	0.6
ST	3+1	15	2	18	50	0.3

(a) Summary Aboxes after filtering

Ontology	I	R.A.	Time	Consistent
Biopax	38	98	0.7	Yes
LUBM-1*	140	102	1	Yes
LUBM-5*	644	466	1.5	Yes
LUBM-10*	1283	938	2	Yes
LUBM-30*	4045	2942	3.5	Yes
NIMD	2	1	0.2	Yes
ST	-	-	0.1	No

(b) Sizes for consistency check

the time for retrieving and checking the image of the inconsistent partition on the original Abox. As shown in Table 3(b), ST was an inconsistent ontology, but we determined this purely based on a concept satisfiability check for partitions with single individuals. We also deliberately injected an inconsistency for one of the Biopax databases (agrocyc), to check if we could detect an inconsistency that could not simply be detected by a concept satisfiability check. We were able to detect that the Abox was inconsistent using our algorithm.

5 Related Work

There are many highly optimized reasoners such as Pellet [10], Racer [11], InstanceStore [12], and Kaon2 [3] designed for consistency checking, but only InstanceStore and Kaon2 can be extended to Aboxes in secondary storage [2]. Kaon2 applies to deductive databases, whereas our techniques work with relational databases. InstanceStore is limited to role-free Aboxes. In theory, Instance Store can handle Aboxes with role assertions through a technique called precompletion [13], but this may not be practical for large Aboxes stored in databases because it could result in an exponential number of Aboxes. Our approach can be compared with optimization techniques such as model caching and Abox contraction [14], and partitioning techniques [15], but again, it is unclear how such techniques can be applied to large Aboxes in databases.

6 Conclusions

We have demonstrated a technique to scale consistency detection to large Aboxes in secondary storage by extracting a small representative Abox. Further, we have shown that, in practice, this technique works efficiently on four large ontologies. Our plan is to extend this approach to apply more accurate analysis techniques, extend its applicability to more expressive languages, and to optimize these techniques for efficient query processing.

---

[2] RacerPro version 1.9.0 does not provide that capability, but its user guide indicates that it will be available in a future version.

References

1. Horrocks, I., Tessaris, S.: Querying the semantic web: a formal approach. In Horrocks, I., Hendler, J., eds.: Proc. of the 1st Int. Semantic Web Conf. (ISWC 2002). Number 2342 in Lecture Notes in Computer Science, Springer-Verlag (2002) 177–191
2. Donini, F.: Complexity of reasoning. In Baader, F., Calvanese, D., McGuinness, D., Nardi, D., Patel-Schneider, P., eds.: Description Logic Handbook. Cambridge University Press (2002) 101–141
3. U.Hustadt, Motik, B., Sattler, U.: Reducing shiq description logic to disjunctive datalog programs. (Proc. of 9th Intl. Conf. on Knowledge Representation and Reasoning (KR2004)) 152–162
4. Horrocks, I., Sattler, U., Tobies, S.: Reasoning with individuals for the description logic SHIQ*. Proc. of 17th Int.Conf. on Automated Deduction (2000) 482–496
5. Fokoue, A., Kershenbaum, A., Ma, L., Schonberg, E., Srinivas, K.: Scalable reasoning: Cutting ontologies down to size. In: http://www.research.ibm.com/iaa/techReport.pdf. (2006)
6. Horrocks, I., Tobies, S.: Reasoning with axioms: Theory and practice. In: KR. (2000) 285–296
7. Guo, Y., Pan, Z., Heflin, J.: An evaluation of knowledge base systems for large owl datasets. Third International Semantic Web Conference (2004) 274–288
8. Ma, L., Yang, Y., Qiu, Z., Xie, G., Pan, Y.: Towards a complete owl ontology benchmark. In: Proc. of the third European Semantic Web Conf.(ESWC 2006). (2006) 124–139
9. Welty, C., Murdock, J.W.: Towards knowledge acquisition from information extraction. In: Proc. of the fifth International Semantic Web Conf.(ISWC 2006). (2006)
10. Sirin, E., Parsia, B.: Pellet: An owl dl reasoner. In: Description Logics. (2004)
11. Haarslev, V., Moller, R.: Racer system description. Conf. on Automated Reasoning (IJCAR 2001) (2001) 701–705
12. Bechhofer, S., Horrocks, I., Turi, D.: The owl instance store: System description. Proc. of 20th Int.Conf. on Automated Deduction (2005) 177–181
13. Tessaris, S., Horrocks, I.: Abox satisfiability reduced to terminological reasoning in expressive description logics. In: LPAR. (2002) 435–449
14. Haarslev, V., Moller, R.: An empirical evaluation of optimization strategies for abox reasoning in expressive description logics. Proc. of the International Workshop on Description Logics (1999) 115–199
15. Grau, B.C., Parsia, B., Sirin, E., Kalyanpur, A.: Automatic partitioning of owl ontologies using e-connections. In: Description Logics. (2005)

Semantic Metadata Generation for Large Scientific Workflows

Jihie Kim, Yolanda Gil, and Varun Ratnakar

Information Sciences Institute, University of Southern California
4676 Admiralty Way, Marina del Rey CA 90292, United States
{jihie, gil, varunr}@isi.edu

Abstract. In recent years, workflows have been increasingly used in scientific applications. This paper presents novel metadata reasoning capabilities that we have developed to support the creation of large workflows. They include 1) use of semantic web technologies in handling metadata constraints on file collections and nested file collections, 2) propagation and validation of metadata constraints from inputs to outputs in a workflow component, and through the links among components in a workflow, and 3) sub-workflows that generate metadata needed for workflow creation. We show how we used these capabilities to support the creation of large executable workflows in an earthquake science application with more than 7,000 jobs, generating metadata for more than 100,000 new files.

Keywords: metadata reasoning, workflow generation, grid workflows.

1 Introduction

Scientists have growing needs to use workflows to manage large distributed computations [13, 5, 2, 24]. In recent years, uses of large workflows have been significantly increased. Often they adopt grid-based environments that enable efficient execution of workflows by making use of distributed shared resources [22]. In such cases, computations in scientific workflows are represented as grid jobs that describe components used, input files required, and output files that will be produced as well as file movements, and deposition to distributed repositories [4].

Metadata describe the data used and generated by workflow components. Semantic web techniques have been applied for metadata reasoning on workflows such as validation of input parameters based on provenance data using component semantics [23], representing and managing dependencies between data products [14], helping scientists relate and annotate data and services through ontology-based generation and management of provenance data [25], etc. However, most of the existing metadata reasoning approaches focus on analyses of provenance data that are created from execution [18] rather than generation of input and output file descriptions needed in the workflow before execution.

The metadata reasoning capabilities of existing systems focus on files and simple collections and cannot effectively handle constraints on nested collections. Existing checks on files are limited to validation of inputs for individual components.

However, often there are global constraints on inputs and outputs of multiple components, and the workflow should be validated against such constraints in order to prevent execution of invalid workflows and wasting of expensive computations. In addition, unnecessary execution of individual components or multiple components in the given workflow should be detected and avoided when datasets that are equivalent to the ones to be produced already exist.

The creation of large workflows in the domains we use required several novel metadata reasoning capabilities:

- Keeping track of constraints on datasets used (i.e. files and file collections), including global constraints among multiple components as well as local constraints within individual components.
- Describing datasets that are used or created by the workflow.
- Detecting equivalent datasets and prevent unnecessary execution of workflow parts when datasets already exist.
- Managing large datasets and their provenance.

This paper presents novel metadata reasoning capabilities that we have developed to support the creation of large workflows. They include 1) use of semantic web technologies in handling metadata constraints on file collections and nested file collections, 2) propagation and validation of metadata constraints from inputs to outputs in a workflow component, and through the links among components in a workflow, and 3) sub-workflows that generate metadata needed for workflow creation. We illustrate these novel capabilities to support the creation of large workflows in an earthquake science application.

2 Motivation

A computational workflow is a set of executable programs (called *components*) that are introduced and linked together to pass data products to each other. The purpose of a computational workflow is to produce a desired end result from the combined computation of the programs. We will call a computational workflow as a *workflow* in this paper for brevity. Whereas a workflow represents a flow of data products among executable components, a *workflow template* is an abstract specification of a workflow, with a set of *nodes* and *links* where each node is a placeholder for a *component* or *component collections* (for iterative execution of a program over a file collection), and each link represents how the input and output parameters are connected. For example, Figure 1-(a) shows a template that has been used by earthquake scientists in SCEC (Southern California Earthquake Center) in Fall 2005. The template has two nodes (seismogram generation and calculation of spectral accelerations), each one containing a component collection. The workflow created from the template is shown in Figure 1-(b). This workflow was used in estimating hazard level of a site with respect to spectral acceleration caused by ruptures and their variations over time.

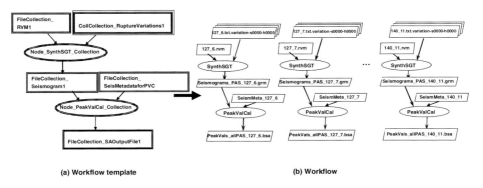

Fig. 1. Workflow creation for seismic hazard analysis in Fall 2005

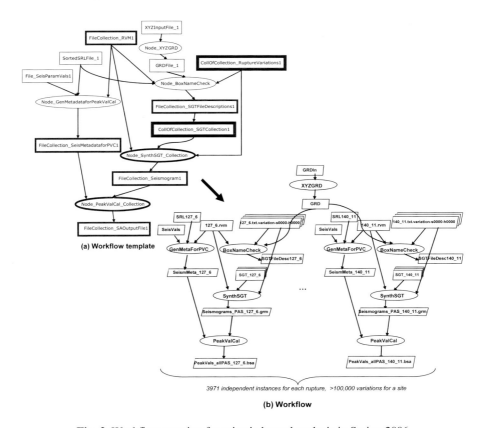

Fig. 2. Workflow creation for seismic hazard analysis in Spring 2006

The workflow was generated from manually created scripts that specify how to bind files to input parameters of the components and what are the expected output file names. An important feature of the workflow is that their data products are stored in files, often organized in directory structures that reflect the structure of the workflows. The names of the files and the directories follow conventions to encode metadata information in the names such as the creation date or the relative area covered by the analysis. Therefore, the scripts that generate the workflow must orchestrate the creation of very particular data identifiers, namely file names that comply with those conventions and are instantiated to the appropriate constants. For example, a file containing the points for a hazard curve would be named using the rupture id and the fault id that were used in the simulation of the wave, as well as the lat-long of the location for the curve. The script included calls to functions or other scripts that generate information needed by the workflow (e.g. seismic parameter values). These manual 'seam' steps were not a part of the workflow. Most of the validation checks on the files and the collections were done by hand.

Figure 2-(a) shows an extension in the template in Spring 2006. This extension was needed to include strain green tensors (SGTs) as additional data input for seismogram generation. As the workflow template and descriptions of components become more complex, the script based approach becomes infeasible. First of all, there are more manual seam steps to handle. For example, since the SGT files that should be used in the workflow are unknown, the function that generates appropriate SGT file names should be executed beforehand. Validation of the workflow requires more checks. For example, now we need to check whether the SGTs use in generating seismogram are consistent with the rupture variations used for calculating peak values. If the seismogram generation step uses ruptures for Pasadena and their corresponding SGTs but the peak value calculation uses a rupture variation map for LA, the execution of the workflow will fail. When there exists a dataset that is equivalent to the expected output from executions of some components (e.g. SGT name datasets for Pasadena already exist), scientists had to identify them by hand.

In summary, generation of large workflows for this type of applications requires flexibility in adding or changing components to the template, systematic identification of files that are needed and generated by the workflow, incorporation of manual 'seam' steps into the workflow (making them a part of the workflow), and automatic validation of files and collections that are input to the workflow.

3 Approach

In developing new metadata reasoning capabilities for workflow creation, we use a workflow creation framework called Wings [6]. Wings takes a workflow template and initial input file descriptions, and creates an abstract workflow called DAX (DAG XML description). A DAX is transformed into an executable concrete workflow through a mapping that assigns available grid resources for execution by Pegasus [4]. Wings uses OWL-DL for representing files and collections, components, workflow templates, and workflows [6]. Currently Jena supports the reasoning.

In this work, Wings was extended to support metadata reasoning and generation. We developed an approach for representing metadata constraints on files and collections, and supporting metadata reasoning capabilities. Figure 3 shows an overview of the relevant components in the system, described in the following subsections. Although the descriptions rely on earthquake science examples, the same approach is used for other applications [6].

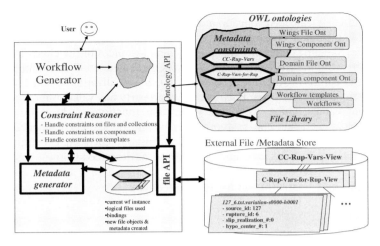

Fig. 3. Metadata reasoning for workflow creation

3.1 Representing Metadata Constraints

One of the novel capabilities addresses the issue of keeping track of constraints on individual files, constraints on collections and their elements, constraints on inputs and outputs of each component, and global constraints among multiple components.

3.1.1 Metadata Constraints on Individual Files

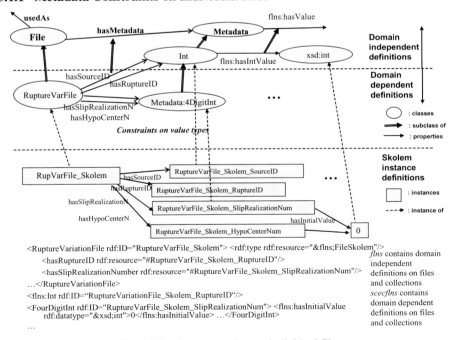

Fig. 4. Metadata constraints on individual files

Each file class can have one or more metadata properties associated with it. In representing metadata constraints of a file class, we use a *skolem* instance (e.g., RupVarFile_Skolem) that represents prototypical instances of the class. The metadata can describe what the file contains, how it was generated, etc. For example, a rupture variation file can have Ruptupre ID, SourceID, SlipRealizationN, and HypoCenterN that represent what it contains. Each metadata property has value ranges and can have some initial values. Other workflow generation functions such as how to derive filenames from metadata can be represented using the skolem instance. The actual metadata property values of file instances can be used in checking constraints on input and output files/collections used in the workflow, as described below.

3.1.2 Handling Constraints on Nested Collections

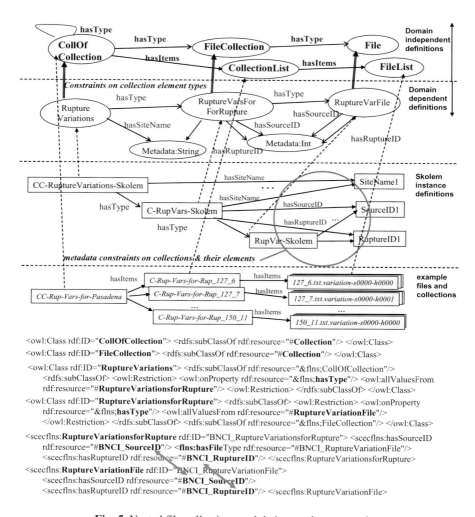

Fig. 5. Nested file collections and their metadata constraints

In general, for a given site (e.g. Pasadena), several ruptures are used in performing the hazard analysis. According to rupture dynamics of earthquakes that depend on hypocenter and slip values, each temporal variation of the stress is described in a rupture variation file. That is, rupture variations for a site are naturally structured as a collection of file collections. In our ontology, the concept *collection* represents both simple file collections and nested collections. Each collection should specify the type for the collection element using the 'hasType' property. There can be constraints between a collection and its elements. For example, for a rupture variation collection for a rupture, the SourceID and the RuptureID of individual rupture variation file should be the same as the rupture's SourceID and RuptureID. That is, if the rupture variation collection for a rupture has SourceID 127 and RuptureID 6, each element (a rupture variation file) should have SourceID 127 and RuptureID 6. Figure 5 shows how these constraints on collections and nested collections are represented with skolem instances.

3.1.3 Constraints on Components: Constraints on Input and Output Files and Collections

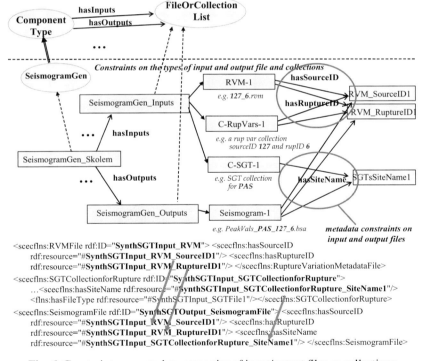

Fig. 6. Constraints on metadata properties of input/output files or collections

Each workflow component is described in terms of its input and output data types. In Figure 6, the SeismogramGen component has three inputs: an RVM (rupture variation map) file, a rupture variation collection, and a SGT file collection. Each

RVM file has a SourceID and a RuptureID of the rupture that it represents. In order to create valid results, their values should be the same as the RuptureID and SourceID of the input rupture variation collection. The input SGT collection should have a site name associated with it. Given these inputs, the SeismogramGen component produces a seismogram file.

The metadata for the generated seismogram file depends on the metadata of the inputs. In the above example, the site name of the SGT collection (PAS), and the SourceID and RuptureID of the RVM file (127 and 6) are propagated to corresponding metadata properties of the output seismogram file. The procedure for metadata validation and propagation during workflow creation is described in Section 3.2.

3.1.4 Global Constraints on Templates: Constraints Among Different Nodes and Links

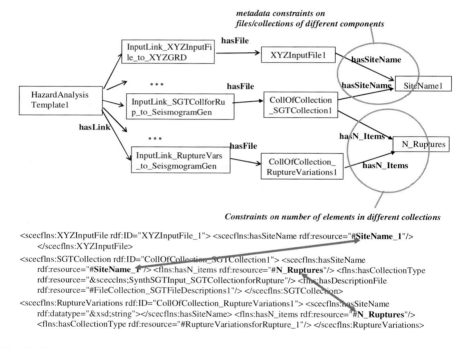

Fig. 7. Global constraints on metadata properties among files and collections used by different components in a template

There are additional validation checks that should be made in order to create a valid workflow. First of all, the components should use seismic data for the same site (e.g. PAS) in performing hazard analysis. In Figure 7, the site name of the XYZinput file used in generating a mesh for simulation should be the same as the site name of the SGT collection of collections. (We also use a isSameAs property in representing equalities of metadata.) In addition, the components should use the same number of ruptures throughout the workflow. For example, the number of elements in a collection of collection rupture variations indicates the number of ruptures used in modeling the site. This number (i.e. the number of ruptures) should be the same as the number of elements (SGT collections) in the collection of collection SGTs that are used. If the specific number of ruptures is known, the value can be given for the N_Ruptures using the flns:hasValue property. Figure 7 shows the current representations. In representing these global constraints, we make use of *link skolems*. Each link skolem is a placeholder for a file or collection that is bound to the input and output parameters of the components associated with the link during workflow creation. If more than one link skolems in a template share the same metadata objects, when the bindings for the links are created their corresponding metadata values should be the same. These constraints are used by metadata reasoner in creating consistent and correct workflows. The details of metadata based validation are described below.

3.2 Metadata Propagation and Validation

Table 1. Steps for propagating metadata and checking constraints during workflow creation

```
Bind&ValidateWorkflow (WorkflowTemplate wt, InputLinks ILinks)
  1. Assign ILinks to LinksToProcess.
  2. While LinksToProcess is not empty
    2.2. Remove one from LinksToProcess and assign it to L1.
    2.2. Let F1 be the link skolem for binding files or collections to L1.
    2.3. If metadata for F1 should be generated from an execution of a component
      2.3.1. if the execution results are not available, continue.
        ;; i.e. exclude this link in the sub-workflow
    2.4. If any metadata of F1 depends on a link L2 that is not bound yet,
      2.4.1. Mark L1 as a dependent of L2 and continue.
    2.5. If L1 is an input link,
      2.5.1. Get metadata of the file from the user or a file server
      2.5.2. Check consistencies with links that L1 depends on
      2.5.3. Check consistencies with existing bindings based on template-level constraints
      2.5.4. If any metadata are inconsistent, report inconsistency and return.
      2.5.5. Bind file/collection name and metadata to F1.
      2.5.6. If the file type for F1 is a collection, recursively get the metadata of its elements
    2.6. Else (i.e. L1 is InOutLink or OuputLink)
      2.6.1. Generate file names and metadata base on the definition of the depending links.
        ;; metadata propagation
    2.7. For each link L2 that is dependent on l1,
      2.7.1. if all the links that L2 is depending on are bound, put L2 in LinksToProcess.
    2.8. If L1 is an output link, continue.
    2.9. Else (L1 is InputLink or InOutLink)
      2.9.1. If all the inputs to the destination node (i.e. the component that L1 provides an input to)
            have been bound,
        2.9.1.1. Add all the OutputLinks and InOutLinks from the destination node to the
              LinksToProcess.
```

Table 1 shows the procedure for propagating metadata constraints and validating workflows created using metadata constraints. The procedure significantly extends the existing Wings algorithm by including steps for metadata propagation and validation checks. It traverses links in the workflow template and generates consistent bindings for link skolems. There are three classes of links: InputLink, InOutLink, and OutputLink. An InputLink is a link from an initial input file or collection to a node. Each InOutLink represents a connection from an output parameter of a node to an input parameter of another node. An OutputLink represents an end result from a node. The procedure specifies how the system starts with the input links of a template, identifies dependencies among the links based on definitions of metadata constraints, binds link skolems to files or collections, propagates and checks constraints of the bindings based on metadata constraints, and traverses the next unbound links based on the dependencies.

A link l1 is dependent on l2 if some of the metadata of l1 needs to be filled in based on some metadata of l2. For example, in Figure 6, the metadata of the output of SeismogramGen step depends on the metadata of the RVM file and the SGT collection. The input link for a rupture variation collection depends on the input link for an RVM, if the SourceID and the RuptureID of the rupture variations are derived from the values in the RVM file. We assume that there are no cyclic dependencies in the definition of metadata constraints.

The file names and the metadata for initial input files or collections can be given from the user or existing file library (in OWL) through a file API. The metadata of the initial inputs can also be retrieved from other external file stores using the same API. Currently we use a web repository, but we are exploring uses of grid catalogs such as MCS (Metadata Catalog Service) [19]. The italicized steps handle sub-workflows, which are explained in the next section.

3.3 Sub-workflows for Generating Metadata Needed for Workflow Creation

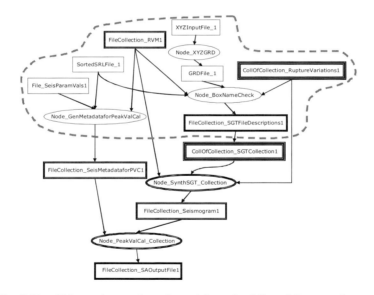

Fig. 8. Identifying and executing sub-workflows for full workflow creation

As described in Section 2, creation of workflows needed manual 'seam' steps that call functions that generate information needed by the workflow, such as file names and parameter values. In order to minimize such manual steps, we have created new workflow components that model such steps. For example, in Figure 8 (an enlargement of Figure 2-(a)), individual files in CollOfCollection_SGTCollection1 are unknown initially and the file names should be generated by executing the BoxNameCheck component. Previously, the execution of BoxNameCheck was done manually. We represent such components as workflow components, and link them to the depending component inputs or outputs (e.g. SGT files needed by SynthSGT) in the template.

In generating grid workflows, for each execution of a component, the names of the inputs and output files for the component should be specified beforehand. That is, what data are created, and what data are staged in and out of the computation should be known before execution. Names (or descriptions) of some of the files in the workflow are not given initially, and their names should be automatically generated from metadata of other files.

As shown in Table 1, our Bind&ValidateWorkflow procedure checks these dependencies, and generates a 'sub'-workflow that includes only the parts that can be instantiated with the currently available data. For the template in Figure 8, a subworkflow with bindings for input and output links of the three components (XYZGRD, GenMetaForPeakValCal and BoxNameCheck), highlighted with dotted lines, is generated. The resulting sub-workflow is mapped to grid resources through Pegasus [5] and executed in a grid environment. The execution of a sub-workflow provides results for dependent input/output links, such as file names needed for component inputs or outputs. The metadata for these new file names are generated and added to our file repository by the metadata generator (shown in Figure 3) so that they can be used in creating an expanded workflow. The creation and execution of sub-workflows can be interleaved until the complete workflow is generated. The above workflow template needs only one iteration of sub-workflow creation and execution.

4 Results

Table 2. Number of files and OWL instances created during workflow generation

	Workflow creation time	Number of file instances created for the workflow	Number of OWL individuals created
A sub workflow for hazard analysis	7 minutes, 59 seconds	15,888	322,473
A full workflow for hazard analysis	22 minutes, 52 seconds	117,379	2,001,972

The above metadata reasoning capabilities are used in creating workflows for seismic hazard analysis. In creating a workflow for an LA site with the template in Figure 8, there were about 3,971 ruptures and 97,228 variations of ruptures to take into account. As the number of files and file collections become large, many OWL objects that represent file and collections and their metadata should be created and queried. The number of files in the workflow we have represented was 117,379, as shown in Table 2. The number of OWL individuals created was over two million. (We excluded the anonymous individuals that are created as a by-product of rdf:list in the count, so the actual number is larger.) For the full workflow, the DAX included 7,945 jobs. Large workflows pose challenges on computational resources (CPUs and memory) used during workflow creation. Currently it takes about 8 minutes to create a sub workflow and about 23 minutes to generate the full workflow on a Pentium 4 3.0GHz with 1GB of RAM. The current system is being used for other applications including statistical natural language processing tasks where parallel processing of a large corpus is needed.

In order to efficiently perform the required metadata reasoning with many objects, we split a workflow into multiple independent workflow parts and create each separately. In splitting, we make use of metadata properties that can divide collections into independent sub-collections. For example, separate sub-trees in Figure 2-(b) can be independently generated. We currently use the SourceID to split rupture file collections into sub-collections. Other collections such as rupture variation collections are divided using the same set of metadata properties. Currently we select such metadata properties by hand, but we are investigating an automatic approach that takes into account sizes of file collections. The independent workflow parts are accumulated in the workflow generator and are automatically merged in the end, creating a complete workflow.

Using the same collection splitting approach described above, we can store the resulting files and collections into separate file library entities. The objects can be selectively loaded and used in creation of new workflows. Equivalent files or collections can be identified using metadata, which enables detection of unnecessary execution of components or workflow parts that will produce equivalent datasets.

5 Related Work

Semantic web techniques have been used in supporting many e-science workflow systems [10, 7]. Applications include semantic description of web services, resource discovery, data management, composition of workflow templates [17, 20, 1], etc. Our work complements existing work by supporting creation of large workflows needed for data and/or compute intensive scientific applications.

Recently various data management and provenance techniques have been developed for e-Science applications [18,8]. Most of the existing work focuses on pedigree or lineage metadata that describes the data resources and the processes used in generating data products. These provenance metadata are often used in qualifying data products and supporting data management and reuse. Our current work focuses on metadata reasoning that support workflow creation and validation. The metadata that are generated during workflow creation can be used in combination with other provenance metadata for supporting file reuse. Our work extends existing approaches for validating workflows in that we take into account constraints on nested collections and global constraints among multiple components as well as constraints on inputs within individual components [23,14]. Another difference is that we make use of metadata in generating valid workflows before execution instead of validating already executed workflows with provenance data, also enabling detection of unnecessary jobs before execution.

6 Conclusion and Future Work

We presented a semantic metadata generation and reasoning approach that supports creation of large workflows. Given the metadata of initial input files, the system propagates metadata constraints from the inputs to the outputs, and through the links among the components during workflow creation. Both global constraints among multiple components and local constraints are used for workflow validation. The files that will be produced from workflow execution as well as the input files are identified during the metadata propagation and validation process. Some of the metadata are generated through creation and execution of sub-workflows when the metadata need to be computationally generated. Because we are able to identify data collections and their properties before the workflow is executed, we can detect whether the data has been generated before by querying an existing data repository. This is important for optimizing execution performance: If some intermediate data product already exists then there is no need to re-execute the portion of the workflow that produces it. We also use the metadata in managing large collections and their provenance.

We are currently working on extensions of the workflow template shown in Figure 2-(a) and they will use more datasets for seismic analysis of different sites in Southern California. In order to further improve the efficiency of the workflow creation and metadata reasoning, we are considering several extensions to our system. One area of improvement is creating a scalable metadata repository. Currently we can store metadata in multiple OWL file libraries, but we are planning to explore its integration with MCS that can store metadata of data products (such as files) published on the Grid [19]. With this approach, when there are new files and metadata added to MCS by a different workflow or system, we will be able to use them in creating new workflows. In order to perform iterative sub-workflow generation and execution more efficiently, we are investigating a client-server style approach where our system can call a workflow execution server with a newly generated sub-workflow, and the execution results can be notified to our system (a client). The newly generated metadata during workflow creation can be used in combination with other metadata for data provenance applications. For example, the metadata can tell whether the two files (or collections) contain the same kind of information, even when they are generated from different workflows. We are exploring various uses of metadata in relating datasets used in scientific workflows.

Acknowledgments. We thank David Okaya, Philip Maechling, Scott Callaghan, Hunter Francoeur, and Li Zhao in the Southern California Earthquake Center (SCEC) for valuable discussions on seismic hazard analysis workflows. We would also like to thank Gaurang Mehta and Ewa Deelman for their help in executing workflows with Pegasus.This research was funded by the National Science Foundation (NSF) with award number EAR-0122464. The SCEC contribution number for this paper is 1016.

References

1. Altintas, I., Berkley, C., Jaeger, E., Jones, M., Ludäscher, B., Mock, S.: Kepler: Towards a Grid-Enabled System for Scientific Workflows. The Workflow in Grid Systems Workshop in GGF10 - The Tenth Global Grid Forum, Berlin, Germany (2004)
2. Campobasso, M., Giles, M.:Stabilization of a Linear Flow Solver for Turbomachinery Aeroelasticity Using Recursive Projection Method. AIAA Journal, 42(9) (2004)

3. Churches, D., Gombas, G., Harrison, A., Maassen, J., Robinson, C., Shields, M., Taylor, I., Wang, I.: Programming Scientific and Distributed Workflow with Triana Services. Grid Workflow Special Issue of Concurrency and Computation: Practice and Experience (2004)
4. Deelman, E., Blythe, J., Gil, Y., Kesselman, C., Mehta, G., Patil, S., Su, M., Vahi, K., Livny, M.: Pegasus: Mapping Scientific Workflows onto the Grid. Across Grids Conference (2004)
5. Deelman, E., Blythe, J., Gil, Y., Kesselman, C.: Workflow Management in GriPhyN. The Grid ResourceManagement, Kluwer (2003)
6. Gil, Y., Ratnakar, V., Deelman, E., Spraragen, M., Kim, J.: Wings for Pegasus: A Semantic Approach to Creating Very Large Scientific Workflows. Internal project report (2006)
7. Goble, C.: Using the Semantic Web for e-Science: Inspiration, Incubation, Irritation. Lecture Notes in Computer Science 3729:1-3, (2005)
8. Goble, C.: Position Statement: Musings on Provenance, Workflow and (Semantic Web) Annotations for Bioinformatics. Workshop on Data Derivation and Provenance (2002)
9. Guo, Y., Pan Z., Heflin, J.: An Evaluation of Knowledge Base Systems for Large OWL Datasets,. Proc. of the Third International Semantic Web Conference (2004)
10. Hendler, J.: Science and the Semantic Web. Science 299 (2003) 520-521
11. Hustadt, U., Motik, B., Sattler, U.: Data Complexity of Reasoning in Very Expressive Description Logics. Proc. of the 19th International Joint Conference on AI (2005)
12. Kim, J., Spraragen, M., Gil, Y.: An Intelligent Assistant for Interactive Workflow Composition. Proceedings of the Intl. Conference on Intelligent User Interfaces(2004)
13. Maechling, P. Chalupsky, H., Dougherty, M., Deelman, E., Gil, Y., Gullapalli, S., Gupta, V., Kesselman, C., Kim, J., Mehta, G., Mendenhall, B., Russ, T., Singh, G., Spraragen, M., Staples, G., Vahi, K.: Simplifying Construction of Complex Workflows for Non-Expert Users of the Southern California Earthquake Center Community Modeling Environment. ACM SIGMOD Record, special issue on Scientific Workflows, 34 (3) (2005)
14. Myers, J., Pancerella, C., Lansing, C., Schuchardt, K., Didier, B.: Multi-scale Science: Supporting Emerging Practice with Semantically-Derived Provenance. Semantic Web Technologies for Searching and Retrieving Scientific Data Workshop (2003)
15. openRDF, 2006: http://www.openrdf.org/ (2006)
16. OWL Web Ontology Language, 2006: http://www.w3.org/TR/owl-features/ (2006)
17. Sabou, M., Wroe, C., Goble, C., Mishne, G.: Learning Domain Ontologies for Web Service Descriptions: an Experiment in Bioinformatics. Intl. Conf. on World Wide Web. (2005)
18. Simmhan Y., Plale B., Gannon, D.: A Survey of Data Provenance in e-Science. SIGMOD Record, vol. 34, 2005, pp. 31-36 (2005)
19. Singh, G., Bharathi, S., Chervenak, A., Deelman, E., Kesselman, C., Manohar, M., Patil, S., Pearlman, L.: A Metadata Catalog Service for Data Intensive Applications. SC (2003)
20. Sirin, E., Parsia, B., Hendler, J.: Filtering and selecting semantic web services with interactive composition techniques. IEEE Intelligent Systems, 19(4) (2004)
21. Sycara, K., Paolucci, M., Ankolekar, A., Srinivasan, N.: Automated Discovery, Interaction and Composition of Semantic Web services. Journal of Web Semantics 1(1) (2003)
22. TeraGrid 2006. NSF Teragrid Project, http://www.teragrid.org/ (2003)
23. Wong, S., Miles, S., Fang, W., Groth, P., Moreau, L.: Validation of E-Science Experiments using a Provenance-based Approach. Proc. of 4th Intl. Semantic Web Conference (2005)
24. Wroe, C., Goble, C., Greenwood, M., Lord, P., Miles, S., Papay, J., Payne, T., Moreau, L.: Automating Experiments Using Semantic Data on a Bioinformatics Grid. IEEE Intelligent Systems special issue on e-Science (2004)
25. Zhao, J., Goble, C., Stevens R., Bechhofer, S: Semantics of a Networked World: Semantics for Grid Databases. Proc. of the First International IFIP Conference, ICSNW (2004)

Reaching Agreement over Ontology Alignments

Loredana Laera[1], Valentina Tamma[1], Jérôme Euzenat[2],
Trevor Bench-Capon[1], and Terry Payne[3]

[1] Department of Computer Science, University of Liverpool, UK
{lori, valli, tbc}@csc.liv.ac.uk
[2] INRIA Rhône-Alpes, Montbonnot, France
Jerome.Euzenat@inrialpes.fr
[3] Department of Electronics and Computer Science, University of Southampton, UK
trp@ecs.soton.ac.uk

Abstract. When agents communicate, they do not necessarily use the same vocabulary or ontology. For them to interact successfully, they must find correspondences (mappings) between the terms used in their respective ontologies. While many proposals for matching two agent ontologies have been presented in the literature, the resulting alignment may not be satisfactory to both agents, and thus may necessitate additional negotiation to identify a mutually agreeable set of correspondences.

We propose an approach for supporting the creation and exchange of different arguments, that support or reject possible correspondences. Each agent can decide, according to its preferences, whether to accept or refuse a candidate correspondence. The proposed framework considers arguments and propositions that are specific to the matching task and are based on the ontology semantics. This argumentation framework relies on a formal argument manipulation schema and on an encoding of the agents' preferences between particular kinds of arguments. Whilst the former does not vary between agents, the latter depends on the interests of each agent. Thus, this approach distinguishes clearly between alignment rationales which are valid for all agents and those specific to a particular agent.

1 Introduction

Ontologies play an important role in inter-agent communication, by providing the definitions of the vocabularies used by agents to describe the world [11]. An agent can use such a vocabulary to express its beliefs and actions, and so communicate about them. Ontologies contribute to semantic interoperability when agents are embedded in open, dynamic environments, such as the Web and its proposed extension, the Semantic Web [4]. However, in this type of environment there cannot be a single universally shared ontology that is agreed upon by all the parties involved, as this would result in imposing a standard communication vocabulary. Instead, every agent will typically use its own private ontology, which may not be understandable by other agents. Interoperability therefore relies on the ability to reconcile different existing ontologies that may be heterogeneous in format and with partially overlapping domains [19]. This reconciliation usually relies on the existence of correspondences (or mappings) between agent ontologies, and using them in order to interpret or translate messages exchanged by agents. The underlying problem is usually termed an *ontology matching* problem [10].

There are many matching algorithms that are able to produce such alignments [14]. In general, alignments can be generated by independent, trustable alignment services that can be invoked in order to obtain an alignment between two ontologies, and use it for translating messages [9]. Alternatively, they can be retrieved from libraries of alignments. However, in an open environment where autonomous agents try to pursue their own objectives, the acceptability of a partial alignment provided by such services cannot be taken for granted. For a given context, agents might have different and inconsistent perspectives; *i.e. interests* and *preferences*, on the acceptability or not of a candidate mapping, each of which may be rationally acceptable. This may be due, for instance, to the subjective nature of ontologies, to the context and the requirement of the alignments and so on. For example, an agent may be interested in accepting only those mappings that have linguistic similarities, since its ontology is too *structurally simple* to realise any other type of mismatch. In addition, any decision on the acceptability of these mappings has to be made dynamically at run time, due to the fact that the agents exist within an open environment, and thus have no prior knowledge of either the existence or constraints of other agents. These constraints are also relevant in Semantic Web Service applications, where services performing the same tasks may advertise their capabilities differently, or where service requests, and service offers may be expressed by using different ontologies, and thus need to be reconciled dynamically at run time.

In order to address this problem, we present a framework that allows agents to reach a consensus on the terminology they use in order to communicate. The framework we present was primarily motivated by open-agent environments, and although in the reminder of the paper we refer to agents, the framework can equally be applied to semantic web services. The framework allows agents to express their preferred choices over candidate correspondences. This is achieved by adapting argument-based negotiation, used in multi-agent systems, to deal specifically with arguments that support or oppose the proposed correspondences between ontologies. The set of potential arguments are clearly identified and grounded on the underlying ontology languages, and the kinds of mapping that can be supported by any such argument are clearly specified. In order to compute the preferred ontology alignments for each agent, we use a value-based argumentation framework [3] allowing each agent to express its preferences between the categories of arguments that are clearly identified in the context of ontology alignment. Our approach is able to give a formal motivation for the selection of any correspondence, and enables consideration of an agents' interests and preferences that may influence the selection of a given correspondence. Therefore, this work provides a concrete instantiation of the "meaning negotiation" process that we would like agents to achieve. Moreover, in contrast to current ontology matching procedures, the choice of alignment is based on two clearly identified elements: (i) the argumentation framework, which is common to all agents, and (ii) the preference relations which are private to each agent.

The remainder of this paper is structured as follows. Section 2 defines the assumptions underlining the framework. In Section 3 we present in detail the argumentation framework and how it can be used. Section 4 defines the various categories of arguments that can support or attack mappings. Section 5 defines the notion of agreed and agreeable alignments for agents, and a procedure to find them is proposed in Section 6. Next, in section 7, an example is provided to illustrate the argumentation process. Section 8 presents some related work, and finally, Section 9 draws some concluding remarks and identifies directions for further exploration.

2 Assumptions Underlining the Framework

In this paper, we focus on autonomous agents situated in an open system. Each agent has a name and a knowledge base, expressed using an ontology. Moreover, we assume that the *mental attitudes* of an agent towards correspondences are represented in terms of *interests* and *preferences*. These represent the motivations of the agent, that determine whatever a mapping is accepted or rejected. Indeed, each agent has a (partial or total) pre-ordering of preferences over different types of ontology mismatches (*Pref*).

In order for agents to communicate, they need to establish alignments between their ontologies[1]. We assume that potential alignments are generated by a dedicated agent, called an *Ontology Alignment Service (OAS)* [10]. The alignment provided will consist of a set of all possible correspondences between the two ontologies. A correspondence (or a mapping) can be described as a tuple: $m = \langle e, e', n, R \rangle$, where e and e' are the entities (concepts, relations or individuals) between which a relation is asserted by the correspondence; n is a degree of confidence in that correspondence; and R is the relation (e.g., equivalence, more general, etc.) holding between e and e' asserted by the correspondence [14]. There are a number of approaches that an Ontology Alignment Service can use for deriving such correspondences. A correspondence which has been provided by an OAS, but for which no agreement has been made by the agents will be called a *candidate mapping*. Moreover, we assume that for each correspondence m, an OAS is able to provide a set of justifications G, that explain why it has generated a candidate mapping. Agents will use such information to exchange arguments supplying the reasons for their mapping choices. In addition, every agent has a private threshold value ε which will be compared to the degree of confidence that an OAS associates with each mapping. Although few approaches for ontology alignment provide such justification [15] [5], tools such as [8] combine different similarity metrics, and these measures can be used to extend the system and provide the required justifications.

An agent will apply its pre-ordering of preferences and threshold, ϵ, when generating the arguments for and against a candidate mapping. Furthermore, we note that the process of reaching agreement should be as automatic as possible and should not require any involvement from human users.

3 Argumentation Framework

In order for the agents to consider potential mappings and the reasons for and against accepting them, we use an argumentation framework. Our framework is based on Value-based Argument Frameworks ($VAFs$) [3].This work is an experimental research and a prototype of the framework is under development. We start with the presentation of Dung work [7], upon which the $VAFs$ rely.

---

[1] Although the agents' ontologies may differ, we assume that ontologies are encoded in the same language, the standard OWL (http://www.w3.org/OWL/), thus eliminating the problem of integrating different ontology languages.

Definition 1. *An Argumentation Framework (AF) is a pair* $AF = \langle AR, A \rangle$, *where* AR *is a set of arguments and* $A \subset AR \times AR$ *is the attack relationship for* AF. A *comprises a set of ordered pairs of distinct arguments in* AR. *A pair* $\langle x, y \rangle$ *is referred to as "x attacks y". We also say that a set of arguments S attacks an argument y if y is attacked by an argument in S.*

An argumentation framework can be simply represented as a directed graph whose vertices are the arguments and whose edges correspond to the elements of A. In Dung's work, arguments are atomic and cannot be analysed further. In this paper, however, we are concerned only with arguments about mappings. We can therefore define arguments as follows:

Definition 2. *An argument* $x \in AF$ *is a triple* $x = \langle G, m, \sigma \rangle$ *where m is a correspondence* $\langle e, e', n, R \rangle$; G *is the grounds justifying a prima facie belief that the correspondence does, or does not hold;* σ *is one of* $\{+, -\}$ *depending on whether the argument is that m does or does not hold.*

An argument x is attacked by the assertion of its negation $\neg x$, namely the *counter-argument*, defined as follows:

Definition 3. *An argument* $y \in AF$ *rebuts an argument* $x \in AF$ *if x and y are arguments for the same mapping but with different signs, e.g. if x and y are in the form* $x = \langle G_1, m, + \rangle$ *and* $y = \langle G_2, m, - \rangle$, *x counter-argues y and vice-versa.*

Moreover, if an argument x supports an argument y, they form the argument $(x \rightarrow y)$ that attacks an argument $\neg y$ and is attacked by argument $\neg x$.

When the set of such arguments and counter arguments have been produced, it is necessary for the agents to consider which of them they should accept. Given an argument framework we can use definitions from [7] to define acceptability of an argument.

Definition 4. *Let* $\langle AR, A \rangle$ *be an argumentation framework. Let R, S, subsets of* AR. *An argument* $s \in S$ *is attacked by R if there is some* $r \in R$ *such that* $\langle r, s \rangle \in A$. *An argument* $x \in AR$ *is acceptable with respect to S if for every* $y \in AR$ *that attacks x there is some* $z \in S$ *that attacks y. S is conflict free if no argument in S is attacked by any other argument in S. A conflict free set S is admissible if every argument in S is acceptable with respect to S. S is a preferred extension if it is a maximal (with respect to set inclusion) admissible subset of* AR.

In addition, an argument x is *credulously accepted* if there is *some* preferred extension containing it; whereas x is *sceptically accepted* if it is a member of *every* preferred extension.

The key notion here is the *preferred extension* which represents a consistent position within AF, which is defensible against all attacks and which cannot be further extended without becoming inconsistent or open to attack.

In Dung's framework, attacks always succeed. This is reasonable when dealing with deductive arguments, but in many domains, including the one under consideration, arguments lack this coercive force: they provide reasons which may be more or less persuasive. Moreover, their persuasiveness may vary according to their audience. To handle such defeasible reasons giving arguments we need to be able to distinguish attacks from successful attacks, those which defeat the attacked argument, therefore we use a Value-based Argumentation Framework, which prescribes different strengths to arguments on the basis of the values they promote and the ranking given to these values by the audience for the argument. This allows us to systematically relate strengths of arguments to their motivations, and to accommodate different audiences with different interests and preferences.

Definition 5. *A* Value-Based Argumentation Framework *(VAF) is defined as* $\langle AR, A, \mathcal{V}, \eta \rangle$, *where* (AR, A) *is an argumentation framework,* $\mathcal{V}$ *is a set of k values which represent the types of arguments and* $\eta: AR \rightarrow \mathcal{V}$ *is a mapping that associates a value* $\eta(x) \in \mathcal{V}$ *with each argument* $x \in AR$

In section 4, the set of values $\mathcal{V}$ will be defined as the different types of ontology mismatch, which we use to define the categories of arguments and to assign to each argument one category.

Definition 6. *An* audience *for a VAF is a binary relation* $\mathcal{R} \subseteq \mathcal{V} \times \mathcal{V}$ *whose (irreflexive) transitive closure,* $\mathcal{R}^*$, *is asymmetric, i.e. at most one of* (v, v'), (v', v) *are members of* $\mathcal{R}^*$ *for any distinct* $v, v' \in \mathcal{V}$. *We say that* v_i *is preferred to* v_j *in the audience* $\mathcal{R}$, *denoted* $v_i \succ_\mathcal{R} v_j$, *if* $(v_i, v_j) \in \mathcal{R}^*$.

Let $\mathcal{R}$ *be an audience,* α *is a* specific audience *(compatible with* $\mathcal{R}$*) if* α *is a total ordering of* $\mathcal{V}$ *and* $\forall v, v' \in \mathcal{V}$, $(v, v') \in \alpha \Rightarrow (v', v) \notin \mathcal{R}^*$

In this way, we take into account that different agents (represented by different audiences) can have different perspectives on the same candidate mapping. Acceptability of an argument is defined in the following way: [2]

Definition 7. *Let* $\langle AR, A, \mathcal{V}, \eta \rangle$ *be a VAF and* $\mathcal{R}$ *an audience.*

a. *For arguments* x, y *in* AR, x *is a* successful attack *on* y *(or* x defeats y*) with respect to the audience* $\mathcal{R}$ *if:* $(x, y) \in \mathcal{A}$ *and it is not the case that* $\eta(y) \succ_\mathcal{R} \eta(x)$.
b. *An argument* x *is* acceptable *to the subset* S *with respect to an audience* $\mathcal{R}$ *if: for every* $y \in AR$ *that successfully attacks* x *with respect to* $\mathcal{R}$, *there is some* $z \in S$ *that successfully attacks* y *with respect to* $\mathcal{R}$.
c. *A subset* S *of* AR *is* conflict-free *with respect to the audience* $\mathcal{R}$ *if: for each* $(x, y) \in S \times S$, *either* $(x, y) \notin \mathcal{A}$ *or* $\eta(y) \succ_\mathcal{R} \eta(x)$.
d. *A subset* S *of* AR *is* admissible *with respect to the audience* $\mathcal{R}$ *if:* S *is conflict free with respect to* $\mathcal{R}$ *and every* $x \in S$ *is acceptable to* S *with respect to* $\mathcal{R}$.
e. *A subset* S *is a* preferred extension *for the audience* $\mathcal{R}$ *if it is a maximal admissible set with respect to* $\mathcal{R}$.
f. *A subset* S *is a* stable extension *for the audience* $\mathcal{R}$ *if* S *is admissible with respect to* $\mathcal{R}$ *and for all* $y \notin S$ *there is some* $x \in S$ *which successfully attacks* y *with respect to* $\mathcal{R}$.

In order to determine whether the dispute is resolvable, and if it is, to determine the preferred extension with respect to a value ordering promoted by distinct audiences, [3] introduces the notion of objective and subjective acceptance as follows:

---
[2] Note that all these notions are now relative to some audience.

Definition 8. *Given a VAF, $\langle AR, A, \mathcal{V}, \eta \rangle$, an argument $x \in AR$ is subjectively acceptable if and only if, x appears in the preferred extension for some specific audiences but not all. An argument $x \in AR$ is objectively acceptable if and only if, x appears in the preferred extension for every specific audience. An argument which is neither objectively nor subjectively acceptable is said to be* indefensible.

4 Categories of Arguments for Correspondences

As we mentioned in Section 2, potential arguments are clearly identified and grounded on the underlying ontology language OWL. Therefore, the grounds justifying correspondences can be extracted from the knowledge in ontologies. This knowledge includes both the extensional and intensional OWL ontology definitions. Our classification of the grounds justifying correspondences is the following:

semantic (M): the sets of models of two entities do or do not compare;
internal structural (IS): two entities share more or less internal structure (e.g., the value range or cardinality of their attributes);
external structural (ES): the set of relations, each of two entities have, with other entities do or do not compare;
terminological (T): the names of two entities share more or less lexical features;
extensional (E): the known extension of two entities do or do not compare.

These categories correspond to the type of categorizations underlying ontology matching algorithms [19].

In our framework, we will use the types of arguments described above as types for the VAF; hence $\mathcal{V} = \{M, IS, ES, T, E\}$. Therefore, for example, an audience may specify that terminological arguments are preferred to semantic arguments, or vice versa. Note that this may vary according to the nature of the ontologies being aligned. Semantic arguments will be given more weight in a fully axiomatised ontology, compared to that in a lightweight ontology where there is very little reliable semantic information on which to base such arguments.

Table 1 summarises a number of reasons capable of justifying candidate OWL ontology alignments. Therefore, the table represents an (extensible) set of argument schemes, instantiations of which will comprise AR. Attacks between these arguments will arise when we have arguments for the same mapping but with conflicting values of σ, thus yielding attacks that can be considered symmetric. Moreover, the relations in the mappings can also give rise to attacks: if relations are not deemed exclusive, an argument against inclusion is a fortiori an argument against equivalence (which is more general).

Example 1. Consider a candidate mapping $m = \langle c, c', \_, \equiv \rangle$ between two OWL ontologies O_1 and O_2, with concepts c and c' respectively. An argument for accepting the mapping m may be that the labels of c and c' are synonymous. An argument against may be that some of their super-concepts are not mapped.

Therefore, in $VAFs$, arguments against or in favour of a candidate mapping are seen as grounded on their type. In this way, we are able to motivate the choice between preferred extensions by reference to the type ordering of the audience concerned. Moreover, as mentioned in section 2, the pre-ordering of preferences *Pref* for each agent will be over $\mathcal{V}$, that corresponds to the determination of an audience. Specifically, for each candidate mapping m, if there exist justification(s) G for m that corresponds to the highest preferences *Pref* (with the respect of the pre-ordering), assuming n is greater than its private threshold ε, an agent will generate arguments $x = \langle G, m, +\rangle$. If not, the agent will generate arguments against: $x = \langle G, m, -\rangle$. The generation is achieved by instantiating the argumentation schema.

Table 1. Argument scheme for OWL ontological alignments

Mapping	σ	Grounds	Comment
$\langle e, e', n, \equiv\rangle$	+	$\exists m_i = \langle ES(e), ES(e'), n', \equiv\rangle$	e and e' have mapped neighbours (e.g., super-entities, sibling-entities, etc.) of e are mapped in those of e'
$\langle e, e', n, \sqsubseteq\rangle$	+	$\exists m_i = \langle ES(e), ES(e'), n', \equiv\rangle$	(some or all) Neighbours (e.g., super-entities, sibling-entities, etc.) of e are mapped in those of e'
$\langle e, e', n, \equiv\rangle$	-	$\not\exists m_i = \langle ES(e), ES(e'), n', \equiv\rangle$	No neighbours of e and e' are mapped
$\langle e, e', n, \sqsubseteq\rangle$	-	$\not\exists m_i = \langle ES(e), ES(e'), n', \equiv\rangle$	No neighbours of e are mapped to those of e'
$\langle e, e', n, \sqsubseteq\rangle$	-	$\exists m_i = \langle ES(e'), ES(e), n', \equiv\rangle$	(some or all) Neighbours of e' are mapped to those of e
$\langle c, c', n, \sqsubseteq\rangle$	+	$\exists m_i = \langle IS(c), IS(c'), n', \equiv\rangle$	(some or all) Properties of concept c are mapped to those of concept c'
$\langle c, c', n, \sqsubseteq\rangle$	-	$\not\exists m_i = \langle IS(c), IS(c'), n', \equiv\rangle$	No properties of c are mapped to those of c'
$\langle c, c', n, \sqsubseteq\rangle$	-	$\exists m_i = \langle IS(c'), IS(c), n', \equiv\rangle$	(some or all) Properties of c' are mapped to those of c
$\langle c, c', n, \equiv\rangle$	+	$\exists m_i = \langle IS(c'), IS(c), n', \equiv\rangle$	The concepts c and c' have mapped properties
$\langle c, c', n, \equiv\rangle$	-	$\not\exists m_i = \langle IS(c'), IS(c), n', \equiv\rangle$	No properties in c and c' are mapped
$\langle p, p', n, \equiv\rangle$	+	$\exists m_i = \langle IS(p), IS(p), n', \equiv\rangle$	The range and/or the domain of the property p is mapped with those of p'
$\langle p, p', n, \sqsubseteq\rangle$			
$\langle p, p', n, \equiv\rangle$	-	$\not\exists m_i = \langle IS(p), IS(p), n', \equiv\rangle$	The range and/or the domain of the properties p and p' are not mapped
$\langle p, p', n, \sqsubseteq\rangle$			
$\langle i, i', n, \equiv\rangle$	+	$\exists m_i = \langle IS(i, i''), IS(i', i''), n', \equiv\rangle$	Each individual i and i' referees to a third instance i'' via two properties that are mapped
$\langle p, p', n, \equiv\rangle$	-	$\not\exists m_i = \langle IS(i, i''), IS(i', i''), n', \equiv\rangle$	The properties that link each individual i and i' to a third instance i'' are not mapped
$\langle p, p', n, \sqsubseteq\rangle$			
$\langle e, e', n, \equiv\rangle$	+	$\exists m_i = \langle E(e), E(e'), n', \equiv\rangle$	(some or all) Instances of e and e' are mapped
$\langle e, e', n, \sqsubseteq\rangle$	+	$\exists m_i = \langle E(e), E(e'), n', \equiv\rangle$	(some or all) Instances of e are mapped to those of e'
$\langle e, e', n, \equiv\rangle$	-	$\not\exists m_i = \langle E(e), E(e'), n', \equiv\rangle$	No instances of e and e' are mapped
$\langle e, e', n, \sqsubseteq\rangle$	-	$\not\exists m_i = \langle E(e), E(e'), n', \equiv\rangle$	No instances of e are mapped to those of e'
$\langle e, e', n, \sqsubseteq\rangle$	-	$\exists m_i = \langle E(e'), E(e), n', \equiv\rangle$	(some or all) Instances of e' are mapped to those of e
$\langle e, e', n, \equiv\rangle$	+	$label(e) \approx_T label(e')$	Entities's labels share lexical features (e.g., synonyms and lexical variants)
$\langle e, e', n, \sqsubseteq\rangle$			
$\langle e, e', n, \equiv\rangle$	-	$label(e) \not\approx_T label(e')$	Entities' labels do not share lexical features (e.g., homonyms)
$\langle e, e', n, \sqsubseteq\rangle$			
$\langle e, e', n, \equiv\rangle$	+	$URI(e) \approx_T URI(e')$	Entities' URIs share lexical features
$\langle e, e', n, \sqsubseteq\rangle$			
$\langle e, e', n, \equiv\rangle$	-	$URI(e) \not\approx_T URI(e')$	Entities' URIs do not share lexical features
$\langle e, e', n, \sqsubseteq\rangle$			

5   Agreed and Agreeable Alignments

Although in $VAFs$ there is always a unique non-empty preferred extension with respect to a specific audience, provided the AF does not contain any cycles in a single argument type, an agent may have multiple preferred extensions either because no preference between two values in a cycle has been expressed, or because a cycle in a single value exists. The first may be eliminated by committing to a specific audience, but the second cannot be eliminated in this way. In our domain, where many attacks are symmetric, two cycles will be frequent and in general an audience may have multiple preferred extensions.

Thus, given a set of arguments justifying mappings organised into an argumentation framework, an agent will be able to determine which mappings are acceptable by computing the preferred extensions with respect to its preferences. If there are multiple preferred extensions, the agent must commit to the arguments present in all preferred extensions, but has some freedom of choice with respect to those in some but not all of them. This will partition arguments into three sets: *desired arguments*, present in all preferred extensions, *optional arguments*, present in some but not all, and *rejected arguments*, present in none. If we have two agents belonging to different audiences, these sets may differ. Doutre et al. [6] describe a means by which agents may negotiate a joint preferred extension on the basis of their partitioned arguments so as to maximise the number of desired arguments included, whilst identifying which optional arguments need to be included to support them.

Based on the above considerations, we thus define an *agreed alignment* and an *agreeable alignment* as follows. An *agreed alignment* is the set of correspondences supported[3] by those arguments which are in every preferred extension of every agent. An *agreeable alignment* extends the agreed alignment with those correspondences supported by arguments which are in some preferred extension of every agent. Whilst the mappings included in the agreed alignments can be considered valid and consensual for all agents, the agreeable alignments have a uncertain background, due to the different alternative positions that each agent can take. However, given our context of agent communication, we seek to accept as many candidate mappings as possible. We will therefore take into consideration both set of alignments - agreed and agreeable.

6 Instantiating Argumentation Frameworks

In order to reach agent consensus about ontology alignments, first we have to build the argumentation frameworks and evaluate them to find which arguments are agreed and agreeble. There are four main steps in applying our argumentation approach:

1. Given a single agent, and for each candidate mapping, we construct an argumentation framework by considering the repertoire of argument schemes available to the agent, and constructing a set of arguments by instantiating these schemes with respect to the interests of the agent. Each argument either supports or rejects the conclusion that the mapping is valid. Internally, an argument is represented by a simple identifier (letter A,B,C, etc.), the type of value which it promoted, and optionally, the agent(s) introducing the argument. Having established the set of arguments, we then determine the attacks between them by considering their mappings and signs, and the other factors discussed above. The formulation of suitable attacks is a key part of representing the different point of views of agents. Arguments may have different strength, which depends on the values they promote. Therefore, an attack can fail, since the attacked argument may be stronger than its attacker.

---
[3] Note that a correspondence m is *supported* by an argument x if x is $\langle G, m, + \rangle$.

2. Given multiple agents, we simply merge their individual frameworks by forming the union of their individual argument sets and attack relations, and then extend the attack relations by computing the attacks between the arguments present in the framework of each agent with the arguments of all the other agents.
3. Then, for each VAF, we determine which of the arguments are undefeated by attacks from other arguments. We employ the algorithm in [2] for computing the preferred extensions of a value-based argumentation framework given a value ordering. The global view is considered by taking the union of these preferred extensions for each audience.
4. Finally, we consider which arguments are in every preferred extension of every audience. The mappings that have only arguments for will be included in the agreed alignments, and the mappings that have only arguments against will be rejected. For those mappings where we cannot establish their acceptability, we extend our search space to consider those arguments which are in some preferred extension of every audience. The mappings supported by those arguments are part of the set of agreeable alignments. An algorithm to find such agreed and agreeable alignments is available in Laera et al. [12].

The dialogue between agents can thus consist simply of the exchange of individual argumentation frameworks, from which they can individually compute acceptable mappings. If necessary and desirable, these can then be reconciled into a mutually acceptable position through a process of negotiation, as suggested in [6] which defines a dialogue process for evaluating the status of arguments in a VAF, and shows how this process can be used to identify mutually acceptable arguments. In the course of constructing a position, an ordering of values best able to satisfy the joint interests of the agents concerned is determined. However, such issues are the subject of ongoing research.

The above technique considers sets of mappings and complete argumentation frameworks. If instead the problem is to determine the acceptability of a single mapping it may be more efficient to proceed by means of a dialectical exchange, in which a mapping is proposed, challenged and defended.

7 A Walk Through Example

Let us assume that some agents or services need to interact with each other using two independent but overlapping ontologies. The first agent, Ag_1 uses the bibliographic ontology[4] from the University of Toronto, based on bibTeX; whereas the second agent, Ag_2, uses the General University Ontology[5] from the French company Mondeca[6]. For space reasons, we will only consider a subset of these ontologies, shown in Table 2, where the first and second ontologies are represented by O_1 and O_2 respectively.

---

[4] http://www.cs.toronto.edu/semanticweb/maponto/ontologies/BibTex.owl
[5] http://www.mondeca.com/owl/moses/univ.owl
[6] Note that ontology O_2 has been slightly modified for the purposes of this example.

Table 2. Excerpts of O_1 and O_2 ontologies

O_1 **Ontology**	O_2 **Ontology**
$Artifact \sqsubseteq \top$	$Document \sqsubseteq \top$
$Print\_Media \sqsubseteq Artifact$	$Publication \sqsubseteq Document$
$Press \sqsubseteq Print\_Media$	$Periodical \sqsubseteq Publication$
$Magazine \sqsubseteq Press$	$Magazine \sqsubseteq Periodical$
$Newspaper \sqsubseteq Press$	$Newspaper \sqsubseteq Periodical$
$publication \sqsubseteq \forall hasPublisher.Publisher$	$Newsletter \sqsubseteq Periodical$
$publication \sqsubseteq Print\_Media$	$Journal \sqsubseteq Periodical$
$Publisher \sqsubseteq Organization$	$Publication \sqsubseteq Document$
	$Publication \sqsubseteq \forall publishedBy.Organization$

We will reason about the following candidate mappings, provided by the OAS:
$m_1 = \langle O_1: Press, O_2: Periodical, n, = \rangle$;[7]
$m_2 = \langle O_1: publication, O_2: Publication, n, = \rangle$;
$m_3 = \langle O_1: hasPublisher, O_2: publishedBy, n, = \rangle$;
$m_4 = \langle O_1: Magazine, O_2: Magazine, n, = \rangle$;
$m_5 = \langle O_1: Newspaper, O_2: Newspaper, n, = \rangle$;
$m_6 = \langle O_1: Organization, O_2: Organization, n, = \rangle$.

As mentioned in Section 2, the generation of the arguments and counter-arguments is based on the agent's preferences and threshold. However, here we assume that all above candidate mappings have a degree of confidence n that is above the threshold of each agent, and so will not influence their acceptability.

Assume now that there are two possible audiences, $\mathcal{R}_1$, which prefers terminology to external structure, $(T \succ_{\mathcal{R}_1} ES)$, and $\mathcal{R}_2$, which prefers external structure to terminology $(ES \succ_{\mathcal{R}_2} T)$. The pre-ordering of preference *Pref* will correspond to the agents's audience.

We can identify a set of arguments and the attacks between them. We assume that a set of arguments is generated by instantiating the argumentation schemes, given in table 1, with respect to the interests and preferences *Pref* of the agents and taking into consideration the justifications G, provided by the OAS. Table 3 shows each argument, labeled with an identifier Id, its type $\mathcal{V}$, and the attacks A that can be made on it by opposing arguments. Based upon these arguments and the attacks, we can construct the argumentation frameworks which bring the arguments together so that they can be evaluated. These are shown in Figure 1, where nodes represent arguments (labelled with their Id) with the respective type value $\mathcal{V}$. The arcs represent the attacks A, whereas the direction of the arcs represents the direction of the attack. By instantiating the general VAF according to their own preferences, Ag_1 and Ag_2 obtain two possible argumentation frameworks, (a) and (b). In the argumentation framework (a), we have two arguments against m_1, and one for it:

– A is against the correspondence m_1, since none of the super-concepts of the $O_1: Press$ are mapped to any super-concept of $O_2: Periodical$.

---

[7] m_1 states an equivalence correspondence with confidence n between the concept $Press$ in the ontology O_1 and the concept $Periodical$ in the ontology O_2.

Table 3. Arguments for and against the correspondences m_1, m_2, m_3, m_4, m_5 and m_6

Id	Argument	$\mathcal{A}$	$\mathcal{V}$
A	$\langle \nexists m = \langle superconcept(Press), superconcept(Periodical), n, \equiv, \rangle, m_1, -\rangle$	B,L,O	ES
B	$\langle \exists m = \langle subconcept(Press), subconcept(Periodical), n, \equiv, \rangle, m_1, +\rangle$	A,C	ES
C	$\langle Label(Press) \not\approx_T Label(Periodical), m_1, -\rangle$	B	T
D	$\langle Label(publication) \approx_T Label(Publication), m_2, +\rangle$	E	T
E	$\langle \nexists m = \langle superconcept(publication), superconcept(Publication), n, \equiv, \rangle, m_2, -\rangle$	D,F	ES
F	$\langle \exists m = \langle property(publication), property(Publication), n, \equiv, \rangle, m_2, +\rangle$	E	IS
G	$\langle \nexists m = \langle range(hasPublisher), range(publishedBy), n, \equiv, \rangle, m_3, -\rangle$	F,H	IS
H	$\langle Label(hasPublisher) \approx_T Label(publishedBy), m_3, +\rangle$	G	T
I	$\langle \exists m = \langle superconcept(Publisher), Organization, n, \equiv, \rangle, m_7, +\rangle$	G	ES
J	$\langle Label(Magazine) \approx_T Label(Magazine), m_4, +\rangle$		T
K	$\langle \exists m = \langle siblingConcept(Magazine), siblingConcept(Magazine), n, \equiv, \rangle, m_4, +\rangle$		ES
L	$\langle \exists m = \langle superconcept(Magazine), superconcept(Magazine), n, \equiv, \rangle, m_4, +\rangle$		ES
M	$\langle Label(Newspaper) \approx_T Label(Newspaper), m_5, +\rangle$		T
N	$\langle \exists m = \langle siblingConcept(Newspaper), siblingConcept(Newspaper), m_5, +\rangle$		ES
O	$\langle \exists m = \langle superconcept(Newspaper), superconcept(Newspaper), n, \equiv, \rangle, m_5, +\rangle$		ES
P	$\langle Label(Organization) \approx_T Label(Organization), m_6, +\rangle$		T

– B argues for m_1 because two sub-concepts of O_1: $Press$, (O_1: $Magazine$ and O_1: $Newspaper$), are mapped to two sub-concepts of O_2: $Periodical$, (O_2: $Magazine$ and O_2: $Newspaper$), as established by m_4 and m_5.
– C argues against m_1, because $Press$ and $Periodical$ do not have any lexical similarity.

Moreover, we have six arguments supporting the correspondences m_4, m_5 and m_6. K, L and M justify the mapping m_4, since, respectively, the labels of O_1: $Magazine$ and O_2: $Magazine$ are lexically similar; their siblings are mapped, as established by m_5 and their super-concepts; O_1: $Press$ and O_2: $Periodical$ are mapped by m_1. There is a similar situation for the arguments M, N and O. Clearly, argument A attacks the arguments L and O.

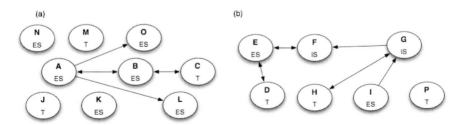

Fig. 1. Value-Based Argumentation Frameworks

In the second argumentation framework (b) we relate the following arguments: D justifies the mapping m_2, since the labels of O_1: $publication$ and O_2: $Publication$ are lexically similar. Their super-concepts, however, are not mapped (argument E). Argument F is based on the fact that O_1: $publication$ and O_2: $Publication$ have mapped properties, O_1: $hasPublisher$ and O_2: $publishedBy$, as defined in m_3. F is then attacked by G, which states that the range of these properties, respectively O_1: $Publisher$ and

O_2: $Organization$, are not mapped. This is in turn counter-attacked by the arguments H and I. The argument H states that the mapping m_3 is correct, since O_1: $hasPublisher$ and O_2: $publishedBy$ are lexically similar. The argument I attacks the justification of G stating that the ranges of these properties are similar, since a super-concept of O_1: $Publisher$, (O_1: $Organization$), is already mapped to O_2: $Organization$. The argument P states that O_1: $Organization$ and O_2: $Organization$ are mapped since their labels are lexically similar.

The above analysis gives different, but sometimes overlapping reasons to argue for and against several candidate mappings. Given the two audiences, $\mathcal{R}_1$ and $\mathcal{R}_2$, the preferred extensions for the union of the argumentation frameworks (a) and (b) is shown in Table 4.

Table 4. Preferred Extensions

Preferred Extensions for the union of (a) and (b)	Audience
$\{A, C, J, K, M, N, D, F, I, H, P\}$	$\mathcal{R}_1$
$\{A, C, J, K, M, N, D, F, I, H, P\}, \{B, O, L, J, K, M, N, D, F, I, H, P\}$	$\mathcal{R}_2$
$\{A, C, J, K, M, N, E, I, H, P\}, \{B, O, L, J, K, M, N, E, I, H, P\}$	

Therefore, the arguments that are accepted by both audiences are $\{I, H, J, K, M, N, P\}$. Arguments A, C, D, E, and F are, however, all potentially acceptable, since both audiences can choose to accept them, as they appear in some preferred extension for each audience. This means that the mapping m_1 will be rejected (since B is unacceptable to $\mathcal{R}_1$), while the mappings m_3, m_4, m_5 and m_6 will be all accepted (they are all accepted by $\mathcal{R}_1$ and all acceptable to $\mathcal{R}_2$). m_2 will be acceptable too, because the arguments supporting it are in some preferred extension for these audiences, as defined in section 5. The *agreed alignment* is then m_3, m_4, m_5 and m_6, while the *agreeable alignment* adds m_2. Interestingly, in this scenario, should an agent wish to reject the mappings m_2 and m_3, it can achieve this by considering a new audience $\mathcal{R}_3$, in which internal structure is valued more than external structure, which is valued more than terminology ($IS \succ_{\mathcal{R}_3} ES \succ_{\mathcal{R}_3} T$). In this case, the preferred extension from framework (b) is $\{E, G, I, P\}$, since the new preference allows G to defeat H and resist I. G will also defeat F leaving E available to defeat D. This clearly shows how the acceptability of an argument crucially depends on the audience to which it is addressed.

8 Related Work

There are few approaches in the literature which have addressed the use of argumentation or negotiation between agents w.r.t. ontology alignments. An ontology mapping negotiation [17] has been proposed to establish a consensus between different agents which use the MAFRA alignment framework. The approach is based on the utility and meta-utility functions used by the agents to establish if a mapping is accepted, rejected or negotiated. However, the approach is highly dependent on the use of the MAFRA framework and cannot be flexibly applied in other environments. van Diggelen et al. [18] present an approach for agreeing on a common grounding ontology in a decentralised way. Rather than being the goal of any one agent, the ontology mapping is a common goal for every agent in the system. Bailin and Truszkowski [1] present an ontology negotiation protocol which enables agents to exchange parts of their ontology, by a process of successive interpretations, clarifications, and explanations. However, the end result of this process is that each agent will converge on a single, shared ontology consisting of the union of all the terms and their relations. In our context, agents keep their own ontologies that they have been designed to reason with, while keeping track of the mappings with other agent's ontologies. Contrastingly, significant research exists in the area of argumentation-based negotiation [16][13] in multi-agent systems. However, none has been apply in area of ontology alignments.

9 Summary and Outlook

In this paper we have outlined a framework that provides a novel way for agents, who use different ontologies, to come to agreement on an alignment. This is achieved using an argumentation process in which candidate correspondences are accepted or rejected, based on the ontological knowledge and the agent's preferences. Argumentation is based on the exchange of arguments, against or in favour of a correspondence, that interact with each other using an *attack* relation. Each argument instantiates an argumentation schema, and utilises domain knowledge, extracted from extensional and intensional ontology definitions. When the full set of arguments and counter-arguments has been produced, the agents consider which of them should be accepted. As we have seen, the acceptability of an argument depends on the ranking - represented by a particular preference ordering on the type of arguments. Our approach is able to give a formal motivation for the selection of a correspondence, and enables consideration of an agent's interests and preferences that may influence the selection of a correspondence. We believe that this approach will aim at reaching more sound and effective mutual understanding and communicative work in agents system.

In the current state of the implementation, the ontology alignments is provided manually. The next step is to extend the developed prototype to utilize an ontology alignment services in oder to obtain the alignment automatically. An empirical evaluation is planned. Moreover, in future work we intend to investigate the use of a negotiation process to enable agents to reach an agreement on a mapping when they differ in their ordering of argument types. Another interesting topic for future work would be to investigate how to argue about the whole alignments, and not only the individual candidate mapping. These arguments could occur when a global similarity measure between the whole ontologies is applied.

Acknowledgements. The research has been partially supported by Knowledge Web (FP6-IST 2004-507482) and PIPS (FP6-IST 2004-507019). Special thanks to Floriana Grasso and Ian Blacoe.

References

1. S. C. Bailin and W. Truszkowski. Ontology Negotiation: How Agents Can Really Get to Know Each Other. In *Proceedings of the WRAC 2002*, 2002.
2. T. Bench-Capon. Value based argumentation frameworks. In *Proceedings of Non Monotonic Reasoning*, pages 444–453, 2002.
3. T. Bench-Capon. Persuasion in Practical Argument Using Value-Based Argumentation Frameworks. In *Journal of Logic and Computation*, volume 13, pages 429–448, 2003.
4. T. Berners-Lee, J. Hendler, and O. Lassila. The Semantic Web. *Scientific American*, 284(5):34–43, 2001.
5. R. Dhamankar, Y. Lee, A. Doan, A. Halevy, and P. Domingos. iMAP: Discovering complex semantic matches between database schemas. In *Proceedings of the International Conference on Management of Data (SIGMOD)*, pages 383–394, 2004.
6. S. Doutre, T. Bench-Capon, and P. E. Dunne. Determining Preferences through Argumentation. In *Proceedings of AI*IA'05*, pages 98–109, 2005.
7. P. Dung. On the Acceptability of Arguments and its Fundamental Role in Nonmonotonic Reasoning, Logic Programming and n-person Games. In *Artificial Intelligence*, volume 77, pages 321–358, 1995.
8. M. Ehrig and S. Staab. QOM - Quick Ontology Mapping. In *Proceedings of the International Semantic Web Conference*, 2004.
9. J. Euzenat. Alignment infrastructure for ontology mediation and other applications. In M. Hepp, A. Polleres, F. van Harmelen, and M. Genesereth, editors, *Proceedings of the First International workshop on Mediation in semantic web services*, pages 81–95, 2005.
10. J. Euzenat and P. Valtchev. Similarity-based ontology alignment in OWL-Lite. In *Proceedings of the European Conference on Artificial Intelligence (ECAI 2006)*, 2004.
11. T. R. Gruber. A Translation Approach to Portable Ontology Specifications. *Knowledge Acquisition*, 5(2):199–220, 1993.
12. L. Laera, V. Tamma, T. Bench-Capon, and J. Euzenat. Agent-based Argumentation for Ontology Alignments. In *Proceedings of the Workshop on Computational Models of Natural Argument (CMNA 2006)*, 2006.
13. I. Rahwan, S. D. Ramchurn, N. R. Jennings, P. McBurney, S. Parsons, and L. Sonenberg. Argumentation-based negotiation. In *The Knowledge Engineering Review*, volume 18, pages 343–375, 2003.
14. P. Shvaiko and J. Euzenat. A survey of schema-based matching approaches. *Journal on data semantics*, 4:146–171, 2005.
15. P. Shvaiko, F. Giunchiglia, P. Pinheiro da Silva, and D. McGuinness. Web explanations for semantic heterogeneity discovery. In *Proceedings of ESWC*, pages 303–317, 2005.
16. C. Sierra, N. R. Jennings, P. Noriega, and S. Parsons. A Framework for Argumentation-Based Negotiation. In *Proceedings of the 4th International Workshop on Intelligent Agents IV, Agent Theories, Architectures, and Languages*, 1997.
17. N. Silva, P. Maio, and J. Rocha. An Approach to Ontology Mapping Negotiation. In *Proceedings of the Workshop on Integrating Ontologies*, 2005.
18. J. van Diggelen, R. Beun, F. Dignum, R. van Eijk, and J.-J. Meyer. A decentralized approach for establishing a shared communication vocabulary. In *Proceedings of the AMKN*, 2005.
19. P. Visser, D. Jones, T. Bench-Capon, and M. Shave. Assessing Heterogeneity by Classifying Ontology Mismatches. In N. Guarino, editor, *Proceedings of the FOIS'98*, 1998.

A Formal Model for Semantic Web Service Composition

Freddy Lécué[1,2] and Alain Léger[1]

[1] France Telecom R&D, France,
4, rue du clos courtel F-35512 Cesson Sévigné
{freddy.lecue, alain.leger}@orange-ft.com
[2] École Nationale Supérieure des Mines de Saint-Étienne, France
158, cours Fauriel F-42023 Saint-Étienne cedex 2

Abstract. Automated composition of Web services or the process of forming new value added Web services is one of the most promising challenges in the semantic Web service research area. Semantics is one of the key elements for the automated composition of Web services because such a process requires rich machine-understandable descriptions of services that can be shared. Semantics enables Web service to describe their capabilities and processes, nevertheless there is still some work to be done. Indeed Web services described at functional level need a formal context to perform the automated composition of Web services. The suggested model (i.e., Causal link matrix) is a necessary starting point to apply problem-solving techniques such as regression-based search for Web service composition. The model supports a semantic context in order to find a correct, complete, consistent and optimal plan as a solution. In this paper an innovative and formal model for an AI planning-oriented composition is presented.

Keywords: Semantic Web, Web service, AI planning, Automated composition, Automated reasoning.

1 Introduction

Web service [1] provides the feature richness, flexibility and scalability needed by enterprises to manage the SOA challenges. By Web services we mean loosely coupled, reusable software components that semantically encapsulate discrete functionality and are distributed and programmatically accessible over standard internet protocols.

Web services proliferation over the web implies difficulties to find specific services that can perform specialized tasks. Nevertheless a combination of existing services is an alternative and promising approach although manual Web service combination from scratch can be difficult and time consuming. That is why new abilities are necessary to support dynamic and automated tasks such as discovery, selection and composition. The main ability is to describe capability (inputs, outputs, preconditions, and effects: IOPEs) and process model (Web services activities, interaction protocol) of Web services. The latter needs are covered by means of semantic Web services. Indeed a semantic Web service [2] is described as a Web service whose internal and external description is in a language that has well-defined semantics.

Composition of Web services is probably the most interesting challenge spawned by this paradigm. Most of the work in semantic Web services composition has focused on two main levels of composition: functional [3,4,5] and process [6,7,8] levels. The former level considers Web services as "atomic" components described in terms of their IOPEs, and executed in a simple request-response step. The latter level supposes Web services as stateful processes with an interaction protocol involving in different sequential, conditional, and iterative steps. The functional and process level composition are complementary methods to propose solutions for composition. In this paper, we study an AI planning-oriented functional composition of Web services through a new formal model i.e., the Causal link matrix (CLM). The CLM aims at not only storing all relevant Web services in a semantic way but also pre-chaining Web services according to a semantic link i.e., the causal link. According to a CLM, the Ra_4C algorithm proposes a **R**egression-based **A**pproach **for** **C**omposition. Thus the issue of the paper is an automated process of chaining Web services according to their functional description.

The rest of the paper is organized as follows. Section 2 introduces a motivating example through an e-healthcare scenario. Section 3 presents the causal link matrix as a formal model to describe Web services at functional level. In section 4, an AI planning-oriented method is presented to solve a Web service composition with a specific CLM. We briefly comment on related work in section 5. Finally in section 6, we draw some conclusions and we talk about possible future directions.

2 A Motivating Example: An e-Healthcare Scenario

One of the most challenging problems in healthcare domain is providing a way to order and compose medical devices. Such a composition does not only improve the patient follow-up but also reduce the number of consultations, examinations, medical check-ups and consequently their price. Indeed a long-standing clinical observation in hospital is no longer a realistic issue for cost reasons since the elderly. In order to tackle this problem and propose an automated process of composition, we propose an AI planning oriented composition approach through the Causal link matrix. For this purpose, the existing applications and medical devices (e.g., sphygmomanometer) are wrapped as Web services. Thus telemedical collaborations are possible through the Web service paradigm. A solution of such a problem consists in implementing a composite and value-added Web service that can automate the patient follow-up by a reliable Web service interoperation, hence a long distance follow-up.

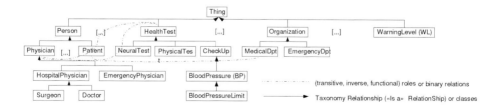

Fig. 1. A sample of an e-healthcare ontology $\mathcal{T}$

Consider the above scenario with six different Web services: S_a returns the blood pressure (BP) of a patient given his PatientID (PID) and DeviceAddress (Add); S_b and $S_{b'}$ return respectively the supervisor (Person) and a physician of an organisation (Org); S_c returns a Warning level (WL) given a blood pressure; S_d returns the Emergency department given a level of Warning; S_e returns the Organization given a Warning level.

3 Formal Model

3.1 Motivation

Algorithms for Web service composition have to not only find feasible plans with relevant Web services, but also find the optimal plan according to an optimization criteria. The latter criteria will be viewed as a quality of semantic connection between Web services (Input and output parameters relation). Indeed the semantic connection between Web services is considered as essential to form new value-added Web services. The formal model (i.e., the Causal link matrices) aims at storing all those connections (i.e., causal links) in order to find the best Web service composition. The CLM pre-computes all semantic links between Web services as an Output-Input matching because a Web service composition is mainly made up of semantic connections. Indeed a solution of a Web service composition have to design and define a plan of Web services wherein all Web services are semantically well ordered and well linked. The latter links are computed and stored in CLMs.

The idea behind the CLM is a formal model to store Web services in an adequate and semantic context for functional level composition of Web services hence a clear formalization of the Web service composition. The CLM aims at proposing a composition model for a finite set of Web services. The latter Web services are supposed to be relevant according to a discovery criteria [9,2]. In such a case, the CLM pre-computes and defines all the possible semantic matching functions between Web services to improve the performance of Web service composition, and also to make Web service composition easier. Moreover CLMs allow us to consider a simpler composition problem i.e., the causal link composition. Thus the Web service composition is mapped to a causal link composition wherein causal links inform about semantic connections between Web service. A composition solution is mainly oriented by the CLM of the domain.

3.2 Semantic Web Context

Parameters (i.e., input and output) of Web services are concepts referred to in an ontology $\mathcal{T}$ (e.g., OWL-S profile [10], WSMO capability [11]). Finding a semantic similarity between two parameters Out_s_y and In_s_x is similar to find a mapping [12] between two knowledge representations encoded using the same ontology $\mathcal{T}$. Causal links store this semantic similarity between parameters of Web services. Indeed a causal link describes a semantic relation between an output parameter $Out\_s_y \in \mathcal{T}$ of a Web service s_y and an input parameter $In\_s_x \in \mathcal{T}$ of a Web service s_x. Thereby s_x and s_y are semantically and partially linked according to a matchmaking function $Sim_{\mathcal{T}}(Out\_s_y, In\_s_x)$ with $\mathcal{T}$ a terminology (e.g., Figure 1).

Table 1. Semantic matching functions described by $Sim_\mathcal{T}$

Match Type	Exact	Plug-in	Subsume	Fail
$Sim_\mathcal{T}(Out\_s_y, In\_s_x)$	1	$\frac{2}{3}$	$\frac{1}{3}$	0
Logic meaning	$Out\_s_y \equiv In\_s_x$	$Out\_s_y \subset In\_s_x$	$Out\_s_y \supset In\_s_x$	Otherwise

Despite some methods [13,14,15], solving a mapping problem is hard because the syntactic form of two knowledge representations rarely matches exactly. Four kinds of semantic matching functions [13] are considered in our model to check semantic similarity between a concept Out_s_y and a concept In_s_x. The semantic similarity is valued by the $Sim_\mathcal{T}$ function (Table 1) in order to estimate the semantic degree of link between parameters of Web services. In other words the semantic similarity valuation is necessary to chain Web services parameters with the most appropriate links. For example, the *Plug-in match* means that an output parameter of a service s_y is subsumed by an input parameter of the succeeding service s_x whereas the *Subsume match* means that an output parameter of a service s_y subsumes an input parameter of the succeeding service s_x. Besides these four semantic matching functions (Table 1), non-empty intersection [14], concept abduction or contraction [15] might be proposed in order to add expressivity of the $Sim_\mathcal{T}$ function.

Suppose two Web services s_y and s_z with a respective output parameter Out_s_y and Out_s_z. In case one finds a Web service s_x such that Out_s_y and Out_s_z semantically match with In_s_x, a semantic similarity function is necessary to value Web services connections. Thus the latter function aims at ordering the different kinds of matching (Out_s_y, In_s_x). The similarity function described as $Sim_\mathcal{T}(Out\_s_y, In\_s_x)$ is clearly analogous to $degreeOfMatch(Out\_s_y, In\_s_x)$ function [13].

3.3 Web Service Composition Formalism

Web service composition is close to function composition in the mathematical area. A trivial Web service composition of two Web services s_y and s_x is considered as a mathematical composition $s_x \circ s_y$. The latter composition means that s_y precedes s_x and there exists a positive value of $Sim_\mathcal{T}$ between all input parameters of s_x and some output parameters of s_y. CLMs (i.e., matrices of semantic connections) are introduced with the aim of finding not only trivial but also more complex composition.

3.4 Causal Link Matrices

The CLMs contribute to the automated process of Web service composition by classifying Web services according to a formal link called "causal link". A causal link is related to a logical dependency among input and output parameters of different Web services.

A causal link[1] [16,17] is refined as a triple $\langle s_y, Sim_\mathcal{T}(Out\_s_y, In\_s_x), s_x \rangle$ such that s_x and s_y refer to two Web services in a set of available Web services S_{Ws}. The concept Out_s_y is an output parameter of the service s_y whereas the concept In_s_x is an input parameter of the service s_x. The function $Sim_\mathcal{T}$ is the function

---
[1] In AI planning area, some authors call causal link **protection intervals** [16].

of semantic similarity described in Table 1. $Sim_\mathcal{T}$ returns a value in $[0,1]$ depending on the matching degree between the concepts $Out\_s_y, In\_s_x \in \mathcal{T}$. A causal link $\langle s_y, Sim_\mathcal{T}(Out\_s_y, In\_s_x), s_x \rangle$ requires that i) s_y precedes s_x, ii) no Web service is interleaved between s_x and s_y.

Definition 1. *(Valid Causal link)*
A causal link $\langle s_y, Sim_\mathcal{T}(Out\_s_y, In\_s_x), s_x \rangle$ is valid iff $Sim_\mathcal{T}(Out\_s_y, In\_s_x) > 0$.

Example 1. *(Valid Causal link illustration)*
According to the motivating example, $\langle S_d, Sim_\mathcal{T}(EmergencyDpt, Organization), S_{b'} \rangle$ is a valid causal links whereas $\langle S_b, Sim_\mathcal{T}(Person, Organization), S_{b'} \rangle$ is not.

A causal link matrix contains all enabled, legal and valid transitions for a composition goal because causal links help to detect inconsistencies (Fail case in Table 1) of semantic link between Web services. Indeed all valid causal links between Web services are explicitly represented with a value pre-computed by the $Sim_\mathcal{T}$ function. The latter value is based on the semantic quality of valid causal links. The Causal link matrix aims at storing all those valid causal links in an appropriate way. The more valid causal links there are, the better it is for a functional composition problem.

Definition 2. *(Causal link matrix CLM)*
The set of $p \times q$ CLMs[2] is defined as $M_{p,q}(\mathcal{P}((S_{Ws} \cup \mathcal{T}) \times (0,1]))$. Columns $c_{j,j \in \{1,...,q\}}$ are labelled by $(Input(S_{Ws}) \cup \beta) \subseteq \mathcal{T}$, the inputs parameters of services in S_{Ws} and/or the concepts described by the goal set $\beta \subseteq \mathcal{T}$. Rows $r_{i,i \in \{1,...,p\}}$ are labelled by $Input(S_{Ws})$, the inputs parameters of services in S_{Ws}. Each entry $m_{i,j}$ of a CLM $\mathcal{M}$ is defined as a set of pairs $(s_y, score) \in (S_{Ws} \cup \mathcal{T}) \times (0,1]$ such that

$$(s_y, score) = \begin{cases} (s_y, Sim_\mathcal{T}(Out\_s_y, c_j)) & if \ s_y \in S_{Ws}, \ Out\_s_y \in Out(s_y) \\ (s_y, 1) & if \ s_y \in \mathcal{T} \end{cases} \quad (1)$$

with $r_i \in \mathcal{T} \cap In(s_y) \subseteq Input(S_{Ws})$ is the label of the ith row.
with $c_j \in \mathcal{T} \cap (Input(S_{Ws}) \cup \beta)$ is the label of the jth column.

$Out(s_y)$ is the set of output parameters of the Web services s_y whereas $In(s_y)$ is its set of input parameters. β contains the set of goals, described as concepts in a terminology $\mathcal{T}$. Those concepts have to be reached. The variable $score$ refers to the degree of match $Sim_\mathcal{T}(Out\_s_y, c_j)$ between an output parameter $Out\_s_y \in \mathcal{T}$ of s_y and $c_j \in Input(S_{Ws}) \cup \beta$ in case $s_y \in S_{Ws}$. In the alternative case $s_y \in \mathcal{T}$, the value $score$ is 1. A CLM pre-computes the semantic similarities between all output and input parameters of a closed set of Web services. All entries defined in $\mathcal{P}((S_{Ws} \cup \mathcal{T}) \times (0,1])$ are valid causal links . Indeed $Sim_\mathcal{T}$ is restricted on $(0,1]$ according to definition 2.

A CLM is seen as a matrix with entries in $\mathcal{P}((S_{Ws} \cup \mathcal{T}) \times (0,1])$. Thus each entry of a CLM refers to a set of pairs $(s_y, score)$ such that the score refers to a semantic similarity between an output parameter of a Web service s_y and an input parameter of another Web service in S_{Ws}. All semantic connections (i.e., Causal links) are precomputed in such a matrix to make Web service composition easier.

---

[2] $\mathcal{P}(S)$ refers to power set of S whereas $\#S$ refers to the Cardinality of S.

Table 2. Labels of the rows r_i and columns c_j of the 5×6 matrix $\mathcal{M}$

i/j index	1	2	3	4	5	6
$r_{i.label}$	Address (Add)	BloodPressure (BP)	Org	Patient (PID)	Warning Level (WL)	
$c_{j.label}$	Address (Add)	BloodPressure (BP)	Org	Patient (PID)	Warning Level (WL)	Person

Table 3. Semantic Web services of S_{Ws} and their capabilities

Web Services	S_a	S_b	S_c	S_d	S_e
Input	PID (r_4, c_4), Add (r_1, c_1)	Org (r_3, c_3)	BP (r_2, c_2)	WL (r_5, c_5)	WL (r_5, c_5)
Output	BP (r_2, c_2)		Person (c_6)	WL (r_5, c_5)	Emerg. Dpt	Org (r_3, c_3)

According to definition 2, Causal link matrices are defined with p rows and q columns, with $\#(\beta)$ is the cardinality of goals:

$$p = \#(Input(S_{Ws})) \quad (2)$$
$$q = p + \#(\beta) - \#(\beta \cap Input(S_{Ws})) \quad (3)$$

The variables p and q refer, respectively, to the cardinality of input parameters of all Web services in S_{Ws} and the cardinality of input parameters of all Web services in S_{Ws} and β. In compliance with [18], dimension of a causal link matrix in $M_{p,q}(\mathcal{P}(S_{Ws} \times (0,1]))$ is defined by $dim_{\mathcal{P}(S_{Ws} \times (0,1])} M_{p,q}(\mathcal{P}(S_{Ws} \times (0,1])) = p \times q$. In the general case, CLMs are not square matrices since $q > p$.

Example 2. *(Illustration of Causal link matrix indexes and labels.)*
Let $\{S_a, S_b, S_c, S_d, S_e\}$ be the set of Web services S_{Ws} (section 2) and $\{Person\}$ be the goal β. p and q are respectively equal to 5 and 6 (Tables 2, 3) according to equalities (2), (3) and Definition 2. Thus rows, columns of the CLM $\mathcal{M}$ are respectively indexed by $\{1,...,5\}$, $\{1,...,6\}$ and labelled by concepts $r_{i,i\in\{1,...,5\}}$, $c_{j,j\in\{1,...,6\}}$ of $\mathcal{T}$. $\mathcal{M}$ refers to a causal link matrix with entries in $\mathcal{P}((S_{Ws} \cup \mathcal{T}) \times \{\frac{1}{3}, \frac{2}{3}, 1\})$.

The causal link matrices construction is function of the cardinality of output and input parameters of Web services in S_{Ws}. Suppose $\#(Output(S_{Ws}))$ and $\#(Input(S_{Ws}))$ be respectively the cardinality of output parameters of Web services in S_{Ws} and the cardinality of input parameters of Web services in S_{Ws}. The algorithmic complexity for the causal link matrix construction is $\theta(\#(Input(S_{Ws})) \times \#(Output(S_{Ws})))$ or $\theta((Max\{\#(Input(S_{Ws})), \#(Output(S_{Ws}))\})^2)$ so square in the worst case [19]. In other words, the CLMs construction consists of finding a semantic similarity *score* between the output parameters of all Web services $s_y \in S_{Ws}$ and the input parameters of another Web service in S_{Ws}. In case *score* is not null, the pair $(s_y, score)$ is added in the CLM according to the Definition 2. For further details, [19] studies the whole process of the CLM construction.

Example 3. *(Causal link matrix illustration with Tables 2, 3)*
The entry $m_{5,3}$ *(i.e.,* $m_{WarningLevel,Organization}$*) is equal to* $\{(S_d, \frac{2}{3}), (S_e, 1)\}$*. Indeed a Web service* S_d *with one input parameter* $WarningLevel$ *and an output*

$EmergencyDpt$ semantically similar to $Organization$ exists in S_{Ws}. $\langle S_d, Sim_\mathcal{T}$ $(EmergencyDpt, Organization), S_b\rangle$ is a valid causal link. The $EmergencyDpt$ and $Orga$-$nization$ concepts match with the **Plug-in match** *according to the definition of $Sim_\mathcal{T}$. According to examples 1 and 2, the causal link matrix $\mathcal{M}$ follows:*

$$\mathcal{M} = \begin{pmatrix} \emptyset & \{(S_a,1)\} & \emptyset & \emptyset & \emptyset & \emptyset \\ \emptyset & \emptyset & \emptyset & \emptyset & \{(S_c,1)\} & \emptyset \\ \emptyset & \emptyset & \emptyset & \{(S_b,\frac{1}{3})\} & \emptyset & \{(S_b,1)\} \\ \emptyset & \{(S_a,1)\} & \emptyset & \emptyset & \emptyset & \emptyset \\ \emptyset & \emptyset & \{(S_d,\frac{2}{3}),(S_e,1)\} & \emptyset & \emptyset & \emptyset \end{pmatrix}$$

Given a set of instantiated concepts in $\mathcal{KB}$, definition 3 initialises a CLM $\mathcal{M}$ and the property 1 follows.

Definition 3. *(Causal link matrix initialisation)*
Let $\mathcal{M}$ be a CLM in $\mathrm{M}_{p,q}(\mathcal{P}((S_{Ws} \cup \mathcal{T}) \times (0,1]))$ and $\mathcal{KB}$ be the set of instantiated concepts $\{C_1, \ldots, C_t\}$ such that $\mathcal{KB} \subseteq Input(S_{Ws}) \cap \mathcal{T}$. $\mathcal{M}$ is initialised with $\mathcal{KB}$ iff

$$m_{i,k} \supseteq (C_k, 1), \forall i \in \{1, \ldots, p\}, \forall k \in \{1, \ldots, t\}$$

Example 4. *(Illustration of a causal link matrix initialisation)*
Let $\{Address, PatientID\}$ be the knowledge base $\mathcal{KB}$ and $\mathcal{M}$ be the CLM (example 3). According to the definition 2, Tables 2 and 3, the initialised CLM is:

$$\mathcal{M}_0 = \begin{pmatrix} \{(Add,1)\} & \{(S_a,1)\} & \emptyset & \{(PID,1)\} & \emptyset & \emptyset \\ \{(Add,1)\} & \emptyset & \emptyset & \{(PID,1)\} & \{(S_c,1)\} & \emptyset \\ \{(Add,1)\} & \emptyset & \emptyset & \{(PID,1),(S_b,\frac{1}{3})\} & \emptyset & \{(S_b,1)\} \\ \{(Add,1)\} & \{(S_a,1)\} & \emptyset & \{(PID,1)\} & \emptyset & \emptyset \\ \{(Add,1)\} & \emptyset & \{(S_d,\frac{2}{3}),(S_e,1)\} & \{(PID,1)\} & \emptyset & \emptyset \end{pmatrix}$$

Property 1. *An entry $m_{i,j}$ from a causal link matrix $\mathcal{M} \in \mathrm{M}_{p,q}(\mathcal{P}((S_{Ws}\cup\mathcal{T})\times(0,1]))$ is different from the empty set if and only if one of the following conditions is satisfied:*

i) $\exists s_y \in S_{Ws}$ with at least one input $r_{i.label} \in \mathcal{T}$ and one output $Out\_s_y \in Out(s_y) \cap \mathcal{T}$ such that $Sim_\mathcal{T}(Out\_s_y, c_{j.label}) \neq 0$ (definition 2);
ii) $c_{j.label}$ is a concept in $\mathcal{KB}$ (definition 3).

Once all Web services in S_{Ws} are semantically chained according to the causal link criteria, the Web service composition problem is mapped to an AI planning problem.

3.5 Causal Link Matrix Issues

The key contribution of the Causal link matrix is a formal and semantic model to control a set of Web services which are relevant for a Web service composition. Web services of S_{Ws} are supposed to be relevantly discovered in a discovery process [2,9]. Thus the set of Web services S_{Ws} is closed in order to limit the dimension of the Causal link matrix. This model allows performance analysis of proposed plans with a concrete view of the composition background: causal links and their semantic dependency. The Causal link matrix aims at pre-chaining Web services according to a semantic similarity based on their Output/Input specification. Thus the CLM describes all possible interactions between all the known Web services in S_{Ws} as semantic connections. Moreover the CLM model in an interesting trade-off to support processes such as Web service verification (valid causal link) or repairing by insertion and deletion of Web services. The Causal link matrix is able to prepare a suitable context for an AI planning problem [7,20] with the purpose of obtaining complete, correct, consistent and optimal plan.

A set of ontologies $\mathcal{T}$, a set of Web services S_{Ws}, a goal β, a knowledge base $\mathcal{KB}$ and a semantic similarity function $Sim_\mathcal{T}$ are required in order to satisfy such a challenging solution. With a terminology $\mathcal{T}$, we deal with conceptual analysis (inference problems) and knowledge representation. A set of Web services refers to a set of actions for a planning problem. β informs about plan directions (as searching concepts). A knowledge base $\mathcal{KB}$ informs about initial conditions (instantiated concepts). Finally the similarity function $Sim_\mathcal{T}$ semantically compares two parameters as concepts in $\mathcal{T}$.

4 AI Planning and Causal Link Matrices

The planning problem is formalized as a triple $\Pi = \langle S_{Ws}, \mathcal{KB}, \beta \rangle$. S_{Ws} refers to a set of possible state transitions, $\mathcal{KB}$ is an *Initial state* and $\beta \subseteq \mathcal{T}$ is an explicit goal representation. The Web service composition method consists of finding a plan that produces the desired outputs β according to a knowledge base $\mathcal{KB}$. The causal link score allows the early detection of impossible, feasible and best links between Web services (Definitions 1 and 2). That is why our method is based on the causal link validity between Web service. The CLM of a specified domain allows to detect all Web service composition with semantic connections. Composition as sequences of Web service is a necessary requirement to propose a solution plan. Such a composition is defined by the sequence-composability. The latter composability defines a composition $s_x \circ s_y$ if an output of s_y is consumed by an input of another Web service s_x. The sequence-composability knowledge is expressed in CLMs according to the Theorem 1.

Theorem 1. *Let $\mathcal{M}$ be a CLM, and s_x, s_y be two Web services in S_{Ws}. s_x and s_y are sequence-composable iff*

- $\exists i \in \{1,..,p\}, \exists j \in \{1,..,q\}, \exists v \in (0,1]$ such that $(s_y, v) \subseteq m_{i,j}$. $c_{j.label}$ and $r_{i.label}$ are respectively inputs of s_x $(In(s_x))$ and s_y $(In(s_y))$.

Proof. Consider the proof of theorem 1 as the following two implications.

($\Rightarrow$) Let s_x, s_y be two Web services in S_{Ws} and $\mathcal{M}$ be a CLM with entries in $\mathcal{P}((S_{Ws} \cup \mathcal{T}) \times (0,1])$. Moreover, we consider the *Sequence-composability* of s_x and s_y such that an output of the Web service s_y is consumed by the input of another Web service s_x i.e., $s_x \circ s_y$. According to the CLM definition, input parameters of s_x are labelled in $\mathcal{M}$ as concepts in $\mathcal{T}$. Thus we may suppose $\{1, ..., p_{s_x}\}$ as the index of the s_x input parameters in $\mathcal{M}$ without loss of generalities. According to the *Sequence-composability* definition, $\exists j \in \{1, ..., q_{s_x}\}$ such that $Sim_\mathcal{T}(Out\_s_y, c_{j.label}) > 0$ since an output $Out\_s_y \in Out(s_y)$ of one Web service s_y is consumed by an input $c_{j.label}$ of another web service s_x. Consequently $\langle s_y, Sim_\mathcal{T}(Out\_s_y, c_{j.label}), s_x \rangle$ is a valid causal link. According to the property 1.i), an entry $m_{i,j}$ from $\mathcal{M}$ is different from the empty set. Finally $\exists i \in \{1, ..., p_{s_x}\} \subseteq \{1, ..., p\}, \exists j \in \{1, ..., q_{s_x}\} \subseteq \{1, ..., q\}$ such that $(s_y, Sim_\mathcal{T}(Out\text{-}\_s_y, c_{j.label})) \subseteq m_{i,j}$ with $c_{j.label} \in In(s_x)$ and $r_{i.label} \in In(s_y)$.

($\Leftarrow$) Suppose $\exists i \in \{1,...,p\}, \exists j \in \{1,...,q\}, \exists score \in (0,1]$ such that $(s_y, score) \subseteq m_{i,j}$ with $c_{j.label} \in In(s_x) \subseteq \mathcal{T}$ and $r_{i.label} \in In(s_y) \subseteq \mathcal{T}$. According to definition 2 and property 1.i), an entry $m_{i,j}$ from $\mathcal{M}$ is different from the empty set. Thus $\exists s_y \in S_{Ws}$ with at least one input $r_{i.label} \in \mathcal{T}$ and one output $Out\_s_y \in \mathcal{T}$ such that $Sim_\mathcal{T}(Out\_s_y, c_{j.label}) \neq 0$. Since $c_{j.label} \in In(s_x)$, two Web services s_x and s_y in S_{Ws} exist such that an output of the Web service s_y is consumed by an input of another Web service s_x. Thus s_x and s_y are sequence-composable.

Remark 1. *In case of more complex composition, more than one Web service needs to be chained with s_x in order to produce input parameters of s_x (in case of a regression-base search). So parallel constructs may be applied. The latter constructs is conceivable in case the entry cardinality (in the CLM) is greater than 1.*

Example 5. *Suppose the CLM $\mathcal{M}$ in section 3. S_c and S_d are sequence-composable in S_{Ws} if and only if $S_d \circ S_c$ (Theorem 1). Indeed there exists $(i,j) = (2,5)$ in $\mathcal{M}$ such that $(r_{i.label}, c_{j.label}) = (BloodPressure, WarningLevel)$. $(S_c, 1) \subseteq m_{i,j}$ with $c_{j.label} \in In(S_d) \subseteq \mathcal{T}$ and $r_{i.label} \in In(S_c) \subseteq \mathcal{T}$. Therefore the output S_c is consumed by the input of S_d because $Sim_\mathcal{T}(Out\_S_c, In\_S_d) \neq 0$ (Table 1).*

4.1 AI Planning Context and Regression-Based Approach

A simpler form of AI planning is introduced to avoid problems [21] from planning-based Web services composition, e.g., non determinism and implicit goal. The set of Web services S_{Ws} (i.e., Actions) is closed by assumption and the *goal* set β refers to a set of concepts in a terminology $\mathcal{T}$. Thus we propose a solution plan in a well-defined domain: goals are explicitly given, initial state is well defined and Web services are strictly defined at functional level. So non determinism, implicit goal, fuzzy Web service description and behaviour are out of the question. Therefore it does seem possible to directly apply current AI planning methods to our specific problem.

The composition process consists of a recursive and regression-based approach. The main idea is to propose a controlled and adequate matrix parsing. Thus each causal link takes place in the solution plan as a semantic link between Web services. According to the Ra_4C algorithm, a goal β needs to be solved. In case the previously goal is fulfilled by the initial condition i.e., the knowledge base $\mathcal{KB}$, the process of consistent plans discovery is stopped. Otherwise a Web service s_x with a goal β as an output parameter should be discovered in S_{Ws}. This discovery process is eased by the CLM of the domain. In case of a discovery success, the process is iterated with the s_x input parameters as new goals. Alternatively, the process is stopped and the (or a part of the) plan is reduced to $\emptyset$. All the process is recursive until all goals and new goals are concepts in $\mathcal{KB}$ (stop condition). The algorithm 1 presents the complete process of composition and returns a disjunction of consistent plans consisted of valid and "*sequence-composable*"causal links. CLMs ease the regression-based search because all Web services are semantically well ordered in a robust and formal model. The solutions are plans wherein Web services are semantically chained by causal links. The complexity of the algorithm 1 depends on the filling rate of the CLM. The more the CLM is sparse the faster the Ra_4C algorithm is. Instead a regression-based approach, other problem-solving techniques - called heuristic reasoning - may be applied [22].

Plan constructs are necessary to describe a partial ordering [23] of Web services in Π, hence $\wedge$ the conjunction operator (parallel construct), $\vee$ the disjunction operator (non determinism construct), $\circ$ the sequence construct, and $\wedge > \vee > \circ$ their priority order. The operator $\circ$ defines the sequence-composability between two Web services.

Algorithm 1. Composition by regression-based approach Ra_4C

Input: A CLM $\mathcal{M}$ ($[m_{i,j}]$), a (or disjunction of) plan(s) π, a planning problem $\langle S_{Ws}, \mathcal{KB}, \beta \rangle$, a set of solved goals G, a set of non valid goals β_{nv}.
Result: A disjunction of consistent plans π.
begin
  $S_c \leftarrow \emptyset$; // *Temporary set of pairs in* $(S_{Ws} \cup \mathcal{T}) \times (0, 1]$.
  // *Stop condition of the* Ra_4C *algorithm.*
  if $((\exists C_k \in \mathcal{KB})$ & $(Sim_{\mathcal{T}}(C_k, \beta) \neq 0))$ **then** $\pi \leftarrow \beta$;
  // *Web services discovery with β output.*
  foreach $I_i \in Input(S_{Ws})$ **do**
    | **if** $\exists (s_y, v) \in m_{I_i, \beta}$ **then** $Add((s_y, v), S_c)$;
  // *Plan for Web service composition.*
  if $S_c \neq \emptyset$ **then**
    | **foreach** *pair* $(s_y, v) \in S_c$ *such that* $s_y \in S_{Ws}$ **do**
    | | $\pi \leftarrow \pi \vee s_y$;
    | | **foreach** $In\_s_y \in In(s_y)$ **do**
    | | | **if** $\beta \in G$ **then** $\pi \leftarrow \pi \wedge \emptyset$; $Add(G, \beta_{nv})$; // *inconsistent plan*
    | | | **else**
    | | | | $Add(\beta, G)$; $\Pi \leftarrow \langle S_{Ws}, \mathcal{KB}, In\_s_y \rangle$;
    | | | | $\pi \leftarrow \pi \vee (\bigwedge_{In(s_y)} Ra_4C(\mathcal{M}, \pi, \Pi, G))$;
  else $\pi \leftarrow \pi \wedge \emptyset$; // *inconsistent plan*
  return π;
end

$s_x \circ s_y$ if $\exists Out\_s_y, In\_s_x \in \mathcal{T} \mid \langle s_y, Sim_{\mathcal{T}}(Out\_s_y, In\_s_x), s_x \rangle$ is a valid causal link. The conjunction operator is used to express parallel plans. Such a situation is possible if a Web service contains more than one input parameter (e.g., $m_{1,2}$, $m_{4,2}$). The latter parameters consider new parallel goals in the Ra_4C algorithm. The disjunction operator is used if more than one output parameter is consumed by the goal (e.g., $m_{5,3}$).

4.2 Consistency, Completeness and Correctness Properties of Solutions

Consistency is a necessary condition for a solution plan. Such a condition is satisfied by plans which contain no cycle in the ordering constraints and no causal link conflicts [17]. The Ra_4C algorithm builds such a plan and avoid cycles and conflicts to dispose of inconsistent causal links. The latter inconsistency is tackled by the Algorithm 1 with an update of solved goals. Thus the Ra_4C algorithm do not solve goals already solved. The correctness proof of algorithm 1 is detailed in [24].

Example 6. *(Set of consistent plans)*
Let $\mathcal{M}_0$ be the CLM (section 3) and $\Pi = \langle \{S_a, S_b, S_c, S_d, S_e\}, \{Add, PatientID\}, \{Person\}\rangle$ be the planning-oriented Web service composition problem. We are looking for a "Person" with skills to understand hypertension troubles. The result is a disjunction of four consistent plans: $\pi_{a1} = S_b \circ ((S_d \circ S_c \circ S_a(Add \wedge PID)))$, $\pi_{b1} = S_b \circ ((S_e \circ S_c \circ S_a(Add \wedge PID)))$, $\pi_{a2} = S_b \circ ((S_d \circ S_c \circ S_a(Add \wedge (S_b \circ \emptyset))))$, $\pi_{b2} = S_b \circ ((S_e \circ S_c \circ S_a(Add \wedge (S_b \circ \emptyset))))$.

Plans suggested by Algorithm 1 do not necessarily satisfy the correctness and completeness properties of plan. Regarding a complete plan [17] as a plan where every input of every Web service is achieved by some other previous Web service, a complete plan is a partial order of well-ordered causal links. By definition, a CLM contains all necessary information about complete plans because a CLM explicitly stores all valid causal links between Web services. Non-complete plans contain empty plan $\emptyset$ (Algorithm 1) hence open goals. Plans with open goals (e.g., π_{a3}, π_{b3}) are removed from the solutions set since those goals can not be satisfied by $\mathcal{KB}$ or the S_{Ws} Web services.

The plans refinement follows a backward chaining strategy from a goal to initial states. In other words the goal $\beta \in \mathcal{T}$ is recursively produced from a (or some) valid causal link(s) $\langle s_y, Sim_{\mathcal{T}}(Out\_s_y, \beta), s_x \rangle$. So correctness of the solution plans is guaranteed by the causal link between the input and output parameters of Web services.

Therefore the algorithm 1 returns a set of correct, complete and consistent plans. However such a set may contain a large number of plans. So pruning strategies for plan-space is necessary to propose a solution. A "causal link"-based optimization criteria is proposed to detect the optimal plan, hence the computation of best causal links in a regression process. The process is recursively executed until the plan is a solution or until the inputs $In(s_y) \subseteq \mathcal{T}$ of the service s_y are concepts in $\mathcal{KB}$. The weight of the optimal plan is computed by means of the CLM and algorithm 1 previously introduced:

$$W_{Max}(\beta) = Max_{S_c}\{\frac{1}{\#In(s_y)^2} \sum_{In(s_y)} m_{I_i,\beta}.score \times (\prod_{In(s_y)} (W_{Max}(I_i)))\} \quad (4)$$

The recursive function W_{Max} returns the weight of the best plan depending on the goal β. (4) is based on the weight of valid causal links of suggested plans. S_c is a set of couple (s_y, v) such that s_y is a Web service with an output β and input I_i. In other words, $\langle s_y, Sim_{\mathcal{T}}(Out\_s_y, \beta), s_x \rangle$ is a valid causal link. The $In(s_y)$ set is the inputs set of $s_y \in S_{Ws}$ whereas I_i is an input of s_y. $\mathcal{M}$ is a CLM with coefficients in $\mathcal{P}((S_{Ws} \cup \mathcal{T}) \times (0,1])$. $m_{I_i,\beta}.score$ is the second component of a couple $(s_y, v) \subseteq m_{I_i,\beta}$. Max_S is a n-arity function which returns the maximum value between n float value(s). Given a CLM, the combination of algorithm 1 and (4) is an interesting trade-off to find an optimal, consistent, correct and complete plan when one exists.

Example 7. *According to example 6, π is divided into a disjunction of four consitent plans $\{\pi_{ai}, \pi_{bi}\}_{1 \leq i \leq 2}$. The plans π_{a2} and π_{b2} are not complete. The weights of different plans have been computed with formula (4). $Weight(\pi_{a1}) = 1 \times \frac{2}{3} \times 1 \times \frac{1}{2^2} \times (1+1) = \frac{1}{3}$ whereas $Weight(\pi_{b1}) = 1 \times 1 \times 1 \times \frac{1}{2^2} \times (1+1) = \frac{1}{2}$. Thus π_{b1} is the optimal plan.*

4.3 The Flexibility and Scalability of the Model

The flexibility of Web service composition models is a fundamental criteria for a relevant evaluation. In particular such models should be as robust as possible in order to evolve in a volatile environment such as the Web services area. The formal model for semantic Web service composition introduced in this paper takes into account this flexibility criteria. Indeed the alteration and modification (e.g., addition, deletion, and the update of Web services in the set S_{Ws}) is the scope of CLMs. Each new update of S_{Ws} is supported by a Causal link matrix revision since the CLM is responsible for storing Web service in a semantic way through the causal relationship. Thus incremental systems wherein new Web services are progressively added, are supported by the previous model of composition and especially the CLMs. For instance the integration of a new Web service is related to the insertion of new labelled rows and columns in the worst case. In the alternative case the integration of a Web service s_y means a simple insertion of s_y in the relevant entry(ies) of the specific CLM. The flexibility of the model allows us to apply a dynamic process of Web service discovery. The only constraint is a simple update of the CLM before applying the Ra_4C algorithm.

Scalability [25] of Web service composition and discovery models is still an open issue. However the formal model scales well in France Telecom scenarios (about twenty Web services) such as the e-healthcare (six Web services and a 5×6 CLM) scenario.

5 Related Work

Two different approaches [26,27] propose matrices to represent the Web services domain. [26] solve an AI planning problem where actions are viewed as tasks. Actions are formally described with Preconditions and Effects. These tasks are executed by concrete Web services, according to a service/task (row/column) matrix. [27] proposes a simple method to store Web service according to an input/output (row/column) matrix. The Matrix model used in [26,27] does not propose reasoning about those matrices. In fact, such the matrices are simply considered as representation models. Moreover no semantic feature is introduced in their models.

From HTNs [28] to regression planning based on extensions of PDDL [29], different planning approaches have been proposed for the composition of Web services. However there is still the issue of how to deal with non determinism in these frameworks. Some composition planners [20] propose output/input mapping with type characteristics of these parameters and initial, final state predicates to generate compositions (i.e., plans). However, services need to be composed using a specification technique that characterizes ongoing behaviour of the service in order to ensure a sound composition. Situation calculus is proposed in [7] to represent Web service and Petri nets for describing the execution behaviours of Web services. A planner is declared as a state chart in [30], and the resulting composite services are executed by replacing the roles in the chart by selected individual services. With the aim of generating a composite service plan out of existing services, [31] propose a composition path, which is a sequence of operators that compute data, and connectors that provide data transport between operators. The search for possible operators to construct a sequence is based on the shortest path algorithm on the graph of operator space. However, they only considered two kinds of services operator and connector with one input and one output parameter (i.e., the simplest case for a service composition). [32] propose a forward chaining approach to solve a planning problem. Their composition process terminates when a set of Web services that matches all expected output parameters given the inputs provided by a user is found.

6 Conclusion and Future Work

Despite the fact that Web service composition is in its infancy some proposals are being studied, but no theoretical model has been proposed to help automation of composition at the best stage of our knowledge. Nevertheless many work directions may need such clearer formalizations, for instance for verification purposes. In this paper we outlined the main challenge faced in semantic Web services. Indeed we showed how the CLM tackles this challenge by providing a necessary formal model which draws a concrete context for automatic Web service composition. This concrete context captures semantic connections between Web services. The composition model has its roots in AI planning domain and takes advantage of causal link expressivity by extending its definition in a semantic context. Semantically weighted by the Sim_T function, the latter link refers to a local optimization criteria in order to find solution plans. Moreover solution plans have properties of completeness, correctness, consistency and optimality. The model of functional level composition is easily applied to Web services which are described according to OWL-S (service profile) or WSMO (capability model) specification. Finally, contrary to [26,27], our matrix model pre-computes the semantic similarities between Web services (individual inputs and outputs) according to causal links. Web service composition is viewed as causal link composition.

For further studies new optimization algorithms and scalability of the model need to be studied. Finally a process level composition needs to be associated to our functional level composition to guarantee a full correctness of the composition process.

References

1. Alonso, G., Casati, F., Kuno, H., Machiraju, V.: Web Services: Concepts, Architectures and Applictions. Springer-Verlag (2004)
2. Sycara, K.P., Paolucci, M., Ankolekar, A., Srinivasan, N.: Automated discovery, interaction and composition of semantic web services. J. Web Sem **1**(1) (2003) 27–46
3. Paolucci, M., Sycara, K.P., Kawamura, T.: Delivering semantic web services. In: Proceedings of the international conference on WWW (Alternate Paper Tracks). (2003) 829–837
4. Sirin, E., Parsia, B., Hendler, J.A.: Filtering and selecting semantic web services with interactive composition techniques. IEEE Intelligent Systems **19**(4) (2004) 42–49
5. Klusch, M., Fries, B., Khalid, M., Sycara, K.: Owls-mx: Hybrid owl-s service matchmaking. In: AAAI Fall Symposium Series. (2005)
6. Berardi, D., Calvanese, D., Giacomo, G.D., Lenzerini, M., Mecella, M.: Automatic composition of e-services that export their behavior. In: 1st ICSOC. (2003) 43–58 volume 2910.
7. Narayanan, S., McIlraith, S.: Simulation, verification and automated composition of web services,. Eleventh International World Wide Web Conference (2002) 7–10
8. Pistore, M., Roberti, P., Traverso, P.: Process-level composition of executable web services: "on-the-fly" versus "once-for-all" composition. In: ESWC. (2005) 62–77

9. Benatallah, B., Hacid, M.S., Leger, A., Rey, C., Toumani, F.: On automating web services discovery. VLDB J **14**(1) (2005) 84–96
10. Ankolenkar, A., Paolucci, M., Srinivasan, N., Sycara, K.: The owl services coalition, owl-s 1.1 beta release. Technical report (2004)
11. Fensel, D., Kifer, M., de Bruijn, J., Domingue, J.: Web service modeling ontology (wsmo) submission, w3c member submission. (2005)
12. Küsters, R.: Non-Standard Inferences in Description Logics. Volume 2100 of Lecture Notes in Computer Science. Springer (2001)
13. Paolucci, M., Kawamura, T., Payne, T., Sycara, K.: Semantic matching of web services capabilities. In: Proceedings of the First International Semantic Web Conference, LNCS 2342, Springer-Verlag (2002) 333–347
14. Li, L., Horrocks, I.: A software framework for matchmaking based on semantic web technology. In: Proceedings of the Twelfth International Conference on WWW. (2003) 331–339
15. Colucci, S., Noia, T.D., Sciascio, E.D., Mongiello, M., Donini, F.M.: Concept abduction and contraction for semantic-based discovery of matches and negotiation spaces in an e-marketplace. In: Proceedings of the 6th ICEC, ACM Press (2004) 41–50
16. McAllester, D., Rosenblitt, D.: Systematic nonlinear planning, Menlo Park, CA, AAAI (1991) 634–639
17. Russell, S., Norvig, P.: Artificial Intelligence: a modern approach. Prentice-Hall (1995)
18. Baker, A.: Matrix Groups: An Introduction to Lie Group Theory. Springer undergraduate mathematics series. Springer-Verlag, London (2002)
19. Lécué, F., Léger, A.: Semantic web service composition through a matchmaking of domain. In: 4th IEEE European Conference on Web Services (ECOWS) (to appear). (2006)
20. Desjardins, M., Sheshagiri, M., Finin, T.: A planner for composing services described in DAML-S. In: AAMAS Workshop on Web Services and Agent-based Engineering. (2003)
21. Srivastava, B., Koehler, J.: Web service composition - current solutions and open problems. In: ICAPS 2003 Workshop on Planning for Web Services. (2003)
22. Ghallab, M., Nau, D., Traverso, P.: Automated Planning: Theory and Practice. Morgan Kaufmann Publishers (2004)
23. Sacerdoti, E.: The nonlinear nature of plan. In: IJCAI-4. (1975) 206–214
24. Lécué, F., Léger, A.: Semantic web service composition based on a closed world assumption. In: 4th IEEE European Conference on Web Services (ECOWS) (to appear). (2006)
25. Constantinescu, I., Faltings, B., Binder, W.: Type-based composition of information services in large scale environments. In: The International Conference on Web Intelligence. (2004)
26. Claro, D.B., Albers, P., Hao, J.K.: Selecting web services for optimal composition. In: ICWS International Workshop on Semantic and Dynamic Web Processes, Orlando - USA (2005)
27. Constantinescu, I., Faltings, B., Binder, W.: Type based service composition. In: WWW (Alternate Track Papers & Posters). (2004) 268–269
28. Wu, D., Parsia, B., Sirin, E., Hendler, J.A., Nau, D.S.: Automating DAML-S web services composition using SHOP2. In: ISWC. (2003) 195–210
29. Dermott, D.M.: PDDL - the planning domain definition language (1997)
30. Benatallah, B., Sheng, Q.Z., Ngu, A.H.H., Dumas, M.: Declarative composition and peer-to-peer provisioning of dynamic web services. In: ICDE. (2002) 297–308
31. Mao, Z.M., Katz, R.H., Brewer, E.A.: Fault-tolerant, scalable, wide-area internet service composition. Technical report (2001)
32. Zhang, R., Arpinar, I.B., Aleman-Meza, B.: Automatic composition of semantic web services. In: ICWS. (2003) 38–41

Evaluating Conjunctive Triple Pattern Queries over Large Structured Overlay Networks*

Erietta Liarou[1], Stratos Idreos[2], and Manolis Koubarakis[3]

[1] Technical University of Crete, Chania, Greece
[2] CWI, Amsterdam, The Netherlands
[3] National and Kapodistrian University of Athens, Athens, Greece

Abstract. We study the problem of evaluating conjunctive queries composed of triple patterns over RDF data stored in distributed hash tables. Our goal is to develop algorithms that scale to large amounts of RDF data, distribute the query processing load evenly and incur little network traffic. We present and evaluate two novel query processing algorithms with these possibly conflicting goals in mind. We discuss the various tradeoffs that occur in our setting through a detailed experimental evaluation of the proposed algorithms.

1 Introduction

Research at the frontiers of P2P networks and Semantic Web has recently received a lot of interest [23]. One of the most interesting open problems in this area is how to evaluate queries expressed in Semantic Web query languages (e.g., RDQL [22], RQL [17], SPARQL [21] or OWL-QL [10]) on top of P2P networks [9,4,19,20,25,18].

In this paper we study the problem of evaluating *conjunctive queries* composed of *triple patterns* on top of RDF data stored in distributed hash tables. *Distributed hash tables (DHTs)* are an important class of P2P networks that offer distributed hash table functionality, and allow one to develop scalable, robust and fault-tolerant distributed applications [2]. DHTs have recently been used for the distributed storage and retrieval of various kinds of data e.g., relational [12,14], textual [27], RDF [9] etc. Conjunctions of triple patterns are core constructs of some RDF query languages (e.g., RDQL [22] and SPARQL [21]) and used implicitly in all others (e.g., in the generalized path expressions of RQL [17]).

The contributions of this paper are the following. We present two novel algorithms for the evaluation of conjunctive RDF queries composed of triple patterns on top of the distributed hash table Chord [24]. This has been an open problem since the proposal of RDFPeers [9] where only *atomic* triple patterns and conjunctions of triple patterns with the *same* variable or constant subject and possibly different *constant* predicates have been studied. Extending these query

---

* This work was supported in part by the European Commission project Ontogrid (http://www.ontogrid.net/).

classes considered by RDFPeers to full conjunctive queries is an important issue if we want to deal effectively with the full functionality of existing RDF query languages [22,17,21]. But notice that the resulting query class is more challenging than the ones considered in RDFPeers. In the terminology of relational databases: we now have to deal with arbitrary *selections, projections* and *joins* on a virtual ternary relation consisting of all triples.

The focus of our work is on the experimental evaluation of the proposed algorithms. We concentrate on three parameters that are critical in a distributed setting: *amount* of data stored in the network, *load distribution* and generated *network traffic*. Our algorithms are designed so that they involve in the query evaluation as many network nodes as possible, store as little date in the network as possible, and minimize the amount of network traffic they create. Trying to achieve all of these goals involves a tradeoff, and we demonstrate how we can sacrifice good load distribution to keep data storage and network traffic low and vice versa.

The rest of the paper is organized as follows. Section 2 presents a synopsis of the underlying assumptions regarding network architecture, data model and query language. Sections 3 and 4 present the alternative data indexing and query processing algorithms. Then, in Section 5, we present an optimization to further reduce the network traffic generated by the algorithms. In Section 6, we show a detailed experimental evaluation and comparison of our algorithms under various parameters that affect performance. Finally, Section 7 discusses related work, and Section 8 presents conclusions and future work directions.

2 System Model and Data Model

System model. We assume an overlay network where all nodes are *equal*, they run the same software and have the same rights and responsibilities. Each node n has a unique key (e.g., its public key), denoted by $key(n)$. Nodes are organized according to the Chord protocol [24] and are assumed to have synchronized clocks. This property is necessary for the time semantics we describe later on in this section. In practice, nodes will run a protocol such as NTP and achieve accuracies within few milliseconds [6]. Each data item i has a unique key, denoted by $key(i)$. Chord uses consistent hashing to map keys to identifiers. Each node and item is assigned an m-bit identifier, that should be large enough to avoid collisions. A cryptographic hash function, such as SHA-1 or MD5 is used: function $Hash(k)$ returns the m-bit identifier of key k. The identifier of a node n is denoted as $id(n)$ and is computed by $id(n) = Hash(key(n))$. Similarly, the identifier of an item i is denoted by $id(i)$ and is computed by $id(i) = Hash(key(i))$. Identifiers are ordered in an *identifier circle (ring)* modulo 2^m, i.e., from 0 to $2^m - 1$. Key k is assigned to the first node which is equal or follows $Hash(k)$ clockwise in the identifier space. This node is called the *successor* node of identifier $Hash(k)$ and is denoted by $Successor(Hash(k))$. We will often say that this node is *responsible* for key k. A query for locating the node responsible for a key k can be done in $O(\log N)$ steps with high probability [24], where N is the number of nodes in the network. Chord is described in more detail in [24].

The algorithms we describe in this paper use the API defined in [26,14,13]. This API provides two functionalities not given by the standard DHT protocols: (i) send a message to multiple nodes (multicast) and (ii) send d messages to d nodes where each node receives exactly one of these messages (this can be thought of as a variation of the multicast operation). Let us now briefly describe this API. Function $send(msg, id)$, where msg is a message and id is an identifier, delivers msg from any node to node $Successor(id)$ in $O(\log N)$ hops. Function $multiSend(msg, I)$, where I is a set of $d > 1$ identifiers $I_1, ..., I_d$, delivers msg to nodes $n_1, n_2, ..., n_d$ such that $n_j = Successor(I_j)$, where $1 < j \leq d$. This happens in $O(d \log N)$ hops. Function $multiSend()$ can also be used as $multiSend(M, I)$, where M is a set of d messages and I is a set of d identifiers. In this case, for each I_j, message M_j is delivered to $Successor(I_j)$ in $O(d \log N)$ hops in total. A detailed description and evaluation of alternative ways to implement this API can be found in [13].

Data model. In the application scenarios we target, each network node is able to describe in RDF the resources that it wants to make available to the rest of the network, by creating and inserting metadata in the form of *RDF triples*. In addition, each node can *submit queries* that describe information that this node wants to receive all possible *answers* that are available at this time. We use a very simple concept of schema equivalent to the notion of a namespace. Thus, we do not deal with RDFS and the associated reasoning about classes and instances. Different schemas can co-exist but we do not support schema mappings. Each node uses some of the available schemas for its descriptions and queries.

We will use the standard RDF concept of a triple[1]. Let D be a countably infinite set of URIs and RDF literals. A triple is used to represent a statement about the application domain and is a formula of the form $(subject, predicate, object)$. The *subject* of a triple identifies the resource that the statement is about, the *predicate* identifies a property or a characteristic of the subject, while the *object* identifies the value of the property. The subject and predicate parts of a triple are URIs from D, while the object is a URI or a literal from D. For a triple t, we will use $subj(t)$, $pred(t)$ and $obj(t)$ to denote the string value of the subject, the predicate and the object of t respectively.

As in RDQL [22], a *triple pattern* is an expression of the form (s, p, o) where s and p are URIs or variables, and o is a URI, a literal or a variable. A *conjunctive query* q is a formula

$$?x_1, \ldots, ?x_n : (s_1, p_1, o_1) \wedge (s_2, p_2, o_2) \wedge \cdots \wedge (s_n, p_n, o_n)$$

where $?x_1, \ldots, ?x_n$ are variables, each (s_i, p_i, o_i) is a triple pattern, and each variable $?x_i$ appears in at least one triple pattern (s_i, p_i, o_i). Variables will always start with the '?' character. Variables $?x_1, \ldots, ?x_n$ will be called *answer variables* when we want to distinguish them from other variables of the query. A query will be called *atomic* if it consists of a single conjunct.

---
[1] http://www.w3.org/RDF/

Let us now define the concept of valuation (so we can talk about values that satisfy a query). Let V be a finite set of variables. A *valuation* v over V is a total function v from V to the set D. In the natural way, we extend a valuation v to be identity on D and to map triple patterns (s_i, p_i, o_i) to triples, and conjunctions of triple patterns to conjunctions of triple patterns.

We will find it useful to use various concepts from relational database theory in the presentation of our work. In particular, the operations of the relational algebra utilized in algorithm QC below follow the *unnamed perspective* of the relational model (i.e., tuples are elements of Cartesian products and co-ordinate numbers are used instead of attribute names) [5].

An *RDF database* is a set of triples. Let DB be an RDF database and q a conjunctive query $q_1 \wedge \cdots \wedge q_n$ where each q_i is a triple pattern. The *answer* to q over database DB consists of all n-tuples $(v(?x_1), \ldots, v(?x_n))$ where v is a valuation over the set of variables of q and $v(q_i) \in DB$ for each $i = 1, \ldots, n$.

In the algorithms we will describe below, each query q has a unique key, denoted by $key(q)$, that is created by concatenating an increasing number to the key of the node that posed q.

3 The QC Algorithm

Let us now describe our first query processing algorithm, the *query chain* algorithm (QC). The main characteristic of QC is that the query is evaluated by a chain of nodes. Intermediate results flow through the nodes of this chain and finally the last node in the chain delivers the result back to the node that submitted the query. We will first describe how triples are stored in the network and then how an incoming query is evaluated by QC.

Indexing a new triple. Assume a node x that wants to make a resource available to the rest of the network. Node x creates an RDF description d that characterizes this resource and publishes it. Since, we are not interested in a centralized solution, we do not store the whole description d to a single node. Instead, we choose to split d into triples and disperse it in the network, trying to distribute responsibility of storing descriptions and answering future conjunctive queries to several nodes. Each triple is handled separately and is indexed to three nodes. Let us explain the exact details for a triple $t = (s, p, o)$. Node x computes the index identifiers of t as follows: $I_1 = Hash(s)$, $I_2 = Hash(p)$ and $I_3 = Hash(o)$. These identifiers are used to locate the nodes r_1, r_2 and r_3, that will store t. In Chord terminology, these nodes are the successors of the relevant identifiers, e.g., $r_1 = Successor(I_1)$. Then, x uses the $multiSend()$ function to index t to these 3 nodes. Each node that receives a triple t stores it in its local *triple table TT*. In the discussion below, TT will be formally treated as a ternary relation (in the sense of the relational model).

Evaluating a query. Assume a node x that poses a conjunctive query q which consists of triple patterns $q_1, \ldots, q_k$. Each triple pattern of q will be evaluated by a (possibly) different node; these nodes form the *query chain* for q. The order we use to evaluate the different triple patterns is crucial and we discuss the issues involved later on. Now, for simplicity, we assume that we first evaluate the first triple pattern, then the second and so on.

Query evaluation proceeds as follows. Node x determines the node that will evaluate triple pattern q_1 by using one of the constants in q_1. For example, if $q_1 = (?s_1, p_1, ?o_1)$ then x computes identifier $I_1 = Hash(pred(q_j))$ since the predicate part is the only constant part of q_j. This identifier is used to locate the node r_1 (the successor of I_1) that may have triples that satisfy q_1, since according to the way we index triples, all triples that have $pred(q_j)$ as their predicate will be stored in r_j. Thus, n sends the message $QEval(q, i, R, IP(x))$ to node r_1 where q is the query, i is the index of the triple pattern to be evaluated by node r_1, $IP(x)$ is the IP address of node x that posed the query, and R is the relation that will be used to accumulate triples that are *intermediate results* towards the computation of the answer to q. In this call, R receives its initial value (formally, the trivial relation $\{()\}$ i.e., the relation that consists of an empty tuple over an empty set of attributes).

In case that q_1 has multiple constants, x will heuristically prefer to use first the subject, then the object and finally the predicate to determine the node that will evaluate q_1. Intuitively, there will be more *distinct* subject or object values than *distinct* predicates values in an instance of a given schema. Thus, our decision help us to achieve a better distribution of the query processing load.

Local processing at each chain node. Assume now that a node n receives a message $QEval(q, i, R, IP(x))$. First, n evaluates the i-th triple pattern of q using its local triple table i.e., it computes the relation $L = \pi_X(\sigma_F(TT))$ where F is a selection condition and X is a (possibly empty) list of natural numbers between 1 and 3. F and X are formed in the natural way by taking into account the constants and variables of q_i e.g., if q_i is $(?s_i, p_i, o_i)$ then $L = \pi_1(\sigma_{2=p_i \wedge 3=o_i}(TT))$. Then, n computes a new relation with intermediate results $R' = \pi_Y(R \bowtie L)$ where Y is the (possibly empty) list of positive integers identifying columns of R and L that correspond to answer variables or variables with values that are needed in the rest of the query evaluation (i.e., variables appearing in a triple pattern q_j of q such that $j > i$). Note that the special case of $i = 1$ (when $R' = \pi_Y(L)$) is covered by the above formula for R', given the initial value $\{()\}$ of R. If R' is not the empty relation then n creates a message $QEval(q, i+1, R', IP(x))$ and sends it to the node that will evaluate triple pattern q_{i+1}. If R' is the empty relation then the computation stops and an empty answer is returned to node x.

In the case that $i = k$, the last triple pattern of q is evaluated. Then, n simply returns relation R' back to x using a message $Answer(q, R')$. Now R' is indeed a relation with arity equal to the number of answer variables and contains the answer to query q over the database of triples in the network.

In the current implementation, $R' = \pi_Y(R \bowtie \pi_X(\sigma_F(TT)))$ is computed as follows. For each tuple t of R, we first rewrite q_i by substituting variables of q_i by their corresponding values in R. Then, we use q_i to probe TT for matching triples. For each matching triple, the appropriate tuple of R' is computed on

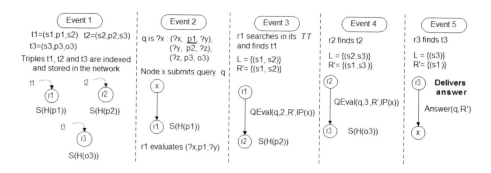

Fig. 1. The algorithm QC in operation

the fly. Access to TT can be made vary fast (essentially constant time) using hashing. In relational terminology, this is a nested loops join using a hash index for the inner relation TT. This is a good implementation strategy given that we expect a good evaluation order for the triple patterns of q to minimize the number of tuples in intermediate relation R (see relevant discussion at the end of this section).

Example. QC is shown in operation in Figure 1. Each *event* in this figure represents an event in the network, i.e., either the arrival of a new triple or the arrival of a new triple pattern. Events are drawn from left to right which represents the chronological order in which these events have happened. In each event, the figure shows the steps of the algorithm that take place due to this event. For readability, in each event we draw only the nodes that do something due to this event, i.e., store or search triples, evaluate a query etc. Finally, note that we use S for the function $Successor()$, H for the function $Hash()$ and we use comma to denote a conjunction between two triple patterns.

In Event 1, node n inserts three triples t_1, t_2 and t_3 in the network. In Event 2, node n submits a conjunctive query q that consists of three triple patterns. The figure shows how the query travels from node n to r_2, then to r_4 and finally to r_7, where the answer is computed and returned to n.

Order of nodes in a query chain. The order in which the different triple patterns of a query are evaluated is crucial, and affects network traffic, query processing load or any other resource that we try to optimize. For example, if we want to minimize message size for QC, we would like to put early in the query chain nodes that are responsible for triple patterns with *low selectivity*. Selectivity information can be made available to each node if statistics regarding the contents of TTs are available. Then, when a node n determines the next triple pattern q_{i+1} to be evaluated, n has enough statistical information to determine a good node to continue the query evaluation. The details of how to make our algorithms *adaptive* in the above sense are the subject of future work.

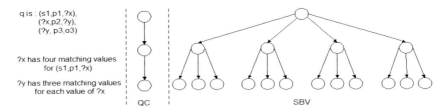

Fig. 2. Comparing the query chains in QC and SBV

4 The SBV Algorithm

Let us now present our second algorithm, the algorithm *spread by value* (SBV). SBV extends the ideas of QC to achieve a better distribution of the query processing load. It does not create a single chain for a query as QC does, but by exploiting the values of matching triples found while processing the query incrementally, it distributes the responsibility of evaluating a query to more nodes than QC. In other words, it is essentially constructing multiple chains for each query. A quick understanding of the difference between QC and SBV can be obtained from Figure 2. There, we draw for each algorithm, all the nodes that participate in query processing for a query q that consists of 3 triple patterns. QC creates a single chain that consists of only 3 nodes and query evaluation is carried out by these nodes only. On the contrary, SBV creates multiple chains which can collectively be seen as a tree. Now the query processing load for q is *spread* among the nodes of this tree. Each path in this tree is determined by the *values* used by triples that match the respective triple patterns at the different nodes (thus the name of the algorithm).

Indexing a new triple. Assume a new triple $t = (s, p, o)$. In SBV t will be stored at the successor nodes of the identifiers $Hash(s)$, $Hash(p)$, $Hash(o)$, $Hash(s + p)$, $Hash(s + o)$, $Hash(p + o)$ and $Hash(s + p + o)$. We will exploit these replicas of triple t to achieve a better query load distribution.

Evaluating a query. As in QC, the node that poses a new query q of the form $q_1 \wedge \cdots \wedge q_k$ sends q to a node r_1 that is able to evaluate the first triple pattern q_1. From this point on, the query plan produced by SBV is created *dynamically* by exploiting the values of the matching triples that nodes find at each step in order to achieve a better distribution of the query processing load. For example, r_1 will use the values for variables of q_1, that it will find in local triples matching q_1, to bind the variables of $q_2 \wedge \cdots \wedge q_k$ that are common with q_1 and produce a new set of queries that will jointly determine the answer to the original query q. Since we expect to have multiple matching values for the variables of q_1, we also expect to have *multiple next nodes* where the new queries will continue their evaluation. Thus, multiple chains of nodes take responsibility for the evaluation of q. The nodes at the leafs of these chains will deliver answers back to the node that submitted q. Our previous discussion on the order of nodes/triple patterns in a query chain is also valid for SBV. For simplicity, in the formal description of SBV below, we assume again that the evaluation order is determined by the order that the triple patterns appear in the query.

To determine which node will evaluate a triple pattern in SBV, we use the constant parts of the triple pattern as in QC. The difference is that if there are multiple constants in a triple pattern, we use the *combination* of all constant parts. For example, if $q_j = (?s_j, p_j, o_j)$, then $I_j = Hash(pred(q_j)+obj(q_j))$ where the operator + denotes *concatenation* of string values. We use the concatenation of constant parts whenever possible, since the number of possible identifiers that can be created by a combination of constant parts is definitely higher and will allow us to achieve a better distribution of the query processing load.

Assume a node x that wants to submit a query q with set of answer variables V. x creates a message $Eval(q, V, u, IP(x))$, where u is the empty valuation. x computes the identifier of the node that will evaluate the first triple pattern and sends the message to it with the $send()$ function in $O(\log N)$ hops.

When a node r receives a message $Eval(q, V, u, IP(x))$ where q is a query $q_1 \wedge \cdots \wedge q_n$ and $n > 1$, r searches its local TT for stored triples that satisfy triple pattern q_1. Assume m matching triples are found. For each satisfying triple t_i, there is a valuation v_i such that $t_i = v_i(q_1)$. For each v_i, r computes a new valuation $v_i' = u \cup v_i$ and a new query $q_i' \equiv v_i(q_2 \wedge \cdots \wedge q_n)$. Then r decides the node that will continue the algorithm with the evaluation of q_i' (as we described in the previous paragraph), and creates a new message $msg_i = Eval(q_i', V, v_i', IP(x))$ for that node. As a result, we have a set of at most m messages and r uses the $multiSend()$ function to deliver them in $O(m \log N)$ hops. Each node that receives one of these messages reacts as described in this paragraph.

In the case that a node r receives a message $Eval(q, V, u, IP(x))$ where q consists of a single triple pattern q_1 (i.e., r is the last node in this query chain), then the evaluation of q finishes at r. Thus, r simply computes all triples t in TT and valuations v such that $t = v(q_n)$ and sends the set of all such valuations v back to node x that posed the original query in one hop (after projecting them on the answer variables of the initial query). These valuations are part of the answer to the query. This case covers the situation where $n = 1$ as well (i.e., q consists of a single conjunct). Figure 3 shows an example of SBV in operation.

5 Optimizing Network Traffic

In this section we introduce a new routing table, called *IP cache* (IPC) [14] that can be used by our algorithms to significantly reduce network traffic. In both our algorithms, the evaluation of a query goes through a number of nodes. The observation is that similar queries will follow a route with some nodes in common and we can exploit this information to decrease network traffic. Assume a node x_j that participates in the evaluation of a query q and needs to send a message to a "next" node x_{j+1} that costs $O(\log N)$ overlay hops. After the first time that node x_j has sent a message to node x_{j+1}, x_j can keep track of the IP address of x_{j+1} and use it in the future when the same query or a similar one obliges it to communicate with the same node. Then, x_j can send a message to x_{j+1} in

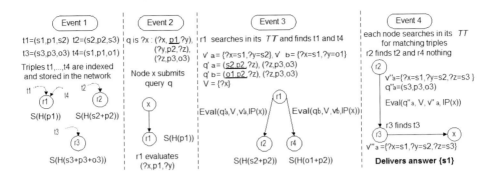

Fig. 3. The algorithm SBV in operation

just 1 hop instead of $O(\log N)$. The cost for the maintenance of the IPC is only local. As we will show in the experiments section, the use of IPCs significantly improves network traffic. Another effect of IPC, is that we reduce the *routing load* incurred by nodes in the network. The routing load of a node n is defined as the number of messages that n receives so as to forward them closer towards their destination, i.e., these are messages not sent to n but through n. Without using the IPC, each message that forwards intermediate results will pass through $O(\log N)$ nodes while with IPCs, it will go directly to the receiver node.

6 Experiments

In this section, we experimentally evaluate the algorithms presented in this paper. We implemented a simulator of Chord in Java on top of which we developed our algorithms. Our metrics are: (a) the amount of network traffic that is created and (b) how well the query processing load and storage load are distributed among the network nodes. Each metric will be carefully described in the relevant experiment. We create a uniform workload of queries and data triples. We synthetically create RDF triples and queries assuming an RDFS schema of the form shown in Figure 4, i.e., a balanced tree with depth d and branching factor k. We assume that each class has a set of k properties. Each property of a class C which is at level $l < d-1$ ranges over another class which belongs to level $l+1$. Each class of level $d-1$ has also k properties which have values that range over XSD datatypes. These data types are located at the last level d.

To create an RDF triple t, we first randomly choose a depth of the tree of our schema. Then, we randomly choose a class C_i among the classes of this depth. After that, we randomly choose an instance of C_i to be $subj(t)$, a property p of C_i to be $pred(t)$ and a value from the range of p to be $obj(t)$. If the range of the selected property p are instances of a class C_j that belongs to the next level, then $obj(t)$ is a resource, otherwise it is a literal.

For our experiments, we use conjunctive *path queries* of the following form:

$$?x : (?x, p_1, ?o_1) \wedge (?o_1, p_2, ?o_2) \wedge \cdots \wedge (?o_{n-1}, p_n, o_n)$$

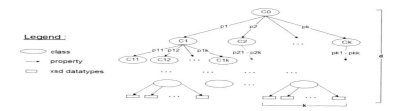

Fig. 4. The schema used in our experiments

In other words, we want to know the nodes in the graph $?x$ for which there is a path of length n to node o_1 labeled by predicates $p_1, \ldots, p_n$. Path queries are an important type of conjunctive queries for which database and query workloads over the schema of Figure 4 can be created easily. To create a query of this type, we randomly choose a property p_1 of class C_0. Property p_1 leads us to a class C_1 from the next level. Then we randomly choose a property p_2 of class C_1. This procedure is repeated until we create n triple patterns. For the last triple pattern, we also randomly choose a value (literal) from the range of p_n to be o_n.

Our experiments use the following parameters. The depth of our schema is $d = 4$. The number of instances of each class is 500, the number of properties that each one has is $k = 3$ while the a literal can take up to 200 different values. Finally, the number of triple patterns in each query we create is 5.

E1: Network traffic and IPC effect. This experiment provides a comparison of our algorithms in terms of the network traffic that they create. To estimate better the network traffic, we use weighted hops, i.e., each hope has as weight the amount of intermediate results that it carries. Furthermore, we investigate the effect of the IPC in each algorithm and the cost of this optimization. We set up this experiment as follows. We create a network of 10^4 nodes and install 10^4 triples. Then, in order to count how expensive it is to insert and evaluate a query, in terms of network traffic, we pose a set Q of 100 queries and calculate the average cost of answering them. In order to understand the effect of IPCs the experiment continues as follows. We train IPCs with a varying number of queries, starting from 5 queries up to 640. After each training phase, we insert the same set of queries Q and count (a) the average amount of network traffic that is created and (b) the average size of IPCs in the network. Each training phase, as we call it, has two effects: query insertions cause the algorithms to work so query chains are created and the rewritten queries are transferred through these chains, but also because of these forwarding actions IPCs are filled with information that can reduce the cost of a subsequent forwarding operation. After each training phase, we measure the cost of inserting a query in the network after all the queries inserted so far, by exploiting the content of IPCs.

In Figure 5(a) we show the network traffic that each algorithm creates. The point 0 on the x-axis has the maximum cost, since it represents the cost to insert the first query in the network. In this case all IPCs are empty and their use has no effect. Thus, this point reflects the cost of the algorithms if we do not use

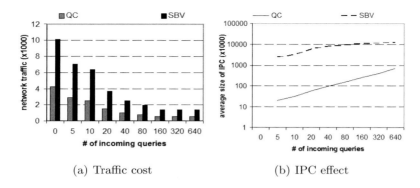

Fig. 5. (E1) Traffic cost and IPC effect as more queries are submitted

IPCs. However, in the next phases where IPCs have information that we can exploit, we see that the network traffic required to answer a query is decreased. For example, observe that after the last phase the cost of QC is 87% lower than it was at point 0. Another important observation is that QC causes less network traffic than SBV. In QC the nodes that participate in query chains are successors of a single value (of the predicate value for the queries we use in these experiments), so it is more possible that a query can use the IPC. SBV always creates more network traffic since the nodes that participate in query chains are successors of the combination of two values (a subject plus a predicate value). Since the combinations of these values are more then just a single one, it is less possible to use the IPC. QC is also cheaper at the point 0 on the x-axis since SBV has to sent the information though multiple chains.

In Figure 5(b) we show the average storage cost of the IPCs. Note, that here for readability we use a logarithmic scale for the y-axis. During the training phases, nodes fill their IPCs so we see that the size of IPC increases, as the number of submitted queries increases. Since even a small IPC size can significantly reduce network traffic, we can allow each node to fill its IPC as long as it can handle its size. The IPC cost in SBV is much more greater than in QC which happens again because SBV creates multiple chains for each query.

E2: Load distribution. In this experiment we compare the algorithms in terms of load distribution. We distinguish between two types of load: query processing load and storage load. The *query processing load* that a node n incurs is defined as the number of triple patterns that arrive to n and are compared against its locally stored triples. Note that for algorithm QC the comparison of a triple pattern with the triples stored in TT happens for each tuple of relation R when R' is computed. Thus, the query processing load of a node n in QC is equal to the number of tuples in R whenever a message $QEval()$ is received. The *storage load* of a node n is defined as the sum of triples that n stores locally. For this experiment, we create a network of 10^4 nodes where we insert $3 * 10^5$ triples. Then we insert 10^3 queries and after that, we count the query processing and the storage load of each node in the network.

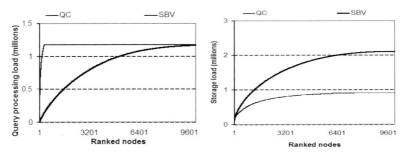

(a) Cumulative query processing load (b) Cumulative storage load

Fig. 6. (E2) Query processing and storage load distribution

In Figure 6(a) we show the query processing load for both algorithms. On the x-axis of this graph, nodes are ranked starting from the node with the highest load. The y-axis represents the cumulative load, i.e, each point (a,b) in the graph represents the sum of load b for the a most loaded nodes. First, we observe that both algorithms create the same total query processing load in the network. SBV achieves to distribute the query processing load to a significantly higher portion of network nodes, i.e, in QC there are 306 nodes (out of 10^4) participating in query processing, while in SBV there are 9666 nodes. SBV achieves this nice distribution since it exploits the values used to create rewritten queries by forwarding the produced intermediate results to nodes that are the successors of a combination of two or three constant parts.

Finally, in Figure 6(b) we present the storage load distribution for both algorithms. As before, nodes are ranked starting from the node with the highest load while the y-axis represents the cumulative storage load. We observe that in QC the total storage load is less than in SBV. This happens because in QC we store each triple according to the values of its subject, its predicate and its object, while in SBV we also use the combinations per two and three of these values. Thus, in SBV a triple is indexed/stored four more times than in QC. The highest total storage load in the network is a price we have to pay for the better distribution of the query processing load in SBV.

Notice that our load balancing techniques are at the *application level*. Thus, they can be used together with DHT-level load balancing techniques, e.g., [16].

7 Related Work

The recent book [23] is an up-to-date collection of papers on work at the frontiers of P2P networks and Semantic Web. In the rest of this section, we only survey works that are closely related to our own.

In [9], Min Cai et al. studied the problem of evaluating RDF queries in a scalable distributed RDF repository, named RDFPeers. RDFPeers is implemented on top of MAAN [8], which extends the Chord protocols [24] to efficiently answer multi-attribute and range queries. [9] was the first work to consider RDF queries on top of a DHT. The authors of [9] propose algorithms for evaluating triple pattern queries, range queries and conjunctive multi-predicate queries for the one-time query processing scenario. Furthermore, a simple replication algorithm is used to improve load distribution. Finally, [9] sketches some ideas regarding publish/subscribe scenarios in RDFPeers. In previous work [18], we have presented algorithms that go beyond the preliminary ideas of [9] regarding publish/subscribe for conjunctive multi-predicate queries.

The ideas in [9] have influenced the design of QC. However, we deal with the full class of conjunctive queries which is an extension of the class of conjunctive multi-predicate queries considered in [9]. In addition, we have presented the more advanced algorithm SBV which achieves efficient load distribution in a novel way.

The other interesting work in the area of RDF query processing on top of DHTs is GridVine [4]. GridVine is built on top of P-Grid [1] and can deal with the same kind of queries as RDFPeers. In addition, it has an original approach to global semantic interoperability by utilizing gossiping techniques [3].

Another distributed RDF repository that provides a general RDF-based metadata infrastructure for P2P applications is the Edutella system [19,20]. Edutella has two differences with our proposal: it is based on super-peers (while our proposal assumes that all nodes are equal) and concentrates on data integration issues (while we do not study this topic). Edutella uses HyperCup in its super-peer layer to achieve efficient routing of messages, but it does not consider issues such as the distribution of triples in the network to achieve scalability, load balancing etc. as in our approach.

The paper [25] is another interesting work on distributed RDF query processing focusing on the optimization of path queries over multiple sources.

Our research is also closely related with work on P2P databases based on the relational model [7,11,12,14]. Currently, one can distinguish two orthogonal research directions in this area: work that emphasizes semantic interoperability of peer databases [7,11] and work that attempts to push the capabilities of current database query processors to new large-scale Internet-wide applications by utilizing DHTs [12]. Our work can be categorized in the latter direction since it studies the processing of a subclass of conjunctive relational queries on top of DHTs. The only existing study of conjunctive relational queries on top of DHTs is [12] where join queries are studied. The ideas in this paper complement the ones in [12] and could also be used profitably in the relational case. This is an avenue that we plan to explore in future work together with extensions of our current results on continuous relational queries [14].

8 Conclusions and Future Work

In this paper we presented two novel algorithms for the distributed evaluation of conjunctive RDF queries composed of triple patterns. The algorithms manage to distribute the query processing load to a large part of the network while trying to minimize network traffic and keep storage cost low. The key idea is to decompose each conjunctive query to the triple patterns that it consists of, and then handle each triple pattern separately at a different node. The first algorithm establishes a chain of nodes that carry out the query evaluation. The second algorithm dynamically exploits matching triples to determine the next node in the query plan and creates multiple node chains that carry out the query evaluation. As a result, it achieves a better distribution of the query processing load at the expense of extra network traffic and storage load in the network.

Our future work concentrates on extending our algorithms so that they can be adaptive to changes in the environment (e.g., changes in the data distribution), be able to handle skewed workloads efficiently, take into account network proximity etc. We also plan to extend our algorithms to deal with RDFS reasoning. Eventually, we want to support the complete functionality of languages such RDQL [22], RQL [17] and SPARQL [21]. The algorithms will be incorporated in our system Atlas [15] which is developed in the context of the Semantic Grid project OntoGrid[2] (Atlas currently implements QC).

References

[1] K. Aberer. P-Grid: A Self-Organizing Access Structure for P2P Information Systems. In *CoopIS '01*.
[2] K. Aberer, L. O. Alima, A. Ghodsi, S. Girdzijauskas, M. Hauswirth, and S. Haridi. The essence of P2P: A reference architecture for overlay networks. In *IEEE P2P 2005*.
[3] K. Aberer, P. Cudré-Mauroux, and M. Hauswirth. Start making sense: The chatty web approach for global semantic agreements. *Journal of Web Semantics*, 1(1), December 2003.
[4] K. Aberer, P. Cudre-Mauroux, M. Hauswirth, and T. V. Pelt. GridVine: Building Internet-Scale Semantic Overlay Networks. In *WWW '04*.
[5] S. Abiteboul, R. Hull, and V. Vianu. *Foundations of Databases*. Addison Wesley, 1995.
[6] M. Bawa, A. Gionis, H. Garcia-Molina, and R. Motwani. The Price of Validity in Dynamic Networks. In *SIGMOD '04*.
[7] P. A. Bernstein, F. Giunchiglia, A. Kementsietsidis, J. Mylopoulos, L. Serafini, and I. Zaihrayeu. Data Management for Peer-to-Peer Computing: A Vision . In *WebDB '02*.
[8] M. Cai, M. Frank, and J. C. P. Szekely. MAAN: A Multi-Attribute Addressable Network for Grid Information Services. In *Grid '03*.
[9] M. Cai, M. R. Frank, B. Yan, and R. M. MacGregor. A Subscribable Peer-to-Peer RDF Repository for Distributed Metadata Management. *Journal of Web Semantics*, 2(2):109–130, December 2004.
[10] R. Fikes, P. Hayes, and I. Horrocks. OWL-QL: A Language for Deductive Query Answering on the Semantic Web. *Journal of Web Semantics*, 2(1):19–29, December 2004.
[11] S. Gribble, A. Halevy, Z. Ives, M. Rodrig, and D. Suciu. What Can Peer-to-Peer Do for Databases, and Vice Versa? In *WebDB '01*.
[12] R. Huebsch, J. M. Hellerstein, N. Lanham, B. T. Loo, S. Shenker, and I. Stoica. Querying the Internet with PIER. In *VLDB '03*.

---

[2] http://www.ontogrid.net

[13] S. Idreos. Distributed evaluation of continuous equi-join queries over large structured overlay networks. Master's thesis, 2005.
[14] S. Idreos, C. Tryfonopoulos, and M. Koubarakis. Distributed Evaluation of Continuous Equi-join Queries over Large Structured Overlay Networks. In *ICDE '06*.
[15] Z. Kaoudi, I. Miliaraki, M. Magiridou, A. Papadakis-Pesaresi, and M. Koubarakis. Storing and querying RDF data in Atlas. In *Demo Papers ESWC '06*.
[16] D. Karger and M. Ruhl. Simple Efficient Load Balancing Algorithms for Peer to Peer Systems. In *SPAA '04*.
[17] G. Karvounarakis, S. Alexaki, V. Christophides, D. Plexousakis, and M. Scholl. RQL: A Declarative Query Language for RDF. In *WWW '02*.
[18] E. Liarou, S. Idreos, and M. Koubarakis. Publish-Subscribe with RDF Data over Large Structured Overlay Networks. In *DBISP2P '05*.
[19] W. Nejdl, B. Wolf, C. Qu, S. Decker, M. Sintek, A. Naeve, M. Nilsson, M. Palmer, and T. Risch. EDUTELLA: A P2P Networking Infrastructure Based on RDF. In *WWW '02*.
[20] W. Nejdl, M. Wolpers, W. Siberski, C. Schmitz, M. Schlosser, I. Brunkhorst, and A. Loser. Super-Peer-Based Routing and Clustering Strategies for RDF-Based Peer-To-Peer Networks. In *WWW '03*.
[21] E. Prud'hommeaux and A. Seaborn. SPARQL Query Language for RDF. http://www.w3.org/TR/rdf-sparql-query/, 2005.
[22] A. Seaborne. Rdql - a query language for RDF. W3C Member Submission, 2004.
[23] S. Staab and H. Stuckenschmidt. *Semantic Web and Peer-to-Peer*. Springer, 2006.
[24] I. Stoica, R. Morris, D. Karger, M. F. Kaashoek, and H. Balakrishnan. Chord: A scalable peer-to-peer lookup service for internet applications. In *SIGCOMM '01*.
[25] H. Stuckenschmidt, R. Vdovjak, J. Broekstra, and G.-J. Houben. Towards Distributed Processing of RDF Path Queries. *International Journal of Web Engineering and Technology*, 2(2/3):207–230, 2005.
[26] C. Tryfonopoulos, S. Idreos, and M. Koubarakis. LibraRing: An Architecture for Distributed Digital Libraries Based on DHTs. In *ECDL '05*.
[27] C. Tryfonopoulos, S. Idreos, and M. Koubarakis. Publish/Subscribe Functionality in IR Environments using Structured Overlay Networks. In *SIGIR '05*.

PowerMap: Mapping the Real Semantic Web on the Fly

Vanessa Lopez, Marta Sabou, and Enrico Motta

Knowledge Media Institute (KMi), The Open University.
Walton Hall, Milton Keynes, MK7 6AA, United Kingdom
{v.lopez, r.m.sabou, e.motta}@open.ac.uk

Abstract. Ontology mapping plays an important role in bridging the semantic gap between distributed and heterogeneous data sources. As the Semantic Web slowly becomes real and the amount of online semantic data increases, a new generation of tools is developed that automatically find and integrate this data. Unlike in the case of earlier tools where mapping has been performed at the design time of the tool, these new tools require mapping techniques that can be performed at run time. The contribution of this paper is twofold. First, we investigate the general requirements for run time mapping techniques. Second, we describe our PowerMap mapping algorithm that was designed to be used at run-time by an ontology based question answering tool.

Keywords: Semantic Web, question answering, heterogeneity, and ontology mapping.

1 Introduction

The Semantic Web (SW) is evolving towards an open, distributed and heterogeneous environment. Core to the information integration tasks that would be supported by SW technology are algorithms that allow matching between the elements of several, distributed ontologies. The importance of mapping for the SW has been widely recognized [1] and a range of techniques and tools have already been developed. However, the predominant view of mapping is that it will be performed at *"design time"*, e.g. when deciding on mapping rules between a set of ontologies [2]. This was a plausible assumption because, until recently, only a limited amount of semantic data was available; therefore, there was little need for run time integration. Indeed, one of the main characteristics of SW based applications built so far is that they tackle the data heterogeneity problem in the context of a given domain or application by integrating a few, a-priori determined sources [3, 4]. As such, they act more as smart, database centered applications rather than tools that truly explore the dynamic and heterogeneous nature of the SW [5].

Recently, things have started to change. There is now a reasonable amount of online semantic data, to such an extent that the need has arisen for a semantic search engine, Swoogle [6], which can crawl and index all these data. Hence, we are now slowly reaching a key point in the history of this very young discipline, where we can start moving away from the early applications characterized by limited heterogeneity and start developing the kind of applications, which will define the SW of the future.

These tools will dynamically find and integrate data from online available sources depending on their current information need. However, mapping still remains an important step. Rather than being performed during the development of the application it now needs to be performed at *"run time"*. Obviously, this new scenario brings novel challenges for ontology mapping techniques.

In this paper we present a mapping algorithm, PowerMap, which is a core component of the PowerAqua ontology based question answering system. PowerAqua belongs to the new generation of SW tools as it tries to answer questions asked in natural language by leveraging on the semantic data available online. As a result, PowerMap needs to be able to create mappings between heterogeneous data on-the-fly and with no pre-determined assumption about the source and the ontological structure of these data.

The paper is organized as follows. Section 2 provides a perspective about the novel scenarios that the evolving SW tools will impose on mapping. Section 3 describes the context in which our own mapping algorithm was developed, the PowerAqua question answering system, and illustrates through an example some of the challenges that such run time mapping operations face. Section 4 details the major design components that underlie PowerMap. In Section 5 we present the details of the algorithm. Finally, we provide an example (Section 6). We summarize in Section 7.

2 Mapping in the Context of Semantic Web Tools

The problem of ontology schema mapping has been investigated by many research groups which have proposed a large variety of approaches [1, 7]. While all this research has produced increasingly complex algorithms, the setting in which the mapping problem was tackled was almost always the same: given two ontologies, find all the possible mappings between their entities attaching a confidence level to the mappings that are returned. One of the challenges in the field of ontology mapping now is not so much perfecting these algorithms, but rather trying to adapt them to novel scenarios, which require SW applications to automatically select and integrate semantic data available online. Obviously, mapping techniques are crucial in achieving this goal. However, the setting in which the mapping would take place is quite different from the "traditional" ontology mapping scenario. Indeed, the focus is not on mapping complete ontologies but rather small snippets that are relevant for a given task. These new scenarios impose a number of requirements:

1) **More ontologies** – when integrating data from online ontologies it is often necessary to map between **several** online ontologies. This is very unlike the traditional scenario where only two ontologies were mapped at a time.
2) **Increased heterogeneity** – traditional mapping techniques often assume that the ontologies to be matched will be similar in structure, describe more or less the same topic domain. For example, S-Match [8] is targeted towards matching classification hierarchies. Or, due to its structure based techniques, Anchor-PROMPT [9] works best if the matched ontologies have structures of similar complexity. Such similarity assumptions fail on the SW: we cannot predict whether relevant information will be provided by a simple FOAF file or by WordNet, or top level ontologies, or combined from these different sources. Mapping techniques should function without any pre-formulated assumptions about the ontological structure.

3) **Time Performance is important** - As already pointed out in [10], the majority of mapping approaches focus on the effectiveness (i.e., quality) of the mapping rather than on its efficiency (i.e., speed). This is a major challenge that needs to be solved in the context of run-time mappings where the speed of the response is a crucial factor. The above mentioned paper also shows that some minor modifications of the mapping strategy can highly improve response time and have only a marginal negative effect on the quality of the mappings. Unfortunately the work presented in [10] is rather unique in the context of mapping research -- although we think that such research is crucial for making mapping techniques usable during run-time.
4) **Consider relation and instance mappings** – much of the work in ontology mapping has focused on matching the concepts in two schemas, while other ontology entities, such as relations and instances, have largely been ignored so far (although relations and instances are taken into account as evidence to support the matching process in some approaches). However, SW tools are often used to find out information about specific entities (traditionally modeled as ontology instances), as well as the relations between entities. Therefore, we think that mapping techniques should be developed to efficiently map also between these kinds of entities, for example, on instance mapping, by reusing earlier work on tuple matching from the database community.
5) **Cross-ontology mapping filtering** - several approaches adopt the model of first generating all possible mappings and then filtering the relevant ones. However, in these approaches mappings are typically created between two ontologies describing the same domain. When performing mappings on the SW, we are also likely to discover several mappings but this time the mapping candidates might be drawn from different ontologies. Therefore we need to be able to reason about ontologies which may only have very few concepts in common. As discussed later in this paper, this requires mechanisms to assess whether or not such 'sparse concepts' are related.
6) **Produce Semantic output** – with the exception of S-Match, most mapping algorithms simply determine a similarity coefficient between the concepts that are mapped. Such coefficients are not very useful if the mappings have to be automatically used by a tool. In the scenario of SW tools, to support automatic processing of the mapping results, it would be more useful to return the semantic relations between the mapped entities (equivalent, more generic/specific) rather than just a number.

3   Motivating Scenario: Question Answering on the Semantic Web

Question answering has been investigated for many years by several different communities [11] (e.g., information retrieval). These approaches have largely been focused on retrieving the answer from raw text[1]. An obvious hypothesis is that QA would become easier if the answers could be retrieved from semantic data.

---

[1] Sponsored by the American National Institute (NIST) and the Defence Advanced Research Projects Agency (DARPA), TREC introduced an open-domain QA track in 1999 (TREC-8).

Based on this hypothesis, we have developed the **AquaLog** [12] ontology-based question answering system. The novelty of the system with respect to traditional QA systems is that it relies on the knowledge encoded in the underlying ontology and its explicit semantics to disambiguate the meaning of the questions and to provide answers. AquaLog has been developed during a period when little semantic data was available online. As a result it only uses one ontology at a time, even though AquaLog is portable from one domain to the other, being agnostic to the domain of the ontology that it exploits. In other words, while AquaLog is ontology independent, the user needs to tell the system which ontology is going to be used to interpret the queries. To briefly illustrate the question answering process, imagine that the system is asked the following question: *"Who are the researchers in KMi that have publications at ISWC?"*. The major task of the system is to bridge between the terminology used by the user and the concepts used by the underlying ontology. In a first step, by using linguistic techniques, the system breaks up the question into the following binary linguistic triples *(person, researcher, Knowledge Media Institute) (?, have publication, ISWC)*. Then, these terms are linked and mapped to ontology elements, generating the following ontology compliant triples *(researcher, works-for, knowledge-media-institute-at-the-open-university) (researcher, has-publications, international-semantic-web-conference)* from where the answer is derived. Obviously, if one of the terms of the question cannot be mapped to the ontology then no answer will be retrieved.

One way to overcome this limited scope is to take advantage of online available semantic data. The new version of AquaLog, **PowerAqua** [13], adopts an "open question answering strategy" by consulting and aggregating information derived from multiple heterogeneous ontologies on the Web. PowerAqua will function in the same way as AquaLog does, with the essential difference that the terms of the question will need to be **dynamically** mapped to **several** online ontologies. This run time mapping brings up several challenges in comparison with Aqualog, which need to be solved by the PowerMap mapping algorithm of PowerAqua:

a) **Finding the right ontologies.** PowerMap matching operations first need to determine the ontology(ies) from where the answer will be derived. Syntactic matching techniques can be used in a first step to identify all those ontologies with potential mappings to the terms in the triples. For example, "researcher" is a concept appearing in almost all ontologies about the academic domain, while "KMi" appears only in one of those ontologies[2]. For the second triple, we find many concepts related to "publication" and "iswc".

b) **Semantic relevance analysis.** When multiple mapping candidates are discovered, only semantically relevant ones should be selected.

c) **Filtering the right mappings.** From the identified ontologies the ones that potentially provide the most information need to be selected. PowerMap relies on two criteria. First, at least a complete mapping coverage for each triple is crucial (i.e., one triple should not be spread over many ontologies. However, triples can be mapped over several ontologies that provide equivalent information, or whose information can be partially combined and integrated through similar

---
[2] This populated ontology can be browsed through at: http://semanticweb.kmi.open.ac.uk.

semantically interoperable classes from different ontologies to provide a complete mapping. In the example above, it is easy to choose the first ontology which completely covers the "researcher" and "KMi" terms. Second, in case of ambiguity (more than one interpretation of the same query term) the correct interpretation for the given term in the context of the user query (triples) and the ontology relatedness should be returned. In case this is not enough to perform disambiguation, the final decision should be left to the target tools or to the user. For the second triple, there are considerably more ontologies that completely cover the triple. However, all of them are semantically equivalent solutions. Nevertheless, only one ontology contains a path between "researcher", "publication" and "iswc".

d) **Composing heterogeneous information.** PowerAqua will use PowerMap mapping results to find the relations that link those entities and the triples, so the resulting ontology triples will be *(researcher, works-in, knowledge-media-institute)* referring to the KMi ontology and, e.g., the triples *(researchers, wrote, publications) (publications, published, iswc)* in a second ontology, although other equivalent triples in other ontologies will also be valid. Finally, PowerAqua needs to combine partial answers from these different ontologies, e.g., to obtain the researchers on KMi and the researchers that have publications at *ISWC*. Among other things, to give an answer this requires the ability to recognize whether two instances from different sources may refer to the same individual. Some co-relation and disambiguation methods to determine if two resources refer to the same individual have been used in Flink [4].

4 PowerMap at a Glance

The requirements imposed by SW applications, like PowerAqua, that open up to harvest the rich ontological knowledge on the Web are the foundations for the design of PowerMap. In PowerMap the **mapping process is driven by the task** that has to be performed, more concretely by the query that is asked by the user. Indeed, this is novel in comparison with traditional approaches where mappings are done prior to the ontology being used for a specific task. An input query is represented by a triple or set of triples that indicated how the words are related together (in fact, better results are expected considering the triples than by only considering isolated words). We envision a scenario where a user may need to interact with thousands of knowledge bases structured according to hundreds of ontologies. However, we believe that good performance could be obtained also at such scale because PowerMap avoids a global interpretation of the mapped ontologies, in which the level of effort is at least linear in the number of matches to be performed [8] (e.g., the Match operator). In this sense only relevant concepts to the user's query are analyzed.

PowerMap is a hybrid matching algorithm comprising *terminological and structural schema matching* techniques with the assistance of large scale ontological or lexical resources. Figure 1 depicts the three main phases of PowerMap.

Phase I: Syntactic Mapping. The role of this phase is to identify candidate mappings for all query terms in different online ontologies (therefore identify potentially relevant ontologies for that particular query). This is the simplest phase as it only considers concept labels (i.e., ignores the structure of ontologies). It relies on simple, *string-based* comparison methods (e.g., *edit distance metrics*) and WordNet to look-up lexically related words (synonyms, hypernyms and hyponyms).

Phase II: Semantic Mapping. This phase operates on the reduced set of ontologies identified in the previous phase. The goal is to verify the syntactic mappings identified previously and exclude those that do not make sense from a semantic perspective (e.g., the intended meaning of the query term differs from the intended meaning of the concept that was proposed as a candidate match). For example, if the term "capital" is matched to concepts with identical labels in a geographical ontology and a financial ontology, these two meanings are not semantically equivalent. Unlike the previous phase, this phase relies on more complex methods. First, it exploits the hierarchical structure of the candidate ontologies to elicit the sense of the candidate concepts. Second, it uses WordNet based methods to compute the *semantic similarity* between the query terms and the ontology classes.

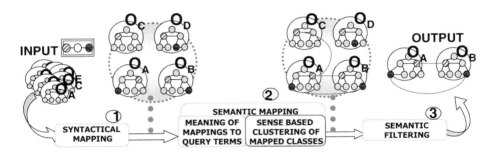

Fig. 1. Mapping process example to obtain potential ontology mappings for a triple

Phase III: Semantic Filtering. The mappings filtered out by the previous phase are spread over several ontologies. The goal of this final phase is to filter out the meaningful mappings that better represent the query domain by (a) determining those ontologies that cover entire triples and not just individual terms of the triples and by (b) studying the ontology relatedness to determine the valid semantic interpretation (e.g. to decide which ontology interpretation of "capital" is valid for the sense of the query term). In this phase we employ relation mapping techniques to match between the predicates of the triples and relations in the identified ontologies. This step will return a small set of ontologies that jointly cover all terms and hopefully contain enough information to deduce the answer to the question.

Note that, in order to optimize performance, the complexity of these phases increases both because of the type of ontology entities that they consider and because of the techniques they use. Hence the most time-consuming techniques are executed last, when the search has been narrowed down to a smaller set of ontologies.

5 Details of the PowerMap Algorithm

We explore each major step of this algorithm that is currently being implemented.

5.1 Phase I: Syntactic Mapping

The syntactic mapping phase identifies candidate entities from different ontologies to be mapped to each input term in the triple(s) by means of syntax driven techniques (SDT) using the labels and local names of the ontology elements. We test our prototype on a collection of ontologies saved into online repositories but in the mean time we are working on adapting it to directly fetch relevant ontologies from Swoogle.

This phase is responsible to bridge the gap between user terminology and the multiple heterogeneous ontologies. This is done through two mechanisms. First, the set of query terms is broadened with semantically equivalent terms using WordNet. We take into account synonyms, hypernyms and hyponyms. Currently we experiment with using the SUMO upper level ontology and extending it with the mappings to the WordNet lexicon [14]. The mappings of SUMO to WordNet avoid the excessive fine-grainedness of WN sense distinctions, which is the most frequently cited problem of WordNet [15]. The second mechanism to ensure a high recall, is to perform so called "fuzzy" syntactic matches between terms and ontology entities (e.g. "PhDStudent" is a fuzzy match to "Student"). We are also considering the use of wikipedia [16] to find similar names, abbreviations, and acronyms in the case of instances.

SDT (fuzzy searches and lexically related words) are good mechanisms to broaden the search space as they can return a lot of hits that contain the term. However, they have two main weaknesses. First, SDT become increasingly computationally expensive as the number of ontologies increases. Second, many of the discovered ontology elements syntactically related with the query terms may be similarly spelled words (labels) that do not have precisely the same meaning.

The first weakness is addressed by using efficient and large-scale ontology repositories [17] in combination with Lucene[3]. Lucene indexes the semantic entities in the online and distributed back-end repositories into one or more indexes, and is used as our fast search engine[4], which supports fuzzy searches based on the Lavenshtein Distance, or Edit Distance algorithm. Moreover, it includes a *Spell Checker* to suggest a list of words close to a misspelled word using the n-gram technique. Also, query terms and in some cases relations are mapped to instances or classes therefore the system searches for classes, instances, properties and literals. Studying relations is computationally expensive and it is done only after the arguments are well know (although if one of the argument is unmapped, they can also be used to broaden the search space of candidate classes, i.e., through the ontology relationships that are valid for the mapped term, we can identify a set of possible candidate classes that can complete the triple). Relations are considered on the third phase to help filtering out the most relevant mapping candidates (Section 5.4).

---

[3] http://lucene.apache.org
[4] A first implementation of the search engine can be found on the KMi semantic web portal: http://semanticweb.kmi.open.ac.uk:8080/ksw/pages/semantic_searching.jsp

The second weakness is addressed in the next semantic phases, where we will focus on the issue of checking the semantic validity of the mappings and disambiguating among the possible interpretations of a query.

5.2 Phase II: Semantic Mapping

Semantic mapping checks the semantic validity of the previously identified syntactic ontology mappings for each query term in the triple. We perform two main steps. In the first step (Section 5.3.1) we discard mappings established between terms and concepts with different meaning. Then, in the next step (Section 5.3.2), we cluster the resulting mappings according to the senses that they cover. These steps rely on two more generic algorithms to determine the similarity between two senses in WN (Section 5.3.3) and to obtain the meaning of a concept and compare the senses of concepts in different ontologies (Section 5.3.4).

5.2.1 Step1: Verifying the Meaning of Mappings Respect to Query Terms

In this step we verify whether a mapping is also valid at a semantic level, i.e., the intended meaning of the term is the same as that of the concept. Mappings between elements with completely different meaning will be discarded (e.g. the "research-area" = "researcher" mapping).

We rely on sense information provided by WordNet to check the semantic similarity between the mapped terms. We perform the following steps:

1) For a term T, we extract all its WordNet senses, S_T
2) For the proposed mapping of T, a concept C, we also extract its senses S_C
3) We compute semantic similarity, using the algorithm in Section 5.3.3, between T and C to obtain the shared senses $S_{T,C}$
4) Based on the value of $S_{T,C}$, we determine the semantic relation between T and C as follows
   a. If $S_{T,C}$ is empty, the terms share no sense, and therefore the mapping is discarded
   b. If $S_{T,C}$ is not empty there is a semantic relation between the two terms which needs to be further investigated ($S_{T,C} \leq S_C$)
   c. If $S_{T,C} = S_T$, then the terms share all senses and they are potentially semantically identical (see "capital" example in Section 6).

Note that in this step we took into account all possible senses for C. However, the true senses of C are determined by its place in the hierarchy of the ontology. Because this sense is more costly to compute, to improve performance we use it only in the next step after the obviously wrong mappings have been discarded in this step.

5.2.2 Step 2: Sense-Based Clustering of Retrieved Mappings

The previous step might result in several mappings for the same term to concepts in different ontologies and these ontologies might have different subject domains (thus enforcing different meaning on their concepts). In this step we compare the concepts to which the term is mapped to determine whether they have the same sense (in case of instances we study the class they belong to). For this we rely on their place in the hierarchy of the ontology.

Apart from the senses being delimited by the query term {$S_{T,C}$}, the senses of the candidate mapped ontology class C are also delimited by its meaning in the ontology. For each concept C, we determine its sense as restricted by its place in the hierarchy S^H_C by using the algorithm presented in Section 5.3.4.. We then intersect this sense with the senses that C and T share according to our previous step, $S_{T,C}$. Obviously, if this intersection ($S^H_C \cap S_{T,C}$) is empty it means that the sense of the concept in the hierarchy is different from the sense that we though it might have in the previous step, and therefore that mapping should be discarded. Otherwise, the intersection represents the sense which is captured by the mapping. For example, if the term "queen" was previously mapped to two concepts Bee/Queen and Royalty/Queen having the same label, after interpreting the meaning of the two concepts according to their parent concept, we deduce that they have two different meanings as their intersection with the senses of the query term contains different senses (in case the two mapped concepts don't share the same label, the intersection or shared senses are computed using the semantic similarity notion on Section 5.3.3). Mappings with different meanings or interpretations are not semantically equivalent and therefore the correct interpretation should be disambiguate and filtered in the next step (5.3.4).

We group the mappings that refer to the same sense together.

5.2.3 Computing Semantic Similarity

In this section we detail the semantic similarity algorithm used to find shared senses of two words by relying on WordNet. In *Hierarchy distance based matchers* [18] the relatedness between words is measured by the distance between the two concept/senses in a given input hierarchy. In particular, similarity between words is measured by looking at the shortest path between two given concepts/sense in the WN *IS-A* taxonomy of concepts. Note that similarity ("bank-trust") is a more specialized notion than association or relatedness (i.e. any kind of functional relationship or frequent association, which cannot always be determined purely from a priori lexical resources such as WN, like "penguin-Antarctica") [19].

We say that **two words are similar** if any of the following hold:

1. They have a synset(s) in common (e.g. "human" and "person")
2. Any of the senses of a word is a hypernym/hyponym in the taxonomy of any of the senses of the other word.
3. If there exists an allowable "is-a" path (in the WN taxonomy) connecting a synset associated with each word. To evaluate this, we make use of two WN indexes: the *depth* and the *common parent index* (C.P.I). The rationale of this point is based on the two criteria of similarity between concepts established by Resnik in [20]. The first one is that the shorter the path between two terms the more similar they are, this is measured using the *depth* index. However, a widely acknowledged problem is that the approach typically "relies on the notion that links in the taxonomy represent uniform distances", but typically this is not true and there is a wide variability in the "distance" covered by a single taxonomic link [19]. As a consequence the second criterion of similarity is the extent to which the concepts share information in common, which in an *IS-A* taxonomy can be determined by inspecting the relative position of the most-specific concept that subsumes them both, which is the *C.P.I* index. With the use of the *C.P.I* we can immediately identify the lowest super-ordinate concept (*lso*) between the two terms, also called

the most specific common subsumer. Apart from point 1 of the algorithm, in which the words have a synset in common, the most immediate case occurs in point 2 (C.P.I = 1, Depth = 1), e.g. while comparing "poultry" and "chicken" we notice that "poultry#2" is the common subsumer (hypernym) of "chicken#1".
4. Additionally, if any of the previous cases is true and the definition (gloss) of one of the synsets of the word (or its direct hypernyms/hyponyms) includes the other word as one of the synonyms, we say they are strongly similar.

For example, for the input triple (investigators, work, akt project) using string algorithms over WordNet synonyms, PowerMap discovers the following candidate mappings for "investigators": "researcher", "research-area". Going back to the step 1 (Section 5.3.1), using the WordNet "IS-A" taxonomy we must find at least one synset in common with the mapped ontology class and the query term or a short/relevant path in the IS-A WordNet taxonomy that relates them together. Otherwise it is discarded as a solution. Here, "researcher" and "investigator" have a synset in common, namely "research-worker, researcher, investigator – a scientist who devotes himself to doing research". However "research-area" will be discarded because not only do they not share any sense in common but also there is not a relevant "IS-A" path that connects "researcher" with "research-area" -- "researcher" is connected to the root through the path "scientist/man of science" and "person", while "research-area" is connected through "investigation" which is connected to "work".

5.2.4 Ontology Structure Based Sense Disambiguation
The meaning of an ontology term should be made explicit by an interpretation of its label through a WordNet sense and its position in the ontology taxonomy.

According to the algorithm presented by Magnini et al. in [21] to make explicit the semantics hidden in schema models, in a nutshell, given a concept c and either one of its ancestors or descendants r all WordNet synsets for both labels are retrieved. Then, if any of the senses for c is related to any of the senses for r either by being a synonym, hypernym, holonym, hyponym or a meronym, then that sense of c is considered the right one.

Our algorithm, originally based on Magnini et al., is adapted to use ontologies rather than catalogues or classifications, therefore we can exploit the use of the notion of similarity *IS-A* given by the ontology taxonomy explicit semantics instead of the notion of relatedness (e.g. "hospital" is not a good match for "nurse" even if they are highly related). The WN senses of an ontology class are obtained by looking at the similarity (as previously defined) between the class and its ascendant/descendant in the ontology. The senses of the class that are similar to at least one of the senses of its ascendant/descendant are retained and the rest of the senses discarded.

5.3 Phase III: Semantic Filtering

Having worked at the level of individual term mappings so far, in this step we select those ontologies that cover *entire* triples (ontologies with better domain coverage). Moreover, we take advantage of the relatedness expressed in the ontology semantics and input triples to filter out the semantically interoperable candidate mappings for the query terms. Also, if different ontologies cover different triples then we must make sure that the concepts that link between the triples have the same sense in those ontologies (semantic interoperable concepts, as studies in Section 5.3.2).

Previous steps have only determined mappings of concepts and instances from the query. The reason for this is based on our experience with AquaLog where mapping relations is more difficult than mapping concepts. In the case of PowerAqua due to the increasing number of heterogeneous ontologies the challenge is to semantically map the terms. Once the terms are mapped the meaning of a relation is given by the type of its domain and its range rather than by its name (typically vaguely defined as e.g. "related to"), so the precondition of a mapping between two relations is that their domain and range classes match to some extent. With the exception of the cases in which some relations are presented in some ontologies as a concept (e.g. *has Author* can be modeled as a concept *Author* in a given ontology), in PowerMap relations are treated as "second class citizens" to help disambiguating the candidate classes, and ontologies, that better cover the query domain.

The following is a disambiguating example considering the coverage criterion. The query "Which wine is appropriate with chicken?" translated into the triple (wine, appropriate, chicken) has syntactic mappings with the class "wine" in an ontology of colors, and in an ontology of food and wines. Similarly, the term "chicken" maps to an ontology of farming and to the same food and wine ontology. Since the food and wine ontology presents a complete potential translation for the triple we retain it, and we discard the partial translations from both the farming and color ontologies. A disambiguating example using ontology relations is described in Section 6.

6 Experimental Example

In this section we present an example run on our prototype. Consider the query "what is the capital of Spain?" translated in a triple without information about the *focus* of the query: (?, capital, Spain). After the execution of phase I we get the following mappings for the terms and their lexical variations:

- Geographical ontology. Contains the class "capital-city" and "Spain" as an instance of "country", "capital-city" and "country" are connected by a direct relation.
- Financial ontology. Contains the class "capital" and "Spain" as an instance of "country", "capital" and "country" are related through the concept "company".
- Country statistics ontology. Contains the term "Spain".

The coverage criterion can be already applied to this stage of the algorithm, however the three interpretations will remain because both ontology 1 and 2 cover the terms "capital" and "Spain", and ontology 3 only covers the term "Spain" but "capital" is considered as a relation and as such it may be mapped into an ontology relation.

There is only one possible sense for "Spain", therefore we only study the semantic similarity for the term "capital". In principle, both interpretations remain (step 1, Section 5.3.1), as the lemma for both terms is the same as the query term, potentially they have all the synset in common. Semantic equivalence between both classes is then determined by studying their ontology meaning (step 2, Section 5.3.2.). When running the similarity algorithm between "capital" and its ancestor "city" in the geographical ontology we obtained the results presented in Table 3.

Table 1. Similarity between "capital" and its ontology ancestor "city"

	City#1: large and densely populated urban area.., metropolis	City#2: an incorporated administrative district ..	City#3: people living in large municipality
Capital#a (assests ..)	*Not an allowable path or depth is too long to be considered relevant*		
Capital#b (wealth ..)			
Capital#c (seat of government)	Depth = 8, lso = region Num_so(common_subsumers) = 3 (region, location, entity)	Depth = 7, lso = region Num_so = 3 (entity, location, region)	
Capital#d (capital letter)			
Capital#e (book by Karl Marx)			
Capital#f (upper part column)	Depth = 8, lso = location Num_so = 2 (entity, location)	Depth = 7, lso = location Num_so=2 (entity,location)	

Analyzing the results of Table 1 we can quickly filter *capital#c, capital#f, city#1, city#2* and discard the others. A deeper study will show that *capital#c* is more likely than *capital#f* because there are only 2 common subsumers in the latter (entity and location), both of them representing abstract top elements of the WordNet taxonomy, while in the former we have 3 common subsumers. We can not study the descendants of "capital" in the ontology because none exist. The study of the next direct ascendant of "city" ("geographical-unit") does not offer additional information. Moreover, the hypernym of *capital#c* is *"seat#5"*, defined as "seat –centre of authority (*city* from which authority is exercised)". The word "city" is used as part of its definition, therefore *capital#c* is strongly related to *"city"*.

After the semantic similarity analysis the sense of "capital" is made explicit as senses #1 and #2 in the financial ontology, while the geographical ontology is referred to sense *#3*. Therefore both terms in different ontologies are not semantically equivalent and the system must select one of them using ontology semantics or query relatedness. Using SUMO's mapping files to WordNet synsets we can identify senses that are not very distinctive (they are mapped to the same SUMO concept), e.g. for city {#1 an incorporated administrative district, #2: metropolis, and #3: people living in large municipality}, all its senses map to the same SUMO class.

A deeper analysis of the ontology relationships to narrow down between the two valid non-equivalent mappings "capital" shows a direct relation that connects any country, e.g. Spain, with its capital for the geographical ontology. However, in the financial ontology there is not a direct relation between countries and capital. There is a mediating concept that represents a company, that has a series of capital goods and it is based in a country. This is a strong indication that the geographical ontology is more related to our query and should be selected. For the country statistics ontology, where capital is considered a relation, a relationship analysis simply using of string distance metrics [22] will uncover the relation "is-capital-of" between "country" and "city". Therefore both mappings in the geographical and statistics ontologies will be valid semantically equivalent representations of the query.

7 Summary

The main message of this paper is that the new context introduced by the evolving SW tools will require mapping techniques that can be used at run-time rather than at the design time of such tools and applications. Our main contribution is to recognize and analyze this need which could present a turning point in the field of ontology mapping. We presented some of the requirements that have to be addressed by such novel mapping techniques. In particular, such techniques need to balance the heterogeneity and large scale of online available semantic data and the requirement of being fast so that they can be used at run-time.

The core of the paper exemplifies the requirements for run time ontology mapping in the context of a concrete application, PowerAqua, an ontology based QA system and then describes the PowerMap algorithm which performs such run-time mappings. Unlike traditional mapping algorithms, PowerMap is focused towards dealing with several, heterogeneous ontologies which are not given a priory but rather discovered depending on the content of the user's query (thus we fulfill requirements 1 and 2). To maintain a good performance, as requested by our third requirement, PowerMap employs three steps that are increasingly complex: we start with syntactic mappings that take into account only concept labels to find potentially useful ontologies, then we rely on WordNet information and on the meaning of the mapped concepts in their hierarchy to verify that the proposed mappings are also semantically sound. Finally, we rely on the structure of the triples and techniques to map between relations in order to filter out a set of relevant ontologies from which PowerAqua will extract the answers (requirement 5).

PowerMap is currently under implementation and our obvious future work is in finalizing the prototype and evaluating it. In particular we are working on extending the technique to work directly with Swoogle and to provide mappings between instances as well (see requirement 4). However, we think that our ideas about run-time ontology mapping and the proposed algorithm could benefit the ontology mapping community in particular, and the SW research in general.

Acknowledgments. This work was partially supported by the AKT project sponsored by UK EPSRC and by the EU OpenKnowledge project (FP6-027253). Thanks to Yuangui Lei and Victoria Uren for all the technical help and relevant input.

References

1. Shvaiko, P., Euzenat, J.: A Survey of Schema-Based Matching Approaches. *J. of Data Semantics IV*, 2005. 146-171.
2. Bouquet P., Serafini L. and Zanobini S. Semantic coordination: a new approach and an application. *In Proc of ISWC,* 2003, 130-145.
3. Hyvonen, E., Makela, E., Salminen, M., Valo, A., Viljanen, K., Saarela, S., Junnila, M., Kettula, S.. MuseumFinland – Finnish Museums on the SemanticWeb. *Journal of Web Semantics*, 3(2), 2005
4. Mika, P. Flink: SemanticWeb Technology for the Extraction and Analysis of Social Networks. *Journal of Web Semantics*, 3(2), 2005

5. Motta, E., Sabou, M., Language Technologies and the Evolution of the Semantic Web. *In Proceedings of LREC*, 2006
6. Ding, L., Pan, R., Finin, T., Joshi, A., Peng, Y., Kolari, P. Finding and Ranking Knowledge on the Semantic Web. *In Proceedings of ISWC*, 2005, p. 156 – 170.
7. Rahm E. and Bernstein P. A. A survey of approaches to automatic schema matching. *The International Journal on Very Large Data Bases* 10(4): 334-350, 2001.
8. Giunchiglia F., Shvaiko P and Yatskevich M. S-Match: an algorithm and an implementation of semantic matching. *In Proc. of the 1st European Semantic Web Symposium*, 2004.
9. N. Noy and M. Musen. Anchor-PROMPT: using non-local context for semantic matching. *In Proceedings of the workshop on Ontologies and Information Sharing at the International Joint Conference on Artificial Intelligence (IJCAI)*, 2001, pages 63–70.
10. M. Ehrig and S. Staab. QOM: Quick ontology mapping. In *Proceedings of ISWC*, 2004, pages 683–697.
11. Hirschman, L., Gaizauskas, R.: Natural Language question answering: the view from here. *Natural Language Engineering, Special Issue on QA*, 7(4) 275-300, 2001
12. Lopez V., Pasin M. and Motta E. AquaLog: An Ontology-portable Question Answering System for the Semantic Web. *In Proc. of ESWC,* 2005.
13. Lopez V., Motta E. and Uren, V. PowerAqua: Fishing the Semantic Web. *In Proc. of ESWC,* 2006.
14. Pease, A., Niles, I., and Li, J. The Suggested Upper Merged Ontology: A Large Ontology for the Semantic Web and its Applications. *In Working Notes of the AAAI Workshop on Ontologies and the Semantic Web*, 2002.
15. Ide N. and Veronis J. Word Sense Disambiguation: The State of the Art. *Computational Linguistics*, 24(1):1-40, 1998.
16. Bunescu, R., Pasca, M. Using Encyclopedic Knowledge for Named Entity Disambiguation. *In Proceedings of the 11th Conference of the European Chapter of the Association for Computational Linguistics (EACL-06)*, 2006.
17. Guo, Y., Pan, Z., Heflin, J. An Evaluation of Knowledge Base Systems for Large OWL Datasets. *In Proc of ISWC*, 2004, pages 274-288.
18. Giunchiglia F. and Yatskevich M. Element Level Semantic Matching. *Meaning Coordination and Negotiation Workshop, ISWC*, 2004.
19. Budanitsky, A. and Hirst, G. Evaluating WordNet-based measures of semantic distance. *Computational Linguistics*, 2006.
20. Resnik P. Disambiguating noun grouping with respect to WordNet senses. *In Proc. of the 3rd Workshop on very Large Corpora*. MIT, 1995.
21. Magnini B., Serafín L., and Speranza M. Making Explicit the Semantics Hidden in Schema Models. *In Proc. of the Workshop on Human Language Technology for the Semantic Web and Web Services*, held at *ISWC-2003*, Sanibel Island, Florida, 2003.
22. Cohen, W., W., Ravikumar, P., Fienberg, S., E.: A Comparison of String Distance Metrics for Name-Matching Tasks. *In Proc. of the 2nd Web Workshop at IJCAI ,2003*.

Ontology-Driven Information Extraction with OntoSyphon

Luke K. McDowell[1] and Michael Cafarella[2]

[1] Computer Science Department, U.S. Naval Academy,
Annapolis MD 21402 USA
lmcdowel@usna.edu
[2] Dept. of Computer Science and Engineering, University of Washington,
Seattle WA 98195 USA
mjc@cs.washington.edu

Abstract. The Semantic Web's need for machine understandable content has led researchers to attempt to automatically acquire such content from a number of sources, including the web. To date, such research has focused on "document-driven" systems that individually process a small set of documents, annotating each with respect to a given ontology. This paper introduces OntoSyphon, an alternative that strives to more fully leverage existing ontological content while scaling to extract comparatively shallow content from millions of documents. OntoSyphon operates in an "ontology-driven" manner: taking any ontology as input, OntoSyphon uses the ontology to specify web searches that identify possible semantic instances, relations, and taxonomic information. Redundancy in the web, together with information from the ontology, is then used to automatically verify these candidate instances and relations, enabling OntoSyphon to operate in a fully automated, unsupervised manner. A prototype of OntoSyphon is fully implemented and we present experimental results that demonstrate substantial instance learning in a variety of domains based on independently constructed ontologies. We also introduce new methods for improving instance verification, and demonstrate that they improve upon previously known techniques.

1 Introduction

The success of the Semantic Web critically depends upon the existence of a sufficient amount of high-quality, relevant semantic content. But to date relatively little such content has emerged. In response, researchers have investigated systems to assist users with producing (or annotating) such content, as well as systems for automatically extracting semantic content from existing unstructured data sources such as web pages.

Most systems for automated content generation work as follows. Given a small to moderate size set of hopefully relevant documents, the system sequentially processes each document. For each document, the system tries to extract relevant information and encode it using the predicates and classes of a given ontology. This extraction might utilize a domain-specific wrapper, constructed by hand [1] or via machine learning techniques [2]. More recent domain-independent approaches have utilized a named entity recognizer to identify interesting terms, then used web searches to try to determine the term's class [3]. In either case, these are *document-driven* systems whose workflow follows the documents.

This paper describes OntoSyphon, an alternative *ontology-driven* information extraction (IE) system. Instead of sequentially handling documents, OntoSyphon processes the ontology in some order. For each ontological class or property, OntoSyphon searches a large corpus for instances and relations than can be extracted. In the simplest case, for instance, a `Mammal` class in the ontology causes our system to search the web for phrases like "mammals such as" in order to identify instances (and subclasses) of `Mammal`. We then use redundancy in the web and information in the ontology to verify the candidate instances, subclasses, and relations that were found. In this paper, we focus on learning instances.

Compared to more traditional document-driven IE, OntoSyphon's ontology-driven IE extracts relatively shallow information from a very large corpus of documents, instead of performing more exhaustive (and expensive) processing of a small set of documents. Hence, the approaches are complementary, and real world systems may profitably utilize both. We note, however, several benefits of ontology-driven IE. First, driving the entire IE process directly from the ontology presents a very natural path for exploiting all kinds of ontological data, e.g., utilizing class labels and synonyms for broader searching and exploiting instances and stated restrictions for verifying candidate facts. Second, a search-based system enables us to consider a much larger set of documents than could be handled via individual, document-driven processing. Only a small fraction of the corpus will be used for any one system execution, but much more potentially relevant information is accessible. Finally, ontology-driven IE can be easily focused on the desired results. Rather than processing all content from some documents and then looking for the desired info, we can instruct the system to search directly for relevant classes.

Our contributions are as follows. First, we introduce the ontology-driven paradigm for information extraction and explain its benefits compared to complementary approaches. Second, we explain how to apply this general paradigm to find instances from the web and demonstrate successful instance population for three different, independently created ontologies. Third, we evaluate several different techniques for improving the accuracy of instance identification and classification. In addition, we introduce two simple but highly effective improvements to previously known assessment techniques for such extractions. These improvements relate to adding or improving upon frequency-based normalization, and can be used even in contexts without an explicit ontology. Finally, we describe techniques for further improving accuracy based on explicitly leveraging the structure of the ontology.

The next section summarizes related work in this area. Section 3 summarizes OntoSyphon's operation, while Section 4 describes our methodology and evaluation metrics. Section 5 describes the existing and new techniques that we use for the key problem of assessing candidate instances. Finally, Section 6 presents experimental results, Section 7 discusses our findings, and Section 8 concludes.

Table 1. A summary of work that attempts to (semi-)automatically extract instance-like content from the web or other text corpora. Note that an ontology-based system almost always utilizes a domain-specific ontology, but may still be a domain-independent *system* if it can easily exploit input ontologies from many different domains.

	Text-based	Ontology-based	
		Document-driven	Ontology-driven
Domain-specific	Crystal[4], Citeseer, Opine[5]	WebKB[6], TAP[1], OntoMiner[7], OntoSophie[8], Armadillo[2], ADEL[9]	Cyc "web population"[10,11], van Hage et al.[12]
Domain-independent	MindNet[13], Snowball[14], Cederberg et al.[15], KnowItAll[16], Pantel et al.[17]	Hahn et al.[18], S-CREAM[19], SemTag[20], KIM[21], PANKOW[3],	**OntoSyphon**

2 Related Work on Information Extraction from the Web

The general task we face is to learn information from some textual source, such as the WWW, and encode that information in a structured language such as RDF. Table 1 provides an interpretation of the most relevant other work in this area. The rows of this table distinguish systems that are domain-independent from those that rely on domain-specific techniques or extraction patterns.

The columns of Table 1 explain the extent to which each system utilizes an explicit ontology. In the leftmost column ("Text-based") are information extraction systems that are not explicitly based on an ontology. For instance, Citeseer automatically extracts metadata about research publications, Opine [5] focuses on product reviews, and Crystal [4] uses a domain-specific lexicon to learn text extraction rules by example. Amongst more domain-independent systems, Mind-Net [13] builds a semantic network based on dictionary and encyclopedia entries, while Snowball [14] learns relations (such as `headquartersOf`) based on an initial set of examples. KnowItAll [16] learns instances and other relations from the web. Many such systems [15,16,17] learn hyponym or is-a relationships based on searching for particular lexical patterns like "cities such as ...," inspired by Hearst's original use of such patterns [22]. Our work uses these same patterns as building blocks, but exploits an ontology to guide the extraction and assessment, and to formally structure the results.

Some of these text-based systems, such as MindNet, use their input corpus to derive an ontology-like structured output. In contrast, we call a system *ontology-based* if it specifies its output in terms of a pre-existing, formal ontology. These systems almost always use a domain-specific ontology in their operation, but we consider a system to be domain-independent if it can operate without modification on ontologies covering a wide range of domains.

The majority of these ontology-based systems are document-driven: starting from a particular document (or set of documents), they try to annotate all of the entities in that document relative to the target ontology. For instance,

TAP [1] exploits a variety of wrappers to extract information about authors, actors, movies, etc. from specifically identified websites such as Amazon.com. WebKB [6] and Armadillo [2] both use supervised techniques to extract information from computer science department websites. Amongst more domain-independent systems, SemTag [20] and KIM [21] scan documents looking for entities corresponding to instances in their input ontology. Likewise, S-CREAM [19] uses machine learning techniques to annotate a particular document with respect to its ontology, given a set of annotated examples. PANKOW [3] annotates a specified document by extracting named entities from the document and querying Google with ontology-based Hearst phrases. For instance, if the entity "South Africa" is found in a document, PANKOW would issues multiples queries like "South Africa is a river" and use hit count results to determine which ontology term (river, country, etc.) was the best match. These systems all use an ontology to specify their output, but make limited use of information that is contained in the ontology beyond the names of classes and properties that may be relevant.

OntoSyphon offers a complementary approach of being ontology-based and *ontology-driven*. Instead of trying to learn all possible information about a particular document, we focus on particular parts of an ontology and try to learn all possible information about those ontological concepts from the web. In addition, we seek to use ontological data and structure to enhance our assessment of the content that is found (see Section 6).

The only work of which we are aware that adopts a somewhat similar approach is that of Matuszek et al. [10,11] and van Hage et al. [12]. Both systems use an ontology to generate web search terms, though neither identifies this ontology-driven approach or examines its merits. van Hage et al. use the searches to find mappings between two given ontologies, whereas Matuszek et al. use the searches to identify instances and relations that could be inserted into the (large) Cyc ontology. Matuszek et al. use more sophisticated natural language processing than we do, and use the existing Cyc ontology to perform more kinds of reasoning. Compared to OntoSyphon, however, the systems of van Hage and Matuszek perform much less accurate verification of content learned from the web, either assuming that a human will perform the final verification [10] or treating all web candidates as correct because of data sparsity [12]. In addition, both systems only discover information about instances or classes that are already present in their ontology, and both are domain-specific. Matuszek's system, for instance, depends upon manually generated search phrases for a few hundred carefully chosen properties.

Ontology learning systems seek to learn or extend an ontology based on examination of a particular relevant corpus [23,24,25,26]. Some such systems [24,25,26] use Hearst-like patterns to identify possible subclass relations. Ontology learning systems, however, presume a particularly relevant corpus and do not focus on learning instances (with some limited document-driven exceptions, e.g., Text2Onto [26]). In addition, the goal of producing a very accurate ontology leads to very different verification techniques, usually including human guidance

Init: **SearchSet = {R} + O.subclassesOf(R)**
SearchSet = {Animal} + {Amphibian, Arthropod, Bird, Fish,...}
1. **C = PickAndRemoveClass (SearchSet)**
   C = Bird
2. **Phrases = ApplyPatterns(C)**
   Phrases = {"birds such as ...", "birds including ...", "birds especially ...",
              "... and other birds", "... or other birds"}
3. **Candidates += FindInstancesFromWeb (Phrases)**
   Candidates = {..., (kookaburra, Bird, 20), (oriole, Bird, 37), ... }
4. **If MoreUsefulWork(SearchSet, Candidates), goto Step 1**
5. **Results = Assess (O, Candidates)**

(kookaburra, Bird, 20)	$Results = \{$	
(kookaburra, Mammal, 1)	(kookaburra, Bird, 0.93),	*LA: 1.00*
(leather, Animal, 1) $\Longrightarrow$	(leather, Animal, 0.01),	*LA: 0.00*
(oriole, Bird, 37)	(oriole, Bird, 0.93),	*LA: 1.00*
(wildebeest, Animal, 56)	(wildebeest, Animal, 0.91)	*LA: 0.67*
(wildebeest, Mammal, 6)	$\}$	

Fig. 1. OntoSyphon's algorithm (bold lines), given a root class R, for populating an ontology O with instances, and partial sample output (other lines). The text (oriole, Bird, 37) describes a candidate instance that was extracted 37 times. Step 5 converts these counts into a confidence score or a probability, and chooses the most likely class for candidates that had more than one possible class (results shown computed via Urns, see Section 5). "LA" is the "Learning Accuracy" of the final pair (see Section 4).

and/or final verification. OntoSyphon instead operates in a fully automatic, unsupervised manner, and uses the web rather than require that a domain-specific corpus be identified.

This paper focuses on demonstrating how a domain-independent, ontology-driven system can reliably extract instances using a few simple techniques. Overall performance could be increased even more by incorporating other techniques such as domain-specific pattern learning [14,27,16], automatic subclass identification [16], non-pattern based extraction [18,24,25,23], and the combination of multiple sources of evidence [28].

3 Overview of OntoSyphon's Operation

Figure 1 gives pseudocode for OntoSyphon's operation. The input to OntoSyphon is an ontology O and a root class R such as Animal. The search set is initialized to hold the root term R and all subclasses of R. OntoSyphon then performs the following steps: pick a "promising" class C from the ontology (step 1), instantiate several lexical phrases to extract instances of that class from the web (steps 2-3), then repeat until a termination condition is met (step 4). Finally, use the ontology and statistics obtained during the extraction to assess the probability of each candidate instance (step 5). Below we explain in more detail.

1. **Identify a Promising Class:** OntoSyphon must decide where to focus its limited resources. For our initial experiments, we pragmatically chose to completely explore all subclasses of the user-provided root class. Future work should consider how best to use OntoSyphon's limited resources when broader explorations are desired. For instance, we might like to chose the class that we know the least about (fewest instances), or instead focus attention on classes that are similar to those that yielded good results in the past. Finally, note that some classes (e.g., zip codes) may produce very large amounts of data that is accurate but uninteresting.
2. **Generate Phrases:** Given a class C, we search for lexico-syntactic phrases that indicate likely instances of C. For instance, phrases like "birds such as" are likely to be followed by instances of the class `Bird`. We use the 5 Hearst phrase templates [22] listed in the sample output of Figure 1. To generate the phrases, we use heuristic processing to convert class IDs such as `SweetDessert` to the search label "sweet desserts." Where present we also exploit alternative class labels that can be inferred from the ontology, e.g., through the definition of an equivalent class.
3. **Search and extract:** Next, we search the web for occurrences of these phrases and extract candidate instances. This could be done by submitting the phrases as queries to a search engine, then downloading the result pages and performing extraction on them. For efficiency, we instead use the Binding Engine (BE) [29]. BE accepts queries like "birds such as <NounPhrase>" and returns all possible fillers for the <NounPhrase> term in about a minute, but for only a 90-million page fragment of the web.
4. **Repeat** (for this paper, until *SearchSet* is empty).
5. **Assess Candidate Instances** (see Section 5).

We focus in this paper on basic instance learning, but this algorithm naturally lends itself to several future enhancements. For instance, in step 3, the candidate instances that are discovered will also discover subclasses. Such subclasses might be added to the *SearchSet* and/or might be used to extend the ontology itself. Our initial experiments have shown that, as is to be expected, such steps will increase recall but at some cost of precision. The next section discusses how we grade discovered subclasses for this work; future work will more fully investigate the benefits of exploiting these candidate subclasses.

4 Methodology

We ran OntoSyphon over the three ontologies shown in Table 2. All three ontologies were created by individuals not associated with OntoSyphon, and were freely available on the web. For each, we selected a prominent class to be the "root class," thereby defining three different domains for evaluation: Animals, Food, and Artists. Note that instances for the first two domains are dominated by common nouns (horses, sushi), whereas the latter yields mostly proper nouns (Michelangelo). These choices encompass a variety of domains and ontology

Table 2. The domains and ontologies used for our experiments. The third column gives the number of subclasses of the chosen root term, followed by the average (and maximum) depth of these subclasses relative to the root term. The last column is the number of candidates that were human-graded for evaluation (5% of the total found).

Domain	Ontology used	# Subs.	Avg. Depth	# Graded
Animals	sweet.jpl.nasa.gov/ontology/biosphere.owl	28	1.04 (max 2)	300
Artists	www.kanzaki.com/ns/music.rdf	39	2.63 (max 4)	940
Food	www.w3.org/TR/owl-guide/food.rdf	31	2.13 (max 3)	170

types. For instance, the Animal ontology was fairly complete but shallow, while the Artist ontology covers artists in general but most classes focus on musical artists. The Food ontology has been used for demonstrating OWL concepts; it contains more complex constructions and classes such as NonSpicyRedMeat.

OntoSyphon operates in a totally unsupervised manner and outputs a ranked list of candidate instances for the ontology. Because there is no accurate, authoritative source for determining the full, correct set of instances for our three domains, we cannot report recall as an absolute percentage, and instead report just the number of distinct, correct instances found. In addition, we must evaluate correctness by hand. To do this, we created a "gold standard" as follows: all system configurations produce the same basic set of candidate instances for a given ontology. A human evaluator (one of the authors) classified a random sample of 5% of this set (see Table 2). For each candidate, the evaluator chose the best, most specific ontology class available, while allowing for multiple senses. So a dog would be marked as a Mammal rather than the less specific Animal, while Franz Liszt would be marked as a Composer, Pianist, and Conductor. Two classes, ExoticSpecies and IndigenousSpecies, were removed from Animals because they were too subjective for a human to evaluate. To reduce bias, the evaluator had no knowledge of what class OntoSyphon assigned to each candidate nor OntoSyphon's assigned probability for that candidate.

Candidates with no correct class for that domain (e.g., truck) were marked as incorrect, as were misspelled or incomplete terms (e.g., the artist "John"). To decide whether a candidate was a proper instance or a subclass, we assumed that the ontology was fairly complete and tried to follow the intent of the ontology. Candidates that could be properly classified as an instance of a leaf node in the ontology were treated as instances. Candidates that were already present in the ontology as a class or that seemed to parallel an existing class (e.g., the discovered "fiddler" and the existing class Pianist) were counted as incorrect. Finally, candidates that did not fit the intent of the ontology were marked incorrect. For instance, we considered the Animal ontology to be about types of animals (dogs, cats), so specific animals like "King Kong" or "Fido" were incorrect; other animal ontologies might make different decisions (see Section 7).

This evaluation produced the function $gold_O()$, where $gold_O(i)$ is the set of classes assigned to candidate instance i by the evaluator for ontology O. Then, given a candidate instance i and a class c, we define the pair (i, c) to be:

- **correct** if $c \in gold_O(i)$,
- **sensible** if $\exists c' \in gold_O(i)$ s.t. $c' \in subclasses(c)$,
- or **incorrect** otherwise.

For instance, if $gold_O(dog) = \{Mammal\}$, then $(dog, Mammal)$ is correct, $(dog, Animal)$ is sensible, and $(dog, Reptile)$ is incorrect.

Let X be the output of the system for some experimental condition, where X consists of a set of pairs of the form (i, c), and where each candidate instance i appears in only one pair.[1] Then the *recall* is the number of pairs in X that are correct, and the *precision* is the fraction of pairs in X that are correct. These metrics are useful, but count only instances that were assigned to the most correct class possible, and thus do not fully reflect the informational content of the result. Consequently, we primarily report our results using the *sensible-recall*, which is the number of pairs in X that are sensible. In addition, we follow the example of several others in using *learning accuracy (LA)* instead of exact precision. The LA measures how close each candidate pair (i, c) was to the gold standard $(i, gold_O(i))$. This measurement is averaged over all pairs to yield a precision-like number ranging from zero to one where $LA(X) = 1$ indicates that all candidate pairs were completely correct.

We follow the general definition of Learning Accuracy from Cimiano et al. [3], which requires the least common superconcept (lcs) of two classes a and b for ontology O:

$$lcs_O(a,b) = \arg\min_{c \in O}(\delta(a,c) + \delta(b,c) + \delta(top,c)) \quad (1)$$

where $\delta(a, b)$ is the number of edges on the shortest path between a and b. Given this definition, the taxonomic similarity $Tsim$ between two classes is:

$$Tsim_O(d,e) = \frac{\delta(top,f) + 1}{\delta(top,f) + 1 + \delta(d,f) + \delta(e,f)} \quad (2)$$

where $f = lcs_O(d, e)$. We then define the average learning accuracy for ontology O of a set X of candidate pairs as:

$$LA_X = \frac{1}{|X|} \sum_{(i,c) \in X} max(0, \max_{c' \in gold(i)} Tsim_O(c,c')) \quad (3)$$

5 Assessing Candidate Instances

Extracting candidate instances from the web is a noisy process. Incorrect instances may be extracted for many reasons including noun phrase segmentation

---

[1] OntoSyphon assigns only a single class to each instance, which is often sufficient but restrictive for domains like Artists. Future work should consider more general techniques.

errors, incorrect or incomplete sentence parsing, or factual errors in the web corpus. Because OntoSyphon operates in an unsupervised manner, it is thus critical to be able to automatically assign a confidence value to the instances that are produced. These values can be then used to expunge instances that are below some confidence threshold and/or to provide reliability estimates to applications that later make use of the output data.

Below we describe the five assessment techniques that we consider in our initial results. Each is used to assign a confidence score or probability to a candidate pair (i, c). In what follows, $count(i, c, p)$ is the number of times that the pair (i, c) was extracted using the pattern p, and $hits(y)$ is the number of hits for the term y alone in the corpus.

1. Strength: Intuitively, if the pair $(dog, Mammal)$ is extracted many times from our web corpus, this redundancy gives more confidence that that pair is correct. The Strength metric thus counts the number of times a candidate pair was observed across all extraction patterns P:

$$Score_{strength}(i, c) = \sum_{p \in P} count(i, c, p) \qquad (4)$$

This metric was also used by PANKOW [3], although the counts were obtained in a different manner.

2. Str-Norm: The Strength metric is biased towards instances that appear very frequently on the web. To compensate, Str-Norm normalizes the pattern count by the number of hits for the instance alone:

$$Score_{str-norm}(i, c) = \frac{\sum_{p \in P} count(i, c, p)}{hits(i)} \qquad (5)$$

Similar normalization techniques are found in many systems (e.g., [16,28]).

3. Str-Norm-Thresh: The normalization performed by Str-Norm can be misleading when the candidate instance is a very rare term or a misspelling. Consequently, we created a modified Str-Norm where the normalization factor is constrained to have at least some minimum value. We found that a variety of such thresholds worked well. For this work we sort the instances by $hits(i)$ and then select Hit_{25}, the hit count that occurs at the 25th percentile:

$$Score_{str-norm-thresh}(i, c) = \frac{\sum_{p \in P} count(i, c, p)}{max(hits(i), Hit_{25})} \qquad (6)$$

4. Urns: OntoSyphon, like some other systems, extracts candidate facts by examining a large number of web pages (though we use the aforementioned Binding Engine to perform this process very efficiently). Prior work has developed the Urns model to apply in such cases [30,31] and has shown it to produce significantly more accurate probabilities than previous methods such as PMI (pointwise mutual information) or noisy-or. The Urns model treats each extraction event as a draw of a single labeled ball from one or more urns, with replacement. Each urn contains both correct labels (from the set C), and incorrect labels (from the set E); where each label may be repeated on a different number of balls. For instance, $num(C)$ is the multi-set giving the number of balls for each label $i \in C$. Urns is designed to answer the following question: given that a candidate i was extracted k times in a set of n draws from the urn (i.e., in n extractions from the corpus), what is the probability that i is a correct instance? For a single urn, if s is the total number of balls in the urn, then this probability is computed as follows:

$$P(i \in C | NumExtractions_i(n) = k) = \frac{\sum_{r \in num(C)} \frac{r}{s}^k (1 - \frac{r}{s})^{n-k}}{\sum_{r' \in num(C \cup E)} \frac{r'}{s}^k (1 - \frac{r'}{s})^{n-k}} \quad (7)$$

Urns operates in two phases. In the first phase, the set of all candidate extractions is used to estimate the needed model parameters ($num(C)$ and $num(C \cup E)$), using Expectation Maximization (EM). In particular, $num(C)$ is estimated by assuming that the frequency of correct extractions is Zipf-distributed, and then estimating the exponent z which parameterizes this distribution. In the second phase, a single pass is made over the extractions and each is assigned a probability using the estimated model parameters and an integral approximation to Equation 7 [30].

Urns was designed to assign probabilities to a set of extractions that were targeting a single class, and the EM phase relies upon having a sufficient number of samples (roughly 500) for estimation. In our context, very few classes yield this many extractions on their own. Fortunately, we found that combining the candidates from all of the classes of a single ontology together for model estimation yielded good results, better than performing per-class model fitting with prior parameters for low-sample classes.

5. Urns-Norm: The Urns model, like Strength, does not exploit the frequency with which a candidate appears in the corpus. Instead, each instance is assumed to occur with equal probability anywhere along the aforementioned Zipf distribution. Introducing an appropriate prior probability of an input candidate's location along this curve would improve accuracy, but would significantly complicate the model and computation.

Fortunately, we can approximate the benefit of such a change with a much simpler approach. We begin by sorting the input data set X by $hits(i)$. We then run EM both on the "lower" half (which contains the less frequent terms), obtaining parameter z_L and on the whole data set, obtaining the aforementioned z. We then compute a parameter z_i for each instance i as follows:

$$z_i = max(z_L, z + log(hits(i)) - \sum_{(j,c) \in X} \frac{log(hits(j))}{|X|}) \quad (8)$$

The probability for candidate (i, c) is then computed using z_i. Intuitively, the log functions increase z_i when a candidate i is more frequent than average, thus forcing i to have more pattern matches to obtain a high probability. On the other hand, the max function ensures that very infrequent words (particularly misspellings) do not obtain an artificially high probability, by insisting that the minimum z_i is a value appropriate for the "lower" half of the inputs (z_L).

Strength, Str-Norm, and Urns have been used in some form in other work, though Urns required some adaption for our multi-class problem. Both Str-Norm-Thresh and Urns-Norm, however, are novel contributions of this work that we found to be very effective, and that should also provide significant improvements in other systems.

6 Experimental Evaluation

In this section we experimentally evaluate OntoSyphon. We first consider its overall performance and the impact of different assessment techniques, then examine how to further improve accuracy by exploiting ontological structure.

6.1 Assessing Instances

Figures 2-4 show the results of executing OntoSyphon on our sample ontologies. Each line represents one output of the system using a particular assessment technique. To create one point on the line, we chose a threshold and then removed from the output set all candidate pairs whose assigned confidence values were below that threshold. The x-axis measures the sensible-recall of this modified set, and the y-axis shows the LA of this set. Varying the threshold thus produces a line with properties similar to a classical precision/recall tradeoff curve.

The data demonstrates that OntoSyphon was able to find a substantial number of sensible instances for all 3 domains. In addition, the data shows that some of our tested assessment techniques are quite effective at identifying the more reliable instances. In particular, the techniques that perform normalization (Str-Norm, Str-Norm-Thresh, and Urns-Norm) show consistent improvements over both techniques that do not (Strength and Urns). Consider, for instance, the "50% recall" point, where each technique has a sensible-recall equal to half of the maximum achieved under any situation (e.g., where sensible-recall equals 900 for Animals). At this point, Urns-Norm and Str-Norm-Thresh increase LA compared to the no-normalization techniques by 82-110% for Animals, 19% for Artists, and 51-56% for Food.

Overall, both Urns-Norm and Str-Norm-Thresh perform consistently well. Str-Norm also performs well, except that it has many false positives at low recall. It gets fooled by many incorrect terms that are very infrequent on the web, and thus have a high score after normalization, even though they were extracted only once or a few times. For instance, Str-Norm incorrectly gives a high score to the misspelled terms "mosquities" for Animals, "Andrea Cotez" for Artists, and "pototato" for Food.

OntoSyphon found the most sensible instances for Artists, but our assessment techniques worked least well on this domain, showing a fairly flat curve. One reason is that the assessment techniques are fooled by a large number of spurious candidates that come from one ambiguous class, Players. This class (intended for musical instrument players), finds mostly sports team participants (e.g. "Greg Maddux") and a few digital music software products ("WinAmp"). Figure 5 shows the results if this class is removed from OntoSyphon's search process

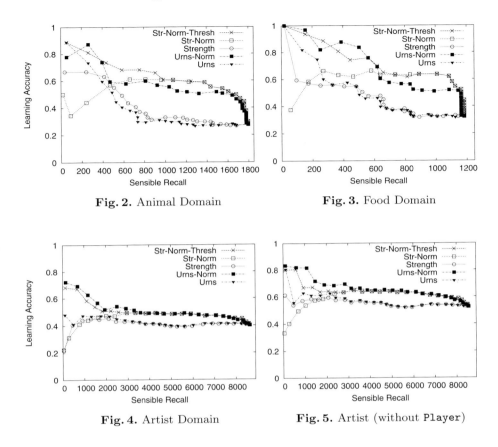

Fig. 2. Animal Domain

Fig. 3. Food Domain

Fig. 4. Artist Domain

Fig. 5. Artist (without `Player`)

(Section 7 describes how this could be done automatically). With Str-Norm-Thresh, LA increases from 0.49 to 0.64 at 50% recall.

A more fundamental problem is the smaller amount of redundancy in our corpus for the Artists domain. For instance, a sensible instance for Animals is extracted by OntoSyphon's patterns on average 10.9 times vs. 2.1 times for an incorrect instance (23.9 vs 3.5 hits for Food). However, Artists, even with `Player` removed, averages only 3.0 hits for sensible instances vs. 2.1 hits for incorrect instances. This smaller split yields a much more difficult assessment task, and additional work is needed to more fully exploit the potential of such domains.

6.2 Leveraging Ontological Structure

When confronted with multiple possible classes for a candidate instance (e.g., is "lemur" an `Animal`, `Mammal`, or `Reptile`?), the results above chose the instance/class pair with the highest score. We also tried normalizing the metrics above by class frequency to influence this choice of classes, but we found that this produced erratic results without improving accuracy. Instead, we found better results by more explicitly leveraging the ontology to pick the best class via an average score computed over all classes. The component that each class contributes is weighted by class frequency and by the taxonomic similarity $Tsim$:[2]

$$Class(i) = \arg\max_{c \in O} \sum_{c' \in O} Score(i, c') \frac{Tsim_O(c, c')}{hits(c')} \quad (9)$$

For our corpus and domains, only about 25% of distinct instance terms were extracted for more than one subclass. Thus, this enhancement had a very small effect on overall results. However, looking only at that 25% of the results where a class decision must be made, we found that this new technique consistently improved LA for both Animals and Artists, and had negligible effect for Food. For instance, for Str-Norm-Thresh at 50% recall, LA improved from 0.88 to 0.95 for Animals and from 0.62 to 0.76 for Artists.

Thus, exploiting taxonomic relationships in the ontology can improve accuracy, though the small number of possible classes found for each instance limits the impact of this technique. There remains room for improvement, because even with this enhancement in the full results only 44-69% (average 60%) of the instances that were assigned a valid class by the evaluator were assigned that same fully correct class by the system. In the future, we would like to explore combining this technique with web-wide statistics computed via pointwise mutual information (PMI) [16]. Using PMI would require a significant number of additional search queries, and would need to be expanded to deal with our multi-class scenario. However, this approach should boost performance by providing additional supporting data while still enabling us to leverage our efficient gathering of candidate instances from our base 90 million page corpus.

7 Discussion and Future Work

Overall, we conclude that OntoSyphon was highly effective at extracting instances from a web corpus, and that our new assessment techniques (Str-Norm-Thresh and Urns-Norm) significantly improved the accuracy of the results. In particular, using Str-Norm-Thresh OntoSyphon was able to achieve a LA of about 0.6 while extracting 1400 sensible Animal instances (78% of the total found), 1100 Food instances (93% of the total), and (after removing `Player`) 7500 Artist instances (87% of the total). Even higher accuracy may be obtained for Animals and Food at a cost of reduced recall.

A Learning Accuracy of 0.6 is on par with the results surveyed by Cimiano et al. [3]. They report LA of between 0.44 and 0.76 (with an average of 0.61 for independent systems) and recall ranging from 0.17 to 0.31 (with an average of 0.24).

---

[2] Maedche et al. previously used a similar, non-normalized technique ("tree ascent") for ontology learning, with some mixed success [24].

These results are not directly comparable with ours, since these systems perform a different task (annotating individual documents rather populating a ontology from many documents), use different ontologies, and in some cases evaluate LA using only those terms marked by the evaluator as valid for some class.[3] Also, these systems generally define recall as the percentage of results from the complete gold standard that was found by the system. For our open-web system, however, recall is reported as a raw number or as a percentage of the set of all answers found by any execution of the system (as with [16]). Nonetheless, the magnitude of these previous results demonstrate that an LA of 0.6 is reasonable, and our results show that OntoSyphon can find many instances at this accuracy level.

Normalization was essential to our results. Such normalization is particularly important for OntoSyphon, as opposed to document-driven systems, because the candidate terms are not guaranteed to come from domain-relevant, somewhat reliable input documents. These same factors caused us to achieve the best, most consistent results only when that normalization was constrained by a minimum threshold to account for very rare or misspelled words.

Our two metrics that performed such normalization, Str-Norm-Thresh and Urns-Norm, both performed well and about comparably. These results are consistent with earlier, non-normalized findings: while Urns was found to be greatly superior to many other techniques in terms of producing accurate probabilities [30], simple Strength-like measures performed almost as well if only a relative confidence ranking, not a probability was required [31]. Because Urns and Urns-Norm are more complex to compute, many situations may thus call for using the simpler Str-Norm-Thresh. On the other hand, users of the final, populated ontology may find actual probabilities very helpful for further processing, in which case Urns-Norm may be best.

Finally, OntoSyphon in its present form is clearly not suited for populating every kind of ontology. For instance, ontologies describing things or events that are mentioned only a handful of times on the web are not well suited to our current strategy of using simple pattern-based extractions followed by redundancy-based assessment. Likewise, classes that are either complex (`NonBlandFish`) or ambiguous (`Player`) will not yield good results. We intend to develop techniques to address these issues, for instance, by recognizing ambiguous classes by the small degree of overlap between a class and its parent (as is the case with `Player` and `Artist`) or by adding additional search terms to disambiguate such classes during extraction. Lastly, deciding whether a term such as "dog" should be a subclass or an instance can be challenging even for human ontologists. More work is needed to help OntoSyphon honor the intent of an ontology, e.g., by considering subclasses and instances already present in that ontology.

---

[3] For instance, C-PANKOW [3] appears to compute LA using only instances that were assigned a class by both the system and an evaluator. For our system (see Equation 3) it seemed more accurate to instead assign a value of zero to a pair (i, c) produced by the system but for which $gold_O(i) = \emptyset$ (e.g. for $(truck, Animal)$). This decision lowers our LA values in comparison.

8 Conclusion

The Semantic Web critically needs a base of structured content to power its applications. Because of the great variety of information, no one approach will provide everything that is needed. Much content can only be created by human annotators, and incentives are needed to motivate this work. Other data is contained in documents that can be effectively leveraged via the document-driven approaches described in Section 2. This paper has focused on an alternative ontology-driven method to extract large amounts of comparatively shallow information from millions of web pages. This approach lets us leverage the existing work of skilled ontology designers, extract information from a very large corpus, and focus extraction efforts where it is most valuable and relevant.

While additional work is needed to demonstrate that OntoSyphon is robust across an even wider range of ontologies and can extract non-instance information, our initial results have demonstrated the feasibility of OntoSyphon's ontology-driven, domain-independent approach. We successfully extracted a large number of instances from a variety of independently-created ontologies. We demonstrated how different assessment techniques affect the accuracy of the output, and introduced simple improvements to existing assessment techniques that significantly improved upon these results. Because these techniques, Str-Norm-Thresh and Urns-Norm, are easy to implement modifications to techniques that have been used for other tasks, our improvements should carry over easily to many other systems (e.g., [3,16,10,17,12]). Future work will examine the many promising directions for further improvements in this area.

Acknowledgements. Thanks to Christopher Brown, Martin Carlisle, Frederick Crabbe, Oren Etzioni, Jeff Heflin, and the anonymous referees for their helpful comments on aspects of this work. This work was partially supported by the Naval Research Council, ONR grants N0001405WR20153 & N00014-02-1-0324, NSF grant IIS-0312988, DARPA contract NBCHD030010, as well as gifts from Google, and carried out in part at the University of Washington's Turing Center.

References

1. Guha, R., McCool, R., Miller, E.: Semantic search. In: World Wide Web. (2003)
2. Chapman, S., Dingli, A., Ciravegna, F.: Armadillo: harvesting information for the semantic web. In: Proc. of the 27th Annual Int. ACM SIGIR conference on Research and development in information retrieval. (2004)
3. Cimiano, P., Ladwig, G., Staab, S.: Gimme' the context: Context-driven automatic semantic annotation with C-PANKOW. In: Proc. of the Fourteenth Int. WWW Conference. (2005)
4. Soderland, S.: Learning to extract text-based information from the World Wide Web. In: Knowledge Discovery and Data Mining. (1997) 251–254
5. Popescu, A.M., Etzioni, O.: Extracting product features and opinions from reviews. In: Proceedings of the Conference on Empirical Methods in Natural Language Processing (EMNLP). (2005)

6. Craven, M., DiPasquo, D., Freitag, D., McCallum, A.K., Mitchell, T.M., Nigam, K., Slattery, S.: Learning to construct knowledge bases from the World Wide Web. Artificial Intelligence **118**(1/2) (2000) 69–113
7. Davalcu, H., Vadrevu, S., Nagarajan, S.: OntoMiner: Bootstrapping and populating ontologies from domain specific web sites. IEEE Intelligent Systems **18**(5) (2003) 24–33
8. Celjuska, D., Vargas-Vera, M.: Ontosophie: A semi-automatic system for ontology population from text. In: International Conference on Natural Language Processing (ICON). (2004)
9. Lerman, K., Gazen, C., Minton, S., Knoblock, C.A.: Populating the semantic web. In: Proceedings of the AAAI 2004 Workshop on Advances in Text Extraction and Mining. (2004)
10. Matuszek, C., Witbrock, M., Kahlert, R., Cabral, J., Schneider, D., Shah, P., Lenat, D.: Searching for common sense: Populating cyc from the web. In: Proc. of AAAI. (2005)
11. Schneider, D., Matuszek, C., Shah, P., Kahlert, R., Baxter, D., Cabral, J., Witbrock, M., Lenat, D.: Gathering and managing facts for intelligence analysis. In: Proceedings of the International Conference on Intelligence Analysis. (2005)
12. van Hage, W., Katrenko, S., Schreiber, G.: A method to combine linguistic ontology-mapping techniques. In: Fourth International Semantic Web Conference (ISWC). (2005)
13. Richardson, S., Dolan, W., Vanderwende, L.: Mindnet: acquiring and structuring semantic information from text. In: COLING. (1998)
14. Agichtein, E., Gravano, L.: Snowball: Extracting relations from large plain-text collections. In: Proceedings of the Fifth ACM International Conference on Digital Libraries. (2000)
15. Cederberg, S., Widdows, D.: Using LSA and noun coordination information to improve the precision and recall of automatic hyponymy extraction. In: Seventh Conference on Computational Natural Language Learning (CoNLL). (2003)
16. Etzioni, O., Cafarella, M., Downey, D., Kok, S., Popescu, A., Shaked, T., Soderland, S., Weld, D., Yates, A.: Unsupervised named-entity extraction from the web: An experimental study. Artificial Intelligence **165**(1) (2005) 91–134
17. Pantel, P., Ravichandran, D., Hovy, E.: Towards terascale knowledge acquisition. In: 20th International Conference on Computational Linguistics (COLING). (2004)
18. Hahn, U., Schnattinger, K.: Towards text knowledge engineering. In: AAAI/IAAI. (1998)
19. Handschuh, S., Staab, S., Ciravegna, F.: S-CREAM - semi-automatic creation of metadata. In: EKAW. (2002)
20. Dill, S., Eiron, N., Gibson, D., Gruhl, D., Guha, R.: Semtag and seeker: Bootstrapping the semantic web via automated semantic annotation. In: Proc. of the Twelth Int. WWW Conference. (2003)
21. Kiryakov, A., Popov, B., Terziev, I., Manov, D., Ognyanoff, D.: Semantic annotation, indexing, and retrieval. Journal of Web Semantics **2**(1) (2004) 49–79
22. Hearst, M.: Automatic acquisition of hyponyms from large text corpora. In: Proc. of the 14th Intl. Conf. on Computational Linguistics. (1992)
23. Cimiano, P., Hotho, A., Staab, S.: Learning concept hierarchies from text corpora using formal concept analysis. Journal of Artificial Intelligence Research **24** (2005) 305–339
24. Maedche, A., Pekar, V., Staab, S.: Ontology learning part one – on discovering taxonomic relations from the web. In: Web Intelligence, Springer (2002)

25. Alfonesca, E., Manandhar, S.: Improving an ontology refinement method with hyponymy patterns. In: Language Resources and Evaluation (LREC). (2002)
26. Cimiano, P., Volker, J.: Text2onto - a framework for ontology learning and data-driven change discovery. In: Int. Conf. on Applications of Natural Language to Information Systems. (2005)
27. Snow, R., Jurafsky, D., Ng, A.Y.: Learning syntactic patterns for automatic hypernym discovery. In: NIPS 17. (2004)
28. Cimiano, P., Pivk, A., Schmidt-Thieme, L., Staab, S.: Learning taxonomic relations from heterogeneous evidence. In: ECAI-2004 Workshop on Ontology Learning and Population. (2004)
29. Cafarella, M., Etzioni, O.: A search engine for natural language applications. In: Proc. of the Fourteenth Int. WWW Conference. (2005)
30. Downey, D., Etzioni, O., Soderland, S.: A probabilistic model of redundancy in information extraction. In: Proc. of IJCAI. (2005)
31. Cafarella, M., Downey, D., Soderland, S., Etzioni, O.: KnowItNow: fast, scalable information extraction from the web. In: Proc. of HLT-EMNLP. (2005)

Ontology Query Answering on Databases

Jing Mei[1,2], Li Ma[2], and Yue Pan[2]

[1] Department of Information Science
Peking University
Beijing 100871, China
mayyam@is.pku.edu.cn
[2] IBM China Research Lab
Beijing 100094, China
{malli, panyue}@cn.ibm.com

Abstract. With the fast development of Semantic Web, more and more RDF and OWL ontologies are created and shared. The effective management, such as storage, inference and query, of these ontologies on databases gains increasing attention. This paper addresses ontology query answering on databases by means of Datalog programs. Via epistemic operators, integrity constraints are introduced, and used for conveying semantic aspects of OWL that are not covered by Datalog-style rule languages. We believe such a processing suitable to capture ontologies in the database flavor, while keeping reasoning tractable. Here, we present a logically equivalent knowledge base whose (sound and complete) inference system appears as a Datalog program. As such, SPARQL query answering on OWL ontologies could be solved in databases. Bi-directional strategies, taking advantage of both forward and backward chaining, are then studied to support this kind of customized Datalog programs, returning exactly answers to the query within our logical framework.

1 Introduction

The Resource Description Framework (RDF) [25] has been recognized as a popular way to represent information in the Semantic Web, accompanying with a standardized query language, SPARQL [27]. An important vocabulary extension of RDF is the Web Ontology Language (OWL) [24], whose formalisms rely closely on the Description Logic (DL) [2]. The Semantic Web Rule Language (SWRL) [28] arises, when rules are considered to work with OWL in a syntactically and semantically coherent manner.

Given an RDF document, having information of ontologies (i.e. upgraded to an OWL document) even rules (i.e. further upgraded to a SWRL document), a SPARQL query is to extract implicit and explicit RDF data, with query answering as an underlying reasoning service. Compared with weak DL query languages, SPARQL is expressible for the union of conjunctive queries on RDF triples, not only concerning traditional DL queries (e.g. instantiation, realization and retrieval [14]), but also allowing predicates (could be DL classes and properties) being queried as variables.

Database (DB) technologies provide a solid support for various data-intensive applications and could be used for ontology management. So, SPARQL queries on ontologies possibly work in a similar way as SQL queries on relational data in databases. Meanwhile, the intention of making the Semantic Web more acceptable to the industry is another underlying promotion to impede the connection to database communities [9]. However, relational DBs are not rich enough to capture semantics implied in ontologies. Thus, Datalog is regarded as a suitable intermedium, and the next section motivates this opinion in detail.

Technically, this paper generalizes a (negation-free) Datalog program P w.r.t. a given DL KB $\Sigma = <\mathcal{T}, \mathcal{A}>$, whose EDB (extensional database) consists of the inferred DL TBox $\mathcal{T}^*$ and the original DL ABox $\mathcal{A}$, and whose IDB (intensional database) is composed of 7 inference rules devised by DL semantics. We state that P is a syntax variant of an inference system Γ, and Γ is proved sound and complete with a specified MKNF-DL [10] KB Σ', where Σ', assuming satisfiable, extends Σ with *integrity constraints* (ICs). By *epistemic interpretations*, those ICs exactly reflect the semantic discrepancy between DL and DB, making query answering in DL accessible to the DB community. As such, we elaborate a strategy, which benefits from the tractable data complexity of Datalog, to address popular SPARQL queries on databases, provided by RDF data obtained from OWL documents. Within such a framework, it is possible to futher support SWRL rules which are user-defined Datalog rules sharing predicates with the ontology classes and properties.

The paper is organized as follows. Section 2 is our motivation including an analysis to encountered problems and existing approaches. Section 3 introduces the preliminaries and notions used in this paper. In Section 4, a so-called DL2DB KB Σ' w.r.t. a given DL KB Σ is defined, along with a natural deduction system Γ consisting of DL-driven inference rules. Also, the correspondence of Σ' to its original Σ, as well as the soundness and completeness of Γ with Σ', are presented. A Datalog program, corresponding to Γ, is demonstrated in Section 5 for query answering in Σ. There, we discuss computation strategies and evaluation approaches as well. Section 6 envisions the desirable extension with user-defined rules, and shows preliminary experiments in our prototype implementation. Finally, the conclusion is drawn in Section 7. (Readers can find more details on the proofs in the paper at http://www.is.pku.edu.cn/~mayyam/appendix.pdf.)

2 Motivation

Our objective is to perform SPARQL query answering on databases which are used to store RDF data (including OWL ontologies). However, it has been studied in DL-Lite [6] that data complexity of query answering in DL has a LOGSPACE boundary, above which query answering is not expressible as a first-order logic formula and hence a SQL query. However, most DLs are more expressive than DL-Lite. The worst case is an unrestricted combination of OWL and rules, such as SWRL, leading to the undecidability of interesting reasoning problems [28]. An EXPTIME complexity is reobtained, for query answering in a less expressive extension to OWL with DL-safe rules [19], but the exponential data complexity greatly weakens the efficiency.

The discrepancy between DL and DB is actually remarkable. As well-known, DL is based on an open world assumption (OWA) permitting incomplete information in an ABox, while DB adopts a closed world assumption (CWA) requiring information always understood as complete. The unique name assumption (UNA) is often emphasized in DB but not in DL. OWL Flight [9], furthermore, clarifies restrictions in DL and constraints in DB, of which the former is to infer and the latter to check. When negation comes, DBs prefer to "non-monotonic negation", while DLs rely on "monotonic negation".

Facing to these open issues, various proposals have been presented. According to the engines which do reasoning indeed, existing ontology persistent systems can be roughly divided into two categories: DL-based and rule-based. The Instance Store [4] is a representative of DL-based systems, where DB serves mainly for voluminous storage and convenient retrieval, and classical DL tableaux algorithms help make implicit information explicit. In the Instance Store, whatever queries are (particularly, those queries involving properties and variables can be handled by rolling-up techniques [14]), a reduction to checking the KB unsatisfiability provides support for query answering. Rule-based approaches are a bit different, which intuitively translate the meaning of DL constructors into rules. Due to the expressive power of rules, those DL constructors (e.g. existential restrictions) are either partially forbidden (as DLP [12] does) or assigned new meanings (as OWL Flight [9] does). Unlike DL tableaux algorithms, the evaluation of queries adopts strategies by forward chaining or backward chaining. More tractably, DL-lite [6] is proposed to execute the ABox using a SQL engine, whose language itself is restrictive while keeping low complexity of reasoning, namely polynomial in the size of instances in the knowledge base.

Since rule-based approaches are more extensible to SWRL, we make an attempt to give inference rules as a translation of DL semantics, while RDF data (from OWL documents) is stored in databases. Concentrating on query answering, this paper introduces a DL2DB deduction system Γ and studies which sub-language of DLs is equivalent to the so-called DL2DB. Surely, DLP (Description Logic Programs [12]) is a nice measure, as cited by most related work. However, inspired by MKNF-DL (Description Logics of Minimal Knowledge and Negation as Failure [10]), also motivated by bridging DL and DB, we exploit integrity constraints to a DL KB Σ, resulting in a special MKNF-DL KB Σ'. Checking satisfiability of (DB) integrity constraints has been well investigated (e.g. in [5]), and our proposed ICs, in the DL setting, admit of $C \sqcup D$ (respectively, $\exists P.C$) being *known* only if holding an autoepistemic belief of either C or D (respectively, P and C). That is, we contribute Σ' as a logically equivalent version of Σ in the sense of query answering. Particularly, the DL2DB system Γ proves sound and complete with Σ' for non-epistemic queries. With a focus on query answering, we assume both Σ and Σ' are satisfiable. Generally speaking, it makes little sense, in classical logics, when everything is possible to be entailed by inconsistent KBs. Also, checking satisfiability of a DL KB or a MKNF-DL KB has been studied in [2] and [10], but not scoped in this paper.

We remark this paper does not propose to "change" or "weaken" the semantics of a DL KB. Instead, for keeping DL in classical first-order semantics, we move to a MKNF-DL "world" whose unique epistemic model is identical to that of DL, provided by integrity constraints on demand. In other words, we capture an epistemic perception for those rule-based approaches, and gain an insight into integrity constraints for DL constructors, rather than tying to change or weaken the classical DL semantics.

On the other hand, we do realize nonmonotonic features are gaining increasing interest in the context of the Semantic Web initiatives [26], and the paper [8] provides a good survey. A latest work is [18], which proposes hybrid MKNF KBs integrating decidable DLs with nonmonotonic rules. However, our paper here belongs to the direction of research for query answering over ontologies relying over database technologies by making use, in a "natural" way as a rational agent does, of well established formalizations and computing mechanisms.

3   Preliminaries

Consider the main layers of the DL family bottom-up [2][13], $\mathcal{ALC}$ is a basic and simple language, permitting class descriptions via $C \sqcap D, C \sqcup D, \neg C, \forall P.C$, and $\exists P.C$, where C, D are classes and P is a property. Augmented by transitive properties, $\mathcal{ALC}$ becomes $\mathcal{ALC}_{R^+}$, denoted by $\mathcal{S}$ in the following. $\mathcal{SI}$ is an extension to $\mathcal{S}$ with inverse properties, followed by $\mathcal{SHI}$ with property hierarchies. It is called $\mathcal{SHIF}$ if extending by functional restrictions, $\mathcal{SHIN}$ if by cardinality restrictions, and $\mathcal{SHIQ}$ if by qualified number restrictions. Support for datatype predicates (e.g. string, integer) brings up the concrete domain of **D**, and using nominals $\mathcal{O}$ helps construct classes with singleton sets.

With the expected pervasive use of OWL, $\mathcal{SHIF}(\mathbf{D})$ and $\mathcal{SHOIN}(\mathbf{D})$ are paid more attention: one is the syntax variant to OWL Lite and the other is to OWL DL. This paper currently takes $\mathcal{SHI}$ into account, and more expressive extensions will be explored in our ongoing work. Alternately, DB built-in features, such as arithmetic operators and aggregate functions, might be considered as a workaround for $\mathcal{F}, \mathcal{N}, \mathcal{Q}$ and **D**, while list operations for $\mathcal{O}$. In the following, if not stated otherwise, C, D denote $\mathcal{SHI}$ classes and P, Q denote $\mathcal{SHI}$ properties.

A DL KB Σ is defined as a pair $\Sigma = <\mathcal{T}, \mathcal{A}>$. The TBox $\mathcal{T}$ is a finite set of class and property subsumptions having the form of $C \sqsubseteq D$ and $P \sqsubseteq Q$, resp. The ABox $\mathcal{A}$ is a finite set of class and property assertions having the form of $C(a)$ and $P(a, b)$. Also, an *interpretation* $\mathcal{I} = (\Delta, \bullet^\mathcal{I})$ consists of a nonempty set Δ (the domain of $\mathcal{I}$) and a function $\bullet^\mathcal{I}$ (the interpretation function of $\mathcal{I}$) that maps every class to a subset of Δ and every property to a subset of $\Delta \times \Delta$. An interpretation $\mathcal{I}$ is a model of a DL KB Σ (denoted as $\mathcal{I} \models \Sigma$) iff every sentence (subsumption or assertion) of Σ is satisfied in $\mathcal{I}$. For a complete presentation of other definitions, such as the satisfiability of sentences, we direct readers to the classical DL handbook [2]. Query answering for $q(\bar{x})$ in Σ attempts to receive all ground substitutions $\bar{t}$ to $\bar{x}$ such that $\Sigma \models q(\bar{t})$, and two KBs Σ and Σ' are equivalent in the sense of query answering iff those obtained results are identical in both Σ and Σ' [6].

Next, a more sophisticated language, namely MKNF-DL [10], is sketched. One epistemic operator **K** works for minimal knowledge, and the other epistemic operator **A** plays a role to default assumption. The syntax of MKNF-DL extends DL with $\mathbf{K}C, \mathbf{K}P, \mathbf{A}C$ and $\mathbf{A}P$, where C is a DL class and P is a DL property. The semantics of MKNF-DL resorts to *epistemic interpretations*. An epistemic interpretation is a triple $(\mathcal{I}, \mathcal{M}, \mathcal{N})$ where $\mathcal{I}$ is a (first-order) interpretation and $\mathcal{M}, \mathcal{N}$ are sets of (first-order) interpretations. Non-epistemic classes and properties are interpreted same as in $\mathcal{I}$, i.e. $C^{\mathcal{I},\mathcal{M},\mathcal{N}} = C^{\mathcal{I}}$ and $P^{\mathcal{I},\mathcal{M},\mathcal{N}} = P^{\mathcal{I}}$. The other semantic conditions state that:

$$\top^{\mathcal{I},\mathcal{M},\mathcal{N}} = \Delta;\ \bot^{\mathcal{I},\mathcal{M},\mathcal{N}} = \emptyset;\ (\neg C)^{\mathcal{I},\mathcal{M},\mathcal{N}} = \Delta \backslash C^{\mathcal{I},\mathcal{M},\mathcal{N}};$$
$$(C \sqcap D)^{\mathcal{I},\mathcal{M},\mathcal{N}} = C^{\mathcal{I},\mathcal{M},\mathcal{N}} \cap D^{\mathcal{I},\mathcal{M},\mathcal{N}};\ (C \sqcup D)^{\mathcal{I},\mathcal{M},\mathcal{N}} = C^{\mathcal{I},\mathcal{M},\mathcal{N}} \cup D^{\mathcal{I},\mathcal{M},\mathcal{N}};$$
$$(\exists P.C)^{\mathcal{I},\mathcal{M},\mathcal{N}} = \{a \in \Delta | \exists b.(a,b) \in P^{\mathcal{I},\mathcal{M},\mathcal{N}}\text{ and }b \in C^{\mathcal{I},\mathcal{M},\mathcal{N}}\};$$
$$(\forall P.C)^{\mathcal{I},\mathcal{M},\mathcal{N}} = \{a \in \Delta | \forall b.(a,b) \in P^{\mathcal{I},\mathcal{M},\mathcal{N}}\text{ implies }b \in C^{\mathcal{I},\mathcal{M},\mathcal{N}}\};$$
$$(\mathbf{K}C)^{\mathcal{I},\mathcal{M},\mathcal{N}} = \bigcap_{\mathcal{J} \in \mathcal{M}}(C^{\mathcal{J},\mathcal{M},\mathcal{N}});\ (\mathbf{K}P)^{\mathcal{I},\mathcal{M},\mathcal{N}} = \bigcap_{\mathcal{J} \in \mathcal{M}}(P^{\mathcal{J},\mathcal{M},\mathcal{N}});$$
$$(\mathbf{A}C)^{\mathcal{I},\mathcal{M},\mathcal{N}} = \bigcap_{\mathcal{J} \in \mathcal{N}}(C^{\mathcal{J},\mathcal{M},\mathcal{N}});\ (\mathbf{A}P)^{\mathcal{I},\mathcal{M},\mathcal{N}} = \bigcap_{\mathcal{J} \in \mathcal{N}}(P^{\mathcal{J},\mathcal{M},\mathcal{N}});$$

For any property Q being the inverse of P, if $(a,b) \in P^{\mathcal{I},\mathcal{M},\mathcal{N}}$ then $(b,a) \in Q^{\mathcal{I},\mathcal{M},\mathcal{N}}$; For any transitive property P, if $(a,b),(b,c) \in P^{\mathcal{I},\mathcal{M},\mathcal{N}}$ then $(a,c) \in P^{\mathcal{I},\mathcal{M},\mathcal{N}}$.

A set of interpretations $\mathcal{M}$ is an epistemic model for Σ (denoted as $\mathcal{M} \models \Sigma$) iff the structure $(\mathcal{M},\mathcal{M})$ satisfies Σ and, for each set of interpretations $\mathcal{M}'$, if $\mathcal{M} \subset \mathcal{M}'$ then $(\mathcal{M}',\mathcal{M})$ does not satisfy Σ. A structure $(\mathcal{M},\mathcal{N})$ satisfies Σ (denoted as $(\mathcal{M},\mathcal{N}) \models \Sigma$) iff each interpretation $\mathcal{I} \in \mathcal{M}$ is such that every sentence (subsumption or assertion) of Σ is satisfied in the epistemic interpretation $(\mathcal{I},\mathcal{M},\mathcal{N})$. The paper of MKNF-DL [10] provides a complete presentation of other definitions, such as the satisfiability of sentences, and we follow its convention. Notice that, for any (non-epistemic) DL KB Σ, it has one and only one epistemic model, i.e. the set of all first-order models for Σ, denoted as $\mathcal{M}(\Sigma)$.

Finally, this paper adopts assumptions that are suitable for the semantics of MKNF (cf. [8][10][18]): (1) Every first-order interpretation is over the same fixed, countably infinite domain; (2) There is a one-to-one correspondence between individuals in the language and elements in the domain. Thus, the set of all individuals $\mathcal{O}$ is fixed to $\mathcal{I}$, i.e., $\Delta = \mathcal{O}$, and we denote the interpretation of $a \in \mathcal{O}$ simply as a itself, i.e., $a^{\mathcal{I}} = a$. The assumption of (2) also implies that two distinct individuals denote two distinct elements, referred as to UNA.

4 Bridging DL and DB

Given a DL KB Σ, a specified MKNF-DL KB, namely the DL2DB KB Σ', is studied. We guarantee the equivalency of Σ' and Σ in the sense of query answering, for non-epistemic queries. And then, we generalize an inference system, namely the DL2DB system Γ, and this contribution of Γ is posed by its soundness and completeness with Σ', building a bridge between DL and DB.

4.1 The DL2DB KB

Inspired by representing integrity constraints (ICs) in MKNF-DL [10], we propose ICs for some DL constructors to strengthen beliefs, meeting the requirement that w.r.t. certain information the KB is prone to be complete.

Before introducing definitions, we recall how to formalize ICs using an example from [10]. For instance, a TBox $\mathcal{T}$: **K**employee$\sqsubseteq$ **A**male$\sqcup$**A**female corresponds to an IC that "each known employee must be known to be either male or female". Having only one assertion in ABox $\mathcal{A}$: employee(Bob), makes this KB $<\mathcal{T}, \mathcal{A}>$ lack of epistemic models. That is, this IC is violated. Turning to a system level, we require each known DL class of $C \sqcup D$ must be known to be either C or D, viz. sub1 as defined below, while sub2 is for $\exists P.C$. Considering the discrepancy between DL and DB, we believe that ICs bridge them in a semantic "pay-as-you-go" manner.

We use $\text{clos}(C)$ for the closure of a class C, and $\text{clos}(C)$ is the smallest set containing C that is closed under subclasses and negation (in Negation Normal Form), while the size of $\text{clos}(C)$ is linear in the length of C [13]. Given a set of classes M, $\text{clos}(M) = \bigcup_{C \in M} \text{clos}(C)$, the size of $\text{clos}(M)$ is polynomial in the size of M.

Definition 1. *Let $\Sigma = <\mathcal{T}, \mathcal{A}>$ be a DL KB, and Σ_C be the set of classes occurring in Σ. A DL2DB KB w.r.t. Σ is $\Sigma' = <\mathcal{T}', \mathcal{A}>$ where $\mathcal{T}' = \mathcal{T} \cup$ sub1 $\sqcup$ sub2,*
sub1=$\{\mathbf{K}(C \sqcup D) \sqsubseteq \mathbf{A}C \sqcup \mathbf{A}D \mid C \sqcup D \in \text{clos}(\Sigma_C)\}$ *and*
sub2=$\{\mathbf{K}(\exists P.C) \sqsubseteq \exists \mathbf{A}P.\mathbf{A}C \mid \exists P.C \in \text{clos}(\Sigma_C)\}$.

The following proposition helps gain insights into the nature of epistemic models for Σ' and Σ. Due to space limitation, the detailed proof can be found at http://www.is.pku.edu.cn/~mayyam/appendix.pdf.

Proposition 1. *Let Σ be a DL KB, and Σ' be a DL2DB KB w.r.t. Σ. A set of interpretations $\mathcal{M}$ is an epistemic model for Σ' iff (1) $\mathcal{M}$ is an epistemic model for Σ; (2) for each subsumption $\varphi \in$sub1$\cup$sub2 in Σ', $(\mathcal{M}, \mathcal{M})$ satisfies φ.*

As pointed out above, the (non-epistemic) DL KB Σ has a unique epistemic model, namely $\mathcal{M}(\Sigma)$, consisting of all first-order models for Σ. This proposition indicates that Σ' has the same unique epistemic model as $\mathcal{M}(\Sigma)$ if the structure $(\mathcal{M}(\Sigma), \mathcal{M}(\Sigma))$ satisfies all subsumptions in sub1$\cup$sub2, otherwise Σ' is unsatisfiable. Thus, under the assumption that both Σ and Σ' are satisfiable, the two KBs Σ and Σ' are equivalent in the sense of query answering.

It possibly happens that Σ is satisfiable but Σ' is not, which implies some of those ICs have been violated. In this case, we fail to returning complete answers to queries via Σ', although incomplete information in Σ would not attack Σ itself. For example, a DL KB Σ, having a TBox $\mathcal{T}$: male$\sqsubseteq$person and female$\sqsubseteq$person in addition to an ABox $\mathcal{A}$: male$\sqcup$female(Bob), is satisfiable and entails person(Bob) but neither male(Bob) nor female(Bob). Obviously, the IC of **K**(male$\sqcup$female)$\sqsubseteq$ **A**male$\sqcup$**A**female is violated, making this Σ' unsatisfiable. In real DB-based applications, it is highly possible to have complete information on Bob's gender, which leads to person(Bob) in Σ' and reobtaining the satisfiability of Σ'.

4.2 The DL2DB System

DL TBox reasoning has been well-developed, but scalable DL ABox reasoning deserves more investigation. Instead of using classical DL tableaux calculus, we aim at exploiting an alternative way to ABox reasoning on databases, which are initialized by an inferred TBox and an original ABox.

Since the complexity of deciding $\mathcal{SHI}$ DL class satisfiability is EXPTIME-complete [13], computing the closure of the TBox is in coEXPTIME, provided that C is subsumed by D iff $C \sqcap \neg D$ is unsatisfiable [2]. Although, such computational impact might be non-negligible, TBoxes are relatively fixed and certain data preprocessing at the back end is feasible for applications, to some extent.

So far, a DL2DB system Γ w.r.t. a DL KB $\Sigma = <\mathcal{T}, \mathcal{A}>$ is constructed as below. Starting by initialization, a TBox taxonomy $\mathcal{T}^* = \{C \sqsubseteq D | \Sigma \models (C \sqsubseteq D)\} \cup \{P \sqsubseteq Q | \Sigma \models (P \sqsubseteq Q)\}$, derived from external DL reasoners, is uploaded to Γ together with the original ABox $\mathcal{A}$.

Initialization:

$TBox$: If $\varphi \in \mathcal{T}^*$, then $\varphi \in \Gamma$.
$ABox$: If $\varphi \in \mathcal{A}$, then $\varphi \in \Gamma$.

Inference rules:

$\in$: If $\varphi \in \Gamma$, then $\Gamma \vdash \varphi$.
$\sqcap$: If $\Gamma \vdash C(a)$ and $\Gamma \vdash D(a)$, then $\Gamma \vdash (C \sqcap D)(a)$.
$\exists$: If $\Gamma \vdash P(a,b)$ and $\Gamma \vdash C(b)$, then $\Gamma \vdash \exists P.C(a)$.
$\forall$: If $\Gamma \vdash P(a,b)$ and $\Gamma \vdash \forall P.C(a)$, then $\Gamma \vdash C(b)$.
$\sqsubseteq_T$: If $\Gamma \vdash (C \sqsubseteq D)$ and $\Gamma \vdash C(a)$, then $\Gamma \vdash D(a)$.
$\sqsubseteq_P$: If $\Gamma \vdash (P \sqsubseteq Q)$ and $\Gamma \vdash P(a,b)$, then $\Gamma \vdash Q(a,b)$.
P_i: If $\Gamma \vdash P(a,b)$, then $\Gamma \vdash Q(b,a)$, where Q is inverse of P.
P_t: If $\Gamma \vdash P(a,b)$ and $\Gamma \vdash P(b,c)$, then $\Gamma \vdash P(a,c)$, where P is transitive.

Symbols of a, b, C, D, P, Q etc. will be instantiated by corresponding individuals, classes and properties in Σ. Classical $\mathcal{SHI}$ DL [13] depicts another rule of $\forall_+$: If $\Gamma \vdash P(a,b)$ and $\Gamma \vdash \forall Q.C(a)$, where P is transitive and $\Gamma \vdash (P \sqsubseteq Q)$, then $\Gamma \vdash \forall P.C(b)$. However, support for TBox reasoning gives $\forall Q.C \sqsubseteq \forall P.(\forall P.C)$, because of $P \sqsubseteq Q$ where P is transitive. As a result, Rule[$\forall$] covers the situation of Rule[$\forall_+$], i.e., if $\Gamma \vdash P(a,b)$ and $\Gamma \vdash \forall P.(\forall P.C)(a)$, then $\Gamma \vdash \forall P.C(b)$.

Applying these inference rules, a sentence φ is called derivable if $\Gamma \vdash \varphi$, and its derivation length n counts in the times of applying inference rules. A conflict is defined in Γ by the facts that $\Gamma \vdash C(a)$ and $\Gamma \vdash \neg C(a)$. In this paper, conflict-free systems are focused, unless otherwise noted.

As far as we know, these above inference rules, more or less, play a role in most "state of the art" Semantic Web reasoning engines, in particular for those which adopt rule-based approaches. Thus, a corresponding KB fit in with this Γ is expected, and Σ' defined previously happens to be the candidate.

Theorem 1. *Let Σ be a DL KB, Σ' be a satisfiable DL2DB KB w.r.t. Σ, Γ be a conflict-free DL2DB system w.r.t. Σ, and φ be a non-epistemic sentence. $\Gamma \vdash \varphi$ if and only if $\Sigma' \models \varphi$.*

For proofs of this theorem (or called as soundness and completeness), please refer to the report at http://www.is.pku.edu.cn/~mayyam/appendix.pdf.

5 Query Answering

Moving the proposed DL2DB system into practice, a (negation-free) Datalog program is presented in this section. Also, we discuss rewriting techniques which make SPARQL queries processable, even those syntactic sugars involving predicates as variables. By implementing a bi-directional strategy of top-down and bottom-up, we believe that, following some optimization techniques, e.g. Magic Set [3] and Tabling [1], scalable ontology query answering is hopeful.

5.1 SPARQL Queries

SPARQL is a query language for obtaining information from RDF graphs. An RDF graph is a set of triples and each triple consists of a subject, a predicate and an object. From DL perspective, a reserved predicate rdf:type, for example, indicates DL class assertions with individuals as the subject and DL classes as the object. Possibly, a SPARQL query concerns the retrieval of those objects standing for DL classes, e.g. asking for all types of a specific individual.

Ignoring non-logical constitutions in SPARQL, such as filters, prefixes and so on, we denote a SPARQL query $q(\bar{x})$ by an expression of the form $\{\bar{x}|\mathtt{dnf}(\bar{x},\bar{y})\}$. Here, $\bar{x}$ are the so-called distinguished variables that will be bound with individuals in the KB, and $\bar{y}$ are the non-distinguished variables which are existentially qualified variables [6]. $\mathtt{dnf}(\bar{x},\bar{y})$ is a disjunctive normal form of $\mathtt{Rel}(sub,pre,obj)$, and $\mathtt{Rel}$, being a logical predicate, has three parameters: sub,pre,obj, each of which is either a constant in the RDF DB or a variable in $\bar{x}$ or $\bar{y}$.

A question naturally arises, facing to "constants in the RDF DB": what the RDF DB is and what the constants are. Rewriting techniques are introduced to address the problem. Given a DL KB, $C(a)$ and $P(a,b)$ in the ABox are rewritten by $\mathtt{Rel}(a,\text{rdf:type},C)$ and $\mathtt{Rel}(a,P,b)$, while $C \sqsubseteq D$ and $P \sqsubseteq Q$ in the TBox are rewritten by $\mathtt{Rel}(C,\text{rdfs:subClassOf},D)$ and $\mathtt{Rel}(P,\text{rdfs:subPropertyOf},Q)$, where rdf:type, rdfs:subClassOf, and rdfs:subPropertyOf are reserved predicates. Actually, rewriting not only provides support for SPARQL queries, but also bridges DL and relational databases. DL constructive classes such as $\exists P.C$ are not straightforwardly expressible inside of DBs. So, we use unique IDs to make them recognizable as for participating in sub,pre,obj. Thus, an RDF DB is a storage of triples w.r.t. a DL KB, where constants are those IDs representing individuals, DL classes and DL properties.

5.2 A Datalog Program

Rewriting techniques, additionally, give our inference rules a new version. For instance, Rule[∃] is depicted as $\mathtt{Rel}(a,\text{rdf:type},\exists P.C) \leftarrow \mathtt{Rel}(a,P,b)$,

Rel(b, rdf:type, C). Attention should be paid for variable bindings of a, b, P, C, and $\exists P.C$, which impose semantic conditions into the rule body such that a, b are individuals and $\exists P.C$ is a pending DL class together with its affiliated DL property P and class C. Other rules are processed similarly. For example, Rule[$\sqsubseteq_T$] turns to Rel(a, rdf:type, D) ← Rel(C, rdfs:subClassOf, D), Rel(a, rdf:type, C).

As such, given a DL KB $\Sigma =<\mathcal{T}, \mathcal{A}>$, the DL2DB system Γ w.r.t. Σ appears as a Datalog program P. The IDB of P consists of those inference rules (except Rule[∈]) in Γ rewritten in triples. The EDB of P is exactly an RDF DB w.r.t. Σ storing triples for the original ABox $\mathcal{A}$ and the inferred TBox $\mathcal{T}^*$, driven by Rule[∈]. With the help of DL reasoners, we regard the computation of TBoxes as a preprocessing. It is $\mathcal{T}^*$ instead of $\mathcal{T}$ that plays a role in this program. Since Datalog has P-complete data complexity [7], query answering in Γ is polynomial in size of the KB $\Sigma^* =<\mathcal{T}^*, \mathcal{A}>$.

Grounding a Datalog program P on the defined RDF DB needs $k \cdot N^M$ binding operations in maximum, where k, M and N are the number of Datalog rules, variables and constants, resp. In the case of our DL2DB system Γ, we have $k = 7$ Datalog rules excluding Rule[∈], each of which has maximally $M = 5$ variables acting as sub, pre, obj. The number N of constants counts those IDs representing individuals, DL classes and DL properties in Σ. Consequently, interpreting Γ in Datalog rules has a computational cost of $O(7 \cdot n^5)$.

5.3 Strategies

Although, a theoretical complexity is tractable, the evaluation strategy in practice is another story. For example, a cyclic DL TBox of $\exists P.C \sqsubseteq C$ indicates the query of $C(x)$ is based on that of $\exists P.C(x)$ which relies on $C(y)$ and $P(x, y)$. The backward chaining becomes $C(x) \leftarrow P(x, y), C(y)$, getting entangled in the recursive retrieval of C. Meanwhile, a pitfall exists when using forward chaining freely in this example. Thinking about an ABox of $P(a, a)$ and $C(a)$, we receive an infinite series of $\exists P.C(a), \exists P.\exists P.C(a), \exists P.\exists P.\exists P.C(a)$, and so on. A straightforward top-down implementation can take exponential time using these rules while a bottom-up approach is faster (generally polynomial), but still wastes time exploring other rules which are never used in the solution of the query [3].

To improve performance, we can use a procedure which collects subgoals of a given query top-down firstly, and then evaluates all subgoals bottom-up. Referring to techniques involved in Deductive Databases [21], the repetition of computing is by all means avoided on the one hand, and the irrelevant goals may as well be ignored on the other hand.

We are now ready to define algorithms, as shown in Table 1. To improve legibility, Rule[*] is presented, where * is the placeholder of every inference rule introduced in the DL2DB system, such as Rule[∃] and Rule[$\sqsubseteq_T$], except for Rule[∈]. For computing the answers to a subgoal g over the KB $\Sigma^* =<\mathcal{T}^*, \mathcal{A}>$, we first exploit the relational DB to obtain $\mathcal{A}(g)$ which means a ground base of g asserted in $\mathcal{A}$, and then answers are propagated until reaching a fixpoint.

In fact, this proposed strategy, to simulate top-down semantics in a bottom-up framework, is not new, tracing back to the Magic Set [3] developed in Deductive

Table 1. Algorithms of TopDown and BottomUp

Algorithm	TopDown($q, \mathcal{T}^*$)	BottomUp($S, \mathcal{T}^*, \mathcal{A}$)
Input	A query q and an inferred TBox $\mathcal{T}^*$	A set S of subgoals for q and an inferred TBox $\mathcal{T}^*$ and an original ABox $\mathcal{A}$
Output	A set S of subgoals for q	A set Ans of answers to subgoals in S

Steps	$S := \{q\}$; $top := 0$;
	while ($top <$ `sizeOf`(S)) **do**
	  for each g in S **do**
	    if g matches the consequent
	    of an instantiated Rule[*]
	    then $top := top + 1$; $S := S\cup$
	    {those antecedents of Rule[*]};
	return S
		$Ans := \{\mathcal{A}(g) \mid g \in S\}$
		do $Ans' := Ans$
		  if an instantiated Rule[*] is settled
		  with its antecedents in Ans'
		  then $Ans' := Ans' \cup$
		  {the consequent of Rule[*]}
		while $Ans = Ans'$;
		return Ans

Databases. Not providing a general magic set transformation, we regard the collection of subgoals as a magic set s.t. Rue1[∃], for example, appears as `Rel`(a, rdf:type, $\exists P.C$) ← `Magic`($\exists P.C$), `Rel`(a, P, b), `Rel`(b, rdf:type, C). Unless required, such class expression $\exists P...\exists P.C$ as mentioned above would not be generated by the Rule[∃] with `Magic`.

Meanwhile, there are various algorithms to address the termination of top-down methods, most of which may be considered as variants of OLDT-resolution [21]. Being a representative and used in XSB Prolog [1], the Tabling method declares tabled predicates (manually or automatically) whose evaluation is by means of a so-called SLG resolution, while non-tabled predicates are resolved as normal, i.e., using the SLD resolution steps, by which the termination reaches without infinite loops. However, complex and large DL TBoxes expect tabled predicates declared automatically. Only to exploring all instantiated rules by a 'compilation' of the TBox, those predicates are detected. It means, a top-down-like static analysis in Tabling looks similar to the collection of subgoals in our approach. Besides, we observe that, in Tabling, the table entry associated with calls to tabled predicates is enriched by inserting new derived answers, step by step. Such a gradual insertion is executed also similarly in our bottom-up computation for obtained subgoals. Briefly, running in our strategy seems not more expensive than in Tabling, equipped with physical optimizations.

So far, we believe that a bi-directional strategy is suitable for query answering in a DL-driven Datalog program. Specifically, the (indirect) cyclic DL TBox is legal which leads to the recursion unavoidable, while the superfluous computation (particularly encountering voluminous data in the Semantic Web) has been cut down by the collection of subgoals. Finally, our bi-directional strategy will terminate for a given DL KB, provided by the facts that

1. A finite number of subgoals is encountered, whose worst case is the collection of all DL classes and DL properties appearing in the KB, and
2. Each of these subgoals has a finite number of instances with the maximum of all individuals in the KB.

5.4 Comparisons

In this section, we summarize and compare systems and approaches for rule-based ontology query answering.

Knowledge compilation, making implicit information explicit in advance, has been widely used in some systems. For example, OWLIM [15], being a semantic repository, builds a materialized RDF database with the inferred closure of an OWL DLP KB. Similarly, Minerva[1] performs entailment rules bottom-up for the DL ABox inferences, plugged with a DL reasoner for precomputing the DL TBox subsumptions [16][29]. Creating DB views has been preprocessed in DLDB-OWL [20], of which each view stands for a DL class. Briefly, this kind of tools fills in DBs with data by a bottom-up precompilation, pushing a direct retrieval to back-end databases, but at the risk of a whole re-computation when updating.

Querying on-the-fly during reasoning alleviates the suffering caused by updating. There are two frameworks, KAON2 [19] and DL-lite [6], getting deserved attention. KAON2 reduces a DL KB to a disjunctive Datalog program, using the magic set algorithm developed for disjunctive programs. DL-lite is less expressive, although, any query is expressible as the union of conjunctive queries in SQL via a KB normalization, making SQL engines responsible to return the exact answers. Thus, our DL2DB stands in the middle of KAON2 and DL-lite. Generally speaking, this kind of tools follows a solid logical language, to address the challenges of expressivity and reasoning power.

It leaves a straightforward way, in which existing (top-down, bottom-up) rule engines are borrowed as a whole. In this trend, a production rule engine Jess is used by OWLJessKB[2] and OWL2Jess [17], while XSB Prolog is preferred in FLORA-2[3] and TRIPLE[4]. Also, SWI-Prolog[5] provides a Semantic Web Library dealing with the RDF data extracted from RDF(S) and OWL documents. Taking negation into account, deduction in ontologies via ASP (Answer Set Programming) has been discussed in [23] but regarding classical negation ¬ as default not, and HEX-Programs [11] provide a hybrid platform integrating ASP rules with external DL atoms, both of which utilize underlying ASP rule engines.

6 Discussions

Not surprising, user-defined rules are expected in real applications. Viewing those inference rules in a system level, we envision a common platform with support for SPARQL query answering in SWRL. Learning from our preliminary experiments, performance problems (e.g. running time and memory space) are discussed below, towards the development of a powerful Semantic Web tool.

---

[1] http://www.alphaworks.ibm.com/tech/semanticstk
[2] http://edge.cs.drexel.edu/assemblies/software/owljesskb/
[3] http://flora.sourceforge.net/
[4] http://triple.semanticweb.org/
[5] http://www.swi-prolog.org/

6.1 Extensions

SWRL [28] is a combination of OWL DL and unary/binary Datalog rules. Technically, let S be a SWRL knowledge base, where O_C is a set of OWL classes, O_P is a set of OWL properties, and S_T is a set of OWL individuals and SWRL variables. A SWRL rule has the form: $h_1 \wedge \cdots \wedge h_n \leftarrow b_1 \wedge \cdots \wedge b_m$, where $h_i, b_j, 1 \leq i \leq n, 1 \leq j \leq m$ are atoms of the form $C(t)$ with $C \in O_C$ and $t \in S_T$, or atoms of the form $P(t_1, t_2)$ with $P \in O_P$ and $t_1, t_2 \in S_T$.

We are more interested in SWRL rules with a unique head atom, and rewriting techniques are still suitable s.t. each SWRL rule appears as: $\mathtt{Rel}(s_0, p_0, o_0) \leftarrow \mathtt{Rel}(s_1, p_1, o_1) \cdots \mathtt{Rel}(s_n, p_n, o_n)$. Facing to a rule body having $\mathtt{Rel}(a, \text{rdf:type}, \exists P.C)$, for instance, a rewritten version of Rule[$\exists$] as mentioned above is applied to obtain corresponding entailments, also Rule[$\sqsubseteq_T$] and others are applicable. Thus, assuming that a Datalog program works for our DL2DB system, the situation is not aggravated when more rules, in the same style, are involved. Being a preliminary work, our prototype is towards support for query answering with SWRL rules, whose semantics appeals, however, for integrity constraints.

A large variety of features have been captured in MKNF-DL [10], such as default rules and epistemic queries. Our future work includes a more general formalization concerning non-monotonic logics and latest work in [8] [11] [18] is well deserved studying.

6.2 Preliminary Experiments

We conducted initial experiments on a DBMS-based OWL repository, Minerva (DB2 in experiments). Test data sets are from the extended LUBM [16], an OWL ontology including 69 atomic classes, 39 intersection classes, 10 existential restrictions, 55 properties, 263 class subsumptions, 16 property subsumptions, 46450 class assertions, 239933 property assertions, and 25461 individuals. These documents involve one terminology file of size 66 KB, one university file of size 207 KB and twenty department files each of which is about 1300 KB.

Not tangling with complex DL class descriptions, such queries as finding instances typed of "Organization" receive answers (counting to 229 none of which is asserted in the ABox) in 0.91 second. However, the query to "Chair", defined as Person $\sqcap \exists$ headOf.Department where Department$\sqsubseteq$Organization, requires the evaluation of "Person" firstly. There are 35 classes being recognized as the subclasses of "Person", inducing totally 90 subgoals. Finally, it counts to 14995 persons (none exists in the ABox) and 40 chairs (half asserted, half inferred) in 29.73 second. As for a certain individual, who is asserted as "Man" and "Full-Professor" in the ABox, our engine further knows him typed of "Professor", "Faculty", "Employee", "Person" and "Chair" in 21.48 second.

We found that how to process intermediate results obtained from subgoals becomes a bottleneck of performance, and the worse case reports "out of memory" if temporary results are carried out in memory. Inserting them into DBs is considered, but it takes minutes since various indexes need to be established and DB needs to write logs. Thus, we turn to declared global temporary tables (without logging in DB2), in which inferred results are cached. At running time, top-down and bottom-up procedures proceed, followed by inserting intermediate answers into temporary tables active in a session. SQL engines serve for the final retrieval, concerning unions of conjunction queries on arbitral RDF triples, from temporary tables (filled by inferred results) together with other physical DB tables.

7 Conclusions

On the Semantic Web, SPARQL is for query answering in the RDF community. An OWL ontology is RDF-based, adopting DL as its logical foundation. Given a DL KB Σ, by introducing integrity constraints inspired by MKNF-DL [10], we present its logically equivalent version, namely the DL2DB KB Σ', in the sense of query answering. Meanwhile, an inference system, the DL2DB system Γ w.r.t. Σ, takes effect, while preserving sound and complete with Σ' for non-epistemic queries. The appearance of a Datalog program moves Γ into practice, getting SPARQL queries solved.

Our proposal, to some extent, is not beyond DLP, where DLP has syntactical expressive restrictions while DL2DB has semantical integrity constraints. We still believe this paper, in an epistemic perspective, generalizes those using rules to perform OWL reasoning. As a preliminary implementation, an engine, coupled with a scalable OWL storage (e.g. Minerva [29] but not committing its ABox inferences), is developed. Answers to SPARQL queries are received in seconds on a data set of a medium size. A better performance is expected by using more optimization techniques from existing Datalog engines (e.g. [21]) and other Semantic Web applications (e.g. [22]).

References

1. *The XSB System Version 2.7.1 Volume 1: Programmer's Manual.*
2. Franz Baader, Diego Calvanese, Deborah McGuinness, Daniele Nardi, and Peter Patel-Schneider. *The Description Logic Handbook: Theory, Implementation, and Applications.* Cambridge University Press, 2003.
3. François Bancilhon, David Maier, Yehoshua Sagiv, and Jeffrey D. Ullman. Magic Sets and Other Strange Ways to Implement Logic Programs. In *Proceedings of the 5th ACM Symposium on Principles of Database Systems*, pages 1–15, 1986.
4. Sean Bechhofer, Ian Horrocks, and Daniele Turi. The OWL Instance Store: System Description. In *Proceedings of CADE-20*, LNCS 3632, pages 177–181, 2005.
5. Francois Bry, Norbert Eisinger, Heribert Schutz, and Sunna Torge. SIC: Satisfiability Checking for Integrity Constraints. In *Proceeding of Deductive Databases and Logic Programming*, pages 25–36, 1998.
6. Diego Calvanese, Giuseppe De Giacomo, Domenico Lembo, Maurizio Lenzerini, and Riccardo Rosati. DL-Lite: Tractable Description Logics for Ontologies. In *Proc. of the 20th Nat. Conf. on Artificial Intelligence*, pages 602–607, 2005.
7. Evgeny Dantsin, Thomas Eiter, Georg Gottlob, and Andrei Voronkov. Complexity and Expressive Power of Logic Programming. *ACM Computing Surveys*, 33(3):374–425, 2001.

8. Jos de Bruijn, Thomas Eiter, Axel Polleres, and Hans Tompits. On Representational Issues About Combinations of Classical Theories with Nonmonotonic Rules. In *Proceedings of KSEM*, LNCS 4092, pages 1–22, 2006.
9. Jos de Bruijn, Axel Polleres, Rubén Lara, and Dieter Fensel. OWL DL vs. OWL Flight: Conceptual Modeling and Reasoning on the Semantic Web. In *Proceedings of the 14th International World Wide Web Conference*, Chiba, Japan, 2005. ACM.
10. Francesco M. Donini, Daniele Nardi, and Riccardo Rosati. Description Logics of Minimal Knowledge and Negation as Failure. *ACM Transactions on Computational Logic*, 3(2):177–225, 2002.
11. Thomas Eiter, Giovambattista Ianni, Roman Schindlauer, and Hans Tompits. Effective Integration of Declarative Rules with External Evaluations for Semantic-Web Reasoning. In *Proceedings of ESWC*, LNCS 4011, pages 273–287, 2006.
12. Benjamin N. Grosof, Ian Horrocks, Raphael Volz, and Stefan Decker. Description Logic Programs: Combining Logic Programs with Description Logic. In *Proceedings of the 12th International World Wide Web Conference*, pages 48–57. ACM, 2003.
13. Ian Horrocks, Ulrike Sattler, and Stephan Tobies. A Description Logic with Transitive and Converse Roles, Role Hierarchies and Qualifying Number Restrictions. LTCS-Report 99-08, RWTH Aachen, Germany, 1999.
14. Ian Horrocks and Sergio Tessaris. Querying the Semantic Web: a Formal Approach. In *Proceedings of ISWC*, LNCS 2342, pages 177–191, 2002.
15. Atanas Kiryakov, Damyan Ognyanov, and Dimitar Manov. OWLIM: A Pragmatic Semantic Repository for OWL. In *Proceeding of International Workshop on WISE*, LNCS 3807, pages 182–192, 2005.
16. Li Ma, Yang Yang, Zhaomin Qiu, Guotong Xie, Yue Pan, and ShengPing Liu. Towards A Complete OWL Ontology Benchmark. In *Proceedings of ESWC*, LNCS 4011, pages 124–139, 2006.
17. Jing Mei, Elena Paslaru Bontas, and Zuoquan Lin. OWL2Jess: A Transformational Implementation of the OWL Semantics. In *Proceedings of International Workshops on ISPA*, LNCS 3759, pages 599–608, 2005.
18. Boris Motik and Riccardo Rosati. Closing Semantic Web Ontologies. Technical report, University of Karlsruhe, May 2006. http://kaon2.semanticweb.org/.
19. Boris Motik, Ulrike Sattler, and Rudi Studer. Query Answering for OWL-DL with Rules. *Journal of Web Semantics*, 3(1):41–60, 2005.
20. Zhengxiang Pan and Jeff Heflin. DLDB: Extending Relational Databases to Support Semantic Web Queries. In *Practical and Scalable Semantic Systems*, 2003.
21. Kotagiri Ramamohanarao and James Harland. An introduction to deductive database languages and systems. *The VLDB Journal*, 3(2):107–122, 1994.
22. Edna Ruckhaus, Eduardo Ruiz, and Maria-Esther Vidal. Query Evaluation and Optimization in the Semantic Web. In *Proc. of ALPSWS*, 2006.
23. Terrance Swift. Deduction in Ontologies via ASP. In *Proceedings of Logic Programming and Nonmonotonic Reasoning*, LNCS 2923, 2004.
24. W3C. OWL: Web Ontology Language. http://www.w3.org/TR/owl-absyn/.
25. W3C. Resource Description Framework (RDF): Concepts and Abstract Syntax. http://www.w3.org/TR/rdf-concepts/.
26. W3C. Rule Interchange Format WG. http://www.w3.org/2005/rules/wg.
27. W3C. SPARQL Query Language. http://www.w3.org/TR/rdf-sparql-query/.
28. W3C. SWRL: A Semantic Web Rule Language Combining OWL and RuleML. http://www.w3.org/Submission/SWRL/.
29. Jian Zhou, Li Ma, Qiaoling Liu, Lei Zhang, Yong Yu, and Yue Pan. Minerva: A Scalable OWL Ontology Storage and Inference System. In *Proceedings of Asia Semantic Web Conference*, To appear, 2006.

Formal Model for Ontology Mapping Creation*

Adrian Mocan, Emilia Cimpian, and Mick Kerrigan

Digital Enterprise Research Institute, University of Innsbruck, Austria
{adrian.mocan, emilia.cimpian, mick.kerrigan}@deri.org

Abstract. In a semantic environment data is described by ontologies and heterogeneity problems have to be solved at the ontological level. This means that alignments between ontologies have to be created, most probably during design-time, and used in various run-time processes. Such alignments describe a set of mappings between the source and target ontologies, where the mappings show how instance data from one ontology can be expressed in terms of another ontology. We propose a formal model for mapping creation. Starting from this model we explore how such a model maps onto a design-time graphical tool that can be used in creating alignments between ontologies. We also investigate how such a model helps in expressing the mappings in a logical language, based on the semantic relationships identified using the graphical tool.

1 Introduction

Ontology mapping is becoming a crucial aspect in solving heterogeneity problems between semantically described data. The benefits of using ontologies, especially in heterogenous environments where more than one ontology is used, can only be realized if this process is effective. The trend is to provide graphical tools capable of creating alignments during design-time in a (semi-)automatic manner [2,10,9]. These alignments consist of mapping rules, frequently described as *statements* in a logical language. One of the main challenges is to fully isolate the domain expert (who is indispensable if 100% accuracy is required) from the burdens of logics using a graphical tool, and in the same time to be able to create complex, complete and correct mappings between the ontologies.

It is absolutely necessary to formally describe the mapping creation process and to link it with the instruments available in a graphical tool and with a mapping representation formalism that can be used later during run-time. This allows the actions performed by the user to be captured in a meaningful way with respect to the visualized ontology structure and to associate the results of these actions (mappings) with concrete statements in a mapping language (mapping rules).

---

* Work funded by the European Commission under the projects ASG, DIP, enIRaF, InfraWebs, Knowledge Web, Musing, Salero, SEKT, Seemp, SemanticGOV, Super, SWING and TripCom; by Science Foundation Ireland under the DERI-Líon Grant No.SFI/02/CE1/I13; by the FFG (Österreichische Forschungsfrderungsgesselleschaft mbH) under the projects Grisino, RW², SemNetMan, SeNSE, TSC, OnTourism.

The document structure is as follows: the next section presents the context and motivation for the work. Section 3 introduces the model we propose expressed using First-Order Logic [4]. Section 4 describes how this model can be applied to WSMO [3] ontologies, while Section 5 presents the creation of mapping rules; the prototype that implements and applies the proposed formal model is described in Section 6. Following, related work and conclusions are presented.

2 Context and Motivation

The work described in this paper has been carried out in the Web Service Execution Environment (WSMX) working group, whose scope is to build a framework that enables discovery, selection, mediation, invocation and interoperation of Semantic Web Services [6]. Web Services are semantically described using ontologies, but as they are generally developed in isolation, heterogeneity problems appear between the underlying ontologies. Without resolving these problems the communication (data exchanged) between Web Services cannot take place. The data mediation process in WSMX includes two phases: a *design-time* and a *run-time* phase. The mismatches between the ontologies are resolved at design-time, while these findings are used at run-time to transform the data passing through the system. The run-time phase can be completely automated, while the design-time phase remains semi-automatic, requiring the inputs of a domain expert.

For the design-time a semi-automatic ontology mapping tool was developed that allows the user to create alignments between ontologies and to make these alignments available for the run-time process. There has been much research in the area of graphical mapping tools, e.g. [9,10], however we believe there are many challenges still to be addressed. In particular, our focus has been on defining strategies that hide the burden of logical languages, that are generally used to express ontology alignments, from the domain expert. The mapping process must remain simple to use but simultaneously allow the creation of complex mappings between two ontologies.

Table 1. Ontology Fragment

```
                                concept gender
concept person                      value ofType xsd:string
  name ofType xsd:string
  age ofType xsd:integer        instance male memberOf gender
  hasGender ofType gender           value hasValue "male"
  hasChild ofType person        instance female memberOf gender
  marriedTo ofType person           value hasValue "female"
```

As described in [8], we noticed that the graphical point of view adopted to visualize the source and target ontologies makes it easier to identify certain types of mappings. The ontology fragment in Table 1 can be visualized using different viewpoints by shifting the focus from one ontology element to another (see Table 2). We call such a viewpoint a *perspective* and argue that only by switching between combinations of these perspectives on the source and target ontologies, can certain types of mappings be created using only one simple operation, *map*, combined with mechanisms for ontology traversal and contextualized visualization strategies.

A formal model that describes the general principles of the perspectives allows a better understanding of the human user actions in the graphical tool and of the effects of these actions on the ontology alignment (i.e. mapping rules) that is being created. This model defines the main principles that support the graphical instruments (e.g. perspectives) and how they fit with the underlying logical mechanism (e.g. decomposition, context updates). The same model is also used to describe how the inputs placed through these graphical instruments by the domain expert effects the generated mappings. Having this formal model as a link between the graphical elements and the mappings, defines precisely the process of hiding from the domain expert the complexity of the underlying logical languages; it also allows some of the mapping properties such as (in)completeness or (in)consistency to be reflected back into the graphical tool. Additionally, such a model allows experts to become more familiar with the tools and to create extensions that are more suited to capturing certain types of mismatches.

Table 2. *PartOf*, *InstanceOf* and *RelatedBy* Perspectives

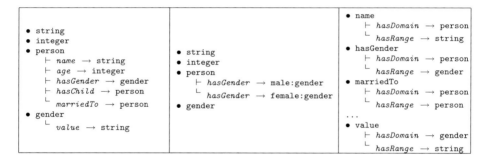

3 A Model for Mapping Creation

This section defines a model to be used in the creation of mappings between ontologies. The roles that appear in the graphical user interface, and which will be later associated with ontological entities, are defined here. First-Order Logic [4] is used as a formalism to represent this model.

3.1 Perspectives

In our approach the ontologies are presented to the user using *perspectives*. A perspective can be seen as a vertical projection of the ontology and it will be used by the domain expert to visualize and browse the ontologies and to define mappings. We can define several perspectives on an ontology as presented in Section 4, all of them characterized by a set of common elements.

Table 3. Types of items for the perspectives in Table 2

	PartOf	InstanceOf	RelatedBy
c_i	person, gender	person	name, hasGender, marriedTo, value
p_i	string, integer	string, integer, gender	-
d_i	name, age, hasChild, marriedTo	hasGender	hasDomain, hasRange
s_i	string, integer, gender, person	male, female	person, string, gender

We identify four types of such elements (items): *compound, primitive, description* and *successor*. We use the following unary relations to denote each of them, $ci(x)$ where x is a compound item, $pi(x)$ where x is a primitive item, $di(x)$ where x is a description item and $si(x)$ where x is a successor item. Both primitive and compound items represent first-class citizens of a perspective while description and successor items link the compound and the primitive items in a graph-based structure. In addition we define a set of general relationships between these items that hold for all perspectives:

- Each compound item is described by at least one description item:

$$\forall x.(ci(x) <=> \exists y.(di(y) \land describes(y,x))) \quad (1)$$

where *describes* is a binary relation that holds between a compound item and one of its description items. The participants in this relation are always a compound item and a description item:

$$\forall x.\forall y.(describes(x,y) => ci(y) \land di(x)) \quad (2)$$

- Each description item points to at least one successor item:

$$\forall x.(di(x) <=> \exists y.(si(y) \land successor(y,x))) \quad (3)$$

where *successor* is a binary relation that holds between a description item and one of its successor items. The participants in this relation are always a description item and a successor item:

$$\forall x.\forall y.(successor(x,y) => di(y) \land si(x)) \quad (4)$$

- The successor items are either primitive or compound items:

$$\forall x.(si(x) => pi(x) \lor ci(x)) \quad (5)$$

- The compound, primitive and description items are mutually exclusive for the same perspective:

$$\forall x.(\neg((ci(x) \land pi(x)) \lor (ci(x) \land di(x)) \lor (di(x) \land pi(x)))) \quad (6)$$

This is a set of minimal descriptions for our model, but by inference other useful consequences can be inferred. For example, note that sentences 1 and 6 imply that primitive items have no description items. Table 4 shows examples of relationships for the perspectives in Table 2.

As a consequence we can define a perspective as being a set $\phi = \{x_1, x_2, ..., x_n\}$ for which we have:

$$\forall x.\forall \phi.(member^1(x,\phi) => pi(x) \lor ci(x) \lor di(x)) \quad (7)$$

---

[1] *member* is a relationships expressing the membership of an element to a list.

Table 4. Relations between items in the perspectives depicted in Table 2

	$successor(\cdot, \cdot)$	$describes(\cdot, \cdot)$
PartOf	(string, name), (gender, hasGender) (person, marriedTo)	(name, person), (hasGender, person) (marriedTo, person)
InstanceOf	(male, hasGender), (female, hasGender)	(hasGender, person)
RelatedBy	(person, hasDomain), (string, hasRange) (gender, hasRange)	(hasDomain, name), (hasRange, name) (hasRange, hasGender)

In addition, for any perspective the following sentences hold:

$$\forall x.\forall y.\forall \phi.(describes(y,x) => (member(x,\phi) <=> member(y,\phi))) \quad (8a)$$

$$\forall x.\forall y.\forall \phi.(successor(y,x) => (member(x,\phi) <=> member(y,\phi))) \quad (8b)$$

Sentences 8a and 8b together with 2 and 4 state that the description of a compound item appears in the perspective *iff* the compound item appears in the perspective as well. Similarly, a successor of a description item appears in a perspective *iff* the description item appears in the perspective too.

3.2 Contexts

Not all of the information modeled in the ontology is useful in all stages of the mapping process. The previous section shows that a perspective represents only a subset of an ontology, but we can go further and define the notion of *context*. A context is a subset of a perspective that contains only those ontological entities, from that perspective, relevant to a concrete operation. We can say that γ_ϕ is a context of the perspective ϕ if:

$$\forall x.(member(x, \gamma_\phi) => member(x, \phi)) \quad (9)$$

For a context from formulas 8a and 8b only 8a holds, such that:

$$\forall x.\forall y.\forall \gamma_\phi.(describes(y,x) => (member(x, \gamma_\phi) <=> member(y, \gamma_\phi))) \quad (10)$$

As a consequence we can say that all perspectives are contexts but not all contexts are perspectives.

A notion tightly related with contexts is the process of *decomposition*. A context can be created from another context (this operation is called *context update*) by applying decomposition on an item from a perspective or a context. Let $decomposition(x, \phi)$ be a binary function which has as value a new context obtained by decomposing x in respect with the context γ_ϕ. We can define the following axioms:

$$\forall x.\forall y.\forall \gamma_\phi.(member(x, \gamma_\phi) \wedge pi(x) =>$$
$$(member(y, decomposition(x, \gamma_\phi)) <=> member(y, \gamma_\phi))) \quad (11)$$

$$\forall x.\forall y.\forall \gamma_\phi.(member(x, \gamma_\phi) \wedge ci(x) =>$$
$$(member(y, decomposition(x, \gamma_\phi)) <=> y = x \vee describes(y, x))) \quad (12)$$

$$\forall x.\forall y.\forall z.\forall \gamma_\phi.(member(x, \gamma_\phi) \wedge di(x) \wedge successor(z,x) \wedge (pi(z) \vee (ci(z) \wedge member(z, \gamma_\phi))) =>$$
$$(member(y, decomposition(x, \gamma_\phi)) <=> member(y, \gamma_\phi))) \quad (13)$$

$$\forall x.\forall y.\forall z.\forall \gamma_\phi.(member(x, \gamma_\phi) \wedge di(x) \wedge successor(z,x) \wedge ci(z) \wedge \neg(member(z, \gamma_\phi)) =>$$
$$(member(y, decomposition(x, \gamma_\phi)) <=> member(y, decomposition(z, \phi)))) \quad (14)$$

Intuitively, formula 11 specifies that the decomposition of a primitive concept does not update the current context (the context remains unchanged). Also, decomposition applied on a description item that has a primitive successor (formula 13) leaves the current context unchanged. The same formula also does not allow the decomposition of those description items that have as successor a compound item already contained by the current context (recursive structures).

Table 5 presents some examples of decompositions and context updates: each column shows how the context changes by decomposing any of the marked items in the top row. The decomposition can be applied simultaneously on multiple items, and the result of decomposing each item is contributing to the new context. Note as described over for column 1 no change occurs as all of the marked items cannot trigger decomposition conforming to formulae 11 and 13.

Table 5. Decomposition and context updates

Original Context		
• string • integer • person ⊢ *name* → string ⊢ *age* → integer ⊢ *hasGender* → gender ⊢ *hasChild* → person └ *marriedTo* → person • gender └ *value* → string	• string • integer • person ⊢ *name* → string ⊢ *age* → integer ⊢ *hasGender* → gender ⊢ *hasChild* → person └ *marriedTo* → person • gender └ *value* → string	• string • integer • person ⊢ *name* → string ⊢ *age* → integer ⊢ *hasGender* → gender ⊢ *hasChild* → person └ *marriedTo* → person • gender └ *value* → string
New Context		
• string • integer • person ⊢ *name* → string ⊢ *age* → integer ⊢ *hasGender* → gender ⊢ *hasChild* → person └ *marriedTo* → person • gender └ *value* → string	• person ⊢ *name* → string ⊢ *age* → integer ⊢ *hasGender* → gender ⊢ *hasChild* → person └ *marriedTo* → person	• gender └ *value* → string

3.3 Mappings

To create mappings between ontologies, a source and target perspective is used to represent the source and target ontologies. We refer to this approach as interactive mapping creation. It means that the mapping creation process relies upon the domain expert, who has the role of choosing an item from the source perspective and one from the target perspective (or contexts) and explicitly marking them as mapped items. We call this action *map* and using this the domain expert states that there is a semantic relationship between the mapped items. Choosing the right pair of items to be mapped is not necessarily a manual task: a semi-automatic solution can offer suggestions that are eventually validated by the domain expert [8].

We define a *mapping context* as a quadruple $Mc = <\phi_S, \gamma_{\phi_S}, \phi_T, \gamma_{\phi_T}>$ where ϕ_S and ϕ_T are the source and target perspectives associated to the source and target ontologies. γ_{ϕ_S} and γ_{ϕ_T} are the current contexts derived out of the two perspectives ϕ_S and ϕ_T. Initially, $\gamma_{\phi_S} \equiv \phi_S$ and $\gamma_{\phi_T} \equiv \phi_T$.

We also define $map_{Mc}(x,y)$ the action of marking the two items x and y as being semantically related with respect to the mapping context Mc. Thus, we have the following axiom:

$$\forall x. \forall y. \forall \phi_S. \forall \phi_T. \forall \gamma_{\phi_S}. \forall \gamma_{\phi_T} map_{Mc}(x,y) \land Mc = <\phi_S, \gamma_{\phi_S}, \phi_T, \gamma_{\phi_T}> \land$$
$$((ci(x) \lor pi(x)) \land (ci(y) \lor pi(y))) \lor (di(x) \land di(y)) =>$$
$$member(x, \gamma_{\phi_S}) \land member(y, \gamma_{\phi_T}) \tag{15}$$

Formula 15 defines the allowed types of mapping. Thus we can have mappings between primitive and/or compound items and between description items. As described in [8] the set of the allowed mappings can be extended or restricted by a particular, concrete perspective.

Each time a *map* action occurs the mapping context is updated; we denote the updates using: $Mc \twoheadrightarrow Mc'$ meaning that at least one element of the quadruple defining Mc has changed and the new mapping context is Mc'. The mapping context updates occur as defined in axiom 16:

$$\forall x. \forall y. map_{Mc}(x,y) \land Mc = <\phi_S, \gamma_{\phi_S}, \phi_T, \gamma_{\phi_T}> \quad => \tag{16}$$
$$Mc' = <\phi_S, decomposition(x, \gamma_{\phi_S}), \phi_T, decompositin(y, \gamma_{\phi_T})> \land Mc \twoheadrightarrow Mc'$$

There are cases when Mc and Mc' are identical; such situations occur when the source and target context remain unchanged, e.g. when creating mappings between primitive items.

4 Grounding the Model to Ontologies

This section explores the way in which the model presented above can be applied to a real ontological model and how we can use it to define concrete perspectives that could be used to create meaningful mappings between ontologies. We first introduce the main aspects of WSMO ontologies and a mechanism to link these ontologies with our model and then we will present the three types of concrete perspectives we identified as being useful in the mapping process.

The Web Service Modeling Ontology (WSMO) defines the main aspects related to Semantic Web Services: Ontologies, Web Services, Goals and Mediators [3], from these only Ontologies are interesting in this work. We will focus only on concepts, attributes and instances in this paper, however we intend to address other ontological elements in the future. WSMO ontologies are expressed using the Web Service Modeling Language (WSML) which is based on different logical formalisms namely, Description Logics, First-Order Logic and Logic Programming [5].

Table 1 presents an example of concepts and their attributes, and some instances of these concepts. The concept *person* is modeled as having 5 attributes, each of them having a type (i.e. a range) that is either another concept or a data type. For the concept *gender* there are two instances defined (i.e. *male* and *female*) that have attributes pointing to values of the corresponding types.

4.1 PartOf Perspective

The *PartOf* perspective is the most common perspective that can be used to display an ontology, focusing on the concepts, attributes and attributes' types hierarchies. To link this perspective with our model we define the unary relations $ci_{PartOf}(x)$, $pi_{PartOf}(x)$ and $di_{PartOf}(x)$ such that:

$$ci(x) \text{ iff } ci_{PartOf}(x) \qquad pi(x) \text{ iff } pi_{PartOf}(x) \qquad di(x) \text{ iff } di_{PartOf}(x) \qquad (17)$$

$ci_{PartOf}(x)$, $pi_{PartOf}(x)$ and $di_{PartOf}(x)$ have to be defined in the logical language used to represent the ontologies to be aligned, in our case WSML[2] as can be seen in 18. In the *PartOf* perspective the role of compound items is taken by those concepts that have at least one attribute - we call them *compound concepts*. Naturally, the description items are in this case attributes, as stated in 19. Primitive items are data types or those concepts that have no attributes, as expressed by axiom 20 where x **subconceptOf** *true* holds iff x is a concept and *naf* stands for negation as failure. Finally we link the *describes* and *successor* relations with the WSML ontologies in 21. The ontology fragment presented in Table 1 can be visualized using the *PartOf* perspective as in Table 2.

$$\text{axiom } ci_{PartOf} \text{ definedBy } ci_{PartOf}(x) \text{ equivalent exists } ?y, ?z(?x[?y \text{ ofType } ?z]) \qquad (18)$$
$$\text{axiom } di_{PartOf} \text{ definedBy } di_{PartOf}(y) \text{ equivalent exists } ?x, ?z(?x[?y \text{ ofType } ?z]) \qquad (19)$$
$$\text{axiom } pi_{PartOf} \text{ definedBy } pi_{PartOf}(x) :\!\!- ?x \text{ subconceptOf } true \text{ and naf } ci_{PartOf}(x) \, (20)$$
$$describes(y,x) \wedge successor(z,y) \text{ iff } ?x[?y \text{ ofType } ?z] \qquad (21)$$

4.2 InstanceOf Perspective

The *InstanceOf* perspective can be used to create conditional mappings based on predefined values and instances. To link this perspective with our model we define $ci_{InstanceOf}(x)$, $pi_{InstanceOf}(x)$ and $di_{InstanceOf}(y,w)$ such that:

$$ci(x) \text{ iff } ci_{InstanceOf}(x) \quad pi(x) \text{ iff } pi_{InstanceOf}(x) \quad di(<y,w>) \text{ iff } di_{InstanceOf}(y,w) \quad (22)$$

The description items are tuples $<y,w>$ where **y** is an attribute matching the above conditions and **w** is an instance member of y's type explicitly defined in the ontology or an anonymous id representing a potential instance of the y's type. In the same way as above, $ci_{InstanceOf}(x)$, $pi_{InstanceOf}(x)$ and $di_{InstanceOf}(x)$ are defined using WSML; also the *describes* and *successor* relations can be linked with the WSML ontologies in a similar manner as presented in the previous section. From space reasons, they are omitted from this paper. The fragment of ontology presented in Table 1 can be visualized using the *InstanceOf* perspective as in Table 2.

---

[2] In WSML $\alpha[\beta \text{ ofType } \gamma]$ is an atomic formulas called *molecule*; in here both α and γ identifies concepts while β identifies an attribute and '?' is used to denote variables. An example of a molecule for the ontology fragment in Table 1 is *person[name* **ofType** *string]*.

4.3 RelatedBy Perspective

The *RelatedBy* perspective focuses on the attributes of the ontology, and describes them from their domain and type perspective.

$$ci(x) \text{ iff } ci_{RelatedBy}(x) \quad pi(x) \text{ iff } pi_{RelatedBy}(x) \quad di(x) \text{ iff } di_{RelatedBy}(x) \qquad (23)$$

In the same way as above, $ci_{RelatedBy}(x), pi_{RelatedBy}(x)$ and $di_{RelatedBy}(x)$ are defined using WSML; also the *describes* and *successor* relations can be linked with the WSML ontologies in a similar manner as presented in Section 4.1. From space reasons, they are omitted from this paper. The fragment of ontology presented in Table 1 can be visualized using the *RelatedBy* perspective as in Table 2.

5 Linking the Model to a Mapping Language

In this section we specify the allowed mappings for each of the perspectives described in Section 4. We start from the following premise $map_{Mc}(x_S, y_T) \wedge Mc =< \phi_S, \gamma_{\phi_S}, \phi_T, \delta_{\phi_T} >$ which means that the elements x_S and y_T from the source and target ontology, respectively, are to be mapped in the mapping context Mc. In the following subsection we will discuss the situations that can occur for a pair of perspectives (due to space reasons we address only those cases when the source and target perspectives are of the same type). The types of mapping that can be created will be analyzed with respect to the Abstract Mapping Language proposed in [1], briefly described in 5.1.

5.1 Abstract Mapping Language

We chose to express the mappings in the abstract mapping language proposed in [1] because it does not commit to any existing ontology representation language. Later, a formal semantic has to be associated with it and to ground the mappings to a concrete language (such a grounding can be found in [8]). We provide only a brief listing of some of the abstract mapping language statements:

- *classMapping* - By using this statement, mappings between classes in the source and the target ontologies are specified. Such a statement can be conditioned by class conditions (*attributeValueConditions, attribuiteTypeConditions, attributeOccurenceConditions*).
- *attributeMapping* - Specifies mappings between attributes. Such statements usually appear together with classMappings and can be conditioned by attribute conditions (*valueConditions, typeConditions*).
- *classAttributeMapping* - It specifies mappings between a class and an attribute (or the other way around) and it can be conditioned by both class conditions and attribute conditions.
- *instanceMapping* - It states a mapping between two individuals, one from the source and the other from the target.

In the next sections we illustrate how these mapping language statements are generated during design time by using a particular combination of perspectives.

5.2 *PartOf* to *PartOf* Mappings

When using the *PartOf* perspective to create mappings for both the source and target ontologies we have the following allowed cases (derived from axiom 15):

- $pi_{PartOf}(x_S) \wedge pi_{PartOf}(x_T)$. In this case, the mapping will generate a *classMapping* statement in the mapping language and leaves the mapping context unchanged (axioms 11 and 16).
- $ci_{PartOf}(x_S) \wedge ci_{PartOf}(x_T)$. Generates a *classMapping* statement and updates the context for the source and target perspectives (axioms 12 and 16).
- $di_{PartOf}(x_S) \wedge di_{PartOf}(x_T)$. In this case $successor(y_S, x_S) \wedge successor(y_T, x_T)$ holds and we can distinguish the following situations:
  - $pi_{PartOf}(y_S) \wedge pi_{PartOf}(y_T)$. An *attributeMapping* is generated between x_S and x_T followed by a *classMapping* between y_S and y_T. Conforming to the axioms 13 and 16, the mapping context remains unchanged.
  - $ci_{PartOf}(y_S) \wedge ci_{PartOf}(y_T)$. An *attributeMapping* is generated having as participants x_S and x_T. The mapping context is updated conform to the axioms 13, 14 and 16.
  - $pi_{PartOf}(y_S) \wedge ci_{PartOf}(y_T)$. Generates a *classAttributeMapping* between z_S and the x_T, where $describes(x_S, z_S)$. The new mapping context keeps the source context unchanged while decomposing the target context over y_T.
  - $ci_{PartOf}(y_S) \wedge pi_{PartOf}(y_T)$. This case is symmetric with the one presented above and it generates a *classAttributeMapping* between x_S and the z_T where $describes(x_T, z_T)$.
- $ci_{PartOf}(x_S) \wedge pi_{PartOf}(x_T)$. It is not allowed for this combination of perspectives. To take an example, such a case would involve a mapping between $ci_{PartOf}(person)$ and $pi_{PartOf}(string)$ where $describes(hasName, person) \wedge successor(string, hasName)$, which does not have any semantic meaning. A correct solution would be a mapping between $ci_{PartOf}(person)$ and $ci_{PartOf}(u_T)$ such as $\exists v_T.(describes(v_T, u_T) \wedge successor(string, v_T)$.
- $pi_{PartOf}(x_S) \wedge ci_{PartOf}(x_T)$. The same explanation applies as above.

5.3 *InstanceOf* to *InstanceOf* Mappings

When using the *InstanceOf* perspectives we can create similar mappings to those created with the *PartOf* perspectives, the difference being that conditions are added to the mappings, and by this, the mappings hold only if the conditions are fulfilled. The mappings between two primitive items or between two compound items in the *InstanceOf* perspective are identical with the ones from the *PartOf* perspective. For the remaining cases we have:

- $di_{InstanceOf}(x_S, w_S) \wedge di_{InstanceOf}(x_T, w_T)$. In this case, we have $successor(<x_S, w_S>, y_S) \wedge successor(<x_T, w_T>, y_T)$ and we can distinguish the following situations:
  - $pi_{InstanceOf}(y_S) \wedge pi_{InstanceOf}(y_T)$. An *attributeMapping* is generated between x_S and x_T conditioned by two *attributeValueCondition*s imposing

the presence of w_S and w_T in the mediated data. Also a *classMapping* between y_S and y_T is generated. Conforming to the axioms 13 and 16 the mapping context remains unchanged.
- $ci_{InstanceOf}(y_S) \wedge ci_{InstanceOf}(y_T)$. An *attributeMapping* is generated having as participants x_S and x_T conditioned by two *typeConditions*. The mapping context is updated conforming to the axioms 13, 14 and 16.
- $pi_{InstanceOf}(y_S) \wedge ci_{InstanceOf}(y_T)$. This case generates a *classAttributeMapping* between z_S and the x_T, where $describes(x_S, z_S)$. A *typeCondition* is added for x_T attribute. The new mapping context keeps the source context unchanged while decomposing the target context over y_T.
- $ci_{InstanceOf}(y_S) \wedge pi_{InstanceOf}(y_T)$. This case is symmetric with the one presented above and it generates a *classAttributeMapping* between x_S and the z_T, where $describes(x_T, z_T)$. A *typeCondition* is added for x_S.
– $di_{InstanceOf}(x_S, w_S) \wedge pi_{InstanceOf}(x_T)$. *InstanceOf* extends the set of allowed mappings as defined in 15. For z_S such that $describes(<x_S, w_S>, z_S)$, a *classMapping* between z_S and x_T is generated, conditioned by an *attributeValueCondition* on the attribute x_S and value w_S.
– $pi_{InstanceOf}(x_S) \wedge di_{InstanceOf}(x_T, w_T)$. Similar with the above case.
– $ci_{InstanceOf}(x_S) \wedge pi_{InstanceOf}(x_T)$. It is not directly allowed for this combination of perspectives, but the intended mapping can be created as described by previous case.
– $pi_{InstanceOf}(x_S) \wedge ci_{InstanceOf}(x_T)$. The same explanation applies as above.

5.4 *RelatedBy* to *RelatedBy* Mappings

In the *RelatedBy* perspective attributes are seen as root elements, having only two descriptions: their domain and their type. We identify the following cases:

– $pi_{RelatedBy}(x_S) \wedge pi_{RelatedBy}(x_T)$. This case does not appear as we do not have primitive items in the *RelatedBy* perspective.
– $ci_{RelatedBy}(x_S) \wedge ci_{RelatedBy}(x_T)$. The mapping will generate an *attributeMapping* statement in the mapping language having as participants x_S and x_T.
– $di_{RelatedBy}(x_S) \wedge di_{RelatedBy}(x_T)$. The source and the target perspectives are changed from *RelatedBy* to *PartOf* and the context is obtained by decomposing the perspectives over z_S and z_T, where $successor(z_S, x_S) \wedge successor(z_T, x_T)$

5.5 Mapping Examples

Table 6 shows examples of mappings in the abstract mapping language and how these mappings look like when grounded to WSML when mapping the person concept in the the source ontology with human (and man) in the target ontology. When evaluated, the WSML mapping rules will generate instances of *man* if the *gender* condition is met, or of *human* otherwise. The construct $mediated(X, C)$ represents the identifier of the newly created target instance, where X is the source instance that is transformed, and C is the target concept we map to.

Table 6. Decomposition and context updates

Abstract Mapping Language	Mapping Rules in WSML

`Mapping(o1#persono2#man`
  `classMapping(`*one-way*
    `person man))`
`Mapping(o1#ageo2#age`
  `attributeMapping(one-way`
    `[(person)age=>integer]`
        `[(human)age=>integer]))`
`Mapping(o1#nameo2#name`
  `attributeMapping(one-way`
    `[(person)name => string]`
        `[(human)name => string]))`
`Mapping(o1#hasGendero2#man`
  `attributeClassMapping(one-way`
    `[(person)hasGender => gender] man))`
  `valueCondition(`
    `[(person)hasGender => gender] male)`
	`axiom mapping001 definedBy`
	  `mediated(X_1, o2#man) memberOf o2#man:-`
	    `X_1 memberOf o1#person.`
	`axiom mapping001 definedBy`
	  `mediated(X_2, o2#human) memberOf o2#human:-`
	    `X_2 memberOf o1#person.`
	`axiom mapping005 definedBy`
	  `mediated(X_5, o2#human)[o2#age hasValue Y_6]:-`
	    `X_5[o1#age hasValue Y_6]:o1#person.`
	`axiom mapping006 definedBy`
	  `mediated(X_7, o2#human)[o2#name hasValue Y_8]:-`
	    `X_7[o1#name hasValue Y_8]:o1#person.`
	`axiom mapping007 definedBy`
	  `mediated(Y_11, o2#man)[A_9 hasValue AR_10]:-`
	    `mediated(Y_11, o2#human)[A_9 hasValue AR_10 ],`
	    `Y_11[o1#hasGender hasValue o1#male].`

6 Implementation and Prototype

The ideas and methods presented in this paper are used in the mediation component of the WSMX architecture. The WSMX Data Mediation component is designed to support data transformation, which means to transform the source ontology instances entering the system into instances expressed in terms of the target ontology. As described above, in order to make this possible the data mediation process consists of a design-time and a run-time phase. Each of these two phases has its own implementations: the *Ontology Mapping Tool* and the *Run-time Data Mediator*.

The *Ontology Mapping Tool* is implemented as an Eclipse plug-in, part of the Web Service Modeling Toolkit (WSMT)[3] [7] an integrated environment for ontology creation, visualization and mapping. The Ontology Mapping Tool is currently compatible with WSMO ontologies (but by providing the appropriate wrappers different ontology languages could be supported); it offers different ways of browsing the ontologies using perspectives and allows the domain expert to create mappings between two ontologies (source and target) and to store them in a persistent mapping storage. Currently only the *PartOf* and *InstanceOf* perspectives are implemented while decomposition and context principles are fully supported. These principles, together with the suggestion mechanisms make the prototype a truly semi-automatic ontology mapping tool.

The *Run-time Data Mediator* plays the role of the data mediation component in WSMX (available together with the WSMX system[4]. It uses the abstract mappings created during design-time, grounds them to WSML and uses a reasoner to evaluate them against the incoming source instances. The storage used is a relational data base. The Run-time Data Mediator is also available as a stand alone application.

---

[3] Open Source Project available at http://sourceforge.net/projects/wsmt
[4] Open Source Project available at http://sourceforge.net/projects/wsmx

7 Related Work

MAFRA [10] proposes a Semantic Bridge Ontology to represent the mappings. This ontology has as central concept, the so called "Semantic bridge" which is the equivalent of our mapping language statements. The main difference to our approach is that MAFRA does not define any explicit relation between the graphical representation of the ontologies in their tool and the generation of these Semantic Bridges or between the user's actions and the particular bridges to be used. The formal abstract model we propose links the graphical elements of the user interface with the mapping representation language, ensuring a clear correspondence between user actions and the generated mappings.

PROMPT[9] is an interactive and semi-automatic algorithm for ontology merging. The user is asked to apply a set of given operations to a set of possible matches, based on which, the algorithm recomputes the set of suggestions and signals the potential inconsistencies. The fundamental difference in our approach is that instead of defining several operations we have only one operation (*map*) which will take two ontology elements as arguments, and multiple *perspectives* to graphically represent the ontologies in the user interface. Based on the particular types of perspectives used and on the roles of the *map* action arguments in that perspective the tool is able to determine the type of mapping to be created. Such that, by switching between perspectives, different ontology mismatches can be addressed by using a single *map* action. An interesting aspect is that PROMPT defines the term *local context* which perfectly matches our *context* definition: the set of descriptions attached to an item together with the items these descriptions point to. While PROMPT uses the local context in decision-making when computing the suggestions, we also use the context when displaying the ontology.

Instead of allowing browsing on multiple hierarchical layers, as PROMPT and MAFRA do, we adopt a context based browsing that allows the identification of the domain experts intentions and generates mappings.

8 Conclusion and Further Work

In this paper we define a formal model for mapping creation. This model sits between the graphical elements used to represent the ontologies and the result of the mapping process, i.e. the ontology alignment. By defining both the graphical instruments and the mapping creation strategies in terms of this model we assure a direct and complete correspondence between human user action and the effect on the generated ontology alignment. In addition we propose a set of different graphical perspectives that can be linked with the same model, each of them offering a different viewpoint on the displayed ontology. By combining this types of perspectives different types of mismatches can be addressed in an identical way from one pair of views to the other.

As future work, we plan to focus in identifying more relevant perspectives and to investigate the possible combination of these perspectives in respect with the types of mappings to be created. These would lead in the end to defining a set of mapping patterns in terms of our model, which will significantly improve the mappings finding mechanism. Another point to be investigated is the mapping with multiple participants from the source and from the target ontology. In this paper we investigated only the cases when exactly one element from the source and exactly one element from the target can be selected at a time to be mapped. We plan to also address transformation functions from the perspective of our model. Such transformation functions (e.g. string concatenation) would allow the creation of new target data based on a combination of given source data.

References

1. J. de Bruijn, D. Foxvog, and K. Zimmerman. Ontology mediation patterns library. SEKT Project Deliverable D4.3.1, Digital Enterprise Research Institute, University of Innsbruck, 2004.
2. M. Ehrig, S. Staab, and Y. Sure. Bootstrapping ontology alignment methods with APFEL. *Fourth International Semantic Web Conference (ISWC-2005)*, 2005.
3. C. Feier, A. Polleres, R. Dumitru, J. Domingue, M. Stollberg, and D. Fensel. Towards intelligent web services: The web service modeling ontology (WSMO). *International Conference on Intelligent Computing (ICIC)*, 2005.
4. M. R. Genesereth and N. J. Nilson. *Logical Foundations of Artificial Inteligence*. Morgan-Kaufmann, 1988.
5. A. Polleres H. Lausen, J. de Bruijn and D. Fensel. WSML - A Language Framework for Semantic Web Services. *W3C Workshop on Rule Languages for Interoperability*, April 2005.
6. A. Haller, E. Cimpian, A. Mocan, E. Oren, and C. Bussler. WSMX - A Semantic Service-Oriented Architecture. *International Conference on Web Services (ICWS 2005)*, July 2005.
7. M. Kerrigan. WSMOViz: An Ontology Visualization Approach for WSMO. *10th International Conference on Information Visualization*, 2006.
8. A. Mocan and E. Cimpian. Mapping creation using a view based approach. *1st International Workshop on Mediation in Semantic Web Services (Mediate 2005)*, December 2005.
9. N.F. Noy and M. A. Munsen. The PROMPT suite: Interactive tools for ontology merging and mapping. *International Journal of Human-Computer Studies*, 6(59), 2003.
10. N. Silva and J. Rocha. Semantic web complex ontology mapping. *Proceedings of the IEEE Web Intelligence (WI2003)*, page 82, 2003.

A Semantic Context-Aware Access Control Framework for Secure Collaborations in Pervasive Computing Environments

Alessandra Toninelli[1], Rebecca Montanari[1], Lalana Kagal[2], and Ora Lassila[3]

[1] Dipartimento di Elettronica, Informatica e Sistemistica
Università di Bologna
Viale Risorgimento, 2 - 40136 Bologna - Italy
{atoninelli, rmontanari}@deis.unibo.it
[2] MIT CSAIL
32 Vassar Street, Cambridge, MA 02139, USA
lkagal@csail.mit.edu
[3] Nokia Research Center Cambridge
3 Cambridge Center, Cambridge, MA 02142, USA
ora.lassila@nokia.com

Abstract. Wireless connectivity and widespread diffusion of portable devices offer novel opportunities for users to share resources anywhere and anytime, and to form ad-hoc coalitions. Resource access control is crucial to leverage these ad-hoc collaborations. In pervasive scenarios, however, collaborating entities cannot be predetermined and resource availability frequently varies, even unpredictably, due to user/device mobility, thus complicating resource access control. Access control policies cannot be defined based on entity's identities/roles, as in traditional access control solutions, or be specified a priori to face any operative run time condition, but require continuous adjustments to adapt to the current situation. To address these issues, this paper advocates the adoption of novel access control policy models that follow two main design guidelines: *context-awareness* to control resource access on the basis of context visibility and to enable dynamic adaptation of policies depending on context changes, and *semantic technologies* for context/policy specification to allow high-level description and reasoning about context and policies. The paper also describes the design of a semantic context-aware policy model that adopts ontologies and rules to express context and context-aware access control policies and supports policy adaptation.

1 Introduction

Telecommunication systems and the Internet are converging towards an integrated pervasive scenario that permits users to access services anytime and anywhere even when they are on the move. Recent technological advances in both computational capabilities and connectivity of portable devices are also enabling mobile users in physical proximity of each other to form ad-hoc networks for spontaneous coalitions and to engage in opportunistic and temporary resource sharing without relying on the availability of a fixed network infrastructure.

However, these ad-hoc collaborations impose several challenges to the secure retrieval of and operation on distributed resources, undermining several assumptions of traditional access control solutions. These solutions usually assign permissions to principals depending on their identity/role. In the new pervasive scenario, however, users typically share services with unknown entities and, more importantly, with entities whose identity may not be sufficiently trustworthy. In addition, since spontaneous collaborations among users are typically established in an impromptu and opportunistic fashion, it may not be possible to rely on formal collaboration agreements to decide who can access which resources and how, thus excluding the possibility to exploit access control policies defined on a contractual basis as in medium or long-term inter-organizational coalitions. Access control in spontaneous coalitions is further complicated by the high dynamicity in resource availability. Each collaborating entity may alternatively play the role of either a service client or provider or both, depending on dynamic conditions and the current status of interaction. When playing the service provider role, an entity may introduce new services into the environment, thus changing the set of available resources. Variations in resource availability occur also because of the transience of ad-hoc coalitions where entities -resource providers- leave and/or enter a coalition, unpredictably, at any time.

Appropriate access control models are needed to enable resource sharing and access in spontaneous coalition scenarios. It is crucial that the definition and enforcement of access control policies take into account the heterogeneity and dynamicity of the environment in terms of available services, computing devices, and user characteristics. To address these issues, this paper advocates a paradigm shift from subject-centric access control models to context-centric ones. Hereinafter, at a high level, the term "context" is defined as any information that is useful for characterizing the state or the activity of an entity or the world in which this entity operates [1]. Differently from subject-centric solutions where context is an optional element of policy definition that is simply used to restrict the applicability scope of the permissions assigned to the subject, in context-centric solutions, context is the first-class principle that explicitly guides both policy specification and enforcement process and it is not possible to define a policy without the explicit specification of the context that makes policy valid. We also claim that context-centric access control solutions need to adopt ontological technologies as key building blocks for supporting expressive policy modeling and reasoning. Semantically-rich policy representations permit description of policies at different levels of abstraction and support reasoning about both the structure and properties of the elements that constitute a pervasive system, i.e., the context and the management policies, thus enabling policy analysis, conflict detection, and harmonization.

This paper describes an implementation of these ideas in a policy model that exploits context-awareness and ontological technologies for the specification and the evaluation of access control policies. In our access control framework the role of context exploitation for controlling access control is twofold. Drawing inspiration from the RBAC model that exploits the concept of role as a mechanism for grouping subjects based on their properties [2], we state that, the same as with role, the concept of context can provide a level of indirection between entities requesting resource access and their permitted set of actions on requested resources. Instead of assigning permissions directly to the subjects and defining the contexts in which these permissions should be considered valid and applicable, a system administrator defines for each resource the contextual conditions that enable one to operate on it. When an entity operates in a specific context, she automatically acquires the ability to perform the set of actions permitted in the current context.

In addition, we consider context crucial for enabling policy adaptation. In pervasive environments the conditions that characterize interactions between users and resources may be largely unpredictable. Consequently, policies cannot all be specified *a priori* to face any operative run-time situations, but may require dynamic adjustments to be able to control access to resources. We use the term "policy adaptation" to describe the ability of the policy-based management system to adjust policy specifications and evaluation mechanisms in order to enable their enforcement in different, possibly unforeseen situations. In this scope, it is crucial to be able to represent the various operative conditions under which policies should be applied, i.e., the context, and to define the expected behaviour of the policy framework on the basis of such context variations.

Another fundamental design guideline of our access control model is the adoption of an ontological approach using Description Logic (DL) to context/policy specification to enable context/policy classification, comparison, and static conflict detection. We also adopt a rule-based approach taking the perspective of Logic Programming (LP) to encode rules that allows policy makers to specify policies based on context variables whose value is unknown at policy definition time, thus enabling the efficient enforcement of policies defined over dynamically determined context values. Let us note that our work does not aim at providing a unifying logical framework for DL and LP, which have well-known crucial logical mismatches, but rather at combining the logical results obtained by means of their respective reasoning features.

The paper is organized as follows. Section 2 outlines some crucial requirements for the definition of access control policies in dynamic scenarios like inter-organizational spontaneous coalitions. Section 3 presents our proposed semantic context-aware policy model, while Section 4 compares it with related state-of-the art access control solutions. Final remarks and future activities follow in Section 5.

2 Policy Requirements for Spontaneous Coalition Scenarios

To point out some unique challenges in dynamic mobile environments, we start by considering the spontaneous coalition scenario of a meeting occurring during a conference among members of different universities working on a common project. In the remainder of the paper, we use this meeting scenario as a running example to illustrate the main access control challenges and our solution guidelines. In this meeting scenario, each participant may wish to grant access to her resources to other participants, in order to enable cooperation and knowledge sharing. Access to personal resources must be regulated in order to protect them from malicious access or misuse. However, the specification of adequate access control policies in the depicted scenario presents us with several challenges. For example, the complete list of participants may not be known in advance or it may be modified just before the meeting starts or even during a meeting, thus making it infeasible to define access control policies based on the requestor's identity.

Even the role-based approach seems cumbersome in controlling access to cross-organizational resources, since role definitions and hierarchies might vary across parties, thus making their interpretation difficult outside the specific boundaries of each organization. A possible solution might be the creation of a common ad-hoc role for all meeting participants, to which each participant delegates her roles, so that others are able to access her resources [3]. However, since roles required to access resources have to be separately assigned by each participant to this ad-hoc role, inconsistencies may arise between the access rights of the different members, e.g., in the case of a member being allowed to access another member's resources, but not vice versa. Moreover, the activation/deactivation of such temporary roles represents a critical security issue.

In order to properly control access to resources, we claim the need for a more general and comprehensive approach that exploits not only identity and role information but also other contextual information, such as location, time, ongoing activities, etc. In particular, we believe that it may be advantageous for each participant to define the access control policies for his managed resources simply according to the current conditions of the requestor, the resource, and of the surrounding environment, i.e., the current resource context. For instance, in an informal meeting, access should be granted to those who are currently located in the same room where the resource owner is located, if they actually participate in the activity/project relating to the meeting, as long as current time corresponds to the time scheduled for the meeting. Access control policies should be associated with the combination of one or more context conditions and users should be instantaneously granted/denied access to resources on the basis of those specific context conditions.

The integration of access control with contextual information has two main characteristics. First, it is an example of an active access control model [4]. Active security models are aware of the context associated with an ongoing activity in providing access control and thus distinguish the passive concept of permission assignment from the active concept of context-based permission activation. Second, the exploitation of context as a mechanism for grouping policies and for evaluating applicable ones simplifies access control management by increasing policy specification reuse and by making policy update and revocation easier. In fact, in subject-based access control solutions, the tight coupling of the identities/roles of principals with their permissions and with the operating conditions in the system to grant permitted actions requires security administrators to foresee all contexts in which each principal is likely to operate. In pervasive environments where principals are typically unknown and where contextual conditions frequently change, this traditional approach may lead to a combinatorial explosion of the number of policies to be written, force a long development time, and even introduce potential bugs. The traditional approach, when applied to pervasive scenarios, also lacks flexibility. New access control policies need to be designed and implemented from scratch for any principal when new context situations occur. In a context-centric access control approach, instead of managing principals and their permissions individually, administrators define the set of permitted actions for each context. When a principal operates in a specific context, the evaluation process of his permissions in that context is triggered.

Another difficulty in dynamic collaboration scenarios is that it is impossible to define in advance all necessary policies for all possible situations. These environments should permit new policies to be dynamically and easily specified on demand as new situations occur as well as allow existing policies to be adapted to meet changing conditions. For example, let us consider the case of a meeting that continues beyond its originally scheduled end time. It is essential to ensure that meeting participants can continue to access each other's resources as long as the meeting is actually taking place. It is therefore necessary to adapt previous policies to reflect the new conditions of the meeting. In the absence of policy adaptation support, access to the policy owner's resources would be denied after the scheduled time, since the conditions that limit the applicability of the policy, specifically the condition concerning time, would be evaluated to be false. In a traditional approach, the policy owner would have to specify another policy to grant access to her resources after the scheduled end time of the meeting. However, this solution presents several disadvantages. First, the resource owner might not be the policy administrator of her resources, and might be unable to specify the policy when needed. In addition, the specification of ad-hoc policies is not a correct approach to policy definition because it does not favor clarity or traceability, thus complicating policy management. Finally, in such a case, efficiency and security might collide. If the policy owner specifies an access control policy that grants access to her resources for a short time interval, e.g., ten minutes, she might possibly be forced to specify the same policy several times because the eventual end time of the meeting is not known in advance. Conversely, a policy granting access for a longer period might allow undesired access to the user's resources after the meeting.

This simple example demonstrates the need for a new approach to policy specification that not only defines policies based on context information, but also allows the seamless adaptation of policies depending on current context. In this example, we need to "instruct" the system such that, if certain context conditions hold, the context activating the policy is still considered active. Essential for policy adaptation is appropriate modeling of contextual information that enables the policy framework to sense and reason about the current situation. This ensures adequate access control even in changing and possibly unforeseen conditions.

Another important principle is the adoption of semantically-rich representations for policy definition. A semantics-based approach allows description of contexts and associated policies at a high level of abstraction, in a form that enables their classification and comparison. This feature is essential, for instance, in order to detect conflicts between policies before they are actually enforced. In addition, semantic techniques can provide the reasoning features needed to deduce new information from existing knowledge. This ability may be exploited by the policy framework when faced with unexpected situations to react in a contextually appropriate way.

3   A Semantic Context-Aware Access Control Policy Model

Our access control model is centered around the concept of context that we consider to be any characterizing information about the controlled resources and about the world surrounding them. We adopt a resource-centric approach to context modeling: contexts are associated with the resources to be controlled and represent all and only those conditions that enable access to the resources. Contexts act as intermediaries between the entities requesting access to resources and the set of operations that can be performed on these resources. Access control policies define for each context how to operate on the associated resource(s). In particular, access control policies can be viewed as one-to-one associations between contexts and allowed actions. Drawing inspiration from Java protection domains [5], we call these contexts hereinafter as *protection contexts*: they provide users with a controlled visibility of the considered resource in terms of performable access actions on it (action view). Protection contexts are determined by the defined policies. Entities can perform only those actions that are associated with the protection contexts currently in effect (*active context*), i.e., the contexts whose defining conditions match the operating conditions of the requesting entity, requested resource, and environment as measured by specific sensors. All entities sharing the same active protection context share the same abilities to operate on the context-related resource.

3.1   Context Model

A protection context consists of all the characterizing information that is considered relevant for access control, logically organized in parts that describe the state of the resource associated with the protection context, such as availability or load (the *resource* part), the entities operating on the resource (the policy/resource owner and the requestor), such as their roles, identities or security credentials (the *actor* part), and the surrounding environment conditions, such as time, or other available resources (the *environment* part).

   A protection context is a set of attributes and predetermined values, labelled in some meaningful way and associated with desirable semantics [6]. Instead of a single value, an attribute could also define constraints for a range of allowed values. Let us note that an attribute value can be assigned to a fixed constant or can be a variable over a value domain. The current state of the surrounding world is also represented in terms of attribute/value pairs where the attribute values represent the output of sensors (with the term "sensor" used loosely). For a protection context to be "in effect", the attribute values that define the current state of the world have to match the definition of the context (as given above).

   We adopt description logics (DL) and associated inferencing to model and process protection context data. In particular, we use Web Ontology Language (OWL) -based ontologies as shown in Figure 1a. A protection context is defined as a subclass of a generic context and consists of the resource, the actor and the environment context elements. Each context element is characterized by an identity property and a location property defining the physical or logical position of an entity. Single context elements are characterized by specific additional properties.

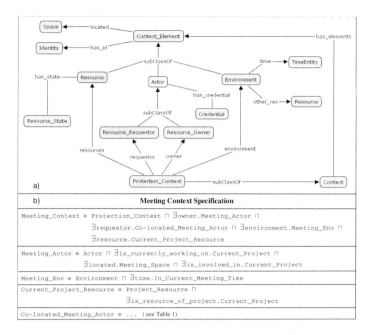

Fig. 1. Context ontology model and an OWL context specification example

Figure 1b shows an OWL-based protection context representation example related to the meeting scenario depicted in Section 2. This example assumes that each actor taking part to the meeting owns a set of resources that relates to the project/activity the meeting is about and shares these resources with the other participants. In particular, the protection context shown in Figure 1b grants access to these resources under certain conditions: the resources must be specifically pertaining the project discussed at the current meeting; the resource owner must be involved in the meeting's project as "project partner", must be currently work on the project-related set of resources, and must be located in the place where the meeting is planned to take place to guarantee that he is attending the meeting. The entities requesting access to resources must be involved in the project as "project partners", co-located with the resource owner, and currently working on project-specific resources on their devices. In addition, resources can be accessed when the time in the environment corresponds to the time scheduled for the meeting. Let us note that the core context ontology has been extended to model the specific meeting-related concepts. For example, a resource is associated with the project it relates to, an actor has attributes describing the project she is involved in or she is currently working on, and the environment time can be expressed in terms of scheduled events in an actor's calendar. The meeting ontology also explicitly defines the concept of "current event", which is an event or activity occurring at the moment of context and policy evaluation. In addition, we make use of a location ontology that is provided within the basic context model[1].

---

[1] All our ontologies are available at http://lia.deis.unibo.it/research/SemanticPolicies.

Let us note that the use of DL in context modeling and reasoning has well-known benefits. For instance, considering protection contexts as classes and a set of sensor inputs (i.e., the current state of the world) as individuals, DL-based reasoning allows one to determine which protection contexts are in effect by verifying which protection context classes the current state is an instance of, and to figure out how defined protection contexts relate to each other (nesting, etc.) [6].

However, DL-based reasoning may not always be sufficient. Our context-aware access control model needs more expressive context reasoning in order to be effective. On the one hand, we need to correlate contexts using not only class definitions (as in pure DL-based reasoning) but also property path relationships between anonymous individuals. For instance, in a meeting context we need to state that if the resource owner is located in a certain place and the resource requestor is located in the same place, the two are co-located. On the other hand, we need to bind the context attribute values to specific instances depending on application-specific context attribute/value relationships. For instance, to enforce the meeting-related policies, we must be able to determine, at each moment, what the actual current project is, so that the corresponding resources belonging to each actor are identified and protected. To overcome some DL-based reasoning restrictions we combine it with LP-based reasoning. In particular, we define two types of rules: context *aggregation rules* to support reasoning using property path relationships and context *instantiation rules* to provide OWL assertions for attribute values. For instance, the condition of co-location between two collaborating entities at a conference is expressed with an aggregation rule, whereas the condition of current project with an instantiation rule. Both types of rules are expressed according to the following pattern:

<u>if</u> context attributes $C_1 ... C_n$ <u>then</u> context attribute C_m

that corresponds to a Horn clause, where predicates in the head and in the body are represented by classes and properties defined in the context and application-specific ontologies.

3.2 Context-Aware Access Control Policy Model

Our policy model consists of three distinct phases (see Figure 2a): policy specification, policy refinement, and policy evaluation. In the *policy specification* phase resource administrators specify OWL-based policies representing ontological associations between actions and protection contexts ontology definitions. Figure 2b shows an example of a policy that controls access to the meeting resources. The protection contexts may have attribute values assigned to constants or may be variables. In the latter case, attributes are assigned proper values by combining DL-based and LP-based reasoning over the context ontology and the context aggregation and activation rules. In particular, the output of LP rules is fed into the DL knowledge base to determine the value of each attribute given the current context. This means that OWL-based policies cannot be directly enforced into the system, but need to be further processed. By adopting an object-oriented terminology, OWL-based policies can be viewed as policy types: they define the actions that are allowed in a set of context types. In order to be enforced in the real world, policy types need to be transformed into policy objects that associate sets of actions with specific instantiated contextual conditions. In the policy specification phase, administrators have to define aggregation and evaluation rules to enable effective enforcement and adaptation of OWL policies. For instance, in the meeting scenario an instantiation rule is needed to instantiate the current project attribute value included in the specification of the Colocated_Meeting_Actor class. The resource administrator could also define an aggregation rule to represent the "co-location" property as a relationship path based on the "location" property by means of variables.

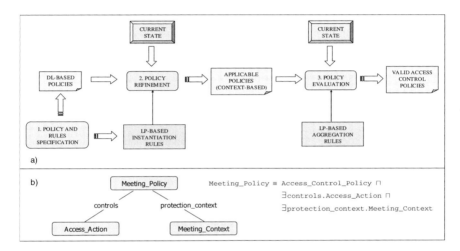

Fig. 2. The Context-Aware Policy Model and the DL-based meeting policy specification

In the *policy refinement* phase, OWL policies are instantiated by adapting them to the particular state of the world, in order to obtain the set of applicable policies. In the *policy evaluation* stage, the protection contexts of applicable policies are verified against the current state of context elements as measured by sensors to determine the set of currently active policies. Let us note that the context-aware transformation process comprising of policy refinement and evaluation may be triggered by any resource context change, such as a new user requesting to access the resource or a significant change in the resource state, e.g., its location.

It is worth noticing that our policy model adopts a combined approach to policy specification and reasoning. DL reasoning is exploited to perform static classification and conflict resolution of context and policy ontologies. LP reasoning is used to adapt the specification of OWL policies to the current state and allow their dynamic evaluation at access request time by means of appropriate rules. Adopting a combined approach allows us to benefit from the advantages of a pure ontology-based approach and those of a pure rule-based approach, both of which exhibit some limitations with respect to the definition and evaluation of policies and contexts [6, 7]. It is worth noting that our context model does not require the tight integration of the DL and the LP logical frameworks, which have well-known logical mismatches, but it is rather a combination of the two aiming at achieving more expressive description and reasoning capabilities about contexts and policies.

In the following subsections we focus on the policy refinement and evaluation phases which characterize our model and distinguish it from other state-of-the art related access control solutions [8, 9, 3].

3.2.1 Policy Refinement

Let us recall the meeting scenario to describe how policy refinement works. In the protection context of the meeting policy, shown before, the resource requestor property must belong to the Co-located_Meeting_Actor class that imposes that the resource requestor is co-located with the resource owner. Table 1 shows the definition of this context element, using a compact DL notation instead of OWL. Let us consider the restrictions applying to the properties is_currently_working_on and is_involved_in. These properties are restricted to a variable value, represented by the Current_Project class. This is an intrinsically variable value since the current project varies over time due to the changing activities of the resource owner and requestor, thus corresponding to different instances at different time instants.

Table 1. Co-located_Meeting_Actor class specification and instantiation and aggregation rules

Colocated Meeting Actor Specification	
`Meeting_Actor ≡ ∃is_currently_working_on.Current_Project ⊓` `∃is_involved_in.Current_Project ⊓ ∃colocated_with.Resource_Owner`	
Instantiation Rules to be applied in case of an ordinary scheduled meeting	
`Current_Meeting_Rule`	`Scheduled_Calendar_Slot(?x) ∧ Meeting(?x) →` `Current_Meeting(?x)`
`Current_Project_Rule`	`Current_Meeting(?x) ∧ Project(?y) ∧` `meeting_on_project(?x,?y) → Current_Project(?y)`
Instantiation Rules to be applied in case of a meeting prolongation	
`Current_Project_Rule-2`	`Actor(?y) ∧ Last_Current_Project(?x) ∧` `is_currently_working_on(?y,?x) ∧` `Scheduled_Calendar_Slot(?z) ∧ Idle(?z) →` `Current_Project(?x)`
`Current_Meeting_Rule-2`	`Scheduled_Calendar_Slot(?x) ∧ Idle(?x) ∧` `Past_Calendar_Slot(?y) ∧ Meeting(?y) Current_Project(?z) ∧` `meeting_on_project(?y,?z) → Current_Meeting(?y)`
Aggregation Rule to determine co-location	
`Colocation_Rule`	`Actor(?x) ∧ Actor(?y) ∧ SymbolicSpace(?z) ∧ located(?x,?z)` `∧ located(?y,?z) → colocated_with(?x,?y)`

The defined context instantiation rules are used to determine the correct instance of the current project class at access request time. In particular, let us consider the first couple of rules shown in Table 1. The first rule establishes that, if the user's calendar shows a meeting for the current time, then that meeting has to be considered the current meeting. The second rule states that the project discussed at the current meeting is the current project. Once the facts about the user's calendar are inserted into the refinement fact base, the first rule is triggered and the inferred current meeting instance is used as a new fact to trigger the second rule. Then, the protection context is instantiated by re-writing it with the inferred context element values. For instance, if SwapMe-Meeting is scheduled on the user calendar, and SwapMe-Project is the corresponding project, then Current_Project is replaced by SwapMe-Project in the Colocated_Meeting_Actor specification. A new protection context is thus instantiated with the SwapMe-Project value and the corresponding policy generated with the instantiated protection context.

The combined adoption of OWL policies and LP rules enables policy adaptation when needed. For example, let us suppose that the meeting has gone beyond the allotted time. Given this state, the first group of rules cannot be applied because there are no valid facts in their head. Therefore, a new set of rules has to be defined during the definition phase to cover the situation of an extended meeting. In particular, the first rule determines the owner's current project on the basis of her past and current activities, independently from her calendar schedule. For instance, if the last instance of current project (determined at pre-defined intervals or at access request time) was the SwapMe-Project, if the calendar does not show any event for the current time, and if the actor is working on the SwapMe-Project, then the SwapMe-Project is still the current project instance. The second rules checks for the last and the current scheduling in the actor calendar. If there is no current event, and the last event was a meeting, and that meeting was about the current project (as determined with the first rule), then the last meeting is also the current one. In our example, the current meeting instance is the SwapMe-Meeting.

3.2.2 Policy Evaluation

We now describe the evaluation phase by using the same meeting scenario. When the current state of context elements, measured by sensors, is matched against the protection context of the meeting applicable policy, it is necessary to determine whether the protection context is currently in effect. During the evaluation phase the Co-located_Meeting_Actor definition of Table 1 is considered as well as the aggregation rule of Table 1 stating that if two actors are located in the same place (defined with the use of variables), they are co-located. Then, the resource owner's and the requestor's location are determined and inserted as facts into the evaluation fact base, which causes the execution of the co-location aggregation rule. Let us suppose that the requestor is co-located with the resource owner. In this case, a new fact is inferred that states that the resource requestor is co-located with the owner. This information is used to build the description of the current state of the world. In particular, an instance of the resource requestor element is created using the resource owner (which is known) as the value for the attribute co-location, and this instance of requestor is used in the protection context instance that describes the current state of the world. The created protection context instance is then compared with the protection context of the meeting policy by making use of ontology classification to recognize whether the former is an instance of the latter.

4 Related Work

Several research efforts have addressed the issue of access control in dynamic environments. We do not intend to provide a general survey of the state-of-the-art access control solutions in dynamic environments, but only to focus on the research that either integrates context-awareness and semantic technologies into access control policy frameworks for pervasive environments or addresses access control issues in similar coalition application scenarios.

Considering context explicitly for access control is a very recent research direction with only few context-dependent policy model proposals. The importance of taking context into account for securing pervasive applications is particularly evident in [8] that allows policy designers to represent contexts through a new type of role called *environment role*. Environment roles capture relevant environmental conditions that are used for restricting and regulating user privileges. Permissions are assigned both to roles (both traditional and environmental ones) and role activation/deactivation mechanisms regulate the access to resources. Environmental roles are similar to our contexts in that they act as intermediaries between users and permissions. However, because environmental roles are statically defined in terms of attribute-constant value pairs their evaluation cannot provide support for policy adaptation as in our proposed semantic context-aware approach. In addition, differently from our approach, in [8] there is no integrated support for representing at a high level of abstraction and reasoning about environmental roles and policies.

By focusing on access control in spontaneous coalitions in pervasive environments, [3] proposes a delegation-based approach, where users participating to a communication session can delegate a set of their permissions to a temporary *session role*, in order to enable access to each other's resources. In particular, one end-point user assigns the session role to the entities he is willing to communicate with. Contextual information is used to define the conditions that must hold in the system in order for the assignment to take place, thus limiting the applicability scope of this process. Only a limited set of contextual information can be specified and no semantic technologies are exploited to represent nor the session role nor the delegation context constraint. In addition, security problems may arise whenever an entity delegated to play the session role leaves the communication session. In fact, unless the user explicitly states she is leaving the session, there is no way for the framework to be aware that the session role must be revoked for the departing user.

The importance of adopting a high level of abstraction for the specification of all security policy building elements (subjects, actions, context, etc..) is starting to emerge in well-known policy frameworks, such as KAoS and Rei [9]. KAoS and Rei represent, respectively, significant examples of DL-based and LP-based policy languages. In particular, KAoS uses OWL as the basis for representing and reasoning about policies within Web Services, Grid Computing, and multi-agent system platforms [10]. Contextual information is represented as ontologies and is used to constrain the applicability of policies. The KAoS approach, however, relying on pure OWL capabilities, encounters some difficulties with regard to the definition of certain kinds of policies, specifically those requiring the definition of variables. Rei adopts OWL-Lite to specify policies and can reason over any domain knowledge expressed in either RDF or OWL [11]. A policy basically consists of a list of rules expressed as OWL properties of the policy and a context represented in terms of ontologies that is used to restrict the policy's applicability. Though represented in OWL-Lite, Rei still allows the definition of variables that are used as placeholders as in Prolog. In this way, Rei overcomes one of the major limitations of the OWL language, and more generally of description logics. i.e., the inability to define variables. On the other hand, the choice of expressing Rei rules similarly to declarative logic programs prevents it from exploiting the full potential of the OWL language. In particular, the Rei engine is able to reason about domain-specific knowledge, but not about policy specification. Our policy model shares some commonalities with regard to context/policy representation with both KAoS and Rei, but differs in how it deals with context. Our approach considers context as the primary basis that allows one to deduce which policies apply to a subject acting in the system whereas KAoS and Rei, similarly to traditional approaches, exploit context to build filtering mechanisms for policy applicability.

5 Conclusions and Future Work

The dynamicity and heterogeneity of pervasive scenarios introduce new access control challenges. A paradigm shift in policy models is needed to move focus from the identity/role of the principal to the context that the principal is operating in. We propose a semantic context-aware policy model, which treats context as a first-class principle for policy specification and adopts a hybrid approach to policy definition based on DL ontologies and LP rules. We are currently working on implementing a prototype for the meeting scenario using OWL to specify ontologies and SWRL to encode rules. For this implementation, we are using Pellet [www.mindswap.org/2003/pellet/] to reason about ontologies and Jess [herzberg.ca.sandia.gov/jess/] for forward-chained reasoning about rules, both accessed through a Java interface (via Jena [jena.sourceforge.net/] with Pellet). We are also working on the design of a deployment model that includes different components in charge of monitoring contexts, installing policies into the system, performing policy refinement and evaluation, and enforcing policies. Future work will include providing alternative implementations of the model using different languages, such as N3Logic [http://www.w3.org/DesignIssues/Notation3.html], which provides a uniform notation for ontology and rule specification, and the cwm reasoner [http://www.w3.org/2000/10/swap/doc/cwm.html]. We also plan to further develop application scenarios in order to analyse the usability and effectiveness of our semantic context-aware model.

References

[1] Dey, A., Abowd, G., and Salber: D.. A conceptual framework and a toolkit for supporting the rapid prototyping of context-aware applications. Human-Computer Interaction, 16:97-166, 2001.
[2] Sandu, R., et al. : "Role based access control models", IEEE Computer, Vol.29, No.2, February (1996).
[3] Liscano, R. and Wang, K.: "A SIP-based Architecture model for Contextual Coalition Access Control for Ubiquitous Computing", In: Proceedings of the Second Annual Conference on Mobile and Ubiquitous Systems (MobiQuitous '05). IEEE Computer Society Press (2005).
[4] Georgiadis, C.K., et al.: "Flexible Team-Based Access Control Using Contexts", In: Proc. of the 6th ACM Symposium on Access Control Models and Technologies (SACMAT 2001), May 3-4, Chantilly, Virginia, USA. ACM (2001).

[5] Gong, L.: "Inside Java 2 Platform Security", Addison Wesley, 1999.
[6] Lassila, O. and Khushraj: D., "Contextualizing Applications via Semantic Middleware", In: Proc. of the Second Annual Conference on Mobile and Ubiquitous Systems (MobiQuitous '05). IEEE Computer Society Press (2005).
[7] Toninelli, A., Kagal, L., Bradshaw, J.M., and Montanari, R.: "Rule-based and Ontology-based Policies: Toward a Hybrid Approach to Control Agents in Pervasive Environments." In: Proc. of the Semantic Web and Policy Workshop (SWPW), in conj. with ISWC 2005, Galway, Ireland, Nov. 7 (2005).
[8] Covington, M.J., et al.: "Securing Context-Aware Applications Using Environmental Roles", In: Proc. of the 6th ACM Symposium on Access Control Models and Technologies (SACMAT 2001), May 3-4, Chantilly, Virginia, USA. ACM (2001).
[9] Tonti, G., Bradshaw, J. M., Jeffers, R., Montanari, R., Suri, N., Uszok, A.: "Semantic Web languages for policy representation and reasoning: A comparison of KAoS, Rei, and Ponder", In: Proc. of the Second International Semantic Web Conference (ISWC2003), LNCS, Vol. 2870. Springer-Verlag, Berlin, pp. 419-437, Sanibel Island, Florida, USA, October 2003.
[10] Uszok, A., et al.: "KAoS policy management for semantic web services". IEEE Intelligent Systems, 19(4), p. 32-41, 2004.
[11] Kagal, L., Finin, T., Joshi, A.: "A Policy Language for Pervasive Computing Environment" In: Proc. of IEEE Fourth International Workshop on Policy (Policy 2003). Lake Como, Italy, pp. 63-76, IEEE Computer Society Press 4-6 June 2003.

Extracting Relations in Social Networks from the Web Using Similarity Between Collective Contexts

Junichiro Mori[1,2], Takumi Tsujishita[1], Yutaka Matsuo[2], and Mitsuru Ishizuka[1]

[1] University of Tokyo, Japan
{jmori, tjstkm, ishizuka}@mi.ci.i.u-tokyo.ac.jp
[2] National Institute of Advanced Industrial Science and Technology, Japan
y.matsuo@aist.go.jp

Abstract. Social networks have recently garnered considerable interest. With the intention of utilizing social networks for the Semantic Web, several studies have examined automatic extraction of social networks. However, most methods have addressed extraction of the strength of relations. Our goal is extracting the underlying relations between entities that are embedded in social networks. To this end, we propose a method that automatically extracts labels that describe relations among entities. Fundamentally, the method clusters similar entity pairs according to their collective contexts in Web documents. The descriptive labels for relations are obtained from results of clustering. The proposed method is entirely unsupervised and is easily incorporated into existing social network extraction methods. Our method also contributes to ontology population by elucidating relations between instances in social networks. Our experiments conducted on entities in political social networks achieved clustering with high precision and recall. We extracted appropriate relation labels to represent the entities.

1 Introduction

Social networks have recently attracted considerable interest. For the Semantic Web, there is great potential to utilize social networks for myriad applications such as trust estimation [1], ontology construction [2], and end-user ontology [3].

Aiming at using social networks for the Semantic Web, several studies have addressed extraction of social networks automatically from various sources of information. Mika developed a system for extraction, aggregation, and visualization of online social networks for a Semantic Web community, called Flink [4]. In that system, social networks are obtained using Web pages, e-mail messages, and publications. Using a similar approach, Matsuo et al. developed a system called Polyphonet [5]. In line with those studies, numerous studies have explored automatic extraction of social networks from the Web [6,7,8,9].

Given social network extraction using the methods described above, the next step would be to explore underlying relations behind superficial connections in those networks. However, most automatic methods to extract social networks merely provide a clue to the strength of relations. For example, a link in Flink [4] is only assigned the strength of its relation. A user might wonder what kind of underlying relation exists behind the link. In the field of social network analysis, it has been shown that rich information about underlying social relationships engenders more sophisticated analysis [10,11].

One reason for the lack of information about underlying relations is that most automatic extraction methods [6,4,8,9] use a superficial approach (e.g. co-occurrence analysis) instead of profound assessment to determine the type of relation. Matsuo et al. defines four kinds of relations in a research community and classifies the extracted relation [5]. They adopt a supervised machine learning method, which requires a large annotated corpus that requires a great deal of time and effort to construct and administer. In addition, it is necessary to gather domain-specific knowledge a priori to define the extracted relations.

Our goal is to extract underlying relations among entities (e.g., person, location, company) from social networks (e.g., person-person, person-location network). Thereby, we are aiming at extracting descriptive labels of relations automatically, such as affiliations, roles, locations, part-whole, and social relationships. In this paper, we propose a method that automatically extracts the labels that describe relations among entities in social networks. We obtain a local context in which two entities co-occur on the Web, and accumulate the context of the entity pair in different Web pages. Given the collective contexts of each entity pair, the key idea is clustering all entity pairs according to the similarity of their collective contexts. This clustering using collective contexts is based on our hypothesis that entity pairs in similar relations tend to occur in similar contexts. The representative terms in context can be regarded as representing a relationship. Therefore, the labels to describe the relations among entities are extracted from the clustering process result. As an exemplary scenario for our approach, we address a political and social network that is composed of two types of entities: politicians and geopolitical entities (GPEs).

Our method uses context information that is obtained during extraction of social networks. Consequently, the proposed method is easily incorporated into existing methods of social network extraction; it serves to enrich such networks by adding relation labels. In addition, the proposed method is entirely unsupervised. For that reason, our method requires neither a priori definition of relations nor preparation of large annotated corpora. It also requires no instances of relations as initial seeds for weakly supervised learning.

Identifying underlying relations is also important in ontology development. Recent studies have shown that social networks and collective knowledge contribute greatly to ontology extraction [2]. Because relation labels assigned to pairs of entities in social network can be regarded as non-taxonomic relations between instances, our work can be regarded as a specific case of ontology population in the context of social networks.

The remainder of this paper is structured as follows. Section 2 describes basic ideas of our approach and detailed steps of the proposed method. Section 3 describes our experiment. Section 4 describes results and evaluation. Section

5 compares our approach to other ongoing relevant research in social network extraction, relation extraction, and ontology population for the Semantic Web. We end our presentation with a discussion of future work, after which we provide concluding remarks in section 6.

2 Method

2.1 Problem Setting

In this paper, as an exemplary scenario for our approach, we use a political social network. Many studies of social network extraction from the Web have addressed researchers or students as entities [4,7,5]. Those individuals are easy for researchers to evaluate: they typically provide more than sufficient relational evidence (e.g., co-authors of a paper, co-members in a project, co-participants in a conference) through Web-based materials. Relations among political entities (e.g., politicians, geopolitical-entities) are also widely various; information for clues of relations is readily available from the Web (e.g., news sites, weblogs). In fact, political and social networks are one research target of social network analyses[1] Therefore, it is worthwhile to examine political social networks.

Figure 1 shows an automatically extracted social network from the Web using Mika and Matsuo's method [4,5]. The social network, including two types of political entities (a politician and a geopolitical location (GPE)), was extracted according to co-occurrence of two types of entities (politician-politician, politician-location) on the Web. In the network, a circular node represents a location entity and an elliptical node represents a political entity. Each edge in the network implies that there is a relation between entities. Given the social network, our task is to extract descriptive relation labels between entities in that social network. In particular, as an example of our approach, we address the relations between politicians and locations. Various relations exist among politicians and locations, for example "born in", "originally from", "elected in", "representing", and so on. These relations between politicians and locations have also been addressed in relation-extraction tasks of natural language processing and information extraction.

Given entity pairs in the social network (e.g., George W. Bush – United States, Junichiro Koizumi – Japan, etc.), our present goal is to extract labels to describe the relations of respective entity pairs (to discover relevant terms that relate a politician to a location). In the following section, we explain our basic idea to this purpose.

2.2 Concept

A simple approach to extract the labels that are useful for describing relations in social networks is to analyze the surrounding local context in which entities of

---

[1] Two focused sessions exist in the international social network conference (Sunbelt): politics and networks, politics and network structures.

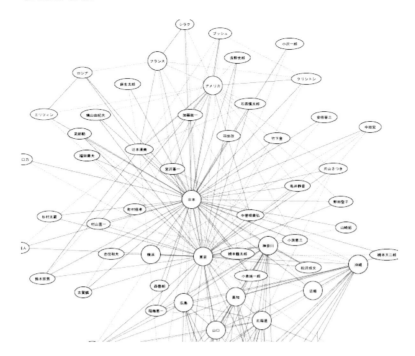

Fig. 1. Political social network extracted from the Web: a circular node represents a location entity and an elliptical node represents a political entity. Each edge in the network implies a relation between entities.

interest co-occur on the Web, and to seek clues to describe that relation. Local context is often used to identify entities or relations among entities in tasks of natural language processing or information extraction [12,13,14].

Table 1 shows keywords [2] that were extracted from local contexts of four entity pairs (Junichiro Koizumi – Japan, Yoshiro Mori – Japan, Junichiro Koizumi – Kanagawa, Yoshiro Mori – Ishizuka [3]). Keywords were extracted from the collective local contexts where co-occurrence of each entity pair was found. For each entity pair, the local contexts from 100 Web pages were collected. The keywords are ordered according to TF-IDF-based scoring, which is a widely used method in many keyword extraction methods to score individual words within text documents to select concepts that accurately represent the documents' contents. The keywords scored by TF-IDF can be considered as a bag-of-words model to represent the local context surrounding an entity pair.

---

[2] In our experiment, we mainly used Web pages in Japanese. Therefore, keywords in the table are translated from their original Japanese. The keyword beginning with a capital letter represents a Japanese proper noun.

[3] Junichiro Koizumi is the current Prime Minister of Japan and Yoshiro Mori is a former Prime Minister. Kanagawa is the prefecture where Koizumi was elected and Ishikawa is the prefecture where Mori was elected.

Table 1. Keywords obtained from each local context of four kinds of entity pairs: Junichiro Koizumi – Japan, Yoshiro Mori – Japan, Junichiro Mori – Kanagawa, and Yoshiro Mori – Ishikawa

(1) Junichiro Koizumi – Japan
pathology, Fujiwara, **prime minister**, Koizumi, Kobun-sha, politics, prime minister, visit, page, **prime minister**, products, **cabinet**, citizen, reform, **minister**, Warsaw, United States, Yasukuni, Yasukuni Shrine, revitalization, society
(2) Yoshiro Mori – Japan
rugby, **prime minister**, chairman, bid, **minister**, association, science, administration, **prime minister**, director, soccer, Africa, world, universe, competition, page, sport, gaffes, media, **cabinet**, director
(3) Junichiro Koizumi – Kanagawa
election, **prime minister**, Yokosuka, **candidate**, **congressional representative**, Saito, **Liberal Democratic Party**, Miura, Koizumi, Democratic Party, lower house, page, fair adversary, politics, endorsement, Liberal Democratic Party, house, president, running in a election, by-elections, constituent
(4) Yoshiro Mori – Ishikawa
Ichikawa, Yasuo, **prime minister**, **election**, Liberal Democratic Party, Okuda, **candidate**, Komatsu, **congressional representative**, **Liberal Democratic Party**, Yuji, Nomi, Kaga, Kanazawa, Nishimura, Page, Shinshin, answer, Matsutou, Komeito, winning in a election

We find that some keywords can serve as relevant labels to describe relations of an entity pair. However, other noise keywords that are irrelevant to describe the relations are also included because the keywords were extracted from collective local contexts of various kinds of Web pages. Using this simple approach, no additional information to decide relevant relation labels for entity pairs exists aside from the TF-IDF scoring. Therefore, we must find another clue to select relevant keywords for relation labels.

From a slightly different perspective, if we examine the common keywords (shown in bold typeface in the table) shared by (1) and (2), we note that the keywords that describe the relations of each entity pair, such as "prime minister" and "cabinet", are commonly shared. In fact, Koizumi and Mori are the current and former prime ministers of Japan. Similarly, if we look at common keywords of (3) and (4), we find that the keywords that describe the relations of each entity pair such as "election" and "candidate" are shared. In fact, Koizumi was elected in Kanagawa, a prefecture, and Mori was elected in Ishikawa. In contrast, if we compare Koizumi's keywords (1) with another of his keywords (3), we find that different keywords appear because of their respective links to different locations: Japan and Kanagawa (although both keywords are Koizumi's.).

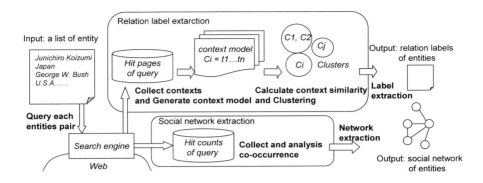

Fig. 2. Outline of the proposed method

Based on the observations described above, we hypothesize that if the local contexts of entity pairs in the Web are similar, then the entity pairs share a similar relation. Our hypothesis resembles previously tested hypotheses related to context [15,14]: words are similar to the extent that their contextual representations are similar. According to that hypothesis, our method clusters entity pairs according to the similarity of their collective contexts. Then, the representative terms in a cluster are extracted as labels to describe the relations of each entity pair in the cluster, assuming that each cluster represents different relations and that the entity pair in a cluster is an instance of a certain relation. The key point of our method is that we determine the relation labels not by examining the local context of one single entity pair, but by the collective local contexts of all entity pairs of interest. In the following section, we explain the precise steps of our proposed method.

2.3 Procedure

Our method for extraction of relation labels in social networks includes the following steps.

1. Collect co-occurrence information and local context of an entity pair
2. Extract a social network that is composed of entity pairs.
3. Generate a context model of each entity pair.
4. Calculate context similarity between entity pairs.
5. Cluster entity pairs.
6. Select representative labels to describe relations from each cluster.

Figure 2 depicts the outline of our method. Our method requires a list of entities (e.g., personal name, location name) to form a social network as the input; it then outputs the social network and a list of relation labels for each entity pair. Although collection of a list of entities is beyond the scope of this paper, one might use named entity recognition to identify entities and thereby generate a list of entities of interest.

The first step is to collect co-occurrence and local contexts of each entity pair from the Web. Many existing methods of social network extraction use a search engine and its resultant query hit counts to obtain co-occurrence information of entities from the Web [Matsuo, Mika]. In line with such methods, we use Google [4] to collect co-occurrence information and generate a social network, as shown in Fig. 1.

Using co-occurrence information, we also collect local contexts in which elements of an entity pair of interest co-occur within a certain contextual distance of one another within the text of a Web page. For this, we downloaded the top 100 web pages included in the search result of corresponding search query to each entity pair (in our example of a politician and location name, the query is "Junichiro Koizumi AND Japan"). This can be accomplished in the process of collecting co-occurrence information, which uses search query hit counts.

2.4 Context Model and Similarity Calculation

For each entity pair, we accumulate the context terms surrounding it; thereby, we obtain the contexts of all entity pairs. As the next step, to calculate the similarity between collective contexts of each entity pair, we require a certain model that represents the collected context. In our method, we propose a context model that represents the context using a bag-of-words and a word vector [16]. We define the context model as a vector of terms that are likely to be used to describe the context of an entity pair (e.g., the keywords list shown in Table 1 can be considered as an example of the context model.). A context model $C_{i,j}$ of an entity pair (e_i, e_j) is defined as the set of N terms $t_1, ..., t_N$ that are extracted from the context of an entity pair as $C_{i,j}(n,m) = t_1, ..., t_N$, where both n and m are parameters of the context window size, which defines the number of terms to be included in the context. In addition, m is the number of intervening terms between e_i and e_j; n is the number of words to the left and right of either entity.

Each term t_i in the context model $C_{i,j}(n,m)$ of an entity pair (e_i, e_j) is assigned a feature weight according to TF-IDF-based scoring defined as $tf(t_i) \cdot idf(t_i)$. Therein, $tf(t_i)$ is defined by the term frequency of term t_i in all the contexts of the entity pair (e_i, e_j). Furthermore, $idf(t_i)$ is defined as $log(|C|/df(t_i))+1$, where $|C|$ is the number of all context models and $df(t_i)$ is the number of context models including term t_i. With the weighted context model, we calculate the similarity $sim(C_{i,j}, C'_{i,j})$ between context models according to the cosine similarity as follows: $sim(C_{i,j}, C'_{i,j}) = C_{i,j} C'_{i,j} / (|C_{i,j}||C'_{i,j}|)$.

In our exploratory experiment, we tried probability distribution-based scoring and several similarities such as L1 norm, Jensen-Shannon and Skew divergence [13]. According to those results, TFIDF-based cosine similarity performs well.

2.5 Clustering and Label Selection

Calculating the similarity between the context models of entity pairs, we cluster all entity pairs according to their similarity. This is based on our hypothesis

---
[4] http://www.google.com

described in Sect. 2.2: the local contexts of entity pairs in the Web are similar, and the entity pairs share a similar relation.

Ideally, the clustering process terminates when it generates a relevant number of clusters that correspond to the number of relations that entity pairs can hold. However, we do not know what kinds of relation pertain. Therefore, we do not know in advance how many clusters we should make. For that reason, we employ hierarchical agglomerative clustering, which is similarity-based and which uses a bottom-up clustering method.

Several clustering methods exist for hierarchical clustering: single linkage, average linkage and complete linkage. We used those different methods in our exploratory experiment. According to those results, complete linkage performs well because it is conservative in producing clusters and does not tend to generate a biased large cluster. In complete linkage, the similarity between the clusters CL_1, CL_2 is evaluated by considering the two most dissimilar elements as follows: $min_{C_{i,j} \in CL_1, C'_{i,j} \in CL_2} sim(C_{i,j}, C'_{i,j})$.

Initially, each entity pair forms its own cluster. Then the clustering algorithm repeats the step that merges the two most similar clusters still available until the cluster quality drops below a predefined threshold. The cluster quality is evaluated according to two measures [17]: the respective degrees of similarity of entity pairs within clusters and among clusters.

After the clustering process terminates and creates a certain number of clusters, we extract the terms from a cluster as labels to describe the relations of each entity pair in the cluster. This is based on the assumption that each cluster represents a different relation and each entity pair in a cluster is an instance of similar relation. The term relevancy, as a cluster label, is evaluated according to a TFIDF-based measure in the same manner as weighting the terms in a context model. However, in this process, the term frequency is determined for all contexts of a cluster. The underlying idea is to extract terms that appear in the cluster, but which do not appear in other clusters. With a cluster CL's labels $l_1, ..., l_n$ scored according to the term relevancy, an entity pair, e_i and e_j, that belongs to the CL can be regarded as holding the relations described by $l_1, ..., l_n$.

3 Experiment

Using our proposed method, we extracted labels to describe relations of each entity pair in a social network. We chose 143 distinct entity pairs (a politician and a GPE) that comprise the social network shown in Fig. 1. The politicians mainly include chiefs of state of Japan and other countries. The GPE includes locations such as country, prefectural district, and city. Examples of entity pairs are "Junichiro Koizumi – Japan", "George W. Bush – United States of America", and "Shintaro Ishihara – Tokyo".

We created a context model of each entity pair using nouns and noun phrases from parts-of-speech (POS) surrounding entity pairs in a Web page. We exclude stop words, symbols, and highly frequent words. For each entity pair, we download

Table 2. Manually assigned relation labels of entity pairs of "Junichiro Koizumi – Japan", "George W. Bush – United States of America"

Junichiro Koizumi-Japan	prime minister
George W. Bush – United States of America	president, chief of state

the top 100 web pages in the process of collecting co-occurrence information for extraction of social network. For the context size, we used two parameters, m and n, as explained in Sect. 2.4. As a baseline of the context size, we assigned 10 and 5, respectively, to m and n.

We used complete-linkage agglomerative clustering to cluster all entity pairs. Thereby, we created five distinct clusters according to the predefined thresholds of two quality measures within the clusters and among the clusters, as explained in Sect. 2.5. To evaluate the clustering results and the extracted labels, two human subjects analyzed the context terms of each entity pair and manually assigned the relation labels (three or fewer possible labels for each). Examples of manually assigned relation labels of the entity pair of "Junichiro Koizumi – Japan", "George W. Bush – United States of America" are shown in Table 2. Then, a cluster label was chosen as the most frequent term among the manually assigned relation labels of entity pairs in the cluster. The manually assigned relation labels are used as ground truth in the subsequent evaluation stage.

In Table 3 [5], the left column shows the label of each cluster. The right column shows the highly scored terms that are extracted automatically from each cluster. They can be considered as the labels that describe relations of each entity pair in the cluster. The terms are sorted by relevancy score.

4 Evaluation

We first evaluated the clustering results. For each cluster cl, we counted the number of entity pairs $EP_{cl,correct}$ whose manually assigned relation labels included the label of cluster cl. We also counted the entity pairs $EP_{cl,total}$ in the cluster cl. Next, for each relation label l, we counted the number of entity pairs $EP_{l,correct}$ that have the relation label l whose cluster label is l. We also counted the entity pairs $EP_{l,total}$ that have the relation label l. Then, precision and recall of the cluster were calculated as:

$$precision = \Sigma_{cl \in CL} \frac{EP_{cl,correct}}{EP_{cl,total}}, \; recall = \Sigma_{l \in L} \frac{EP_{l,correct}}{EP_{l,total}}.$$

According to $precision$ and $recall$, we evaluated clusters based on the F measure as $F = 2 * precision * reall/(precision + recall)$.

The graph depicted in Fig. 3 shows that the clustering results vary depending on the context size. Consequently, to find the optimal context size, we calculate

---
[5] In our experiment, we mainly used Web pages in Japanese. Therefore, keywords in the table are translated from their original Japanese.

Table 3. Cluster label and automatically extracted relation labels from a cluster

1 mayor	mayor, citizen, hosting, president, affairs, officer, matter, answer, city, conference
2 president	president, administration, world, Japan, economics, policy, war, principle, politics, Iraq
3 prime minister	prime minister, administration, politics, article, election, prime minister, government, peace
4 governor	prefectural governor, governor, president, prefectural-government, committee, Heisei, prefectural administration, mayor, comment, prefectural assembly
5 congressional representative	congressional representative, election, Liberal Democratic Party, candidate, lower house, Democratic Party, proportional representation

the F-measure by changing two size parameters: m and n. Expanding the context size from the minimum, the F-measure takes an optimal value when m is around 30 and n is around 10 (Fig. 3 and Table 4) . We employed this optimal context size to extract the relation labels in our experiment. After reaching the peak, the value of the F-measure decreases as the context size increases. The wider context window tends to include noise terms that are not appropriate to represent the context, thus rendering the similarity calculation between the contexts irrelevant. The optimal context size depends on the structural nature of language. Consequently, we must choose the context size carefully when applying our methods to a different language.

To evaluate the automatically extracted relation labels, we compared the cluster label (left column of Table 3) with the automatically extracted relation labels (right column of Table 3). We found that the relation label that has the highest score is equal to the corresponding cluster's relation label. Precision of the clustering results in our experiment is quite high, as shown above. Therefore, we can say that each entity pair in a cluster is represented properly by the highest-scored relation label from the cluster. In addition, if we examine other automatically extracted relation labels, we find that various terms that represent the relations are extracted.

5 Related Work

Aiming at extracting underlying relations in social networks from the Web, our method is related closely to existing extraction methods of social networks. Several studies have addressed extraction of social networks automatically from various sources of information such as the Web, e-mail, and contacts [6,7,8,9,4]. While most approaches for social network extraction have focused on the strength of the relation, few studies have addressed automatic identification of underlying relations. Matsuo et al. employed a supervised machine learning method to classify four types of relations in a research community [5]. There have also been several important works that have examined supervised learning of relation extraction

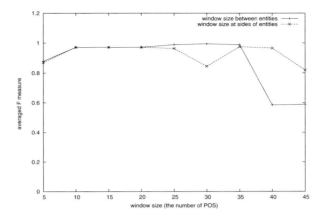

Fig. 3. F measure of clustering results vs. Context window size with two parameters: one is the number of intervening terms between entities and another is the number of words to the left and right of either entity

Table 4. Clustering performance in parameters of context window size with two parameters: m and n

Context window size n, m	Precision	Recall	F-measure
$n = 10$, $m = 30$	0.992	0.995	0.994
$n = 5$, $m = 10$	0.88	0.85	0.86
All terms in a Web page	0.76	0.677	0.716

in the field of natural language processing and information extraction [18,19,20]. However, a supervised method requires large annotated corpora, which cost a great deal of time and effort. In addition, it is necessary to know the domain specific knowledge to define extracted relations a priori. Our method is fully unsupervised and requires no annotated corpora. Furthermore, our method works domain independently and requires no pre-defined relations. For further improvement of our method, it might be worth considering exploitation of weakly supervised and bootstrapping methods [21,22] that rely on a small set of pre-defined initial seeds instead of a large annotated corpus.

Because recent studies have shown that social networks greatly contribute to ontology extraction [2], identifying underlying relations is important for ontology development. Currently, several studies are examining the use of relation extraction for ontology learning and population [23]. Although ontology learning and population share the common goal of facilitating ontology construction, they differ slightly. Whereas ontology learning mainly addresses extraction of taxonomic relations among concepts, the goal of ontology population is extraction of non-taxonomic relations among instances of concepts [24]. In our case, because the labels (non-taxonomic relations) of relations are assigned to pairs of entities of social networks (relation instances), our work can be regarded as a specific case of ontology population in the context of social networks.

Relation extraction for ontology population is typically an unsupervised approach. Because ontology population is usually intended to extract information about instances from large and heterogeneous sources such as the Web, a fully supervised approach that assumes numerous training instances is not feasible for large-scale exploitation, as pointed out in some precedent studies [25]. Therefore, several studies have exploited unsupervised or semi-supervised approaches. Particularly, the current approaches for relation extraction in ontology population are classifiable into two types: those that exploit certain patterns or structures, and those that rely on contextual features.

Pattern-based approaches [26,27,28] seek phrases or sentence structures that explicitly show relations between instances. However, most Web documents have a very heterogeneous structure, even within individual web pages. Therefore, the effectiveness of the pattern-based approach depends on the domain to which it is applied. Rather than exploiting patterns or structures, context-based approaches [29,30,31] assess contextual syntactic, semantic, and co-occurrence features. Several studies have employed contextual verb arguments to identify relations in text [29,31], assuming that verbs express a relation between two ontology classes that specify a domain and range. Although verbs are relevant features to identify relations, we assume that syntactic and dependency analyses are applicable to text collections. Because the Web is highly heterogeneous and often unstructured, syntactic and dependency structures are not always available. For that reason, we employed a contextual model that uses a bag-of-words to assess context. Therefore, the method is applicable to any unstructured documents in the Web. As shown in our experiment, the simple context model performed well to extract descriptive relation labels without depending on any syntactic features in text.

Aiming at extraction of the relation labels in automatically extracted social network from the Web, our method is a Web mining method. Recent approaches of Web mining toward the Semantic Web use the Web as a huge language corpus and combine it with a search engine. This trend is observed not only in recent social network extraction [4,5] but also in ontology population for entities [32,33] and relations [27,34]. The underlying concept of these methods is that it uses globally available Web data and structures to annotate local resources semantically to bootstrap the Semantic Web. In line with this, our approach utilizes the Web to obtain the collective contexts that engender extracting representative relations in social network. As pointed in [35], we claim that relations should be defined not by local information, but rather by a global viewpoint of a network composed of individual relations.

6 Conclusions and Future Work

We propose a method that automatically extracts labels that describe relations between entities in social networks. The proposed method is entirely unsupervised and domain-independent; it is easily incorporated into existing extraction methods of social networks.

Future studies will explore the possibilities of extending the proposed method to relations in other types of social networks. Enriching social networks by adding relation labels, our method might contribute to several social network applications such as finding experts and authorities, trust calculation, community-based ontology extraction, and end-user ontology.

References

1. Golbeck, J., Hendler, J.: Accuracy of metrics for inferring trust and reputation in semantic web-based social networks. In: Proceedings of the 14th International Conference on Knowledge Engineering and Knowledge Management (EKAW). (2004)
2. Mika, P.: Ontologies are us: A unified model of social networks and semantics. In: Proceedings of the 4th International Semantic Web Conference (ISWC). (2005)
3. Brickley, D., Miller, L.: Foaf vocabulary specification. namespace document. (2005)
4. Mika, P.: Flink:semantic web technology for the extraction and analysis of social networks. Journal of Web Semantics **3**(2) (2005)
5. Matsuo, Y., Mori, J., Hamasaki, M., Ishida, K., Nishimura, T., Takeda, H., Hashida, K., Ishizuka, M.: Polyphonet: An advanced social network extraction system. In: Proceednings of the 15th International Word Wide Web Conference (WWW). (2006)
6. Kautz, H., Selman, B., Shah, M.: The hidden web. AI Magazine **18**(2) (1997) 27–36
7. Adamic, L.A., Adar, E.: Friends and neighbors on the web. Social Networks **23**(3) (2003)
8. Harada, M., Sato, S., Kazama, K.: Finding authoritative people from the web. In: Proceedings of the Joint Conference on Digital Libraries (JCDL). (2004)
9. Culotta, A., Bekkerman, R., McCallum, A.: Extracting social networks and contact information from email and the web. In: Proceedings of the 1st Conference on Email and Anti-Spam (CEAS). (2004)
10. Scott, J.: Social Network Analysis: A Handbook. Sage Publications, London (2000)
11. Wasserman, S., Faust, K.: Social network analysis. Methods and Applications. Cambridge University Press, Cambridge (1994)
12. Grefenstette, G.: Explorations in Automatic Thesaurus Construction. Kluwer (1994)
13. Lin, D.: Automatic retrieval and clustering of similar words. In: Proceedings of COLING-ACL98. (1998)
14. Schutze, H.: Automatic word sense dicrimination. Computational Linguistics **24**(1) (1998)
15. Harris, Z.: Mathematical Structures of Language. Wiley (1968)
16. Raghavan, V., Wong, S.: A critical analysis of vector space model for information retrieval. Journal of the American Society for Information Retrieval **35**(5) (1998)
17. Kannan, R., Vempala, S., Vetta, A.: On clustering: Good, bad and spectral. Computer Science (2000)
18. Zelenko, D., Aone, C., Richardella, A.: Kernel methods for relation extraction. Machine Learning Research **2003**(2) (2003)
19. Culotta, A., Sorensen, J.: Dependency tree kernel for relation extraction. In: Proceedings of the 42nd Annual Meeting of the Association for Computational Linguistics (ACL). (2004)

20. Kambhatla, N.: Combining lexical, syntactic, and semantic features with maximum entropy models for extracting relations. In: Proceedings of ACL. (2004)
21. Brin, S.: Extracting patterns and relations from the world wide web. In: Proceedings of the WebDB Workshop at 6th International Conference on Extending Database Technology (EDBT). (1998)
22. Agichtein, E., Gravano, L.: Extracting relations from large plain-text collections. In: Proc. of the 5th ACM International Conference on Digital Libraries (ACMDL00). (2000) 85–94
23. Buitelaar, P., Cimiano, P., Magnini, B.: Ontology Learning from Text: Methods, Evaluation and Applications. IOS Press, Amsterdam (2005)
24. Maedche, A.: Ontology Learning for the Semantic Web. Kluwer (2002)
25. Cimiano, P.: Ontology learning and populations. In: Proceedings of the Dagstuhl Seminar Machne Learning for the Semantic Web. (2005)
26. Velardi, P., Navigli, R., Cuchiarelli, A., Neri, F.: Evaluation of ontolearn, a methodology for automatic population of domain ontologies. In: P. Cimiano, and B. Magnini, editors, Ontology Learning from Text: Methods, Applications and Evaluation. IOS Press. (2005)
27. Geleijnse, G., Korst, J.: Automatic ontology population by googling. In: Proceedings of the 17th Belgium-Netherlands Conference on Artificial Intelligence (BNAIC). (2005)
28. Ciravegna, F., Chapman, S., Dingli, A., Wilks, Y.: Learning to harvest information for the semantic web. In: Proceednings of the 1st European Semantic Web Symposium. (2004)
29. Kavalec, M., Maedche, A., Svatek, V.: Discovery of lexical entries for nontaxonomic relations in ontology learning. In: Van Emde Boas, P., Pokorny, J.,Bielikova, M.,Stuller, J. (eds.). SOFSEM 2004. (2004)
30. Cimiano, P., Volker, J.: Towards large-scale open-domain and ontology-based named entity classification. In: Proceedings of the International Conference on Recent Advances in Natural Language Processing (RANLP). (2005)
31. Schutz, A., P.Buitelaar: Relext: A tool for relation extraction from text in ontology extension. In: Proceedings of the 4th International Semantic Web Conference (ISWC). (2005)
32. Cimiano, P., Ladwig, G., Staab, S.: Gimme' the context: Context-driven automatic. semantic annotation with c-pankow. In: Proceednings of the 14th International Word Wide Web Conference (WWW). (2005)
33. Etzioni, O., Cafarella, M., Downey, D., Kok, S., Popescu, A., Shaked, T., Soderland, S., Weld, D., Yates, A.: Web-scale information extraction in knowitall(preliminary results). In: Proceedings of the 13th International Word Wide Web Conference (WWW). (2004)
34. Boer, V., Someren, M., Wielinga, B.: Extracting instances of relations from web documents using redundancy. In: Proceedings of the 3rd European Semantic Web Conference (ESWC). (2006)
35. Matsuo, Y., Hamasaki, M., Takeda, H., Mori, J., Danushka, B., Nakamura, H., Nishimura, T., Hashida, K., Ishizuka, M.: Spinning multiple social network for semantic web. In: Proceedings of the 21st National Conference on Artificial Intelligence (AAAI). (2006)

Can OWL and Logic Programming Live Together Happily Ever After?

Boris Motik[1], Ian Horrocks[1],
Riccardo Rosati[2], and Ulrike Sattler[1]

[1] University of Manchester, Manchester, UK
[2] Università di Roma "La Sapienza", Rome, Italy

Abstract. Logic programming (LP) is often seen as a way to overcome several shortcomings of the Web Ontology Language (OWL), such as the inability to model integrity constraints or perform closed-world querying. However, the open-world semantics of OWL seems to be fundamentally incompatible with the closed-world semantics of LP. This has sparked a heated debate in the Semantic Web community, resulting in proposals for alternative ontology languages based entirely on logic programming. To help resolving this debate, we investigate the practical use cases which seem to be addressed by logic programming. In fact, many of these requirements have already been addressed outside the Semantic Web. By drawing inspiration from these existing formalisms, we present a novel logic of *hybrid MKNF knowledge bases*, which seamlessly integrates OWL with LP. We are thus capable of addressing the identified use cases without a radical change in the architecture of the Semantic Web.

1 Introduction

In the past couple of years, a significant body of Semantic Web research was devoted to defining a suitable language for ontology modeling. In 2004, this endeavor resulted in the Web Ontology Language (OWL). OWL is based on Description Logics (DLs) [1]—a family of knowledge representation formalisms based on first-order logic and exhibiting well-understood computational properties. OWL has been successfully applied to numerous problems in computer science, such as information integration or metadata management. Prototypes of OWL reasoners,[1] such as RACER, FaCT++, Pellet, or KAON2, have been implemented and applied in research projects; commercial implementations and projects using them are currently emerging.

However, the experience in building practical applications has revealed several shortcomings of OWL. For example, OWL does not allow for integrity constraints or closed-world reasoning. Rule-based formalisms grounded in logic programming have repeatedly been proposed as a possible solution, so adding a rule layer on top of OWL is nowadays seen as a central task in the development of the Semantic Web language stack. The Rule Interchange Format (RIF)

---

[1] A list of reasoners is available at http://www.cs.man.ac.uk/~sattler/reasoners.html.

working group[2] of the World Wide Web Consortium (W3C) is currently working on standardizing such a language.

Responding to popular demand, the Semantic Web Rule Language (SWRL) was proposed in [13]. However, as the authors point out, SWRL is a simple extension of OWL with material (first-order) implication and, due to the straightforward way in which the rules are integrated with OWL, it is trivially undecidable. Furthermore, SWRL was designed as a first-order language, so it does not address nonmonotonic reasoning tasks, such as expressing integrity constraints. OWL and SWRL were criticized on these accounts in [4], and an alternative ontology language OWL-Flight, based entirely on logic programming, was proposed. In [14], the authors go even further by saying that a true rule formalism grounded in logic programming is intrinsically incompatible with OWL. They propose to change the layering architecture of the Semantic Web: instead of building rules on top of OWL, they propose OWL and rules to exist side-by-side, with semantic interoperability grounded in Description Logic Programs (DLP) [11]—a straightforward intersection of DLs and LP. Furthermore, the authors propose the Web Service Modeling Language (WSML) [3] or F-Logic [15] as suitable ontology languages based on logic programming. These approaches were criticized in [12] on the grounds that separating OWL and rules creates two Semantic Webs with little or no semantic interoperability.

To help in resolving this debate, in Section 3 we investigate the practical use cases which are difficult or impossible to realize in OWL, but seem to be addressed by logic programming. These use cases are not novel to knowledge representation: numerous formalisms addressing different subsets of these requirements have already been developed, so we present an overview of the most relevant ones in Section 4. Many existing proposals are based on description logics, so analyzing them provides valuable insights into integrating logic programming with OWL without sacrificing backwards compatibility.

By combining the ideas from the existing formalisms with the principles of logic programming, we developed a novel formalism of *hybrid MKNF knowledge bases*, which we overview in Section 5. This formalism, based on the logic MKNF by Lifschitz [18], is fully compatible with both OWL and logic programming, and thus addresses the identified use cases without sacrificing backwards compatibility. Because it subsumes logic programming, our logic provides a foundation for integrating OWL with languages such as WSML and F-Logic. Thus, it is possible to obtain a coherent stack of logical languages without establishing the "twin towers of the Semantic Web" [12], and our formalism provides a framework for integrating several proposals considered within RIF.

Due to space constraints, we present hybrid MKNF knowledge bases only at a high level by means of an example. For precise definitions and decision procedures, please refer to [19].

---
[2] http://www.w3.org/2005/rules/

2 Preliminaries

2.1 The OWL Family of Languages

OWL is actually a family of three ontology languages: OWL-Lite, OWL-DL, and OWL-Full. The first two languages can be considered syntactic variants of the $\mathcal{SHIF}(\mathbf{D})$ and $\mathcal{SHOIN}(\mathbf{D})$ description logics, respectively, whereas the third language was designed to provide full compatibility with RDF(S). We focus mainly on the first two variants of OWL because OWL-Full has a nonstandard semantics that makes the language undecidable and therefore difficult to implement. OWL comes with several syntaxes, all of which are rather verbose. Hence, in this paper we use the standard DL syntax, which we overview next. For a full introduction to the syntax and the semantics of DLs, please refer to [1].

The main building blocks of DL knowledge bases are *concepts* (or *classes*), representing sets of objects, *roles* (or *properties*), representing relationships between objects, and *individuals*, representing specific objects. Concepts such as *Person* are *atomic*. Using a rich set of concept constructors, one can construct *complex* concepts, which describe the conditions on concept membership. For example, the concept $\exists hasFather.Person$ describes those objects that are related through the *hasFather* role with an object from the concept *Person*. A DL knowledge base $\mathcal{O}$ typically consists of a TBox $\mathcal{T}$ and an ABox $\mathcal{A}$. A TBox contains axioms about the general structure of all allowed worlds, and is therefore akin to a database schema. For example, the TBox axiom (1) states that each instance of the concept *Person* must be related by the role *hasFather* with an instance of the concept *Person*. An ABox contains axioms that describe the structure of a particular world. For example, the axiom (2) states that *Peter* is a *Person*, and (3) states that *Paul* is a brother of *Peter*.

(1) $$Person \sqsubseteq \exists hasFather.Person$$
(2) $$Person(Peter)$$
(3) $$hasBrother(Peter, Paul)$$

A DL knowledge base can be given semantics by translating it into first-order logic with equality. Atomic concepts are translated into unary predicates, complex concepts into formulae with one free variable, and roles into binary predicates. The basic reasoning problems for OWL are checking if an individual a is an instance of a concept C (written $\mathcal{O} \models C(a)$) or if the a concept C is subsumed by another concept D (written $\mathcal{O} \models C \sqsubseteq D$). These problems are decidable for OWL-Lite and OWL-DL in ExpTime and NExpTime, respectively.

The concept-centric style of modeling endorsed by OWL has proven to be particularly suitable for modeling taxonomic knowledge. Furthermore, the open-world semantics of OWL grounded in first-order logic allows one to state general truths, and not only statements about known objects. In fact, in OWL one can introduce new, unknown individuals to express such truths, which provides an elegant way of modeling incomplete information.

2.2 Logic Programming

Logic programming (LP) is a family of KR formalisms centered around the notion of rules—statements of the following form:

$$(4) \qquad H \leftarrow B_1^+, \ldots, B_n^+, \mathbf{not}\ B_1^-, \ldots, \mathbf{not}\ B_k^-$$

Different semantics for LP have been considered in practice, with stable models [9] being the most widely accepted one: a set of atoms M is a *stable model* of a set of rules P if it is the minimal model of a program P^M, where the latter is obtained by replacing each atom $\mathbf{not}\ B_i^-$ with its value in M. A set of rules P can have zero, one, or several stable models, and checking satisfiability of P is an NP-complete problem, assuming P is function-free. Numerous variants of these basic formalisms have been considered, such as rules with disjunctions in the rule heads or extensions with classical negation; a combination of these two features is commonly known as *answer set programming* [10].

F-Logic [15] is a language layered on top of logic programming, providing object-oriented primitives for modeling concept hierarchies, concept instantiation, relationships between individuals, and inheritance. For execution, F-Logic theories can be compiled into logic programming; hence, the relationship between F-Logic and LP is somewhat similar to the relationship between C++ and assembler. OWL-Flight [4] and the Web Service Modeling Language (WSML) [3] are other notable object-oriented front-ends for logic programming.

Logic programming partly evolved as an extension of relational databases with deductive features. Therefore, LP typically focuses on efficient query answering over a bounded data set, and is often used in data-intensive applications that require managing large amounts of data. With the introduction of answer set programming, LP is increasingly seen as a general problem-solving formalism, capable of succinctly expressing hard computational problems.

3 Why Integrate OWL with Logic Programming?

In this section we motivate the need for integrating OWL and LP. In particular, we present several important modeling problems that are hard, if not impossible to solve using OWL alone, but can easily be addressed using logic programming.

Higher Relational Expressivity. OWL provides a rich set of primitives for expressing concepts; however, the set of primitives regarding roles is often not sufficient for practical applications. Roughly speaking, OWL can model only domains where objects are connected in a tree-like manner; however, many real-world applications require modeling general relational structures. For example, saying that "an uncle of a person is a brother of that person's father" requires expressing a triangle between the person, the father, and the uncle. An in-depth discussion about the relational expressivity of OWL can be found in [20].

Polyadic Predicates. The basic modeling constructs of OWL are concepts and roles, which correspond to unary and binary predicates. However, many relationships encountered in practice are of arity larger than two. For example, flight connections between cities together with the airline providing the service can naturally be represented using a ternary predicate, so $flight(MAN, STR, HLX)$ might mean that HLX offers flights between Manchester and Stuttgart.

Closed-World Reasoning. Consider an OWL knowledge base $\mathcal{O}$ containing an assertion $flight(a, b)$ for each pair of cities connected by a flight. Due to the *open-world* semantics of OWL, we can use $\mathcal{O}$ to answer positive queries—that is, queries about which cities are connected by a flight. However, we cannot use $\mathcal{O}$ to answer negative queries: $\mathcal{O}$ does not contain explicit information about not connected cities, so, for each c and d, we have $\mathcal{O} \not\models \neg flight(c, d)$. Answering queries about negative information in an intuitive way usually requires some form of *closed-world* reasoning.

The difference between open- and closed-world reasoning can be intuitively described as follows. In first-order logic, if a fact α holds only in a subset of the models of $\mathcal{O}$, then we can conclude neither $\mathcal{O} \models \alpha$ nor $\mathcal{O} \not\models \alpha$; in a way, $\mathcal{O}$ is *underspecified* with respect to α. In contrast, closed-world formalisms make the common-sense conjecture that all relevant information is explicitly known, so all unprovable facts should be assumed not to hold in $\mathcal{O}$. Hence, closed-world reasoning can be understood as reasoning where $\mathcal{O} \not\models \alpha$ implies $\mathcal{O} \models \neg\alpha$.

The requirement for closed-world reasoning comes in practice in two distinct forms. Certain applications require only *closed-world querying* of open-world knowledge bases. A closed-world query language can be layered on top of OWL without changing the semantics of OWL itself.

Alternatively, closed-world reasoning can be integrated into the reasoning process itself. For example, after determining that c and d are not connected by a flight, a travel planning application might check for a train connection. This is usually enabled through a form of *default* or *weak* negation, commonly denoted with **not**. Default negation is closely related to closed-world reasoning: intuitively, from $\mathcal{O} \not\models \alpha$ one concludes $\mathcal{O} \models \mathbf{not}\,\alpha$. Unlike a closed-world query language, default negation must be built into the foundations of the knowledge representation formalism, affecting its semantics significantly.

We point out two common misconceptions about closed-world reasoning. The first one is that closed-world reasoning can be emulated within first-order logic by specifying complete information—for example, using a form of *role closure*. The following axiom states that flights exist only between cities a and b, and b and c, thus making the role *flight* closed:

$$(5) \qquad \forall x, y : flight(x, y) \leftrightarrow (x \approx a \land y \approx b) \lor (x \approx b \land y \approx c)$$

Assuming that $\mathcal{O}$ contains only (5), we can now conclude $\mathcal{O} \models \neg flight(a, d)$, so role closure seems to solve the problem. However, such a solution is not satisfactory since it does not provide the required support for inferencing. For example, it is natural to query $\mathcal{O}$ for nondirect flights between cities—that is, to query the transitive closure of *flight*. A natural solution is to add a transitive role *anyLengthFlight* and the axiom *flight* $\sqsubseteq$ *anyLengthFlight*. However, $\mathcal{O}$ can again answer only positive queries, since we did not say that *anyLengthFlight* is a *minimal* transitive relation containing *flight*. In fact, transitive closure is not axiomatizable in first-order logic, so answering our (quite natural) query requires some form of closed-world, non-first-order reasoning.

Furthermore, closed-world reasoning is often confused with closed-domain reasoning. Consider a knowledge base $\mathcal{O}$ containing axioms (1)–(3). Axioms (1) and (2) state that *Peter* has a father without saying who the father is. The only persons known in $\mathcal{O}$ are *Peter* and *Paul*, but in open-domain reasoning the unnamed father of *Peter* is not required to be either of them: the existential quantifier in (1) can refer to an object not explicitly mentioned by name. However, the fact that the existential quantifier makes the *domain* of the ontology open is unrelated to the problems of open- or closed-world reasoning. As explained earlier, closed-world reasoning is about drawing common-sense conjectures regarding explicit or implicit objects; it has nothing to do with the ability to refer to new individuals. In fact, closing the domain of $\mathcal{O}$ can be done without leaving first-order logic, by including the axiom $\top \sqsubseteq \{Peter, Paul\}$. Now, the father of *Peter* is either *Paul* or *Peter* (note that we did not say that fatherhood is acyclic), so the domain of $\mathcal{O}$ is closed. However, closing the domain does not provide any new default consequences. For example, the sex of *Peter* has not been explicitly specified, so $\mathcal{O} \not\models Man(Peter)$ and $\mathcal{O} \not\models \neg Man(Peter)$. It is also possible to combine closed-world reasoning with the ability to refer to unknown individuals. For example, if we additionally state that *Peter*, *Paul*, and the unnamed father are different objects, by closed-world reasoning we can deduce that the domain contains exactly three objects, even though only two individuals are known by name. The domain in this example is open in the (weaker) sense that it is not restricted to named individuals.

Integrity Constraints. In OWL, domain and range restrictions constrain the type of objects that can be related by a role. For example, (6) states that fatherhood is defined only for persons and animals. Also, participation restrictions specify that certain objects have relationships to other objects. For example, (7) states that each person has a social security number.

(6) $\qquad\qquad\exists hasFather.\top \sqsubseteq Person \sqcup Animal$
(7) $\qquad\qquad Person \sqsubseteq \exists hasSSN.SSN$

Under standard first-order semantics, (6) and (7) imply new facts: from $\mathcal{O} = \{hasFather(Peter, Paul), Person(Ann)\}$, we conclude $Person \sqcup Animal(Peter)$ and that *Ann* has a social security number (we do not know which one).

Axioms (6) and (7) describe the structure of the world being modeled. However, one often wants to describe the required structure of the knowledge base. In traditional object-oriented modeling, (6) means "fatherhood can be stated only for objects known to be persons or animals"; similarly, (7) means "a social security number must be known for each person." Under such an interpretation, the axioms (6) and (7) would be interpreted as *integrity constraints*. Now $\mathcal{O}$ would invalidate the integrity constraints, since it is incomplete. It is well-known that integrity constraints cannot be realized within first-order logic [22].

Modeling Exceptions. Exceptions abound in the natural world. For example, most people have the heart on the left, but some people (called dextrocardiacs) have it on the right side of the body. Such a domain cannot be modeled in OWL: the axioms $Human \sqsubseteq HeartOnLeft$, $Dextrocardiac \sqsubseteq Human$, and $Dextrocardiac \sqsubseteq \neg HeartOnLeft$ make the concept $Dextrocardiac$ unsatisfiable. To enable exception modeling, one must go beyond first-order logic and apply a nonmonotonic formalism, usually involving some form of default negation.

One might argue that exceptions should be handled extralogically: one could preprocess a knowledge base and add an assertion $HeartOnLeft(\alpha)$ to each object α that is provably a $Human$ and not an $Dextrocardiac$. However, this solution is far from ideal. The preprocessing algorithm would be defined in an ad-hoc way, thus destroying the well-defined semantics—something deemed to be a crucial feature of OWL. Also, it would be difficult to describe the interaction between preprocessing and the actual reasoning. Nonmonotonic formalisms provide a coherent framework for studying such issues.

4 Existing Solutions to the Problems Mentioned

The use cases from Section 3 are not novel to knowledge representation, and they have been addressed previously by different formalisms. Many of them are based on DLs, so they provide important guidelines for integrating OWL with logic programming without introducing backwards incompatibility.

4.1 First-Order Rule Formalisms for DLs

Many different proposals exist for extending DLs with first-order rules.[3] The general idea is quite simple: one allows for the axioms of the form $H \leftarrow B_1, \ldots, B_n$ where H (the rule *head*) and B_i (the rule *body*) can be of the form $C(s)$ or $R(s,t)$, for C a concept, R a role, and s and t terms (i.e., variables or individuals). The rules are interpreted under standard first-order semantics as $\forall \mathbf{x} : H \vee \neg B_1 \vee \ldots \vee \neg B_n$, where $\mathbf{x}$ is the set of free variables of all H and B_i. The Semantic Web Rule Language (SWRL) [13] was layered on top of OWL based on these principles. The following rule models the relationship about uncles from Section 3:

(8) $\qquad hasUncle(x,z) \leftarrow hasFather(x,y), hasBrother(y,z)$

It is straightforward to extended SWRL with n-ary predicates, in which case one usually distinguishes the *DL-predicates* (the predicates allowed to occur in DL axioms) from the *non-DL-predicates* (the predicates occurring solely in rules).

---

[3] Some authors insist on calling first-order rules *clauses*, reserving the term "rules" for nonmonotonic formalisms. This has not established itself in the Semantic Web.

First-order extensions of DLs with rules are quite straightforward from the standpoint of the semantics: the rules are actually standard first-order material implications, just like standard DL inclusion axioms. All first-order properties, such as contrapositive inferences, apply to the rules as well: from $A(x) \leftarrow B(x)$ and $\neg A(a)$ we can derive $\neg B(a)$.

Unfortunately, extending DLs with rules significantly affects the computational properties of the resulting formalism. In [17], it was shown that integrating recursive Horn rules with even moderately expressive DLs makes reasoning undecidable. Hence, various syntactic restrictions on the rules and the DL have been investigated to regain decidability. For example, CARIN [17] proposes *role safety*, according to which at least one variable from a literal with a role predicate must also occur in a non-DL-literal in the rule body. $\mathcal{AL}$-log [6] and DL-safe rules [20] explore a related notion, which was recently generalized in $\mathcal{DL}$+log [23] to *weak safety*: each variable from the *rule head* must occur in a non-DL-literal in the rule body. Weakly safe rules can derive facts only about explicitly known individuals; however, in contrast to $\mathcal{AL}$-log and DL-safe rules, the body literals of $\mathcal{DL}$+log rules can be matched to existentially introduced individuals. Thus, $\mathcal{DL}$+log generalizes conjunctive queries over DL knowledge bases.

Note that the shortcomings in relational expressivity have been partially addressed in the DL $\mathcal{SROIQ}$ [16]. This logic extends OWL-DL with *complex role inclusion* axioms, such as *hasFather* ∘ *hasBrother* ⊑ *hasUncle*, where ∘ stands for role concatenation. To make reasoning decidable, these axioms must be *regular*—that is, compatible with a certain acyclic ordering. For example, the previous axiom alone is allowed, but it cannot be used together with the axiom *hasChild* ∘ *hasUncle* ⊑ *hasBrother*, as this would create a cycle in the definitions of *hasBrother* and *hasUncle*. We discuss the relationship between $\mathcal{SROIQ}$ and rule-based solutions on an example in Section 5.

4.2 Autoepistemic Nonmonotonic Extensions of DLs

Many extensions of DLs with nonmonotonic features are based on autoepistemic logics, as they allow for *introspection*—the ability to reason about one's own beliefs. In these proposals, DLs are extended with an *autoepistemic knowledge operator* **K**, which can be applied to concepts and roles with an intuitive meaning "is known to hold." Consider again the example from Section 3 of asking whether two cities are not connected by a flight: whereas $\mathcal{O} \not\models \neg\mathit{flight}(c, d)$ holds due to the open-world semantics of OWL, we have $\mathcal{O} \models \neg\mathbf{K}\,\mathit{flight}(c, d)$, intuitively meaning that "c and d are not *known* to be connected by a flight." A formula $\mathbf{K}\,\alpha$ is true if α is true in each first-order model I of a knowledge base $\mathcal{O}$. Autoepistemic reasoning can be integrated with DLs in two distinct ways.

Epistemic Operators in Queries. An approach to autoepistemic querying of DL knowledge bases[4] was presented in [5], and it was recently generalized to the

---

[4] Actually, a more general KR formalism was presented in [5], in which **K** can also occur in the DL knowledge base. However, a reasoning algorithm has been presented only for the case of ordinary knowledge bases and epistemic queries.

Epistemic Query Language (EQL) [2]. We overview here EQL-Lite($\mathcal{Q}$)—a fragment of EQL with favorable computational properties. Given a first-order DL query language $\mathcal{Q}$, EQL-Lite($\mathcal{Q}$) queries are first-order formulae built over the atoms of the form $\mathbf{K}\,q$, where q is a query expressed in the language $\mathcal{Q}$. For example, the cities not connected by a flight can be retrieved using the query $q[x,y] = \neg\,\mathbf{K}\,q'[x,y]$, where $q'[x,y] = hasFlight(x,y)$ is a first-order (conjunctive) query. Since $\mathbf{K}$ can occur only in queries, the semantics of $\mathbf{K}$ is layered on top of the standard DL semantics in a nonintrusive way. In fact, $\mathbf{K}$ can be understood as the *consequence* operator, and EQL-Lite($\mathcal{Q}$) can be understood as an algebra for manipulating first-order consequences of $\mathcal{O}$.

Epistemic Operators in the Knowledge Base. Autoepistemic query languages do not provide default negation or exception modeling; to enable such features, autoepistemic reasoning must be tightly integrated with ordinary DL reasoning. This can be achieved by allowing $\mathbf{K}$ to occur in DL axioms. Usually, a negation-as-failure operator **not**—intuitively understood as "can be false"—is added as well. The first-order version of such a logic is known as the logic of minimal knowledge and negation-as-failure (MKNF) [18], and it generalizes several important nonmonotonic formalisms, such as logic programming under stable model semantics [9] and default logic [21].

Based on these principles, the authors extend in [7] the DL $\mathcal{ALC}$ with an autoepistemic knowledge operator $\mathbf{K}$ and an autoepistemic assumption operator $\mathbf{A}$ (which is semantically equivalent to $\neg\,\mathbf{not}$ from the first-order MKNF). The authors also present a decision procedure for an expressive fragment of this logic. Such a logic elegantly addresses the problems from Section 3 related to nonmonotonic reasoning, while being fully compatible with the underlying semantics of DLs. It clearly provides for closed-world querying, and $\mathbf{A}$ directly corresponds to default negation. It also enables defining integrity constraints and provides for exception modeling. For example, the problem of dextrocardiacs from Section 3 can be modeled as $\mathbf{K}\,Human \sqcap \neg\,\mathbf{A}\,Dextrocardiac \sqsubseteq \mathbf{K}\,HeartOnLeft$.

5 Integrating OWL and LP by Hybrid MKNF KBs

Related approaches presented in Section 4 may give us important clues on how to seamlessly integrate OWL with logic programming. On the one hand, a rule formalism layered on top of a DL may address the problems related to relational expressivity and the lack of polyadic predicates. On the other hand, the autoepistemic extensions of DLs integrate closed- and open-world reasoning and thus provide a common logical framework for nonmonotonic extensions of DLs. By integrating these two formalisms, we have developed a novel approach that can be used to seamlessly integrate any DL with LP-style rules. Due to space constraints, we give here only a high-level overview of our proposal; for a complete definition, complexity, and decision algorithms, please see [19].

A *hybrid MKNF knowledge base* $\mathcal{K}$ consists of a knowledge base $\mathcal{O}$ in any decidable description logic $\mathcal{DL}$ and a set $\mathcal{P}$ of MKNF rules of the following form:

(9) $\quad\quad \mathbf{K}\, H_1 \vee \ldots \vee \mathbf{K}\, H_n \leftarrow \mathbf{K}\, B_1^+, \ldots, \mathbf{K}\, B_m^+, \mathbf{not}\, B_1^-, \ldots, \mathbf{not}\, B_k^-$

As in SWRL, H_i, B_i^+, and B_i^- are first-order atoms of the form $P(t_1, \ldots, t_n)$. For $P = \approx$ or a predicate occurring in $\mathcal{O}$, the atom is a DL-atom; otherwise, it is a non-DL-atom. We assume that $\mathcal{DL}$ comes with an operator π that translates any DL knowledge base $\mathcal{O}$ into a formula $\pi(\mathcal{O})$ of first-order logic with equality. The semantics of our formalism is defined by mapping $\mathcal{K}$ into the following first-order MKNF formula, where $\mathbf{x}$ is the set of free variables of a rule r:

$$\pi(\mathcal{K}) = \mathbf{K}\, \pi(\mathcal{O}) \wedge \bigwedge_{r \in \mathcal{P}} \forall \mathbf{x} : r$$

To obtain a logic with intuitive consequences, we make the *standard names assumption*, which imposes certain restrictions on the models of $\pi(\mathcal{K})$; for more details, please refer to [19]. All inference problems for $\mathcal{K}$, such as satisfiability or entailment, are defined w.r.t. $\pi(\mathcal{K})$ in the obvious way.

As we discuss in [19], such a formalism can fully capture the semantics of SWRL and $\mathcal{DL}$+log [23]. The only approach for combining (possibly nonmonotonic) rules with DLs that we are aware of and that cannot be captured using hybrid MKNF rules is the one by Eiter et al. [8]

Similarly to related extensions of DLs with rules, our logic is undecidable in the general case. We address this using the well-known concept of DL-safety: an MKNF rule is DL-safe if each variable in the rule occurs in a non-DL-atom of the form $\mathbf{K}\, A$ in the rule body. Notice that a rule r can automatically be made DL-safe by appending to its body a special literal $\mathbf{K}\, O(x)$ for each variable x, and by adding an assertion $\mathbf{K}\, O(\alpha)$ for each individual α occurring in $\mathcal{K}$. We shall discuss the consequences of this transformation on the semantics of r shortly; moreover, an in-depth discussion of this issue can be found in [20]. We believe that our approach can easily be extended to handle weakly safe rules.

In [19] we present decision procedures for different types of rules. Furthermore, we analyze the data complexity of reasoning (the complexity under the assumption that the TBox and the rules are fixed, but the ABox varies). Assuming that reasoning in $\mathcal{DL}$ is data complete for NP (which is the case for expressive DLs such as $\mathcal{SHIQ}$), our logic has the same complexity as the corresponding fragment of logic programming. Furthermore, we identify fragments with polynomial data complexity, which are particularly interesting for practice.

The semantics of hybrid MKNF knowledge bases exhibits two important properties. On the one hand, it is fully compatible with OWL: if $\mathcal{P} = \emptyset$, then $\mathcal{K} \models \alpha$ if and only if $\mathcal{O} \models \alpha$ for any first-order formula α. In other words, all standard DL questions are answered in the usual way. On the other hand, MKNF is also fully compatible with logic programming: in [18] it was shown that a disjunctive logic program under stable model semantics is equivalent to the MKNF theory where each rule is replaced by an MKNF implication (9). Hence, our formalism reduces to logic programming for $\mathcal{O} = \emptyset$. Function symbols are not allowed to occur in the rules, since this would make query answering undecidable. However, from

Table 1. A Hybrid MKNF Knowledge Base about Cities

(10) $historicCity \sqsubseteq \exists hasChurch.church$	Historic cities have churches.
(11) $church \sqsubseteq \exists designedBy.architect$	Churches are designed by architects.
(12) $\mathbf{K}\, famousCitizen(x,z) \leftarrow$ $\mathbf{K}\, hasChurch(x,y), \mathbf{K}\, designedBy(y,z),$ $\mathbf{K}\, O(x), \mathbf{K}\, O(y), \mathbf{K}\, O(z)$	Architects are famous citizens in cities where they build their churches.
(13) $\exists famousCitizen.\top \sqsubseteq interestingCity$	Cities with famous people are interesting.
(14) $historicCity(Barcelona)$	Barcelona is a historic city.
(15) $hasChurch(Barcelona, SagradaFamilia)$	The famous church in Barcelona...
(16) $designedBy(SagradaFamilia, Gaudi)$	...was designed by Antonio Gaudi.
(17) $seasideCity \sqsubseteq \exists hasRegion.beach$	Seaside cities have a beach.
(18) $beach \sqsubseteq recreational$	Beaches are for recreation.
(19) $\exists hasRegion.recreational \equiv livableCity$	Livable cities provide for recreation.
(20) $portCity(Barcelona)$	Barcelona is a city with a port.
(21) $portCity(Hamburg)$	Hamburg is a city with a port.
(22) $\neg seasideCity(Hamburg)$	Hamburg is not a seaside city.
(23) $\mathbf{K}\, DesignOK(x) \leftarrow \mathbf{K}\, designedBy(x,y),$ $\mathbf{K}\, O(x), \mathbf{K}\, O(y)$	Auxiliary for the following rule.
(24) $\leftarrow \mathbf{K}\, church(x), \mathbf{not}\, DesignOK(x), \mathbf{K}\, O(x)$	Each church must have an architect.
(25) $church(HolyFamily)$	Holy Family is a church.
(26) $HolyFamily \approx SagradaFamilia$	Definition of synonyms.
(27) $\neg seasideCity \equiv notSC$	An atomic name for $\neg seasideCity$.
(28) $\mathbf{K}\, seasideCity(x) \leftarrow$ $\mathbf{K}\, portCity(x), \mathbf{not}\, notSC(x), \mathbf{K}\, O(x)$	Port cities are usually at the seaside.
(29) $\mathbf{K}\, Suggest(x) \leftarrow$ $\mathbf{K}\, livableCity(x), \mathbf{K}\, historicCity(x)$	Suggest to visit livable and historic cities.
(30) $\neg livableCity \equiv notLivableCity$	An atomic name for $\neg livable$.
(31) $\mathbf{K}\, Consider(x) \leftarrow$ $\mathbf{not}\, notLivableCity(x), \mathbf{K}\, O(x)$	Take cities that are not known to be unlivable into consideration as well.

Note: DL-predicates start with a lowercase, and non-DL-predicates with an uppercase letter. There is an assertion $O(\alpha)$ for each object α.

the standpoint of the semantics, extending the formalism with function symbols is straightforward, and identifying decidable fragments is an interesting topic for future research. Finally, MKNF rules can also be used to integrate OWL with languages providing an object-oriented view over logic programming, such as F-Logic or WSML.

At first glance, our proposal may seem to be difficult to use and understand. However, we believe MKNF rules to be quite intuitive: just read $\mathbf{K}\, A$ as "A is known to hold" and $\mathbf{not}\, A$ as "it is possible for A not to hold." We demonstrate this on the following example, which also shows how MKNF rules address the requirements from Section 3. Imagine a system helping us to decide where to go on holiday, based on the tourism ontology $\mathcal{K}$ shown in Table 1.

The impact of DL-safety is demonstrated by axioms (10)–(13). By (10) and (11), each historic city α has at least one church β, which has at least one architect γ. By (12), γ is a famous citizen of α so, by (13), α is an interesting city. Now if (12) were a normal (non-DL-safe, first-order) rule, one might perform this inference for *any* individuals α, β, and γ, which would thus imply $\mathcal{K} \models historicCity \sqsubseteq interestingCity$. However, (12) is DL-safe—all variables occur in an atom with the predicate O. Hence, it is applicable only to the individuals *known in the ABox by name*, and not to those introduced by the existential quantifier, so we cannot conclude that *interestingCity* subsumes *historicCity*. Note that (12) could be stated in $\mathcal{SROIQ}$ using a "non-DL-safe" role inclusion axiom, and this would correctly imply the subsumption relationship.

Whereas making rules DL-safe usually restricts the subsumption inferences, it typically has less impact on ABox query answering. Namely, (14)–(16) specify the names of a church in Barcelona and its architect. All variables in (12) can now be bound to known individuals, so $\mathcal{K} \models \mathit{famousCitizen}(\mathit{Barcelona}, \mathit{Gaudi})$; by (13), we derive $\mathcal{K} \models \mathit{interestingCity}(\mathit{Barcelona})$. Hence, DL-safety is a compromise that provides for ABox query answering at the expense of some subsumption inferences if expressivity beyond $\mathcal{SROIQ}$ is needed, but without losing decidability. DL-safety is crucial for nonmonotonic reasoning: without it, most nonmonotonic logics with existential quantification are not even semidecidable.

Consider an integrity constraint requiring that an architect should be explicitly specified for each explicitly mentioned church. One might intuitively write the rule $\leftarrow \mathbf{K}\, church(x), \mathbf{not}\, designedBy(x,y), \mathbf{K}\, O(x), \mathbf{K}\, O(y)$ (paraphrased as "it is an error to have a known church without a known designer"). However, this rule is incorrect: all variables in rules are universally quantified, so this rule requires each church to be connected through *designedBy* to each other object. To formulate the integrity constraint correctly, we introduce the auxiliary rule (23) which projects the variable y from $designedBy(x,y)$, and then use the result in (24) to identify the churches without a designer.

Nonmonotonic formalisms usually assume that distinct constants mean different things—a feature known as *unique name assumption* (UNA). Let us for the moment assume that $\mathcal{K}$ does not contain (26). We would then intuitively expect (24) to be violated, since the designer of *HolyFamily* has not been specified. However, without UNA, $\mathcal{K}$ would be satisfiable, and it would entail that *HolyFamily* and *SagradaFamilia* are the same things. To avoid such counterintuitive consequences, logic programming assumes UNA by default.

In contrast, OWL does not employ UNA: explicit equality statements can be used to define synonyms. We integrate OWL with logic programming by using the standard names assumption. Roughly speaking, we allow that two individuals are equal only if there is explicit evidence for doing so. For more information on this issue, please refer to [19]; we just note here that such a semantics does not change any standard OWL consequences. Returning to our example, we make *HolyFamily* and *SagradaFamilia* synonyms by (26), which then makes (24) satisfied for (16) and (25).

Rule (28) asserts the common-sense knowledge that port cities are usually at the seaside, allowing us to conclude $\mathcal{K} \models \mathit{seasideCity}(\mathit{Barcelona})$. However, (28) allows for exceptions: the atom $\mathbf{not}\, notSC(x)$ basically says "if not proven not to be at the seaside." (Axiom (27) is needed because only atomic concepts can occur in MKNF rules.) According to (22), Hamburg is an exception (it is located on the river Elbe), so the default conclusion $\mathcal{K} \models \mathit{seasideCity}(\mathit{Hamburg})$ of (28) is suppressed, as it would lead to contradiction.

The rule (29) is intended as a query that suggests which cities to visit. Even though the conclusion *seasideCity(Barcelona)* was derived by nonmonotonic reasoning, it implies further conclusions through monotonic reasoning. Namely, axioms (17)–(19) imply $\mathcal{K} \models livableCity(Barcelona)$, which is derived by standard DL reasoning involving unnamed individuals (introduced by $\exists hasRegion.Beach$). Hence, $\mathcal{K} \models Suggest(Barcelona)$.

Finally, (31) shows how default negation is layered over open-world semantics. Intuitively, MKNF performs open- and closed-world inferences "in parallel." For example, $\mathcal{K} \not\models livableCity(Hamburg)$ and $\mathcal{K} \not\models \neg livableCity(Hamburg)$ hold according to the usual DL semantics. By reformulating these questions with closed-world interpretation in mind, we get $\mathcal{K} \models \mathbf{not}\ livableCity(Hamburg)$ (Hamburg is not known to be livable) and $\mathcal{K} \models \mathbf{not}\ notLivable(Hamburg)$ (Hamburg is not known not to be livable either). Hence, (31) allows us to conclude $Consider(Hamburg)$—even though we do not know for sure that Hamburg is a livable city, we do not know the opposite either, so it might still be worth a visit. Intuitively speaking, the DL part of $\mathcal{K}$ is interpreted under open-world semantics; however, $\mathbf{K}$ and $\mathbf{not}$ allow the user to put on "closed-world glasses" and examine the nonmonotonic consequences of the DL part. By using these consequences in rules, one can enforce new nonmonotonic conclusions.

6 Conclusion

Motivated by the ongoing controversy in the Semantic Web community about the proper layering of a nonmonotonic rule formalism on top of OWL, we analyze the shortcomings of OWL that are deemed to be solvable using logic programming. Furthermore, we overview existing formalisms that address these requirements. We thus gain insight into how OWL could be integrated with rules without sacrificing semantic compatibility with either formalism.

By combining the ideas of SWRL and DL-safe rules with the approaches for autoepistemic extensions of DLs, we propose a new formalism of hybrid MKNF knowledge bases that seamlessly integrates OWL with logic programming. We present the features of our formalism on a nontrivial example. Under the standard DL-safety assumption, our formalism is decidable, and its data complexity is not higher than for plain logic programming. Therefore, our formalism provides a solid foundation for the integration of OWL and logic programming, as well as a framework for integrating several considered proposals within RIF.

The main challenge for our future work is to implement our approach in the KAON2[5] reasoner and thus validate the usefulness of our formalism in practice.

References

1. F. Baader, D. Calvanese, D. McGuinness, D. Nardi, and P. F. Patel-Schneider, editors. *The Description Logic Handbook: Theory, Implementation and Applications*. Cambridge University Press, January 2003.
2. D. Calvanese, G. De Giacomo, D. Lembo, M. Lenzerini, and R. Rosati. Epistemic First-Order Queries over Description Logic Knowledge Bases. In *Proc. DL 2006*, Lake District, UK, May 30–June 1 2006.

---

[5] http://kaon2.semanticweb.org/

3. J. de Bruijn, H. Lausen, A. Polleres, and D. Fensel. The Web Service Modeling Language: An Overview. In *Proc. ESWC2006*, Budva, Serbia and Montenegro, June 11–14 2006. 590–604.
4. J. de Bruijn, A. Polleres, R. Lara, and D. Fensel. OWL DL vs. OWL Flight: Conceptual Modeling and Reasoning on the Semantic Web. In *Proc. WWW2005*, pages 623–632, Chiba, Japan, May 10–14 2005.
5. F. M. Donini, M. Lenzerini, D. Nardi, W. Nutt, and A. Schaerf. An Epistemic Operator for Description Logics. *Artificial Intelligence*, 100(1–2):225–274, 1998.
6. F. M. Donini, M. Lenzerini, D. Nardi, and A. Schaerf. AL-log: Integrating Datalog and Description Logics. *Journal of Intelligent Information Systems*, 10(3), 1998.
7. F. M. Donini, D. Nardi, and R. Rosati. Description Logics of Minimal Knowledge and Negation as Failure. *ACM Transactions on Computational Logic*, 3(2):177–225, 2002.
8. T. Eiter, T. Lukasiewicz, R. Schindlauer, and H. Tompits. Combining Answer Set Programming with Description Logics for the Semantic Web. In *Proc. KR 2004*, pages 141–151, Whistler, Canada, June 2–5, 2004 2004.
9. M. Gelfond and V. Lifschitz. The Stable Model Semantics for Logic Programming. In *Proc. ICLP '88*, pages 1070–1080, Seattle, WA, USA, August 15–19 1988.
10. M. Gelfond and V. Lifschitz. Classical Negation in Logic Programs and Disjunctive Databases. *New Generation Computing*, 9(3–4):365–386, 1991.
11. B. N. Grosof, I. Horrocks, R. Volz, and S. Decker. Description Logic Programs: Combining Logic Programs with Description Logic. In *Proc. WWW 2003*, pages 48–57, Budapest, Hungary, May 20–24 2003.
12. I. Horrocks, B. Parsia, P. F. Patel-Schneider, and J. Hendler. Semantic web architecture: Stack or two towers? In *Proc. PPSWR 2005*, pages 37–41, Dagstuhl Castle, Germany, September 11–16 2005.
13. I. Horrocks and P. F. Patel-Schneider. A Proposal for an OWL Rules Language. In *Proc. WWW 2004*, pages 723–731, New York, NY, USA, May 17–22 2004.
14. M. Kifer, J. de Bruijn, H. Boley, and D. Fensel. A Realistic Architecture for the Semantic Web. In *Proc. RuleML 2005*, pages 17–29, Galway, Ireland, 2005.
15. M. Kifer, G. Lausen, and J. Wu. Logical foundations of object-oriented and frame-based languages. *Journal of the ACM*, 42(4):741–843, 1995.
16. O. Kutz, I. Horrocks, and U. Sattler. The Even More Irresistible SROIQ. In *Proc. KR 2006*, Lake District, UK, June 2–5 2006. 57–67.
17. A. Y. Levy and M.-C. Rousset. Combining Horn Rules and Description Logics in CARIN. *Artificial Intelligence*, 104(1–2):165–209, 1998.
18. V. Lifschitz. Nonmonotonic Databases and Epistemic Queries. In *Proc. IJCAI '91*, pages 381–386, Sydney, Australia, August 24–30 1991.
19. B. Motik and R. Rosati. Closing Semantic Web Ontologies. Technical report, University of Manchester, UK, 2006.
http://www.cs.man.ac.uk/~bmotik/publications/papers/mr06closing-report.pdf.
20. B. Motik, U. Sattler, and R. Studer. Query Answering for OWL-DL with rules. *Journal of Web Semantics*, 3(1):41–60, 2005.
21. R. Reiter. A Logic for Default Reasoning. *Artificial Intelligence*, 13(1–2), 1980.
22. R. Reiter. What Should a Database Know? *Journal of Logic Programming*, 14(1–2):127–153, 1992.
23. R. Rosati. $\mathcal{DL} + log$: A Tight Integration of Description Logics and Disjunctive Datalog. In *Proc. KR 2006*, pages 68–78, Lake District, UK, June 2–5 2006.

Innovation Detection Based on User-Interest Ontology of Blog Community

Makoto Nakatsuji, Yu Miyoshi, and Yoshihiro Otsuka

NTT Network Service Systems Laboratories, NTT Corporation,
9-11 Midori-Cho 3-Chome, Musashino-Shi, Tokyo 180-8585, Japan
{nakatsuji.makoto, miyoshi.yu, otsuka.yoshihiro}@lab.ntt.co.jp

Abstract. Recently, the use of blogs has been a remarkable means to publish user interests. In order to find suitable information resources from a large amount of blog entries which are published every day, we need an information filtering technique to automatically transcribe user interests to a user profile in detail. In this paper, we first classify user blog entries into service domain ontologies and extract interest ontologies that express a user's interests semantically as a hierarchy of classes according to interest weight by a top-down approach. Next, with a bottom-up approach, users modify their interest ontologies to update their interests in more detail. Furthermore, we propose a similarity measurement between ontologies considering the interest weight assigned to each class and instance. Then, we detect innovative blog entries that include concepts that the user has not thought about in the past based on the analysis of approximated ontologies of a user's interests. We present experimental results that demonstrate the performance of our proposed methods using a large-scale blog entries and music domain ontologies.

1 Introduction

Blogs are becoming more popular for publishing and discussing interests among users who share interests between each other. In blog search, users can automatically pull blog entries from RDF Site Summary (RSS)[1] feed by entering keywords about their interests beforehand. Information-sharing systems of this type have the potential to enable users to expand their interests by browsing collected blog entries published by other users in blog communities.

However, information retrieval in current blog services relies only on keyword searches of blogs using Google or based on simple metadata such as that of an RSS. Moreover, there is no function to generate personalized searches easily, so users need to consider and enter search keywords that suit their own interests appropriately. Such a keyword search is time consuming and troublesome. Moreover, users cannot perform a keyword search if they do not understand what they want to search for to some degree beforehand. Thus, when keywords cannot be specified, information retrieval from blog entries often cannot be performed even if users might become interested in a topic.

---

[1] http://blogs.law.harvard.edu/tech/rss

To counteract the above problems, in the research on Adaptive Information Filtering (AIF) [2], the user profile is constructed cooperatively with a user, and recommendations based on the profile are offered. Making a user profile interactively beforehand is good for offering recommendations to users, as indicated by the high-accuracy performance of AIF. A common complaint about AIF is the user's task of making his/her own profiles, and a user often encounters known information many times because he/she cannot distinguish documents including new information in the recommendation results.

For filtering these redundant documents, researchers on novelty detection [7] define novelty as a document that includes new information that is relevant to a user profile. They extract relevant documents from a document stream. Then, they classify the documents as novel or not, and provide novelty documents to users. However, detecting novelty provides documents with information that includes concepts only in a user profile.

In this paper, we define *innovation* as new concepts which seem to be interesting to the user even though they are not included in a user profile. Then, we try to expand user interests significantly by recommending innovative information. Especially, we adopt innovation detection to blogs because they become a popular architecture of publishing and searching information that expands user interests.

For achieving above-mentioned purpose, we first construct user profile automatically as a user-interest ontology, which is a class hierarchy of user interests with interest weights. Then, we propose measuring the similarity of interest ontologies considering the degree of interest agreement to each class and instance. We apply our techniques to help users create a blog community by browsing innovative blog entries which include information unknown to users with a high probability of being interesting.

The specific contributions of this paper are the following.

– First, in order to analyze user interests in detail, we propose an automatic extraction of an interest ontology with an interest weight assigned to each class and instance. Bloggers are apt to describe their interests about topics in several service domains freely. Thus, we use blog entries for specifying user interests by introducing a template ontology, which is a domain ontology of each service. We classify user entries according to a template ontology, and remove classification mistakes by using class characteristics and continuity of descriptions about user interests. This mechanism of improving entry classification is one of the reasons for applying the ontology technique to our research.

– We propose measuring the similarity between interest ontologies that have interest weight. By introducing interest ontologies, we can help users create interest-based communities considering the width and depth of concepts of users' interests. Furthermore, we can calculate the similarity between ontologies more accurately than in previous ontology mapping techniques from the viewpoint of the agreement of the weights of user interests. Then, we can detect innovative blog entries for each user u by analyzing the classes

C of other users' ontologies that have a high similarity to the ontology of the user u though the interest ontology of user u lacks those classes C. This new approach of recommending innovative information is another reason for applying the ontology technique to our research.
– We describe a comprehensive set of experiments. Our experimental results are based on a large number of blog entries (1,600,000 entries of 55,000 users) and a music template ontology (114 classes and 4,300 instances). We confirm that our automatic ontology extraction and innovation detection have potential for creating a user-oriented blog community according to user interests. We also investigate the appropriate granularity of a community by analyzing the similarity of users' interests among the community extracted by our similarity measurements.

The paper is organized as follows. Section 2 introduces related works. Section 3 describes our automatic user-interest ontology-extraction, and Section 4 describes innovative blog-entry detection by our similarity measurement. Section 5 describes our experimental study, and Section 6 concludes this paper.

2 Related Works

Many online content providers such as Amazon[2], offer recommendations based on collaborative filtering (CF) [5] which is a broad term for the process of recommending items to users based on the intuition that users within a particular group tend to behave similarly under similar circumstances. One advantage of previous CF techniques is that they can recommend relevant items that are different from those in a user's profile. However, they cannot detect innovative blog entries because only the similarity between user profiles based on instances such as selling items is measured. Therefore, CF often offers items that have the same concept to users. We want blog users to expand their interests by detecting innovative blog entries whose information is not included in the concepts (classes) of their interest ontology.

For applying a semantic approach to retrieving information from a blog, semblog [6] tries to construct a user profile using a personal ontology which is a manual construction of a users' classification of blog entries in a category directory of the ontology according to their interests. A category directory is built by users beforehand to construct an ontology-mapping-based search framework. However, manual ontology creation is a time-consuming and troublesome task for users, and applying a semantic ontology to a blog community is difficult. We automatically extract a user-interest ontology; thus, creating and updating ontologies is easy for users.

In researches of ontology mapping [1, 3], similarity measurements considering approximation of classes and class topologies are proposed in [3]. In addition to class topology, we consider each user's weighted interest in each class and instance. Furthermore, in analyzing conjunctions in class topologies of ontologies

---
[2] http://www.amazon.com

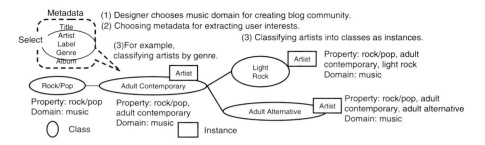

Fig. 1. Procedure for designing template ontology

with high similarity scores, we detect innovative instances that a user does not have in his/her ontology, though other users have them with a high probability.

3 Interest Ontology Extraction

We first explain the template ontology design of each service domain such as those of content delivery services of music and movies and then describe an automatic method of extracting interest ontologies.

3.1 Design for Template Ontology

We use OWL (Web Ontology Language) [4] for describing a template ontology. We can express a domain ontology in detail using OWL. However, the generation and spread of a detailed ontology is obstructed because users have difficulty of designing it. Therefore, we design template ontologies as lightweight ontologies that only use a hierarchical relationship among the classes and a property description restricts the succession condition of a class hierarchy. Then, we automatically extract an interest ontology by classifying user blog entries into template ontologies without user intervention in Section 3.2.

As shown in Fig. 1, first, the ontology designer chooses a service domain for extracting user interests. Then, the designer chooses metadata that reflects user interests. In a music domain, the designer chooses metadata of genres or artists, considering the exsisting community is generated with such metadata. Finally, the designer chooses metadata as a restriction property of a class hierarchy and classifies other metadata as instances of classes. For example, the designer chooses genres as a property and classifies artists as instances of classes. In this way, we distinguish classes from instances and define the characteristics of classes based on the restriction properties of a class hierarchy and classified instances. We make use of these class characteristics to improve the accuracy of interest ontology generation in Section 3.2.

The service designers only has to construct a template ontology with the intended domains and gradually increase the number of ontologies along with expanding the service. Designers also should adjust granularity of the end classes

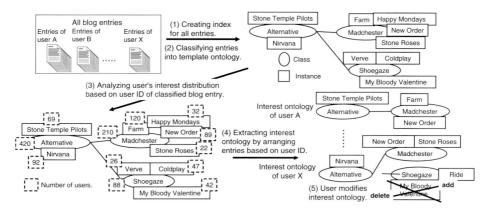

Fig. 2. Procedure for generating interest ontologies

for reflecting user interests in detail. Fortunately, content directories such as goo music[3] set granularity in detail for users to browse contents according to their interests. Therefore, we first construct template ontologies according to these directories and evaluate the granularity through the analysis in Section 5.

3.2 Interest Ontology Generation Algorithm

We explain our interest ontology generation algorithm by analyzing the interest distribution of users, as shown in Fig. 2.

Basic ontology generation algorithm. First, we describe the basic ontology generation algorithm (BOGA) as follows.

(1) First, we make index files for all blog entries collected through the ping server. Here, we assume that collected blog entries have a unique user ID.

(2) Second, we classify all collected blog entries into a template ontology. We classify blog entry E_i into class C_i if there is a name attribute value of C_i in E_i. We also classify blog entry E_i into instance $I_i (\in C_i)$ if there is a name attribute value of I_i in E_i. We permit the blog entries to be classified into two or more classes. For example, consider the template ontology in Fig. 2. We classify the blog entry into instance "Happy Mondays" of class "Madchester" when there is a "Happy Mondays" character string in the description in the blog entry.

(3) Then, we measure the number of interested users in each instance of C_e, which is one of the end classes in the template ontology. On calculating the number of interested users, we count the number of users as one, even if the same user is describing the same instance or class in two or more blog entries. We calculate the number of interested users in class C_e by obtaining the number of interested users in all instances in C_e and in class C_e. Thus, the interested user distribution in the domain can be measured by recurrently counting the number of users from C_e to the root class C_r.

---

[3] http://music.goo.ne.jp/

(4) Next, by extracting only the classification results about a user ID from all classification results, we can extract an interest ontology for this user ID. In Fig. 2, we can extract an interest ontology of user A when the blog entries of this user describe instances of "Stone Temple Pilots", "New Order", and "Farm".

(5) Finally, the user inspects and updates the interest ontology according to their interests. Furthermore, we can develop a template ontology that is more suitable by merging this modified information into a template ontology.

Ontology filtering algorithms. For example, BOGA classifies blog entries that describe "Farm", which means an agricultural farm, into the instance "Farm" of class "Madchester". For filtering these mistakes caused by words with several meanings, we make use of the following characteristics such as class relationships in ontologies and durability of user interests in a blog.

– Instances that belong to the same class have the same characteristics.
– Adjacent classes have similar characteristics. Instances of those classes also have similar characteristics.
– User interests that continue for a certain period and describe an interest for two or more days.

We propose two filtering algorithms FA1 and FA2. First, we explain FA1.

Filtering algorithm 1. We subdivide procedure (2) of BOGA for performing FA1.

(2-1) When the name attribute value $n(I_i)$ of instance $I_i (\in C_i)$ is described in blog entry E_i, FA1 checks whether a name attribute value of an instance of the same class (concept) $I_k\{(I_k \in C_i) \cap (I_k \neq I_i)\}$ or C_i is described in all blog entries that the user accumulates. We call instances I_k and C_i classification decision elements(CDEs).

(2-2) Entry E_i is classified as mentioning instance I_i when there is a description of CDEs, and not classified in I_i when there is no description. In Fig. 3, when the description of "Farm" exists in E_i, and "New Order" is described among all accumulation blog entries of a user, E_i is assumed to be a blog entry about instance "Farm" of "Madchester" and classified.

Filtering algorithm 2. We propose filtering algorithm 2 (FA2) whose classification is stronger than FA1. In procedure (2-1) of FA1, FA2 checks whether CDEs are described in blog entry E_i. Then, blog entry E_i is classified in I_i when there is a description of CDEs, and not classified in I_i when there is no description.

Adjusting the range of CDEs0. We give a mechanism that adjusts the range of CDEs by using the class hierarchy. We consider that descriptions of classes and instances of interest often appear with instances of the neighboring classes. We add a new adjustment parameter, hop, which defines the range of CDEs. In Fig. 3-(a), we assume brother classes, the grandfather class, and instances that belong to each of CDEs when there are two hops from end classes.

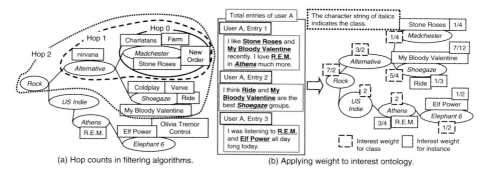

Fig. 3. (a) hops in filtering algorithms, and (b) applying interest weight to ontology

3.3 Introducing Interest Weight to Ontology

In addition, we introduce the interest weight as a parameter that shows the degree of a user's interest in each class and instance of an interest ontology. By using this parameter, we can create a community among users who have almost the same degree of interest in the same classes or instances.

Here, we define interest weight, as shown in Fig. 3-(b). First, the interest weight of every blog entry is one. Second, if there are $N(E_i)$ kinds of name attribute values of interest classes and instances that appear in blog entry E_i, the interest weight of each class and instance in E_i becomes $1/N(E_i)$. Third, when we define the set of all accumulation blog entries of a user as E, the interest weight $S(I_i)$ of each instance I_i is $S(I_i) = \sum_{(I_i \in E_i)}^{|E|} (1/N(E_i))$, and the interest weight $S(C_i)$ of each class C_i is $S(C_i) = \sum_{(C_i \in E_i)}^{|E|} (1/N(E_i)) + \sum_{I_i \in C_i} S(I_i)$. Fourth, the interest weight of the instances is reflected in that of the class that includes the instance. The interest weight of the classes is reflected in that of the super class. For example, in Fig. 3-(b), we give the interest weight of instance "Elf Power" as $1/2$, instance "R.E.M." as $1/4 + 1/2 = 3/4$, class "Elephant 6" as $1/2$, and class "Athens" as $1/2 + 3/4 + 1/2 + 1/4 = 2$.

4 Detecting Innovative Blog Entries Using Similarity Measurements

We propose measuring the similarity between ontologies considering interest weight. Then, we describe innovative blog-entry detection and community creation support based on the analysis of interest ontologies with high similarity.

4.1 Interest-Weight-Based Similarity Measurement

We now explain our similarity measurement in detail by using Fig. 4.

We first define terminologies. We give interest ontology O_A of user A and O_B of user B, topology T_1, which is defined as the relation between a class and

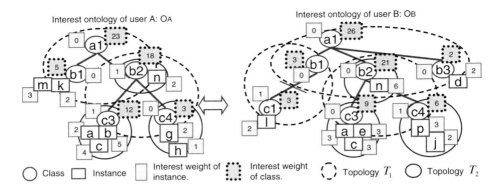

Fig. 4. Measuring similarity based on the degree of interest agreement

subclasses, and topology T_2, which is defined as the relation between a class and instances. Furthermore, we define common classes of both ontologies as C_i, and common instances as I_i. In particular, we define common class set, $C(T_1)$, as that which characterizes topology T_1, and common class set, $C(T_2)$, as that which characterizes topology T_2. For example, in Fig. 4, $C(T_1)$ has common classes $a1$ and $b2$, and $C(T_2)$ has common classes $b2$, $b3$, and $c4$. We also give the degree of interest agreement of common instance I_i as $I(I_i)$, that of common class C_i as $I(C_i)$, and that of common topology created by common class C_i as $I_t(C_i)$.

In [3], the authors calculate the similarity between ontologies considering the degree of similarity between class topologies T_1. In addition, we take the following ideas from the view point of creating a user-interest-based community.

- Evaluating the degree of interest agreement between C_is and I_is as a smaller value of interest weight. This idea is for filtering users who only enumerate a lot of instances in an entry, and creating a community among users who have similar or larger interest weight values from the viewpoint of each user.
- Separately treating topologies T_1 and T_2 because we consider that T_1 reflects the width and depth of a user's interests and T_2 reflects the objects in which users are interested.
- Achieving a low computational complexity by generating the class schema of user-interest ontologies accroding to that of template ontologies. This is important for ontology mapping to adopt large-scale dataset of blog community such as that of our experiments in Section 5.

(1) We analyze classes common to O_A and O_B and extract common classes which belong to $C(T_1)$ and $C(T_2)$.

(2) When common class C_i has common instance I_i between ontologies, we assign the smaller value of the interest weight of common instances I_i to $I(I_i)$. For example, $I(a)$ is 2.

(3) Similarly, we assign the smaller value of the interest weight of common class C_i to $I(C_i)$. For example, $I(b1)$ is 3.

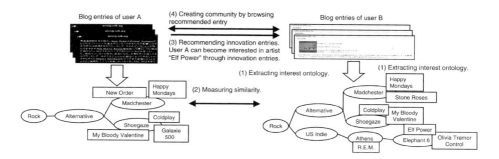

Fig. 5. Community creation service of recommending innovative blog entries

(4) We define product sets of subclasses of C_i, which are common to a class set, as $N(C_i)$, and the set union of subclasses of C_i among $C_i \in C(T_1)$ as $U(C_i)$. For example, $N(a1) = \{b1, b2\}$ and $U(a1) = \{b1, b2, b3\}$. Then, we give $I_t(C_i)$ as $\frac{\sum_{C_j \in N(C_i)} I(C_j)}{|U(C_i)|}$. For example, $I_t(a1)$ is given by $(3 + 18 + 0)/3 = 7$. Thus, we obtain degree of interest agreement $S(T_1)$ of $C(T_1)$ as $\sum_{C_i \in C(T_1)} I_t(C_i)$. In Fig. 4, $S(T_1) = (3 + 18 + 0)/3 + (9 + 3)/2$.

(5) We also define an instance set of C_i in ontology O_A as $I_A(C_i)$, and an instance set of C_i in ontology O_B as $I_B(C_i)$ among $C_i \in C(T_2)$. Then, we give $I_t(C_i)$ as $\frac{\sum_{I_i \in C_i} I(I_i)}{|I_A(C_i) \cup I_B(C_i)|}$. For example, $I_t(c3)$ is given by $((2 + 0 + 3 + 0)/4) = 5/4$. Thus, we assign the degree of interest agreement $S(T_2)$ of $C(T_2)$ as $\sum_{C_i \in C(T_2)} I_t(C_i)$. In Fig. 4, $S(T_2) = 2/1 + 5/4 + 0$.

(6) By using evaluation function $f(X)$ corresponding to the relative degree of importance of a topology, we finally assign the similarity score between ontologies $S_O(AB)$ as $S(T_1) + f(S(T_2))$.

4.2 Innovative Blog-Entry Detection

We adopt our similarity measurement to innovative blog-entry detection.

(1) We calculate the similarity between the ontology of user A and ontologies of other users in set U. By using the heuristic threshold X, we derive X users who have a high similarity to user A as an interest-sharing community G_U.

(2) Then, we analyze difference instances between the ontology of user A and ontologies of G_U. We also define a parameter, degree of innovation, which indicates how many hops we need to get from difference instances of an ontology of G_U to the class of the ontology of user A. In Fig. 5, we need 3 hops to go from difference instance "Elf Power" of ontology of user B to class "Rock" of ontology of user A. By recommending blog entries with a high degree of innovation, users may significantly expand their interests. Otherwise, users may receive new concept with a low degree of innovation comparatively more acceptable.

(3) Finally, we extract innovative instances G_I, which user A does not have, even though users in G_U have with a high possibility, and recommend innovative blog entries about G_I for user A with innovation degree.

Fig. 5 depicts an example of our community creation. We can analyze whether a user who is interested in instance "Happy Mondays" of class "Madchester" and so on has a possibility to become interested in instance "Elf Power" of class "Elephant 6". By browsing blog entries concerning these innovative instances, users expand their interests and share interests with each other.

5 Experimental Results

We now present experimental results that show the performance of interest ontology extraction and innovative blog-entry detection.

5.1 Datasets and Methodology

We evaluated the performance of our proposed methods based on the large-scale blog portal Doblog[4], which has 1,600,000 blog entries of 55,000 users. We also used the template ontology of the music domain, as shown in Fig. 2, which was created referring to public information about web portals such as goo music. Our experimental template ontology contains 114 classes as genres and 4,300 artists as instances, and each class and instance have two or more name attribute values. For example, the instance "R.E.M." has the name attribute values of "R.E.M." and "REM". Thus, we gave 7,600 name attribute values to 4,300 instances.

For evaluating accuracy, we defined correct answers as blog entries that have descriptions of classified classes or instances and evaluated the generated interest ontology by using precision and recall in classified results. In this paper, precision means the proportion of correct answers in classified results and recall means that of correct answers in all blog entries. When the recall is high, extracted interest ontologies cover user interests better. However, when the precision is lower, created interest ontologies include classified mistakes, and innovation detection for the user becomes unreliable. Thus, achieving high precision is indispensable. In evaluation, we adopted filtering algorithms to instances with one word such as "police", because we considered one word has a high possibility of having several meanings. For generating index files of blog entries, we used Namazu[5].

5.2 Measuring Interest Distributions of Blog Users

Graphs of user distributions in the music domain of our experiment are depicted in Fig. 6-(a). There are about 200 users, even in end classes. By checking the blog entries classified in end classes, we confirmed that these blog entries frequently have unique words, which describe the features of these classes. For example, blog entries classified into the end class "Death Metal" have the phrase "death voice" with a high probability. This is because the end classes in our template ontology have an appropriate granularity to extract the feature of the blog entries classified into these classes. The granularity of end classes is important because it affects whether we can determine if a user is interested in the community.

---

[4] http://www.doblog.com
[5] http://www.namazu.org/

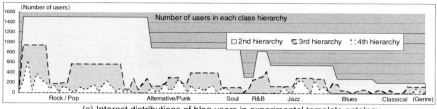
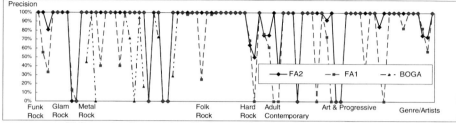

Fig. 6. Experimental results of user distributions and ontology extraction

5.3 Measuring Performance of Extracted Interest Ontology

We evaluated the accuracy of FA2 by checking 1/4 of classified blog entries, which were randomly selected. As shown in Table. 1-(a), the achieved precision is higher than 90% with a high recall of 80%. Thus, our filtering algorithm is effective for generating suitable user-interest ontologies.

5.4 Comparing Filtering Algorithms

Then, we compared BOGA and filtering algorithms by randomly checking 1/4 of the blog entries, which were classified into instances with one word.

Graphs of the precision of BOGA, FA1, and FA2 over 83 instances, which were randomly selected among 827 instances with one word, are shown in Fig. 6-(b). The accuracy between BOGA and filtering algorithms is compared in Table. 1-(b). These results indicate that precision improves in the order of BOGA, FA1, and FA2, and recall decreases significantly in FA2, even though FA1 drops only slightly from BA. For improving recall with high precision in FA2, we will add a method that checks for CDEs in the blog entries with a high probability of appearing these elements such as entries near each other in a time series.

Analyzing Fig. 6-(b) in more detail, there are eight instances in which the precision cannot be improved even with FA2, and they lower the overall precision. Then, we extracted instances in which the number of classifications increases by ten times or more when changing from FA2 to FA1. As a result, we extracted 28 instances and the precisions of 5 of those instances were 0. The reason is that they do not co-occur in the same blog entry with CDEs, even though the user was interested in them and described the name attribute value of these

Table 1. Experimental results of our ontology extraction and innovation detection

(a) Accuracy of extracted interest ontology (FA2, hop 2).

Precision	Recall
94.9%	80.3%

(b) Comparing accuracy of instances with one word.

	FA2	FA1	BOGA
Precision	70.0%	57.9%	18.9%
Recall	32.6%	93.0%	100.0%

(c) Comparing accuracy by changing hop counts.

	Hop 0	Hop 2	Hop 4
Precision	89.1%	91.0%	85.6%

(d) Recall of innovation detection.

	X=30	X=60	X=90
Recall	64.8%	76.7%	80.1%

(e) Comparing degree of innovation in recommendation lists.

Degree of innovation	0	1	2	3
Proportion	57.6%	15.2%	23.2%	4.0%

(f) Comparing degree of innovation in our detections.

Degree of innovation	0	1	2	3
Proportion	23.4%	23.1%	44.3%	9.2%

instances often. Thus, to improve the precision, deleting these instances from template ontology is effective.

We also evaluated the accuracy of FA2 based on the change in the hop number. Hop 2 is better than hop 0 with respect to the number of correct answers and precision, as shown in Table. 1-(c). However, hop 4 is lower than hop 2 in precision, although the number of correct answers is slightly better. That is because our template ontology has a large number of instances in end classes, and the relationship between end classes and super classes is closer than the relationship between super classes and grandfather classes. For example, end class "Acid Metal" has the super class "Metal" and grandfather class "Rock". In this case, the relationship between "Acid Metal" and "Metal" is closer than the relationship between "Metal" and "Rock". Thus, hop 2 has a better precision than hop 0 because hop 2 has many CDEs, and hop 4 has a lower precision than hop 2 because we consider CDEs in hop 4 as instances that are far from end classes.

5.5 Measuring Performance of Innovation Detection

We evaluated innovative blog-entry detection. In the evaluation, we defined correct answers for each instance by referring to recommendation lists such as "you might like these artists" in a music portal like goo music. Designers of music portals in this evaluation manually defined artists (A_n) that are relevant to another artist (A_i) for recommending relevant artists (A_n) to users who are interested in artist (A_i). Then, we evaluated our technique by checking the recall of 1/20 of 1503 users who were judged to be interested in the music domain of our template ontology. In this evaluation, recall means the proportion of correct answers in our recommended instances.

We evaluated recall in the change of X described in Section 4.2. Table. 1-(d) indicates that recall of our recommendation was about 80%. In particular, recall improves significantly when $X = 30 - 60$, even though $X = 90$ improves slightly from $X = 60$. This result indicates that we can extract innovative instances by only checking 60 high-rank interest ontologies among interest ontologies of 1503 users from the viewpoint of the user who receives the recommendation. Table. 1-(e) and (f) compare the proportion of degree of innovation in extracted instances

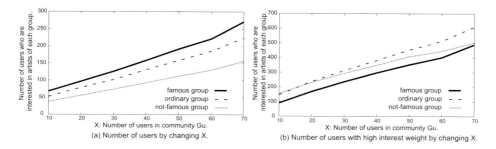

Fig 7. (a) number of users obtained by changing X. (b) number of users obtained that have high interest weight by changing X.

between recommendation lists in a music portal and our detected instances. These results indicate that our technique detects instances with high degree of innovation more in number than recommendation lists.

5.6 Analyzing the Suitable Granularity of User-Oriented Community

We also investigated suitable number of users for creating a community. First, we selected a user among all users extracted by our template ontology and analyzed suitable granularities of G_U by changing parameter X described in Section 4.2. In this evaluation, we divided innovative instances G_I into 3 instance groups in order of the appearance rate of instances when we set X to 70: a famous group, an ordinary group, and a not-famous group. We calculated the number of users who are interested in the artists of each group by changing X from 10 to 70.

Graphs of the number of users who are interested in each group obtained by changing X are shown in Fig. 7-(a). Next, we focused on users who have a high interest weight in their interest ontologies. Graphs of the number of such users obtained by changing X are shown in Fig. 7-(b). A famous group is recommended to users in spite of changes in X in Fig. 7-(a). On the other hand, in Fig. 7-(b), a not-famous group is recommended most when X is 10, and a normal group comes to be recommended gradually as X grows. This is because users with a high interest weight have a tendency of discussing not-famous instances, in spite of discussing famous instances. Furthermore, the number of users of each group increases suddenly when X is greater than 60. This is because the gap between a user's ontology and ontologies of G_u is larger when X is greater than 60, and instances with a low possibility of being interesting come to be recommended more often. From the results of Section 5.5 and 5.6, our innovation detection is effective according to detailed user interests when X is smaller than 60.

6 Conclusion

We proposed an interest ontology generation method and similarity measurement considering interest weight. Then, we adapted our technique to detect innovative blog entries in a blog community. We also performed large-scale experiments and confirmed that our techniques achieved automatic ontology extraction and detection of innovative blog entries with high accuracy.

We offer an experimental service DoblogMusic[6] for Doblog users and confirm the effectiveness of our innovative blog-entry recommendation method for creating a blog community by analyzing user access during a period of time.

Acknowledgments

In the verification of this research we used data from blog portal Doblog of NTT DATA Corporation. I wish to express my gratitude to the Doblog team and Hottolink Corporation, which pleasantly cooperated in offering the data and discussing the blog community creation service.

References

1. Doan, A., Madhavan, J., Domingos, P., and Halevy, A.: Learning to map between ontologies on the semantic web, in *The 11th International WWW Conference* (2002).
2. Godoy, D. and Amandi, A.: User Profiling in Personal Information Agents: A Survey, *Knowledge Engineering Review, Cambridge University Press* (2005).
3. Maedche, A. and Staab, S.: Measuring Similarity between Ontologies, *Proc. Of the European Conference on Knowledge Acquisition and Management - EKAW-2002. Madrid, Spain, LNCS/LNAI 2473, Springer*, pp. 251–263 (2002).
4. McGuinness, D. L. and v. Harmelen, F.: Web Ontology Language (OWL): Overview, W3C Recommendation, http://www.w3.org/TR/owlfeatures/ (2004).
5. O'Donovan, J. and Dunnion, J.: Evaluating Information Filtering Techniques in an Adaptive Recommender System, *Proceedings of Adaptive Hypermedia and Adaptive Web-Based Systems*, pp. 312–315 (2004).
6. Ohmukai, I. and Takeda, H.: Metadata-Driven Personal Knowledge Publishing., *International Semantic Web Conference*, pp. 591–604 (2004).
7. Zhang, Y., Callan, J. and, Minka, T.: Novelty and redundancy detection in adaptive filtering, *Proceedings of the 25th annual international ACM SIGIR conference on research and development in information retrieval*, pp. 81–88 (2002).

---

[6] http://music.doblog.com/exp/index

Modeling Social Attitudes on the Web

Matthias Nickles

AI/Cognition Group, Department of Computer Science,
Technical University of Munich
D-85748 Garching b. München, Germany
nickles@cs.tum.edu

Abstract. This paper argues that in order to allow for the representation, comparison and assessment of possibly controversial or uncertain information on the web, the semantic web effort requires capabilities for the social reasoning about web ontologies and other information acquired from multiple heterogeneous sources. As an approach to this, we propose formal means for the representation of possibly controversial opinions of groups and individuals, and of several other social attitudes regarding information on the web. Doing so, we integrate concepts from distributed artificial intelligence with approaches to web semantics, aiming for a *social semantics* of web content.

Keywords: Semantic Web, Description Logic, Information Integration, Agent Communication, Modal Logic.

1 Introduction

Social aspects of the web have attracted increased attention in the field of semantic web research recently. This development is certainly driven in part by the tremendously growing interest in web-based collaboration by means of *social software* (e.g., for blogging, collaborative tagging, wiki creation etc.). But the increasing interest in sociality also seems to be stemming from the general insight, that the semantic web can never become some kind of huge distributed knowledge base in the traditional sense. Instead, it will in our opinion become a more and more realistic emergent image of the current "non-semantic" web, i.e., an open environment with heterogenous groups of information sources and users, both with different and often conflicting viewpoints and interests, and with a high amount of personal interaction. This development will likely accelerate with new interaction-oriented developments like *semantic blogging*.

Approaches like *emergent semantics* [1], *dynamic ontologies* [14] and advances in the field of information integration in general and ontology mapping and merging specifically (e.g., [13,2]) already provide strong responses to some of the challenges posed by open information environments. But nevertheless, to their major part, current approaches to web semantics are concerned with the modeling of homogenous information, or the assessment and filtering of heterogenous information in terms of trustability and suitability. What is still widely missing are formal means for the modeling of (knowledge-related) sociality on the web itself, especially the simultaneous and comparative representation of heterogeneous and possibly inconsistent viewpoints of multiple information sources. Such means would not only allow for a rich modeling of social (i.e., communication) structures of web information (providing meta-information useful for, e.g., a subsequent resolution of conflicts and credibility issues). They would also allow for the social reasoning about the social meaning of information contributions on a logical level (as opposed to semi-formal approaches like *social networks* or *provenance information*). In this regard, the annotation of web information with meta-information denoting their provenance already received significant attention, but provenance modeling is to its main part strongly tailored to the problem of trustability, and it usually provides "only" meta-data (i.e., identifiers of the information sources), not an integrated logical model suitable for social reasoning.

As a response to the described issues, the main contribution of this paper is a general approach to a social semantics for the web by introducing a formal framework for a "social" multi-modal description logic, as informally outlined in the next section, and formally presented in Section 3 (including the semantics and decidability results). 3.4 introduces a social semantics of web publishing acts building on the formal framework, and Section 4 demonstrates our approach by means of a case study. Section 5 concludes.

2 A Communication-Oriented Model of Web Semantics

The basic concept underlying our approach is that of the integration of ("first-level") information with ("second-level") information about the social meaning of the former. This can in principle be done by the assignment of appropriate second-level meta-data to first-level information artifacts, using various techniques (e.g., higher-order logic, modal logic, or even RDF's reification). Henceforth, this way of reifying information is called *social reification* (or *social higher-order modeling*, if a higher-order logic shall be used). In demarcation from more informal ways of annotating information with meta-data (and the problematic and semantically extremely weak reification facility of RDF), we focus in this work on the formal integration of first-level and second-level information items which correspond (as a compound pair) to formulas and expressions of logic languages, e.g., axioms and facts represented in description logic (DL). E.g., a simple form of such a socially reified statement could look like "Frank *informs*: Sheep are pink" (or "Frank informs us that sheep are pink"), in contrast to the un-reified and hopefully highly controversial first-level statement "Sheep are pink".

Supposedly, it is easier for agents (including humans) to agree on a statement which quotes the opinion of someone else, compared to the less likely agreement with that opinion content itself ("agree to disagree" probably, so to say). Thus we believe that the (selective) social reification of web statements would achieve a great deal of increased semantic consistency of the web. In addition, social reification provides in many cases a rather safe way of semantic linkage among different information sources or documents (like different ontologies), and is thus expected to provide a means for information integration in case there exists not enough meta-knowledge (like trust) in order to decide about the alignment and merging of the information into a consistent set of un-reified axioms and facts. Although, e.g., OWL already allows for the inclusion of foreign ontologies and class descriptions, this works on a syntactical, constraint-less level, possibly leading to inconsistencies. Information integration using social reification in contrast allows to integrate foreign information in a relatively "safe" manner even if some reified first-level information is mutually inconsistent, and later integration steps can use the meta-information about the social meaning of the reified information for tasks like conflict resolution or credibility assignment.

Most important, social reification enables social reasoning about web information *within* a logic-based knowledge representation framework itself, not needing the help of "external", non-logical approaches (although we expect that a combination of such approaches - especially that of social networks - with social reification could be very fruitful).

So, the question is how such meta-knowledge about the social meaning of web information should look like in detail. In this work, we claim that - independently of technical information authorship or message-passing means - authoring information on the web is implicitly and unavoidably a *communication* performed by an autonomous, self-interested source, namely an assertive or informational speech act performed in order to express a subjective opinion (probably about some formerly published opinion). Thereby, it is not even necessary to make either the authorship or the propositional attitude towards the act content explicit. But we find a formal account to such second-order information highly useful, namely to have a means for its representation using semantic web languages.

To this end, the direct inclusion of speech act locutions as with agent communication languages would not be adequate for languages like OWL or RDF since speech acts are on a different conceptual level. Therefore, we propose a logical means for the modeling of asserted information. Intuitively, we want to express that, after uttering, the knowledge source (human, agent, web service...) is committed to his assertion. To represent such states, we have chosen the approach introduced in [7,4] and the more or less equivalent approach presented in [6,5] as a starting point for the semantics of web communication. Our approach demarcates itself strongly both from the well-known BDI agent model and from multiagent belief modeling (including dynamic epistemic models such as *public announcement logic*, which is not concerned with opinions in our sense but with the effects of announcements on beliefs [3]). At this, we distinguish sincere individual and group beliefs (which might be not visible on the web) from publicly visible *alleged* beliefs and subjective claims (the latter also to be distinguished from objective knowledge), and from public intentions.

Observe in this respect that it would not be sufficient to extend web knowledge representation languages with modal operators for belief or epistemic knowledge modalities. The former denotes a mentalistic concept, which cannot be extended to information publishing since information sources in open environments like the web are autonomous actors with opaque beliefs and intentions. A certain publisher might assert some statement a to audience A, assert at the same time $\neg a$ to another audience B, while believing neither a nor $\neg a$. In contrast, the modality of knowing would provide epistemic introspection, but would not be particularly useful in regard to the mentioned issues stemming from opinion controversies and the absence of an authoritative "truth" in the web.

In order to model public[1] attitudes of web actors towards information (and thus assign second-order information about social meaning), we introduce the modalities *public assertion and belief* and *public intention* as communication-level pendants to the mental attitudes belief and intention, and thus lift mental attitudes to the "social stage".

Examples demonstrating the high expressivity of a DL language with social attitudes are:

- $\Box_{\{s_1,s_4,s_5\},\{a_1,a_7\}} \exists loves.\top = \top$
  (The group of web actors $\{s_1, s_4, s_5\}$ (e.g., bloggers) publicly express facing $\{a_1, a_7\}$ the opinion that everybody loves somebody)
- $\Box_{\{a_1,a_5\}} Asserts_{\text{Frank} \mapsto all}(\exists loves.\top = \top)$
  (Group $\{a_1, a_5\}$ publicly believes that Frank asserts that everybody loves someone)
- $PInt_{\text{Frank} \mapsto \{a_1,a_5\}}(\exists loves.\top = \top)$
  (Frank publicly intends towards group $\{a_1, a_5\}$ that everybody shall love someone)
- $PInt_{\text{Frank} \mapsto \{a_1\}}(Asserts_{a_1 \mapsto all}^{expr}(\exists loves.\top = \top))$
  (Frank publicly intends that a_1 publicly announces that everybody shall love someone (while probably privately intending the opposite))
- $\Box_{\{Sarah\}} Customer = \Box_{\{Frank\}} Customer \wedge \exists has.Money$
  (Sarah's customers are Frank's customers, but only those with money. Modalities for social attitudes are thus also attachable to concept names (and role names), not only to axioms.)

Social attitudes will be given an intuitive but precise formal semantics which resembles the modalities of an actor's belief and intention in many ways [9]. They are nevertheless cleanly separated from mental attitudes (as in the BDI agent model and related multiagent belief frameworks), and can thus be used together with these without any interference. An agent might, e.g., reason simultaneously about the "real" beliefs of another agent and about the information this other agent gave to the public communicatively, which is not possible using BDI. Note in this respect that our approach is to its main part settled on a different conceptual level than related fields like multi-agent belief revision and information integration: Whereas these are mainly concerned with the determination of correct, consistent and useful information, the primary purpose of social attitudes is to represent communicatory properties of and differences among semantically heterogeneous attitudes, possibly preceding their assessment in terms of trustability and reliability.

---

[1] We use the term "public" not necessarily in the sense of "everyone attending", but to refer to communicatively disclosed information within specific closed or open groups (including "the web public"), as well as single persons (in form of singleton groups).

What mainly distinguishes an agents social attitude of *public* belief from her mental attitude of belief is that the former is an *ostensible* belief expressed communicatively (maybe restricted to a specific *audience*), and triggered and revised by social conditions (in our context namely web publishing and reception). Different groups and even subgroups of some groups can hold different public beliefs without causing logical inconsistencies. Public assertions in addition aim at ostensibly convincing their addressees. While public assertions and beliefs might as well reflect the true beliefs of benevolent, trustworthy information sources, this should be considered a special case for autonomous, self-interested sources in open environments. Also, uttering a public assertion doesn't necessarily mean that the agent truthfully intends to make someone adopt this public assertion as a mentalistic belief (that would be unrealistic), but as a *public* belief. Essentially this denotes that the release of information on the web is understood to an important part as a request which asks the readers of the information to show a positive attitude regarding the released information (i.e., implicit or explicit approval).

The general provision of meaning for data found on the web in terms of social attitudes as described in the next sections is henceforth called *social web semantics* (or just *social semantics*).

In a nutshell, we see the main benefits of modeling social attitudes in the provision of means for:

- Representation of and reasoning about public opinions (with sub-types such as agreement and disagreement), as opposed to mental beliefs, and also as opposed to ("objective") knowledge. We claim that virtually *any* kind of information published on the (semantic) web *initially* falls in the category of opinion, since such information is initially (from an observers point of view without any meta-knowledge such as about reliability) neither known as sincere subjective belief of the publisher nor knowledge. But quite surprisingly, to our knowledge no explicit, sufficiently powerful formal means for the modeling of opinions existed so far (i.e., with a required expressivity higher than BDI or other Kripke-style multi-belief frameworks).
- Representation of and reasoning about public intentions (like the intentions behind web publishing acts, e.g., the intention to make others agree with the respective claims)
- Modeling of different audiences. E.g., someone (using different nicknames) might utter inconsistent information depending on the addressees of these opinions. Such issues will likely become increasingly important with the rise of social software and the use of semantic web technology for the representation of discourses like in web blogs or web-based negotiation platforms.

  All social attitudes introduced in this paper can be restricted to specific audiences (part-publics, so to say).
- A social semantics of web publishing acts (and some other internet-relevant communication acts such as *request*) in terms of social attitudes.

2.1 Related Works

Apart from the related research field of ontology integration, the storage of heterogeneous information from multiple sources also has some tradition in the fields of *data warehousing* and view-generation for distributed and enterprise database systems [15,2], whereby such approaches do not take a social or communication-oriented perspective. *Contexts* are also used for the integration of heterogeneous information [12], but contexts in this sense originate from McCarthy's *truth contexts*, as opposed to the essentially pragmatic "social contexts" implicitly used for social reification. The assignment of provenance information is mostly based on annotation, or makes use of the reification facility found in RDF, which also lacks a social semantics of course. Approaches to provenance are already very useful if it is required to specify who contributed some information artifact (which is also done with a similar intent on the basis of social networks [11]), but they do not provide a logic model of the meaning of being an opinion source. Precisely, they allow to specify that someone asserts some information, but they do not handle what asserting (requesting, denying...) actually means, in contrast to the semantics introduced in this paper.

3 A Description Logic with Social Modalities

This section presents a description logic enhanced with modalities for the previously introduced social attitudes public assertion, public belief and public intention. The latter modality is mainly introduced for the purpose of providing a web publishing semantics later in this work; since we omit the specification of cross-modality axioms in this paper, it could be safely removed from the language in case one only wants to model public assertions and beliefs.

Our language is based on the "standard" DL $\mathcal{ALC}$ (Attributive concept description Language with Complements) [8], with modal extensions in the style of [9,10]. A further extension with additional features found in $\mathcal{SHOIN}(D)$ (the description logic equivalent to OWL-DL) is omitted here as being not relevant in the context of this work, but should be completely straightforward, since they do not affect the model-based semantics of our modalities (see below).

3.1 The Language $\mathcal{S} - \mathcal{ALC}$

Definition 1. The language $\mathcal{S} - \mathcal{ALC}$ (*Social ALC*) is defined as follows. The syntax allows both to specify terminological knowledge about concepts and roles ("TBox"), and assertional knowledge[2] about their instances ("ABox"). Modalities can be attached not only to formulas, but also to roles and concepts.
Atomic concepts: $C = \{C_0, C_1, ...\}$
Atomic Roles: $R = \{R_0, R_1, ...\}$
Individuals: $I = \{o_0, o_1, ...\}$

---

[2] The double meaning of "assertion" in this paper is unfortunate, but we wanted to stick with the usual DL terminology.

Inductively, we define (compound) *concepts* and *roles* now. Let R be a role and C and D concepts. Then $\Box_i R$, $\boxdot_i R$ and atomic roles are roles, and $\top$, $C \sqcap D$, $\neg D$, $\exists R.C$, $\boxdot_i C$, $\Box_i C$ and atomic concepts are concepts ($i \in \mathbb{N}$). Observe that in our framework $\Box$ is not he dual of $\boxdot$.

Formulas (in other DLs often called *axioms*) are either the atomic formulas $\top$, $C = D$, aRb, $a : C$ (with $a, b \in I$), or compound formulas $\Box_i \phi$, $\boxdot_i \phi$, $\neg \phi$, $\phi \wedge \psi$, with ϕ and ψ being formulas.

For convenience, we also define $\phi \rightarrow \psi = \neg(\phi \wedge \neg \psi)$.

Let $authors = \{s_1, ..., s_n\}$ be a finite set of information sources (web actors, publishers, web sites, peers...), and $addressees = \{a_1, ..., a_m\}$ the set of recipients (possibly overlapping or identical with $authors$). Let $actors = authors \cup addressees$ be the set of all participants.

Then we define the following *social attitudes*, where $\theta : 2^{authors} \times 2^{addressees} \rightarrow \mathbb{N}$ maps elements of the cartesian product of the powerset of authors and the powerset of addressees unequivocally to a multi-modality index number (e.g., $(\{s_5, s_7\}, \{a_1, a_6\}) \mapsto 570160$), $s \in authors$, $S \subseteq authors$, and $A \subseteq addressees$. Possibly empty or singleton subsets of $authors \cup addressees$ are called *groups*.

Opinion / Public weak assertion:
$\Box_{S,A} \phi = \Box_{\theta((S,A))} \phi$ (analogously for $\Box_{S,A} C$ and $\Box_{S,A} R$).

This attitude denotes that group S holds towards group A the opinion that ϕ is true. Opinions need not to be honest (thus they are also called *ostensible beliefs* [7]), and a certain author or a group can hold mutually inconsistent opinions (precisely: inconsistent propositional contents of the resp. opinions) facing different addressees.

In case S and A are identical in the definition of opinion, we use the following abbreviation:

Ostensible group belief:
$\Box_I \phi = \Box_{I,I} \phi$,
with $I \subseteq actors$, $|I| > 1$, denoting that in a group I ϕ is the ostensibly accepted group belief (while it is possible that a member or a subgroup of I ostensibly or sincerely believes $\neg \phi$ - an example for such a subgroup would be some politically dissident group which can articulate its true beliefs only in the underground). This important special case is close to the notion of *grounding* [5,6].
(Analogously for $\Box_I C$ and $\Box_I R$)

Public intention: $PInt_{s,A}(\phi) = \boxdot_{\theta((\{s\},A))} \phi$
This modality denotes that s publicly (i.e., facing A) intends that ϕ becomes true. A public intention is also ostensible only, and might have nothing in common with any true (i.e., mental) intention of s. Again, "public" means group A plus s.

Public assertion:
$Asserts_{s,A}(\phi) = \Box_{\{s\},A} \phi \wedge PInt_{s,A}(\Box_{A,\{s\}} \phi)$
(analogously for classes and roles instead of ϕ.)
Thus, informally, a public assertion modality states that an actor *ostensibly* believes some content, and *ostensibly* intends other actors to adopt his viewpoint in this regard (not necessarily explicitly)).

The difference of assertion (*Asserts*) and weak assertion / opinion is simply that the latter attitude does by itself not include convincing the addressee from its propositional content but the information source just expresses herself. For a simplified notation for the expression of *disagreement* with some given information cf. 3.4.

Upon these definitions, various constraints extending the well-known KD45 axioms scheme could be imposed optionally, which is omitted here for lack of space (but see [4,7] for an - non-terminological - approach to this issue).

Private belief: $Bel_s(\phi) = \Box_{\{s\},\{s\}}\phi$
(analogously for classes and roles instead of ϕ.)

Private intention: $Int_s(\phi) = PInt_{s,\{s\}}(\phi)$.

Maybe surprisingly at a first glance, the ordinary mental (i.e., private) belief Bel_s of a single actor can be modeled as a special case of the former public belief, namely the ostensible belief of a singleton group. Informally, one can imagine that actor s always expresses her honest private belief if she is within a group consisting of herself only (talking to herself, so to say). Although we don't encourage the use of this operator without being prefixed with another modality (denoting, e.g., that it is publicly believed that someone privately believes something), it allows $\mathcal{S} - \mathcal{ALC}$ to model multi-agent beliefs also.

Note that while the *Asserts* operator distinguishes information source and addressee, this differentiation is not required for the semantics of the public belief operator $\Box_I$. The latter just expresses that a certain proposition (concept, role) is *ostensibly* (but not necessarily sincerely or correctly) believed by a certain group of agents (not to be confused with the traditional concepts of multiagent *group belief* and *common belief*, which have a different meaning - recall that ostensible group belief does *not* entail that any of the group members or subgroups believes the respective statement). E.g., $Asserts_{s_3,\{a_1,a_5\}}(\phi)$ denotes that ϕ is asserted by source s_3, addressing recipients a_1 and a_5, which is equivalent to saying that i) $\Box_{\{s_3\},\{a_1,a_5\}}\phi$ (i.e., s_3 ostensibly believes ϕ) and ii) $PInt_{s_3,\{a_1,a_5\}}(\Box_{\{a_1,a_5\},s_3}\phi)$. We will later describe in detail the semantics of *making* public assertions (i.e., *announcing* ostensible beliefs) in a speech act -sense.

3.2 Model-Based Semantics

The following provides a model-based semantics for $\mathcal{S} - \mathcal{ALC}$, with an integration of multi-modalities $\Box_i$ and $\boxdot_i$ using a multiple-world approach (a.k.a. Kripke-style semantics) enhancing [9]. For details on modal description logics in general please refer to [9,10].

Definition 2. A model (of $\mathcal{S} - \mathcal{ALC}$) is a pair $M = (F, I)$ with $F = (W, \rhd_{PI}, \rhd_{PB})$. W is a non-empty set of worlds, $\rhd^i_{PI} \subseteq W \times W$ and $\rhd^i_{PB} \subseteq W \times W$ are a so-called binary *accessibility relations* for public intentions and beliefs respectively, with each element linking one world to another, $i \in \mathbb{N}$. Each $\rhd^i_{PB}$ shall be serial, transitive and euclidian, $\rhd^i_{PI}$ shall be serial. Moreover, for each $\rhd^i_{PB}$ shall exist one irreflexive predecessor element (thus this relation shall reflect the axioms of a KD45 modal logic - cf. [4] for details on these axioms).

I is an interpreting function which associates with each world in W an $\mathcal{ALC}$ model $I(w) = (D, R_0^{I,w}, ..., C_0^{I,w}, ..., o_0^{I,w}, ...)$. At this, D is the *domain* of the model, $R_i^{I,w} \subseteq D \times D$, $C_i^{I,w} \subseteq D$, and $o_i^{I,w} \in D$ (i.e., the o_i's are objects within the domain).

Definition 3. The values of concepts and roles, and truth-relation $(M, w) \models \phi$ for formulas are defined as follows:

1. $\top^{I,w} = D$, $C^{I,w} = C_i^{I,w}$, $R^{I,w} = R_j^{I,w}$ for $C = C_i, R = R_j$
2. $x(\Box_i R)^{I,w} y$ iff $\forall v \triangleright_{PI}^i w : xR^{I,v}y$
3. $x(\Box_i R)^{I,w} y$ iff $\forall v \triangleright_{PB}^i w : xR^{I,v}y$
4. $(C \sqcap D)^{I,w} = C^{I,w} \cap D^{I,w}$
5. $(\neg C)^{I,w} = D - C^{I,w}$
6. $x \in (\Box_i C)^{I,w}$ iff $\exists v \triangleright_{PI}^i w : x \in C^{I,v}$
7. $x \in (\Box_i C)^{I,w}$ iff $\exists v \triangleright_{PB}^i w : x \in C^{I,v}$
8. $x \in (\exists R.C)^{I,w}$ iff $\exists y \in C^{I,w} : xR^{I,w}y$
9. $(M, w) \models C = D$ iff $C^{I,w} = D^{I,w}$
10. $(M, w) \models a : C$ iff $a^{I,w} \in C^{I,w}$
11. $(M, w) \models aRb$ iff $a^{I,w} R^{I,w} b^{I,w}$
12. $(M, w) \models \Box_i \phi$ iff $\forall v \triangleright_{PI}^i w : (M, v) \models \phi$
13. $(M, w) \models \Box_i \phi$ iff $\forall v \triangleright_{PB}^i w : (M, v) \models \phi$
14. $(M, w) \models \phi \wedge \psi$ iff $(M, w) \models \phi$ and $(M, w) \models \psi$
15. $(M, w) \models \neg \phi$ iff $(M, w) \not\models \phi$

3.3 Decidability

A formula ϕ is *satisfiable* w.r.t. the semantic above if there exists a pair (M, w) such that $(M, w) \models \phi$.

Theorem 1. *The satisfaction problem for $\mathcal{S} - \mathcal{ALC}$ formulas is decidable.*

As shown in [9], the satisfaction problem (i.e, whether there exists a model and a world such that $(M, w) \models \phi$) is decidable for $\mathcal{ALC}_M$, which apart from the multi-modalities has an identical semantics. $\mathcal{ALC}_M$ uses arbitrary models, as well as such models which have two constrained accessibility relations corresponding to the modal logics $S5$ and $KD45$, the latter commonly used to model agent belief (as well as multi-agent belief when using multi-modalities $\Box_i$ (KD45$_n$). Since our accessibility relations $\triangleright_{PI/PB}^i$ observe S5$_n$ respectively KD45$_n$, and we are effectively mapping agent and group beliefs to single pseudo-agent beliefs (of pseudo-agents representing groups and ostensible attitudes) using θ, $\mathcal{S} - \mathcal{ALC}$ is decidable as well.

Related to this, it can be also easily seen that in the case we would allow only singletons for indexing the multi-modalities $\Box_i$, we would gain multi-agent belief modalities (in the sense of [10]). If we would additionally do the same with $\Box_i$, and also remove all constraints on the accessibility relation $\triangleright$, $\mathcal{S} - \mathcal{ALC}$ would "deflate" to a syntactic variant of $\mathcal{ALC}_\mathcal{M}$. The former is expressed with

Theorem 2. *Public singleton group belief corresponds to private individual belief.*

Thus, mental propositional attitudes can be written as a special case of social attitudes.

3.4 Social Semantics of Web Publishing

The data found on web pages or any other content on the web is in general, if taken "as is", neither knowledge nor private belief. Instead, web content needs to be interpreted as the content of communication acts. By means of such an interpretation (which essentially unfolds the semantics in the semantic web), the recipient can then classify the web artifact as knowledge (e.g., via trust), and, usually in a previous step, as opinions and other social attitudes. The step from the respective speech act of publishing (asserting, requesting, denying...) web content to its meaning in terms of social attitudes is specified in the following. Note that although we use an action notation, it would of course not be necessary to rewrite web pages as speech acts, since the speech act meaning of publishing web content is implicit. A web page claiming that "sheep are pink" is essentially nothing else than the description of an assertive speech act.

But technically, the following acts could also be used more or less directly within a document as "social semantics links" to external content (similar to the import-directive of OWL).

The following provides both a semantics for typical publishing acts in terms of their pre- and post-conditions, and at the same time an alternative (but under-specified) operational semantics for social attitudes in terms of those acts which are allowed to take place when certain attitudes hold. We achieve both by using the formal style (but not the content) of mentalistic semantics of agent communication languages, i.e., by specifying for each act its so-called *feasibility precondition* (FP) and its *rational effect* (RE) [6]. The former denotes what needs to hold (in terms of social attitudes in this work), the latter denotes both guaranteed illocutionary and perlocutionary effect(s) of the respective act. Publishing acts are denoted as

identifier$_1$: *author.Performative*(*audience*, $\phi|C|R|$*identifier$_2$*), with *author* $\in$ *authors*, *audience* $\subseteq$ *addressees*, and *identifier* $\in \mathbb{N}$.

If *audience* is omitted, the respective act is either not addressed at someone, or at an unspecified group of potential recipients (as it is usually in case when the locution is asynchronously given in form of a web site, which addresses potentially the whole internet).

identifier optionally assigns the act an unequivocal number (or a time stamp or an URI), or refers to another act. The helper function *content* maps an identifier to the propositional or terminological content of the respective act.

The content of an act (class, role or axiom) is denoted as ω.

Note that in regard to the semantics of speech acts it is not of importance whether the acts are technically performed asynchronously with its potential reception (like it is the usual case on the web), or synchronously, e.g., as steps in an interactive argumentation process.

- $id : s.assert(A, \omega)$ (author s asserts ω towards the recipients A)
  FP: $\neg Asserts_{s,A}(\omega)$ and $\neg Asserts_{s,A}(\neg \omega)$ and $\neg \Box_{A \cup \{s\}} \Box_A \omega$
  RE: $Asserts_{s,A}(\omega)$
  The feasibility preconditions (FP) here express that in order to perform an assert act, neither the information source nor the audience have already publicly announced their alleged belief in ω already (otherwise the act would not make sense). $\neg Asserts_{s,A}(\neg \omega)$ ensures that the information source does not contradict herself communicating with A (but she might expose a public assertion inconsistent with ω towards a different audience).
  The postcondition expresses that it became public that s asserts ω (which includes the public intention of s to convince A that ω). In the case that no trustability or other expectations are existing in regard to ω and/or its provenance a_1, the postcondition makes the assert-act essentially a request do adopt a public assertion, with a more or less uncertain effect on the addressee.
- $id : s.inform(A, \omega)$ (author s informs the recipients A that ω)

  FP: $\neg \Box_{\{s\},A}(\omega)$ and $\neg \Box_{\{s\},A}(\neg \omega)$
  RE: $\Box_{\{s\},A}(\omega)$
  The inform act is thus a weaker form of the assert act in that the author does not necessarily aim to convince the receivers.

Note that we can not simply define similar publishing acts for the utterance of group belief corresponding to $\Box_{group}$ (except in the case that the group is in fact a single actor on the web, like an organization - but this is already covered with *assert* and *inform*). Uttering such a group belief would require some judgement aggregation procedure (like voting), and can for principle reasons not be successful in all cases.

In order to provide convenient means for the agreement or disagreement with certain information, the following macro acts are proposed. We suppose they are particularly useful if the implemented language provides some sort of linkage facility, such as OWL's `owl:imports` and class or property descriptions in form of URI references. Interpreting the interlinked items (documents, class descriptions, meta-data etc.) as assertions, the graph formed from such items related by URL/URL references effectively maps to a communication process.

- $id_0 : s.agree(a, id_1) \equiv s.assert(\{a\}, content(id_1))$
- $id_0 : s.deny(a, id_1) \equiv s.assert(\{a\}, \neg content(id_1))$

We also propose the following *intend* and *request* acts, which (e.g.) allow to announce that a certain proposition is intended to be true, or to ask someone to publish a certain information. Note that our notion of intending includes as a special case *desiring* that another actor makes something true (like on request):

- $id : s.intend(A, \omega)$ (author s announces to an audience A that she intends that ω)
  FP: $\neg PInt_{s,A}(\omega)$
  RE: $PInt_{s,A}(\omega)$
- $id : s.request(a, \omega) \equiv s.intend(\{a\}, PInt_{a,\{s\}}(\omega))$
- $id : s.requestEach(A, \omega) \equiv \forall a \in A : s.intend(\{a\}, PInt_{a,\{s\}}(\omega))$ The latter two acts express requests directed to another agent (or a group thereof) to make some desired state come true. The act types *agree* and *deny* can be used to utter positive or negative replies to such requests, by asserting to intend resp. not to intend the requested act/state.

These makro acts are not unproblematic, since they request a potentially insincere intention ($PInt_{a,\{s\}}$). Instead, we could write $PInt_{a,\{a\}}$ to demand a sincere intention, but this would also be problematic.

4 Case Study

In order to demonstrate the properties and one possible application of our approach, this section presents a brief case study in form of a shortened *purchase negotiation* scenario (adapted from a scenario presented in [6]), which should be quite typical for the semantic modeling of, e.g., seller/buyer platforms on the web.

The interaction roughly follows protocols for *purchase negotiation dialogue games*, but we omit some details which are not relevant for our purposes (e.g., specification of selling options). Although the example deals with negotiation, the approach is expected to be usable for the modeling of other types of interaction on the (semantic) web also (such as argumentation).

Our scenario consists of four participants $\{s_1, s_2, c_1, c_2\}$, representing potential car sellers and customers (implemented, e.g., in form of two seller web services and two agents of the customers). In the discourse universe exists two instances ϑ_1 and ϑ_2 of some car type ϑ (e.g., specimen of the Alfa Romeo 159).

The interaction course is presented as a sequence of steps in the following form. Note that the interaction course consists of multiple interlaced conversations among different sender/receiver pairs. In particular, c_2 is involved in two selling dialogues at the same time. The different dialogues shall be visible only for the participants (senders and receivers of the respective communication acts).

Utterance id. sender→receiver(-s): Descriptive act title
Message
Effect (optionally) gives the effect of the act in terms of social attitudes.

In contrast to *Effect*, *Private information (PI)* optionally unveils relevant mental attitudes before or after an act has been uttered and understood by the respective agents. The PIs are not determined by preceding communication acts, due to agent autonomy. They are also of course usually not available to observers on the web, and thus just given here for the reader's information.

PI_{s_1}: Bel_{s_1} discounts
U1 $s_1 \to \{c_1, c_2\}$: **Information about discount**
  s_1.assert($\{c_1, c_2\}, \neg discounts$)
  Effect: $\Box_{\{s_1\},\{c_1,c_2\}} \neg discounts$
  $\land PInt_{s_1,\{c_1,c_2\}} \Box_{\{c_1,c_2\},\{s_1\}} \neg discount$
  Seller s_1 asserts that no discounts can be given while believing that the opposite is true (there might be the company policy that discounts should be given, but that might reduce the seller's individual profit).
  Note that such a contradiction between private and public (communicated) beliefs or intentions could not be modeled using BDI or known semantic web languages, although being, as already pointed out, crucial for the semantic web as a public opinions platform.
  Intentions can also not be modeled with any current web semantics framework known to us, including the highly relevant ostensible public intentions ($PInt...$).
U2 $s_1 \to \{c_2\}$: **Information about discount**
  s_1.assert($\{c_2\}, discounts$)
  Effect: $\Box_{\{s_1\},\{c_2\}} discounts \land PInt_{s_1,c_2} \Box_{\{c_2\},\{s_1\}} discount$
  While seller s_1 informed group $\{c_1, c_2\}$ that there would be no price discounts, he informs customer c_2 that this is not true (likely because s_1 thinks that c_2 is a valued customer whereas c_1 is not).
  Such different, inconsistent assertions addressed to different (even nested) groups of addressees can not be modeled using any current web semantics language (and also not by means of the BDI framework).
U3 $c_2 \to \{s_1\}$: **Query if car type has high accident rate**
  c_2.request($\{s_1\}, InformIfAccidentRateHigh$)
  Effect: $PInt_{c_2,s_1} Done(s_1 : InformIfAccidentRateHigh) \land ...$, with
  $InformIfAccidentRateHigh \stackrel{def}{=}$
  s_1.inform($\{c_2\}, accidentRateHigh(\vartheta)) \lor s_1$.inform($\{c_2\}, \neg accidentRateHigh(\vartheta)$)
PI_{s_1} : Bel_{s_1} $accidentRateHigh(\vartheta)$
U4 $s_1 \to \{c_2\}$: **Information about accident rate**
  s_1.assert($\{c_2\}, \neg accidentRateHigh(\vartheta)$)
  Effect: $\Box_{\{s_1\},\{c_2\}} \neg accidentRateHigh(\vartheta)$
  Seller s_1 asserted $\neg accidentRateHigh(\vartheta)$ while thinking the opposite. Privately, c_2 believes this information (see PI_{c_2} below) and publicly agrees in the next step, but will revise her private (but not her public) belief this later.
U5 $c_1 \to \{s_2\}$: **Expression of belief**
  c_2.inform($\{s_1\}, \neg accidentRateHigh(\vartheta)$)
  Effect: $\Box_{\{c_2\},\{s_1\}} \neg accidentRateHigh(\vartheta)$
  Since c_2 has himself asked s_1 to provide him the information uttered in the previous step, he publicly believes it.
PI_{c_2} : Bel_{c_2} $\neg accidentRateHigh(\vartheta)$
U6 $c_2 \to \{s_2\}$: **Query if car type has high accident rate**
  c_2.request($\{s_2\}, InformIfAccidentRateHigh$)
  To make sure, the potential buyer c_2 asks s_2 the same question.
U7 $s_2 \to \{c_2\}$: **Information about accident rate**
  s_2.assert($\{c_2\}, accidentRateHigh(\vartheta)$)
  Effect: c_2 publicly believes the information facing s_2, and even trusts it for some reason privately more than the information given by seller s_1 earlier. Nevertheless, it remains true that he also still publicly believes the opposite towards the other seller (i.e., that $\Box_{\{c_2\},\{s_1\}} \neg accidentRateHigh(\vartheta)$).

$PI_{c_2} : Bel_{c_2}\, accidentRateHigh(\vartheta)$
U8 $c_2 \to \{s_2\}$: **Propose to buy at a low price**
   $c_2.\mathsf{intend}(\{s_2\}, buy(\vartheta_2, 4000\pounds))$
U9 $s_2 \to \{c_2\}$: **Accept proposal**
   $s_2.\mathsf{intend}(\{c_2\}, sell(\vartheta_2, 4000\pounds))$
   Effect (together with the previous act):
   $PInt_{c_2,s_2} buy(\vartheta_2, 4000\pounds) \wedge PInt_{s_2,c_2} sell(\vartheta_2, 4000\pounds)$ (i.e., c_2 and s_2 are publicly committed to buy resp. sell ϑ_2 at the price of $4000\pounds$ now).

5 Conclusion

This paper argued that in order to allow for the logical representation of possibly controversial or uncertain web information on the web, current formal representation frameworks for web knowledge need to be enhanced for the modeling of the social meaning of information. To this end, we proposed a socially-enhanced description logic for the foundational modeling of socially acquired knowledge on the web, and a social semantics of web publishing acts in terms of the dynamics of social (i.e., communication) attitudes. Next steps will concentrate on a practical evaluation, the enhancement of other relevant languages such as $\mathcal{SHOIN}(D)$ with operators for social attitudes, and a full axiomatization of the modal logic.

Acknowledgements. This work is funded by Deutsche Forschungsgemeinschaft (DFG) (research project *Open Ontologies and Open Knowledge Bases*, contract BR609/13-1). I would also like to thank the anonymous reviewers for their very valuable comments.

References

1. A. Maedche, F. Nack, S. Santini, S. Staab, L. Steels. Emergent Semantics. IEEE Intelligent Systems, Trends & Controversies, 17(2), 2002.
2. D. Calvanese, G. De Giacomo, M. Lenzerini. Ontology of Integration and Integration of Ontologies. Procs. of the 2001 Description Logic Workshop (DL 2001), 2001.
3. J. A. Plaza. Logics of Public Communications. In M. L. Emrich et al (eds.). Procs. of the 4th International Symposium on Methodologies for Intelligent Systems, 1989.
4. F. Fischer, M. Nickles. Computational Opinions. Procs. of the 17th European Conference on Artificial Intelligence (ECAI-06), 2006.
5. B. Gaudou, A. Herzig, D. Longin. Grounding and the expression of belief. Procs. of the 10th Intl. Conf. on Principles of Knowledge Representation and Reasoning (KR 2006), 2006.
6. B. Gaudou, A. Herzig, D. Longin, M. Nickles. A New Semantics for the FIPA Agent Communication Language based on Social Attitudes. Procs. of the 17th European Conference on Artificial Intelligence (ECAI'06), 2006.
7. M. Nickles, F. Fischer, G. Weiss. Communication Attitudes: A Formal Approach to Ostensible Intentions, and Individual and Group Opinions. Procs. of the 3rd Intl. Workshop on Logic and Communication in Multiagent Systems (LCMAS-05), 2005.

8. M. Schmidt-Schau, G. Smolka. Attributive concept descriptions with complements. Articial Intelligence, 48(1):1-26, 1991.
9. F. Wolter, M. Zakharyaschev. Modal description logics: Modalizing Roles. Fundamenta Informaticae, v.39 n.4, p.411-438, 1999.
10. A. Laux. Beliefs in multi-agent worlds: A terminological approach. In Procs. of the 11th European Conference on Artificial Intelligence, 1994.
11. J. Golbeck, B. Parsia, J. Hendler. Trust networks on the semantic web. Procs. of the 7th International Workshop on Cooperative Information Agents (CIA), 2003.
12. A. Farquhar, A. Dappert, R. Fikes, W. Pratt. Integrating Information Sources using Context Logic. Procs. of the AAAI Spring Symposium on Information Gathering from Distributed Heterogeneous Environments, 1995.
13. V.A.M. Tamma. An Ontology Model Supporting Multiple Ontologies for Knowledge Sharing. PhD Thesis, The University of Liverpool, 2002.
14. J. Heflin, J. A. Hendler. Dynamic Ontologies on the Web. Procs. of the Seventeenth National Conference on Artificial Intelligence and Twelfth Conference on Innovative Applications of Artificial Intelligence, 2000.
15. R. Hull. Managing semantic heterogeneity in databases: A theoretical perspective. In Procs. of PODS-97, 1997.

A Framework for Ontology Evolution in Collaborative Environments

Natalya F. Noy, Abhita Chugh, William Liu, and Mark A. Musen

Stanford University, Stanford, CA 94305
{noy, abhita, wsliu, musen}@stanford.edu

Abstract. With the wider use of ontologies in the Semantic Web and as part of production systems, multiple scenarios for ontology maintenance and evolution are emerging. For example, successive ontology versions can be posted on the (Semantic) Web, with users discovering the new versions serendipitously; ontology-development in a collaborative environment can be synchronous or asynchronous; managers of projects may exercise quality control, examining changes from previous baseline versions and accepting or rejecting them before a new baseline is published, and so on. In this paper, we present different scenarios for ontology maintenance and evolution that we have encountered in our own projects and in those of our collaborators. We define several features that categorize these scenarios. For each scenario, we discuss the high-level tasks that an editing environment must support. We then present a unified comprehensive set of tools to support different scenarios in a single framework, allowing users to switch between different modes easily.

1 Evolution of Ontology Evolution

Acceptance of ontologies as an integral part of knowledge-intensive applications has been growing steadily. The word *ontology* became a recognized substrate in fields outside the computer science, from bioinformatics to intelligence analysis. With such acceptance, came the use of ontologies in industrial systems and active publishing of ontologies on the (Semantic) Web. More and more often, developing an ontology is not a project undertaken by a single person or a small group of people in a research laboratory, but rather it is a large project with numerous participants, who are often geographically distributed, where the resulting ontologies are used in production environments with paying customers counting on robustness and reliability of the system.

The Protégé ontology-development environment[1] has become a widely used tool for developing ontologies, with more than 50,000 registered users. The Protégé group works closely with some of the tool's users and we have a continuous stream of requests from them on the features that they would like to have supported in terms of managing and developing ontologies collaboratively. The configurations for collaborative development differ significantly however. For instance, Perot Systems[2] uses a client–server

---
[1] http://protege.stanford.edu
[2] http://www.perotsystems.com

mode of Protégé with multiple users simultaneously accessing the same copy of the ontology on the server. The NCI Center for Bioinformatics, which develops the NCI Thesaurus[3] has a different configuration: a baseline version of the Thesaurus is published regularly and between the baselines, multiple editors work asynchronously on their own versions. At the end of the cycle, the changes are reconciled. In the OBO project,[4] ontology developers post their ontologies on a sourceforge site, using the sourceforge version-control system to publish successive versions. In addition to specific requirements to support each of these collaboration models, users universally request the ability to annotate their changes, to hold discussions about the changes, to see the change history with respective annotations, and so on.

When developing tool support for all the different modes and tasks in the process of ontology evolution, we started with separate and unrelated sets of Protégé plugins that supported each of the collaborative editing modes. This approach, however, was difficult to maintain; besides, we saw that tools developed for one mode (such as change annotation) will be useful in other modes. Therefore, we have developed a single unified framework that is flexible enough to work in either synchronous or asynchronous mode, in those environments where Protégé and our plugins are used to track changes and in those environments where there is no record of the change steps. At the center of the system is a *Change and Annotation Ontology* (CHAO) with instances recording specific changes and meta-information about them (author, timestamp, annotations, acceptance status, etc.). When Protégé and its change-management plugins are used for ontology editing, these tools create CHAO instances as a side product of the editing process. Otherwise, the CHAO instances are created from a structural diff produced by comparing two versions. The CHAO instances then drive the user interface that displays changes between versions to a user, allows him to accept and reject changes, to view concept history, to generate a new baseline, to publish a history of changes that other applications can use, and so on.

This paper makes the following contributions:

- analysis and categorization of different scenarios for ontology maintenance and evolution and their functional requirements (Section 2)
- development of a comprehensive solution that addresses most of the functional requirements from the different scenarios in a single unified framework (Section 3)
- implementation of the solution as a set of open-source Protégé plugins (Section 4)

2 Ontology-Evolution Scenarios and Tasks

We will now discuss different scenarios for ontology maintenance and evolution, their attributes, and functional requirements.

2.1 Case Studies

We now describe briefly some specific scenarios that we encountered in studying various collaborative projects which members work closely with the Protégé group. Most of

---

[3] http://nciterms.nci.nih.gov/NCIBrowser/
[4] http://obo.sourceforge.net

these projects focus on developing ontologies in biomedical domain and thus represent scenarios that occur when domain experts develop ontologies collaboratively.

Perot Systems[5] provides technology solutions for organizations. In one of their projects, they are developing an ontology for a Hospital Enterprise Architecture using Protégé. There are almost 100 editors involved in ontology development. These editors use a client–server version of Protégé. The ontology resides on a central server that all editors access remotely. Changes made by one user are immediately visible to everyone. Therefore, there is no separate conflict-resolution stage or maintenance of various archived versions.

Another team with which we work closely is the team developing the NCI Thesaurus at the NCI Center for Bioinformatics [1]. NCI regularly publishes *baseline* versions of the NCI Thesaurus. Users access the Thesaurus through an API or browse it using the NCI's Terminology Browser.[6] Intermediate versions between the baselines are for internal editing only. Currently, each editor edits his own copy of the Thesaurus and checks in his changes regularly. The tools then merge the changes from different editors and identify conflicts. A conflict in this context is any class that was edited by more than one person. A curator then examines the merged ontology and the changes performed by all the editors, resolves the conflicts, and accepts or rejects the changes.

Currently, NCI is switching to producing the NCI Thesaurus directly in OWL and to using Protégé for this purpose. In the new workflow, editors will use the Protégé client–server mode and access the same version of the ontology. Therefore, the merging step will no longer be needed. The curation step will still be present, as the curator still needs to perform quality control and to approve the changes.

The Open Biomedical Ontology repository[7] (OBO) is our final example of an approach to ontology development. OBO is a Web site established by the Gene Ontology Consortium to enable biologists to share their ontologies. The OBO site is a sourceforge site that serves many biological ontologies and vocabularies. Ontology developers post successive versions of their ontologies in the repository, without posting a specific list of changes between the versions. Developers use different tools to edit the ontologies in their local environments (e.g., Protégé, OBO-Edit, Swoop) and create the ontologies in different languages. In many cases, the tools do not create any record of changes and when they do create such a record, the authors do not make it accessible to the outside world when they post their ontology in a repository.

2.2 Attributes of Collaborative Development

Analyzing various scenarios (like the ones described in Section 2.1), we identified several dimensions that we can use to classify scenarios for collaborative ontology evolution. Depending on the values for each of these dimensions, projects have different functional requirements, which we discuss in Section 2.3

Synchronous vs asynchronous editing. In synchronous editing, collaborators work on the *same* version of an ontology that resides on a server accessible to all members of the team. Changes made by one editor are immediately visible to others. Thus,

---
[5] http://www.perotsystems.com
[6] http://nciterms.nci.nih.gov/NCIBrowser
[7] http://obo.sourceforge.net

the possibility of conflicts is reduced or, essentially, eliminated since users know what changes others have made to the concept they are editing. With proper transaction support, where operations are wrapped in a transaction and two users cannot, for example, overwrite each others' values without knowing about it, conflicts are technically impossible. In asynchronous editing, collaborators check out an ontology or a part of it and edit it off-line. Then they merge their changes into the common version. In this case, conflicts may occur and need to be resolved during the merge.

Continuous editing vs periodic archiving. In continuous editing, there is no separate step of archiving a particular version, giving it a name, making it accessible. In this case, the only version of an ontology that exists is the latest one, and any rollback is performed using an undo operation. Alternatively, versions can be archived periodically, and one can roll back to any of the archived versions.

Curation vs no curation. In many centralized environments, new versions of an ontology do not get published externally until a designated curator or curators had a chance to examine all the changes and accept or reject them, and to resolve conflicts. In these scenarios, after editors perform a set of edits, a separate curation step takes place. By its nature, curation almost always happens in the scenarios with periodic versions, as the creation of a new archived version is a natural point for the curation step.

Monitored vs non-monitored. In monitored editing, the tools record the changes and, possibly, metadata about these changes, making the declarative description of changes available to other tools. In non-monitored development, the tools either do not log the changes, or these records are not readily available to other tools. For instance, any case where successive versions are published in a repository without change logs being available could be considered non-monitored editing.

2.3 Functional Requirements for Collaborative Ontology Development

We start by discussing the functional requirements that are relevant for all modes of ontology evolution and maintenance. Essentially in any collaborative project users request the following features:

– *Change annotations* that explain the rationale for each change, and refer to citations or Web links that precipitated the change.
– *Change history for a concept* that describes all the changes that were made to the concept, who performed the changes, when, what was the rationale for the change. Programmatic access to such information is particularly important as tools may rely on earlier versions of the concept definition and they must be able to process the changes and adjust to them.
– *Representation of changes* from one version to the next, including information on
  • which classes were changed, added, deleted, split, merged, retired;
  • which elements of each class definitions where added, deleted, changed;
  • who edited each change (possibly simply a list of editors that have altered a class since the previous version; ideally, a more detailed account, with complete trace of how each editor changed the class, with old and new values, etc);
  • which classes have more than one editor.

- Definition of *access privileges* where each author can edit only a particular subset of an ontology, thus avoiding clashes with other editors.
- The ability to *query* an old version using the vocabulary of the new version.
- A *printed summary* of changes and a programmatically accessible record of changes between an old and a new baseline.

If ontology editing by multiple authors is **asynchronous**, with each author editing his own copy of the ontology, additional requirements ensure that authors can resolve conflicts afterwards when the different copies are merged back together:

- *Identification of conflicts* between the local version being checked in and the shared version This identification must include treatment of "indirect" conflicts: it is not sufficient to identify concepts that were edited by more than one person. One person may have edited a class A, and another person may have edited its subclass B. While only one person has edited B, there may still be a conflict at B with the changes it inherited from A.
- *Negotiation mechanism to resolve conflicts* if they are caused by someone else's changes. Since check-ins are usually prevented until conflicts are resolved, mechanisms such as chats and emails (integrated with the ontology-development environment) can enable users to resolve conflicts efficiently.

In **continuous editing**, where essentially only a single version of the ontology exists (the current one) and there is no archiving, the main additional requirement is being able to revert back to an earlier version. Since in continuous editing no archives exist, this capability is usually implemented through the undo mechanism and earlier versions are *virtual versions* since they can be generated on demand, but are not explicitly saved. In other words, the following key feature is required for continuous editing:

- An ability to *roll-back* to a particular state of the ontology, for example, to the state of affairs in a particular date.

The following features provide support for **curated editing** by enabling the curator to perform quality control before a new version of an ontology is made public or is used in production:

- A mechanism to *accept and reject* individual changes and groups of changes; groups can be identified structurally (e.g., accept all changes in a subtree) or based on who performed the change and when (e.g., accept all changes from a particular editor);
- Ability to *save the current state of reviewing* (in the middle of the curation process) and to come back to it to continue reviewing the changes;
- *Specialized views of changes*, such as changes from specific editors or views that display only conflicts between editors.

In **non-monitored editing**, there is no explicit record of changes and all that the user has available are two successive versions. Therefore, in this mode there are a number of requirements that deal with comparing the versions and identifying and describing the changes. More specifically, the following features support change management in non-monitored mode:

- *Version comparison* at the structural level, understanding what was added, what was deleted, and what was modified.
- Ability to *post and describe new versions*, specify where the previous version is, and whether the new version is backwards compatible (see, for example, work by Heflin and colleagues on backwards compatibility of ontology versions [4]).

3 Components of a Comprehensive Ontology-Evolution System

Figure 1 presents the architecture for an ontology-evolution system that we developed and that provides support for most of the tasks that we have outlined in Section 2. At the center of the system is the *Change and Annotation Ontology* (CHAO) [8]. Instances in this ontology represent changes between two versions of an ontology and user annotations related to these changes. For each change, the ontology describes the following information: its type; the class, property, or instance that was changed; the user who performed the change; the date and time when the change was performed. In addition to change information, we also record annotations on changes. In our implementation (Section 4), we store the annotations as part of the change ontology, but the annotations can be as easily separated into a different ontology with cross-references between the two.[8] Annotations are stored as instances that refer to the change instances (Figure 2). Our representation of annotations extends the Annotea schema.[9] Therefore, the annotations can be saved to an Annotea store and be accessible to applications that process Annotea data.

3.1 CHAO: The Change and Annotations Ontology

Our Change and Annotation Ontology (CHAO) is based on our earlier work [8] and on the work of our colleagues [7]. In this paper, we highlight only the most relevant features of the ontology. We suggest that the interested reader downloads the plugin and examines the ontology that comes with it for specific details.

The ontology contains two main classes, the class Change represents changes in the ontology and the class Annotation stores related annotations on changes. These two classes are linked by a pair of inverse properties (Figure 2). Subclasses of the Change class describe changes at a more fine-grained level. These subclasses include changes to classes such as adding, deleting, or modifying class properties, subclasses, or restrictions; changes to properties; changes to individuals, and changes to a whole ontology, such as creating or deleting classes. There is also a class to group multiple changes into a higher-order change. Changes performed by users are represented as instances of the corresponding subclass of the class Change. These instances contain the information describing the change as well as the class, property, or individual to which the change is applied. For example, if a superclass C_{super} is added to a class C_{sub}, we record that a Superclass_Added change is applied to the class C_{sub}.

---

[8] In Figure 1 we show the two parts—changes and annotations—separately.
[9] http://www.w3.org/2001/Annotea

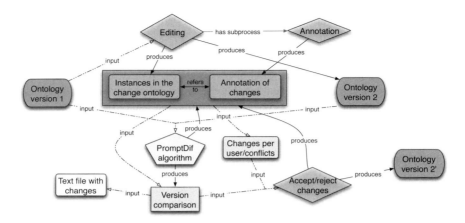

Fig. 1. Components of the ontology-evolution framework. The rounded rectangles represent versions of an ontology. The diamonds represent processes performed by a user. Through the Editing and Annotation processes, an ontology version 1 becomes ontology version 2. The CHAO instances are created as by-product of the editing process. If the CHAO instances are not present, the two versions themselves serve as input to the PROMPTDIFF algorithm that creates a version comparison, from which CHAO instances are generated. The CHAO instances and author, timestamp, and annotation information contained therein are used in the process of accepting and rejecting changes. Each accept or reject operation is recorded as a Boolean flag on the corresponding change instance.

3.2 Generation of the CHAO Instances

We must use different mechanisms to generate instances in CHAO, depending on whether editing is monitored or not (Section 2.2). With monitored editing, the tools can generate CHAO instances as a by-product of the ontology-editing process. Therefore, when users look at a new version of an ontology, they (or the tools they use) also have access to the CHAO instances describing all the changes, and the corresponding annotations.

In many cases, however, particularly in the de-centralized environment of the Semantic Web, tools have access only to successive versions of an ontology, and not to the description of changes from one version to another. In this case, we need to compare the two versions first in order to understand what the differences are. We then can save the differences as instances in CHAO. Naturally, we will not have specific author and timestamp information for each change.

3.3 Using CHAO Instances in Ontology-Evolution Tasks

The instances in CHAO provide input for many of the tasks that support functional requirements that we identified in Section 2.3.

Examining changes Many of the scenarios that we discuss involve having a user examine changes between versions. Users need to understand what changed between versions and what changes others have performed. The task is similar to tracking changes

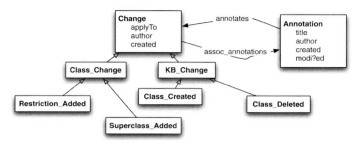

Fig. 2. The `Change` and `Annotation` classes in the change and annotations ontologies, a selection of their properties, and some examples of subclasses of `Change`

in Microsoft Word. The instances in CHAO provide data that inform the display of changes. Some examples of such a display include a table that lists concepts that have been changed and what has been changed for each of the concepts and a tree of classes with deleted, added, or moved classes marked in different fonts and colors and, possibly, underlined or crossed-out (see Figure 3).

Accepting and rejecting changes. In curated ontology-evolution in particular, but also in other modes, one may want not only to examine changes between two versions, but also to accept or reject these changes (not unlike accepting or rejecting changes in a Word document). We also need to save the state of the reviewing process (i.e, what has been accepted or rejected) so that the user may come back to it. We use CHAO to record the state of accept/reject decisions if the user wants to save a session and come back to it later. Consider a non-monitored editing where CHAO instances are generated by comparing the old and the new version of the ontology. Note that accepting a change does not involve any actual change to the new version, it is just a decision approving a change that has already been made. Therefore, if we start a new session and compare the two versions again (the old one and the version with which the editor had been working), the accepted change will appear as a change again. To avoid this behavior, any time a user accepts or rejects a change, we record the decision in the corresponding instance of CHAO. So, for instance, a change instance can be flagged as "accepted." A rejection of a change is an actual change, and we record this as another instance in CHAO. The link to the annotation instances enables the user to put additional annotations that, for example, explain his acceptance or rejection decision.

Viewing concept history. For each change, CHAO contains the information on the concept to which the change was applied and author and timestamp of the change (if the editing was monitored). We can readily process this information to provide concept history. Thus, for each concept, we can present the history of its changes, who performed them and when. Because CHAO links the changes to the annotations where users can describe rationale for and make other comments about each change or a group of changes, we can also provide annotations in the concept history. As a result, the user can see not only what changes where made to the concept, but also the explanation of why the changes were made, and, if available, the discussion about these changes.

Fig. 3. Comparison of versions in PROMPTDIFF. Classes that were added are underlined; deleted classes are crossed out; moved classes are grayed out.

Providing auditing information. We can compile the information about authors and timestamps for the changes to create auditing information for a curator. For instance, a curator can see which editors have performed changes in a particular time period, how many concepts each editor has edited, how many concepts where edited by more than one editor in a particular time period.

The use of an ontology to record changes and annotations enables us to have a modular system that supports multiple tasks. For instance, regardless of how the CHAO instance are generated (as a by-product of monitored editing or through version comparison in non-monitored editing), once we have it, we can use it in other tasks, such as presenting concept history, displaying changes between versions, and so on. When the user accepts or rejects a change, we can again use the same set of structures to record his decisions and corresponding annotations. As a result, when a user, for instance, accepts a change to a concept C and records his rationale for this decision, this comment appears in the concept history for C. Furthermore, the use of an ontology to record changes and annotations can potentially enable sharing of this information between ontology-editing tools.

4 Implementation Details

We have implemented a system to support the different modes of ontology evolution in a single comprehensive framework that we described in Section 3 as a set of plugins to the Protégé ontology-development environment. The framework is implemented as two related Protégé plugins:

The Change-management plugin provides access to a list of changes and enables users to add annotations to individual changes or groups of changes; when this plugin is activated, the changes are stored as instances in CHAO. Further, this plugin enables users to see a concept history for the class and the corresponding annotations, when they are examining the classes in the standard Classes tab.

The PROMPT plugin for ontology management provides comparisons of two versions of an ontology and facilities to examine a list of users who performed changes and to accept and reject changes [9].

In addition, the Protégé environment itself provides many of the facilities necessary to support the scenarios we outlined in Section 2, such as synchronous editing in a client–server mode, transaction support, undo facilities, and other features. The Protégé API provides convenient access to changes as they are performed, to facilities to create and edit ontologies, and to the user interface components that the plugins use.

We now describe these components and where they fall in the overall framework.

4.1 The Change-Management Plugin

The Change-management plugin to Protégé performs several functions. First, when the user enables the plugin, each ontology change is recorded as an instance in CHAO with the timestamp and the author of the change. Thus, with this plugin in place, the editing is monitored and a declarative record of changes is stored. CHAO instances are saved when the user saves the project. If needed, users can open CHAO in Protégé or access it through the Protégé knowledge-base API, just as they would any other ontology.

Second, users can see the "Changes" tab that provides an overview of changes and corresponding annotations (Figure 4). There are two views for the changes: the "detailed" view shows low-level changes that correspond to each operation in the ontology. The "summary" view (the default) groups the low-level changes into higher-level ones that roughly correspond to the operations that the user performs in the user interface. For instance, when a user creates an OWL restriction for a class, a series of low-level operations happen: an anonymous class is created, property values for this class are assigned, and this class becomes a superclass for the class that it restricts. This set of operations corresponds to a single high-level operation "Restriction added."

The user can select a change and view annotations for this change and any of the groups of changes that involve the selected change. The user can also provide annotations for the selected change or select a group of changes and provide annotation for the whole group. For example, a user can describe the rationale for adding a set of classes. The tab also provides search capabilities.

In the Classes tab (the standard Protégé tab for browsing and editing classes), an additional menu item—"Change info"—appears when the Change-management plugin is activated. Through this menu, the user can view the concept history and the corresponding annotations for the class selected in the Classes tab. The display is similar to the change and annotation display in Figure 4, but the list of changes is limited to the changes that pertain to the class of interest. The user can also create additional annotations here.

4.2 The PROMPT Tab

PROMPT is a Protégé plugin that provides a number of ontology-management functions. Here we discuss only the functionality that is relevant for ontology evolution.

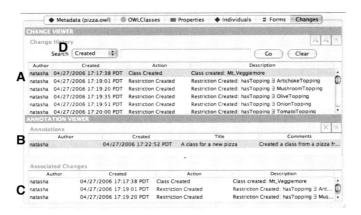

Fig. 4. The Change-management tab in Protégé. The table at the top (A) displays all the changes to the current project. When the user selects a change in the top table, the middle table(B) shows all annotations associated with this change. For selected annotation, the bottom table (C) shows other changes in the group if annotation applied to a group of changes rather than a single change. The user can create new annotations, examine the details of existing ones through this display, and search through annotations (D).

When the user activates the PROMPT tab and instructs it to compare two versions of an ontology, one of the two things happens: (1) If instances of CHAO are present (the editing was monitored), PROMPT uses these instances to compile the changes and to present them to the user. (2) If there are no CHAO instances and the user has only the two version of the ontology, and no record of the changes between them, the PROMPT-DIFF algorithm compares the two versions and creates a *structural diff*, using a set of heuristics to determine what has changed between the versions. It determines, for example, when classes are renamed, when classes are moved in the class hierarchy, or when their definitions change. Recall that we designed the architecture for ontology evolution to have CHAO drive all other components in order to have a modularized structure and to have the same components work in different editing modes. Thus, if there is no declarative record of changes in the form of CHAO, PROMPT generates these instances from the results of the PROMPTDIFF algorithm.

One of the unique features of version comparison in PROMPT, is the ability to examine changes using an intuitive interface, based on the Protégé interface for class editing (Figure 3), and to accept and reject changes. In the class hierarchy, the users can see which classes and subtrees were deleted or added, which were changed, moved, and so on. For each class, PROMPT provides a list of changes for that class. Users can also view the old and the new definitions of the class side-by-side. Users then can accept or reject each specific change, all changes for a class, or all changes for a particular subtree.

If CHAO exists, PROMPT also generates a list of users who changed the ontology. For each user, PROMPT displays the number of concepts he created or modified, and the number of concepts that are in conflict with modification performed by others. Here we define a conflict (something that a curator might want to verify) as one concept modified by more than one user. Curators can also accept or reject all changes performed by a specific user in a single click or all changes that are not in conflict with others.

4.3 Client–Server Mode for Ontology Editing in Protégé

Of the many features of the Protégé core system that support ontology evolution, we focus on the one that specifically addresses one of the modes of ontology editing: synchronous editing by multiple users. The multi-user mode in Protégé uses a client–server architecture, with the ontologies being stored on the machine running the Protégé server. Users then remotely connect to this server using a thick Protégé client. All users editing an ontology always see the same version of it, and changes made by one user are visible immediately to other users. If the Change-management plugin is installed on the server, it records all the changes that happen on the server machine made by different users.

Most of the features described in this Section are already available for beta-testing at the time of this writing as part of the Protégé beta distribution. A small number of features, such as saving to Annotea, are currently in alpha-testing or under development.

5 Related Work

We have developed initial ideas on how a change ontology can drive various ontology-evolution tasks in our earlier work [8]. We have borrowed many ideas on the CHAO structure from there, but extended it with additional pragmatic information such as identification of a concept to which the change applies, author and timestamp of the change, and link to relevant annotations. Thus, in this paper, we have not focused on the representation of changes per se using the detailed work by others in this area [7].

Many ontology-development tools support monitored ontology evolution by recording change logs. However, in most cases, the changes are recorded as sequences of changes rather than a set of instances in a change ontology [6,11]. While one form of representation can be inferred from the other and vice versa, representation in the form of ontology instances facilitates querying for concept histories and enables attaching annotations to changes.

The SWOOP ontology editor [6] supports an extensive set of annotations, distinguishing between comments, advices, examples, and so on. We currently do not enable users to categorize annotations in different ways, but plan to add such capability in the future. As a practical matter, since our annotation ontology already extends the Annotea RDF Schema, we need to develop only the user interface for such support.

The ontology-evolution support in KAON [13,3] focuses on the effects of changes. Users can specify their desired strategies for ontology evolution in terms of handling of changes. Recent work [3] focuses on maintaining consistency during evolution for DL-based ontologies. The authors consider various scenarios, such as maintaining consistency as the ontology changes, repairing inconsistencies, or answering queries over inconsistent ontologies.

There is one aspect of ontology evolution and versioning that we do not currently deal with in this work—effects of changes on applications. This analysis requires an understanding of which version of an ontology an application is compatible with, in particular in the context of ongoing ontology development where newer versions may not be consistent. The issue of compatibility is addressed in the MORE framework for reasoning with multi-version ontologies [5] and in the work of Heflin and colleagues on declarative specifications of compatibility between versions [4].

6 Discussion

In summary, the two plugins—the Change-management plugin and the PROMPT plugin—in combination with Protégé's own facilities, provide support for all modes of ontology evolution that we have identified among our projects.

Because Protégé can import ontologies developed by other tools (in OWL, RDFS, and a number of other formats), developers can benefit from the Protégé change-management facilities even if they first develop their ontologies in a different tool. For example, if an OWL ontology was originally developed in SWOOP, the developer can still use PROMPT to compare its versions, accept or reject changes, create a new baseline, and then continue editing in SWOOP.

While we have not yet performed a summative evaluation of our tools, we have run formative evaluations with the developers of NCI Thesaurus. In these evaluations, five NCI Thesaurus editors and a curator used Protégé and some of the tools we described here to edit portions of the Thesaurus in parallel with their regular environment (Apelon's TDE). Mainly, the curator used the PROMPT plugin to examine the changes performed by the editors and to accept or reject them. We also used the PROMPT representation of changes to generate the concept-history output in a database format that the APIs for accessing the NCI Thesaurus expect. Many of the features we discussed here (e.g., side-by-side views of the old and the new version of the class, the ability to save the status of the accept/reject process, the ability to annotate changes and curation decisions, etc.) resulted from usability studies during these evaluations. As the result of the studies, NCI is moving towards switching to Protégé and its change-management plugins as their primary editing environment for NCI Thesaurus.

There are several limitations of our current work that we plan to address in the future. First, we currently assume that when there is a record of changes between two versions, this record is *complete*. In many cases, however, this record will not be complete. For instance, a user may disable the change-management support, perform edits, and then enable it again or he may edit a portion of the ontology in a different tool and then import it back into Protégé. We need to address two questions to deal with incomplete change records: (1) how do we determine automatically that a record is indeed incomplete; and (2) in the case of incomplete change record, can we have a hybrid solution that uses the author, date, annotation, and other pertinent information that is available in the incomplete record and combines it with the record generated by PROMPTDIFF.

Migration of instances from one version of an ontology to the next is a critical issue in the context of evolving ontologies. Some ontology changes, such as creating new classes or properties, do not affect instances; when these changes occur, instances that were valid in the old version are still valid ini the new version. However, a large number of changes may potentially affect instances. In this latter case, some strategies can include having tools take their best guess as to how instances should be transformed, allowing users to specify what to do for a specific class of changes (e.g., similar to evolution strategies [13]), or flagging instances that might be invalidated by changes.

Ontology modularization [12,2] is also critical for support of ontology evolution, in particular in the asynchronous mode. It will be impractical if the whole ontology is the only unit that users can check out. Rather, editing in asynchronous mode would be much more effective if ontology consists of well-delineated modules that cross-reference one another. Users must be able to check out a specific module rather than a whole ontology.

Finally, consistency checking and ontology debugging [14,10], while important for ontology development in general, are particularly critical in the collaborative setting. Users must be able to understand what the effects changes performed by others have, to understand the rationale for those changes, and to check consistency of the ontology when all the changes are brought together.

We continue to work with our collaborators that use Protégé in large collaborative ontology-development projects to identify new requirements and modes of collaboration. As it exists today, however, we believe that the environment that we described in this paper is one of the most complete sets of components to support ontology evolution today. And the framework that underlies our implementation provides for flexible and modular development of ontology-evolution support.

Acknowledgments

This work was supported in part by a contract from the U.S. National Cancer Institute. Protégé is a national resource supported by grant LM007885 from the United States National Library of Medicine.

References

1. G. Fragoso, S. de Coronado, M. Haber, F. Hartel, and L. Wright. Overview and utilization of the nci thesaurus. *Comparative and Functional Genomics*, 5(8):648–654, 2004.
2. B. C. Grau, B. Parsia, and E. Sirin. Working with multiple ontologies on the semantic web. In *Third Internatonal Semantic Web Conference (ISWC2004)*, 2004.
3. P. Haase, F. van Harmelen, Z. Huang, H. Stuckenschmidt, and Y. Sure. A framework for handling inconsistency in changing ontologies. In *Fourth International Semantic Web Conference (ISWC2005)*, 2005.
4. J. Heflin and Z. Pan. A model theoretic semantics for ontology versioning. In *Third International Semantic Web Conference*, page 6276. Springer, 2004.
5. Z. Huang and H. Stuckenschmidt. Reasoning with multiversion ontologies: a temporal logic approach. In *Fourth International Semantic Web Conference (ISWC2005)*, 2005.
6. A. Kalyanpur, B. Parsia, E. Sirin, B. Cuenca-Grau, and J. Hendler. SWOOP: A web ontology editing browser. *Journal of Web Semantics*, 2005.
7. M. Klein. *Change Management for Distributed Ontologies*. PhD thesis, Vrije Universiteit Amsterdam, 2004.
8. M. Klein and N. F. Noy. A component-based framework for ontology evolution. In *Workshop on Ontologies and Distributed Systems at IJCAI-03*, Acapulco, Mexico, 2003.

9. N. F. Noy and M. A. Musen. The PROMPT suite: Interactive tools for ontology merging and mapping. *International Journal of Human-Computer Studies*, 59(6):983–1024, 2003.
10. B. Parsia, E. Sirin, and A. Kalyanpur. Debugging OWL ontologies. In *14th Intl Conference on World Wide Web*, pages 633–640, New York, NY, 2005. ACM Press.
11. P. Plessers and O. De Troyer. Ontology change detection using a version log. In *Fourth International Semantic Web Conference (ISWC2005)*, 2005.
12. J. Seidenberg and A. Rector. Web ontology segmentation: Analysis, classification and use. In *15th International World Wide Web Conference*, Edinburgh, Scotland, 2006.
13. L. Stojanovic. *Methods and Tools for Ontology Evolution*. PhD thesis, University of Karlsruhe, 2004.
14. H. Wang, M. Horridge, A. Rector, N. Drummond, and J. Seidenberg. Debugging OWL-DL ontologies: A heuristic approach. In *4th International Semantic Web Conference (ISWC2005)*, Galway, Ireland, 2005. Springer.

Extending Faceted Navigation for RDF Data

Eyal Oren, Renaud Delbru, and Stefan Decker

DERI Galway, Ireland
firstname.lastname@deri.org

Abstract. Data on the Semantic Web is semi-structured and does not follow one fixed schema. Faceted browsing [23] is a natural technique for navigating such data, partitioning the information space into orthogonal conceptual dimensions. Current faceted interfaces are manually constructed and have limited query expressiveness. We develop an expressive faceted interface for semi-structured data and formally show the improvement over existing interfaces. Secondly, we develop metrics for automatic ranking of facet quality, bypassing the need for manual construction of the interface. We develop a prototype for faceted navigation of arbitrary RDF data. Experimental evaluation shows improved usability over current interfaces.

1 Introduction

As Semantic Web data emerges, techniques for browsing and navigating this data are necessary. Semantic Web data, expressed in RDF[1], is typically very large, highly interconnected, and heterogeneous without following one fixed schema [1]. Any technique for navigating such datasets should therefore be scalable; should support graph-based navigation; and should be generic, not depend on a fixed schema, and allow exploration of the dataset without a-priori knowledge of its structure.

We identified four existing interface types for navigating RDF data: (1) keyword search, e.g. Swoogle[2], (2) explicit queries, e.g. Sesame[3], (3) graph visualisation, e.g. IsaViz[4] , and (4) faceted browsing [12, 19, 23]. None of these fulfill the above requirements: *keyword search* suffices for simple information lookup, but not for higher search activities such as learning and investigating [13]; writing *explicit queries* is difficult and requires schema knowledge; *graph visualisation* does not scale to large datasets [7]; and existing *faceted interfaces* are manually constructed and domain-dependent, and do not fully support graph-based navigation.

In this paper we 1. improve faceted browsing techniques for RDF data, 2. develop a technique for automatic facet ranking, 3. develop a formal model of faceted browsing, allowing for precise comparison of interfaces, and 4. support our conclusions with a formal analysis and an experimental evaluation.

---

[1] http://www.w3.org/RDF/
[2] http://swoogle.umbc.edu/
[3] http://www.openrdf.org/
[4] http://www.w3.org/2001/11/IsaViz/

2 Faceted Browsing

An exploratory interface allows users to find information without a-priori knowledge of its schema. Especially when the structure or schema of the data is unknown, an exploration technique is necessary [21]. Faceted browsing [23] is an exploration technique for structured datasets based on the facet theory [17].

In faceted browsing the information space is partitioned using orthogonal conceptual dimensions of the data. These dimensions are called facets and represent important characteristics of the information elements. Each facet has multiple restriction values and the user selects a restriction value to constrain relevant items in the information space. The facet theory can be directly mapped to navigation in semi-structured RDF data: information elements are RDF subjects, facets are RDF predicates and restriction-values are RDF objects.

A collection of art works can for example have facets such as type of work, time periods, artist names and geographical locations. Users are able to constrain each facet to a restriction value, such as "created in the 20th century", to limit the visible collection to a subset. Step by step other restrictions can be applied to further constrain the information space.

A faceted interface has several advantages over keyword search or explicit queries: it allows exploration of an unknown dataset since the system suggests restriction values at each step; it is a visual interface, removing the need to write explicit queries; and it prevents dead-end queries, by only offering restriction values that do not lead to empty results.

3 A Faceted Interface for RDF Data

In this section we introduce our faceted interface for arbitrary RDF data, explain its functionality, and formally describe its expressive power. The formal treatment allows us to clearly show the improvement in expressive power over existing interfaces, which we will do in Sec. 5.1.

3.1 Overview

A screenshot of our BrowseRDF prototype[5], automatically generated for arbitrary data, is shown in Fig. 1. This particular screenshot shows the FBI's most wanted fugitives[6]. These people are described by various properties, such as their weight, their eye-color, and the crime that they are wanted for. These properties form the facets of the dataset, and are shown on the left-hand side of the screenshot.

Users can browse the dataset by constraining one or several of these facets. At the top-center of the screenshot we see that the user constrained the dataset to all fugitives that weigh 150 pounds, and in the middle of the interface we see that three people have been found conforming to that constraint. These people

---
[5] available at `http://browserdf.org`.
[6] `http://sp11.stanford.edu/kbs/fbi.zip`

Fig. 1. Faceted browsing prototype

are shown (we see only the first), with all information known about them (their alias, their nationality, their eye-color, and so forth). The user could now apply additional constraints, by selecting another facet (such as citizenship) to see only the fugitives that weigh 150 pounds and speak French.

3.2 Functionality

The goal of faceted browsing is to restrict the search space to a set of relevant resources (in the above example, a set of fugitives). Faceted browsing is a visual query paradigm [15, 9]: the user constructs a selection query by browsing and adding constraints; each step in the interface constitutes a step in the query construction, and the user sees intermediate results and possible future steps while constructing the query.

We now describe the functionality of our interface more systematically, by describing the various operators that users can use. Each operator results in a constraint on the dataset; operators can be combined to further restrict the results to the set of interest. Each operator returns a subset of the information space; an exact definition is given in Sec. 3.3.

Basic selection. The basic selection is the most simple operator. It selects nodes that have a direct restriction value. The basic selection allows for example to "find all resources of thirty-year-olds", as shown in Fig. 2a. It selects all nodes that have an outgoing edge, labelled "age", that leads to the node "30". In the interface, the user first selects a facet (on the left-hand side) and then chooses a constraining restriction value.

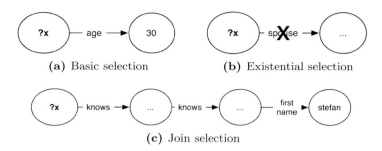

Fig. 2. Selection operators

Existential Selection. There might be cases when one is interested in the existence of a property, but not in its exact value, or one may be interested simply in the non-existence of some property. For example, we can ask for "all resources without a spouse" (all unmarried people), as shown in Fig. 2b. In the interface, instead of selecting a restriction value for the facet, the user clicks on "any" or "none" (on the left-hand side, after the facet name).

Join Selection. Given that RDF data forms a graph, we often want to select some resources based on the properties of the nodes that they are connected to. For example, we are looking for "all resources who know somebody, who in turn knows somebody named Stefan", as shown in Fig. 2c. Using the join-operator recursively, we can create a path of arbitrary length[7], where joins can occur on arbitrary predicates. In the interface, the user first selects a facet (on the left-hand side), and then in turn restricts the facet of that resource. In the given example, the user would first click on "knows", click again on "knows" and then click on "first-name", and only then select the value "Stefan".

Intersection. When we define two or more selections, these are evaluated in conjunction. For example, we can use the three previous examples to restrict the resources to "all unmarried thirty-years old who know some other resource that knows a resource named Stefan Decker", as shown in Fig. 3. In the interface, all constraints are automatically intersected.

Inverse Selection. All operators have an inverse version that selects resources by their inverse properties. For example, imagine a dataset that specifies companies and their employees (through the "employs" predicate). When we select a person, we might be interested in his employer, but this data is not directly

---

[7] The path can have arbitrary length, but the length must be specified; we, or any RDF store [1], do not support regular expression queries, as in e.g. GraphLog [3].

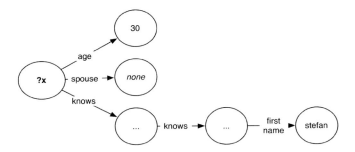

Fig. 3. Intersection operator

available. Instead, we have to follow the inverse property: we have to look for those companies who employ this person. In the user interface, after all regular facets, the user sees all inverse facets. The inverse versions of the operators are:

Inverse basic selection. For example, when the graph only contains statements such as "DERI employs ?x", we can ask for "all resources employed by DERI", as shown in Fig. 4a.

Inverse existential selection. We could also find all employed people, regardless of their employer, as shown in Fig. 4b.

Inverse join selection. The inverse join selection allows us to find "all resources employed by a resource located in Ireland", as shown in Fig. 4c.

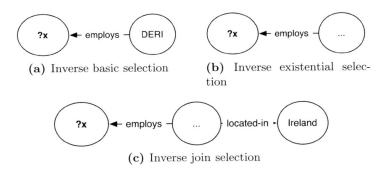

(a) Inverse basic selection (b) Inverse existential selection

(c) Inverse join selection

Fig. 4. Inverse operators

We can merge the last example with the intersection example to find "all unmarried thirty-year-olds who know somebody –working in Ireland– who knows Stefan", as shown in Fig. 5.

3.3 Expressiveness

In this section we formalise our operators as functions on an RDF graph. The formalisation precisely defines the possibilities of our faceted interface, and allows us to compare our approach to existing approaches (which we will do in Sect. 5.1).

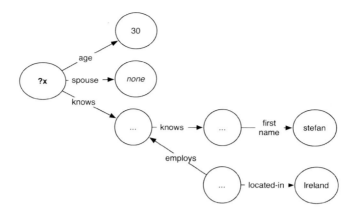

Fig. 5. Full selection

First, we define the graph on which the operations are applied. Our notion of an RDF graph differs from the standard one[8]: we only consider the explicit statements in an RDF document and do not infer additional information as mandated by the RDF semantics. The latter is not a "violation" of the semantics, because we assume the RDF store to perform the necessary inferences already; we regard a given RDF graph simply as the graph itself.

Definition 1 (RDF Graph). *An RDF graph G is defined as $G = (V, E, L, l)$ where V is the set of vertices (subjects and objects), E is the set of edges (predicates), L is the set of labels, $l : E \to label$ is the labelling function for predicates and with V and E disjoint[9]. The projections, source $: E \to V$ and target $: E \to V$, return the source and target nodes of edges.*

Table 1 gives a formal definition for each of the earlier operators. The operators describe faceted browsing in terms of set manipulations: each operator is a function, taking some constraint as input and returning a subset of the resources that conform to that constraint. The definition is not intended as a new query language, but to demonstrate the relation between the interface actions in the faceted browser and the selection queries on the RDF graph. In our prototype, each user interface action is translated into the corresponding SPARQL[10] query and executed on the RDF store.

The primitive operators are the basic and existential selection, and their inverse forms. The basic selection returns resources with a certain property value. The existential selection returns resources that have a certain property, irrespective of its value. These primitives can be combined using the join and the intersection operator. The join returns resources with a property, whose value is

---

[8] http://www.w3.org/TR/rdf-mt/
[9] In RDF E and V are not necessarily disjoint but we restrict ourselves to graphs in which they actually are.
[10] http://www.w3.org/TR/rdf-sparql-query/

part of the joint set. The intersection combines constraints conjunctively. The join and intersection operators have closure: they have sets as input and output and can thus be recursively composed. As an example, all thirty-year-olds without a spouse would be selected by: $intersect(select(age, 30), not(spouse))$.

Table 1. Operator definitions

operator	definition
basic selection	$select(l, v') = \{v \in V \mid \forall e \in E : label(e) = l, source(e) = v$ $target(e) = v'\}$
inv. basic selection	$select^-(l, v') = \{v \in V \mid \forall e \in E : label(e) = l, source(e) = v'$ $target(e) = v\}$
existential	$exists(l) = \{v \in V \mid \forall e \in E : label(e) = l, source(e) = v\}$
inv. existential	$exists^-(l) = \{v \in V \mid \forall e \in E : label(e) = l, target(e) = v\}$
not-existential	$not(l) = V - exists(l)$
inv. not-existential	$not^-(l) = V - exists^-(l)$
join	$join(l, V') = \{v \in V \mid \forall e \in E : label(e) = l, source(e) = v$ $target(e) \in V'\}$
inv. join	$join^-(l, V') = \{v \in V \mid \forall e \in E : label(e) = l, source(e) \in V'$ $target(e) = v\}$
intersection	$intersect(V', V'') = V' \cap V''$

4 Automatic Facet Ranking

By applying the previous definitions a faceted browser for arbitrary data can be built. But if the dataset is very large, the number of facets will typically also be large (especially with heterogeneous data) and users will not be able to navigate through the data efficiently. Therefore, we need an automated technique to determine which facets are more useful and more important than others. In this section, we develop such a technique.

To automatically construct facets, we need to understand what characteristics constitute a suitable facet. A facet should only represent one important characteristic of the classified entity [17], which in our context is given by its predicates. We need to find therefore, among all predicates, those that best represent the dataset (the best descriptors), and those that most efficiently navigate the dataset (the best navigators).

In this section, we introduce facet ranking metrics. We first analyse what constitutes suitable descriptors and suitable navigators, and then derive metrics to compute the suitability of a facet in an dataset. We demonstrate these metrics on a sample dataset.

4.1 Descriptors

What are suitable descriptors of a data set? For example, for most people the "page number" of articles is not very useful: we do not remember papers by their page-number. According to Ranganathan [17], intuitive facets describe a property that is either temporal (e.g. year-of-publication, date-of-birth), spatial (conference-location, place-of-birth), personal (author, friend), material (topic, color) or energetic (activity, action).

Ranganathan's theory could help us to automatically determine intuitive facets: we could say that facets belonging to either of these categories are likely to be intuitive for most people, while facets that do not are likely to be unintuitive. However, we usually lack background knowledge about the kind of facet we are dealing with since this metadata is usually not specified in datasets. Ontologies, containing such background knowledge, might be used, but that is outside the scope of this paper.

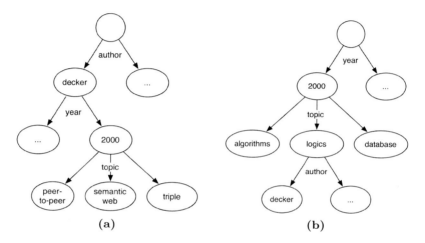

Fig. 6. Faceted browsing as decision tree traversal

4.2 Navigators

A suitable facet allows efficient navigation through the dataset. Faceted browsing can be considered as simultaneously constructing and traversing a decision tree whose branches represent predicates and whose nodes represent restriction values. For example, Fig. 6a shows a tree for browsing a collection of publications by first constraining the author, then the year and finally the topic. Since the facets are orthogonal they can be applied in any order: one can also first constrain the year and topic of publication, and only then select some author, as shown in Fig. 6b.

A path in the tree represents a set of constraints that select the resources of interest. The tree is constructed dynamically, e.g. the available restriction values for "topic" are different in both trees: Fig. 6b shows all topics from publications in 2000, but Fig. 6a shows only Stefan Decker's topics.

4.3 Facet Metrics

Regarding faceted browsing as constructing and traversing a decision tree helps to select and use those facets that allow the most efficient navigation in the tree.

In this section we define this "navigation quality" of a facet in terms of three measurable properties (metrics) of the dataset. All metrics range from [0..1]; we combine them into a final score through (weighted) multiplication. We scale the font-size of facets by their rank, allowing highlighting without disturbing the alphabetical order[11].

The metrics need to be recomputed at each step of the decision tree, since the information space changes (shrinks) at each decision step. We give examples for each metric, using a sample[12] of the Citeseer[13] dataset for scientific publications and citations, but these example metrics only apply on the top-level (at the root of the decision-tree).

We would like to rank facets not only on their navigational value, but also on their descriptive value, but we have not yet found a way to do so. As a result, the metrics are only an indication of usefulness; badly ranked facets should not disappear completely, since even when inefficient they could still be intuitive.

Predicate Balance. Tree navigation is most efficient when the tree is well-balanced because each branching decision optimises the decision power [20, p. 543]. We therefore use the balance of a predicate to indicate its navigation efficiency.

For example, we see in Table 2a that *institution* and *label* are well balanced, but publication *type* is not, with a normalised balance of 0.3. Table 2b shows in more detail why the type of publications is unbalanced: among the 13 different types of publications, only three occur frequently (proceeding papers, miscellaneous and journal articles); the rest of the publication types occur only rarely. Being a relatively unbalanced predicate, constraining the publication type would not be the most economic decision.

We compute the predicate balance $balance(p)$ from the distribution $n_s(o_i)$ of the subjects over the objects as the average inverted deviation from the vector mean μ. The balance is normalised to [0..1] using the deviation in the worst-case distribution (where N_s is the total number of subjects and n is the number of different objects values for predicate p):

$$balance(p) = 1 - \frac{\sum_{i=1}^{n} |\, n_s(o_i) - \mu \,|}{(n-1)\mu + (N_s - \mu)}$$

Object Cardinality. A suitable predicate has a limited (but higher than one) amount of object values to choose from. Otherwise, when there are too many choices, the options are difficult to display and the choice might confuse the user.

For example, as shown in Table 2c, the predicate *type* is very usable since it has only 13 object values to choose from, but the predicate *author* or *title* would not be directly usable, since they have around 4000 different values. One

---

[11] font scaling has not yet been implemented.
[12] http://www.csd.abdn.ac.uk/~ggrimnes/swdataset.php
[13] http://citeseer.ist.psu.edu/

solution for reducing the object cardinality is object clustering [11, 22], but that is outside the scope of this paper.

We compute the object cardinality metric $card(p)$ as the number of different objects (restriction values) $n_o(p)$ for the predicate p and normalise it using the a function based on the Gaussian density. For displaying and usability purposes the number of different options should be approximately between two and twenty, which can be regulated through the μ and σ parameters.

$$card(p) = \begin{cases} 0 & \text{if } n_o(p) \leq 1 \\ \exp^{-\frac{(n_o(p)-\mu)^2}{2\sigma^2}} & \text{otherwise} \end{cases}$$

Predicate Frequency. A suitable predicate occurs frequently inside the collection: the more distinct resources covered by the predicate, the more useful it is in dividing the information space [4]. If a predicate occurs infrequently, selecting a restriction value for that predicate would only affect a small subset of the resources.

For example, in Table 2d we see that all publications have a type, author, title, and URL, but that most do not have a volume, number, or journal.

We compute the predicate frequency $freq(p)$ as the number of subjects $n_s(p) = |exists(p)|$ in the dataset for which the predicate p has been defined, and normalise it as a fraction of the total number of resources n_s: $freq(p) = \frac{n_s(p)}{n_s}$.

Table 2. Sample metrics in Citeseer dataset

predicate	balance
institute	1.00
label	1.00
url	1.00
title	1.00
text	0.99
author	0.96
pages	0.92
editor	0.82
isbn	0.76
⋮	⋮
type	0.30

(a) balance

type	perc.
inproc.	40.78%
misc	28.52%
article	19.44%
techrep.	7.59%
incoll.	2.66%
phd	0.47%
book	0.21%
unpub.	0.19%
msc	0.07%
inbook	0.05%
proc.	0.02%

(b) objects in *type*

predicate	objects
title	4215
url	4211
author	4037
pages	2168
text	1069
booktitle	1010
number	349
address	341
journal	312
editor	284
⋮	⋮
type	13

(c) cardinality

predicate	freq.
type	100%
author	99%
title	99%
url	99%
year	91%
pages	55%
booktitle	37%
text	25%
number	23%
volume	22%
journal	20%
⋮	⋮

(d) frequency

5 Evaluation

We first evaluate our approach formally, by comparing the expressiveness of our interface to existing faceted browsers. We then report on an experimental evaluation.

5.1 Formal Evaluation

Several approaches exist for faceted navigation of (semi-)structured data, such as Flamenco [23], mSpace [19], Ontogator [12], Aduna Spectacle[14], Siderean Seamark Navigator[15] and Longwell[16]. Our formal model provides a way to compare their functionality explicitly.

Existing approaches cannot navigate arbitrary datasets: the facets are manually constructed and work only on fixed data structures. Furthermore, they assume data homogeneity, focus on a single type of resource, and represent other resources with one fixed label. One can for example search for publications written by an author with a certain name, but not by an author of a certain age, since authors are always represented by their name.

Table 3 explicitly shows the difference in expressive power, indicating the level of support for each operator. The existing faceted browsers support the basic selection and intersection operators; they also support joins but only with a predefined and fixed join-path, and only on predefined join-predicates. The commercial tools are more polished but have in essence the same functionality. Our interface adds the existential operator, the more flexible join operator and the inverse operators. Together these significantly improve the query expressiveness.

Table 3. Expressiveness of faceted browsing interfaces

operator	BrowseRDF	Flamenco	mSpace	Ontogator	Spectacle	Seamark
selection	+	+	+	+	+	+
inv. selection	+	−	−	−	−	−
existential	+	−	−	−	−	−
inv. exist.	+	−	−	−	−	−
not-exist.	+	−	−	−	−	−
inv. not-exist.	+	−	−	−	−	−
join	+	±	±	±	±	±
inv. join	+	−	−	−	−	−
intersection	+	+	+	+	+	+

Other related work. Some non-faceted, domain-independent, browsers for RDF data exist, most notably Noadster [18] and Haystack [16]. Noadster (and its predecessor Topia) focuses on resource presentation and clustering, as opposed to navigation and search, and relies on manual specification of property weights, whereas we automatically compute facet quality. Haystack does not offer faceted browsing, but focuses on data visualisation and resource presentation.

Several approaches exist for generic visual exploration of RDF graphs [6, 5] but none scale for large graphs: OntoViz[17] cannot generate good layouts for more than 10 nodes and IsaViz[18] is ineffective for more than 100 nodes [7].

---

[14] http://www.aduna-software.com/products/spectacle/
[15] http://www.siderean.com/
[16] http://simile.mit.edu/longwell
[17] http://protege.stanford.edu/plugins/ontoviz/
[18] http://www.w3.org/2001/11/IsaViz/

Related to our facet ranking approach, a technique for automatic classification of new data under existing facets has been developed [4], but requires a predefined training set of data and facets and only works for textual data; another technique [2], based on lexical dispersion, does not require training but it is also limited to textual data.

5.2 Experimental Evaluation

We have performed an experimental evaluation to compare our interface to alternative generic interfaces, namely keyword-search and manual queries.

Prototype. The evaluation was performed on our prototype, shown earlier in Fig. 1. The prototype is a web application, accessible with any browser. We use the Ruby on Rails[19] web application framework to construct the web interface. The prototype uses ActiveRDF[20] [14], an object-oriented API for arbitrary RDF data, to abstract the RDF store and translate the interface operators into RDF queries. The abstraction layer of ActiveRDF uses the appropriate query language transparently depending on the RDF datastore. We used the YARS [10] RDF store because its index structure allows it to answer our typical queries quickly.

Methodology. Mimicking the setup of Yee *et al.* [23], we evaluated[21] 15 test subjects, ranging in RDF expertise from beginner (8), good (3) to expert (4). None were familiar with the dataset used in the evaluation.

We offered them three interfaces, keyword search (through literals), manual (N3) query construction, and our faceted browser. All interfaces contained the same FBI fugitives data mentioned earlier. To be able to write queries, the test subjects also received the data-schema.

In each interface, they were asked to perform a set of small tasks, such as "find the number of people with brown eyes", or "find the people with Kenyan nationality". In each interface the tasks were similar (so that we could compare in which interface the task would be solved fastest and most correctly) but not exactly the same (to prevent reuse of earlier answers). The questions did not involve the inverse operator as it was not yet implemented at the time. We filmed all subjects and noted the time required for each answer; we set a two minute time-limit per task.

Results. Overall, our results confirm earlier results [23]: people overwhelmingly (87%) prefer the faceted interface, finding it useful (93%) and easy-to-use (87%).

As shown in Table 4, on the keyword search, only 16% of the questions were answered correctly, probably because the RDF datastore allows keyword search only for literals. Using the N3 query language, again only 16% of the questions were answered correctly, probably due to unfamiliarity with N3 and the unforgiving nature of queries. In the faceted interface 74% of the questions were answered correctly.

---

[19] http://rubyonrails.org
[20] http://activerdf.org
[21] evaluation details available on http://m3pe.org/browserdf/evaluation.

Where correct answers were given, the faceted interface was on average 30% faster than the keyword search in performing similar tasks, and 356% faster than the query interface. Please note that only 10 comparisons could be made due to the low number of correct answers in the keyword and query interfaces.

Questions involving the existential operator took the longest to answer, indicating difficulty understanding that operator, while questions involving the basic selection proved easiest to answer — suggesting that arbitrarily adding query expressiveness might have limited benefit, if users cannot use the added functionality.

Table 4. Evaluation results

	solved	unsolved
keyword	15.55%	84.45%
query	15.55%	84.45%
faceted	74.29%	25.71%

(a) Task solution rate

	keyword	query	faceted
easiest to use	13.33%	0%	86.66%
most flexible	13.33%	26.66%	60%
most dead-ends	53.33%	33.33%	13.33%
most helpful	6.66%	0%	93.33%
preference	6.66%	6.66%	86.66%

(b) Post-test preferences

6 Conclusion

Faceted browsing [23] is a data exploration technique for large datasets. We have shown how this technique can be employed for arbitrary semi-structured content. We have extended the expressiveness of existing faceted browsing techniques and have developed metrics for automatic facet ranking, resulting in an automatically constructed faceted interface for arbitrary semi-structured data. Our faceted navigation has improved query expressiveness over existing approaches and experimental evaluation shows better usability than current interfaces.

Future work. Our additional expressiveness does not necessarily result in higher usability; future research is needed to evaluate the practical benefits of our approach against existing work. Concerning the ranking metrics, we performed an initial unpublished evaluation showing that although the search space is divided optimally, the ranking does not always correspond to the intuitive importance people assign to some facets; again, further research is needed.

Acknowledgements. This material is based upon works supported by the Science Foundation Ireland under Grants No. SFI/02/CE1/I131 and SFI/04/BR/CS0694. We thank Jos de Bruijn and the anonymous reviewers for valuable comments on a previous version.

References

[1] R. Angles and C. Gutierrez. Querying RDF data from a graph database perspective. In *ESWC*, pp. 346–360. 2005.
[2] P. Anick and S. Tipirneni. Interactive document retrieval using faceted terminological feedback. In *HICSS*. 1999.

[3] M. P. Consens and A. O. Mendelzon. Graphlog: a visual formalism for real life recursion. In *PODS*, pp. 404–416. 1990.
[4] W. Dakka, P. Ipeirotis, and K. Wood. Automatic construction of multifaceted browsing interfaces. In *CIKM*. 2005.
[5] C. Fluit, M. Sabou, and F. van Harmelen. Ontology-based information visualization. In [8], pp. 45–58.
[6] C. Fluit, M. Sabou, and F. van Harmelen. Supporting user tasks through visualisation of light-weight ontologies. In S. Staab and R. Studer, (eds.) *Handbook on Ontologies*, pp. 415–434. Springer-Verlag, Berlin, 2004.
[7] F. Frasincar, A. Telea, and G.-J. Houben. Adapting graph visualization techniques for the visualization of RDF data. In [8], pp. 154–171.
[8] V. Geroimenko and C. Chen, (eds.) *Visualizing the Semantic Web*. Springer-Verlag, Berlin, second edn., 2006.
[9] N. Gibbins, S. Harris, A. Dix, and mc schraefel. Applying mspace interfaces to the semantic web. Tech. Rep. 8639, ECS, Southampton, 2004.
[10] A. Harth and S. Decker. Optimized index structures for querying RDF from the web. In *LA-WEB*. 2005.
[11] M. A. Hearst. Clustering versus faceted categories for information exploration. *Comm. of the ACM*, 46(4), 2006.
[12] E. Hyvönen, S. Saarela, and K. Viljanen. Ontogator: Combining view- and ontology-based search with semantic browsing. In *Proc. of XML Finland*. 2003.
[13] G. Marchionini. Exploratory search: From finding to understanding. *Comm. of the ACM*, 49(4), 2006.
[14] E. Oren and R. Delbru. ActiveRDF: Object-oriented RDF in Ruby. In *Scripting for Semantic Web (ESWC)*. 2006.
[15] C. Plaisant, B. Shneiderman, K. Doan, and T. Bruns. Interface and data architecture for query preview in networked information systems. *ACM Trans. Inf. Syst.*, 17(3):320–341, 1999.
[16] D. Quan and D. R. Karger. How to make a semantic web browser. In *WWW*. 2004.
[17] S. R. Ranganathan. *Elements of library classification*. Bombay: Asia Publishing House, 1962.
[18] L. Rutledge, J. van Ossenbruggen, and L. Hardman. Making RDF presentable: integrated global and local semantic Web browsing. In *WWW*. 2005.
[19] m. schraefel, M. Wilson, A. Russell, and D. A. Smith. mSpace: Improving information access to multimedia domains with multimodal exploratory search. *Comm. of the ACM*, 49(4), 2006.
[20] R. Sedgewick. *Algorithms in C++*. Addison-Wesley, 1998.
[21] R. W. White, B. Kules, S. M. Drucker, and mc schraefel. Supporting exploratory search. *Comm. of the ACM*, 49(4), 2006.
[22] R. Xu and D. W. II. Survey of clustering algorithms. *IEEE Trans. on Neural Networks*, 16(3):645–678, 2005.
[23] K.-P. Yee, K. Swearingen, K. Li, and M. Hearst. Faceted metadata for image search and browsing. In *CHI*. 2003.

Reducing the Inferred Type Statements with Individual Grouping Constructs

Övünç Öztürk, Tuğba Özacar, and Murat Osman Ünalır

Department of Computer Engineering,
Ege University
Bornova, 35100, Izmir, Turkey
{ovunc.ozturk, tugba.ozacar, murat.osman.unalir}@ege.edu.tr

Abstract. A common approach for reasoning is to compute the deductive closure of an ontology using the rules specified and to work on the closure at query time. This approach reduces the run time complexity but increases the space requirements. The main reason of this increase is the type and subclass statements in the ontology. Type statements show a significant percentage in most ontologies. Since subclass is a transitive property, derivation of other statements, in particular type statements relying on it, gives rise to cyclic repetition and an excess of inferred type statements. In brief, a major part of closure computation is deriving the type statements relying on subclass statements. In this paper, we propose a syntactic transformation that is based on novel individual grouping constructs. This transformation reduces the number of inferred type statements relying on subclass relations. Thus, the space requirement of reasoning is reduced without affecting the soundness and the completeness.

1 Introduction

Semantic web applications will require multiple large ontologies for querying [1]. Although current reasoners are capable of schema reasoning with these real world ontologies, they break down for reasoning and retrieving the individuals in an ontology when the number of instances becomes large [2] [3]. It is a common and space consuming approach to compute the deductive closure of these large ontologies and to work on the closure at query time. This approach is known as offline reasoning that reduces run time complexity but increases space requirements.

Present work focusses at query-rewriting techniques. For example, [4] presents the *true RDF processor*. This processor provides *a slot access function* which allows the underlying graph to be viewed as if its RDFS-closure had been generated. This model has problems in dealing with domain and range restrictions and does not cover the complete RDF semantics. Another query rewriting approach for RDF reasoning [5], computes a small part of the implied statements offline thereby reducing space requirements, upload time and maintenance overhead. The computed fragment is chosen in such a way that the problem of inferring implied statements at run time can be reduced to a simple query rewriting. In contrast to [4], [5] covers the complete RDF semantics by precomputing the transitive closure of hierarchical relations. These approaches do not compute complete closure offline thus they require online reasoning, which increases the runtime complexity.

In this paper, we propose a model that introduces novel individual grouping constructs for reducing the number of inferred type statements. The major problem with reasoning about individuals is deriving type statements relying on subclass relations between the classes. Our approach solves this problem with only a syntactic transformation. Instead of relating the class with each of its instances, this transformation relates the class with a group of sets where each set is a partial extension of that class. The advantages of our approach are listed below:

- covers complete semantics of RDF-based languages, since it is only a syntactic transformation
- does not affect the soundness and the completeness of the reasoning
- does not require query-rewriting and online reasoning
- does not require online reasoning

The rest of the paper is organized as follows: Section 2 introduces the model in detail and its subsections describe the transformations required by the model. Section 3 formulates the utilization rate of the model and evaluates utilization with large scale ontologies by means of ontology metrics in [6]. Finally Section 4 concludes the paper with an outline of some potential future research.

2 A Model with Individual Grouping Constructs

In this paper we propose a model that introduces individual grouping constructs for reducing the number of inferred type statements without affecting the soundness and the completeness of the reasoning.

An individual grouping construct is a partial extension of a class. The union of these partial extensions defines the exact list of class individuals. An individual of a class may be in one or more partial extensions of that class. These partial extensions are called *subExtensions*. A *subExtension* is related to one or more classes via *hasSubExt* predicate and it is related to individuals of the class with *contains* predicate. A *subExtension* is *direct* or *inherited* according to its relation with the class.

All individuals of a class, except the ones derived through a subclass relation, are added to the *directSubExtension* of that class. Each anonymous and non-anonymous class in the ontology has zero or one *directSubExtension*. Any class that has at least one individual has a *directSubExtension*. A class is related with its *directSubExtension* with *hasDirectSubExt* predicate. A *subExtension* can be related to one and only one class via *hasDirectSubExt* predicate.

An *inheritedSubExtension* of a class is the *directSubExtension* of a subclass of that class. In other words, an *inheritedSubExtension* holds the class individuals that are inherited to that class from one of its subclasses. A class is related to one or more *inheritedSubExtensions* with *hasInheritedSubExt* predicate. A *subExtension* is related to one or more classes via an inferred *hasInheritedSubExt* relation. Note that, since every class is a subclass of itself, the *directSubExtension* of the class is also one of its *inheritedSubExtensions*. Thus every *subExtension* of a class is also an *inheritedSubExtension* of that class.

In our model the ontology is syntactically transformed to a semantically equivalent ontology with newly introduced individual grouping constructs. In order to preserve the completeness and the soundness of the reasoning, rules and queries are transformed in needs of these grouping constructs. These transformations [1] are described in the following subsections.

2.1 Triple Transformation

Let O be the set of triples in the ontology to be transformed, t be a type statement with subject I and object C then t is replaced with triple set S where;

$$S = \begin{cases} \{contains(E,I)\}, & \text{if } hasDirectSubExt(C,E) \in O \\ \{contains(E,I), hasDirectSubExt(C,E)\}, & \text{otherwise.} \end{cases}$$

It is worth to note that the same replacement is done whenever a type statement is added to or removed from ontology.

2.2 Rule/Query Transformation

Transforming rules is necessary to derive new statements with the transformed ontology without changing the completeness and the soundness of the reasoning. After the transformation, some rules have a form like $head :- body1 \vee body2$. These rules can be transformed easily via the following Lloyd-Topor transformation [7]:

$$head :- body1 \vee body2 \Rightarrow head :- body1 \text{ and } head :- body2$$

Note that it is necessary to extend the rule set to include the following rule, which specifies that every *directSubExtension* and *inheritedSubExtension* of a class is also a *subExtension* of that class:

$$\frac{hasDirectSubExt(B,E) \vee hasInheritedSubExt(B,E)}{hasSubExt(B,E)}$$

The following is *the standard rule transformation*, which is valid for all rules other than *RDF Rule 7*:

- A rule having a body condition with a type predicate is transformed in the following way :

$$\frac{...\wedge type(U,B) \wedge ...}{h_1} \Rightarrow \frac{...\wedge hasSubExt(B,E) \wedge contains(E,U) \wedge ...}{h_1}$$

- A rule having a head condition with a type predicate is transformed in the following way :

$$\frac{b_1 \wedge ... \wedge b_n}{type(U,B)} \Rightarrow \frac{b_1 \wedge ... \wedge b_n \wedge hasDirectSubExt(B,E)}{contains(E,U)}$$

---

[1] The transformation overhead is small enough to be considered negligible.

RDF Rule 7 computes the type statements relying on subclass relations. In order to reduce the number of inferred type statements, this rule is transformed in a different manner than the *standart rule transformation*. Instead of deriving a type relation between every individual of subclass and its superclass (Fig. 1a), *RDF Rule 7* simply derives only one relation with predicate *hasInheritedSubExt* between the *directSubExtension* and each *inheritedSubExtension* of subclass and its superclass (Fig. 1b). Table 1 demonstrates the transformation of some RDF rules from RDF Semantics [8], including *RDF Rule 7*.

Table 1. Transformation of RDF Rules

Rule No	RDFS Rule	Transformed Rule
(1)	$\dfrac{A(X,Y)}{type(A,Property)}$	$\dfrac{A(X,Y) \land hasDirectSubExt(Property,E)}{contains(E,A)}$
(2)	$\dfrac{domain(A,X) \land A(U,Y)}{type(U,X)}$	$\dfrac{domain(A,X) \land A(U,Y) \land hasDirectSubExt(X,E)}{contains(E,U)}$
(3)	$\dfrac{range(A,X) \land A(Y,V)}{type(V,X)}$	$\dfrac{range(A,X) \land A(Y,V) \land hasDirectSubExt(X,E)}{contains(E,V)}$
(4)	$\dfrac{A(U,B) \lor A(B,U)}{type(U,Resource)}$	$\dfrac{(A(U,B) \lor A(B,U)) \land hasDirectSubExt(Resource,E)}{contains(E,U)}$
(5)	$\dfrac{type(U,Property)}{subPropertyOf(U,U)}$	$\dfrac{hasSubExt(Property,E) \land contains(E,U)}{subPropertyOf(U,U)}$
(6)	$\dfrac{type(U,Class)}{subClassOf(U,Resource)}$	$\dfrac{hasSubExt(Class,E) \land contains(E,U)}{subClassOf(U,Resource)}$
(7)	$\dfrac{subClassOf(U,X) \land type(V,U)}{type(V,X)}$	$\dfrac{subClassOf(U,X) \land hasSubExt(U,E)}{hasInheritedSubExt(X,E)}$
(8)	$\dfrac{type(U,Class)}{subClassOf(U,U)}$	$\dfrac{hasDirectSubExt(Class,E) \land contains(E,U)}{subClassOf(U,U)}$

A query is a rule without a head thus the standard rule transformation is also applicable to queries. The queries are transformed in the following way where h_1 is an empty set:

$$\frac{...\land type(U,B) \land ...}{h_1} \Rightarrow \frac{...\land hasSubExt(B,E) \land contains(E,U) \land ...}{h_1}$$

It is also important to represent the answer in the standard way. Let S be the set of all triples in the answer set then replace the following triple sets with triple $type(U, B)$:

- $\{hasDirectSubExt(B,E), contains(E,U)\}$
- $\{hasInheritedSubExt(B,E), contains(E,U)\}$
- $\{hasSubExt(B,E), contains(E,U)\}$

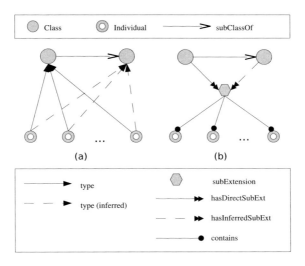

Fig. 1. Reducing the inferred type statements relying on subclass relations

3 Analyzing the Utilization of the Model

3.1 Computation of the Utilization Rate

Computation of the utilization rate reveals whether the model is valuable to use with a specific ontology. In order to calculate the utilization rate, the number of type statements in the ontology and the number of subclass relations in the closure of the ontology must be known. Since it is necessary to know only the number of subclass statements in the closure, it is enough to find the closure of the schema of the ontology.

The following formula calculates the decrease in the inferred triple count by applying the proposed model. Let Δ be the decrease in the inferred triple count by applying the model. The formula finds Δ by calculating the difference between the decrease in inferred type statements and the newly added or inferred triples related with grouping constructs. Before applying the model, every individual of a subclass is added to the individuals of its every superclass if the superclass does not have this individual. The number of these additions is $\mathcal{T}$. This value is the decrease in inferred type statements. In order to calculate the exact decrease in the inferred statements by applying the model, we have to minus the number of newly added *hasDirectSubExt*, *hasInferredSubExt* and *hasSubExt* statements from this value. Let $\mathcal{D}$ be the number of newly added *hasDirectSubExt* statements, $\mathcal{I}$ be the number of inferred *hasInferredSubExt* statements and $\mathcal{S}$ be the number of *hasSubExt* statements, then;

$$\Delta = \mathcal{T} - (\mathcal{I} + \mathcal{D} + \mathcal{S}) \qquad (1)$$

Let n be the number of classes in the ontology, $\mathcal{E}_{C_x}$ be the set of all explicit individuals of class C_x where $1 \leq x \leq n$, $|X|$ be the number of elements in set

X, \ be the set minus operator and $\delta(C_x, C_y)$ be a function which returns 1 if C_x is an explicit or implicit subclass of C_y. Otherwise the returned value is 0. And let $\phi(C_x)$ be a function, which computes the number of elements in the set-theoretic difference of $\mathcal{U}$ and C_x, where $\mathcal{U}$ is the union of all explicit and implicit subclasses of C_x.

$$\mathcal{T} = \sum_{i=1}^{n} \Phi(C_i) \tag{2}$$

$$\Phi(C_x) = |\bigcup_{i=1}^{n} \sigma(C_i, C_x)|$$

$$\sigma(C_x, C_y) = \begin{cases} \mathcal{E}_{C_x} \setminus \mathcal{E}_{C_y}, & \text{if } C_x \text{ is a subclass of } C_y \\ \emptyset, & \text{otherwise.} \end{cases}$$

$$\mathcal{I} = \sum_{i=1}^{n} \sum_{j=1}^{n} \delta(C_i, C_j) \tag{3}$$

$$\delta(C_x, C_y) = \begin{cases} 1, & \text{if } C_x \text{ is a subclass of } C_y \\ 0, & \text{otherwise.} \end{cases}$$

Let $\gamma(C_x)$ be a function which returns 0, if C_x is an empty set. Otherwise the returned value is 1. Each non-empty class in the ontology has one and only one *directSubExtension*, thus

$$\mathcal{D} = \sum_{i=1}^{n} \gamma(C_i) \tag{4}$$

$$\gamma(C_x) = \begin{cases} 0, & \text{if } \mathcal{E}_{C_x} = \emptyset \\ 1, & \text{otherwise.} \end{cases}$$

One and only one *subExtension* of a class is related to that class with *hasDirectSubExt* predicate. All the other *subExtensions* are related to the class with *hasInheritedSubExt* predicate. Since every class is a subclass of itself, the only *subExtension* that is related to the class with *hasDirectSubExt* predicate is also related to that class with *hasInheritedSubExt* predicate. Thus, all *subExtensions* of a class are also related to the class with *hasInheritedSubExt* predicate. Then, we can conclude that:

$$\mathcal{S} = \mathcal{I} \tag{5}$$

The utilization rate is the ratio between the reduction in inferred statements and the number of statements in the closure without implementing the model. Let t be the number of statements in the ontology before inference, ρ be the number of inferred statements without implementing the model, then the utilization rate of the model $\mathcal{U}$ is;

$$\mathcal{U} = 1 - \frac{\Delta}{t + \rho}$$

If the model is useful and reduces the number of inferred statements, the utilization rate is in the interval of $(0, 1]$. The closer the value is to 0, the higher the utilization of the model. If the utilization rate is equal to 1, then applying the model shows no impact. If the utilization rate is greater than 1, then applying the model shows a negative impact (i.e., the number of inferred statements increases).

3.2 Estimation of the Utilization Rate Using Ontology Metrics

The model shows a negative impact when the ontology has no subclass relation or the number of type statements in the ontology is less than the number of class definitions and subclass relations in the ontology. These two factors result in a relatively low number of inferred type statements in the closure of the ontology. In this case, the number of additional statements required by the technique is greater than the decrease in the number of inferred type statements.

Obviously, this case is not very common in real world ontologies and also is not meaningful from the perspective of knowledge representation. Table 2 depicts this issue by supplementing the number of subclass and type relations in representative ontologies. The common characteristics of ontologies in Table 2 are the reasonable amount of type and subclass statements and a significant increase in type statements in their corresponding closures [5]. Consequently, the model is valuable enough with these ontologies, but we enumerate the factors that increase the utilization rate in order to figure out when the model is applicable. These factors are:

- high number of subclass relations
- high number of individuals

Table 2. Behaviour of realistic data

	CIA WFB		TAP KB		SUMO		WordNet	
	orig.	closure	orig.	closure	orig.	closure	orig.	closure
type	376	4150	36988	191972	6709	18198	99653	277267
subClassOf	9	60	283	1491	3797	18439	78446	606418
other	25899	26077	71148	71253	8637	10584	295529	374032

In order to estimate whether the model is suitable for a particular ontology, the preceding factors can be associated with ontological metrics. Ontological metrics are used to assess the quality of an ontology. The quality of an ontology can be valuated in different aspects. These aspects are mainly grouped according to their relevance with ontology, they are related either with schema or with knowledge base, or both. Previous work in the literature is classified in [6], and one dimension of this classification is the relevance with ontology. In accordance with the classification, we decided to use metrics defined in OntoQA [6].

OntoQA metrics are mainly divided into schema metrics and instance metrics. Schema metrics are about the structure of the ontology. Instance metrics are about the population and its distribution over the classes. We selected two metrics from the OntoQA metric set: *inheritance richness* and *average population*. In [6], *inheritance richness* is defined as "the average number of subclasses per class", and *average population* is defined as "the number of instances of the knowledge base divided by the number of classes defined in the ontology schema". These metrics are proportional to the utilization of the model. Although an increase in average population results in an increase in the utilization of the model, it is necessary to note that the population intensifying in the leaf classes has a greater effect.

3.3 Evaluation of the Utilization Rate with Large Scale Ontologies

We also applied the model on a RETE based inference engine [9], with Lehigh University Benchmark (LUBM) in order to exemplify utilization of the model [10]. LUBM is developed to evaluate the inference and query performance of semantic web repositories over a large data set. The data set is generated according to one ontology, named *univ-bench*, using the synthetic data generation tool provided with the benchmark. LUBM can generate datasets with chosen size using the schema, for example LUBM(2,0) means the ontology includes two university instances with their corresponding dataset.

We conducted the test using four different rule sets. The first two sets are related with RDF semantics. The first one contains rules covering the semantics of *partial rdfs* [11], where some of the normative RDFS entailments are discharged for performance reasons. The second one is the transformed form of the previous rule set in needs of the proposed model. The remaining two sets are related with OWL semantics [12]. The first one contains rules covering the semantics of a DL that is between OWL Lite and OWL DL. This set contains 30 rules, which satisfy completeness and soundness of LUBM queries by 100 percent. Finally,

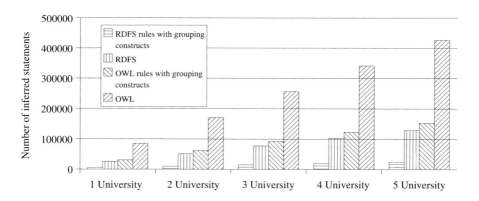

Fig. 2. Number of inferred statements in LUBM ontologies

the last rule set is the transformed form of the rule set having 30 OWL rules, in needs of the proposed model.

As can be seen from Figure 2, the model significantly reduces the number of inferred triples and also the number of total triples in the closure of the ontology. Therefore, the inferencing time of the ontology and the memory required to open the ontology decrease. The utilization is higher in RDFS level because in RDFS the ratio between inferred type statements and inferred statements is greater than in OWL. Also query time is not affected because there is no need to make backward chaining as in [5].

4 Conclusion and Future Work

This work is an attempt to reduce the number of inferred statements in the closure of web ontologies. It is just a syntactic transformation that does not change the soundness or the completeness of the reasoning. Instead of relating a class with each of its instances, this transformation relates the class with a group of sets where each set is a partial extension of that class.

The model is valuable with real world ontologies having a reasonable amount of individuals. This work formulates the utilization and also tries to associate it with ontology metrics in literature to estimate the utilization with a specific ontology. Since there is not enough work related with ontology metrics and the values of existent metrics with well known ontologies are not presented, we couldn't give a detailed work on the association of the utilization and the metrics. It will be an interesting future work to define the intervals of metrics in which the utilization is best.

Another potential future work is to reduce the semantic coverage of the model and specialize it to a specific ontology language, in order to gain additional utilization rate. This will be possible by defining not only individual grouping constructs, but also additional specific grouping constructs for a specific ontology language (e.g. grouping constructs specific for RDF).

References

1. Wielemaker, J., Schreiber, G., Wielinga, B.J.: Prolog-based infrastructure for rdf: Scalability and performance. In: International Semantic Web Conference. (2003) 644–658
2. Haarslev, V., Möller, R.: High performance reasoning with very large knowledge bases: A practical case study. In: IJCAI. (2001) 161–168
3. Horrocks, I., Li, L., Turi, D., Bechhofer, S.: The instance store: Dl reasoning with large numbers of individuals. In: Description Logics. (2004)
4. Lassila, O.: Taking the rdf model theory out for a spin. In: International Semantic Web Conference. (2002) 307–317
5. Stuckenschmidt, H., Broekstra, J.: Time - space trade-offs in scaling up rdf schema reasoning. In: WISE Workshops. (2005) 172–181

6. Tartir, S., Arpinar, I.B., Moore, M., Sheth, A.P., Aleman-Meza, B.: Ontoqa: Metric-based ontology quality analysis. In: Proceedings of IEEE ICDM 2005 Workshop on Knowledge Acquisition from Distributed, Autonomous, Semantically Heterogeneous Data and Knowledge Sources. (2005)
7. Lloyd, J.W.: Foundations of Logic Programming, 2nd Edition. Springer (1987)
8. Hayes, P.: Rdf semantics (2004)
9. Ünalir, M., Özacar, T., Öztürk, Ö.: Reordering query and rule patterns for query answering in a rete-based inference engine. In: WISE Workshops. (2005) 255–265
10. Guo, Y., Pan, Z., Heflin, J.: An evaluation of knowledge base systems for large owl datasets. In: International Semantic Web Conference. (2004) 274–288
11. Horst, H.J.: Combining rdf and part of owl with rules: Semantics, decidability, complexity. In: International Semantic Web Conference. (2005) 668–684
12. Patel-Schneider, P.F., Hayes, P., Horrocks, I.: Rdf semantics (2004)

A Framework for Schema-Driven Relationship Discovery from Unstructured Text

Cartic Ramakrishnan, Krys J. Kochut, and Amit P. Sheth

LSDIS Lab, Dept. of Computer Science, University of Georgia, Athens, GA
{cartic, kochut, amit}@cs.uga.edu

Abstract. We address the issue of extracting implicit and explicit relationships between entities in biomedical text. We argue that entities seldom occur in text in their simple form and that relationships in text relate the modified, complex forms of entities with each other. We present a rule-based method for (1) extraction of such complex entities and (2) relationships between them and (3) the conversion of such relationships into RDF. Furthermore, we present results that clearly demonstrate the utility of the generated RDF in discovering knowledge from text corpora by means of locating paths composed of the extracted relationships.

Keywords: Relationship Extraction, Knowledge-Driven Text mining.

1 Introduction

Dr. Vannevar Bush, in 1945 [1], referring to the human brain said, "*It operates by association. With one item in its grasp, it snaps instantly to the next that is suggested by the association of thoughts, in accordance with some intricate web of trails carried by the cells of the brain.*" This vision may seem anachronistic given that topic hierarchies are used extensively today to index and retrieve documents (non-hyperlinked) in many domains. But as we demonstrate in this paper, this vision emphasizing relationships and associations continues to be highly relevant, and can indeed drive the next generation of search and analysis capabilities.

A good quality hierarchical organization of topics can serve as a very effective method to index and search for documents. A great example in the biomedical domain is the PubMed [2] database which contains over 16 million *manually classified* abstracts of scientific publications. In this domain, it is rare that the information sought by the user is completely contained in one document. The nature of biomedical research is such that each scientific publication in this domain serves to corroborate or refute a fact. Let us assume for the sake of argument that some publication asserts that "*stress can lead to loss of magnesium in the human body*". Another publication might present evidence of the fact that "*Migraine Patients seem to be experiencing stress*". It is therefore implicitly expected that the user of PubMed will piece together the *partial information* from *relevant documents* returned by PubMed searches to conclude that, for instance, "*Migraine could lead to cause a loss of Magnesium*".

One major drawback of this expectation was pointed out by Dr. D.R. Swanson in 1986. By searching biomedical literature manually, he discovered previously unknown connections between Fish Oils and Raynaud's Syndrome [3], which were implicit in the literature. He followed this up with several more examples such as the association between Magnesium and Migraine [4]. In fact, the paper revealed eleven neglected, potentially beneficial effects that Magnesium might have in alleviating Migraine. These discovered connections have since been validated by clinical trials and experiments. Such hidden, valuable relationships have been termed *Undiscovered Public Knowledge*. However, there is practically no support in contemporary information systems for users to unearth such undiscovered knowledge from public text in an automated manner.

2 Background and Motivation

It is clear that there are large bodies of knowledge in textual form that need to be utilized effectively (*e.g.* PubMed [2]). The creation of MeSH and UMLS are steps aimed at making such textual knowledge more accessible. PubMed, however, has been growing at a phenomenal rate. Consequently, the amount of *Undiscovered Public Knowledge* is also likely to increase at a comparable rate. Meanwhile, in the Semantic Web community analytical operators over semi-structured data have been receiving increased attention. Notable among these are *Semantic Association* [5] and *Relevant sub-graph Discovery* [6]. Both are aimed at discovering named relationships between entities in RDF data. Guha et. al. [7] introduced the notion of a *"Research Search"* as a type of Semantic Search. Users start with a search phrase which refers to an entity. The *"Research Search"* then helps users to gather pieces of information from multiple documents which collectively satisfy their information need.

It is critical to support such search, query and analytics paradigms over text data. Currently, these paradigms assume the existence of a rich variety of named relationships connecting entities in an instance base. Our aim, and indeed one of the aims of the Semantic Web community, is to apply these search and analytics paradigms to text data. It is clear that to enable this, we need to bridge the gap between unstructured data (free text) and semi-structured data (such as that represented in RDF, a W3C standard). As a step towards bridging this gap, in this paper, we address the challenge of **extracting implicit and explicit relationships between known entities in text.**

Recently, relationship extraction from biomedical text has received a lot of attention among several research communities. A comprehensive survey of current approaches to biomedical text mining is presented in [8]. Particular attention has been paid to surveying Named Entity Recognition. Most of the attention in this sub-area has focused on identifying gene names. One very effective method is AbGene [9]. This method uses training data in the form of hand-tagged sentences that contain known gene and protein names and is combined with the Brill Tagger [10] to extract names of genes and proteins. According to the authors in [8], most approaches to the relationship extraction consider very specific entities (such as genes), while relationships vary from general (e.g., any biochemical relationship) to specific (e.g., regulatory relationships). This becomes clear when we look at the approaches to relationship extraction surveyed in [8]. These include pattern based approaches [11] where patterns such as "also known as" are used to identify synonymy in protein and gene names. Template based approaches have also been investigated in the PASTA system [12]. Natural Language Processing (NLP) methods have been used in [13] and [14]. In [13] the authors focus their attention on cellular pathways and extract structured information from biomedical literature. Since they focus on cellular pathways their GENESIS system processes the entire article as opposed to just the abstract. Their system considers 125 fine-grained verbs that are classified into 14 broad semantic classes. The critical difference between GENESIS and our system is that our system uses empirical rules as opposed to grammatical rules to extract relationships between entities. In [14], the author uses NLP techniques to generate underspecified parses of sentences in biomedical text. Semantics from UMLS are then used to extract assertions from these parses. Our technique is most similar to this approach. The difference, however, is that our approach extracts modified and composite entities and relationships between them. This allows us to extract variants of known entities and assertions involving these variants.

From our perspective, all relationships of interest in these approaches are very specific. One obvious reason for this is that there is a dire need for such specific relationships to be extracted. In this paper, our approach focuses on more general relationships that are defined in UMLS and is not dependent on any specific type of relationship. The reasons for this are two-fold. First, our long-term goal is to support semantic browsing, searching and analysis of biomedical abstracts. The intended users of such a system could range from a layperson to domain experts. The second reason is that once instances of genes, proteins, etc. and relationships among them are extracted (by approaches discussed above) these could be integrated with clinical trials data which is arguably at the same level of specificity. Such integration would only be possible if the more general entities and the relationships between them were known.

The main difference between our work in this paper and all previous work aimed at relationship extraction is, that our extraction mechanism, in contrast with most past work, can easily be applied to any domain where a well defined ontology schema and set of know entity instances is available. For this project, we choose the biomedical domain since it has all the characteristics that are required to demonstrate the usefulness of the structured data we extract.

3 Our Approach

The general problem of relationship extraction from text is very hard. Our approach recognizes and takes the advantage of special circumstances associated with the biomedical domain. More specifically, we leverage the availability of a controlled vocabulary called the Medical Subject Headings (MeSH) [15] and domain knowledge in the form of the Unified Medical Language System (UMLS) [16]. We combine this domain knowledge with some of the established NLP techniques for relationship extraction. The use of domain knowledge eliminates the need for two key constituent, but challenging steps, namely Named Entity Identification and Named Entity Disambiguation/Reference Reconciliation, both of which are required before relationships can be extracted.

MeSH is a controlled vocabulary organized as a taxonomy, which is currently used to index and retrieve biomedical abstracts from the PubMed database. We treat MeSH terms as entities. These entities may be mentioned in several different contexts in PubMed abstracts. MeSH terms (*simple entities*) may be combined with other *simple entities* to form *composite entities* or may occur as *modified entities*. They may be related to each other by *complex relationships*. Our aim in this paper is to identify and extract these three types of entities and relationship between them occurring in biomedical text. In this paper:

1. We use an off-the-shelf part-of-speech tagger [17] and a chunk parser [18] to produce parse trees of sentences in biomedical abstracts. This is described briefly in Section 4.2.1.
2. We present a rule-based post-processing technique to enrich the generated parse trees. The rules serve to identify complex entities and known relationships between them. This is described in detail in Section 4.2.2.
3. The conversion of these processed trees to the corresponding RDF structures is described in Section 4.3. Sample sentences from PubMed abstracts are used to illustrate the effectiveness of our methodology.
4. An evaluation of the effectiveness of our post-processing rules in terms of precision and recall is presented in Section 5. The dataset which provides the framework for this study is also discussed in Section 5.
5. Finally, we demonstrate the usefulness of our results in the context of Semantic Analytics, presented in Section 5.

4 Relationship Discovery

In this section we describe the features of our dataset used in our research. We then detail the methodology for relationship extraction.

4.1 Dataset

As mentioned earlier, PubMed contains over 16 million abstracts of biomedical publications. Each abstract is uniquely identified by a PubMed ID (PMID). These abstracts are manually classified by domain experts and annotated as pertaining to one or more entities in the MeSH hierarchy. MeSH contains 22,807 named entities which include 316 pharmacological names. UMLS contains a Semantic Network containing 136 classes which are related to each other by one or more of 49 named relationships. Each named entity in MeSH has been manually asserted as an instance of one or more classes in UMLS. Furthermore, MeSH contains synonyms of entities. For instance, *"Neoplasms"* has the synonym *"Tumors"*. This obviates the need for Named Entity Identification and Disambiguation for the purposes of this paper. Further, UMLS also contains synonyms of the 49 relationships. These synonyms have been created by domain experts and used in biomedical abstracts indexed by PubMed. We use this information to spot named relationships occurring in PubMed abstracts. We split biomedical abstracts into sentences and generate RDF on a per-sentence basis. Therefore, in this paper we do not address the problem of Co-Reference Resolution or Pronominal Anaphora Resolution.

4.2 Methodology

Throughout this section, we will use a sample abstract from PubMed to illustrate the steps of our methodology. We chose this abstracts at random. The only criterion was that it should contain known entities (MeSH terms) and known relationships (from UMLS) so as to allow us to illustrate all structure types that we extract. The sentence listing of this abstract is shown below.

> [1254239-1] An excessive endogenous or exogenous stimulation by estrogen induces adenomatous hyperplasia of the endometrium.
> [1254239-2] The age of the patient and the origin of the estrogenic stimulus however influence the morphology of the hyperplasia.
> [1254239-3] Those resulting from exogenous estrogen rapidly regress after the estrogen is discontinued.
> [1254239-4] To cure hyperplasias brought on by endogenous estrogen, however, therapy with high doses of gestagen is required.

Fig. 1. Sample sentences from abstract of PMID-1254239 for illustration (Numbers in the figure indicate PubMed ID-Sentence Number)

4.2.1 Part-of-Speech Tagging and Parsing

Given a sentence, our first step is to tag parts-of-speech in the sentence and parse it to generate a parse tree. We use the SS-Tagger [17] to tag sentences, which claims to offer fast tagging (2400 tokens/sec) with state-of-the-art accuracy (97.10% on the Wall Street Journal corpus). This tagger uses an extension of Maximum Entropy Markov Models (MEMM), in which tags are determined in the easiest-first manner. To parse the result of this tagger and produce a parse tree we use the SS-parser [18]. According to the authors, this CFG parser offers a reasonable performance (an f-score of 85%) with high-speed parsing (71 sentences/sec). Although there are possibly more accurate parsers available [19-21], the speed of this parser makes it a better choice for us. A comparison of our results obtained by using each of these parsers is something we plan to investigate in the future. We also plan to consider domain specific parsers [22].

The output of the SS-Parser is converted into a main-memory tree representation. The figure below shows such a tree for the sentence 1254239-1. As is shown in Fig. 2, known entities (MeSH terms) and relationships (from UMLS) are identified in the parse tree. In this example, *estrogen* (D004967), *hyperplasia* (D006965) and *endometrium* (D004717) are the simple entities spotted. The verb *induces* turns out to be a synonym of the relationship *causes* (UMLS ID-T147). Besides recording the known entities and relationships occurring in each node, pointers are maintained to their siblings. For ease of discussion, we group the nodes in the tree into terminal nodes (referred to as *_T* henceforth) and non-terminal nodes (referred to as *_NT* henceforth). The text corresponding to a *_T* node is a single word and that for a *_NT* node is the phrase formed by its children. This text for each node will be referred to as the *token* of that node throughout this paper.

4.2.2 Rule Based Post Processing

Entities that occur in biomedical text (or in any text for that matter) seldom occur in their simple unmodified form. They typically occur in a sentence, combined with other entities to form a *composite entity* or are combined with some *modifier* to form a *modified entity*. Consequently, relationships in such sentences may connect two entities which may be either *composite entities*, *modified entities* or just *simple entities*. In the following sub-sections, we define the three types of entities. We present the rules for identifying them in a sentence along with an algorithm for applying these rules. Finally, we present an algorithm for extracting relationships between the identified entities in the sentence.

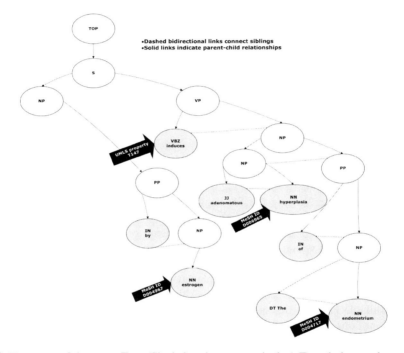

Fig. 2. Fragment of the parse Tree (Shaded nodes are terminals (_T) and clear nodes are non-terminals (_NT))

4.2.2.1 Entity Types. We define simple entities as MeSH terms. Modifiers are siblings of any entity type which are not entities themselves and have one of the following linguistic types:
- determiners (except the words "the", "an" or "a")
- noun/noun-phrases
- adjectives/adjective-phrases
- prepositions/prepositional-phrases.

Determiners are included in the definition of modifiers to account for negative modifiers such as the words *no, not,* etc. which identify negative facts. *Modified*

Entities are *Simple Entities* or other *Modified Entities* that have a sibling which is a *Modifier*. *Composite Entities* are those that are composed of one or more *Simple* or *Modified Entities*.

Table 1. Symbols used and their definitions

Symbols	Definitions
SE	Simple Entity
M	Modifier
ME	Modified Entity
CE	Composite Entity
R	Relationship
_T	Terminal node in parse tree
_NT	Non-Terminal node in parse tree

The definitions discussed above form a rather simple model that can be used to describe the patterns that trigger the extraction of entities and relationships from text. In some ways, our model is very similar to the one in [23] which the author uses to learn linguistic structures from text. In [23], the model described treats certain linguistic types (Noun Phrases, Personal pronouns,etc.) occurring in parse trees as *nuclei* to which *adjuncts* (Adjectival Phrases) may be attached. Furthermore, *linkers* are defined as either conjunctions or punctuations. The purpose of this model is the induction of rules that capture linguistic structure. However, it does not account for named relationships connecting entities. Therefore, although some of our ideas are similar to the ones in [23], the overall purpose is very different.

4.2.2.2 Rules for entity identification. We use the following rules to identify the defined entity types in sentences.

Rule 1: Modifiers attach themselves to Simple Entities in sentences forming Modified Entities. Therefore, if a Modifier M is a sibling of a Simple Entity SE a Modified Entity is produced.
Rule 2: Modifiers can attach themselves to other Modified Entities to form other modified entities. Therefore, if a Modifier M is a sibling of a Modified Entity ME another Modified Entity is produced.
Rule 3: Any number of modified or simple entities can form a composite. Therefore, if one or more Modified Entities ME and Simple Entities SE are siblings then a Composite Entity CE comprising of all these siblings is produced.

4.2.3 Algorithm for Modified and Composite Entity Identification
In this section we describe the algorithm for systematic application of the rules discussed above. The algorithm (*Identify_Entities*) makes two passes over the parse tree in a bottom-up manner.

Pass 1
Step 1: The first pass of *Identify_Entities* begins with *Simple Entities* found in terminal nodes. It propagates this information about identified simple entities up the

parse tree recording this information in all _NT nodes till a sentence node is reached. This information will later be useful when identifying modified non-terminal entities. Instances of relationships found in _T nodes are also propagated up in a similar manner. This information will later be useful when identifying the subject and object of a relationship in that sentence.

Step 2: The next step in the first pass is to look at siblings of all _T nodes carrying simple entities to identify modifiers. For every identified modifier *Rule 1* is triggered and the parent node is marked as containing a modified entity.

Pass 2

Step 1: Next, the set of non-terminal (_NT) nodes which were marked as carrying entities in Pass 1 is considered. For each node in this set which is not a Verb Phrase (VP) or an Adverb Phrase (ADVP), its siblings are checked.

Case 1: If modifiers are found in the siblings *Rule 2* is triggered and the parent of the current node is marked as containing a Modified Entity.

Case 2: If Simple entities or other Modified entities are found *Rule 3* is triggered and the parent node is marked as a Composite Entity.

4.2.4 Algorithm for Relationship Identification

After *Identify_Entities* has processed a parse tree, the children of the node marked S (Sentence) contain the information necessary to produce a relationship between the entities involved. To identify this relationship, we use the following algorithm.

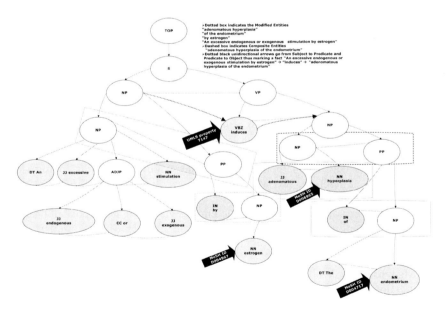

Fig. 3. Processed tree showing modified entities, composite entities and a relationship "induces"

If the children of the node marked S contain an entity followed by a relationship and another entity then such a pattern suggests the existence of a relationship between those entities. To guarantee that this relationship *R* is indeed valid, we use the information from the UMLS schema. Note that a candidate subject (Subject) and object (Object) of the suggested relationships could be composite or modified entities as per our definitions. Further, note that RDFS allows a property to have multiple domains and ranges. Let the domain and the range of R be the sets $domain(R) = \{C_1, C_2, \ldots, C_n\}$ and $range(R) = \{C_1, C_2, \ldots, C_m\}$. If $\exists C_i, C_j$ for $1 \leq i \leq n$ and $1 \leq j \leq m$ such that $C_i \in Subject$ and $C_j \in Object$ then we say that the Subject and Object are related by the relationship R. Fig.3. shows the relationship *"induces"* between the modified entity *"An excessive endogenous or exogenous stimulation by estrogen"* and *"adenomatous hyperplasia of the endometrium"*.

4.3 Serializing Identified Structures in RDF

In this section we use the running example of sentence 1254239-1 to describe the RDF resources generated by our method.

4.3.1 Simple Entities in RDF
Fig. 4. shows the RDF generated for simple entities. Note that the MeSH term identifiers are used here as URIs for the resources corresponding to each simple entity.

```
<rdf:Description rdf:about="#D004967">
    <rdfs:label xml:lang="en">estrogen</rdfs:label>
    <rdf:type rdf:resource="#Organic_Chemical"/>
    <rdf:type rdf:resource="#Pharmacologic_Substance"/>
    <rdf:type rdf:resource="#Hormone"/>
    <umls:hasSource>1254239-1</umls:hasSource>
</rdf:Description>

<rdf:Description rdf:about="#D006965">
    <rdfs:label xml:lang="en">hyperplasia</rdfs:label>
    <rdf:type rdf:resource="#Pathologic_Function"/>
    <umls:hasSource>1254239-1</umls:hasSource>
</rdf:Description>

<rdf:Description rdf:about="#D004717">
    <rdfs:label xml:lang="en">endometrium</rdfs:label>
    <rdf:type rdf:resource="#Body_Part_Organ_or_Organ_Component"/>
    <umls:hasSource>1254239-1</umls:hasSource>
</rdf:Description>
```

Fig. 4. RDF serialization of Simple Entities

4.3.2 Modified Entities in RDF
To generate RDF for the modified entities we need to create a resource corresponding to each modifier. Therefore, we have augmented the UMLS schema with a generic class which we call *umls:ModifierClass*. In addition, we have created a special property *umls:hasModifier*. This property has domain *rdf:resource* and range *umls:ModifierClass*. Using this property. instances of *umls:ModifierClass* are attached to instances of *rdf:resource* that are entities. Fig. 5(a). shows the RDF resources generated for the modified entities in sentence 1254239-1.

4.3.3 Composite Entities in RDF
By definition, composite entities are made up of one or more simple of modified entities. To create such composites, we had to further augment the UMLS schema to include a new class *umls:CompositeEntityClass* and a new property *umls:hasPart*.

The new property has as its domain and range *rdf:resource* and therefore serves to connect the parts of a composite to the resource that represents the composite entity. Fig. 5(b) shows the composite extracted from sentence 1254239-1.

4.3.4 Property Instances in RDF

Each of the 49 relationship in UMLS has been defined with its appropriate domain and range in the UMLS schema. For instance, the verb *induces* is a synonym of the property *umls:causes*. This property has several domains and ranges. One pair of classes that this property relates is *umls:Pharmacologic_Substance* and *umls:Pathologic_Function*. Since *estrogen* is an instance of *umls:Pharmacologic_Substance* (Fig. 5(a)) and "hyperplasia" is an instance of class *umls:Pathologic_Function*, we generate the RDF shown in Fig. 5(c).

```
<rdf:Description rdf:about="#m_1">
    <rdfs:label xml:lang="en">adenomatous</rdfs:label>
    <rdf:type rdf:resource="#ModifierClass"/>
    <umls:hasSource>1254239-1</umls:hasSource>
</rdf:Description>

<rdf:Description rdf:about="#me_1">
    <rdfs:label xml:lang="en">adenomatous_hyperplasia</rdfs:label>
    <umls:hasModifier rdf:resource="#m_1"/>
    <umls:hasPart rdf:resource="#D006965"/>
    <umls:hasSource>1254239-1</umls:hasSource>
</rdf:Description>

<rdf:Description rdf:about="#m_2">
    <rdfs:label xml:lang="en">of</rdfs:label>
    <rdf:type rdf:resource="#ModifierClass"/>
    <umls:hasSource>1254239-1</umls:hasSource>
</rdf:Description>

<rdf:Description rdf:about="#me_2">
    <rdfs:label xml:lang="en">of_the_endometrium</rdfs:label>
    <umls:hasModifier rdf:resource="#m_2"/>
    <umls:hasPart rdf:resource="#D004717"/>
    <umls:hasSource>1254239-1</umls:hasSource>
</rdf:Description>
```
(a)

```
<rdf:Description rdf:about="#ce_1">
    <rdfs:label xml:lang="en">me_1|me_2</rdfs:label>
    <rdf:type rdf:resource="#CompositeEntitiesClass"/>
    <umls:hasPart rdf:resource="#me_1"/>
    <umls:hasPart rdf:resource="#me_2"/>
    <umls:hasSource>1254239-1</umls:hasSource>
</rdf:Description>
```
(b)

```
<rdf:Statement rdf:about="#triple_1">
    <rdfs:label xml:lang="en">me_4|induces|ce_1</rdfs:label>
    <rdf:subject rdf:resource="#me_4"/>
    <rdf:predicate rdf:resource="#induces"/>
    <rdf:object rdf:resource="#ce_1"/>
    <umls:hasSource>1254239-1</umls:hasSource>
</rdf:Statement>
```
(c)

Fig. 5. RDF serialization of (a) Modifiers and Modified entities (b) Composite Entities and (c) Instance of a relationship between entities

5 Discussion of Results

In our experiments, we tested our methodology for relationship extraction on two datasets. Both datasets are subsets of PubMed. The first is the set of abstracts obtained by querying PubMed with the keyword *"Neoplasms"*. Unless otherwise specified, PubMed returns all abstracts annotated with a MeSH term as well as its descendants defined in MeSH. As of today, such a query returns over 500,000 abstracts. This forms the dataset which we refer to as ALLNEOPLASMS in this paper. The second dataset is a more focused, smaller set containing abstracts of papers that describe the various roles of *Magnesium* in alleviating *Migraine*. Among the eleven neglected connections described in [4], we focus our attention on four connections. These involve the intermediate entities *Stress, Calcium Channel Blockers, Platelet Aggregation* and *Cortical Spreading Depression*. To retrieve documents pertaining to these intermediate entities and either Migraine or Magnesium we searched PubMed with pair-wise combinations of each intermediate entity with both Migraine and Magnesium, respectively. This resulted in a set of approximately 800 abstracts. We call this set MAGNESIUMMIGRAINE. Our objective in extracting triples from the ALLNEOPLASM set at this point is to test the scalability of our system. In the future, we plan to sample the generated triples to evaluate our methodology in terms of precision and recall. Processing approximately 1.6 million candidate sentences from the ALLNEOPLASM set resulted in over 200,000 triples. In the case of the MIGRAINEMAGNESIUM test our objective was to investigate two aspects of our results. They can be characterized by the following questions.

Question 1: How effective are our rules in extracting relationships and the entities involved from text?
Questions 2: How useful is the extracted RDF data?

We identify candidate sentences for relationship extraction as those that contain at least two instances of MeSH terms and at least one instance of a named relationship (or its synonym). In the MIGRAINEMAGNESIUM set, we identified 798 candidate sentences. These sentences are therefore the ones which we expect to generate instances of relationships. In our results, these relationships never relate simple entities but always seem to relate modified or composite entities. The number of entities of each type and the relationship instances extracted for the MIGRAINEMAGNESIUM set are as follows: Simple Entities (752), Modifiers (2522), Modified Entities (4762), Composite Entities (377) and Relationships (122). We found that 122 relationship instances were extracted from the 798 candidate sentences. To measure recall accurately, a domain expert would have to read each of the 798 sentences manually to see if they should generate a relationship. We plan to conduct just such an experiment in the future. This is however infeasible for larger datasets. We analyzed those candidate sentences that did not produce relationship instances. In our approach to relationship extraction we used the fairly simple rule which expected the subject and the object entity in the same sentence. Close to 90% of the candidate sentences that failed to generate relationships were of a more complex form where the subject is an entity and the object is a sentence itself. Such a structure is an ideal candidate for a reified statement in RDF. We plan to increase the recall of our system by adding a rule to generate such a structure.

Of the 122 relationships, 5 were incorrect extractions resulting in 95% precision. Precision directly affects the usefulness of the extracted relationships. We therefore study the usefulness of the extracted relationships in the context of the Undiscovered Public Knowledge.

In the RDF produced, every modified entity is "connected" to its constituent modifiers by the *umls:hasModifier* relationship and to its constituent simple or modified entities by the *umls:hasPart* relationship. In the case of a composite entity, each of its constituents are *"connected"* to it by the *umls:hasPart* relationships. Besides these *"connections"* there are named relationships connecting entities (SE, ME and CE). As described earlier, the entities Stress, Platelet Aggregation, Spreading Cortical Depression and Calcium Channel Blockers are some of the intermediate entities that serve to describe the beneficial affect that Magnesium has in alleviating Migraine. The usefulness of the RDF extracted from the MIGRAINEMAGNESIUM could therefore be demonstrated if the abovementioned intermediate entities occur in paths connecting Migraine and Magnesium in the RDF. To test for this, we run a simple bidirectional length-limited breadth first search for paths connecting Migraine and Magnesium. We decided to limit the path length since we expected the number of paths to be prohibitively large, and since very long paths are seldom of interest. As expected, there are a very large number of paths and this number increases exponentially with path length. Only the paths that contain named relationships (besides *umls:hasPart* and *umls:hasModifier*) are considered interesting to us. The results of these length-limited searches on the MIGRAINEMAGNESIUM RDF data are shown below.

Table 2. Paths between Migraine and Magnesium

Paths between Migraine and Magnesium			
Path length	Total Number of paths found	# of interesting paths	Max. # of named relationships in any path
6	260	54	4
8	4103	1864	5
10	106450	33403	5

To see the value of these paths, we examined some of the paths among those of length 6. We focused our attention on the ones that had 2-3 named relationships. Fig. 6 below shows an example of such a path. This path indicates that migraine is caused by abnormality of platelet behavior (PMID 2701286, sentence number 1), collagen stimulates platelets (PMID 8933990, sentence number 9) and Magnesium has an inhibitory effect on collagen induced platelet aggregation (PMID 10357321, sentence number 7). We have included here the pointers to the specific sentences in each abstract that corroborates each of the 3 facts above to form the said path. This example clearly demonstrates that our extraction process was successful in extracting relationship instances from PubMed abstracts. It further demonstrates that by virtue of the *umls:hasPart* and *umls:hasModifier* these **relationship instances extracted from different documents can be chained together** to form paths.

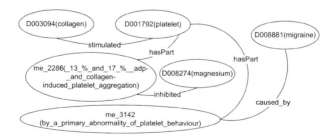

Fig. 6. Example path between Magnesium and Migraine

The edges in the figure are left undirected although the relationships are directed in the generated RDF. Directionality of these relationships can be deduced from the schema. The generated RDF can serve as the foundation for applying analytical operators such as those in [5] and [6] to provide support for discovering Undiscovered Public Knowledge. All the generated data from our experiments in this paper is available at http://lsdis.cs.uga.edu/projects/semdis/relationExt/.

6 Applications and Future Work

In order to thoroughly evaluate the accuracy of our extracted relationships and consequently that of the resulting paths, we plan to enlist the help of a domain expert. We plan to do this for the MIGRAINEMAGNSIUM dataset. We also plan to test this on the Fish Oils and Raynaud's disease associations. We plan to investigate the following potential applications resulting from our work:

"Semantic" Browsing - Our next natural step is to superimpose the extracted RDF back onto the original text and annotate biomedical abstracts with entities and relationships between them. We envision a Semantic Browsing paradigm in which the user of such a Semantic Browser will be able to traverse a space of documents based on named relationships between entities of interest. This vision is in line with the *"trailblazing"* idea posited by Dr. Vannevar Bush [1].

Knowledge-Driven ("Semantic") Document Retrieval - Paths between entities in our generated RDF instance base can be used as a query for documents. A simple example of such a query can be seen in the association between Migraine and Magnesium, where intermediate entities like Stress or Calcium Channel Blockers would serve to constrain the returned documents to only that set which corroborates the said associations.

Semantic Analytics over Literature - The operators described in [5] return paths between entities in the query. The sub-graph discovery operator described in [6] takes as input two entities in an RDF instance base and returns a set of paths between them that are not vertex-disjoint (i.e. forming a sub-graph). Applying these queries to RDF generated by mining biomedical literature will allow us to quantify the relevance of the returned paths. This gives rise to a very powerful mechanism for exploratory analysis of large document sets.

7 Conclusions

Our experiments have demonstrated the utility of extracting relationships from biomedical text to support analytical queries. The effectiveness of our method augmented with rules to extract more complex structures remains to be investigated. It is however clear that domain knowledge can be effectively combined with NLP techniques to good effect. We intend to continue this work and investigate the use of other vocabularies in addition to MeSH to aid in relationship extraction. The relationship-centric view of document organization, in our opinion, will mark the next generation of search and analytics over document corpora. This work is funded by NSF-ITR-IDM Award#0325464 (SemDIS: Discovering Complex Relationships in the Semantic Web).

References

1. Bush, V., *As We May Think*. The Atlantic Monthly, 1945. **176**(1): p. 101-108.
2. NLM, *PubMed*, The National Library Of Medicine, Bethesda MD.
3. Swanson, D.R., *Fish Oil, Raynaud's Syndrome, and Undiscovered Public Knowledge*. Perspectives in Biology and Medicine, 1986. **30**(1): p. 7-18.

4. Swanson, D.R., *Migraine and Magnesium: Eleven Neglected Connections.* Perspectives in Biology and Medicine, 1988. **31**(4): p. 526-557.
5. Anyanwu, K. and A. Sheth, *ρ-Queries: enabling querying for semantic associations on the semantic web*, in *Proceedings WWW*. 2003, ACM Press: Budapest, Hungary.
6. Ramakrishnan, C., et al., *Discovering informative connection subgraphs in multi-relational graphs.* SIGKDD Explor. Newsl., 2005. **7**(2): p. 56-63.
7. Guha, R., R. McCool, and E. Miller, *Semantic search*, in *WWW '03* p. 700-709.
8. Cohen, A.M. and W.R. Hersh, *A survey of current work in biomedical text mining.* Brief Bioinform, 2005. **6**(1): p. 57-71.
9. Tanabe, L. and W.J. Wilbur, *Tagging gene and protein names in biomedical text.* Bioinformatics, 2002. **18**(8): p. 1124-1132.
10. Brill, E., *Transformation-based error-driven learning and natural language processing: a case study in part-of-speech tagging.* Comput. Linguist., 1995. **21**(4): p. 543-565.
11. Yu, H., et al., *Automatically identifying gene/protein terms in MEDLINE abstracts.* J. of Biomedical Informatics, 2002. **35**(5/6): p. 322-330.
12. Gaizauskas, R., et al., *Protein structures and information extraction from biological texts: the PASTA system.* Bioinformatics, 2003. **19**(1): p. 135-143.
13. Friedman, C., et al., *GENIES: a natural-language processing system for the extraction of molecular pathways from journal articles.* Bioinformatics, 2001. **17 Suppl 1**: p. 1367-4803.
14. Rindflesch, T.C., et al., *EDGAR: extraction of drugs, genes and relations from the biomedical literature.* Pac Symp Biocomput, 2000: p. 517-528.
15. NLM, *Medical Subject Heading (MeSH)*, The National Library Of Medicine, Bethesda, MD.
16. NLM, *Unified Medical Language System (UMLS)*, The National Library Of Medicine, Bethesda, MD.
17. Tsuruoka, Y. and J.i. Tsujii, *Bidirectional Inference with the Easiest-First Strategy for Tagging Sequence Data*, in *Proceedings of Human Language Technology Conference and Conference on Empirical Methods in Natural Language Processing*. 2005, Association. p. 467-474.
18. Tsuruoka, Y. and J.i. Tsujii, *Chunk Parsing Revisited*, in *Proceedings of the 9th International Workshop on Parsing Technologies (IWPT 2005)*. 2005. p. 133-140.
19. Charniak, E., *A maximum-entropy-inspired parser*, in *Proceedings of the first conference on North American chapter of the ACL*. 2000, Morgan. p. 132-139.
20. Collins, M., *Head-driven statistical models for natural language parsing.* 1999.
21. Collins, M. and N. Duffy, *New ranking algorithms for parsing and tagging: kernels over discrete structures, and the voted perceptron*, in *ACL '02* p. 263-270.
22. Tsuruoka, Y., et al., *Developing a Robust Part-of-Speech Tagger for Biomedical Text.* Lecture Notes in Computer Science. 2005. 382-392.
23. Déjean, H., *Learning rules and their exceptions.* J. Mach. Learn. Res., 2002. **2**: p. 669-693.

Web Service Composition Via Generic Procedures and Customizing User Preferences

Shirin Sohrabi, Nataliya Prokoshyna, and Sheila A. McIlraith

Department of Computer Science, University of Toronto, Toronto, Canada
{shirin, nataliya, sheila}@cs.toronto.edu

Abstract. We claim that user preferences are a key component of Web service composition – a component that has largely been ignored. In this paper we propose a means of specifying and intergrating user preferences into Web service composition. To this end, we propose a means of performing automated Web service composition by exploiting generic procedures together with rich qualitative user preferences. We exploit the agent programming language Golog to represent our generic procedures and a first-order preference language to represent rich qualitative temporal user preferences. From these we generate Web service compositions that realize the generic procedure, satisfying the user's hard constraints and optimizing for the user's preferences. We prove our approach sound and optimal. Our system, GologPref, is implemented and interacting with services on the Web. The language and techniques proposed in this paper can be integrated into a variety of approaches to Web or Grid service composition.

1 Introduction

Web services provide a standardized means for diverse, distributed software applications to be published on the Web and to interoperate seamlessly. Simple Web accessible programs are described using machine-processable descriptions and can be loosely composed together to achieve complex behaviour. The weather service at www.weather.com and the flight-booking services at www.aircanada.ca, are examples of Web applications that can be described and composed as Web services. They might be coupled as part of a travel-booking service, for example.

Automated Web service composition is one of many interesting challenges facing the Semantic Web. Given computer-interpretable descriptions of: the task to be performed, the properties and capabilities of available Web services, and possibly some information about the client or user's specific constraints, *automated Web service composition* requires a computer program to automatically select, integrate and invoke multiple Web services in order to achieve the specified task in accordance with any user-specific constraints. Compositions of Web or Grid services are necessary for realizing both routine and complex tasks on the Web (resp. Grid) without the need for time-consuming manual composition and integration of information. Compositions are also a useful way of enforcing business rules and policies in both Web and Grid computing.

Fully automated Web service composition has been characterized as akin to both an artificial intelligence (AI) planning task and to a restricted software synthesis task (e.g., [1]). A composition can be achieved using classical AI planning techniques by conceiving services as primitive or complex actions and the task description specified as a (final state) goal (e.g., [2,3]). This approach has its drawbacks when dealing with data. In general, the search space for a composition (aka plan) is huge because of the large number of available services (actions), which grow far larger with grounding for data.

A reasonable middle ground which we originally proposed in [4,1] is to use *generic procedures* to specify the task to be performed and to customize these procedures with *user constraints*. We argued that many of the tasks performed on the Web or on intranets are repeated routinely, and the basic steps to achieving these tasks are well understood, at least at an abstract level – travel planning is one such example. Nevertheless, the realization of such tasks varies as it is tailored to individual users. As such, our proposal was to specify such tasks using a workflow or generic procedure and to customize the procedure with user constraints at run time. Such an approach is generally of the same complexity as planning but the search space is greatly reduced, and as such significantly more efficient than planning without such generic advice.

In [1] we proposed to use an augmented version of the agent programming language Golog [5] to specify our generic procedures or workflows with sufficient nondeterminism to allow for customization. (E.g., *"book inter-city transportation, local transportation and accommodations in any order"*). User constraints (e.g., *"I want to fly with Air Canada."*) were limited to hard constraints (as opposed to "soft"), were specified in first-order logic (FOL), and were applied to the generic procedure at run-time to generate a user-specific composition of services. A similar approach was adopted using hierarchical task networks (HTNs) to represent generic procedures or templates, and realized using SHOP2 (e.g., [6]) without user customization of the procedures.

In this paper, we extend our Golog framework for Web service composition, customizing Golog generic procedures not only with hard constraints but with *soft* user constraints (henceforth referred to as *preferences*). These preferences are defeasible and may not be mutually achievable. We argue that user preferences are a critical and missing component of most existing approaches to Web service composition. User preferences are key for at least two reasons. First, the user's task (specified as a goal and/or generic procedure with user constraints) is often under constrained. As such, it induces a family of solutions. User preferences enable a user to specify properties of solutions that make them more or less desirable. The composition system can use these to generate preferred solutions.

A second reason why user preferences are critical to Web service composition is with respect to *how* the composition is performed. A key component of Web service composition is the selection of specific services used to realize the composition. In AI planning, primitive actions (the analogue of services) are selected for composition based on their preconditions and effects, and there is often only one primitive action that realizes a particular effect. Like actions, services are selected for composition based on functional properties such as inputs, output, preconditions and effects, but they are also selected based on domain-specific nonfunctional properties such as, in the case of airline ticket booking, whether they book flights with a carrier the user prefers, what credit cards they accept, how trusted they are, etc. By integrating user preferences into Web service composition, preferences over services (the *how*) can be specified and considered along side preferences over the solutions (the *what*).

In this paper we recast the problem of Web service composition as the task of finding a composition of services that achieves the task description (specified as a generic procedure in Golog), that achieves the user's hard constraints, and that is *optimal* with respect to the user's preferences. To specify user preferences, we exploit a rich qualitative preference language, recently proposed by Bienvenu et al. to specify users' preferences in a variant of linear temporal logic (LTL) [7]. We prove the soundness of our approach and the optimality of our compositions with respect to the user's preferences. Our system can be used to select the optimal solution from among families of solutions that achieve the user's stated objective. Our system is implemented in Prolog and integrated with a selection of scraped Web services that are appropriate to our test domain of travel planning.

The work presented here is cast in terms of FOL, *not* in terms of one of the typical Semantic Web languages such as OWL [8] nor more specifically in terms of a semantic Web service ontology such as OWL-S [9], WSMO [10] or SWSO [11]. Nevertheless, it is of direct significance to semantic Web services. As noted in (e.g., [9]) process models, necessary for Web service composition, cannot be expressed in OWL while preserving all and only the intended interpretations of the process model. OWL (and thus OWL-S) is not sufficiently expressive. Further OWL reasoners are not designed for the type of inference necessary for Web service composition. For both these reasons, Web service composition systems generally translate the relevant aspects of service ontologies such as OWL-S into internal representations such as PDDL that are more amenable to AI planning (e.g., [6,12]). Golog served as one of the inspirations for what is now OWL-S [4] and all the OWL-S constructs have translations into Golog [13]. Further, the semantics of the OWL-S process model has been specified in situation calculus [11,14]. Thus, our Golog generic procedures can be expressed in OWL-S and likewise, OWL-S ontologies can be translated into our formalism. We do not have a current implementation of this translation, but it is conceptually straightforward.

2 Situation Calculus and Golog

We use the situation calculus and FOL to describe the functional and nonfunctional properties of our Web services. We use the agent programming language Golog to specify composite Web services and to specify our generic procedures. In this section, we review the essentials of situation calculus and Golog.

The situation calculus is a logical language for specifying and reasoning about dynamical systems [5]. In the situation calculus, the *state* of the world is expressed in terms of functions and relations (fluents) relativized to a particular *situation* s, e.g., $F(\boldsymbol{x},s)$. In this paper, we distinguish between the set of fluent predicates, $\mathcal{F}$, and the set of non-fluent predicates, $\mathcal{R}$, representing properties that do not change over time. A situation s is a *history* of the primitive actions, $a \in \mathcal{A}$, performed from a distinguished initial situation S_0. The function $do(a,s)$ maps a situation and an action into a new situation thus inducing a tree of situations rooted in S_0. Poss(a,s) is true if action a is possible in situation s.

Web services such as the Web exposed application at www.weather.com are viewed as actions in the situation calculus and are described as actions in terms of a situation calculus basic action theory, $\mathcal{D}$. The details of $\mathcal{D}$ are not essential to this paper but the interested reader is directed to [5,14,1] for further details.

Golog [5] is a high-level logic programming language for the specification and execution of complex actions in dynamical domains. It builds on top of the situation calculus by providing Algol-inspired extralogical constructs for assembling primitive situation calculus actions into complex actions (aka *programs*) δ. These complex actions simply serve as constraints upon the situation tree. Complex action constructs include the following:

a — primitive actions	if ϕ then δ_1 else δ_2 – conditionals
$\delta_1;\delta_2$ — sequences	$\delta_1\|\delta_2$ — nondeterministic cho ice of actions
ϕ? — tests	$\pi(x)\delta$ — nondeterministic choice of arguments
while ϕ **do** δ — while loops	**proc** $P(\boldsymbol{v})$ δ **endProc** — procedure

We also include the construct **anyorder**$[\delta_1,\ldots,\delta_n]$ which allows any permutation of the actions listed. The conditional and while-loop constructs are defined in terms of other constructs. For the purposes of Web service composition we generally treat iteration as finitely bounded by a parameter k. Such finitely bounded programs are called *tree programs*.

$$\textbf{if } \phi \textbf{ then } \delta_1 \textbf{ else } \delta_2 \stackrel{\text{def}}{=} [\phi?;\delta_1] \mid [\neg\phi?;\delta_2]$$

$$\textbf{while}_1(\phi) \ \delta \stackrel{\text{def}}{=} \textbf{ if } \phi \textbf{ then } \delta \textbf{ endIf }\ ^1$$

$$\textbf{while}_k(\phi) \ \delta \stackrel{\text{def}}{=} \textbf{ if } \phi \textbf{ then } [\delta;\textbf{while }_{k-1}(\phi)\delta] \textbf{ endIf}$$

These constructs can be used to write programs in the language of the domain theory, or more specifically, they can be used to specify both composite Web services and also generic procedures for Web service composition. E.g.[2],

bookAirTicket($\boldsymbol{x}$) ; **if** far **then** bookCar($\boldsymbol{y}$) **else** bookTaxi($\boldsymbol{y}$) **endIf**
bookCar($\boldsymbol{x}$) ; bookHotel($\boldsymbol{y}$).

In order to understand how we modify Golog to incorporate user preferences, the reader must understand the basics of Golog semantics. There are two popular semantics for Golog programs: the original evaluation semantics [5] and a related single-step transition semantics that was proposed for on-line execution of concurrent Golog programs [15]. The transition semantics is axiomatized through

---

[1] **if-then-endIf** is the obvious variant of **if-then-else-endIf**.
[2] Following convention we will generally refer to fluents in situation-suppressed form, e.g., $at(toronto)$ rather than $at(toronto,s)$. Reintroduction of the situation term is denoted by $[s]$. Variables are universally quantified unless otherwise noted.

two predicates $Trans(\delta, s, \delta', s')$ and $Final(\delta, s)$. Given an action theory $\mathcal{D}$, a program δ and a situation s, $Trans$ defines the set of possible successor configurations (δ', s') according to the action theory. $Final$ defines whether a program successfully terminated, in a given situation. $Trans$ and $Final$ are defined for every complex action. A few examples follow. (See [15] for details):

$$Trans(nil, s, \delta', s') \equiv False$$
$$Trans(a, s, \delta', s') \equiv Poss(a[s], s) \wedge \delta' = nil \wedge s' = do(a[s], s)$$
$$Trans(\phi?, s, \delta', s') \equiv \phi[s] \wedge \delta' = nil \wedge s' = s$$
$$Trans([\delta_1; \delta_2], s, \delta', s') \equiv Final(\delta_1, s) \wedge Trans(\delta_2, s, \delta', s')$$
$$\vee \exists \delta''. \delta' = (\delta''; \delta_2) \wedge Trans(\delta_1, s, \delta'', s')$$
$$Trans([\delta_1 \mid \delta_2], s, \delta', s') \equiv Trans(\delta_1, s, \delta', s') \vee Trans(\delta_2, s, \delta', s')$$
$$Trans(\pi(x)\delta, s, \delta', s') \equiv \exists x. Trans(\delta_x^v, s, \delta', s')$$
$$Final(nil, s) \equiv \text{TRUE} \qquad Final(a, s) \equiv \text{FALSE}$$
$$Final([\delta_1; \delta_2], s) \equiv Final(\delta_1, s) \wedge Final(\delta_2, s)$$

Thus, given the program $bookCar(\boldsymbol{x}); bookHotel(\boldsymbol{y})$, if the action $bookCar(\boldsymbol{x})$ is possible in situation s, then
$$Trans([bookCar(\boldsymbol{x}); bookHotel(\boldsymbol{y})], s, bookHotel(\boldsymbol{y}), do(bookCar(\boldsymbol{x}), s))$$
describes the only possible transition according to the action theory. $do(bookCar(\boldsymbol{x}), s)$ is the transition and $bookHotel(\boldsymbol{y})$ is the remaining program to be executed. Using the transitive closure of $Trans$, denoted $Trans^*$, one can define a Do predicate as follows. This Do is equivalent to the original evaluation semantics Do [15].

$$Do(\delta, s, s') \stackrel{def}{=} \exists \delta'. Trans^*(\delta, s, \delta', s') \wedge Final(\delta', s'). \tag{1}$$

Given a domain theory, $\mathcal{D}$ and Golog program δ, program execution must find a sequence of actions $\boldsymbol{a}$ (where $\boldsymbol{a}$ is a vector of actions) such that: $\mathcal{D} \models Do(\delta, S_0, do(\boldsymbol{a}, S_0))$. $Do(\delta, S_0, do(\boldsymbol{a}, S_0))$ denotes that the Golog program δ, starting execution in S_0 will legally terminate in situation $do(\boldsymbol{a}, S_0)$, where $do(\boldsymbol{a}, S_0)$ abbreviates $do(a_n, do(a_{n-1}, \ldots, do(a_1, S_0)))$. Thus, given a generic procedure, described as a Golog program δ, and an initial situation S_0, we would like to infer a terminating situation $do(\boldsymbol{a}, S_0)$ such that the vector $\boldsymbol{a}$ denotes a sequence of Web services that can be performed to realize the generic procedure.

3 Specifying User Preferences

In this section, we describe the syntax of the first-order language we use for specifying user preferences. This description follows the language we proposed in [7] for preference-based planning. The semantics of the language is described in the situation calculus. We provide an informal description here, directing the reader to [7] for further details. Our language is richly expressive, enabling the expression of static as well as temporal preferences. Unlike many preference languages, it provides a total order on preferences. It is qualitative in nature, facilitating elicitation. Unlike many ordinal preference languages, our language provides a facility to stipulate the relative strength of preferences.

Illustrative example: To help illustrate our preference language, consider the task of travel planning. A generic procedure, easily specified in Golog, might say: *In any order, book inter-city transportation, book local accommodations and book local transportation.* With this generic procedure in hand an individual user can specify their hard constraints (e.g., *Lara needs to be in Chicago July 29-Aug 5, 2006.*) together with a list of preferences described in the language to follow.

To understand the preference language, consider the composition we are trying to generate to be a situation – a sequence of actions or Web services executed from the initial situation. A user specifies his or her preferences in terms of a single, so-called *General Preference Formula*. This formula is an aggregation of preferences over constituent properties of situations (i.e., compositions). The basic building block of our preference formula is a *Basic Desire Formula* which describes properties of (partial) situations (i.e., compositions).

Definition 1 (Basic Desire Formula (BDF)). *A basic desire formula is a sentence drawn from the smallest set $\mathcal{B}$ where:*
1. $\mathcal{F} \subset \mathcal{B}$
2. $\mathcal{R} \subset \mathcal{B}$
3. $f \in \mathcal{F}$, then **final**$(f) \in \mathcal{B}$
4. If $a \in \mathcal{A}$, then **occ**$(a) \in \mathcal{B}$
5. If φ_1 and φ_2 are in $\mathcal{B}$, then so are $\neg\varphi_1$, $\varphi_1 \wedge \varphi_2$, $\varphi_1 \vee \varphi_2$, $(\exists x)\varphi_1$, $(\forall x)\varphi_1$, **next**(φ_1), **always**(φ_1), **eventually**(φ_1), *and* **until**(φ_1, φ_2).

final(f) states that fluent f holds in the final situation, **occ**(a) states that action a occurs in the present situation, and **next**(φ_1), **always**(φ_1), **eventually**(φ_1), and **until**(φ_1, φ_2) are basic LTL constructs.

BDFs establish properties of preferred situations (i.e., compositions of services). By combining BDFs using boolean connectives we are able to express a wide variety of properties of situations. E.g.[3]

$$\textbf{final}(at(home)) \tag{P1}$$

$$(\exists\ \boldsymbol{c}).\textbf{occ}'(bookAir(\boldsymbol{c}, economy, direct)) \wedge member(\boldsymbol{c}, starAlliance) \tag{P2}$$

$$\textbf{always}(\neg((\exists\ \boldsymbol{h}).hotelBooked(\boldsymbol{h}) \wedge hilton(\boldsymbol{h}))) \tag{P3}$$

$$(\exists\ \boldsymbol{h}, \boldsymbol{r}).(\textbf{occ}'(bookHotel(\boldsymbol{h}, \boldsymbol{r})) \wedge paymentOption(\boldsymbol{h}, visa)$$
$$\wedge\ starsGE(\boldsymbol{r}, 3) \tag{P4}$$

P1 says that in the final situation Lara prefers to be at home. P2 says that Lara prefers to eventually book direct economy air travel with a Star Alliance carrier. Recall there was no stipulation in the generic procedure regarding the mode of transportation between cities or locally. P3 expresses the preference

---
[3] To simplify the examples many parameters have been suppressed. For legibility, variables are bold faced, we abbreviate **eventually**(**occ**(φ)) by **occ**$'(\varphi)$, and we refer to the preference formulae by their labels.

that a Hilton hotel never be booked while P4 expresses a preference for hotels that accept visa credit cards and have a rating of 3 stars or more.

To define a preference ordering over alternative properties of situations, we define *Atomic Preference Formulae* (APFs). Each alternative being ordered comprises 2 components: the property of the situation, specified by a BDF, and a *value* term which stipulates the relative strength of the preference.

Definition 2 (Atomic Preference Formula (APF)). *Let $\mathcal{V}$ be a totally ordered set with minimal element v_{min} and maximal element v_{max}. An atomic preference formula is a formula $\varphi_0[v_0] \gg \varphi_1[v_1] \gg ... \gg \varphi_n[v_n]$, where each φ_i is a BDF, each $v_i \in \mathcal{V}$, $v_i < v_j$ for $i < j$, and $v_0 = v_{min}$. When $n = 0$, atomic preference formulae correspond to BDFs.*

An APF expresses a preference over alternatives. In what follows, we let $\mathcal{V} = [0, 1]$, but we could instead choose a strictly qualitative set like {*best* < *good* < *indifferent* < *bad* < *worst*} since the operations on these values are limited to max and min. The following APFs express an ordering over Lara's preferences.

$$P2[0]$$
$$\gg (\exists \, \boldsymbol{c}, \boldsymbol{w}).\mathbf{occ}'(bookAir(\boldsymbol{c}, economy, \boldsymbol{w}) \wedge member(\boldsymbol{c}, starAlliance)[0.2]$$
$$\gg \mathbf{occ}'(bookAir(delta, economy, direct))[0.5] \qquad (P5)$$
$$(\exists \, \boldsymbol{t}).\mathbf{occ}'(bookCar(national, \boldsymbol{t}))[0] \gg (\exists \, \boldsymbol{t}).\mathbf{occ}'(bookCar(alamo, \boldsymbol{t}))[0.2]$$
$$\gg (\exists \, \boldsymbol{t}).\mathbf{occ}'(bookCar(avis, \boldsymbol{t}))[0.8] \qquad (P6)$$
$$(\exists \, \boldsymbol{c}).\mathbf{occ}'(bookCar(\boldsymbol{c}, suv))[0] \gg (\exists \, \boldsymbol{c}).\mathbf{occ}'(bookCar(\boldsymbol{c}, compact))[0.2] \qquad (P7)$$

P5 states that Lara prefers direct economy flights with a Star Alliance carrier, followed by economy flights with a Star Alliance carrier, followed by direct economy flights with Delta airlines. P6 and P7 are preference over cars. Lara strongly prefers National and then Alamo over Avis, followed by any other car-rental companies. Finally she slightly prefers an SUV over a compact with any other type of car a distant third.

To allow the user to specify more complex preferences and to aggregate preferences, General Preference Formulae (GFPs) extend our language to conditional, conjunctive, and disjunctive preferences.

Definition 3 (General Preference Formula (GPF)). *A formula Φ is a general preference formula if one of the following holds:*

- *Φ is an APF*
- *Φ is $\gamma : \Psi$, where γ is a BDF and Ψ is a GPF [Conditional]*
- *Φ is one of*
  - *$\Psi_0 \, \& \, \Psi_1 \, \& \, ... \, \& \, \Psi_n$ [General Conjunction]*
  - *$\Psi_0 \mid \Psi_1 \mid ... \mid \Psi_n$ [General Disjunction]*

where $n \geq 1$ and each Ψ_i is a GPF.

Continuing our example:

$(\forall\ h, c, e, w).\mathbf{always}(\neg hotelBooked(h) : \neg\mathbf{occ}'(bookAir(c, e, w)))$ (P8)

$far\ :\ \text{P5}$ (P9)

P3 & P4 & P6 & P7 & P8 & P9 (P10)

P8 states that Lara prefers not to book her air ticket until she has a hotel booked. P9 conditions Lara's airline preferences on her destination being far away. (If it is not far, she will not fly and the preferences are irrelevant.) Finally, P10 aggregates previous preferences into one formula.

Semantics: Informally, the semantics of our preference language is achieved through assigning a weight to a situation s with respect to a GPF, Φ, written $w_s(\Phi)$. This weight is a composition of its constituents. For BDFs, a situation s is assigned the value v_{min} if the BDF is satisfied in s, v_{max} otherwise. Recall that in our example above $v_{min} = 0$ and $v_{max} = 1$, though they could equally well have been a qualitative e.g., [excellent, abysmal]. Similarly, given an APF, and a situation s, s is assigned the weight of the best BDF that it satisfies within the defined APF. Returning to our example above, for P6 if a situation (composition) booked a car from Alamo rental car, it would get a weight of 0.2. Finally GPF semantics follow the natural semantics of boolean connectives. As such General Conjunction yields the maximum of its constituent GPF weights and General Disjunction yields the minimum of its constituent GPF weights. For a full explanation of the situation calculus semantics, please see [7]. Here we also define further aggregations that can be performed. These are mostly syntactic sugar that are compelling to the user and we omit them for space.

We conclude this section with the following definition which shows us how to compare two situations (and thus two compositions) with respect to a GPF:

Definition 4 (Preferred Situations). *A situation s_1 is at least as preferred as a situation s_2 with respect to a GPF Φ, written $pref(s_1, s_2, \Phi)$ if $w_{s_1}(\Phi) \leq w_{s_2}(\Phi)$.*

4 Web Service Composition

In this section, we define the notion of web service composition with generic procedures and customizing user preferences, present an algorithm for computing these compositions and prove properties of our algorithm. Our definition relies on the definition of *Do* from (1) in Section 2.

Definition 5 (Web Service Composition w/User Preferences (WSCP)). *A Web service composition problem with user preferences is described as a 5-tuple $(\mathcal{D}, O, \delta, C, \Phi)$ where:*

- *$\mathcal{D}$ is a situation calculus basic action theory describing functional properties of the Web services,*
- *O is a FOL theory describing the non-functional properties of the Web services[4],*

---
[4] The content of $\mathcal{D}$ and O would typically come from an OWL-S, SWSO, or other semantic Web service ontology.

- δ is a generic procedure described in Golog,
- C is a formula expressing hard user constraints, and
- Φ is a GPF describing user preferences.

A Web Service Composition (WSC) is a sequence of Web services $\boldsymbol{a}$ such that

$$\mathcal{D} \wedge O \models \exists s.Do(\delta, S_0, s) \wedge s = do(\boldsymbol{a}, S_0) \wedge C(s)$$

A preferred WSC (WSCP) is a sequence of Web services $\boldsymbol{a}$ such that

$$\mathcal{D} \wedge O \models \exists s.Do(\delta, S_0, s, \Phi) \wedge s = do(\boldsymbol{a}, S_0) \wedge C(s)$$
$$\wedge \ \nexists s'.[Do(\delta, S_0, s', \Phi) \wedge C(s') \wedge pref(s', s, \Phi)]$$

I.e., a WSC is a sequence of Web services, $\boldsymbol{a}$, whose execution starting in the initial situation enforces the generic procedure and hard constraints terminating successfully in $do(\boldsymbol{a}, s)$. A WSCP yields a most preferred terminating situation.

4.1 Computing Preferred Compositions

A Golog program places constraints on the situation tree that evolves from S_0. As such, any implementation of Golog is effectively doing planning in a constrained search space, searching for a legal termination of the Golog program. The actions that define this terminating situation are the plan. In the case of composing web services, this plan is a web service composition.

To compute a preferred composition, WSCP, we search through this same constrained search space to find the *most preferred* terminating situation. Our approach, embodied in a system called GologPref, searches for this optimal terminating situation by modifying the PPLAN approach to planning with preferences proposed in [7]. In particular, GologPref performs best-first search through the constrained search space resulting from the Golog program, $\delta; C$. The search is guided by an admissible evaluation function that evaluates partial plans with respect to whether they satisfy the preference formula, Φ. The admissible evaluation function is the optimistic evaluation of the preference formula, with the pessimistic evaluation and the plan length used as tie breakers where necessary, in that order.

The preference formula is evaluated over intermediate situations (partial compositions) by exploiting *progression* as described in [7]. Informally, progression takes a situation and a temporal logic formula (TLF), evaluates the TLF with respect to the state of the situation, and generates a new formula representing those aspects of the TLF that remain to be satisfied in subsequent situations.

Fig 1 provides a sketch of the basic GologPref algorithm following from PPLAN. The full GologPref algorithm takes as input a 5-tuple $(\mathcal{D}, O, \delta, C, \Phi)$. For ease of explication, our algorithm sketch in Fig 1 explictly identifies the initial situation of $\mathcal{D}$, *init*, the Golog program, $\delta; C$ which we refer to as *pgm* and Φ, which we refer to as *pref*. GologPref returns a sequence of Web services, i.e. a plan, and the weight of that plan. The *frontier* is a list of nodes of the form [*optW, pessW, pgm, partialPlan, state, pref*], sorted by optimistic weight, pessimistic weight, and then by length. The frontier is initialized to the input program and the empty partial

---

GologPref(*init, pgm, pref*)
frontier ← **initFrontier**(*init, pgm, pref*)
while *frontier* ≠ ∅
    current ← **removeFirst**(*frontier*)
    % establishes current values for *progPgm, partialPlan, state, progPref*
    if *progPgm=nil* and *optW=pessW*
        return *partialPlan, optW*
    end if
    neighbours ← **expand**(*progPgm, partialPlan, state, progPref*)
    frontier ← **sortNmergeByVal**(*neighbours, frontier*)
end while
return [], ∞

expand(*progPgm, partialPlan, state, progPref*) returns a list of new nodes to add to the frontier. If *partialPlan=nil* then **expand** returns [ ]. Otherwise, **expand** uses Golog's *Trans* to determine all the executable actions that are legal transitions of *progPgm* in *state* and to compute the remaining program for each.
It returns a list which contains, for each of these executable actions *a* a node
    (*optW, pessW, newProgPgm, newPartialPlan, newState, newProgPref*)
and for each *a* leading to a terminating state, a second node
    (*realW, realW, nil, newPartialPlan, newState, newProgPref*).

Fig. 1. A sketch of the GologPref algorithm

plan, its *optW*, *pessW*, and *pref* corresponding to the progression and evaluation of the input preference formula in the initial state.

On each iteration of the **while** loop, GologPref removes the first node from the frontier and places it in *current*. If the Golog program of *current* is *nil* then the situation associated with this node is a terminating situation. If it is also the case that *optW=pessW*, then GologPref returns *current*'s partial plan and weight. Otherwise, it calls the function **expand** with *current's* node as input.

expand returns a new list of nodes to add to the frontier. If *progPgm* is *nil* then no new nodes are added to the frontier. Otherwise, **expand** generates a new set of nodes of the form [*optW, pessW, prog, partialPlan, state, pref*], one for each action that is a legal Golog transition of *pgm* in *state*. For actions leading to terminating states, **expand** also generates a second node of the same form but with *optW* and *pessW* replaced by the actual weight achieved by the plan. The new nodes generated by **expand** are then sorted by *optW*, *pessW*, then length and merged with the remainder of the frontier. If we reach the empty frontier, we exit the **while** loop and return the empty plan.

We now prove the correctness of our algorithm.

Theorem 1 (Soundness and Optimality). *Let* $\mathcal{P}=(\mathcal{D}, O, \delta, C, \Phi)$ *be a Web service composition problem, where* δ *is a tree program. Let* **a** *be the plan returned by GologPref from input* $\mathcal{P}$. *Then* **a** *is a WSCP of* $(\mathcal{D}, O, \delta, C, \Phi)$.

Proof sketch: We prove that the algorithm terminates appealing to the fact that δ is a tree program. Then we prove that $\boldsymbol{a}$ is a WSC by cases over *Trans* and *Final*. Finally we prove that $\boldsymbol{a}$ is also optimal, by exploiting the correctness of progression of preference formuale proven in [7], the admissibility of our evaluation function, and the bounded size of the search space generated by the Golog program $\delta; C$.

4.2 Integrated Optimal Web Service Selection

Most Web service composition systems use AI planning techniques and as such generally ignore the important problem of Web service selection or discovery, assuming it will be done by a separate matchmaker. The work presented here is significant because it enables the selection of services for composition based, not only on their inputs, outputs, preconditions and effects but also based on other nonfunctional properties. As such, users are able to specify properties of services that they desire along side other properties of their preferred solution, and services are selected that optimize for the users preferences in the context of the overall composition.

To see how selection of services can be encoded in our system, we reintroduce the service parameter $\boldsymbol{u}$ which was suppressed from the example preferences in Section 3. Revisiting P2, we see how the selection of a service $\boldsymbol{u}$ is easily realized within our preference framework with preference P2'.

$$(\exists\ \boldsymbol{c}, \boldsymbol{u}).\mathbf{occ}'(bookAir(\boldsymbol{c}, economy, direct, \boldsymbol{u})) \land member(\boldsymbol{c}, starAlliance)$$
$$\land\ serviceType(\boldsymbol{u}, airTicketVendor) \land sellsTickets(\boldsymbol{u}, \boldsymbol{c}) \qquad \text{(P2')}$$

5 Implementation and Application

We have implemented the generation of Web Service compositions using generic procedures and customizing user preferences as described in previous sections. Our implementation, GologPref, builds on an implementation of PPLAN [7] and an implementation of IndiGolog [5] both in SWI Prolog[5].

GologPref interfaces with Web services on the Web through the implementation of domain-specific scrapers developed using AgentBuilder 3.2, and AgentRunner 3.2, Web agent design applications developed by Fetch Technologies ©. Among the sites we have scraped are Mapquest, and several air, car and hotel services. The information gathered is collected in XML and then processed by GologPref.

We tested GologPref in the domain of travel planning. Our tests serve predominantly as a proof of the concept and to illustrate the utility of GologPref.

Our generic procedure which is represented in Golog was very simple, allowing flexibility in how it could be instantiated. What follows is an example of the Prolog encoding of a GologPref generic procedure.

---
[5] See [5] for a description of the translation of $\mathcal{D}$ to Prolog.

```
anyorder [bookAcc, bookCityToCityTranspo, bookLocalTranspo]

proc(bookAcc(Location, Day, Num),
[ stayWithFriends(Location) | bookHotel(Location, Day, Num) ]).

proc(bookLocalTranspo(Location, StartDay, ReturnDay),
[       getRide(Location, StartDay, ReturnDay)   |
        walk(Location)     |    bookCar(Location, StartDay, ReturnDay) ]).

proc(bookCityToCityTranspo(Location, Des, StartDay, ReturnDay),
[       getRide(Location, Des, StartDay, ReturnDay) |
        bookAir(Location, Des, StartDay, ReturnDay) |
        bookCar(Location, Des, StartDay, ReturnDay) ]).
```

We tested our GologPref generic procedure with 3 different user profiles: Jack the impoverished university student, Lara the picky frequent flyer, and Conrad the corporate executive who likes timely luxury travel. Each user lived in Toronto and wanted to be in Chicago for specific days. A set of rich user preferences were defined for each user along the lines of those illustrated in Section 3. These preferences often required access to different Web information, such as driving distances. Space precludes listing of the preferences, code and full test results, but these are available at http://www.cs.toronto.edu/~sheila/gologpref/.

Not surprisingly, in all cases, GologPref found the optimal WSC for the user. Compositions varied greatly ranging from Jack who arranged accommodations with friends; checked out the distance to his local destinations and then arranged his local transportation (walking since his local destination was close to where he was staying); then once his accommodations were confirmed, booking an economy air ticket Toronto-Chicago with one stop on US Airways with Expedia. Lara on the other hand, booked a hotel (not Hilton), booked an intermediate-sized car with National, and a direct economy air ticket with Star Alliance partner Air Canada via the Air Canada Web site. The optimality and the diversity of the compositions, all from the same generic procedure, illustrate the flexibility afforded by the WSCP approach.

Figure 2 shows the number of nodes expanded relative to the search space size for 6 test scenarios. The full search space represents all possible combinations of city-to-city transportation, accommodations and local transportation available to the users which could have been considered. These results illustrate the effectiveness of the heuristic used to find optimal compositions.

6 Summary and Related Work

In this paper we argued that the integration of user preferences into Web service composition was a key missing component of Web service composition. Building on our previous framework for Web service composition via generic procedures [1] and our more recent work on preference-based planning [7], we proposed a system for Web service composition with user preferences. Key contributions of this paper include: characterization of the task of Web service composition with

Case Number	Nodes Expanded	Nodes Considered	Time (sec)	Nodes in Full Search Space
1	104	1700	20.97	28,512
2	102	1647	19.93	28,512
3	27	371	2.88	28,512
4	27	368	2.92	28,512
5	99	1692	21.48	28,512
6	108	1761	21.29	28,512

Fig. 2. Test results for 6 scenarios run under Windows XP with a 593MHz processor and 512 MB of RAM. The times shown are five run averages.

generic procedures and user preferences, provision of a previously developed language for specifying user preferences, provision of the GologPref algorithm that integrates preference-based reasoning into Golog, a proof of the soundness and optimality of GologPref with respect to the user's preferences, and a working implementation of our GologPref algorithm. A notable side effect of our framework is the seamless integration of Web service selection with the composition process.

We tested GologPref on 6 diverse scenarios applied to the same generic procedure. Results illustrated the diversity of compositions that could be generated from the same generic procedure. The number of nodes expanded by the heuristic search was several orders of magnitude smaller than the grounded search space, illustrating the effectiveness of the heuristic and the Golog program in guiding search.

A number of researchers have advocated using AI planning techniques to address the task of Web service composition including using regression-based planners [2], planners based on model checking (e.g., [3]), highly optimized hierarchical task network (HTN) planners such as SHOP2 (e.g., [16]), and most recently a combination of classical and HTN planning called XPLAN [12]. Like Golog, HTNs afford the user the ability to define a generic procedure or *template* of how to perform a task.

Recently Sirin et al. incorporated simple service preferences into the SHOP2 HTN planner to achieve dynamic service binding [6]. Their preference language is significantly less expressive than the one presented here and is restricted to the task of service selection rather than solution optimization. Nevertheless, it is a promising start. The most related previous work was performed by Fritz and the third author in which they *precompiled* a subset of the preference language presented here into Golog programs that were then integrated with a decision-theoretic Golog (DTGolog) program [17]. The main objective of this work was to provide a means of integrating qualitative and quantitative preferences for agent programming. While both used a form of Golog, the form and processing of preferences was quite different. We know of no other work integrating preferences into Web service composition. Nevertheless, there is a recent focus on preference-based planning. Early preference-based planners include PPLAN [7] and an approach to preference-based planning using answer set programming [18]. A number of preference-based planners were developed for the 2006 International Planning Competition (IPC-5) and are yet to be published. Preliminary descriptions of these planners can be found at http://zeus.ing.unibs.it/ipc-5/.

Acknowledgements

Thanks to Meghyn Bienvenu for her work on PPLAN which was fundamental to the realization of this work. Thanks to Christian Fritz for useful discussions and to Fetch Technologies for allowing us to use their AgentBuilder software. We also gratefully acknowledge the Natural Sciences and Engineering Research Council of Canada (NSERC) and the CRA's Canadian Distributed Mentorship Project (CDMP) for partially funding this research.

References

1. McIlraith, S., Son, T.C.: Adapting Golog for composition of semantic web services. In: Proceedings of the Eighth International Conference on Knowledge Representation and Reasoning (KR02), Toulouse, France (2002) 482–493
2. McDermott, D.V.: Estimated-regression planning for interactions with web services. In: Proceedings of the Sixth International Conference on AI Planning and Scheduling (AIPS-02). (2002) 204–211
3. Traverso, P., Pistore, M.: Automatic composition of semantic web services into executable processes. In: Proceedings of the Third International Semantic Web Conference (ISWC2004). (2004)
4. McIlraith, S., Son, T., Zeng, H.: Semantic Web services. In: IEEE Intelligent Systems (Special Issue on the Semantic Web). Volume 16. (2001)
5. Reiter, R.: Knowledge in Action: Logical Foundations for Specifying and Implementing Dynamical Systems. MIT Press, Cambridge, MA (2001)
6. Sirin, E., Parsia, B., Wu, D., Hendler, J., Nau, D.: HTN planning for web service composition using SHOP2. Journal of Web Semantics **1**(4) (2005) 377–396
7. Bienvenu, M., Fritz, C., McIlraith, S.: Planning with qualitative temporal preferences. In: Proceedings of the Tenth International Conference on Knowledge Representation and Reasoning (KR06). (2006) 134–144
8. Horrocks, I., Patel-Schneider, P., van Harmelen, F.: From $\mathcal{SHIQ}$ and RDF to OWL: The making of a web ontology language. Journal of Web Semantics **1**(1) (2003) 7–26
9. Martin, D., Burstein, M., McDermott, D., McIlraith, S., Paolucci, M., Sycara, K., McGuinness, D., Sirin, E., Srinivasan, N.: Bringing semantics to web services with owl-s. World Wide Web Journal (2006) To appear.
10. Bruijn, J.D., Lausen, H., Polleres, A., Fensel, D.: The web service modeling language WSML: An overview. Technical report, DERI (2006)
11. Battle, S., Bernstein, A., Boley, H., Grosof, B., and R. Hull, M.G., Kifer, M., Martin, D., McIlraith, S., McGuinness, D., Su, J., Tabet, S.: Semantic web service ontology (SWSO) first-order logic ontology for web services (FLOWS) (2005) http://www.daml.org/services/swsl/report/.

12. Klusch, M., Gerber, A., Schmidt, M.: Semantic web service composition planning with OWLS-Xplan. In: Working notes of the AAAI-05 Fall Symposium on Agents and the Semantic Web, Arlington VA, USA (2005)
13. McIlraith, S.A., Fadel, R.: Planning with complex actions. In: 9th International Workshop on Non-Monotonic Reasoning (NMR), Toulouse, France (2002) 356–364
14. Narayanan, S., McIlraith, S.: Simulation, verification and automated composition of web services. In: Proceedings of the Eleventh International World Wide Web Conference (WWW-2002). (2002)
15. de Giacomo, G., Lespérance, Y., Levesque, H.: ConGolog, a concurrent programming language based on the situation calculus. Artificial Intelligence **121**(1–2) (2000) 109–169
16. Sirin, E., Parsia, B., Hendler, J.: Template-based composition of semantic web services. In: Working notes of the AAAI-05 Fall Symposium on Agents and the Semantic Web. (2005)
17. Fritz, C., McIlraith, S.: Decision-theoretic GOLOG with qualitative preferences. In: Proceedings of the Tenth International Conference on Principles of Knowledge Representation and Reasoning (KR06). (2006)
18. Son, T., Pontelli, E.: Planning with preferences using logic programming (2007) Theory and Practice of Logic Programming. To appear.

Querying the Semantic Web with Preferences

Wolf Siberski[1], Jeff Z. Pan[2], and Uwe Thaden[1]

[1] L3S and University of Hannover, Hannover
{siberski, thaden}@l3s.de
[2] University of Aberdeen
jpan@csd.abdn.ac.uk

Abstract. Ranking is an important concept to avoid empty or overfull and unordered result sets. However, such scoring can only express total orders, which restricts its usefulness when several factors influence result relevance. A more flexible way to express relevance is the notion of preferences. Users state which kind of answers they 'prefer' by adding soft constraints to their queries.

Current approaches in the Semantic Web offer only limited facilities for specification of scoring and result ordering. There is no common language element to express and formalize ranking and preferences. We present a comprehensive extension of SPARQL which directly supports the expression of preferences. This includes formal syntax and semantics of preference expressions for SPARQL. Additionally, we report our implementation of preference query processing, which is based on the ARQ query engine.

Keywords: preferences, query language, semantic web.

1 Introduction

With the abundance of available information, the issue of information filtering becomes more and more pressing. Instead of receiving empty or possibly huge and unordered result sets, users want to get just a manageable set of 'best' answers, which satisfy the query best, even if there are no exact matches.

As widely established in information retrieval and other areas, ranking has shown to be useful to improve the quality of result lists. As more and more Semantic Web applications emerge, this aspects gains importance for the information available in that context. However, the current Web solutions for 'best' answers are not easily applicable to this new context. User queries usually consist of a set of words that have to appear in the document and/or in some metadata of the documents. The support for structured search is very limited; only very first steps in the direction of integrating structured information, such as taxonomies, have been taken.

On the other hand, the benefit of introducing the 'best match' notion has already been identified for several Semantic Web applications (e.g., [1,2,3]). For example, Bibster [3] allows to search for publications by topic and ranks results according to their similarity to the requested topic. However, the preferences used in these systems typically apply to specific properties, and hard-coded, unmodifiable scoring functions are used.

The same issue has been tackled in database research in the last years. Top-k queries have been introduced which allow to identify the 'best matches' according to a numerical score [4]. Skyline queries have extended this notion to contexts where multiple independent scores have to be taken into account [5]. The most general notion developed in the database area is the notion of *preference-based querying* [6,7], where logic formulas can be used to specify which items are preferred.

Preference queries are based on the observation that expressions of the form "I like A more than B" are easily stated by users when asked for their wishes. For example, when buying a car, it is easy for one to say which colors he prefers, that he likes cars more for which he has to pay less, that he likes automatic transmission more than manual gear change, etc. Therefore, it should be optimal if a query engine can derive best matches directly from such preference expressions.

The notion of preference is very important in the Semantic Web context, too. Actually, we show in Section 2 that the motivating example from the seminal Semantic Web article [8] written by Tim Berners-Lee et al. can in fact be easily interpreted as preference-based search. A variety of potential Semantic Web applications can benefit from preference queries, e.g. advanced document search or service matchmaking (cf. Section 6).

Therefore, we propose to add preference-based querying capabilities to Semantic Web query languages. As SPARQL is currently the most important of these query languages, we have used it as basis to formally integrate and implement such capabilities as language extension.

2 Motivating Example

In this section we revisit the motivating scenario from [8] in detail. We use this example to show how preferences fit into the Semantic Web vision, and what is needed to specify preferences as part of a query in an informal fashion.

Let us first summarize the scenario: Lucy and Pete are looking for suitable appointments at a physical therapist for their Mom[1]. They have some hard constraints for their search with respect to therapist rating, location, etc., which are not relevant in our context. We therefore only keep the constraint that the therapist's rating must be *very good* or *excellent*.

When Pete sees the first answer to this search, it turns out that there are also some soft constraints he did not consider yet. Therefore, he has to reformulate his query with "stricter preferences". The following preferences can be identified:

1. prefer a nearer therapist over one more far away.
2. prefer *excellent* therapists over *very good* ones.
3. prefer an appointment which does not overlap with the rush hour.
4. prefer appointments with a late starting time over early ones, to avoid the necessity to leave during the work hours.

If these preferences would be expressed as hard constraints, this would most likely lead to an empty result set, because it happens rarely that a result matches exactly to the optimal values with respect to each single preference in the query. The usual case is a trade-off, i.e. results optimal with respect to one dimension tend to have disadvantages

---
[1] Note that here we do not aim at providing an agent environment as sketched in [8].

in other dimensions. Therefore, a user would have to adapt to the system and relax his query manually (typically by try and error), until some suitable results are found.

Furthermore, in multidimensional queries a user normally is not able to prioritize his different preferences, since he does not know how this will affect the outcome. Is it more important to to have a nearby appointment or is it more important to avoid rush-hour? Is it more important to have an excellent therapist, or more important to get a late appointment? Typically these trade-offs are not weighed by the user in advance, but only when he sees the different options with their concrete advantages and disadvantages. Therefore, it has to be possible to specify multiple (independent) preference dimensions. Note that with current Semantic Web query languages such as SPARQL this is not possible (cf. Section 3.2).

To specify the mentioned preferences, we need atomic preference expressions and facilities for combination. For atomic preferences, two types can be distinguished:

- *Boolean preferences* expressed by a boolean condition (preference 2 and 3 from the example). Results satisfying that condition are preferred over results which do not satisfy it.
- *Scoring preferences* specified by a value expression (preferences 1 and 4) . Results for which this expression leads to a higher value are preferred over results with a lower value (rsp. the other way round).

While we do not want to force the user to prioritize all of his preferences, for some preferences it might be desired to specify priorities. For example, it might be more important to Pete to avoid rush hour than to get a late appointment. Therefore we need two different ways to combine preferences, one for *independent* preferences and one for *prioritized* ones.

Now we take a look at what results a user would actually expect for given preferences. To simplify the presentation, we omit some hard constraints and preferences of the example, and continue with a reduced query:

Return all excellent and very good therapists, with the following preferences:
    Prefer excellent therapists over very good ones (preference 2).
    Prefer appointments outside rush hour over appointments overlapping it
    (preference 3).
      Prefer the later appointment over an earlier one, if both are equal
      with respect to rush hour (preference 4).

Note that this removes no complexity with respect to preference specification.

A sample knowledge base on which the query can be executed is shown in Figure 1. Physical therapists have an associated rating and associated appointments. Appointments have start and end time.

Based on this knowledge base, let us analyze what a user would expect as results. Definitely, he does not want to get any result A which is worse than another one B with respect to one preference dimension, and not better in any other dimension. If this is the case, we say that A is *dominated* by B. The interesting results are therefore those which are *not* dominated by others.

We assume that rush hour is from 16:00 to 18:00. Then, as Figure 2 shows, the non-dominated results are *appointment1* and *appointment5*. *appointment1* is in every preference dimension better or equal to *appointment2* and *appointment3*. The same

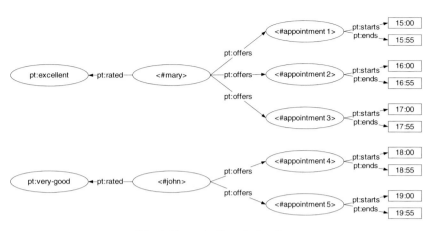

Fig. 1. Example Knowledge Base

applies to *appointment5* with respect to *appointment4*. The hatched regions denote the domination areas of these results: all answers lying in these areas are dominated and thus not optimal. On the other hand, *appointment1* and *appointment5* can't dominate each other, because *appointment1* is better with respect to rating, but *appointment5* is superior with respect to appointment time. Therefore, these two should be returned as result to the user.

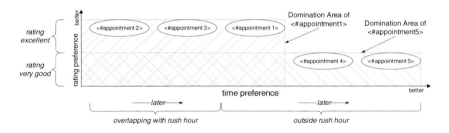

Fig. 2. Appointment Preference Relations

We will show in Section 3.2 what part of the requirements derived from the example SPARQL can cover, and pick up the scenario to illustrate our proposed language extension in Section 4.

3 Background

3.1 Querying with Preferences

Preferences have one of their origins in decision theory, as a way to support complex, multifactorial decision processes [9]. Another important source are personalized systems (e.g. [10]), where preferences capture a users likings and dislikes. In databases, this thread was picked up by Lacroix and Lavency [11].

Following Chomicki [7], we distinguish between quantitative and qualitative approaches to preferences. In quantitative approaches, each preference is associated with an atomic scoring function, and combination operations are used to compute a score for each result tuple [12]. This restricts the approach to total orderings of result tuples. Top-k queries return the k best matches according to such a score [4]. A formal extension of relational algebra by a specific top-k operator has been proposed in [13]. The qualitative approach is more general than the quantitative one. It does not impose a total order on the result tuples, but allows treating preferences independently, which results in a partial preference order. For relational databases, the qualitative approach has been formalized independently by Kießling [6] and Chomicki [7].

In the following we rely on Chomicki's preference query formalization [7]. In this extension to relational algebra, preferences are expressed as binary relations between tuples from the same database relation. The central concept is the notion of domination (as introduced informally in the previous section).

Definition 1. *Given a relation schema $R(A_1, \ldots, A_n)$ such that U_i, $1 \leq i \leq n$, is the domain of the attribute A_i, a relation $\succ$ is a* preference relation *over R if it is a subset of $(U_1 \times \cdots \times U_n) \times (U_1 \times \cdots \times U_n)$. A result tuple t_1 is said to be dominated by t_2, if $t_1 \succ t_2$.*

We restrict this very general notion to relations that are defined by so-called *intrinsic preference formulas*, first order logic expressions in which a limited set of constraint operators occur.

Definition 2. *Given a relation schema R, an intrinisic preference formula $C(t_1, t_2)$ is a first order formula over two tuples of R which only uses equality and rational order $(<, >)$ constraints. Such a preference formula C defines a preference relation $\succ_C$: $t_1 \succ_C t_2 \equiv C(t_1, t_2)$.*

For a more convenient notation, we introduce an additional operator to denote incomparability between two result tuples.

Definition 3. *Given a preference formula C and two tuples t_1 and t_2, the incomparability operator $\sim_C$ is defined as*
$$t_1 \sim_C t_2 \equiv t_1 \not\succ_C t_2 \wedge t_2 \not\succ_C t_1.$$
If t_1 either dominates t_2 or is incomparable with it, this is denoted as
$$t_1 \succeq_C t_2 \equiv t_1 \succ_C t_2 \vee t_1 \sim_C t_2.$$

Now we can define the new operator, called *winnow operator*, that selects all non-dominated objects from a set of tuples.

Definition 4. *If R is a relation schema and C a preference formula defining a preference relation $\succ_C$ over R, the winnow operator ω_C is defined as $\omega_C(R)$, and for every instance r of R:*
$$\omega_C(r) = \{t \in r | \neg \exists t' \in r.\ t' \succ_C t\}.$$

ω_C therefore selects all non-dominated objects from a set of tuples. In Section 4, we show how to apply these concepts for our extension of SPARQL.

3.2 Ontology Querying

An *ontology* [14] typically consists of a set of important classes, important properties, and constraints about these classes and properties. An ontology language provides some constructors to construct class and property descriptions based on named classes and properties, as well as some forms of axioms about classes, properties and individuals. For example, RDFS [15] provides some axioms (such as domain and range axioms), but no class or property constructors. OWL DL [16] provides class constructors (e.g. conjunction $C \sqcap D$ and number restriction $\leqslant n\, R$), property constructors (e.g. inverse properties R^-) and more kinds of axioms (such as individual equality axioms a $\approx$ b) than RDFS. Furthermore, OWL DL distinguishes *individual* properties (properties relating individuals to individuals) from *datatype* properties (properties relating individual to data literals). Data literals are literal forms of data values. Due to space limitation, the reader is referred to [15] and [16] for details of the RDFS and OWL DL languages, respectively.

A conjunctive query (CQ) q is of the form

$$q(X) \leftarrow \exists Y.conj(X,Y,Z)$$

or simply $q(X) \leftarrow conj(X,Y,Z)$, where $q(X)$ is called the head, $conj(X,Y,Z)$ is called the body, X are called the distinguished variables, Y are existentially quantified variables called the non-distinguished variables, Z are individual names or data literals, and $conj(X,Y,Z)$ is a conjunction of atoms of the form $C(v)$, $r(v_1,v_2)$, $s(v,t)$, or $\mathrm{E}(t_1,\ldots,t_n)$, where C, r, s, E are respectively classes, object properties, datatype properties and datatype built-ins, v, v_1 and v_2 are *individual* variables in X and Y or individual names in Z, and t, $t_1,\ldots,t_n$ are *data* variables in X and Y or data literals in Z. As usual, an interpretation $\mathcal{I}$ satisfies an ontology $\mathcal{O}$ if it satisfies all the axioms in $\mathcal{O}$; in this case, we say $\mathcal{I}$ is a model of $\mathcal{O}$. Given an evaluation $[X \mapsto S]$, if every model $\mathcal{I}$ of $\mathcal{O}$ satisfies $q_{[X \mapsto S]}$, we say $\mathcal{O}$ entails $q_{[X \mapsto S]}$; in this case, S is called a *solution* of q. A solution sequence $\mathbf{S} = (S_1,\ldots,S_n)$ is a list of solutions. A disjunctive query (DQ) is a set of conjunctive queries sharing the same head.

SPARQL. SPARQL [17] is a query language (W3C candidate recommendation) for getting information from such RDF graphs. It introduces a notion of *E-entailment regime*, which is a binary relation between subsets of RDF graphs. The default SPARQL setting is simple entailment [18]; examples of other E-entailment regime are RDF entailment [18], RDFS entailment [18] and OWL entailment [18].

SPARQL provides *solution modifiers* which allow to transform the solution list derived from a CQ in several ways. The following solution modifiers are available: Distinct, Order, Limit and Offset. Here is the SPARQL syntax for the last three solution modifiers.

```
SolutionModifier::= OrderClause? LimitClause? OffsetClause?
OrderClause      ::= 'ORDER' 'BY' OrderCondition+
OrderCondition   ::= ( ( 'ASC' | 'DESC' ) '(' Expression ')' ) |
                     ( FunctionCall | Var | '(' Expression ')')
LimitClause      ::= 'LIMIT' INTEGER
OffsetClause     ::= 'OFFSET' INTEGER
```

Distinct. The Distinct solution sequence modifier D (used in the SELECT clause) ensures solutions in the sequence are unique; i.e., $D(\mathbf{S}) = \mathbf{S}' = (S'_1, \ldots, S'_k)$ so that $\{S'_1, \ldots, S'_k\} \subseteq \{S_1, \ldots, S_n\}$ and $S'_i \neq S'_j$ for all $1 \leq i < j \leq k$.

OrderClause. The Order solution sequence modifier O applies ordering conditions to a solution sequence, and thus provides a limited form of preference expressions. An ordering condition can be a variable or a function call, and it can be explicitly set to ascending or descending by enclosing the condition in ASC() or DESC() respectively.[2] In general, an expression is a disjunctive normal form of numeric expression (see [17] for details) but typically is a variable. Given an order condition C, we have $O(\mathbf{S}, C) = \mathbf{S}' = (S'_1, \ldots, S'_n)$ so that $\{S'_1, \ldots, S'_n\} = \{S_1, \ldots, S_n\}$ and $S'_i \succeq_C S'_j$ or $S'_i \sim_C S'_j$ for all $1 \leq i < j \leq n$. We say that S'_i dominates S'_j w.r.t. C if $S'_i \succ_C S'_j$ holds. The semantics of multiple order conditions (ORDER BY C_1, C_2, ...) are treated as prioritised composition (cf. 4.2):

$$S'_i \succ_{C_1, C_2} S'_j \equiv S'_i \succ_{C_1} S'_j \vee (S'_i \sim_{C_1} S'_j \wedge S'_i \succ_{C_2} S'_j)$$

i.e., ordering according to C_2 unless C_1 is applicable. To sum up, with the OrderingClause SPARQL supports only unidimensional (prioritized) composition of ordering expressions.

LimitClause. The Limit solution sequence modifier L puts an upper bound m on the number of solutions returned; i.e., $L(\mathbf{S}, m) = \mathbf{S}' = (S_1, \ldots, S_k)$ where $k = m$ if $n \geq m$ and $k = n$ otherwise.

OffsetClause. The Offset solution sequence modifier OS causes the solutions generated to start after the specified number of solutions; i.e., $OS(\mathbf{S}, m) = \mathbf{S}' = (S_m, \ldots, S_n)$, where $m \leq n$, and $OS(\mathbf{S}, m) = \mathbf{S}' = ()$, otherwise. The combination of the Order, Limit and Offset solution sequence modifiers can result in returning partial results.

Example. Now let us take a look at what we can achieve with respect to the example from Section 2 using the current solution modifiers. As we cannot specify independent preferences, we have to decide for either rating preference or time preference. Here, we show the query for the latter:

```
PREFIX pt: <http://physical-therapists.org/schema>

SELECT ?t ?app ?start ?end ?rating
WHERE ?t pt:offers-appointment ?app .
    ?t pt:rating ?rating .
    ?app pt:starts ?start .
    ?app pt:ends ?end .
    ?t pt:has-rating ?rating
FILTER (?rating = pt:very-good || ?rating = pt:excellent) .
ORDER BY DESC(?end <= '16' || ?start >= '18' ) DESC(?start)
```

---

[2] The default is ascending.

As we can see, expression of prioritized preferences is possible using several order conditions. In contrast to the discussion in Section 2, the shown query will also return dominated appointments, but only at the bottom of the solution list.

4 Preference-Based Querying for SPARQL

In this section, we will introduce our formal extension of SPARQL solution modifiers to support the kind of preference that we need in ontology querying answering. For illustrative purposes we start with an informal description of our sample preference query according to the proposed extension:

```
1 SELECT ?t, ?app
2 WHERE {?t pt:offers-appointment ?app .
3        ?t pt:has-rating ?rating .
4        ?app pt:starts ?start .
5        ?app pt:ends ?end .
6 FILTER (?rating = pt:very-good || ?rating = pt:excellent)}
7 PREFERRING
8        ?rating = pt:excellent
9      AND
10       (?end <= '16:00' || ?start >= 18:00)
11          CASCADE HIGHEST(?start)
```

Line 1–6 of the query contains the solution pattern and hard constraints, defined as usual. The PREFERRING keyword on line 7 starts the preference definition. Line 8 specifies that results where *?rating = pt:excellent* is true are preferred over the ones where this is not the case. The 'AND' keyword (line 9) is used to separate independent preference dimensions. The *avoid rush hour* preference is expressed in line 10, and line 11 contains the the *late appointment* preference. The 'CASCADE' keyword expresses that the left-hand preference (*avoid rush hour*) takes priority over the right hand preference (*late appointment*).

4.1 The *Preferring* Solution Sequence Modifier

Now we extend SPARQL with a new *Preferring* solution sequence modifier, in order to facilitate the representation of preference motivated by the examples presented in Section 2. Our extension covers the following two features:

1. Skyline queries: find all the solutions that are *not* dominated by any other solutions.
2. Soft constraints: Preferably return only the solutions that satisfy all the (hard and soft) constraints; otherwise, relax some or all soft constraints and return only the best answers.

In our extension, preference is a first-class construct in the query language. The extended SPARQL syntax is listed below.

```
SolutionModifier ::= PreferringClause? OrderClause? LimitClause?
                     OffsetClause?
PreferringClause ::= 'PREFERRING' MultidimensionalPreference
MultidimensionalPreference ::= CascadedPreference
```

```
                      ('AND' CascadedPreference)*
CascadedPreference ::= AtomicPreference
                      ('CASCADE' AtomicPreference)*
AtomicPreference   ::= BooleanPreference
                      | HighestPreference | LowestPreference
BooleanPreference  ::= Expression
HighestPreference  ::= 'HIGHEST' Expression
LowestPreference   ::= 'LOWEST' Expression
```

Intuitively, users can specify preferences that do not overwrite each other, by using the Preferring clauses with the definitions independent preference separated by the 'AND' construct. In each of these dimensions, atomic preferences can be nested using the 'CASCADE' construct. Here, the leftmost part of the preference expression is evaluated first, and only if two solutions are equal with respect to this part, the next atomic preference expression is evaluated.

4.2 Semantics of the *Preferring* Modifier

Formally, we define the semantics of atomic and combined preference relations, as follows:

Boolean preferences. Boolean preferences are specified by a boolean expression BE. For any solutions S_i and S_j, the domination relation for such a preference, $\succ_{C_{BE}}$ is defined as

$$S_i \succ_{C_{BE}} S_j \equiv BE(S_i) \land \neg BE(S_j).$$

Scoring preferences. They are specified by an expression which evaluates to a number or a value in other SPARQL domains that have total ordering. For such an ordering $<$ and any solutions S_i and S_j, the domination relation $\succ_{C_{LOWEST,<}}$ is defined as

$$S_i \succ_{C_{LOWEST,<}} S_j \equiv S_i < S_j,$$

and $\succ_{C_{HIGHEST,<}}$ is defined as

$$S_i \succ_{C_{HIGHEST,<}} S_j \equiv S_j < S_i.$$

Multidimensional Preferences. For any solutions S_i and S_j, the domination relation to combine independent preferences $\succ_{[C_1 \text{ AND } C_2]}$ is defined as

$$S_i \succ_{[C_1 \text{ AND } C_2]} S_j \equiv S_i \succeq_{C_1} S_j \land S_i \succeq_{C_2} S_j \land (S_i \succ_{C_1} S_j \lor S_i \succ_{C_2} S_j).$$

Intuitively, this says that S_i is dominated by S_j in neither C_1 nor C_2, and that S_i dominates S_j in either C_1 or C_2.

CascadedPreference. For any solutions S_i and S_j, the domination relation to combine prioritized preferences $\succ_{[C_1 \text{ CASCADE } C_2]}$ is defined as

$S_i \succ_{[C_1 \text{ CASCADE } C_2]} S_j \equiv S_i \succ_{C_1} S_j \vee (S_i \sim_{C_1} S_j \wedge S_i \succ_{C_2} S_j).$

With these definitions, we can now define the preferring solution modifier PS: Given a domination relation C, $PS(\mathbf{S}, C) = \mathbf{S}' = (S'_1, \ldots, S'_n)$ so that, for any $S'_i \in \mathbf{S}'$, there exists no $S_j \in \mathbf{S}$ such that $S_j \succ_C S'_i$. Thus, the solution modifier PS gives us exactly the non-dominated solutions in $\mathbf{S}$.

Depending on the given preferences and solutions, PS may deliver just one (the best) solution. We iteratively define the next best solutions as follows:

$PS^1(\mathbf{S}, C) = PS(\mathbf{S}, C)$
$PS^{n+1}(\mathbf{S}, C) = concat\,(PS^n(\mathbf{S}, C), PS(\mathbf{S} \setminus PS^n(\mathbf{S}, C), C))$

When combined with the LIMIT k solution modifier, n is selected such that $|PS^n(\mathbf{S}, C)| > k$.

5 Implementation

As a proof of concept, the SPARQL implementation ARQ [19] has been extended. ARQ is based on a query operator approach, where an operator class is implemented for each solution modifier. This architecture allows to plug in additional solution modifiers easily. Query processing in ARQ is a three-stage process (see 'Query Engine' in Fig. 3):

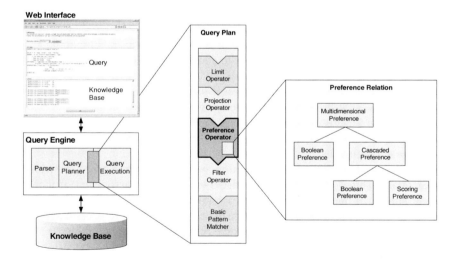

Fig. 3. ARQ Query Engine with Sample Query Plan and Preference Expression

First, the query is *parsed* and converted into an internal representation. To enable preference handling for this step, productions according to the syntax specified in the previous section have been added to the parser. Preference expression classes which are responsible for evaluating the different preference constructs have been implemented. The extended parser instantiates objects from these classes and assembles them to a preference relation representation (see right-hand side of Fig. 3).

Second, ARQ creates a *query plan* for each incoming query, consisting of accordingly chained operators. Such an operator for preference handling, has been added which which contains the algorithm for determining dominating objects, based on the given preference relation representation. The structure of an example query plan is shown in the middle of Fig. 3. The planning algorithm has been extended to insert the preference operator into the plan if a preference clause is present.

Finally, the query is *executed* on the given knowledge base. During this execution, the preference operator filters all dominated solutions. In our prototype, we use the BNL (Blocked Nested Loop) algorithm [5] for this purpose. The computation of the preference relation is delegated to its representation which was generated during query planning.

The ARQ query engine interface can be used by applications as before, and we have implemented a Web interface to test applications of our extension which calls the modified query engine to evaluate preference queries.[3]

6 Related Work

Most of the approaches that deal with ranking in the Semantic Web offer very specific (hard-coded) ways to specify some of the properties and scoring functions, which are not editable by the users.

Bibster [3] is a system for storing and sharing information about publications. It allows to search for publications by topic and uses a very specific and unmodifiable preference function, which makes it impossible to define scores and constraints on arbitrary properties.

More domain dependent is the Textpresso-system [1], a system that allows for ontology-based search for biological literature. Textpresso focuses on optimized ontology-creation for this domain. Querying can be done combining fulltext and concept search, i.e., using known associations or the combination of concepts. Explicit rankings are not definable.

Aleman-Meza et al. [20] present a ranking approach which is based on measuring complex relationships. Two entities are related (semantically associated) if there is at least one binding property. They present several ways to rank the complex relationships, but also do not propose a query language extension. A more general approach is the Corese Search Engine [2], a search engine based on conceptual graphs. It is based on RDF, and its expressivity is comparable to RQL or SqishQL. The extension for approximate search is not done by extending one of the existing query languages but is designed as a completely new language.

A more flexible solution is proposed in [21]. Here, the way in which a result of a query is derived is used to rank the results of that query (based on how the results "relate"). The relevance is defined on the level of the relation instances, while the

---

[3] available at `http://prefs.l3s.uni-hannover.de`

results are a set of concept instances. The scoring functions used are in IR-style, but not definable by the user.

The only approach known to the authors that also extends a query language is Imprecise RDQL [22]. This approach introduces the concept of similarity to enable ranking on arbitrary properties. Their idea of similarity joins is based on the work of [23]. The specification of soft constraints is still rather limited: IMPRECISE defines the variable that shouldn't be matched exactly. The measure to be used for an imprecise variable is specified by the SIMMEASURE clause, but the measures which can be used are constrained to a set of predefined metrics which the authors defined in a library. Furthermore, like the previous approaches Imprecise RDQL offers only scoring for one dimension.

Often, users won't express their preferences directly, but the application might infer preferences from a user profile or other context information, and amend an explicit query accordingly (e.g. [24]). Various techniques for preference mining and elicitation have already been developed, e.g. [25,26], which can be used in Semantic Web applications as well.

7 Conclusion

In this paper we showed that ranking and preferences as established concepts in relational databases also play an important role in querying the Semantic Web. We discussed why preferences are needed and how this concept can be transferred to Semantic Web query languages such as SPARQL. The presented formal model can be used as unifying framework for of a wide variety of ranking specifications. Finally, we described our ARQ implementation of the SPARQL extension. Thus, the solution presented here provides the basis for combining the strengths of logic-based precise querying and benefits of ranking-based retrieval.

References

1. Müller, H., Kenny, E., Sternberg, P.: Textpresso: An ontology-based information retrieval and extraction system for biological literature. PLoS Biol **2** (2004)
2. Corby, O., Dieng-Kuntz, R., Faron-Zucker, C.: Querying the semantic web with corese search engine. In: Proceedings of the 16th Eureopean Conference on Artificial Intelligence (ECAI). (2004) 705–709
3. Haase, P., Broekstra, J., Ehrig, M., Menken, M., Mika, P., Olko, M., Plechawski, M., Pyszlak, P., Schnizler, B., Siebes, R., Staab, S., Tempich, C.: Bibster – a semantics-based bibliographic peer-to-peer system. In: Proceedings of 3rd International Semantic Web Conference (ISWC). (2004) 122 – 136
4. Fagin, R., Lotem, A., Naor, M.: Optimal aggregation algorithms for middleware. In: Proceedings of the Twentieth ACM SIGACT-SIGMOD-SIGART Symposium on Principles of Database Systems (PODS), Santa Barbara, California, USA (2001)
5. Börzsönyi, S., Kossmann, D., Stocker, K.: The skyline operator. In: Proceedings of the 17th International Conference on Data Engineering (ICDE), Heidelberg, Germany (2001) 421–430

6. Kießling, W.: Foundations of preferences in database systems. In: Proceedings of the 28th International Conference on Very Large Data Bases (VLDB), Hong Kong, China (2002) 311–322
7. Chomicki, J.: Preference formulas in relational queries. ACM Trans. Database Syst. **28** (2003) 427–466
8. Berners-Lee, T., Hendler, J., Lassila, O.: The semantic web. Scientific American (2001)
9. Fishburn, P.C.: Utility Theory for Decision Making. Wiley, New York (1970)
10. Riecken, D.: Introduction: personalized views of personalization. Commun. ACM **43** (2000) 26–28 (Introduction to Special Issue on Personalization).
11. Lacroix, M., Lavency, P.: Preferences; putting more knowledge into queries. In: Proceedings of 13th International Conference on Very Large Data Bases (VLDB), Brighton, UK (1987) 217–225
12. Agrawal, R., Wimmers, E.L.: A framework for expressing and combining preferences. In: Proceedings of the ACM SIGMOD International Conference on Management of Data (SIGMOD), Dallas, TX, USA (2000) 297–306
13. Li, C., Soliman, M.A., Chang, K.C.C., Ilyas, I.F.: Ranksql: Supporting ranking queries in relational database management systems. In: Proceedings of the 31st International Conference on Very Large Data Bases (VLDB), Trondheim, Norway (2005) 1342–1345
14. Uschold, M., Gruninger, M.: Ontologies: Principles, Methods and Applications. The Knowledge Engineering Review (1996)
15. Brickley, D., Guha, R.: RDF Vocabulary Description Language 1.0: RDF Schema (2004) W3C recommendation, http://www.w3.org/TR/rdf-schema/.
16. Patel-Schneider, P.F., Hayes, P., Horrocks, I.: OWL Web Ontology Language Semantics and Abstract Syntax (2004) W3C Recommendation, http://www.w3.org/TR/owl-semantics/.
17. Prud'hommeaux, E., Seaborne, A.: SPARQL query language for RDF (2006) W3C Candidate Recommendation, http://www.w3.org/TR/rdf-sparql-query/.
18. Hayes, P.: RDF Semantics (2004) W3C recommendation, http://www.w3.org/TR/rdf-mt/.
19. Seaborne, A.: An open source implementation of SPARQL (2006) WWW2006 Developers track presentation, http://www2006.org/programme/item.php?id=d18.
20. Aleman-Meza, B., Halaschek-Wiener, C., Arpinar, I.B., Ramakrishnan, C., Sheth, A.P.: Ranking complex relationships on the semantic web. IEEE Internet Computing **9** (2005) 37–44
21. Stojanovic, N.: An approach for defining relevance in the ontology-based information retrieval. In: Proceedings of the International Conference on Web Intelligence (WI), Compiegne, France (2005) 359–365
22. Bernstein, A., Kiefer, C.: Imprecise RDQL: Towards Generic Retrieval in Ontologies Using Similarity Joins. In: 21th Annual ACM Symposium on Applied Computing (SAC), New York, NY, USA, ACM Press (2006)
23. Cohen, W.W.: Data integration using similarity joins and a word-based information representation language. ACM Trans. Inf. Syst. **18** (2000) 288–321
24. Dolog, P., Henze, N., Nejdl, W., Sintek, M.: The personal reader: Personalizing and enriching learning resources using semantic web technologies. In: Proceedings of the Third International Conference on Adaptive Hypermedia and Adaptive Web-Based Systems (AH), Eindhoven, Netherlands (2004) 85–94
25. Sai, Y., Yao, Y., Zhong, N.: Data analysis and mining in ordered information tables. In: Proceedings of the International Conference on Data Mining (ICDM), San Jose, CA, USA (2001) 497–504
26. Blum, A., Jackson, J.C., Sandholm, T., Zinkevich, M.: Preference elicitation and query learning. Journal of Machine Learning Research **5** (2004) 649–667

ONTOCOM: A Cost Estimation Model for Ontology Engineering

Elena Paslaru Bontas Simperl[1], Christoph Tempich[2], and York Sure[2]

[1] Free University of Berlin, Takustr. 9, 14195 Berlin, Germany
paslaru@inf.fu-berlin.de
[2] Institute AIFB, University of Karlsruhe, 76128 Karlsruhe, Germany
{tempich, sure}@aifb.uni-karlsruhe.de

Abstract. The technical challenges associated with the development and deployment of ontologies have been subject to a considerable number of research initiatives since the beginning of the nineties. The economical aspects of these processes are, however, still poorly exploited, impeding the dissemination of ontology-driven technologies beyond the boundaries of the academic community. This paper aims at contributing to the alleviation of this situation by proposing ONTOCOM (Ontology Cost Model), a model to predict the costs arising in ontology engineering processes. We introduce a methodology to generate a cost model adapted to a particular ontology development strategy, and an inventory of cost drivers which influence the amount of effort invested in activities performed during an ontology life cycle. We further present the results of the model validation procedure, which covered an expert-driven evaluation and a statistical calibration on 36 data points collected from real-world projects. The validation revealed that ontology engineering processes have a high learning rate, indicating that the building of very large ontologies is feasible from an economic point of view. Moreover, the complexity of ontology evaluation, domain analysis and conceptualization activities proved to have a major impact on the final ontology engineering process duration.

1 Introduction

The popularity of ontologies grows with the emergence of the Semantic Web. Nevertheless, their large scale dissemination – in particular beyond the boundaries of the academic community – is inconceivable in the absence of methods which address the *economic* challenges of ontology engineering processes in addition to the *technical* and *organizational* ones. A wide range of ontology engineering methodologies have been elaborated in the Semantic Web community [6]. They define ontology development as a well-structured process, which shows major similarities with established models from the neighboring area of software engineering. Unlike adjacent engineering disciplines these methodologies, however, ignore the economic aspects of engineering processes, which are fundamental in real-world business contexts. Topics such as costs estimation, quality assurance procedures, process maturity models, or means to monitor the business value and the impact of semantic technologies at corporate level have been marginally exploited so far.

This paper aims at contributing to the alleviation of this situation. We introduce ONTOCOM (Ontology Cost Model), a model for predicting the costs related to ontology engineering processes. In this context we describe a *methodology* to generate a cost model suitable for particular ontology development strategies, and an inventory of *cost drivers* for which we demonstrate to have a direct impact on the amount of effort invested during an ontology life cycle. ONTOCOM has been subject to an extensive validation procedure. This covered two phases: an expert-driven evaluation and a statistical calibration, which adjusted the predictions of the model according to 36 data points collected from empirical ontology engineering processes.

The remaining of this paper is organized as follows: Section 2 examines general-purpose cost estimation methods w.r.t. their relevance for the ontology engineering field. Building upon the results of this analysis Section 3 gives a detailed description of the ONTOCOM cost prediction model and explains how it can be applied to arbitrary ontology engineering processes. Section 4 discusses the results of the evaluation. We conclude the paper with related and future work (Section 5).

2 Cost Estimation Methodologies

In order to reliably approximate the development efforts the engineering team needs to specify a method for cost estimation in accordance with the particularities of the current project as regarding product, personnel and process aspects. This specification task can be accomplished either by building a new cost model with the help of dedicated methodologies or by adapting existing general-purpose ones to the characteristics of a specific setting.

Due to its high relevance in real-world situations cost estimation is approached by a wide range of methods, often used in conjunction in business context due to their optimal applicability to particular classes of situations. We give an overview of some of the most important ones [1,10,15]:

1) Analogy Method. The main idea of this method is the extrapolation of available data from similar projects to estimate the costs of the proposed project. The method is suitable in situations where empirical data from previous projects is available and trustworthy. It highly depends on the accuracy in establishing real differences between completed and current projects.

2) Bottom-Up Method. This method involves identifying and estimating costs of individual project components separately and subsequently combining the outcomes to produce an estimation for the overall project. It can not be applied early in the life cycle of the process because of the lack of necessary information related to the project components. Nevertheless since the costs to be estimated are related to more manageable work units, the method is likely to produce more accurate results than the other approaches.

3) Top-Down Method. This method relies on overall project parameters. For this purpose the project is partitioned top-down into lower-level components and life cycle phases (so-called *work breakdown structures* [1,10]). The method is applicable to early cost estimates when only global properties are known, but it can be less accurate due to the decreased focus on lower-level parameters and technical challenges. These are usually predictable later in the process life cycle, at most.

4) Expert Judgment/Delphi Method. This approach is based on a structured process for collecting and distilling knowledge from a group of human experts by means of a series of questionnaires interspersed with controlled opinion feedback. The involvement of human experts using their past project experiences is a significant advantage of this approach. The most extensive critique point is related to the subjectivity of the estimations and the difficulties to explicitly state the decision criteria used by the contributors.

5) Parametric/Algorithmic Method. This method involves the usage of mathematical equations based on research and previous project data. The method analyzes main cost drivers of a specific class of projects and their dependencies, and uses statistical techniques to adjust the corresponding formulas. The generation of a proved and tested cost model using the parametric method is directly related to the availability of reliable project data to be used in calibrating the model.

Given the current state of the art in ontology engineering the **top-down**, **parametric** and **expert-based** methods form a viable basis for the development of a cost estimation model in this field.[1] A combination of the three is considered in many established engineering disciplines as a feasible means to reach a balance between the low amount of reliable historical data and the accuracy of the cost estimations [1,15]. The work breakdown structure for ontology engineering is to a great extent described by existing ontology engineering methodologies. Further on, the cost drivers associated with the parametric method can be derived from the high number of case studies available in the literature. The limited amount of accurate empirical data can be counterbalanced by taking into account the significant body of expert knowledge available in the Semantic Web community. The next section describes how the three methods were jointly applied to create ONTOCOM.

3 The ONTOCOM Model

The cost estimation model is realized in three steps. First a *top-down* work breakdown structure for ontology engineering processes is defined in order to reduce the complexity of project budgetary planning and controlling operations down to more manageable units [1,10]. The associated costs are then elaborated using the *parametric* method. The result of the second step is a statistical prediction model (i.e. a parameterized mathematical formula). Its parameters are given start values in pre-defined intervals, but need to be calibrated on the basis of previous project data. This empirical information complemented by expert estimations is used to evaluate and revise the predictions of the initial *a-priori model*, thus creating a validated *a-posteriori model*.

3.1 The Work Breakdown Structure

The top-level partitioning of a generic ontology engineering process can be realized by taking into account available process-driven methodologies in this field.[2] According to them ontology building consists of the following core steps (cf. Figure 1):

---

[1] By contrast the bottom-up method can not be applied in early stages of the ontology engineering process, while the analogy method requires means to compare among ontologies and associated development processes.

[2] Refer, for instance, to [6] for a recent overview on ontology engineering methodologies.

1) Requirements Analysis. The engineering team consisting of domain experts and ontology engineers performs a deep analysis of the project setting w.r.t. a set of pre-defined requirements. This step might also include **knowledge acquisition** activities in terms of the re-usage of existing ontological sources or by extracting domain information from text corpora, databases etc. If such techniques are being used to aid the engineering process, the resulting ontologies are to be subsequently customized to the application setting in the conceptualization/implementation phases. The result of this step is an ontology requirements specification document [16]. In particular this contains a set of competency questions describing the domain to be modelled by the prospected ontology, as well as information about its use cases, the expected size, the information sources used, the process participants and the engineering methodology.

2) Conceptualization. The application domain is modelled in terms of ontological primitives, e. g. concepts, relations, axioms.[3]

3) Implementation. The conceptual model is implemented in a (formal) representation language, whose expressivity is appropriate for the richness of the conceptualization. If required reused ontologies and those generated from other information sources are translated to the target representation language and integrated to the final context.

4) Evaluation. The ontology is evaluated against the set of competency questions. The evaluation may be performed automatically, if the competency questions are represented formally, or semi-automatically, using specific heuristics or human judgement. The result of the evaluation is reflected in a set of modifications/refinements at the requirements, conceptualization or implementation level.

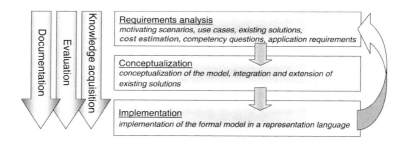

Fig. 1. Typical Ontology Engineering Process

Depending on the ontology life cycle underlying the process-driven methodology, the aforementioned four steps are to be seen as a sequential workflow or as parallel activities. Methontology [6], which applies prototypical engineering principles, considers **knowledge acquisition**, **evaluation** and **documentation** as being complementary *support activities* performed in parallel to the main development process. Other methodologies, usually following a classical waterfall model, consider these support activities as part of a sequential engineering process. The OTK-Methodology [16] additionally introduces an initial **feasibility study** in order to assess the risks associated with an

---
[3] Depending on methodology and representation language these ontological primitives might have different names, e.g. class or concept, relation or relationship, slot, axiom, constraint.

ontology building attempt. Other optional steps are **ontology population/instantiation** and **ontology evolution/maintenance**. The former deals with the alignment of concrete application data to the implemented ontology. The latter relates to modifications of the ontology performed according to new user requirements, updates of the reused sources or changes in the modelled domain. Further on, likewise related engineering disciplines, reusing existing knowledge sources—in particular ontologies—is a central topic of ontology development. In terms of the process model introduced above, **ontology reuse** is considered a **knowledge acquisition** task.

The parametric method integrates the efforts associated with each component of this work breakdown structure to a mathematical formula as described below.

3.2 The Parametric Equation

ONTOCOM calculates the necessary person-months effort using the following equation:

$$PM = A * Size^\alpha * \prod CD_i \tag{1}$$

According to the parametric method the total development efforts are associated with cost drivers specific for the ontology engineering process and its main activities. Experiences in related engineering areas [1,7] let us assume that the most significant factor is the *size of the ontology* (in kilo entities) involved in the corresponding process or process phase. In Equation 1 the parameter $Size$ corresponds to the size of the ontology i.e. the number of primitives which are expected to result from the conceptualization phase (including fragments built by reuse or other knowledge acquisition methods). The possibility of a non-linear behavior of the model w.r.t. the size of the ontology is covered by parameter α. The constant A represents a baseline multiplicative calibration constant in person months, i.e. costs which occur "if everything is normal". The *cost drivers* CD_i have a rating level (from Very Low to Very High) that expresses their impact on the development effort. For the purpose of a quantitative analysis each rating level of each cost driver is associated to a weight (*effort multiplier* EM_i). The *productivity range* PR_i of a cost driver (i.e. the ratio between the highest and the lowest effort multiplier of a cost driver $PR_i = \frac{max(EM_i)}{min(EM_i)}$) is an indicator for the relative importance of a cost driver for the effort estimation [1]. In the a-priori cost model a team of five ontology engineering experts assigned productivity ranges between 1.75 and 9 to the effort multipliers, depending on the perceived contribution of the corresponding cost driver to the overall development costs. The final effort multipliers assigned to the rating levels are calculated such that the contribution of an individual rating level is linear and the resulting productivity range for a cost driver corresponds to the average calculated from the expert judgements. In the same manner, the start value of the A parameter was set to 3.12. These values were subject to further calibration on the basis of the statistical analysis of real-world project data (cf. Section 4).

3.3 The ONTOCOM Cost Drivers

The ONTOCOM cost drivers, which are expected to have a direct impact on the total development efforts, can be roughly divided into three categories:

1) PRODUCT-RELATED COST DRIVERS account for the impact of the characteristics of the product to be engineered (i.e. the ontology) on the overall costs. The following cost drivers were identified for the task of ontology building:

- **Domain Analysis Complexity (DCPLX)** to account for those features of the application setting which influence the complexity of the engineering outcomes,
- **Conceptualization Complexity (CCPLX)** to account for the impact of a complex conceptual model on the overall costs,
- **Implementation Complexity (ICPLX)** to take into consideration the additional efforts arisen from the usage of a specific implementation language,
- **Instantiation Complexity (DATA)** to capture the effects that the instance data requirements have on the overall process,
- **Required Reusability (REUSE)** to capture the additional effort associated with the development of a reusable ontology,
- **Evaluation Complexity (OE)** to account for the additional efforts eventually invested in generating test cases and evaluating test results, and
- **Documentation Needs (DOCU)** to state for the additional costs caused by high documentation requirements.

2) PERSONNEL-RELATED COST DRIVERS emphasize the role of team experience, ability and continuity w.r.t. the effort invested in the engineering process:

- **Ontologist/Domain Expert Capability (OCAP/DECAP)** to account for the perceived ability and efficiency of the single actors involved in the process (ontologist and domain expert) as well as their teamwork capabilities,
- **Ontologist/Domain Expert Experience (OEXP/DEEXP)** to measure the level of experience of the engineering team w.r.t. performing ontology engineering activities,
- **Language/Tool Experience (LEXP/TEXP)** to measure the level experience of the project team w.r.t. the representation language and the ontology management tools,
- **Personnel Continuity (PCON)** to mirror the frequency of the personnel changes in the team.

3) PROJECT-RELATED COST DRIVERS relate to overall characteristics of an ontology engineering process and their impact on the total costs:

- **Support tools for Ontology Engineering (TOOL)** to measure the effects of using ontology management tools in the engineering process, and
- **Multisite Development (SITE)** to mirror the usage of the communication support tools in a location-distributed team.

The ONTOCOM cost drivers were defined after extensively surveying recent ontology engineering literature and conducting expert interviews, and from empirical findings of numerous case studies in the field.[4] For each cost driver we specified in detail the decision criteria which are relevant for the model user in order for him to determine the concrete rating of the driver in a particular situation. For example for the cost driver CCPLX—accounting for costs produced by a particularly complex conceptualization—we pre-defined the meaning of the rating levels as depicted in Table 1. The human experts assigned in average a productivity range of 6.17 to this cost driver. The resulting

---

[4] See [11,12] for a detailed explanation of the approach.

non-calibrated values of the corresponding effort multipliers are as follows: 0.28 (Very Low), 0.64 (Low), 1 (Nominal), 1.36 (High) and 1.72 (Very High) [11]. The appropriate value should be selected during the cost estimation procedure and used as a multiplier in equation 1. Depending on their impact on the overall development effort, if a particular activity increases the nominal efforts, then it would be rated with values such as High and Very High. Otherwise, if it causes a decrease of the nominal costs, then it would be rated with values such as Low and Very Low.

Table 1. The Conceptualization Complexity Cost Driver **CCPLX**

Rating Level	Effort multiplier	Description
Very Low	0.28	concept list
Low	0.64	taxonomy, high nr. of patterns, no constraints
Nominal	1.0	properties, general patterns available, some constraints
High	1.36	axioms, few modelling patterns, considerable nr. of constraints
Very High	1.72	instances, no patterns, considerable nr. of constraints

The decision criteria associated with a cost driver are typically more complex than in the previous example and might be sub-divided into further sub-categories, whose impact is aggregated to the final effort multiplier of the corresponding cost driver by means of normalized weights [11,12].

3.4 Using ONTOCOM in Ontology Engineering Processes

ONTOCOM is intended to be applied in early stages of an ontology engineering process. In accordance to the process model introduced above the prediction of the arising costs can be performed during the feasibility study or, more reliably, during the requirements analysis. Many of the input parameters required to exercise the cost estimation are expected to be accurately approximated during this phase: the expected size of the ontology, the engineering team, the tools to be used, the implementation language etc.[5]

The high-level work breakdown structure foreseen by **ONTOCOM** can be further refined depending of the ontology development strategy applied in an organization in a certain application scenario. As explained in Section 3.1 **ONTOCOM** distinguishes solely between the most important phases of ontology building: requirements analysis, conceptualization, implementation, population, evaluation and documentation. Further on, it focuses on *sequential* development processes (as opposed to, for instance, rapid prototyping, or iterations of the building workflow). In case the model is applied to a different ontology development process, the relevant cost drivers are to be aligned (or even re-defined) to the new sub-phases and activities, while the parametric equation needs to be adapted to the new activity breakdown. An example of how **ONTOCOM** can be applied to an ontology development methodology targeted at rapid prototyping in distributed scenarios is provided in [12].

---
[5] Ontology engineering methodologies foresee this information to be collected in a ontology requirements document at the end of this phase [16].

After this optional customization step the model can be utilized for cost predictions.[6] For this purpose the engineering team needs to specify the rating levels associated with each cost driver. This task is accomplished with the help of decision criteria which have been elaborated for each of the cost driver rating levels (such as those for the CCPLX cost driver illustrated in Figure 2). Cost drivers which are not relevant for a particular scenario should be rated with the nominal value 1, which does not influence the result of the prediction equation.

4 Evaluation

For the evaluation of the model we relied on the quality framework for cost models by Boehm[1], which was adapted to the particularities of ontology engineering. The framework consists of 10 evaluation criteria covering a wide range of quality aspects, from the reliability of the predictions to the model ease-of-use and its relevance for arbitrary ontology engineering scenarios (Table 2).

Table 2. The ONTOCOM Evaluation Framework

No	Criterion	Description
1	Definition	- clear definition of the estimated and the excluded costs - clear definition of the decision criteria used to specify the cost drivers - intuitive and non-ambiguous terms to denominate the cost drivers
2	Objectivity	- objectivity of the cost drivers and their decision criteria
3	Constructiveness	- human understandability of the model predictions
4	Detail	- accurate phase and activity breakdowns
5	Scope	- usability for a wide class of ontology engineering processes
6	Ease of use	- easily understandable inputs and options - easily assessable cost driver ratings based on the decision criteria
7	Prospectiveness	- model applicability in early phases of the project
8	Stability	- small differences in inputs produce small differences in outputs
9	Parsimony	- lack of highly redundant cost drivers - lack of cost drivers with no appreciable contribution to the results
10	Fidelity	- reliability of the predictions

The evaluation was conducted in two steps. First a team of experts in ontology engineering evaluated the a-priori model, in particular the ONTOCOM cost drivers, w.r.t. their relevance to cost issues (Criteria 1 to 8 in the table above). Second the predictions of the model were compared with 36 observations from real world projects (Criteria 9 and 10 of the quality framework).

4.1 The Expert-Based Evaluation

The evaluation of the a-priori model was performed by conducting interviews with two groups of independent experts in the area of ontology engineering. Considering that the

---

[6] However, if new cost drivers have been defined in addition to the ones foreseen by ONTOCOM, these should be calibrated using empirical data.

people best placed to give a comprehensive assessment of the cost estimation model are IT practitioners or researchers being directly involved in theoretical or practical issues of ontology engineering, we organized two experts groups affiliated in both communities, which evaluated the model sequentially. The first group consisted of 4 academics whose research was in the area of Semantic Web and Ontology Engineering. The second group brought together 4 researchers and 4 IT senior managers from companies with a Semantic Web profile. Participants were given a one hour overview of the ONTOCOM approach, followed by individual interviews. We summarize the key findings of the conducted interviews categorized according to the criteria depicted in Table 2:

- **Definition/Constructiveness.** The first draft of the model did not include the ontology evaluation activity. The cost driver **Evaluation Complexity (OE)** was introduced to the model for this purpose. The **Ontology Instantiation (OI)** cost driver was extended with new decision criteria and minor modifications of the terminology were performed.
- **Objectivity.** The objectivity of the cost drivers and the associated decision criteria were evaluated by the participants favorably. Both suffered minor modifications. W.r.t. the size of the ontology, a key parameter of the model, some of the participants expressed the need for a more careful distinction between the impact of the different types of ontological primitives (e.g. concepts, axioms, relationships) w.r.t. the total efforts. In particular, as axioms and relationships between concepts are more challenging to be modelled than simple concepts and taxonomical structures, they recommended that this difference should be reflected by the parametric model. While the current version of **ONTOCOM** does not include this option, we are investigating the possibility of introducing a revised size formula which associates particular ontology primitives' categories to normalized weights:

$$Size = w_1 * NoClasses^{\alpha_1} + w_2 * NoRelations^{\alpha_2} + (1 - w_1 - w_2) * NoAxioms^{\alpha_3} \quad (2)$$

A final direction w.r.t this issue is planed for the a-posteriori model, as we require a significant set of empirical data in order to prove the validity of the experts' recommendations.
- **Detail/Scope.** The cost drivers covered by the model were unanimously estimated to be relevant for the ontology engineering area. The collection of empirical data demonstrated that the model accommodates well to many real-world settings, situation which was also confirmed by applying **ONTOCOM** to the **DILIGENT** ontology engineering methodology[12]. However, the majority of the evaluators emphasized the need of a revised model for reuse and evolution purposes, an issue which will be investigated in the future. W.r.t. the detail of the cost drivers covered by the model, three new product drivers stating for the complexity of the domain analysis, conceptualization and implementation (DCPLX, CCPLX and ICPLX, see Section 3.3) were introduced in return to an original cost driver **Ontology Complexity** (OCPLX). Some of the participants also expressed the need for a more detailed coverage of the ontology evaluation task in engineering processes, so as to distinguish between the evaluation of an ontology against a set of competency questions and its fitness of use within a particular software system. A final decision w.r.t. this modification requires, however, a more significant set of empirical data.
- **Ease of use.** The goal and the scope of the model were easily understood by the interviewees. During the data collection procedure, the only factor which seemed to require additional clarification was the size of the ontology, which was conceived to cover all types of ontological primitives (e.g. concepts/classes, properties, axioms, rules,

constraints, manually built instances). Further on, the experiments revealed that there is no clear understanding between the re-usage of existing ontologies and the acquisition of ontologies from more un-structured knowledge sources such as text documents. However, this latter issue can not be necessarily considered as a weakness of the model itself, but as the result of a potentially ambiguous definition of the two activities in current ontology engineering methodologies.

- **Prospectiveness.** Some of the participants manifested concerns w.r.t. the availability of particular model parameters in early phases of the engineering process. However, as underlined in a previous section, many of the input parameters are foreseen to be specified in the ontology requirements specification document in the last part of the requirements analysis phase.
- **Stability.** This is ensured by the mathematical model underlying ONTOCOM.

4.2 Evaluation of the Prediction Quality

The remaining two evaluation criteria **Fidelity** and **Parsimony** were approached after the statistical calibration of the model. In order to determine the effort multipliers associated with the rating levels and to select non-redundant cost drivers we followed a three-stage approach: First experts estimated the a-priori effort multipliers based on their experience as regarding ontology engineering. Second we applied linear regression to real world project data to obtain a second estimation of the effort multipliers.[7] Third we combined the expert estimations and the results of the linear regression in a statistically sound way using Bayesian analysis [2].

Data Collection. The results reported in this paper are based on 36 structured interviews with ontology engineering experts [13]. The interviews were conducted within a three months period and covered 35 pre-defined questions related to the aforementioned cost drivers. The survey participants are representative for the community of users and developers of semantic technologies. The group consisted of individuals affiliated to industry or academia, who were involved in the last 3 to 4 years in ontology building projects in areas such as skill management, human resources, medical information systems, legal information systems, multimedia, Web services, and digital libraries.[8] The average number of ontology entities in the surveyed ontologies is 830 with a median at 330. It took the engineers in average 5.3 month (median 2.5) to build the ontologies. 40% of the ontologies were built from scratch. Reused ontologies contributed in average 50% (median 50%) of ontology entities to the remaining 60% of the surveyed ontologies.

Data Analysis. In order to adapt the prediction model in accordance to experiences from previous ontology engineering processes we derived estimates of the cost driver productivity ranges from the collected data set. The estimates were calculated following a linear regression approach combined with Bayesian analysis. This approach allows the usage of human judgement and data-driven estimations in a statistically consistent way,

---

[7] Linear regression is a mathematical method to calculate the parameters of a linear equation so that the squared differences between the predictions from the linear equation and the observations are minimal [14].
[8] Around 50% of the interviewees were affiliated to industry.

such that the variance observed in either of the two determines its impact to the final values.[9] Linear regression models perform better with an increasing number of incorporated observations and a decreasing number of parameters to estimate. Its drawbacks can be compensated with the help of human estimations [4] and by excluding those parameters which have an insignificant influence on the final prediction value or are highly correlated.

In order to select relevant cost drivers for the ONTOCOM model we performed a correlation analysis on the historical data (Table 3). We excluded the following cost drivers

Table 3. Selection of Relevant Cost Drivers using Correlation Analysis

Cost driver	Correlation with PM	Cost driver	Correlation with PM	Comment
SIZE	0.50	DATA	0.31	strong correlation with DCPLX
OE	0.44	SITE	0.27	low number of different data points
DCPLX	0.39	DOCU	0.22	moderated influence; strong correlation with OE
REUSE	0.38			
ICPLX	0.29	LEXP/TEXP	0.13	little influence; strong correlation with OXEP/DEEXP
CCPLX	0.24			
OCAP/DECAP	-0.19	PCON	0.04	low number of different data points
OXEP/DEEXP	-0.36	$\frac{Size_{Reused}}{Size_{Total}}$	-0.10	little influence

in order to get more accurate results. The cost driver **DATA** is strongly correlated with the cost driver **DCPLX**. Most of the surveyed projects took place at one site resulting in limited information about the actual influence of the **SITE** parameter, which was therefore excluded. The cost driver **DOCU** highly correlates with the **OE** cost driver and has only moderate influence on the effort. A similar line of reasoning applies to the cost drivers **LEXP/TEXP** which are highly correlated with **OXEP/DEEXP** while modestly contributing to the prediction variable. The surveyed projects did not experience a permanent personnel turnover, resulting in a very low correlation coefficient for the cost driver **PCON**. Intriguingly, reusing ontologies had only a limited effect on the ontology building effort as indicated by the small negative correlation between $\frac{Size_{Reused}}{Size_{Total}}$ and the effort. Most interviewees reported major difficulties translating and modifying reused ontologies, which obviously offset most of the time savings expected from ontology reuse. The cost driver **TOOL** was not considered in the calibration, because it did not differentiate the projects (i.e. all data points utilized only ontology editors).

The exclusion of the mentioned cost drivers from the current ONTOCOM calibration does not mean, that those cost drivers are not relevant for predicting the ontology building effort. With the currently available data set it is, however, not possible to provide accurate estimates for these cost drivers. The prediction quality for multi-site developments and projects with a high personal turnover might suffer from the exclusion of the corresponding drivers. However, the accuracy of the prediction for the remaining cost drivers increases.

---

[9] Refer to [4] for an exhaustive explanation of the application of Bayesian analysis for cost estimation purposes.

Calibration Results. The approximation of the effort multipliers with the linear regression approach implies a reformulation of equation 1. After applying the logarithm function and introducing the parameters β_i as exponents for the cost drivers we obtained the equivalent equation 3.[10] β_i are scaling factors by which the existing effort multipliers should be scaled in order to fit the model. We recall that α is a learning rate factor also used to model economies of scale.

$$\ln(PM_X) = \ln(A) + \alpha * \ln(Size_X) + \sum \beta_i * ln(CD_{Xi}) \qquad (3)$$

The linear regression delivers a best fit for the effort multipliers w.r.t. to the surveyed empirical data. However, the relatively small sample size results in a limited accuracy of the estimated effort multipliers. This drawback can be overcome with the help of the a-priori estimations of the parameters, which were defined by human experts. A linear combination of expert estimations and historical data is, however, sub-optimal. The combination should take into account the number of data points used for the linear regression and the variance observed in the expert ratings as well as in the data points. A mulitplier which all experts have given the same rating, while the linear regression results in a high variance should be influenced less by the data than by the experts. Bayesian analysis is a way to achieve the desired outcome [4].

$$\beta^{**} = [\frac{1}{s^2}X'X + H^*]^{-1} \times [\frac{1}{s^2}X'X\beta + H^*b^*] \qquad (4)$$

Equation 4 delivers the estimations of the scaling factor β^{**} combining expert knowledge and empirical data in a statistically sound way. s^2 is the variance of the residual data of the sample; X is the matrix of observations; and H^* and b^* is the inverse of the covariance matrix and the mean of the expert estimations, respectively. Figure 2 exemplifies the approach. The lines depict the probability distribution of the productivity range estimations for the expert judgement, the data analysis and the Bayesian combination, respectively. The arrows point to the corresponding means. We note that the experts judgement indicates a productivity range for the cost driver CCPLX of 6.17 with a small variance. Estimating the productivity range based on the data results in a mean of 7.05 with a higher variance, though. The Bayesian analysis induces a shift of the estimation towards the data-driven estimation, but only with a small fraction because its higher data variance.

Table 4 summarizes the results of the Bayesian analysis. In column *Correlation with PM* we list the correlation coefficients for the reduced number of cost drivers with the effort in person months (PM). In the *Significance* column we plot the confidence level for the estimation. Not all effort multipliers could be determined with the same accuracy. A lower confidence level indicates a better estimation. The calibration is very good for, for instance, the exponent α (**SIZE**), but less accurate for the effort multipliers related to **OCAP/DECAP**. The *Productivity range* column lists the relative influence a cost driver has on the final prediction.

Based on the results of the calibration Figure 4.2 compares the predictions from the calibrated model with the observations. In order to visualize the results we have

---

[10] This step is only possible if the data is distributed exponentially, thus we have significantly more data points with a low number of entities than with a high number of entities. This holds true for the collected data.

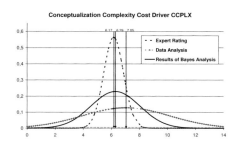 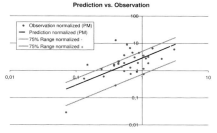

Fig. 2. Productivity Range: Conceptualization Complexity

Fig. 3. Comparison of Observed Data with Predictions

Table 4. Statistical Data and Productivity Range of the Effort Multipliers

Cost Driver	Correlation with PM	Significance	Productivity range
SIZE	0.50	0.001	$\alpha = 0.5$
OE	0.44	0.034	4.0
DCPLX	0.39	0.063	3.2
REUSE	0.38	0.528	5.2
CCPLX	0.24	0.311	6.3
OXEP/DEEXP	-0.36	0.060	1.5
ICPLX	0.29	0.299	0.6
OCAP/DECAP	-0.19	0.925	1.5

normalized the data with the product of the corresponding cost drivers. The gray lines indicate a range around the prediction adding and subtracting 75% of the estimated effort. 75% of the historical data points lie within this range. For the corresponding 30% range the model covers 32% of the real-world data. This indicates a linear behavior of deviation which we consider quite accurate for a very first model. Our goal is that 75% of the data lie in the range of adding and subtracting 20% of the estimated effort.

Discussion of the Calibration Results. Although any prediction model provides solely an approximation of the true building efforts, this calibration is already helpful to get an early impression on the expected values. Experiences with cost estimation models in established engineering disciplines suggest that a calibration for a particular company or project team yields more accurate estimations than a general-purpose calibration. Our calibration may therefore predominantly serve as an example for a more context-specific calibration process and may help to identify the resource-intensive activities in a generic ontology engineering process. Moreover, project teams can compare their estimations against a general average value as provided by us. Note also that a calibration uses historical data to estimate future outcomes. Although the average and the variation observed in the historical data may remain constant in future projects, the predicted effort for any specific project may still significantly differ from the actual effort.

Regarding the quality of our model w.r.t. the calibration accuracy it is important to note that the estimations for the cost drivers **OCAP/DECAP** and **REUSE** have a low significance. For the cost drivers **OCAP/DECAP** this leaves room for improvement, as the data analysis counterintuitively suggests that more capable project teams need longer to develop an ontology. We obtained the same result for the cost driver **OEXP/DEEXP**. The main reason for this artefact may be the fact that ontology engineers from academia were more experienced, implying that they invested more time in developing ontologies than people from industry, whose mode of operation might have been motivated by different factors as in academic projects.

Another interesting finding of the analysis is the relative importance of the cost drivers **Ontology evaluation (OE)**, **Domain complexity (DCPLX)** and **Conceptualization complexity (CCPLX)** in correlation with the observed significance. This indicates that any facilitation in those areas may result in major efficiency gains w.r.t. the overall ontology engineering effort. Moreover, the very high learning rate indicates that the building of very large ontologies is feasible from an economic point of view, although we admit that the number of data points for ontologies larger than 1.000 ontology entities is comparatively low.

5 Related Work

Cost estimation methods have a long-standing tradition in more mature engineering disciplines such as software engineering or industrial production [1,7,15]. Although the importance of cost issues is well-acknowledged in the community, as to the best knowledge of the authors, no cost estimation model for ontology engineering has been published so far. Analogue models for the development of knowledge-based systems (e.g., [5]) implicitly assume the availability of the underlying conceptual structures. [9] provides a qualitative analysis of the costs and benefits of ontology usage in application systems, but does not offer any model to estimate the efforts. [3] presents empirical results for quantifying ontology reuse. [8] adjusts the cost drivers defined in a cost estimation model for Web applications w.r.t. the usage of ontologies. The cost drivers, however, are not adapted to the requirements of ontology engineering and no evaluation is provided. We present an evaluated cost estimation model, introducing cost drivers with a proved relevance for ontology engineering, which can be applied in the early stages of an ontology development process.

6 Conclusion

The application of ontologies in commercial applications depends on the availability of appropriate methodologies guiding the ontology development process and on methods for an effective cost management. We propose a parametric cost estimation model for ontologies by identifying relevant cost drivers having a direct impact on the effort invested in ontology building. We evaluate the model a-priori and a-posteriori.

The a-priori evaluation shows the validity of the approach to cost estimation and the meaningful selection of the cost drivers. The a-posteriori evaluation results in high quality estimations for the learning rate α and the cost drivers related to the ontology evaluation and the requirements complexity. These are also among the more relevant cost drivers. Provision of tool support for these two areas of ontology engineering may thus be particularly effective to facilitate the ontology engineering process. The collection of data will continue towards a more accurate calibration of the model. In particular we intend to approach the suggestions received during the a-priori evaluation w.r.t. a more differentiated size parameter and w.r.t. the support for ontology reuse activities on the basis of a larger number of data points. In the near future we also plan to make the results of our survey public and to provide a service which offers on-the-fly cost estimations for ontology engineering processes based on the available data.

Acknowledgements. This work has been partially supported by the European Network of Excellence "KnowledgeWeb-Realizing the Semantic Web" (FP6-507482), as part of the KnowledgeWeb researcher exchange program **T-REX**, and by the European project "Sekt-Semantically-Enabled Knowledge Technologies"(EU IP IST-2003-506826) and "NeOn - Lifecycle Support for Networked Ontologies" (EU IP IST-2005-027595). We thank all interviewees for the valuable input without which this paper could not have been produced.

We encourage the community to participate and contribute experiences from ontology engineering projects at `http://ontocom.ag-nbi.de`.

References

1. B. W. Boehm. *Software Engineering Economics*. Prentice-Hall, 1981.
2. G. Box and G. Tiao. *Bayesian Inference in Statistical Analysis*. Addison Wesley, 1973.
3. P. R. Cohen, V. K. Chaudhri, A. Pease, and R. Schrag. Does Prior Knowledge Facilitate the Development of Knowledge-based Systems? In *AAAI/IAAI*, pages 221–226, 1999.
4. S. Devnani-Chulani. *Bayesian Analysis of the Software Cost and Quality Models*. PhD thesis, Faculty of the Graduate School University of Southern California, 1999.
5. A. Felfernig. Effort Estimation for Knowledge-based Configuration Systems. In *Proc. of the 16th Int. Conf. of Software Engineering and Knowledge Engineering SEKE04*, 2004.
6. A. Gomez-Perez, M. Fernandez-Lopez, and O. Corcho. *Ontological Engineering – with examples form the areas of Knowledge Management, e-Commerce and the Semantic Web*. Springer Verlag, 2004.
7. C. F. Kemerer. An Empirical Validation of Software Cost Estimation Models. *Communications of the ACM*, 30(5), 1987.
8. M. Korotkiy. On the Effect of Ontologies on Web Application Development Effort. In *Proc. of the Knowledge Engineering and Software Engineering Workshop*, 2005.
9. T. Menzies. Cost benefits of ontologies. *Intelligence*, 10(3):26–32, 1999.
10. National Aeronautics and Space Administration. NASA Cost Estimating Handbook, 2004.
11. E. Paslaru Bontas and M. Mochol. Ontology Engineering Cost Estimation with ONTOCOM. Technical Report TR-B-06-01, Free University of Berlin, January 2006.
12. E. Paslaru Bontas and C. Tempich. How Much Does It Cost? Applying ONTOCOM to DILIGENT. Technical Report TR-B-05-20, Free University of Berlin, October 2005.
13. E. Paslaru Bontas and C. Tempich. Ontology Engineering: A Reality Check. In *5th Int. Conf. on Ontologies, DataBases, and Applications of Semantics (ODBASE2006)*, 2006.
14. G.A.F. Seber. *Linear Regression Analysis*. Wiley, New York, 1977.
15. R. D. Stewart, R. M. Wyskida, and J. D. Johannes. *Cost Estimator's Reference Manual*. Wiley, 1995.
16. Y. Sure, S. Staab, and R. Studer. Methodology for Development and Employment of Ontology based Knowledge Management Applications. *SIGMOD Record*, 31(4), 2002.

Tree-Structured Conditional Random Fields for Semantic Annotation*

Jie Tang[1], Mingcai Hong[1], Juanzi Li[1], and Bangyong Liang[2]

[1] Department of Computer Science, Tsinghua University
12#109, Tsinghua University, Beijing, 100084. China
j-tang02@mails.tsinghua.edu.cn,
{hmc, ljz}@keg.cs.tsinghua.edu.cn
[2] NEC Labs China
11th Floor, Innovation Plaza, Tsinghua Science Park, Beijing, 100084, China
liangbangyong@research.nec.com.cn

Abstract. The large volume of web content needs to be annotated by ontologies (called Semantic Annotation), and our empirical study shows that strong dependencies exist across different types of information (it means that identification of one kind of information can be used for identifying the other kind of information). Conditional Random Fields (CRFs) are the state-of-the-art approaches for modeling the dependencies to do better annotation. However, as information on a Web page is not necessarily linearly laid-out, the previous linear-chain CRFs have their limitations in semantic annotation. This paper is concerned with semantic annotation on hierarchically dependent data (*hierarchical semantic annotation*). We propose a Tree-structured Conditional Random Field (TCRF) model to better incorporate dependencies across the hierarchically laid-out information. Methods for performing the tasks of model-parameter estimation and annotation in TCRFs have been proposed. Experimental results indicate that the proposed TCRFs for hierarchical semantic annotation can significantly outperform the existing linear-chain CRF model.

1 Introduction

Semantic web requires annotating existing web content according to particular ontologies, which define the meaning of the words or concepts in the content [1].

In recent years, automatic semantic annotation has received much attention in the research community. Many prototype systems have been developed using information extraction methods. The methods usually convert a document into an 'object' sequence and then identify a sub-sequence of the objects that we want to annotate (i.e. targeted instance). (Here, the object can be either natural language units like token and text line, or structured units indicated by HTML tags like "<table>" and "<image>"). The methods make use of the contexts information that is previous to and next to the target instances for the identification task.

Empirical study shows that strong dependencies exist across different types of targeted instances. The type of dependencies varies in different kinds of documents

---

* Supported by the National Natural Science Foundation of China under Grant No. 90604025.

and different applications, for instance, in Part-Of-Speech (POS) tagging from NLP, the dependencies between POS labels can be linear-chain [20]; while in object extraction from web pages, the dependencies can be two-dimensional [26].

Conditional Random Fields (CRFs) are the state-of-the-art approaches in information extraction taking advantage of the dependencies to do better annotation, compared with Hidden Markov Model (HMMs) [8] and Maximum Entropy Markov Model (MEMMs) [17]. However, the previous linear-chain CRFs only model the linear-dependencies in a sequence of information, and is not able to model hierarchical dependencies [14] [26].

In this paper, we study the problem of *hierarchical semantic annotation*. In hierarchical semantic annotation, targeted instances on a web page can have hierarchical dependencies with each other, for example, an instance may have a dependency with another instance in the upper level (i.e. child-parent dependency), have a dependency with one in the lower level (i.e. parent-child dependency), or have a dependency with one in the same level (i.e. sibling dependency).

To better incorporate dependencies across hierarchically laid-out information, a Tree-structured Conditional Random Field (TCRF) model has been proposed in this paper. We present the graphical structure of the TCRF model as a tree (see Figure 3) and reformulate the conditional distribution by defining three kinds of edge features. As the tree structure can be cyclable, exact inference in TCRFs is expensive. We propose to use the Tree Reparameterization algorithm to compute the approximate marginal probabilities for edges and vertices. Experimental results indicate that the proposed TCRF models perform significantly better than the baseline methods for hierarchical semantic annotation.

The rest of the paper is organized as follows. In Section 2, we introduce related work. In Section 3, we formalize the problem of hierarchical semantic annotation. In Section 4, we describe our approach to the problem. Section 5 gives our experimental results. We make some concluding remarks in Section 6.

2 Related Work

Semantic annotation is an important area in semantic web. Many research efforts have been made so far. However, much of the previous work views web page as an 'object' sequence and focuses on annotating web page by using existing information extraction techniques. To the best of our knowledge, no previous work has been done on semantic annotation of hierarchically laid-out information.

1. Semantic Annotation Using Rule Induction
Many semantic annotation systems employ rule induction to automate the annotation process (also called as 'wrapper' induction, see [13]).

For example, Ciravegna et al propose a rule learning algorithm, called LP^2, and have implemented an automatic annotation module: Amilcare [4]. The module can learn annotation rules from the training data. Amilcare has been used in several annotation systems, for instance, S-CREAM [12]. See also [18] [22].

The rule induction based method can achieve good results on the template based web pages. However, it cannot utilize dependencies across targeted instances.

2. Semantic Annotation as Classification

The method views semantic annotation as a problem of classification, and automates the process by employing statistical learning approaches. It defines features for candidate instances and learns a classifier that can detect the targeted instance from the candidate ones.

For example, SCORE Enhancement Engine (SEE) supports web page annotation by using classification model [11]. It first classifies the web page into a predefined taxonomy; then identifies name entities in the classified web pages; finally recognizes the relationships between the entities via analysis of the web content.

The classification based method can obtain good results on many annotation tasks. However, it cannot also use the dependencies across different targeted instances.

3. Semantic Annotation as Sequential Labeling

Different from the rule induction and the classification methods, sequential labeling enables describing dependencies between targeted instances. The dependencies can be utilized to improve the accuracy of the annotation.

For instance, Reeve et al propose to utilize Hidden Markov Model (HMM) in semantic annotation [19]. As a generative model, HMM needs enumerate all possible observation sequences, and thus requires the independence assumption to ease the computation. Despite of its usefulness, limited research has been done using the sequential labeling method in semantic annotation.

4. Information Extraction Methods

Many information extraction methods have been proposed. Hidden Markov Model (HMM) [8], Maximum Entropy Markov Model (MEMM) [17], Conditional Random Field (CRF) [14], Support Vector Machines (SVM) [6], and Voted Perceptron [5] are widely used information extraction models.

Some of the methods only model the distribution of contexts of target instances and do not model dependencies between the instances, for example, SVM and Voted Perceptron. Some other methods can model the linear-chain dependencies, for example, HMM, MEMM, and CRF.

Recently, several research efforts have been also made for modeling the non-linear dependencies. For instance, Sutton et al propose Dynamic Conditional Random Fields (DCRFs) [21]. As a particular case, a factorial CRF (FCRF) was used to jointly solve two NLP tasks (noun phrase chunking and Part-Of-Speech tagging) on the same observation sequence. Zhu et al propose 2D Conditional Random Fields (2D CRFs) [26]. 2D CRFs is also a particular case of CRFs. It is aimed at extracting object information from two-dimensionally laid-out web pages. See also [3].

3 Hierarchical Semantic Annotation

For semantic annotation, we target at detecting targeted instances from a document and annotating each of the instances by concepts/attributes of a particular ontology.

Information on a web page can be laid-out differently, for example, product information on a web page is typically two-dimensionally laid-out [26]; and in Natural Language Processing, word's POS (Part-Of-Speech) can be organized as a sequence, and thus viewed as linearly laid-out [20]. In this paper, we concentrate on

Fig. 1. Example of Hierarchical laid-out information

semantic annotation on hierarchically laid-out information that we name as *hierarchical semantic annotation*. In hierarchical semantic annotation, information is laid-out hierarchically. An example is shown in Figure 1.

In Figure 1, there are two emails. One is the email of the company directorate secretary and the other is the email of the company registration office. Previous linear-chain models such as linear-chain CRFs view the text as a token-sequence (or text-line sequence) and assign a label to each token in the sequence by using neighborhood contexts (i.e. information previous to and next to the targeted instance).

However, the neighborhood contexts of the two emails are the same with each other in the linear-chain token-sequence. The neighborhood contexts include tokens previous to and next to the emails. Tokens previous to the two emails are both "Email: " and tokens next to them are also identical "<return>Phone:". It is inevitable that the linear-chain CRF models will fail to distinguish them from each other.

By further investigation, we found that the information is hierarchically laid-out: the two emails are respectively located in two sections and each section has a heading, i.e. "3. Company directorate Info" and "4. Company Registration Info". The two headings can be used to distinguish the two emails from each other. We call it as hierarchically laid-out information when existing hierarchical dependencies across information and call the task of semantic annotation on hierarchically laid-out information as *hierarchical semantic annotation*. In hierarchical semantic annotation, we target at improving the accuracy of semantic annotation by incorporating hierarchical dependencies. For instance, in Figure 1, we can use the upper level information "3. Company directorate Info" to help identify the email "ajcoob@mail2.online.sh.cn".

4 Tree-Structured Conditional Random Fields

In this section, we first introduce the basic concepts of Conditional Random Fields (CRFs) and introduce the linear-chain CRFs, and then we explain a Tree-structured CRF model for hierarchically laid-out information. Finally we discuss how to perform parameter estimation and annotation in TCRFs.

4.1 Linear-Chain CRFs

Conditional Random Fields are undirected graphical models [14]. As defined before, X is a random variable over data sequences to be labeled, and Y is a random variable over corresponding label sequences. All components Y_i of Y are assumed to range over a finite label alphabet Y. CRFs construct a conditional model $p(Y|X)$ with a given set of features from paired observation and label sequences.

CRF Definition. *Let $G = (V, E)$ be a graph such that $Y=(Y_v)_{v \in V}$, so that Y is indexed by the vertices of G. Then (X, Y) is a conditional random field in case, when conditioned on X, the random variable Y_v obey the Markov property with respect to the graph: $p(Y_v|X, Y_w, w \neq v) = p(Y_v|X, Y_w, w \sim v)$, where $w \sim v$ means that w and v are neighbors in G.*

Thus, a CRF is a random field globally conditioned on the observation X. Linear-chain CRFs were first introduced by Lafferty et al [14]. The graphical structure of linear-chain CRFs is shown in Figure 2.

By the fundamental theorem of random fields [10], the conditional distribution of the labels y given the observations data x has the form

$$p(y \mid x) = \frac{1}{Z(x)} \exp\left(\sum_{e \in E, j} \lambda_j t_j(e, y|_e, x) + \sum_{v \in V, k} \mu_k s_k(v, y|_v, x) \right) \quad (1)$$

where x is a data sequence, y is a label sequence, and $y|_e$ and $y|_v$ are the set of components of y associated with edge e and vertex v in the linear chain respectively; t_j and s_k are feature functions; parameters λ_j and μ_k correspond to the feature functions t_j and s_k respectively, and are to be estimated from the training data; $Z(x)$ is the normalization factor, also known as partition function.

4.2 Tree-Structured Conditional Random Fields (TCRFs)

Linear-chain CRFs cannot model dependencies across hierarchically laid-out information. This paper proposes a Tree-structured Conditional Random Field (TCRF) model which is also a particular case of CRFs. The graphical structure of TCRFs is a tree (see Figure 3).

From Figure 3, we see that y_4 is the parent vertex of y_2 and y_{n-1} (for simplifying description, hereafter we use parent-vertex to represent the upper-level vertex and use child-vertex to represent the lower-level vertex of the current vertex). TCRFs can model the parent-child dependencies, e.g. y_4-y_2 and y_4-y_{n-1}. Furthermore, y_2 and y_{n-1} are in the same level, which are represented as a sibling dependency in TCRFs.

Here we also use X to denote the random variable over observations, and Y to denote the random variable over the corresponding labels. Y_i is a component of Y at the vertex i. Same as the linear-chain CRFs, we consider one vertex or two vertices as a clique in TCRFs. TCRFs can also be viewed as a finite-state model. Each variable Y_i has a finite set of state values and we assume the one-to-one mapping between states and labels. And thus dependencies across components Y_i can be viewed as transitions between states.

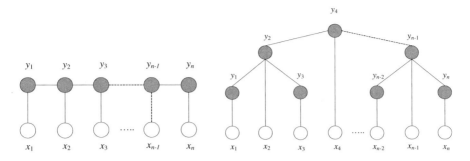

Fig. 2. The Graphical structure of Linear-chain CRFs

Fig. 3. The Graphical structure of TCRFs

Let (y_p, y_c) be the dependency between a parent- and a child-vertices, (y_c, y_p) be the dependency between a child- and a parent-vertices, and (y_s, y_s) be the dependency between sibling vertices. A TCRF model, as a particular case of CRFs, has the form

$$p(y \mid x) = \frac{1}{Z(x)} \exp\left(\sum_{e \in \{E^{pc}, E^{cp}, E^{ss}\}, j} \lambda_j t_j(e, y\mid_e, x) + \sum_{v \in V, k} \mu_k s_k(v, y\mid_v, x) \right) \quad (2)$$

where E^{pc} denotes the set of (y_p, y_c), E^{cp} denotes the set of (y_c, y_p), and E^{ss} denotes the set of (y_s, y_s). t_j and s_k are feature functions.

TCRFs have the same form as that of linear-chain CRFs except that in TCRFs the edges include parent-child edges, child-parent edges, and sibling-vertices edges while in CRFs the edges mean the transitions from the previous-state to the current-state.

In semantic annotation, the observation x in TCRFs can correspond to a document (as the example shown in Figure 1). The label y thus corresponds to the annotation result for the document. Specifically, x_i is a token in the document, and label y_i is the annotation result (called label) to the token, where the label corresponds to either one of the concept/attribute from a particular ontology or none.

4.3 Parameter Estimation

The parameter estimation problem is to determine the parameters $\Theta = \{\lambda_1, \lambda_2, \ldots; \mu_k, \mu_{k+1}, \ldots\}$ from training data $D = \{(x^{(i)}, y^{(i)})\}$ with empirical distribution $\tilde{p}(x, y)$. More specifically, we optimize the log-likelihood objective function with respect to a conditional model $p(y \mid x, \Theta)$:

$$L_\Theta = \sum_i \tilde{p}(x^{(i)}, y^{(i)}) \log p_\Theta(y^{(i)} \mid x^{(i)}) \quad (3)$$

In the following, to facilitate the description, we use f to denote both the edge feature function t and the vertex feature function s; use c to denote both edge e and vertex v; and use λ to denote the two kinds of parameters λ and μ. Thus, the derivative of the object function with respect to a parameter λ_j associated with clique index c is:

$$\frac{\delta L_\Theta}{\delta \lambda_j} = \sum_i \left[\sum_c f_j(c, y_{(c)}^{(i)}, x^{(i)}) - \sum_y \sum_c p(y_{(c)} | x^{(i)}) f_j(c, y_{(c)}, x^{(i)}) \right] \quad (4)$$

where $y^i_{(c)}$ is the label assignment to clique c in $x^{(i)}$, and $y_{(c)}$ ranges over label assignments to the clique c. We see that it is the factors $p(y_{(c)}|x^{(i)})$ that require us to compute the marginal probabilities. The factors $p(y_{(c)}|x^{(i)})$ can be again decomposed into four types of factors: $p(y_p, y_c|x^{(i)})$, $p(y_c, y_p|x^{(i)})$, $p(y_s, y_s|x^{(i)})$, and $p(y_i|x^{(i)})$, as we have three types of dependencies (described as edges here) and one type of vertex. Moreover, we also need to compute the global conditional probability $p(y^{(i)}|x^{(i)})$.

The marginal probabilities can be done using many inference algorithms for undirected model (for example, Belief Propagation [25]). However, as the graphical structure in TCRFs can be a tree with cycles, exact inference can be expensive in TCRFs. We propose utilizing the Tree Reparameterization (TRP) algorithm [24] to compute the approximate probabilities of the factors. TRP is based on the fact that any exact algorithm for optimal inference on trees actually computes marginal distributions for pairs of neighboring vertices. For an undirected graphical model over variables x, this results in an alternative parameterization of the distribution as:

$$p(x) = \frac{1}{Z} \prod_{s \in V} \varphi_s(x_s) \prod_{(s,t) \in V} \varphi_{st}(x_s, x_t) \Rightarrow p(x) = \prod_{s \in V} p_s(x_s) \prod_{(s,t) \in V} \frac{p_{st}(x_s, x_t)}{p_s(x_s) p_t(x_t)} \quad (5)$$

where $\varphi_s(x_s)$ is the potential function on single-vertex x_s and $\varphi_{st}(x_s, x_t)$ is the potential function on edge (x_s, x_t); and Z is the normalization factor.

TRP consists of two main steps: Initialization and Updates. The updates are a sequence of $T^n \to T^{n+1}$ on the undirected graph with edge set E, where T represents the set of marginal probabilities maintained by TRP including single-vertex marginals $T_u^{n+1}(x_u)$ and pairwise joint distribution $T_{uv}^{n+1}(x_u, x_v)$; and n denotes the iteration number. The TRP algorithm is summarized in Figure 4. (The algorithm is adopted from [21]).

---

1. Initialization: for every node u and every pair of nodes (u, v), initialize T^0 by $T_u^0 = \kappa \varphi_u$ and $T_{uv}^0 = \kappa \varphi_{uv}$, with κ being a normalization factor.

1. TRP Updates: for $i=1, 2, \ldots$, do:

- Select some spanning tree $\Gamma^i \in R$ with edge set E^i, where $R=\{\Gamma^i\}$ is a set of spanning trees.
- Use any exact algorithm, such as belief propagation, to compute exact marginals $p^i(x)$ on Γ^i. For all $(u, v) \in E^i$, set

$$T_u^{i+1}(x_u) = p^i(x_u), \quad T_{uv}^{i+1}(x_u, x_v) = \frac{p^i(x_u, x_v)}{p^i(x_u) p^i(x_v)}$$

- Set $T_{uv}^{i+1} = T_{uv}^i$ for all $(u, v) \in E/E^i$ (i.e. all the edges not included in the spanning tree Γ^i).
- Stop if termination conditions are met.

Fig. 4. The TRP Algorithm

So far, the termination conditions are defined as: if the maximal change of the marginals is below a predefined threshold or the update times exceed a predefined number (defined as 1000 in our experiments), then stop the updates. When selecting spanning trees $R=\{T^i\}$, the only constraint is that the trees in R cover the edge set of the original undirected graph U. In practice, we select trees randomly, but we select first edges that have never been used in any previous iteration.

Finally, to reduce overfitting, we define a spherical Gaussian weight prior $p(\Theta)$ over parameters, and penalize the log-likelihood object function as:

$$L_\Theta = \sum_i p(x^{(i)}, y^{(i)}) \log p_\Theta(y^{(i)} | x^{(i)}) - \frac{\|\lambda\|^2}{2\sigma^2} + const \tag{6}$$

with gradient

$$\frac{\delta L_\Theta}{\delta \lambda_j} = \sum_i \left[\sum_c f_j(c, y^{(i)}_{(c)}, x^{(i)}) - \log Z(x^{(i)}) \right] - \frac{\lambda_j}{\sigma^2} \tag{7}$$

where *const* is a constant.

The function L_Θ is convex, and can be optimized by any number of techniques, as in other maximum-entropy models [14] [2]. In the result below, we used gradient-based L-BFGS [15], which has previously outperformed other optimization algorithms for linear-chain CRFs [20].

4.4 Annotation

Annotation (also called as 'labeling') is the task to find labels y^* that best describe the observations x, that is, $y^*=\max_y p(y|x)$. Dynamic programming algorithms are the most popular methods for this problem. However, it is difficult to directly adopt it for annotation in TCRFs. Two modes exist in the annotation of TCRFs: known structure and unknown structure. In the first mode, the hierarchical structure is known, for example, one can use the document logic structure to infer the hierarchical structure. Hence, we can use the TRP algorithm to compute the maximal value of $p(y|x)$. In the second mode, the hierarchical structure is unknown. We used a heuristics based method and performed the annotation for a given observation x_i as follows: (1) use vertex features to preliminary identify the possible labels for each vertex; (2) incorporate the edge features to compute all possible label results (that is, to enumerate all possible hierarchical structures) for an observations x_i; (3) use equation (6) to compute the log-likelihood for each structure and choose one as the annotation result y^* that has the largest log-likelihood. (The annotation in the second mode can be expensive, the issue and some of the related problems are currently researching, and will be reported elsewhere.)

4.5 Using TCRFs for Semantic Annotation

Currently, there is still not sufficient Semantic Web content available. Existing web content should be upgraded to Semantic Web content. Our proposed TCRFs can be used to create an annotation service, especially for the hierarchically laid-out data.

The output of the service will be generated according to the language pyramid of Semantic Web, so that agents can automatically handle the semantic information.

TCRFs can be used in two ways. One is to extract the web content (that we are interested) from its source, annotate it by an ontology, and store it in knowledge base. The other is to add the annotation results into the web page.

5 Experimental Results

5.1 Data Sets and Evaluation Measures

1. Data Sets

We carried out the experiments on two data sets, one synthetic and one real. For the real data set, we collected company annual reports from Shanghai Stock Exchange (http://www.sse.com.cn). We randomly chose in total 3,726 annual reports (in Chinese) from 1999 to 2004. To evaluate the effectiveness of our approach, we extracted the Section "Introduction to Company" from each annual report for experiments. For Chinese tokenization, we used a toolkit proposed in [16].

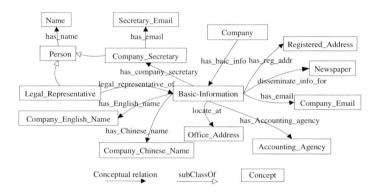

Fig. 5. Ontology of company annual report

Figure 5 shows the ontological information (that is we need to annotate) defined for the annual report. In total, fourteen concepts were defined in the ontology and the annotation task is to find instances for the fourteen concepts. Most of the concepts have hierarchical dependencies. Human annotators conducted annotation on all annual reports.

We also constructed a synthetic data set. The data set contains 62 company annual reports chosen from the real data set. In this data set, four concepts are defined only: "Company_Secretary", "Secretary_Email", "Registered_Address", and "Company_ Email". Where the first two concepts and the last two concepts have the parent-child dependencies respectively and the concepts "Company_Secretary", "Registered-_Address" have the sibling dependency. Every report in the data set exclusively has the four types of instances and the four instances are organized hierarchically.

2. Features in Annotation Models
Table 1 indicates the features used in the annotation models.

Table 1. Features used in the annotation models

Category	Feature
Edge Feature	$f(y_p, y_c), f(y_c, y_p), f(y_s, y_s)$
Vertex Feature	$\{w_i\}, \{w_p\}, \{w_c\}, \{w_s\}$
	$\{w_p, w_i\}, \{w_c, w_i\}, \{w_s, w_i\}$

Given the j-th vertex in the observation x_i, $f(y_p, y_c)$, $f(y_c, y_p)$, and $f(y_s, y_s)$ represent whether the current vertex has a parent-child dependency with a parent vertex, whether it has a child-parent dependency with a child vertex, and whether it has a sibling dependency with a sibling vertex, respectively. For vertex features, each element in $\{w_i\}$ represents whether the current vertex contains the word w_i. Similarly, each element in $\{w_p\}$, $\{w_c\}$, and $\{w_s\}$ represents whether the parent vertex of the current vertex contains word w_p whether its child vertices contain w_c, and whether its sibling vertices contain w_s, respectively. $\{w_p, w_i\}$ represents whether the current vertex contains word w_i and its parent vertex contains word w_p. To save time in some of our experiments, we omitted the vertex features that appear only once.

3. Evaluation Measures
In all the experiments of annotation, we conducted evaluations in terms of precision, recall, and F1-measure. By comparison of the previous work, we also give statistical significance estimates using Sign Test [9].

4. Baselines
To evaluate our model's effectiveness of incorporating hierarchical dependencies for semantic annotation, we choose linear-chain CRFs as the baseline models for their outstanding performance over other sequential models. The linear-chain CRF models are trained using the same features as those in table 1 (the only difference is that the linear-chain CRFs uses the linear edge features and the TCRFs uses the hierarchical edge features).

We also compared the proposed method with the classification based annotation method, which is another popular annotation method. The classification based method treats a company annual report as a sequence of text lines, employs two classification models to respectively identify the start line and the end line of a target instance, and then view lines that between the start line and the end line as a target (see [7] and [23] for details). In the experiments, we use Support Vector Machines (SVMs) as the classification models. In the SVMs models, we use the same features as those in table 1 (excluding the edge features).

5.2 Experiments

We evaluated the proposed method on the two data sets. We conducted the experiments in the following way. First, we converted each company annual report into a sequence of text lines; for the SVMs base method, we use the vertex features and train two SVM models for each concept; for the linear-chain CRFs, we use the vertex features and the linear edge features to train the models; for TCRFs, we use the vertex features and the hierarchical edge features to train the models. For training SVM models we use SVM-light, which is available at http://svmlight.joachims.org/. For training linear-chain CRF models, we use KEG_CRFs, which is available at http://keg.cs.tsinghua.edu.cn/persons/tj/.

5.2.1 Experimental Results on the Synthetic Data Set

Table 2 shows the five-fold cross-validation results on the synthetic data set. SVM, CRF, and TCRF respectively represent the SVMs based method, the linear-chain CRFs method, and the proposed TCRFs method. Prec., Rec., and F1 respectively represent the scores of precision, recall, and F1-measure.

Table 2. Performance of semantic annotation on the synthetic data set (%)

Annotation Task	SVM			CRF			TCRF		
	Prec.	Rec.	F1	Prec.	Rec.	F1	Prec.	Rec.	F1
Company_Secretary	99.26	88.74	93.71	100.0	100.0	100.0	100.0	100.0	100.0
Secretary_Email	50.00	7.52	13.07	50.00	42.86	46.15	100.0	100.0	100.0
Registered_Address	97.46	89.84	93.50	100.0	100.0	100.0	100.0	100.0	100.0
Company_Email	0.00	0.00	0.00	46.15	50.00	48.00	100.0	100.0	100.0
Average	61.68	46.53	50.07	89.15	89.15	89.15	100.0	100.0	100.0

We see that for both "Company_Secretary" and "Registered_Address", all of the three methods can achieve high accuracy of annotation. Compared with the SVMs based method, CRF and TCRF can obtain better results. We can also see that for "Secretary_Email" and "Company_Email", the proposed method TCRF significantly outperforms the SVMs based method and the linear-chain CRFs based method. We conducted sign tests on the results. The p values are much smaller than 0.01, indicating that the improvements are statistically significant.

5.2.2 Experimental Results on the Real Data Set

Table 3 shows the five-fold cross-validation results on the real data set. In the table, we also use SVM, CRF, and TCRF to respectively represent the SVMs based method, the linear-chain CRFs method, and the proposed TCRFs method; and use Prec., Rec., and F1 to respectively represent the scores of precision, recall, and F1-measure.

From the results we see that TCRF can achieve the best performance 89.87% in terms of F1-measure (outperforming CRF+7.67% and SVM+14.10% on average). In terms of both precision and recall, CRF can outperform SVM. TCRF again outperform CRF +3.14% in terms of precision and +12.08% in terms of recall. We conducted sign tests on the results. The p values are much smaller than 0.01, indicating that the improvements are statistically significant.

5.2.3 Discussions

(1) Effectiveness of TCRF. In the synthetic data set, the data are hierarchically organized. TCRF can indeed improve the annotation performance. On annotation of "Secretary_Email" and "Company_Email", the SVMs based method only uses the neighborhood contexts and thus cannot disambiguate them from each other (only 13.07% and 0.00% in terms of F1-measure). The linear-chain CRFs based method can improve the annotation result by making use of linear dependencies (46.15% and 48.00% respectively). However, as the linear-chain CRFs cannot model hierarchical dependencies, the improvements are limited. The proposed TCRFs based method can model the hierarchical dependencies, and obtain the best performance (100.00% and 100.00% respectively). This indicates that the proposed Tree-structured Conditional Random Fields are effective for the problem of hierarchical semantic annotation.

Table 3. Performance of semantic annotation on the real data set (%)

Annotation Task	SVM			CRF			TCRF		
	Prec.	Rec.	F1	Prec.	Rec.	F1	Prec.	Rec.	F1
Company_Chinese_Name	88.82	89.40	89.11	82.10	80.69	81.37	84.34	92.72	88.33
Company_English_Name	90.51	95.33	92.86	71.68	80.14	75.66	89.26	88.67	88.96
Legal_Representative	94.84	97.35	96.08	92.86	96.60	94.66	94.84	97.35	96.08
Company_Secretary	99.29	93.33	96.22	91.65	96.99	94.23	77.96	96.67	86.31
Secretary_Email	57.14	8.89	15.39	69.94	56.53	62.34	73.86	97.01	83.87
Registered_Address	98.66	96.71	97.68	94.75	87.20	90.80	84.05	90.13	86.98
Office_Address	70.41	97.54	81.78	77.41	87.06	81.94	86.93	89.86	88.37
Company_Email	0.00	0.00	0.00	84.57	85.64	85.09	95.20	90.84	92.97
Newspaper	100.0	99.34	99.67	94.51	91.97	93.21	98.69	100.0	99.34
Accounting_Agency	83.15	95.63	88.95	73.81	56.77	62.73	79.57	97.19	87.50
Average	78.28	77.35	75.77	83.33	81.96	82.20	86.47	94.04	89.87

(2) Improvements over CRF. In the real data set, TCRF significantly outperforms the linear-chain CRF for the annotation of most concepts. For the concepts that have strong hierarchical dependencies, TCRF can achieve much better results than CRF, for example, on "Secretary_Email" and "Company_Email" TCRF outperforms CRF by +21.53% and +7.88%, respectively.

(3) Improvements over SVM. In the real data set, TCRF outperforms SVM +8.19% in terms of precision and +16.69% in terms of recall. The SVMs based method suffers from the extremely bad results on the annotation of "Secretary_Email" and "Company_Email". This is due to that the SVMs based method considers only neighborhood contexts. Besides the two concepts, TCRF also outperforms SVM on annotation of some other concepts, for example "Office_Address". We need notice that in some cases, TCRF underperforms SVM. For example on "Company_Chinese_Name" and "Company_English_Name", TCRF underperforms SVM by -0.78% and -2.9%, respectively. This is because instances of such concepts seem to be independent and do not have dependencies with instances of the other concepts.

(4) Time complexity. We conducted analysis of time complexity of our approach. We tested the three methods on a computer with two 2.8G Dual-Core CPUs and three Gigabyte memory. In total, for training and annotating the fourteen concepts, the SVMs based method takes about 96 seconds and 30 seconds respectively, while the CRF method takes about 5 minutes 25 seconds and 5 seconds respectively. Our current implementation of the TCRF method used more time for training and annotation (about 50 minutes 40 seconds and 50 seconds respectively.) This indicates that the efficiency of TCRF still needs improvements.

(5) Error analysis. We conducted error analysis on the results of our approach.

There are mainly three types of errors. The first type of errors (about 34.85% of the errors) is that in some concepts, there are no hierarchical dependencies, for example "Company_Chinese_Name" and "Company_English_Name". In such cases, the proposed TCRFs contrarily result in worse performance than the SVMs based method that does not consider dependencies. About 28.05% of the errors occur when there are extra email addresses in the text. The third type of errors was due to extra line breaks in the text, which mistakenly breaks the targeted instance into multiple lines.

6 Conclusions

In this paper, we investigated the problem of hierarchical semantic annotation. We proposed a Tree-structured Conditional Random Field (TCRF) model. This model provides a novel way of incorporating the dependencies across the hierarchical structure to improve the performance of hierarchical semantic annotation. Using an approximate algorithm, i.e. Tree Reparameterization (TRP), efficient parameter estimation and annotation can be performed. Experimental results on two data sets show that the proposed model significantly outperforms the linear-chain CRF models and the SVMs based models for annotating hierarchically laid-out data. We also found that the efficiency of the proposed TCRF model still needs improvements.

References

[1] R. Benjamins and J. Contreras. Six challenges for the semantic web. Intelligent Software Components. Intelligent Software for the Networked Economy (isoco). 2002.
[2] A. L. Berger, S. A. Della Pietra, and V. J. Della Pietra. A maximum entropy approach to natural language processing. Computational Linguistics, Vol,22,1996. pp. 39-71
[3] R. C. Bunescu, R. J. Mooney. Collective information extraction with relational Markov networks. In Proceedings of the 42nd Annual Meeting of the Association for Computational Linguistics (ACL'04), 2004. pp. 439-446
[4] F. Ciravegna. (LP)2, an adaptive algorithm for information extraction from web-related texts. In Proceedings of the IJCAI'2001 Workshop on Adaptive Text Extraction and Mining held in conjunction with 17th IJCAI'2001, Seattle, USA. 2001. pp. 1251-1256
[5] M. Collins. Discriminative training methods for hidden Markov models: Theory and Experiments with Perceptron Algorithms. In Proceedings of EMNLP'02. 2002.
[6] C. Cortes and V. Vapnik. Support-Vector Networks. Machine Learning, Vol. 20, 1995, pp. 273-297

[7] A. Finn and N. Kushmerick. Multi-level boundary classification for information extraction. In Proceedings of the ECML'2004, Pisa, 2004. pp.156-167
[8] Z. Ghahramani and M. I. Jordan. Factorial hidden Markov models. Machine Learning, Vol.29, 1997, pp. 245-273
[9] L. Gillick and S. Cox. Some statistical issues in the compairson of speech recognition algorithms. In International Conference on Acoustics Speech and Signal Processing, 1989, Vol. 1: 532-535
[10] J. Hammersley and P. Clifford. Markov fields on finite graphs and lattices. Unpublished manuscript. 1971.
[11] B. Hammond, A. Sheth, and K. Kochut. Semantic enhancement engine: a modular document enhancement platform for semantic applications over heterogeneous content, in real world semantic web applications. IOS Press, 2002. pp. 29-49
[12] S. Handschuh, S. Staab, and F. Ciravegna. S-CREAM - semi-automatic creation of metadata. In Proceedings of the 13th International Conference on Knowledge Engineering and Management (EKAW'2002), Siguenza, Spain, 2002. pp. 358-372
[13] N. Kushmerick, D. S. Weld, and R. B. Doorenbos. Wrapper induction for information extraction. In Proceedings of the International Joint Conference on Artificial Intelligence (IJCAI). Nagoya, Japan, 1997. pp. 729-737
[14] J. Lafferty, A. McCallum, and F. Pereira. Conditional random fields: probabilistic models for segmenting and labeling sequence data. In Proceedings of the 18th International Conference on Machine Learning (ICML'01), 2001. pp. 282-289
[15] D. C. Liu and J. Nocedal. On the limited memory BFGS method for large scale optimization. Mathematical Programming, 1989. pp. 503-528
[16] T. Lou, R. Song, W.L. Li, and Z.Y. Luo. The design and implementation of a modern general purpose segmentation system, Journal of Chinese Information Processing, (5), 2001.
[17] A. McCallum, D. Freitag, and F. Pereira. Maximum entropy Markov models for information extraction and segmentation. In Proceedings of the 17th International Conference on Machine Learning (ICML'00), 2000. pp. 591-598
[18] B. Popov, A. Kiryakov, A. Kirilov, D. Manov, D. Ognyanoff, and M. Goranov. KIM - semantic annotation platform. In Proceedings of 2nd International Semantic Web Conference (ISWC'2003), Florida, USA, 2003. pp. 834-849
[19] L. Reeve. Integrating hidden Markov models into semantic web annotation platforms. Technique Report. 2004.
[20] F. Sha and F. Pereira. Shallow parsing with conditional random fields. In Proceedings of Human Language Technology, NAACL. 2003.
[21] C. Sutton, K. Rohanimanesh, and A. McCallum. Dynamic conditional random fields: factorized probabilistic models for labeling and segmenting sequence data. In Proceedings of ICML'2004. 2004.
[22] J. Tang, J. Li, H. Lu, B. Liang, and K. Wang. 2005a. iASA: learning to annotate the semantic web. Journal on Data Semantic, IV. Springer Press. pp. 110-145
[23] J. Tang, H. Li, Y. Cao, and Z. Tang. Email data cleaning. In Proceedings of SIGKDD'2005. August 21-24, 2005, Chicago, Illinois, USA. Full paper. pp. 489-499
[24] M. Wainwright, T. Jaakkola, and A. Willsky. Tree-based reparameterization for approximate estimation on graphs with cycles. In Proceedings of Advances in Neural Information Processing Systems (NIPS'2001), 2001. pp. 1001-1008
[25] J. Yedidia, W. Freeman, and Y. Weiss. Generalized belief propagation. Advances in Neural Information Processing Systems (NIPS). 2000.
[26] J. Zhu, Z. Nie, J. Wen, B. Zhang, and W. Ma. 2D conditional random fields for web information extraction. In Proceedings of ICML'2005.

Framework for an Automated Comparison of Description Logic Reasoners

Tom Gardiner, Dmitry Tsarkov, and Ian Horrocks*

University of Manchester
Manchester, UK
{gardiner, tsarkov, horrocks}@cs.man.ac.uk

Abstract. OWL is an ontology language developed by the W3C, and although initially developed for the Semantic Web, OWL has rapidly become a de facto standard for ontology development in general. The design of OWL was heavily influenced by research in description logics, and the specification includes a formal semantics. One of the goals of this formal approach was to provide interoperability: different OWL reasoners should provide the same results when processing the same ontologies. In this paper we present a system that allows users: (a) to test and compare OWL reasoners using an extensible library of real-life ontologies; (b) to check the "correctness" of the reasoners by comparing the computed class hierarchy; (c) to compare the performance of the reasoners when performing this task; and (d) to use SQL queries to analyse and present the results in any way they see fit.

1 Introduction

OWL is an ontology language (or rather a family of three languages) developed by the World Wide Web Consortium (W3C) [21]. Although initially developed in order to satisfy requirements deriving from Semantic Web research [13], OWL has rapidly become a de facto standard for ontology development in general, and OWL ontologies are now under development and/or in use in areas as diverse as e-Science, medicine, biology, geography, astronomy, defence, and the automotive and aerospace industries.

The design of OWL was heavily influenced by research in description logics (DLs); investigations of (combinations of) DL language constructors provided a detailed understanding of the semantics and computational properties of, and reasoning techniques for, various ontology language designs [1,10,14,15]; this understanding was used to ensure that, for two of the three OWL dialects (OWL DL and OWL Lite), key reasoning problems would be decidable. Basing the language on a suitable DL also allowed for the exploitation of existing DL implementations in order to provide reasoning services for OWL applications [11,20,7].

The standardisation of OWL has led to the development and adaption of a wide range of tools and services, including reasoners such as FaCT++ [26], Racer-Pro [7], Pellet [24] and KAON2 (http://kaon2.semanticweb.org/). Reasoners

---
* This work was partially supported by EPSRC, project IST-2006-027269 "Sealife".

are often used with editing tools, e.g., Protégé [23] and Swoop [17], in order to compute the class hierarchy and alert users to problems such as inconsistent classes.

One of the key benefits that a formal language standard provides to users of web-based technologies is *interoperability*. In the case of OWL, this should mean that users can load ontologies from the internet and use them in applications, possibly answering queries against them using one of the available OWL reasoners. One of the goals of standardisation is that the result of this process is independent of the chosen reasoner. Up to now, however, relatively little attention has been given to checking if this goal is indeed satisfied by available OWL reasoners—the OWL standard includes a test suite [4], but this mainly focuses on small tests that isolate some particular language feature; it does not include many complex cases that involve interactions between different features, nor tests that use realistic ontologies.

This kind of comparison is also of great value to implementors of DL reasoning systems, who typically use testing in order to check the correctness of their implementations. This may be relatively easy for small examples, where manual checking is possible, but will usually not be feasible for realistic ontologies. In such cases, the best (perhaps the only) way to check the correctness of an implementation may be by checking for consistency with the reasoning of other systems.

Once we have confirmed that some or all reasoners are correct (or at least consistent), we may also want to compare their performance. Reasoning with expressive DLs (like those underlying OWL-DL) has high worst case complexity, and this means that, in general, reasoning is highly intractable for these logics. The hope/claim is, however, that modern highly optimised systems perform well in "realistic" ontology applications. To check the validity of this claim it is necessary to test the performance of these systems with (the widest possible range of) ontologies derived from applications.

Real-world ontologies vary considerably in their size and expressivity. While they are all valuable test cases, it is still important to understand each ontology's properties in order to provide efficient and relevant testing. For example, a user (or potential user) of OWL may have some particular application in mind, and might like to know which of the available OWL reasoners is most suitable. In this case, it would be useful if they could compare the performance of reasoners with ontologies having similar characteristics to those that will be used in their application. System developers might also find this kind of testing useful, as it can help them to identify weaknesses in their systems and to devise and test new optimisations.

In this paper we present a system that allows users:

- to test and compare OWL reasoners using an extensible library of real-life ontologies;
- to check the "correctness" of the reasoners by comparing the computed class hierarchy;

- to compare the performance of the reasoners when performing this task;
- to use SQL queries to analyse and present the results in any way they see fit.

2 Background and Related Work

There is extensive existing work on benchmarking DL (as well as modal logic) reasoners. E.g., the TANCS comparisons and benchmark suites [18], the DL comparisons and benchmark suite [12], the OWL benchmark suite and test results, and various test results from papers describing systems such as M-SPASS [16], FaCT and DLP [9,8], FaCT++ [25], KAON2, Pellet [24], Racer [6], Vampire [27], etc.

Due to the fact that relatively few (large and/or interesting) ontologies were available, earlier tests often used artificially generated test data. For some tests of this kind (e.g. the DL-98 tests, [12]) are hand crafted, or constructed according to a pattern, in such a way that a correct answer is known; in this case they can be used both to test correctness and to measure the performance of reasoners on a certain class of tasks. Other artificial benchmarks (like [22]) are randomly generated, so no correct answer is known for them; in this case they can only be used for performance testing (or for comparing results from more than one reasoner). The Lehigh University Benchmark [5] has been developed specifically for testing OWL reasoners, and uses a synthetic ontology and randomly generated data to test their capabilities using specific weightings to compare systems on characteristics of interest. Results from such tests are, however, of doubtful relevance when gauging performance on real-life ontologies. The popularity of OWL means that many more real-life ontologies are now available, and recent benchmarking work has focused on testing performance with such ontologies.

One such example involved benchmarking of a number of reasoners against a broad range of realistic ontologies [19]. Note that only performance was tested in that work; no results regarding any comparison of the outputs of the reasoner are known. Additionally, not all reasoners used in that comparison supported OWL as an input language, so quantitative comparison of performance would have been difficult/un-justified. This latter problem is eased by the popularity of the DIG (DL Implementation Group) interface [2], which is widely used by application developers and has thus been implemented in most modern DL Reasoners.

Our work builds on these earlier efforts, taking advantage of the DIG standard to provide a generic benchmarking suite that allows the automatic quantitative testing and comparison of DL Reasoners on real-world ontologies with a wide range of different characteristics, e.g., with respect to size and the subset of OWL actually used in the ontology. We aim to make the testing process as automatic as possible, taking care, for example, of (re)starting and stopping reasoners as necessary, to make the results available as and when required by storing them in a database, and to make the analysis of results as easy and flexible as possible by allowing for arbitrary SQL queries against the collected data. We also aim to provide (in the form of a publicly available resource) a library of test ontologies where each ontology has been checked for expressivity (i.e., the subset of OWL actually used) and syntactic conformance, translated into DIG syntax (which is much easier to work with for the benchmarking purposes than OWL's RDF/XML syntax), and includes (where possible) results (such as the class hierarchy) that can be used for testing the correctness of reasoning systems.

3 Methodology

The system we present here has three main functions. The first is to collect real-world OWL ontologies (e.g., from the Web), process them and add them to a library of ontologies which can be used as a test suite. The second is to automatically run benchmarking tests for one or more reasoners, using the ontology library and storing the results (both performance data and reasoning results) in a database. The third is to allow users to analyse and compare saved results for one or more reasoners.

When processing ontologies, the system takes as an input a list of OWL ontology URIs. Before they can be used in testing, some preprocessing of these ontologies is required. The process involves generating of valuable meta-data about each ontology, as well as converting each of the OWL ontologies into DIG.

The meta-data is generated using code written for SWOOP [17], and specifies some details w.r.t. the expressivity (i.e. the constructs present in the ontology) together with the number of classes, object properties, data properties, individuals, class axioms, property axioms and individual axioms present. This is invaluable information in helping to understand and analyse the results obtained through testing; it can be used, e.g., to study the strengths and weaknesses of particular systems, or to identify ontologies with similar characteristics to those that will be used in a given application.

The OWL-to-DIG conversion uses the OWL-API (http://sourceforge.net/projects/owlapi). This process is far from being trivial as OWL's RDF syntax is complex, and it is easy to (inadvertently) cause ontologies to fall outside OWL-DL, e.g., by simply forgetting to explicitly type every object. Moreover, the current DIG interface supports only the most basic of datatypes, such as <xsd:string> and <xsd:integer>.[1] The result is that many of the available OWL ontologies we found could not be successfully converted to DIG, due to either being OWL-Full or to using more expressive data types than those that are allowed in DIG. In the former case, i.e., OWL-Full ontologies, it is almost *always* the case that they are OWL-Full only as the result of some trivial syntax error; usually missing typing information. Such ontologies can easily be "repaired" and added to the library.

Local copies of both the OWL ontology and the DIG version are stored in a database. This is done not only for efficiency during the testing, but also to ensure consistency (as online ontologies rarely remain static). Moreover, this allows us to fix trivial errors (like missing type information for an object) in

---

[1] A new DIG standard, DIG 2.0, is currently under development, and will provide support for all OWL compatible datatypes.

OWL ontologies in order to ensure that they are in OWL-DL. This can be done by using a technique described in [3]. Such "repaired" ontologies can be successfully translated into DIG, and thus can be used for testing purposes. These files, together with their properties/meta-data, are stored as database entries for easy access and manipulation.

The main function of the benchmark suite itself is to gather the classification information for each ontology and each reasoner. This information includes the time spent by a reasoner in performing certain queries, and the query answer returned by the reasoner.

To promote fairness, each reasoner is terminated and then restarted before loading each ontology. This ensures that every reasoner is in the same "state" when working on a given ontology, regardless of how successful previous attempts were. This also simplifies the management of cases for which the time-out limit was exceeded.

One problem that arises when trying to compare the performance of different reasoners is that they may perform reasoning tasks in different ways. For example, some may take an "eager" approach, fully classifying the whole ontology and caching the results as soon as it is received; others may take a "lazy" approach, only performing reasoning tasks as required in order to answer queries. To try to get around this problem, we use a five step test, for each ontology, that forces reasoners to fully classify the ontology, whether eagerly or lazily. The steps are as follows:

1. Load the ontology into the reasoner;
2. Query the reasoner for all the named (atomic) classes in the ontology;
3. Query the reasoner for the consistency of the ontology by checking the satisfiability of the class owl:Thing;
4. Query the reasoner for the satisfiability of each of the named classes in the ontology;
5. Query the reasoner for the ontology taxonomy (i.e., the parents and children of all named classes).

Each of these individual steps is timed, providing interesting information about when different reasoners do their work. It is, however, the total time for this complete (classification) test that is probably of most interest.

Each test can end in one of three ways. It can either complete successfully, fail due to lack of resources (either time or memory), or fail because the reasoner could not parse/process the ontology and/or query successfully. In case of success, the answers given by the reasoner are saved in the database. These answers can be used for testing the correctness of reasoning (or at least comparing results with those obtained from other reasoners).

The benchmarking process is fully automatic, dealing with most errors autonomously, meaning that the testing can be left to run over-night or over a week-end (which may be necessary when using a large time-out). All data is recorded in a database, making it easy for the user to view and analyse the data in a variety of ways.

As discussed in Section 1, in order to get a clearer indication of how DL Reasoners perform in the real world, we aim to build a large library of OWL ontologies from those that are publicly available. Currently, our library contains over 300 OWL ontologies, but so far only 172 of these have been successfully converted to DIG. This has, however, provided us with a total of just under 72,000 classes and over 30,000 individuals in a DIG format. Only 18% of the ontologies had the expressivity corresponding to the DL $\mathcal{ALC}$ or higher, which suggests that the majority of real-world ontologies are not, in fact, very complex, but it also means that we have a useful number of "interesting" examples.

4 Data Storage

As we have mentioned on several occasions, the database is used to store all processed data. We have used a database as it provides persistence, and allows the user to quickly summarize data and to analyse it in any way that is deemed appropriate. The database contains a wealth of information about both the ontologies and the behaviour of the reasoners, allowing users to produce high level summaries or to focus on and investigate results of particular interest.

Moreover, the database is designed so that any data obtained through our tests is stored with a normalised layout. For example, the responses to the queries in our 5 step test are returned by the reasoners as large XML documents (in DIG format) which can represent the same information in a number of different ways. Our system parses these responses and records them as simple class names, along with information such as satisfiability status (i.e., satisfiable or not), parents (i.e., named classes that are direct subsumers) and children (i.e., named classes that are direct subsumees). This makes it easy to use SQL queries to look for similarities or differences between different reasoner's responses.

The advantages of our approach are demonstrated in Section 5 below, where we show examples of the kind of query that we could issue and the resulting information that would be extracted from the database.

5 Testing

Our system as it stands is fully automatic and runs the classification tests successfully through our whole library. The times taken by each reasoner, for each step and for each ontology are recorded, together with the parsed and normalised version of the responses returned by each reasoner.

We have performed tests using our system with several state-of-the-art DIG reasoners, and we provide here some examples of the kinds of information that the system can produce. It is important to note that we simply set up our benchmarking system to run overnight for each ontology with each reasoner. All the information described in the following sub-sections was then obtained by querying the resulting database to extract the information that we were interested in.

FaCT++ v1.1.3, KAON2, Pellet v1.3 and RacerPro v1.8.1 are four of the most widely used OWL/DIG reasoners, and we therefore decided to use these to test the current capabilities of our system. The tests were performed using an Intel Pentium-M processor 1.60 GHz and 1Gb of main memory on Windows XP. The time-out period was set to 10 minutes (in real time). Pellet and KAON2 are Java applications, and for these tests were run with a maximum heap space of 200Mb. RacerPro and FaCT++ were left to run at their default settings. Our system does not try to optimise the performance of the reasoners for particular ontologies, as we believe this is the job of the reasoners themselves: users of OWL reasoners cannot be expected to be experts in how to tune them in order to optimise their performance.

5.1 Correctness

Every step of our benchmarking is timed to allow performance comparison of the reasoners in question. However, this data only becomes relevant if we can confirm the correctness of the responses returned by these systems when answering the queries we put to them (test steps 2-5): a reasoner that quickly but incorrectly answers queries is of little use (or at least cannot be fairly compared to one that gives correct answers).

When reasoner implementors test the correctness of their systems, they typically use small artificially generated examples and manually check the correctness of their system's responses. Due to the sheer size of the ontologies in our library, it is not feasible to check responses by hand, so we needed a way of automating this task.

It is impossible to say any one reasoner is universally correct, and we are therefore unable to base correctness on any one reasoner's answers. Our solution was to base our measure of correctness on tests of consistency of different reasoner's answers. Our claim is that consistency between multiple reasoners implies a high probability of correctness, especially when the reasoners have been designed and implemented independently, and in some cases even use different reasoning techniques.[2]

With normalised entries of the parsed responses stored in our database, checking for consistency was a simple matter of writing a few short SQL queries to see if each reasoner had symmetrical entries for each of the DIG queries. Naturally, this required that at least two reasoners had successfully completed the 5-step classification test. Of our 172 DIG ontologies, 148 had this property; of the remaining 24 ontologies, more than half were not successfully classified by *any* of the reasoners.

We started by checking for 100% consistency on each of the classification steps, where 100% consistency meant that all reasoners that successfully completed the test gave the same answers w.r.t. the class hierarchy. Where there were conflicts, we used more specific SQL queries to analyse the reason in detail, allowing us to see exactly how big the differences were.

---

[2] KAON2 uses a resolution based technique; the other reasoners tested here use a tableaux based technique.

Our findings were surprisingly impressive, with only 7 of the 148 ontologies (that were fully classified by at least two reasoners) not being 100% consistent on all tests. This reflects very positively on the OWL standardisation process (and on the developers of these reasoners), and shows that the OWL standard really does result in a high degree of interoperability.

The inconsistencies between reasoners on the seven aforementioned ontologies raised some interesting issues.

Starting with step 2 (querying for the list of classes in each ontology), there were only three ontologies on which there were inconsistencies. The reason for the inconsistencies was due to the existence of nominals (i.e., extensionally defined classes resulting, e.g., from the use of the OWL *oneOf* or *hasValue* constructors). RacerPro was actually returning nominals as classes, while the other three reasoners were not. (These three ontologies were also the only three ontologies containing nominals that RacerPro successfully classified). We assume that this happens because RacerPro does not claim to be sound and complete in the presence of nominals, but instead tries to approximate them using classes to represent them.

Step 3 (querying for the satisfiability of owl:Thing) was 100% consistent for all ontologies. This is, however, not surprising as owl:Thing is satisfiable for all of the ontologies in the library.

Step 4 (querying for the satisfiability of each named class in the ontology) found only two ontologies with inconsistent answers. Interestingly, they were both only successfully classified by FaCT++ and Pellet, and on one of the ontologies they disagreed about the satisfiability of over 2/3 of the classes present.

The first ontology was in $\mathcal{SHIN}$ (Tambis) and the other was in DL-Lite with Datatypes and Inverse roles. Other properties of these ontologies suggested no obvious challenges. We therefore selected a few of the classes on which there was disagreement, and used SWOOP to analyse them. Using this tool we found that FaCT++ was clearly inconsistent in its reasoning w.r.t. these classes.

Taking one class as an example: FaCT++ answered that the class *RNA* was satisfiable, while Pellet disagreed. SWOOP showed that the definition of *RNA* consisted of the intersection of the class *Macromolecular-compound* and a number of other classes. However, FaCT++ and Pellet both agreed that *Macromolecular-compound* was not satisfiable, hence implying that *RNA* was definitely unsatisfiable. As a result of this investigation, a bug in FaCT++ has been identified and is now in the process of being fixed. This demonstrates how valuable the information provided by our system can be to system developers as well as to users of OWL reasoners.

As hoped, step 5 (querying for the parents and children of each named class in the ontology) found that the taxonomies defined by the parent and children relations were consistent in the vast majority of cases, and there were only three ontologies on which the reasoners were not in agreement. In each of these cases, FaCT++ was not in agreement with the other reasoners. Due to the detailed information recorded by our system holds, we are easily able to identify the classes that are causing this problem, and thus investigate it more closely. In this way we can not only find bugs that have not been discovered before, but the detailed analysis allows a system implementor to quickly find exactly what is causing the bug, and hopefully to fix it.

5.2 Efficiency

We present here some examples of the kinds of performance related information that can be extracted from the database using suitable SQL queries. Table 1 provides an overview of the performance of the four reasoners: it shows how many of the test ontologies they were able to classify within the specified time limit, and then breaks this information down by focussing on sets of ontologies using particular language features. Finally, it also shows their performance on OWL-Lite ontologies, i.e., all those with expressivity up to and including $\mathcal{SHIF}$. Note that only 100% consistent ontologies are compared here; as we mentioned before, the performance analysis is of doubtful value when different reasoners do not agree on query results.

It is important to note that "Could not process" most often means that the reasoner does not support the constructs present within that particular ontology (and does not claim to either).

Table 1. Sample of Overall Performance for 100% Consistent Ontologies

Type	Status	FaCT++	KAON2	Pellet	RacerPro
All	Success	137	43	143	105
All	CouldNotProcess	24	119	20	60
All	ResourcesExceeded	4	3	2	0
Nominals	Success	4	0	2	0
Nominals	CouldNotProcess	0	5	3	5
Nominals	ResourcesExceeded	1	0	0	0
TransRoles	Success	9	5	9	6
TransRoles	CouldNotProcess	2	6	3	7
TransRoles	ResourcesExceeded	2	2	1	0
Datatypes	Success	91	0	98	62
Datatypes	CouldNotProcess	19	112	14	50
Datatypes	ResourcesExceeded	2	0	0	0
OWL-Lite	Success	43	41	42	43
OWL-Lite	CouldNotProcess	5	6	6	7
OWL-Lite	ResourcesExceeded	2	3	2	0

The SQL statement below shows how easily we filled the transitive-roles part of Table 1. Here, "name" refers to the name of the reasoner, "status" is a choice of "Succes", "CouldNotProcess" or "ResourcesExceeded" and the COUNT function returns a count of the number of ontologies that meet the given criteria.

```
SELECT name, status, COUNT(status)
FROM resultsview
WHERE rplus
AND ontology IN
(
  /*Get the list of ontologies that had full consistency on all steps*/
  SELECT ontology
  FROM consistency
  WHERE clist AND topsat AND allsat AND parents
)
GROUP BY name, status;
```

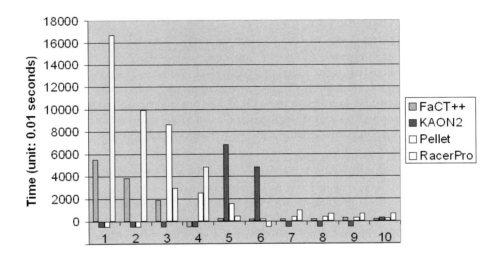

Fig. 1. Comparison of Reasoners on the Top 10 Most Challenging Ontologies

Table 2 presents some information describing the features of the the 10 most "challenging" (w.r.t. reasoning) ontologies in the library. We did this by selecting all those ontologies that were successfully classified by at least two reasoners, and then ordering these ontologies by the average classification time for those reasoners that successfully classified them. Note that this is just an example of the way in which the data can be analysed, and we do not claim this to be the "correct" way to select challenging ontologies.

This table is useful in helping us understand what makes these particular Ontologies so time-consuming to reason over. In the case of the NCI and Gene Ontologies (1st and 2nd), it can be clearly seen that it is their sheer size that provides the challenge. The Hydrolic Units ontologies (7th and 10th) have very few classes (only 5 and 6 respectively), but relatively large numbers of individuals. The world-fact-book ontology (4th) uses only a minimal subset of the ontology language (no more than the DL subset of RDFS), but has a reasonably large

Table 2. Properties of Top 10 Most Challenging Ontologies

	Expressivity	nClass	nIndiv	Ontology
1	DLLite	27652	0	NCI
2	$\mathcal{ALR+}$	20526	0	GeneOntology
3	$\mathcal{SHF}$	2749	0	Galen
4	RDFS(DL)	1108	3635	WorldFactBook
5	RDFS(DL)	1514	0	DataCenter
6	$\mathcal{SHIF}$	37	0	DolceLite
7	$\mathcal{ALR+HI(D)}$	5	2744	HydrolicUnits2003
8	RDFS(DL)	382	1872	Tambis
9	RDFS(DL)	98	0	MovieDatabase
10	RDFS(DL)	6	2744	HydrolicUnits

number of both classes and individuals. Finally, the Galen ontology (2nd) has a moderately large number of classes, and also uses a relatively rich subset of OWL. This demonstrates the kinds of insight that can be achieved using suitable queries. In this case we examined just three properties (specifically expressivity, number of classes and number of individuals) of our chosen ontologies; we could easily have extended our analysis to include available information such as the number of object/data properties, kinds of axiom occurring, etc.

In Figure 1, we present a graphical view of the amount of time each Reasoner took to classify the 10 most challenging ontologies according to the above mentioned measure (where negative time represents unsuccessful classification). It is interesting to note that there is no clear "winner" here; for example, FaCT++ performs well on the ontologies with very large numbers of classes (the NCI and Gene Ontologies), but relatively poorly on some ontologies with large numbers of individuals (e.g., the world-fact-book ontology).

Regarding the ontologies that include large numbers of individuals, it is important to note that our testing procedure (the 5-step classification) does not yet include any ABox queries (adding this kind of testing will be part of future work). This is clearly disadvantageous to systems such as KAON2 that are mainly designed to optimise ABox query answering rather than classification.

Table 3. Average Division of Task Time

Reasoner	Load	ClassList	SatofTop	SatOfClasses	Hierarchy
FaCT++	16%	26%	16%	21%	21%
KAON2	48%	44%	1%	2%	5%
Pellet	69%	21%	1%	2%	7%
RacerPro	57%	10%	4%	9%	19%

Finally, in Table 3, we present the average proportion of the classification time that the reasoners spent on each of the five steps. This shows, for example, that

Pellet performs a lot of work as soon as it receives the Ontology (the `Load` step), while `FaCT++` does relatively little work until the first query (the `ClassList` step).

Note that the reason for the `Load` step taking such a large proportion of the total time may be the result of the relatively high overhead of loading an ontology into a reasoner via the DIG interface; it is not necessarily due to time taken performing "eager" reasoning.

6 Discussion

As we mentioned in Section 1, testing is useful for reasoner and tool developers as well as for application users. Building on existing work, we have developed a system for testing reasoners with real-life ontologies. The benefits of our approach include autonomous testing, flexible analysis of results, correctness/consistency checking and the development of a test library that should be a valuable resource for both the DL and ontology community. We will continue to extend the library, and will publish the computed class hierarchy in case a consistent answer is obtained. We will also continue to analyse the reasons for the inconsistencies we have found, and would eventually like to analyse which implementation strategies and optimisations seem to be most effective for particular kinds of ontology and reasoning problems.

While there are an increasingly large array of OWL ontologies available for public use, other Ontology formats (e.g. OBO: the Open Biomedical Ontologies, http://obo.sourceforge.net) are still in widespread use, and would make a valuable addition to our test examples. It is also the case, as described in [3], that a large proportion of the available OWL-Full ontologies, could relatively easily be "repaired" so as to be OWL-DL; adding a few extra typing statements is all that is typically required. In the future we hope to use semi-automated repair of OWL-Full ontologies and translation from formats such as OBO to increase the size and scope of our ontology library.

So far we have focused on testing TBox reasoning (classification). Although the use of nominals in OWL-DL blurs the separation between TBox and ABox, it would still be useful to explicitly test ABox reasoning, e.g., by asking for the instances of some query class. In fact, for ontologies that include far more individuals than classes (such as the world-fact-book, Tambis and Hydrolic Units ontologies), it makes little sense to test classification and not to test query answering. Focusing on classification also fails to give a fair picture of the performance of systems such as KAON2 that aim to optimise query answering. Extending the testing regime to include querying will be part of our future work.

Apart from the future work described above, there are a number of extensions to our benchmarking system that would enhance its utility. Allowing users to define their own customised tests would help reasoner developers to test specific optimisations and implementations as they are developed. It would also be useful to be able to investigate how multiple concurrent queries affect reasoner performance, and whether reasoners perform better or worse if they are *not* restarted between tests.

Both the testing system and the ontology library are publicly available resources, and can be downloaded from http://www.cs.man.ac.uk/ horrocks/ testing/.

References

1. Franz Baader and Ulrike Sattler. An overview of tableau algorithms for description logics. *Studia Logica*, 69(1):5–40, October 2001.
2. Sean Bechhofer, Ralf Möller, and Peter Crowther. The DIG description logic interface. In *Proceedings of DL2003 International Workshop on Description Logics*, September 2003.
3. Sean Bechhofer, Raphael Volz, and Phillip Lord. Cooking the semantic web with the OWL API. In Dieter Fensel, Katia Sycara, and John Mylopoulos, editors, *Proc. of the 2003 International Semantic Web Conference (ISWC 2003)*, number 2870 in Lecture Notes in Computer Science. Springer, 2003.
4. Jeremy J. Carroll and Jos De Roo. OWL web ontology language test cases. W3C Recommendation, 10 February 2004. Available at http://www.w3.org/TR/owl-test/.
5. Yuanbo Guo, Zhengxiang Pan, and Jeff Heflin. An evaluation of knowledge base systems for large OWL datasets. In Sheila A. McIlraith, Dimitris Plexousakis, and Frank van Harmelen, editors, *Proc. of the 2004 International Semantic Web Conference (ISWC 2004)*, number 3298 in Lecture Notes in Computer Science, pages 274–288. Springer, 2004.
6. Volker Haarslev and Ralf Möller. High performance reasoning with very large knowledge bases: A practical case study. In *Proc. of the 17th Int. Joint Conf. on Artificial Intelligence (IJCAI 2001)*, pages 161–168, 2001.
7. Volker Haarslev and Ralf Möller. RACER system description. In *Proc. of the Int. Joint Conf. on Automated Reasoning (IJCAR 2001)*, volume 2083 of *Lecture Notes in Artificial Intelligence*, pages 701–705. Springer, 2001.
8. I. Horrocks. Benchmark analysis with FaCT. In *Proc. of the 4th Int. Conf. on Analytic Tableaux and Related Methods (TABLEAUX 2000)*, number 1847 in Lecture Notes in Artificial Intelligence, pages 62–66. Springer-Verlag, 2000.
9. I. Horrocks and P. F. Patel-Schneider. FaCT and DLP. In *Proc. of Tableaux'98*, pages 27–30, 1998.
10. I. Horrocks, U. Sattler, and S. Tobies. Practical reasoning for expressive description logics. In H. Ganzinger, D. McAllester, and A. Voronkov, editors, *Proc. of the 6th Int. Conf. on Logic for Programming and Automated Reasoning (LPAR'99)*, number 1705 in Lecture Notes in Artificial Intelligence, pages 161–180. Springer, 1999.
11. Ian Horrocks. The FaCT system. In Harrie de Swart, editor, *Proc. of the 2nd Int. Conf. on Analytic Tableaux and Related Methods (TABLEAUX'98)*, volume 1397 of *Lecture Notes in Artificial Intelligence*, pages 307–312. Springer, 1998.
12. Ian Horrocks and Peter F. Patel-Schneider. DL systems comparison. In *Proc. of the 1998 Description Logic Workshop (DL'98)*, pages 55–57. CEUR Electronic Workshop Proceedings, http://ceur-ws.org/Vol-11/, 1998.

13. Ian Horrocks, Peter F. Patel-Schneider, and Frank van Harmelen. From $\mathcal{SHIQ}$ and RDF to OWL: The making of a web ontology language. *J. of Web Semantics*, 1(1):7–26, 2003.
14. Ian Horrocks and Ulrike Sattler. Ontology reasoning in the $\mathcal{SHOQ}$(D) description logic. In *Proc. of the 17th Int. Joint Conf. on Artificial Intelligence (IJCAI 2001)*, pages 199–204, 2001.
15. Ian Horrocks and Ulrike Sattler. A tableaux decision procedure for $\mathcal{SHOIQ}$. In *Proc. of the 19th Int. Joint Conf. on Artificial Intelligence (IJCAI 2005)*, pages 448–453, 2005.
16. U. Hustadt and R. A. Schmidt. Using resolution for testing modal satisfiability and building models. In I. P. Gent, H. van Maaren, and T. Walsh, editors, *SAT 2000: Highlights of Satisfiability Research in the Year 2000*, volume 63 of *Frontiers in Artificial Intelligence and Applications*. IOS Press, Amsterdam, 2000. Also to appear in a special issue of *Journal of Automated Reasoning*.
17. A. Kalyanpur, Bijan Parsia, Evren Sirin, Bernardo Cuenca-Grau, and James Hendler. SWOOP: a web ontology editing browser. *J. of Web Semantics*, 4(2), 2005.
18. Fabio Massacci and Francesco M. Donini. Design and results of TANCS-00. In R. Dyckhoff, editor, *Proc. of the 4th Int. Conf. on Analytic Tableaux and Related Methods (TABLEAUX 2000)*, volume 1847 of *Lecture Notes in Artificial Intelligence*. Springer, 2000.
19. Zhengxiang Pan. Benchmarking DL reasoners using realistic ontologies. In *Proc. of the First OWL Experiences and Directions Workshop*, 2005.
20. P. F. Patel-Schneider. DLP system description. In *Proc. of the 1998 Description Logic Workshop (DL'98)*, pages 87–89. CEUR Electronic Workshop Proceedings, http://ceur-ws.org/Vol-11/, 1998.
21. Peter F. Patel-Schneider, Patrick Hayes, and Ian Horrocks. OWL web ontology language semantics and abstract syntax. W3C Recommendation, 10 February 2004. Available at http://www.w3.org/TR/owl-semantics/.
22. Peter F. Patel-Schneider and Roberto Sebastiani. A new general method to generate random modal formulae for testing decision procedures. *J. of Artificial Intelligence Research*, 18:351–389, 2003.
23. Protégé. http://protege.stanford.edu/, 2003.
24. E. Sirin, B. Parsia, B. Cuenca Grau, A. Kalyanpur, and Y. Katz. Pellet: A practical OWL-DL reasoner. Submitted for publication to Journal of Web Semantics, 2005.
25. Dmitry Tsarkov and Ian Horrocks. Ordering heuristics for description logic reasoning. In *Proc. of the 19th Int. Joint Conf. on Artificial Intelligence (IJCAI 2005)*, pages 609–614, 2005.
26. Dmitry Tsarkov and Ian Horrocks. FaCT++ description logic reasoner: System description. In *Proc. of the Int. Joint Conf. on Automated Reasoning (IJCAR 2006)*, volume 4130 of *Lecture Notes in Artificial Intelligence*, pages 292–297, 2006.
27. Dmitry Tsarkov, Alexandre Riazanov, Sean Bechhofer, and Ian Horrocks. Using Vampire to reason with OWL. In Sheila A. McIlraith, Dimitris Plexousakis, and Frank van Harmelen, editors, *Proc. of the 2004 International Semantic Web Conference (ISWC 2004)*, number 3298 in Lecture Notes in Computer Science, pages 471–485. Springer, 2004.

Integrating and Querying Parallel Leaf Shape Descriptions

Shenghui Wang[1] and Jeff Z. Pan[2]

[1] School of Computer Science, University of Manchester, UK
[2] Department of Computing Science, University of Aberdeen, UK

Abstract. Information integration and retrieval have been important problems for many information systems — it is hard to combine new information with any other piece of related information we already possess, and to make them both available for application queries. Many ontology-based applications are still cautious about integrating and retrieving information from natural language (NL) documents, preferring structured or semi-structured sources. In this paper, we investigate how to use ontologies to facilitate integrating and querying information on parallel leaf shape descriptions from NL documents. Our approach takes advantage of ontologies to precisely represent the semantics in shape description, to integrates parallel descriptions according to their semantic distances, and to answer shape-related species identification queries. From this highly specialised domain, we learn a set of more general methodological rules, which could be useful in other domains.

1 Introduction

Information integration and retrieval have been important problems for many information systems [1] — it is hard to combine new information with any other piece of related information we already possess, and to make them both available for application queries. Most information in *descriptive* domains is only available in natural language (NL) form and often comes *parallel, i.e.*, the same objects or phenomena are described in multiple free-styled documents [2]. With ontologies being shared understandings of application domains, ontology-based integration and retrieval [3] is a promising direction. However, many ontology-based applications avoiding integrating and retrieving information from NL documents, preferring structured or semi-structured sources, such as databases and XML documents.

In this paper, we investigate how to use ontologies to facilitate integrating and querying information on parallel leaf shape descriptions from botanical documents. As one of the premier descriptive sciences, botany offers a wealth of material on which to test our methods. Our observation is that if the parallel information can be extracted and represented in a uniform ontology, the explicitly written information can be accessed easily and the implicit knowledge can also be deduced naturally by applying reasoning on the whole ontology. We have recently demonstrated that it is feasible for an ontology-based system to use this method to capture, represent and use the semantics of colour descriptions from botanical documents [4]. In this paper, we focus on another specialised aspect — leaf shape descriptions.

As a highly domain-dependent property, shapes are not easily described in NL. Unlike colours, a specialist terminology is used to describe shapes that naturally occur in each domain, combined with general NL syntax. For instance, the leaves of the aspen trees are described differently in five floras:[1]

- broadly ovate to suborbicular or oblate-orbicular
- broadly ovate to orbicular
- kidney-shaped, reniform or oblate
- suborbicular
- almost round

To capture the semantics in these descriptions and formalise them into an ontology system is our concern. Our approach takes advantage of ontologies to represent the semantics in shape descriptions precisely, to integrate parallel descriptions according to their semantic distances, and to answer shape-related species identification queries.

1. Firstly, we need an appropriate semantic model in which the semantics in shape descriptions can be captured and the compatibility between descriptions can be measured. We adopt a known shape model, called SuperFormula [5], to model common leaf shape terms. Based on this we derive a domain-dependent four-feature leaf shape model. The semantics of complex descriptions are precisely constructed from those of simple terms by applying a small number of morpho-syntactic rules. The quantitative semantics is then represented in the OWL-Eu ontology language [6].
2. Secondly, we propose a distance function, based on the four-feature leaf shape model, to calculate distances between parallel information (*e.g.*, the distance between "linear to ovate" and "narrowly elliptic"), so as to facilitate a proper strategy of integrating such information.
3. Thirdly, we use the OWL-Eu subsumption reasoning to check if one shape description is more general than another one. Such a reasoning service is helpful in answering species identification queries, for example, to search all species which have "ovate to elliptic" leaves (more examples in Section 5) over the integrated information.

In order to check the feasibility of the above approach, we develop and implement a shape reasoner, based on the FaCT-DG Description Logic reasoner [7,8]. The shape reasoner integrates parallel shape information based on their semantic distances; it also answers queries over the integrated information. We will show that semantic distances can also improve the presentation of the query results: they help by (i) measuring how well the results match the query, and (ii) presenting the best results first. We evaluate our approach in two steps. Firstly, we ask a domain expert to check how good our proposed semantic model and

---

[1] A flora is a treatise on or list of the plants of an area or a period.

semantic distance function are. Secondly, we evaluate the query results from our shape reasoner based on the reliable semantic distance function.

The rest of the paper is structured as follows. Section 2 introduces a known shape model and our four-feature leaf shape model. In Section 3, we show how the semantics in a complex leaf shape description is constructed and represented formally. Section 4 introduces distance-based integration and some experimental results. Section 5 investigates how to query on the integrated information and improve the presentation of returned results by ranking them, based on their degree of match to a particular query. Section 6 discusses related work and Section 7 concludes this paper.

2 A Multi-parametric Semantic Model for Leaf Shapes

Shape modelling is not easy, in the sense that it is highly domain dependent. People have tried to use cylinders [9] or superquadrics [10] as primitives to model abstract shapes. For real shapes in nature, several modelling methods have also been tried, such as interpolation methods which use polynomials or splines to fit curves. Since the pioneering work of D'Arcy Thompson [11], bio-mathematicians have investigated describing natural shapes and forms by using morphometric methods [12]. Outlines and landmark-based patterns are used to represent natural shapes. However, their high-dimensional representation cannot be interpreted easily and is not suitable in a logic-based system.

Gielis [5] recently proposed the Superformula, which in polar co-ordinates (r, θ), is:

$$r(\theta) = \frac{1}{\sqrt[n_1]{(|\frac{1}{a}\cos(\frac{m}{4}\theta)|)^{n_2} + (|\frac{1}{b}\sin(\frac{m}{4}\theta)|)^{n_3}}} \tag{1}$$

This can generate approximations to many naturally occurring shapes and forms. Although it is not easy to find the precise parameters (m, a, b, n_1, n_2, n_3) for a particular shape, the simplicity and expressiveness of this formula encouraged us to use it for modelling leaf shapes.

Here, we consider only *simple* leaves[2] for demonstrating the feasibility of our method. We selected 21 common simple leaf shape terms from *Botanical Latin* [13]. Based on our experiments and experts' evaluation, for each term, we found a 6D vector (m, a, b, n_1, n_2, n_3) which generates its prototypical shape. For instance, the parameters $(2, 1, 1, 1, -0.5, 0.5)$ generates a "cordate" shape. Figure 1 (a) shows some other shapes.

The terminology is limited while real shape variations are continuous. Therefore, in order to describe continuous shape variations, one has to compare the real shapes with prototypical ones. If a real shape S_i is *similar* enough to the prototypical shape S of a shape term T, i.e., their distance $d(S_i, S) < \epsilon$, then it can be named by term T. Thus each term does not correspond to a point but a region around that point in the multi-parametric space.[3] Complex leaf shape

---

[2] Simple leaves are entire (without teeth or lobes) and bilaterally symmetric about their main vein.

[3] According to the conceptual space theory [14], this region must be convex.

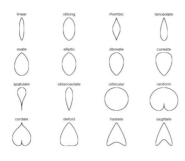 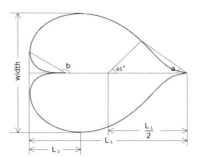

(a) Common leaf shapes generated by the SuperFormula

(b) 4-feature leaf shape model derived from the SuperFormula

Fig. 1. Leaf shape modelling

descriptions, such as "narrowly ovate to elliptic", also correspond to certain regions. Since the shape of such regions is still unknown [14], we use a simple definition: the region for a shape term contains all points whose distance to its prototype point is smaller than a predefined threshold.

Unfortunately, the six parameters of the Superformula are not directly related to any visible leaf features, which makes it extremely difficult to measure shape distance directly based on the 6D vectors. Therefore, we devised a special leaf shape model. Four basic features are calculated from the shape generated by the Superformula, see Figure 1 (b):

- length-width ratio: $f_1 = \frac{L_1}{width}$;
- the position of the widest part: $f_2 = \frac{L_2}{L_1}$;
- the apex angle: $f_3 = a$;
- the base angle: $f_4 = b$.

In this four-feature shape model, each term corresponds to a region with a small range in each feature while the region of a complex shape description is constructed from those of simple terms (see next section for details). The distance function between shape regions is defined in Section 4.

3 From NL Phrases to Ontological Representation

3.1 Morpho-syntactic Rules

One term is usually not enough to cover the natural shape variations of one species, hence complex descriptions have to be used (as shown in Section 1). In order to capture the semantics of these descriptions, we need to know how they are constructed from basic terms. We carried out a morpho-syntactic analysis

Table 1. Leaf shape description patterns

Leaf Shape Description Pattern	Example
1. Single term	"ovate"
2. Modified term	"broadly elliptic"
3. Hyphenated expression	"linear-lanceolate"
4. Range built by "to"	"oblong to elliptic"
5. Multiple ranges connected by coordinators ("and","or"), or punctuations	"linear, lanceolate or narrowly elliptic" "ovate and cordate"

on 362 leaf shape descriptions of 291 species from five floras.[4] The description patterns are summarised in Table 1.

3.2 Semantics for Complex Descriptions

The semantics of complex descriptions is constructed by applying certain operations on that of basic terms. Firstly, basic shape regions are generated, including:

Single term: Given the 6D vector of a simple term, we calculate its four features (f_1, f_2, f_3, f_4), then we generate a region with a small range in each feature, i.e., $(r_{f_1}, r_{f_2}, r_{f_3}, r_{f_4})$, where $r_{f_i} = [f_i \times 0.9, f_i \times 1.1]$, for $i = 1, \ldots, 4$.

Modified term: Leaf shapes are normally modified in terms of their length-width ratio, e.g., "narrowly" and "broadly." As side effects, apex and base angle also change. According to our experiments, if "narrowly" and "broadly" are defined as:

"narrowly:" $f_1' = f_1 \times 1.2$
$f_i' = f_i \times 0.9$, for $i = 3, 4$
"broadly:" $f_1' = f_1 \times 0.8$
$f_i' = f_i \times 1.1$, for $i = 3, 4$

then the region around the new point (f_1', f_2, f_3', f_4') represents the best "narrowly" and "broadly" shape of this term.

Hyphenated expression: According to the experts we consulted, a hyphenated expression "X-Y" means an intermediate shape between X and Y. The intermediate features between X and Y are calculated as follows:

$$hf_i = \frac{f_{X_i} + f_{Y_i}}{2}, \text{ for } i = 1, \ldots, 4 \qquad (2)$$

The region is generated correspondingly.

Secondly, we combine basic regions to construct the region for the complex descriptions.

1. If basic shapes are connected by one or more "to"s, the final region should be the whole range from the first one to the last one. That is, the range which covers two basic regions $(r_{f_1}^1, r_{f_2}^1, r_{f_3}^1, r_{f_4}^1)$ and $(r_{f_1}^2, r_{f_2}^2, r_{f_3}^2, r_{f_4}^2)$ is $(R_{f_1}, R_{f_2}, R_{f_3}, R_{f_4})$, where $R_{f_i} = [\min(r_{f_i}^1, r_{f_i}^2), \max(r_{f_i}^1, r_{f_i}^2)]$.

---

[4] They are *Flora of the British Isles* [15], *New Flora of the British Isles* [16], *Flora Europaea* [17], *The Wild Flower Key* [18] and *Gray's Manual of Botany* [19].

2. If basic shapes are connected by any of these symbols: "or," "and," comma (",") or slash ("/"), they are kept as separate regions, *i.e.*, disjoint from each other. Notice that "and" is treated as a disjunction symbol, because it does not indicate a logical conjunction in a NL scenario [20]. Instead, it normally indicates that the shapes could both be found in nature for the same species, similar to the meaning of "or".

By using an NL parser with corresponding operations, the semantics of a complex description can be constructed into a multi-parametric representation. Next, we need to formalise the semantics in our plant ontology.

3.3 Representing Shape Descriptions in Ontologies

As the W3C standard ontology language OWL DL [21] does not support XML Schema user-defined datatypes, we use the OWL-Eu language [6] suggested by a W3C Note [22] from the Semantic Web Best Practice and Deployment Working Group. OWL-Eu supports customised datatypes through unary datatype expressions (or simply datatype expressions) based on unary datatype groups. This support of customised datatypes is just what we need here to capture feature information of leave shapes. Like an OWL DL ontology, an OWL-Eu ontology typically contains a set of class axioms, property axioms and individual axioms.[5] Here we use the FaCT-DG ontology reasoner, a Datatype Group extension of the FaCT reasoner, which supports reasoning in OWL-Eu ontologies that do not contain nominals.[6]

The fragment of our plant ontology $\mathcal{O}_s$ contains Species, Leaf and LeafShape as primitive classes; important object properties include *hasPart* and *hasShape*; important datatype properties include *hasLengthWidthRatio*, *hasBroadestPosition*, *hasApexAngle* and *hasBaseAngle*, which are all *functional* properties.[7] Each datatype property and its range is also defined, for example,

`DatatypeProperty(`*hasBaseAngle* `Functional range(and(`$\geq 0, \leq 180$`)))`,

where `and`($\geq 0, \leq 180$) is a unary conjunctive datatype expression representing the sub-type [0,180] of Integer. Typical relations between classes include:

Species $\sqsubseteq \exists hasPart$.Leaf (Each species has a part: leaf)
Leaf $\sqsubseteq \exists hasShape$.LeafShape (Each leaf has a property: leafshape)

Actual leaf shapes are defined using the above primitive classes and properties, where datatype expressions are used to restrict the values of four features. For example, the shape "ovate" is defined as the following OWL-Eu class:

Ovate $\equiv$ LeafShape $\sqcap$
  $\exists hasLengthWidthRatio$.(`and`($\geq 15, \leq 18$)) $\sqcap$ $\exists hasApexAngle$.(`and`($\geq 41, \leq 50$))
  $\exists hasBroadestPosition$.(`and`($\geq 39, \leq 43$)) $\sqcap$ $\exists hasBaseAngle$.(`and`($\geq 59, \leq 73$))

---
[5] See [6] for more details on datatype expressions and unary datatype groups.
[6] Details of the FaCT-DG reasoner as well as its flexible reasoning architecture can be found in [8] and `http://www.csd.abdn.ac.uk/$\sim$jpan/factdg/`.
[7] A functional datatype property relates an object with at most one data value.

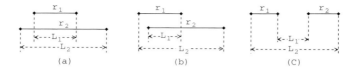

Fig. 2. Three relations between two ranges

Similarly, complex shape descriptions are also represented as OWL-Eu classes based on the regions with constraints on the four features. Ontological representations of shape descriptions enable us to carry out species identification queries based on their leaf shapes (see Section 5 for more details).

4 Distance-Based Integration

The example in Section 1 shows that parallel descriptions are very common among existing floras. In this section, we present a distance-based integration approach for parallel shape descriptions.

4.1 Distance Definition for Leaf Shape Descriptions

Parallel information is assumed to be complementary, possibly with a certain degree of overlap.[8] It is not appropriate to simply combine two or more pieces of information without carefully studying how similar or how different they are. However, measuring the distances between shape descriptions is not easy, while defining the distance between shapes itself is already an inherently ill-defined problem. For example, how far is "linear to ovate" from "linear to elliptic"?

As introduced in Section 3, a complex shape description is translated into a vector, and each element is a range in one feature, $i.e.$, $(R_{f_1}, R_{f_2}, R_{f_3}, R_{f_4})$. In order to calculate the distance between such vectors, distances in each element range should first be calculated. There are three different types of relations between two ranges, shown in Figure 2. We define the following distance function for two arbitrary ranges r_1 and r_2:

$$d(r_1, r_2) = \begin{cases} 1 - \frac{L_1}{L_2} & \text{if } r_1 \text{ and } r_2 \text{ overlap} \\ 1 + \frac{L_1}{L_2} & \text{otherwise;} \end{cases} \quad (3)$$

where L_2 is the length of minimal super-range which contains both r_1 and r_2, and L_1 is defined as follows: when r_1 and r_2 overlap (see (a) and (b)), L_1 is the length of the overlapping part; otherwise, for (c), L_1 is the length of the gap between two ranges. If two ranges r_1 and r_2 only share one point, we say they *meet* each other and $L_1 = 0$.

The distance $d(r_1, r_2)$ is nicely scaled into the range $[0, 2]$: if $d(r_1, r_2) = 0$, r_1 equals r_2; if $0 < d(r_1, r_2) < 1$, r_1 and r_2 overlap; if $d(r_1, r_2) = 1$, r_1 meets r_2; if

---

[8] [23] showed that, when information was collected from six parallel descriptions of a representative sample of plant species, over half the data points came from a single source, while only 2% showed outright disagreement between sources.

$1 < d(r_1, r_2) < 2$, r_1 and r_2 are disjoint; as two ranges move further apart from each other, the distance gets closer to 2.

The distance along each feature is calculated by using Formula (3). The whole distance between two shape regions R_1 and R_2 is then calculated as:

$$d(R_1, R_2) = \sum_{i=1}^{4} w_i \times d_{f_i} \qquad (4)$$

where d_{f_i} is the distance in the feature f_i, w_i is the corresponding weight for the feature f_i, and $\sum_{i=1}^{4} w_i = 1$ holds.[9] The $d(R_1, R_2)$ has similar mathematical properties to $d(r_1, r_2)$, but is harder to interpret due to the influence of the weighting. According to our experiments with a domain expert from the Museum of Manchester,[10] this similarity distance function is valid and corresponds closely to how experts judge similarity between shapes.

4.2 Integration Based on Semantic Distances

We can now compute the distance between two descriptions, as calculated by Formula 4. If two descriptions are "close" or "similar" enough, although they might not be identical (for various reasons), it is better to combine them into one single "super-description" so that redundancies can be removed. Otherwise, it is safer to leave them separate because they are likely to provide complementary information of the same object. If a reasonable threshold is chosen, our integration process can automatically combine similar descriptions and keep others separate.

So, for a single species, the recursive integration process on the collections of shape regions from parallel descriptions is as follows:

Step 1 Calculate the distances between any pair of regions.

Step 2 Select two closest regions and check whether they are similar enough, *i.e.*, whether their distance is less than the threshold. If they are not similar enough then the integration stops; otherwise, the smallest region containing both of them is generated (this is same operation as building "to" ranges). This new region replaces the original two as their integrated result.

Step 3 Go back to Step 1 to check the updated collection of regions to see whether there are any further pairs of regions requiring integration.

4.3 Experiments on Integration

We selected 410 species from the floras mentioned in Section 3 and the online efloras,[11] so that each of the selected species is described in at least two flo-

---

[9] From our statistical analysis on real text data, f_2 is the most distinguishing feature. However, there is no satisfactory way to find the optimal weights.

[10] The contact information for our domain expert is available on request.

[11] This is an international project (http://www.efloras.org/) which collects plant taxonomy data from several main floras, such as *Flora of China*, *Flora of North America*, *Flora of Pakistan*, etc. Plant species descriptions are available in electronic form, but are still written in the common style of floras, *i.e.*, semi-NL.

Table 2. Examples of integration results, where R_{f_1} is the range of the length-width ratio, R_{f_2} is the range of the position of the widest part, R_{f_3} is the range of the apex angle; R_{f_4} is the range of the base angle

Species	Leaf Shape Descriptions	Integration Results			
		R_{f_1}	R_{f_2}	R_{f_3}	R_{f_4}
Salix pentandra (Laurel willow)	ovate or ovate-elliptical to elliptical- or obovate-lanceolate broadly lanceolate to ovate-oblong broadly elliptical broadly lanceolate, ovate-oblong, or elliptic-lanceolate	1.21–2.87	0.27–0.57	0.10–0.35	0.27–0.37
Glinus lotoides	obovate or orbiculate to broadly spatulate obovate to oblong-spatulate orbiculate or more or less cuneate	0.90–2.33	0.46–0.80	0.34–0.47	0.04–0.44
Spinacia oleracea	hastate to ovate	1.22–1.63	0.08–0.39	0.17–0.25	0.37–0.63
	ovate to triangular-hastate oblong	1.81–2.21	0.45–0.55	0.27–0.33	0.27–0.33
Alternanthera paronychioides	oblanceolate or spatulate	2.83–3.46	0.62–0.76	0.28–0.34	0.09–0.11
	elliptic, ovate-rhombic, or oval	2.39–2.92	0.72–0.88	0.34–0.42	0.03–0.04
	elliptic, oval or obovate	1.45–2.57	0.40–0.69	0.17–0.38	0.22–0.32

ras. Some species only exist in particular regions, so parallel information is not guaranteed for each species.

In order to calculate the threshold for the integration, we selected a group of parallel descriptions from the dataset, which are not identical yet are still considered to be similar enough to be combined. The average distance of these parallel descriptions is used as the threshold, which turned out to be 0.98.

In Table 2, we list the original descriptions of several species with their integrated results. An overview of these parallel data is presented clearly. Some species' leaves, such as the first two, are described differently but all descriptions more or less agree with each other, therefore they are integrated into a single region with combined constraints on its four features. Here, the integration reduces the redundancies among the parallel information.

Other species, such as the last two, have quite different leaf shapes. These shapes are "dissimilar" enough to be kept as complementary information. If the species itself has wide variations, one author might not capture them all. Integration of parallel information makes the whole knowledge as nearly complete as possible. By comparing original descriptions and integrated ones, we can easily find some geographically-caused variations.

5 Results on Ranking of Responses to Queries

One of the advantages of putting NL information into a formal ontology is to make the knowledge in NL documents easier to access. After leaf shape information is represented formally, we can query species based on their leaf shapes. Similar to the method used in [4], firstly, the queried shape is represented by an OWL-Eu class Q. The shape reasoner interacts with FaCT-DG reasoner and returns a list of species, whose leaf shapes (in terms of the four features) either exactly match Q, are subsumed by Q, subsume Q (also called plugin matching), or intersect with Q.

Table 3. Query results for "lanceolate to elliptic" (partial)

Species	Leaf Shape Descriptions	Matching Type	Distance	Ranking
Comastoma muliense	lanceolate to elliptic	Exact	0.00	1
Polygonatum biflorum	narrowly lanceolate to broadly elliptic	Plugin	0.23	6
Hydrangea longifolia	lanceolate	Subsume	0.85	453
Rhodiola smithii	linear to oblong narrowly ovate to ovate-linear	Intersection	0.44	64

Some results for the query: "any possible species with lanceolate to elliptic leaves," is shown in Table 3. The matching type indicates the logic relations between the matched species and the query. Because our method uses the real semantics for querying, it can find some hidden results which are ignored by keyword matching, *e.g.*, the last species in Table 3. However, the problem is that it is not clear how well a result matches the query. The user has to go through the whole list and judge by himself.

Since our distance measure has been confirmed to be valid (see Section 4.1), we can use this distance as a criterion to quantify how well a logically matched species matches the query. A shorter distance means a better match. We sort the whole list based on the distance between each species' leaf shape and the queried one. Based on the matching ranks, as those in the last column of Table 3, the better matched results can be recovered easily.

We further enlarged our dataset from the eFloras, including 1154 species, some of which were described in more than one flora. Parallel descriptions were integrated first and then all queries are based on integrated knowledge. If one species has more than one shape region which matches the query, only the "best-match" (with the smallest distance to the query) is selected to join the ranking. We carried out 10 queries on basic terms and range phrases. Most queries finished in 1–2 seconds, the others took less than 5 seconds, on a 2G Hz Pentium 4 PC.

We compared our method with the keyword-based method over the 10 queries. For each query, results returned by both methods were merged into a single list, in the ascending order of their distances to the query. The ordered list was then divided into five groups, representing top 20% matched species, 20–40% matched ones, and so on. In each group, we counted the number of the species that the keyword-based method missed and that our method missed, respectively (see Figure 3 (a)). The numbers above each pair of columns is the mean similarity distance of that group. It shows that our method is able to find some well matched results (with small similarity distances) which are not matched by keyword search.

Due to the strictness of logic reasoning, our method failed to find some good results (judged by the expert). Therefore, we decreased the strictness level; if there are at least three features matched, the species is also returned if its distance to the query is less than the threshold which was used for integration. The performance was evaluated similarly, shown in Figure 3 (b). More hidden results were returned by our method while the quality (*i.e.*, mean distances) keeps stable.

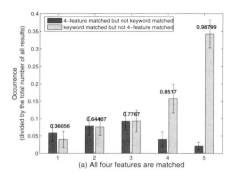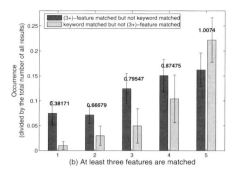

Fig. 3. Comparison of semantic-based query and keyword-based query

Table 4. Comparison between different levels of matching

Condition	Semantic matching		Keyword matching	
	Precision	Recall	Precision	Recall
4 features are perfectly matched	0.99888	0.55237	0.84474	0.65417
At least 3 features are matched	0.96642	0.72727	0.84430	0.65327

We use the standard precision/recall[12] to measure the performance of our method against keyword-based querying. From Table 4, we can see that when the strictness of matching criterion is loosened the precision decreases while the recall increases; this is a typical balancing problem.

In short, our approach outperforms the keyword-based method; this is because the former takes the real semantic of shape descriptions into account, while the latter simply checks the word matching of the descriptions.

6 Related Work

Sharing information among multiple sources occurs at many different levels. Access to a semantics is crucial for successful information integration and retrieval [1,3]. Instead of working on structured or semi-structured data, our work focuses mainly on integrating parallel NL information extracted from homogeneous monolingual (English) documents.

Many information integration systems have adopted ontologies as their working platform because of the various semantic expression of domain knowledge contained in ontologies [3,24,25] and powerful formal-logical reasoning tools supported by them [26,27,28]. Unfortunately, most systems stop at collecting and

---

[12] The precision indicates the proportion of answers in the returned list that were correct, while the recall is the proportion of correct answers in the whole data set that were found. Here, the correctness of a species is judged by whether the distance of its leaf shape description to the query is less than the integration threshold.

re-organising information from multiple sources instead of really integrating them based on their meanings.

The main obstacle for an ontology-based system to process NL documents is that the NL semantics is difficult to interpret. Many methods to capture and represent the semantics in NL have been tried, such as those multi-dimensional concept modelling including Osgood's semantic differential [29], lexical decomposition [30], etc. Using spatial or geometrical structures to model concepts has also been exploited in the cognitive sciences [31,14]. The limitations of their methods are either the dimensions are difficult to interpret or they are qualitative which prevents the semantics to be precisely captured.

It is not easy for a logic system to represent continuous ranges. OWL-Eu supports representing numerical ranges but still cannot express other ranges, *e.g.*, "ovate to elliptic". Using a semantic model to some extend helps the ontology system to represent such ranges. Furthermore, our work shows that datatype-enabled ontology reasoning can be very useful for real world applications.

Similarity measurement has been investigated in different knowledge representation systems and used in many applications [14,32], while similarity ranking is still one of the new ideas for current ontology techniques [33]. Traditionally, only subsumption checking is used to answer queries. Until recently, some other types of matching, such as intersection matching, are also considered for special cases [34]. However, there is little effort to integrate logic reasoning and similarity measuring. Such integration can determine how well results match the query and therefore can improve the usability of final results.

7 Conclusion

Ontology-based information integration in descriptive domains often comes to grief when comparison and integration have to be based on real semantics. Encouraged by our earlier work on processing parallel colour descriptions [4], we have applied the same methodology on leaf shape descriptions, where we introduced the notion of semantic distance to help parallel information integration and improve the usability of query results.

It turns out that the distances between shape descriptions are very hard to define. To solve the problem, we have derived a domain-dependent four feature leaf shape model. In our model, distances between the shapes are very well captured by the distances between the features, which has been evaluated by our domain expert. Besides the support of distance-based integration, our ontology-based approach (OA) outperforms the keyword-based approach (KA) because OA considers both the syntax and semantics of shape descriptions, while KA considers neither.

Most importantly, from the experiments in colour and leaf shape domain, we have learnt a set of more general methodological rules for processing parallel descriptive information in an ontology-based system. Key tasks we have identified include: (i) it is unlikely that a universal semantic model for all different domains exists, so for each domain, an appropriate (no need to be perfect) model has to be chosen in order to get useful results; (ii) based on the semantic model, single terms have to be located, the effect of modifiers has to be defined and ranges have to be built properly; (iii) in order to integrate parallel information, a proper distance measurement is crucial to quantify the similarities among information from multiple sources; (iv) depending on the application, more expressive representation and additional reasoning may be necessary to solve real problems.

References

1. Stuckenschmidt, H., van Harmelen, F.: Information Sharing on the Semantic Web. Springer-Verlag (2004)
2. Ceusters, W., Smith, B., Fielding, J.M.: Linksuite: Formally robust ontology-based data and information integration. In: Proceedings of First International Workshop of Data Integration in the Life Sciences (DILS'04). Volume 2994 of Lecture Notes in Computer Science., Springer (2004) 124–139
3. Wache, H., Voegele, T., Visser, U., Stuckenschmidt, H., Schuster, G., Neumann, H., Huebner, S.: Ontology-based integration of information - a survey of existing approaches. In: Proceedings of the IJCAI-01 Workshop: Ontologies and Information Sharing, Seattle, WA (2001) 108–117
4. Wang, S., Pan, J.Z.: Ontology-based representation and query colour descriptions from botanical documents. In: Proceedings of OTM Confederated International Conferences. Volume 3761 of Lecture Notes in Computer Science., Springer (2005) 1279–1295
5. Gielis, J.: A generic geometric transformation that unifies a wide range of natural and abstract shapes. American Journal of Botany **90** (2003) 333–338
6. Pan, J.Z., Horrocks, I.: OWL-Eu: Adding Customised Datatypes into OWL. In: Proceedings of Second European Semantic Web Conference (ESWC 2005). (2005) An extended and revised version is published in the Journal of Web Semantics, 4(1). 29-39.
7. Pan, J.Z.: Description Logics: Reasoning Support for the Semantic Web. PhD thesis, School of Computer Science, The University of Manchester (2004)
8. Pan, J.Z.: A Flexible Ontology Reasoning Architecture for the Semantic Web. In: IEEE Transactions on Knowledge and Data Engineering, Specail Issue on the Semantic Web. (2006) To appear.
9. Marr, D., Nishihara, H.: Representation and recognition of the spatial organization of three-dimensional shapes. In: Proceedings of the Royal Society B 200, London (1978) 269–294
10. Pentland, A.: Perceptual organization and the representation of natural form. Artificial Intelligence **28** (1986) 293–331
11. Thompson, D.: On growth and form. Cambridge University Press, London (1917)
12. Adams, D.C., Rohlf, F.J., Slice, D.E.: Geometric morphometrics: Ten years of progress following the "revolution". Italian Journal of Zoology **71** (2004) 5–16
13. Stearn, W.T.: Botanical Latin: history, grammar, syntax, terminology and vocabulary. David and Charles, Newton Abbot, England (1973)
14. Gärdenfors, P.: Conceptual Spaces: the geometry of thought. The MIT Press, Cambridge, Massachusetts (2000)
15. Clapham, A., Tutin, T., Moore., D.: Flora of the British Isles. Cambridge University Press (1987)

16. Stace, C.: New Flora of the British Isles. Cambridge University Press (1997)
17. Tutin, T.G., Heywood, V.H., Burges, N.A., Valentine, D.H., Moore(eds), D.M.: Flora Europaea. Cambridge University Press (1993)
18. Rose, F.: The Wild Flower Key: British Isles and North West Europe. Frederick Warne (1981)
19. Fernald, M.: Gray's Manual of Botany. American Book Company, New York (1950)
20. Dik, S.C.: Coordination: Its implications for the theory of general linguistics. North-Holland, Amsterdam (1968)
21. Bechhofer, S., van Harmelen, F., Hendler, J., Horrocks, I., McGuinness, D.L., Patel-Schneider, P.F., eds., L.A.S.: OWL Web Ontology Language Reference. http://www.w3.org/TR/owl-ref/ (2004)
22. Carroll, J.J., Pan, J.Z.: XML Schema Datatypes in RDF and OWL. Technical report, W3C Semantic Web Best Practices and Development Group (2006) W3C Working Group Note, http://www.w3.org/TR/swbp-xsch-datatypes/.
23. Lydon, S.J., Wood, M.M., Huxley, R., Sutton, D.: Data patterns in multiple botanical descriptions: implications for automatic processing of legacy data. Systematics and Biodiversity (2003) 151–157
24. Goble, C., Stevens, R., Ng, G., Bechhofer, S., Paton, N., Baker, P., Peim, M., Brass, A.: Transparent access to multiple bioinformatics information sources. IBM Systems Journal Special issue on deep computing for the life sciences **40** (2001) 532 – 552
25. Williams, D., Poulovassilis, A.: Combining data integration with natural language technology for the semantic web. In: Proceedings of Workshop on Human Language Technology for the Semantic Web and Web Services, at ISWC'03. (2003)
26. Calvanese, D., Giuseppe, D.G., Lenzerini, M.: Description logics for information integration. In Kakas, A., Sadri, F., eds.: Computational Logic: Logic Programming and Beyond, Essays in Honour of Robert A. Kowalski. Volume 2408 of Lecture Notes in Computer Science. Springer (2002) 41–60
27. Maier, A., Schnurr, H.P., Sure, Y.: Ontology-based information integration in the automotive industry. In: Proceedings of the 2nd International Semantic Web Conference (ISWC2003), Sanibel Island, Florida, USA, Springer (2003) 897–912
28. Ferrucci, D., Lally, A.: UIMA: an architectural approach to unstructured information processing in the corporate research environment. Journal of Natural Language Engineering **10** (2004) 327–348
29. Osgood, C., Suci, G., Tannenbaum, P.: The Measurement of Meaning. University of Illinois Press, Urbana, IL (1957)
30. Dowty, D.R.: Word Meaning and Montague Grammar. D. Reidel Publishing Co., Dordrecht, Holland (1979)
31. Lakoff, G.: Women, Fire, and Dangerous Things: What Categories Reveal about the Mind. University of Chicago Press (1987)
32. Schwering, A.: Hybrid models for semantics similarity measurement. In: Proceedings of OTM Confederated International Conferences. Volume 3761 of Lecture Notes in Computer Science., Springer (2005) 1449–1465
33. Anyanwu, K., Maduko, A., Sheth, A.P.: Semrank: ranking complex relationship search results on the semantic web. In Ellis, A., Hagino, T., eds.: WWW, ACM (2005) 117–127
34. Li, L., Horrocks, I.: A Software Framework For Matchmaking Based on Semantic Web Technology. In: Proceedings of the Twelfth International World Wide Web Conference (WWW 2003), ACM (2003) 331–339

A Survey of the Web Ontology Landscape

Taowei David Wang[1], Bijan Parsia[2], and James Hendler[1]

[1] Department of Computer Science,
University of Maryland, College Park, MD 20742, USA
{tw7, hendler}@cs.umd.edu
[2] The University of Manchester, UK
bparsia@cs.man.ac.uk

Abstract. We survey nearly 1300 OWL ontologies and RDFS schemas. The collection of statistical data allows us to perform analysis and report some trends. Though most of the documents are syntactically OWL Full, very few stay in OWL Full when they are syntactically patched by adding type triples. We also report the frequency of occurrences of OWL language constructs and the shape of class hierarchies in the ontologies. Finally, we note that of the largest ontologies surveyed here, most do not exceed the description logic expressivity of $\mathcal{ALC}$.

1 Introduction

The Semantic Web envisions a metadata-rich Web where presently human-readable content will have machine-understandable semantics. The Web Ontology Language (OWL) from W3C is an expressive formalism for modelers to define various logical concepts and relations. OWL ontologies come in three species: Lite, DL, and Full, ordered in increasing expressivity. Every Lite ontology is also a DL ontology, and every DL ontology is also a Full ontology. OWL Lite and OWL DL are the species that use only the OWL language features in the way that complete and sound reasoning procedures exist. OWL Full, on the other hand, is undecidable. While OWL recently became a W3C recommendation in 2004, people have been working with it a few years, and many interesting ontologies already exist on the Web. We are interested in evaluating these ontologies and see if there are interesting trends in modeling practices, OWL construct usages, and OWL species utilization.

2 Related Work

Using statistics to assess ontologies is not a new idea. Several approaches to create benchmarking for Semantic Web applications have exploited the statistical measures to create better benchmarks. Wang and collegues describe an algorithm to extract features of instances in a real ontology in order to generate domain-specific data benchmark that resembles the real ontology [16]. A method to count the types of triples of instances is employed, and the distribution of these triples is used to create the synthetic data. Tempich and Volz surveyed 95 DAML ontologies and collected various usage information regarding classes, properties, individuals, and restrictions [15]. By examining these numbers, they were able to cluster the ontologies into 3 categories of significant difference.

In [11], Magkannaraki et al. looked at a collection of existing RDFS schemas and extracted statistical data for size and morphology of the RDFS vocabularies. Here we attempt a similar survey for both OWL and RDFS files. However, our focus is primarily on OWL, and the data from RDFS documents serve as a good measuring stick for comparisons.

Bechhofer and Volz studied a sample of 277 OWL ontologies and found that most of them are, surprisingly, OWL Full files [2]. They showed that many of these OWL Full ontologies are OWL Full because of missing type triples, and can be easily patched syntactically. Here we collect a much larger size of samples, and we apply similar analysis to attempt to patch these OWL Full files. In addition, we show how many OWL Full files can be coerced into OWL Lite and OWL DL files. With the expressivity binning of the surveyed ontologies, we show that the number of OWL Lite files that makes use of OWL Lite's full expressivity is relatively small.

3 Methodology

Here we describe the steps taken to collect the ontologies from the Web, how the data was then gleaned, and how we analyzed the data. Our goal was to analyze the various aspects of ontological documents, not RDF documents that make use of ontologies or schemas. Inspite of FOAF [1] (and DOAP [2] and RSS) being a large percentage of the semweb documents out there, they exhibit almost no ontological variance, being primarily data with a thin schema, and are not in the scope of this study.

3.1 Ontology Collection

We used several Web resources to collect the ontologies and schemas. We collected just the URIs at this stage, as our analysis tools will retrieve documents from the web given dereferenceable URIs. First, we used the Semantic Web Search engine Swoogle [7] to obtain a large number of semantic documents that Swoogle classify as ontologies. Using `sort:ontology` [3] as the search term, we were able to crawl on the list 4000+ files. They were a mixture of OWL, DAML, RDF, and RDFS documents. Since we are interested primarily in OWL ontologies, and wanted to get a representatively large sample to perform our analysis, we also searched on Google [4]. Using the search term `owl ext:owl`, we were able to obtain 218 hits [5] at the time of data collection (February 9, 2006). We also collected OWL ontologies from well-known repositories: Protégé OWL

---
[1] http://xmlns.com/foaf/0.1/index.rdf
[2] http://usefulinc.com/doap
[3] Swoogle 2005 http://swoogle.umbc.edu/2005/ allows this type of search. The new Swoogle 2006, which was released after the survey was completed, does not.
[4] http://www.google.com
[5] As noted in [2], the number of search results returned by Google is only an estimate. Furthermore, Google has since changed how OWL files are indexed, and the numbers returned today are orders of magnitudes larger.

Library [6], DAML Ontology Library, [7], Open Biological Ontologies repository [8], and SchemaWeb [9].

Since we collected our URIs from several resources, some URIs appeared more than once in our collection. We first pruned off these duplicate URIs. Next, we threw away the unsuitable data for our analysis. We pruned off all the DAML files as they are not the focus of this study. We threw away the various test files for OWL from W3G and test files for Jena [4]. Though these are valid ontologies or schema files, they were created specifically for the purpose of testing, and do not resemble realistic ontological documents. Around 1000 WordNet RDFS files were also dropped. While WordNet as a whole is useful, each separate WordNet RDFS file does not preserve the meaning of that specific fragment. Finally, we discard any URIs that no longer existed. At the end, we had 1276 files. We looked at each of the documents to see if the OWL or the RDFS namespaces are defined to determine whether they are OWL ontologies or RDFS schemas. Of the 1275 collected, 688 are OWL ontologies, and 587 are RDFS schemas. Resolving these URIs, We keep local copies of these documents for future references.

Table 1. Sample Statistics Collected

Basic Statistics	Dynamic Statistics
No. Defined/Imported Classes	No. Subsumptions
No. Defined/Imported Properties	No. Multiple Inheritance in Class Hierarchy
No. Defined/Imported Instances	Graph Morphology of the Class Hierarchy
DL Expressivity	Depth, Bushiness of the Class Hierarchy
No. Individual (Type/Property) Assertions	Depth, Bushiness of the Property Hierarchy
OWL Species	Whether the Ontology is Consistent
No. of Symmetric Properties	No. Unsatisfiable Classes

3.2 Statistics Collection

We used the OWL ontology editor SWOOP [9] as a framework for automating the analysis tasks. For each URI we collected a set of statistics of that document. There were two types of statistics we collected. The first set contains the statistics that do not change when a reasoner processes the ontology. We call this set static statistics, and it includes, for example, number of defined classes, what ontologies are imported (if any), or which of the OWL species the document belongs to. On the other hand, a second set of statistics changes depending on whether a reasoning service is present. We call this set dynamic statistics. For example, the number of concepts that have more than one parent may change when reasoning is applied since new subsumption relationships can be discovered by the reasoner. Because dynamic statistics change, we collected both the told (without reasoning), and the inferred (with reasoning) versions. Our method is to load each URI into SWOOP, collect the static statistics and the told dynamic statistics,

---
[6] http://protege.stanford.edu/plugins/owl/owl-library/
[7] http://www.daml.org/ontologies/
[8] http://obo.sourceforge.net/main.html
[9] http://www.schemaweb.info/

then turn on the Pellet [13] reasoner and collect the inferred dynamic statistics. We list a few selected categories that are relevant to our discussion in Table 1.

For each OWL ontology, we also collect what OWL constructs are used. We do this by inserting each ontology into a Jena model and check all triples for OWL vocabulary. There are 38 boolean values, one for each OWL construct, for each ontology. Note that we are not keeping track of the usage of OWL:Thing and OWL:Nothing. RDF and RFDS vocabulary such as `rdfs:subClassOf` are also not collected.

4 Results

Here we report the analysis performed, results from our analysis, and what trends we discover.

4.1 OWL Species, DL Expressiveness, Consistency

There are several reasons that make an ontology OWL Full. Bechhofer and Volz discusses each reason in detail in [2]. Here we summarize them into 4 categories to facilitate discussion.

1. **(Syntactic OWL Full).** In this category, the document contains some syntactic features that make the ontology OWL Full. This category includes ontologies that are missing `rdf:type` assertions for its classes, properties, individuals, or itself (untyped ontology). Missing type triples is easily amended as proposed in [2]. Our tool Pellet can generate a patch in RDF/XML to add to the original document to eliminate this type of OWL Fullness.
   Another way to be in OWL Full is to have structural sharing. Here we discuss the sharing of a restriction as an example, but any bnode sharing is likely to lead to OWL Full. An OWL Restriction in RDF is represented as a bnode. A modeler can reuse an existing restriction by referring to the bnode ID. However, doing so will make the ontology OWL Full. On the other hand, if the same modeler creates a new restriction with the same semantics instead of referring to the existing one, structural sharing is avoided.
2. **(Redefinition of Built-In Vocabulary).** Documents that attempt to redefine known vocabulary (such as those in the OWL or RDFS specification) will be in OWL Full. Attempting to add new terms in known namespaces (OWL, RDF, RDFS, etc.) will place the document under OWL Full as well, even innocuous statements such as subclassing `rdf:label`.
3. **(Mixing Classes, Properties, and Individuals).** In OWL DL, the sets of `owl:Class`, `owl:Property`, and `owl:Individual` must be disjoint. The ontologies that use, for example, classes as instances or classes as properties do not respect such disjointness, and are classified as OWL Full documents. Some authors do intend to use instances as classes, for example, for metamodeling purposes. However, there are many other cases where simply an oversight had occurred. We also mention that in RDFS semantics, the set of `rdfs:Class` and `rdf:Property` are not assumed to be disjoint, therefore any RDFS schema will be considered as a

OWL Full file. Though if the schema does not use classes and properties interchangeably, patching up with type triples will likely take the RDFS document out of OWL Full.
4. **(Need for Beyond OWL DL).** This group uses OWL constructs to create an ontology that has expressivity going beyond what OWL DL has to offer. Examples are those that declare a DatatypeProperty to be inverse functional (e.g. `FOAF`), or those that declare cardinality restrictions on transitive properties.

Table 2. Number of Documents in Each Species (species determined by Pellet)

Species	RDFS	Lite	DL	Full	Error
Count	587	199	149	337	3

Now we have a better idea of the syntactic and semantic elements that make an OWL ontology OWL Full, we are ready to look at our data. By looking at the namespaces declared in each document, we decide which files are in RDFS, and which ones in OWL. Using Pellet as an OWL species validation tool, we obtain the distribution of each OWL species in Table 2. Note that since RDFS does not enforce the disjointness of the set of classes, the set of properties, and the set of instances, the RDFS files are technically OWL Full.

We inspected the results Pellet outputs. Out of 924 OWL Full files (including RDFS), 863 can be patched. 30 OWL and 31 RDFS documents can not. Of the 863 patchable ones, 115 become OWL DL, 192 become OWL Lite, and the remaining 556 documents are RDFS. Table 3 shows the updated counts.

Table 3. Number of Documents in Each Species (After Patching)

Species	RDFS(DL)	Lite	DL	Full	Error
Count	556	391	264	61	3

Though Table 3 resembles Table 2, there is one important difference. Note that we use RDFS(DL) [5] instead of RDFS in this case to emphasize that RDFS(DL) assumes the disjointness of classes and properties, and is a proper subset of OWL Lite. Of the 307 OWL Full documents that can be patched, 63% become OWL Lite documents, and just 37% become OWL DL. Two observations can be made. First, The majority (91%) of the OWL Full documents (from Table 2) can be turned into a decideable portions of the languages by adding type triples. Secondly, the majority of RDFS documents (95%) can transition to OWL easily by adding type triples and use OWL vocabulary instead of RDFS vocabulary.

Of the 30 OWL documents that cannot be patched, nearly all of them contain problems of redefining built-in vocabulary. One ontology contains structural sharing. There are 8 ontologies that mix the usage of instances, classes, or properties. And there are 2 cases where beyond OWL DL features are detected. In both of these cases, a DatatypeProperty is defined to be inverse functional.

Of the 31 RDFS documents that cannot be patched, most contain wrong vocabulary, redefinition of known vocabulary, or liberal use built-in vocabulary (such as using `rdfs:subClassOf` on `xsd:time`).

Although species validation gives us a rough idea of the distribution of expressivity among ontologies, it is not a fine enough measure. OWL Lite has the same expressivity as the description logic $\mathcal{SHIF}(\mathcal{D})$, and OWL DL is equivalent to $\mathcal{SHOIN}(\mathcal{D})$. There is a large expressivity gap between RDFS(DL) and OWL Lite. We group the DL expressivity of the documents into bins in atttempt to find out how many ontologies make full use of OWL Lite's features.

We bin the expressivity of the documents as follows. For simplicity, we ignore the presence of datatype, so $\mathcal{SHIF}(\mathcal{D})$ is considered the same as $\mathcal{SHIF}$. For all ontologies that contain nominals $\mathcal{O}$ or number restrictions $\mathcal{N}$, we put them in the most expressive bin (Bin 4). For example, $\mathcal{SHOIN}$ belongs to Bin 4. The next group Bin 3 contains the ones that make use of inverses $\mathcal{I}$ or complements $\mathcal{C}$ but not nominals or number restrictions. $\mathcal{SHIF}$ belongs to this group. Bin 2 consists of role hierarchies $\mathcal{H}$ or functional properties $\mathcal{F}$, but not the features Bin 4 or Bin 3 care about. Bin 2 would contain $\mathcal{ALHF}$, which is more expressive than RDFS(DL). Lastly, everything else will fall into the Bin 1, e.g. $\mathcal{AL}$. We expect the first two bins to contain all of the RDFS(DL) documents and some OWL Lite documents. The question is, of course, how many?

Table 4. Expressivity Binning

Bin	Bin 1 ($\mathcal{AL}$)	Bin 2 ($\mathcal{ALHF}$)	Bin 3 ($\mathcal{SHIF}$)	Bin 4 ($\mathcal{SHOIN}$)
Count	793	55	262	151

Table 4 shows the count of each expressivity bin. 14 OWL documents cannot be processed and are not included in this part of the analysis. The 848 documents in bin 1 and 2 consists of those that are less expressive than $\mathcal{SHIF}$. Subtracting 848 by the number of RDFS documents from Table 2, we reveal 261 documents that are OWL Lite. This is the number of OWL Lite files that do not make use of its full language expressivity. If we subtract this number from the number of OWL Lite documents in Table 3, we get 130. Therefore, the number of ontologies that make good use of OWL Lite features is less than 20% of the total number of OWL ontologies we surveyed here. This is an indication that the OWL Lite vocabulary guides users to create ontologies that are far less expressive than what OWL Lite can express. In fact, of the total number of OWL Lite documents (after patching), 67% use very little above RDFS(DL).

Out of the 688 OWL ontologies, 21 are inconsistent. 18 of the inconsistent ontologies are due to missing type on literal values. These are simple causes for inconsistency that can be detected syntactically. Data type reasoners should have a way to automatically fix it. The other three contain actual logical contradictions. There are also 17 consistent ontologies that contain unsatisfiable classes. 12 belong to bin 4, while the rest belong to bin 3.

4.2 Usage of OWL Constructs

In Table 5, we show, for each OWL construct, the number of ontologies that use it. The table is organized in 5 sections: Ontology, Class, Property, Individual, or

Restriction-Related. Not surprisingly, `owl:Class`, `owl:ObjectProperty`, and `owl:Data-typeProperty` are used in many ontologies. `owl:ObjectProperty` occurs in 185 more ontologies than `owl:DatatypeProperty` does. One possible explanation is that modelers wish to use the semantically rich property types in OWL such as `owl:InverseFunctionalProperty`, `owl:SymmetricProperty`, `owl:TransitiveProperty`, and `owl:InverseOf`, which can only be used with `owl:ObjectProperty` in OWL DL. The fact that `owl:InverseOf` alone is used in 128 ontologies seem to support this hypothesis.

Looking at the Class-Related Constructs, we note that `owl:Union` (109) is used more often than `owl:IntersectionOf` (69). We believe the difference stems from the fact that OWL semantics assumes intersection by default when a modeler says 'A is a subclass of B' and in a different part of the document 'A is a subclass of C'. This is semantically equivalent to saying 'A is a subclass of (B and C)' in OWL. This means in these non-nested boolean cases, one can express an AND relationship without explicitly using 'owl:IntersectionOf'. Another possible contribution to the higher number of `owl:Union` is tool artifact. It is well-known that Protégé assumes union semantics for multiple range and domain axioms. That is, if one were to say 'R has domain A' and 'R has domain B', then Protégé assumes that the user means 'R has domain (A OR B)' and uses `owl:Union`. However, we are not sure how many ontologies were created by using Protégé.

`owl:Imports` appears in 221 OWL documents. This seems to suggest that a good number of ontologies are being reused. However, we do not know how widely an ontology is being imported, nor do we know how many ontologies are being imported. Many institutions that create a suite of ontologies often have heavy use of imports among these ontologies (e.g. SWEET JPL [10]). However cross-institutional ontology sharing seems less common.

There are 253 OWL ontologies that have at least 1 defined individual in this survey. However, Table 5 shows that very few Individual-Related OWL constructs are used. Though `owl:SameAs` is used much more often than the others.

4.3 Tractable Fragments of OWL

There has recently been interest in finding useful yet tractable fragments of OWL in the community [11]. Recent proposals for tractable Description Logics include $\mathcal{EL}++$ [1] and *DL-Lite* [3]. $\mathcal{EL}++$ is an extension of $\mathcal{EL}$, which is used to model certain medical domains. *DL-Lite*, on the other hand, is designed for query answering. We inspect our OWL ontologies to see how many fall into the expressivities the two languages provide. We also look at how many OWL ontologies fall into RDFS(DL). Because Pellet's DL expressivity checker checks on normalized models, and is not very fine grained (starts with $\mathcal{AL}$), we use expressivity as reported by SWOOP.

Table 6 confirms that many OWL files are in RDFS(DL). Of the other two more expressive fragments, the number of *DL-Lite* documents nearly doubles that of $\mathcal{EL}$++. We also look at the OWL constructs for the ontologies that fall into these two fragments. Table 7 shows the highlight. Although conjunction is the only logical connective the two

---

[10] http://sweet.jpl.nasa.gov/ontology/
[11] http://owl-workshop.man.ac.uk/Tractable.html

Table 5. OWL Construct Usage

Construct	Count	Construct	Count
Ontology-Related Constructs		*Class-Related Constructs*	
owl:Ontology	567	owl:Class	580
owl:OntologyProperty	0	owl:ComplementOf	21
owl:BackwardCompatibleWith	0	owl:DeprecatedClass	2
owl:Imports	221	owl:DisjointWith	97
owl:InCompatibleWith:	1	owl:EquivalentClass	77
owl:PriorVersion	8	owl:IntersectionOf	69
owl:VersionInfo	305	owl:OneOf	43
Individual-Related Constructs		owl:Union	109
owl:AllDifferentFrom	6	*Property-Related Constructs*	
owl:DifferentFrom	5	owl:AnnotationProperty	28
owl:DistinctMembers	6	owl:DataRange	14
owl:SameAs	18	owl:DatatypeProperty	277
Restriction-Related Constructs		owl:DeprecatedProperty	2
owl:AllValuesFrom	118	owl:EquivalentProperty	25
owl:Cardinality	120	owl:FunctionalProperty	114
owl:hasValue	48	owl:InverseFunctionalProperty	30
owl:MaxCardinality	60	owl:InverseOf	128
owl:MinCardinality	99	owl:ObjectProperty	462
owl:onProperty	263	owl:SymmetricProperty	20
owl:Restriction	263	owl:TransitiveProperty	39
owl:SomeValuesFrom	85		

Table 6. Tractable fragments of OWL and how many of each fragment appears in this survey

Fragment	RDFS(DL)	DL-Lite	$\mathcal{EL}++$	Non-Tractable
Count	230	94	56	287

fragments allow fully, `owl:Intersection` not widely used. The $\mathcal{EL}$++ ontologies have a much higher percentage in using restrictions and object Properties than *DL-Lite*. However, much higher percentage of *DL-Lite* files use datatype property. The large disparity in the number of $\mathcal{EL}$s++ that use datatype property and object property is surprising. Finally, we note that *DL-Lite* does not allow cardinality greater than one.

Table 7. OWL construct usage for *DL-Lite* and $\mathcal{EL}++$

Constructs	DL-Lite	$\mathcal{EL}++$
owl:Intersection	1(1%)	3(5%)
owl:Restriction	35 (37%)	36 (64%)
owl:ObjectProperty	45 (48%)	43(77%)
owl:DatatypeProperty	44 (0.47%)	4 (7%
owl:FunctionalProperty	20 (20%)	0 (0%)
owl:Cardinality	21 (22%)	0 (0%)
owl:SomeValuesFrom	0(0%)	33(60%)

However, it does allow for functionality. All the *DL-Lite* documents that make use of cardinality restrictions are only using cardinality of 1.

4.4 Shape of Class Hierarchy

When we think of defined vocabularies in schemas and ontologies, we often think of the structure as a tree, where each class is a node, and each directed edge from a parent to a node denotes subsumption. It may be because of our experience as seeing the terms being displayed as tree widgets in our ontology editing tools such as SWOOP or Proétegé or because trees are easier to mentally visualize. However, the vocabulary hierarchy can be all kinds of more general graph structures. In Figure 1 we show the kinds of graph structure a defined set of vocabulary can take shape. The black-dotted circle denotes the top concept (e.g. owl:Thing in OWL ontologies). List, lists, tree, and trees should be familiar to the reader. Multitrees can be seen as a directed acyclic graph (DAG) where each node can have a tree of ancestors and a tree of children. There cannot be a diamond structure in a mulitree [8]. If a diamond structure exists, then it is a general DAG. We can consider the categories list, lists, tree, trees, multitree, and DAG as a strictly ordered list in increasing order of graph complexity.

We point out that a general graph (where cycles exist) is possible. However, because the edges represent subsumptions, all the nodes on the cycle are semantically equivalent. Some paths on the cycle may not be obvious, but sound and complete reasoners will always discover them. Therefore when a reasoner is present, no cyclic graphs of subsumption hierarchies can appear. There can be cycles in a told structure, though these are easy to detect syntactically. In addition, because turning on reasoning services will discover these equivalences and more subsumptions, the graph morphology may change between the told and the inferred structure. Below we show scatterplots of the graph morphological changes in the OWL documents. The scatterplots are fashioned using Spotfire [12].

In Figure 2, each square represents an OWL document, and the size of the square indicates how many classes are in the document. Using the grid point (x,y) closest to each document and referring to the two axes, we can find out what morphology the class hierarchy is in. The vertical axis indicates the morphology in the told structure. The horizontal axis indicates the morphology in the inferred structure. The data points do not lie strictly on an intersection of the grid lines because we have jittered the positions of the data points to avoid occlusions. The jittering also gives a better idea of how many datapoints are in each grid intersection.

If an ontology is inconsistent when reasoner is turned on, the class hierarchy will collapse, and there are no structures. We use the category INCONSISTENT to denote this case. The None structure denotes that the ontology contains no classes, hence there are no structures. In Figure 2, note the clusters along the diagonal. These indicate that most ontologies retain their told morphology after a reasoner has been applied. However, 75 of them did change, 21 of which became inconsistent. 42 ontologies went up to a more complex structure (e.g. from trees to multitrees). Of the 42 that went up in graph complexity, 25 came from trees to either DAGs or multitrees. 3 multitrees and 3 lists became DAGs. 5 ontologies that had lists as the told strucure had the tree or

---

[12] http://www.spotfire.com/

trees strucure when reasoning is turned on. 6 lists became multitrees. The graph morphological changes in increasing graph complexity indicate that more subsumptions are discovered. The ones in decreasing graph complexity means that equivalences are discovered. The most interesting ones are the ontologies that discover multiple inheritance in the inferred structure when there was none in the told structure. These are the list, lists, tree, and trees that became multrees or DAGs. This indicates that some interesting modeling is at work here, and there are 34 of them.

Figure 2 shows the same scatterplot, but for the RDFS documents. We do not expect there to be many, if any, changes in graph morphology because every subclass relationship must be explicitly asserted. In this graph, we clearly see that no RDFS class strucure has changed as a result of a reasoning service.

Because the morphology changes between the told and the inferred structures can give indication on which classes are undermodeled or heavily modeled, to be able to compare them side-by-side and interactively explore them can be potentially useful to modelers and users. Current ontology editors and visualizers, such as the ones described in [9] [12] [10] [14], do not directly support this task.

Here we look at the distribution of the largest ontologies in this survey. Of the 19 ontologies that have more than 2000 classes, 14 have the expressivity of $\mathcal{ALC}$ or lower. 2 have the expressivity $\mathcal{SHF}$, 2 have $\mathcal{S}$, and 1 has $\mathcal{SHOIF(D)}$. In the top right corner of Figure 2, we see that there are a number of large OWL ontologies sitting in the (DAG, DAG) position. To explore further, we plotted the inferred graph morphology against OWL species in Figure 3. The upper right corner shows that many large ontologies belong to the OWL Lite species, and their class structures are DAGs. There are 6 ontologies with more than 10000 classes in this survey, 5 of the 6 are in the (DAG, Lite) cluster. Of these 5, 4 have DL expressivity of $\mathcal{ALC}$, 1 has the the expressivity of $\mathcal{S}$. The combination of the most generalized graph structure and the least expressive species is interesting because it suggests that these ontologies are modeling fairly complex domains where the class structures are DAGS. However, none of the OWL DL features are used in the modeling process. Whether the modelers purposely intended to stay in OWL Lite (for fear of computational complexity in reasoning), or that OWL Lite provides all the constructs they needed is unclear.

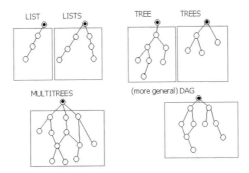

Fig. 1. Possible graph morphology of class hierarchies

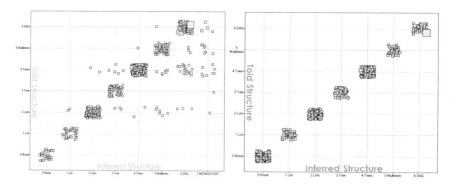

Fig. 2. Scatterplots of the graph morphology of OWL documents (on left), and the RDFS documents (right)

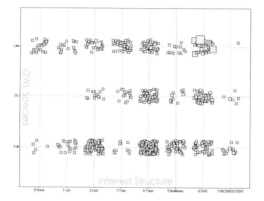

Fig. 3. Scatterplot of the graph morphology of OWL documents against OWL species

5 Future Work

The future work includes a survey on a larger pool of ontologies. For example, many DAML files can be converted to OWL without any loss of semantics. The only major difference between the two languages is that DAML has qualified number restrictions. It would be an interesting to see how many DAML files uses qualified number restrictions. In addition, the newly released Swoogle 2006 claims to have indexed many more semantic documents, including over 10000+ ontologies.

We see in this study that a fairly large number of ontologies use imports. It would be interesting to find out which ontologies are being imported and by how many others, what percentage of imports are not used by ontologies developed in the same institution. Related to this issue is finding out which are the most popularly used ontologies by RDF files (such as people's FOAF files). Another issue related to imports is to find out how many terms are being used in an ontology without importing the ontologies the terms are defined in.

It would also be interesting to attempt to partition the OWL ontologies using the modularity framework outlined in [6]. Partitionability of an ontology indicates that there are, informally, self-contained domains that can be separated, and possibly reused by other ontologies. The number of ontologies that can be partitioned and the distribution of the sizes of the partitions can shed some light about practitioners' modeling practices in terms of how often/many disjoint domains are used in an ontology.

6 Conclusions

As use OWL grows, assessments of how the language is being used and how modeling trends begin to emerge is both useful and interesting to the community. By collection nearly 1300 ontological documents from the Web and analyzing the statistics collected from them, we were able to note several trends and make interesting observations. There are higher percentage of OWL DL and OWL Lite files than it was previously reported in [2]. Most of the OWL Full files surveyed here can be syntactically patched. Of the patched OWL Full files, roughly one-third becomes OWL DL two-thirds become OWL Lite. In addition, by adding type triples, most of the RDFS files can easily transition to OWL files.

We showed that majority of OWL Lite documents fall into the bins of very inexpressive ontologies. The number of ontologies that contain interesting logical contradictions in this survey is small. But they all have high expressivity. In OWL construct analysis, we showed that `owl:intersection` is used in fewer ontologies than `owl:union`. `owl:ObjectProperty` is more prevalent than `owl:DatatypeProperty`. Though about one-third of the ontologies contain instances, very few instance constructs are being used currently. Looking at the graph morphologies, we are able to see where the interesting modeling practices occur. In addition, we conjecture that tools that presents/exploits the changes between told and inferred structures may allow users to gain understanding otherwise hard to obtain. We also observe that the largest of the OWL files have the characteristic that they have a high graph-morphological complexity and relatively low DL expressivity.

Acknowledgments

This work was supported in part by grants from Fujitsu, Lockheed Martin, NTT Corp., Kevric Corp., SAIC, the National Science Foundation, the National Geospatial Intelligence Agency, DARPA, US Army Research Laboratory, and NIST. Special thanks to Evren Sirin and Aditya Kalyanpur for their insightful discussions.

References

1. Franz Baader, Sebastian Brandt, and Carsten Lutz. Pushing the el envelope. *Proceedings of the 19th International Joint Conference on Artificial Intelligence (IJCAI-05)*, 2005.
2. Sean Bechhofer and Raphael Volz. Patching syntax in owl ontologies. *Proceedings of the 3rd International International Semantic Web Conference*, 2004.

3. Diego Calvanese, Giuseppe De Giacomo, Domenico Lembo, Maurizio Lenzerini, and Riccardo Rosati. *DL-Lite*: Tractable description logics for ontologies. *Proceedings of American Association for Artificial Intelligence (AAAI05)*, 2005.
4. J. Carroll, I. Dickinson, C. Dollin, D. Reynolds, A. Seaborne, and K. Wilkinson. Jena: Implementing the semantic web recommendations. *Proceedings of the 13th World Wide Web Conference*, 2004.
5. Bernardo Cuenca Grau. A possible simplification of the semantic web architecture. *Proceedings of the 13th International World Wide Web Conference (WWW2004)*, 2004.
6. Bernardo Cuenca-Grau, Bijan Parsia, Evren Sirin, and Aditya Kalyanpur. Modularity and web ontologies. 2006. To Appear in Proceedings of the 10th *International Conference on Principles of Knowledge Representation and Reasoning (KR2006)*.
7. Li Ding et al. Swoogle: A search and metadata engine for the semantic web. *Proceedings of the Thirteenth ACM Conference on Information and Knowledge Management*, 2004.
8. G. W. Furnas and J.Zacks. Multitrees: Enriching and reusing hierarchical structure. *Proceedings of ACM CHI 1994 Conference on Human Factors in Computing Systems*, 1994.
9. A. Kalyanpur, B. Parsia, and J. Hendler. A tool for working with web ontologies. *Int. J. on Semantic Web and Info. Syst.*, 1(1), 2004.
10. Thorsten Liebig and Olaf Noppens. OntoTrack: Combining browsing and editing with reasoning and explaining for OWL Lite ontologies. *Proceedings of the 3rd International International Semantic Web Conference*, 2004.
11. A. Magkanaraki, S. Alexaki, V. Christophides, and D. Plexousakis. Benchmarking rdf schemas for the semantic web. *Proceedings of the 1rd International International Semantic Web Conference*, 2002.
12. Natalya F. Noy, Michael Sintek, Stefan Decker, Monica Crubézy, Ray W. Fergerson, and Mark A. Musen. Creating semantic web content with protégé-2000. *IEEE Intelligent Systems*, 16(11):60–71, 2001.
13. Evren Sirin, Bijan Parsia, Bernardo Cuenca Grau, Aditya Kalyanpur, and Yarden Katz. Pellet: A practical owl-dl reasoner. Submitted for publication to Journal of Web Semantics.
14. M.-A. D. Storey, M. A. Musen, J. Silva, C. Best, N. Ernst, R. Fergerson, and N. F. Noy. Jambalaya: Interactive visualization to enhance ontology authoring and knowledge acquisition in Protégé. *Workshop on Interactive Tools for Knowledge Capture (K-CAP-2001)*, 2001.
15. Christoph Tempich and Raphael Volz. Towards a benchmark for semantic web reasoners - an analysis of the daml ontology library.
16. Sui-Yu Wang, Yuanbo Guo, Abir Qasem, and Jeff Heflin. Rapid benchmarking for semantic web knowledge base systems. *Proceedings of the 4th International Semantic Web Conference(ISWC2005)*, 2004.

CropCircles: Topology Sensitive Visualization of OWL Class Hierarchies

Taowei David Wang[1] and Bijan Parsia[2]

[1] Department of Computer Science,
University of Maryland, College Park, MD 20742, USA
tw7@cs.umd.edu
[2] The University of Manchester, UK
bparsia@cs.man.ac.uk

Abstract. OWL ontologies present many interesting visualization challenges. Here we present CropCircles, a technique designed to view the class hierarchies in ontologies as trees. We place special emphasis on topology understanding when designing the tool. We drew inspiration from treemaps, but made substantial changes in the representation and layout. Most notably, the spacefillingness of treemap is relaxed in exchange for visual clarity. We outline the problem scape of visualizing ontology hierarchies, note the requirements that go into the design of the tool, and discuss the interface and implementation. Finally, through a controlled experiment involving tasks common to understanding ontologies, we show the benefits of our design.

1 Introduction

The vision of the Semantic Web is a meta-data rich Web where presently human-readable content will have machine-understandable semantics. The Web Ontology Language (OWL) is a W3C recommendation that allows modelers to use its expressive formalism to define various logical concepts and relations[1]. A content-creator can use appropriate ontologies to, for example, annotate existing Web content. The enriched content can then be consumed by machines to assist humans in various tasks.

However, expressive ontologies can be difficult to understand. Content-creators often need to locate and inspect concepts of interest in detail to determine whether specific concepts are suitable for their use. The hierarchical structure of the concepts in an ontology can reveal a great deal about how these concepts are organized and how they are intended to be used. Effective presentation of the hierarchies can be a big win for the users.

In an OWL ontology, if we ignore `owl:Thing` as the root of the tree, and view the structure starting at the second level, an OWL ontology hierarchy can take the form of list(s), tree(s), multitrees [9], or a direct acyclic graph. One may believe that cycles of subclasses can occur. However, since the classes define sets, a cycle of subsets indicate that all classes in the cycle are equivalent. In OWL ontology editors such as Protégé [17] or SWOOP [14] the class trees are shown as standard tree widgets. Although the

---

[1] In this paper, we will use the term concept and class interchangeably.

widget is adequate for browsing node labels, it gives no additional information on how bushy or how deep a subtree is without further expanding it.

We present CropCircles, a technique to enhance user's ability to view the class structure at a glance. CropCircles is a tree visualizer, and like a treemap [13], CropCircles uses containment to represent the parent-child relationship. However, CropCircles sacrifices the space-fillingness for better visual clarity, enhancing understanding of the topology. This paper presents the design goals of CropCircles, the interface, and a validation of our design through a controlled experiment with treemap and SpaceTree.

2 Related Work

There are a number of ontology visualization tools available. Most of them are derivatives of tree visualizers. There are two major types of representations of trees. One is the traditional node-link diagram. The other is using geometric containment. Trees represented by node-link diagrams typically suffer from inefficient use of space. The root of the tree is usually situated where there is a lot of unused space. On the other hand, the nodes in the deep part of the tree have little room among themselves.

To remedy the inefficient use of space, hyperbolic tree viewer [15] places the hierarchy on a hyperbolic plane, and then maps the plane onto a circular region. User's focus on the tree will be given more space, accentuating the structures around it. The layout of the tree smoothly animates as the user clicks and drags at different parts of the tree. OntoRama [8] uses a hyperbolic approach to view RDF graphs. OntoRama can visualize RDF serialization of an OWL ontology, which is more verbose and consequently makes it more difficult to understand the hierarchy. One problem with the hyperbolic representation is that the constant relayout makes it difficult to maintain a mental map of where the nodes are or what the structure is.

SpaceTree [18] is a tree browser combined with a rich set of interactions to help users explore the tree. The dynamic rescaling of branches to fit the available screen space minimizes user interaction. Preview icons and miniature trees are used to give users a sense of the depth, breadth, and size of the subtrees. The smooth 3-stage animation to expand/contract subtrees help keeping the context without overwhelming users. Though it is possible to view 2 subtrees simultaneously using SpaceTree, it requires some careful user interaction. OntoTrack [16] builds on SpaceTree to browse and edit the ontology. It augments SpaceTree to use cross links to represent multiple inheritance. The implementation of the cross links, however, is awkward. Sharp bends of the links occur. Link occlusion by node labels often arise, and no optimization is done to minimize edge crossings.

Instead of using edges to represent the parent-child relationship in trees, a second type of tree representation uses geometric containment. Treemap [13] is a spacefilling representation of a tree using nested rectangles. The leaf nodes can use color and size to indicate their associated attributes. Labels for the nodes are displayed in place when there is enough room. The original treemap uses the slice-and-dice algorithm [13], which often produces elongated rectangles that are difficult to see and interact with. Squarified treemaps [5] and ordered treemaps [4] have been proposed to explicitly maintain good aspect ratio of the rectangles. Although treemaps were first applied to visualize directory structures, they have been widely applied to other areas, among them, stock market [2], news [3], sports reporting [12], microarray analysis using hierarchies from the gene ontology [1], and digital photo management system [3]. As widely as used treemaps are, they are most effective when the main focus is to understand the attribute distributions of the leaf nodes. Topological understanding is not one of its strengths.

Jambalaya [19] uses nested rectangles to show the hierarchy of classes and instances. It has a treemap view option. Different relations among the classes and instances are represented via edges between them. Users can filter both node and edge types. The visualization typically can show only 3 levels deep without serious user intervention.

There have been attempts to use geometric shapes other than rectangles to implement treemaps. Voronoi treemaps [2] use iterative relaxation of Voronoi tesselation to compute a layout of arbitrary polygons to fill a screenspace. The approach aims to address the high aspect ratio problem in treemaps and to better delineate boundaries among polygons. Kai Wetzel created a circular treemap to visualize Linux directories [4]. There is also recent work focusing on circle packing in directory viewing [20]. Though these algorithms are used to pack in the circles as tight as possible, nested circles can obviously not fill a space. However, this extra space makes it easier to distinguish the different levels of a tree.

3 Design and Implementation

Given an ontology, users typically want to find out whether some classes in the ontology is suitable for their use. They are interested in how many subclasses a paticular class has, as these subclasses are more specific than their parents and are differentiated from their siblings. In an unknown ontology, by exploring the larger branches of the hierarchy, a user is more likely to find out what the ontology is about. Likewise, in an inferred tree, one can tell that classes that lack subclasses and are children of `owl:Thing` are often undermodeled. By comparing the structural differences between the told the inferred class hierarchies, a user can also tell whether an ontology is mostly asserted, or is intricately modeled. An effective visualization should allow users to comparatively distinguish depth, bushiness, and size of subtrees.

The subsumption hierarchy in OWL is a directed graph, and to visualize it as a graph is natural and has the advantage that we do not need to duplicate nodes that have multiple parents. However, this often creates nonplanar graphs where intersecting edges cannot be avoided. Cross links are not desirable for both aesthetic and usability issues. As a result many graph drawing approaches name minimal edge-crossing as a requirement [6] [11]. Matrix representations of graphs represent edges implicitly, avoiding messy edge crossings and occlusions. But it is difficult to, for example, find how many subclasses a concept C has. This is a natural task in a tree, however. A user only needs to explore the subtree rooted at C. In a tree structure, users can better recoginze the

---

[2] http://www.smartmoney.com/marketmap/
[3] http://www.marumushi.com/apps/newsmap/newsmap.cfm
[4] http://lip.sourceforge.net/ctreemap.html

bushiness at a certain node and whether a branch can lead to a deep node. By imposing tree structures onto a graph, we believe this will enable users to perform these tasks better.

Treemap's ability to show multiple branches and multiple levels simultaneously is attractive. It allows users to compare depth, bushiness, and size of several subtrees at once. However, despite adjustable border size and depth filters, it is still difficult to gather topological information. In particular, treemaps emphasize on visualizing leaf node attributes. The intermediate nodes are deemphasized. In visualizing ontology hierarchies, however, intermediate nodes are as important as leaf nodes. Scanning for a node's children is also problem, as they are scattered in 2D space, and labels can be cropped or completely hidden.

Our visualization design requirements are aimed to address the problems and tasks outlined above. They are summarized below.

- **Topology Overview.** In supporting the tasks to discern size, depth, and bushiness, we aim to show multiple subtrees and multiple levels at once in a tree structure. This should allow users to better comparatively gauge the subtrees. But unlike treemaps, we sacrifice spacefillingness to increase clarity.
- **Linearity in Node Reading.** At any level of the tree, the user should be able to quickly read the labels of the children. Node-link representation of trees usually have sibling nodes arranged closely on a line or a curve. Reading and counting node labels in such situations is easy.
- **Node Duplication Detection.** Because we are imposing a graph structure onto a graph, we need to support users to detect duplications due to multiple inheritance.
- **Aesthetics.** Though not the most important requirement, we feel that a visually pleasing presentation would encourage users to look at the data and gain insights from the visualization.

3.1 Layout

In CropCircles circles represent nodes in a tree. Every child circle is nested inside its parent circle. Every circle's diameter is proportional to the size of the subtree rooted at that node. The smallest subtrees (the leaf nodes) have the minimum size of all circles. For every node, CropCircles sorts its children in descending order according to their subtree sizes, and then lays them out in that order. The sorting creates a sense of order in an otherwise unorderd 2D space within a circle. The larger nodes occupy more space, showing more importance, and encourage users to explore them first.

Depending on the size distribution of the children nodes, we employ 4 different layout strategies. These layout strategies are aimed to allow users to quickly gauge how the subtree sizes are distributed. To recognize whether a node has subtrees of equal size, a single subtree, or a predominant subtree can aid users' decisions on whether to explore such node further. When there is only one single child, the child node is concentrically placed inside its parent. When there are a number of equal sized children nodes, they are laid out on a concentric circle inside the parent, uniformly distributed. When there are no dominant children (a subtree that has more than 37% of the total number of descendents the parent subtree contains), all children are laid out along the lower arc of its parent, the largest node first. When at least one dominant child is present, smaller children are laid out on an arc, equidistant from the center of the largest child. The layout for dominant child introduces a deviation from the philosophy of the other 3 layouts. In this case, the arc the layout relies on does not depend on the parent node. It brings focus to the dominant child, and gives users a visual cue that something different is there. The four layout strategies can be seen in Figure 1[5].

In addition to the layout strategies, every child is rotated by an amount , proportional to its size-sorted rank, with respect to the either the center of of the parent, or the center of its largest child. This lessens the regularity of the layout, and the result is more visually pleasing. Because of these intricately nested circles, we name our tool CropCircles. We believe the sorting of child nodes and the regularity in layout can facilitate user's understanding of the structures where the current circle-packing approaches such as Kai Wetzel's circular treepmaps and [20] are not placing emphasis on.

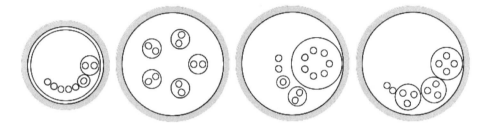

Fig. 1. From left to right, the figure shows the different layout strategies: single-child, all-children-of-equal-size, dominant-child, and no-dominant-child

3.2 Interface

The interface for CropCircles has two major components: a visualization area to the right, and a panel serving both nagivation needs and detailed views to the left (see Figure 2). The visualization area shows the tree as nested circles. Users can left click on any circle to highlight that subtree in white. Each double click on a circle will pan and fit that subtree to the screen. All the zooming and panning are done in one step (no animation). Mousing over any circle will show its statistics: label of the node, depth at which it is rooted, and how large its subtree is. To effectively support multiple inheritance, when users select a circle, all other duplicated circles will be highlighted, making it easy to spot all the parents of the selected node.

For each selected node, all its immediate children are displayed on a list to the left of the visualization. Above the list, user can utilize the navigation buttons to move forward and backward to previously selected nodes. If multiple ontologies are being visualized, users can select to view any subset of them in the ontology list on top of the nagivation buttons. Instead of seeing a list of immediate children, users may elect to see

---

[5] We note that the colors in the screen shots have been altered to ensure readability. For unaltered images, please see http://www.mindswap.org/~tw7/work/iswc2006/CropCircles/

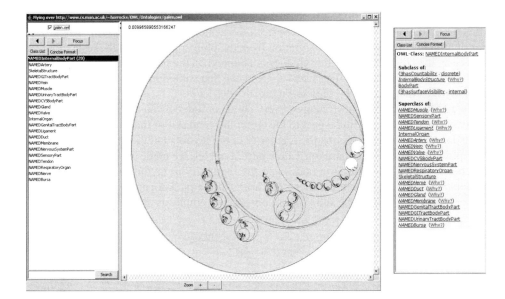

Fig. 2. This figure on the left shows the CropCircles interface. The visualization on shows the *inferred* class tree of galen. Note that the class "NAMEDInternalBodyPart" is multiply inherited in two places (hence the highlights). The left panel shows the children of the class. Alternatively, user can select the Concise Format tab to see the definition and inferred facts about the class, as shown in the right figure.

its definitions by click on the tab "Concise Format". Finally, there is a search box for name lookup. The current implementation of CropCircles uses the JUNG [6] framwork, and is downloadable as part of the open source OWL ontology editor SWOOP [7].

4 Empirical Evaluation

4.1 Choice of Tools

In the controlled experiemnt, we chose to compare the following 3 tree visualizers: CropCircles, treemap (Treemap 4.1 [8]), and SpaceTree (SpaceTree 1.6 [9]). Although treemaps are best when used to visualize node attributes at the leaf level, because much of our design decision was derived from treemap, we want to show that CropCircles is an improvement over treemaps on topological tasks. On the other hand, SpaceTree has been shown to be effective in conveying the structure of trees well in several tasks, though not without its own weaknesses [18]. We show that CropCircles is effective in conveying topological information and addresses the weaknesses of the other two

---

[6] http://jung.sourceforge.net/
[7] http://www.mindswap.org/2004/SWOOP/
[8] from http://www.cs.umd.edu/hcil/treemap/
[9] from http://www.cs.umd.edu/hcil/spacetree/

tools. We used the default settings on Treemaps in our experiment. SpaceTree uses a left-to-right layout and triangle and miniature trees as visual cues. Figure 3 shows visualizations of the experimental data using the three tools.

4.2 Choice of Tasks

For each tool, we ask users to perform the following tasks.

- **Find Unknown Node.** Users are asked to find a node in the hierarchy. They are not allowed to use search boxes. Users must rely on the visual representation of the trees and labels to find the node, and have up to 2 minutes to complete the task. If they are unable to finish the task within the time limit, the experiment administrator shows the user the steps to find the node. Users are asked to perform this task twice, each time with a different target node.
- **Return to Previously Visited Node.** Users are asked to locate a node that they found in a previous node-finding task. Users are asked to click on the node to show that they have found it. They can rely on their memory of the location of the node or any nagivational interfaces the tool supports. Users have up to 2 minutes to complete the task.
- **Comparison of Subtrees.** Users are asked to compare and contrast two subtrees. The experiment administrator brings the tool to a state where both subtrees are visible. Users are then free to explore the subtrees to state any structural similarities and differences of the two subtrees. Users are told to ignore label similarities, but are welcome to use them as references.
- **Find the Bushiest Child Node.** Given a node, users are asked to identify which one of its child nodes has the most immediate children. Users have up to 2 minutes to complete the task.
- **Find the Largest Subtree.** Given a node, users are asked to identify which one of its child nodes has the most descendents. Users have up to 2 minutes to complete the task. The node given to the participants has 18 immediate children, and total of 207 descendents.
- **Find a Deepest Node.** Given a subtree, users are asked to find a node that resides at the deepest level they can find. A time limit of 3 minutes is enforced.
- **Find 3 Nodes with at Least 10 Children.** Users are instructed to find 3 nodes that have at least 10 immediate descendents. Time limit is 2 minutes.
- **Find 3 Top-level Nodes that Root a subtree of Depth of at Least 5.** Users are asked to find 3 top level nodes (children of OWL:Thing) that root a subtree with depth of at least 5. Two minute limit is enforced.

Node-finding is an elementary task for any tree visualizer. When ontology users wish to use an ontology that is potentially suitable for their purposes, they must locate the class(es) they are interested in in order to examine if the modeling of these classes are compatible with the users' intended usage.

Ontology browsing often requires successive browsing of semantically related concepts. However, these related concepts often are not closely related in the hierarchy. That is, these concepts may not have an ancestor-descendent or even a sibling relationship.

One concept may be related to multiple concepts semantically. Users may need to adopt a breadth-first browsing pattern on the semantic relations to gain understanding of the specific concept semantically. A tool that allows users to quickly return to previously visited nodes would be favored.

Structural similarities are not uncommon in ontologies. The obvious case are the concepts that have multiple parents. These subtrees would be duplicated within an ontology. However, when an ontology imports another, and builds on top of the imported ontology, subtrees of different parents may no longer be the same. To be able to visually recognize similar trees is a plus. For example, the Federal Enterprise Architecture Reference Model (FEARMO) ontology [10] makes heavy reuse of imported concepts. By inspecting the structure alone and knowing where subtrees are reused, one can quickly grasp the modeling patterns.

The last five tasks have to do with topology of the tree. Tree topology in an ontology conveys information about where in the ontology the most well-defined parts are. The number of immediate children of a node indicate how fine-grained this particular concept is being modeled. The depth of a subtree indicates how specific a particular concept is modeled. Of course, the size of the subtree is a reflection of the above two measures.

4.3 Choice of Data

We use an older version of NASA SWEET JPL ontologies as our data [11]. Since the ontologies import one another, we stitched them together into a single file without changing the semantics. There are a total of 1537 defined classes. Adding the duplicate subtrees due to multiple inheritance creates a tree of 2104 nodes. We use this told tree for the first 3 tasks we described above. We then turn on an OWL reasoner to obtain the inferred tree, which contains 2007 total nodes. These two trees have sufficiently different topology. The told tree has a maximum depth of 11, average depth of leaf nodes 4.2, maximum branching factor 154, average branching factor of non-leaf nodes 3.9, and 103 nodes that have multiple inheritance. The inferred tree has the following, respectively, statistics: 12, 5.1, 74, 3.7, 125. We use the inferred tree to carry out the experiments on the topological tasks to prevent the effect of user learning the topology of the tree performing the first 3 tasks.

To mitigate users' possible prior familiarity with the ontology and the domain knowledge, we obfuscate the ontology by renaming the classes. The class are renamed in a pre-order traversal fashion. Given a starting integer N, the root of a subtree is given the name "CN". Then a pre-order traversal takes place to rename all its descendents recursively by incrementing N everytime a new node is encountered. We keep track of which number has been assigned to which node, so when duplicate nodes are encounterd multiples in the traversal they can be assigned the same names. We create 3 pairs of the told tree and the inferred tree, every pair using a different starting N. We then cross-pair a told tree and an inferred tree so that each tree in every pair has different

---

[10] http://www.topquadrant.com/owl/2004/11/fea/FEA.owl
[11] http://www.mindswap.org/ontologies/debug-sweet-jpl.owl. The most current version can be obtained via http://sweet.jpl.nasa.gov/ontology/

starting N. One pair is used for one tool in the experiment. We explain how the nodes are numbered prior to the experiment so users can search for nodes they have not seen before.

4.4 Experimental Setup

There are 18 subjects in our study. They are computer science graduate or undergraduate students or researchers who are familiar with tree structures. We give an overview to each subject on what they will be asked to do, and begin 3 sessions of training and experimentation phases, one session per tool. In each session, we spend up to 10 minutes training the subject on how to use the specific tool in that session. We make sure the subject understands the visual representation of the tree, whatever visual cues are available in the specific tool, ways to nagivate the tree, and how to obtain vital tree topology statistics (depth of a node, size of a subtree, etc.). We show users how to use features in the tools to help them accomplish the tasks effectively. In particular, we train users to use the depth filter in treemap, and to use bookmarks in SpaceTree. After the directed instructions are done, the user is allowed to freely experiment with the tool. When a user is comfortable with the tool, or when the 10 minute time is up, we proceed to the experimental phase. After each experimental phase, we ask users to fill out a section of a survey pertaining to the tool they just used with respect to the tasks they just performed. After the experiment, users are asked to complete the survey for other feedback and background information.

The order in which the tools are presented to the users are counterbalanced to eliminate learning effects and fatigue. All experiments are done on an IBM T41 laptop with 1.4GHz CPU 1.28GB of RAM running Windows XP. Each tool occupies 1240x740 pixels. The entire experiment does not exceed 75 minutes.

5 Results

We analyze each task separately. For each continuous dependent variable (e.g. time), we use a repeated measures one-way ANOVA. We check for the sphericity condition and then perform a modified F test in the ANOVA as suggested by [10]. This means that we first conduct an unmodifed univariate F test, and if the test is not significant, we accept the null hypothesis that the means obtained across the three tools are not different. If this first test is significant, we then lower the degrees of freedom and perform a conservative F test, which relies on, in our case, $F_{1,17}$ distribution. Tukey's HSD method is used for multiple comparisons when spheiricity is not grossly violated. Otherwise we use Bonferroni correction on subsequent pairwise two-tailed t-tests. We use $p = 0.05$ for the ANOVA and the post hoc procedures (note that the Bonferroni correction will lower p to ensure the overall significance is 0.05). For binomial variables (e.g. success/failure), we use Cochran-Mantel-Haenzsel general association statistic (which follows χ^2 distribution) to test whether the response profiles of the three tools are different [7]. We then use Bonferroni correction on the pairwise comparisons. Here we also use $p = 0.05$ for the CMH test and the pairwise comparisons. In the following sections, we present the experimental results, observations, and offers possible explanation to the observed

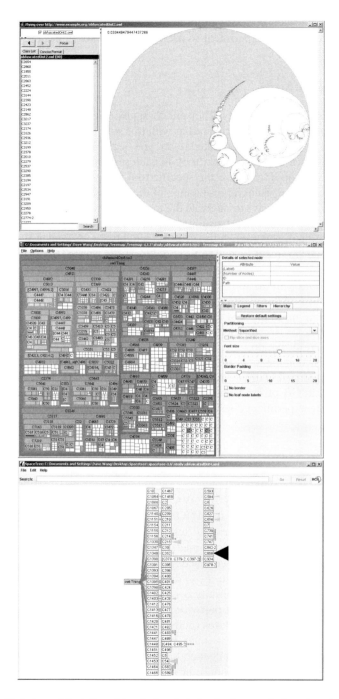

Fig. 3. The initial view of the inferred tree in the study by the three tools (top-down): CropCircles, Treemap 4.11, and SpaceTree 1.6

results. The results are summarized in Table 1. Unless otherwise specified, units used on performance is time in seconds.

Table 1. Results of the experiments. Each cell shows the recorded mean and the standard deviation of the dependent variable for a particular task and a particular tool. The statistic column shows the relevant statistics used and the level of significance obtained (if the test is significant). * denotes $p < 0.01$, + denotes $p < 0.05$. The last column shows only the statistically significant findings of the three tools: (C)ropcircles, (T)reemap, (S)paceTree. X > Y indicates that X outperforms Y with statistical significance.

Task	C		T		S		Statistic	significance
	mean	SD	mean	SD	mean	SD		
Node Finding 1	87.6	34.24	77.87	37.9	30.40	13.58	$F_{1,17} = 20.53^*$	S > C, S > T
Node Finding 2	62.31	34.0	63.42	31.6	28.91	13.13	$F_{1,17} = 15.85^*$	S > C, S > T
Return to Visited Node	19.94	7.64	59.75	41.23	17.44	5.34	$F_{1,17} = 15.86^*$	C > T, S > T
Subtree Compare (succ. rate)	1.0	0.0	0.78	0.43	0.83	0.38	$\chi^2_2 = 5.2$	none
Bushiest Child	27.42	19.04	55.45	31.70	12.15	7.88	$F_{1,17} = 19.08^*$	C > T, S > T
Largest Subtree	26.09	16.25	39.23	17.88	34.66	17.54	$F_{2,34} = 2.97$	none
A Deepest Node (error rate)	0.22	0.43	0.67	0.49	0.33	0.49	$\chi^2_2 = 6.93^+$	C > T
3 Nodes with ≥ 10 Children	19.56	6.14	26.14	23.39	53.59	27.27	$F_{1,17} = 15.26^*$	C > S, T > S
3 Subtrees of Depth ≥ 5	47.90	20.4	54.09	27.81	50.84	11.86	$F_{2,34} = 0.40$	none

5.1 Navigational Tasks

- **(First Time Node-Finding)** SpaceTree performed significantly better than Crop-Circles and treemap. However, there was no statistically significant difference between CropCircles and Treemap. Seven participants used the depth slider in Treemap to help reduce visual clutter. Participants also used the fact that they can read labels at multiple levels of tree simultaneously to their advantage in Treemap. Participands had problems finding nodes in CropCircles. The list of size-sorted labels is difficult to digest, particularly at the root level, where there are 154 branches to explore.
- **(Return to Visited Node)** In returning to a previously visited node, both CropCircles and SpaceTree outperformed Treemap with statistical significance. There was no significant difference between CropCircles and SpaceTree. Treemap's representation does not seem to help users much in this task. In fact, the relayout to achieve space-fillingness at each zoom disorients users even though they have already done the same traversal once before. Though CropCircle users can use history to navigate backwards, only 3 participants used it. Most participants used their memory on the traversal process on the class list to accomplish this task. Participants associated well with the steps they had taken to find the node using SpaceTree. Many remembered where to look at each stage of tree expansion.

5.2 Topology Recognition Tasks

- **(Subtree Comparison)** Although all participants were successful in making the observation using CropCircles, and some portions of participants failed in Treemap and SpaceTree, the differences among the tools are not statistically significant.

- **(Finding the Child Node that has the Most Immediate Children)** CropCircles and SpaceTree allowed users to complete this task significantly faster than Treemap. But there is no statistical sigificance between CropCircles and SpaceTree. When the target node was expanded in SpaceTree, it fully expanded both its child and its grand child level, but not its great-grand child level. This is exactly the right amount of information users needed to complete the task. The children nodes are presented in a linear list, making it easy to count. Many participants were observed to use the depth slider in treemap to filter out unnecessary nodes to quickly obtain the answer.
- **(Finding the Largest Subtree)** There was no statistical significance among the three tools. This was a surprising result. We observed that although participants are told that the nodes were sorted by size in CropCircles, users would spend time to verify the sizes as if they do not trust the visual representation. Similar situation is observed in SpaceTree. Users moused over all children to read the size of the subtree reported in the tooltips when only the subtrees with dark preview triangles should require closer inspection.
- **(Finding a Deepest Node)** We measured how successful users were at finding a node that is at the deepest level of the given subtree. We performed analyses on the error rate. CropCircles had significantly lower error rate than treemap, but the difference between SpaceTree and CropCircles was not significant. There was also no significant difference between SpaceTree and treemap.
- **(Finding 3 Nodes with at Least 10 Immediate Descendents)** Both CropCricles and Treemap outperformed SpaceTree significantly, but there was no statistically significant difference between the two. The nodes that CropCircles users reported tend to be at the upper levels of the tree, as they took no additional zooming to see. On the contrary, all nodes reported by Treemap users are the ones that contain many leaf nodes, which are white, and are easy to see.
- **(Finding 3 Top-Level Nodes that Root Subtrees of Depth of at Least 5)** There were no statistically significant differences among the three tools.

6 Discussion

Ignoring statistically insignificant results, CropCircles performed well against Treemap and SpaceTree in topological tasks. CropCircles edged SpaceTree in finding 3 nodes with at least 10 children, and was better than Treemap in finding a deepest node and finding the bushiest child. Although there was no one task that CropCircles was better than both of the other two tools, there was also no one topology task that CropCircles performed unsatisfactorily. In this sense CropCircles is the most balanced of the three tools in topology recognition tasks. By avoiding Treemap's and SpaceTree's weaknesses, CropCircles is an appropriate visualization for class hierarchy. For example, ontology modelers who wish to visually explore where an ontology is undermodeled (characterized by subtrees that lack depth and bushiness in the inferred tree), CropCircles would be a good choice. The results also suggest that ontology hierarchy visualizers that use SpaceTree or treemap as the underlying technique should be aware of their shortcomings and address them.

On the other hand, not all of our design decisions were validated. Although listing children in a list that enables level-traversal allows users to remember the path they took to a particular visited node, the list is inadequate to support label browsing. An option to sort the labels alphabetically would have helped the users a great deal in node-finding tasks. We were also not able to show that CropCircles can outperform the other tools with statistical significance in finding the largest subtree, even though the subtrees are ranked by size.

Our participants gave us valuable feedbacks on how to improve CropCircles in our post experimental survey. Many mentioned better context support when details are focused. Several users suggested a more tightly integrated history with the visualization. Almost all participants commented on the lack of support to sort node labels alphabetically. Information density in CropCircles is a concern, and several users have mentioned the desire to see the space utilized better. These comments and our experimental results are observed, and will be the main focus in the next step of our iterative design process.

7 Conclusions

We describe CropCircles and our requirements in designing a tool to visualize the topology of OWL class hierarchy. While our design exploited several useful principles, not all design decisions are helpful in completing the tasks in the experiments. However, we are able to show that in topological tasks, CropCircles's performance is comparable to strengths of the two other tools, and is an improvement over their known weaknesses. This result makes CropCircles an attractive alternative in viewing class hierarchies in OWL.

Acknowledgments

This work was supported in part by grants from Fujitsu, Lockheed Martin, NTT Corp., Kevric Corp., SAIC, the National Science Foundation, the National Geospatial Intelligence Agency, DARPA, US Army Research Laboratory, and NIST. Special thanks to Jennifer Golbeck for her helpful comments and suggestions.

References

1. Eric H Baehrecke, Niem Dang, Ketan Babaria, and Ben Shneiderman. Visualization and analysis of microarray and gene ontology data with treemaps. *BMC Bioinformatics*, 84(5), 2004.
2. Michael Balzer, Oliver Deussen, and Claus Lewerentz. Voronoi treemaps for the visualization of software metrics. *In Proceedings of the IEEE Symposium on Information Visualization*, 2005.
3. Benjamin B. Bederson. Quantum treemaps and bubblemaps for a zoomable image browser. *In Proceedings of User Interface Systems and Technology*, pages 71–80, 2001.
4. Benjamin B. Bederson, Ben Shneiderman, and Martin Wattenberg. Ordered and quantum treemaps: Making effective use of 2d space to display hierarchies. *ACM Transations on Graphics*, 21(4):833–854, 2002.

5. Mark Bruls, Kees Huizing, and Jarke J. van Wijk. Squarified treemaps. *Proc. IEEE Symposium on Information Visualization '99*, pages 284–291, 2000.
6. Ron Davidson and David Harel. Drawing graphs nicely using simulated annealing. *ACM Tran. on Graphics*, 15:301–331, 1996.
7. Charles S. Davis. *Statistical Methods for the Analysis of Repeated Measurements*. Springer, 2002.
8. P. Eklund, N. Roberts, and S. P. Green. Ontorama: Browsing an rdf ontology using a hyperbolic-like browser. *In Proceedings of the 1st International Symposium on CuberWorlds (CW2002)*, pages 405–411, 2002.
9. G. W. Furnas and J.Zacks. Multitrees: Enriching and reusing hierarchical structure. *Proceedings of ACM CHI 1994 Conference on Human Factors in Computing Systems*, 1994.
10. S. W. Greenhouse and S. Geisser. On methods in the analysis of profile data. *Psychometrika*, 29:95–112, 1959.
11. David Harel and Meir Sardas. Randomized graph drawing with heavy-duty preprocessing. *Journal of Visual Language and Computing*, 6:233–253, 1995.
12. Liquin Jin and David C. Banks. Tennisviewer: A browser for competition trees. *IEEE Computer Graphics and Applications*, 17(4):63–65, 1997.
13. Brian Johnson and Ben Shneiderman. Tree-maps: A space-filling approach to the visualization of hierarchical information structures. *In Proceedings of the 2nd International IEEE Visualization Conference*, pages 284–291, 1991.
14. A. Kalyanpur, B. Parsia, and J. Hendler. A tool for working with web ontologies. *Int. J. on Semantic Web and Info. Syst.*, 1(1), 2004.
15. J. Lamping, R. Rao, and P. Pirolli. A focus+context technique based on hyperbolic geometry for visualizing large hierarchies. *Conference Proceedings on Human factors in computing systems*, pages 401–408, 1995.
16. Thorsten Liebig and Olaf Noppens. OntoTrack: Combining browsing and editing with reasoning and explaining for OWL Lite ontologies. *In Proceedings of the 3rd International International Semantic Web Conference*, 2004.
17. Natalya F. Noy, Michael Sintek, Stefan Decker, Monica Crubézy, Ray W. Fergerson, and Mark A. Musen. Creating semantic web content with protégé-2000. *IEEE Intelligent Systems*, pages 60–71, 2000.
18. Catherine Plaisant, Jesse Grosjean, and Benjamin B. Bederson. Spacetree: Supporting exploration in large node link tree, design evolution and empirical evaluation. *In Proceedings of IEEE Symposium on Information Visualization*, pages 57–64, 2002.
19. M.-A. D. Storey, M. A. Musen, J. Silva, C. Best, N. Ernst, R. Fergerson, and N. F. Noy. Jambalaya: Interactive visualization to enhance ontology authoring and knowledge acquisition in Protégé. *Workshop on Interactive Tools for Knowledge Capture (K-CAP-2001)*, 2001.
20. Weixin Wang, Hui Wang, Guozhong Dai, and Hongan Wang. Visualization of large hierarchical data by circle packing. *In Proceedings of SIGCHI Conference on Human Factors in Computing Systems (CHI'06)*, pages 517–520, 2006.

Towards Knowledge Acquisition from Information Extraction

Chris Welty and J. William Murdock

IBM Watson Research Center
Hawthorne, NY 10532
{welty, murdock}@us.ibm.com

Abstract. In our research to use information extraction to help populate the semantic web, we have encountered significant obstacles to interoperability between the technologies. We believe these obstacles to be endemic to the basic paradigms, and not quirks of the specific implementations we have worked with. In particular, we identify five dimensions of interoperability that must be addressed to successfully populate semantic web knowledge bases from information extraction systems that are *suitable for reasoning*. We call the task of transforming IE data into knowledge-bases *knowledge integration*, and briefly present a framework called KITE in which we are exploring these dimensions. Finally, we report on the initial results of an experiment in which the knowledge integration process uses the deeper semantics of OWL ontologies to improve the precision of relation extraction from text.

Keywords: Information Extraction, Applications of OWL DL Reasoning.

1 Introduction

Ontologies describe the kinds of phenomena (e.g., people, places, events, relationships, etc.) that can exist. Reasoning systems typically rely on ontologies to provide extensive formal semantics that enable the systems to draw complex conclusions or identify unintended models. In contrast, systems that extract information from text (as well as other unstructured sources such as audio, images, and video) typically use much lighter-weight ontologies to encode their results, because those systems are generally *not* designed to enable complex reasoning.

We are working on a project that is exploring the use of large-scale information extraction from text to address the "knowledge acquisition bottleneck" in populating large knowledge-bases. This is by no means a new idea, however our focus is less on theoretical properties of NLP or KR systems in general, and more on the realities of these technologies *today*, and how they can be used together. In particular, we have focused on state-of-the art text extraction components, many of which consistently rank in the top three at competitions such as ACE (Luo, et al, 2004) and TREC (Chu-Carroll, et al, 2005), that have been embedded in the open-source Unstructured Information Management Architecture (UIMA) (Ferrucci & Lally, 2004), and used to populate semantic-web knowledge-bases.

This, too, is not a particularly new idea; recent systems based on GATE (e.g. (Popov, et al 2004)) have been exploring the production of large RDF repositories from text. In our project, however, we are specifically focused on the *nature of the data* produced by information extraction techniques, and its *suitability for reasoning*. Most systems that we have come across (see the related work section) do not perform reasoning (or perform at best the most simplistic reasoning) over the extracted knowledge stored in RDF, as the data is either too large or too imprecise. This has led many potential adopters of semantic web technology, as well as many people in the information extraction community, to question the value of the semantic web (at least for this purpose). We believe this community can be important in helping drive adoption of the semantic web.

In this paper we will discuss our general approach to generating OWL knowledge-bases from text, present some of the major obstacles to using these knowledge-bases with OWL- and RDF-based reasoners, and describe some solutions we have used. Our research is not in information extraction, ontologies, nor reasoning, but in their combination. Our primary goal is to raise awareness of the real problems presented by trying to use these technologies together, and while we present some solutions, the problems are far from solved and require a lot more attention by the community.

2 Related Work

Research on extraction of formal knowledge from text (e.g., Dill, et al. 2003) typically assumes that text analytics are written for the ontology that the knowledge should be encoded in. Building extraction directly on formal ontologies is particularly valuable when the extraction is intended to construct or modify the original ontology (Maynard, Yankova, et al. 2005; Cimiano & Völker, 2005). However, there is a substantial cost to requiring text analytics to be consistent with formal ontology languages. There are many existing systems that extract entities and relations from text using informal ontologies that make minimal semantic commitments (e.g., Marsh, 1998; Byrd & Ravin, 1999; Liddy, 2000; Miller, et al., 2001; Doddington, et al., 2004). These systems use these informal ontologies because those ontologies are relatively consistent with the ambiguous ways concepts are expressed in human language and are well-suited for their intended applications (e.g., document search, content browsing). However, those ontologies are not well-suited to applications that require complex inference.

Work on so-called *ontology-based* information extraction, such as compete in the ACE program, (e.g. (Cunningham, 2005), (Bontcheva, 2004)) and other semantic-web approaches like (Maynard, 2005), (Maynard, et al, 2005), and (Popov, et al, 2004), focus on directly populating small ontologies that have a rich and well-thought out semantics, but very little if any formally specified semantics (e.g. using axioms). The ontologies are extensively described in English, and the results are apparently used mainly for evaluation and search, not to enable reasoning. Our work differs in that we provide an explicit knowledge integration step that allows us to populate fully axiomatized ontologies from information extraction.

Our emphasis actually makes our work similar to work in semantic integration or schema matching (e.g., Milo & Zohar, 1998; Noy & Musen, 2001), which typically focuses on finding very simple (e.g., one-to-one) mappings among terms in ontologies. Schema matching is useful when the ontologies are large and complex, so that these mappings, while individually simple, are numerous and challenging to find. Our work however focuses on the opposite circumstance: We assume that the ontologies are small and manageable enough that one can find the correspondences manually and that the mappings may be more complex (conditional, many-to-many, etc.) than an automated matching system can handle.

Schema-matching technologies have typically been used when the applications that the source and target ontologies were designed for are identical or at least quite similar; e.g., matching one e-commerce database schema to another. In those cases, the assumption that individual mappings will tend to be very simple can be valid; since the designers of the ontologies had the same basic purpose in mind. Mapping extracted information into formal reasoning ontologies does not have this characteristic; these applications are radically different and tend to lead to radically different conceptualizations of basic content. For these sorts of differences, it is not feasible to restrict the mappings between terms to be sufficiently simple and obvious enough that they can be discovered by state-of-the-art fully-automated matching techniques.

We use in our work components implemented within the Unstructured Information Mangagement Architecture (UIMA). UIMA is an open-source middleware platform for integrating components that analyze unstructured sources such as text documents. UIMA-based systems define "type systems" (i.e., ontologies with extremely limited semantic commitments) to specify the kinds of information that they manipulate (Götz & Suhre, 2004). UIMA type systems include no more than a single-inheritance type/subtype hierarchy, thus to do substantive reasoning over the results of UIMA-based extraction, one needs to convert results into a more expressive representation.

3   Generating RDF from Text

The context of our application deserves some attention, as our results are somewhat dependent on the assumptions that arise from it. First of all, we are taking the approach that analytics are more expensive to produce than ontologies. This presumes, of course, that we are talking about smaller, lightweight ontologies of no more than 100 classes and 100 object properties, which makes sense if they are to be populated from text analysis, as typical information extraction ontologies are extremely small. Analytics are available in reusable components that can be embedded in frameworks like UIMA, in which they are composed into larger aggregate analysis engines. The individual components overlap to varying degrees in the types of entities and relations they discover, and in the cases of overlap, need to have their results combined. While this has in general been shown to improve overall precision and recall, it does create interesting anomalies in the non-overlapping types of data (which we will discuss below). The individual analytic components we treat as black boxes, their operation is for the most part functional (producing the same output for the same input). Ontologies therefore are custom built to suit particular application needs, whereas analytics are reused and composed off the shelf. Our experiences are that this characterizes hundreds, if not thousands, of users today looking to populate their part of the semantic web from textual sources. These users are in the medical domain, national and business intelligence, compliance, etc., and many have resources to fund research in the area. The work described here was funded jointly by IBM and the U.S. Government.

3.1 Text to Knowledge Pipeline

In our evaluation prototype, we produce knowledge-bases from text in a pipeline that proceeds through several stages:

Keyword Indexing. The simplest and most scalable processing is the generation of an inverted index to support keyword search. Although techniques such as link analysis, query expansion, etc., can offer minor improvements, this approach is generally very low in precision. In addition to its current established usage, we consider the function of keyword search to be *domain corpus production.* We employ recall-improving techniques such as query expansion to reduce the size of the target corpus to the scale required by the next stage of processing (information extraction) – this is typically 1-2 orders of magnitude.

Information Extraction. Information extraction (IE) in general can be viewed as the analysis of unstructured information to assign labels (or *annotations*) that carry some semantics to regions of the data. The canonical example would be to label the text "George Bush" with *Person*. The field has advanced considerably since these beginnings, and are well represented by the ACE program (Doddington, et al, 2004), participants in which produce annotations for entities (*Person, Organization*, etc.), relations (*partOf, citizenOf,* etc.), and coreference analysis. While almost any kind of information processing can be folded into an information extraction view, in our system, IE components play the role of providing relatively shallow processing in order to be scalable. In particular, this stage limits itself to processing data in documents, and performs the same analysis on each document independently. As a result, IE processing scales linearly with the size of the domain corpus.

Coreference Across Documents. The annotations produced in the IE stage are used as input to *corpus-level processing*, the most important to our purposes of which is coreference analysis – the identification of individual entities that are mentioned (and annotated) in multiple places. Many of our IE components produce coreference analysis within documents, but connecting these results across the entire corpus clearly requires processing that can collect information across the documents, and thus will typically scale at a polynomial rate. In our experiece, the most critical properties of co-reference are recognition of aliases and nicknames, common spelling variations of names (especially in other languages), common diminutives, abbreviations, etc. This is a wide-open research area that requires significant attention.

Knowledge Integration. Although it is not required, the data produced in the first three stages of our system are all based on the same underlying format (discussed in Ferrucci&Lally, 2004), which is a simple extension of an OO programming model with a tight programmatic API and a loose semantics (that is, the semantics of a data model can be interpreted by software as the programmers choose). The process of mapping the information from the previous stages into OWL is analogous to the general problem of semantic integration (schema matching, ontology alignment, etc.) with some additional challenges, which we discuss below. We call this stage knowledge integration. The result of knowledge integration, an OWL knowledge-base that can be viewed as a graph, provides the ability to use OWL-based reasoning to perform more sophisticated *deductive search*. For example, we can express axioms of spatial or temporal containment in OWL, and conclude obvious (but nevertheless implicit) results, such as a person in Paris is also in France.

3.2 Knowledge Integration Challenges

Knowledge Integration is analogous to semantic integration. The basic problem is to align the type system of the analytic components with the ontology of the reasoning components (see the beginning of this section for a discussion of why they are not the same), such that the data produced by the analytic components can "instantiate" the ontology. Knowledge integration is difficult however, and to our knowledge is not often attempted, due to the vastly different requirements, and different communities, on each side. As a result, what seems on the surface to be a natural connection – producing structured representations from unstructured information and then reasoning over those structures – turns out to be a difficult challenge. Below we list the five dimensions of interoperability we have identified and brief notes on how we are addressing them:

Precision. Formal reasoning systems are notoriously intolerant of errors, and IE systems are notoriously prone to producing them. This is probably the most fundamental problem in putting them together. In particular, logical reasoning becomes meaningless in the face of contradiction, most inference engines will prove any statement to be true if the knowledge-base is inconsistent to begin with. Although improving precision is an obvious approach to this problem, we take it as a given that IE processes will never be perfect, and furthermore even in the presence of perfect IE, data sources can contradict each other intentionally (e.g. reports from CNN and the pre-war Iraqi News Agency), and instead we focus on making the reasoning systems more tolerant of errorful data. Our simplest technique is to perform limited reasoning such as semantic constraints that can be checked rapidly, and that in our evaluations we find to be indicative of IE errors and not intended contradictions. We discuss this further below.

Recall. Imperfect recall is another significant obstacle to interoperability. The amount of knowledge we typically get from documents is quite small compared to what a human might produce from the same document. The reasoning system is, therefore, crippled by major gaps in the input. Using inference can actually help improve recall, however it is a different sense than is typically used in IE measurements. Recall measurements are based on comparison to a "ground truth" (i.e. a human annotated corpus), in which implicit information does not appear. For example, in the sentence

"Joe arrived in Paris", we would not expect a test corpus to include the relationship that Joe arrived in France, yet this inferred information clearly increases the recall.

Relationships. Simple IE systems that produce type annotations (such as Person, Organization, etc.) are not of much use as input to a reasoning system. These end up in a knowledge base as assertions that something is an instance of something else. There is very little reasoning that can be done with only that information. In order for reasoning to produce useful results, we need relationships to be extracted as well. For example, there is not much to conclude from the sentence, "Joe was in Paris," if all that was produced was that "Joe" is a person and "Paris" is a place. In this case, a located-in relation would be useful as well, as simple spatial containment axioms plus basic world knowledge (e.g. that Paris is in France) would allow a reasoner to conclude that Joe was in France. We use a number of IE components that produce relations over text, however the state-of-the-art in relation extraction is very poor on precision and recall.

Annotations vs. Entities. In our experience, relation annotation by itself creates another problem. Every relation annotation creates a tuple whose elements are the spans of text that participate in the relation, and thus do not appear in other relations. This severely limits the usefulness of reasoning, since the elements of the relation tuples are the *mentions* not the entities. For example, from the sentences, "Joe was in Paris. Fred was in Paris, too," relation annotation would produce two tuples, however the elements of the tuples are not the strings, "Joe", "Fred", and "Paris", but the regions containing those strings in the original text, and as a result we have four elements identified by their position in text, *not* by their contents. Thus the first and second occurrences of "Paris" are different elements, and we could not conclude in a reasoner that, e.g. Joe and Fred are in the same place. In fact, without connecting these two mentions of Paris (both within and across documents), we end up with a large list of unconnected relation tuples. We address this problem with coreference analysis, and although we do not discuss it in this paper, *coreference analysis is an essential task in populating knowledge-bases from text.* In particular, consider that the output of knowledge integration is a graph – the graph without coreference analysis would be a disconnected set of connected pairs.

Scalability. IE techniques scale far better than KR techniques, and as a result we also need to limit the amount of data that any reasoning component has to deal with. In our experience, documents provide an excellent and reliable heuristic for KB size, as well as for consistency. We have found that, excluding IE errors, in excess of 90% of the documents we process are internally consistent, and thus far all documents (we focus mainly on news articles, intelligence reports and abstracts) have been the basis of small enough KBs for any of our advanced reasoning systems. Still, document-based partitioning is inadequate for a lot of information gathering tasks that we have focused on, so a variety of incremental capabilities are required, as are efforts at more scalable reasoning.

We attempt to address these dimensions in a component-based framework for supporting knowledge integration, discussed in the next section. Due to space considerations we cannot discuss all five dimensions, and will focus mainly on

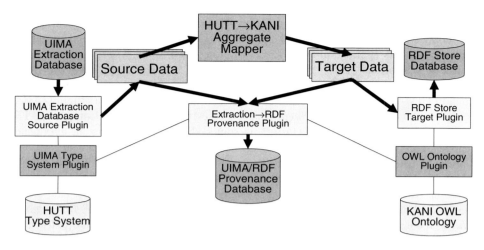

Fig. 1. Example KITE-based application

experiments we have performed to use deeper semantics expressed in OWL-DL to improve precision.

4 Knowledge Integration and Transformation Engine (KITE)

KITE (Murdock & Welty, 2006) is a middleware platform for use by developers of knowledge integration applications. KITE consists of two major components:

- **KITE Core Framework:** Java interfaces, data structures, and a central control mechanism for mapping entities and relationships from one ontology to another.
- **KITE Commons:** A set of broadly applicable plugins that comply with the interfaces specified in the core framework.

A KITE-based integrator takes as input a *Source Repository* (e.g., a database, an RDF/XML file). Information in that repository is encoded in the *Source Ontology* (which is accessed via an *Ontology Language Plugin*). The *Source Plugin* reads from the source repository and outputs *Source Data* encoded in KITE data structures for instances and tuples. *Mapper Plugins* may be primitive or aggregate. Aggregate mapper plugins are composed of other (primitive or aggregate) mapper plugins. Primitive mapper plugins are Java objects that take *Source Data* as input and output *Target Data* (which consist of the same data structures, but are encoded in the *Target Ontology*). The *Target Plugin* writes that data to a *Target Repository* and the *Provenance Plugin* writes the mappings from source to target data into a *Provenance Repository*.

Figure 1 shows an example of a KITE-based knowledge integrator. Source data for this application is encoded in HUTT (Hierarchical Unified Type Taxonomy), a UIMA type system based on a variety of established information extraction taxonomies (e.g., Doddington, et al., 2004; Sauri, Litman, et al., 2004). The output ontology for this application is the OWL ontology used in the KANI project (Fikes, Ferrucci, & Thurman, 2005).

The input data for the example application is stored in a database designed to contain UIMA extracted information. The KITE Commons includes a plugin (*UIMA Extraction Database Source Plugin*) that accesses this database and outputs KITE instances and tuples (*Source Data*). This source data is provided to an aggregate mapper composed of an assortment of both generic mappers from the KITE Commons and specialized mappers that were written for the HUTT to KANI integrator. These mappers output target data. That data is consumed by two plugins from the KITE Commons: the *RDF Store Target Plugin* writes the target data alone into a relational database for RDF triples, and the *Extraction → RDF Provenance Plugin* records (potentially complex) mappings from source data in the extraction database to target data in the RDF database; these mappings are stored in the *UIMA/RDF Provenance Database*.

Systems that access instances and triples from the RDF store can request traces of the information extraction and knowledge integration processes that created those instances and triples. The provenance database is able to return that information either as database entries or in the OWL-based Proof Markup Language, PML (Pinheiro da Silva, McGuinness & Fikes, 2006). Systems that perform additional reasoning over the extracted knowledge can provide integrated end-to-end PML traces that explain their conclusions as a combination of logical inferences from the RDF knowledge and extraction inferences used to obtain that knowledge from text (Murdock, et al., 2006).

The most complex mappers that were written for this application involve the handling of temporal information. The representation of time in HUTT is based on TimeML (Sauri & Littman, 2004), a language for marking up expressions of time in natural-language text. The representation of time in the KANI ontology is OWL-Time (Hobbs, 2004), a semantic web ontology. OWL-Time makes relatively subtle distinctions that are usually implicit in text (e.g., distinguishing between time intervals and time interval descriptions). Furthermore, OWL-Time has distinct properties to encode different aspects of a description of a time (year, month, day, hour, etc.). In contrast, TimeML does not encode a time and its expression separately, and uses a relatively compact normalized form to encode a full time description in a single string. These differences are motivated by the different applications that these ontologies were designed for; OWL-Time directly enables a wide variety of logical inferences about times, while TimeML provides a convenient and compact formalism for identifying, normalizing, and linking expressions of time in text. A generic mapping component that was expressive enough to handle the mapping between these two portions of the HUTT and KANI ontologies would be extremely complicated to develop and to use. However, many of the other terms in HUTT and KANI *are* handled easily by simple, generic mappers from the KITE Commons.

5 Improving Annotator Precision & Recall Using OWL

One particularly promising result of our knowledge integration efforts supported by the KITE framework has been using the kind of deep, axiomatic, semantics that OWL enables, to help improve precision and recall in the results. We present here our technique and a preliminary evaluation of its effectiveness with a large UIMA-based application that includes dozens of "off the shelf" analytic components run on a corpus of news articles.

5.1 Technique and Evaluation for Improving Precision

The most problematic kind of extraction produced by analytic components we have experienced is relation extraction. A common type of error we see in extracted relations is the violation of simple domain and range constraints. For example, in the following sentence:

> In February 1993, US officials said that US President Bush's decision in September 1991 to withdraw tactical <u>nuclear bombs</u>, missiles and torpedoes from US Navy ships has caused the impetus for naval arms control to whither.

our analytics extract an ownership relation in the underlined text between "nuclear" (annotated as a weapon), and "bombs" (also a weapon), which maps to a *ownerOf* relation in the ontology. The *ownerOf* relation has a restriction limiting the domain to *Person* or *Organization* or *GPE* and a disjointness constraint between each of these and *Weapon*.

Our approach is a simple one. During knowledge integration, we construct an intermediate knowledge base (in fact, a Jena model) consisting of only the mapped entities and their type information. Then, during the mapping process producing relations, we add resulting triples to this KB one at a time. With each addition, we run the KB through a consistency check using Pellet. If the KB is not consistent, we "drop" the triple, if it is consistent, we add the triple to the output of the transformation. Obviously this technique does not scale particularly well and is entirely dependent on the degree to which the ontology is axiomatized. In preliminary experiments, however, the technique appears promising and does quite well – offering a clear improvement in precision by dropping incorrect triples. We are still exploring how these results generalize, but we present here some concrete examples, analysis, and discussion:

Ontology. The ontology we tested consists of 56 classes and 62 object properties in the domain of nuclear arms proliferation. Other than a few specific classes for weapons, the classes and properties are fairly generic (people, places, facilities, etc.). All properties have global domain and range constraints, however some are not that restrictive. Five classes have local range constraints. Cardinality constraints are not of use in our domain. The most effort was spent assigning appropriate disjointness constraints, as these are key to the technique.

Analytics. Our analytics are 42 off-the-shelf components that were developed for other projects such as TREC and ACE, and that we aggregated using the composition capabilities of UIMA. The merged type system contains 205 entity and 79 relation types; most of our analytic components overlap on common types such as *PERSON* and *ORGANIZATION*, etc., but each adds some unique functionality to the overall aggregate. We have special purpose components for arbitrating between conflicting annotation assignments and for computing co-reference across documents.

Corpus. The corpus contains over 30K documents that average about a page in length. Most are news articles or summaries of news articles in the domain of interest. Due to the extensive cost of evaluation (which must be done by hand), the experiments were performed on 10, 41, and 378 documents. We report here the results of the 378 document test. On average our analytics produce 322 entity annotations and 21 relation annotations per document, and coreference merges an average of 15 annotations per entity and 1.8 annotations per relation. The KITE-based knowledge integrator maps those entities and relations into instances and tuples in the KB. For the 378 document corpus, the end result is a KB of 6281 individuals and 834 object property triples. These numbers clearly demonstrate the significance of recall in this process, only a fraction of the generated knowledge base is of any real use to the semantic web, more than 70% of the entities simply have a label and a type.

Results. Our technique dropped 67 (object property) triples of the 834 produced by the mapping process. Of the 67 dropped, 2 were actually correct and should not have been dropped (see the analysis below). This is a *relative* improvement in precision of 8.7%., which is considerably more than the difference between the first and fifth place competitors in the ACE competition relation extraction task (for which this scale is also appropriate). The cost of this improvement is high; the system without this check takes about 5 minutes to generate a KB from 378 documents, and with the reasoning check takes over an hour. There is a lot that can be done to improve this, however, and our precision improvement results are encouraging enough that we are exploring alternatives, such as a much more rapid heuristic consistency checker (Fokue, et al, 2006), partitioning the KB by document instead of checking global consistency, and others.

5.2 Analysis of Evaluation

Of the 67 triples we reported dropped, 2 should not have been dropped. A further 11 triples fell into a special category in which the triples themselves were correct, but the coreference resolution or type assignments for relation arguments were wrong, so a more robust solution would have been to amend the coreference or typing.

Many (but not all) of the correct filtering of incorrect relations is a result of the combination of multiple independent annotators to determine the type of an entity. An example of this occurred in the following phrase:

> With the use of these pits, landmines, and guerrilla attacks, <u>Khmer Rouge forces</u> allegedly drove off the personnel sent to repair the road.

One of our entity and relation annotators incorrectly determines that "Khmer Rouge" is a person who is the leader of the "forces." However, the combination of annotators concludes that "Khmer Rouge" is actually an organization. Since the OWL ontology indicates that an organization can't be the leader of another organization, this triple is correctly dropped.

The two erroneously dropped triples were due to a combination of weak typing of entities and errors in another relation that did not manifest as inconsistencies until the triple in question was added to the KB. For example, consider the phrase:

> ... of countries like Pakistan, <u>India, Iran</u>, and North Korea, who are building ...

A comma between two geopolitical entities often indicates a subPlace relation (e.g., "Delhi, India"), and one of our annotators incorrectly extracts a subPlace relation between India and Iran. The cross-document coreference process is unable to authoritatively assign the "Country" label to the entity corresponding to "India", so it ends up as a GPE (geopolitical entity), a superclass of Country. The entity corresponding to "Iran", however, is correctly typed as a Country. In the ontology, there is a local range restriction on the *Country* class that prevents it from being a *subPlace* of another country. So, if the entity corresponding to "India" had been correctly labeled as a country, our technique would have dropped the "India subPlace Iran" relation when it was mapped, however since some countries are subplaces of GPEs (e.g. France subPlace EU), the weaker GPE assignment for India allows the erroneous triple through. By happenstance, a subsequent triple in the mapping process results from this passage,

> ... were seized by <u>Indian authorities</u> after a raid on a suspected weapons lab ...

where our analytics correctly extract a *citizenOf* relation in the underlined text between "authorities" and "Indian", correctly coreference "Indian" with the entity for "India" in the previous passage, and correctly assign the type Person to the entity corresponding to "authorities". The ontology contains a global range restriction for the *citizenOf* relation to instances of Country. Since the erroneous *subPlace* triple added previously prevents India from being a country (since a country cannot be a subPlace of a country), adding this correct triple causes an inconsistent KB. This shows the technique has some order dependences, had these triples been added in a different order the correct one would have been dropped. Fortunately our initial results indicate these circumstances to be rare (2 erroneous drops out of 834 triples).

There were eleven examples of dropped triples where problems were actually in the assignment of types to the entities or in coreference, so that a better approach would have been to fix the type assignments or undo a coreference merge. For example:

> ... and the increase in organized criminal <u>groups in the FSU</u> and Eastern Europe.

In this case, the analytics produce a *basedIn* relation between "groups" and "FSU" in the underlined text, but multiple annotators disagree on the type of "FSU" (some correctly say GPE, some incorrectly say Organization), and the incorrect label (Organization) ends up winning. Overall our technique for combining annotations does improve precision, but like all IE techniques it isn't perfect, as in this case. Therefore we end up with an organization being *basedIn* an organization, and the ontology requires organizations to be *basedIn* GPEs, and specifies that GPEs and Organizations are disjoint.

It is somewhat debatable whether dropping this triple is a mistake – clearly it would be *better* to fix the type, but the entity corresponding to "FSU", as presented to the KB, is an organization and cannot be the object of a *basedIn* relation. Thus the KB does end up cleaner without it.

5.3 Techniques for Improving Recall

Our initial motivation for combining IE with semantic technology in general was the possibility of improving information access beyond keyword-based approaches through inference. For example, in the passage "Joe arrived in Paris", no keyword search, nor search enhanced by semantic markup, would retrieve this passage in response to the query, "Who is in France?" Clearly with some world knowledge (that Paris is in France) and the ability to accurately recognize the relation in the passage (& query), we could employ reasoning to catch it.

OWL-DL is not particularly strong in its ability to perform the kinds of "A-box" reasoning that would be needed to make a significant improvement in this kind of recall. Other choices are RDF rules and translating the KBs into more expressive languages (like KIF). A semantic web rules language would obviously help here as well.

An interesting challenge is in measuring the impact of this kind of reasoning. It makes sense to call this an improvement in recall; in the simple example above clearly the passage in question contains an answer to the query, and clearly keyword search would not find it. However, it is a different sense of recall than is typically used in IE measurements. Recall measurements are based on comparison to a "ground truth" (i.e. a human annotated corpus), in which implicit information does not appear. In textual entailment (Dagan et al, 2005) the measurement problem is similar, however they address this in evaluations by always making the determination based on pairs of text passages. So we can show improvement in recall by selecting meaningful queries and determining if and how reasoning improves the recall for each query, but measuring recall improvements in the KB itself is more difficult.

6 Conclusions

In our research to use information extraction to help populate the semantic web, we have encountered significant obstacles to interoperability between the technologies. We believe these obstacles to be endemic to the basic paradigms, and not quirks of the specific implementations we have worked with. In particular, we identified five dimensions of interoperability that must be addressed to successfully populate semantic web knowledge bases from information extraction systems that are *suitable for reasoning*. We called the task of transforming IE data into knowledge-bases *knowledge integration*, and briefly presented a framework called KITE in which we are exploring these dimensions. Finally, we reported on the initial results of an experiment in which the knowledge integration process used the deeper semantics of OWL ontologies to improve the precision of relation extraction from text. By adding a simplistic consistency-checking step, we showed an 8.7% relative improvement in precision over a very robust IE application without that checking.

This work is still in the beginning stages, but we do have results and conclusions, the most important of which is to address a long-standing problem that presents an obstacle to interoperability: being realistic. IE and NLP systems do not produce perfect output of the sort that KR systems deal with, and KR systems are not capable of handling the scale, precision, and recall that NLP and IE systems produce. These are not criticisms but realities. We cannot just sit back and wait for the two technologies to eventually meet, rather we must begin exploring how to realistically integrate them.

We should also point out that none of the implemented systems we used were baseline "strawman" systems, but reportedly state-of-the-art systems in each area. It is not our intention to advance research in information extraction nor in knowledge representation and reasoning, but rather in the combination of the two. We believe that the combination will be better than either individually, and have demonstrated one example of how this is so, using deeper semantics and reasoning to improve precision of relation extraction.

Acknowledgements

This work was supported in part by the ARDA/NIMD program.

References

K. Bontcheva. 2004. Open-source Tools for Creation, Maintenance, and Storage of Lexical Resources for Language Generation from Ontologies. *Fourth International Conference on Language Resources and Evaluation (LREC'2004)*. Lisbon, Portugal. 2004.

Roy Byrd & Yael Ravin. 1999. Identifying and Extracting Relations in Text. *4th International Conference on Applications of Natural Language to Information Systems* (NLDB). Klagenfurt, Austria.

Jennifer Chu-Carroll, Krzysztof Czuba, Pablo Duboue, and John Prager. 2005. IBM's PIQUANT II in TREC2005. *The Fourteenth Text REtrieval Conference (TREC 2005)*.

Philipp Cimiano, Johanna Völker. 2005. Text2Onto - A Framework for Ontology Learning and Data-driven Change Discovery. *10th International Conference on Applications of Natural Language to Information Systems* (NLDB). Alicante, Spain.

Ido Dagan, Oren Glickman and Bernardo Magnini. The PASCAL Recognising Textual Entailment Challenge. *In Proceedings of the PASCAL Challenges Workshop on Recognising Textual Entailment*, 2005.

Hamish Cunningham. 2005. Automatic Information Extraction. *Encyclopedia of Language and Linguistics, 2cnd ed.* Elsevier.

Stephen Dill, Nadav Eiron, David Gibson, Daniel Gruhl, R. Guha, Anant Jhingran, Tapas Kanungo, Sridhar Rajagopalan, Andrew Tomkins, John A. Tomlin, & Jason Y. Zien. 2003. SemTag and Seeker: Bootstrapping the semantic web via automated semantic annotation. *12th International World Wide Web Conference* (WWW), Budapest, Hungary.

George Doddington, Alexis Mitchell, Mark Przybocki, Lance Ramshaw, Stephanie Strassel, & Ralph Weischedel. 2004. Automatic Content Extraction (ACE) program - task definitions and performance measures. *Fourth International Conference on Language Resources and Evaluation* (LREC).

David Ferrucci & Adam Lally. 2004. UIMA: an architectural approach to unstructured information processing in the corporate research environment. *Natural Language Engineering* 10 (3/4): 327–348.

Richard Fikes, David Ferrucci, & David Thurman. 2005. Knowledge Associates for Novel Intelligence (KANI). *2005 International Conference on Intelligence Analysis* McClean, VA.

Achille Fokoue, Aaron Kershenbaum, Li Ma, Edith Schonberg and Kavitha Srinivas. 2006. The Summary Abox: Cutting Ontologies Down to Size. *Proceedings of the 5th International Semantic Web Conference.* Springer-Verlag.

T. Götz & O. Suhre. 2004. Design and implementation of the UIMA Common Analysis System. *IBM Systems Journal* 43 (3): 476-489.

Jerry R. Hobbs and Feng Pan. 2004. An OWL Ontology of Time. http://www.isi.edu/~pan/time/owl-time-july04.txt

Elizabeth D. Liddy. 2000. Text Mining. *Bulletin of American Society for Information Science & Technology.*

Xiaoqiang Luo, Abraham Ittycheriah, Hongyan Jing, Nanda Kambhatla, Salim Roukos: A Mention-Synchronous Coreference Resolution Algorithm Based On the Bell Tree. *ACL 2004*: 135-142.

Elaine Marsh. 1998. *TIPSTER information extraction evaluation: the MUC-7 workshop.*

D. Maynard. 2005. Benchmarking ontology-based annotation tools for the Semantic Web. AHM2005 Workshop "Text Mining, e-Research and Grid-enabled Language Technology", Nottingham, UK, 2005.

Diana Maynard, Milena Yankova, Alexandros Kourakis, and Antonis Kokossis. 2005. Ontology-based information extraction for market monitoring and technology watch. ESWC Workshop "End User Apects of the Semantic Web," Heraklion, Crete, May, 2005.

Scott Miller, Sergey Bratus, Lance Ramshaw, Ralph Weischedel, Alex Zamanian. 2001. FactBrowser demonstration. *First international conference on Human language technology research* HLT '01.

T. Milo, S. Zohar. 1998. Using Schema Matching to Simplify Heterogeneous Data Translation. VLDB 98, August 1998.

J. William Murdock & Chris Welty. 2006. Obtaining Formal Knowledge from Informal Text Analysis. IBM Research Report RC23961.

J. William Murdock, Deborah L. McGuinness, Paulo Pinheiro da Silva, Christopher Welty, David Ferrucci. 2006. Explaining Conclusions from Diverse Knowledge Sources. *Proceedings of the 5th International Semantic Web Conference.* Springer-Verlag.

N. F. Noy & M. A. Musen. 2001. Anchor-PROMPT: Using Non-Local Context for Semantic Matching. *Workshop on Ontologies and Information Sharing*, Seattle, WA.

Paulo Pinheiro da Silva, Deborah L. McGuinness & Richard Fikes. A proof markup language for Semantic Web services. 2006. *Information Systems* 31(4-5): 381-395.

Borislav Popov, Atanas Kiryakov, Damyan Ognyanoff, Dimitar Manov, Angel Kirilov. 2004. KIM - A Semantic Platform for Information Extraction and Retrieval. *Journal of Natural Language Engineering*, 10(3-4): 375-392.

Roser Sauri, Jessica Littman, Robert Gaizauskas, Andrea Setzer, & James Pustejovsky. 2004. TimeML Annotation Guidelines, Version 1.1. http://www.cs.brandeis.edu/%7Ejamesp/arda/time/timeMLdocs/guidetest.pdf

Alexander Schutz and Paul Buitelaar. 2005. RelExt: A Tool for Relation Extraction from Text in Ontology Extension. *Proceedings of ISWC-05.*

Johanna Voelker, Denny Vrandecic, York Sure. 2005. Automatic Evaluation of Ontologies (AEON). In *Proceedings of ISWC-05.*

A Method for Learning Part-Whole Relations

Willem Robert van Hage[1,2], Hap Kolb[1], and Guus Schreiber[2]

[1] TNO Science & Industry Delft
wrvhage@few.vu.nl, hap.kolb@tno.nl
[2] Vrije Universiteit Amsterdam
schreiber@cs.vu.nl

Abstract. Part-whole relations are important in many domains, but typically receive less attention than subsumption relation. In this paper we describe a method for finding part-whole relations. The method consists of two steps: (i) finding phrase patterns for both explicit and implicit part-whole relations, and (ii) applying these patterns to find part-whole relation instances. We show results of applying this method to a domain of finding sources of carcinogens.

1 Introduction

A plethora of existing vocabularies, terminologies and thesauri provide key knowledge needed to make the Semantic Web work. However, in using these sources witinin one context, a process of alignment is needed. This has already been identified as a central problem in semantic-web research. Most aligment approaches focus on finding equivalence and or subclass relations between concepts in diffeent sources. The objective of this paper is to identifying alignment relations of the part-whole type. Part-whole relations play a key role in many application domains. For example, part-whole is a central structuring principle in artefact design (ships, cars), in chemistry (structure of a substance) and medicine (anatomy). The nature of part-whole has been studied in the area of formal ontology (*e.g.*, [1]). Traditionally, part-whole receives much less attention than the subclass/subsumption relation.

The main objective of this paper is to develop a method for learning part-whole relations from existing vocabularies and text sources. Our sample domain is concerned with food ingredients. We discuss a method to learn part-whole relations by first learning phrase patterns that connect parts to wholes from a training set of known part-whole pairs using a search engine, and then applying the patterns to find new part-whole relations, again using a search engine. We apply this method in a use case of assisting safety and health researchers in finding sources of carcinogenic substances using Google. We evaluate the performance of the pattern-learning and the relation-learning steps, with special attention to the performance of patterns that implicitly mention part-whole relations. Furthermore we perform an end-to-end task evaluation to establish whether our method accomplishes the task.

In Sec. 2 we describe the use case on which we evaluate end-to-end performance and pose performance criteria. In Sec. 3 we discuss the experimental set-up we use to learn part-whole relations. In Secs. 4 and 5 we describe the learning and application of patterns to find part-whole relations and evaluate the performance of the patterns in terms of Precision. In Sec. 6 we evaluate Recall on four sample carcinogens. Sec. 7 discusses related work. We conclude with a discussion of the results and open research questions in Sec. 8.

2 Use Case

An important application area of part-whole learning is health and safety research. Experts in this field are faced with hard information retrieval tasks on a regular bases. News of a benzene spill in a river, for example, will trigger questions like "Is the general public's health in danger?", "Are there any foodstuffs we should avoid?", and "Are there any occupational risks, fishermen perhaps?". The first task the health and safety researchers are faced with is to find out via which pathways the substance in question can reach humans. Only then can they investigate if any of these pathways apply to the current situation. A sizable part of this problem can be reduced to finding all part-whole relations between the substance and initially unknown wholes in scientific literature and reports from authorities in the field such as the United States Food and Drugs Administration[1] (FDA) and Environmental Protection Agency[2] (EPA), and the World Health Organization[3] (WHO).

The wholes should be possible routes through which humans can be exposed to the substance. For example, tap water, exhaust fumes, or fish. We will not go into detail discussing the roles these concepts play that leads to the actual exposure. For example, when humans are exposed to benzene in fish by eating the fish, fish assumes the role of food. Relevant part-whole relations can be of any of the types described by Winston, Chaffin, and Herrmann [12].

component/integral object "Residents might have been exposed to *benzene* in their *drinking water*."
member/collection "*Benzene* belongs in the group of *BTX-aromatics*."
portion/mass "*3 tons* of the *benzene emissions* can be attributed to the dehydrator."
stuff/object "*Aftershave* used to contain *benzene*."
feature/activity "*Benzene* is used in the *dehydration process*." The part in this case is not benzene itself, but the application of benzene, which is abstracted over with the word "used".
place/area "*Benzene* was found in the *river*." The part in this case is the location where the benzene was found, which is left anonymous.

The automation of the knowledge discovery task described above is a success if and only if the following criteria are met:

1. The key concepts of each important pathway through with a carcinogen can reach humans should be found. (*i.e.,* Recall should be very high.)
2. The researchers should not be distracted by too many red herrings. (*i.e.,* Precision should be sufficient.)

---

[1] http://www.fda.gov
[2] http://www.epa.gov
[3] http://www.who.int

Precision can be evaluated in a straightforward manner by counting how many of the returned part-whole relations are valid. The evaluation of Recall however poses a greater problem. We are attempting to learn unknown facts. How can one measure which percentage of the unknown facts has been learnt when the facts are unknown? For this use case we will solve this problem by looking at exposure crises for four substances (acrylamide, asbestos, benzene, and dioxins) that have been documented in the past. We know now which pathways led to the exposure in the past. This means we can construct sets of pathways we should have known at the time of these crises and use these sets to evaluate Recall.

3 Experimental Set-Up

In this paper we will use two-step method to learn part-whole relations. First we learn lexical patterns from known part-whole pairs, using search engine queries. Then we apply these patterns to a set of parts to find wholes that are related to these parts, also using search engine queries. To constrain the size of the search space we will constrain both the set of parts and the set of wholes to controlled vocabularies. In more detail, the method works as follows:

1. **Learning part-whole patterns.**
   (a) Construct a search query for each part-whole pair in a training set.
   (b) Collect phrases from the search results that contain the part-whole pair.
   (c) Abstract over the parts and wholes in the phrases to get patterns.
   (d) Sort the patterns by frequency of occurrence. Discard the bottom of the list.
2. **Learning wholes by applying the patterns.**
   (a) Fill in each pattern with all parts from a set of part instances, while keeping the wholes free.
   (b) Construct search queries for each filled in pattern.
   (c) Collect phrases from the search result that contain the filled in pattern.
   (d) Extract the part-whole pairs from the phrases.
   (e) Constrain the pairs to those with wholes from a controlled vocabulary.
   (f) Sort the pairs by frequency of occurrence. Discard the bottom of the list.

In the following two sections we will describe the details of the data sets we used and we will motivate the decisions we made.

4 Learning Part-Whole Patterns

In this section we will describe the details of step 1 in our part-whole learning method, described in the previous section. We will describe the training set we used and the details of the application of step 1 on this training set, and analyze the resulting patterns.

Our training set consists of 503 part-whole pairs, derived from a list of various kinds of food additives and food product types they can occur in created by the International Food Information Council[4] (IFIC) and the FDA.[5] The list contains 58 additives (parts) and 113 food products (wholes), grouped together in 18 classes of additives such as sweeteners and preservatives. An example is shown in Fig. 1. It is not specified which additives occur

---
[4] http://www.ific.org
[5] http://www.cfsan.fda.gov/~dms/foodic.html

in which food products. To discover this, we took the cartesian product of the additives and the food products and filtered out the pairs that yielded no hits on Google[6] when put together in a wildcard query. For example, the pair ⟨table-top sugar, aspartame⟩ is filtered out, because the query `"table-top sugar * aspartame"` or `"aspartame * table-top sugar"` yields no hits.

Type	Sweeteners
What They Do	Add sweetness with or without the extra calories.
Examples of Uses	Beverages, baked goods, confections, table-top sugar, substitutes, many processed foods.
Product Label Names	Sucrose (sugar), glucose, fructose, sorbitol, mannitol, corn syrup, high fructose corn syrup, saccharin, aspartame, sucralose, acesulfame potassium (acesulfame-K), neotame

Fig. 1. An excerpt from the IFIC and FDA list of food additives

For all 503 part-whole pairs that did yield results we collected the first 1000 snippets (or as many snippets as were available). We attempted to part-of-speech tag these snippets. This did not produce good results, because nearly all snippets were incomplete sentences and many were lists of substances. For example, "...Water)*, Xanthan Gum, Brassica Campestris (Rapeseed), Essential Oils [+/- CI 77491,CI...". None of the part-of-speech taggers we tried were able to deal with this. Therefore we used the untagged snippets and looked up all consistent phrases that connected the part and whole from the query. In these phrases we substituted all parts and wholes by the variables "part and whole". This yielded 4502 unique patterns, which we sorted by frequency of occurrence. The frequencies of the patterns are shown in Fig. 2.

Due to the fact that there were many lists of substances in our data there were also many patterns that did not describe a part-whole relation, but that were merely part of a list of substances containing the part and the whole. These patterns can be easily recognized, because they contain names of substances. For example, for the pair ⟨cheese, enzymes⟩ the following snippet was returned: "*cheese* (pasteurized milk, cheese cultures, salt, *enzymes*)". An example of a good snippet is: "All *cheese* contains *enzymes*.". To exclude lists we removed all patterns that contain, apart from the part and whole, labels of concepts in agricultural thesauri. The thesauri we used are the NAL Agricultural Thesaurus[7] and the AGROVOC Thesaurus[8]. (We used the SKOS[9] version of these thesauri.) This filtered out 1491 patterns, of which only 12 were correct part-whole patterns. Fig. 2 shows a Precision graph of the list of patterns before and after the filtering step.

To restrict the number of Google queries needed to find wholes for parts we decided not to use all of the remaining 3011 patterns, but to select the most productive patterns. We analyzed the 300 patterns that produce the most results. For each pattern we looked

---

[6] http://www.google.com
[7] http://agclass.nal.usda.gov/agt
[8] http://www.fao.org/agrovoc
[9] http://www.w3.org/2004/02/skos

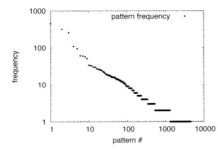
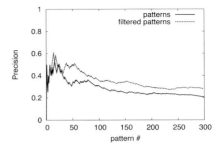

Fig. 2. (left) Frequency distribution in the training set of the learnt patterns. Referred to as T in Table 3. (right) Precision@n (*i.e.*, # correct part of patterns in the top-n / n) graph over the top-300 most frequent patterns, before and after filtering out patterns that contain labels of AGROVOC or NALT concepts.

at the snippets it returned. If the majority of the occurrences of the pattern described a proper part-whole relation (*i.e.*, Precision $\geq$ .5) we classified the pattern as part-whole. Otherwise we classified it as not part-whole.

We distinguished the following groups of patterns, based on the most common types of errors that led to the classification of the pattern as not part-whole. A pattern can yield more than one type of false relations, but the classification is based on the most common of the error types.

too specific Too training-set specific to be useful. Either the pattern contains adjectives or it yields no hits due to over-training.
too generic The pattern matches part-whole relations, but also too many non-part-whole relations to be useful. For example, the pattern "whole part", as in "barn door", can match any type of collocation.
is a The pattern primarily matches hyponyms. The language used to describe member/collection relations is also used for hyponyms.
conjunction/disjunction The pattern primarily matches conjunctions / disjunctions.
related The pattern connects terms that are related, but not part-whole related.
wrong Not a proper pattern for any other reason. Most of the errors in the wrong category can be attributed to the lack of sophisticated linguistic analysis of the phrases.

Table 2 shows the build-up of the different error types.

We corrected 6 patterns that were classified as not part-whole, and added them to the part-whole patterns. These patterns are not counted in Table 2. They are listed in Table 1. Notice that in the English grammar, hyphenation turns a part-whole relation into its inverse. For example, "sugar-containing cake" and "cake containing sugar".

While analyzing the correct part-whole patterns we noticed that the phrases that deal with part-whole relations do not always explicitly state that relation. Often, the part-whole relation has to be inferred from the description of a process that led to the inclusion of the part in the whole or the extraction of the part from the whole. For example, from the sentence "I add *honey* to my *tea*." we can infer that honey is part of the tea, even though the sentence only mentions the process of adding it. In addition to explicit

Table 1. Manually corrected patterns

"part to whole"	→ "add part to whole", "added part to whole"
"part to the whole"	→ "add part to the whole", "added part to the whole"
"part gives the whole"	→ "part gives the whole its"
"part containing whole"	→ "part-containing whole"
"part reduced whole"	→ "part-reduced whole"
"part increased whole"	→ "part-increased whole"

descriptions of part-whole relations we distinguish two types of phrases that mention part-whole relations implicitly.

part of The phrase explicitly describes a part-whole relation. For example, "There's alcohol in beer.".

source of The phrase implicitly describes a part-whole relation by describing the action of acquiring the part from the whole. For example, "Go get some *water* from the *well*.".

made with The phrase implicitly describes a part-whole relation by describing a (construction) process that leads to a part-whole relation. For example, "I add *honey* to my *tea*".

Table 2 shows that together, the implicit patterns account for a third of the total number of part-whole pairs.

When applying patterns to learn part-whole relations it is useful to make this distinction into three types, because it turns out that these three types have rather different Precision and Recall properties, listed in Table 3. The patterns in the part of class yield the most results with high Precision. The patterns in the made with class also yield many results, but—somewhat surprisingly—with much lower Precision, while the patterns in the source of class yield few results, but with high Precision.

The 91 patterns we used for the discovery for wholes are the 83 classified as part-whole in Table 2 and the 8 listed in Table 1 on the right side. They are listed in Table 6.

5 Finding Wholes

In this section we will describe the details of step 2 in our part-whole learning method, described in the previous section. We will describe the sets of part and whole instances we used, and analyze the resulting part-whole relations.

In the use case we focus on finding wholes that contain a specific substance. Initially, any concept name is a valid candidate for a whole. We tackle this problem by first reducing the set of valid wholes to those that occur in a phrase that matches one of the patterns learnt in step 1 of our method. This corresponds to step 2c and 2d of our method. Then we prune this set of potential wholes using two large, agricultural, and environmental thesauri that are geared to indexing documents relevant to our use case. We remove all wholes that do not match a concept label in either thesaurus. This

Table 2. Analysis of the top-300 most frequently occurring patterns

pattern class	example pattern	# patterns in class
part-whole		83
part of	whole containing part	40
made with	part added to whole	36
source of	part found in whole	7
not part-whole		217
wrong	part these whole, part organic whole	186
too specific	part in commercial whole	10
too generic	part of whole	7
is a	whole such as part	5
related	part as well as whole	4
conjunction	part and whole, whole and part	3
disjunction	part or whole, whole or part	2

corresponds to step 2e of our method. The former reduction step asserts that there is a part-whole relation. The latter that the whole is on topic.

We select the possible part instances from a list of carcinogens provided by the International Agency for Research on Cancer[10] (IARC). In the IARC Monographs on the Evaluation of Carcinogenic Risks to Humans[11] carcinogenic agents, mixtures and exposures are classified into four groups: positively carcinogenic to humans, probably or possibly carcinogenic to humans, not classifiable as carcinogenic to humans, and probably not carcinogenic to humans. We took the agents and mixtures from the group of positively carcinogenic factors. We interpreted each line in the list as a description of a concept. We removed the references and expanded the conjunctions, interpreting each conjunct as a label of the concept. i.e., For example, we transform the list entry "Arsenic [7440-38-2] and arsenic compounds (Vol. 23, Suppl. 7;1987)" into a concept arsenic with the labels "Arsenic" and "arsenic compounds". The resulting list contains 73 concepts, with 109 labels in total. We applied the 91 patterns that resulted from the process described Sec. 4 on these 109 labels to discover wholes. We allow for words—generally articles and adjectives—to appear in between the whole and the rest of the pattern. For example, the pattern "part in whole" can be interpreted as "part in ∗ whole", and hence will match "part in deep-sea whole" and "part in the whole". This also means there can be overlap between the sets of part-whole pairs retrieved by patterns. From the resulting filled-in patterns we extracted the wholes. We filtered out all wholes from this list that do not appear in the UN FAO AGROVOC Thesaurus and the USDA NAL Agricultural Thesaurus. When put together, these thesauri contain 69,746 concepts with 87,357 labels in total. Thus limiting the set of discoverable wholes to 69,746 concepts. For each remaining whole in the list we construct a part-whole relation.

An assessment of the part-whole results is shown in Table 6. We approximated Precision for the 91 patterns we used to find wholes based on a random sample of 25 discovered pairs. The results are shown under "Precision". The number of hits per pattern are listed under D. This number includes duplicate phrases and multiple phrases

---
[10] http://www.iarc.fr
[11] http://monographs.iarc.fr/ENG/Classification

describing the same part-whole pair. Table 4 in Sec. 6 shows how many unique wholes are found for four example parts.

Table 3. Average pattern performance per pattern class. T is the number of times patterns in the class occur in the training set. D is the number of discovered part-whole phrases.

pattern class	# patterns in class	T	D	avg. Precision
part of	40	744	84852	.81
made with	36	525	33408	.69
source of	7	111	8497	.83

6 Analysis

In Sec. 2 we stated two criteria that have to be met for the application of our part-whole learning method to be a success. Precision has to be sufficient, and Recall has to be very high. In Secs. 4 and 5 we analyzed the results in terms of frequency and Precision. We achieved an average Precision of .74. In this section we will assess Recall.

Since even the knowledge of experts of whether or not a substance is contained in some whole is far from complete we can not create a complete gold standard to measure Recall. It is simply infeasible. We can, however, approximate Recall by computing it on samples.

We set up four test cases centered towards discovering possible causes of exposure to a specific carcinogenic agent. The agents we chose are acrylamide, asbestos, benzene, and dioxins. These substances have all caused health safety crises in the past and possible exposure to them has been extensively documented. For each case we decided on 15 important concepts that contain the carcinogen and define a possible exposure route. For example, you can be exposed to acrylamide by eating fried food such as french fries, because acrylamide can be formed in the frying process. The selection of the wholes was based on reports from the United States Environmental Protection Agency (EPA) and the Netherlands Organization for Applied Scientific Research (TNO) Quality of Life. The cases were set up without knowledge of the data set and the learning system, to minimize the hindsight bias, but with knowledge of the concepts in the AGROVOC and NALT thesauri. The sets of wholes are shown in Table 5, along with the rank at which the whole occurs in the list of discovered wholes. Recall and the total number of discovered wholes are shown in Table 4.

For all of the cases we found a large majority of the important concepts. For half of the missed concepts we found concepts that are very closely related. For example, we

Table 4. Recall on four sample substances

concept (part)	# of wholes found	Recall
acrylamide	350	13/15 (.86)
asbestos	402	11/15 (.73)
benzene	479	13/15 (.86)
dioxins	439	12/15 (.80)

did not find the concept "cement pipes", but we did find "cement" and "pipes", and we did not find "air", but we did find "air pollution" and "atmosphere".

The data sets and the results can be found at the following web location: http://www.few.vu.nl/~wrvhage/carcinogens.

7 Related Work

The method of automatic learning of relations by first learning patterns and then applying these patterns on a large corpus is widely used. An example in the domain of business mergers and production is described in the 1999 article by Finkelstein-Landau and Morin [5]. Their work on extracting companies-product relations touches lightly upon the subject of this paper. Another example of pattern-based relation learning on the web is the KnowItAll system of Etzioni et al. [4]. The learning of part-whole relations however is quite rare. Two examples, are the work of Berland and Charniak in 1999 [2] and Girju, Badulescu and Moldovan in 2003 [6].

Berland and Charniak learn part-whole patterns from a part-of-speech tagged corpus, the Linguistic Data Consortium's (LDC) North American News Corpus (NANC). To illustrate the pattern learning phase they mention five example patterns. "whole's part", "part of {the|a} whole", "part in {the|a} whole", "parts of wholes", and "parts in wholes". The domain they used for evaluation is component/integral object relations between artifacts such as cars and windshields. Even though our domain is quite different, we found all five of their example patterns using our training data, respectively at rank 294, 290, 12, 128, and 2 (of 4502 learnt patterns).

Girju, Badulescu, and Moldovan, used the SemCor 1.7 corpus and the LA Times corpus from the Ninth Text Retrieval Conference (TREC-9). They used the meronyms from WordNet [9], mainly component/integral object and member/collection relations. Girju, Badulescu, and Moldovan also make the distinction between explicit and implicit part-whole constructions, but the implicit constructions they focus on are mainly possessive forms like "the girl's mouth", "eyes of the baby", "oxygen-rich water", and "high heel shoes". They list the three most frequent patterns, which also contain part-of-speech tags. "part of whole", "whole's part", and "part *Verb* whole". We found the first two patterns, as mentioned above, and many instances of the third pattern, such as "part fortified whole" at rank 4.

Other applications of part-whole relations than discovering sources of substances are query expansion for image retrieval [8, Ch. 6], and geographical retrieval [3].

8 Discussion

Our experimental setup assumes that all interesting information pertaining to some carcinogenic substance can be obtained in one single retrieval step. The construction of complex paths from the substance to the eventual exposure has to happen in the mind of the user—and depends solely on his expertise and ingenuity. This is a severe limitation that leaves room for considerable improvement. A relatively straightforward extension would be to iterate the retrieval step using suitable wholes found in retrieval step $n-1$ in the part slot in retrieval step n. Separation of roles, classes, etc. amongst the wholes

Table 5. Recall bases for four sample substances

Acrylamide

concept (whole)	rank
coffee	18
fried food	22
plastics industry	39
smoke	42
drinking water	43
olives	103
paper	109
dyes	114
soil	144
fish	158
herbicide	181
water treatment	195
textiles	275
air	not found
baked food	not found

Benzene

concept (whole)	rank
leaded gasoline	1
water	4
solvents	9
smoke	10
dyes	32
pesticides	68
soil	69
detergents	76
cola	84[a]
rubber	161
bottled water	191
rivers	228
lubricants	340
air	not found[b]
fats	not found

[a] soft drinks appear at rank 5
[b] found air pollution and atmosphere

Asbestos

concept (whole)	rank
insulation	5
vermiculite	9
roofing	12
building materials	16
flooring	23
rocks	37
water	47
brakes	67
adhesives	127
cars	160
mucus	211
cement pipes	not found[a]
sewage	not found[b]
air	not found
feces	not found

[a] found cement and pipes
[b] found refuse and wastewater

Dioxins

concept (whole)	rank
fish	2[a]
paper	3
soil	7
herbicides	8
defoliants	17[b]
water	32
smoke	38
bleach	39
chickens	75
animal fat	106
animal feed	138
waste incineration	142
pigs	not found[c]
air	not found[d]
diesel trucks	not found[e]

[a] also found fishermen
[b] also found vietnam
[c] found cattle and livestock
[d] found air quality
[e] found exhaust gases

Table 6. The 91 patterns used for the learning of wholes, ordered by the number of correct pairs it yielded. Prec. is Precision approximated on a sample of 25 occurrences (or less if freq. < 25). D is the number of discovered part-whole phrases.

Prec.	D	pattern	Prec.	D	pattern
.84	26799	part in whole	.76	980	part content in the whole
.68	8787	whole with part	.96	745	part-treated whole
.84	5266	part in the whole	.84	786	part derived from whole
.96	4249	part from whole	.76	852	whole rich in part
.68	5917	part for whole	.28	2306	whole high part
.60	5794	part content whole	.88	617	part-containing whole
.88	3949	whole contain part	.20	2571	whole add part
1	2934	whole containing part	.72	700	part in most whole
.64	4415	part based whole	.80	623	part for use in whole
.72	3558	whole using part	.40	1169	part to make whole
.92	2591	part levels in whole	.72	630	add part to the whole
1	2336	part-laden whole	.72	580	part enriched whole
.84	2327	part content in whole	.56	703	part in many whole
1	1945	whole contains part	.96	404	part-enriched whole
.76	2536	whole have part	.72	527	part contents in whole
.72	2622	part into whole	.52	608	added part to whole
.88	2035	part is used in whole	.92	314	part occurs naturally in whole
1	1760	part found in whole	.84	288	part extracted from whole
.52	3217	part free whole	.96	226	whole enriched with part
1	1672	part is found in whole	.68	310	part to our whole
.88	1834	part-rich whole	.16	1160	whole provide part
.80	1994	part used in whole	.68	247	added part to the whole
.92	1680	part content of whole	.72	220	whole with added part
.20	7711	whole for part	.96	137	part found in many whole
.96	1497	part is present in whole	1	124	whole containing high part
.84	1600	add part to whole	.76	134	part replacement in whole
.88	1496	part added to whole	.60	133	part for making whole
.80	1597	part in their whole	.88	64	whole fortified with part
.92	1372	part-based whole	.76	74	whole have part added
.88	1421	part in these whole	.96	54	part-fortified whole
1	1218	whole that contain part	.36	120	part compound for whole
1	1203	part levels in the whole	.36	120	part fortified whole
.84	1361	part in all whole	1	24	whole sweetened with part
1	1112	part contained in whole	.16	89	whole preserves part
.76	1455	part in some whole	.91	11	part-reduced whole
.84	1301	part in your whole	.90	10	part gives the whole its
1	1058	part present in whole	.04	85	part sweetened whole
.76	1350	part in our whole	.27	11	part-increased whole
1	985	part laden whole	.67	3	part-added whole
.32	3052	whole use part	1	1	part-sweetened whole
.52	1648	whole mit part	1	1	part to sweeten their whole
.84	930	whole made with part	1	1	part fortification of whole
.88	885	part-free whole	0	0	part additions in various whole
.52	1477	part is in whole	0	0	part used in making whole
.80	945	part is added to whole	0	242	part hydrogenated whole
.92	811	whole high in part			

by means of classification (*cf., e.g.,* [7]) might be necessary to limit the inevitable loss of precision. For example, if step $n-1$ yielded that there is benzene in some fish, then proceeding to investigate in step n whether these fish are part of people's diet. If, however, step $n-1$ yielded that benzene is part of a group of carbon-based chemicals, then proceeding to investigate these chemicals might lead to excessive topic drift.

The usefulness of such an extension depends to a large extent on the validity of some sort of transitive reasoning over the paths. Yet, the transitivity characteristics of part-whole expressions are notoriously quirky. Existing accounts actually either take the classical route set out by Stanislaw Lesniewski in the 1920's, defining the relations in question axiomatically and with little consideration for actual usage, or they formulate reasoning patterns for specific application domains and expressions (*cf., e.g.,* [10]). Neither approach is applicable to the mixed bags of "interesting" token relations our setup derives from natural language usage. A rare attempt to ground reasoning patterns in the general usage of part-whole expressions is contained in [12]. Even though our lay-out is orthogonal (and not even coextensive) to their influential classification of part-whole relations, their basic intuition w.r.t. transitivity does carry over to our case. In short:

1. The part-whole relations, P, expressed in natural language form a partial order $\mathscr{P} = \langle P, \geq \rangle$;
2. The weakest link determines the interpretation of a chain of part-whole pairs w.r.t. transitivity;
3. Transitivity fails if the chain contains uncomparable relation instances (w.r.t. $\geq$).

Contrary to [12] we assume that there is some weakest mereological relation, i.e., the poset $\mathscr{P}$ has a minimum element. (2) can then be generalized as follows:

2' Any element of $\mathscr{P}$ which is compatible with (i.e., as least as weak as) every relation used to form a chain of part-whole pairs determines a transitive interpretation of that chain.

This means that for every chain of part-whole pairs there is a meaningful, albeit sometimes rather weak, transitive interpretation available. It depends solely on the intended utilization whether the information obtained in this way is specific enough to be useful. What has its merits in a task with a strong element of exploration and novelty detection like our use case, may well be a show stopper for tasks such as diagnosis in a process control environment. Refinements, especially concerning the classification of relation types and the properties of the poset of relations are necessary to extend the general applicability of this approach.

This is especially true when our work is placed in the more general context of vocabulary and ontology alignment. Most ontology-alignment systems aim at finding equivalence relations. Yet, many real-world alignment cases have to deal with vocabularies that have a different level of aggregation. (*cf.*, [11]) In such cases equivalent concepts are quite rare, while aggregation relations, such as broader/narrower term, subclass and part-whole, are common. The carcinogen-source discovery case can be seen as an ontology-alignment problem where the alignment relation is the part-whole relation and the vocabularies are the controlled vocabulary of IARC group 1 carcinogens, and the AGROVOC and NALT thesauri. Under this perspective our work describes a first step towards a novel approach to ontology alignment. The influence part-whole alignment relations have on the consistency of the resulting aligned ontologies is unknown.

Acknowledgements

Margherita Sini and Johannes Keizer (FAO), Lori Finch (NAL), Fred van de Brug (TNO), Dean Allemang (BU), Alistair Miles (CCLRC) and Dan Brickley (W3C), the IARC, EPA, IFIC, and FDA, Vera Hollink (UvA), Sophia Katrenko (UvA), Mark van Assem (VUA), Laura Hollink (VUA), Véronique Malaisé (VUA). This work is part of the Virtual Lab e-Science project[12].

References

1. Alessandro Artale, Enrico Franconi, Nicola Guarino, and Luca Pazzi. Part-whole relations in object-centered systems: an overview. *Data & Knowledge Engineering*, 20(3):347–383, 1996.
2. Matthew Berland and Eugene Charniak. Finding parts in very large corpora. In *Proc. of the 37th Annual Meeting of the Association for Computational Linguistics*, 1999.
3. Davide Buscaldi, Paolo Rosso, and Emilio Sanchis Arnal. A wordnet-based query expansion method for geographical information retrieval. In *Working Notes for the CLEF 2005 Workshop*, 2005.
4. Oren Etzioni, Michael Cafarella, Doug Downey, Ana-Maria Popescu Tal Shaked, Stephen Soderland, Daniel S. Weld, and Alexander Yates. Methods for domain-independent information extraction from the web: An experimental comparison. In *Proc. of the AAAI Conference*, 2004.
5. Michal Finkelstein-Landau and Emmanuel Morin. Extracting semantic relationships between terms: Supervised vs. unsupervised methods. In *International Workshop on Ontological Engineering on the Global Information Infrastructure*, pages 71–80, 1999.
6. Roxana Girju, Adriana Badulescu, and Dan Moldovan. Learning semantic constraints for the automatic discovery of part-whole relations. In *Proc. of the HLT-NAACL*, 2003.
7. Nicola Guarino and Christopher Welty. An overview of ontoclean. In Steffen Staab and Rudi Studer, editors, *Handbook on Ontologies*, pages 151–171. Springer Verlag, 2004.
8. Laura Hollink. *Semantic Annotation for Retrieval of Visual Resources*. PhD thesis, Free University Amsterdam, 2006. Submitted. URI: http://www.cs.vu.nl/~laurah/thesis/thesis.pdf.
9. George A. Miller. Wordnet: a lexical database for english. *Communications of the ACM (CACM)*, 38(11):39–41, 1995.
10. Stefan Schulz and Udo Hahn. Part-whole representation and reasoning in formal biomedical ontologies. *Artificial Intelligence in Medicine*, 34(3):179–200, 2005.
11. Willem Robert van Hage, Sophia Katrenko, and Guus Schreiber. A method to combine linguistic ontology-mapping techniques. In *International Semantic Web Conference*, pages 732–744, 2005.
12. Morton E. Winston, Roger Chaffin, and Douglas Herrmann. A taxonomy of part-whole relations. *Cognitive Science*, 11:417–444, 1987.

---

[12] http://www.vl-e.org

OntoWiki – A Tool for Social, Semantic Collaboration

Sören Auer[1,2], Sebastian Dietzold[2], and Thomas Riechert[2]

[1] University of Pennsylvania, Department of Computer and Information Science
Philadelphia, PA 19104, USA
auer@seas.upenn.edu

[2] Universität Leipzig, Institut für Informatik, Augustusplatz 10-11,
D-04109 Leipzig, Germany
{lastname}@informatik.uni-leipzig.de

Abstract. We present OntoWiki, a tool providing support for agile, distributed knowledge engineering scenarios. OntoWiki facilitates the visual presentation of a knowledge base as an information map, with different views on instance data. It enables intuitive authoring of semantic content, with an inline editing mode for editing RDF content, similar to WYSIWYG for text documents. It fosters social collaboration aspects by keeping track of changes, allowing to comment and discuss every single part of a knowledge base, enabling to rate and measure the popularity of content and honoring the activity of users. Ontowiki enhances the browsing and retrieval by offering semantic enhanced search strategies. All these techniques are applied with the ultimate goal of decreasing the entrance barrier for projects and domain experts to collaborate using semantic technologies. In the spirit of the Web 2.0 OntoWiki implements an "architecture of participation" that allows users to add value to the application as they use it. It is available as open-source software and a demonstration platform can be accessed at http://3ba.se.

We present a tool supporting agile Knowledge Engineering in a pure Web environment. It is called OntoWiki since it is close in the spirit to existing Wiki systems. Technologically however, the OntoWiki design is independent and complementary to conventional Wiki technologies. As such, the OntoWiki approach differs from recently emerged strategies to integrate Wiki systems and the Semantic Web (cf. [6,5,8,11,12]). In these works it is proposed to integrate RDF triples into Wiki texts in a special syntax. It is a straightforward combination of existing Wiki systems and the Semantic Web knowledge representation paradigms. However, we see the following obstacles:

- *Usability:* The main advantage of Wiki systems is their unbeatable usability. Adding more and more syntactic possibilities counteracts ease of use for editors.
- *Redundancy:* To allow the answering of real-time queries to the knowledge base statements have to be stored additionally in a triple store. This introduces a redundancy complicating the implementation.

– *Scalability:* Knowledge base changes which involve statements with different subjects will scale very bad since all corresponding Wiki texts have to be parsed and changed.

The OntoWiki strategy presented in this paper, on the contrary, does not try to mix text editing with knowledge engineering, instead it applies the Wiki paradigm of "making it easy to correct mistakes, rather than making it hard to make them"[9] to collaborative knowledge engineering. The main goal of the OntoWiki approach thus is to rapidly simplify the presentation and acquisition of instance data from and for end users. This is achieved by regarding knowledge bases as "information maps". Each node at the information map is represented visually and intuitively for end users in a generic but configurable way and interlinked to related digital resources. Users are further enabled to enhance the knowledge schema incrementally as well as to contribute instance data agreeing on it as easy as possible to provide more detailed descriptions and modelings. Consequently, the following requirements have been determined for OntoWiki:

– *Intuitive display and editing* of instance data should be provided in generic ways, yet enabling means for domains specific views.
– *Semantic views* allow the generation of different views and aggregations of the knowledge base.
– *Versioning and Evolution* provides the opportunity to track, review and selectively roll-back changes.
– *Semantic search* facilitates easy-to-use full-text searches on all literal data, search results can be filtered and sorted (using semantic relations).
– *Community support* enables discussions about small information chunks. Users are encouraged to vote about distinct facts or prospective changes.
– *Online statistics* interactively measures the popularity of content and activity of users.
– *Semantic syndication* supports the distribution of information and their integration into desktop applications.

In the remainder of the paper we propose strategies on how to put these requirements into effect in a real-life system and report about implementation in a prototypical OntoWiki on the basis of Powl [1], a framework for Semantic Web application development. To stress the generic character of OntoWiki, the figures in this paper show screenshots of the OntoWiki prototype with a knowledge base collaboratively developed[1] and containing information about scientific conferences, as well as another publicly available knowledge base[2] containing information about research projects, people and publications at a research institute.

1 Visual Representation of Semantic Content

The compromise of, on the one hand, providing a generic user interface for arbitrary RDF knowledge bases and, on the other hand, aiming at being as

---
[1] at http://3ba.se
[2] http://www.aifb.uni-karlsruhe.de/viewAIFB_OWL.owl

intuitive as possible is tackled by regarding knowledge bases as "information maps". Each node at the information map, i.e. RDF resource, is represented as a Web accessible page and interlinked to related digital resources. These Web pages representing nodes in the information map are divided into three parts: a left sidebar, a main content section and a right sidebar. The left sidebar offers the selection of content to display in the main content section. Selection opportunities include the set of available knowledge bases, a class hierarchy browser and a full-text search. Once a selection is made, the main content section will arrange matching content in a *list view* linking to *individual views* for individual instances (cf. 1). The right sidebar offers tools and complementary information specific to the selected content.

Fig. 1. List view (left) and view of an individual instance with expanded inline reference view (right)

List views allow to view a selection of several instances in a combined view. The selection of instances to display can be either based on class membership or on the result of a selection by facet or full-text search. OntoWiki identifies those properties used in conjunction with the instances of the selection. The display of the corresponding property values for each instance can be switched on, thus resulting in a tabular view. Furthermore, each individual instance displayed is linked to an individual view of that instance.

Individual views combine all the properties attached to an particular instance. Property values pointing to other individuals are rendered as HTML links to the corresponding individual view. Alternatively, to get information about the referenced individual without having to load the complete individual view it is possible to expand a short summary (loaded per AJAX) right where the reference is shown. The right sidebar provides additionally information about similar instances (of the same type) and incoming links (i.e. references from other instances).

Different Views on Instance Data. The OntoWiki prototype facilitates different views on instance data. Such views can be either domain specific or generic. Domain specific views have to be implemented as plug-ins. Generic views provide visual representations of instance data according to certain property values. The following views are currently implemented:

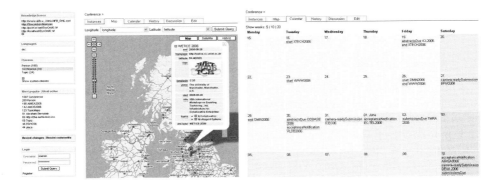

Fig. 2. Map view (left) and calendar view (right) of instance data

Map View. If the selected data (either a single instance or a list of instances) contains property values representing geographical information (i.e. longitude and latitude coordinates) a map view provides information about the geographical location of the selected data (cf. Figure 2). Technically, this view is realized by integrating the Google Maps API[3]. However, the integration is bi-directional, since objects displayed in the map can be expanded and instance details are dynamically fetched from the knowledge base and displayed directly within the map view. The selection of instances to be displayed can be furthermore the result of a facet-based filtering (cf. Section 4).

Calendar View. Instances having property values with the associated datatype `xsd:date` can be displayed in a calendar view (cf. Figure 2). As for the map view the selection of instances displayed in the calendar view can be the result of a facet-based filtering. Each item displayed is linked to the individual view of the corresponding instance. The sidebar offers a link to export calendar items in iCal format, which enables to import the selected calendar items into a desktop calender application.

2 Collaborative Authoring

To enable users to edit information presented by the OntoWiki system as intuitively as possible, the OntoWiki approach supports two complementary edit strategies for the knowledge base:

---

[3] http://www.google.com/apis/maps/

- *Inline editing*, the smallest possible information chunks (i.e. statements) presented in the OntoWiki user interface are editable for users.
- *View editing*, common combinations of information (such as an instance of a distinct class) are editable in one single step.

Both editing strategies are supported by a mixed client and server side *concept identification and reuse technology and a library of* generic editing widgets. In the remainder of this section the editing strategies and their supporting technologies are presented in more detail.

2.1 Inline Editing

For human users it is important that the statements of a knowledge base are presented on the user interface in a way facilitating the efficient reception of this information. To achieve this goal information should be ordered and grouped and as a result of this information appearing redundant should be omitted. If the context clarifies, for example, that some information describes a distinct concept (e.g. since the OntoWiki page for a person was accessed) the concept will be displayed only once on the OntoWiki user interface, even though all the statements describing the concept contain the concepts URI reference as subject. If furthermore a property (e.g. referencing publications) occurs multiple times (e.g. since the person described is author of multiple publications) those statements should be grouped together and the label of the property should be displayed only once (cf. Figure 3).

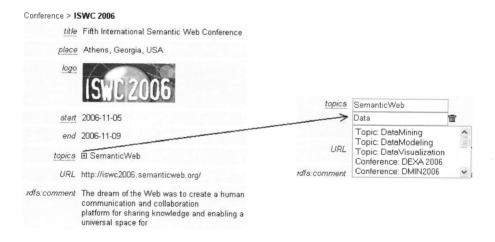

Fig. 3. OntoWiki instance display with statement edit buttons (left). Statement editor with interactive search for predefined individuals based on AJAX technology (right).

Even though such a human friendly representation of the statements contained in the knowledge bases conceals the original statement structure the OntoWiki system is aware which information displayed on the user interface originated from what statements. To enable users to rapidly edit or add statements as soon as they notice mistakes or missing information OntoWiki features an inline editing mode. This means that all information originating from statements presented on the OntoWiki user interface is equipped with a small edit button as well as an add button (cf. Figure 3). After clicking one of those buttons a resource editor (cf. Figure 4) is loaded and the corresponding statement can be easily edited or a similar content (i.e. a statement with same subject and predicate) can be added.

This strategy can be seen analogous to the WYSIWYG (What You See Is What You Get) editing strategy for text editing, since information can be edited in the same environment as it is presented to users.

2.2 Concept Identification and Reuse

Knowledge bases become increasingly advantageous, if once defined concepts (e.g. classes, properties, or instances) are as much reused and interlinked as possible. This especially eases the task of rearranging, extracting and aggregating knowledge. To become part of the daily routine for even inexperienced and rare users of the OntoWiki system already defined concepts should be suggested to the user, whenever he is requested to contribute new information. In a Web based environment and for highly scalable knowledge bases conventional Web technologies were the major obstacles for this.

Conventional Web technologies do not support large data sets to be handled at the client (browser) side. But this is usually needed when working with large knowledge bases. To overcome this limitation, reloading of web pages becomes necessary. This approach is time consuming and requires multiple user interactions. Recently, with the deployment of more sophisticated Web browsers, supporting modern JavaScript and XML technologies, mixed server and client side web applications became possible. These were recently named AJAX (Asynchronous JavaScript and XML) and early adopters such as Google-Maps[4] or Flickr[5] make extensive use of them.

The OntoWiki uses the AJAX technology to interactively propose already defined concepts while the user types in new information to be added to the knowledge base (cf. Figure 3). To realize this interactive search, all URI references and literals are indexed for full-text searches in the statement repository.

2.3 Editing Widgets

For convenient editing of differently typed literal data the OntoWiki system provides a library of reusable user interface components for data editing, called widgets. Such widgets are implemented in a server side programming language (e.g. PHP), they generate HTML fragments together with appropriate Cascading Style Sheet definitions and optionally JavaScript code. They may be customized for usage in specific contexts by widget configurations. The following widgets are currently provided by the prototypical OntoWiki implementation:

---

[4] http://maps.google.com
[5] http://www.flickr.com

- *Statements*: allows editing of subject, predicate, and object.
- *Nodes*: edit literals or resources.
- *Resources*: select and search from/for existing resources
- *Literals*: literal data in conjunction with a data type or a language identifier.
- *Widgets for specific literal data types*: e.g. dates, HTML fragments.
- *File widget*: allows uploading of files to the OntoWiki system.

All widgets can be configured. The OntoWiki system allows to define and attach certain sets of configurations to a specific widget. In addition to widget specific configurations, generic widget configuration which should be applicable to all widgets includes HTML attributes such as `class`, height and width of the widget, or arbitrary CSS styles.

A widget selection connects a widget configuration with a context. Contexts are the data type of the literal to be edited, the property of the statement which's object is edited, the property in conjunction with a specific class, the knowledge base the node to be edited belongs to, as well as the editing user and her group.

2.4 View Editing

Editable views are combinations of widgets to edit a specific view on the knowledge base in one single step. The OntoWiki system provides the following types of editable views:

- *Metadata*: comments, labels, and annotations (such as versioning and compatibility information) which can be attached to arbitrary resources are combined in a metadata view.
- *Instances*: An instance view combines all properties attached to the instance's class or one of the super-classes. For large knowledge bases this

Fig. 4. Editing of a property's values at many instances at once (left). Dynamically generated form combining different widgets based on an OWL class definition (right).

might include a large amount of properties. The OntoWiki system thus allows to restrict the view to such properties which are really used in conjunction with other instances of the same class. On the basis of range definitions for the property, OntoWiki selects appropriate editing widgets. Additional properties can be added on-the-fly, the system will ask the user in a next step to specify the property's characteristics (e.g. domain, range, cardinality restrictions).
- *Views*: The earlier described inline-editing technique allows to edit arbitrary views. The columns of list views arranging many instances in a tabular way for example can be easily edited at once, thus allowing to rapidly add "horizontal" knowledge (across several instances) to the knowledge base (cf. Figure 4).

3 Enabling Social Collaboration

A major aim of OntoWiki is to foster and employ social interactions for the development of knowledge bases. This eases the structured exchange of meta-information about the knowledge base drastically and promotes collaboration scenarios where face-to-face communication is hard. Making means of social interactions as easy as possible furthermore contributes in creating an "architecture of participation" that allows users to add value to the system as they use it. Social collaboration within OntoWiki is in particular supported by:

Change tracking. All changes applied to a knowledge base are tracked. OntoWiki enables the review of changes on different levels of detail (see also [3]) and optionally restricted to a specific context, such as changes on a specific instance, changes on instances of a class, or changes made by a distinct user. In addition to present such change sets on the Web, users can subscribe to get information about the most recent changes on objects of their interest by email or RSS/Atom feeds.

Commenting. All statements presented to the user by the OntoWiki system may be annotated, commented, and their usefulness can be rated. This enables community driven discussions, for example about the validity of certain statements. Technically, this is implemented on the basis of RDF reifications, which allow to make statements about statements. Small icons attached to an object of a statement within the OntoWiki user interface indicate that such reifications exist (cf. Figure 5). Positioning the mouse pointer on such an icon will immediately show up a tool tip with the most recent annotations; clicking on the icon will display them all.

Rating. OntoWiki allows to rate instances. Users have to be registered and logged into the system to participate in order to avoid duplicate ratings by the same user. However, a user may change his rating for a certain instance. Special annotation properties allow the creation of rating categories with respect

Fig. 5. Comments attached to statements

to a certain class. Instances of the class can then be rated according to these categories, thus allowing for example the rating of instances of a class publication according to categories originality, quality and presentation.

Popularity. All accesses to the knowledge base are logged thus allowing to arrange views on the content based on popularity. As with ratings or user activity, the popularity of content can be measured with respect to a certain knowledge base or fragment of it (e.g. popularity with respect to class membership). This enables users to add value to the system as they use it.

Activity/Provenance. The system keeps record of what was contributed by whom. This includes contributions to the ontology schema, additions of instance data or commenting. This information can be used to honor active users in the context of the overall system, a specific knowledge base or a fragment of it (e.g. instance additions to some class). This way it contributes to instantly gratify users for their efforts and helps building a community related to certain semantic content.

4 Semantic Search

To realize the full potential of a semantic browsing experience the semantic structuring and representation of content should be employed to enhance the retrieval of information for human users. OntoWiki implements two complementary strategies to achieve this goal.

4.1 Facet-Based Browsing

Taxonomic structures give users exactly one way to access the information. Furthermore, the development of appropriate taxonomic structures (whether e.g. class or SKOS keyword hierarchies) requires significant initial efforts. As a pay-as-you-go strategy, facet-based browsing allows to reduce the efforts for a priori knowledge structuring, while still offering efficient means to retrieve information. Facet-based browsing was also implemented by the Longwell Browser[6] for RDF data and it is widely deployed in the shape of tagging systems of the Web 2.0 folksonomies. To enable users to select objects according to certain facets,

---

[6] http://simile.mit.edu/longwell/

all property values (facets) of a set of selected instances are analyzed. If for a certain property the instances have only a limited set of values, those values are offered to restrict the instance selection further. Hence, this way of navigation through data will never lead to empty results. The analyzing of property values though can be very resource demanding. To still enable fast response times the OntoWiki system caches the results of of a property value analysis for later reuse and invalidates those cache objects selectively if values of the respective property are updated (see [2, Chapter 5] for details).

4.2 Semantically Enhanced Full-Text Search

OntoWiki provides a full-text search for one or multiple keywords occurring in literal property values. Since there can be several property values of a single individual containing the search string the results are grouped by instances. They are ordered by frequency of occurrence of the search string. Search results may be filtered to contain only individuals which are instances of a distinct class or which are described by the literal only in conjunction with a distinct property (cf. Figure 6).

A semantic search has significant advantages compared to conventional full-text searches. By detecting classes and properties, contain matching instances, the semantic search delivers important feedback to the user how the search may be successfully refined.

The semantic search is currently implemented as a search in the local RDF store. In conjunction with a crawler, which searches, downloads, and stores arbitrary RDF documents from the web, OntoWiki can be easily transformed in a Semantic Web search engine.

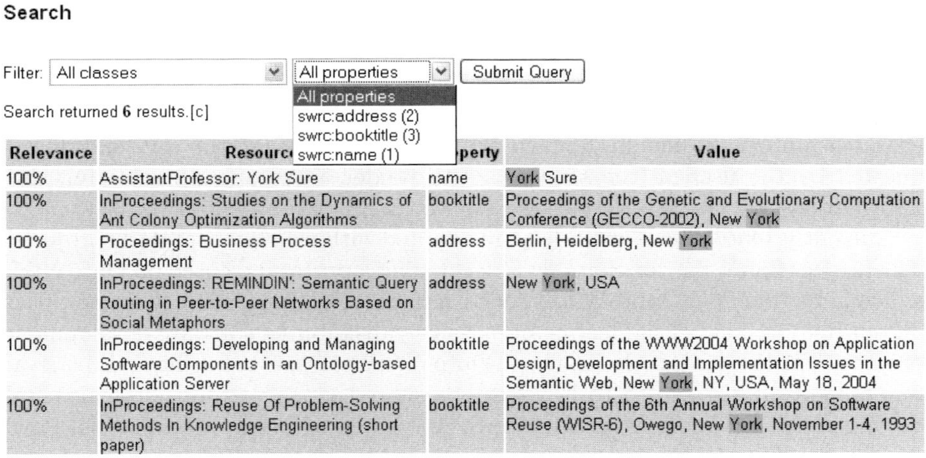

Fig. 6. User interface for the semantic search in the OntoWiki system. After a search for "York" it suggested to refine his search to instances with one of the properties swrc:address, swrc:booktitle or swrc:name.

5 Implementation and Status

OntoWiki is implemented as an alternative user interface to the schema editor integrated in Powl. Powl is a platform for Semantic Web application development realized in a 3-tier architecture consisting of storage tier, object-oriented API and user interfaces (cf. Figure 7). Many of the requirements for OntoWiki were gathered from use cases of Powl.

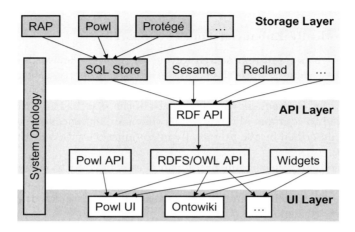

Fig. 7. Architecture of Powl and OntoWiki

OntoWiki was implemented in the scripting language PHP, thus allowing to be easily deployed on most Web hosting environments. The application is available as open-source software from SourceForge[7]. A publicly available knowledge repository on the basis of OntoWiki is available at http://3ba.se.

The system is designed to work with knowledge bases of arbitrary size (only limited by disk space). This is achieved by loading only those parts of the knowledge base into main memory which are required to display the information requested by the user on the screen (i.e. to render a Web page containing this information).

Currently, OntoWiki is extended and adopted within a variety of R&D projects. The project SoftWiki[8] for example is developing a prototype based on OntoWiki, which aims to employ OntoWiki's social collaboration functionality for end-user driven Requirements Engineering of massively distributed software development projects. For the project Orchestra [7] OntoWiki's storage, browsing and retrieval functionality is envisioned to be used as a shared repository for ontologies and queries in the bio-informatics domain. In the project "Vernetzte Kirche" [4] Powl and parts of OntoWiki were applied to foster a meta-data initiative for social, cultural and religious content.

---

[7] http://powl.sf.net
[8] http://softwiki.de

6 Conclusion

In this paper we presented the OntoWiki approach, exemplary exhibiting how tool support for agile, collaborative knowledge engineering scenarios can be provided. Since the OntoWiki system is based technologically on Powl, we stressed in this paper especially aspects facilitating the usage of the OntoWiki system. These include the visual presentation of a knowledge base as an information map, social collaboration aspects as well as a semantic search strategy. Such efforts, which decrease the entrance barrier for domain experts to collaborate using semantic technologies, are in particular crucial to gain a maximized impact on collaborative knowledge engineering. Examples from other domains, such as Community Content Management and Software Development, showed that such efforts can have an enormous impact on distributed collaboration, thus enabling completely new products and services. Conventional Wiki technologies for example radically simplified the editing process and enabled the Wikipedia project[9] to attract a multitude of editors finally succeeding in the creation of the worlds largest encyclopedia. Technologies for distributed collaborative software development as CVS and Subversion[10] or the SourceForge[11] platform made it possible to develop almost any standard software for private or business needs largely in absence of strong, centralized, commercial corporations. The aim of OntoWiki is to contribute giving the Semantic Web a much broader basis.

Application domain. The OntoWiki system is technologically independent of and complementary to conventional text Wiki systems. It enables the easy creation of highly structured content by distributed communities. The following points summarize some limitations and weaknesses of OntoWiki and thus characterize the application domain:

- *Environment*: OntoWiki is a Web application and presumes all collaborators working in a Web environment, possibly spatially distributed.
- *Usage Scenario*: OntoWiki focuses on knowledge engineering projects where a single, precise usage scenario is either initially not (yet) known or not (easily) definable.
- *Reasoning*: Application of reasoning services is (initially) not mission critical.
- *Budget*: Only a small amount of financial and personnel resources are available.

Open issues and potential future work.

- Implement a privilege system and access control for and on the basis of the RDF data model with support for rights management on higher conceptual levels than that of statements.
- Obtain more case studies, in particular independent comparisons, are needed to provide further evidence to see whether OntoWiki lives up to its promises.

---

[9] http://wikipedia.org
[10] http://subversion.tigris.org
[11] http://sf.net

- Examine possibilities to tighter integrate the Description Logic reasoning services into OntoWiki.
- Establish better methods of interaction with existing content and knowledge management systems.

Further related work. In addition to the affinity with Wiki systems and Web portals in general the OntoWiki approach can be seen as a representative of a new class of semantic portals (cf. [13]). The SEAL SEmantic portAL [10] for example exploits semantics for providing and accessing information at a portal as well as constructing and maintaining the portal. Due being based on a rather static methodology [14] it focuses less on spontaneous, incremental enhancements of the knowledge base than OntoWiki. Another approach to develop a semantic portal is the website of the Mindswap project[12]. Semantic Web knowledge representation standards are used as primary data source and for interoperability, the editing and publishing process as well as collaboration aspects however seem to be either not tackled or publicised.

Acknowledgments

This research was supported in part by the following grants: BMBF (SE2006 #01ISF02B), NSF (CAREER #IIS-0477972 and SEIII #IIS-0513778).

References

1. Sören Auer. Powl: A Web Based Platform for Collaborative Semantic Web Development. In Sören Auer, Chris Bizer, and Libby Miller, editors, *Proceedings of the Workshop Scripting for the Semantic Web*, number 135 in CEUR Workshop Proceedings, Heraklion, Greece, 05 2005.
2. Sören Auer. *Towards Agile Knowledge Engineering: Methodology, Concepts and Applications*. PhD thesis, Universität Leipzig, 2006.
3. Sören Auer and Heinrich Herre. A Versioning and Evolution Framework for RDF Knowledge Bases. In *Proceedings of Ershov Memorial Conference*, 2006.
4. Sören Auer and Bart Pieterse. "Vernetzte Kirche": Building a Semantic Web. In *Proceedings of ISWC Workshop Semantic Web Case Studies and Best Practices for eBusiness (SWCASE05)*, 2005.
5. David Aumüller. Semantic Authoring and Retrieval within a Wiki (WikSAR). In Demo Session at the Second European Semantic Web Conference (ESWC2005), May 2005. Available at http://wiksar.sf.net, 2005.
6. David Aumüller. SHAWN: Structure Helps a Wiki Navigate. In *Proceedings of the BTW-Workshop "WebDB Meets IR"*, 2005.
7. Zachary G. Ives, Nitin Khandelwal, Aneesh Kapur, and Murat Cakir. ORCHESTRA: Rapid, collaborative sharing of dynamic data. In *CIDR*, pages 107–118, 2005.
8. Markus Krötzsch, Denny Vrandecic, and Max Völkel. Wikipedia and the Semantic Web - The Missing Links. In Jakob Voss and Andrew Lih, editors, *Proceedings of Wikimania 2005, Frankfurt, Germany*, 2005.

---
[12] http://www.mindswap.org/first.shtml

9. Bo Leuf and Ward Cunningham. *The Wiki Way: Collaboration and Sharing on the Internet*. Addison-Wesley Professional, 2001.
10. Alexander Maedche, Steffen Staab, Nenad Stojanovic, Rudi Studer, and York Sure. SEmantic portAL: The SEAL approach. In Dieter Fensel, James A. Hendler, Henry Lieberman, and Wolfgang Wahlster, editors, *Spinning the Semantic Web*, pages 317–359. MIT Press, 2003.
11. Eyal Oren. SemperWiki: A Semantic Personal Wiki. In Stefan Decker, Jack Park, Dennis Quan, and Leo Sauermann, editors, *Proc. of Semantic Desktop Workshop at the ISWC, Galway, Ireland, November 6*, volume 175, November 2005.
12. Adam Souzis. Building a Semantic Wiki. *IEEE Intelligent Systems*, 20(5):87–91, 2005.
13. Steffen Staab, Jürgen Angele, Stefan Decker, Michael Erdmann, Andreas Hotho, Alexander Maedche, Rudi Studer, and York Sure. Semantic Community Web Portals. In *Proc. of the 9th World Wide Web Conference (WWW-9)*, Amsterdam, Netherlands, 2000.
14. Steffen Staab, Rudi Studer, Hans-Peter Schnurr, and York Sure. Knowledge processes and ontologies. *IEEE Intelligent Systems*, 16(1):26–34, 2001.

Towards a Semantic Web of Relational Databases: A Practical Semantic Toolkit and an In-Use Case from Traditional Chinese Medicine

Huajun Chen[1], Yimin Wang[2], Heng Wang[1], Yuxin Mao[1],
Jinmin Tang[1], Cunyin Zhou[1], Ainin Yin[3], and Zhaohui Wu[1]

[1] College of Computer Science, Zhejiang University, Hangzhou, 310027, China
{huajunsir, paulwang, maoyx, jmtang981, 02rjgczcy, wzh}@zju.edu.cn
[2] Institute AIFB, University of Karlsruhe, D-76128, Germany
ywa@aifb.uni-karlsruhe.de
[3] China Academy of Traditional Chinese Medicine, Beijing, 100700, China
yinan@mail.cintcm.ac.cn
http://ccnt.zju.edu.cn/projects/dartgrid

Abstract. Integrating relational databases is recently acknowledged as an important vision of the Semantic Web research, however there are not many well-implemented tools and not many applications that are in large-scale real use either. This paper introduces the Dartgrid which is an application development framework together with a set of semantic tools to facilitate the integration of heterogenous relational databases using semantic web technologies. For examples, DartMapping is a visualized mapping tool to help DBA in defining semantic mappings from heterogeneous relational schemas to ontologies. DartQuery is an ontology-based query interface helping user to construct semantic queries, and capable of rewriting SPARQL semantic queries to a set of SQL queries. DartSearch is an ontology-based search engine enabling user to make full-text search over all databases and to navigate across the search results semantically. It is also enriched with a concept ranking mechanism to enable user to find more accurate and reliable results. This toolkit has been used to develop an currently in-use application for China Academy of Traditional Chinese Medicine (CATCM). In this application, over 70 legacy relational databases are semantically interconnected by an ontology with over 70 classes and 800 properties, providing integrated semantic-enriched query, search and navigation services to TCM communities.

1 Introduction

Up to date, many killer applications reported by the Semantic Web community often focus on processing the unstructured document data, using semantic annotation or various of learning, mining, and natural language processing techniques [1]. However, data in big organizations is normally stored in relational databases or other appropriately formatted documents. Over emphasizing on those applications, which handles unstructured document, may obscure the community from the fact that the essence of the Semantic Web comes from its similarity to a huge distributed database. To back up this idea, consider the following statements made by Tim Berners-Lee in 2005 about his vision of the future Semantic Web[1].

> ...The Semantic Web is not about the meaning of documents. It's not about marking up existing HTML documents to let a computer understand what they say. It's not about the artificial intelligence areas of machine learning or natural language understanding... **It is about the data which currently is in relational databases, XML documents, spreadsheets, and proprietary format data files, and all of which would be useful to have access to as one huge database**...

From this point of view, one of the way to realize the vision of Semantic Web is (i) to interconnect distributed located legacy databases using richer semantics, (ii) to provide ontology-based query, search and navigation as one huge distributed database, and (iii) to add additional deductive capabilities on the top to increase the usability and reusability of data.

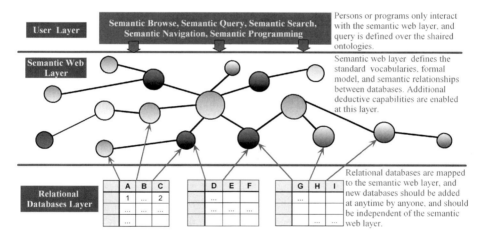

Fig. 1. Towards a semantic web of relational databases

Besides, since most of the data is currently stored in relational databases, for semantic web to be really useful and successful, great efforts are required to offer methods and tools to support integration of heterogeneous relational databases. Dartgrid is an application development framework together with a set of practical semantic tools to facilitate the integration of heterogenous relational databases using semantic web technologies. In specific, DartMapping is a visualized mapping tool to help DBA in defining semantic mappings from heterogeneous relational schemas to ontologies. DartQuery is an ontology-based query interface helping user to construct semantic queries, and capable of rewriting SPARQL semantic queries to a set of SQL queries. DartSearch is an

---

[1] http://www.consortiuminfo.org/bulletins/semanticweb.php

ontology-based search engine enabling user to make full-text search over all databases and to navigate across the search results semantically. It is also enriched with a concept ranking mechanism to enable user to find more accurate and reliable results.

Building upon Dartgrid, we have developed and deployed a semantic web application for China Academy of Traditional Chinese Medicine (CATCM)[2][3]. It semantically interconnects over 70 legacy TCM databases by a formal TCM ontology with over 70 classes and 800 properties. The TCM ontology acts as a separate semantic layer to fill up the gaps among legacy databases with heterogeneous structures, which might be semantically interconnected. Users and machines only need to interact with the semantic layer, and the semantic interconnections allow them to start in one database, and then move around an extendable set of databases. The semantic layer also enables the system to answer semantic queries across several databases such as "What diseases does this drug treat? " or "What kind of drugs can treat this disease?", not like the keyword-based searching mechanism provide by conventional search engines.

The paper is organized as follows. Section 2 talks about the system architecture and technical features. Section 3 elaborates on the implementation of the semantic mediator and the visualized semantic mapping tool. Section 4 introduces the TCM semantic portals which provides semantic query and search services. Section 5 reports the user evaluation and lessons learned from this developing life-cycle. Section 6 mentions some related works. Section 7 gives the summary and our future directions.

Please also note due to the special character of TCM research, in which the Chinese terminologies and definitions are not always interpretable, some figures in this paper contain Chinese search results and web interface. We have annotated all the necessary parts of the figures in English, and we would expect it would be sufficient to understand the functionalities of this application.

2 System Architecture and Technical Features

2.1 System Architecture

As Fig. 2 depicted, there are four key components in the core of DartGrid.

1. **Ontology Service** is used to expose the shared ontologies that are defined using web ontology languages. Typically, the ontology is specified by a domain expert who is also in charge of the publishing, revision, extension of the ontology.
2. **Semantic Registration Service** maintains the semantic mapping information. Typically, database providers define the mappings from relational schema to domain ontology, and submit the registration entry to this service.
3. **Semantic Query Service** is used to process SPARQL semantic queries. Firstly, it gets mapping information from semantic registration service. Afterward, it translates the semantic queries into a set of SQL queries and dispatch them into specific databases. Finally, the results of SQL queries will be merged and transformed back to semantically-enriched format.

---

[2] http://ccnt.zju.edu.cn/projects/dartgrid/tcmgrid.html
[3] Demo videos http://ccnt.zju.edu.cn/projects/dartgrid/demo

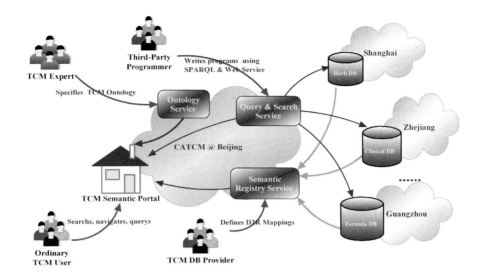

Fig. 2. System Architecture and Usage Senario

4. **Search Service** supports full-text search in all databases. The search results will be statistically calculated to yield a *concepts ranking*, which help user to get more appropriate and accurate results.

2.2 Technical Features

The following four features that distinguish this application from other similar semantic data integration tools, which will be introduced in detail in Section 6.

Semantic View and Visualized Semantic Mapping Tool. In our system, an ontology acts as the semantic mediator for heterogenous databases. Relational database schemas are mapped into corresponding classes or properties, and related by semantic relationship defined in this ontology. To be specific, the mappings are defined as *semantic views*, that is, each relational table is defined as a *view* over this shared ontology. Defining mappings is a labor-intensive and error-prone task. In our system, new database could be added into the system by using a visualized mapping tool. It provides many easy-of-use functionalities such as drag-and-drop mapping, mapping visualization, data source annotation and so on.

SPARQL Query Rewriting with Additional Inference Capabilities. A view-based query rewriting algorithm is implemented to rewrite the SPARQL queries into a set of SQL queries. This algorithm extends earlier relational and XML techniques for rewriting queries using views, with consideration of the features of web ontology languages. Otherwise, this algorithm is also enriched by additional inference capabilities on predicates such as *subClassOf* and *subPropertyOf*.

Ontology-based Semantic Query User Interface. A form-based query interface is offered to construct semantic queries over shared ontologies. It is automatically generated at runtime according to property definitions of classes, and will finally generate a SPARQL query.

Intuitive Search Interface with Concepts Ranking and Semantic Navigation. This Google-like search interface accepts one or more keywords and makes a complete full-text search in all databases. Users could semantically navigate in the search results, and move around an extendable set of databases based on the semantic relationships defined in the semantic layer. Meanwhile, the search system could generate a suggested list of concepts which are ranked based on their relevance to the keywords. Thereafter, users could explore into the semantic query interface of those concepts, and specify a semantic query on them to get more accurate and appropriate information.

3 Semantic Mediation

3.1 Semantic View and View-Based Mapping

In our system, databases are mediated and related by a shared ontology, and each relational table is mapped into one or more classes. For example, the mapping scenario in Fig. 3 illustrates relational schemas from two sources(W3C and ZJU), and a shared ontology (a part of the foaf ontology).

Mappings are typically defined as views in conventional data integration systems in the form of GAV (global-as-view), LAV (local-as-view) [2]. Considering the case in this paper, GAV is to define each class or property as a view over relational tables, and LAV is to define each relational table as a view (or query) over the shared ontology. The experiences from conventional data integration systems tell us that LAV provides greater extensibility than GAV: the addition of new sources is less likely to require a change to the mediated schema [2]. In our TCM case, new databases are regularly added so total number of databases is increasing gradually. Therefore, the LAV approach is employed in our system, that is, each relational table is defined as a view over the ontologies. We call such kind of views as *Semantic View*.

The lower part of Fig. 3 showcases how to represent the mappings as *semantic views* in a Datalog-like syntax. Like in conventional data integration, a typical *semantic view* consists of two parts. The left part is called the view head, and is a relational predicate. The right part is called the view body, and is a set of RDF triples. There are two kinds of variables in the view definitions. Those variables such as "?en,?em,?eh,?pn,?ph" are called distinguished variables, which will be assigned by an data or instance values from the database. Those variables such as "?y1, ?y2" are called existential variables.

In general, the body can be viewed as a query over the ontology, and it defines the semantics of the relational predicate from the perspective of the ontology. The meaning of semantic view would be more clear if we construct a *Target Instance* based on the semantic mapping specified by these views. For example, given a relational tuple as below, applying the View-4 in Fig. 3 on this tuple will yield a set of RDF triples.

```
Relational Tuple:
    w3c:emp("DanBrickley","danbri@w3.org",
            "SWAD","http://swad.org","EU");
```

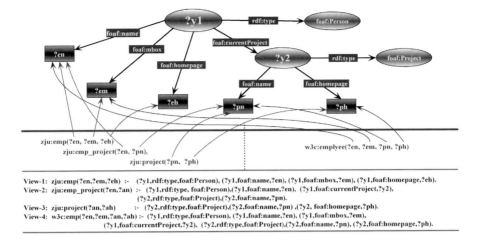

Fig. 3. Mappings from two relational databases with different structures to an ontology. "?en,?em,?eh,?pn,?ph" are variables and represent "employee name", "employee email", "employee homepage", "project name", "project homepage", respectively.

```
Yielded RDF triples by Applying View-4:
    _:bn1 rdf:type foaf:Person;
          foaf:name "Dan Brickley";
          foaf:mbox "danbri@w3.org";
          foaf:currentProject _:bn2.
    _:bn2 rdf:type  foaf:Project;
          foaf:name "SWAD";
          foaf:homepage "http://swad.org".
```

One of the key notion is the newly generated blank node ID. As illustrated, corresponding to each existential variable $?y$ in the view, a new blank node ID is generated. For examples, $\_:bn1, \_:bn2$ are both newly generated blank node IDs corresponding to the variables $?y1, ?y2$ in View-4 respectively. This treatment of existential variable is in accordance with the RDF semantics, since blank nodes can be viewed as existential variables. We give the formal definition of the semantic view as below. More detailed Foudermental aspects about *semantic view* could be found in another paper [3].

Definition 1. Semantic View. Let Var be a set of variable names . A typical semantic view is like the form $:R(\bar{X}) : -G(\bar{X}, \bar{Y}), where :$
1. $R(\bar{X})$ is called the head of the view, and R is a relational predicate ;
2. $G(\bar{X}, \bar{Y})$ is called the body of the view, and G is a RDF graph with some nodes replaced by variables in Var;
3. The $\bar{X}, \bar{Y}$ contain either variables or constants.The variables in $\bar{X}$ are called distinguished variables , and the variables in $\bar{Y}$ are called existential variables.

3.2 Visualized Semantic Mapping Tool

The task of defining semantic mappings from relational schema to ontologies is burdensome and erroneous. Although we could develop tools to automate this process, it still can not be fully automated and requires humans involvement, especially for integration of databases with different schema structures.

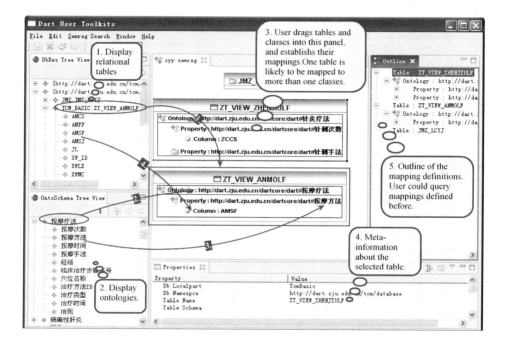

Fig. 4. Visualized Semantic Mapping Tool

Fig. 4 displays the visualized mapping tool we developed to facilitate the task of defining semantic views. It has five panels. The *DBRes* panel displays the relational schemas, and the *OntoSchem* panel displays the shared ontology. The *Mapping Panel* visually displays the mappings from relational schemas to ontologies. Typically, user drag tables or columns from DBRes panel, and drag classes or properties from OntoSchem panel, then drop them into the mapping panel to establish the mappings. By simple drag-and-drop operations, users could easily specify which classes should be mapped into a table and which property should be mapped into a table column. After these operations, the tool automatically generates a registration entry, which is submit to the semantic registration service. Besides, user could use the *Outline* panel to browse and query previously defined mapping information, and use the *Properties* panel to specify some global information, such as namespace, or view the meta-information about the table.

Towards a Semantic Web of Relational Databases 757

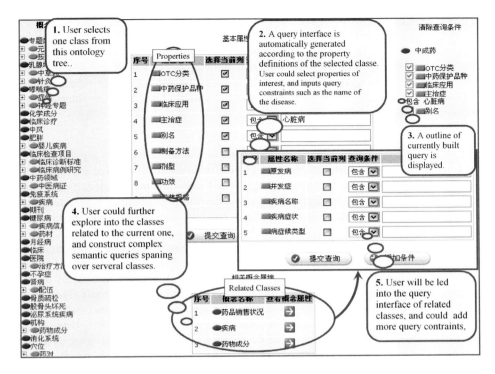

Fig. 5. Dynamic Semantic Query Portal. Please note: because many Chinese medical terminologies are only available in Chinese language and they are not always interpretable, we have annotated all the necessary parts of the figures in English.

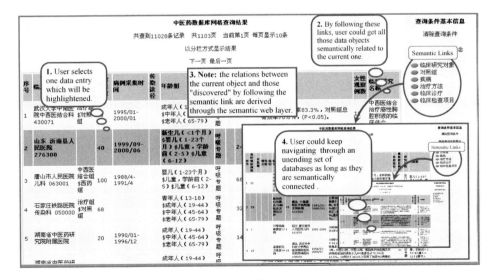

Fig. 6. Semantic navigation through the query results

4 TCM Semantic Portals

The semantic mediator is designed to separate data providers and data consumers so that they only need to interact with the semantic layer. For example, developers could write applications using the shared ontology without the need of any knowledge about databases. Besides that, our system also offer two different kinds of user interfaces to support query and search services.

4.1 Dynamic Semantic Query Interface

This form-like query interface is intended to facilitate users in constructing semantic queries. The query form is automatically generated according to class definitions. This design provides the extensibility of the whole system – when ontology is updated with the changes of database schema, the interface could dynamically adapt to the updated shared ontology.

Fig. 5 shows the situation how a TCM user constructs a semantic query. Starting from the *ontology view panel* on the left, user can browse the ontology tree and select the classes of interest. A query form corresponding to the property definitions of the selected class will be automatically generated and displayed in the middle. Then user can check and select the properties of interests or input query constraints into the text boxes. Accordingly, a SPARQL query is constructed and could be submit to the semantic query service, where the query will be rewritten into a set of SQL queries using mapping views contained in the semantic registration service. The query rewriting is a somewhat complicated process, and [3] gives the detailed introduction on the rewriting algorithm. In addition, user could define more complex queries. For example, depicted in the lower-middle part of Fig. 5, user could follow the links leading to related classes of the current class, and select more properties or input new query constraints.

Fig. 6 shows the situation in which a TCM user is navigating the query results. Starting from selecting one result highlighted, the user can find out all of the related data entries by following the semantic links. Please note that in this example, the relations between the search results and those "discovered" by following the semantic links, are derived from the semantic layer.

4.2 Intuitive Search Interface with Concepts Ranking and Semantic Navigation

Unlike the semantic query interface, this Google-like search interface just accepts one or more keywords and makes a complete full-text search in all databases. Fig. 7 shows the situation where a TCM user performs some search operations. Starting from inputting a keyword, the user can retrieve all of those data entries containing one or more hits of that keyword. Being similar to the case of the query interface, user could also semantically navigate the search results by following the semantic links listed with each entries.

Meanwhile, the search system generates a list of suggested concepts which are displayed on the right part of the portal. They are ranked based on their relevance to the keywords. These concept links will lead the users to the dynamic query interface introduced in previous section. Thereafter, users could specify a semantic query on them to get more accurate and appropriate information. We call it as intuitive search because it could generate a list of concept suggestions to help user improve the search results.

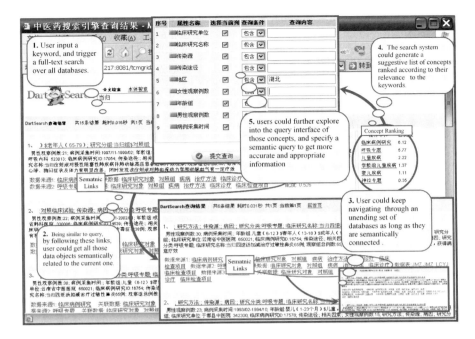

Fig. 7. Intuitive Search Portal with Concept Ranking and Semantic Navigation

5 User Evaluation and Lesson Learned

5.1 Feedbacks from CATCM

The first proof-of-concepts prototype was deployed during fall 2004. By using that prototype, we convinced CATCM partner to take the semantic web technologies to help them in managing their fast increasing TCM databases. After a thorough requirements analysis and with a careful redesign and re-engineering of the entire system, a more stable and user-friendly version was released in September 2005, and deployed at CATCM for open evaluation and real use.

Currently, the system deployed at CATCM provides access to over 70 databases including TCM herbal medicine databases, TCM compound formula databases, clinical symptom databases, traditional Chinese drug database, traditional Tibetan drug database, TCM product and enterprise databases, and so on. The TCM shared ontology includes over 70 classes, 800 data or object properties.

In general, users from CATCM reacted positively to the entire semantic web approach and our system. They indicated that the system provided an amazing solution for the semantic heterogeneity problem which had been troubling them for a long time. In particular, they gave high praise to the visualized semantic registration tool, and indicated that the features of semantic registration of new database considerably save them a lot of time when new database were developed and needed to be integrated.

They also gave positive comments to the semantic portals as well, especially the semantic navigation functionality. They indicated that semantic interconnections among different databases was indeed what they wanted. Nevertheless, we found most of the users prefer Google-like search to semantic query interface. Some of them complained that the learning cycle of using the semantic query interface was too long, although it could return more accurate results. They also said they would very like to use the concepts ranking functionality to get more accurate result by constructing further queries when the entries returned from search was overwhelming.

5.2 A Survey on the Usage of RDF/OWL Predicates

RDF/OWL has offered us a range of predicates, but not all of them are useful for relational data integration. We made a survey on the usage of RDF/OWL predicates for relational database integration, and the results are indicated in table 1.

In this survey, we invited ten developers who are familiar with both semantic web technologies and our system. They are asked with the same questions: "From a practical view, what are those most important constructs do you think for relational data integration in semantic web", and are requested to write down some explanation for the reason of their choice. We summarize their comments and the score result as follows.

Table 1. The results for the survey of predicates usage

Predicate	E1	E2	E3	E4	E5	E6	E7	E8	E9	E10	AVG
rdf:datatype	9	10	8	9	10	10	9	7	10	9	9.1
rdfs:subClassOf	8	8	7	9	9	8	8	9	10	7	8.3
rdfs:subPropertyOf	8	8	8	7	8	8	9	9	9	8	8.2
owl:inverseOf	8	8	7	8	7	9	8	9	7	9	8.0
owl:cardinality	7	8	7	7	6	7	9	7	7	9	7.4

Data type support was considered to be important, because most commercial RDBMS has well-defined and unique data type system. RDFS predicates *rdfs:subClassOf* and *rdfs:subPropertyOf* have higher scores because they could enhance the query processing with additional inference capabilities. OWL predicate *owl:inverseOf* is useful when defining relations in both directions which is a usual case in relation database integration. One of the developer indicated that predicate *owl:inverseOf* could help to find more efficient rewritings in some cases. Predicate *owl:cardinality* is useful in adding more constraints to ensure the data integrity.

Some other predicates are considered as useful include: *owl:TransitiveProperty, owl:SymmetricProperty, owl:DatatypeProperty, owl:ObjectProperty*. Some of them thought both *owl:TransitiveProperty* and *owl:SymmetricProperty* could add additional deductive capabilities on top to yield more query results. *owl:DatatypeProperty* and *owl:ObjectProperty* could be used to distinguish simple data value column and foreign key column.

6 Related Works

6.1 Semantic Web Context

In the Semantic Web community, semantic data integration has been always a noticeable research topic. In particular, there have been a number of works dealing with how to make contents of existing or legacy database available for semantic web applications. A typical one is D2RQ[4]. D2RQ is a declarative language to describe mappings between relational database schemata and OWL/RDFS ontologies, and is implemented as a Jena plugin that rewrites RDQL queries into SQL queries. The result sets of these SQL queries are transformed into RDF triples that are passed up to the higher layers of the Jena framework. RDF Gateway[5] is a commercial software having similar functionalities. It connects legacy database resources to the Semantic Web via its *SQL Data Service Interface*. The *SQL Data Service* translates a RDF based query to a SQL query and returns the results as RDF data. Our system is different from D2RQ and RDF Gateway. We take the view-based mapping approach which has sound theoretical foundation, and we have visualized mapping tool and ontology-based query and search tool which are not offered by these two systems.

Some other works propose direct manipulation of relational data to RDF/OWL format, and then the data could be processed by OWL reasoners or be integrated by ontological mapping tool. D2RMap, KAON REVERSE[6] and many other toolkits offer such kind of reverse engineering functionality. Cristian Perez de Laborda and colleagues [4] propose an ontology called "Relation OWL" to describe the relational schema as OWL, and then use this OWL-representation to transform relational data items into RDF/OWL and provide query service by RDQL. The shortcoming of this kind of approaches is that they have to dump all the relational data into RDF/OWL format before querying, which would be impractical if the RDBMS contains huge volume of data. Moreover, they did not consider the issue of integrating heterogeneous databases using formal ontologies, which is one of the focuses of our solution.

Yuan An and colleagues [5] present an interesting paper concerning about defining semantic mappings between relational tables and ontologies within semantic web context. They introduce a tool which could automatically infer the LAV mapping formulas from simple predicate correspondences between relational schema and formal ontologies. Although completely automatic approach to define semantic mapping is difficult, it would be great enhancement to our visualized tool if some candidate mapping suggestions could be provided beforehand. That will be one of our future work.

The DOPE project (Drug Ontology Project for Elsevier) [6] explores ways to provide access to multiple life science information sources through a single semantic interface called DOPE browser. However, it is still a document management system, mainly concerning on thesaurus-based search, RDF-based querying, and concept-based visualization of large online document repositories. It can not answer semantic queries such as "What diseases does this drug treat?" or "What kind of drugs can treat this disease?". We've seen the authors of DOPE are considering it as one of their future work.

---
[4] `http://www.wiwiss.fu-berlin.de/suhl/bizer/D2RQ/`
[5] `http://www.intellidimension.com`
[6] `http://kaon.semanticweb.org/alphaworld/reverse/view`

Piazza [7] is an interesting P2P-based data integration system with consideration of semantic web vision. But the current system has been implemented with the XML data model for its mapping language and query answering. However, we think P2P architecture would be a promising direction, and we are considering to extend our system to support P2P working mode and test its scalability and usability.

For other related works, Dejing Dou and colleagues [8] propose an ontology-based framework called OntoGrate. It can automatically transform relational schema into ontological representation, and users can define the mappings at the ontological level using bridge-axioms. Francois [9] considers theoretic aspect of answering query using views for semantic web and Peter Haase and Boris Motik introduces a mapping system for OWL-DL ontology integration [10].

6.2 Conventional Data Integration Context

Without considering the semantic web technologies, our solution can be categorized to the topic "answering query using view", which has been extensively studied in database community [2] [11]. Most previous works has been focused on the relational case [2], and XML case [12].

On the one hand, we believe it would be valuable for the semantic web community to take more consideration of the techniques that have been well studied in the database community such as answering query using view. On the other hand, we think that the semantic web research does raise a lot of new issues and challenges for database researchers. From our experiences, the challenges include: From our experiences, the challenges include: how to rank the data object just like the page rank of google? how to maintain highly evolvable and changeable schema mappings among an great number of and open-ended set of databases with no centralized control?

Moreover, a lot of works have been done in the area of ontology-based data integration [13]. Many of them took some ontological formalism such as DL to mediate heterogenous databases, and used the view-based mapping approach. In comparison with them, our implementation is the case of RDF/OWL-based relational data integration with a *semantic web vision in mind*.

7 Summary and Future Work

In this paper, we presented an in-use application of Traditional Chinese Medicine enhanced by a range of semantic web technologies, including RDF/OWL semantics and reasoning tools. The ultimate goal of this system is to realize the "web of structured data" vision by semantically interconnecting legacy databases, that allows a person, or a machine, to start in one database, and then move around an unending set of databases which are connected by rich semantics. To achieve this demanding goal, a set of convenient tools were developed, such as visualized semantic mapping tool, dynamic semantic query tool, and intuitive search tool with concepts ranking. Domain users from CATCM indicated that the system provided an amazing solution for the semantic heterogeneity problem troubling them for a long time.

Currently, although this project is complete, several updated functionalities are still in our consideration. To be specific, we are going to enhance the mapping tools with some heuristic rules to automate the mapping task as far as possible, just like the approach proposed by Yuan An and colleagues [5]. Otherwise, we will develop a more sophisticated mechanism to rank the data objects just like the page rank technology provided by popular search engines.

Acknowledgements

The authors' research is supported by China 973 subprogram "Semantic Grid for Traditional Chinese Medicine" (NO.2003CB316906), China NSF program (NO. NSFC60503018) and the EU-IST-027595 NeOn project. We would thank the fruitful discussion and first hand evaluation from our colleagues and partners.

References

1. Buitelaar, P., Olejnik, D., Sintek, M.: OntoLT: A protégé plug-in for ontology extraction from text. In: Proceedings of the International Semantic Web Conference (ISWC). (2003)
2. Halevy, A.Y.: Answering queries using views: A survey. The VLDB Journal. **10** (2001) 270–294
3. Chen, H., Wu, Z., Wang, H., Mao, Y.: Rdf/rdfs-based relational database integration. In: ICDE. (2006) 94
4. de Laborda, C.P., Conrad, S.: Bringing relational data into the semantic web using sparql and relational owl. In: International Workshop on Semantic Web and Database at ICDE 2006. (2006) 55–60
5. An, Y., Borgida, A., Mylopoulos, J.: Inferring complex semantic mappings between relational tables and ontologies from simple correspondences. In: International Semantic Web Conference. (2005) 6–20
6. Stuckenschmidt, H., van Harmelen, F., de Waard et al, A.: Exploring large document repositories with rdf technology: The dope project. IEEE Intelligent Systems. **19** (2004) 34–40
7. Halevy, A.Y., Ives, Z.G., Madhavan, J., Mork, P., Suciu, D., Tatarinov, I.: The piazza peer data management system. IEEE Trans. Knowl. Data Eng. **16-7** (2004) 787–798
8. Dou, D., LePendu, P., Kim, S., Qi, P.: Integrating databases into the semantic web through an ontology-based framework. In: International Workshop on Semantic Web and Database at ICDE 2006. (2006) 33–50
9. Goasdoue, F.: Answering queries using views: a krdb perspective for the semantic web. ACM Transaction on Internet Technology. (2003) 1–22
10. Haase, P., Motik, B.: A mapping system for the integration of owl-dl ontologies. In: IHIS '05: Proceedings of the first international workshop on Interoperability of heterogeneous information systems. (2005) 9–16
11. Abiteboul, S., Duschka, O.M.: Complexity of answering queries using materialized views,. In: The Seventeenth ACM SIGACT-SIGMOD-SIGART symposium on Principles of database systems,. (1998) 254–263
12. Yu, C., Popa, L.: Constraint-based xml query rewriting for data integration. In: 2004 ACM SIGMOD international conference on Management of data. (2004) 371–382
13. Wache, H., Vögele, T., Visser, U., Stuckenschmidt, H., Schuster, G., Neumann, H., Hubner, S.: Ontology-based integration of information - a survey of existing approaches. In Stuckenschmidt, H., ed.: IJCAI01 Workshop: Ontologies and Information Sharing. (2001) 108–117

Information Integration Via an End-to-End Distributed Semantic Web System

Dimitre A. Dimitrov[1], Jeff Heflin[2], Abir Qasem[2], and Nanbor Wang[1]

[1] Tech-X Corporation, 5621 Arapahoe Avenue, Suite A, Boulder, CO 80303
{dad, nanbor}@txcorp.com
[2] Lehigh University, 19 Memorial Drive West, Bethlehem, PA 18015
{heflin, abir.qasem}@cse.lehigh.edu

Abstract. A distributed, end-to-end information integration system that is based on the Semantic Web architecture is of considerable interest to both commercial and government organizations. However, there are a number of challenges that have to be resolved to build such a system given the currently available Semantic Web technologies. We describe here the ISENS prototype system we designed, implemented, and tested (on a small scale) to address this problem. We discuss certain system limitations (some coming from underlying technologies used) and future ISENS development to resolve them and to enable an extended set of capabilities.

1 Introduction

Different groups or subdivisions of a large organization often develop data management solutions semi-independently from each other with their own data schemas. Moreover, the data is often semi-structured, contains large binary (e.g. images) entities, dynamically evolves, grows, and is distributed over a number of data servers on a network. The efficient extraction of relevant information from all available and diverse data sources require the solution of a number of problems related to data representation and information integration in a distributed environment [1]. We describe here our initial implementation of the ISENS system that we designed as a test case to address these problems. We integrated and extended emerging Semantic Web [2,3] technologies to handle information integration (based on logical views [4]) and querying of distributed metadata. We have developed the ISENS system prototype during a Phase I Small Business Inovation Research (SBIR) project.

At the user (top) level, the service that ISENS is to provide consists of answering queries over distributed metadata repositories that describe underlying semi-structured data. Moreover, ISENS is designed to address a number of challenges in information representation that cannot be solved with markup languages such as HTML and XML. ISENS is built on top of specific Semantic Web technologies that support relations over different concepts expressed in the metadata. This allows the use of logical reasoners to derive semantic information from the metadata and its representation (markup). Furthermore, a language is needed to represent queries for computer programs to be able to parse, process, and extract relevant answers from the available metadata.

In a distributed environment of data centers that generate metadata on the same domain of knowledge, the syntax of the markup that each data center uses will generally be different from the syntax that each of the other centers are using to encode their data. The modeling of the data may be different too. For example, one data center modeler may see manufacturer as a property of a device, i.e. a device has a manufacturer, another modeler may see it as a property related to order, i.e. an order from a manufacturer. Then, the problem is how to provide information integration over metadata that each data center provides. Specifically, how can a user query the metadata from the distributed data centers using a uniform syntax even though the different data centers might be using their own syntax to markup the data they provide and how can the syntactic/semantic differences be resolved?

To encode metadata and address its representation we used the Resource Description Framework (RDF) and the OWL Web Ontology Language. This also includes the technologies that RDF and OWL extend and their associated schemas (XML, XMLS, and RDFS). For query representation, parsing, and processing, we selected and implemented a solution based on the SPARQL [5] query language for RDF. SPARQL is specifically designed to represent information for the Semantic Web. It provides to users and developers an extensible and flexible framework to construct queries over the extended set of RDF/RDFS capabilities. Finally, to address the third problem (uniform query over heterogeneous metadata from different and distributed data centers) we adopted the MiniCon algorithm [6]. This is a scalable algorithm for answering queries using views over different databases. We have enhanced it to work with a Semantic Web data model (as opposed to a relational data model in databases).

For testing of the implementation in a distributed, heterogeneous environment, and to simulate a plausible real-world scenario, we developed independently two different ontologies, one by the group at Tech-X Corp. and one by the Lehigh University group, on the same domain of knowledge. The two ontologies, while describing the same knowledge base, have different markup syntax. And furthermore, they model concepts differently from one another. To resolve syntactic and semantic heterogeneity we have used OWL axioms to describe a map between them. The axioms relate concepts from one ontology to the other. ISENS consults this map to retrieve information from sources that may have otherwise appeared to be providing differing information. In our framework, a map is an ontology that imports these ontologies whose terms it will align.

In the rest of the paper, we discuss first the architecture of the ISENS prototype we designed and implemented. Then, we describe the approach we developed for information integration with mapping ontologies and illustrate it with a number of example test queries. Finally, we summarize our experience from the implementation and testing of ISENS, discuss current limitations (some inherited from underlying technologies we used) and future development to extend the system.

2   Prototype System Architecture

The ISENS system prototype consists of three main components: the Web Interface Component (WIC), the Distributed Querying System (DQS), and the Distributed Enabling Component (DEC). For the purpose of driving the development of the prototype system, we developed two ontologies on a specific domain of knowledge. However, the issues addressed by the ontologies are representative of the general case about managing business related information faced by commercial organizations, e.g. for tracking on-going performance and/or forecasting future developments. Additionally, we created data individuals based on the two ontologies, configured two remotely located Sesame [7,8] RDF/OWL metadata repositories, and stored in them the ontology individuals. The overall architecture of ISENS is represented in Fig. 1.

The WIC provides a basic user interface to ISENS that is accessible via a Web browser. This user interface allows submission of SPARQL queries and displays the returned results. The WIC takes the user input in the form of a SPARQL query and passes it to the DQS for processing. The DQS returns the answers it finds in response to the query. The answers are encoded in XML and passed back to the WIC. The WIC then parses the returned XML and presents it to the user in a certain format.

The DQS component processes each SPARQL query and enables data integration over different, distributedly located, ontologies. The DQS contains a set of source descriptions. A source description specifies the attributes that can be found in the data source and the constraints on the contents of the source. One of the approaches for specifying source descriptions is to represent the contents of a data source as a view over a mediated schema [4]. This approach is known as Local as a View (LAV) in the database literature.

A mediated schema is a set of virtual relations that provide a uniform interface to the user. The LAV approach facilitates the addition of new data sources since existing views do not have to change when a source is added to the system. Although we use LAV as a foundation, in the DQS system the ontology of the query plays the role of the mediated schema. Thus, either of our two ontologies can serve as the mediated schema. In this sense, we are more general than LAV-based information integration (there is no need to construct a mediated schema in our system). The DQS relies on KAON2 [9] for its description logic reasoning functionality. The mapping ontologies that the DQS needs to do its information integration tasks are written in a subset of OWL DL.

In order to answer a query, a data integration system needs to translate a query in terms of the mediated schema into one that refers directly to the schemas in the data sources. Since the contents of the data sources in LAV are described as views, the translation problem amounts to finding a way to answer a query using a set of views. MiniCon [6] is one of the more scalable LAV algorithms.

The basic idea of the MiniCon algorithm is to examine each query sub goal against each view and check if the view can be used to "answer" the query sub goal and if so, in what "form"? It also treats "shared" variables carefully for certain optimizations. Finally, it combines views to answer all query sub goals.

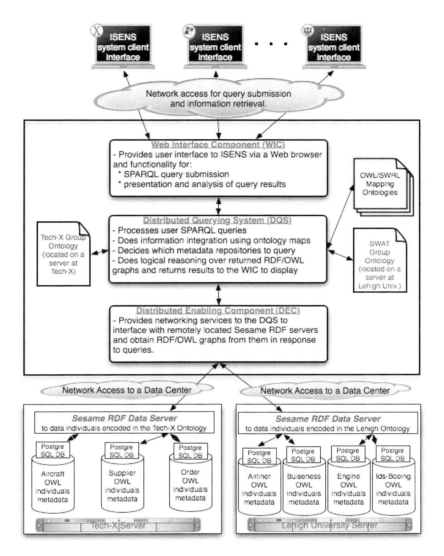

Fig. 1. The architecture of the ISENS prototype system is currently configured for querying of distributed RDF/OWL metadata at two data centers: one at Tech-X Corporation and the other at Lehigh University. The OWL individuals data is stored in multiple PostgreSQL databases that are managed by Sesame RDF servers. The Sesame servers provide remote access to the OWL individuals data. This set up allows testing of ISENS in a distributed and heterogeneous environment.

The DQS uses network services that are provided by the DEC to retrieve RDF/OWL graphs from distributedly located Sesame RDF servers. In the current configuration, the DEC can remotely query Sesame RDF servers. The DEC is also being designed to provide authentication and security services in ISENS per user/customer requirements.

For the ISENS prototype testing, we separated the OWL data individuals into seven different parts. These were then loaded into two Sesame RDF servers configured to use PostgreSQL databases. The Sesame RDF server at Tech-X Corporation stores the data individuals encoded in the Tech-X group ontology into three PostgreSQL databases. The data individuals encoded in the Lehigh University group ontology syntax are stored on a Sesame server at Lehigh University into four PostgreSQL databases.

3 Information Integration with Mapping Ontologies

In this Section, we use a top-down approach to describe an information integration solution that incorporates Semantic Web technologies. First, we consider a general way to address the problem. Then, we report on our current implementation in the ISENS system.

3.1 General Approach

In the general case, an operational environment consists of a set of ontologies and a set of data sources.

Each data source commits to one or more ontologies. The ontologies may include axioms which augment the data sources that commit to them with additional semantic information. Each ontology may extend other ontologies in order to refine the semantic definitions of the concepts in them. This model can be applied to legacy data sources if we assume that each data source has an ontology associated with it. Minimally, the ontology can just be a database schema. Integration is enabled by special ontologies called mapping ontologies. This model is represented in Fig. 2.

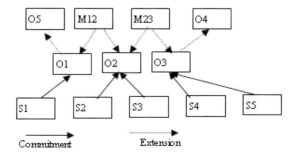

Fig. 2. Information integration using Semantic Web ontologies. Here, O1-O5 represent ontologies, S1-S5 represent data sources, and M12 and M23 are mapping ontologies.

The key problem here is that a query may be formulated using the language of one ontology but the relevant data may be in a data source that commits to a different ontology. The DQS will solve this problem by using the mapping ontologies to decompose the query into a set of queries that can be directly sent to some subset of the data sources. If there is no direct mapping, it will traverse through a semantic connection of maps to determine relevant ontologies and data sources. Consider our example described above. There is a direct map M12 between the O1 and O2 ontologies. Therefore, a query q using terms from O1 can access data in the S2 and S3 data sources using the map. There is, however, no direct map between O1 and O3 but by combining M12 and M23 we can now retrieve answers from S1, S2, S3, S4 and S5.

3.2 Implementation in the DQS

The basic structure of the implemented DQS architecture is shown in Figure 3. It involves two separate processes. The Map Processor reads the source descriptions and the mapping ontologies in order to load a meta-information knowledge base. Source descriptions identify sources that have relevant information with respect to classes and/or properties. If a source can express that it has relevant information we can choose to query it as opposed to other sources that do not express this information. In this way we can locate the desired information without querying every possible source. Having relevant information for a query, however, does not mean that the source is capable of answering the query completely. It only indicates that the source has some useful information on the query.

To implement source descriptions in OWL, we introduce a `isRelevantFor` predicate in our framework. We use a new namespace `meta` for this predicate. For example, a data source may have the following OWL statement to assert that it has relevant information on individuals of the class `Aircraft`.

```
<meta:isRelevantFor>
  <owl:Class rdf:ID="Aircraft"/>
</meta:isRelevantFor>
```

The load is done asynchronously from the query process. It can check for updates periodically or receive updates directly at a users request. The meta-information is augmented with ontological information in order to ease the reformulation process.

When the DQS receives a query, it will be processed by the Reformulator. Using the meta-information knowledge base, the Reformulator determines which data sources should be queried and what queries should be sent to them. This is currently based on the MiniCon algorithm for relational data sources. In a future development, we will extend the DQS with a peer data management algorithm [10] that generalizes the two common mapping schemes from information integration: local-as-view (LAV), where the local source schemas are defined as views over a global mediated schema, and global-as-view where the global

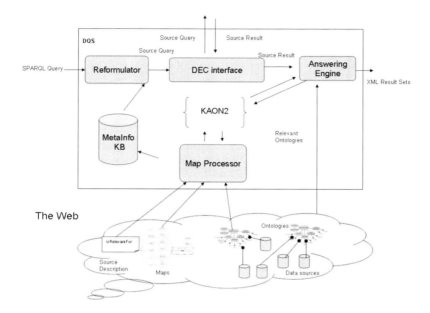

Fig. 3. Architecture of the DQS

mediated schema is defined as a view over the local source schemas. Note, this will reuse much of the MiniCon algorithm we already implemented.

The Reformulator produces a set of ⟨*source id, query*⟩ pairs that are given to the DEC. Using this information, the DEC queries the data sources using their native interfaces and returns the results in a standard format.

The answers returned by the DEC are processed by the Answering Engine. The answering engine loads these answers into the KAON2 knowledge base system. It also loads all relevant ontologies, so that the KAON2 knowledge base represents the subset of data that is relevant to the query. The Answering Engine issues the original query to the knowledge base and outputs the answers in XML format. *Note, by using a knowledge base system here, we are able to benefit from the inferences that KAON2 can derive.* For example, KAON2 can determine the sub classes of a given class. If some of the data is described in terms of a sub class (as opposed to the class mentioned in the query), we will still obtain them in our results. We implemented the DQS (the code for the MiniCon algorithm is part of it) in Java.

3.3 Aircraft Ontologies and Data Individuals

The two ontologies were created independently (one by the Tech-X group and the other by the Lehigh University group) to drive the development and testing of the ISENS system. They consist of about 30/35 classes each, four levels deep, and of about 30/35 object and data properties each. We developed the two ontologies on aircraft and related manufacturers. The rationale for this decision is that information for this domain of knowledge is very easy to obtain off the Internet. Moreover, issues for integrating information relevant to the aircraft industry will, in general, be similar to other enterprise-related domains of knowledge. We show a graph structure for one of the ontologies in Fig. 4.

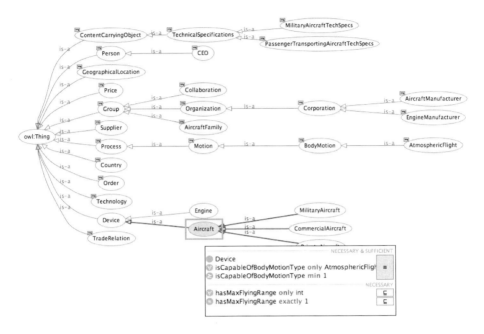

Fig. 4. The asserted model for the Tech-X group ontology and its hierarchy shows how we have modeled the domain of knowledge on aircraft manufacturers and related conceptual entities

We developed the ontologies independently to simulate a real-world scenario where different data centers will generally provide different encoding syntax to the metadata they provide. The integrated access to the data from such heterogeneous sources will then require a system to enable translation among the different encodings. The translation will have to be smart enough to support not only the equivalent object/data types, but also the relations among them.

For the current ISENS set up, the Tech-X ontology[1] (without its related data individuals) and the corresponding Lehigh University group ontology[2] are available on-line.

After a model for the concepts in the ontology has been developed, one can start creating data individuals of the different types supported. Moreover, once

---

[1] http://fusion.txcorp.com/~dad/isens/onto/txcorp/aircraft.owl (the URLs cited here were last accessed in May 2006).

[2] http://swat.cse.lehigh.edu/onto/airdata.owl

we have developed the ontologies to model the domains of knowledge that are of interest, we can design and implement computer programs to automate the generation of RDF/OWL data individuals that describe existing and/or dynamically evolving raw data. We created seven data sets and stored them in seven different PostgreSQL databases that were accessible via our two Sesame RDF servers (see Fig. 1). For each data set, we created one source description file that summarizes the kind of data that can be found in it.

3.4 ISENS Map Ontologies

Since the two ontologies were developed separately, many similar concepts have been modeled using different terms. For example, the Tech-X group defined the concept of commercial aircraft as the class `CommercialAircraft`, whereas the Lehigh University group defined it as `Airliner`. To integrate data sources that commit to these ontologies one needs to formally specify the fact that `CommercialAircraft` is equivalent to `Airliner`. We achieve this in our solution as follows:

```
<owl:Class rdf:about="&txcorp;CommercialAircraft">
  <owl:equivalentClass rdf:resource="&swat;Airliner"/>
</owl:Class>
```

Object and datatype property equivalence is expressed with similar syntax in the map ontology, e.g.:

```
<owl:ObjectProperty rdf:about="&txcorp;wasOrderedBy">
  <owl:equivalentProperty rdf:resource="&swat;soldTo"/>
</owl:ObjectProperty>
<owl:DatatypeProperty rdf:about="&txcorp;wasOrderedOn">
  <owl:equivalentProperty rdf:resource="&swat;sellDate"/>
</owl:DatatypeProperty>
```

An ontology that is a collection of this type of axioms is herein after called a map ontology and each of these axioms is referred to as a map. The complete source code of our map ontology is available[3] on-line.

Mapping ontologies are published using the same OWL syntax that is used to define ontologies that are being mapped. The maps are then available for use by anyone authorized to use the system. *As such, the mapping work performed by one organization can be easily shared with others.* This is in stark contrast to many contemporary integration efforts in which custom code is written for each integration effort.

The use of OWL as a mapping language combined with a suitable description logic reasoner KAON2, allowed us to express more complex maps than mere equivalences. In addition to constructing taxonomical correspondences where we map classes and properties to their sub classes and sub properties, we could also use OWL restrictions to map a defined class with an inferred class. For example:

---

[3] Map ontology URL: http://swat.cse.lehigh.edu/onto/txcorp-swat-map.owl

```xml
<owl:Class rdf:about="&swat;IDS">
  <owl:intersectionOf rdf:parseType="Collection">
    <owl:Class rdf:about="&txcorp;Aircraft"/>
    <owl:Restriction>
      <owl:onProperty rdf:resource="txcorp;hasApplication"/>
      <owl:someValueFrom rdf:resource="txcorp;Military"/>
    </owl:Restriction>
  </owl:intersectionOf>
</owl:Class>
```

While OWL allowed us to achieve an acceptable amount of integration, it should be noted that there were some concepts in the two ontologies that, although similar, were impossible to map using OWL. Consider the property "maximum thrust" of an engine. In the Lehigh group (`swat`) ontology it has been defined as a property of the class `Engine`. However, in the txcorp ontology, an `Engine` is related to its maximum thrust via the `TechnicalSpecifications` class (it models a technical specification document). In First Order Logic, the relationship can be specified as:

$$\texttt{txcorp}:\texttt{Engine}(X) \wedge \texttt{txcorp}:\texttt{hasEngineTechSpec}(X, S) \wedge$$
$$\texttt{txcorp}:\texttt{hasEngineMaxThrustTechSpec}(S, Z) \Leftrightarrow$$
$$\texttt{swat}:\texttt{Engine}(X) \wedge \texttt{swat}:\texttt{maxThrust}(X, S)$$

However, this axiom cannot be expressed in OWL (and most description logics, for that matter) because it requires role composition. Note, this kind of mapping can be supported in certain OWL-compatible rule-based Semantic Web languages such as SWRL, and is likely to be supported in the Rule Interchange Format (RIF) currently being developed by a W3C working group.

3.5 Information Integration Query Test Cases

Here, we consider how information integration over two separately developed ontologies on the same domain of knowledge and data individuals that are distributedly located over multiple databases is handled by the ISENS system prototype. Specifically, we can compare SPARQL queries that can be executed only on one of the separate ontologies to extract the relevant answers from each of them to queries executed by the ISENS system to obtain the answers from both sources at the same time. We used such comparisons to test the data integration achieved by the ISENS system to retrieve data encoded with different ontologies from remotely located data servers.

Moreover, users can query (using specific syntax) distributed RDF/OWL metadata repositories that are encoded with different syntax (from each of the two different ontologies in this case). The ISENS system uses its map ontology in the process of integrating information from the different ontologies. We start with a "simple" mapping example to show this capability. Consider, querying ISENS to find the commercial aircraft it has information about.

The SPARQL query[4]:

```
SELECT ?Aircraft
WHERE { ?Aircraft rdf:type tx:CommercialAircraft .}
```

is in the Tech-X ontology syntax. The DQS uses its ontology maps to determine which data repositories contain relevant data to solve the query from both the Tech-X and the Lehigh University data individuals, thus achieving the desired information integration. The results from executing this query[5] contain the commercial aircraft from both ontologies.

The DQS does the needed logical reasoning to decide to which of the two Sesame RDF servers (and their specific PostgreSQL databases) to issue network calls in order to obtain relevant data for a query from all available RDF/OWL data repositories. The commercial aircraft encoded in the Tech-X ontology syntax are extracted from the Sesame RDF server at Tech-X that stores such data in its "Aircraft" data individuals PostgreSQL database. The commercial aircraft encoded in the Lehigh University group ontology are extracted from their Sesame RDF server and its "Airliner" PostgreSQL database.

Since the DQS has ontology maps to translate concepts between the two ontologies, we can also use the syntax from the Lehigh University group ontology to search for the same information with the following SPARQL query:

```
SELECT ?Aircraft
WHERE { ?Aircraft rdf:type ac:Airliner .}
```

Running this query[6] returns the same results (only in different order) as the ones from the query that used the Tech-X group ontology syntax. These two queries demonstrate that one can publish the ontologies separately from their RDF/OWL data individuals.

The two SPARQL queries above demonstrated the ability of the ISENS system prototype to handle information integration over an OWL object type. In the next example, we show that ISENS provides integration over RDF/OWL object predicates (properties) as well. If one executes[7] the SPARQL query:

---

[4] We present the example SPARQL queries here in a concise form. For each query, we have omitted the appropriate explicit prefix definitions from the set:
PREFIX rdf: <http://www.w3.org/1999/02/22-rdf-syntax-ns#>
PREFIX ac: <http://swat.cse.lehigh.edu/onto/airdata.owl#>
PREFIX tx:
  <http://fusion.txcorp.com/~dad/isens/onto/txcorp/aircraft.owl#>

[5] We have set up a test version of the ISENS system prototype that is available online. We provide here URLs to PHP scripts that can directly execute some of the queries here and display the results ISENS found together with the submitted query (to enable further interaction with the system if necessary). The URL for the above query is:
http://fusion.txcorp.com/~dad/isens/wic/run-dqs-q6.php

[6] http://fusion.txcorp.com/~dad/isens/wic/run-dqs-q6-reversed.php

[7] http://fusion.txcorp.com/~dad/isens/wic/run-dqs-q5.php

```
SELECT ?Aircraft ?Manufacturer
WHERE {
  ?Aircraft rdf:type ac:Airliner .
  ?Aircraft ac:manufacturedBy ?Manufacturer .
}
```

using the Lehigh group ontology syntax, then the data individuals that correspond to aircraft and their manufacturers are properly extracted from the data repository encoded with the Tech-X group ontology syntax (there are currently no such RDF/OWL data individuals in the Lehigh University group ontology). Again, the DQS reasons using its map ontologies to do the data integration/translation and decides from which RDF/OWL data repositories to obtain the relevant answers. For this case, ISENS supports data integration over the `tx:isMadeBy` predicate.

The next SPARQL query:

```
SELECT ?sellOrder ?soldProduct
WHERE {
  ?sellOrder rdf:type ac:Sell .
  ?sellOrder ac:soldProduct ?soldProduct .
  ?sellOrder ac:soldTo
     <http://.../isens/onto/txcorp/aircraft.owl#DeltaAirlines>.
}
```

also uses the Lehigh University group ontology syntax to search for all sell orders to the `DeltaAirlines` data individual. Notice that this individual is in the Tech-X ontology namespace. Only one of the Tech-X RDF/OWL repositories has relevant data for this query. The ISENS prototype again relies on the information integration algorithm in the DQS to find[8] the proper answer.

We have also used KAON2's reasoning capability over numerical datatypes (e.g. ordering) to implement filtering in our queries. When a query has a filtering request, we remove the filtering part of the query and decompose the rest. After we generate the reformulation and load the KAON2 knowledge base, we reinsert the filtering part and issue the whole query. In the future, we plan to implement a variation of MiniCon that supports comparison predicates, which should allow the system to scale to larger datasets.

The final query we consider here:

```
SELECT ?sellOrderID ?sellPriceInUSDollars
WHERE {
  ?sellOrderID rdf:type ac:Sell .
  ?sellOrderID ac:sellAmount ?sellPriceInUSDollars .
  FILTER (?sellPriceInUSDollars > 10 &&
     ?sellPriceInUSDollars < 40)
}
```

---

[8] http://fusion.txcorp.com/~dad/isens/wic/run-dqs-q1-4m.php

shows support for filters over XMLS integer type data properties together with information integration in ISENS. Running[9] this query shows the data individuals that match the imposed constraints. There are, however, current limitations with the support for XMLS data types that we discuss in Section 4.

All of the above queries completed in under two seconds, including network latency. Although this was only a prototype and extensive evaluation is yet to be conducted, we consider these results to be promising.

4 Summary and Future Development

We developed a prototype application, ISENS, based on Semantic Web (including RDF/OWL/SPARQL/SWRL) technologies. The system demonstrates how information integration can be accomplished over two remotely located RDF/OWL data repositories that are encoded with syntax from different ontologies. This was implemented in the DQS component of the ISENS system. It is important to note that for its reasoning tasks the DQS uses the KAON2 logical reasoner [9]. We used the LUBM [11] to evaluate three candidate reasoners (Sesame, OWLIM and KAON2) for use in the DQS. Of these, KAON2 is the only reasoner that is complete. Moreover, KAON2's ability to handle both description logic and rules was one of the key factors that led us to select it. In addition KAON2 is light weight and is available for free if used for research purposes.

The current limitations of the ISENS system prototype are:

1. KAON2 is unable to handle XML schema date data type correctly. As a consequence, the DQS fails to use FILTER queries on the date data type. We have been informed by KAON2's developers that a future release will be able to handle such cases.
2. The system relies on a compilation of the map ontologies and the source descriptions into an intermediate form. In order, to get the prototype working with limited resources, this compilation was performed manually. A full system will need an algorithm to perform this translation automatically.
3. The prototype is designed to work with a two-ontology architecture. However, in the general setting there may be many ontologies, and sometimes multiple maps will need to be composed in order to achieve complete integration.

In future development, we will generalize the DQS to address the current two-ontology architecture limitation. We will use the schema mediation in peer data management systems (PDMS) idea by Halevy *et al.* [10] to design and implement such a system. This is a natural extension to our system because a key component of the PDMS rewriting algorithm is the MiniCon algorithm. However, the PDMS algorithms will have to be extended to be used in a Semantic Web context.

---

[9] http://fusion.txcorp.com/~dad/isens/wic/run-dqs-q2.php

Our experience in implementing the ISENS system prototype and the results from its testing show that this is a feasible approach to build a system for information integration, managing, and sharing of RDF/OWL data that could provide important, new, Semantic Web capabilities.

Acknowledgements

We are grateful to the Department of Energy for supporting this work under a Phase I SBIR grant.

References

1. Halevy, A.Y., Ashish, N., Bitton, D., Carey, M., Draper, D., Pollock, J., Rosenthal, A., Sikka, V.: Enterprise information integration: successes, challenges and controversies. In: SIGMOD '05: Proceedings of the 2005 ACM SIGMOD international conference on Management of data, New York, NY, USA, ACM Press (2005) 778–787
2. Berners-Lee, T., Hendler, J., Lassila, O.: The semantic web. Sci. Am. (2001)
3. Heflin, J.: Towards the Semantic Web: Knowledge Representation in a Dynamic, Distributed Environment. PhD thesis, University of Maryland (2001)
4. Ullman, J.D.: Information integration using logical views. In: Proc. of ICDT, Delphi, Greece (1997) 19–40
5. SPARQL: Query Language for RDF, W3C Working Draft. ("http://www.w3.org/TR/rdf-sparql-query/")
6. Pottinger, R., Halevy, A.: MiniCon: A scalable algorithm for answering queries using views. VLDB Journal: Very Large Data Bases **10**(2–3) (2001) 182–198
7. Broekstra, J., Kampman, A.: Sesame: A generic architecture for storing and querying rdf and rdf schema. In: Proceedings of the 2nd International Semantic Web Conference (IAWC2003), Sanibel Island, Florida. (2002)
8. Aduna: Sesame RDF Framework. ("http://www.openrdf.org")
9. Motik, B.: KAON2: infrastructure for managing OWL-DL and SWRL ontologies. ("http://kaon2.semanticweb.org/")
10. Halevy, A., Ives, Z., Suciu, D., Tatarinov, I.: Schema mediation in peer data management systems. In: Proc. of ICDE. (2003)
11. Guo, Y., Pan, Z., Heflin, J.: An evaluation of knowledge base systems for large owl datasets. In: Proceedings of the 3rd International Semantic Web Conference (IAWC2004), Hiroshima, Japan. (2004) 274–288

NEWS: Bringing Semantic Web Technologies into News Agencies

Norberto Fernández, José M. Blázquez, Jesús A. Fisteus, Luis Sánchez,
Michael Sintek, Ansgar Bernardi, Manuel Fuentes,
Angelo Marrara, and Zohar Ben-Asher

The NEWS Consortium*
info@news-project.com

Abstract. In the current Information Society, being informed is a basic necessity. As one of the main news bussiness actors, news agencies are required to provide fresh, relevant, high-quality information to their customers. Dealing with this requirement is not an easy task, but, as partners of the NEWS (News Engine Web Services) project, we believe that the usage of Semantic Web technologies could help news agencies in achieving that objective. In this paper we will describe the aims and main achievements of the NEWS project, that was just completed.

1 Introduction

The news business is based on producing news items about current events and delivering them to customers. Customers want to receive information about events as soon as they occur. Customers do not want to be bothered with useless information, that is, they want to get information only about events of interest.

Dealing with both requirements, information freshness and relevance, is not easy to do. For instance, state of the art workflows at the news agencies try to address the relevance requirement by adding metadata to news items. These metadata are used to filter the news items according to the interests of each customer. But currently the metadata are added manually by the journalists and this is a time consuming task. Of course the negative effect of this metadata addition overhead can be reduced by restricting the metadata to be added to a few, easy to add, items: news item priority, keywords, editing location, category (economy, sports, ...), etc. This is the approach currently followed by the agencies. For instance, the categorisation is currently done based on small ($\simeq 10$ categories), in-house, category systems, easy to learn and use by the journalists. Finer grained annotations of the news items' contents (like basic entities occurrence) are not currently added. The effect of these restrictions on the set

---

* The NEWS Consortium is composed of news agencies *Agencia EFE S.A.* and *Agenzia ANSA S.C.R.A.L.*, the *Deutsches Forschungszentrum für Künstliche Intelligenz GmbH* Research Institute, *Ontology Ltd.* and *Universidad Carlos III de Madrid* university.

of annotations to be added, is that high quality information filtering services are difficult to implement, which is opposite to the relevance requirement.

So, the current situation at news agencies as the Spanish EFE or the Italian ANSA is that customers access the news content either as a streaming according to their profiles (categories and other basic metadata), *push distribution mode*, or making free text queries over a news item repository, *pull distribution mode*. This of course results in receiving a lot of non-relevant content that the customer should manually filter. Additionally due to the fact that queries over news agencies' repositories are keyword-based, multilingual information retrieval is not feasible: the customer gets news items in the language of the terms (s)he has introduced in the free text query.

The NEWS [1] EU IST project aims at providing solutions which help news agencies to overcome limitations in their current workflows and increase their productiveness and revenues. In order to reach this aim, the NEWS project makes use of state-of-the-art Semantic Web technologies. In that sense, the work developed in this project covers mainly three topics:

Annotation: Implementing a semantic annotation component which automatically produces metadata annotations for news items. In the context of NEWS, the core of this semantic annotation component is the natural language processing (NLP) engine of Ontology Ltd.
Intelligent Information Retrieval: Developing intelligent components for the news domain, with multilingual and multimedia capabilities, which use semantic annotations and ontologies to allow the development of intelligent services for the news domain. In the context of NEWS we have developed a Heuristic and Deductive Database (HDDB) component and the NEWS Ontology [2], which covers the main concepts required in the news domain.
User Interface: We have developed a Web based interface that allows the journalists to access to all the system functionalities.

The components of the NEWS system interact by means of Web Services. The combination of Semantic Web technologies with Web Services results in a quite flexible and open architecture easy to extend, to integrate into the legacy agencies' workflows and with good interoperability properties with other systems. In this paper, we will describe all the NEWS components. A first version of them is currently being tested in real conditions in EFE news agency. The rest of this paper is organized as follows: section 2 describes the annotation component, section 3 describes the HDDB component and section 4 describes the NEWS GUI. Finally, sections 5, with references on some related work, and 6, with concluding remarks, close this paper.

2 Annotation Engine

NEWS realized the automated annotation of news items using NLP engines for several languages. While originally focussed on text this can also support multimedia news item processing. The next two subsections provide a brief technical introduction to the annotation engines and to some experiments that we have performed in the context of NEWS with multimedia news item processing.

2.1 Natural Language Processing Engine

In the context of the NEWS project we are using the natural language processing engine of Ontology Ltd., which provides news item categorization, abstract generation and named entity recognition (persons, organizations, locations). This engine categorizes into the International Press Telecommunication Council [3] (IPTC) categorization system known as Subject Code NewsCodes, (a.k.a. Subject Reference System or SRS) which contains more than 1300 categories.

The engine is based on a hybrid approach to natural language processing, which combines linguistic techniques, based on patterns and linguistic rules, with statistical techniques, used to automatically identify and evolve the linguistic rules. There are a diversity of features that the statistical model of Ontology Ltd. learns and later uses to process texts:

Word stems: The Ontology Ltd. annotation engine performs the linguistic tasks of stemming and part-of-speech tagging (a.k.a morphological normalization).
Complex features: These are pairs, triples and higher-order tuples of related words, e.g. the verb *buy* with the noun *company* serving as its object. Such pair of words conveys a more specific notion than the isolated terms *buy* and *company* and should be treated as one complex feature. The detection of this and other syntatic role dependencies in a large variety of phrase structures is performed using linguistic processing.
Concept classes: Words and expressions that in a specific context play similar roles are grouped into one class and are analyzed statistically as a collective feature (in addition to their treatment as individual features). In the context of *Mergers & Acquisitions*, for example, one may want to consider the shared meaning of the verbs *buy*, *sell*, and *purchase* and the noun *acquisition*. Concept classes can be organized in a hierarchy, either as a tree or as a more general graph, allowing a class to have more than one conceptual parent.

All types of features coexist in the categorization and extraction engines of Ontology Ltd. and interact with each other. In the NEWS project, Ontology's engines process news in Spanish, English and Italian languages.

2.2 Dealing with Multimedia News Items

News agencies not only produce textual news items, but also multimedia items such as photographs, audio and video. In the context of the NEWS project, we have analyzed how these multimedia items can be processed by the natural language processing engine in order to generate automatic annotations about them.

Photographs in a news agency have normally attached a textual description, and some management metadata, such as the date, categories, location or author. The NEWS system can analyze the textual description and annotate persons, locations and organizations related to the photograph. We are evaluating the integration of the NEWS system with the photograph archive of the Spanish news agency EFE, called *Fototeca*. The archive contains now over 2 million photographs and about 1500 new ones are added daily into it.

Regarding audio and video news items, our approach consists in using a speech–to–text tool to transcribe the content of the audio track. The resulting text can be processed by the natural language processing engine. The state–of–the–art speech–to–text tools provide high–quality transcriptions and support many languages. In the environment of NEWS, however, there are some drawbacks: major speech–to–text tools require the system to be previously trained by the speaker, but training for every journalist is not possible; audio tracks of news items are normally recorded in noisy environments with portable equipment, and transferred to the agencies by low–quality channels (e.g. conventional or cellular telephone lines); punctuation marks and capital letters normally need to be dictated in the speech, which is impossible in recorded news items.

We have performed two experiments in order to evaluate the impact of the above–mentioned drawbacks in the quality of the annotations, using a commercial speech–to–text tool: *Dragon Naturally Speaking*. In the first experiment, we trained *Dragon* for one male user and one female user. We applied it to five different audio news items provided by the EFE news agency. When the gender of training and the one of the analysed speaker match we obtained a rate of 70%–80% of correctly transcribed words. Gender mismatch however lead to very poor results.

In a second experiment, we evaluated the impact of the loss of punctuation marks. Our experiment was run over a collection of 171 news items. Each news item was processed twice: once the original version and once without punctuation marks. Comparing annotations of the two versions of each news item, we found that the average error rate is about 20%, considering that an error is an annotation in the original item nor present in the modified one, or vice versa.

Although not perfect, experiments show that our approach produces medium–quality annotations without human intervention, and is a feasible alternative to a high–cost manual annotation system.

3 Heuristic and Deductive Database

The Heuristic and Deductive Database component has three main functions in the NEWS system architecture:

– It acts as a Deductive Database (DDB) which stores the news items and their metadata. This repository can be queried by users (pull distribution mode), or used to implement subscription-based push services. It consist basically of three elements:

- A relational database, which stores the information in the NEWS Ontology and the metadata of the news items.
- A text indexing engine, Lucene [4], used to allow keyword-based queries over the textual contents of news items.
- An inference engine which allows basic reasoning (transitive closure computation) with the NEWS Ontology.

– It uses some heuristics in order to perform context-aware instance identification (so the H in HDDB), mapping entities found by the natural language processing tool to instances in the NEWS Ontology.
– It uses the information inside the NEWS Ontology and the Lucene index in providing basic event recognition features.

The next three subsections will describe in more detail some of the key components of the HDDB: the NEWS Ontology, the instance identification algorithm and the event recognition feature.

3.1 The NEWS Ontology

As stated in section 1, the main objective of the NEWS project is to apply Semantic Web technologies in the journalism domain. Applying Semantic Web technologies to a certain domain of interest requires the definition of ontologies to model such domain. In the context of the NEWS project, we have developed the NEWS Ontology. It is a lightweight RDFS [5] ontology which is composed of three modules:

Categorization Module: Provides the vocabulary for automatic news categorization. It is based on IPTC's Subject Code NewsCodes. The Subject Codes set is a three level hierarchy that consists of Subjects, Subject Matters and Subject Details. The top level contains 17 different Subjects. The full set has about 1300 categories. In the categorization taxonomy module, concrete categories from NewsCodes are defined as RDFS classes.

Management Metadata Module: Taking as basis DC [6], PRISM [7], the management metadata included in news representation standards as NITF [8] or NewsML [9] and the management metadata currently used by news agencies, we have developed a vocabulary to be used in annotating news items with management metadata. It covers, among others, topics like authorship information, news item priority and news item media type.

Content Annotation Module: Provides the basic vocabulary for news content annotation. As in principle almost anything in the world can appear in a piece of news, we have decided to rely on a generic top-level ontology. It is inspired in SUMO/MILO [10] and consist of more than 200 classes and about 100 properties. The module was also populated with instances taken from different information sources like ISO country codes standard ISO 3166:1997-1, CIA WorldFact Book [11], NASDAQ companies codes, SUMO/MILO instances, Web sources as Wikipedia [12], etc. As a result the current version contains more than 11,000 instances of different classes: countries, cities, companies, persons, etc. In order to deal with multilingualism, we have added to the different components in the ontology labels in Italian, Spanish and English. To relate the labels with the ontology elements, we are using Simple Knowledge Organization System, SKOS [13] properties (preferred label, alternative label, description).

3.2 Context-Aware Instance Identification

As we have seen, the NLP engines are able to extract basic entities from text. But in order to achieve fine-grained retrieval results it is not enough to figure out, that the extracted text string *Bush* represents a person, we need to know who is that person by mapping the entity with an instance in the NEWS Ontology.

In order to deal with this problem, the NEWS consortium has developed the IdentityRank algorithm based on PageRank [14]. Basically this algorithm exploits all the information provided by the natural language processing engine (categories, entities) and the news item timestamp as context for entity disambiguation. It is based on two principles:

Semantic coherence: Instances typically occur in news items of certain SRS categories, e.g. president *Bush* in news items of politics category. Also the occurrence of a certain instance gives information about the occurrence of other instances. For example, the spanish F1 driver *Fernando Alonso* usually appears in news items where the F1 Team *Renault* is also mentioned.

News trends: Important events typically are described with several news items covering a certain period of time. For instance when the former Pope died, news items describing such event where composed during several days, most of them including instances as *Vatican* or *John Paul II*.

The process to run the algorithm starts by defining a set of candidate instances for each entity detected in the news item by the natural language processing engine. This can be done by matching the entity text with the labels (in the appropriate language) of the NEWS Ontology's instances. The entity type should also be matched with the instance class to define a candidate instance, so for example we do not considered an instance of class *Region* to be a candidate for an entity of type person.

Once we have all candidate instances of all the entities, we define a semantic network with all these instances. In such semantic network nodes represent candidate instances for the entities in a news item and arcs between two nodes appear when the two instances have cooccured in the past in at least one news item. The category and the timestamp information are taken into account in giving initial weight to the nodes in the semantic network, so if an instance has recently appeared in news items, its node is given more weight. If the instance usually appears in news items of the same SRS category/ies as the news item being considered, its node is also given more weight.

Once the semantic network is defined, we apply the IdentityRank to it. In contrast to classical PageRank, the weight of a node or instance is not divided uniformly between all adjacent nodes, but we give weights to arcs. If two instances typically cooccur, a bigger weight is given to the arc which connects these instances. In any case, both algorithms deliver a ranking of the nodes in the network. By looking at such ranking, we can find in our case the most relevant instances which can be mapped to the entities in the news item.

We have carried out a basic experiment with 30 news items from EFE news agency where the entity *Georgia* of type location appears with an ambiguous meaning, representing either the US state or the Asian country. The results of the experiment indicate that the algorithm produces a correct mapping entity-instance in about the 80% of the situations, but of course more extensive tests need to be performed.

3.3 Event Recognition

News agencies produce news items that describe events, so automatic event recognition is an attractive feature for them. In order to deal with this requirement, in NEWS we had to deal with two complementary aspects: defining what an event type is at the NEWS Ontology and implementing an event type recognition facility.

In NEWS, an event type definition includes a set of SRS categories, which are expected to be associated with the event, and a set of language dependant patterns manually defined by the ontology maintainer. These patterns have an SPO (Subject-Predicate-Object) structure, where subject and object are defined as one of the following three entity types: person, organization or location, and the predicate can include a verb and/or some free text. The P part of the SPO pattern is compulsory, but S and O are optional. Examples of valid patterns could be the following:

S-P-O ORG - (buy|bought|has_bought) - ORG
S-P PER - (say|said|has_said)
P-O (visit|visited|has_visited) - LOC

The event recognition software is based on the Lucene *span query* facility, so uses the information in the Lucene index at the HDDB. Basically a *span* provides information about where a match of a certain token (piece of text, usually a word) has taken place in a document. That position information can be used later in queries. For the purposes of this paper we are mainly interested in the following kinds of Lucene span queries[1]:

SpanTermQuery: Matches spans containing a term. Basically allows to find a certain term or token in a document and its position/s.
SpanNearQuery: Matches spans which are near one another. Developers could specify the *slop*, the maximum number of intervening unmatched positions, as well as whether matches are required to be in-order. For instance, a *span near* query could be built by combining two *span term* queries and providing the slop, the maximum number of positions between the results of such queries.

---
[1] See the Lucene 1.9.1 package org.apache.lucene.search.spans.

SpanOrQuery: Matches the union of its clauses. It is used to combine (with OR logical operator) other span queries.

So, the patterns that we have introduced previously are converted inside the HDDB to rules, each of which consists of a set of span queries to Lucene of the types described above. For instance given the pattern:

ORG buys|bought|has_bought|will_buy ORG

and assuming that the natural language processing engine has found the following entities of type organization: *Intel Corporation* and *Microsoft* inside a news item, the following query would be generated to check the news item for occurrences of the pattern and the corresponding event type:

```
SpanNear(
  SpanNear(SpanTerm(Intel), SpanTerm(Corporation), SLOP=1),
  SpanOr(
    SpanTerm(buy),
    SpanTerm(bought),
    SpanNear(SpanTerm(has), SpanTerm(bought), SLOP=1),
    SpanNear(SpanTerm(will), SpanTerm(buy), SLOP=1)
  ),
  SpanTerm(Microsoft),
  SLOP=15
)
```

If the news item matches the query and is an instance of one of the SRS categories associated to the event (or of one of their subcategories) then an association between the event type and the news item is stored in the relational database of the HDDB.

Note that the mechanism that we have described is based on text queries, so it is language dependent. We make it compatible with our requirement of multilinguality by providing versions in spanish, english and italian for each pattern. In order to make the process of pattern definition simpler to the ontology maintainer, we have implemented a Web Service which receives as input a pattern with a verb in infinitive form and generates variants for the pattern and translations to the different languages. For instance, given the pattern in italian: *bambini vb:giocare calcio* (note that the infinitive in the initial pattern is marked with *vb:*) the suggestion service provides the following alternatives:

en: children (play|played|has_played) soccer
es: niños (juega|jugó|ha_jugado) fútbol
it: bambini (gioca|ha_giocato) calcio

As automatic translation is used in pattern generation, the ontology maintainer should carefully check the results of the process.

4 Graphical User Interface

In order to allow the journalists to access all the NEWS system functionalities, we have developed a Web based graphical user interface accessible via conventional browser. This interface is implemented using Java Server Pages which are served by an Apache Tomcat [15] engine.

The first step that the journalist should perform in order to access the system is authentication. After that, (s)he will have some tabs organized according to the functionalities offered by the system. These tabs are:

Latest News: Push news item retrieval based on user profile.
Browse Knowledge Base: Pull news item retrieval by browsing the NEWS knowledge base.
Query: Pull news item retrieval by querying.
Create NewsItem: News item creation.
Edit Profile: Personalization and user profile definition.

4.1 Latest News

This is the tab being shown by default when the user logs in into the system. Basically its role is to show the latest news items stored in the HDDB filtered according to the information on the user profile (categories, languages, date ranges). These news items are sorted by timestamp, so the first being shown to the user is the most recent one. The information in this tab is refreshed periodically with a period defined by the user in his/her profile.

4.2 Browse Knowledge Base

The NEWS GUI allows different possibilities for browsing the knowledge stored into the HDDB. These are:

Browse by Categories: Allows the user to find the news items that belong to a set of categories of the IPTC categorization system and that have occurred in a specific date range. The user can select one or more categories from any of the levels and (s)he will get the news items that belong to any of those levels or to one of their sublevels, and that occurred in the specified date range.
Browse by Instances: Allows the user to get news items that contain a concrete instance. The tree with the classes of the NEWS Ontology content module is displayed. The user can browse this tree to select the class that contains the instance (s)he looks for. After clicking on the name of the class, (s)he has to click on a "Find Instances" button. This will retrieve all the instances that appear in any news item stored in the database in the selected date range. Finally, the user has to select one of the instances in order to get the news items that contain this instance in the selected date range.
Browse by Properties: Performs a function similar to that of the previous one: find news items that contain instances. However, in this case, these instances are not selected directly, but through the use of properties. First of all the user selects the class of the instance (s)he looks for (for example the class *Human*). When clicking on that class a list of the properties which have

the class as domain or range (for instance *Human works_at Organization*) appears. By selecting a certain property (like *works_at*) a set of instances are shown to the user. If the initially selected class is the domain of the property, the instances are those in the range (*Organizations* in our example) and vice versa. By clicking on an instance (for example *Ferrari*) the user is looking for news items which mention the instance/s of the initially selected class which are related with the selected instance by the selected property (that is, news items talking about *Humans* that *work_at Ferrari* in our example).

Browse by Events: This tab (see figure 1) allows users to get news items related to a concrete event. Events (see 3.3) are related to the IPTC categorization system so the tree with these categories is shown in order to ease the task of finding them. Once the category is selected, a query is sent to the HDDB to get the events that are related to the category. Finally, the user has to choose one of the available events before sending the query and retrieving news items.

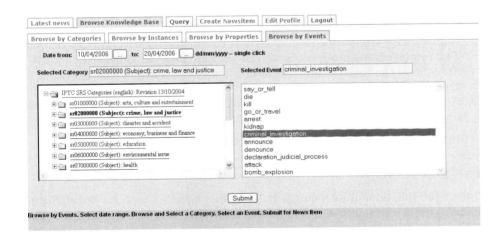

Fig. 1. NEWS Browse by Events Window

4.3 Query

This tab allows the user to introduce queries in order to retrieve news items that satisfy certain criteria. Two kinds of queries can be performed: keyword-based basic queries and advanced queries, where additional restrictions on metadata information can also be specified. The process of performing a basic query is the following:

1. The user enters the terms of the query in the text field.
2. The system tries to match the terms of the query with known instances or entities in the knowledge base in order to perform a semantic search. If there are several possibilities, the user is requested to disambiguate the query.

3. The system looks in the knowledge base for news items that match the entities/instances selected in the previous step. If there are not selected entities nor instances, a full text search is performed.
4. The user can click on a result in order to retrieve the full text of the news item and its metadata, including the entities and instances it is related to.

The advanced query interface permits restricting these results by filtering them by SRS category, news agency, etc.

4.4 Create NewsItem

This tab guides the journalist through the news item creation process, which includes:

1. Manual typing of the content of the news item and some management metadata like priority or edition location.
2. Automatic categorization and annotation of the news item. The results are shown to the user who can validate both the categories and the entities recognized by the annotation engine. During this step the instance identification process takes also place using the information provided by the NLP engine and a Web service at the HDDB to run the IdentityRank algorithm. The results of this process can also be validated by the journalist. The GUI also allows the manual addition of new categories, entities and instances to the news item.
3. Automatic recognition of event types using a Web service at the HDDB and event type validation (and/or addition) by the journalist.

Finally, the news item is sent to the HDDB where it is stored.

4.5 Edit Profile

One of the functionalities required by the news agencies was the possibility of adapting the system to the user. In order to achieve this task the GUI provides the Edit Profile tab. In this tab the user can modify, among others, the following properties:

- Language of the user interface.
- Refresh time of the Latest News tab.
- Preferred categories, language/s and date range for news item filtering in Latest News tab.

5 State of the Art

The news domain has a number of features that make it interesting for running experiences using Semantic Web technologies in real business: data heterogeneity, huge amounts of information to manage, multilinguality, etc. Taking this into account it is not strange to find in the state of the art several projects related with the topic of applying Semantic Web technologies to the journalism domain, like for instance:

NAMIC. The News Agencies Multilingual Information Categorisation project [16] had as main objective to develop and bring to marketable stage advanced NLP technologies for multilingual news customisation and broadcasting throughout distributed services. Though dealing with multilingual and categorization issues in the context of professional journalism, as NEWS, the application of technologies as ontology-based reasoning or a Web Service based architecture were not considered.

KIM. The KIM Platform [17] provides a Knowledge and Information Management (KIM) infrastructure for automatic semantic annotation, indexing, and retrieval of unstructured and semi-structured content. Though the KIM platform can be integrated in different contexts, it has not been designed taking news agencies' specific requirements, as compatibility with journalism standards like SRS, into account.

PENG. The Personalized News Content Programming project [18,?] aims at defining a news content composition and programming environment that provides news professionals with a flexible tool for a user customizable filtering, retrieval and composition of news. Though dealing with the news domain, this is done from a general perspective so again some specific requirements of the news agencies like multilinguism are not directly covered.

MESH. The Multimedia Semantic Syndication for Enhanced News Services project [20] will create multimedia content brokers acting on behalf of users to acquire, process, create and present multimedia information personalized (to user) and adapted (to usage environment). It is an EU funded project that has just started (march 2006) so at the moment there are not available results that can be compared with NEWS achievements.

6 Conclusions and Lessons Learned

In this paper we have described the main achievements of the NEWS project, which has as main objective to bring the Semantic Web technologies into the news domain. Among these achievements we can cite:

1. The development of an ontology for the domain of interest.
2. The design and implementation of annotation mechanisms (categorization, entity extraction and event recognition) in the languages of interest (English, Spanish and Italian).
3. The development of algorithms which allow to match entities detected by the annotation engine to instances in an ontology.
4. The development of intelligent components which exploit the annotations and the information in the NEWS Ontology to perform semantic information retrieval dealing with the multilingualism requirement.
5. The design and implementation of proper user interfaces that allow the journalists to access all the system functionalities in a personalized manner.

A first prototype of the NEWS system has been recently deployed at EFE. We refer the interested reader to [21] for more information on that. Another prototype is available for public access at [22]. As main lessons learned during the project lifecicle we can cite the following:

Integration into existent workflow: NEWS components were required to be easily integrable and interoperable with legacy tools and workflows. In order to do so, we have developed our components as Web services, which provide a modular and flexible solution. For instance, in principle it is possible that the agencies use only some components, or replace in the future ours with others performing similar operations.

Response time: It is crucial in the news domain, where freshness information is a very important concern. In the context of NEWS this requirement of news agencies had one important consequence: reduce reasoning process, which is complex and time consuming. In our case, we have reduced reasoning to query expansion over the NEWS Ontology.

Scalability: Our applications should be able to handle thousands of new news items each day, and to manage repositories containing millions of items. The consequences in NEWS were clear:
- Use as much as possible well-known scalable technologies as relational databases and classical text indexing engines.
- Avoid reasoning to do things which can be easily implemented and performed by classical procedural mechanisms.
- Use offline mechanisms to perform complex operations if possible. For instance, the training process of Ontology Ltd. engine is performed previously to deployment in news agency.

Human Interface: If, as it is the case of NEWS tools, a non technician human user is going to interact with our systems, the design of the human interface is a crucial issue. Multilingual issues, usability, reliability and completeness (it has sufficient options to access all the available functionalities) are all factors to be taken into account. In that sense our experience when deploying the system in news agencies was that classical tree-based ontology browsing mechanisms (that for instance we provide at the GUI to browse the SRS tree and the NEWS Ontology content module tree) were not well accepted by journalists because for them it is sometimes difficult to know where to find the class that they need. As a possible workaround to this problem we provided keyword based navigation to allow to the journalists to look for a specific class by name, but using personalized views of the ontologies is a possibility to be explored in the future.

Acknowledgements

This work has been partially funded by the European Comission under contract FP6-001906 in the framework of the Information Society Technologies (IST) programme.

References

1. NEWS Home: http://www.news-project.com
2. Fernández-García, N.; Sánchez-Fernández, L.; Building an Ontology for NEWS Applications. Poster in the 3rd International Semantic Web Conference, ISWC04.
3. IPTC Home: http://www.iptc.org/
4. Apache Lucene Home: http://lucene.apache.org/
5. RDF Vocabulary Description Language 1.0: RDF Schema. http://www.w3.org/TR/rdf-schema/
6. Dublin Core Metadata Initiative (DCMI). http://dublincore.org/
7. PRISM: Publishing Requirements for Industry Standard Metadata. http://www.prismstandard.org/
8. NITF: News Industry Text Format. http://www.nitf.org/
9. IPTC NewsML Web. http://www.newsml.org/
10. Niles, I. and Pease, A.; Towards a Standard Upper Ontology. In Proceedings of the 2nd International Conference on Formal Ontology in Information Systems (FOIS-2001), Ogunquit, Maine, October 17-19, 2001.
11. CIA WorldFact Book. http://www.cia.gov/cia/publications/factbook/
12. Wikipedia Home: http://wikipedia.org/
13. Simple Knowledge Organisation System, SKOS. http://www.w3.org/2004/02/skos/
14. Page, L.; Brin, S.; Motwani, R and Winograd, T.; The PageRank Citation Ranking: Bringing Order to the Web. http://dbpubs.stanford.edu/pub/1999-66.
15. Apache Tomcat Home: http://tomcat.apache.org/
16. NAMIC: News Agencies Multilingual Information Categorisation. http://www.dcs.shef.ac.uk/nlp/namic/
17. Kiryakov, A.; Popov, B.; Ognyanoff, D.; Manov, D.; Kirilov, A. and Goranov, M.; Semantic Annotation, Indexing and Retrieval. In Proceedings of the 2nd International Semantic Web Conference, ISWC 2003, LNCS 2870, pp 485-499.
18. PENG: Personalized News Content Programming. http://www.peng-project.org/
19. Pasi, G. and Villa, R.; Personalized News Content Programming (PENG): A System Architecture. In proceedings of the 16th International Workshop on Database and Expert Systems Applications (DEXA'05).
20. MESH: Multimedia Semantic Syndication for Enhanced News Services. http://cordis.europa.eu/ist/kct/fp6_mesh.htm
21. Sánchez-Fernández, L.; Fernández-García, N.; Bernardi, A.; Zapf, L.; Peñas, A. and Fuentes, M.; An experience with Semantic Web technologies in the news domain. In Proceedings of the ISWC 2005 Workshop on Semantic Web Case Studies and Best Practices for eBusiness, SWCASE05, CEUR-WS, Vol. 155.
22. NEWS Web Demo. http://corelli.gast.it.uc3m.es:8081/NEWS/ (login: guest, password: guest)

Semantically-Enabled Large-Scale Science Data Repositories

Peter Fox[1], Deborah McGuinness[2,3], Don Middleton[4], Luca Cinquini[4],
J. Anthony Darnell[1], Jose Garcia[1], Patrick West[1],
James Benedict[3], and Stan Solomon[1]

[1] High Altitude Observatory, ESSL/NCAR
PO Box 3000, Boulder CO 80307-3000
pfox@ucar.edu
[2] Knowledge Systems, Artificial Intelligence Lab
353 Serra Mall, Stanford University, Stanford, CA 94305
[3] McGuinness Associates
20 Peter Coutts Circle, Stanford, CA 94305
dlm@cs.stanford.edu
[4] Scientific Computing Division, CISL/NCAR
PO Box 3000, Boulder CO 80307-3000

Abstract. Large heterogeneous online repositories of scientific information have the potential to change the way science is done today. In order for this potential to be realized, numerous challenges must be addressed concerning access to and interoperability of the online scientific data. In our work, we are using semantic web technologies to improve access and interoperability by providing a framework for collaboration and a basis for building and distributing advanced data simulation tools. Our initial scientific focus area is the solar terrestrial physics community. In this paper, we will present our work on the Virtual Solar Terrestrial Observatory (VSTO). We will present the emerging trend of the virtual observatory - a virtual integrated evolving scientific data repository - and describe the general use case and our semantically-enabled architecture. We will also present our specific implementation and describe the benefits of the semantic web in this setting. Further, we speculate on the future of the growing adoption of semantic technologies in this important application area of scientific cyberinfrastructure and semantically enabled scientific data repositories.

1 Introduction

Semantic Web technology has the potential to enable new work paradigms and make vast changes to existing and/or emerging paradigms. One emerging area of scientific work practice where semantic technologies are starting to be used is the area of Virtual Observatories (VOs). VOs [3] are distributed resources that may contain vast amounts of scientific observational data, theoretical models, and analysis programs and results from a broad range of disciplines. Semantics in VOs resemble efforts in the Semantic Grid efforts [5] and science more generally[2].

Currently semantics are mostly usable with the aid of an experienced researcher and only in a narrow domain. One goal of Virtual Observatories is to enable not just expert researchers working in narrow domains to make progress but also to make young researchers and interdisciplinary researchers much more efficient and enable new, global problems to be solved as researchers may now access vast amounts of data that they or others have created. The key to the new efficiency is that users (humans and agents) must now be able to understand what the data is describing, how the data (and topic area) relates to other data (and other topic areas), how the data was collected, and what assumptions are being used. These problems are a perfect match for semantic technologies.

We are using semantic technologies to create an interdisciplinary Virtual Solar Terrestrial Observatory (VSTO) [15]. The work to create a scalable environment for searching, integrating, and analyzing databases distributed over the Internet requires a higher level of semantic interoperability than was previously required by most (if not all) distributed data systems or discipline specific virtual observatories. We leveraged existing background domain ontologies (SWEET) [13] and generated our own ontologies in OWL [10] covering the required subject areas. We leverage the precise formal definitions of the terms in supporting semantic search and interoperability.

Our science domain area - solar and solar-terrestrial physics - utilizes a balance of observational data, theoretical models and analysis/interpretation to make effective progress. Since many of the data collections are increasingly growing in volume and complexity, the task of truly making them a research resource that is easy to find, access, compare and utilize is still a very significant challenge to discipline researchers. The datasets can be highly interdisciplinary as well as complex and provide a good initial focus for virtual observatory work since the datasets are of significant scientific value to a set of researchers and capture many, if not all, of the challenges inherent complex, diverse scientific data.

VSTO addresses the next logical and intellectual challenge for scientific cyberinfrastructure work: that of an interdisciplinary virtual observatory which requires advances both in computer science areas such as knowledge representation and ontology development as well as depth in the science areas of concern to provide an appropriate scientific infrastructure that is usable and extensible.

In this article we describe our Virtual Observatory project, including the vision, our design and implementation. We will describe where we are using Semantic Web technologies and discuss our motivation for using them and some benefits we are realizing. We will also briefly describe our deployment setting which started production late summmer of 2006.

2 Virtual Observatories

The virtual observatory (VO) vision includes a distributed, virtual, ubiquitous, semantically integrated scientific repository where scientists (and possibly lay people) can access data. The VO data repository appears to be local and integrated. In the VO vision, tools exist that make it easy for users to access the data they want.

Additionally, support exists for helping them understand the data, its embedded assumptions, and any inherent uncertainties in a discpline-specific context.

3 The Virtual Solar Terrestrial Observatory

Our VSTO project inherits all of the goals of a general virtual observatory project [8,14] while focusing on the domains of solar and space physics. Our goal is to provide virtual access to specific data, model, tool and material archives containing items from a variety of space- and ground-based instruments experiments, as well as individual and community modeling and software efforts bridging research and educational use.

We have developed a series of use cases sampling the solar-terrestrial problem domain, drawing on existing experience and either fully or partially developed capabilities in existing domain-relevant scientific services. Prior to beginning this project, the National Center for Atmospheric Research already had the CEDAR-WEB [4] (CEDAR - Coupled Energetics and Dynamics of Atmospheric Regions; an NSF focused program covering aeronomy and terrestrial upper-atmosphere studies), Center for Integrated Space-Weather Modeling at Boston and funded by an NSF Science and Technology Center grant, and the Advanced Coronal Observing System (ACOS) at the Mauna Loa Solar Observatory (MLSO) operated by the National Center for Atmospheric Research's High Altitude Observatory. Our team includes members who are key contributors to those existing efforts, some of whom started and/or maintain those systems. This team makeup helps with our efforts involved both in gathering requirements as well as in providing a transition plan for deployment and acceptance in the communities.

3.1 Solar-Terrestrial Use Cases

We have developed a number of use cases for VSTO and in this section we will present the first of these which addresses the state of the neutral terrestrial upper atmosphere. We will describe how this use case (and how some aspects of the other use cases) have contributed to our ontology and semantic web architecture requirements.

Our general use case is of the form "Plot values of a particular parameter as recorded by a particular instrument subject to certain constraints in a particular time period, in a manner that makes sense for the data." An instantiation of this pattern that may be asked of our implemented system is: "Plot the observed/measured Neutral Temperature as recorded by the Millstone Hill Fabry-Perot interferometer while looking in the vertical direction during January 2000 in a way that makes sense for the data."

This use case serves as a prototypical example for our target scientific community, that if answered will help the scientists do their research more efficiently and in a more collaborative manner. Our goal from a semantic web perspective is to demonstrate the development of the semantic framework for a virtual observatory while leveraging existing data sources and (catalog and plotting) services.

The anticipated result is a successful return of a graphical representation of the specified data.

The second use case is in the field of solar physics, specifically assisting a user in finding images of the solar atmosphere from the advanced coronal observing system during a particular time period. This process involves a series of selections similar to the first use case but includes an additional stage of finding preview images prior to the actual data selection. Our goal is the successful identification and selection of solar image data with the successful outcome that the user finds preview images and downloads image data.

In the analysis of the second use case, a substantial similarity with the first use case - observatory, instrument, parameter, dataset, etc. was identified and we added only a few properties and sub-classes to the instrument ontology. As a result of this conceptual similiarity in the workflow we were able to generalize the workflow interface. Figure 1 displays the general workflow within the context of the semantic web framework, including connections to information sources.

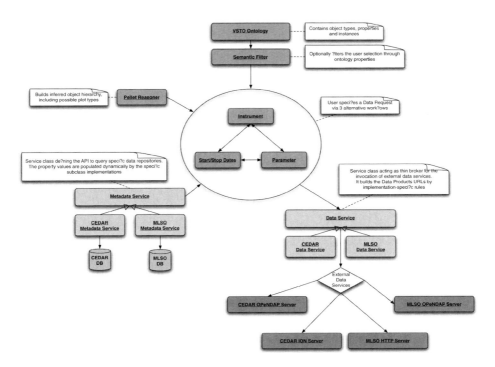

Fig. 1. Generalized workflow for VSTO production release - integrating two use cases from two different disciplines

1. User accesses the portal application (or otherwise accesses application with or without authenticating)
2. User may select from three generic workflows (combination of instrument selection, date-time selection and parameter selection) which are first class

objects in the ontology. At each step, the user selection determines the range of available options in the subsequent steps. The remainder of the information to proceed to a catalog query and thus a data selection request is inferred (using Pellet) from the ontology. At the final stage of the request, we inferred the return data types and possible ways of plotting the data, which includes whether they are time-series, height and time, images, etc.
3. The framework validates the user request: first it verifies that the user is authorized to access the specific kind of data, then it verifies the logical correctness of the request, i.e. that Millstone Hill is an observatory that operates a type of instrument that measures neutral temperature (i.e. check that Millstone Hill is an observatory and check that the range of the measures property on the Millstone Hill Fabry Perot Interferometer subsumes neutral temperature).
4. The application processes the user request to locate the physical storage of the data, returning for example a URL-like expression: find Millstone Hill Fabry-Perot Interferometer data of the correct type (operating mode; defined by a specific operating model since the instrument has two operating modes) in the given time range.
5. The application plots the data in the specified plot type (inferred to be a time series). This step involves extracting the data from records of one or more files, creating an aggregate array of data with independent variable time (of day or day+time depending on time range selected) and passing this to a procedure to create the resulting image.

3.2 Architecture

One of the overriding principles to virtual observatories is to be able to find and retrieve a wide variety of data sources. As a result, the ability to rapidly develop the semantic framework, deploy and test it is essential. Fortunately, the availability of the OWL language, and software tools and plug-ins such as Protégé supported rapid ontology building and additional tools, such as Pellet [11] also supported reasoning and queries for testing.

In Figure 2 the current VSTO architecture is represented graphically. It utilizes the Jena [7] and Eclipse [6] plug-ins for Protégé to generate the Java stub code for the ontology classes and allows the incorporation of existing calls to the CEDAR catalog service for the date and time coverage for the data from the instruments (the remainder of the previous calls to the catalog, implemented in mySQL, are encoded as individuals in the ontology).

The user interface is built on the Spring [12] framework, which enocdes the workflow and navigation features. The examples of the prototype implementation are displayed in later figures. The initial implementation includes the need for reasoning which is implemented via the Pellet reasoning engine which will operate on over 10,000 triples and typically returns results in a few seconds on our deployment platform.

As a part of the implementation, we utilize an existing set of services for returning selections over a large number (over 60 million records) of date/time

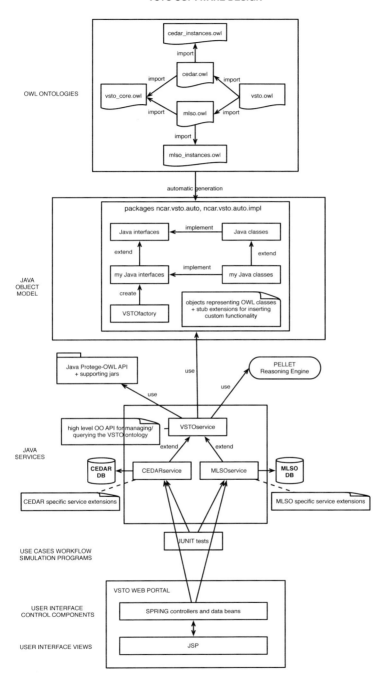

Fig. 2. Overall VSTO software architecture

information in the CEDAR database. We also utilize a set of existing serivces for plotting the returned data which are currently operating in the production CEDARWEB. These services utilize the Interactive Date Language as well as the Open Source Project for Network Data Access Protocol [9] to access the relevant data elements from the data archive. The ability to rapidly re-use these services is an essential and effective tool in our effort to deploy a production data-driven virtual observatory environment.

3.3 Ontology Focus Areas

We began our ontology development process after carefully analyzing our use cases to look for important classes, instances, and relationships between terms. We also looked at critical controlled vocabulary starting points that were either already included in our base implementations of the existing CEDAR and Mauna Loa Solar Observatory services. One such starting point was the controlled vocabulary associated with the CEDAR database which has a long history in the upper atmospheric and aeronomy communities. For a history of the CEDAR program and the CEDAR database, visit the current website - http://cedarweb.hao.ucar.edu. Data in the CEDAR database was arranged around date of observation and a combined observatory/instrument classification. Within each dataset, a series of tables is encoded in a so-called CEDAR binary format which holds the parameters. Each observatory/instrument and parameter has a long name, a mneumonic name and a numeric code.

In developing the ontology, we drew upon the vocabulary of the use case, the existing vocabulary of CEDAR and wherever possible the terms and concepts in the semantic web for earth and environmental terminology (SWEET) ontology. In the case of SWEET, to date there has been limited application to the earth's upper atmosphere (i.e. realms in SWEET terminology) so we adopted parts of SWEET that applied to our needs and for the time being, developed our ontology separately from SWEET but keeping in mind that our aim is to merge much of what we develop back into SWEET for broad use. Our goal was to keep our ontology development separate until we believed it was stable and vetted at two different workshops which brought together domain scientists to discuss foundational earth and space science ontologies and related issues.

One of the first classes to be discussed in the use case was the concept of an instrument, in this case a Fabry-Perot Interferometer (see description below). One of our contributions both to our domain specific work on VSTO and to general work on virtual observatories is our work on the instrument ontology. We constructed a class hierarchy of Instrument (see Figure 3), OpticalInstrument, Interferometer and then Fabry-Perot Interferometer (as known as FPI, for which the Millstone Hill FPI is an individual of the last class). With each class for the initial prototype we added the minimal set of properties at each level in the class hierarchy. The production release features a more complete but still evolving set of properties. across all classes. In the next few paragraphs, we elaborate on a few of the ontology classes in order to give enough background for the impact discussion later.

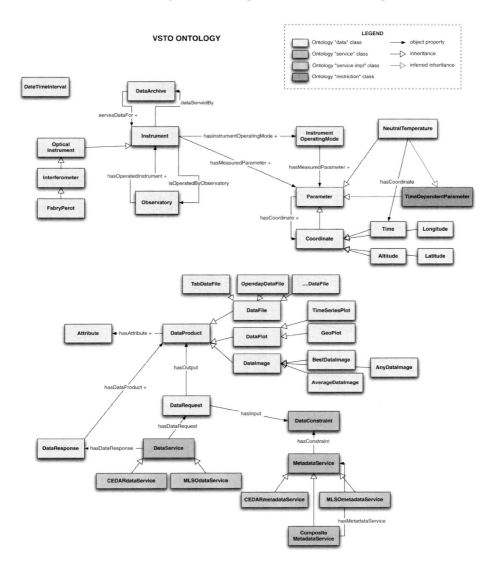

Fig. 3. Schematic of VSTO Ontology 1.0 indicating a variety of classes: for data, service, service implementation and value restrictions. We also indicate a few properties/associations, inheritance and inference.

Instrument: description - A device that measures a physical phenomenon or parameter. At a minimum, it possesses a detector which produces a signal from which the desired quantity is calculated or inferred.

OpticalInstrument: description - Instrument that utilizes optical elements, i.e. passing photons (light) through the system elements which may be reflective and transmissive and may include filters.

Interferometer: description - An instrument that uses the principle of interference of electromagnetic waves for purposes of measurement. Note: Interferometers may be used to measure a variety of physical variables, such as displacement (distance), temperature, pressure, and strain.

Fabry-PerotInterferometer: description - A multiple-beam interferometer. Due to their optical and mechanical configuration, Fabry-Perot interferometers can also be used as spectrometers with high resolution. This description highlights one important attribute of this instrument sub-class which we highlight in a later section: that a "Fabry-Perot interferometer scan be used as a spectrometer with high resolution".

We also have built an initial Instrument class hierarchy as a result of all the instruments utilized in generating the CEDAR and MLSO data holdings. This hierarchy is encoded in OWL and is part of the VSTO framework. Below is an excerpt from the list of the OpticalInstrument class with some subclasses abbreviated in parentheses.

- OpticalInstrument
  - Heliograph {SpectroHeliograph, ... }
  - Interferometer
    * Fabry-PerotInterferometer
    * MichelsonInterferometer   {InfraredMichelsonInterferometer, DopplerMichelsonInterferometer, ...}
  - Imager {AirGlowImager, AllSkyImager ...}
  - Lidar {AerosolLidar, CalciumLidar, DifferentialAbsorptionLidar, DopplerLidar, IonLidar, OzoneLidar, RamanLidar, RayleighLidar, SodiumLidar, StrontiumLidar, ...}
  - Photometer {SingleChannelPhotometer, MultiChannelPhotometer, SpectroPhotometer, ...}
  - Polarimeter {SpectroPolarimeter, ... }
  - Spectrometer {SpectroPhotometer, SpectroHeliograph, SpectroPolarimeter, ...}

In all cases, the class properties are associated with value restrictions, but these are not discussed here.

The next important class is the InstrumentOperatingMode with depends on the Instrument and leads to a particular type of physical quantity (parameter) being measured and an indication of its domain of applicability and how it should be interpreted. Its description is: A configuration which allows the instrument to produce the required signal.

In practice for terrestrial atmosphere use case the instrument operating mode indicates which direction the FPI is pointing, i.e. vertical, or "horizontal" - actually 30° or 45°. Knowing these modes is critical for understanding and using the data as different quantities are measured in each mode and geometric projection, i.e. north component of neutral wind has to be calculated correctly depending on the mode.

Also shown in Figure 3 is the Observatory class, whose description for the sub-class GroundBasedObservatory is: A facility which houses and operates one or more instruments either synoptically or periodically. It has a physical location and operating hours. It can be either manned or remote.

An important part of the use case is the actual quantity that a user (scientist) is seeking. This entity is captured in the class Parameter (also known as PhysicalQuantity in SWEET). Its description is: A measured physical property in signal units. It has units and possibly a timestamp. The signal units are not the physical ones, like Gauss or Kelvin, but are something inherent in the detector, like volts. The physical units are either calculated or inferred from the signal units.

In developing a production implementation of the VSTO it has been essential to make the connection between the high-level concepts of the ontology classes all the way to the data itself. This entails the data files, the data constraints, and the underlying catalogs, and data and plotting services - all of which have been in existence for some time and are made available from distributed network sites and accessed via common internet protocols (ftp, http, web services, etc.). Thus we fill out the ontology with data-related classes (see Figure 3).

Dataset: description - A collection of observations of the physical quantity of interest. They usually have a location, observatory, instrument, and parameter (or set of parameters) associated with them. They also have a format along with an epoch over which they were taken.

Perhaps the most important property of the Dataset class is: hasContainedParameter, which is the asserted association with the Parameter class which in turn connects to the instrument, etc.

For a user of the VSTO, the creation of a data product based on the series of user choices and available data constraints. We represent this at the DataProduct (and associated Request, Service and Metadata) classes which we will not give details on in this paper.

Additional, data-related classes are as follows:

DataRequest: description - Generic class representing a request for data. The class contains both the information necessary to define the data to be extracted (input), and the form of the resulting data product (output).

Dataservice: description - Generic class representing the outcome of a data request to a service. It acts as a wrapper for a collection of DataProduct objects.

MetadataService: description - Generic class that defines the functionality for querying metadata information from a data archive. The results of the query may be constrained by an associated DataConstraint object. Instances of MetadataService and DataConstraint are created on demand to support a transient query session.

As a final integrating theme, the parameters and instruments of interest have a physical domain of influence which needs to represented. In use case for the terrestrial atmosphere, the SWEET-equivalent class AtmosphereLayer: contains layers known as: Thermosphere which ranges from 80-85 km (i.e. the upper boundary of the Mesosphere) to greater than $\approx$ 640 km.

A final note for the ontology development is that for the classes included in the current implementation, we encode all the individuals within the ontology except for the date and time (class: DateTime). The latter is a practical choice due to the large number of specific instances of date and time records associated with the diverse set of instrument datasets associated with both use cases. Thus, we implement a set of service classes to execute queries and retrieve results from the underlying (SQL) catalogs for each set of data holdings.

3.4 Discussion

Ontologies are used throughout the workflow to guide the user through the consecutive selection steps leading to the final service request. By representing physical instruments and their output streams as concrete instances of classes the application is able to follow the relationships between classes so to always present to the user a range of sensible valid options that greatly reduces the amount of specific knowledge the user needs to already posses about the data.

Our application includes an ontology covering important domain concepts (observatories, instruments, operating modes and parameters). We have found that the ontology can be easily reused in related efforts and additionally found it to be more flexible and extensible than a traditional database-like system.

Our ontologies include annotations at the class, instance, and property level and these annotations contain formal as well as informal descriptions. These descriptions may be used by domain experts (scientists and researchers) as well as by other application users (other scientists from the same or different domain as well as teachers, students, etc.).

We are not simply using ontologies for straightforward class subsumption and instance recognition. With the help of a reasoning engine we are also using them to infer the possible plot type based on the selected parameter. Plot type possibility deduction reduces the level of knowledge required from users and is possible because of the combination of reasoning and declarative background knowledge encoding.

In addition to this simple inference, there are many related and valuable inferential requirements for our application areas. One example inference is the selection of instruments that measure the 'same' parameter. Previously, users needed to know a significant amount of domain-specific information to be able to guess or choose which other classes of instruments or specific instruments were relevant. The semantic framework can not only infer this information but also explain how the inference was made.

A second example of inference is highlighted by our first use case (see the description of FPI above) where the FPI is able to operate as a spectrometer, i.e. an interferometer operates as something else in the OpticalInstrument class hierarchy. As a result, we can infer this in such a way that the framework uses inheritance but does not give up or need to override any properties on the spectrometer. Thus, a user seeking a particular type of spectral intensity (parameter) measurement, e.g. over a certain wavelength with high spectral resolution would be able to find not only data from spectrometers but also from Fabry-Perot Interferometers, the latter being an unknown source of data.

Our work in ontology-supported virtual observatories in two fairly distinct discipline-specific use cases has come together to allow us to produce an integrated ontology for semantic integration of solar terrestrial scientific integration. The resulting overall ontology which is used to generate the semantic framework is thus based on the core set of ontologies and then includes discipline-specific classes and instances for each of the solar and terrestrial upper atmospheres.

Prior to the production release we made the new portal available for internal testing to a group of science and data literate users who were very familiar with the existing services and had specific functional requirements. We also solicited input and evaluations from domain experts on our ontology developments both at small workshop and large national and international conferences where we presented, talks, posters and demonstrations. Now that the portal is released we will perform an evaluation study in about six months.

3.5 Status

The generalized workflow for our use cases (see Figure 1) implement data service capabilities for two significant scientific overlapping but distinct communities. The CEDAR community has over 1200 participants, ≈ 600 of which are registered and active users of the CEDAR data holdings which comprise ~ 1370 datasets, and over 320 distinct instruments/data sources. The ACOS instrument suite has an active user community base (ranging from individuals to agencies) of ≈ 120 and features $\sim 300,000$ datasets with a total archive size of ≈ 10 TBytes.

The VSTO portal supercedes the existing operation of both the CEDAR instruments and ACOS web-based data search and retrieval. As such, the semantic framework described above and implemented within the initial VSTO immediately has a large user base and delivers a wider range of functionality over the existing datasets.

After initial work on designing use cases and our architecture, and identifying existing data services that could be leveraged (such as the CEDARWEB data retrieval services), we implemented a prototype interface. After testing and demoing that prototype, we implemented a second use case and continued to populate the ontology and add the required additional services to support the production implementation.

The production interface features a full population of the ontology classes in Figure3, including all individuals (except date and time). As a result of encoding these parts of the ontology the performance of the interface to progression through the workflow is much faster than the existing CEDARWEB interface which queries the SQL catalog as required for all steps in the workflow.

The production VSTO portal also accommodates the security and audit mechanisms in place for the existing CEDARWEB site. At present, we utilize existing data and plotting services for the production VSTO portal and document these services in OWL-S.

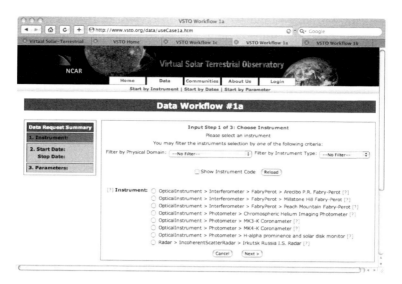

Fig. 4. VSTO 1.0 production portal for instrument selection, with possible domain and semantic filter operations

3.6 Conclusion

We have prototyped and deployed a production quality semantically-enabled data framework to support two large, heterogeneous, online repositories in the area of solar, and solar-terrestrial physics. We have utilized numerous semantic web technologies in the process of searching and accessing the data and created an interoperable and dynamically configurable framework. We see this as a major step toward a virtual integrated evolving scientific data repository.

We have found significant benefit in encoding the formal descriptions of terms in OWL and using inference to provide completion. The primary benefits are (i) reducing input specification requirements thus decreasing input burden and more importantly (ii) allowing users to be able to create correct (and non-over constrained) queries without needing to have expert-level knowledge. Previously, we noticed non-experts having dificulty generating error data requests.

In this implementation we also made practical choices as to what level of detail of the science and processing concepts we encoded in OWL and what aspects of the search, access and services we defer to, and thus re-use, existing services.

We are presently implementing the next series of use cases which are enabling us to further populate the ontologies and validate them. For example, on instantiation of the next use case is: "Find data which represents the state of the neutral atmosphere anywhere above 100km and toward the arctic circle (above 45N) at any time of high geomagnetic activity." The vocabulary of this use case has much less direct mapping to the classes in the first use case and thus additional terms and additional reasoning based on properties of the existing classes is required.

Finally, in the medium term we are exploring options for using our semantic framework and rapid prototyping environment to develop a configurator within specific disciplines to enable the assembly of a virtual observatory within that discipline, or specific to a project/task based using a subset of our ontology.

Acknowledgements

VSTO is an NSF Shared Cyberinfrastructure project under award 0431153 and SESDI is a semantic science data integration project sponsored by NASA Advancing Collaborative Connections for Earth-Sun System Science (ACCESS) and NASA Earth-Sun System Technology Office (ESTO) under award AIST-QRS-06-0016.

References

1. Advanced Coronal Observing System (ACOS), http://mlso.hao.ucar.edu
2. Tim Berners-Lee, Wendy Hall, James Hendler, Nigel Shadbolt, and Daniel J. Weitzner 2006, Enhanced: Creating a Science of the Web, *Science*, **313** #5788, pp. 769-771, DOI: 10.1126/science.1126902
3. The US NVO White Paper: Toward a National Virtual Observatory: Science Goals, Technical Challenges, and Implementation Plan, 2001, Virtual Observatories of the Future, *ASP Conference Proceedings*, **225**, Ed.; Robert J. Brunner, S. George Djorgovski, and Alex S. Szalay, San Francisco: Astronomical Society of the Pacific, p.353
4. http://cedarweb.hao.ucar.edu
5. De Roure, D. Jennings, N.R. Shadbolt, N.R. 2005, The semantic grid: past, present, and future, *Proceedings of the IEEE*, **93**, Issue: 3, pp. 669-681, DOI: 10.1109/JPROC.2004.842781
6. http://www.eclipse.org/
7. http://jena.sourceforge.net/
8. http://www.us-vo.org
9. Open source Project for Network Data Access Protocol (OPeNDAP), http://www.opendap.org
10. Deborah L. McGuinness and Frank van Harmelen. OWL Web Ontology Language Overview. World Wide Web Consortium (W3C) Recommendation. February 10, 2004. Available from http://www.w3.org/TR/owl-features/
11. http://www.mindswap.org/2003/pellet/
12. http://www.springframework.org/
13. http://sweet.jpl.nasa.gov
14. http://virtualsolar.org
15. http://www.vsto.org, http://vsto.hao.ucar.edu

Construction and Use of Role-Ontology for Task-Based Service Navigation System

Yusuke Fukazawa, Takefumi Naganuma, Kunihiro Fujii, and Shoji Kurakake

Service & Solution Development Department, NTT DoCoMo, Inc.
NTT DoCoMo R&D Center, 3-5 Hikari-no-oka, Yokosuka, Kanagawa, 239-8536 Japan
{fukazawayuu, naganuma, fujiiku, kurakake}@nttdocomo.co.jp

Abstract. We have been developing a task-based service navigation system that offers to the user for his selected services relevant to the task the user wants to perform. We observed that the tasks likely to be performed in a given situation depend on the user's role such as businessman or father. To further our research, we constructed a role-ontology and utilized it to improve the usability of task-based service navigation. We have enhanced a basic task-model by associating tasks with role-concepts defined in the new role-ontology. We can generate a task-list that is precisely tuned to the user's current role. In addition, we can generate a personalized task-list from the task-model based on the user's task selection history. Because services are associated with tasks, our approach makes it much easier to navigate a user to the most appropriate services. In this paper, we describe the construction of our role-ontology and the task-based service navigation system based on the role-ontology.

1 Introduction

The mobile Internet is expanding dramatically from various viewpoints, such as the number of subscribers and the volume of mobile contents[2]. As the mobile Internet gains in popularity, information retrieval must be made easier and more efficient. Towards this goal, we proposed a task-based service navigation system[1][3] that supports the user in finding appropriate services. Naganuma et al. proposed a method for constructing a rich task-model that represents a wide variety of user activities in the real world. Part of the task-model is shown in Fig.1. The connection between tasks is expressed by the *is-achieved-by* relation. The upper nodes of the task-model have generic tasks, while the lower nodes have more concrete tasks; the end nodes provide associations to services or contents via their URI. To use the task-model for service navigation, the user enters a task-oriented query such as "Go to theme park" and a list of tasks that match the query is sent to the mobile device. The user selects the most appropriate task and, in turn, the corresponding detailed sub-tasks are shown to the user. By repeatedly selecting a task and its sub-tasks, the user can clarify the demand or problem, and when the user reaches an end-node task, appropriate services associated with the selected task in the service DB are shown; a service is invoked by clicking its URI link.

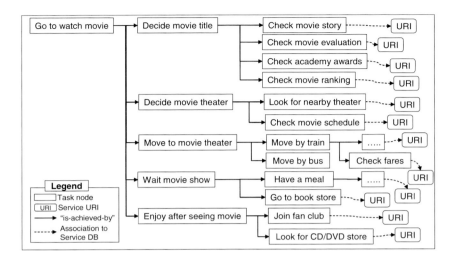

Fig. 1. View of a part of task-model[1]

The above task-model aims at modeling general real world activities that could be performed by the average mobile user. In order for an individual user to access the task-model more effectively, we need to generate a task-list appropriate for the individual user, which would make the user's task-selection process easier. Achieving this goal is particularly important when the user uses a mobile phone since mobile phones have small displays and poor input devices.

Our proposal for generating the task-list appropriate for the individual user is to use the role-concept as the most important factor in selecting tasks or services from the task-model and service DB. In order to use role-concept appropriately, we must categorize the many different roles user can play in the real world and make their relations clear. For this purpose, we have constructed a role-ontology. We have also designed an enhanced service navigation system that uses the role-ontology.

We briefly explain the idea of role-concept in the following. As per Masolo's definition[4], humans can play several roles simultaneously, "FamilyRole" and "ShoppingCustomerRole", and a role can change dynamically in the real world such as "ShoppingCustomerRole" to "TrainPassengerRole" when the user leaves the shop and takes a train. We use this idea of roles in the real world to realize task-based service navigation. That is, we assume that the user can play several roles simultaneously when selecting a task. We define two types of roles; **task-roles** depend on the task selected by the user (i.e. "ShoppingCustomerRole") while **social-roles** depend on the relationship to the surrounding people (i.e. "FamilyRole"). By storing the user's history of tasks selected under both social-roles and task-roles, we can generate a personalized task list and services that match the user's current social-role and task-role.

The remainder of this paper is organized as follows. Section 2 describes our constructed role-ontology and shows how the task-model can be enhanced by the roles defined in the role-ontology. Section 3 describes our task-based service navigation system that can generate a personalized task-list and services according to the current user's role. Section 4 concludes this paper.

2 Role-Ontology for Task-Based Service Navigation System

In this chapter, we describe our role-ontology, which is used together with the task-model to guide the user to most appropriate services. Prior work is described in the next section. How we represent the role-concept is described in Section 2.2. The constructed role-ontology is described in Section 2.3 and the enhanced task-model is shown in Section 2.4.

2.1 Prior Work

In the knowledge representation field, role-ontology has been studied in order to construct an accurate domain-ontology (conceptualization of knowledge domain) by strictly separating the role concept from the objective domain.

Sowa distinguished between natural types "that relate to the essence of the entities" and role types "that depend on an accidental relationship to some other entity"[5]. In his subsequent work, he asserts that role types are subtypes of natural types[6]. For example, the role types *Child*, *Pet* and *Quotient* are subtypes of the natural types *Person*, *Animal* and *Number*, respectively.

In developing Sowa's ideas further, Guarino makes an ontological distinction between role and natural types, and this has been adopted as the basic notion by other researchers in handling the role-concept in ontology[7]. In his notion, a role is a concept that is supported by other concepts while, on the other hand, a natural type is characterized by being free to stand independent from any relationship with others. For example, *Person* is a natural type since to be a person is independent of any relationships with other concepts and an individual person will always remain a person. On the other hand, *Student* is a role since to be a student requires entrance to university and a student stops being a student when he/she drops out or graduates.

Fan et al. noticed that role is heavily dependent on events, and stated that "the representation of role-concept is an extensional features of an entity that are due to its participation in some event"[8]. Sunagawa et al. noted that the relationship between context and role was decided by the context and proposed two relations, the *part-of* relation and the *participant-in* relation, and developed the ontology construction tool named *Hozo*, which can represent these relations[9].

Work to date has discussed how the role-concept and its relation to other concepts (such as natural type, instance, and other role concepts) must be represented in a knowledge-base or ontology. However, no approaches utilizing the role-ontology to generate a UI that can reduce the user's effort in reaching the

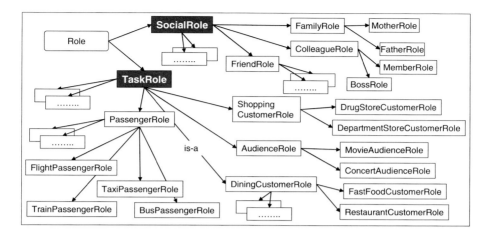

Fig. 2. Role-ontology for task-based service navigation system

objective resource have been published so far. In this paper, we construct a role-ontology appropriate for the task-based service navigation systems explored in our previous work[1]. We then propose a new task-based service navigation system that can generate a task-list according to the current user's role and personalize it appropriately.

2.2 Representation of Role-Concept

The role-concept continues to attract researchers from different areas such as linguistics[10], knowledge representation[5], relational database[11], and access control[12]; a significant amount of research has been done to date.

Despite the many different ways in which the role-concept has been used, the number of ways roles have been represented is rather small. Steimann[13] examined more than 50 papers and identified three common ways of representing roles. In the following, we explain two role representations. First, the role can be represented by the relationships between roles. In the examples above, the relation *is-a* can represent the relationship between "PassengerRole" and "TrainPassengerRole". Second, the role can be expressed by the relationship between role-concept and another concept. For example, the relation *is-played-by* can represent the relationship between task-concept "Go to watch movie" and the role "MovieAudienceRole".

One aim of this paper is to construct a role-ontology and then enhance the task-model through the addition of the role-concept. We use the first way of representing role-concept to represent the relationship between role-concepts in role-ontology. We use the second way of representing role-concept to represent the relationship between task (defined in task-model) and role-concept.

2.3 Discussion of Role-Concept and Constructed Role-Ontology

In this section, we discuss how the user can play several roles in the task-selection process, and then the constructed role-ontology is explained. We start by adapting the definition of roles given in[4]; 1) role is a property assigned to humans, roles can change dynamically, and 2) humans can have multiple roles simultaneously. We adapt the 1st property by supposing that the user changes a role when selecting a task, which we call the task-selection process. For example, the user plays "MovieAudienceRole" when the user selects "Go to watch movie", and if the user selects "Move to movie theater" from the child nodes of the previously selected task, the user's role changes to "PassengerRole". We define these roles that can change during the task-selection process as **task-roles**.

We adapt the 2nd property by supposing that user can play multiple roles during the task-selection process. In the task-selection process, the user can select just one task from the task-list; therefore the user has only one task-role as per the above definition. Other than the task-role, we define the **social-role**; it is decided by the people the user wants to do the task with, such as family or friends. The user can play both a task-role and a social-role simultaneously. For example, if the user selects the task for planning to go to watch movie at the weekend with Family, the user plays both "FamilyRole" and "MovieAudienceRole" simultaneously in the task-selection process.

We have constructed the role-ontology by using both of these defined role-concepts; task-role and social-role, and the relationships introduced in the previous section. The constructed role-ontology is shown in Fig.2. The concept "role" has two top-level role concepts: "social-role" and "task-role". As mentioned in the previous section, the relationships between role-concepts are expressed using *is-a* relation. For example, task-role has role-concepts such as "PassengerRole", "AudienceRole", "ShoppingCustomerRole" and "DiningCustomerRole" as its child nodes. On the other hand, social-role has role-concepts such as "FamilyRole", "FriendRole" and "ColleagueRole" as its child nodes.

2.4 Enhancing Task-Model with Roles

In this section, we explain the enhancement of the task-model through application of the constructed role-ontology. As we described in the previous section, the task-role can change according to the task selected by the user. Therefore, in order to catch the change in task-roles and recommend the services appropriate for the current task-role, we need to express the relationship between the task and the task-role. For this we use the relation *is-played-by* introduced in Section 2.2.

Fig.3 shows a part of the task-model in which task-roles are related to task nodes. The node "Go to watch movie" has five children nodes, one of which is "Move to movie theater". The node "Go to watch movie" is associated with the task-role "MovieAudienceRole" by the *is-played-by* relation. This relation indicates that the task is performed by the user who plays the designated task-role. The node "Move to movie theater", on the other hand, is associated with

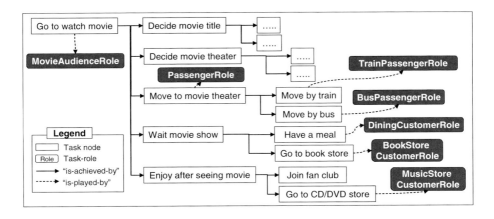

Fig. 3. Enhancement of task-model using role-concept defined in role-ontology

the task-role "PassengerRole". By associating the task with the task-role, we can recognize that the user plays "MovieAudienceRole" when the user selects "Go to watch movie". In addition, we can capture the change in user's role to "PassengerRole" if the user selects "Move to movie theater" from the child nodes of the previously selected task. Note that some nodes in Fig.3 have no corresponding task-roles; these nodes take the task-role of their parent.

2.5 Reasoning Functionality of Role-Ontology

Our proposed role-ontology is not only used for clearly distinguishing between the various kinds of roles, but also for supporting determining task candidates, their order, and recommended services appropriate for current user's social-role/task-role by using the *is-a* relation defined in role-ontology. Basically, these determinations can be done based on the relationship between task and current user's social-role/task-role, which can be found in enhanced task model shown in Fig.3 and user's task selection log, see Table 1. However, there is a possibility that we cannot find the task that has relationships to the current task-role or current social-role, and as a result, we cannot make the above determinations. We deal with this problem by using the *is-a* relation defined in role-ontology and make the above determination by reasoning from the relationship between the task and the child/parent role of current task-role or social-role. Details of these determination of the task candidates, their order, and recommended services for each task candidate are described in Sections 3.2, 3.3 and 3.4, respectively.

3 Enhanced Task-Based Service Navigation

In this chapter, we propose task-based service navigation as realized by the enhanced task-model and the role-ontology. The overall process of enhanced task-based service navigation is shown in Fig.4.

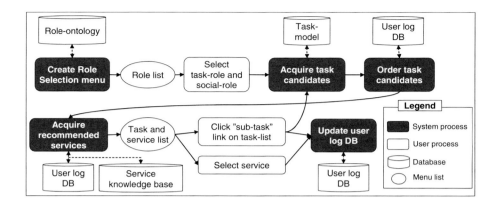

Fig. 4. Overall processes of enhanced task-based service navigation

In the following section, we explain the system processes in the figure, acquisition of user's current social-role and task-role in Section 3.1, acquisition of task candidates in Section 3.2, acquisition of recommended services for each task candidates in Section 3.3, and personalization of task-list including updating user log DB and ordering task candidates in Section 3.4.

3.1 Acquisition of User's Current Social-Role and Task-Role

The role-selection menu is generated in order to acquire the user's current social-role and task-role. A screenshot of a generated social-role selection menu is shown in the upper part of Fig.5(a). The social-role selection menu consists of the child nodes of the social-role as defined in the role-ontology such as "FamilyRole", "FriendRole" and "ColleagueRole". "None" is not a role-concept but means that the user is considering to do the task by himself. A screenshot of a generated task-role selection menu is shown in the lower part of Fig.5(a). This role-selection menu is customizable. By selecting "edit this menu" link on the role selection menu, social-roles and task-roles can be added to the role-selection menu by selecting additional roles from the role list.

3.2 Acquisition of Task Candidates

This section describes the generation of task-candidates. The "Determine task candidates" step in Fig.4 has two inputs from other processes; 1)"select task-role and social-role", and 2)"click sub-tasks", as explained below.

After the user selects task-role, tasks associated with either the selected task-role or child node role-concept of the selected task-role, are acquired from the enhanced task-model. For example, if the user selects "Audience" from the

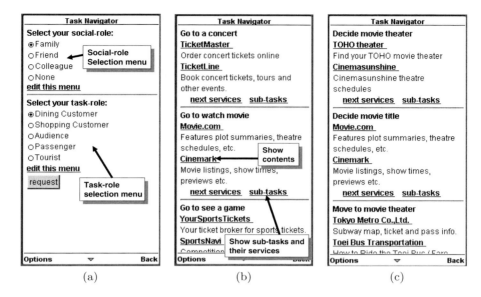

Fig. 5. Screenshots of service navigation;(a)role-selection menu, (b) task-list and recommended services when user selected "Audience Role" from the role-selection menu shown in (a), (c)task-list and recommended services when user clicks "sub-tasks" link of "Go to watch movie" from the task-list shown in (b)

task-role menu, the user's current task-role is judged as "AudienceRole". We acquire the task candidates; "Go to watch movie", "Go to see a play", "Go to a concert" and "Go to see a game", which are associated with the child roles of "AudienceRole" such as "MovieAudienceRole", "PlayAudienceRole", "ConcertAudienceRole", and "GameAudienceRole", respectively.

We create the task selection menu list (task-list) as shown in Fig.5(b). Each task candidate in the task-list has two kinds of links to the other task-list; the links named "sub-tasks", and the links to recommended services for each task candidate. The links to the recommended services take the user to the mobile contents, which user can use to accomplish the user's task. The links named "sub-tasks" can refine the user's demand by showing a list of the sub-tasks of the task candidate and their services. If user clicks "sub-tasks", sub-tasks associated with the task of clicked "sub-task" are extracted from the enhanced task-model as new task candidates. For example, if the user selects "Go to watch movie" from the task-list shown in Fig.5(b), the new task candidates; "Decide movie title", "Decide movie theater", "Move to movie theater" and "Enjoy after seeing movie", which are associated with the task "Go to watch movie", are acquired. We create the task-list using the acquired task candidates, and their recommended services as shown in Fig.5(c).

3.3 Determining Services for Each Task Candidate

This section presents the process of determining the recommended services for each task candidate. In the system proposed by Naganuma et al., the user first selects the generic task, which is an upper node of the task-model such as "Go to watch movie", and gradually refines the demand by repeatedly selecting the specific task associated with the generic task in a tree structure. When user reaches the end-node task, user can find the services to accomplish the task. In our method, we recommend the typical services together with generic tasks (task candidates shown at the beginning) which can reduce the number of operations the user must perform in finding and selecting the desired task.

While refining the task candidates, the user can play not only the task-role associated with the task-candidates but also other task-roles associated with the sub-tasks of the task-candidate. For example, the user can play not only "MovieAudienceRole" but also task-roles such as "PassengerRole", "MusicStoreCustomerRole", "DiningCustomerRole" while refining the task candidate "Go to watch movie" as shown in Fig.3.

It is clear that the task-role played most frequently while refining the task candidates will depend on the individual. Therefore, we realize the personalization of recommended services by determining services according to the task-role history, which is different among individual users. Our method of using the user's history of task-selection to acquire this task-role is described in the next section. After determining the task-role, we acquire the services associated with the end-node task, which is associated with the determined task-role, from the end-node sub-tasks of the task candidate. If there are no such end-node tasks, we use *is-a* relations defined in the role-ontology to determine the recommended services. Concretely, we search for end-node tasks whose associated task-role is a child task-role of the determined task-role.

We show here an example of acquiring the recommended services for the task candidate "Go to watch movie" assuming that the determined task-role played most frequently while refining the task candidate is "MovieAudienceRole". At first, the end-node sub-tasks of the task candidate "Go to watch movie", are acquired such as "Check movie evaluation", "Check movie schedule", "Check fares", "Look for CD/ DVD store" etc. from the enhanced task-model shown in Fig.3. Next, we acquire the tasks associated with the determined task-role "MovieAudienceRole" from the acquired end-node tasks. In this case, both "Check movie evaluation" and "Check movie schedule", which inherit the task-role of "MovieAudienceRole" from their parent task node, are acquired. Next, we acquire the services associated with these acquired end-node sub-tasks and present the services as recommended services for the task candidate "Go to watch movie" such as "Movie.com" and "Cinemark". We show the recommended services below the links of each task candidate as shown in Fig.5(b).

We show here another example of acquiring the recommended services "Move to movie theater" whose task-role is "PassengerRole" in Fig.5(c), we must find the end-node tasks whose task-role is "PassengerRole" and acquire the services

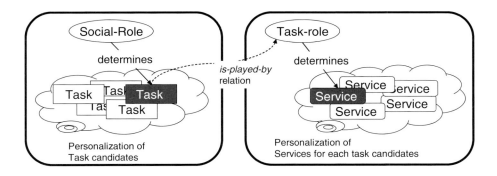

Fig. 6. Personalization of task and services in terms of role-concept

associated with the tasks. However, there are no such end-node tasks whose task-role is "PassengerRole" as shown in Fig.3. Instead, we search for end-node tasks whose task-role is a child task-role of "PassengerRole" such as "TaxiPassengerRole" and "TrainPassengerRole", and acquire the services associated with these end-node tasks.

3.4 Personalization Based on User's Task-Selection Log

We observe that the social-role the user plays determines the user's task, which is socially limited, and the task-role, on the other hand, determines the services or lower level tasks that the user needs to accomplish the task determined by the social-role (Fig.6). For example, when the user is with family, the user sometimes go to see a movie, and always uses the services "Tokyo metro" to check train timetable and "Cinemasunshine" to check movie schedule. In this case, the user is prone to executing the task "Go to see a movie" while playing "FamilyRole" and is prone to use the services of the lower level task "Check train timetable" and "Check movie schedule" while playing "MovieAudienceRole", which is the task-role of "Go to see a movie". We use this observation to personalize the task-list and services. We use social-role to determine priority order between multiple task candidates, and use task-role to determine the recommended services. In the following, we first describe the method of storing user's log of task-selection, and then propose the personalization of the task-list and recommended services; examples are provided.

Storing User's Log of Task-Selection. This section describes how the task-selection actions are stored and updated. The "Update user log DB" step in Fig.4 has two kinds of input from other processes; 1)"Click sub-tasks", and 2)"Select services", as explained below. In the following, we call the task candidate of the links and services user has clicked or selected the target-task.

If the user clicks a "sub-tasks" entry, the target-task is stored in the user log DB together with the user's social-role. On the other hand, if user selects service,

Table 1. An example of user log DB

Social-role	Selected task	Frequency
FriendRole	Go to watch movie	4
	Enjoy after seeing movie	4
	Look for CD/DVD store	4
FamilyRole	Go to a concert	2
	Move to a concert hall	2
Task-role	**Selected task**	**Frequency**
MovieAudienceRole	Look for CD/DVD store	4
ConcertAudienceRole	Move to a concert hall	2

the target-task is stored in the user log DB together with both user's social-role and task-role since selection of the service includes both selection of target-task from task candidates and selection of service of target-task simultaneously. This process is a reflection of the facts that social-role determines the task and task-role determines services to accomplish the task (Fig.6). We show an example below. The stored log for the following explanation is shown in Table 1.

The user selects "AudienceRole" as task-role and "FriendRole" as social-role from the role selection menu yielding Fig.5(a). If the user then clicks the link "sub-tasks" of "Go to watch movie", see Fig.5(b), the target-task "Go to watch movie" is stored together with current user's social-role "FriendRole". The user's current task-role changes to "MovieAudienceRole". Next, if the user selects "sub-tasks" of "Enjoy after seeing movie" from the task-list shown in Fig.5(c), "Enjoy after seeing movie" is stored together with user's social role "FriendRole". Next, if user selects service "HMV.com" of the task "Look for CD/DVD store" from the newly shown task-list, "Look for CD/DVD store" is stored together with both user's task-role "MovieAudienceRole" and social-role "FriendRole".

As another example, the user selects "AudienceRole" as task-role and "FamilyRole" as social-role from the role selection menu. If the user then clicks "sub-tasks" of "Go to a concert" from the task-list, the task "Go to a concert" is stored together with "FamilyRole". The user's current task-role changes to "ConcertAudienceRole". Next, if the user clicks the link of the service of "Move to a concert hall" from the task-list, the target-task "Move to a concert hall" is stored together with both user's task-role "ConcertAudienceRole" and social-role "FamilyRole".

Personalization of Task-List and Their Services. We realize personalization of the task-list by ordering the task candidates according to the frequency with which the user selected the tasks under the current user's social-role. We first acquire task candidates according to the flow described in Section 3.2. Next, the user log DB is checked and if a task candidate is stored under the **user's current social-role**, we acquire the number of times the user selected the task. If no such prior information is held in the DB, we use *is-a* relations defined in the role-ontology to order task candidates. Concretely, task candidates are ordered by referring to the task selection log of parent or child social-role of the current social-role. If no task selection log of both parent or child social-role is held in the DB, we treat the number of times that the task candidate was selected as 0. We acquire this data for all task candidates and use it to order the task candidates in descending order of the number of times selected.

Next, the recommended services for each task candidate are determined. As per Section 3.3, we determine the recommended services by acquiring the task-role the user has played most frequently while refining the objective task, which we call target task-role in the below. We determine the target task-role by acquiring the task-role of the task user has selected most frequently while playing the **task-role of each task candidates** from the user log DB. If there is no task selection log stored together with the task-role of the task candidate, we determine the target task-role as the task-role of the task candidate. Next, the services associated with all end-node sub-tasks whose associated task-role is the same as the target task-role or the child role-concept of the acquired task-role is determined. Detail of the acquisition of recommended services after target task-role is determined is given in Section 3.3. Finally the ordered task candidates and their recommended services are shown to the user.

Example of Generating Personalized Task-List. We show an example of generating a personalized task-list. If the user selects "FriendRole" as social-role and "AudienceRole" as task-role from the role selection menu, the task candidates; "Go to watch movie", "Go to see a play", "Go to a concert" and "Go to see a game", all associated with the child nodes of "AudienceRole", are selected from the task-model. After acquiring the task candidates, the system refers to the user log DB shown in Table 1, and finds that the most frequent task candidate associated with "FriendRole" is "Go to watch movie". Accordingly, "Go to watch movie" is given highest priority when ordering the task candidates.

Next, the recommended services for each task candidate are determined. We explain here the determination of services for "Go to watch movie". The system refers to the user log DB shown in Table 1, and finds that "Look for CD/DVD store" is the most frequently selected task under "MovieAudienceRole", which is the task-role associated with "Go to watch movie". Therefore, the task-role user played most frequently while refining the task candidate "Go to watch movie" is judged to be "MusicStoreCustomerRole", which is associated to "Look for CD/DVD store". Next, the services associated with all end-node sub-tasks whose task-role is "MusicStoreCustomerRole" are acquired such as "HMV.com" and "iTunes music store". Finally the ordered task candidates and their recommended services are shown to the user as shown in Fig.7(left).

As another example, if the user selects "FamilyRole" as social-role and "AudienceRole" as task-role from the role selection menu, the same task candidates as described in above are acquired. After acquiring the task candidates, the system refers to the user log DB shown in Table 1, and finds that the most frequent task candidate associated with "FamilyRole" is "Go to a concert". Accordingly, "Go to a concert" is given the highest priority when ordering the task candidates.

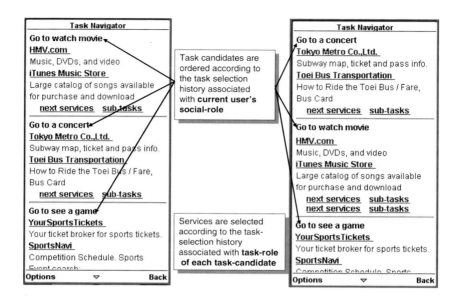

Fig. 7. Screenshots of personalized task-list and services; left: task-list and services tuned for a user with friend, right: task-list and services tuned for a user with family

Next, the recommended services for each task candidate are determined. We explain the determination of services for "Go to a concert" below. The system refers to the user log DB shown in Table 1, and finds that "Move to a concert hall" is the most frequently selected task under "ConcertAudienceRole", which is the task-role of "Go to a concert". Therefore, the task-role the user played most frequently while refining the task candidate "Go to a concert" is "PassengerRole", which is the task-role associated with "Move to a concert hall". Next, the services associated with all end-node sub-tasks whose task-role is child role of "PassengerRole" are acquired, since there are no end-node sub-tasks whose task-role is "PassengerRole", such as "Tokyo metro" and "Toei bus". Finally the ordered task candidates and their recommended services are shown to the user as shown in Fig.7(right).

We show an example when the social-role is first designated and there is no associated task selection log entry. Here, we consider that the user customizes his role selection menu using the "edit this menu" link on the role selection menu shown in Fig.5(a) and designates the social-role as "Brother". In this case, we cannot order task candidates using the task-selection log since there are no such log entries (See Table 1). Instead of using the task selection log associated with "Brother", we use the task selection log associated with "Family", which is the parent node of "Brother". As a result, even if the user manually designates the "Brother" role, the user is presented with the same order of task candidates as for "Family" as shown in Fig.7(right). Here, if user clicks a "sub-task" link on the task-list, the new user task selection log entry shows "Brother", not "Family".

4 Conclusion

In this paper, we constructed a role-ontology and applied it to realize improved task-based service navigation. For this application, we enhanced the basic task-model by associating tasks with role-concepts defined in a role-ontology. By acquiring the user's current role and watching the role changes, we can generate a personalized task-list that allows the user to perform the task-selection process more efficiently. The system can also recommend services for each task candidate appropriate for the task-role associated with each task candidate, which provides the user with more chances of reaching the desired service as soon as possible. In future work, we will construct a rich role-ontology that can express the relation to other concepts; such as situation and context (place, time, etc.) so as to reason the user's current social-role and task-role from the user's situation.

References

1. T. Naganuma and S. Kurakake. Task knowledge based retrieval for service relevant to mobile user's activity. In Y. Gil et al., editor, *4th International Semantic Web Conference: ISWC 2005, LNCS 3729*, pages 959–973, 2005.
2. A. Serenko and N. Bontis. A model of user adoption of mobile portals. *Quarterly Journal of Electronic Commerce*, 4(1):69–98, 2004.
3. Y. Fukazawa, T. Naganuma, K. Fujii, and S. Kurakake. A framework for task retrieval in task-oriented service navigation system. In R. Meersman et al., editor, *Int. Workshop on Web Semantics, LNCS 3762*, pages 876–885, 2005.
4. C. Masolo, L. Vieu, E. Bottazzi, C. Catenacci, R. Ferrario, A. Gangemi, and N. Guarino. Social roles and their descriptions. In *Proc. of the 9th Int. Conf. on the Principles of Knowledge Representation and Reasoning*, pages 267–277, 2004.
5. J.F. Sowa. *Conceptual Structures: Information Processing in Mind and Machine*. Addison-Wesley, New York, 1984.
6. J.F. Sowa. Using a lexicon of canonical graphs in a semantic interpreter. In M.W. Evens, editor, *Relational Models of the Lexicon: Representing Knowledge in Semantic Networks*, pages 113–137. Cambridge University Press, 1988.
7. N. Guarino. Concepts, attributes and arbitrary relations. *Data & Knowledge Engineering*, 8:249–261, 1992.
8. J. Fan, K. Barker, B. Porter, and P. Clark. Representing roles and purpose. In *Proc. of the Int. Conf. on Knowledge Capture*, pages 38–43, 2001.
9. E. Sunagawa, K. Kozaki, Y. Kitamura, and R. Mizoguchi. Organizing role-concepts in ontology development environment: Hozo. In *AI Technical Report*, volume 4 of *1*, pages 453–468. Artificial Intelligence Research Group, I.S.I.R., Osaka Univ., 2004.
10. C.J. Fillmore. Types of lexical information, ausztige abgedruckt. In R. Dirven and G. Radden, editors, *Fillmore's Case Grammar: A Reader*. Julius Groos Verlag, 1987.
11. E.F. Codd. A relational model of data for large shared data banks. *Communications of the ACM*, 13(6):377–387, 1970.
12. R. S. Sandhu, E.J. Coyne, H.L. Feinstein, and C.E. Youman. Role-based access control models. *IEEE Computer*, 29(2):38–47, 1996.
13. F. Steimann. On the representation of roles in object-oriented and conceptual modelling. *Data and Knowledge Engineering*, 35:83–106, 2000.

Enabling an Online Community for Sharing Oral Medicine Cases Using Semantic Web Technologies[*]

Marie Gustafsson[1,2], Göran Falkman[1], Fredrik Lindahl[2], and Olof Torgersson[2]

[1] School of Humanities and Informatics, University of Skövde,
PO Box 408, SE–541 28 Skövde, Sweden
{marie.gustafsson, goran.falkman}@his.se
[2] Computer Science and Engineering, Chalmers University of Technology
SE-412 96 Göteborg, Sweden
{lindahlf, oloft}@cs.chalmers.se

Abstract. This paper describes how Semantic Web technologies have been used in an online community for knowledge sharing between clinicians in oral medicine in Sweden. The main purpose of this community is to serve as repository of interesting and difficult cases, and as a support for monthly teleconferences. All information regarding users, meetings, news, and cases is stored in RDF. The community was built using the Struts framework and Jena was used for interacting with RDF.

1 Introduction

For a community to learn, ongoing learning by its members is vital. One means of supporting the transfer of individual knowledge into community knowledge is using computer supported tools, which can aid in making the knowledge communicable, consensual, and integrated into the community [1,2]. Further, tools supporting remote collaboration and consultation are important to all specialties of medicine [3,4], but especially for smaller fields, such as oral medicine, where specialists may be geographically dispersed.

The members of the Swedish Oral Medicine Network (SOMNet) are clinicians located at about ten different care-giving facilities throughout Sweden. They hold monthly teleconferences to discuss difficult and interesting cases. These remote meetings are currently supported by PowerPoint presentations. The clinicians have identified a need for a more structured online bank of cases covered at meetings, to serve as a collective memory for the group, and to provide better support for follow-ups of the discussed cases. It is believed that in creating, maintaining, and using this bank of cases, community learning will be enhanced.

The building of an online community for SOMNet is part of the SOMWeb (Swedish Oral Medicine Web) project. The project aims to obtain further knowledge about how interactive, user-centred knowledge-based systems supporting

---

[*] The work presented in this paper was supported by the Swedish Agency for Innovation Systems.

evidence-based oral medicine should be designed, implemented and introduced in the daily clinical work [5]. Work on achieving the above aim is divided into three partially overlapping objectives: (1) The formalization of clinical processes and knowledge, (2) the development of web services for oral medicine, and (3) the construction of an intelligent web community.

To further frame the work of this online community, SOMWeb is in turn based on a medical information system called MedView, which contains the basis of SOMWeb in the form of elaborated content when it comes to services for knowledge management, together with an established user community [6]. To provide rapid prototyping and deployment of applications in daily clinical work, and to support the harmonization of clinical processes and knowledge within oral medicine, MedView has been developed in collaboration between experts within SOMNet and experts in computer science.

This paper describes an online community supporting processes of sharing and discussing cases in oral medicine. Previous work on objective one above, the formalization of clinical processes and knowledge in oral medicine [7], has described how Semantic Web technologies can be used to describe and encode medical examinations in oral medicine. This representation of cases will be underlying to the examinations stored in the online community. Semantic Web languages will also be used to describe other parts of the community, such as users, meetings, and news. A general description of the SOMWeb community, with no focus on the use of Semantic Web technology, has been shown as a software demonstration [8].

We begin by giving some background on use of Semantic Web technologies in the life sciences and in online communities. After a description of the current forms of collaboration in SOMNet and a survey of the clinicians desires of a more advanced system, we will present design choices we have made in constructing the SOMWeb community. The implementation of the community is described and some initial results reported. This is followed a short discussion, conclusions, and future work.

2   Semantic Web Technologies

This section will cover arguments for using Semantic Web technologies in medical informatics and in online communities. By Semantic Web technologies we refer foremost to using ontologies and the Web Ontology Language[1] (OWL), describing data using Resource Description Framework[2] (RDF), and using SPARQL[3] as a query language and data access protocol for RDF data. Connected with these are other Semantic Web technologies, such as use of inference and rules.

2.1   Semantic Web and the Life Sciences

The life sciences are often mentioned as an area where Semantic Web technologies could give great improvements. Indeed, the W3C has an interest group devoted

---
[1] http://www.w3.org/2004/OWL
[2] http://www.w3.org/RDF
[3] http://www.w3.org/TR/rdf-sparql-query/

to the subject[4]. Areas where Semantic Web technologies can be applied include integration of heterogeneous data, locating relevant data sources and tools, retrieving relevant information, using inference to gather new insights, sharing formal annotations, creating rich and well-defined models of biological systems, and embedding models and semantics within online publications [9,10].

2.2 Semantic Web and Online Communities

A web portal "collects information for a group of users that have common interests" [11], and using Semantic Web technologies can help portals increase the consistency of information and quality of information processing [12]. In relation to online communities and web portals it is also relevant to mention Content Management System (CMS), which is software for facilitating collaborative creation and organization of documents and other content.

When describing people using Semantic Web technologies, the Friend of a Friend (FOAF) vocabulary[5] is often used. FOAF as a project aims to create a Web of machine-readable homepages "describing people, the links between them and the things they create and do." Indeed, several initiatives for online Semantic Web communities use FOAF in one way or another.

Semantic Web Advanced Development for Europe (SWAD-Europe) presents how Semantic Web tools and standards can be used to build a decentralized information portal [13], as used in the Semantic Web Environmental Directory (SWED) demonstrator. Each of the environmental organizations that want to be in the directory provides RDF descriptions of their organizations, constructed using a web-based data entry tool. The data is then hosted on the organization's own web site (similar to FOAF).

Another approach to adding Semantic Web technology support for communities has been to enable the sharing of forum posts and such between different communities, by defining a common format for these posts, as is done in the Semantically Interlinked Online Communities (SIOC) [14]. Its goal is to interconnect online communities in helping to locate relevant and related information. The ontology and interface will let users searching in one forum find information on forums from other sites using a SIOC-based system architecture. The SIOC ontology outlines main classes, such as Site, Forum, Post, Event, Group, and User and properties of these. Mappings to e.g., FOAF are also provided.

SEmantic portAL (SEAL) [15] uses ontologies for dealing with the requirements of typical community web sites. Such requirements are information integration and web site management. The system architecture of SEAL includes a knowledge warehouse and the Ontobroker [16] system for inferencing. Community users and software agents access the Ontobroker through modules for navigation, query, templates for adding data, and an RDF generator.

The Semantic Web Research Community (SWRC) ontology [17] is an ontology for representing knowledge about researchers and research communities.

---

[4] http://www.w3.org/2001/sw/hcls/
[5] http://www.foaf-project.org/

Main concepts of this ontology are, among others, Organization, Project, Person, Topic, Publication, and Event. The SWRC ontology is used and extended by several portals based on the SEAL approach.

3 An Analysis of Current Forms of Collaboration in SOMNet

SOMNet aims to act as a hub and filter for knowledge in oral medicine, by providing a forum where cases in oral medicine can be presented and discussed in distributed meetings. SOMNet meetings are organized around monthly teleconferences, where about ten clinics participate. The majority of the attendants are experts in oral medicine and the individual clinician has the opportunity to get feedback from colleagues from all over Sweden. Mainly two kinds of cases are presented: cases considered interesting for a wider audience and cases where the submitting clinician wants advice regarding diagnosis and treatment.

The forms of cooperation and opinions of SOMNet have been investigated by observing their meetings and through informal interviews with selected participants and the secretary who coordinates the meetings. Before the SOMWeb initiative, submission of cases was handled by e-mailing PowerPoint presentations to the meeting coordinator, who then e-mailed submitted cases to clinics intending to participate. During the teleconference meeting, each clinic opened their local copy of the file presenting the case. The clinician who had submitted the case presented the details of the case, after which the community discussed it. When a case had been presented and discussed, the file was closed and attendants opened their local copy of the next case. They repeated this process until all submitted cases had been discussed or the time allotted to the meeting was up. At the meetings, no collective written notes were taken, and there was no central repository of handled cases.

The described procedure had several major problems: (1) The opportunities for collective and individual learning were limited by the lack of shared written notes from the meetings. (2) It was difficult to go back and check previously discussed cases as there was no shared record of treated cases. (3) Relevant information may be lacking in the case presentation, as there was no agreed upon template of what had to be included. It was left entirely up to the submitting individual what text and image information to include. (4) There were recurring problems of cases that could not be opened by all attendees, due to differences in versions of the software and platform used to produce the presentations.

Learning from earlier meetings is thus hindered by the lack of access to and reminders of previous cases, and by difficulties in structured comparison of different cases. Even with these problems, the participating clinicians value the opportunity to share experiences with other experts in the field enough to keep participating in the meetings, both by sending in cases and joining for discussion.

The introduction of a common web-based repository was a first step towards improving the IT-maturity of the SOMNet meetings. In this repository, the presentations are stored as HTML documents rather than as PowerPoint presentations.

The new practice makes administration simpler and provides a bank of difficult and interesting cases. Since December 2003, when the clinicians first started using the repository, eighty-four cases from seventeen SOMNet meetings have been added.

A web-based questionnaire was distributed to all SOMNet participants to further examine the needs a wishes of the users. The results indicated that the participants considered SOMNet valuable and wanted it to continue in a similar way: as a forum for the most part dedicated to the discussion of submitted cases. Around seventy-five percent of the respondents also said that they wanted to be able to have access to the collection of treated cases. Ability to share cases and treatment methods and papers directly with other clinicians was of interest to a majority of the respondents. When the questionnaire was discussed at a later meeting, participants agreed that it was important to introduce a system that would allow the community to in a more organized manner follow up previously discussed cases. They also emphasized the importance of means to search the database of cases.

4 System Design

This section begins with the requirements we have previously identified for an ontology in oral medicine. We then present design choices for the oral medicine community which have lead us to use Semantic Web technologies and to build our own system, rather than using an existing Content Management System.

In [7], we presented the following requirements for an ontology for oral medicine, based on experience with the MedView system and interviews with domain experts and developers:

- We need the possibility and ability to utilize external sources of knowledge.
- The relation between the conceptual models of fundamental clinical concepts in use, e.g., examination templates, lists of approved values for terms and groups of related terms and their corresponding concrete entities must be formally examined.
- Relations and interactions between different entities of the ontology must be captured, e.g., that a certain answer to a specific question in a given examination template triggers another question.
- A stronger typing of elements is needed.
- We need to be able to capture different kinds of meta-data, e.g., who is the creator of a specific examination template and what the purpose (scientific or clinical) is of the introduction of a specific examination template.
- The localization of data has to be addressed rigorously: How to provide different language-based versions of the defined concepts, definitions and terms?
- We need to differentiate between different 'views' of the underlying data, to be utilized for, e.g., information visualization and intelligent user interfaces.

Based on these requirements an ontology for examinations in oral medicine was designed in OWL. Individual examination instances are encoded in RDF. Given that the examinations are an important part of the oral medicine community, and that these have Semantic Web representations, using such technologies for other relevant community concepts seems natural. Based on this, along with the analysis given in Sec. 3 we have made the following design choices:

- The community should be constructed in cooperation with its users, foremost to adapt it to the users needs, but also as the development of the online community can be seen as part of a learning process in the SOMNet users.
- The examinations should have a central role in the community and be represented in RDF, motivations for which are given above.
- The examinations to be presented at meetings should be entered online, using forms created from user-defined examinations, represented in OWL.
- Community data should be stored in RDF, to allow interaction with e.g., examination data and hopefully other related online communities in medicine.
- Community data will be stored centrally, rather than distributed as in e.g., [13], as the member clinicians and clinics cannot be expected to have access to local hosting.
- Where possible, existing ontologies for representing community data should be reused.
- To allow integration with the existing tools of the project, Java technologies should be used in realizing the community.
- The constructed community should allow for browsing and visualizing cases, as well as query support and search.
- To adapt to the needs of the users, the community should have basic user modeling support, with the long term goal of providing a more intelligent user interface.
- Our plans to use intelligent user interfaces and to keep a high degree of user customizability of the web interface in order to increase the clinicians trust in the system [18], point away from using a CMS in favor of using a lower-level framework with greater flexibility and end-user control.

While using a CMS would have given us a framework enabling rapid development of some aspects of our system, other aspects, e.g., generating web-based case entry forms from user-defined specifications, would still have to be custom-made from scratch.

5 Implementation

This section describes how the community data is represented using Semantic Web technologies and how Java web technologies are used to create the community framework.

5.1 Semantic Web Technologies

One part of the SOMWeb project is the formalization of clinical concepts and processes in oral medicine. Taking the knowledge model of MedView as a starting point, initial ontologies for examinations in oral medicine has been constructed [7] using OWL. There is one ontology for describing examination templates and one for classes of values that the examination templates use. The examination instances constructed using the ontology are stored as separate RDF-files.

The description of examination templates is further divided so that one 'central' OWL-file describes aspects common to all MedView examinations. This describes general things: classes such as `Examination`, `ExaminationCategory`, and a property `hasExaminationCategory` for connecting an `Examination` instance to `ExaminationCategory` instances. We also have properties corresponding to the different input-types, such as `MultipleExaminationProperty`, and `VASExaminationProperty`. The reason for explicitly representing things that could be handled using cardinality constraints in OWL is to be able to use older MedView datahandling classes to handle examinations. Until those modules can be rewritten, we are using both cardinality constraints and the explicit properties such as `SingleExaminationProperty`.

All individual examination templates refer to this 'central' OWL-file. In SOMWeb the main templates used right now describes what to enter when first entering the case into the system, as well as templates for consultations from the teleconference meeting and for consultations held after the initial examination data was entered. Such an examination template OWL-file contains definitions of the categories that can or need to be included in an examination constructed from that template. Examples of subclasses of `ExaminationCategory` in current use are `PatientData`, `GeneralAnamnesis`, and `MucosChangeAnamnesis`. In each examination template we also describe properties associated with the template, such as `hasAllergy`, as subproperties of the properties described in the general examination description OWL-file, such as `MultipleExaminationProperty`. For each property, there are also properties pertaining to description and instructions, to be shown to the user. Any relevant cardinality constraints are described, as well as the ordering of the categories and the properties within the categories, using `rdf:list`. Properties are connected to an `ExaminationCategory` subclass and a value class using `owl:allValuesFrom` restrictions.

The value list ontology is very simple, right now it only contains classes, with no subhierarchies, and their instances. Thus, we have classes such as `Allergy` and `Diagnosis`, with instances such as `peanutAllergy` and `hairyTongue`, respectively. It can be argued that this means that two patients who have examinations that assert that `hasDiagnosis hairyTongue` have the same hairy tongue, and that it would be more correct to have a class `HairyTongue` with separate instances for all patients with a diagnosis of hairy tongue. However, it was decided that the added complexity of this approach was not compensated by its benefits.

There is currently no use of inference, and the ontologies are not very complex. The examination templates are constructed by a Java program that takes a template in the old XML format and outputs one in OWL. The value list ontology is created by reading the old text file of values and constructing corresponding classes and instances. At first there were attempts to structure this value list so that there were more subclasses, for example for different kinds of diagnoses and allergies. However, this process meant dealing with large amounts of instances

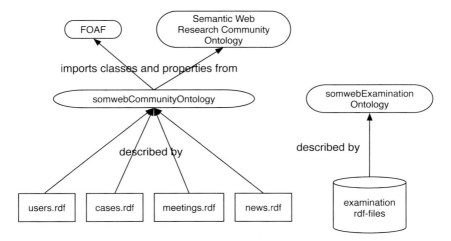

Fig. 1. The figure shows how the different RDF-files and OWL ontologies are related. The RDF-files for persons, meetings, cases (examination metadata), and news are described in the somwebCommunityOntology. The examinations are stored in separate RDF-files, and are described in the somwebExaminationOntology. The examination ontology consists of one OWL-file describing general concepts and then one for each kind of examination used in the community.

and needed much end-user input. Our end-users have not yet had the time to look at this, and we have no good interface for them to do it in. Therefore we decided to go ahead with the unstructured value classes, with the argument that we can add more subclasses later.

In addition to storing the examinations in RDF, other community data, regarding users, meetings, news, and case metadata, is also represented in RDF. What should be included in descriptions of users, meetings, and case metadata is described in OWL. Some of the user-descriptions are related to relevant FOAF-classes and properties. Meeting-descriptions make use of classes and properties of the Semantic Web Research Community ontology [17]. For interacting with the Java parts of the community, Jena[6] is used. Figure 1 shows how these components are related.

5.2 Java Web Technologies

SOMWeb is built on Java Enterprise technology, using Apache Tomcat[7] as the core web container. The system is an extension of the Apache Struts Model-2 web application framework[8]. Model-2 frameworks (a variation of the classic Model-View-Controller (MVC) design paradigm) are based on the idea that Java Servlets execute business logic while presentation resides mainly in server pages. As stated

---

[6] http://jena.sourceforge.net/
[7] http://tomcat.apache.org
[8] http://struts.apache.org/

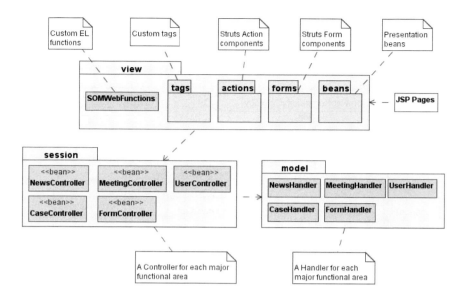

Fig. 2. Overview of the SOMWeb system architecture. The model layer contains persistence classes that read RDF-files for users, meetings, cases, and news and constructs objects of the corresponding Java classes used by the system. These classes are also used for making changes to the RDF model and writing to file.

in [12], reusing mature technology gives a Semantic Web portal improved usability, reliability, and scalability.

The SOMWeb system is a layered architecture, conceptually divided into four main layers – the view layer, the session layer, the model layer, and the foundation layer as depicted in Fig. 2. The view layer is comprised of Java Server Pages (JSP) using Expression Language (EL) constructs, with custom tags and functions in addition to tags from the Java Standards Tag Library (JSTL) and the various Apache Struts tag libraries. Styling and layout of content is done using Cascading Style Sheets (CSS). The session layer has components dealing with the current user session, and is responsible for transforming the application's internal state into the presentation JavaBeans used by the server pages. The model layer has components making up the application's internal state, and is roughly divided into the major functional areas provided by the system. Here we also have persistence classes, which read the RDF-files for users, meetings, cases, and news and creates objects of the corresponding Java-classes used by the system. These persistence classes are manually constructed, but in the future we are considering using Jastor[9] to simplify their updating. While the generation of user input forms from OWL is handled by the SOMWeb system, for handling examination data we use the previously developed MedView system and its datahandling functions, which have been adapted to using OWL and RDF.

---

[9] http://jastor.sourceforge.net/

6 Results

The initial SOMWeb community supports case data entry according to user-defined templates, managing online meetings and assigning cases to these, viewing upcoming and archived meetings and their corresponding cases, and adding comments to cases. Users can use free text search over examination data. Administrators are provided basic user handling, create an manage meetings, and post news.

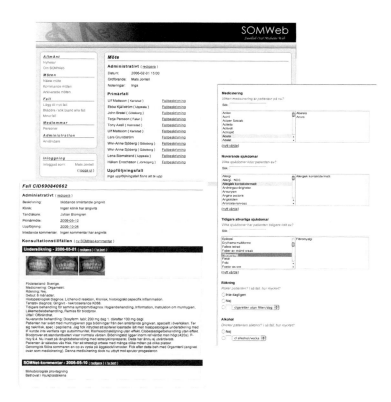

Fig. 3. The figure shows screenshots of some key parts of SOMWeb: overview of cases at a meeting (top), case presentation with pictures and text description generated from examination data (left), and part of an examination data entry form (right). All text is in Swedish.

Figure 3 shows screenshots of core system aspects, such as structured case entry – the user is presented with a blank form based on a user-defined OWL description of the examination, in which the user enters case data. The examination description is created in a separate editor for specifying the content of the examination, and the user never interacts with the OWL representation. The types of questions posed and the allowed values are determined by the underlying OWL description. After submission, the case data is stored as RDF and a summary of the case information can be presented (also shown in Fig. 3).

Shown in the case presentation is administrative information along with a system-generated medical record. The record is constructed from the submitted case data and generated by the mGen document generator, using natural language processing technology, as described in [19]. If more information about a case becomes available, the owner can use forms specifically tailored for this purpose to add new data. Each such data occasion is reflected in the case summary and a record is generated for each occasion. The owner of a case can also schedule the case for initial discussion at a SOMNet meeting, as well as selecting a meeting at which the case should be considered again, for possible follow-up and re-evaluation.

7 Discussion

While the ontologies used in the SOMWeb community are fairly simple, we believe that it is still motivated to use OWL and RDF in our application, both because it, among other things, gives us access to tools for interacting with the RDF content and because we can return in the future and refine our ontology. In the old MedView representation there was no support for refining the knowledge model by subclassing the value classes, and a separate 'aggregation' representation was used for this. When instead using OWL, this can be achieved using one representation. Indeed, Knublauch et al. [20] argue that "the breadth of the OWL language offers a migration route from entry level, hand-crafted taxonomies of terms, to well defined, normalized ontologies capable of supporting reasoning." Thus, at first a semantically simple ontologies such as these is enough to make a Web application able to generate user interface forms from class definitions and describe schema useful for integration. Then, later in the ontology's life cycle, additional expressivity can be added as developers find they need it.

However, OWL and RDF are still fairly young technologies, with the effect that developers are not as familiar with it as with for example regular XML, which means that initially more time is spent getting familiar with new nomenclature and new API's. In designing the larger examination template ontologies, the initial barriers were larger than for the community data ontology. We were faced with confusion in the usage of domain and range, as well as a lack of support for representing for example numeric ranges. Also, for the examination template ontology there was more of a feeling that the 'right' choices had to be made, which sometimes lead to stalled progress.

SOMWeb has been designed to support the collaborative work in SOMNet (and similar organisations), especially the tasks of setting up and holding meetings, from the perspectives of the different types of users. Focusing on behavioural aspects of clinical research – modelling and implementing the 'workflows' of SOMNet, makes SOMWeb more of a workflow management system [21] than a traditional CMS.

While this project has the goal of constructing an online community, it was found that what the clinicians wanted was not so much to discuss the cases online, but to have a common memory there, where they could contribute and find cases. The informal communication was less sought after, and was taken care of in teleconferences and in person or by phone. A drawback of this is that no trail is left after these conversations, which might have benefited those not present.

8 Conclusions and Future Work

We have shown how Semantic Web technologies can be used to support online collaborative work in a small medical speciality. The SOMWeb online community uses RDF for representing central components such as medical examinations and case metadata, community users, scheduled teleconference meetings, and news messages. Where relevant, classes and properties from the FOAF and SWRC ontologies have been reused. These RDF representations interact with the larger Apache Struts framework through the Jena API.

By using RDF for representing the underlying information of SOMWeb we hope to gain increased interoperability, and the ability to use SPARQL. Future work includes allowing users to pose structured queries on the collected data, rather than using free text search, allowing precise answers rather than pieces of documents that match the keyword. However, the users of SOMWeb have little knowledge that the underlying representation of their online community is RDF, and there should not be a need for them knowing this. Therefore, the structured queries need to be characterized in a manner graspable without understanding a more complex underlying design.

There is currently no support in the community for informal communication, through for example online forums, but such features will soon be provided and eventually be compatible with SIOC. While the information of SOMWeb is only available by password identification, we believe that using RDF is still very useful, since we get the possiblity of reusing concepts from larger community ontologies such SIOC. An enticing possibility is to connect several related medical online communities of practice through SPARQL web services.

References

1. Jim Q. Chen, J.H., Ted E. Lee, J.H., Zhang, R.: Systems requirements for organizational learning. Communications of the ACM **46**(12) (2003) 73–79
2. Bose, R.: Knowledge management-enabled health care management systems: capabilities, infrastructure, and decision-support. Expert Systems with Applications **24**(1) (2003) 59–71
3. Dawes, M., Sampson, U.: Knowledge management in clinical practice: a systematic review of information seeking behavior in physicians. International Journal of Medical Informatics **71**(1) (2003) 9–15
4. Ryu, S., Ho, S., Han, I.: Knowledge sharing behavior of physicians in hospitals. Expert Systems with Applications **25**(1) (2003) 113–122
5. Falkman, G., Torgersson, O., Jontell, M., Gustafsson, M.: SOMWeb – Towards an infrastructure for knowledge sharing. In: Proc. Medical Informatics Europe, IOS Press (2005) 527–32

6. Jontell, M., Mattsson, U., Torgersson, O.: MedView: An instrument for clinical research and education in oral medicine. Oral Surg. Oral Med. Oral Pathol. Oral Radiol. Endod. **99** (2005) 55–63
7. Gustafsson, M., Falkman, G.: Representing clinical knowledge in oral medicine using ontologies. In: Proc. Medical Informatics Europe, IOS Press (2005) 743–8
8. Gustafsson, M., Lindahl, F., Falkman, G., Torgersson, O.: An online community for oral medicine supporting structured case entry. In: Poster and Demonstration Proc. MIE 2006. (2006) 469–474
9. Neumann, E.K., Miller, E., Wilbanks, J.: What the semantic web could do for the life sciences. Drug Discovery Today BioSilico **2**(6) (2004) 228–236
10. Lambrix, P.: Towards a semanticweb for bioinformatics using ontology-based annotation. In: WETICE '05: Proceedings of the 14th IEEE International Workshops on Enabling Technologies: Infrastructure for Collaborative Enterprise, Washington, DC, USA, IEEE Computer Society (2005) 3–7
11. Heflin, J.: Web Ontology Language (OWL): use cases and requirements. W3C Recommendation 10 February 2004 (2004)
12. Lausen, H., Ding, Y., Stollberg, M., Fensel, D., Hernandez, R.L., Han, S.K.: Semantic web portals: state-of-the-art survey. Journal of Knowledge Management **9**(5) (2005) 40–49
13. Reynolds, D., Shabajee, P., Cayzer, S., Steer, D.: SWAD-Europe deliverable 12.1.7: Semantic portals demonstrator – lessons learnt (2004)
14. Breslin, J.G., Harth, A., Bojars, U., Decker, S.: Towards semantically-interlinked online communities. In Gómez-Pérez, A., Euzenat, J., eds.: The Semantic Web: Research and Applications, Second European Semantic Web Conference, ESWC 2005, Heraklion, Crete, Greece, May 29 - June 1, 2005, Proceedings. (2005) 500–514
15. Stojanovic, N., Maedche, A., Staab, S., Studer, R., Sure, Y.: SEAL – A framework for developing SEmantic portALs. In: K-CAP 2001 - First Intenational Conference on Knowledge Capture, Victoria, Canada, Oct. 21-23, 2001, ACM (2001)
16. Decker, S., Erdmann, M., Fensel, D., Studer, R.: Ontobroker: Ontology based access to distributed and semi-structured information. In Meersman, R., ed.: Database Semantics: Semantic Issues in Multimedia Systems, Proceedings TC2/WG 2.6 8th Working Conference on Database Semantics (DS-8), Rotorua, New Zealand, Kluwer Academic Publishers, Boston (1999)
17. Sure, Y., Bloehdorn, S., Haase, P., Hartmann, J., Oberle, D.: The SWRC ontology - Semantic Web for research communities. In Bento, C., Cardoso, A., Dias, G., eds.: Proceedings of the 12th Portuguese Conference on Artificial Intelligence – Progress in Artificial Intelligence (EPIA 2005). Volume 3803 of LNCS., Covilha, Portugal, Springer (2005) 218–231
18. Wetter, T.: Lessons learnt from bringing knowledge-based systems into routine use. Artif. Intell. Med. **24**(3) (2002) 195–203
19. Lindahl, F., Torgersson, O.: mGen – An open source framework for generating clinical documents. In: Proc. Medical Informatics Europe, IOS Press (2005) 107–12
20. Knublauch, H., Horridge, M., Musen, M., Rector, A., Stevens, R., Drummond, N., Lord, P., Noy, N.F., Seidenberg, J., Wang, H.: The Protégé OWL Experience. In: Proc. of the Workshop on OWL Experiences and Directions 2005, Galway, Ireland (2005)
21. Pratt, W., Reddy, M., McDonald, D., Tarczy-Hornoch, P., Gennari, J.: Incorporating ideas from computer-supported cooperative work. Journal of Biomedical Informatics **37**(2) (2004) 128–137

EKOSS: A Knowledge-User Centered Approach to Knowledge Sharing, Discovery, and Integration on the Semantic Web

Steven Kraines[1], Weisen Guo[2,1], Brian Kemper[1], and Yutaka Nakamura[1]

[1] Division of Project Coordination of the University of Tokyo, Tokyo 277-8568, Japan
{sk, gws, bkemper, yutaka}@cb.k.u-tokyo.ac.jp
[2] Inst. of Systems Eng. of Dalian University of Technology, Dalian 116024, China
guows@dlut.edu.cn

Abstract. The scientific enterprise depends on the effective transfer of knowledge from creator to user. Recently the rate of scientific knowledge production is overwhelming the ability for researchers to process it. Semantic web technologies may help to handle this vast amount of scientific knowledge. However, automatic computerized techniques that extract semantics from natural language text for use in matching with the requests of knowledge seekers achieve only mediocre results. Clearly, semantic descriptions of expert knowledge that are constructed by the knowledge creators themselves will be more accurate. We report an approach and software implementation of a knowledge sharing platform based on semantic web technologies, called EKOSS for expert knowledge ontology-based semantic search, that helps knowledge creators construct semantic descriptions of their knowledge. The EKOSS system enables knowledge creators to construct computer-interpretable semantically rich statements describing their knowledge with minimal effort and without any knowledge of semantic web technologies.

Keywords: semantic search, knowledge sharing, inference, ontology.

1 Introduction

The scientific enterprise has brought enormous wealth to society in the form of expert scientific knowledge. However, recently concern has been raised that knowledge is being produced in scientific research much faster than we can process it. Some writers have called this a "knowledge explosion", pointing to indicators such as an exponential increase in papers written in specific fields of scientific research [1], [2]. Semantic web technologies are being looked to as a potential approach for better handling this vast amount of scientific knowledge [3]. We report an approach and software implementation, called EKOSS for expert knowledge ontology-based semantic search, to support knowledge sharing by using semantic web technologies. EKOSS takes the approach of enabling the knowledge creators to construct semantic descriptions of their knowledge that are better suited for computer-based processing and matching. In this paper, we describe the basic approach and architecture of the EKOSS system. An accompanying paper gives details on the EKOSS system implementation [28].

We have described the scientific enterprise as a knowledge cycle where knowledge generated by research scientists is continually returned to a global repository of scientific knowledge that forms the basis for further scientific research [5]. The cycle proceeds through stages of problem identification, experimental design, data analysis, and knowledge synthesis. At each stage of the process, the research scientist looks to the existing repository of scientific knowledge in the form of media such as papers and conference proceedings in order to discover previous research findings or hints that could help to achieve the goal of synthesizing useful new knowledge. Finally, the research scientist must input this new knowledge into the repository of scientific knowledge so that it is available to other research scientists for their research activities as well as to members of society for addressing various societal needs.

In the past, a diligent researcher could have read all of the papers in a particular field of scientific knowledge or at least scan abstracts of all potentially interesting papers. However, as the quantity of published results continues its exponential growth, researchers face the difficult problem of deciding which of the current research to invest time reading. Various techniques such as Google Scholar and the Web of Science can help researchers identify which scientific papers are most likely to be useful. However, despite remarkable progress in establishing computer-searchable electronic repositories of scientific papers and algorithms for extracting keywords automatically from those papers, the effectiveness of these techniques remains limited.

The fundamental problem is that scientific papers, in the way that they are published today, do not lend themselves well to computer-based techniques for matching papers with searches for knowledge. While scientific papers a century ago could be seen as a form of correspondence between people, writing a paper today can be compared to putting a message in a bottle and hoping that someone will find it on the Internet sea. Researchers cast a wide net using search engines such as Web of Science, but invariably they end up with many unrelated bottles, false positives, and they end up missing many important messages, false negatives. For example, we conducted a search on Google Scholar for a paper titled "a flexible model integration approach for evaluating tradeoffs between CO_2 emissions and cost in solid oxide fuel cell-based building energy systems" that was published by one of us in the International Journal of Energy Research using the keywords "building" "distributed", "energy systems", "fuel cell", "gas turbine", and "electricity demand" that were contained in the paper's abstract. Only four papers in the top thirty hits had any reference to distributed energy systems in buildings that combine a fuel-cell with a gas turbine. The paper that we had wanted to find was the only paper that was actually about distributed energy systems contained in buildings that combine a fuel-cell with a gas turbine to supply electricity demand of buildings, and it ranked twenty-seventh out of thirty.

2 Using Semantics for More Accurate Searching

By using tools and protocols developed for the realization of the Semantic Web, such as ontologies implemented in OWL-DL, statements with computer-interpretable semantics can be constructed. Logical inference and rule-based reasoning can be used to evaluate matches between such semantic statements, potentially resulting in a far more accurate mechanism for identifying what knowledge is most likely to be useful to a person who is seeking knowledge related to a particular condition, object, or design. For example, we could specify that the knowledge contained in the paper referred to above describes a study of a "building" containing a "distributed energy system" having as a part a "fuel cell" and as another part a "gas turbine" that is used to supply "electricity demand" of the "building". Using the predefined T-box structure of the ontology, a logical reasoning engine could reduce false negatives by knowing, for example, that "office building" is a type of "building" and that a "fuel cell" is a type of "energy device". Furthermore, by using an A-box to specify that both the "fuel cell" and the "gas turbine" are parts of the "energy system", which in turn is a part of the "building", we can reduce false positives. The role of semantics in reducing false positives and false negatives is illustrated in Fig. 1.

The effectiveness of this kind of semantic search is dependent on the accuracy and richness of the semantic statements. In particular, while natural language

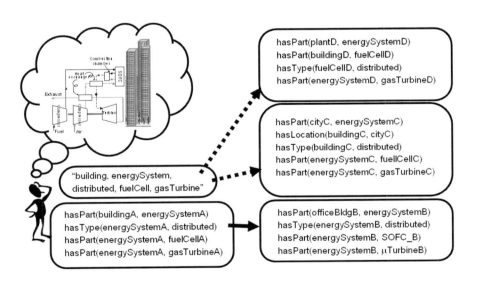

Fig. 1. Semantic matching versus keyword search. A researcher is looking for knowledge related to a "building" that has a part "energy system" with type "distributed", which in turn has parts "fuel cell" and "gas turbine". A simple keyword list matches with the wrong knowledge contents (broken lines). Only the semantic description with declared relationships between the instances of the keywords matches with the correct knowledge contents (solid line).

processing (NLP) techniques can help to extract useful semantics from scientific papers [6], [7], [8], even the best NLP methods still do not perform well in terms of precision and recall of scientific papers [9], [10].

Semantic statements made by the researchers who created the knowledge could be expected to be more accurate. We argue that researchers would be willing to make at least a small effort to publish their knowledge in a particular format if that format could be guaranteed to be significantly more effective at reaching the people who can most benefit from the knowledge. This is analogous to attaching a transmitter that sends out a signal "advertising" the content of the bottle. Authors of papers and conference abstracts do this when they choose keywords to attach to their manuscript that they feel most accurately represent the knowledge contained, and using a controlled vocabulary for keywords helps make the transmission more clear. We believe that, with only a small additional effort, researchers could attach far more effective transmissions to their papers through the use of semantic statements based on formal ontologies. Alternatively, reviewers or editors could attach semantic descriptions of the papers based on their objective understanding of the main messages in the paper. The key requirements in our approach are that the process of authoring the semantic descriptions be decentralized and that the authoring process not require any special expertise on knowledge engineering or semantic technologies.

We have developed a prototype web-based system, called EKOSS for Expert Knowledge Ontology-based Semantic Search, to support this kind of semantic markup of both scientific papers and other knowledge resources that describe some expert knowledge and search requests for scientific knowledge related to specific conditions and/or problems. We use ontologies based on description logics to provide simplified languages in specific domains of knowledge that can be reasoned against using DL reasoning software. The EKOSS system lets users make both semantic descriptions of knowledge and semantic queries to express search requests for that domain. We also support the reverse: that is semantic queries to express conditions that must be filled for particular knowledge to be applicable and semantic descriptions of the particular conditions for which knowledge is being sought. We use the RacerPro reasoner to evaluate the matches between knowledge descriptions and search requests as well as to evaluate the consistency of semantic descriptions and queries for both knowledge and searches [11]. The EKOSS system supports the use of multiple distinct ontologies. A set of administrator tools are provided for loading new ontologies and modifying existing ones, and we are developing user interfaces for modifying the existing ontologies as described in the last section of this paper.

3 The Role of EKOSS in Scientific Knowledge Sharing

The EKOSS system is being developed as a part of a four level architecture for scientific knowledge sharing, discovery, and integration that we have described in previous publications [5], [13], [12]. Briefly, the four levels of the architecture framework, shown in Fig. 2, are as follows. Knowledge resources, including scientific papers, databases and simulation models, created by knowledge experts around the world form the base level of the framework. Tools are provided at the second level to each knowledge expert in order to publish semantic descriptions of that person's expert knowledge. At the third level, software agents representing each of the knowledge experts communicate to identify potentially useful knowledge sharing opportunities based on the semantic descriptions constructed at the second level [13], [14]. The fourth level holds knowledge integration technologies, such as the semantic distance matrix generation tools that we describe at the end of this paper and the distributed object-based modeling environment DOME being developed at the CAD laboratory of the Massachusetts Institute of Technology. DOME can be used to integrate the knowledge discovered at the third level over the Internet in order to rapidly synthesize new integrated knowledge through scenario analyses and optimization [15].

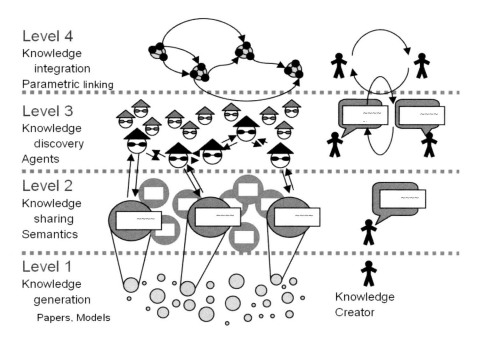

Fig. 2. The four level architecture for knowledge sharing, discovery and integration proposed by the authors

The EKOSS system is intended to implement the second level of this framework. Specifically, the EKOSS system provides a web-accessible knowledge sharing platform with the following features:

- an ontology browser for examining the available ontologies and supporting dialogue concerning ontology development,
- a personal repository of Knowledge Projects that contain semantic descriptions and queries for representing specific expert knowledge of a user,

- a personal repository of Search Projects that contain semantic descriptions and queries that represent knowledge interests or requirements of a user,
- a semantic search engine based on the RacerPro DL reasoner with extensions for rule-based reasoning and datatype reasoning.

EKOSS Knowledge Projects and Search Projects have essentially the same structure. Each project can contain one or more semantic descriptions that represent the details of that project, i.e. the knowledge contained or the conditions behind the search. Projects also can contain several generalized semantic queries to represent the conditions that should be filled in order to establish a match. Often, the Search Projects will contain semantic queries, such as "find me all knowledge projects that mention buildings that contain fuel cells", and the Knowledge Projects will contain semantic descriptions, such as "this is knowledge about a office building that contains an energy system that in turn contains a polymer electrolyte fuel cell". However, the reverse is also useful. For example, a semantic query can be used to specify a particular condition that must hold for the knowledge represented by a Knowledge Project to be applicable: "this knowledge is applicable to situations where there exists a building whose energy demand is supplied by a local energy device". Search Projects can then make use of semantic descriptions to describe the particular conditions for which knowledge is being sought: "we are designing an office building with a microturbine as an energy supply device".

We give a simple example here of creating a semantic description for the matching knowledge shown in Fig. 1. A researcher seeking to share her knowledge regarding buildings with energy systems that have fuel cells and gas turbines logs in to her local EKOSS server and creates a new knowledge project. After entering a name and other information for the project, she clicks a button to add a semantic description to the project and selects one of the ontologies available on the EKOSS server to create an A-box describing the object of her knowledge. The EKOSS ontology browser is displayed, and the researcher navigates the subsumption taxonomy of the selected ontology to find the concept for building. After navigating the subsumption tree to the class in the ontology that best represents the concept that she wants, she presses the "Add" button to create an instance of the selected class, "building", in her A-box and optionally adds a text label to the instance.

The researcher can repeat the process above to add another instance or use the "Add Property" interface to add an object or datatype property to an existing instance. Selecting "Add Property" displays a tree of properties that can take "building" as a domain class (Fig. 3). The researcher wants to indicate that the building has as a part an energy system with a fuel cell and a gas turbine, so she finds the property "has_part", which is a subproperty of "composition_of_individual". The "Add Property" interface shows a subsumption tree of the classes that can be ranges of "has_part". The researcher finds the class "energy_system" and sets it to be the range of "has_part". The EKOSS system creates an instance of "energy_system" and again lets the user label the instance if desired. The user continues to create instances and properties until the A-box for the knowledge description is completed. An interactive directed graph of the A-box can be displayed by selecting "graph view" (Fig. 4).

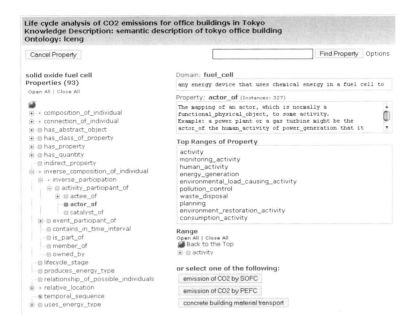

Fig. 3. The "add property" page for adding properties to an instance of the class "fuel_cell"

Semantic descriptions and semantic queries are completely interchangeable, that is a semantic description of one particular project can be declared to be a semantic query or description of another Knowledge or Search Project. Moreover, a Knowledge Project can function as a Search Project and vice versa. This feature of EKOSS both enhances its effectiveness and reduces the learning curve. Each Knowledge and Search Project serves as a node on a directed graph of knowledge, with links between project nodes directed from the queries of the origin project to the descriptions of the destination project (Fig. 5). For example, a directed link from project A to project B means that the abstraction of the knowledge (or request for knowledge) represented by queries in project A is matched, at least in part, by the detailed semantic representation of the knowledge (or search conditions) in project B.

Multiplicity of semantic queries has a special meaning – by creating multiple versions, that is subsets, of a template query, it is possible to evaluate partial matches and special conditions for a match between that project and the semantic description of another project (see [4] for more details). For each semantic query in a Knowledge or Search Project, the project creator can set a matching weight value and a "match type" flag. The "match type" flag specifies whether

840   S. Kraines et al.

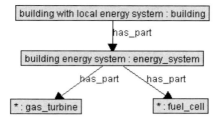

Fig. 4. Graph view of the completed semantic knowledge query. Boxes indicate instances, and arrows show the property connections. The actual instance class is shown to the right of the colon; the user defined instance label is shown to the left of the colon.

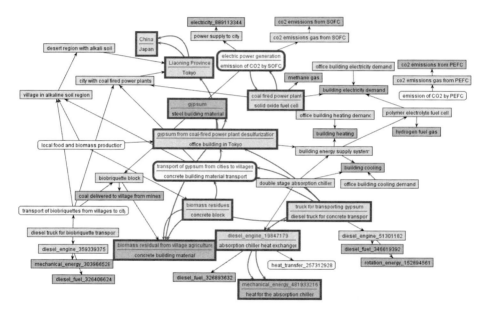

Fig. 5. Example of a match between two semantic knowledge description A-boxes. The instances in A-box used as the search condition are shown with black labels, and the instances in the A-box used as the matching knowledge description are shown with blue labels. The color of the instances indicates the type of instance. Arrows show the properties in the A-boxes connecting the different instances. The matching instances are shown with thick red borders.

(a) all of the instances in the query must bind with instances in the description in order to score a successful match and contribute the weight of the query to the overall match score (the default behavior) or (b) at least one of the instances must not bind with any instances in the description in order to score the successful match. For example, we can represent the following search condition: "I am looking for a building that should contain an energy system, preferably contains a fuel cell, must not contain a diesel engine, and should not contain any kind of engine" using the four queries and settings shown in Table 1.

Table 1. Search queries, match types, and weights for the example given in the text

Search Query	Match Type	Weight
building physically_contains energy_system	Must Match	1
building physically_contains fuel_cell	Must Match	-2
building physically_contains diesel_engine	Must Not Match	5
building physically_contains engine	Must Not Match	1

4 Approaches for Constructing Semantic Descriptions Based on the EKOSS Experience

We are currently employing over 30 students from both undergraduate and graduate courses in fields of environmental technologies and life sciences at the University of Tokyo to create semantic descriptions for the EKOSS server that we have deployed at http://www.ekoss.org. From our own experiences in creating semantic descriptions of knowledge and search conditions for the EKOSS system together with student feedback, we have found that three approaches are particularly effective. The first approach to constructing a semantic description is to begin by making a list of about 10 to 20 keywords that describe the knowledge or search conditions you are considering. Then, for each of the keywords, use the ontology browser function of the "Add Instance" tool to find the class in the ontology that best expresses that keyword. After you have created instances of the ontology classes for each of the keywords, use the "Add Connection" tool to determine the ontology properties that best express the binary relationships between the instances you have created. Finally, you can add additional instances and properties to describe particular attributes of the keywords. A typical example is a keyword that is really best expressed by two classes in the ontology, such as "building energy system". This keyword could be expressed by the A-box ("energy_systemA" "is_part_of" "buildingB").

The second approach that we have found to be effective for constructing semantic descriptions is to begin with a single instance of an ontology class that best describes the object of the knowledge or search. Properties can then be added to connect to other classes in the ontology in order to indicate the attributes that make the object special. For example, knowledge about an office building located in Tokyo that contains a fuel cell used for energy supply could be described by first creating an instance of the class "office_bldg" and then adding the property "physically_contains" pointing to an instance of "fuel_cell", "has_location" pointing to an instance of "city" labeled "Tokyo", and so on.

The third approach that we have used is to start with a relatively clear image of what the graph of instances and properties should look like and then build

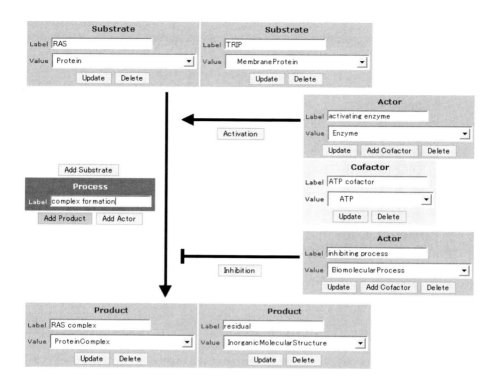

Fig. 6. The biology interface wizard for constructing descriptions of biomolecular processes

that graph. We have found that several common patterns appear in semantic descriptions from particular knowledge domains. For example, in the field of metabolic pathways, much of the knowledge centers on a particular biomolecular process, such as phosphorylation, that has one or more substrates and one or more products. Furthermore, most processes in cellular biology have one or more "actors" that either activate or inhibit the process. This simple model of metabolic pathway knowledge can be expressed by a basic template for semantic descriptions of that knowledge, as shown in Fig. 6. We are developing a number of such templates for commonly occurring patterns in knowledge from different domains that are supported by our system, as described in the section "Future Directions".

5 Comparison of EKOSS with Existing Systems

There are a number of web platforms that have been developed to make use of semantic web technologies for supporting knowledge sharing. Each platform uses different degrees of structure in the computer-interpretable semantics, provides different types of services to its users, and offers different features for assisting users in the process of adding semantics to their knowledge resources. Here, we compare some of these semantic knowledge sharing systems with EKOSS.

Mangrove, developed at the University of Washington, aims to provide a semantic-enabled knowledge sharing platform for communities of "non-technical" people. The philosophy of the Mangrove Project is that non-technical users could be enticed to semantically annotate their web pages if they were provided with useful services that gave them a sense of "instant gratification" [16]. The semantics used by the Mangrove system are therefore necessarily simplistic, and there is no underlying knowledge model or ontology for supporting logical reasoning. Although a proprietary reasoning engine is mentioned, it is unclear what reasoning capabilities are supported.

Dspace has been developed through the collaboration of the W3C, the MIT libraries, and the MIT CSAIL (Computer Science and Artificial Intelligence Laboratory) as a digital library that uses semantic tags to help with cataloging and retrieval [17]. DSpace is being augmented by the SIMILE (Semantic Interoperability of Metadata and Information in unLike Environments) project to support arbitrary metadata schemata in the form of RDF markup [18]. However, while EKOSS provides tools for using DL ontologies to create semantic A-boxes that describe knowledge resources in a way that can be reasoned against with DL reasoners for more accurate matching and retrieval, the semantics supported by Dspace with SIMILE is limited to RDFS so that only reasoning based on class subsumption is possible.

Magpie is a product of the Advanced Knowledge Technologies project that takes the form of a browser plugin providing users with tools for displaying terms in web pages that are found to match with terms from the ontology loaded in the system [22]. As the goal is to provide semantic web services with near-zero overhead costs, speed and minimization of user input requirements are emphasized. The EKOSS system, on the other hand, aims to empower knowledge creators interested in sharing their knowledge with the capacity to create semantic descriptions of that knowledge themselves with only a small amount of effort, trading off a small increase in overhead costs for the potential benefits from the greatly increased semantic richness.

SMORE (Semantic Markup, Ontology, and RDF Editor) is a set of tools created by MINDSWAP and integrated with the SWOOP ontology browser and the pellet OWL-DL reasoner that are intended to help users annotate their own web documents in OWL using ontologies on the web, without requiring the users to know OWL terms and syntax [24]. SMORE also provides limited capabilities for creating new ontologies and modifying existing ontologies to incorporate terms from the user's web documents. In this sense, the SMORE tools are designed for ontology building and annotation of web documents rather than actually describing knowledge resources with computer interpretable semantics.

CONFOTO supports the semantic annotation and browsing of conference photographs with RDF tags that are based on keyword-based classifications or folksonomies [19]. Folksonomies have been hypothesized to be easier for users to use in creating metadata than formal ontologies. However, we believe that through the tools and interfaces provided by the EKOSS system, a significant number of users particularly in the sciences would be willing to make the investment in time and effort to create semantic descriptions that would be far more useful for semantic analysis due to their solid foundation in formal ontologies.

Other related technologies include Cyc and other ontologies that are intended to function as centralized knowledge bases [21], the SEKT (Semantically-Enabled Knowledge Technologies) EU initiative that aims to realize a European Knowledge Society through development of core semantic technologies for knowledge management based on the KAON reasoner [20], the Tucana Knowledge Discovery Platform and its open source versions Kowari and Mulgara that target semantic databases and knowledge discovery platforms for enterprises [23], the SWOOGLE web search engine for searching and analyzing web documents having semantic markup [25], the Ont-O-Mat implementation of the CREAM framework for helping web page authors create semantic annotations in the form of relational metadata [27], and the web-based Annotea system for supporting the creating and sharing of RDF annotations [26].

6 Future Directions

In future research work, we plan to continue the development of the EKOSS system along three paths. First, we will develop domain specific wizards for creating semantic descriptions. These wizards will include 1) pictorial visualizations of ontology for helping users to identify the class in the ontology that best describes a concept that they want to include in an A-box and 2) template wizards for supporting construction of A-boxes for common semantic patterns in particular domains. An example of the second type of wizard was shown in Fig. 6.

We will also extend the functionality of the ontology browser in order to support user dialogue about the classes and structures of the ontologies available in the system, including examples of uses, suggestions for modifications to the ontologies, and addition of new classes. In doing so, we intend to offer expert users the opportunity to "bootstrap" the process of development and refinement of the ontologies on a particular EKOSS server. Furthermore, we will investigate the effectiveness of techniques for ontology translation and alignment based on the A-boxes that are created using the different domain ontologies supported by the EKOSS system.

Finally, on the semantic matching side, as we begin to accumulate a sufficient number of Knowledge Projects in the EKOSS system, we will develop methods for determining the semantic distance between pairs of semantic descriptions representing the Knowledge Projects. One approach that we are using is to create tools for automatically generating interesting subsets of the relatively large semantic description A-boxes and using those subsets as queries for matching with the semantic descriptions of other Knowledge Projects. The result is an indication of the degree of overlap between the two semantic descriptions (Fig. 5). We can use these measured distances between sets of Knowledge Projects to construct different semantic distance matrices depending on the conditions used for generating the queries from the semantic description of the first Knowledge Project. These semantic distance matrices can be used for a variety of knowledge integration applications. For example, we are developing graphic interface tools for visualizing the overall knowledge network that is represented by these semantic distance matrices as two dimensional knowledge maps or as three dimensional visualizations of Knowledge Project distributions around a particular project.

Acknowledgement. We gratefully acknowledge contributions and advice from Rafael Batres, Hiroshi Komiyama, Toshihisa Takagi, and David Wallace. Funding support was provided by the Knowledge Failure Database project at the Japan Science and Technology Agency.

References

1. Beasley, S.W.: The value of medical publications: 'To read them would ... burden the memory to no useful purpose'. Australian and New Zealand Journal of Surgery **70** (2000) 870–874
2. Ziman, J. M.: The proliferation of scientific literature: a natural process. Science **208** (2004) 369–371
3. Berners-Lee, T., Hendler, J.: Publishing on the Semantic Web. Nature **410** (2001), 1023–1024
4. Guo, W., Kraines, S.B.: Achieving Scalability of Semantic Searching and Matching based on OWL-DL, Rules and Datatype Property Reasoning. Submitted to SSWS2006
5. Kraines, S.B., Kemper, B.E., Wallace, D.R., Komiyama, H.: Scientific knowledge sharing through ontologies and computational models. Submitted to Communications of the ACM
6. Craven, M., Kumlien, J.: Constructing biological knowledge bases by extracting information from text sources. Proceedings of the 7th Intl Conf. on Intelligent Systems for Molecular Biology (ISMB-99) (1999)
7. Huang, M., Zhu, X., Hao, Y., Payan, D.G., Qu, K., Li, M.: Discovering patterns to extract protein-protein interactions from full texts. Bioinformatics **20** (2004) 3604–3612
8. Rzhetsky, A., Koike, T., Kalachikov, S., Gomez, S.M., Krauthammer, M., Kaplan, S.H., Kra, P., Russo, J.J., Friedman, C.: A knowledge model for analysis and simulation of regulatory networks. Bioinformatics Ontology **16** (2000) 1120–1128
9. Abbott, R.: Subjectivity as a concern for information science: a Popperian perspective. Journal of Information Science **30** (2004) 95–106
10. Swanson, D.R.: Medical literature as a potential source of new knowledge. Bull. Med. Libr. Assoc. **78** (1990) 29–37
11. Racer Systems GmbH & Co. KG.: World Wide Web site http://www.racer-systems.com
12. Kraines S.B., Batres, R., Koyama, M., Wallace, D.R., Komiyama, H.: Internet-Based Integrated Environmental Assessment: Using Ontologies to Share Computational Models. J. Industrial Ecology **9** (2005) 31–50
13. Kraines S.B., Wolowski, V., Koyama, M., Kemper, B.E., Muraki, R., Batres, R.: A semantic search engine for discovering engineering models using ontologies and agents. J. Industrial Ecology. In press

14. Guo, W., Kraines, S.B.: Knowledge sharing on a multi-agent reputation-based trust network. In preparation
15. Wallace, D.R., Abrahamson, S., Senin, N., Sferro, P.: Integrated design in a service marketplace. Computer-aided Design **32** (2000), 97–107
16. McDowell, L., Etzioni, O., Gribble, S., Halevy, A., Levy, H., Pentney, W., Verma, D., Vlasseva, S.: Mangrove: enticing ordinary people onto the semantic web via instant gratification. In Second International Semantic Web Conference (ISWC 2003), October 2003
17. Dspace website: http://www.dspace.org/
18. Mazzocchi, S., Garland, S., Lee, R.: SIMILE: Practical Metadata for the Semantic Web. XML.com, O'Reilly Media, Inc. January 26, 2005, http://www.xml.com/pub/a/2005/01/26/simile.html
19. Nowack, B.: CONFOTO: A semantic browsing and annotation service for conference photos. In Fourth International Semantic Web Conference (ISWC 2005) Y. Gil et al. (Eds.), LNCS 3729, pp. 1067–1070, 2005
20. SEKT website: http://www.sekt-project.org/
21. cyc website: http://www.opencyc.org/
22. Dzbor, M., Motta, E., Domingue, J.: Opening up magpie via semantic services. In Third International Semantic Web Conference (ISWC 2004), LNCS 3298, pp. 635–649, 2004
23. tucana website: http://tucana.es.northropgrumman.com/
24. Kalyanpur, A., Parsia, B., Hendler, J., Golbeck, J.: SMORE – semantic markup, ontology, and RDF editor. http://www.mindswap.org/papers/SMORE.pdf
25. swoogle website: http://swoogle.umbc.edu
26. Kahan, J., Koivunen, M.: Annotea: an open RDF infrastructure for shared web annotations. WWW2001, Proceedings of the Tenth International World Wide Web Conference. Hong Kong, May 2001.
27. Handschuh, S., Staab, S.: Authoring and annotation of web pages in CREAM. WWW2002, Proceedings of the Eleventh International World Wide Web Conference. Honolulu, Hawaii, USA, May 2002.
28. Kraines, S.B., Guo, W., Kemper, B., Nakamura, Y.: A semantic web application for expert knowledge sharing, discovery, and integration. ISWC2006. In press

Ontogator — A Semantic View-Based Search Engine Service for Web Applications

Eetu Mäkelä[1], Eero Hyvönen[1], and Samppa Saarela[1,2]

[1] Semantic Computing Research Group (SeCo),
Helsinki University of Technology (TKK), Laboratory of Media Technology
University of Helsinki, Department of Computer Science
firstname.lastname@tkk.fi
http://www.seco.tkk.fi/
[2] Mysema Ltd
samppa.saarela@mysema.com

Abstract. View-based search provides a promising paradigm for formulating complex semantic queries and representing results on the Semantic Web. A challenge for the application of the paradigm is the complexity of providing view-based search services through application programming interfaces (API) and web services. This paper presents a solution on how semantic view-based search can be provided efficiently through an API or as web service to external applications. The approach has been implemented as the open source tool Ontogator, that has been applied successfully in several practical semantic portals on the web.

Keywords: semantic view-based search, view projection, Semantic Web middleware.

1 Interfacing Search Services

The Semantic Web enables querying data based on various combinations of semantic relationships. Because of the RDF data model, these queries are usually drafted as possibly complex sets of semantic relation patterns. An example would be "Find all toys manufactured in Europe in the 19th century, used by someone born in the 20th century". Here "toys", "Europe", "the 18th century", "someone" and "the 19th century" are ontological class restrictions on nodes and "manufactured in", "used by" and "time of birth" are the required connecting arcs in the pattern. While such queries are easy to formalize and query as graph patterns, they remain problematic because they are not easy for users to formulate. Therefore, much of the research in complex semantic queries has been on user interfaces [1,2] for creating complex query patterns as intuitively as possible.

View-based search [3,4] is a search interface paradigm based on a long-running library tradition of faceted classification [5]. Usability studies done on view-based search systems, such as Flamenco [6,4] and Relation Browser++ [7] have proved the paradigm both powerful and intuitive for end-users, particularly in drafting complex queries. Thus, view-based search presents a promising direction for semantic search interface design, if it can be successfully combined with Semantic Web technologies.

The core idea of view-based search is to provide multiple, simultaneous views to an information collection, each showing the collection categorized according to some distinct, orthogonal aspect. A search in the system then proceeds by selecting subsets of values from the views, constraining the search based on the aspects selected. As an example, figure 1 shows the view-based search interface of the Veturi [8] yellow pages service discovery portal. Here, the user is looking for sweets, and has specified "marmalade", "buy" and "Helsinki" as the Patient (Mitä), Process (Prosessi) and Place (Paikka) aspects of the service, respectively.

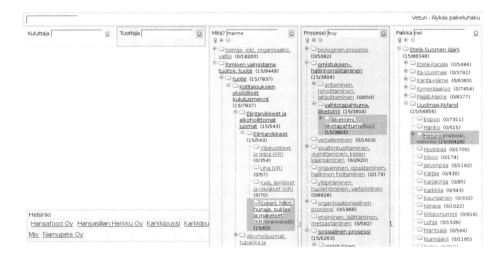

Fig. 1. Locating shops that sell marmalade in Helsinki

A key feature that differentiates view-based search from traditional keyword and Boolean search is the use of a preselected group of categorizing views in both formulating queries and in representing the results. The views give the user the query vocabulary and content classification scheme in an intuitive format. In addition, at each step, the number of hits belonging to each category is shown. Because the search proceeds by selecting these categories as further constraints, the user always knows beforehand exactly how many items will be in the result set after her next move. This prevents the user from making selections that lead to empty or very large result sets, and guides her effectively in constraining the search.

View-based search has been integrated with the Semantic Web in [9,10,11]. In this *semantic view-based search*, the facets are constructed algorithmically from a set of underlying ontologies that are used as the basis for annotating search items. Furthermore, the mapping of search items onto search facets is defined using logic rules. This facilitates more intelligent search of indirectly related items. Another benefit is that the logic layer of rules make it possible to use the same search engine for content of different kinds and annotated using different annotation schemes.

As part of the work, five view-based semantic portals were created. Previous research on the interfaces of the portals [10,11,12] have proved that regarding interface flexibility and extensibility with other semantic techniques, the view-based paradigm provides a versatile base for search on the Semantic Web. The functionalities of the interfaces developed span the whole range of search tasks identified in recent search behavior research[13,14].

Underlying all these portals is the semantic portal tool OntoViews [15], available open source under the MIT license[1]. The tool is based on the Service Oriented Architecture (SOA) approach, combining independent Semantic Web Services into a working whole. This article presents the most important of these services: the general semantic view-based search service Ontogator.

Ontogator presents a solution to the following problem: what kind of search engine service and Application Programming Interface (API) are needed for supporting a variety of semantic view-based search interfaces? For a traditional Boolean logic or keyword based search engine such as Google, the API is fairly simple[2]. The functionalities needed of a general view-based search API are much more complex. It should support facet visualization, including hit counting, facet selection, and result visualization in different ways in addition to the search logic.

Ontogator is a service with an XML/RDF-based API that provides an external software agent with all the services needed for performing view-based search. The system with its query language and implementation is described in detail in [16]. In the following, we focus in more detail on the design principles underlying the system, and the issues faced in general while designing and implementing semantic view-based search as an independent, general service.

2 Requirements for a View-Based Search API

Below are listed some services needed from the engine in a view-based semantic portal, such as MuseumFinland [11], for providing the user with a useful view-based user interface (UI).

1. Facets are exposed to the end-user in the UI for making category selections. Therefore, querying facets with hit counts projected on categories is needed.
2. On the view-based UI, clicking on a category link in a facet activates view-based search. The API therefore supports querying by Boolean category search with term expansion along facets, i.e., basic view-based search.
3. Depending on the situation, some metadata of the RDF repository, such as confidential information, should be filtered and consequently not be shown on the UI. Therefore, a mechanism for specifying the form and content of the results is useful.

---

[1] http://www.seco.tkk.fi/projects/semweb/dist.php
[2] see e.g. http://www.google.com/apis/reference.html#searchrequest

4. Reclassifying the result set along different facets and depths is needed when inspecting the hit list. In MuseumFinland, for example, the UI provides the user a link button for each view facet. By clicking it the museum collection artifacts in the hit result set are reclassified along the selected facet, such as Artifact type, Material type, Place of Manufacture, etc. A query mechanism for this is needed.
5. Combining traditional keyword search with view-based search. Research has shown [6,4] that keyword search and view-based search complement each other. In practice, both search paradigms have to be supported simultaneously, and a method for combining the paradigms is needed.
6. Support for knowledge-based semantic search. The search should be intelligent in the sense that the engine can find, using domain knowledge, also content that is only implicitly related with search categories. For example, the underlying knowledge base of MuseumFinland has some 300 rules of common knowledge that tell how artifacts are related to other concepts. If a rule tells that doctor's hats are used in academic ceremonial events, then a search with the category "Ceremonies" in the "Events" facet should retrieve all doctor's hats even when the actual metadata of the hats in the underlying databases does not directly mention ceremonies.

Generalizing these requirements and adding architectural constraints, in the end the following design goals for the system were set:

1. Adaptability and domain independence. Ontogator should easily adapt to variant domains and make use of the semantics of any data.
2. Standards. The query and response interfaces of Ontogator should conform to established Semantic Web standards as independent semantic components.
3. Extensibility. The system architecture should be extensible, especially with regard to querying functionality.
4. Scalability. The system should scale to handle large amounts of semantic metadata (millions of search items).

The challenge in designing the Ontogator search service was to find out how to support these various needs of semantic view-based search in a computationally scalable way. During design, it also became apparent that on the Semantic Web, view category identification poses certain questions in itself. In the following, these points will be discussed in their own sections.

3 Adaptability to Different Domains

A major issue in applying the view-based search paradigm is in how to create the views used in the application as flexibly as possible. On the Semantic Web, domains are described richly using ontologies. However, as in traditional classification systems, hierarchical hyponymy and meronymy relationships are still important for structuring a domain. Therefore, these ontologies typically contain a rich variety of such elements, most often defined with explicit relations, such as "part-of" and "subclass-of". This naturally leads to the idea of using these hierarchical structures as bases for views in view-based searching. To carry this out, Ontogator introduces a preprocessing phase termed *view projection*.

The transformation consists of two important parts: projecting a view tree from the RDF graph, and linking items to the categories projected. Originally, these tasks were performed by the Ontodella logic server [17], but recently have been incorporated into Ontogator itself. For both tasks, Ontogator relies on traversing the RDF graph guided by specified rules, picking up relevant concepts and linking them into a view tree based on the relations they have in the underlying knowledge base. The result of this phase is a set of indexed facet structures linked with the actual content items to be searched for. The domain dependent reasoning part of search is performed at this phase and means in practice mapping search items to the search categories.

For describing the view projections, Ontogator uses an RDF-based configuration format. The projection interface was designed to be modular and extensible, so that new projection rule styles and constructs could be created and used interchangeably in the system. Currently, the interface supports rules defined in a simple RDF path language, as well as the Prova[3] language, a Java version of Prolog. This makes it possible to keep simple rule definitions simple, but also, if needed, take advantage of the expression power of Prolog.

As an example of the configuration format, a snippet from the Veturi portal, slightly adapted for demonstration purposes, is provided:

```
<ogt:HierarchyDefinition rdf:nodeID="patient">
  <ogt:root rdf:resource="&object;Object"/>
  <ogt:incProperty rdf:resource="&rdfs;label"/>
  <ogt:subCategoryLink>
    <ogt:ProvaLink rdf:nodeID="coicopSubClasses">
      <ogt:isLeaf>false</ogt:isLeaf>
      <ogt:linkRule>
        rdf(Target,'coicop:hasParent',Source).
      </ogt:linkRule>
    </ogt:ProvaLink>
  </ogt:subCategoryLink>
  <ogt:subCategoryLink rdf:nodeID="sumoSubClasses"/>
  <ogt:itemLink rdf:nodeID="sumoItems"/>
</ogt:HierarchyDefinition>
```

In the example, in the tree projection phase a "Patient" hierarchy is projected, using two "subCategoryLink" rules for recursively adding subcategories to the view. The first is a simple Prova rule for the COICOP [18] product hierarchy. The second subcategory rule for projecting the Suggested Upper Merged Ontology (SUMO) [19] -based process hierarchy is not actually defined here, but refers to a Prova definition elsewhere in the RDF document. This possibility for rule reuse is a nice property of the RDF model. As an example of a more complex rule, consider the actual definition of the linked rule:

```
% base case, handle categories where we're not told to stop, nor to skip
sumo_sub_category(Source,Target) :-
```

---

[3] http://www.prova.ws/

```
Skip = 'http://www.cs.helsinki.fi/group/iwebs/ns/process.owl#skip',
rdf(Target,'rdfs:subClassOf', Source),
not(rdf(Target,'sumo_ui:display',Skip)),
not(sumo_subcategory_not_acceptable(Target)).

% if we're told to skip a category, then do it.
sumo_sub_category(Source,Target) :-
  Skip = 'http://www.cs.helsinki.fi/group/iwebs/ns/process.owl#skip',
  rdf(SubClass,'rdfs:subClassOf', Source),
  rdf(SubClass,'sumo_ui:display', Skip ),
  sumo_sub_category(SubClass,Target).

% don't process MILO categories
sumo_subcategory_not_acceptable(SubClass) :-
  Milo = 'http://reliant.teknowledge.com/DAML/MILO.owl#',
  not(rdf_split_url(Milo,Prop,SubClass)).

% don't process if we're told to stop
sumo_subcategory_not_acceptable(SubClass) :-
  Stop = 'http://www.cs.helsinki.fi/group/iwebs/ns/process.owl#stop',
  rdf( SubClass, 'sumo_ui:display', Stop).

% don't process if someone above us told us to stop
sumo_subcategory_not_acceptable(SubClass) :-
  Stop = 'http://www.cs.helsinki.fi/group/iwebs/ns/process.owl#stop',
  rdf( Y, 'sumo_ui:display', Stop ),
  not( rdf_transitive(SubClass,'rdfs:subClassOf',Y)).
```

Here, while the basis for hierarchy formulation is still the "rdfs:subClassOf" relationship, complexity arises because it is not used as-is. The class hierarchy of the SUMO ontology is designed mainly to support computerized inference, and is not necessarily intuitive to a human end user. To make the hierarchy less off-putting for a user, two additional rules are used, based on configuration information encoded directly into the RDF data model. First, categories in the middle of the tree that make sense ontologically but not to the user should be skipped, bumping subcategories up one level. Second, sometimes whole subtrees should be eliminated. In addition, in the data model there are also classes of the Mid Level Ontology (MILO) [20] extending the SUMO tree. These are used elsewhere to add textual material to the categories for text-based matching, but are not to be directly processed into the tree.

From an algorithmical perspective, in projecting a tree from a directed graph, there are always two things that must be considered. First, possible loops in the source data must be dealt with to produce a Directed Acyclic Graph (DAG). This usually means just dismissing arcs that would form cycles in the projection process. Second, classes with multiple superclasses must be dealt with to project the DAG into a tree. Usually such classes are either assigned to a single superclass or cloned, which results in cloning also the whole subtree below.

The second phase of view projection is associating the actual information items searched for with the categories. Most often, this is just a simple case of selecting a property that links the items to the categories, but it can get more complex than that here, too. Back in the first listing, the third link rule is an "itemLink", referring to the following rule:

```
<ogt:RDFPathLink rdf:nodeID="sumoItems">
  <ogt:isLeaf>true</ogt:isLeaf>
  <ogt:linkRule>
```

```
      ^sumo:patient^process:subProcess
    </ogt:linkRule>
  </ogt:RDFPathLink>
```

This rule is again defined using the simple RDF path format. The backwards path in the example specifies that to locate the service processes associated with a category of objects, one should first locate all processes where the category is specified as the patient type. From there, one can then find the services that contain those subprocesses.

The reason for introducing the projection preprocessing phase is two-fold. First, in this way the Ontogator search engine can be made completely independent of the domain knowledge and of the annotation schema used. It does not know anything about the domain semantics of the original knowledge base or the annotation schema used, but only about semantics of view-based search. Second, during knowledge compilation, efficient indices facilitating computationally scalable semantic view-based search to millions of search items can be created. A problem of the preprocessing approach is that the contents cannot, at least in the current implementation, be updated gradually.

The extensibility of the Ontogator projection architecture is based on combining only a few well defined component roles to create more complex structures. There are in essence only two types of components in the architecture: those linking individual resources to each other, and those producing resource trees. Based on these roles it is easy to reuse components, for example using the same linkers both for item and subcategory links, or creating a compound hierarchy by including individual hierarchies. Using the RDF data model for configuring the projection further supports this, giving a clear format for expressing these combinatory structures, and even making it possible to refer to and reuse common component instances.

4   Category Identification

Because of the projection, categories in semantic view-based search cannot be identified by the URIs of the original resources. First, the same resources may feature in multiple views, such as when a place is used in both a "Place of Use" and a "Place of Manufacture" view. Second, even inside one view, breaking multiple inheritance may result in cloning resources. Therefore, some method for generating category identifiers is needed.

An important consideration in this is how persistent the created identifiers need to be. In a web application for example, it is often useful for identifiers to stay the same as long as possible, to allow the user to long-term bookmark their search state in their browser. A simple approach for generating persistent category identifiers would start by just concatenating the URIs of categories in the full path from the tree root to the current category to account for multiple inheritance. Then an additional URI would have to be added, for differentiating between the semantic sense by which the actual information items are related to the categories, e.g. "Place of Use" and "Place of Manufacture" again.

This will create identifiers resilient to all changes in the underlying ontology knowledge base other than adding or moving categories in the middle of an existing hierarchy. And even in that case, good heuristics would be available for relocating lost categories. This will, however, result in very long category identifiers.

If persistence is not critical, many schemes can be applied to generate shorter category identifiers. In Ontogator, a prefix labeling scheme [21] based on subcategory relationships is used: the subcategories of a will be identified as aa, ab and so on. This scheme was selected because it makes finding out the subcategories of a given category very easy, a useful property in result set calculation, described later. The potential problem here is that even if the order in which subcategories are projected is preserved, adding resources to, or removing them from the ontology may result in categories with different identifiers. That is, a category with the identifier aba that used to represent e.g. "Finland" could turn out to represent "Norway", with no means for the system to know about the change. As the original portals created on top of OntoViews were fairly static, this was not judged to be a problem outweighing the benefits.

5 Standards: Interfacing with Other Semantic Components

On the Semantic Web, it is important that the interfaces of programs conform to established standards, particularly for semantic services intended to be of general use. To this end, both the queries and results of Ontogator are expressed in RDF. The query interface is defined as an OWL ontology[4], and is therefore immediately usable by any application capable of producing either RDF, or XML conforming to the RDF/XML serialization.

As for conforming to different functional needs, the interface itself then contains plenty of options to filter, group, cut, annotate and otherwise modify the results returned. These options allow the basic interface to efficiently meet different demands, as evidenced by the wide variety of interfaces[11,8,12] created using the system. For example, when constructing a view-based query for an UI page depicting the facets, one can specify that only the facet structure with hit counts but without the actual hits is returned. On a hit list page the attributes can be selected so that the actual hits are returned classified along the direct subcategories of an arbitrary facet category.

Because Ontogator mainly works with tree hierarchies inherent in ontologies, it is only natural that also the result of the search engine is expressed as an RDF tree. This tree structure also conforms to a fixed XML-structure. This is done to allow the use of XML tools such as XSLT to process the results. This provides both a fall-back to well established technologies, and allows for the use of tools especially designed to process hierarchical document structures. In OntoViews, for example, the XML/RDF results of Ontogator are transformed into XHTML UI pages by using XSLT.

---

[4] http://www.cs.helsinki.fi/group/seco/ns/2004/03/ontogator#

The need for defining a new kind of tree-based query language, and not using existing query schemes for relational databases, XML, or RDF is due to the nature of the view-based search and to reasons of computational efficiency. In view-based search, the UI is heavily based of tree structures exposing to the end-user versatile information about the search categories and results. Supporting the creation of such structures by a search engine makes application development easier. The search and result construction is also more efficient this way. Firstly, the needed structures can be constructed at the time of the search where the information needed is easily available. Secondly, in this way the indices and search algorithms can be optimized for view-based search in particular. In our first implementation tests, some generic Semantic Web tools such as Jena were used for implementing the search operations, but in the end, special purpose Java programs were developed leading to a much more efficient implementation.

6 Extensibility

The RDF-based query language created for Ontogator was designed to be as flexible and extensible as possible also with regard to querying functionality. The basic query format is based on two components: an items clause for selecting items for the result set, and a categories clause for selecting a subtree of categories to be used in grouping the results for presentation. This format enables flexibly grouping the results using any category clause, for example organizing items based on a keyword query according to geolocations near the user.

The way both clauses work is based on an extensible set of selectors, components that produce a list of matching resource identifiers based on some criteria particular to them. The current implementation allows searching for view categories using 1) the category identifier, 2) the resource URI of which the category is projected and 3) a keyword, possibly targeted at a specific property value of the category. These category selectors can also be used also to select items. In this case the selector selects all items that relate to the found categories. Items can additionally directly be queried using their own keyword and URI selectors. Different selectors can be combined to form more complex queries using special union and intersection selectors.

Ontogator can be extended by defining and implementing new selectors. This provides a lot of freedom, as the only requirement for a selector is that it produce a list of matching items. The selector itself can implement its functionality in any way desired. For example, a selector selecting items based on location could act as a mere proxy, relaying the request to a GIS server using the user's current location as a parameter and returning results directly for further processing.

7 Scalability

The full vision of the Semantic Web requires search engines to be able to process large amounts of data. Therefore, the scalability of the system was an important consideration in the design of Ontogator. With testing on fabricated data, it was deduced that in general, Ontogator performance degrades linearly with respect to both increasing the average number of items related to a category and increasing the amount of categories as a whole, with the amount of items in isolation not having much effect. As for real-world performance, table 1 lists the results of search performance tests done on the major portals developed. Because the queries used in the different portals differ in complexity, the results do not scale directly with regard to size, but still approximately conform to the results of the earlier tests.

Table 1. Ontogator performance comparison

Portal	Views	Categories	Items	Avg. items / category	Avg. response time
dmoz.org test	21	275,707	2,300,000	8.91	3.50 seconds
Veturi	5	2,637	196,166	128.80	2.70 seconds
MuseumFinland	9	7,637	4,132	5.10	0.22 seconds
SW-Suomi.fi	6	229	152	3.55	0.10 seconds
Orava	5	139	2,142	84.00	0.06 seconds

Of the performance test results, the ones done on the dmoz.org Open Directory Project website catalog data provide an obvious comparison point with current web portals, and confirm that this implementation of view-based search is sufficiently scalable for even large amounts of real life data. This scalability in Ontogator has been achieved using a fast memory-resident prefix label indexing scheme [21], as well as query options restricting result size and necessary processing complexity. These considerations taken are detailed below:

7.1 Indexing

The tree hierarchy -based search as presented here requires that related to a category, direct subcategories, directly linked items, the transitive closure of linked items and the path to the tree root can be computed efficiently. The reverse relation of mapping an item to all categories it belongs to also needs to be efficiently calculated.

Ontogator uses custom Java objects (in memory) to model the direct relations of categories and items. All other data related to the categories and items, such as labels or descriptions are retrieved from an associated Jena[5] RDF model.

Both direct subcategories and directly linked items are recorded in memory for each category to allow for speedy retrieval. A full closure of linked items is not recorded, but calculated at runtime. To do this, Ontogator makes use of a subcategory closure, gathering together all items in all the found subcategories. The subcategory closure itself is acquired efficiently by making use of the prefix labeling scheme used for the categories. After generation, the labels are stored in a lexically sorted index, so that the subcategories of any given category are

---

[5] http://jena.sourceforge.net/, the leading Java RDF toolkit, developed under an open source licence at HP labs

placed immediately after it in the index. This way, any subcategory closure can be listed in $O(log(n) + n)$ time, by enumerating all categories in the index after the queried resource, until a prefix not matching the current resource is found. The use of prefix labeling also means that the whole path from view root to a given category is directly recorded in its label. Another advantage is that the identifiers are short, and easy to handle using standard Java utility classes.

7.2 Result Complexity Management

To decrease result file size as well as result computation complexity, Ontogator provides many options to turn off various result components. If grouping is not wanted, inclusion of categories can be turned off and respectively if items are not desired, their inclusion can be turned off. Turning both off can be used to gain metadata of the query's results, such as number of item or category hits.

The most important of these options, with regards to query efficiency, deals with the hit counts. Turning item hit counting off for categories speeds up the search by a fair amount. Used generally, however, this deprives the tree-views of their important function as categorizations of the data. Therefore, the option makes most sense in pre-queries and background queries, as well as a last effort to increase throughput when dealing with massive amounts of data.

7.3 Result Breadth Management

Result breadth options in Ontogator deal with limiting the maximum number of items or categories returned in a single query. They can either be defined globally, or to apply only to specified categories. With options to skip categories or items, this functionality can also be used for (sub)paging.

In MuseumFinland, a metadata-generating pre-query is used before the actual search query, to optimize the result breadth options used. The query results are used to specify the maximum number of items returned for each shown category — if the result contains only a few categories, more items can be fitted in each category in the user interface.

7.4 Result Depth Management

Depending on the nature of the view-based user interface, hierarchies of different depths are needed. Currently Ontogator supports three subhierarchy inclusion options. These are

none. No subcategories of found categories are included in the result. This option is used in category keyword queries: only categories directly matching the given keyword will be returned.

direct. Direct subcategories of found categories will be included in the result. This option is used to build the basic views in MuseumFinland.

all. The whole subhierarchy of found categories will be included in the result. This option is used to show the whole classification page in MuseumFinland, as well as the main view in Veturi, which give the user an overview of how the items are distributed in the hierarchy.

Similar options are available for controlling if and how paths to the selected category from the view root are to be returned.

With result breadth limits, these options can be used to limit the maximum size of the result set. This is especially important in limited bandwidth environments.

8 Discussion

Several lessons were learned in designing and implementing Ontogator. First, the projection formalism, particularly coupled with the expressive power of Prolog rules provide a flexible base on which to build view projection. However, Prolog is unfamiliar to many programmers. To counter this, projection configuration in Ontogator also allows defining and using simpler formalisms for cases where not so much expressive power is needed.

Second, to increase adaptability and component reuse, the old UNIX motto for creating distinct components that do one thing well, but can be connected to perform complex operations continues to apply. On the Semantic Web, it makes sense for the components to both consume and produce, as well as define their API in RDF and/or OWL.

Third, for scalable tree hierarchy-based search, an efficient index for calculating a transitive closure of items is needed, and it should be possible to curtail result calculation complexity with options. Also, problems of category identification need to be sorted out.

A limitation of the approach was also noted. Ontogator was designed as a stateless SOA service with the expectation that queries would be largely independent of each other. However, for some applications, such as the Veturi interface presented, this expectation does not hold. When navigating the tree hierarchies in Veturi, most queries are just opening further branches in a result tree that is already partially calculated. Currently, the whole visible tree needs to be recalculated and returned. A possible solution using the current architecture would be to maintain in Ontogator a cache of recently calculated result sets for reuse. This would not be a large task, as the API already uses such a cache in calculating category hit counts for the various views inside a single query.

9 Related Implementations

During the timeframe of this research, other implementations of view-based search for the Semantic Web have also surfaced. The Longwell RDF browser[6] provides a general view-based search interface for any data. However, it supports only flat, RDF-property-based views. The SWED directory portal [22] is a semantic view hierarchy-based search portal for environmental organisations and projects. However, the view hierarchies used in the portal are not projections from full-fledged ontologies, but are manually crafted using the W3C SKOS [23]

---

[6] http://simile.mit.edu/longwell/

schema for simple thesauri. The portal does, however, support distributed maintenance of the portal data. The Seamark Navigator[7] by Siderean Software, Inc. is a commercial implementation of view-based semantic search. It also, however, only supports simple flat categorizations.

Acknowledgements

This research was mostly funded by the Finnish Funding Agency for Technology and Innovation Tekes.

References

1. Athanasis, N., Christophides, V., Kotzinos, D.: Generating on the fly queries for the semantic web: The ICS-FORTH graphical RQL interface (GRQL). In: Proceedings of the Third International Semantic Web Conference. (2004) 486–501
2. Catarci, T., Dongilli, P., Mascio, T.D., Franconi, E., Santucci, G., Tessaris, S.: An ontology based visual tool for query formulation support. In: Proceedings of the 16th Eureopean Conference on Artificial Intelligence, IOS Press (2004) 308–312
3. Pollitt, A.S.: The key role of classification and indexing in view-based searching. Technical report, University of Huddersfield, UK (1998)
4. Hearst, M., Elliott, A., English, J., Sinha, R., Swearingen, K., Lee, K.P.: Finding the flow in web site search. CACM **45**(9) (2002) 42–49
5. Maple, A.: Faceted access: A review of the literature. Technical report, Working Group on Faceted Access to Music, Music Library Association (1995)
6. Lee, K.P., Swearingen, K., Li, K., Hearst, M.: Faceted metadata for image search and browsing. In: Proceedings of CHI 2003, April 5-10, Fort Lauderdale, USA, Association for Computing Machinery (ACM), USA (2003)
7. Zhang, J., Marchionini, G.: Evaluation and evolution of a browse and search interface: Relation Browser++. In: dg.o2005: Proceedings of the 2005 national conference on Digital government research, Digital Government Research Center (2005) 179–188
8. Mäkelä, E., Viljanen, K., Lindgren, P., Laukkanen, M., Hyvönen, E.: Semantic yellow page service discovery: The Veturi portal. In: Poster paper, 4th International Semantic Web Conference. (2005)
9. Hyvönen, E., Saarela, S., Viljanen, K.: Application of ontology techniques to view-based semantic search and browsing. In: The Semantic Web: Research and Applications. Proceedings of the First European Semantic Web Symposium (ESWS 2004). (2004)
10. Mäkelä, E., Hyvönen, E., Sidoroff, T.: View-based user interfaces for information retrieval on the semantic web. In: Proceedings of the ISWC-2005 Workshop End User Semantic Web Interaction. (2005)
11. Hyvönen, E., Mäkelä, E., Salminen, M., Valo, A., Viljanen, K., Saarela, S., Junnila, M., Kettula, S.: MuseumFinland – Finnish museums on the semantic web. Journal of Web Semantics **3**(2) (2005) 25
12. Sidoroff, T., Hyvönen, E.: Semantic e-goverment portals - a case study. In: Proceedings of the ISWC-2005 Workshop Semantic Web Case Studies and Best Practices for eBusiness SWCASE05. (2005)

---

[7] http://siderean.com/products.html

13. Sellen, A., Murphy, R., Shaw, K.L.: How Knowledge Workers Use the Web. In: Proceedings of the SIGCHI conference on Human factors in computing systems, CHI Letters 4(1), ACM (2002)
14. Teevan, J., Alvarado, C., Ackerman, M.S., Karger, D.R.: The perfect search engine is not enough: a study of orienteering behavior in directed search. In: Proceedings of the Conference on Human Factors in Computing Systems, CHI. (2004) 415–422
15. Mäkelä, E., Hyvönen, E., Saarela, S., Viljanen, K.: OntoViews - A Tool for Creating Semantic Web Portals. In: Proceedings of the Third Internation Semantic Web Conference, Springer Verlag (2004)
16. Saarela, S.: Näkymäpohjainen rdf-haku. Master's thesis, University of Helsinki (2004)
17. Viljanen, K., Känsälä, T., Hyvönen, E., Mäkelä, E.: Ontodella - a projection and linking service for semantic web applications. In: Proceedings of the 17th International Conference on Database and Expert Systems Applications (DEXA 2006), Krakow, Poland, IEEE (2006) To be published.
18. United Nations, Statistics Division: Classification of Individual Consumption by Purpose (COICOP). United Nations, New York, USA (1999)
19. Pease, A., Niles, I., Li, J.: The suggested upper merged ontology: A large ontology for the semantic web and its applications. In: Working Notes of the AAAI-2002 Workshop on Ontologies and the Semantic Web. (2002)
20. Niles, I., Terry, A.: The MILO: A general-purpose, mid-level ontology. In Arabnia, H.R., ed.: IKE, CSREA Press (2004) 15–19
21. Christophides, V., Karvounarakis, G., Plexousakis, D., Scholl, M., Tourtounis, S.: Optimizing taxonomic semantic web queries using labeling schemes. Journal of Web Semantics 1(2) (2004) 207–228
22. Reynolds, D., Shabajee, P., Cayzer, S.: Semantic Information Portals. In: Proceedings of the 13th International World Wide Web Conference on Alternate track papers & posters, ACM Press (2004)
23. Miles, A., Brickley, D., eds.: SKOS Core Guide. World Wide Web Consortium (2005) W3C Recommendation Working Draft.

Explaining Conclusions from Diverse Knowledge Sources

J. William Murdock[1], Deborah L. McGuinness[2], Paulo Pinheiro da Silva[3,*],
Chris Welty[1], and David Ferrucci[1]

[1] IBM Watson Research Center
19 Skyline Drive
Hawthorn, NY 10532
[2] Knowledge Systems, Artificial Intelligence Laboratory
Stanford University
Stanford, CA 94305
[3] Department of Computer Science
The University of Texas at El Paso
500 W University Ave
El Paso TX 79968-0518

Abstract. The ubiquitous non-semantic web includes a vast array of unstructured information such as HTML documents. The semantic web provides more structured knowledge such as hand-built ontologies and semantically aware databases. To leverage the full power of both the semantic and non-semantic portions of the web, software systems need to be able to reason over both kinds of information. Systems that use both structured and unstructured information face a significant challenge when trying to convince a user to believe their results: the sources *and* the kinds of reasoning that are applied to the sources are radically different in their nature and their reliability. Our work aims at explaining conclusions derived from a combination of structured and unstructured sources. We present our solution that provides an infrastructure capable of encoding justifications for conclusions in a single format. This integration provides an end-to-end description of the knowledge derivation process including access to text or HTML documents, descriptions of the analytic processes used for extraction, as well as descriptions of the ontologies and many kinds of information manipulation processes, including standard deduction. We produce unified traces of extraction and deduction processes in the Proof Markup Language (PML), an OWL-based formalism for encoding provenance for inferred information. We provide a browser for exploring PML and thus enabling a user to understand how some conclusion was reached.

1 Introduction

It has been recognized since at least the early days of expert systems research that systems should be able to provide information about how answers were obtained if users are expected to understand, trust, and use conclusions. In these early systems, conclusions may have been obtained by using sound inference procedures applied to

---

* This work was done while at the Knowledge Systems, Artificial Intelligence Laboratory at Stanford University.

knowledge bases of logical statements that were hand coded by experts. Under these conditions, the knowledge bases may have contained correct and trustworthy information and the reasoners may have been correct. The information about the answer generation process typically focused on the derivation path, and it was typically referred to as an explanation. Sometimes the explanations included some limited information about facts from the knowledge bases. Sometimes there was additional focus on taking the information concerning the derivation path and making it more understandable to the end user.

Modern semantic web systems also require this kind of support, however now they also have additional needs. There are two characteristics that our work addresses:

1. Semantic web systems can have **different kinds of information** that form the basis of their reasoning, e.g., unstructured HTML, manually generated OWL ontologies, RDF stores, etc.
2. Semantic web systems that use different kinds of information will need to use **different kinds of processing** to manipulate that information.

In other words, semantic web systems may use *distributed* knowledge bases constructed by *different organizations* from *many sources* using *multiple reasoning components*.

Systems that process input information in the form of HTML and text typically operate in two phases. First, they *extract* logical statements from the text automatically or semi-automatically. Next those logical statements are combined with existing structured knowledge (if any) to form a knowledge-base used for additional reasoning.

Information extraction techniques are known to produce conclusions that are not sound. In an integrated system in which such statements are input directly into a knowledge base, from which reasoning may derive further incorrect information, there is an increased need to provide thorough and integrated explanations; they need to have access to the raw sources of information and its meta information (recency, authoritativeness, etc.) and they need to provide insight into how the knowledge base statements were obtained.

In this paper, we describe a solution infrastructure that provides meta-information for integrated Natural Language Processing / Knowledge Base systems that includes the sources of information (including documents, passages, linguistic markup, semi-structured and structured data- and knowledge-bases), the nature of the information (documents, annotations, facts), the epistemological status (extracted, derived, asserted), and the sources (people, articles, automated reasoning components, text extraction components). This meta-information, or *knowledge provenance*, is integrated with our explanation infrastructure so that conclusions can be traced to their sources along a derivation path.

This paper is not addressing the issue of presentation techniques for knowledge provenance that may include abstractions and dialogues, and thus is not about explanation in the traditional sense. The primary contributions of the paper are the *uniform framework* that provides the basis for explanations over a much broader range of systems than any known previous work, and a view of *extraction as inference* [Ferrucci, 2004] that allows the integration of proof-based explanations with the field of text analytics.

2 Solution Architecture

Our solution relies on integration work between research on unstructured and structured information. The primary integration work is between two foundational components: The Unstructured Information Management Architecture (UIMA) and the Inference Web (IW). UIMA is a framework for integrating software components that analyze unstructured information such as text [Ferrucci and Lally, 2004]. IW is a framework for explaining systems that manipulate structured information and now unstructured information [McGuinness and Pinheiro da Silva, 2004]. We have developed new capabilities supporting the combination of IW and UIMA, enabling the former to present explanations of analysis performed within the latter.

2.1 UIMA

UIMA provides an infrastructure for integrating analysis components. The components use a declarative formalism. The specifications are hierarchical, i.e., aggregate components may be constructed out of a combination of primitive components and/or other aggregate components. At each level of the component hierarchy, the specification describes input requirements and output capabilities using a simple ontology. By describing analysis systems in terms of inputs and outputs at multiple levels of abstraction, UIMA provides an effective and convenient starting point for explaining analysis.

To support explanation, UIMA now provides a scalable repository for storing the final results of the knowledge extraction processes. This repository is known as the EKDB (Extracted Knowledge Database). The EKDB stores not only the content of the extracted knowledge (i.e., the set of entities and relations that the analysis system concluded from the corpus) but also some intermediate analysis results (such as assigning types to spans of text) and links among the intermediate and final results.

2.2 Inference Web

Inference Web provides an infrastructure for providing explanations from distributed hybrid reasoning systems. It utilizes a proof Interlingua – the Proof Markup Language (PML) [Pinheiro da Silva, McGuinness, Fikes, 2004] to encode justifications of information manipulations. It also provides numerous services for manipulating PML documents. It includes a browser for viewing information manipulation traces, an abstractor for rewriting PML documents so that the low level machine-oriented proofs can be transformed into higher level human-oriented explanations, an explainer to interact with users by presenting explanations and corresponding follow-up questions, a registrar[McGuinness, et al., 2005] for storing and maintaining proof related meta-information, and new search and trust [McGuinness, et al, 2006, Zaihrayeu, et al, 2005] components. It also includes services for helping systems to generate PML, check PML documents for valid applications of inferences[Pinheiro da Silva, et al., 2005], and services for automatic registration of sources and meta-information.

2.3 Text Analytic Information Manipulations

Our explanation solution framework uses a proof interlingua to encode justifications of answers. We can view all information manipulation steps as a kind of inference. One contribution of our work is the design and specification of a taxonomy of text analytic processes and tasks that can be viewed as inferences.

We generated a taxonomy motivated by the need to describe and explain the dominant extraction tasks in UIMA, without overloading the system with more information than would be useful. One key was to generate a taxonomy that is adequate to accurately describe extraction task functionalities and simultaneously abstract enough to be able to hide details of the tasks from end users. Another key was to support explanations to end users of the integrated system, not authors of software components debugging their products.

First we will describe the taxonomy and later we will discuss issues related to its granularity, size, reusability, and extensibility.

We divided text extraction into three primitive areas: annotation, coreference, and integration. We will describe each briefly and provide examples of a few tasks used in a later example. Annotation tasks make assertions about spans of text that recognize a type or argument. Annotation inferences include:

1) **Entity Recognition:** determines that some span of text refers to an entity of a specified type. For example, a component could take the sentence "Joseph Gradgrind is the owner of Gradgrind Foods" and conclude that characters 0 to 16 of that sentence refer to some entity of type *Person*.

2) **Relation Recognition:** assigns a relation type to a span (e.g., a sentence describes a relation of type *Owner*).

3) **Relation Annotation Argument Identification:** determines and assigns values to the roles of a relation (e.g., a particular person is a participant in a given ownership relation instance).

Coreference inferences utilize annotation inferences and further identify that multiple text spans actually refer to the same entity or relation.

4) **Entity Identification:** determines that a set of entity annotations refer to a particular instance.

5) **Relation Identification:** determines that a set of relation annotations refer to a particular relation instance.

6) **Extracted Entity Classification:** determines that a particular coreferenced entity has a particular type. (e.g., the type of the entity referred to by "Gradgrind" is Person).

Knowledge integration inferences include mapping inferences providing access to provenance.

7) **Entity Mapping:** determines that an entity instance in the KB is derived from a set of entities and relation instances.

8) **Relation Mapping:** determines that a relationship in the target KB is derived from a set of entity and relation instances.

9) **Target Entity Classification:** determines that an entity instance is an instance of an entity type in the target ontology.

We have registered these inferences in the IW registry and we use these information manipulation steps to explain all of the UIMA components used in our prototype system, which provides intelligence analyst support for analyzing documents and evaluating results of text statements.

2.4 Text Analytic Manipulation Descriptions

We use our taxonomy of text analytic manipulations in declarative descriptions encoding what was done to generate the extracted knowledge bases. UIMA generates a large extracted knowledge database containing its conclusions. We needed to take that as input (potentially augmented) and generate interoperable proof descriptions (a PML document) as an output.

The software component that produces PML documents for UIMA-based analysis processes begins with a specified result from a specified EKDB (e.g., *JosephGradgrind* is the *Owner* of *GradgrindFoods*). It follows the links in the EKDB from that conclusion back to the intermediate results and raw input that led to it. From these intermediate results, it is able to produce inference steps encoded in PML that refer to the corresponding tasks in the taxonomy. For example, if the EKDB records that characters 0 to 16 of some sentence were labeled as a *Person* and that this labeling was identified as specifying an occurrence of *JosephGradgrind* then the component would create an **Entity Recognition** inference step in PML for that labeling as well as coreference step for the result that the labeling is an occurrence of *JosephGradgrind*.

3 Example in Action

Figure 1 provides an example showing how our new end-to-end explanation infrastructure can provide explanations annotated with meta-information using knowledge bases that may contain facts extracted by UIMA analytics from raw text. This example is similar to, but simpler than the examples produced by our system. In the example, the system is attempting to determine who manages some aspect of Mississippi law enforcement and safety data infrastructure. The answer is derived by a combination of the JTP theorem prover and a set of extraction components. The original sources for the proof include a press release (http://www.ibm.com/industries/government/doc/content/news/pressrelease/1107628109.html) and a knowledge base containing some direct assertions. The format shown in Figure 1 is approximately the same format that the Inference Web Browser uses to present proofs.

The initial data (i.e., the nodes in Figure 1 that have no parents) include assertions from a knowledge base, **KB1.owl** and a sentence from the press release. A fact asserted in the KB is that the Mississippi Automated System Project (*MASProject1*) manages some Mississippi data infrastructure (*MissDataInfrastructure1*), as stated in node (C). An axiom asserted from the KB and encoded in node (B) says that management is transitive.

Node (D) in the figure concludes that *MJAllen1* is the manager of *MASProject1*. This result was derived by a knowledge extraction process that began with a passage in a press release. The process involved the consecutive use of three UIMA-compliant components. IBM EAnnotator [Ando, 2004] assigns entity types to text spans in the document, i.e., it produces entity annotations. An IBM relation recognizer determines relates those spans via a *managerOf* relation. Finally, IBM Coreference

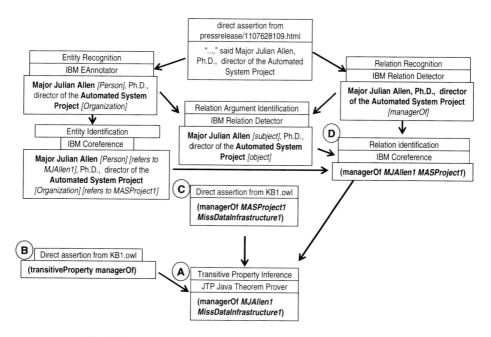

Fig. 1. Example of an integrated proof of extraction and reasoning

concludes that those annotations correspond to particular entities (*MJAllen1* and *MASProject1*) and a relationship between them (*managerOf*). From (B), (C), and (D), the reasoner can deduce (A), that *MJAllen1* is the manager of *MissDataInfrastructure1*. Some end-users may only be interested in that result, but others may wish to see the full derivation of the result from the KB and the raw text.

Figure 2 shows a partial/ablated screen capture of Inference Web's WWW-based browser displaying a portion of the automatically-generated extraction proof for the assertion that Major Julian Allen is the director of the Mississippi Automated System Project. As you can see, the proof is a slightly more complicated version of the one described above. The Inference Web browser interface allows users to show and hide individual steps in the proof in order to see the proof at varying levels of detail. The conclusion can also be explored in detail to determine for example that *uid184* refers to Major Julian Allen and *uid199* refers to the Mississippi Automated System Project. Additional summary views and follow-up options are available in the implemented system. Interested users can explore this proof at:

http://iw4.stanford.edu/iwbrowser/NodeSetBrowser?url=http%3A%2F%2Fiw4.stanford.edu%2F proofs%2FMississippiAutomatedSystem%2Fns36.owl%23ns36

The raw OWL for the final conclusion of that proof (which links to its antecedents, etc.) is at:

http://iw4.stanford.edu/proofs/MississippiAutomatedSystem/ns36.owl

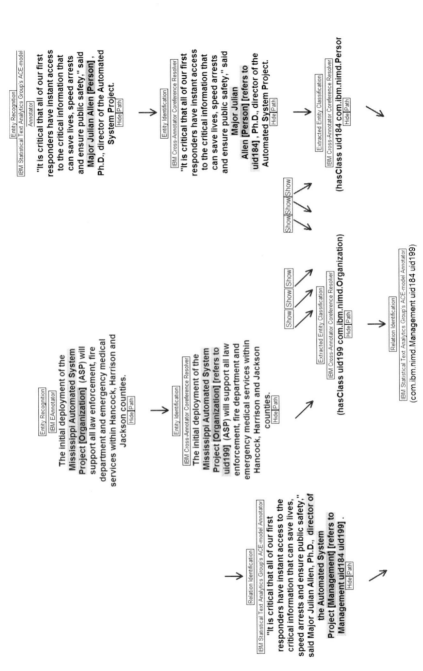

Fig. 2. Partial Inference Web screen capture showing an extraction proof

4 Discussion

We are using a proof-oriented approach to provide the foundation for supporting explanation in a broad range of systems. Our work provides an encoding and infrastructure that allows explanations to include information beyond typical knowledge bases, for example, including unstructured portions of raw text used to generate knowledge base statements. Explanations can also point to knowledge bases that were used along with inference rules to generate conclusions. Utilizing Inference Web, we can also provide multiple views of the explanations, including source document summaries (what documents were used), KB summaries (what knowledge bases were used and what statements in those knowledge bases were used), summaries of trusted sources, assumption summaries, as well as information manipulation (deductive) summaries (what inference rules were used). The fact that the justification foundation is based on declarative specifications of information manipulation rules enables our work to be precise and extensible.

One contribution of our integration work is a more complete exposition of an integrated extraction and deduction process. The exposition of the appropriate portion(s) of original sources instead of or in addition to derived sources allows users to better evaluate the trustworthiness of answers. In our example, the answer was derived from KB1.owl in combination with a portion of the press release. The exposition of extraction rules helps focus the user's attention on the fact that the process may not be entirely based on sound rules. Our example proof uses the *Entity Recognition*, *Relation Recognition, and Relation Identification* rules (from extraction engines that may be unsound) in addition to *Transitive Property Inference* (from a theorem prover expected to be sound).

Another contribution of our work is the design and integrated use of a taxonomy of text analytic tasks along with rules describing tasks performed by other kinds of systems. The new work connecting to text analytic components provides the foundation for transparent integration of knowledge-based question answering systems with information retrieval and text analysis. Within the Inference Web framework, that now enables text analytic components to be integrated with theorem provers (such as Stanford's JTP, SRI's SNARK, etc.), expert systems (such as UFPE's JEOPS), information integrators (such as ISI's Prometheus), web service composition discovery services (such as Stanford's SDS), and task processing (such as SRI's SPARK).

The work provides the possibility to interact more with applications that use automatic and semi-automatic methods to generate knowledge bases. In the past, most explanation systems have focused on knowledge bases that were carefully constructed by hand with authoritative data. As more reasoning systems rely on semi-automatic and automatic generation of knowledge support for understanding the question answering process becomes more critical. With our explainable text analytic platform, we can now expose imprecision in the knowledge base building process and help users understand and probe the system to make appropriate decisions. When imprecise methods are used, it becomes more critical to provide access to meta-information such as source, author, recency, etc. If users (humans and agents) can request this information along with the answer or filter answers based on this information, they can make more informed decisions about what information to rely on. Tools such as ours may be a key differentiator in situations such as those cited in the Select Senate Committee Report on Iraq[1], where recommendations were made to provide judgments that are not overstated, that are supported by underlying intelligence, expose assumptions, and expose uncertainties in the judgments. We claim that our infrastructure provides the key to explanations that may be used with applications that use knowledge bases built manually, semi-automatically, or automatically by providing ways to filter, understand, and evaluate answers.

We have a prototype implementation of the integration between twelve UIMA text analytic components, the explanation system, and a theorem prover. We are exploring issues including granularity of inference and coverage. Our work is being used to explain answers in intelligence tasks in DTO's NIMD program. The explanations are available through the Inference Web interface and are also being exposed through a customized interface designed for analysts. We believe the work is reusable and extensible. The taxonomy of text analytic tasks has provided coverage adequate to explain the text analytic needs that arise from the intelligence tasks addressed to date in the program. Additionally, the taxonomy provides a level of abstraction that has been useful to date in explanations. This paper's contribution is the taxonomy and architecture. A preliminary evaluation of the explanation representation and reasoning infrastructure along with its services for intelligence analysts is described in [Cowell, et. al, 2006].

We provide access to meta-information associated with nodes in PML documents. Thus, if meta-information concerning confidence level, authoritativeness, recency, etc. is encoded, users will have an option of displaying it in explanation presentations and summaries. We have recently begun integration with algorithms for composing answer confidence levels from confidence levels associated with other sentences, such as in [Zaihrayeu *et al.*, 2005, McGuinness et al., 2006]. We are integrating this work with social networks to provide a more complete solution to explaining and propagating trust information.

Finally, an interesting practical use of this work is the ability to use the inference web as a repository for information that is *hidden* from some resource-limited component, but may be needed later. One example of this is a general undo facility. In many of our components that need to process large amounts of data in memory, we do not have the resources to handle all the information leading to a particular conclusion, however on occasion we need that information, e.g. when conclusions are found to be incorrect and should be undone. Rather than keep that information in memory in all cases, we can load it back in from the inference web when needed.

5 Related Work

The idea that information extraction can be used to provide valuable information to supplement the structured sources available on the semantic web is relatively well-established (e.g., [Dill, Eiron, et al. 2003; Maynard, Yankova, et al. 2005; Cimiano & Völker, 2005; Welty and Murdock, 2006]). However, relatively little work exists on explaining information extraction.

There is significant work concerning building causal and/or explanatory representations of text analysis *results* (e.g., [Ram, 1994; Mahesh, *et al.*, 1994; Moldovan and Russ, 2001]). However, representing analysis *processes* is less

---

[1] intelligence.senate.gov/conclusions.pdf (conclusions 1&2).

common. One system that does reason about text analysis processes is Meta-AQUA [Cox and Ram 1999], which generates explanations of reasoning failures in the domain of story understanding in order to facilitate automated learning. However, the tasks of interest in Meta-AQUA are ones such as retrieving scripts and predicting outcomes that are relevant to extracting implicit information from text. These tasks are complementary to the tasks we have modeled, which involve extracting information that is explicitly stated in text.

Significant work also exists concerning support for answer provenance. Work exists on *Knowledge provenance* including *source meta-information*, which is a description of the origin of a piece of knowledge, and *knowledge process information*, which is a description of the information manipulation process used to generate the answer [Pinheiro da Silva *et al.*, 2003]. *Data provenance* and *data lineage,* the database community analog to knowledge provenance, typically includes both a description of the origin of the information and the process by which it arrived in the database [Buneman *et al.*, 2001; Cui *et al.* 2000]. Our work focusing on including extracted knowledge includes enhanced provenance information and thus provides a more complete solution to problems for which users need provenance information.

Finally, there has been a long history of work on explanation, from communities such as expert systems [Davis, 1979; Buchanan and Shortliffe, 1984; Swartout *et al*, 1991] and case-based reasoning [Leake, 1992; Aleven and Ashley, 1996; Goel and Murdock, 1996]. Inference Web continues that tradition and provides a standards-based method for declaratively specifying the types of inference and information manipulation steps one is interested in explaining. The existing Inference Web registry contains a specification of many of the inference types needed for traditional theorem proving and expert system style deduction. Our work integrating Inference Web with UIMA extends the reach of the potential explanations since we provide an infrastructure that supports inclusion of knowledge bases built with extraction techniques.

6 Conclusion

It is generally not acceptable for semantic web systems to present conclusions without additionally being able to provide details about how those conclusions were produced and ultimately why they should be believed. As systems rely more on facts that may have been built with semi-automatic or automatic methods potentially using web sources that are unknown to users, techniques must be included for exposing information concerning sources and a broad range of information manipulation methods. Our work provides a solution to the problem where answers may rely on facts extracted from source text using text extraction techniques. The answers may also rely on information manipulation steps executed by reasoning engines. A set of information sources supporting answers can include raw text in addition to typical ontologies and knowledge bases. A set of information manipulators may include extractors in addition to theorem provers, information integrators, service composition discovery engines, or any other kind of manipulator able to encode justifications in the Proof Markup Language. A set of information manipulation rules may include extraction rules providing an infrastructure capable of explaining text analytic processes as well as standard deduction processes. Our solution bridges a gap between traditional reasoning engine-based solutions and text-analytic-based solutions. Our infrastructure is available for use and individual components such as the taxonomy of inferences, text analytic components, registry, browsers, etc. may be used individually. We have implemented our approach and are using it in several sponsored projects and are interested in additional users.

Acknowledgements

This work was substantially supported by DTO contract number 2003*H278000*000. The authors also gratefully acknowledge collaborators on the KANI project, particularly Cynthia Chang, Alan Chappell, Richard Fikes, and Dave Thurman. This paper is an updated version of a technical report [McGuinness, et al, 2005].

References

Ando, R. 2004. Exploiting Unannotated Corpora for Tagging and Chunking. *Proc. of ACL.*
B.G. Buchanan and E. H. Shortliffe, editors, 1984. Rule-Based Expert Systems: The MYCIN Experiments of the Stanford Heuristic Programming Project. Addison-Wesley Publishing Company, Reading, Mass.
Buneman, P, Khanna, S., and Tan, W. 2001. Why and Where: A Characterization of Data Provenance. *Proc. of 8th International Conference on Database Theory.*
Philipp Cimiano, Johanna Völker. 2005. Text2Onto - A Framework for Ontology Learning and Data-driven Change Discovery. *10th International Conference on Applications of Natural Language to Information Systems (NLDB)*. Alicante, Spain.
Cowell, A., McGuinness, D., Varley, C. and Thurman, D. 2006. Knowledge-Worker Requirements for Next Generation Query Answering and Explanation Systems. *Proc. of the Workshop on Intelligent User Interfaces for Intelligence Analysis, International Conference on Intelligent User Interfaces* (IUI 2006), Sydney, Australia.
Cui, Y., Widom, J. and Wiener, J. 2000. Tracing the Lineage of View Data in a Warehousing Environment. *ACM Trans. on Database Systems*, 25(2), 179-227.
Davis, R. 1979. Interactive Transfer of Expertise: Acquisition of New Inference Rules. *Artificial Intelligence* 12(2):121-157.
Stephen Dill, Nadav Eiron, David Gibson, Daniel Gruhl, R. Guha, Anant Jhingran, Tapas Kanungo, Sridhar Rajagopalan, Andrew Tomkins, John A. Tomlin, & Jason Y. Zien. 2003. SemTag and Seeker: Bootstrapping the semantic web via automated semantic annotation. 12th *International World Wide Web Conference (WWW)*, Budapest, Hungary.
Ferrucci, D. 2004. Text Analysis as Formal Inference for the Purposes of Uniform Tracing and Explanation Generation. IBM Research Report RC23372.
Ferrucci, D. and Lally, A. 2004. UIMA by Example. *IBM Systems Journal* 43, No. 3, 455-475.
Goel, A. and Murdock, J. W. 1996. Meta-Cases: Explaining Case-Based Reasoning. Ashok K. Goel and J. William Murdock. *3rd European Workshop on Case-Based Reasoning*, Lausanne, Switzerland
Leake, D. 1992. *Evaluating Explanations: A Content Theory.* Lawrence Earlbaum.
McGuinness,D.1996. *Explaining Reasoning in Description Logics.* Ph.D. Thesis, Rutgers University. Tech Report LCSR-TR-277.
McGuinness, D. and Pinheiro da Silva, P.2004. Explaining Answers from the Semantic Web: The Inference Web Approach. *Journal of Web Semantics* 1(4):397-413.

Deborah L. McGuinness, Paulo Pinheiro da Silva, Cynthia Chang. IWBase: Provenance Metadata Infrastructure for Explaining and Trusting Answers from the Web. Technical Report KSL-04-07, Knowledge Systems Laboratory, Stanford University, USA, 2004.

McGuinness, D. Pinheiro da Silva, P., Murdock, J. W., Ferrucci, D., 2005. Exposing Extracted Knowledge Supporting Answers. Stanford Knowledge Systems Laboratory Technical Report KSL-05-03, Knowledge Systems Laboratory, Stanford University, USA, 2005. http://www.ksl.stanford.edu/KSL_Abstracts/KSL-05-03.html.

McGuinness, D. L., Zeng, H., Pinheiro da Silva, P., Ding, L., Narayanan, D., and Bhaowal, M. Investigations into Trust for Collaborative Information Repositories: A Wikipedia Case Study. WWW2006 Workshop on the Models of Trust for the Web (MTW'06), Edinburgh, Scotland, May 22, 2006.

Diana Maynard, Milena Yankova, Alexandros Kourakis, and Antonis Kokossis. 2005. Ontology-based information extraction for market monitoring and technology watch. ESWC Workshop "End User Apects of the Semantic Web," Heraklion, Crete, May, 2005.

Moldovan, D. I., Rus, V. 2001. Transformation of WordNet Glosses into Logic Forms. 14th International Florida Artificial Intelligence Research Society Conference, Key West, Florida, 459-463.

Pinheiro da Silva, P, McGuinness, D. and Fikes, R. 2006. A Proof Markup Language for Semantic Web Services. *Information Systems* 31(4-5): 381-395.

Pinheiro da Silva, P., Hayes, P., McGuinness, D. L., Fikes, R. E., and Deshwal. P. 2005 Towards Checking Hybrid Proofs. Technical Report KSL-05-01, Knowledge Systems Laboratory, Stanford University, USA.

Pinheiro da Silva, P., McGuinness, D., and McCool, R. 2003. Knowledge Provenance Infrastructure. *IEEE Data Engineering Bulletin* 26(4), 26-32.

Swartout, W., Paris, C. and Moore, J. 1991. Explanations in Knowledge Systems: Design for Explainable Expert Systems. *IEEE Expert Systems*, 6:3, 58-64.

Welty, C. and Murdock, J. W. 2006. Towards Knowledge Acquisition from Information Extraction. *5th International Semantic Web Conference*.

Zaihrayeu, I., Pinheiro da Silva, P., and McGuinness, D. 2005. IWTrust: Improving User Trust in Answers from the Web. *3rd Intl. Conference on Trust Management*.

A Mixed Initiative Semantic Web Framework for Process Composition

Jinghai Rao[1], Dimitar Dimitrov[2], Paul Hofmann[2], and Norman Sadeh[1]

[1] School of Computer Science, Carnegie Mellon University
5000 Forbes Avenue, Pittsburgh, PA, 15213, USA
{sadeh, jinghai}@cs.cmu.edu
[2] SAP AG
Dietmar-Hopp-Allee 16, D-69190, Walldorf, Germany
{paul.hofmann, dimitar.dimitrov}@sap.com

Abstract. Semantic Web technologies offer the prospect of significantly reducing the amount of effort required to integrate existing enterprise functionality in support of new composite processes.– whether within a given organization or across multiple ones. A significant body of work in this area has aimed to fully automate this process, while assuming that all functionality has already been encapsulated in the form of semantic web services with rich and accurate annotations. In this article, we argue that this assumption is often unrealistic. Instead, we describe a mixed initiative framework for semantic web service discovery and composition that aims at flexibly interleaving human decision making and automated functionality in environments where annotations may be incomplete and even inconsistent. An initial version of this framework has been implemented in SAP's Guided Procedures, a key element of SAP's Enterpise Service Architecture (ESA).

1 Introduction

Service Oriented Architectures (SOAs) provide a framework within which enterprises expose functionality in the form of loosely coupled services that can be integrated and consolidated in response to demand for new applications (or services). Over the past several years, languages and frameworks have been proposed to develop and leverage rich semantic service annotations in support of both service discovery and composition functionality - e.g. [5, 7, 8]. A significant portion of this work has been devoted to scenarios aimed at automating service discovery and composition functionality (see surveys in [12, 13]) – notable exceptions include the semi-automated web services composition approaches reported in [14, 15, 16]. While valuable, this work does not address the challenges involved in training personnel to efficiently and accurately develop the necessary service annotations and ontologies. Nor does it fully recognize the amount of effort involved in annotating legacy applications in use in both small and large organizations. What is needed for enterprises to be able to exploit the power of semantic web service technologies are tools that can effectively support their personnel from day one with significantly incomplete and possibly inconsistent annotations. These tools therefore need to be highly interactive in nature. They need to support users through suggestion, completion and verification functionality, while always allowing them to override their recommendations. In other words, situations where recommendations are ignored by the user are potential indicators of inconsistencies in the underlying model.

In this article, we present a *mixed initiative framework* for semantic web service discovery and composition intended for that purpose. Research in mixed initiative planning and scheduling has a rich history of its own, starting with the work of Allen and others [27, 28]. This also includes our own work on integrating process planning and production scheduling and on supporting coordinated supply chain planning and scheduling across supply chains [3, 4]. In contrast to this prior work, the tools presented in this paper do not assume complete or even consistent ontologies and annotations. Instead they are based on the premise that users should retain close control over many decisions while having the ability to selectively delegate tedious aspects of their tasks. Automated service discovery and composition functionality is merely used to selectively intervene and assist users in some of their tasks by providing suggestions, verification, and completing some of the user's decisions. This enables the user to dynamically choose how much of the discovery and composition process to delegate and how much of it to retain control over.

The framework we present has been validated in the context of SAP's Guided Procedures, a key element of SAP's Enterprise Service Architecture (ESA) [17] and its Composite Application Framework (CAF) [18]. Specifically, CAF is built into SAP's NetWeaver [19] to support the development of cross-functional applications and business processes. Guided Procedures (GP) [20] is the tool developed as part of CAF to enable lay users (i.e. users without software development skills) to set up and execute new collaborative business processes out of existing functionality and applications. Target users include SAP personnel as well as SAP consultants and "analyst" users responsible for the customization, refinement and composition of applications and services at client organizations. It should be pointed out that the mixed initiative framework presented in this paper is not specific to GP and that it could be applied across a broad range of other service discovery and composition scenarios.

The remainder of this paper is organized as follows. Section 2 introduces Guided Procedures and our mixed initiative framework for semantic service discovery and composition. Section 3 details our modeling framework, Section 4 discusses the underlying semantic web reasoning and service discovery and composition functionality used in our framework. This includes the way in which some of this functionality has been broken down in support of our mixed initiative framework. Section 5 revisits the Guided Procedures scenario introduced earlier. Section 6 discusses the framework's current implementation and presents an initial set of empirical results. Concluding remarks are provided in Section 7.

2 A Mixed Initiative Framework for Service Discovery and Composition

SAP's **Guided Procedures** (GP) allow users to define new composite applications and processes by re-using, integrating and orchestrating existing functionality encapsulated in the form of *composable elements*. In GP, composable elements comprise primitive functionality ("callable objects" and "actions" in the GP jargon) as well as composite functionality (or "blocks" in the GP jargon), including complex processes and services.

Usage scenarios range from assisting SAP consultants as they tailor and combine existing SAP modules and functionality to capture the **processes and policies of a particular company**, to scenarios where analyst users build new **composite applications** that leverage functionality exposed by third party partners in the form of **web services**.

The mixed initiative framework for semantic web service discovery and composition described in this paper has been implemented as a recent addition to SAP's Guided Procedures, though its applicability extends beyond this particular environment. It enables users to annotate composable elements with semantic profiles that refer to concepts in an open collection of ontologies. These annotations are used by mixed initiative functionality to support users at **design time** as they specify abstract requests for composite applications, search for, select among, and compose available services to satisfy these requests. This functionality is presented to users in the form of simple services that can selectively intervene at different points in this often highly iterative process (Fig. 1). They provide suggestions, offer to complete tedious steps and verify decisions made by users, while always allowing them to manually override their recommendations and regain control.

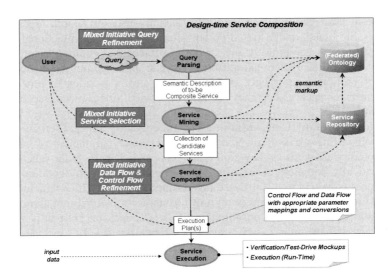

Fig. 1. Simplified Workflow – Mixed initiative design-time functionality supports users as they refine the specification of composite services, identify and select relevant services and compose them. Actual workflows often involve multiple iterations.

The development of composite services tends to be an iterative process, where users successively specify and relax requirements while tailoring and combining existing functionality to satisfy these requirements. The GP framework is intended to accommodate different work styles ranging from "top down" approaches, where a user specifies an abstract description of a desired composite service to more serendipitous or "bottom-up" approaches where users directly edit and compose existing services – and anything in between. Abstract descriptions of composite services will be in the form of constraints on desired input and output parameters as well as on the state of affairs both prior to and after invoking the composite service. A simple example of such an abstract description could read "I want a service that takes a RFQ as input and generates a Quote as output". A more complex description could be of the form "I want a service that takes care of all RFQs that have not yet been processed".

While relying on semantic annotations to guide mixed initiative service discovery and composition, our framework recognizes that **GP users cannot be expected to be experts in annotating composable functionality**. Instead, it is understood that typical users will often fail to initially identify (or specify) relevant annotations. Accordingly our framework is designed to **operate with partial annotations** and help users become better at annotating composable functionality over time. As annotations become richer and more accurate, the quality of the guidance provided by our framework also improves and users gradually learn to take advantage of it. Because mixed initiative functionality is provided in an unobtrusive way, it never hinders users.

Broadly speaking, our framework's mixed initiative functionality consists of simple, often customizable, services capable of providing suggestions and feedback to users as they deal with each of the following three sets of key decisions:

1. **Semantic Discovery:** This functionality enables users to search repositories of composable functionality, based on both functional and non-functional attributes (e.g. [9]) – e.g. searching for one or more services that could help build a composite application. Functional attributes include input, output parameters as well as preconditions and effects. Non-functional attributes refer to other relevant characteristics such as accuracy, quality of service, price, owner, access control restrictions, etc.
2. **Semantic Dataflow Consolidation:** This functionality assists users by automatically suggesting ways of mapping input and output parameters of composable functionality elements as they are being composed. This includes functionality to automatically complete an existing step – this is similar to "code completion" functionality except that it is based on semantic reasoning. It also includes verification functionality that flags seemingly erroneous or inconsistent assignments.
3. **Semantic Control Flow Consolidation:** This is similar, except that here were are concerned with the order in which services will be executed. This includes reasoning about the availability of necessary input variables and, more generally, about the preconditions and effects associated with the execution of different services. Again this functionality can be provided in the form of suggestions or to help verify the correctness of decisions made by users. It can be invoked for an entire process or just for two or more steps in a process currently under construction. Suggestions can include the introduction or removal of particular sequencing constraints. It may also involve identifying and adding one or more additional steps to a partial process. In general, users should be able to specify how much they want to delegate at any point in time, e.g. whether to request help with a small subproblem or with a more extensive portion of an existing solution.

As users interact with the above functionality, they should always have the flexibility to selectively revise and complete existing annotations. Over time, we also envision adding global analysis functionality. This would go beyond just verifying the correctness of composite applications to include identifying redundancies and inefficiencies in processes.

3 Underlying Representation Model

Below, we briefly review the way in which ontologies and semantic web technologies are organized and provide an overview of the underlying service model and annotations used in our framework.

3.1 Ontologies

An ontology is simply a description of concepts relevant to a given domain along with attributes/properties characterizing these concepts. By relying on shared ontologies, namely by agreeing on the definition of common concepts, developers within a given organization can define composable functionality elements that refer to the concepts in these ontologies. So can enterprises as they selectively expose composable functionality elements to business partners in the form of (semantic) web services. It is notable that we use OWL language to annotate the concepts in describing the components in the GP. Although the upper model for the components is very similar to OWL-S, our framework is not restricted to OWL-S language. This services can also be described by other semantic web service description languages, like METEOR-S [23], WSDL-S [24] or WSMO[21].

A composable (functionality) element can be either an atomic service (e.g. a GP Callable Object, Action, including external services wrapped as such) or a composite service (e.g. a GP Block or Process). It is described (or "annotated") by its Input parameters, Output parameters, Preconditions, Effects and Non-functional attributes.

Both preconditions and effects are currently represented using "status" objects. The preconditions are currently interpreted as being part of a conjunction, namely all preconditions need to hold before activating the composable element. A composable element can have multiple conditional effects, each representing different mutually exclusive possible outcomes. In other words, the particular conditional effects that will hold following the execution of a composable element will depend on the actual execution of that component (e.g. whether a request is approved or rejected or whether execution of a service is successful or not). A conditional effect is itself a collection of actions, each either asserting or deleting status objects. Status objects are defined in relation to OWL classes. A status class can have several properties. For example, in describing a *purchase order processing*, service a "submitted" class can be used to indicate that a purchase order has been submitted. These properties are instantiated at runtime based on bindings (defined at design time) to relevant input and output parameters.

A composite process is described in terms of a process model. The model details both its control structure and data flow structure. A process is recursively defined as either a "Composable Element" or a "Composite Process". A "Composite Process" contains one or more sub-processes. Sub-processes are to be executed according to control constructs. Examples of control constructs include "sequence", "choice" and "parallel". Each process has a set of parameters, including "inputs", "outputs", "preconditions" and "effects". A "Composite Process" is also described in terms of "Perform" constructs that specify how data flows across the process. This is done using a "Consolidation" construct that maps input and output parameters of composable elements onto one another ("dataflow consolidation").

3.2 Annotations: Cost-Benefit Tradeoffs

Legacy GP elements already include input and output parameter descriptions that are defined in relation to a small set of possible types (e.g. *string, integer, business object*). Minimally these types can automatically be converted into corresponding ontology elements. At the same time our framework allows users to optionally refine these descriptions and to map service parameters onto more specific classes. For instance, rather than specifying an input parameter as a string, one might define it as an *employee_name*, which itself may be defined as a subclass of *string* in a domain specific ontology. While optional, more detailed descriptions enable more sophisticated reasoning functionality thereby leading to more and better support for the user.

There are however cost-benefit tradeoffs associated with the development of rich ontologies and annotations and it would be unrealistic to assume their existence from day one. Instead our expectation is that over time users will learn to appreciate the better support provided by these annotations and will be more willing and able to invest the necessary effort to develop them. Our mixed initiative framework does not assume the existence of rich and accurate ontologies and annotations. Clearly in the absence of such annotations, the support provided by our framework is not as powerful and may occasionally be itself inaccurate. It is therefore critical for this support to never hinder the user but rather to let the user choose when to invoke it and whether or not to follow its recommendations. As users invoke mixed initiative functionality and identify what appear to be inaccurate or incomplete annotations, it is critical to enable them to easily examine and, if necessary, modify these annotations (subject to proper approval procedures). As annotations become more complete and accurate, we expect GP users to increasingly rely on our mixed initiative support and to make fewer errors as they build composite applications and services (e.g. fewer mismatches between input and output parameters, fewer step omissions in the construction of composite processes, etc.). This in turn should translate into higher quality processes and an overall increase in productivity.

4 Overall Architecture and Underlying Reasoning

4.1 Overall Architecture

The implementation of our mixed initiative semantic web service discovery and composition framework in the context of SAP's Guided Procedures comprises (Fig. 2):

1. Enhancements of the GP graphical user interface with access not just to core GP functionality (e.g. editing callable objects, actions and blocks) but also to a growing collection of mixed initiative service discovery and composition functionality. Invoking this mixed initiative functionality results in requests being sent to a mixed initiative semantic web service discovery and composition reasoner.

2. Services to (de)register both services and ontologies
3. The mixed initiative semantic web service and discovery reasoner itself, which is implemented as an independent module. As already indicated, while an initial version of this module has been integrated in GP, the module itself has been designed so that it could play a similar role in other service composition/process development environments

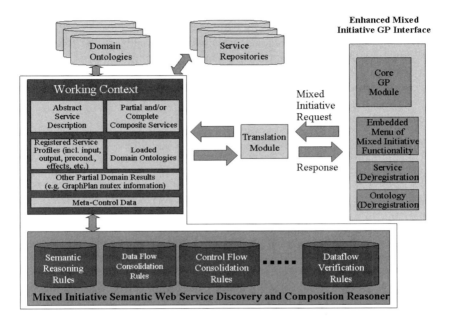

Fig. 2. Overall architecture

This latter module is implemented in the form of a rule-based engine (currently using JESS, a high-performance Java-based rule engine [7]). Rules in the engine implement a growing collection of mixed initiative service discovery and composition functionality, which itself combines two forms of reasoning:

1. **semantic reasoning** (e.g. reasoning about classes and subclasses as well as about more complex constructs supported by the OWL language)
2. **service composition planning** functionality implementing extensions of the highly efficient GraphPlan algorithm [10,11] – itself reimplemented using JESS rules.

This underlying reasoning functionality is further discussed in Subsections 4.2 and 4.3. Facts in the rule-based reasoner are organized in a **working context** (Fig. 2). They include:

– An abstract description of the desired composite service
– A description of partial or complete service(s) generated to satisfy the user's request – these composite services may also include inconsistencies

- Profiles describing registered composable elements (or "services")
- Facts contained in or inferred from registered ontologies
- Partial domain results, produced while processing mixed initiative requests. This information, while dynamic, is maintained as it tends to change only slightly from one user request to the next (during the composition of a given service). Housekeeping rules, not depicted in Fig. 2, help remove facts that have been invalidated. Examples of partial results include nodes, edges, levels and "mutex" information derived as part of the Graphplan algorithm (see 4.3) or candidate matches for dataflow consolidation between two consecutive services.
- Meta-control data is also maintained in the working context in the form of predicates corresponding to different mixed initiative requests. These facts in turn trigger rules associated with the corresponding mixed initiative functionality, e.g rules implementing service discovery, parameter consolidation, dataflow verification, etc.

4.2 Semantic Reasoning

This functionality enables our module to load OWL ontologies and annotations and reason about them. This is done using an OWL-Lite Meta-Model, expressed in CLIPS, the modeling language used by JESS. An example of such a meta-model can be found in [22]. A translator is used to convert OWL-Lite ontologies into JESS triples. Our current implementation is based on Jena's RDF/XML Parser, ARP [25].

4.3 Service Composition Planning

This functionality is implemented using extensions of the GraphPlan algorithm. This is an algorithm that combines:

- **reachability analysis** to determine whether a given state (e.g. a combination of effects) can be reached from another state (e.g. the state reached after invoking an initial set of services), and
- **disjunctive refinement**, namely the addition of constraints between steps to resolve possible inconsistencies

In this algorithm, services and propositions (i.e. input, output, preconditions and effects in our model) are organized in layers in a "graphplan" that is iteratively analyzed and refined to obtain one or more service composition plans – if such plans exist. The graphplan consists of nodes, edges and layers (or levels). Possible inconsistencies are represented in the form of "mutex" information. This information in turn can be used to support mixed initiative functionality such as recommending possible ways in which to sequence services ("control flow"). Clearly, when used in one step, the GraphPlan algorithm can help identify all possible composite services satisfying an abstract description. Instead, we use a variation of this algorithm that enables us to find one or more plans at a time. This approach allows users to specify how many composite services they want to evaluate at a time and is also more practical, given the potentially large computational effort involved in identifying all possible composite services compatible with a given request. Other examples of mixed initiative functionality supported by this planning algorithm include:

- Identifying some or all services capable of producing a given effect or a given output
- Identifying all services that could be invoked following the execution of a given service
- Detecting conflicts between a selected service and other services already selected as part of a partial solution and suggesting ways of resolving these conflicts (using mutex information)
- Suggesting modifications to the abstract description of a desired composite service if no plan can be can be found for the current description – Note that our approach does not require that an abstract description be provided: some users may provide such a description and others may not.

Graphplan expansion and the mutex generation are implemented as Jess rules, while plan extraction is implemented as a combination of Jess queries and Java functions.

The following scenarios further illustrate ways in which mixed initiative functionality can assist users as they work on developing new composite applications.

Scenario 1: Examples of user-oriented services based on dataflow consolidation functionality

A user has added a new service (or step) to a partial process and now attempts to map the new service's input parameters onto the outputs of services already present in the partial process. The following are examples of user-oriented services based on dataflow consolidation functionality

- o One such service can be provided to suggest possible mappings
- o A similar service can also help identify input parameters that cannot be mapped, which in turn can help the user identify missing steps in the current process (e.g. a request for approval has to be submitted in order to generate a particular input value such as the employee ID of the person required to authorize the new step).
- o Alternatively, the user might decide to manually map the new service's input parameters onto the output parameters of other steps in the partial process. She can then invoke dataflow consolidation functionality to verify her choices. An indication that one of the mappings is inconsistent means either of two things: (a) she made a mistake; (b) an annotation is incorrect. In the latter case, the user can decide to override the system's recommendation and, optionally, submit a request for the conflicting annotation to be corrected – or a more general record can be created for future inspection by an annotation specialist.

Scenario 2: Examples of user-oriented services based on service discovery functionality

The partial process created by a user does not yet satisfy some of the desired effects (or produce some of the desired outputs) specified in the abstract process description she has specified. The following are examples of user-oriented services based on service discovery functionality that can assist the user:

- o The user can select one or more of the not-yet-satisfied desired effects and request a list of services capable of producing them

- Alternatively, she can select a particular step in the current partial process (e.g. the last step) and request a list of all services that can potentially be invoked at that point
- More complex versions of the above services could eventually be provided. An example would be a service that allows users to request a list of services that satisfy additional constraints (e.g. find me a service that does X from one of the company's preferred service providers)

Scenario 3: Examples of user-oriented services based on mutex information
The user has just added a new step to the current working process Examples of user-oriented services based on mutex information:

- Mutex information can be used to help the user identify valid places where to insert the new step/service into the existing process
- It can also be used to verify sequencing decisions made by the user

By now, it should be obvious that, by breaking down service discovery and composition functionality into finer, user-oriented services, it becomes possible to effectively support a vast number of possible scenarios, each corresponding to somewhat different situations and work styles. It should also be clear that the same functionality (e.g. computing mutex information, or supporting data consolidation) can be repackaged in a number of different ways. Often the underlying functionality does not even have to be complex. The key is in presenting it to the user at the right time and in a usable, non-obtrusive way. Our approach is to incrementally add more such services, evaluate their usefulness and, if necessary, refine the ways in which they are presented to users.

5 Guided Procedure Scenario Revisited

In a typical interaction with the semantically enhanced version of GP, a user will provide a high level description of a desired composite service. This description can be entered using a wizard that allows users to specify desired service profile attributes (e.g. input/output parameters, preconditions and effects) in relation to loaded ontologies (e.g. see screen shot in Fig. 3). This specification is loaded into the semantic service discovery and composition reasoner's working context, where it will help constrain future mixed initiative requests from the user. A simple (and admittedly naive) request might be to automatically search for one or more composite services that match the user's composite service description. Other more typical requests are in the form of incremental steps, where users iteratively look for composable elements that help satisfy part of the service description, refine the control flow and data flow of selected composable elements, and possibly revise the original composite service until a satisfactory solution is obtained.

Fig. 4 displays a typical screen shot, where a user invokes mixed initiative functionality to obtain suggestions on how to consolidate the input and output of two consecutive services intended to be part of a composite process referred to as "Purchase Order Scenario". Here, based on sub-class relationships in a domain ontology, the system recommends consolidating an output parameter called "warehouse address" with the "ship to location" input parameter of a subsequent service.

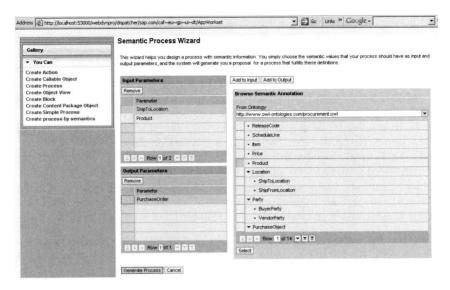

Fig. 3. Specifying an abstract composite service profile in relation to concepts in an ontology

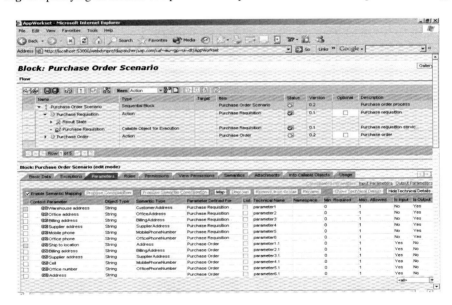

Fig. 4. Suggestions on consolidating input and output parameters of two consecutive services

6 Implementation Details and Evaluation

Our mixed initiative semantic service discovery and composition reasoner has been implemented using Jess. Ontologies are expressed in OWL, while the services are described using a slightly modified fragment of OWL-S. An OWL metamodel [22] is loaded into Jess as facts. We use Jena to translate OWL documents into triples – also represented in Jess facts. Mixed initiative rules based on the GraphPlan algorithm have been implemented to support an initial set of mixed initiative functionality, including service discovery, dataflow consolidation, control flow and verification functionality.

The resulting system has been integrated with SAP's Guided Procedure framework and evaluated on an IBM laptop with a 1.80GHz Pentium M CPU and 1.50GB of RAM. The laptop was running Windows XP Professional OS, Java SDK 1.4.1 and Jess 6.1. Below, we report results obtained using ontologies from the Lehigh University Benchmark (LUBM) [26]. The results are based on the university example with around 50000 triples. Results are reported for repositories of 100, 500 and 1000 randomly generated semantic web services. Each randomly generated service had up to 5 inputs and 5 outputs. Input and output parameter types were randomly selected from the classes in the domain ontology. Performance, measured in the term of CPU times (in milliseconds), has been broken down as follows:

- **Service and ontology loading time** – this is typically done once when launching the system. Registering a single new service is an incremental process that only requires a tiny fraction of this time.
- **Semantic reasoning time**, which mainly involves completing domain ontologies once they have been loaded, is also typically performed just when launching the system
- **Request processing**: This is the time required to automatically generate composite services that match a randomly generated abstract composite service description. This time depends on the number of valid composite services one wishes to generate. For each service repository size, performance for two such values (number between parentheses) is reported.

As can be seen, the time it takes to produce multiple composite services ranges between 0.5 and 4 seconds. This seems quite acceptable, especially given that most of the time users will submit more incremental, and hence less time consuming, requests. The time it takes to load the system is higher than we would like, though we believe that, with some code optimization and possibly more powerful hardware, it will prove to be quite acceptable as well.

	CPU time (in milliseconds)		
Nb. Services (Nb. Sol.)	Ontology and service loading	Semantic Reasoning	Request Processing
100 (12)	54468	86475	1041
100 (211)	52445	89035	3141
500 (2)	52465	206687	511
500 (40)	53166	220227	1702
1000 (3)	54689	477467	1235
1000(78)	57944	457207	4116

While encouraging, these are only preliminary results and further testing is needed to fully evaluate the scalability of our approach. In addition, detailed experimentation with actual users will be needed to fine tune the way in which mixed initiative functionality is presented and to eventually evaluate the full benefits of our approach from a productivity and solution quality standpoint.

7 Summary and Concluding Remarks

In this article, we have summarized ongoing work on the development of a mixed initiative semantic web service discovery and composition framework. In contrast to most work on semantic web service discovery and composition, our approach does not assume the existence of rich and accurate annotations from day one. Instead, it is intended to selectively intervene and assist users in some of their tasks by providing suggestions, identifying inconsistencies, and completing some of the user's decisions. Users are always in control and decide when and how much to delegate to supporting functionality. The quality and accuracy of the support provided by our framework is intended to improve over time, as users learn to develop richer and more accurate annotations.

An initial version of this framework has been integrated and evaluated in the context of SAP's Guided Procedures, a central element of the company's Enterprise Service Architecture. Initial empirical results have confirmed the viability of our underlying reasoning framework, which leverages a combination of semantic reasoning functionality and of service composition planning functionality based on the GraphPlan algorithm Rather than being implemented in a monolithic manner, this functionality has been broken down and extended to support an initial collection of user-oriented, mixed initiative services. Over time, we plan to further extend and refine this collection of services. While our initial results are promising, we recognize that additional testing (and fine tuning) will be needed to fully realize and evaluate the potential of our approach and to measure actual improvements in both user productivity and solution quality.

Acknowledgements

The "Smart Service Discovery and Composition" work reported herein has been conducted in collaboration by Sadeh Consulting and SAP Inspire The authors would like to thank Lutz Heuser and Claudia Alsdorf for supporting this project. Special thanks to Shuyuan Chen, Horst Werner, Kiril Bratanov and Daniel Hutzel for their contributions to the project and to Heinz Wuerth, Frank Schertel and Stamen Kotchkov for many helpful interactions and for their help integrating this technology into SAP's GP framework.

References

[1] W3C: OWL Web Ontology Language Overview, W3C Recommendation, Feb. 2004, http://www.w3.org/TR/owl-features/
[2] Martin et al., OWL-S: Semantic Markup for Web Services, W3C member submission, Nov. 2004. http://www.w3.org/Submission/OWL-S/
[3] D. Hildum, N. Sadeh, T.J. Laliberty, S. Smith, J. McA'Nulty, and D. Kjenstad, Mixed-initiative Management of Integrated Process-Planning and Production-Scheduling Solutions, Proceedings of NSF Research Planning Workshop on Artificial Intelligence and Manufacturing, June, 1996.

[4] N. M. Sadeh, D. W. Hildum, T. J. Laliberty, J. McA'Nulty, D. Kjenstad, and A. Tseng. "A Blackboard Architecture for Integrating Process Planning and Production Scheduling". Concurrent Engineering: Research and Applications, Vol. 6, No. 2, June 1998.
[5] J. Rao. Semantic Web Service Composition via Logic-based Program Synthesis. PhD Thesis. December 2004..
[6] E. Friedman-Hill. Jess in Action: Java Rule-based Systems, Manning Publications Company, June 2003, http://herzberg.ca.sandia.gov/jess/.
[7] F. Gandon and N. Sadeh, "Semantic Web Technologies to Reconcile Privacy and Context Awareness", Web Semantics Journal. 1(3), 2004.
[8] K. Sycara, S.Widoff, M. Klusch, and J. Lu. Larks: Dynamic matchmaking among heterogeneous software agents in cyberspace. Autonomous Agents and Multi-Agent Systems, 5(3), September 2002.
[9] J. O'Sullivan, D. Edmond, and A. T. Hofstede. What's in a service? Towards accurate description of non-functional service properties. Distributed and Parallel Databases, 12:117.133, 2002.
[10] A. Blum and M. Furst, "Fast Planning Through Planning Graph Analysis", Artificial Intelligence, 90:281—300, 1997.
[11] C. Anderson, D. Smith and D. Weld. Conditional Effects in Graphplan, The 4th Intl. Conference on AI Planning Systems (AIPS-98), Pittsburgh, PA, 1998.
[12] J. Rao and X. Su. "A Survey of Automated Web Service Composition Methods". Proceedings of the 1st Intl. Workshop on Semantic Web Services and Web Process Composition, San Diego, 2004.
[13] J. Peer, Web Service Composition as AI Planning - a Survey, Technical Report Univ. of St. Gallen, 2005 http://elektra.mcm.unisg.ch/pbwsc/docs/pfwsc.pdf
[14] F. Casati, S. Ilnicki, and L. Jin. Adaptive and dynamic service composition in EFlow. In Proceedings of 12th International Conference on Advanced Information Systems Engineering(CAiSE), Stockholm, Sweden, June 2000. Springer Verlag.
[15] E. Sirin, J. Hendler, and B. Parsia. Semi-automatic composition of Web services using semantic descriptions. In Proceedings of Web Services: Modeling, Architecture and Infrastructure, 2002.
[16] Rainer Anzboeck and Schahram Dustdar, Semi-automatic generation of Web services and BPEL processes - A Model-Driven approach, Third International Conference on Business Process Management, Nancy, September 2005
[17] SAP ESA http://www.sap.com/solutions/esa/index.epx
[18] SAP NetWeaver http://www.sap.com/solutions/netweaver/index.epx
[19] SAP Composite Application Framework http://www.sap.com/solutions/netweaver/components/caf/index.epx
[20] SAP Guided Procedures http://www.sap.com/solutions/netweaver/cafindex.epx
[21] Web Service Modeling Ontology, http://www.wsmo.org/
[22] Gandon, F and Sadeh, N. "OWL Inference Engine Using XSLT and JESS", 2003. Available at: http://www.cs.cmu.edu/~sadeh/MyCampusMirror/OWLEngine.html
[23] METEOR-S. http://lsdis.cs.uga.edu/Projects/METEOR-S/
[24] WSDL-S http://lsdis.cs.uga.edu/library/download/WSDL-S-V1.html
[25] The Jena RDF/XML Parser, http://www.hpl.hp.com/personal/jjc/arp/
[26] The Lehigh Univeristy Benchmark, http://swat.cse.lehigh.edu/projects/lubm/
[27] J.F. Allen, Mixed initiative planning: Position paper. ARPA/Rome Labs Planning Initiative Workshop, 1994.
[28] M.H. Burstein and D.V. McDermott. Issues in the development of human-computer mixed-initiative planning. In Cognitive Technology: In Search of a Humane Interface, 285–303. Elsevier, 1996.

Semantic Desktop 2.0: The Gnowsis Experience

Leo Sauermann[1], Gunnar Aastrand Grimnes[1], Malte Kiesel[1],
Christiaan Fluit[3], Heiko Maus[1], Dominik Heim[2], Danish Nadeem[4],
Benjamin Horak[2], and Andreas Dengel[1][2]

[1] Knowledge Management Department
German Research Center for Artificial Intelligence DFKI GmbH,
Kaiserslautern, Germany
{firstname.surname}@dfki.de
[2] Knowledge-Based Systems Group, Department of Computer Science,
University of Kaiserslautern, Germany
[3] Aduna BV, Amersfoort, The Netherlands
christiaan.fluit@aduna.biz
[4] University of Osnabrueck, Germany
danzinde@gmail.com

Abstract. In this paper we present lessons learned from building a Semantic Desktop system, the gnowsis beta. On desktop computers, semantic software has to provide stable services and has to reflect the personal view of the user. Our approach to ontologies, the *Personal Information Model* PIMO allows to create tagging services like del.icio.us on the desktop. A semantic wiki allows further annotations. Continuous evaluations of the system helped to improve it. These results were created in the EPOS research project and are available in the open source projects Aperture, kaukoluwiki, and gnowsis and will be continued in the Nepomuk project. By using these components, other developers can create new desktop applications the web 2.0 way.

1 Introduction

A characteristic of human nature is to *collect*. In the information age we have moved from the basic collection of food, books and paintings to collecting websites, documents, e-mails, ideas, tasks and sometimes arguments and facts. We gather information and store them on our desktop computers, but once stored the satisfaction of possessing something is soon distorted by the task of finding information in our personal data swamp [9]. In this paper we present parts of the gnowsis semantic desktop framework, a tool for personal information management (PIM). In addition to providing an interface for managing your personal data it also provides interfaces for other applications to access this, acting as a central hub for semantic information on the desktop. The described *gnowsis* system is a prototype of a *Semantic Desktop* [17], aiming to integrate desktop applications and the data managed on desktop computers using semantic web technology. Previous work published about Semantic Desktop applications [5,12,15] did show that this approach is promising to support users in finding and reminding information, and to work with information in new ways. The architecture was improved during the last years, taking inspiration from the current advanced and popularity of the *web 2.0* (See Section 3). The new architecture and new ontology policies for gnowsis version 0.9 is described in Section 2. In Section 3 we will discuss what semantic desktop applications can learn from the web 2.0, in particular we discuss how semantic wikis provide an ideal lightweight solution for ad-hoc creating of meta-data, and how such semantic wikis and tagging were integrated into gnowsis. In section 4, a short description of the information integration framework *Aperture* is given. A summary on our evaluation efforts and lessons learned is given in Section 5, indicating best practices and other remarks on practical semantic web engineering. The system has been deployed in several evaluation settings, gathering user feedback to further improve it, and an active community is now building around the gnowsis semantic desktop. As the system is now part of the EU-funded Integrated Project Nepomuk[1], which develops a comprehensive solution for a *Social Semantic Desktop*, we expect that the service oriented approach to the semantic desktop will have more impact in the future, which is the conclusion of this paper.

2 The Gnowsis Approach

Gnowsis is a semantic desktop with a strong focus on extensibility and integration. The goal of gnowsis is to enhance existing desktop applications and the desktop operating system with Semantic Web features. The primary use for such a system is *Personal Information Management* (PIM), technically realized by representing the user's data in RDF.Although the technology used is the same, communication, collaboration, and the integration with the global semantic web is not addressed by the gnowsis system. The gnowsis project was created 2003 in Leo Sauermann's diploma thesis [14] and continued in the DFKI research project EPOS[2] [7].

Gnowsis can be coarsely split into two parts, the gnowsis-server which does all the data processing, storage and interaction with native applications; and the graphical user interface (GUI) part, currently implemented as Swing GUI and some web-interfaces (See the gnowsis web-page for illustrative screenshots[3]). The interface between the server and GUI is clearly specified, making it easy to develop alternative interfaces. It is also possible to run gnowsis-server standalone, without a GUI. Gnowsis uses a *Service Oriented Architecture* (SOA), where each component defines a certain interface, after the server started the component the interface is available as XML/RPC service[4], to be used by other applications, for more detail refer to Section 3.

External applications like Microsoft Outlook or Mozilla Thunderbird are integrated via Aperture data-source (See Section 4), their data is imported and mirrored in gnowsis. Some new features were also added to these applications

---

[1] http://nepomuk.semanticdesktop.org
[2] http://www.dfki.uni-kl.de/epos
[3] http://www.gnowsis.opendfki.de/
[4] http://www.xmlrpc.com/

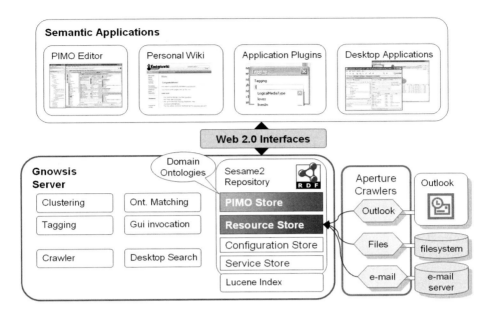

Fig. 1. The Gnowsis Architecture

using plugins, for example, in Thunderbird users can relate e-mails to concepts within their personal ontology (See Section 3.1).

The whole gnowsis framework is free software, published under a BSD compatible license. It is implemented in Java to be platform-independent and reuses well-known tools like Jena, Sesame, Servlets, Swing, and XML-RPC. Gnowsis can be downloaded from http://www.gnowsis.org/.

The Gnowsis Server. The architecture of the *gnowsis-server* service is shown in Figure 1. Its central component is naturally an RDF storage repository. Gnowsis uses four different stores for this purpose. The PIMO store handles the information in the user's *Personal Information Model* (See Section 2.1), the resource store handles the data crawled from Aperture data-sources (See Section 4), the configuration store handles the data about available data-sources, log-levels, crawl-intervals, etc., and finally, the service store handles data created by various gnowsis modules, such as user profiling data or metadata for the crawling of data-sources.

Separating the PIMO store from the resource store was an important decision for the gnowsis architecture, and it was made for several reasons: The resource store is inherently chaotic, since it mirrors the structure of the user's applications (consider your email inbox), whereas the thoughts (eg, concepts and relations) can be structured separately in the PIMO. Another reason was efficiency, while a user's PIMO may contain a few thousand instances for a very frequent user, it is not uncommon for people to have an archive of 100,000 emails. By separating the two we can save time and resources by only performing inference on the

PIMO store. We also note that a similar approach was taken in many other projects, for instance the topic maps community, where topics and occurrences are separated [13]. A discussion of cognitive justification for such a split can be found in Section 2.1.

The storage modules in gnowsis are currently based on Sesame 2 [2] and are using Sesame's native Storage And Inference Layer (SAIL) to store the data on disk. In the previous gnowsis versions we used MySQL in combination with Jena as triple store, but this enforced users to install the database server on their desktops and also the performance of fulltext-searching in MySQL/Jena was not satisfying. By using Sesame2 with the embedded native SAIL we simplified the installation significantly. In addition to the raw RDF the PIMO and resource stores use an additional SAIL layer which utilizes Lucene[5] to index the text of RDF literals, providing extremely fast full-text search capabilities on our RDF stores. Lucene indexing operates on the level of documents. Our LuceneSail has two modes for mapping RDF to logical documents: one is used with Aperture and will index each Aperture data-object (for example files, webpages, emails, etc.) as a document. The other mode does not require Aperture. Instead one Lucene document is created for each named RDF resource in the store. The resulting Lucene Index can be accessed either explicitly through java-code, or by using special predicates when querying the RDF store. Figure 2 shows an example SPARQL query for PIMO documents containing the word "rome". The LuceneSail will rewrite this query to access the Lucene index and remove the special predicates from the triple patterns. This method for full-text querying of RDF stores is equivalent to the method used in Aduna MetaData server and Aduna AutoFocus [6].

```
SELECT ?X WHERE {
    ?X rdf:type pimo:Document ;
       lucene:matches ?Q.
    ?Q lucene:query "rome".
}
```

Fig. 2. A Query using special predicates for full-text searching

2.1 Open Source, Open Standards, Open Minds

A key to success for a future semantic desktop is making it extendable. Partitioning the framework into services and making it possibile to add new services is one way to support this. Another contributor is exposing all programming interfaces based on the XML-RPC standard, allowing new applications can use the data and services of gnowsis.

> Open standards are important to help create interoperable and affordable solutions for everybody. They also promote competition by setting up a technical playing field that is level to all market players. This means lower costs for enterprises and, ultimately, the consumer. EU Commissioner Erkki Liikanen, World Standards Day, 14 October 2003

---

[5] http://lucene.apache.org/

To create an *open standard*, others have to be able to provide a competing implementation of the standardized interfaces. The basis for this process is already laid in the commitment to HTTP interfaces and open source. The gnowsis project will be changed to a subsidiary of the bigger Nepomuk project, and all interfaces and services will be subject to a standardization and re-implementation process in the next years. By opening the project to this community, it is possible to define open standards that can be implemented by competitors, drawing new players to this market. We want to attract *open minds* to the semantic desktop, that combine existing tools creatively and can both rely on a stable platform and stable interfaces. The *web 2.0* has attracted many users. Developers recognize that by opening the data of applications and reusing existing services, new systems can be built and value can be added. We aim to transfer some of this experience to the semantic desktop creating a *semantic desktop 2.0* environment.

2.2 PIMO Ontology Approach

An interesting challenge that semantic web technologies created on desktop computers is the integration of the stored data into a coherent view. In the *Personal Information Model* (PIMO) [16] approach we focus on the fact that all information is related to the user's personal view of the world. Whenever a user writes a document, reads his e-mails, or browses the web, a terminology addressing the same people, projects, places, and organizations is involved. It is connected by the interests and the tasks of the user: if the person "Paul" is working to open a new office in Rome, Italy, many documents, e-mails and files will relate to Rome and the new office. The example user Paul and parts of his PIMO are described in [16], they will be used throughout this document.

The PIMO ontology framework was initially developed in the EPOS project and consists of six components (Figure 3). The first half of these components represent mental models on a conceptual layer using formalized domain ontologies. It consists of three layers: upper-level, mid-level and domain ontologies.

PIMO-Basic, PIMO-Upper, PIMO-Mid and Domain Ontologies. Apart from the native resources, the mental models are represented using a multi-layer approach. Here we transferred the 3 layer approach taken in the KnowMore-project for organizational memories (application layer, knowledge description layer, information object layer; [3]) to the individual desktop. A similar approach was used by Huiyong Xiao and Isabel F. Cruz, they differentiate between *Application Layer, Domain Layer and Resource Layer* [23].

In the PIMO, the ontology layers consist of the following parts:

- PIMO-Basic: defines the basic language constructs. The class pimo-basic: Thing represents a super-class of other classes.
- PIMO-Upper: A domain-independent ontology defining abstract sub-classes of Thing. Such abstract classes are PersonConcept, OrganizationalConcept, LocationConcept, Document, etc.

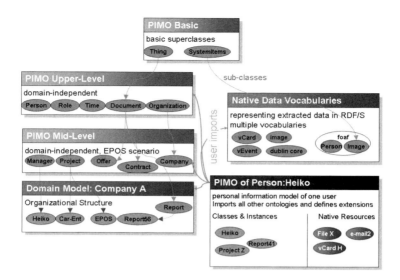

Fig. 3. PIMO ontology components

- PIMO-Mid: More concrete sub-classes of upper-classes. The PIMO mid-level ontology serves to integrate various domain ontologies and provides classes for Person, Project, Company, etc.
- Domain ontologies: A set of domain ontologies where each describes a concrete domain of interest of the user. The user's company and its organizational structure may be such a domain, or it might be a shared public ontology. Domain ontologies should sub-class from PIMO-Mid and PIMO-Upper to allow integration.
- PIMO-User: the extensions of above models created by an individual for personal use.

The first three layers were created once by members of the EPOS team and are well suited for knowledge work scenarios, the domain ontologies are created for real domains and change frequently. For example, a domain ontology was created to represent the organizational structures at the DFKI KM lab, named *"Organizational Repository"*.

The PIMO of an individual user. The personal mental model of the user is represented in the user's own model, called PIMO-User. Personal concepts, ideas, projects, contacts etc. are put there by the user creating classes and instances extending from the higher level PIMO classes and relations. The complete PIMO of a user is now defined as the sum of imported upper and mid-level ontologies, domain ontologies, PIMO-User, and relations to native resources found on the desktop.

Native resources and data. Native resources are desktop data like existing files, e-mails, the calendar, and address book. They reflect the worker's personal view of his or her information space. A framework was created to transform several native structures to the RDF format, for example, data from Microsoft Outlook, IMAP e-mail servers, and many file formats which can be converted to RDF (See Section 4). The data extracted from these native sources is then described using a set of data-oriented RDF/S vocabularies, represented in the layer of *Native Data Vocabularies*. This data is then stored in the resource store of gnowsis.

3 Web 2.0 on the Semantic Desktop

The Web 2.0 [11] is seen as a new generation of web applications and services. Although, dismissed by many as a marketing hype and criticised for being an empty buzzword, there are several features that are generally considered to be central to the idea:

- Open data – when using some particular web-site the user should be in control of his own data, and should be able to export it and move it to an alternative service.
- Open APIs – access to site services should be possible for machine as well as for the user.
- Participatory web-sites – Known as the "architecture of participation", the idea that users create the real value of a web-site is crucial to the web 2.0. Many sites also put heavy emphasise on the social aspect of their services.
- Common features – Wikis, tagging, tag-clouds, blogs, etc. are some features are wide spread among sites considering themselves web 2.0.
- Common technology – web services (SOAP[6], XML-RPC) provide a good basis for exposing a web-site's API, AJAX (Asynchronous Javascript and XML) provides means to build fluid and elegant interfaces using HTML and RSS provides the means to stay up-to-date with a huge number of information sources without having to manually check them all.

With gnowsis we are trying to take these web 2.0 features one step further and bring them "home" to the user's desktop. By having gnowsis data-sources for popular tagging web-sites, such as del.icio.us[7], Flickr[8] and BibSonomy[9], a user can import their existing tags from these sites, and integrate their personal "folksonomy" into their PIMO Ontology. This allows the user to reuse their existing classification schemes for tagging their resource, and has the added advantage of converting what used to be a flat tag list into a first-class ontology.

3.1 Tagging

Modern Tagging Systems are designed to support users in collecting new resources. Nowadays we are able to tag and manage our private pictures in Flickr,

---

[6] http://www.w3.org/TR/soap/
[7] http://del.icio.us
[8] http://www.flickr.com
[9] http://bibsonomy.org

our browser bookmarks in Delicious and our scientific bibliography in BibSonomy. For these three web 2.0 services, we have developed Aperture crawlers and can integrate tag information to the resource store.

The "Ontology matcher" described in Section 4.1 allows morphing these crawled tags into personalized tags in the user's PIMO. To simplify the access to the information stored in the PIMO, we developed a tagging API which can be accessed via XML-RPC and a tagging extension for the Mozilla Thunderbird email client to use it. This enabled the user to connect incoming mails with existing tags in the user's PIMO. A similar approach in the web domain was developed by technorati[10]. The gnowsis tagging API can be seen as *technorati for an individual*.

Further development of the tagging approach in gnowsis is being done by Benjamin Horak in his diploma thesis [8]. The project, called "Contag", contains several new features for a tagging environment: It should be possible to automatically propose new instances and classes as tags for a given resource. By invoking different web 2.0 services such as those developed by Yahoo, TagTheNet[11] and Wikipedia, we can get more information about the resource at hand, and statistical analysis of these sources should allow us to propose correct tags, even if the tag is not explicitly mentioned in the resource itself.

3.2 Open Data, Open APIs

All services and APIs available in gnowsis are also exposed as XML-RPC services, meaning all the gnowsis functionality can be accessed from outside the core Java part of gnowsis. The is extremely beneficial because it opens up gnowsis to a big section of other programming languages and developers. Internally we have used these interfaces to quickly develop testing interfaces for various gnowsis components using HTML, Javascript and AJAX. Using the "JavaScript O Lait" library[12] calling gnowsis function from javascript is trivial. For example, consider this code-snippet from our debug interface, which uses XML-RPC to perform full-text searches on the user's PIMO:

```
<h2 class="header">query pimo</h2>
<div class="container">
q:<input type="text" id="queryFulltext" size="20">
<button onclick="gnowsis_callXmlMethod('gnowsis-server','dataaccess','querySelect',
    document.getElementById('queryFulltext').value,'fulltext');">query!</button>
</div>
```

3.3 Semantic Wiki

Traditional wikis enable people to collaboratively author a set of interlinked texts (*wiki pages*). The idea of semantic wikis is not only to edit texts but author information that can be processed by automatic means. In practice, this means that semantic wikis aim to support advanced queries ("What semantic

---

[10] http://www.technorati.com
[11] http://www.tagthe.net
[12] http://jsolait.net/

web researchers wrote more than 60 papers?") and advanced search ("Search for *ant* as in *software*.").

Gnowsis integrates with the semantic wiki *Kaukolu*[13] [10]. The main idea is that a wiki page can be created for every instance in the PIMO-User ontology. In Paul's PIMO, there would be wiki pages for *Rome, Italy and Paul*. Note that each wiki-page is automatically a *tag*. This means that every gnowsis resource can be browsed in Kaukolu and vice versa. The same is true for relations between resources which can be created either gnowsis or Kaukolu. In gnowsis, relations are created using the standard GUI, while in Kaukolu, relations are written in a plain text syntax that is similar to N3. The user gets supported interactively with an autocompletion feature when entering data. This relieves him from having to know every relation's name or URI. The autocompletion feature bases its suggestions on ontologies stored in the PIMO-storage.The integration of Kaukolu with gnowsis opened up for several interesting features:

- **Browser integration:** With the wiki, it is possible to use the browser as a simple frontend to the gnowsis system. We even plan to move some of gnowsis' more advanced features to the wiki by way of using wiki plugins.
- **Collaborative authoring:** You can set up public spaces in the wiki to which other people are allowed to contribute. Since Kaukolu pages may also contain ontologies, this allows (simple) collaborative ontology authoring.
- **Simple data input:** Wikis are a well-known tool for authoring texts without the need to adhere to rigid templates. This can be used in the semantic desktop context, too, as with the wiki it is possible to add unstructured information (for which either no schemas exist, which are too costly to formalize, or no benefit in formalization can be thought of) to any desktop resource present in the gnowsis system.

4 Aperture to Extract Resources

To interface with applications that are not semantically enabled gnowsis uses a framework called Aperture [4]. Harvesting as much existing semantic information as possible from legacy applications benefits the user as it lowers the entry barrier to use semantic applications, e.g., when compared to approaches that rely on manual annotations. For example, information such as folder names, document authors, and creation dates can be used to provide a semantic information space with little effort required from the user, even though this information may often be shallow or imprecise.

Obtaining this information is a complex engineering task. The information is spread among a variety of source types and file formats and can often not be queried fast enough in their native format to realize the responsiveness and metadata-richness we needed for gnowsis. Crawling and indexing this information does give us these capabilities at the cost of having to keep the extracted

---

[13] http://kaukoluwiki.opendfki.de

metadata in sync with the original sources. Recently we see a tendency to incorporate such functionality in the file system [20,22], but these approaches are still limited and operating system-specific.

The Aperture project provides various open source components for building semantic applications that harvest and index semantically rich information from various sources. Even though Aperture is still in its early stages, a growing number of applications are already making use of it. To enable this extraction Aperture offers a number of services that can be used independently or combined: *Crawlers* access an information source such as a file system, website or mail-boxes and locate all uniquely identifiable objects such as files or e-mails, identifying them by URL. Scheme-specific *DataAccessors* access these URLs and create a data structure for each of them, holding the binary data as well as any metadata provided by that scheme, e.g. file names and last modification dates. MIME type-specific *Extractors* are capable of interpreting the binary data and extracting any information supported by that file type, such as the full-text and metadata contained in a document. Finally, Aperture provides a number of utility classes for MIME type identification of binary resources, hyperlink extraction and handling of secure connections. Interfaces for crawling the contents of archives, viewing resources in their native application and storage and querying of metadata are still under development.

We have designed Aperture with the intention to provide a light-weight, expandable and adaptable framework for handling information sources. Aperture is initiated by DFKI and Aduna as a collaborative opensource project. One of the core decisions that has provided this flexibility is the use of RDF to exchange metadata between Aperture components and between Aperture and the surrounding application.

The use of RDF may have its price as programmers may find it relatively hard to handle RDF models, compared to simple Java Maps with key-value pairs. To alleviate this problem we have designed a simple Java interface called RDFContainer for handling small RDF models. RDFContainer instances are typically used to move metadata from the extractors to other components. In gnowsis, the extracted data is stored directly (without further inference) in the resource storage RDF database. The Aperture project is independent from the semantic desktop and published at sourceforge. And it's use is encourage for anyone wishing to generate RDF datasets from external applications and sources. At the moment, Aperture supports various file types (PDF, Powerpoint, MS-Word, ...) and complex data sources like IMAP e-mail servers, Microsoft Outlook, crawling websites, flickr, del.icio.us, etc.

4.1 Ontology Matcher

Once the data is represented as RDF by Aperture, it has to be aligned with the user's PIMO. As an example, the user already has an instance of class "City" which is labeled "Rome". Aperture crawled the flickr photos of the user and found a photo of an office building, tagged with "Office and Rome". The ontology matcher will now *create a relation* between the existing city "Rome" and this photo. It can also *create new instances* in the user's PIMO, if necessary. For example, the tag "Office" may be unknown, then a new instance in the ontology will be created for this tag, guessing the right class for it. When Aperture crawls larger structures, like a file system, the ontology matcher can *synchronize* parts of the user's PIMO with the file system. For example, when the users has created a list of folders for each of his projects, instances of class "Project" can be created.

In previous work published on this topic [21], term-based matching, structure-based matching, and instance-based matching algorithms were used in combination to implement such services for peer-to-peer ontology alignment and organizational memory (OM) wide ontology management. We are working to port this previous work to the current gnowsis system. In the current software package, only simple algorithms are bundled to realize the basic functionality. We want to encourage others to find more algorithms that work on this existing data.

5 Evaluation

Evaluation of Semantic Desktop that supports user with information finding and reminding with high-level PIM tasks, such as organising resources according to their mental model, needs a naturalistic flexible approach and valid and reliable methods for evaluation [1].

Gnowsis development maps closely to the spiral model of software development: our approach has been to define initial use-cases, write a prototype, and evaluate it with domain experts. A user evaluation of gnowsis based on a structured questionnaire has been made on power users to elicit their experiences, efforts have been made to enhance usability features which could be compared between different versions. We evaluated gnowsis version 0.8 in the EPOS project with domain experts [18], and this provided an important input to modify several features for the new gnowsis 0.9 architecture described in this paper.

- The possibility to add multiple tags to a document was used, in the mean 2.5 tags were attached to a file, which is significantly more than the single category a hierarchical file system provides.
- The gnowsis desktop search was used very frequently. Users answered in the questionnaire that they found unexpected information and that the categories provided by the PIMO helped during retrieval.
- The participants agreed that the PIMO reflects their personal mental models

The gnowsis 0.8 prototype had a Firefox-plugin to support link and browse from within the browser. Gnowsis version 0.9 will come include with a tagging plugin that can be seen as a replacement for today's bookmarks. The possibility to move and classify files (which we call "DropBox") as well as a semantic search are provided in both prototypes because it turned out to be a feature frequently used by the users. Only the Peer-to-Peer search was abandoned for version 0.9 (Although this will be reintroduced in the Nepomuk project). Completely new features in version 0.9 are the installation wizard that is indispensable in todays software and the PIMO. The possibility of relating resources has been completely reconsiderd. The previous linker reflected the technical nature of RDF directly in user interface, thus has been replaced by the annotator, a process-support approach on how to support linking items. Drag and drop support has also been enhanced, as it is an intuitive mechanism for invoking certain operations and its pervasive support adds flexibility in information manipulation.

5.1 Lessons Learned

Building the first gnowsis prototypes has helped us to understand typical problems that arise in semantic web projects, and in this section we will enumerate our main problems. The first problem was that we had *no clear strategy regarding ontologies*. During the version 0.8 prototypes, we did allow both OWL and RDF/S semantics. Through this mixture, the inference engine of Jena had scalability problems and we disabled it. In the 0.9 version, we separated resource store from PIMO store and inference support is now only enabled for the PIMO store and there is a clear policy for the use of ontologies. The PIMO ontology approach is well documented [16] and developers can check the data model for validity, using a convenient web interface. We provided an example ontology (*Paul's Pimo*) which models the example user Paul, and because we created it before the software developments started, all developers could use it to create JUnit tests and user interface Java-Beans. Paul's Pimo accelerated development speed and improved code quality, as we had test data right from the start.

The second problem was the approach to *data extraction*. Two different approaches were evaluated [19], the first based on virtual graphs and live access to data sources. Using virtual graphs, a RDQL query to the system was translated to calls to the datasource, for example a query to list persons with certain properties was forwarded to be handled by Microsoft Outlook. This approach was complicated to implement, and the response times were unacceptable for complex queries. The second alternative was to crawl all data into a RDF database and do the queries on that database. Clearly, the second alternative had lower programming effort and better response times. In version 0.9 the database backend was also changed from Jena with MySQL storage to Sesame2 with storage to binary files, removing the dependency of MySQL. For an end-user application, it was not acceptable to install and configure MySQL together with gnowsis.

The third problem was the attempt to *create a generic RDF interface* that allows both editing and browsing of information. Inspired by Haystack, several prototypes were build for gnowsis to edit RDF in a generic way, and the results were not accepted by end-users and abandoned. The current decision is to use *special purpose applications*; for each task a separate, specialized user interface, like the Drop-Box, linker and desktop search tools mentioned above.

Many problems were solved with approaches that resemble web 2.0 ideas — open data, open apis and a service oriented architecture.

6 Conclusion

Existing semantic desktop implementations like gnowsis version 0.8, Haystack, DBIN, or Mindraider lack the ability to integrate external applications. In theory, they are extensible but in practice programming barriers and monolithic architecture limit the extensibility. The approach taken in gnowsis 0.9 and the future Nepomuk Semantic Desktop framework aims at a service-oriented architecture. Based on interfaces to the core parts and a clear separation of components, we could improve the extensibility of the system. The use of the common database Sesame2 and its web interface allowed developers to understand the system faster and access the data through known interfaces. Also a clear guideline on managing ontologies is needed, and the PIMO approach provided this. It combines findings published by several other authors: a layered ontology, separation of native resources from ontology concepts and a personal model that can be freely edited by the user. Using web 2.0 philosophy in combination with semantic web technology, we propose the semantic desktop framework gnowsis as useful basis for future semantic desktops. An evaluation with knowledge workers and our own experience with the system has shown that the service-oriented approach supports knowledge workers.

Gnowsis will continue as part of the Integrated Project Nepomuk, where we will see more innovation on the Semantic Desktop in the next years.

Acknowledgements. The PIMO ontology system was designed, and created by Ludger van Elst. We want to thank Man Luo from TU Berlin for her input in her meeting management diploma thesis. This work was supported by the German Federal Ministry of Education, Science, Research and Technology (bmb+f), (Grant 01 IW C01, Project EPOS: Evolving Personal to Organizational Memories) and by the European Union IST fund (Grant FP6-027705, project Nepomuk).

References

1. *Evaluating Personal Information Management Behaviors and Tools.* Vol.49.No.1,Communications of ACM, 2006.
2. Seseame 2. http://www.openrdf.org/, 2006.
3. Andreas Abecker, Ansgar Bernardi, Knut Hinkelmann, Otto Kühn, and Michael Sintek. Toward a Technology for Organizational Memories. *IEEE Intelligent Systems*, June 1998.
4. Aperture. http://aperture.sourceforge.net, 2005.
5. Adam Cheyer, Jack Park, and Richard Giuli. Iris: Integrate. relate. infer. share. In *Proc. of Semantic Desktop Workshop at the ISWC, Galway, Ireland*, 2005.
6. Christiaan Fluit. Autofocus: Semantic search for the desktop. In *9th Int. Conf. on Information Visualisation, London, UK*, pages 480–487, 2005.
7. H. Holz, H. Maus, A. Bernardi, and O. Rostanin. From Lightweight, Proactive Information Delivery to Business Process-Oriented Knowledge Management. *Journal of Universal Knowledge Management*, 0(2):101–127, 2005.

8. Benajmin Horak. Contag : Atagging system linking the semantic desktop with web 2.0. Master's thesis, University of Kaiserslautern, 2006.
9. Aura Lippincott Jason Frand. Personal knowledge management: A strategy for controlling information overload. 2002. draft.
10. Malte Kiesel. Kaukolu – hub of the semantic corporate intranet. In *Proc. of Semantic Wiki Workshop at the ESWC 2006*, 2006.
11. Tim O'Reilly. What is web 2.0, design patterns and business models for the next generation of software.
12. Dennis Quan, David Huynh, and David R. Karger. Haystack: A platform for authoring end user semantic web applications. In *International Semantic Web Conference*, pages 738–753, 2003.
13. Holger Rath. The Topic Maps Handbook. empolis white paper, empolis GmbH, 2003.
14. Leo Sauermann. The gnowsis-using semantic web technologies to build a semantic desktop. Diploma thesis, Technical University of Vienna, 2003.
15. Leo Sauermann. The semantic desktop - a basis for personal knowledge management. In *Proceedings of the I-KNOW 2005.*, pages 294 – 301, 2005.
16. Leo Sauermann. Pimo-a pim ontology for the semantic desktop (draft). Draft, DFKI, 2006.
17. Leo Sauermann, Ansgar Bernardi, and Andreas Dengel. Overview and outlook on the semantic desktop. In *Proc. of Semantic Desktop Workshop at the ISWC, Galway, Ireland, November 6*.
18. Leo Sauermann, Andreas Dengel, Ludger van Elst, Andreas Lauer, Heiko Maus, and Sven Schwarz. Personalization in the EPOS project. In *Proc. of the Semantic Web Personalization Workshop at the ESWC Conference*, 2006.
19. Leo Sauermann and Sven Schwarz. Gnowsis adapter framework: Treating structured data sources as virtual rdf graphs. In *Proceedings of the ISWC 2005*, 2005.
20. Apple Spotlight. http://www.apple.com/macosx/features/spotlight/, 2004.
21. Ludger van Elst and Malte Kiesel. Generating and integrating evidence for ontology mappings. In *Proc. of the 14th EKAW*, volume 3257 of *LNAI*, pages 15–29, Heidelberg, 2004. Springer.
22. Microsoft WinFS. http://msdn.microsoft.com/data/winfs/default.aspx, 2006.
23. Huiyong Xiao and Isabel F. Cruz. A multi-ontology approach for personal information management. In *Proc. of Semantic Desktop Workshop at the ISWC, Galway, Ireland*, 2005.

Towards Semantic Interoperability in a Clinical Trials Management System

Ravi D. Shankar[1], Susana B. Martins[1], Martin J. O'Connor[1], David B. Parrish[2], and Amar K. Das[1]

[1] Stanford Medical Informatics, Stanford University School of Medicine,
Stanford, CA 94305
`ravi.shankar@stanford.edu`
[2] The Immune Tolerance Network, Pittsburgh, PA

Abstract. Clinical trials are studies in human patients to evaluate the safety and effectiveness of new therapies. Managing a clinical trial from its inception to completion typically involves multiple disparate applications facilitating activities such as trial design specification, clinical sites management, participants tracking, and trial data analysis. There remains however a strong impetus to integrate these diverse applications – each supporting different but related functions of clinical trial management – at syntactic and semantic levels so as to improve clarity, consistency and correctness in specifying clinical trials, and in acquiring and analyzing clinical data. The situation becomes especially critical with the need to manage multiple clinical trials at various sites, and to facilitate meta-analyses on trials. This paper introduces a knowledge-based framework that we are building to support a suite of clinical trial management applications. Our initiative uses semantic technologies to provide a consistent basis for the applications to interoperate. We are adapting this approach to the Immune Tolerance Network (ITN), an international research consortium developing new therapeutics in immune-mediated disorders.

1 Introduction

Clinical trials are carefully-controlled research studies in human patients to systematically evaluate the safety and efficacy of new or unproven approaches in the prevention and treatment of medical conditions. The lifecycle management of a complex clinical trial typically involves multiple applications facilitating activities such as trial design specification, clinical sites management, laboratory management, and participants tracking. These disparate applications are banded together as a clinical trial management system. The information generated by these applications along with data from loosely controlled sources such as spreadsheets, documents and email messages are then assembled to determine the operational state of the clinical trial. The lack of common nomenclature among the different sources of the tracking information and the unreliable nature of the data generation can lead to significant operational and maintenance challenges. The applications support different but related aspects of a clinical trial, and require clinical trial data flow and knowledge exchange between the applications. Thus, there is a strong impetus to integrate these diverse applications at syntactic, structural and semantic levels so as to improve clarity, consistency and correctness in specifying clinical trials, and in acquiring and analyzing clinical data. The situation becomes especially critical with the need to manage complex clinical trials at various sites, and to facilitate meta-analyses on across the different trials.

We present, Epoch, a knowledge-based approach to support a suite of clinical trial management applications. Our initiative uses semantic technologies to provide a consistent basis for the applications to interoperate. We are adapting this approach to the Immune Tolerance Network[1,2] (ITN), an international consortium that aims to accelerate the development of immune tolerance therapies through clinical trials and integrated mechanistic (biological) studies. The ITN is involved in planning, developing and conducting clinical trials in autoimmune diseases, islet, kidney and liver transplantation, allergy and asthma, and operates more than a dozen core facilities that conduct bioassay services. Many groups, internal and external to ITN, collaborate in facilitating the specification and implementation of the trials and related biological assay studies. Therefore, the successful conduct of a clinical trial depends upon the interaction of professionals working for various entities, including the ITN, contract research organizations, clinical study sites, and core laboratories. Studies need to be tracked for the purposes of general planning, gauging progression, monitoring patient safety, and managing personnel and clinical resources. The management effort is especially compounded by the fact that an ITN trial often is carried out at multiple sites, geographically distributed, sometimes across the world.

The Epoch framework is being collaboratively developed by the Stanford Medical Informatics (SMI) and the ITN in addressing the informatics needs of collecting, managing, integrating and analyzing clinical trial and immunoassay —a special laboratory procedure— data. Figure 1 illustrates a set of clinical trial management applications that we have identified to manage ITN's clinical trials. At the core of our framework is a suite of ontologies that conceptualizes the clinical trial domain. The ontologies along with semantic inferences and rules provide a common protocol definition for the applications to use to interoperate semantically. In this paper, we

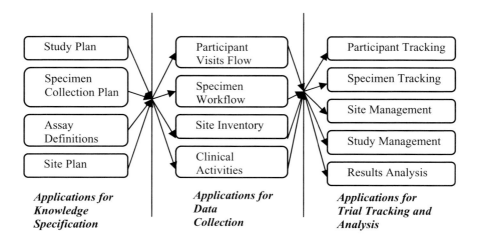

Fig. 1. A set of clinical trial management applications. The arrows indicate knowledge exchange and data flow.

present the strong ontological foundation of our approach, and describe the Epoch components. We illustrate the use of our framework in supporting the semantic interoperability of a subset of the clinical trial management applications to support specimen tracking.

2 The Epoch Core Ontologies

A clinical trial protocol (the plan for a trial) lays out specification, implementation and data analysis details. For example, it includes the reason for undertaking the study, the number of participants that will be in the study and the recruitment process, the sites (clinical and laboratory) where the study will be conducted, the study drug that the participants will take, the medical tests that the participants will undergo, the data that will be collected, and the statistical analyses that will be performed on the data. We highlight four pieces of protocol definitions that are required to support these activities. The *protocol schema* divides the temporal span of the study into phases such as the treatment phase and follow-up phase, and specifies the temporal sequence of the phases. It also includes information on the arms of the protocol. The *schedule of events* enumerates a sequence of protocol visits that are planned at each phase, and, for each visit, specifies the time window when the visit should happen and a list of protocol events (assessments, procedures and tests) that are planned at that visit. The *specimen table* lists the clinical specimens that will be collected from the participant, the visits at which they will be collected, the processing and storage conditions, and the assays —special tests— that will be performed on them. The *specimen flow* describes the workflow associated with the processing of the specimens. The specimens are typically shipped from the collection sites to biorepository sites and, from there to the core laboratories where they are assayed.

We recognize that a structured and standardized knowledge representation that conceptualizes the protocol entities relevant to our management applications is crucial to the interoperability of these applications. We created a suite of ontologies that provide a common nomenclature and semantics of protocol elements and that spans the entire clinical trials process:

- The *clinical ontology* includes terms that specify clinical and biological knowledge on immune tolerance disorders and other concepts relevant to ITN clinical trials.
- The *protocol ontology* is a knowledge model of the clinical trial protocol. It simplifies the complexity inherent in the full structure of the protocol by focusing only on concepts required to support clinical trial management. Other concepts are either ignored or partially represented. The main concepts represented in the protocol ontology are the protocol schema and the schedule of events.
- The *assay ontology* models characteristics of mechanistic studies relevant to immune disorders. An assay specification includes the clinical specimen that can be analyzed using that assay, and the processing instructions at the core laboratories.
- The *specimen ontology* models the workflow of specimens – collection, shipping and processing workflow of specimens at the clinical, laboratory, and biorepository sites.

- The *specimen container* ontology catalogs the different specimen containers such as tubes and slides, and the attributes of each container such as material, size, manufacturer, specimen types, additives, etc. Ancillary ontologies define different specimen types and additives.
- The *site ontology* provides a structure to store site-related data such as protocols implemented at the site, participants on each protocol, relevant clinical resources and personnel.
- The *virtual data ontology* encapsulates the study data that is being collected, such as participant clinical record, specimen workflow logs, and site related data. A mapping component can then map clinical trial data (found in a relational database) to these virtual data records using a mapping ontology. The data model concept is similar to the Virtual Medical Record[3] (VMR) specification promoted in the clinical guideline modeling efforts.
- The *temporal ontology*[4] provides a uniform representation of all temporal information in our models.

We have developed these ontologies in OWL[5] —the Web Ontology Language proposed by W3C— by building hierarchies of *classes* describing concepts in the ontologies and relating the classes to each other using *properties*. OWL can also represent data as instances of OWL classes —referred to as *individuals*— and also provides mechanisms for reasoning with the data and manipulating it. OWL also provides a powerful constraint language for precisely defining how concepts in ontology should be interpreted. The Semantic Web Rule Language[6] (SWRL) allows

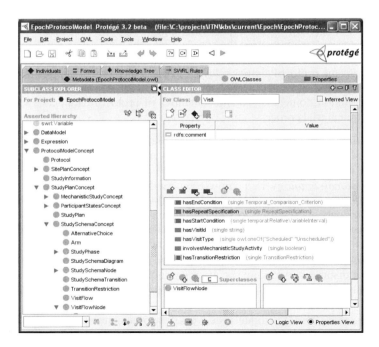

Fig. 2. The Protégé-OWL editor displaying part of the *Protocol ontology*

users to write Horn-like rules that can be expressed in terms of OWL concepts and that can reason about OWL individuals. SWRL provides deductive reasoning capabilities that can infer new knowledge from an existing OWL knowledge base. We use SWRL to specify temporal constraints and rules found in our ontologies in terms of the temporal model. Using SWRL's built-in extension facility, we have implemented a rich library of temporal operators to write rules to express complex temporal constraints. Protégé[7,8] is a software tool that supports the specification and maintenance of terminologies, ontologies and knowledge-bases in OWL. It has a plug-in called SWRL Tab[9], an editor for SWRL rules. We used Protégé to create the ontologies in OWL and SWRL (Figure 2). We, then, entered specific protocols and assays using Protégé's knowledge-acquisition facilities.

3 Components of the Epoch Framework

The Epoch framework broadly supports three types of methods that applications can use to support clinical trial management activities. The knowledge acquisition methods allow users to encode specific protocols and related operational elements, and thus, to create the protocol knowledge base. Ontology-database mapping methods integrate the protocol and biomedical knowledge with clinical trial data including clinical results and operational data stored in the ITN data repository. Concept-driven querying methods support integrated data management, and can be used to create high-level abstractions of clinical data during analysis of clinical results. At the center of all these methods and the applications that use these methods is the suite of Epoch ontologies that we have described in Section 2.

The *Epoch Knowledge Base* contains the ontologies enumerated in Section 2. It also stores specific instantiations of the ontologies for different clinical trials. The repository uses a file backend to store the OWL ontologies in XML format. The SWRL rules are stored as part of the knowledge base. Here is an example of a SWRL rule that is used to set a participant's time of transplant:

> *Observation(?o)* ∧
> *associatedVisitRecord(?o, ?vrecord)* ∧
> *hasParticipantId(?vrecord, ?pid)* ∧
> *hasCode(?o, ?code)* ∧
> *swrlb:equal(?code, "transplant")* ∧
> *temporal:hasValidTime(?o, ?vtO)* ∧
> *TemporalAnchorPoint(?a)* ∧
> *hasName(?a, "Transplant")*
>   → *temporal:hasValidTime(?a, ?vtO)*

Significant events in a protocol such as the transplant time are annotated as temporal anchor points. By definition, other events are temporally constrained by anchor points. For e.g., a visit time window (when the visit should happen) can be specified as a temporal constraint based on the anchor point 'transplant'. The example SWRL rule associates data model concepts such as Observation and VisitRecord to protocol model concepts such as TemporalAnchorPoint. The execution of the rule will set the value of the temporal anchor point 'transplant' with the transplant time for the participant found in the clinical trial database.

A *Knowledge Base Server* provides a programmatic interface (API) that other components can use to access the contents of the ontology repository. We are developing a protocol domain specific API on top of the generic Protégé-OWL API. We have developed a tool to generate XML renditions of the OWL knowledge base based on custom XML Schema. In Section 4, we show how we employed this tool to configure a data collection application with information in the knowledge base. We are building other utility tools to support querying and rule execution. These tools will eventually be integrated with the knowledge base server.

The *Clinical Trial Database* is a relational database system that stores data related to the implementation and execution of clinical trials. The types of data include participant enrollment data, specimen shipping and receiving logs, participant visits and activities, and clinical results.

The *Model-Data Mapper* facilitates runtime access to relational data in the clinical trial database as instances of the Epoch data model. It uses a mapping ontology to connect data model concepts to database entities i.e. properties of an OWL class are mapped to columns of a relational table.

The *Inference / Rule Engine* executes temporal and non-temporal constraints – that have been expressed as SWRL rules – in Epoch ontologies. We have developed a SWRL *built-in* deployment module[9] that provides a general mechanism to define Java implementations of SWRL built-ins, dynamically load them, and invoke them from a rule engine. We used this mechanism to define a set of temporal predicates to operate on temporal values. These predicates support the standard Allen[10] temporal operators such as before *during, starts, ends, inside, overlaps, before and after*. The interface with the Model-Data Mapper allows SWRL rules to be executed on data stored in the clinical trial database. Here is an example of a SWRL rule to check if a participant's visit time fell within that visit's time window:

> *VisitRecord(?vrecord) ^*
> *hasVisitId(?vrecord, ?vid1) ^*
> *hasParticipantId(?vrecord, ?pid) ^*
> *temporal:hasValidTime(?vrecord, ?vtO) ^*
> *Visit(?v) ^*
> *hasVisitId(?v, ?vid2) ^*
> *swrlb:equal(?vid1, ?vid2) ^*
> *hasStartCondition(?v, ?vsc) ^*
> *temporal:inside(?vtO, ?vsc)*
> $\rightarrow$

The empty head of the rule indicates that this rule is formulated as a query. This rule uses a built-in *temporal:inside* that takes in as arguments a time and a relative variable interval, and returns *true* if the time point is within the interval, and returns *false* otherwise. The *relative variable interval* concept is expressed in terms of a temporal anchor point. It is defined as

> *temporal anchor point + offset (+ high variance/- low variance)*

Using the relative variable interval, we can specify visit time windows like

> *transplant time + 28 days with a variance of plus or minus 3 days*

We are currently using JESS[11], a production rule-engine, to selectively execute the rules based on the context. For example, the rule that specifies the constraint on a visit time window will alone need to be executed when checking if a specific participant's visit satisfied the constraint.

The *Clinical Trial Management Applications* are a suite of applications as shown in Figure 1. These applications interoperate via the Epoch components at syntactic, structural and semantic levels to support the management of clinical trials.

4 An Example Usage Scenario – Specimen Collection and Tracking

Clinical specimens are collected from participants at different visits based on clinical assessments and clinical studies (biological assays) planned in the protocol. These specimens are then processed and stored in pre-determined containers and shipped to bio-repositories. The specimens (or portions of them) are shipped to the core laboratories that can perform specific assays on the specimens. The assay results are then sent to a data warehouse for storage and subsequent analysis. The bio-repositories may also archive portions of the specimens for future interrogation. The trials managed by ITN generate enormous amount of specimen traffic across different sites. Tracking the specimen from the point of collection to the point of processing and archival becomes paramount to maintain the integrity of the operation. Appropriate type and number of specimen containers should be stocked at the clinical

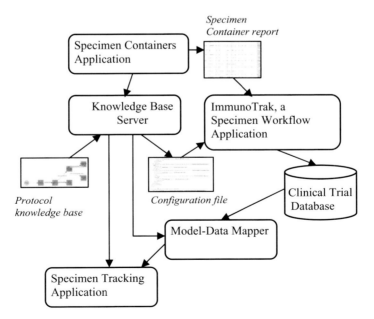

Fig. 3. A high-level view of semantic interoperation among Epoch architectural components and applications

sites in preparation for the anticipated participant visits. At the time of a participant's visit, appropriate specimens should be collected and stored in matching containers. The containers are shipped to the bio-repositories, and then to the core laboratories based on the shipping instructions in the specimen table and the specimen flow of the protocol. Specimens have to be accounted for at all times using shipping and receiving logs.

The ITN has contracted with Cimarron Software, Inc.[12] to build a specimen workflow system called ImmunoTrak based on Cimarron's Laboratory Workflow Systems product. Clinical trial personnel at the sites will use the system to log participant's visit, specimen collection, shipping and receiving of bar-coded specimen containers, etc. ImmunoTrak can be configured using a graphical user interface or via an XML specification. The configuration parameters include, the participant visit flow, the specimen container specification, list of participants, list of clinical and laboratory sites, and specimen workflow. The system should also be configured with the container manufacturer's report on the empty specimen containers shipped to the collection sites. The specimen tracking data that is collected by the system during the course of the trial is stored in a relational database. A Specimen Tracking application can then access the database to monitor the status of the specimen collection and processing.

Figure 3 shows the usage scenario employing the Epoch framework to specimen tracking. The first step is to specify the specimen workflow in the Protégé-OWL editor using relevant Epoch ontologies. Next, the Knowledge Base Server uses an XML Schema file to generate the configuration file for ImmunoTrak, the Specimen Workflow System. The Specimen Container application generates container specifications that form the basis of the manufacturer's report. During the course of the clinical trial, research coordinators at different clinical sites access ImmunoTrak to enter specimen collection data which is stored in the Clinical Trial Database. The Specimen Tracking Application employs the Model-Data Mapper to access the data via the Epoch data models. It can then satisfy user queries for specific specimen processing status, specimen collection inventory. It can also execute any validation rules or temporal constraints as specified in the ontologies on the tracking data using the production rule engine.

All the applications in this example work on the same set of semantic descriptions of specimen workflow concepts found in the Epoch knowledge base. The applications are built by different vendors, and are pressed into service at different stages – specification, execution and monitoring – of the clinical trial. The Epoch ontologies are the foundation that scans across these disparate applications. The semantic chaining of the applications, from protocol specification, to data collection, to data analysis can improve standardization, data integrity, data integration and data analysis.

5 Related Work

In the past few years, we have seen considerable interest in building knowledge-based systems that automate clinical trial protocols and clinical practice guidelines. The Epoch framework employs a task-based paradigm that combines an explicit representation of the clinical trial domain with rules that capture the logical conditions found in the trial management process. There have been a number of proposals on task-based clinical guideline representation formats – EON[13], PRO*forma*[14], GLIF[15], etc. In our laboratory, at Stanford Medical Informatics, we have developed the EON guideline models that are used to build guideline-based decision support systems. These advisory systems provide patient care that is informed by the guidelines. The Epoch models have adapted some of the representational formalisms – workflow, expressions, and coded concepts – found in the EON models. In the area of clinical trials, several modeling efforts have addressed different requirements of trial management activities. The Trial Bank Project[16] is a trial registry that captures information on randomized clinical trials such as intervention, outcomes, and eligibility criteria. The underlying knowledge base can support systematic reviewing and evidence-based practice. Design-A-Trial[17] (DAT) enables the design and specification of protocols that can be exported to software tools for management of clinical trials. DAT presents users with forms in which to enter data describing a trial. It critiques the data entry using a trial domain knowledge base and guides the user to design a clean protocol devoid of inconsistencies. Currently, the Epoch users interact with the generic knowledge-acquisition forms that Protégé provides to specify a protocol. We plan to create rich graphical user interfaces coupled with DAT-like guidance mechanism that will lead our users on custom design pathways based on the restrictions and rules defined in the Epoch knowledge base. The PRO*forma* language, just like the EON models, can capture the structure and content of a clinical guideline, and has been embedded in a commercially available clinical trial management system. The intent of the PRO*forma* knowledge base is mainly to drive patient therapy during clinical trials, in contrast to the Epoch knowledge base that supports trial management activities.

There is an ongoing effort by CDISC[18], an industry-lead, multidisciplinary organization, to develop and support the electronic acquisition, exchange, submission and archiving of clinical trials data. As part of this effort, CDISC is developing the Trial Design Model (TDM) that identifies standard elements of a clinical trial protocol that can be codified to facilitate the data interchange among systems and stakeholders including regulatory authorities, biopharmaceutical industry, statisticians, project managers, etc. A parallel effort is the BRIDG[19] project, a partnership of several organizations including CDISC, the HL7[20] standards body, the National Cancer Institute and the Federal Drug Administration, that consumes the Trial Design Model work to build a comprehensive domain analysis model representing protocol-driven biomedical/clinical research. The BRIDG model is a work in progress to elaborately define functions and behaviors throughout clinical trials, and uses the Unified Modeling Language (UML) for representation. The model, in its current state, cannot fully support the requirements of ITN's trial management. However, we are closely following the development of the BRIDG model, and incorporating the model's semantic descriptions of clinical trials – concepts relevant to our trial management activities – within Epoch.

6 Discussion

The increasing complexity of clinical trials has generated an enormous requirement for knowledge and information management at all stages of the trials – planning, specification, implementation, and analysis. Our focus is currently on two application areas: (1) tracking participants of the trial as they advance through the studies, and (2) tracking clinical specimens as they are processed at the trial laboratories. The core of the Epoch framework is a suite of ontologies that encodes knowledge about the clinical trial domain that is relevant to trial management activities. We used OWL to specify the ontologies, and SWRL rules written in terms of concepts in these ontologies to express any constraints. The Epoch ontologies, especially the *Protocol ontology*, have been influenced by past and ongoing modeling work. Our laboratory has demonstrated in previous projects, the viability of frame-based languages to build knowledge based systems. So, it begs the question: *How does our current approach of using OWL/SWRL to build knowledge based systems compare to our experience with frame-based languages?* A recent work[21] compares the two knowledge-representation languages at the syntactic and semantic levels, and suggests appropriate usage situations. The EON guideline decision support architecture uses a frame-based language to specify guidelines, and an interpreter to execute the guidelines on specific patient data. We spent significant effort in developing custom interpreters to execute domain-specific logic. We do not know if the combination of OWL, SWRL, Jena, and JESS will obviate the need to build custom interpreters for our clinical trial management applications. However, we view the growing interest in the OWL standards, and the plethora of tools and software packages as a significant practical advantage of using OWL and SWRL over frame-based languages.

Native RDF Store (storing data as RDF triples) has advanced recently in performance and scalability. It would have been a natural solution for us to use RDF store for storing clinical trial data, and then seamlessly operate on the data using our OWL ontologies and SWRL rules. ITN uses a legacy relational database system to store clinical trial data, and therefore, prevents us from using native RDF Stores as our backend. We have to devise ways to map the database tables to our data model OWL classes. In a previous project, the BioSTORM disease-surveillance framework[22] employs techniques to map disparate data sources to a data model. These techniques were developed using a frame-based language and we are translating these methodologies to use OWL and SWRL. We are also actively investigating the possibility of using the D2RQ[23], a language to describe mappings between relational database schema and OWL/RDFS ontologies. With these solutions, our virtual data model remains flexible and independent of the structure of the data sources.

Currently, we use the Protégé-OWL editor to build the Epoch models. Based on the class and property definitions, Protégé automatically generates graphical user interface (GUI) forms that can be used to create instances of these classes (OWL *individuals*). Thus, domain specialists can use to enter a specification of a protocol, say for a transplant clinical trial, using these Protégé-generated forms. Unfortunately, domain specialists find it cumbersome and non-intuitive to use the generic user interfaces as they are exposed to the complexities of the Epoch models, the OWL expressions and SWRL rules. We are building custom graphical user interfaces that hide the complexities of the knowledge models, and that facilitate guided knowledge-acquisition. Providing a friendly user interface to enter SWRL rules can be challenging.

A major concern in building and maintaining a knowledge repository of several clinical trial protocols over long periods of time is the versioning of ontologies. Specifications can change even after the trial has started. Protégé-OWL provides some limited versioning capability. It also provides some tool support for comparing and merging different versions of ontology. With continued interest in building and maintaining large OWL-based biomedical ontologies[24], we can expect improved tool and methodology support. It is not clear if the existing and proposed tools can fully address the issues of ontology changes during the execution of a clinical trial and the resulting complexities in collating and analyzing trial data.

The knowledge representation and reasoning requirements borne out of the need for semantic interoperability in our clinical trial management system align well with the touted strengths of semantic technologies – uniform domain-specific semantics, flexible information models, and inference technology. Using semantic approaches, we will be able to integrate existing software applications and databases with our knowledge based framework with greater transparency and dynamic communication.

Acknowledgements. This work was supported in part by the Immune Tolerance Network, which is funded by the National Institutes of Health under Grant NO1-AI-15416.

References

1. Rotrosen, D., Matthews, J.B., Bluestone, J.A. The Immune Tolerance Network: a New Paradigm for Developing Tolerance-Inducing Therapies. J Allergy Clinical Immunology, Jul;110(1):17-23 (2002)
2. ITN: http://www.immunetolerance.org/
3. Johnson, P.D., Tu, S. W., Musen, M. A., Purves, I. A Virtual Medical Record for Guideline-Based Decision Support. AMIA Annual Symposium, Washington, DC, 294-298 (2001).
4. O'Connor, M.J., Shankar, R.D. Das, A.K. An Ontology-Driven Mediator for Querying Time-Oriented Biomedical Data. 19th IEEE International Symposium on Computer-Based Medical Systems, Salt Lake City, Utah, 264-269 (2006)
5. OWL Specification: http://www.w3.org/2004/OWL/
6. SWRL Specification: http://www.w3.org/Submission/SWRL/
7. Protégé: http://protege.stanford.edu/
8. Knublauch, H. Fergerson, R.W., Noy, N.F. and Musen, M.A. The Protégé OWL Plugin: An Open Development Environment for Semantic Web applications Proc Third ISWC (ISWC 2004), Hiroshima, Japan, 229-243 (2004)
9. O'Connor, M.J., Knublauch, H., Tu, S.W., Grossof, B., Dean, M., Grosso, W.E., Musen, M.A. Supporting Rule System Interoperability on the Semantic Web with SWRL. Fourth International Semantic Web Conference (ISWC2005), Galway, Ireland, 974-986 (2005)
10. Allen, J.F. Maintaining knowledge about temporal intervals. Communications of the ACM, 26(11): 832-843 (1993)
11. JESS: http://www.jessrules.com/
12. Cimarron: http://www.cimsoft.com/
13. Musen, M.A., Tu, S.W., Das, A.K., Shahar, Y. EON: A component-based approach to automation of protocol-directed therapy. Journal of the American Medical Informatics Association, 3(6), 367–388 (1996)
14. Fox, J., Johns, N., Rahmanzadeh, A., Thomson, R. PROfarma: A method and language for specifying clinical guidelines and protocols. Proceedings of Medical Informatics Europe, Amsterdam (1996)

15. Boxwala, A.A., Peleg, M., Tu, S. W., Ogunyemi, O., Zeng, Q. T., Wang, D., Patel, V. L., Greenes, R. A., Shortliffe, E. H. GLIF3: A Representation Format for Sharable Computer-Interpretable Clinical Practice. Journal of Biomedical Informatics, 37(3):147-161 (2004)
16. Sim, I., Olasov, B., and Carini, S. The Trial Bank system: capturing randomized trials for evidence-based medicine. Proceedings of the AMIA Annual Symposium, 1076 (2003)
17. Modgil, S., Hammond, P. Decision support tools for clinical trial design. Artificial Intelligence in Medicine, 27(2):181-200. (2003)
18. CDISC: http://www.cdisc.org/standards/
19. BRIDG: http://www.bridgproject.org/
20. HL7: http://www.hl7.org/
21. Wang, H., Rector, A., Drummond, N., et al. Frames and OWL Side by Side. 9th International Protégé Conference, Stanford, CA (2006)
22. Crubezy, M., O'Connor, M.J., Buckeridge, D.L., Pincus, Z.S., Musen, M.A. Ontology-Centered Syndromic Surveillance for Bioterrorism. IEEE Intelligent Systems,20(5):26-35 (2005)
23. D2RQ: http://www.wiwiss.fu-berlin.de/suhl/bizer/d2rq/
24. CBIO: http://www.bioontology.org/

Active Semantic Electronic Medical Record

A. Sheth[1], S. Agrawal[2], J. Lathem[1], N. Oldham[2], H. Wingate[2], P. Yadav[2], and K. Gallagher[2]

[1] LSDIS Lab, University of Georgia
Athens, Georgia 30602
{amit, lathem}@cs.uga.edu
[2] Athens Heart Center
Athens, Georgia 30606
{subodh, noldham, ppyadav, kgallagher}@athensheartcenter.com

Abstract. The healthcare industry is rapidly advancing towards the widespread use of electronic medical records systems to manage the increasingly large amount of patient data and reduce medical errors. In addition to patient data there is a large amount of data describing procedures, treatments, diagnoses, drugs, insurance plans, coverage, formularies and the relationships between these data sets. While practices have benefited from the use of EMRs, infusing these essential programs with rich domain knowledge and rules can greatly enhance their performance and ability to support clinical decisions. Active Semantic Electronic Medical Record (ASEMR) application discussed here uses Semantic Web technologies to reduce medical errors, improve physician efficiency with accurate completion of patient charts, improve patient safety and satisfaction in medical practice, and improve billing due to more accurate coding. This results in practice efficiency and growth by enabling physicians to see more patients with improved care. ASEMR has been deployed and in daily use for managing all patient records at the Athens Heart Center since December 2005. This showcases an application of Semantic Web in health care, especially small clinics.

Keywords: Ontology, Rules, Electronic Medical Record (EMR), Electronic Health Record, Clinical Decision Support, RDQL, Web Services, Semantic Annotation, Active Semantic Document.

1 Introduction

The most cumbersome aspect of health care is the extensive documentation which is legally required for each patient. For these reasons, physicians and their assistants spend about 30% of their time documenting encounters. Paper charts are slowly being phased out due to inconvenience, inability to mine data, costs and safety concerns. Many practices are now investing in electronic medical records (EMR) systems which allow them to have all patient data at their fingertips. Although current adoption by medical groups (based on a 2005 survey [1]) is still below 15% with even less adoption rate for smaller practices, the trend is clearly towards increasing adoption. This trend will accelerate as regulatory pressures such as "Pay-4-Performance" become mandatory thus enhancing the ROI sophisticated systems can achieve. This paper focuses on the first known development and deployment[1] of a comprehensive EMR system that utilizes semantic Web and Web service/process technologies. It is based on substantial collaboration between practicing physicians (Dr. Agrawal is a cardiologists and a fellow of the American Cardiology Association, Dr. Wingate is an emergency room physician) at the Athens Heart Center and the LSDIS lab at UGA. More specifically, we leverage the concept and technology of Active Semantic Documents (ASDs) developed at the LSDIS lab. ASDs get their *semantic* feature by automatic semantic annotation of documents with respect to one or more ontologies. These documents are termed *active* since they support automatic and dynamic validation and decision making on the content of the document by applying contextually relevant rules to components of the documents. This is accomplished by executing rules on semantic annotations and relationships that span across ontologies.

Specifically, Active Semantic Electronic Medical Record (ASEMR) is an application of ASDs in health care which aims to reduce medical errors, improve physician efficiency, improve patient safety and satisfaction in medical practice, improve quality of billing records leading be better payment, and make it easier to capture and analyze health outcome measures. In ASMER, rules specified in conjunction with ontologies play a key role. Examples of the rules include prevention of drug interaction (i.e., not allowing a patient to be prescribed two severely interacting drugs, or alerting the doctor and requiring his/her to make specific exceptions when low or moderate degree of interactions are acceptable) or ensuring the procedure performed has supporting diagnoses. ASDs display the semantic (for entities defined in the ontologies) and lexical (for terms and phrases that are part of specialist lexicon , specific items related to the clinics, and other relevant parts of speech) annotations in document displaced in a browser, show results of rule execution, and provide the ability to modify semantic and lexical components of its content in an ontology-supported and otherwise constrained manner such as through lists, bags of terms, specialized reference sources, or a thesaurus or lexical reference system such as WordNet [11]. This feature allows for better and more efficient patient care and because of the ability of ASDs to offer suggestions when rules are broken or exceptions made.

ASEMR is currently in daily and routine use by the Athens Heart Center (AHC) and eight other sites in Georgia. ASEMRs have been implemented as an enhancement of AHC's Panacea electronic medical management system. Panacea is a web-based, end-to-end medical records and management system, and hence it is used with respect to each patent seen at AHC. This has enhanced the collaborative environment and has provided insights into the components of electronic medical records and the kinds of data available in these systems. The preliminary version was implemented during Summer 2005 and tested in early fall. The current version was deployed and has been fully functional since January 2006. Parts of ASMER we will focus on in this paper are:

- the development of populated ontologies in the healthcare (specifically cardiology) domain

---

[1] Preliminary deployment in September 2005, full deployment in January 2006.

- the development of an annotation tool that utilizes the developed ontologies for annotation of patient records
- the development of decision support algorithms that support rule and ontology based checking/validation and evaluation.

The remainder of this paper is organized as follows. Section 2 makes a case for semantics through a motivating scenario (for brevity, only one example is given). Section 3 describes the knowledge and rules representation. The application is detailed in Sections 4 and the implementation details are given in Section 5. Section 6 evaluates the approach and provides statistics which support the growth of the practice since the use of the EMR. Section 7 lists related work and Section 8 concludes with future work.

2 Motivating Scenario and Benefits

In addition to the complexity of today's healthcare, medical practitioners face a number of challenges in managing their practices. One of the challenges is the need to improve the quality of care, adhere to evolving clinical care pathways, reduce waste and reduce errors (with associated need to develop and report quality of care measures). Another challenge is that of medical billing. Let's investigate the latter further. Each insurance company follows Local Medical Review Policy (LMRP) which are policies specifying which diagnosis justify the medical necessity of a procedure. If the appropriate codes are not given in accordance with these LMRPs, the insurance will not pay for the charge. Because of these rigid requirements many claims are rejected and the amount of time for receiving a payment is prolonged and in many cases the physicians are not reimbursed for their services. If correct coding compliance is enforced by the system at the point of charge entry on the superbill (the bill of all charges and diagnoses for a visit) the problem of procedures without supporting diagnosis codes is eliminated. Table 1 contains a partial list of ICD9CM codes that support medical necessity for CPT 93000 EKG which were taken from the Centers for Medicare and Medicaid Services [3][2].

The primary diagnosis code selected for the EKG must be one of the supporting diagnosis codes listed above. There are additional complex rules such as certain ICD9CM codes should not be selected together and certain procedures should not be billed for in the same claim. In section 4.2, we will present our approach which uses a combination of OWL ontologies and rules to validate data in a superbill to ensure coding compliance by presenting the appropriate subset of linking diagnosis codes when a procedure is selected. Due to the creation of more accurate and compliant claims, this approach has the potential to eliminate coding errors which would result in improved financials.

---

[2] ICD9-CM stands for "The International Classification of Diseases, 9th Revision, Clinical Modification"; these codes are used to denote the diagnosis. CPT (Current Procedural Terminology) codes are used to denote treatments. Payment is done based on the treatment, but the bill must contain acceptable diagnosis for that treatment.

Table 1. Medical Necessity for EKG

ICD9CM	Diagnosis Name
244.9	HYPOTHYROIDISM
250.00	DIABETES MELLITUS TYPE II
250.01	DIABETES MELLITUS TYPE I
242.9	HYPERTHYROIDISM
272.2	MIXED HYPERLIPIDEMIA
414.01	CAD-NATIVE
780.2-780.4	SYNCOPE AND COLLAPSE - DIZZINESS AND GIDDINESS
780.79	OTHER MALAISE AND FATIGUE
785.0-785.3	TACHYCARDIA UNSPECIFIED - OTHER ABNORMAL HEART SOUNDS
786.50-786.51	UNSPECIFIED CHEST PAIN - PRECORDIAL PAIN
786.59	OTHER CHEST PAIN

In addition to greater facilitation of billing process, physicians benefit from the clinical decision support that can be provided by a system which has rich domain understanding through the use of ontologies and rules. Patients benefit as well as this ability allows better patient care, increased safety and satisfaction. Checks such as preferred drug recommendations lead to prescription drug savings for patients leading to improved satisfaction. The most important benefit we seek from ASEMR with its proactive semantic annotations and rule-based evaluation is the reduction of medical errors that could occur as an oversight. Ultimately the proof of these support features will be manifest by improved outcome data for example better Medpar scores (medicare beneficiary morbidity and mortality data) for Physicians.

3 Knowledge and Rules Representation

We employ a combination of OWL [6] ontologies with RDQL[9] rules in order to supply the document with rich domain knowledge. The rules provide additional domain knowledge and compensate for the limitations of the OWL language.2.1 Ontologies. A more complex rule specification (and corresponding rule processing) capabilities may be needed in future, but for our current purpose this was more than adequate and this choice also provided efficient implementation alternative.

We utilize three ontologies to represent aspects of the domain. The practice ontology contains concepts which represent the medical practice such as facility, physician, physician assistant, and nurse. The infrastructure of the medical practice is given by the concepts and relationships. The practice ontology was created in conjunction with experts in the medical field. Parts of our own databases were the source for populating this ontology.

The Drug ontology contains all of the drugs and classes of drugs, drug interactions, drug allergies, and formularies. Capturing such information reduces medical errors and increases patient safety. Furthermore, prescribing drugs from the formularies of the patient's insurance plans improves patient satisfaction. License content (Gold Standard Media) equivalent to physican's drug reference was the primary source for populating this ontology which is shown, in part, in figure 1.

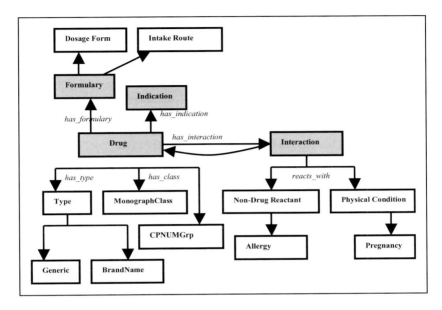

Fig. 1. Partial View of Drug Ontology

The Diagnosis/Procedure ontology includes concepts such as medical conditions, treatments, diagnoses (ICD-9), and procedures (CPT). Licensed SNOMED (Systematized Nomenclature of Medicine--Clinical Terms) [8] content is used for populating this ontology. A key enhancement involved linking this ontology to the drug ontology. This allows powerful decision support by giving the system specialized domain knowledge. We will use this representation to enable the system to suggest treatments and drugs based on the patient's condition or diagnosis. User or user group specific frequently used codes lists are supported by this ontology. This allows customizability such that each area of the practice will be given procedures and diagnosis codes which frequently apply to their area.

For example, procedures such as Dipiridamol injections and Muga scans are generally administered in the area of Nuclear medicine and should therefore the remainder of the clinical staff should not be bothered with those procedures cluttering their view. Each area has customizable frequent lists such as Nuclear, Pacemaker Evaluation, Echocardiograph, etc.

Medical records of patients are automatically annotated using the ontologies listed above and are displayed in a browser. Drugs, allergies, physicians and facilities (e.g., physicians or facilities the patient is referred to), treatments, diagnosis, etc. are automatically annotated. The physician has the ability to pull up a contextual list or even a visual subset of the relevant ontology and pick alternative choices. In some cases, alternatives are provided in ranked order list (e.g., other physicians with the same specialty in the same area and accepting the same insurance as the patient).

3.1 Rules

ASEMRs support active features by executing relevant rules over semantic annotations to support the following initial sets of capabilities:

- drug-drug interaction check,
- drug formulary check (e.g., whether the drug is covered by the insurance company of the patient, and if not what the alternative drugs in the same class of drug are),
- drug dosage range check,
- drug-allergy interaction check,
- ICD-9 annotations choice for the physician to validate and choose the best possible code for the treatment type, and
- preferred drug recommendation based on drug and patient insurance information

The benefits of combining the use of ontologies and rules are two-fold. First, the rules allow the system to make decisions. Second, using rules the system can become declarative to the extent that additional relationships and facts can be added at any time without changing the code. For example, if the relationship "cancels_the_effect" is added to the ontology coupled with a rule indicating which drug or combinations of drugs cancel the effect of drugX, then the capability of the system is enhanced without any code modifications. This allows for a great deal of extensibility and flexibility such that one could even define classes of drugs, such as blood thinners, which cancels the effects of other classes of drugs. **Rules allow for more flexibility, enhanced reasoning power and extensibility.**

4 Application

The following section details two components which utilize semantic web technologies and are currently deployed and in use by at least eight beta sites. The evaluation section contains an analysis of the effect of this semantic health record application on one practice.

4.1 Active Semantic Documents

Physicians are required to thoroughly document each patient encounter. Reports usually contain a problem list, family history, history of present illness, review of symptoms, impressions and plans. Data acquisition and data entry is a painstaking process which usually results in late hours for the physician. One alternative is dictation. While dictation maybe faster for the physician, it has many negative drawbacks including lack of structured data for analysis and mistakes in transcription that have to be corrected. It is clear from our experience that a better solution is an application which "understands the domain" thus facilitates the structured entry of data by offering relevant suggestions in a customizable point and click interface l generating complete and coherent reports. The Active Semantic Documents (ASD) EMR both expedites and enhances the patient documentation process. The support and speed provided by them enables physicians and physician assistants to complete all of their patient documentation while the patient is still in the room allowing the physician to provide better care with a greater volume of patients.

The annotation view pictured in figure 2 is an Active Semantic Document. The annotations facilitate the creation of the document by performing annotations of ICD9s, words and sentences within the report, and drugs. Three drug related annotations can be seen in figure 2 under the "Current Medications" section. The drug Coumadin has a level three interaction warning. Holding the cursor over this warning displays the name of the drug with which it interacts. The yellow *F* annotation warns that the drug is not covered under the patient's insurance formulary. The annotations can also be extended to also semantically enhance the monograph. The green *A* annotation warns that the patient is allergic to this drug. Clicking on the *E*xplore button allows the user to write a prescription for this drug, change quantities, or view the monograph for this drug. Exploring the drug allows for semantic browsing, querying for such details as how many patients are using this class of drug, and for performing decision support. Figure 3 shows the exploration of the drug Tasmar.

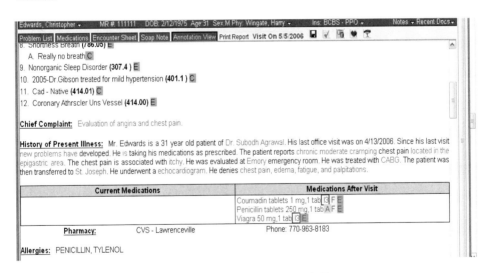

Fig. 2. An application of Active Semantic Documents

4.2 Coding of Impressions

Section 2 described a scenario in which the complexity of medical billing is remedied by enforcing correct coding at the point of data entry by the nurse, physician, or assistant. As a patient is seen, orders and diagnoses are marked by the healthcare provider on an 'encounter sheet' or 'superbill'. It is imperative at this time that a diagnosis which supports medical necessity for a procedure be given in order to facilitate the billing process. This application employs a novel semantic approach for entering charges into the encounter sheet based on domain knowledge taken from the procedure and diagnosis ontology. This application allows for diagnoses to be taken directly from the documentation described in the previous section. Furthermore, when orders are placed the subset of diagnoses codes which are defined to support medical necessity for that order are shown. This method ensures that the charges will be entered correctly at the very beginning of the process. The semantic encounter sheet is shown in figure 4. As users select orders from the right column, the left column automatically populates with the linking diagnosis codes which support medical necessity. The doctor is required to validate this choice, and ontology enables him/her to easily consider alternatives.

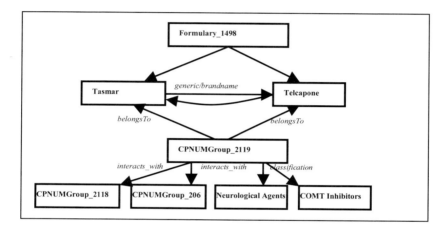

Fig. 3. Exploration of the neighborhood of the drug Tasmar

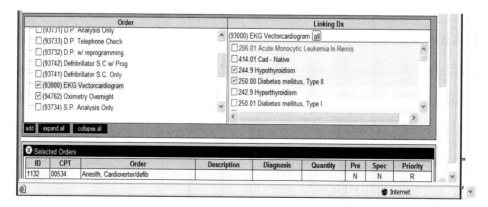

Fig. 4. Semantic Encounter Sheet

5 Implementation Details

The Panacea database holds all information about a patient and the patient's visits including the patient demographics, medications before the visit, medications added during the visit, past and present problems, diagnoses, treatment, doctors seen, insurance information, and a text description of the visit. The method of data entry and data storage ensures that it is well structured and can trivially be converted into a single large XML. It is important to note that the text description is not simply stored as one large string but as a tree structure which can be lexically annotated far faster and with better accuracy compared with using natural language processing. A detailed discussion of this is out of the scope of this paper.

After the XML is created annotations must be applied in order to assert the rules. Since the structure and schema of the XML is known a priori, annotation is simply performed by adding metadata to the correct tags. The correct tags are identified using XPath. This approach has a much higher accuracy them most types of semantic annotation techniques. This is a result of knowing the structure of the XML prior to the annotation.

The module that creates the XML and the module that annotates the XML are separate entities on different servers and implemented in different languages. This was necessary as the legacy code is in ASP and most wide spread tools for XML and ontology querying are written in Java. The two modules communicate by passing the XML from the ASP to the Java server via a REST based web service. The addition of Web 2.0 technologies such as REST services allows much of the requests to generate from the client instead of the server. This gives the application the ability to mask latency and allow easy integration in to client side scripting. This solution offers much more than fixing the heterogeneity created by the two languages. This solution also offers scalability and extensibility. Allowing the memory and IO intensive ontology querying to be done independently of the application server frees up resources which may be used elsewhere.

After annotation a third module applies rules to the annotations. The rules used are written in RDQL. A rule either checks for the existence of an edge or its absence. For example, an 'interaction' relationship should not exist between two drugs or there should be a relationship, 'covered', between a drug and patient's insurance. When these rules are broken metadata is added to the previously added annotations in the form of properties. Once all of the annotations have been applied and the rules are asserted, the annotated XML makes its way back to the client where an XSLT is applied. The XSLT turns the XML into HTML which can be made interactive and presented to the user for review and edits.

Currently Panacea annotates doctors, problems, diagnosis, drugs, and patient demographics semantically. The rest of the document is annotated lexically. Queries that could be ran against these annotation include but are not limited to:

- drug-drug interaction check,
- drug formulary check (e.g., whether the drug is covered by the insurance company of the patient, and if not what the alternative drugs in the same class of drug are),
- drug dosage range check,

- drug-allergy interaction check,
- ICD-9 annotations choice for the physician to validate and choose the best possible code for the treatment type, and
- preferred drug recommendation based on drug and patient insurance information

Figure 5 depicts the architecture of the Active Semantic Document component of Panacea.

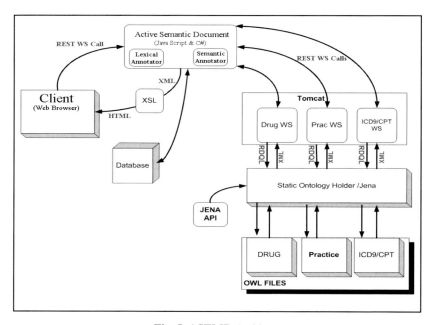

Fig. 5. ASEMR Architecture

6 Deployment and Evaluation

At AHC, the main site of deployment, the application accommodates between 78 and 80 patient encounters per day, most of which are seen within a four hour time frame. The AHC, with two physicians, two to four mid-level providers, eight nurses, and four nuclear and echo technicians, relies on Panacea/ASEMR for fully Web-based paperless operations for all functions except for billing (which is currently under development). The semantically annotated document creation in conjunction with workflow solutions such as patient tracking has allowed the AHC to operate in 'real time' mode such that the physicians and their assistants are able to complete all documentation for the patient's visit during the encounter. Prior to deploying ASEMR, majority of charts were completed in Panacea after patient hours, often requiring mid-level providers to complete them over the weekend.

As a result of Panacea deployment first, followed by its ASEMR extension, the AHC has greatly increased the volume of patients which they are able to care for, and importantly, without increasing its clinical staff. Figure 6 shows the growth of the AHC since March of 2004. This data was obtained by querying the database for the number of appointments scheduled. The development of Panacea began in the year 2002 and the ASEMR was deployed in December 2005; it became fully operational in January 2006. In other words, data prior to December 2005 reflects pre-semantic situation (as Panacea did not have any semantic/ontological/rule support, and the data after January 2006 reflect situation after deploying the semantic technology. The number of clinical staff members and facility remained relatively consistent throughout the entire sample period. The AHC saw growth in 2005 as they scheduled around 1000-1200 patients per month. The patient volume for the year 2006 has started at a consistent growth rate of 25-30%, with March peaking around 1400 appointments scheduled per month. Even with this increase in patient volume, the physician assistants are able to accompany the physicians to the hospital immediately after clinic hours instead of charting until late evening hours. Before the deployment of the new annotation view supported in ASEMR the mid-level providers remained in the office an additional 4-5 hours charting after the clinic closed. Main reason for the work remaining after clinical hours related to the need to insure consistency, completeness and correctness of the patient record (e.g., the CPT and ICD9 codes that form parts of billing information captured as part of coding of impressions). Since ASEMR addressed these issues through semantics and rules. Since the time we completed the training of clinical staff, all charts are completed before the clinic closes, and in most cases a chart is completed while the patient is still in the office.

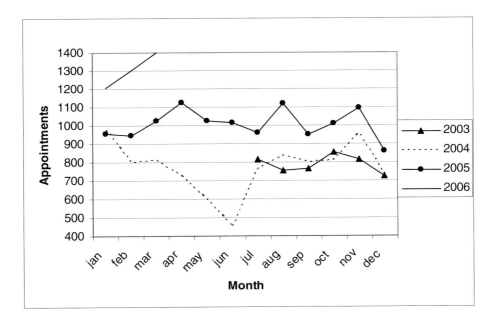

Fig. 6. Athens Heart Center Practice Growth

Even with this increase in patient volume, the physician assistants are able to accompany the physicians to the hospital immediately after clinic hours instead of charting until late evening hours. Before the deployment of the new annotation view supported in ASEMR the mid-level providers remained in the office an additional 4-5 hours charting after the clinic closed. Figures 7 and 8 show the dramatic change in the number of charts completed on the same day versus the number of charts backlogged at the end of the day for pre-deployment and post-deployment months respectively.

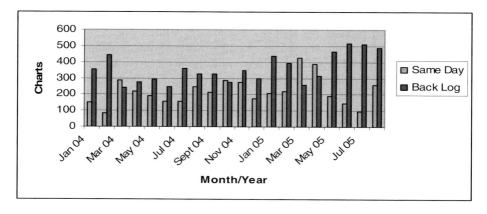

Fig. 7. Chart Completion before the preliminary deployment of the ASMER

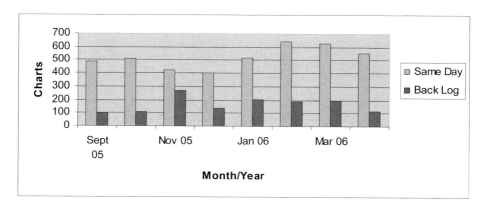

Fig. 8. Chart Completion after the preliminary deployment of the ASMER

We have observed improvement in the patient satisfaction such as through the use formulary check as this could reduce patient costs through the check for medication with lower co-payments and insurance coverage, and the benefits associated with the use coding impression on improved billing as the basis of improved medical records and billing. Our next challenge is to measure these improvements and benefits quantitatively as part of an effort to develop and share return on investment (ROI) measures. As an aside, this work has in part enabled us to be an active member of

W3C's interest Group on Semantic Web for Heath Care and Life Sciences, and provide the perspective of semantic Web applications and deployments in health care arena with a focus on smaller practices [10].

Given that this work was done in a live, operational environment, it is nearly impossible to evaluate this system in a "clean room" fashion, with completely controlled environment – no doctors' office has resources or inclination to subject to such an intrusive, controlled and multistage trial. Evaluation of an operational system also presents many complexities, such as perturbations due to change in medical personnel and associated training. In this context, we believe we have been able to present convincing evaluation of the benefits of a semantic technology.

7 Related Work

Some other healthcare applications have benefited from the use of ontologies. Chen et al. have experimented with step-wise automation of clinical pathways for each patient, in particular, according to the patient's personal health condition at the time of consultation in [4]. Their approach uses ontologies and web services; however, this approach does not propose the use of rules to supplement domain knowledge to compensate for the limitations of OWL. BioDASH [2] is a Semantic Web prototype of a Drug Development Dashboard that associates disease, compounds, drug progression stages, molecular biology, and pathway knowledge for a team of users. This work mentions use of rule-based processing using off-the-shelf RDF inference engines, and the use of rules to filter and merge data. Kashyap et al present a semantics-based approach to automate structured clinical documentation based on a description logics (DL) system for ontology management in [5]. This paper describes the use of document and domain ontologies. Onto-Med Research Group has designed Onto-Builder [7], a tool designed to support the construction and administration of Data Dictionaries in the field of clinical trials. This standard Data Dictionary is then used in the collection and analysis of clinical trials data. Quality assurance in carrying out clinical trials and uniformity are some benefits to such ontology.

We also note that as a "SW in Use" track paper, we focus on discussing a deployed system demonstrating the use of semantic web, rather than attempt to distinguish research contributions with respect to years of research in AI and decision support in healthcare, some of which took much longer to mature and find operational use than the new newer technologies. The newer technologies encompassing Semantic Web, SOA and Web 2.0 offer many practical advantages, including ease of use, deployment and maintenance, which we have not discussed in detail due to space limitations. Resources such as OpenClinical (http://www.openclinical.org/), where this system is also listed, provide extensive complementary material covering research, applications and demonstrations.

8 Conclusion and Future Work

The approach proposed in this paper combines three ontologies with rules in order to enhancing the accuracy of EMRs both by providing clinical decision support and improving the correctness of medical coding therefore reducing the number of rejected claims. We have presented a semantic approach which improves patient care and satisfaction, and enables healthcare providers to complete all charge entry and documentation before the patient has left the office. At this time, we are unaware of any application similar to ASEMR that is in daily use, especially at small practices in any field of health care. During ISWC 2006, we have planned to organize group visits to AHC (which is 5 minutes from the conference venue) to enable all interested persons to observe the use of ASEMR in person (a canned demo is at http://lsdis.cs.uga.edu/projects/asdoc/). This work also demonstrate successful collaboration between academic research and small medical clinics. For business and legal reasons, we are unable to present some details such as error detection and reduction in this paper.

The ASEMR approach can be extended to provide decision support on a deeper level. For example, semantic associations [12] can be discovered to find even obscure relationships between symptoms, patient details, and treatments. Semantic alerts will also be explored in future versions such as when a physician scrolls down on the list of drugs and clicks on the desired drug, any study, clinical trial, or news item about the drug and other related drugs in the same category can be displayed. In addition ontologies can be utilized to find contradictions and mistakes in the medical report. Another key area of extension that we are also working on include coupling this system with a billing system with higher degree of automation (e.g., with better workflow and better validation of billing data) than current state of the art in medical billing.

Acknowledgements. We thank M. Eavenson, C. Henson, and D. Palaniswami at LSDIS for their effort in ontology design and population.

References

1. Agency for Healthcare Research & Quality http://ahrq.gov/news/press/pr2005/lowehrpr.htm
2. E. Neumann and D. Quan, BioDASH: A Semantic Web Dashboard for Drug Development, Pacific Symposium on Biocomputing 11:176-187(2006) Also, http://www.w3.org/2005/04/swls/BioDash/Demo/
3. Centers for Medicare and Medicaid Services http://www.cms.hhs.gov/
4. H. Chen, D. Colaert, J. De Roo, Towards Adaptable Clinical Pathway Using Semantic Web Technology, W3C Workshop Semantic Web for Life Science, 2004.
5. V. Kashyap, A. Morales, T. Hongsermeier and Q. Li Definitions Management: A semantics-based approach for Clinical Documentation in Healthcare DeliveryIndustrial Track, Proceedings of the 4th International Semantic Web Conference, November 2005
6. D. McGuinness, and F. Harmelen, eds. OWL Web Ontology Language Overview http://www.w3.org/TR/owl-features/
7. Open Clinical http://www.openclinical.org/dm_ontobuilder.html
8. SNOMED http://www.snomed.org/
9. A. Seaborne, RDQL - A Query Language for RDFW3C Member Submission 9 January 2004, http://www.w3.org/Submission/RDQL/
10. W3, Semantic Web in Health-care and Life Sciences, www.w3.org/2005/04/swls/
11. Wordnet http://wordnet.princeton.edu/
12. K. Anyanwu and A. Sheth, "The ρ Operator: Discovering and Ranking Associations on the Semantic Web," The Twelfth International World Wide Web Conference, Budapest, Hungary, May 2003, pp. 690-699.

Foafing the Music: Bridging the Semantic Gap in Music Recommendation

Òscar Celma

Music Technology Group, Universitat Pompeu Fabra, Barcelona, Spain
http://mtg.upf.edu

Abstract. In this paper we give an overview of the *Foafing the Music* system. The system uses the *Friend of a Friend* (FOAF) and *RDF Site Summary* (RSS) vocabularies for recommending music to a user, depending on the user's musical tastes and listening habits. Music information (new album releases, podcast sessions, audio from MP3 blogs, related artists' news and upcoming gigs) is gathered from thousands of RSS feeds.

The presented system provides music discovery by means of: user profiling (defined in the user's FOAF description), context based information (extracted from music related RSS feeds) and content based descriptions (extracted from the audio itself), based on a common ontology (OWL DL) that describes the music domain.

The system is available at: **http://foafing-the-music.iua.upf.edu**

1 Introduction

The World Wide Web has become the host and distribution channel of a broad variety of digital multimedia assets. Although the Internet infrastructure allows simple straightforward acquisition, the value of these resources lacks of powerful content management, retrieval and visualization tools. Music content is no exception: although there is a sizeable amount of text–based information about music (album reviews, artist biographies, etc.) this information is hardly associated to the objects they refer to, that is music music files (MIDI and/or audio). Moreover, music is an important vehicle for communicating other people something relevant about our personality, history, etc.

In the context of the Semantic Web, there is a clear interest to create a Web of machine-readable homepages describing people, the links among them, and the things they create and do. The FOAF (*Friend Of A Friend*) project[1] provides conventions and a language to describe homepage–like content and social networks. FOAF is based on the RDF/XML[2] vocabulary. We can foresee that with the user's FOAF profile, a system would get a better representation of the user's musical needs. On the other hand, the RSS vocabulary[3] allows to syndicate Web content on Internet. Syndicated content includes data such as news,

---

[1] http://www.foaf-project.org
[2] http://www.w3.org/RDF
[3] http://web.resource.org/rss/1.0/

events listings, headlines, project updates, as well as music related information, such as new music releases, album reviews, podcast sessions, upcoming gigs, etc.

2 Background

The main goal of a music recommendation system is to propose, to the end-user, interesting and unknown music artists (and their available tracks, if possible), based on user's musical taste. But musical taste and music preferences are affected by several factors, even demographic and personality traits. Then, the combination of music preferences and personal aspects —such as: age, gender, origin, occupation, musical education, etc.— could improve music recommendations [7]. Some of this information can be denoted using FOAF descriptions.

Moreover, a desirable property of a music recommendation system should be the ability of dynamically getting new music related information, as it should recommend new items to the user once in a while. In this sense, there is a lot of freely available (in terms of licensing) music on Internet, performed by "unknown" artists that can suit perfectly for new recommendations. Nowadays, music websites are noticing the user about new releases or artist's related news, mostly in the form of RSS feeds. For instance, iTunes Music Store[4] provides an RSS (version 2.0) feed generator[5], updated once a week, that publishes new releases of artists' albums. A music recommendation system should take advantage of these publishing services, as well as integrating them into the system, in order to filter and recommend new music to the user.

2.1 Collaborative Filtering Versus Content Based Filtering

Collaborative filtering method consists of making use of feedback from users to improve the quality of recommended material presented to users. Obtaining feedback can be explicit or implicit. Explicit feedback comes in the form of user ratings or annotations, whereas implicit feedback can be extracted from user's habits. The main caveats of this approach are the following: the *cold-start* problem, the novelty detection problem, the item popularity bias, and the enormous amount of data (i.e users and items) needed to get some reasonable results [3]. Thus, this approach to recommend music can generate some "silly" (or obvious) answers. Anyway, there are some examples that succeed based on this approach. For instance, Last.fm[6] or Amazon [4] are good illustration systems.

On the other hand, content based filtering tries to extract useful information from the items data collection, that could be useful to represent user's musical taste. This approach solves the limitation of collaborative filtering as it can recommend new items (even before the system does not know anything about that item), by comparing the actual set of user's items and calculating a distance with some sort of similarity measure. In the music field, extracting musical semantics

---

[4] http://www.apple.com/itunes
[5] http://phobos.apple.com/WebObjects/MZSearch.woa/wo/0.1
[6] http://www.last.fm

from the raw audio and computing similarities between music pieces is a challenging problem. In [5], Pachet proposes a classification of musical metadata, and how this classification affects music content management, as well as the problems to face when elaborating a ground truth reference for music similarity (both in collaborative and content based filtering).

2.2 Related Systems

Most of the current music recommenders are based on collaborative filtering approach. Examples of such systems are: Last.fm, MyStrands[7], MusicMobs[8], Goombah Emergent Music[9], iRate[10], and inDiscover[11]. The basic idea of a music recommender system based on collaborative filtering is:

1. To keep track of which artists (and songs) a user listens to —through iTunes, WinAmp, Amarok, XMMS, etc. plugins,
2. To search for other users with similar tastes, and
3. To recommend artists (or songs) to the user, according to these similar listeners' taste.

On the other hand, the most noticeable system using (manual) content based descriptions to recommend music is Pandora[12]. The main problem of the system is the scalability, because all the music annotation process is done manually.

Contrastingly, the main goal of the *Foafing the Music* system is to recommend, to discover and to explore music content; based on user profiling (via FOAF descriptions), context based information (extracted from music related RSS feeds), and content based descriptions (automatically extracted from the audio itself [1]). All of that being based on a common ontology that describes the musical domain. To our knowledge, nowadays it does not exist any system that recommends items to a user, based on FOAF profiles. Yet, there is the *FilmTrust* system[13]. It is a part of a research study aimed to understanding how social preferences might help web sites to present information in a more useful way. The system collects user reviews and ratings about movies, and holds them into the user's FOAF profile.

3 System Overview

The overview of the system is depicted in Fig. 1. The next two sections explain the main components of the system, that is how to gather data from third party sources, and how to recommend music to the user based on crawled data, semantic description of music titles, and audio similarity.

---

[7] http://www.mystrands.com
[8] http://www.musicmobs.com
[9] http://goombah.emergentmusic.com/
[10] http://irate.sourceforge.net
[11] http://www.indiscover.net/
[12] http://www.pandora.com/
[13] http://trust.mindswap.org/FilmTrust

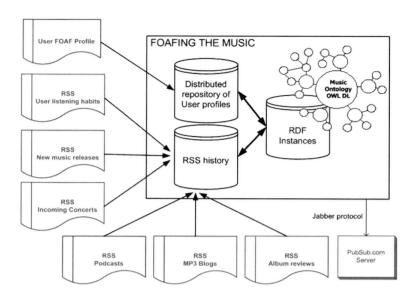

Fig. 1. Architecture of the *Foafing the Music* system

3.1 Gathering Music Related Information

Personalized services can raise privacy concerns, due to the acquisition, storage and application of sensitive personal information [6]. A novelty approach is used in our system: information about the users is not stored into the system in any way. Users' profiles are based on the FOAF initiative, and the system has only a link pointing to the user's FOAF URL. Thus, the sensitivity of this data is up to the user, not to the system. Users' profiles in *Foafing the Music* are distributed over the net.

Regarding music related information, our system exploits the mashup approach. The system uses a set of public available APIs and web services sourced from third party websites. This information can come in any of the different RSS family (v2.0, v1.0, v0.92 and mRSS), as well as in the Atom format. Thus, the system has to deal with syntactically and structurally heterogeneous data. Moreover, the system keeps track of all the new items that are published in the feeds, and stores the new incoming data into a historic relational database. Input data of the system is based on the following information sources:

– **User listening habits.** To keep track of the user's listening habits, the system uses the services provided by Last.fm. This system offers a web–based API — as well as a list of RSS feeds— that provide the most recent tracks a user has played. Each item feed includes, then, the artist name, the song title, and a timestamp —indicating when the user has listened to the track.
– **New music releases.** The system uses a set of RSS that notifies new music releases. Next table shows the contribution of each RSS feed into the historic database of the system:

RSS Source	Percent
iTunes	45.67%
Amazon	42.33%
Oldies.com	2.92%
Yahoo Shopping	0.29%
Others	8.79%

- **Upcoming concerts.** The system uses a set of RSS feeds that syndicates music related events. The websites are: *Eventful.com, Upcoming.org, San Diego Reader*[14] and *Sub Pop* record label[15]. Once the system has gathered all the new items, it queries to the Google Maps API to get the geographic location of the venues.
- **Podcast sessions.** The system gathers information from a list of RSS feeds that publish podcasts sessions.
- **MP3 Blogs.** The system gathers information from a list of MP3 blogs that talk about artists and songs. Each item feed contains a list of links to the audio files.
- **Album reviews.** Information about album reviews are crawled from the RSS published by *Rateyourmusic.com, Pitchforkmedia.com, 75 or less records*[16], and *Rolling Stone* online magazine[17].

Table 1. Information gathered from RSS feeds is stored into a historic relational database

RSS Source	# Seed feeds	# Items crawled per week	# Items stored
New releases	44	980	58,850
Concerts	14	470	28,112
Podcasts	830	575	34,535
MP3 blogs	86	2486 (avg. of 19 audios per item)	149,161
Reviews	8	458	23,374

Table 1 shows some basic statistics of the data that has been gathered since mid April, 2005 until the first week of July, 2006 (except for the album reviews that started in mid June, 2005). These numbers show that the system has to deal with a daily fresh incoming data.

On the other hand, we have defined a music ontology[18] (OWL DL) that describes basic properties of the artists and the music titles, as well as some descriptors extracted from the audio (e.g. tonality —key and mode—, ryhthm —tempo and measure —, intensity, danceability, etc.). In [2] we propose a way to

---

[14] http://www.sdreader.com/
[15] http://www.subpop.com/
[16] http://www.75orless.com/
[17] http://www.rollingstone.com/
[18] The OWL DL music ontology is available at: http://foafing-the-music.iua.upf.edu/music-ontology#

map our ontology and the MusicBrainz ontology, within the MPEG-7 standard, that acts as an upper-ontology for multimedia description.

A focused web crawler has been implemented in order to add instances to the music ontology. The crawler extracts metadata of artists and songs, and the relationships between artists (such as: "related with", "influenced by", "followers of", etc.). The seed sites to start the crawling process are music metadata providers[19], and independent music labels[20]. Thus, the music repository does not consist only of mainstream artists.

Based on the music ontology, the example 1.1 shows the RDF/XML description of an artist from *Garageband.com*.

```
<rdf:Description rdf:about="http://www.garageband.com/artist/
    randycoleman">
 <rdf:type rdf:resource="&music;Artist"/>
 <music:name>Randy Coleman</music:name>
 <music:decade>1990</music:decade>
 <music:decade>2000</music:decade>
 <music:genre>Pop</music:genre>
 <music:city>Los Angeles</music:city>
 <music:nationality>US</music:nationality>
 <geo:Point>
   <geo:lat>34.052</geo:lat>
   <geo:long>-118.243</geo:long>
 </geo:Point>
 <music:influencedBy
     rdf:resource="http://www.coldplay.com"/>
 <music:influencedBy
     rdf:resource="http://www.jeffbuckley.com"/>
 <music:influencedBy
     rdf:resource="http://www.radiohead.com"/>
</rdf:Description>
```

Listing 1.1. Example of an artist individual

Example 1.2 shows the description of a track individual of the above artist:

```
<rdf:Description rdf:about="http://www.garageband.com/song?|
    pe1|S8LTM0LdsaSkaFeyYG0">
 <rdf:type rdf:resource="&music;Track"/>
 <music:title>Last Salutation</music:title>
 <music:playedBy rdf:resource="http://www.garageband.com/
     artist/randycoleman" />
 <music:duration>247</music:duration>
 <music:key>D</music:key>
 <music:keyMode>Major</music:keyMode>
 <music:tonalness>0.84</music:tonalness>
 <music:tempo>72</music:tempo>
</rdf:Description>
```

Listing 1.2. Example of a track individual

---

[19] Such as http://www.mp3.com, http://music.yahoo.com, http://www.rockdetector.com, etc.

[20] E.g. http://www.magnatune.com, http://www.cdbaby.com and http://www.garageband.com

These individuals are used in the recommendation process, to retrieve artists and songs related with user's musical taste.

3.2 Music Recomendation Process

This section explains the music recommendation process, based on all the information that is continuously been gathered. Music recommendations, in the *Foafing the Music* system, are generated according to the following steps:

1. Get music related information from user's FOAF interests, and user's listening habits
2. Detect artists and bands
3. Compute similar artists, and
4. Rate results by relevance.

In order to gather music related information from a FOAF profile, the system extracts the information from the FOAF interest property (if dc:title is given then it gets the text, otherwise it gathers the text from the title tag of the resource).

Based on the music related information gathered from the user's profile and listening habits, the system detects the artists and bands that the user is interested in (by doing a SPARQL query to the artists' individuals repository). Once the user's artists have been detected, artist similarity is computed. This process is achieved by exploiting the RDF graph of artists' relationships.

The system offers two ways of recommending music information. *Static* recommendations are based on the favourite artists encountered in the FOAF profile. We assume that a FOAF profile would be barely updated or modified. On the other hand, *dynamic* recommendations are based on user's listening habits, which is updated much more often that the user's profile. With this approach the user can discover a wide range of new music and artists.

Once the recommended artists have been computed, *Foafing the Music* filters music related information coming from the gathered information (see section 3.1) in order to:

- Get new music releases from iTunes, Amazon, Yahoo Shopping, etc.
- Download (or stream) audio from MP3–blogs and Podcast sessions,
- Create, automatically, XSPF[21] playlists based on audio similarity,
- Read Artists' related news, via the PubSub.com server[22]
- View upcoming gigs happening near to the user's location, and
- Read album reviews.

Syndication of the website content is done via an RSS 1.0 feed. For most of the above mentioned functionalities, there is a feed subscription option to get the results in the RSS format.

---

[21] http://www.xspf.org/. XSPF is playlist format based on XML syntax
[22] http://www.pubsub.com

4 Conclusions

We have proposed a system that filters music related information, based on a given user's profile and user's listening habits. A system based on FOAF profiles and user's listening habits allows to "understand" a user in two complementary ways; psychological factors —personality, demographic preferences, socio-economics, situation, social relationships— and explicit musical preferences. In the music field context, we expect that filtering information about new music releases, artists' interviews, album reviews, etc. can improve a recommendation system in a dynamic way.

Foafing the Music is accessible through http://foafing-the-music.iua.upf.edu

Acknowledgements

This work is partially funded by the SIMAC IST-FP6-507142, and the SALERO IST-FP6-027122 European projects.

References

1. O. Celma, P. Cano, and P. Herrera. Search sounds: An audio crawler focused on weblogs. In *Proceedings of 7th International Conference on Music Information Retrieval*, Victoria, Canada, 2006.
2. R. Garcia and O. Celma. Semantic integration and retrieval of multimedia metadata. In *Proceedings of 4rd International Semantic Web Conference. Knowledge Markup and Semantic Annotation Workshop*, Galway, Ireland, 2005.
3. J. L. Herlocker, J. A. Konstan, L. G. Terveen, and J. T. Riedl. Evaluating collaborative filtering recommender systems. *ACM Trans. Inf. Syst.*, 22(1):5–53, 2004.
4. G. Linden, B. Smith, and J. York. Amazon.com recommendations: Item-to-item collaborative filtering. *IEEE Internet Computing*, 4(1), 2003.
5. F. Pachet. *Knowledge Management and Musical Metadata*. Idea Group, 2005.
6. E. Perik, B. de Ruyter, P. Markopoulos, and B. Eggen. The sensitivities of user profile information in music recommender systems. In *Proceedings of Private, Security, Trust*, 2004.
7. A. Uitdenbogerd and R. van Schnydel. A review of factors affecting music recommender success. In *Proceedings of 3rd International Conference on Music Information Retrieval*, Paris, France, 2002.

Semantic MediaWiki

Markus Krötzsch[1], Denny Vrandečić[1], and Max Völkel[2]

[1] AIFB, Universität Karlsruhe, Germany
[2] FZI Karlsruhe, Germany

Abstract. Semantic MediaWiki is an extension of *MediaWiki* – a widely used wiki-engine that also powers *Wikipedia*. Its aim is to make semantic technologies available to a broad community by smoothly integrating them with the established usage of MediaWiki. The software is already used on a number of productive installations world-wide, but the main target remains to establish "Semantic Wikipedia" as an early adopter of semantic technologies on the web. Thus usability and scalability are as important as powerful semantic features.

1 Introduction

Wikis have become popular tools for collaboration on the web, and many vibrant online communities employ wikis to exchange knowledge. For a majority of wikis – public or not – primary goals are to organise the collected knowledge and to share this information. We present the novel wiki-engine Semantic MediaWiki [1] that leverages semantic technologies to address those challenges.

Wikis are usually viewed as tools to manage online content in a quick and easy way, by editing some simple syntax known as wiki-text. This is mainly plain text with some occasional markup elements. For example, a link to another page is created by enclosing the page's name in brackets, e.g. by writing [[Danny Ayers]]. To enhance usability, we introduce new features by gently extending such known syntactical elements.

2 System Overview

Semantic MediaWiki (SMW)[1] is a semantically enhanced wiki engine that enables users to annotate the wiki's contents with explicit, machine-readable information. Using this semantic data, SMW addresses core problems of today's wikis:

- *Consistency of content:* The same information often occurs on many pages. How can one ensure that information in different parts of the system is consistent, especially as it can be changed in a distributed way?
- *Accessing knowledge:* Large wikis have thousands of pages. Finding and *comparing* information from different pages is a challenging and time-consuming task.
- *Reusing knowledge:* Many wikis are driven by the wish to make information accessible to many people. But the rigid, text-based content of classical wikis can only be used by reading pages in a browser or similar application.

---

[1] SMW is free software, and can be downloaded at http://sourceforge.net/projects/semediawiki/ (current version 0.5). Sites on which SMW is already running are given below.

But for a wiki it does not suffice to provide some technologies to solve these problems – the key is to make those technologies *accessible* to a broad community of non-expert users. The primary objective for SMW therefore is the seamless integration of semantic technologies into the established usage patterns of the existing MediaWiki system. For this reason, SMW also is available in multiple languages and was designed to easily support further localisation.

Semantic wikis are technologically interesting due to their similarity with certain characteristics of the Web in general. Most importantly, information is dynamic and changes in a decentralised way, and there is no central control of the wiki's content. In our case, this even extends to the available annotations: there is no central control for the annotation schema. Decentralisation leads to heterogeneity, but wikis still have had tremendous success in integrating heterogeneous views. SMW ensures that existing processes of consensus finding can also be applied to the novel semantic parts. While usually not its primary use, wikis contain not only text but also uploaded files, especially pictures and similar multimedia content. All functions described below are also available for such extended content.

Details of practical usage are discussed in the next Sect. 3. SMW is based on a simple and unobtrusive mechanism for semantic annotation (Sect. 3.1). Users provide special markup within a page's wiki-text, and SMW unambiguously maps those annotations into a formal description using the OWL DL ontology language. To make immediate use of the semantic data, the wiki supports a simple yet powerful query language (Sect. 3.2). By embedding queries into wiki-text, users can create dynamic pages that incorporate current query results (Sect. 3.3).

As we will see Sect. 4, SMW also provides various interfaces to data and tools on the Semantic Web. To enable external reuse, formal descriptions for one or more articles can be obtained via a web interface in OWL/RDF format (Sect. 4.1). As reviewed in Sect. 4.2, it is also possible to import data from OWL ontologies and to map wiki-annotations to existing vocabularies such as FOAF. Since SMW strictly adheres to the OWL DL standard, the exported information can be reused in a variety of tools (Sect. 4.3). As a demonstration, we provide an external SPARQL query service that is synchronised with the wiki's semantic content.

Semantic wikis have many possible applications, but the main goal of SMW is to provide the basis for creating a *Semantic Wikipedia*. Consequently, the software has a particular focus on scalability and performance. Basic operations such as saving and displaying of articles require only little resources. Even evaluation of queries can usually be achieved in linear time wrt. the number of annotations [2]. In Sect. 5, we give examples that illustrate the high practical relevance of the problems we claimed above, and we sketch the fascinating opportunities that semantic information in Wikipedia would bring. Finally, we present some further current practical uses of SMW in Sect. 6, and give a brief summary and outlook on upcoming developments in Sect. 7.

3 Practical Usage: Ontoworld.org

We illustrate the practical use of SMW via the example of http://ontoworld.org, which is a community wiki for the Semantic Web and related research areas. It contains information about community members, upcoming events, tools and developments. Recently, SMW was also used as a social wiki for various conferences[2], and the evaluation and user feedback made it clear that a single long-term wiki like ontoworld.org would be more advantageous than many short-living conference wikis.

In the following, we introduce the main novelties that a user encounters when using SMW instead of a simple MediaWiki.

3.1 Annotating Pages

The necessary collection of semantic data in SMW is achieved by letting users add annotations to the wiki-text of articles via a special markup. Every article corresponds to exactly one ontological element (including classes and properties), and every annotation in an article makes statements about this single element. This locality is crucial for maintenance: if knowledge is reused in many places, users must still be able to understand where the information originally came from. Furthermore, all annotations refer to the (abstract) concept represented by a page, not to the HTML document. Formally, this is implemented by choosing appropriate URIs for articles.

Most of the annotations that occur in SMW correspond to simple *ABox statements* in OWL DL, i.e. they describe certain individuals by asserting relations between them, annotating them with data values, or classifying them. The schematic information (*TBox*) representable in SMW is intentionally shallow. The wiki is not intended as a general purpose ontology editor, since distributed ontology engineering and large-scale reasoning are currently problematic.[3]

Categories are a simple form of annotation that allows users to classify pages. Categories are already available in MediaWiki, and SMW merely endows them with a formal interpretation as OWL classes. To state that the article `ESWC2006` belongs to the category `Conference`, one just writes `[[Category:Conference]]` within the article `ESWC2006`.

Relations describe relationships between two articles by assigning annotations to existing links. For example, there is a relation `program chair` between `ESWC2006` and `York Sure`. To express this, users just edit the page `ESWC2006` to change the normal link `[[York Sure]]` into `[[program chair::York Sure]]`.

Attributes allow users to specify relationships of articles to things that are not articles. For example, one can state that `ESWC2006` started at June 11 2006 by writing `[[start date:=June 11 2006]]`. In most cases, a relation to a new page `June 11 2006` would not be desired. Also, the system should understand the meaning of the given date, and recognise equivalent values such as `2006-06-11`.

Annotations are usually not shown at the place where they are inserted. Category links appear only at the bottom of a page, relations are displayed like normal links, and attributes just show the given value. A *factbox* at the bottom of each page enables users to view all extracted annotations, but the main text remains undisturbed.

---

[2] WWW 2006, Edinburgh, Scotland and ESWC 2006, Budva, Montenegro.
[3] However, SMW has been used in conjunction with more expressive background ontologies, which are then evaluated by external OWL inference engines [3].

It is obvious that the processing of Attributes requires some further information about the *Type* of the annotations. Integer numbers, strings, and dates all require different handling, and one needs to state that an attribute has a certain type. As explained above, every ontological element is represented as an article, and the same is true for categories, relations, and attributes. This also has the advantage that a *user documentation* can be written for each element of the vocabulary, which is crucial to enable consistent use of annotations.

The types that are available for attributes also have dedicated articles. In order to assign a type in the above example, we just need to state a relationship between `Attribute:start date` and `Type:Date`. This relation is called `has type` (in English SMW) and has a special built-in meaning.[4] SMW has a number of similar *special properties* that are used to specify certain technical aspects of the system, but most users can reuse existing annotations and do not have to worry about underlying definitions.

3.2 Querying and Searching

Nobody will spend time on annotating a wiki if there is no immediate benefit for usage. We already mentioned that a factbox is displayed in each article, and this factbox also features quicklinks for browsing and searching. For example, attributes that denote geographic coordinates will produce links to online map services. However, the main advantage for users *within* the wiki is SMW's querying capability.

Users can search for articles using a simple query language that was developed based on the known syntax of the wiki. Indeed, the query for retrieving all articles that have York Sure as a program chair, one simply writes `[[program chair::York Sure]]`. In other words, the syntax for specifying an annotation is identical with the syntax for searching it. Multiple such query statements are interpreted conjunctively.

The query language becomes more powerful by allowing searches that include wildcards, ranges, and subqueries. For example, the query

```
[[Category:Conference]] [[start date:=>May 14 2006]]
[[program chair::<q>[[member of::AIFB]]</q>]]
```

displays all conferences that started *after* May 14 2006 and which had a program chair from AIFB. We also remark that queries for category membership do a limited (sound but not complete) form of reasoning to take subclass relationships into account. Further information on the query language is found in the online documentation.[5]

3.3 Dynamic Pages

The query functionality of SMW can be used to embed dynamic content into pages, which is a major advantage over traditional wikis. To do so, an *inline query* is written in wiki-text and enclosed in `<ask>` and `</ask>`. The article then shows the results of the given query at this position. Moreover, the query syntax involves statements for displaying further properties of the retrieved results, and for modifying the appearance within the page.

---

[4] Also, it is treated as an owl:AnnotationProperty in order to stay in OWL DL.
[5] `http://ontoworld.org/wiki/Help:Inline_queries`

Events

You can find information about many events and calls for papers within this wiki. Using semantic annotation, it is possible to query for particular events.

Upcoming events: ICCS 2006 (Aalborg, 2006-07-16), EKAW 2006 (Podebrady, 2006-10-02), AST 2006 (Dresden, 2006-10-05), SemanticDesktopWS 2006 (Athens, Georgia, 2006-11-05), SWESE 2006 (Athens, Georgia, 2006-11-06) *full list*

Fig. 1. Dynamic content on the main page of ontoworld.org

For example, the *Main Page* of ontoworld.org displays upcoming events, their dates and locations (see Fig. 1). Those results are generated dynamically by looking for conferences starting after the *current* date, ordering them according to their dates, and printing the first five results.

Many other forms of inline queries can be found in the online documentation.

4 Reuse in the Semantic Web

4.1 Mapping to OWL DL

In this section, we describe how annotations in SMW are formally grounded in OWL. As explained above, every article represents an ontological element, i.e. an element of one of the RDF classes `Thing`, `Class`, `ObjectProperty`, `DatatypeProperty`, and `AnnotationProperty`. Moreover, every article needs a URI which is different from its URL in order to prevent confusion of concepts and HTML pages. We map each URL injectively to a URI which, when requested in a browser, will still be redirected to the original URL.[6]

The type of the elements is fixed for most kind of annotations. Normal articles are just OWL individuals, categories become classes, and relations become object properties between articles. Attributes might be datatype, annotation, or object properties, depending on their type within the wiki.

Based on this mapping, SMW generates OWL/RDF for any page on request. The simplest way to access this RDF is to use the link "View as RDF" at the bottom of each annotated page. More elaborate export settings, which also allow bulk export, backlink inclusion, and recursive export, are found on a dedicated special page.[7] This page also serves as an endpoint for external services that want to access the wiki's semantic data.

4.2 Reusing Existing Ontologies

Since SMW is compatible with the OWL DL knowledge model, it is also feasible to use existing ontologies within the wiki. This is possible in two ways: *ontology import* is a feature that allows to create and modify pages in the wiki to represent the relationships

---

[6] This does not work in all cases, since OWL/RDF requires the use of URIs as XML ids, which in turn cannot use all characters allowed in URLs.
[7] See http://ontoworld.org/wiki/Special:ExportRDF.

that are given in some existing OWL DL document; *vocabulary reuse* allows users to map wiki pages to elements of existing ontologies.

The ontology import feature employs the RAP[8] toolkit for reading RDF documents, and extracts statements that can be represented in the wiki. Article names for imported elements are derived from their labels, or, if no labels are available, from the section identifier of their URI. The main purpose of the import is to bootstrap a skeleton for filling the wiki. Also, ontology import inserts special annotations that generate equivalence statements in the OWL export (i.e. owl:sameAs, owl:equivalentClass, or owl:equivalentProperty). Importing ontologies is only allowed for site administrators, since it could otherwise be used to spam the wiki with thousands of new articles.

Importing vocabulary allows users to identify elements of the wiki with elements of existing ontologies. For example, the `Category:Person` in our online example is directly exported as the class `foaf:Person` of the Friend-Of-A-Friend vocabulary. Wiki users can decide which pages of the wiki should have an external semantics, but the set of available external elements is explicitly provided by administrator users. By making some vocabulary element known to the wiki, they ensure that vocabulary reuse respects the type constraints of OWL DL. For example external classes such as `foaf:Person` cannot be imported as Relations.

4.3 External Reuse in Practice

OWL/RDF export is a means of allowing external reuse of wiki data, but only practical application of this feature can show the quality of the generated RDF. To this end, we have employed a number of Semantic Web tools to the RDF output. SMW cooperates nicely with most tested applications, such as *FOAF Explorer*, the *Tabulator* RDF browser, or the *Piggy Bank* RDF browser extension. Details on the tested tools, including their basic functionality and URL, are given at ontoworld.org.[9]

Moreover, we provide an externally hosted SPARQL querying service.[10] The system is based on the stand-alone RDF server *Joseki*[11] that is synchronised with the semantic content of the wiki. Synchronisation employs the wiki's RSS feed for reporting recent changes to reload changed articles quickly. The SPARQL endpoint thus demonstrates that it is feasible to mirror the wiki's RDF content via small incremental updates, and offers another access point for semantic technologies to reuse the data.

5 Wikipedia

The most important usage scenario for SMW are the various project sites of the *Wikimedia foundation*, especially the different language versions of *Wikipedia*. We already mentioned that ease of use and scalability are central for this application, and SMW has been built to fulfil these requirements. On the other hand, Wikipedia has no reason to use a novel extension at all if it does not bring immediate advantages. However, the

---

[8] RDF API for PHP, http://www.wiwiss.fu-berlin.de/suhl/bizer/rdfapi/
[9] See http://ontoworld.org/wiki/SMW_reuse
[10] See http://ontoworld.org/wiki/SPARQL_endpoint
[11] See http://www.joseki.org/

Workshops					[edit]
↑	Title	abstracts	deadline	date	
WOMO2006	First International Workshop on Modular Ontologies		2006-08-03	2006-11-06	
WCMHLT2006	Web Content Mining with Human Language Technologies workshop 2006		2006-08-01	2006-11-06	
URSW2006	Uncertainty Reasoning for the Web 2006 Workshop		2006-07-20	2006-11-06	
Terra Cognita 2006	Terra Cognita 2006 - Directions to the Geospatial Semantic Web		2006-07-21	2006-11-06	
SWUI2006	The 3rd International Semantic Web User Interaction Workshop	2006-08-04	2006-08-11	2006-11-06	
SWPW2006	2nd International Semantic Web Policy Workshop		2006-08-11	2006-11-06	

Fig. 2. Excerpt of an automatically generated list on ontoworld.org

core wiki problems presented in Sect. 2 all have very concrete consequences for today's Wikipedia.

Consistency of content is a major aspect of the overall quality of Wikipedia. Currently, articles like the "List of cities in Russia by population" are edited manually. If any of the given population numbers changes, a number of articles have to be updated. The dynamic creation of pages described in Sect. 3.3 solves many instances of this problem, e.g. by generating tables as in Fig. 2.

Accessing knowledge in Wikipedia can be extremely difficult due to its sheer size. For example, the reader may want to try to find a list of all *female physicists* in Wikipedia. Keyword searches fail miserably at this task: *Marie Curie* does not appear at all when the term "female" is used, but the majority of the returned articles do not even describe people at all. A simple query as described in Sect. 3.2 would immediately solve the problem.

Reusing knowledge contained in Wikipedia is very desirable as it is the largest human-edited source of information. Currently, tools such as the media player *Amarok* (amarok.kde.org) embed whole articles into their GUI to allow users to access the information. While those implementations show the need for external reuse, they are currently limited to the mere reproduction of Wikipedia's page content.

We thus believe that we address core problems of Wikipedia as a whole, and hope that the extension can be introduced to Wikipedia soon. SMW was discussed among Wikipedians and developers at the recent 2nd International Wikimedia Conference in Boston (Wikimania2006), and large-scale evaluations with a copy of Wikipedia are now being made.

The opportunities of a semantic Wikipedia are huge. Wikipedia covers a large number of knowledge areas, and even the use of Wikipedia as a resource for thoroughly documented URIs would be helpful. With the added semantic information, Wikipedia's knowledge could be exploited in numerous applications. The scientific relevance of large annotated text corpora, and of real-life knowledge models that really represent "shared conceptualisations" would be enormous. Formalised knowledge in different language Wikipedias can be a basis for investigating cultural differences, but independent semantic wikis also provide intersting sources of data for ontology alignment.

While SMW currently uses only simple annotations, users start to articulate the need for more expressive features. However, integration is not trivial at all, and tractability, explanation components, local closed world assumption, paraconsistent reasoning, and other issues might play an important role in extending the expressive power of the wiki.

Beyond such scientific challenges, Wikipedia can also enable a new range of tools based on semantic technologies. As mentioned in Sect. 4.3 we employed a number of tools, but we were also disappointed by the immature state of many of them. We assume that this is due to the lack of interesting semantic data on the web, and believe that Wikipedia can stimulate much more intensive development of semantic tools.

6 Further Use Cases

SMW is currently used in a number of real-life applications and has an active user community. This can also be seen from the many requests to our public mailing lists and the more than 200 registered users of ontoworld.org (not counting the spammers). Moreover, a number of external sites have already introduced SMW into their wikis. Examples are provided online [4], but not all SMW installations are open to public access (e.g. AIFB and FZI use SMW for internal knowledge management). Finally, SMW has been used as a local tool for personal information management on the desktop.

7 Outlook

In this short note, we could only sketch the core features and uses of the Semantic MediaWiki system. Other features, such as the use of *semantic templates* or the support for *units of measurement*, could not be introduced at all. We therefore suggest the reader to refer to the more detailed online documentation [4]. Semantic MediaWiki currently is developed very actively. At the time of this writing, improved browsing capabilities, easy generation of RDF dumps, and support for Timeline[12] output are planned for the next version. Yet, the overall focus remains on producing a stable, scalable, and usable implementation of the core features that will be employed in Wikipedia.

Acknowledgements. We wish to thank all past and present contributors and users of SMW, in particular the volunteer developers S Page and Kai Hüner, and *doccheck* GmbH, Germany. Research reported in this work has been partially supported by the European Union in projects SEKT (IST-2003-506826) and NEPOMUK (IST 027705).

References

1. Völkel, M., Krötzsch, M., Vrandečić, D., Haller, H., Studer, R.: Semantic Wikipedia. In: Proc. of the 15th International WWW Conference, Edinburgh, Scotland. (2006)
2. Krötzsch, M., Vrandečić, D., Völkel, M.: Wikipedia and the Semantic Web, Part II. In: Proc. of the 2nd International Wikimedia Conference, Wikimania, Cambridge, MA, USA. (2006)
3. Vrandečić, D., Krötzsch, M.: Reusing ontological background knowledge in semantic wikis. In Völkel, M., Schaffert, S., Decker, S., eds.: Proc. of the 1st Workshop on Semantic Wikis – From Wikis to Semantics, Budva, Montenegro. (2006)
4. Semantic MediaWiki: Online documentation (August 21 2006) http://ontoworld.org/wiki/Semantic_MediaWiki.

---

[12] See http://simile.mit.edu/timeline/

Enabling Semantic Web Communities with DBin: An Overview

Giovanni Tummarello, Christian Morbidoni, and Michele Nucci

Dipartimento di Elettronica, Intelligenza Artificiale e Telecomunicazioni
Università Politecnica delle Marche, Via Brecce Bianche – 60131 Ancona (Italy)
{g.tummarello, c.morbidoni}@deit.univpm.it, mik.nucci@gmail.com

Abstract. In this paper we give an overview of the DBin Semantic Web information manager. Then we describe how it enables users to create and experience the Semantic Web by exchanging RDF knowledge in P2P "topic" channels. Once sufficient information has been collected locally, rich and fast browsing of the Semantic Web becomes possible without generating external traffic or computational load. In this way each client builds and populates a 'personal semantic space' on which user defined rules, trust metrics and filtering can be freely applied. We also discuss issues such as end user interaction and the social aggregation model induced by this novel application.

1 Introduction

In this paper we present a novel kind of Semantic Web scenario which we call "Semantic Web Communities". The idea is to enable end users to create and experience the Semantic Web by exchanging knowledge in P2P "topic" channels.

Such an application model can in a sense be though of as a file-sharing for metadata with on-top "community configurable" user interfaces (Brainlets). Similar to a file-sharing client, in fact, such application connects directly to other peers; instead of files, however, it downloads and shares RDF metadata about resources which the group has defined "of interest". This creates a flow of RDF information which ultimately allows the participants to build rich personal Semantic Web databases therefore supporting high speed local browsing, searching, personalized filtering and processing of information.

In implementing this idea in our prototype of Rich Semantic Web Client (RSWC), DBin ([1]), it became immediately clear that a number of issues had to be resolved, relating to a great number of independent yet interconnected aspects.

For example, once data has been collected, the real issue becomes how to allow the user to interact with it in a natural way, e.g. in a way much more attractive and meaningful than a list of "properties" and "resources". While this "visualization problem" seems a separately treatable problem, we claim that in this scenario it is not. We propose, for example, to leverage the existence of "groups" by providing a way for a "group leader" to suggest "interaction profiles" with the data that is exchanged within that context.

Upon joining a group, the user is then advised to download what we call a Brainlet, that is a package of configuration settings and a priori knowledge providing editing and browsing facilities to best interact with the information shared in the group.

2 Use Scenario

A typical use of DBin might be similar to that of popular file sharing programs, the purpose however being completely different. While usual P2P applications "grow" the local availability of data, DBin grows RDF knowledge.

Once a user has selected the topic of interest and has connected to a semantic web P2P group, RDF annotations just start flowing in and out "piece by piece" in a scalable fashion. Such operations are clearly topic-agnostic, but for the sake of the demonstration let us take an example of possible use of DBin by a Semantic Web researcher.

For example, a user, let us call him Bob, who expresses interest in a particular topic and related papers (say "Semantic Web P2P"), will keep a DBin open (possibly minimized) connected with a related P2P knowledge exchange group. Bob will then be able to review, from time to time, new pieces of relevant "information" that DBin collects from other participants. Such information might be pure metadata annotations (e.g. "the deadline for on-topic conference X has been set to Y"), but also advanced annotations pointing at rich data posted on the web (e.g. pictures, documents, long texts, etc.). He could then reply or further annotate each of this incoming pieces of information either for his personal use or for public knowledge. If such replies include attachment data, DBin automatically takes care of the needed web publishing. At database level all this information is coherently stored as RDF. At the user level, however, the common operations and views are grouped in domain specific user interfaces, which are called "Brainlets".

3 Brainlets

Brainlets can be though of as "configuration packages" preparing DBin to operate on a specific domain (e.g. Wine lovers, Italian Opera fans etc..). Given that Brainlet include customized user interface, the user might perceive them as full *"domain applications run inside DBin"* which can be installed as plug-ins. In short Brainlets define settings for:

- The ontologies to be used for annotations in the domain
- A general GUI layout;. which components to visualize and how they are cascaded in terms of selection/reaction
- Templates for domain specific "annotations", e.g., a "Movie" Brainlet might have a "review" template that users fill.
- Templates for readily available "pre cooked" domain queries.
- Templates for wizards which guide the user when inserting new domain elements (to avoid duplicated URIs etc)
- A suggested trust model and information filtering rules for the domain. e.g. Public keys of well known "founding members" or authorities,
- Basic RDF knowledge package for the domain

Creating Brainlets doesn't require programming skills, as it is just a matter of knowledge engineering (e.g. selecting the appropriate Ontologies) and editing of XML configuration files.

To create a new Brainlet, one copies from a given empty template which configures an eclipse plug-in to append a new "Brainlet" to the list of those known by DBin.

Enabling Semantic Web Communities with DBin: An Overview

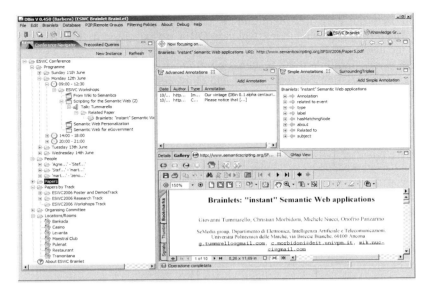

Fig. 1. A screen shot of the ESWC 2006 Brainlet, dialing with presented papers, delegates and so on

This is done by means of an Eclipse RCP [2] extension point, which enables to install a plug-in with specified APIs and properties. Then, each Brainlet has its own XML configuration file, which, in addition to purely layout configuration (e.g. the positioning of the GUI blocks), allows one to define the Brainlet's core properties and facilities. The basic properties are the Brainlet name, version and URI, which usually indicates the web site from which to download the package. An overview of the other configurations and features follows.

3.1 Ontologies and Default RDF Knowledge

Probably the most important step in creating a new Brainlet is the choice of appropriate ontologies to represent the domain of interest. Once they have been identified, the corresponding OWL files are usually included and shipped in the Brainlet itself although they could be placed on the Web. Each of them will be declared in the XML file, specifying the location of the OWL file, a unique name for the ontology and it's base namespace. In the same way basic knowledge of the domain can be included.

3.2 Navigation of Resources

The way concepts and instances are presented and browsed is crucial to the usability of the interface and the effectiveness in finding relevant information. Graph based visualizers are notably problematic when dealing with a relevant number of resources. For this reason, the solution provided by the main DBin Navigator is based on flexible and dynamic tree structures. Such approach can be seen to scale very well with respect to the number of resources, e.g. in Brainlets such as the SW Research one. The peculiarity of the approach is that the Brainlet creator can specify which is the 'relation' between each tree item and its children by associating them a semantic query. The results of such queries, which in DBin are expressed in SeRQL syntax [3], will be the item's children.

There can be multiple topic branches configured in the Navigator, specifying different kinds of relation between parent and child items. This enables the user to explore the resources of the domain under different points of view.

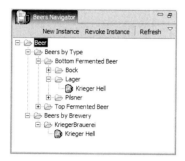

Fig. 2. The navigator view can show different branches which organize concepts in different ways

Figure 2 shows the Navigator view configured to display two branches, one (*beers by type*) gives an ontology driven hierarchical view on the domain, the other (*beers by brewery*) is a custom classification of the beers according the specific brewery producing them.

3.3 Selection Flows

At user interface level, a Brainlet is composed by a set of 'view parts', as defined in the Eclipse platform terminology (Figure 1). Usually, each part takes a resource as a main "focus" and shows a 'something about' it (e.g. it's properties, images associated, etc...). Selection flows among these parts are also scripted at this point; it is possible to establish the precise cause effect chain by which selecting an icon on a view will cause other views to change. This is done specifying, for each view part, which other ones will be notified when a resource has been selected.

3.4 "Precooked Queries"

Within a specific domain there are often some queries that are frequently used to fulfill relevant use cases. Continuing our "Beer" example, such a query could be "find beers [stronger|lighter] than X degrees". The "Precooked queries" facility gives the Brainlet creators the ability to provide such "fill in the blanks" queries to end users.

3.5 URI Wizards

It is very important to avoid different users to choose different URIs to indicate the very same concept. This can cause problems, for example, when two users have inserted the same beer while being off-line and later on they share their knowledge in the same P2P group. For this purpose we introduce the concept of URI Wizard, which defies procedures for assisting the user in the process of assigning identifiers to instances. Different procedures can be associated to different type of objects of the domain. For example, an intuitive procedure for choosing an identifier for Peroni beer might be to visit an authoritative web site (e.g. RateBeer.com), full-text search for 'Peroni' and then use the URL of the resulting web page.

Brainlets creators can choose among different preset procedures by XML configuration of various kinds of URI Wizards. Some of them, for example, creates a URI given a string that can represent the user nick, the time of creation, a well known name and so on, depending on the nature of the concepts (e.g. an MD5 for a file, the name a person, etc.).

This is a very simple methodology for choosing URI, and of course gives not absolute grantees, but we believe it to be very powerful and somehow sound, as it leverages the work of existing and established web communities.

3.6 Custom Domain Dependent Annotation Templates

Brainlets use the ontologies to assist the users in creating simple annotations (e.g suggesting which properties can be associated to a resource based on its type). A Brainlet creator can however also choose to create "complex annotation types" using an ad hoc OWL ontology. An example of such complex annotations is the "Beer Comparison", which directly compares beers, saying which one is better or worse and why. Upon selecting "Add advanced annotation" in DBin the system determines which advanced annotations can be applied to the specified resource and provides a wizard.

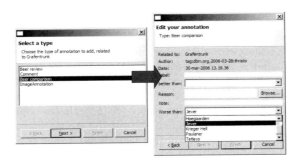

Fig. 3. Advanced annotations are defined in OWL and auto generate property visualization and editing interfaces

3.7 Ontology Issue and Social Model

Brainlets are therefore preloaded by power users with domain specific user interaction facilities, as well as with domain ontologies suggested by the Brainlet creator. This seems to induce an interesting social model, mostly based on consensus upon Brainlets choice, which can help some of the well known issues in distributed metadata environments, a central one being the ontology mismatch problem. Brainlets, by providing an aggregation medium for ontologies, users and data representation structures, are therefore good catalyst of the overall semantic interoperability process. As users gather around popular Brainlets for their topic of choice, the respective suggested ontologies and data representation practice will form an increasingly important reality. If someone decided to create a new Brainlet or Semantic Web application in general which could target the same user group as the said popular Brainlet, there would be an evident incentive in using compatible data structures and ontologies.

4 The RDFGrowth P2P Engine: Basic Concepts

The RDFGrowth P2P algorithm, an early version of which is described in [4], constitutes the main channel by which a DBin client collects RDF data coming from other DBin users.

Previous P2P Semantic Web applications, such as [5] and [6], have explored interactions among groups of trusted and committed peers. In such systems peers rely on each other to forward query requests, collect and return results. In contrast, we consider the real world scenario of peers where cooperation is relatively frail. By this we mean that peers are certainly expected to provide some external service, but commitment should be minimal and in a "best effort" fashion.

The RDFGrowth algorithm has been designed to address this requirement of scalability and minimum commitment among peers, and is based on the peculiar philosophy of minimum external burden. Therefore peers are not required to perform any complex or time consuming operation such as query routing, replication, collecting and merging. As it is not in the scope of this paper to discuss in detail RDFGrowth, in this section we just give an overview of it.

As a design principle, given that a complex graph query could hog any machine's resources, we assumed that individual peers would not, in general, be willing to answer arbitrary external queries. In RDFGrowth any single peer would, if at all, answer just very basic ones, which are defined by the "RDF Neighbours" operator(RDFN).

The RDFN of a resource *a* within a graph *G,* is the closure on blank nodes of the triples of *G* surrounding *a,* and represents what is known about *a* at a given peer. This type of query is not only very fast to execute but can also be cached very effectively.

RDFGrowth uses the group metaphor to enable users to aggregate around topics of interest. When a user joins a particular group, DBin begins to collect and share only that kind of information which is of interest within the group. Such a topic's definition is given by the GUED(Group URI Exposing Definition), which is an operator capable of selecting from a triplestore a set of resources with common characteristics. A GUEDs can be implemented as simple sets of schema queries (e.g. all resources of type *ex:Paper* where *ex:topic* property value is "Semantic Web") and each group relays on one of them for advertising what can be shared within the community.

Once a group has been joined, the algorithm cycles over the set of 'on topic' resources locally known (the result of the GUED operator applied to the local DB) and, for each resource, searches other peers having new knowledge 'about' it. This is done by looking into a sort of Distributed Hash Table(DHT), in which each peer publishes the hashes of its RDFN (say simple MD5). When a certain condition on the RDFN hash is verified an actual metadata exchange is initiated with the other pee. In a simple version one can simply choose the first hash which is different from the local one, but more advanced methods can be used to try to guess the most profitable peer to ask to.

No "active information hunt" such as query routing, replication, collecting and merging is done. Such operations would require peers to do work on behalf of others that is again allowing peers to cause a potentially large external burden.

So, instead of querying around, in DBin a user browses only on a local and potentially very large metadata database, while the RDFGrowth algorithm "keeps it alive" by updating it in a sustainable, "best effort" fashion. A complete discussion is outside the scope of this introduction to the Demo, those interested can refer to [4] and other papers available from the DBin web site. As a result, keeping DBin open and connected to P2P groups with moderate traffic requires absolutely minimal network and computational resources.

5 URI Bridge Component

As we said before, the RDFGrowth algorithm enables the exchange of pure RDF metadata, so it is clear that some facility is needed in DBin to provide the user with the digital content referred by this metadata. Also an 'upload' mechanism is needed to allow users to be able to share his/her digital data (e.g. Images, text etc).

While the download mechanism is straightforward once a URL is available for a specific resource, as it can be retrieved, for example, over standard HTTP protocol, the uploading part requires some further considerations. The URIBridge is based on upload servers where users can store files they want to share (e.g. pictures, text, mp3s). After having uploaded a resource, the user is provided with a URL which can be used to create annotations about the data as well as to retrieve that data in order to visualize it.

DBin clients can be configured to work with one or more upload servers, much like an E-Mail client requires a SMTP server. While the default installation of DBin comes with a simple upload server, this limits the users to small files. For power users, installing a personal upload server is trivial, just deploying a simple PHP script.

6 Identities and Authorship of Annotations

In such a system, which deals with potentially large and unregulated communities, it is important to have information about who said what, in particular which user is the author of a particular annotation received from the network. To do this we use a methodology based on the notion of MSG (Minimum Self Contained Graph), defined in [7] and enabling the decomposition of a graph in atomic units, and on the canonical serialization of RDF graphs suggested in [8].

This methodology enables RDF data to be signed at a fine granularity level and in an efficient way (MSGs are composed by more triples but it can be signed just by reifying a single one of them). It also assures that the context (in this case the authorship) will remain within the metadata when they will be exchanged over the network, as well as enable multiple signature to be attached to the same MSG, also at different times. As it is impossible to discuss in detail the digital signature process due to space limitation, please refer to [7].

When started up for the first time, DBin clients require the users to provide a valid URI which will act as an identifier for the user itself (for example a mailto URL or a web page). Then a public and a private keys are generated; the private key is stored locally, while the public one is uploaded by means of the URIBridge, just as it happens for files. Every time a user will add an annotation to the system it will contain the user's identifier as well as the URL of the public key, and will be signed using the user's private key. In this way, after having received a piece of metadata from the P2P group, clients are able to retrieve the public key and to identify the author of the annotation, without caring about the provenance of the metadata itself.

Once the authorship of a MSG can be verified, a variety of filtering rules can be applied at will. These, in our system, are always non-destructive; information that does not match certain trust criteria can be hidden away but does not get deleted. It is straightforward, for example, to implement a local 'black list' policy, allowing users to add authors to that list and to filter the local knowledge in order to hide all the information signed by the same user's identity.

7 Conclusions and Related Works

Aspects of DBin can be compared with [9], [10] and [11]. Details of this comparison are not possible due to lack of space, but DBin stands out as a end user centered application which provides an all round and integrated Semantic Web experience. By this we mean that, albeit in perfectible forms, DBin provides a single interface that entirely cover the needs of complex use cases. Users can browse, query, publish and cooperatively create Semantic Web databases. Media inserts can be seen together with the relative metadata, incoming knowledge can be filtered based on local policies and information locally produced is digitally signed. More than this, users are given the ability to create "Semantic Web Communities" by creating both application environments, Brainlets, and exchange and meeting places, RDFGrowth channels. DBin is an Open Source project (GPL). Further documentation and compiled executables can be downloaded at http://dbin.org, where a few minutes screen demo is also available.

References

[1] "The DBin project" http://www.dbin.org
[2] "Eclipse Rich Client Platform", http://www.eclipse.org/rcp
[3] J. Broekstra, A. Kampman , "SeRQL: An RDF Query and Transformation Language", ISWC, 2004
[4] G. Tummarello, C. Morbidoni, J. Petersson, P. Puliti, F. Piazza, "RDFGrowth, a P2P annotation exchange algorithm for scalable Semantic Web applications", P2PKM Workshop, 2004
[5] W. Nejdl, B. Wolf , "EDUTELLA: A P2P Networking Infrastructure Based on RDF", WWW, 2002
[6] P.A. Chirita, S. Idreos, M. Koubarakis, W. Nejdl, "Publish/Subscribe for RDF-based P2P Networks", ESWS, 2004
[7] G. Tummarello, C. Morbidoni, P. Puliti, F. Piazza , "Signing individual fragments of an RDF graph", WWW, 2005
[8] J. Carroll, "Signing RDF Graphs", ISWC, 2003
[9] D. Huynh, S. Mazzocchi, D. Karger , "Piggy Bank: Experience the Semantic Web Inside Your Web Browser",ISWC, 2005
[10] J. Broekstra, M. Ehrig, P. Haase, F. van Harmelen, M. Menken, P. Mika, B. Schnizler, R Siebes , "Bibster - A Semantics-Based Bibliographic Peer-to-Peer System." SemPGrid Workshop, 2004
[11] D. Quan, D. Karger, "How to Make a Semantic Web Browser", WWW , 2004

MultimediaN E-Culture Demonstrator

Guus Schreiber[1], Alia Amin[2], Mark van Assem[1], Victor de Boer[3],
Lynda Hardman[2,5], Michiel Hildebrand[2], Laura Hollink[1], Zhisheng Huang[2],
Janneke van Kersen[4], Marco de Niet[4], Borys Omelayenko[1],
Jacco van Ossenbruggen[2], Ronny Siebes[1], Jos Taekema[4],
Jan Wielemaker[3], and Bob Wielinga[3]

[1] Vrije Universiteit Amsterdam (VU), Computer Science
http://www.cs.vu.nl
[2] Center for Math. and Computer Science CWI, Amsterdam
http://www.cwi.nl/ins2
[3] Universiteit van Amsterdam (UvA), HCS Lab
http://hcs.science.uva.nl/
[4] Digital Heritage Netherlands (DEN), The Hague
http://www.den.nl
[5] Technical University Eindhoven (TU/e)
http://w3.win.tue.nl/en/

1 Introduction

The main objective of the MultimediaN E-Culture project is to demonstrate how novel semantic-web and presentation technologies can be deployed to provide better indexing and search support within large virtual collections of cultural-heritage resources. The architecture is fully based on open web standards, in particular XML, SVG, RDF/OWL and SPARQL. One basic hypothesis underlying this work is that the use of explicit background knowledge in the form of ontologies/vocabularies/thesauri is in particular useful in information retrieval in knowledge-rich domains.

This paper gives some details about the internals of the demonstrator. The online version of the demonstrator can be found at:

http://e-culture.multimedian.nl/demo/search

Readers are encouraged to first take a look at the demonstrator before reading on. As a teaser we have included a short description of basic search facilities in the next section. We suggest you consult the tutorial (linked from the online demo page) which provides a sample walk-through of the search functionality. Make sure your browser has adequate SVG support.[1]

---

[1] The current version of the demonstrator runs under Firefox version 1.5.0.4 with the Adobe SVG plugin (v 6.0 38363, see the demonstrator FAQ for installation instructions) and has been tested on Windows, Macintosh and Linux. Support for Internet Explorer is planned for future versions of the demo. Firefox 2 is expected to make the plugin installtions unneccessary (you can try the beta-release). As a project we are committed to web standards (such as SVG) and are not willing to digress to (and spend time on) special-purpose solutions.

Please note that this is a product of an ongoing project. Visitors should expect the demonstrator to change[2]. We are incorporating more collections and vocabularies and are also extending the annotation, search and presentation functionality.

2 A Peek at the Demonstrator

Figure 1 shows a query for `Art Nouveau`. This query will retrieve images that are related to Art Nouveau in some way. The results shown in the figure are 'created by an artist with a matching style". So, these images are paintings by artists who have painted in the Art-Nouveau style, but the style is not part of the metadata of the image itself. This may retrieve some paintings which are not really Art Nouveau, but it is a reasonable strategy if there are no (or only few) images directly annotated with Art Nouveau. We view the use of such indirect semantic links as a potential for semantic search (for more details on path search in the demonstrator see Section 8).

Fig. 1. Results of query for `Art Nouveau`

The lower part of the figure shows a listing of painters who are known to have worked in the Art-Nouveau style. The time line indicates years in which they have created art works (you can click on them to get information).

---
[2] The project has a duration of 4 years and is at the time of writing 18 months underway.

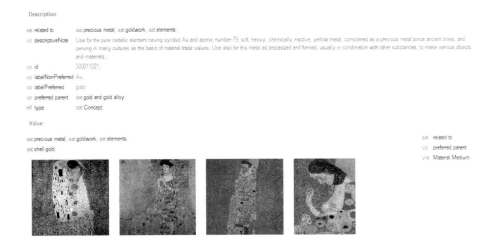

Fig. 2. Information about the indexing term Gold, showing also images that are related to Gold

Images have annotations in which terms from various thesauri are used. Figure 2 shows the information a user gets when selecting such an indexing term, here Gold material from the Art & Architecture Thesaurus. We also show images that have been annotated with this indexing term (or semantically related terms).

These are some basic search- and presentation functions. See the online demo for information about more search options, such as time-based search and faceted search. We also have an experimental search function for finding the semantic relations between two URIs, e.g. for posing the question "How are Van Gogh and Gauguin related?". In fact, this leads to a whole avenue of new search possibilities and related issues with respect to which semantic paths are most relevant, which we hope to explore in more detail in the coming years.

3 Technical Architecture

The foundation of the demo is formed by SWI-Prolog and its (Semantic) Web libraries (for detailed information, see [1,2]). SPARQL-based access is a recent feature. The *Application Logic* module defines searching and clustering algorithms using Prolog as query language, returning the results as Prolog Herbrand terms. The *Presentation Generation* module generates web documents from the raw answers represented as Herbrand terms.

From the user perspective, the architecture provides (i) annotation facilities for web resources representing images, and (ii) search and presentation/visualization facilities for finding images.

4 Vocabularies

Currently, the demonstrator hosts four thesauri, namely the three Getty vocabularies[3], i.e., the Art & Architecture Thesaurus (AAT), Union List of Artists Names (ULAN) and the Thesaurus of Geographical Names (TGN), as well as the lexical resource WordNet, version 2.0. The Getty thesauri were converted from their original XML format into an RDF/OWL representation using the conversion methods principles as formulated in [3]. The RDF/OWL version of the data models is available online[4]. The Getty thesauri are licensed[5].

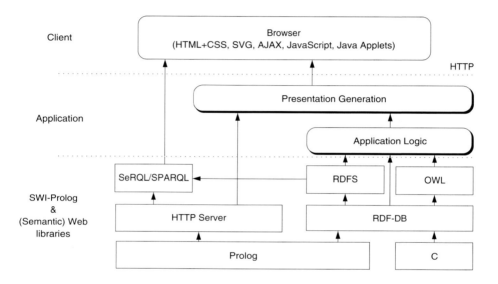

Fig. 3. Technical architecture of the demonstrator

The RDF/OWL conversion of WordNet is documented in a publication of the W3C Semantic Web Best Practices and Deployment Working Group [4]. It is an instructive example of the issues involved in this conversion process, in particular the recipes for publishing RDF vocabularies [5].

The architecture is independent of the particular thesauri being used. We are currently in the process of adding the Dutch version of AAT, amongst others to support a multi-lingual interface. Integration of other (multi-lingual) thesauri is planned.

---

[3] http://www.getty.edu/research/conducting_research/vocabularies/
[4] http://e-culture.multimedian.nl/resources/
[5] The partners in the project have acquired licenses for the thesauri. People using the demonstrator do not have access to the full thesauri sources, but can use them to annotate and/or search the collections.

Using multiple vocabularies is a baseline principle of our approach. It also raises the issue of alignment between the vocabularies. Basically, semantic interoperability will increase when semantic links between vocabularies are added. Within the Getty vocabularies one set of links is systematically maintained: places in ULAN (e.g., place of birth of an artist) refer to terms in TGN. Within the project we are adding additional sets of links. One example is links between art styles in AAT (e.g. "Impressionism") and artists in ULAN (e.g., "Monet"). De Boer [6] has worked on deriving these semi-automatically from texts on art history.

5 Annotation Template

For annotation and search purposes the tool provides the user with a description template derived from the VRA 3.0 Core Categories [7]. The VRA template is defined as a specialization of the Dublin Core set of metadata elements, tailored to the needs of art images. The VRA Core Categories follow the "dumb-down" principle, i.e., a tool can interpret the VRA data elements as Dublin Core data elements.[6].

6 Collection Data and Metadata

In principle, every web resource with a URI can be included and annotated in the virtual collection of our demonstrator. As a test set of data we have included three web collections:

- The Artchive collection[7] contains around 4,000 images of paintings, mainly from the 19th and 20th century.
- The ARIA collection[8] of the Rijksmuseum in Amsterdam contains images of some 750 master pieces.
- The RMV collection[9] of the Rijksmuseum voor Volkenkunde in Leiden describes about 80,000 images of ethnographic objects that belong to various cultures worldwide.

For the Artchive items we have used a parsing technique to transform the existing textual annotation in a semantic annotation, i.e. matching strings from the text to concepts from the various thesauri.

The metadata that accompagnies the Artchive collection consists of a short file holding textual values for title, creator, dimensions, material, year of creation, location and comments. Unfortunately the descriptor name is not specified with the value and not all descriptions have the same values in the same order. We used a grammar to parse and canonise the date of creation and dimension fields. Author and material are matched to ULAN and AAT using a syntactic distance measure and selecting the best match.

---

[6] An unofficial OWL specification of the VRA elements, including links to Dublin Core, can be found at http://e-culture.multimedian.nl/resources/
[7] http://www.artchive.com/
[8] http://rijksmuseum.nl/aria/
[9] http://www.rmv.nl

For the other collections we used similar strategies for enriching the original metadata with semantic categories. Adding a collection thus involves some information-extraction work on the metadata. In addition, the demonstartor supplies an manual-annotation interface which can be used to annotate any image on the Web.

7 Distributed vs. Centralized Collection Data

The architecture is constructed to support multiple distributed image collections. Data (i.e. images) must have an external URI (we keep local copies, but that's only for caching). Ideally, we would like to get the original metadata also from external sources using standard protocols such as OAI[10]. In practice however, we encountered several problems with the quality of metadata retrieved via OAI, so for the moment we still depend on the local copy of the original metadata. Metadata extensions are also stored locally. In the future we hope to feed these back to the collection owners.

Vocabularies form a separate problem. The Getty vocabularies are licensed, so we cannot publish the full vocabulary as is. However, the information in the Getty vocabularies is freely accessible through the Getty online facilities[11]. We hope that these vocabularies will become publicly available. In the meantime, our demonstrator allows you to browse the vocabularies as a semantic structure and search for images semantically related to a vocabulary item (e.g. see Figure 2 for an example for the concept `Gold` from AAT). An RDF/OWL version of WordNet has recently been published (see above). We will move within the next months to this version (the same version as we are now using but with a different base URI).

8 Keyword Search with Semantic Clustering

One of the goals of the demonstrator is to provide users with a familiar and simple keyword search, but still allow the user to benefit from all background knowledge from the underlying thesauri and taxonomies. The underlying search algorithm consists of several steps, that can be summarized as follows. First, it checks all RDF literals in the repository for matches on the given keyword. Second, from each match, it traverses the RDF graph until a resource of interest is found, we refer to this as a *target resource*. Finally, based on the paths from the matching literals to their target resources, the results are clustered.

To improve performance in finding the RDF literals that form the starting points, the RDF database maintains a btree index of words appearing in literals to the full literal, as well as a Porter-stem and metaphone (sounds-like) index to words. Based on these indexes, the set of literals can be searched efficiently on any logical combination of word, prefix, by-stem and by-sound matches[12].

---

[10] http://www.openarchives.org/
[11] See e.g. http://www.getty.edu/research/conducting_research/vocabularies/aat/ for access to the AAT.
[12] See http://www.swi-prolog.org/packages/semweb.html#sec:3.8

In the second step, whichresources are considered of interest is currently determined by their type. The default settings return only resources of type artwork (`vra:Work`), but this can be overridden by the user. To avoid a combinatorial explosion of the search space, a number of measures had to be taken. Graph traversal is done in one direction only: always from the object in the triple to the corresponding subject. Only for properties with an explicit `owl:inverseOf` relation is the graph also traversed in the other direction. While this theoretically allows the algorithm to miss out many relevant results, in practice we found that this is hardly an issue. In addition to the direction, the search space is kept under control by setting a threshold. Starting with the score of the literal match, this score is multiplied by the weight assigned to the property being traversed (all properties have been assigned a (default) weight between 0 and 1), and the search stops when the score falls under the given threshold. This approach not only improves the efficiency of the search, it also allows filtering out results with paths that are too long (which tend to be semantically so far apart, that users do not consider them relevant anymore). By setting the weights to non-default values, the search can also be fine tuned to a particular application domain.

In the final step, all results are clustered based on the path between the matching literal and the target result. When the paths are considered on the instance level, this leads to many different clusters with similar content. We found that clustering the paths on the schema level provides more meaningful results. For example, searching on keyword "fauve" matches works from Fauve painters Matisse and Derain. On the instance level, this results in different paths:

```
dc:creator -> ulan:Derain   -> glink:hasStyle -> aat:fauve -> rdfs:label -> "Fauve"
dc:creator -> ulan:Matisse  -> glink:hasStyle -> aat:fauve -> rdfs:label -> "Fauve"
```

while on the schema level, this becomes a single path:

```
dc:creator -> ulan:Person -> glink:hasStyle -> aat:Concept -> rdfs:label -> "Fauve"
```

The paths are translated to English headers that mark the start of each cluster, and this already gives users an indication why the results match their keyword. The path given above results in the cluster title "Works created by an artist with matching AAT style". To explain the exact semantic relation between the result and the keyword searched on, the instance level path is displayed when hovering over a resulting image.

9 Vocabulary and Metadata Statistics

Table 1 shows the number of triples that are part of the vocabularies and metadata currently being used by the demonstrator. The table has three parts: (i) the schemas (e.g. the RDF/OWL schema for WordNet defining notions such as **SynSet**), (ii) the vocabulary entries and their relationships, and (iii) the collection metadata. In total, these constitute a triple set of roughly 9,000,000 triples. We plan to extend this continuously as more collections (and corresponding vocabularies) are being added.

Table 1. Number of triples for the different sources of vocabularies and collection metadata

Document	# Sources	# Triples
Schemas		
RDFS/OWL	2	358
Annotation	6	769
Vocabularies	9	1,225
Collections	1	29,889
Vocabularies		
TGN	4	425,517
ULAN	16	1,896,936
AAT	1	249,162
WordNet	18	2,579,206
Collections		
Artchive	4	74,414
Rijkmuseum	1	27,933
RVM	1	3,662,257

Acknowledgements. The E-Culture project is an application subproject within the context of the MultimediaN ("Multimedia Netherlands"[13]) project funded by the Dutch BSIK Programme.

References

1. Wielemaker, J., Schreiber, A.T., Wielinga, B.J.: Prolog-based infrastructure for rdf: performance and scalability. In Fensel, D., Sycara, K., Mylopoulos, J., eds.: The Semantic Web - Proceedings ISWC'03, Sanibel Island, Florida. Volume 2870 of Lecture Notes in Computer Science., Berlin/Heidelberg, Sringer Verlag (2003) 644–658 ISSN 0302-9743.
2. Wielemaker, J., Schreiber, G., Wielinga, B.: Using triples for implementation: the Triple20 ontology-manipulation tool. In Gil, Y., Motta, E., Benjamins, R., Musen, M., eds.: The Semantic Web – ISWC 2005: 4th International Semantic Web Conference, Galway, Ireland, November 6-10, 2005. Proceedings. Volume 3729 of Lecture Notes in Computer Science., Springer-Verlag (2005) 773–785
3. van Assem, M., Menken, M., Schreiber, G., Wielemaker, J., Wielinga, B.: A method for converting thesauri to RDF/OWL. In McLlraith, S.A., Plexousakis, D., van Harmelen, F., eds.: Proc. Third Inte. Semantic Web Conference ISWC 2004, Hiroshima, Japan. Volume 3298 of LNCS., Berlin/Heidelberg, Springer Verlag (2004) 17–31
4. van Assem, M., Gamgemi, A., Schreiber, G.: Conversion of wordnet to a standard rdf/owl representation. In: Proc. LREC 2006. (2006) Accepted for publication. http://www.cs.vu.nl/ guus/papers/Assem06a.pdf.
5. Miles, A., Baker, T., Swick, R.: Best practice recipes for publishing RDF vocabularies. Working draft, W3C (2006) http://www.w3.org/TR/2006/WD-swbp-vocab-pub-20060314/.
6. de Boer, V., van Someren, M., Wielinga, B.: Extracting instances of relations from web documents using redundancy. In: Proc. Third European Semantic Web Conference (ESWC'06), Budvar, Montenegro. (2006) Accepted for publication. http://staff.science.uva.nl/ vdeboer/publications/eswc06paper.pdf.
7. Visual Resources Association Standards Committee: VRA Core Categories, Version 3.0. Technical report, Visual Resources Association (2000) URL: http://www.vraweb.org/vracore3.htm.

---

[13] http://www.multimedian.nl

A Semantic Web Services GIS Based Emergency Management Application

Vlad Tanasescu[1], Alessio Gugliotta[1], John Domingue[1], Rob Davies[2],
Leticia Gutiérrez-Villarías[2], Mary Rowlatt[2], Marc Richardson[3], and Sandra Stinčić[3]

[1] Knowledge Media Institute, The Open University,
Walton Hall, Milton Keynes, MK7 6AA, UK
{v.tanasescu, a.gugliotta, j.b.domingue}@open.ac.uk
[2] Essex County Council, County Hall,
Chelmsford, CM1 1LX, UK
{Leticia.gutierrez, maryr}@essexcc.gov.uk,
rob.davies@mdrpartners.com
[3] BT Group
Adastral Park Martlesham, Ipswich IP5 3RE, UK
{marc.richardson, sandra.stincic}@bt.com

1 Introduction

In an emergency situation, relevant information about involved elements is required. This information ranges from demographic data, weather forecasts and sensor data, available transportation means, presence of helpful agents, land use and cover statistics or values, etc. Moreover, the emergency management process is dynamic as it involves several definite steps, described in standard procedures from which the Emergency Officer (EO) should not depart without good reason. Multiple agencies own the relevant data and possess parts of emergency related knowledge.

Exchanging this information by interacting on a personal/phone/fax basis is slow and may even be error prone. Using traditional Geographical Information Systems (GIS) to handle specifically Spatial-Related Data (SRD) is not always satisfactory, since data sources are not always suitable exposed and often present various semantics. In an emergency situation, such barriers are unacceptable and the whish of a more complete interoperability through the network is often expressed[1].

The proposed Emergency Management Application (EMA) is a decision support system based on Semantic Web Services (SWS) technology, which assists the EO in the tasks of retrieving, processing, displaying, and interacting with only emergency relevant information, more quickly and accurately. As a result, the involved agencies become able to extend their knowledge about the emergency situation by making use of different functionalities based on date held by other agencies which otherwise might not be accessible to them or slow to obtain manually.

Our work represents a practical e-Government application, where the stakeholders are the governmental agencies, and the end-users are governmental employees. The application has been designed for the Emergency Planning Department of the Essex County Council (ECC) – a large local authority in UK, but can be adopted by other public authorities and rescue corps dealing with emergency response situations.

---

[1] e.g. http://www.technewsworld.com/story/33927.html

2   Design Choices and Development Methodology

Any information system can gain advantage from the use of semantics [4]. In GIS, the use of semantic layers, although not yet firmly established, is being investigated in a number of research studies [1], [2], [3]. Having ontologies describing a SRD repository and its functionalities is believed to make cooperation with other systems easier and to better match user needs. In particular, SWS technology may provide an infrastructure in which new services can be added, discovered and composed continually, by combining the flexibility, reusability, and universal access that typically characterize a Web Service, with the expressivity of semantic markup and reasoning. This will allow the automatic invocation, composition, mediation, and execution of complex services with multiple paths of execution, and levels of process nesting. In order to provide semantic and step toward the creation of added value services, we adopt WSMO[2] – a promising SWS framework – and IRS-III [5] – a tested implementation of this standard. The reference language for creating ontologies is OCML [6].

Our development process firstly enables the data and functionalities provided by existing legacy systems to be exposed as Web Services (WS). Then, the latter are semantically annotated and published using IRS-III SWS infrastructure. The following layered architecture of the application reflects and explains this double stage process:

- *Legacy System layer:* consists of existing data sources and IT systems provided by each of the involved governmental parties.
- *Service Abstraction layer:* exposes the functionalities of the legacy systems as WS, abstracting from the hardware and software platforms of the legacy systems. Whenever a new service is available at this layer, it will be semantically described and properly linked to existing semantic descriptions.
- *Semantic Web Service layer*: given a goal request this layer, implemented in IRS-III, will (i) discover a candidate set of Web services, (ii) select the most appropriate, (iii) mediate any mismatches at the data, ontological or business process level, and (iv) invoke the selected Web services whilst adhering to any data, control flow and Web service invocation requirements. To achieve this, IRS-III utilises the set of WSMO descriptions, which are composed of goals, mediators, and Web services, supported by relevant domain ontologies. This layer provides the flexibility and scalability of our application. Managing the semantic description, the semantic developer can introduce new functionalities of the application (e.g. new EO goals that can be invoked by the user interface) or updating existing ones.
- *Presentation layer:* is a Web application accessible through a standard Web browser. The goals defined within the previous layer are reflected in the structure of the interface and can be invoked either through the IRS-III API or as an HTTP request. The goal requests are filled with data provided by the user and sent to the Semantic Web Service layer.

In our approach, we aimed to obtain a development process that might be *pragmatic* - in order to quickly lead to a working outcome – as well as *flexible* - in order to easily respond to eventually changes/improvements and meet the multiple

---

[2] http://www.wsmo.org/2004/d2/v1.0/

actors' viewpoints. For these reasons, we followed a prototyping approach composed of the following three straightforward phases: *Requirements capture*, *SWS description*, and *Evaluation*. The last phase triggers the prototyping iterations of the SWS description phase on the basis of involved actors' feedback. At this stage, the application has been shown to the Planning Department Officers and other people dealing with emergency situations in the ECC area (e.g. officers of the London Stansted Airport). Future improvements and changes have been mainly planned on the basis of their feedback, such as accessing to traffic cameras in the affected area.

3 The Emergency Management Application

Following several interviews with SRD holders in ECC, it was decided to focus the application on a real past emergency situation: a snowstorm which affected the M11 motorway on 31st January 2003[3]. To present the application, we follow the layered architecture introduced in the previous section.

Legacy System Layer. The EMA aggregates data and functionalities from three structurally independent and heterogeneous, real world sources:

- *Meteorological Office*: a national UK organization which provides environmental resources and in particular weather forecast data.
- *ViewEssex*: a collaboration between ECC and British Telecommunications (BT) which has created a single corporate spatial data warehouse. As can be expected ViewEssex contains a wide range of data including data for roads, administrative boundaries, buildings, and Ordnance survey maps, as well as environmental and social care data. Within the application we used building related data to support searches for suitable rest centres.
- *BuddySpace* is an Instant Messaging client facilitating lightweight communication, collaboration, and presence management [7] built on top of the instant messaging protocol Jabber[4]. The BuddySpace client can be accessed on standard PCs, as well as on PDAs and on mobile phones which in an emergency situation may be the only hardware device available.

Service Abstraction Layer. We distinguish between two classes of services: *data* and *smart*. The former refers to the three data sources introduced above, and are exposed by means of WS:

- *Meteorological service:* this service provides weather information (e.g. snowfall) over a specific rectangular spatial area.
- *ECC Emergency Planning services*: using the ViewEssex data each service in this set returns detailed information on a specific type of rest centre within a given circular area. For example, the *'getHospitals'* Web service returns a list of relevant hospitals.
- *BuddySpace services*: these services allow presence information on online users to be accessed.

---

[3] BBC news web site: http://news.bbc.co.uk/2/hi/talking_point/2711291.stm
[4] Jabber. http://www.jabber.org/

Smart services represent specific emergency planning reasoning and operations on the data provided by the data services. They are implemented in a mixture of Common Lisp and OCML and make use of the EMA ontologies. In particular, we created a number of filter services that manipulate GIS data according to emergency-specific requirements semantically described (e.g. rest centres with heating system, hotels with at least 40 beds, easier accessible hospital, etc.). The criteria used were gained from our discussions with the EOs.

Domain Ontologies for the Semantic Web Service Layer. The following ontologies reflecting the client and provider domains were developed to support WSMO descriptions:

- *Meteorology, Emergency Planning and Jabber Domain Ontology*: representing the concepts used to describe the services attached to the data sources, such as *snow* and *rain* for Met Office, *hospitals* and *supermarkets* for ECC Emergency Planning, *session* and *presences* for Jabber. If a new source and the Web services exposing its data and functionalities are integrated, a new domain ontology has to be introduced[5]. The services, composed of the data types involved as well as its interface, have to be described in such a ontology usually at a level low enough to remain close from the data.

To get the information provided by web services up to the semantic level, we introduce *lifting operations* that allows the passage of data types instances from a syntactic level (xml) to an ontological one (OCML) specified in the domain ontology definitions. We found that this process can be automated every time the domain ontology one can be.

- *HCI Ontology*: part of the user layer, this ontology is composed of HCI and user-oriented concepts. It allows to lower from the semantic level results for the particular interface which is used (e.g. stating that Google Maps API is used, defining "pretty names" for ontology elements, etc.). Note that although the choice of the resulting syntactic format depends of the chosen lowering process, concepts from the HCI ontology are used in order to achieve this transformation in a suitable way.
- *Archetypes Ontology*: part of the user layer, this is a minimal ontological commitment ontology aiming to provide a cognitively meaningful insight into the nature of a specialized object; for example, by conveying the cognitive ("naïve") feeling that for example an hospital, as a "container" of people and provider of "shelter" can be assimilated to the more universal concept of "house", which we consider to be as an *archetypal* concept, i.e. based on image schemata and therefore supposed to convey meaning immediately. It is moreover assumed that any client, whilst maybe lacking the specific representation for a specific basic level concept, knows its archetypal representation.
- *Spatial Ontology*: a part of the mediation layer, it describes GIS concepts of location, such as coordinates, points, polygonal areas, and fields. It also allows describing spatial objects as entities with a set of attributes, and a location.

---

[5] Here existing ontologies can be reused.

The purpose of the HCI, Archetypes and Spatial ontologies is the aggregation of different data sources on, respectively, a representation, a cognitive and a spatial level. Therefore we can group them under the appellation *aggregation* ontologies. They allow the different data sources to be handled and presented in a similar way. Inversely to the lifting operations, *lowering operations* transform instances of aggregation ontologies into syntactic documents to be used by the server and client applications. This step is usually fully automated since aggregation ontologies are, by definition, quite stable and unique.

- *Context Ontology*: the context ontology allows describing *context n-uples* which represent a particular situation. In the emergency planning application, context n-uples have up to four components, the use case, the user role, the location, and the type of object. Contexts are linked with goals, i.e. if this type of user accesses this type of object around this particular location, these particular goals will be presented. Contexts also help to inform goals, e.g. if a goal provides information about petrol stations in an area, the location part of the context is used to define this area, and input from the user is therefore not needed. Each time an object is displayed by a user at a particular location, a function of the context ontology provides the goals which need to be displayed and what inputs are implicit.

WSMO descriptions for the Semantic Web Service Layer. As introduced in the previous section, the goals, mediators, and Web services descriptions of our application link the Met Office, ECC Emergency Planning, and BuddySpace Web services to the user interface. Correspondingly, the Web service goal descriptions use the SGIS spatial, meteorology, ECC Emergency Planning and Jabber domain ontologies whilst the goal encodings rely on the HCI and archetypes ontologies. Mismatches are resolved by the defined mediators.

A small portion of emergency management process (workflow) represented in terms of SWS descriptions is shown in Figure 1. *Get-Polygon-GIS-data-with-Filter-Goal* represents a request for available shelters within a delimited area. The user specifies the requirements as a target area, a sequence of at least three points (a polygon), and a shelter type (e.g. hospitals, inns, hotels). As mentioned above the set of ECC Emergency Planning Web services each return potential shelters of a specific type with a circular query area. The obtained results need to be filtered in order to return only shelters correlated to emergency-specific requirements (for example a snowstorm). From a SWS point of view the problems to be solved by this particular portion of the SWS layer included: (i) *discovering* the appropriate ECC Emergency Planning Web service; (ii) *meditating* the difference in area representations (polygon vs. circular) between the goal and Web services; (iii) *composing* the retrieve and filter data operations. Below we outline how the WSMO representations in Figure 1 address these problems.

- *Web service discovery:* each SWS description of a ECC Emergency Planning service defines, in its capability, the specific class of shelter that the service provides. Each definition is linked to the *Get-Circle-GIS-Data-Goal* by means of a unique WG-mediator (shown as wgM). The inputs of the goal specify the class of shelter, and the circular query area. At invocation IRS-III discovers through the WG-mediator all associated Web services, and selects one on the basis of the specific class of shelter described in the Web service capability.

- *Area mediation and orchestration*: the *Get-Polygon-GIS-data-with-Filter-Goal* is associated with a unique Web service that orchestrates, by simply invoking three sub-goals in sequence. The first gets the list of polygon points from the input; the second is *Get-Circle-GIS-Data-Goal* described above; finally, the third invokes the smart service that filters the list of GIS data. The first two sub-goals are linked by means of three GG-mediators (depicted as ggM) that return the centre, as a latitude and longitude, and radius of the smallest circle which circumscribes the given polygon. To accomplish this, we created three mediation services invoked through: *Polygon-to-Circle-Lat-Goal*, *Polygon-to-Circle-Lon-Goal*, and *Polygon-to-Circle-Rad-Goal* (the related WG-mediator and Web service ovals were omitted to avoid cluttering the diagram). The results of the mediation services and the class of shelter required are provided as inputs to the second sub-goal. A unique GG-mediator connects the output of the second to the input of the third sub-goal. In this instance no mediation service is necessary.

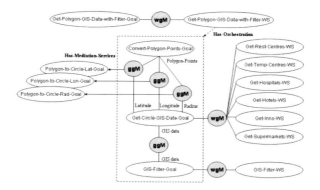

Fig. 1. A portion of the WSMO descriptions for the EMS application

It is important to note that if new WS – for instance providing further SRD from other GIS are available, new Web Service descriptions will be simply introduced, and linked to the *Get-Circle-GIS-Goal* by the proper mediators (even reusing the existing ones, if semantic mismatches do not exist), without affecting the existing structure. In the same way, new GIS filter services (e.g. more efficient ones) may be introduced. The effective workflow – i.e. which services are invoked – is known at run-time only.

Presentation Layer. The application user interface is based on Web standards. XHTML and CSS are used for presentation and JavaScript is used to handle user interaction together with AJAX techniques to communicate with IRS-III. One of the main components of the interface is a map, which uses the Google Maps API to display polygons and objects (custom images) at specific coordinates and zoom level. Goals and attributes are attached to such objects; they are displayed in a pop up window or in a hovering transparent region above the main interface.

Although easy to extend, the actual prototype handles only snow storms and hazards emergency types in the context of the Essex County, according to our real past reference scenario. When the application is launched, a goal is invoked for the

Essex region, and snow hazard or storm polygons are drawn according to data from the meteorological office. The value from which snow values can constitute a hazard or a storm are heuristic and as emergency knowledge is gathered it can easily improved, by modifying the smart services which are composed with weather information, while the goal visible to the user remains the same.

As an example of practical usage, we describe how an EO describes and emergency situation, before trying to contact relevant agents. The procedure is as follows:

1. The EO clicks within the displayed hazard region to bring up a menu of available goals. In this case (Figure 2a) three goals are available: show available shelters, login to BuddySpace and get the presence information for related staff.
2. The EO asks for the available Rest Centres inside the region, and then inspects the detailed attributes for the Rest Centre returned (Figure 2b).
3. The EO requests to see the presence status for all staff within the region and then initiates an online discussion the closest online agency worker (Figure 2c).

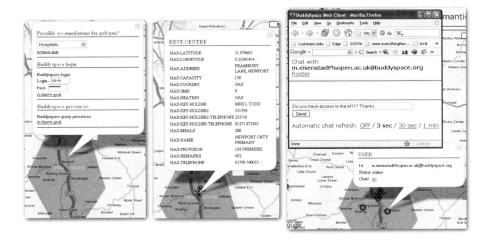

Fig. 2. Showing three screenshots of our application in use

To a comprehensive description of the operations provided to the user, please refer to our on-line screencast tutorial and live demo[6].

4 Lesson Learned

In our approach, the integration of new data sources results relatively simple; the steps involved in the process of adding new data sources can be summarized as follow: ontological description of the service; lifting operations definition; mapping to aggregation ontologies; goal description; mediation description; lowering definition;

---

[6] http://irs-test.open.ac.uk/sgis-dev/

and context linking. Although this procedure may seem tedious, and can actually only be performed by a knowledge expert, it presents many advantages compared to standard based approaches as the one demonstrated in the OWS-3 Initiative[7]:

- *Framework openness*: standards are helpful but not necessary. For example, if querying sensor data, the use of standards – e.g. SensorML[8] – helps the reuse of service ontologies and lifting procedures since they can be applied to any service using a similar schema. However any other schema can be integrated with the same results.
- *High level services support*: since services are described as SWS, they inherit all benefits of the underlying SWS execution platform, such as discovery and composition, and are updated as more features are added to the platform (e.g. trust based invocation). In other solutions support for composition and discovery is imbedded in syntactic standards themselves, which implies specific parsing features and adding ad hoc reasoning capabilities to standard software applications, which is time consuming and error prone. Moreover, SWS introduce a minimalist approach in the description of a domain, by modeling the concepts used by Web Services only, and allowing on-the-fly creation of instances when Web Services are invoked (lifting).
- *Support of the Emergency Handling Process*: also, the constant use of context to link goals and situations greatly enhances the decision process. Indeed, actions are oriented depending on the use case, the object, user role and location. With the help of explanations of the utility of each goal in each context, the Emergency Officer's task is greatly simplified. A future development of the context ontology will include feedback from goal invocation history, and allow workflow definitions, i.e. this goal only appears after these two have been invoked. Note that all goals are also accessible independently of any context which allows non directed queries to occur, if needed.

References

1. Casati, R., Smith, B., Varzi, A. C.: Ontological tools for geographic representation. (1998) 77–85.
2. Peuquet, D., Smith, B., Brogaard B.: The ontology of fields. (1999).
3. Fonseca, F. T., Egenhofer, M. J.: Ontology-Driven Geographic Information Systems. ACM-GIS (1999) 14-19.
4. Semantic Interoperability Community of Practice (SICoP). Introducing Semantic Technologies and the Vision of the Semantic Web. (2005).
5. Cabral, L., Domingue, J., Galizia, S., Gugliotta, A., Norton, B., Tanasescu, V., Pedrinaci, C.: IRS-III: A Broker for Semantic Web Services based Applications. In proceedings of the 5th International Semantic Web Conference (ISWC 2006), Athens, USA (2006).
6. Motta, E.: An Overview of the OCML Modelling Language. (1998).
7. Eisenstadt, M., Komzak, J., Dzbor, M.: Instant messaging+maps = powerful collaboration tools for distance learning. In proceedings of TelEduc03, Havana, Cuba (2003).

---

[7] http://www.opengeospatial.org/initiatives/?iid=162
[8] http://vast.nsstc.uah.edu/SensorML/

Package-Based Description Logics - Preliminary Results

Jie Bao[1], Doina Caragea[2], and Vasant G. Honavar[1]

[1] Artificial Intelligence Research Laboratory, Department of Computer Science,
Iowa State University, Ames, IA 50011-1040, USA
{baojie, honavar}@cs.iastate.edu
[2] Department of Computing and Information Sciences
Kansas State University, Manhattan, KS 66506, USA
dcaragea@ksu.edu

Many representative applications on the semantic web, including collaborative ontology building, partial ontology reuse, selective knowledge hiding and distributed data management, call for modular ontologies,. However, although OWL allows using `owl:imports` to connect multiple ontologies, its current semantics requires all involved ontologies to have a single global semantics, thus providing only a syntactical solution to modularity. As a result, there is a growing interest in modular ontology languages such as Distributed Description Logics (DDL) [7] and $\mathcal{E}$-connections [8]. However, these proposals are also limited in expressivity and reasoning soundness [2,3].

Package-based Description Logics (P-DL) [4] is aimed at solving several problems presented in existing approaches, by offering a tradeoff between the strong *module disjointness* assumption of DDL and $\mathcal{E}$-connections, and the *complete overlapping* of models required by the OWL importing mechanics. P-DL language features are aimed at providing fine-grained modular organization and controllable selective knowledge sharing of an ontology.

P-DL syntax adopts a selective "importing" approach that allows a subset of terms defined in one ontology module to be directly used in another module. In a P-DL ontology, an ontology is composed of a set of packages. A package can use terms defined other packages i.e., an existing package or some of the terms defined in an existing package can be *imported* into another package. Foreign terms can be used to construct local concepts.

P-DL also allows selective knowledge hiding in ontology modules to address the needs of privacy, copyright, security concerns in ontologies. P-DL supports *scope limitation modifiers* (SLM) that can be associated with terms and axioms defined in a package [4]. A SLM (such as *public* and *private*) controls the visibility of the corresponding term or axiom to entities (e.g. a user, a reasoner) on the web, in particular, to other packages. Different from the encryption of ontology which is aimed at safe access of ontologies on a *syntactic* level, SLM in P-DL aims at knowledge hiding on a *semantic* level, where the hiding is *partial*, i.e., hidden parts of an ontology can be used in *safe* indirect inferences [5].

The semantic importing approach adopted by P-DL is different from the "linking" approach adopted by DDL and $\mathcal{E}$-Connections in that it partially relaxes the local model disjointness assumption of the other two formalisms. Such a relaxation enables P-DL to obtain stronger expressivity power. Concept bridge rules in DDL and $\mathcal{E}$-Connection links can be easily reduced to P-DL axioms [3]. P-DL also offers the possibility of avoiding semantic difficulties of DDL and $\mathcal{E}$-Connections. For example, knowledge in one P-DL package can be transitively reused by other packages. The answer to a P-DL reasoning problem is the same as that obtained by reasoning over the integrated ontology [3].

The reasoning procedure for P-DL can be extended from existing DL tableau algorithms [1]. We adopt a tableau-based federated reasoning approach to strictly avoid reasoning with an integrated ontology, thus ensure the autonomy of constituting modules. The whole reasoning process is preformed by a federation of local reasoners, each for a specific package, to construct a collection of local tableaux instead of a single global tableau. The connection between local tableaux is enabled by a set of messages and a local tableau may share nodes with other local tableaux. It is shown that this approach can solve many reasoning difficulties presented in existing approaches [1].

P-DL provides language features needed for efficient *collaborative* construction of large, modular ontologies. We have developed COB-Editor [6] that provides 'proof of concept' of this approach. COB-Editor is a modular ontology editor that enables building biological ontologies such as Gene Ontology. The editor allows ontology developers to create a community-shared ontology server, with the support for concurrent browsing and editing of the ontology. Multiple users can work on the same ontology on different packages (through locking mechanisms), without inadvertent overwriting the work of others.

Work in progress includes reasoning for more expressive P-DL languages and with knowledge hiding, and improved collaborative ontology building tools.

Acknowledgement. This research is supported by grants from US NSF (0219699, 0639230) and NIH (GM066387).

References

1. J. Bao, D. Caragea, and V. Honavar. A distributed tableau algorithm for package-based description logics. In *the 2nd International Workshop On Context Representation And Reasoning (CRR 2006), co-located with ECAI 2006*. 2006.
2. J. Bao, D. Caragea, and V. Honavar. Modular ontologies - a formal investigation of semantics and expressivity. In *R. Mizoguchi, Z. Shi, and F. Giunchiglia (Eds.): Asian Semantic Web Conference 2006, LNCS 4185*, pages 616–631, 2006.
3. J. Bao, D. Caragea, and V. Honavar. On the semantics of linking and importing in modular ontologies. In *accepted by ISWC 2006 (In Press)*. 2006.
4. J. Bao, D. Caragea, and V. Honavar. Towards collaborative environments for ontology construction and sharing. In *International Symposium on Collaborative Technologies and Systems (CTS 2006)*, pages 99–108. IEEE Press, 2006.
5. J. Bao and V. Honavar. Representing and reasoning with modular ontologies. In *AAAI Fall Symposium on Semantic Web for Collaborative Knowledge Acquisition (SWeCKa 2006), Arlington, VA, USA, October 2006*, 2006.

6. J. Bao, Z. Hu, D. Caragea, J. Reecy, and V. Honavar. Developing frameworks and tools for collaborative building of large biological ontologies. In *the 4th International Workshop on Biological Data Management (BIDM'06), @ DEXA'06*. 2006.
7. A. Borgida and L. Serafini. Distributed description logics: Directed domain correspondences in federated information sources. In *CoopIS*, pages 36–53, 2002.
8. B. C. Grau. *Combination and Integration of Ontologies on the Semantic Web*. PhD thesis, Dpto. de Informatica, Universitat de Valencia, Spain, 2005.

Distributed Policy Management in Semantic Web

Özgü Can and Murat Osman Ünalır

Department of Computer Engineering, Ege University,
35100 Bornova, İzmir, Turkey
{ozgu.can, murat.osman.unalir}@ege.edu.tr

Abstract. With the growth of Internet and the fast development of semantic web technologies, the access and usage of information will become much more easier. However, the security of information gathering for both information suppliers and demanders is a critical issue. Policies determine the ideal behaviors for web concepts. The concepts of policy, policy languages and policy ontologies must be determined, effective tools for policy definition and management must be developed.

1 Introduction

In the web environment some concepts are very important: which resources can users or the services access *(security)*, how will the user information going to be used *(privacy)* and if these users are trusted or not *(trust)*. Policies specify who can use a service and under which conditions, how information should be provided to the service, and how the provided information will be used [1]. Two main components exist to secure the semantic web: a policy language which defines security requirements and distributed policy management approach [2]. A security framework based on distributed policy management can be developed with using a semantic policy language.

In the literature, there are various policy ontology and policy language projects. The most popular ones are KAoS[1], Rei[2] and Ponder[3] policy languages, and a framework, Rein[4], which uses the Rei policy language concepts for policies.

2 Research Approach

In our work, we are going to examine existing policy ontologies, KAoS, Rei and Ponder, then we will determine the requirements of policy ontologies and the missing points of the existing policy ontologies. Through these requirements we will constitute a new policy ontology. Our aim is to create an effective new policy ontology which overcomes the missing points of the existing policies and answers the

---

[1] http://ontology.ihmc.us/kaos.html
[2] http://rei.umbc.edu/
[3] http://www-dse.doc.ic.ac.uk/Research/policies/ponder.shtml
[4] http://groups.csail.mit.edu/dig/2005/05/rein/

user's requests in a better manner. Authorizations and obligations are the policy concepts in KAoS; rights, prohibitions, obligations and dispensations are Rei policy language concepts and Ponder has authorizations, obligations, refrains and delegations. In the policy ontology we will have *rights*, *prohibitions*, *obligations*, *dispensations* and *speech acts: delegate, revoke, cancel* and *request* .

One of the existing works is a plug-in application, POLICYTAB [3], which is compatible with Protégé. In this thesis, we want to develop an OWL based plug-in for Protégé Ontology Editor to define policy specifications. Policy rules will be expressed by using Semantic Web Rule Language (SWRL). We will also develop a policy engine to interpret and reason over policies.

There are three policy approaches: rule-based, ontology-based and hybrid [4]. We are going to use hybrid approach in our work. Hybrid approach is based on both rule-based and ontology-based approaches. We will also focus on policy conflicts and policy validation.

Our ontology will be developed with OWL ontology language on Protégé ontology editor. We will use SWRL for rules, RACER reasoning engine, OWL-QL for queries and Java.

3 Conclusions and Future Work

Our prerequisite work is to create our policy ontology and to work on a resource sharing scenario where policies can be applied. Our scenario is based on our university's academic rules and regulations. Now we are constituting our ontology concepts. After that we are going to create our ontology by using Rei. We also want to develop our policy engine and effective mechanisms to solve policy conflicts. Finally we will work on policy validation methods.

References

1. L. Kagal, T. Finin, M. Paolucci, N. Srinivasen, K. Sycara, G. Denker: Authorization and Privacy for Semantic Web Services. IEEE Intelligent Systems, Vol. 19 (2004) 50-56
2. L. Kagal, T. Finin, A. Joshi: A Policy Based Approach to Security for the Semantic Web. 2nd International Semantic Web Conference (ISWC 2003), Sanibal Island, Florida, USA (2003) 402-418
3. W. Nejdl, D. Olmedilla, M. Winslett, C. C. Zhang; Ontology-based Policy Specification and Management. European Semantic Web Conference (ESWC 2005), Heraklion, Greece (2005)
4. A. Toninelli, J. M. Bradshaw, L. Kagal, R. Montanari; Rule-based and Ontology-based Policies: Toward a Hybrid Approach to Control Agents in Pervasive Environments. 4th International Semantic Web Conference, Proceedings of the Semantic Web and Policy Workshop, Galway, Ireland (2005)

Evaluation of SPARQL Queries Using Relational Databases *

Jiří Dokulil

Department of Software Engineering,
Faculty of Mathematics and Physics,
Charles University in Prague, Czech Republic
Jiri.Dokulil@mff.cuni.cz

Abstract. Basic storage and querying of RDF data using a relational database can be done in a very simple manner. Such approach can run into trouble when used on large and complex data. This paper presents such data and several sample queries together with analysis of their performance. It also describes two possible ways of improving the performance based on this analysis.

1 Introduction

The RDF [2] is a key part of the Semantic Web. It defines the format and semantics of such data but does not provide query capabilities. Several query languages have been created or modified to support RDF querying. One of the languages is SPARQL [5]. We have created an experimental implementation of SPARQL.

We used a straightforward way of storing RDF data in a relational database. This allowed us to evaluate SPARQL queries by translating them to SQL queries. Although it worked nicely for small or simple RDF data, we suspected that evaluation times may turn bad with large and complex data. We have been able to obtain such data [4].

2 Experiments, RDF Indexes and Statistics

The data is complex. The RDFS schema consists of 226 classes and 1898 properties and contains 26 million tripes.

Simple test queries showed that no SPARQL feature creates a bottleneck of the system. But when the features were combined in complex queries the performance decreased greatly. After examining the execution plans of the queries, we came up with a possible explanation for this undesirable behavior. The SQL optimizer makes wrong assumptions about the size of the intermediate data produced during the evaluation of the query.

---

* This research was supported in part by the National programme of research (Information society project 1ET100300419).

Major weakness of our system is the fact that for every triple used in the query one table join is added to the result SQL query. This means that a more complex SPARQL query is evaluated using many joins that are usually expensive because large sets are being joined.

We designed a so called *RDF indexes* to overcome this problem. An RDF index is a pre-evaluated SPARQL query and the result of the evaluation is stored inside the database to speed up evaluation of similar queries. Experiments have shown that the RDF indexes improve the performance of the query evaluation.

The Oracle database contains a general way of collecting statistics about the data they contain. But the RDF data have several characteristics that can be used to gather more precise statistics. For instance the system can store precise number of triples for each predicate. This information could be used to help the optimizer build better execution plans via Oracle SQL hints. We plan to implement this function in the future.

3 Conclusion

Large and complex RDF data are not yet widely available. Although large data such as WordNet or DBLP libraries are available [6], their structure is simple. WordNet is commonly used to test performance of RDF databases, for instance in [3]. We feel that the real data of the Semantic Web will be more complex.

The complex data we used in out tests helped us develop two methods of improving the query performance. The methods are in very early stage of development and should be compared to other systems like Sesame [1]. We used much more complex data and encountered problems that would not show up if tests were run on simple data even if the data was very large. This led us to development of two methods of fighting the problems. We implemented one of the methods and measurements confirmed that it has the desired impact on query evaluation performance.

References

1. Broekstra J., Kampman A., Harmelen F. (2002): *Sesame: A Generic Architecture for Storing and Querying RDF and RDF Schema*, in Proceedings of the First International Semantic Web Conference, Italy, 2002, 54-68
2. Carroll J. J., Klyne G. (2004): *Resource Description Framework: Concepts and Abstract Syntax*, W3C Recommendation, 10 February 2004
3. Chong E. I., Das S., Eadon G., Srinivasan J. (2005): *An Efficient SQL-based RDF Querying Scheme*, in Proc. of the 31st International Conference on Very Large Data Bases, Trondheim, Norway, August 30 - September 2, 2005, 1216-1227
4. Dokulil J. (2006): *Transforming Data from DataPile Structure into RDF*, in Proceedings of the Dateso 2006 Workshop, Desna, Czech Republic, 2006, 54-62 http://sunsite.informatik.rwth-aachen.de/Publications/CEUR-WS//Vol-176/paper8.pdf
5. Prud'hommeaux E., Seaborne A. (2005): SPARQL Query Language for RDF, W3C Working Draft, 23 November 2005
6. http://www.semanticweb.org/library/

Dynamic Contextual Regulations in Open Multi-agent Systems

Carolina Howard Felicíssimo

DI – PUC-RIO, Rua Marquês de São Vicente 225, Gávea, RJ, Brazil
cfelicissimo@inf.puc-rio.br

1 Introduction

Following software engineering approaches for the Semantic Web (SW) and also Hendler's vision [3], I believe that the SW will not be a unique large complex Web, but it will be composed, mainly, of several small contextualized domain applications. These domain applications will be, in my opinion, Multi-Agent Systems (MAS) [5]. MAS have emerged as a promising approach for the development of information systems, which are constituted of cooperative goal-oriented problem-solving entities (named agents) [6]. Agent-based computing is rapidly emerging as a powerful technology for the development of distributed and complex information systems.

Information systems for a very dynamic, open and distributed domain (like the SW one) are always subject to unanticipated events [4] caused by their members that may not be compliant with to recommendations of correct behaviors. This risk imposes the necessity for regulatory mechanisms to prevent undesirable actions to happen and to inspire trust to its members. However, in open domains, no centralized control is feasible. Key characteristics of such domains are: agent heterogeneity, conflicting individual goals and limited trust [1]. Heterogeneity and autonomy rule out any assumption concerning the way agents are constructed and behave. So, an external control, dynamically created or modified, and not hard coded into agent implementations, may be the only viable solution for regulations in open systems [2].

2 Contextual Regulations in Open MAS with DynaCROM

My Ph.D. proposal is a novel regulatory approach for dynamic contextual regulations in open multi-agent systems, called DynaCROM. Toward dynamic compositions of contextual laws, from four levels of abstractions (Environment, Organization, Role and Interaction), I propose to easily oversee agent actions. Thus, cooperation among agents, playing the same or different roles, from the same or different organizations and environments, is enhanced with a confidence layer of laws.

DynaCROM is based on top-down modeling of contextual laws, on a normative meta-ontology for law semantics and on a rule support for composing and inferring contextual laws. Developers aiming to use DynaCROM, should perform the following steps: classify and organize user defined laws according to its top-down modeling; explicitly represent these laws into an instance of the DynaCROM meta-ontology; and define compositions of contextual laws by activating and deactivating rules. In DynaCROM, an ontology instance represents the regulatory contexts (expressed by related concepts in the ontology structure) and also represents the user defined environment, organization, role and interaction laws (expressed by instances in the ontology data). Contextual laws are automatically composed and deduced by a rule-based inference engine, according to the ontology instance and active rules.

The main asset of organizing laws into regulatory contexts, from different levels of abstractions, and use rules and a rule-based inference engine is to permit flexibility while enforcing laws. Doing so, system regulations can be dynamically relaxed or restricted by simply changing sets of rules for new compositions of contextual laws. DynaCROM rules are *ontology-based*, i.e. they are created according to the ontology structure by only linking related concepts. Consequently, the numbers of rules and possible customized compositions of contextual law, for each regulatory context, are finite. For instance, 349 customized compositions of environment, organization, role and interaction laws are achieved with 19 rules (1 rule for the environment context, 5 for the organization context, 6 for the role context and 7 for the interaction context). All these rules are provided by the DynaCROM implementation, which is summarized as a JADE behavior [7]. Agents enhanced with the DynaCROM behavior are aware of the system regulation and, so, can take more precise decisions.

3 Conclusion

In this paper, I present DynaCROM – a straightforward method to, smoothly, apply and manage regulatory dynamics in open applications (like the SW ones). For future work, I am currently studying four main research lines: context-aware systems; action ontologies; simulations of regulated open MAS; and libraries of agent behaviors. The idea is to explore, independently, each of these research lines and to enhance DynaCROM, if good results appear. My Ph.D. research aims to contribute to the fields of regulation and cooperation in open MAS, enabling their agent societies. Thus, I believe that the SW represents a perfect scenario.

References

1. Artikis, A.; Pitt, J. and Sergot, M. *Animated specifications of computational societies*. In Proc. of AAMAS-2002, Part III, p. 1053-1061, Italy.
2. Grizard, A.; Vercouter, L.; Stratulat, T. and Muller, G.; *A peer-to-peer normative system to achieve social order*. In Proc. of COIN@AAMAS-2006, Japan.
3. Hendler, J.; *Agents and the Semantic Web*. In IEEE Intelligent Systems & their applications. 2001.16(2)30-37.
4. Hewitt, C.; *Open Information Systems Semantics for Distributed Artificial Intelligence*. AI. V.47, I.1-3, p.79-106. 1991. ISSN: 0004-3702.
5. Huhns, M. and Stephens, L.; *Multi-Agent Systems and Societies of Agents*. G. Weiss (ed.), Multi-Agent Systems, ISBN 0-262-23203-0, MIT Press. 1999.
6. Jennings, N.; Sycara, K. and Wooldridge, M.; *A Roadmap of Agent Research and Development*. Journal of Agents and Multi-Agent Systems, 1:p.7-38, 1998.
7. Tilab Company. (2006) JADE. In: <http://jade.tilab.com/>.

From Typed-Functional Semantic Web Services to Proofs

Harry Halpin

School of Informatics
University of Edinburgh
2 Buccleuch Place
EH8 9LW Edinburgh
Scotland, UK
H.Halpin@ed.ac.uk

Keywords: Semantic Web Services, Proofs, Type Theory, Functional Programming, Curry-Howard Isomorphism.

1 Ontologies, Types, and Functions

Web standards are currently seen as increasingly fragmented between colloquial XML, the Semantic Web, and Web Services. Semantic Web Services, while an immensely productive area of research, has yet to reach in-roads and a large user-base. We propose a minimalist, yet powerful, unifying framework built upon solid computational and philosophical foundations: Web Services are *functions*, ontologies are *types*, and therefore Semantic Web Services are *typed functions*.

Unlike OWL-S and WSMO that focus on automatic omposition, we focus on users will want to manually create their service compositions using an actual programming language, like WS-BPEL provides (Business Process Execution Language, formerly BPEL4WS). However, WS-BPEL is a vast, sprawling imperative language that is difficult to analyze, much less prove anything about. The W3C appears increasingly ready to endorse an approach (SAWSDL) based on annotating input and outputs with RDF. What is needed is a minimal programming language, with a straightforward formal semantics, that builds upon SAWSDL and goes beyond workflows. Workflow tools are notoriously limited to finite state automata so that while termination on the workflow level is guaranteed, they lack common constructs like iteration and recursion. In previous work, we suggest that XML pipeline processing can be thought of as being "inside" an XML document itself. The processing can be contained in a special namespace that can then be mixed in arbitrary XML content. Using this syntax, an example is given below in Figure 1.

2 The Curry Howard Isomorphism

While there has been extensive work using XML types, it makes sense to use RDF as a typing regime since it allows both subtyping and propositions to be stated about types. The Curry-Howard Isomorphism states that there is a tight

```
<fx:let xmlns:fx="http://www.ltg.ed.ac.uk/~ht/functionalXML">
  <fx:bind name="myvariable">
    <fx:include href="document.xml"/>
  </fx:bind>
  <fx:cond>
    <fx:case test="$myvariable/document[@version = 1.0]">
      <fx:transform stylesheet="http://www.example.com/xhtmlout.xsl">
        <fx:decrypt>
          <fx:include href="$myvariable"/>
        </fx:decrypt>
      </fx:transform>
    </fx:case>
  </fx:cond>
</fx:let>
```

Fig. 1. FunctionalXML

coupling between logics and type systems, and can be given the slogan "Proofs are Programs." It was originally formulated as a correspondence between the typed lambda calculus and intuitionistic logic by the logician Curry and the computer scientist Howard. They called it "Propositions are Types" since the types of programs can be seen as formulae. So 'p is a proof of proposition P' is equivalent to 'p is of type P' and both can be written as $p : P$.

For our example we use natural deduction-style proofs to determine proofs about a Semantic Web Service composition. For example, if we have a service that decrypts an XML document ($E \Rightarrow U$) and then we have another service that taken a decrypted XML document transforms it into HTML ($U \Rightarrow H$), we can then prove that if we have these two services we can take an encrypted document and produce the HTML version ($E \Rightarrow H$), i.e. transitivity of implication. Assuming we have an encrypted document x (of type E), we can create the proof that we can transform it into HTML as given in Figure 2.

$$\frac{h:(U \Rightarrow H) \quad \frac{\dfrac{[x:E]^1 \quad u:(E \Rightarrow U)}{(ax):U}(\Rightarrow E)}{(h(ax)):H}(\Rightarrow E)}{\lambda x_E.(h(ax)):(U \Rightarrow H)}(\Rightarrow I)_1$$

Fig. 2. Example Proof using Curry Howard Isomorphism

While the proof assumes the existence of a particular XML document (x), it discharges the assumption by *abstracting over the XML document x* using λ-abstraction, proving the proof for any XML document of type E (any encrypted document). The functional approach offers a principled way to compose Web Services that takes full advantage of semantics and allows your ordinary XML hacker in the street to get real value from Web Services and the Semantic Web.

Towards a Usable Group Editor for Ontologies

Jan Henke

Digital Enterprise Research Institute (DERI)
Technikerstraße 21a
6020 Innsbruck
jan.henke@deri.org

Abstract. Ontologies represent a shared understanding of some domain of interest. Therefore, tools to develop ontologies have to support this sharing in some way. However, current tools lack support of this important aspect, if they tackle it at all. Beyond this, each interactive system cannot be limited to its utility but must also make sure that this is provided in a usable way. However, current ontology editors mostly make the impression of research prototypes, thus not caring too much about this aspect. These two problems are crucial: If we don't support collaborative ontology development, produced ontologies will always lack being product of a social process. Also if the tool support lacks usability, the ontology engineering community cannot expect to spread their ideas to a wider non-expert audience. Therefore the PhD thesis in process tries to tackle these problems and to advance the state of the art. It combines these two aspects as they intervene with each other thus making an integrated approach more promising. The improvements will be thoroughly evaluated with regard to both utility and usability.

Ontology development is a collaborative effort [1]. Although a number of tools like e.g. [2] support this idea, these approaches never really reached maturity.
Ontology development is also an interactive task, thus tool support can't be limited to utility but has to be sufficiently usable as well. Unfortunately current tools have a clear lack in this respect.

The combined existence of these two problems makes ontology development at present-day a cumbersome task. This is a major issue as it makes hardly sense to talk about the potential and the exploitation of ontologies as long as the basic step of their creation is so poorly supported.

The focus of the PhD thesis in progress is to advance the state of the art by tackling both the collaborative and the usability aspects. Respectively, the evaluation of the approach will concentrate on both usability and collaboration support. User tests as well as heuristic evaluations will be performed.

Integrating high usability and sufficient collaboration support into a single ontology editing environment has driven this research in the direction of ontological, groupware, and usability engineering. The overlap between these areas shapes the domain of this thesis.

The three foci of the thesis are applied to each other. In the respective sections, requirements are identified and matched against the current state of the art. Among others, **OilEd** [3], **Protégé** [4], **OntoEdit** [5], **Ontolingua** [1] **CES** [6] and **Quilt** [7] are considered.

Design principles to be followed are elaborated. Successively, the architecture components are addressed.

As proof of concept, a reference implementation will be provided. The tools are selected before the actual realization is addressed.

It shall be evaluated if the state of the art could really be advanced. Both collaboration support and usability of the developed tool have to be considered for this purpose.

The here described PhD thesis will show how the current state of the art of ontology editors can be improved by allowing for collaboration and increasing overall usability. The approach will be prototypically implemented. This prototype again will be evaluated thoroughly.

The prototype implementation is a currently ongoing endeavor. Main future work is to realize the collaboration support and to setup and run the user tests.

References

1. Farquhar, A.F., Richard; Rice, : The Ontolingua Server: a Tool for Collaborative Ontology Construction. (1996)
2. Domingue, J.: Tadzebao and WebOnto: Discussing, Browsing, and Editing Ontologies on the Web. 11th Knowledge Acquisition for Knowledge-Based Systems Workshop, Banff, Canada (1998) 1-20
3. Bechhofer, S.e.a.: OilEd: a Reason-able Ontology Editor for the Semantic Web. KI2001 (2001)
4. Noy, N.F.e.a.: Creating Semantic Web Contents with Protégé-2000. IEEE Intelligent Systems (2001)
5. Sure, Y.E., Michael; Angele, Juergen; Staab, Steffen; Studer; Rudi; Wenke, Dirk OntoEdit: Collaborative Ontology Development for the SemanticWeb. In: I. Horrocks, J.H. (ed.): International Semantic Web Conference, Vol. 2342 / 2002. Springer-Verlag GmbH, Sardinia, Italy (2002)
6. Greif, I., Seliger, R., Weihl, W.E.: Atomic data abstractions in a distributed collaborative editing system. 13th ACM SIGACT-SIGPLAN symposium on Principles of programming languages. ACM Press, St. Petersburg Beach, Florida (1986)
7. Fish, R.S., Kraut, R.E., Leland, M.D.P.: Quilt: a collaborative tool for cooperative writing. ACM SIGOIS and IEEECS TC-OA 1988 conference on Office information systems. ACM Press, Palo Alto, California, United States (1988)

Talking to the Semantic Web - Query Interfaces to Ontologies for the Casual User

Esther Kaufmann

University of Zurich, Dynamic and Distributed Information Systems, Switzerland
kaufmann@ifi.unizh.ch

1 Introduction

The Semantic Web presents the vision of a dynamically growing knowledge base that should allow users to draw on and combine distributed information sources specified in languages based on formal logic. Common users, however, were shown to have problems even with the simplest Boolean expressions [4]; the use of the logic formalism underlying the Semantic Web is beyond their understanding. So how can we bridge the gap between the logic-based Semantic Web and real-world users, who are ill at ease and, oftentimes, unable to use formal logic concepts?

An often proposed solution to address this problem is the use of natural language interfaces (NLIs). Most NLIs, however, only understand some subset of natural language (NL), but often suggest full understanding, which leads to confusing interaction with users [1]. This mismatch between the users' expectations and the capabilities of a NLI is called the *habitability problem* [5]. Furthermore, the development of NL tools requires computationally intensive algorithms relying on large amounts of background knowledge making the tools highly domain-dependent and inapplicable to new domains or applications [1].

This project proposes to break the dichotomy between full NLIs and formal query approaches regarding them as ends of a *Formality Continuum*. It argues that query interfaces should impose some structure on the user's input to guide the entry but not overly restrict the user with an excessively formalistic language. In this way, we hypothesize that the best solutions for the casual and occasional user lie between the freedom of a full NLI and the structuredness of a formal query language. Furthermore, the use of controlled NLs facilitates to overcome both the habitability problem and the adaptivity barrier of full NLIs. The overarching goal is to turn the vision of the Semantic Web into realization, which can only happen if we bridge the gap between the end-users and the logic-based scaffolding of the Semantic Web.

2 Current State of the Project and Future Research

To support our proposition we have developed two different controlled language interfaces to the Semantic Web that lie in the middle of the Formality Continuum: Ginseng [2] and SWAT [3]. Both allow users to formulate queries in a language akin to English. To preliminarily evaluate our interfaces, we confronted users with the Ginseng prototype, with the SWAT prototype, and with a SQL interface as well as a keyword-based text search engine as competitors. Using a standardized usability test, we found that both Ginseng and SWAT significantly outperformed the SQL interface. Both interfaces also yielded much better retrieval performances than the competitors.

While the results of our preliminary usability evaluation are promising, many challenges remain. At the current state, the project provides a good basis for a deeper exploration and evaluation of NLIs to Semantic Web knowledge bases. More specifically, we would like to investigate our hypotheses regarding the Formality Continuum to the fullest extent. We, therefore, intend to (1) develop and implement a total of four different NLIs (two of which are extensions of Ginseng and SWAT) for the casual users to query ontologies, (2) thoroughly evaluate the usability and performance of these NLIs by conducting a comprehensive user study allowing us to generate conclusive evidence regarding our hypotheses.

As a first step, we will design and implement two more NLIs. The new interfaces are intended to "veer" towards both ends of the continuum. Consequently, one new interface will allow full NL input, whereas the other one tends to follow the ideas of the formal approaches. The interfaces will be as domain-independent and easily customizable for different ontologies as possible by extracting the necessary underlying frameworks from the knowledge bases. We pursue to avoid complex and tedious full NLP scaffolds on the one hand as well as a formal query interface that shifts all "intellectual" work to the user on the other hand.

As the second step, we plan to perform a thorough evaluation of the interfaces according to well-established methodologies. The evaluation will comprise three elements: (1) a test set evaluation showing the retrieval performance of our interfaces as well a other NLIs, (2) a heuristic usability evaluation to systematically inspect our interfaces to detect their usability problems, and (3) a comprehensive usability study (benchmarking the tools against each other as well as to other existing NLIs). These evaluation elements should provide us with sufficient evidence to answer the question where on the Formality Continuum the best query interface solutions for the casual and occasional user lie.

References

1. I. Androutsopoulos, G. D. Ritchie, and P. Thanisch. Natural language interfaces to databases - an introduction. *Natural Language Engineering*, 1(1):29–81, 1995.
2. A. Bernstein and E. Kaufmann. Making the semantic web accessible to the casual user: Empirical evidence on the usefulness of semiformal query languages. *IEEE Transactions on Knowlwdge and Data Engineering*, under review.
3. A. Bernstein, E. Kaufmann, A. Göhring, and C. Kiefer. Querying ontologies: A controlled english interface for end-users. In *4th Intl. Semantic Web Conf. (ISWC 2005)*, pages 112–126, 2005.
4. A. Spink, W. Dietmar, B. J. Jansen, and T. Saracevic. Searching the web: The public and their queries. *Journal of the American Society for Information Science and Technology*, 52(3):226–234, 2001.
5. C. W. Thompson, P. Pazandak, and H. R. Tennant. Talk to your semantic web. *IEEE Internet Computing*, 9(6):75–78, 2005.

Changing Ontology Breaks Queries

Yaozhong Liang, Harith Alani, and Nigel Shadbolt

Intelligence, Agents and Multimedia Group
School of Electronics and Computer Science
University of Southampton
Highfield, Southampton
England, United Kingdom
yl504r@ecs.soton.ac.uk
ha@ecs.soton.ac.uk
nrs@ecs.soton.ac.uk

Abstract. Updating an ontology that is in use may result in inconsistencies between the ontology and the knowledge base, dependent ontologies and applications/services. Current research concentrates on the creation of ontologies and how to manage ontology changes in terms of mapping ontology versions and keeping consistent with the instances. Very little work investigated controlling the impact on dependent applications/services; which is the aim of the system presented in this paper. The approach we propose is to make use of ontology change logs to analyse incoming RDQL queries and amend them as necessary. Revised queries can then be used to query the ontology and knowledge base as requested by the applications and services. We describe our prototype system and discuss related problems and future directions.

General Terms. Ontology Management.

Keywords. Ontology Change Management, Ontology Versioning, Knowledge Management, Semantic Web.

1 Introduction and Related Work

Ontologies are quickly becoming indispensable parts of the Semantic Web. The number of ontologies that are being developed and used by various applications is continuously increasing. One of the major problems with ontologies is change. Ontology changes may cause serious problems to its data instantiations (the knowledge base), the applications and services that might be dependent on the ontology, as well as any ontologies that import that changed ontology [3].

Most work so far has focused on ways to handle ontology change, such as change characterisation [3], ontology evolution [4], ontology versioning [2], and consistency maintenance [5, 6, 7]. However, not much has been done with respect to using change-tracks to eliminate or reduce any impact that ontology change can have on any dependent applications and services. It would be very costly and perhaps even unrealistic to expect all parties that could be affected by a change to coordinate any such changes [1]. Therefore, we believe that it would be very beneficial to have a system that could track such changes, relate changes to incoming queries, amend such queries accordingly, and inform the query source of those changes and actions taken.

In this paper we describe a prototype system that targets these problems. The system uses a semantic log of ontology change to amend RDQL queries sent to the ontology as necessary. Such a system could save many hours of application re-development by not only updating queries automatically and maintaining the flow of knowledge to the applications as much as possible, but also to inform the developers of such changes in the ontology that relates to their queries.

2 System Description

The solution shown in Figure 1 to tackle the identified problems is described as a series of steps as follows:

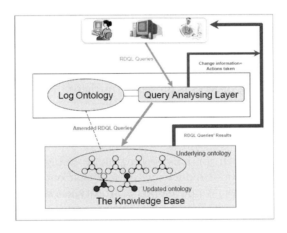

Fig. 1. An overview of the Approach

1. **Capture:** The changes made between two versions of the same ontology is captured at this stage. Currently, we identify changes by comparing two versions using PromptDiff in Protégé [4].
2. **Instantiate:** The *Log Ontology* is populated with cha- nge information identified in step 1.
3. **Analyse:** Queries submitted by the applications are analysed to find out whether any of the entities within the queries could be affected by the changes stored in the Log Ontology.
4. **Update:** If entities within the queries are found to have been changed, they are replaced with their changes to form the new queries with updated entities, and then resubmitted to the queried ontology.

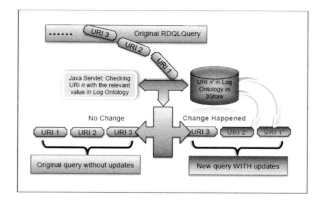

Fig. 2. The working process of the Middle Layer System

5. **Respond:** After the new-formed queries are submitted to the ontology for processing, the results are returned back to the application. At the same time, a summary of change/update information will also be returned back to the end-users with the query results so as to inform users of the updates.

Analyse, Update and Respond are implemented in the Middle Layer System in Figure 1. Its working process is presented in Figure 2.

3 Conclusions and Future Work

We proposed an approach for handling ontology changes by means of using change-tracks to eliminate or reduce any impact that ontology change can have on the application queries. We developed a prototype system that analyses the incoming queries, amends the entities within the queries according to the change information stored in the Log Ontology built to store and manage change information between ontology versions, and informs the end-user of any changes and actions taken. We showed that with the extra support of the middle layer, some of the queries that are targeting parts of the ontology that have changed can be updated and processed properly.

In our next stage work, Enabling *Log Ontology* to capture a series of changes between multiple versions of the same ontology would be a necessity to assist our system to cope with more complex changes. In addition, (semi-)automatic collecting ontology change information between ontology versions would make our system usable in a large scale. Providing the mechanism to inform the end-user of the correlated changes appropriately besides those directly related to the entities explicitly mentioned in the query, and the ability to decide the order of changes happened on the ontology are our next stage work. This would enhance the system to handle more complex changes as well as help us understand deeply the ontology change.

Acknowledgments

This work has been supported under the Advanced Knowledge Technologies Interdisciplinary Research Collaboration (AKT IRC), which is sponsored by the UK Engineering and Physical Science Research Council under grant number GR/N15764/01. Special thanks for the excellent technical supports from my colleague David Dupplaw (dpd@ecs.soton.ac.uk).

References

[1] Heflin, J. and Hendler, J. Dynamic ontologies on the web. In *Proceeding of the 17th American Association for Artificial Intelligence Conference (AAAI)*, pages 443–449, Menlo Park, CA, US, 2000. AAAI/MIT Press.

[2] Huang, Z. and Stuckenschmidt, H. Reasoning with multi-version ontologies: A temporal logic approach. In *Proceeding of the 4th International Semantic Web Conference (ISWC)*, Galway, Ireland, 2005.

[3] Klein, M. and Fensel, D. Ontology versioning on the semantic web. In *Proceeding of International Semantic Web Working Symposium (SWWS)*, Stanford University, California, U.S.A, 2001.

[4] N. K. Klein, M., and Musen, M.A. Tracking changes during ontology evolution. In *Proceeding of the 3rd International Semantic Web Conference (ISWC2004)*, Hiroshima, Japan, November 2004.

[5] Noy, N.F., and Musen, M.A. Promptdiff: A fixed-point algorithm for comparing ontology versions. In *Proceeding of the 18th National Conference of Artificial Intelligence (AAAI)*, pages 744–750, Edmonton, Alberta, Canada, 2002.

[6] K. K. Ognyanov, D., and Fensel, D. Ontology versioning and change detection on the web. In *Proceeding of 13th International Conference on Knowledge Engineering and Management*, Siguenza, Spain, 2002.

[7] H. H. H. Stuckenschmidt, H., and Sure, Y. A framework for handling inconsistency in changing ontologies. In *Proceeding of the 4th International Semantic Web Conference (ISWC)*, Galway, Ireland, 2005.

Towards a Global Scale Semantic Web

Zhengxiang Pan

Department of Computer Science and Engineering, Lehigh University
19 Memorial Dr. West, Bethlehem, PA 18015, U.S.A.
zhp2@lehigh.edu

1 Introduction

By transforming the Web from a collection of documents to a collection of semantically rich data sources, the Semantic Web promises an unprecedented benefit of a global knowledge infrastructure. My PhD research will try to help make that happen at a global scale by doing the following proposed work:

1. Design and implement a highly scalable Semantic Web knowledge base system by exploiting modern relational database technologies combined with the state-of-the-art description logics reasoners.
2. Build and empirically verify a framework that handles ontology evolution and the reuse of data on top of the perspective theory [1]. This framework should be able to relieve inconsistency and heterogeneity in a global scale Semantic Web.
3. Systematically evaluate the resulting system's capability and scalability in processing, integrating and querying data under the real world environment.

2 Problem Statement

Traditionally Semantic Web knowledge bases are based on description logic reasoners. These reasoners usually employ tableaux algorithms to do reasoning. Since most of the inferences are performed in main memory, their scalability are limited by the size of available physical memory. There has been a growing interest in the development of systems that will store and process large amount of Semantic Web data. However, most of these systems are geared towards RDF and RDF(S) data and therefore focus less on OWL reasoning. The above two types of systems represent two conflicting requirements on knowledge bases: completeness and scalability. The trade-off between these must be decided by each application. Nevertheless, an approach that could scale well and keep essential reasoning powers is highly desired in the Semantic Web at global scale.

The Semantic Web at global scale is also dynamic, inconsistent and heterogeneous. A framework that can handle ontology evolution, including ontology extension and the reuse of data, should be able to relieve these issues by integrating various ontologies and data sources.

3 Methodology

My proposed research will combine relational database techniques and description logic reasoning services to archive high scalability with essential inference capabilities. Generally, TBox reasonings will be handled by the DL reasoners and some ABox reasonings will be implemented using database techniques. The relational database management systems (RDBMS) will be used to persistently store processed Semantic Web data and its high availability and scalability will also be employed to support queries at large volumes.

Typical ABox reasoning includes "realization", which is to infer the implicit class memberships for individuals. I believe some of the cases can be handled in the form of database queries. The feasibility of this method has been initially investigated in [2], except that they focused on loading the data in the opposite direction.

I will also construct a framework to support ontology evolution and data reuse. The framework will be built on top of ontology perspectives [1]. This framework could reduce the occurrence of inconsistency since only a relevant subset of the Semantic Web is involved in processing a query. It can also facilitate the integration of information resources by creating new perspectives that include different ontologies and data sources.

Unbiased Semantic Web benchmarks such as LUBM [3] will be employed to make and validate design decisions when building the system. Real Semantic Web data will be used to evaluate the performance of the system comparing to similar existing systems, including those use deductive databases.

My prior work includes DLDB, a knowledge base system that extends a RDBMS with additional capabilities for partial OWL reasoning. The queries supported by current DLDB fall under extensional conjunctive queries. Our experiments with DLDB have demonstrated encouraging scalability [3]. In a recent work of our lab [4], we have used Swoogle's 2005 index as our dataset (45 million triples). We also showed that by adding the mapping ontologies and using them as query perspectives, we retrieve more results with a slight increase in query time.

4 Conclusion

I have proposed a PhD research in building a Semantic Web knowledge base system at global scale. This work faces a couple of challenges. First, the sheer size of Semantic Web poses a critical requirement on scalability. Existing techniques found in artificial intelligence area do not seem to be capable of handling that large scale; whereas existing techniques in database area do not seem to capable of reasoning on that rich semantics. Second, the inherently inconsistent and heterogeneous Semantic Web makes it very difficult to answer queries in a complete and sound fashion.

References

1. Heflin, J., Pan, Z.: A model theoretic semantics for ontology versioning. In: Proc. of the 3rd International Semantic Web Conference. (2004) 62–76
2. Borgida, A., Brachman, R.J.: Loading data into description reasoners. In: SIGMOD Conference. (1993) 217–226
3. Guo, Y., Pan, Z., Heflin, J.: LUBM: A benchmark for owl knowledge base systems. Journal of Web Semantics **3**(2) (2005) 158–182
4. Pan, Z., Qasem, A., Heflin, J.: An investigation into the feasibility of the semantic web. In: Proc. of the Twenty First National Conference on Artificial Intelligence (AAAI-06). (2006) 1394–1399

Schema Mappings for the Web

François Scharffe

Digital Enterprise Research Institute
University of Innsbruck
francois.scharffe@deri.org

Abstract. Current solutions to data integration present many inconvenients. The bottleneck seems to be the impossible automation of the whole process. Human intervention will always be needed at some point, and the problem is to find where and how this intervention can be performed the most efficiently. In traditional mediator approaches the global schema and mappings between the global and local schemas are designed by hand. This is not the way to go if we want to see emerging a "semantic web". The collaborative development of one-to-one mappings driven by application needs has much more chance to rapidly create a network of schemas. We propose to build on top on this view, shifting the human intervention from the global schema elaboration to the one-to-one mapping between local schemas. This repartition of efforts associated with publication of the local mappings is the only solution if we want to see the deep web rising up and the semantic web vision becoming true. I propose to contribute to this paradigm at two levels. First, mappings between heterogeneous schemas must be universally understandable, as schema descriptions may be of various natures (XML, relational, Ontologies, Semi structured, . . .). An independant language able to model correspondences between two schemas is then needed. This language also serves as an exchange format for matching algorithms as well as graphical mapping tools. A global schema is still necessary in order to provide a unified view over resources. We propose in the following to study how from a network of related schemas can we extract a global schema together with the associated mapping rules.

Triple Space Computing for Semantic Web Services – A PhD Roadmap

M. Omair Shafiq

Digital Enterprise Research Institute (DERI),
University of Innsbruck (UIBK)
6020 Innsbruck, Austria.
`omair.shafiq@deri.org`

Abstract. This thesis will address how to enable Triple Space Computing as a communication paradigm for Semantic Web Services. Currently, Semantic Web Services are following a message based communication paradigm. Triple Space Computing is envisioned as communication and coordination paradigm for Semantic Web Services which is an extension of tuple space computing to support RDF and then use it for communication based on the principle of persistent publication and read of data. Web Service Modeling Ontology (WSMO) is our conceptual model for Semantic Web Services. Web Service Execution Environment (WSMX) is one of the reference implementations of the WSMO conceptual model. The paper presents an overview of technical insights about integration of WSMX with Triple Space Computing and proposes that how WSMX can use Triple Space computing for its communication and coordination in terms of dynamic components management, external communication management, resource management and coordination of different interconnected WSMXs.

1 A Roadmap to Enable Triple Space Computing in Semantic Web Services

The communication paradigm in Semantic Web Services (SWS) is synchronous, i.e. users communicate with SWS and SWS communicate with real world Web Services synchronously by sending direct messages. The synchronous communication requires quick response as its makes sender halt until response is received, which is not possible in case of execution process in SWS as it involves a heavy processing of semantic descriptions in terms of discovery, selection, composition, mediation, execution. This problem is to be overcome by introducing asynchronous communication and Triple Space Computing is perfect solution as being semantic based asynchronous communication paradigm. In this thesis we take Web Service Execution Environment (WSMX) [2] as reference implementation of Web Service Modeling Ontology (WSMO) to concretely solve the concerned issues. Using Triple Space Computing for asynchronous communication between different WSMXs enables and brings them a step closer to their architectural goal, i.e. to support greater modularization, flexibility and decoupling in communication of different WSMX nodes. Similarly, it enables WSMX to be highly distributed and easily accessible.

This thesis will address the integration of Triple Space Computing [1] with WSMX by analyzing that how and where exactly the two technologies fit together. The integration has been proposed as three major entry points which are (1) enabling components management in WSMX using Triple Space Computing, (2) External communication grounding in WSMX using Triple Space Computing, (3) Resource Management in WSMX using Triple Space Computing and (4) enabling communication of different inter-connected WSMX. After achieving these integration aspects, the goal will be then to build an application scenario to show its viability. Each of the integration aspect has been described in details below:

WSMX has a management component [6] that manages the over all execution by enabling coordination of different components based on some execution scenario [4] specified by user in Goal. In this way there is a clear separation between business and management logic in WSMX. The individual components have clearly defined interfaces and have component implementation well separated with communication issues. Each component in WSMX have wrapper to handle the communication. WSMX manager and the individual components wrappers are needed to be interfaced with Triple Space in order to enable the WSMX manager manage the coordination of the components over Triple Space. The communication between manager and wrappers of the components will be carried out by publishing and subscribing the data as a set of RDF triples over Triple Space. The wrappers of components that handle communication will be interfaced with Triple Space middleware.

WSMX acts as a semantic middleware between users and real world web services. Currently, due to existence of message oriented communication paradigm, users communicate with WSMX and WSMX communicate with Web Services synchronously. The external communication manager of WSMX is needed to provide a support to communicate over Triple Space. The interfaces for sending and receiving external messages by WSMX are needed provide a grounding support to alternatively communicate over Triple Space. This needs to be resolved by addressing several issues, i.e. invoker component in WSMX is needed to support Web Services Description Language (WSDL) and Simple Object Access Protocol (SOAP) communication binding over Triple Space. The Entry point interfaces will be interfaced with Triple Space middleware in order to provide the glue between existing Web Services standards and Triple Space Computing.

WSMX contains different repositories to store ontologies, goals, mediators and web services descriptions as WSML based files. The internal repositories of WSMX are needed to be made optional and enable to store the WSML based data as set of RDF named graphs in Triple Space Storage. This is mainly concerned with transforming the existing representation of data in form of WSML into RDF representation. The repository interfaces are needed to be interfaced with Triple Space middleware.

After enabling WSMX with Triple Space Computing, the next step will be to enable the communication and coordination of different WSMXs over Triple Space, i.e. forming a cluster of different interconnected WSMX nodes to support distributed service discovery, selection, composition, mediation, invocation etc. The management component in WSMX is will be enhanced to coordinate with WSMX managers in other WSMXs over Triple Space to form a cluster. After the implementation of integration of Triple Space Computing in WSMX, an application scenario will be analyzed, designed and developed over WSMX to show the usefulness of the new communication paradigm in WSMX. It will be a travel agent based application that will use semantic descriptions of several real life Web Services, like Amazon, Google, currency converter, money transfer etc. and would require extensive and distributed discovery, selection, composition, mediation and invocation of Semantic Web Services to fulfill the user's requirements.

Acknowledgements. Author acknowledges the guidance support from Michal Zaremba being the chief architect of Web Services Execution Environment (WSMX), Dieter Fensel being the initiator of WSMX and Triple Space Computing and Ying Ding for reviews, suggestions and further guidelines.

References

1. D. Fensel, Triple-space computing: Semantic Web Services based on persistent publication of informatio: In Proceedings of the IFIP International Conference on Intelligence in Communication Systems, INTELLCOMM 2004, Bangkok, Thailand, November 23-26, 2004.
2. C. Bussler et al, Web Service Execution Environment (WSMX), W3C Member Submission, June 2005. Available at http://www.w3.org/Submission/WSMX
3. Michal Zaremba, Matthew Moran, Thomas Haselwanter, WSMX Architecture, D13.4v0.2 WSMX Working Draft.
4. M. Zaremba, C. Bussler: Towards Dynamic Execution Semantics in Semantic Web Services, In Proceedings of the Workshop on Web Service Semantics: Towards Dynamic Business Integration, International Conference on the World Wide Web (WWW2005). Chiba, Japan, 2005.
5. R. Krummenacher, M. Hepp, A. Polleres, C. Bussler, and D. Fensel: WWW or What Is Wrong with Web Services. In Proc. of the 2005 IEEE European Conf on Web Services (ECOWS 2005), Växjö, Sweden, November 14-16, 2005.
6. T. Haselwanter, Maciej Zaremba and Michal Zaremba. Enabling Components Management and Dynamic Execution Semantic in WSMX. WSMO Implementation Workshop 2005 (WIW 2005), 6-7 June, Innsbruck, Austria.

Toward Making Online Biological Data Machine Understandable

Cui Tao

Brigham Young University, Provo, Utah 84602, U.S.A.
ctao@cs.byu.edu

Abstract. Huge amounts of biological data are available online. To obtain needed information, biologists sometimes have to traverse different Web sources and combine their data manually. We introduce a system that can automatically interpret the structures of heterogeneous Web pages, extract useful information from them, and also transform them to machine-understandable pages for the Semantic Web, so that a Semantic Web agent can automatically find the information of interest.

Huge and growing amounts of biological data reside in various online repositories. Most of them only focus on some specific areas or only allow limited types of user queries. Sometimes the information a user needs spans multiple sources. A system that traverses only one source may not answer user queries completely. A system that can automatically retrieve, understand, and extract online biological data independent of the source is needed. In this research, I propose a system that can automatically interpret, extract, and annotate biological data with respect to an ontology and make it machine understandable as Semantic Web data. This research interweaves many different areas in information technology and bioinformatics. In [3], I surveyed different approaches in Information Extraction, Schema Matching, the Semantic Web, Data Integration, and Bioinformatics, in order to prepare for my own research.

The first step is to understand heterogeneous source pages automatically, which means to recognize attribute-value pairs and to map these attribute-value pairs to the concepts in the domain extraction ontology[1]. We proposed two techniques to resolve this problem, *sibling-page comparison* and *Sample-Ontology-Object recognition*. The sibling page comparison technique compares *sibling pages*, which are the pages commonly generated by underlying web databases, and identifies and connects non-varying components as category labels and varying components as

---

[1] The system works based on a data extraction ontology, which is a conceptual-model instance that serves as a wrapper for a domain of interest [2]. When an extraction ontology is applied to a Web page, the ontology identifies objects and relationships and associates them with named object sets and relationship sets in the ontology's conceptual-model instance and thus wraps the recognized strings on a page and makes them "understandable" in terms of the schema specified in the conceptual-model instance.

data values. Experimental results show that it can successfully identify sibling tables, generate structure patterns, and interpret different tables using the generated patterns. An alternate way to discover attribute-value pairs and map them to concepts in the ontology is through the use of a sample ontology object. A *sample ontology object* contains as much information as we can collect for one object in a specified application domain with respect to the extraction ontology. For a sample ontology object to be useful, it must commonly appear in many sites. Instead of attributes, our sample-ontology-object recognition technique depends on values to detect structural patterns and tries to infer the structure pattern of a page by observing the layout of the page with respect to the sample ontology object.

If we can interpret a source page and have already matched attribute value pairs in the source page to target concept(s) in the ontology, it is not hard to semantically annotate values for each page in the site using the ontology as the annotation ontology since the machine has already "understood" it [1]. This means that we can transform a source page to a Semantic Web page, which is machine-understandable.

The system is partially implemented. I have implemented tools to interpret source tables and finished a few papers related to this topic [4]. I am currently working on generating a set of sample ontology objects, implementing the sample-ontology-object recognition technique, and building a tool that can semi-automatically generate ontologies in the molecular biology domain from source tables and a few sample ontology objects. To build an ontology in such a broad domain is not easy, not to mention that it should to be automatic. I am currently facing many challenges such as how to better resolve the scalability issues and inter-sources conflicts; and what kind of information we should cover.

The prototype system is to be built for research purposes. It will not do any integration beyond synchronization with the target extraction ontology. The extraction ontology will not cover all the concepts, relationships, and values in the molecular biology domain. Although I will implement and test the system in the molecular biology domain, this approach will likely be general to all application domains that have similar characteristics.

References

1. Y. Ding, D. W. Embley, and S. W. Liddle. Automatic creation and simplified querying of semantic Web content: An approach based on information-extraction ontologies. In *Proceedings of the 1st Asian Semantic Web Conference (ASWC'06)*, 2006. to Appear.
2. D.W. Embley, D.M. Campbell, Y.S. Jiang, S.W. Liddle, D.W. Lonsdale, Y.-K. Ng, and R.D. Smith. Conceptual-model-based data extraction from multiple-record Web pages. *Data & Knowledge Engineering*, 31(3):227–251, November 1999.
3. C. Tao. Biological data extraction and integration — a research area background study. Technical report, Brigham Young University, UT, USA, May 2005.
4. C. Tao and D. W. Embley. Table intepretation by sibling page comparison. 2006. submitted.

Where the Social Web Meets the Semantic Web

Tom Gruber

tomgruber.org
RealTravel.com

Abstract. The Semantic Web is an ecosystem of interaction among computer systems. The social web is an ecosystem of conversation among people. Both are enabled by conventions for layered services and data exchange. Both are driven by human-generated content and made scalable by machine-readable data. Yet there is a popular misconception that the two worlds are alternative, opposing ideologies about how the web ought to be. Folksonomy vs. ontology. Practical vs. formalistic. Humans vs. machines. This is nonsense, and it is time to embrace a unified view. I subscribe to the vision of the Semantic Web as a substrate for collective intelligence. The best shot we have of collective intelligence in our lifetimes is large, distributed human-computer systems. The best way to get there is to harness the "people power" of the Web with the techniques of the Semantic Web. In this presentation I will show several ways that this can be, and is, happening.

1 About the Speaker

Tom Gruber is a researcher, inventor, and entrepreneur with a focus on systems for knowledge sharing and collective intelligence. He did foundational work in ontology engineering and is well-known for his definition of ontologies in the context of Artificial Intelligence. The approaches and technologies from this work are precursors to the infrastructure for today's Semantic Web. At Stanford University in the early 1990's, Tom was a pioneer in the use of the Web for collaboration and knowledge sharing. He invented HyperMail, a widely-used open source application that turns email conversations into collective memories, which chronicled many of the early discussions that helped define the Web. He built ontology engineering tools and established the first web-based public exchange for ontologies, software, and knowledge bases. During the rise of the Web, Dr. Gruber founded Intraspect, an enterprise software company that pioneered the space of collaborative knowledge management. Intraspect applications help professional people collaborate in large distributed communities, continuously contributing to a collective body of knowledge. His current project is RealTravel.com, which aspires to be the best place on the web to share knowledge and experiences about travel. RealTravel provides an environment for a community of travel enthusiasts to create beautiful travel journals of their adventures, share them with friends and family, and learn from other like-minded travelers.

The Semantic Web: Suppliers and Customers

Rudi Studer

Institute AIFB, Universität Karlsruhe (TH)
D-76128 Karlsruhe, Germany
studer@aifb.uni-karlsruhe.de

Abstract. The notion of the Semantic Web can be coined as a Web of data when bringing database content to the Web or as a Web of enriched human-readable content when encoding the semantics of web-resources in a machine-interpretable form.

It has been clear from the beginning that realizing the Semantic Web vision will require interdisciplinary research. At this the fifth ISWC, it is time to re-examine the extent to which interdisciplinary work has played and can play a role in Semantic Web research, and even how Semantic Web research can contribute to other disciplines. Core Semantic Web research has drawn from various disciplines, such as knowledge representation and formal ontologies, reusing and further developing their techniques in a new context.

However, there are several other disciplines that explore research issues very relevant to the Semantic Web in different guises and to differing extents. As a community, we can benefit by also recognizing and drawing from the research in these different disciplines. On the other hand, Semantic Web research also has much to contribute to these disciplines and communities. For example, the Semantic Web offers scenario that often ask for unprecedented scalability of techniques from other disciplines. Throughout the talk, I will illustrate these points through examples from disciplines such as natural language processing, databases, software engineering and automated reasoning.

The industry also has a major role to play in the realization of the Semantic Web vision. I will therefore additionally examine the added value of Semantic Web technologies for commercial applications and discuss issues that should be addressed for broadening the market for Semantic Web technologies.

1 About the Speaker

Rudi Studer is Full Professor in Applied Informatics at the University of Karlsruhe, Institute AIFB (www.aifb.uni-karlsruhe.de/WBS). His research interests include knowledge management, Semantic Web technologies and applications, ontology management, data and text mining, service-oriented architectures, peer-to-peer systems, and Semantic Grid.

Rudi Studer is also director in the research department Information Process Engineering at the FZI Research Center for Information Technologies at the

University of Karlsruhe (www.fzi.de/ipe) and one of the presidents of the FZI Research Center, as well as co-founder of the spin-off company ontoprise GmbH (www.ontoprise.de) that develops semantic applications. He is the current president of the Semantic Web Science Association (www.iswsa.org) and Editor-in-chief of the journal Web Semantics: Science, Services, and Agents on the World Wide Web (www.websemanticsjournal.org).

He is also engaged in various national and international cooperation projects being funded by various agencies such as Deutsche Forschungsgemeinschaft (DFG), the European Commission, the German Ministry of Education and Research, and by industry.

The Semantic Web and Networked Governance: Promise and Challenges

Jane E. Fountain

National Center for Digital Government
University of Massachusetts at Amherst
fountain@polsci.umass.edu

Abstract. The virtual state is a metaphor meant to draw attention to the structures and processes of the state that are becoming increasingly aligned with the structures and processes of the semantic web. Semantic Web researchers understand the potential for information sharing, enhanced search, improved collaboration, innovation, and other direct implications of contemporary informatics. Yet many of the broader democratic and governmental implications of increasingly networked governance remain elusive, even in the world of public policy and politics.

Governments, not businesses, remain the major information processing entities in the world. But where do they stand as knowledge managers, bridge builders and creators? As they strive to become not simply information-based but also knowledge-creating organizations, public agencies and institutions face a set of striking challenges. These include threats to privacy, to intellectual property, to identity, and to traditional processes of review and accountability. From the perspective of the organization of government, what are some of the key challenges faced by governments as they seek to become networked? What best practices are emerging globally? And in the networked world that is rapidly emerging and becoming institutionalized, how can public, private and nonprofit sectors learn from one another?

1 About the Speaker

Jane E. Fountain is Professor of Political Science and Public Policy and the Director of the Center for Public Policy and Administration at the University of Massachusetts Amherst. She is also the founder and director of the National Center for Digital Government which was established with support from the National Science Foundation to build research and infrastructure in the field of research on technology and governance.

Fountain is the author of Building the Virtual State: Information Technology and Institutional Change (Brookings Institution Press, 2001) which was awarded an Outstanding Academic Title in 2002 by Choice. The book has become a classic text in the field and has been translated into and published in Chinese, Japanese and Portuguese. Fountain is currently researching the successor volume to Building the Virtual State, which will examine technology-based cross-agency innovations in the U.S. federal government and their implications for governance and democratic processes, and Women in the Information Age (to be published by Cambridge University Press), which focuses on gender, information technology, and institutional behavior.

Professor Fountain also directs the Science, Technology, and Society Initiative (STS) and the Women in the Information Age Project (WITIA). The STS Initiative serves as a catalyst for collaborative, multi-disciplinary research partnerships among social, natural and physical scientists. WITIA examines the participation of women in computing and information-technology related fields and, with its partner institutions, seeks to increase the number of women experts and designers in information and communication technology fields.

She has served on several governing bodies and advisory groups in the public, private and nonprofit sectors in the U.S. and abroad. Her executive teaching and invited lectures have taken her to several developing countries and governments in transition including those of Saudi Arabia, the United Arab Emirates, Nicaragua, Chile, Estonia, Hungary, and Slovenia as well as to countries including Japan, Canada, New Zealand, Australia and the countries of the European Union.

Author Index

Agrawal, S.   913
Alani, Harith   1, 982
Aleman-Meza, Boanerges   44
Amin, Alia   951
Arenas, Marcelo   30
Arpinar, I. Budak   44
Aswani, Niraj   329
Auer, Sören   736
Aurnhammer, Melanie   58

Bao, Jie   72, 967
Basters, Ulrich   87
Bechhofer, Sean   101
Belhajjame, Khalid   116
Ben Hassine, Ahlem   130
Ben-Asher, Zohar   778
Bench-Capon, Trevor   371
Benedict, James   792
Bernardi, Ansgar   778
Bernstein, Abraham   144
Bizer, Christian   158
Blázquez, José M.   778
Bontcheva, Kalina   329
Brambilla, Marco   172
Brewster, Christopher   1
Brockmans, Saartje   187

Cabral, Liliana   201
Cafarella, Michael   428
Can, Özgü   970
Caragea, Doina   72, 967
Celino, Irene   172
Celma, Òscar   927
Ceri, Stefano   172
Cerizza, Dario   172
Chen, Huajun   750
Cheung, Kwok   215
Chugh, Abhita   544
Cimpian, Emilia   459
Cinquini, Luca   792
Colomb, Robert M.   187
Cunningham, Hamish   329

Darnell, J. Anthony   792
Das, Amar K.   901

Davies, Rob   959
de Boer, Victor   951
de Niet, Marco   951
Decker, Stefan   258, 559
Delbru, Renaud   559
Della Valle, Emanuele   172
Dellschaft, Klaas   228
Dengel, Andreas   887
Dietzold, Sebastian   736
Dimitrov, Dimitar   873
Dimitrov, Dimitre A.   764
Ding, Li   242
Dokulil, Jiří   972
Domingue, John   201, 959

Embury, Suzanne M.   116
Euzenat, Jérôme   16, 371

Facca, Federico Michele   172
Falkman, Göran   820
Felicíssimo, Carolina Howard   974
Fernández, Norberto   778
Ferrucci, David   861
Finin, Tim   242
Fisteus, Jesús A.   778
Fluit, Christiaan   887
Fokoue, Achille   343
Fountain, Jane E.   997
Fox, Peter   792
Fuentes, Manuel   778
Fujii, Kunihiro   806
Fukazawa, Yusuke   806

Galizia, Stefania   201
Gallagher, K.   913
Garcia, Jose   792
Gardiner, Tom   654
Gil, Yolanda   357
Goble, Carole A.   116
Grimnes, Gunnar Aastrand   887
Gruber, Tom   994
Gugliotta, Alessio   201, 959
Guo, Weisen   833
Gustafsson, Marie   820

Author Index

Gutierrez, Claudio 30
Gutiérrez-Villarías, Leticia 959

Haase, Peter 187
Halpin, Harry 976
Hanappe, Peter 58
Hardman, Lynda 272, 951
Harper, Simon 101
Harth, Andreas 258
Hassell, Joseph 44
Heflin, Jeff 764
Heim, Dominik 887
Hendler, James 682
Henke, Jan 978
Herzog, Marcus 286
Hildebrand, Michiel 272, 951
Hofmann, Paul 873
Hollink, Laura 951
Holzinger, Wolfgang 286
Honavar, Vasant G. 72, 967
Hong, Mingcai 640
Horak, Benjamin 887
Horrocks, Ian 501, 654
Hu, Wei 300
Huang, Zhisheng 951
Hunter, Jane 215
Hurtado, Carlos A. 314
Hyvönen, Eero 847

Idreos, Stratos 399
Ishida, Toru 130
Ishizuka, Mitsuru 487

Kagal, Lalana 473
Karger, David 158
Kaufmann, Esther 144, 980
Kemper, Brian 833
Kendall, Elisa F. 187
Kerrigan, Mick 459
Kershenbaum, Aaron 343
Kiesel, Malte 887
Kim, Jihie 357
Klusch, Matthias 87
Kochut, Krys J. 583
Kolb, Hap 723
Koubarakis, Manolis 399
Kraines, Steven 833
Krötzsch, Markus 935
Krüpl, Bernhard 286
Kurakake, Shoji 806

Laera, Loredana 371
Lassila, Ora 473
Lathem, J. 913
Lécué, Freddy 385
Lee, Ryan 158
Léger, Alain 385
Li, Juanzi 640
Liang, Bangyong 640
Liang, Yaozhong 982
Liarou, Erietta 399
Lindahl, Fredrik 820
Liu, William 544
Lopez, Vanessa 414
Lunn, Darren 101

Ma, Li 343, 445
Mäkelä, Eetu 847
Mao, Yuxin 750
Marrara, Angelo 778
Martins, Susana B. 901
Matsubara, Shigeo 130
Matsuo, Yutaka 487
Maus, Heiko 887
McDowell, Luke K. 428
McGuinness, Deborah L. 792, 861
McIlraith, Sheila A. 597
Mei, Jing 445
Middleton, Don 792
Miyoshi, Yu 515
Mocan, Adrian 459
Montanari, Rebecca 473
Morbidoni, Christian 943
Mori, Junichiro 487
Motik, Boris 501
Motta, Enrico 414
Murdock, J. William 709, 861
Musen, Mark A. 544

Nadeem, Danish 887
Naganuma, Takefumi 806
Nakamura, Yutaka 833
Nakatsuji, Makoto 515
Nickles, Matthias 529
Norton, Barry 201
Noy, Natalya F. 544
Nucci, Michele 943

O'Connor, Martin J. 901
Oldham, N. 913
Omelayenko, Borys 951

Oren, Eyal   559
Otsuka, Yoshihiro   515
Özacar, Tuğba   573
Öztürk, Övünç   573

Pan, Jeff Z.   612, 668
Pan, Yue   445
Pan, Zhengxiang   986
Parrish, David B.   901
Parsia, Bijan   682, 695
Paslaru Bontas Simperl, Elena   625
Paton, Norman W.   116
Payne, Terry   371
Pedrinaci, Carlos   201
Pérez, Jorge A.   30
Pietriga, Emmanuel   158
Pinheiro da Silva, Paulo   861
Poulovassilis, Alexandra   314
Prokoshyna, Nataliya   597

Qasem, Abir   764
Qu, Yuzhong   300

Ramakrishnan, Cartic   583
Rao, Jinghai   873
Ratnakar, Varun   357
Richardson, Marc   959
Riechert, Thomas   736
Rosati, Riccardo   501
Rowlatt, Mary   959

Saarela, Samppa   847
Sabou, Marta   414
Sadeh, Norman   873
Sánchez, Luis   778
Sattler, Ulrike   501
Sauermann, Leo   887
Scharffe, François   988
Schonberg, Edith   343
Schreiber, Guus   723, 951
Shadbolt, Nigel   1, 982
Shafiq, M. Omair   989
Shankar, Ravi D.   901
Sheth, Amit P.   583, 913
Siberski, Wolf   612
Siebes, Ronny   951
Sintek, Michael   778
Sohrabi, Shirin   597
Solomon, Stan   792
Srinivas, Kavitha   343
Staab, Steffen   228

Steels, Luc   58
Stevens, Robert   116
Stinčić, Sandra   959
Studer, Rudi   995
Sure, York   625

Taekema, Jos   951
Tamma, Valentina   371
Tanasescu, Vlad   201, 959
Tang, Jie   640
Tang, Jinmin   750
Tao, Cui   992
Tempich, Christoph   625
Thaden, Uwe   612
Toninelli, Alessandra   473
Torgersson, Olof   820
Tsarkov, Dmitry   654
Tsujishita, Takumi   487
Tummarello, Giovanni   943

Umbrich, Jürgen   258
Ünalır, Murat Osman   573, 970

van Assem, Mark   951
van Hage, Willem Robert   723
van Kersen, Janneke   951
van Ossenbruggen, Jacco   272, 951
Völkel, Max   935
Vrandečić, Denny   935

Wallace, Evan K.   187
Wang, Heng   750
Wang, Nanbor   764
Wang, Shenghui   668
Wang, Taowei David   682, 695
Wang, Yimin   750
Welty, Chris   187, 709, 861
West, Patrick   792
Wielemaker, Jan   951
Wielinga, Bob   951
Wingate, H.   913
Wood, Peter T.   314
Wu, Zhaohui   750

Xie, Guo Tong   187

Yadav, P.   913
Yin, Ainin   750

Zhou, Cunyin   750
Zimmermann, Antoine   16

Printing: Mercedes-Druck, Berlin
Binding: Stein+Lehmann, Berlin

Lecture Notes in Computer Science

For information about Vols. 1–4202

please contact your bookseller or Springer

Vol. 4292: G. Bebis, R. Boyle, B. Parvin, D. Koracin, P. Remagnino, A. Nefian, G. Meenakshisundaram, V. Pascucci, J. Zara, J. Molineros, H. Theisel, T. Malzbender (Eds.), Advances in Visual Computing, Part II. XXXII, 906 pages. 2006.

Vol. 4291: G. Bebis, R. Boyle, B. Parvin, D. Koracin, P. Remagnino, A. Nefian, G. Meenakshisundaram, V. Pascucci, J. Zara, J. Molineros, H. Theisel, T. Malzbender (Eds.), Advances in Visual Computing, Part I. XXXI, 916 pages. 2006.

Vol. 4283: Y.Q. Shi, B. Jeon (Eds.), Digital Watermarking. XII, 474 pages. 2006.

Vol. 4281: K. Barkaoui, A. Cavalcanti, A. Cerone (Eds.), Theoretical Aspects of Computing - ICTAC. XV, 371 pages. 2006.

Vol. 4279: N. Kobayashi (Ed.), Programming Languages and Systems. XI, 423 pages. 2006.

Vol. 4278: R. Meersman, Z. Tari, P. Herrero (Eds.), On the Move to Meaningful Internet Systems 2006: OTM 2006 Workshops, Part II. XLV, 1004 pages. 2006.

Vol. 4277: R. Meersman, Z. Tari, P. Herrero (Eds.), On the Move to Meaningful Internet Systems 2006: OTM 2006 Workshops, Part I. XLV, 1009 pages. 2006.

Vol. 4276: R. Meersman, Z. Tari (Eds.), On the Move to Meaningful Internet Systems 2006: CoopIS, DOA, GADA, and ODBASE, Part II. XXXII, 752 pages. 2006.

Vol. 4275: R. Meersman, Z. Tari (Eds.), On the Move to Meaningful Internet Systems 2006: CoopIS, DOA, GADA, and ODBASE, Part I. XXXI, 1115 pages. 2006.

Vol. 4273: I. Cruz, S. Decker, D. Allemang, C. Preist, D. Schwabe, P. Mika, M. Uschold, L. Aroyo (Eds.), The Semantic Web - ISWC 2006. XXIV, 1001 pages. 2006.

Vol. 4272: P. Havinga, M. Lijding, N. Meratnia, M. Wegdam (Eds.), Smart Sensing and Context. XI, 267 pages. 2006.

Vol. 4271: F.V. Fomin (Ed.), Graph-Theoretic Concepts in Computer Science. XIII, 358 pages. 2006.

Vol. 4270: H. Zha, Z. Pan, H. Thwaites, A.C. Addison, M. Forte (Eds.), Interactive Technologies and Sociotechnical Systems. XVI, 547 pages. 2006.

Vol. 4269: R. State, S. van der Meer, D. O'Sullivan, T. Pfeifer (Eds.), Large Scale Management of Distributed Systems. XIII, 282 pages. 2006.

Vol. 4268: G. Parr, D. Malone, M. Ó Foghlú (Eds.), Autonomic Principles of IP Operations and Management. XIII, 237 pages. 2006.

Vol. 4267: A. Helmy, B. Jennings, L. Murphy, T. Pfeifer (Eds.), Autonomic Management of Mobile Multimedia Services. XIII, 257 pages. 2006.

Vol. 4266: H. Yoshiura, K. Sakurai, K. Rannenberg, Y. Murayama, S. Kawamura (Eds.), Advances in Information and Computer Security. XIII, 438 pages. 2006.

Vol. 4265: N. Lavrač, L. Todorovski, K.P. Jantke (Eds.), Discovery Science. XIV, 384 pages. 2006. (Sublibrary LNAI).

Vol. 4264: J.L. Balcázar, P.M. Long, F. Stephan (Eds.), Algorithmic Learning Theory. XIII, 393 pages. 2006. (Sublibrary LNAI).

Vol. 4263: A. Levi, E. Savas, H. Yenigün, S. Balcisoy, Y. Saygin (Eds.), Computer and Information Sciences – ISCIS 2006. XXIII, 1084 pages. 2006.

Vol. 4261: Y. Zhuang, S. Yang, Y. Rui, Q. He (Eds.), Advances in Multimedia Information Processing - PCM 2006. XXII, 1040 pages. 2006.

Vol. 4260: Z. Liu, J. He (Eds.), Formal Methods and Software Engineering. XII, 778 pages. 2006.

Vol. 4259: S. Greco, Y. Hata, S. Hirano, M. Inuiguchi, S. Miyamoto, H.S. Nguyen, R. Słowiński (Eds.), Rough Sets and Current Trends in Computing. XXII, 951 pages. 2006. (Sublibrary LNAI).

Vol. 4257: I. Richardson, P. Runeson, R. Messnarz (Eds.), Software Process Improvement. XI, 219 pages. 2006.

Vol. 4256: L. Feng, G. Wang, C. Zeng, R. Huang (Eds.), Web Information Systems – WISE 2006 Workshops. XIV, 320 pages. 2006.

Vol. 4255: K. Aberer, Z. Peng, E.A. Rundensteiner, Y. Zhang, X. Li (Eds.), Web Information Systems – WISE 2006. XIV, 563 pages. 2006.

Vol. 4254: T. Grust, H. Höpfner, A. Illarramendi, S. Jablonski, M. Mesiti, S. Müller, P.-L. Patranjan, K.-U. Sattler, M. Spiliopoulou (Eds.), Current Trends in Database Technology – EDBT 2006. XXXI, 932 pages. 2006.

Vol. 4253: B. Gabrys, R.J. Howlett, L.C. Jain (Eds.), Knowledge-Based Intelligent Information and Engineering Systems, Part III. XXXII, 1301 pages. 2006. (Sublibrary LNAI).

Vol. 4252: B. Gabrys, R.J. Howlett, L.C. Jain (Eds.), Knowledge-Based Intelligent Information and Engineering Systems, Part II. XXXIII, 1335 pages. 2006. (Sublibrary LNAI).

Vol. 4251: B. Gabrys, R.J. Howlett, L.C. Jain (Eds.), Knowledge-Based Intelligent Information and Engineering Systems, Part I. LXVI, 1297 pages. 2006. (Sublibrary LNAI).

Vol. 4249: L. Goubin, M. Matsui (Eds.), Cryptographic Hardware and Embedded Systems - CHES 2006. XII, 462 pages. 2006.

Vol. 4248: S. Staab, V. Svátek (Eds.), Managing Knowledge in a World of Networks. XIV, 400 pages. 2006. (Sublibrary LNAI).

Vol. 4247: T.-D. Wang, X. Li, S.-H. Chen, X. Wang, H. Abbass, H. Iba, G. Chen, X. Yao (Eds.), Simulated Evolution and Learning. XXI, 940 pages. 2006.

Vol. 4246: M. Hermann, A. Voronkov (Eds.), Logic for Programming, Artificial Intelligence, and Reasoning. XIII, 588 pages. 2006. (Sublibrary LNAI).

Vol. 4245: A. Kuba, L.G. Nyúl, K. Palágyi (Eds.), Discrete Geometry for Computer Imagery. XIII, 688 pages. 2006.

Vol. 4244: S. Spaccapietra (Ed.), Journal on Data Semantics VII. XI, 267 pages. 2006.

Vol. 4243: T. Yakhno, E.J. Neuhold (Eds.), Advances in Information Systems. XIII, 420 pages. 2006.

Vol. 4241: R.R. Beichel, M. Sonka (Eds.), Computer Vision Approaches to Medical Image Analysis. XI, 262 pages. 2006.

Vol. 4239: H.Y. Youn, M. Kim, H. Morikawa (Eds.), Ubiquitous Computing Systems. XVI, 548 pages. 2006.

Vol. 4238: Y.-T. Kim, M. Takano (Eds.), Management of Convergence Networks and Services. XVIII, 605 pages. 2006.

Vol. 4237: H. Leitold, E. Markatos (Eds.), Communications and Multimedia Security. XII, 253 pages. 2006.

Vol. 4236: L. Breveglieri, I. Koren, D. Naccache, J.-P. Seifert (Eds.), Fault Diagnosis and Tolerance in Cryptography. XIII, 253 pages. 2006.

Vol. 4234: I. King, J. Wang, L. Chan, D. Wang (Eds.), Neural Information Processing, Part III. XXII, 1227 pages. 2006.

Vol. 4233: I. King, J. Wang, L. Chan, D. Wang (Eds.), Neural Information Processing, Part II. XXII, 1203 pages. 2006.

Vol. 4232: I. King, J. Wang, L. Chan, D. Wang (Eds.), Neural Information Processing, Part I. XLVI, 1153 pages. 2006.

Vol. 4231: J. F. Roddick, R. Benjamins, S. Si-Saïd Cherfi, R. Chiang, C. Claramunt, R. Elmasri, F. Grandi, H. Han, M. Hepp, M. Hepp, M. Lytras, V.B. Mišić, G. Poels, I.-Y. Song, J. Trujillo, C. Vangenot (Eds.), Advances in Conceptual Modeling - Theory and Practice. XXII, 456 pages. 2006.

Vol. 4230: C. Priami, A. Ingólfsdóttir, B. Mishra, H.R. Nielson (Eds.), Transactions on Computational Systems Biology VII. VII, 185 pages. 2006. (Sublibrary LNBI).

Vol. 4229: E. Najm, J.F. Pradat-Peyre, V.V. Donzeau-Gouge (Eds.), Formal Techniques for Networked and Distributed Systems - FORTE 2006. X, 486 pages. 2006.

Vol. 4228: D.E. Lightfoot, C.A. Szyperski (Eds.), Modular Programming Languages. X, 415 pages. 2006.

Vol. 4227: W. Nejdl, K. Tochtermann (Eds.), Innovative Approaches for Learning and Knowledge Sharing. XVII, 721 pages. 2006.

Vol. 4226: R.T. Mittermeir (Ed.), Informatics Education – The Bridge between Using and Understanding Computers. XVII, 319 pages. 2006.

Vol. 4225: J.F. Martínez-Trinidad, J.A. Carrasco Ochoa, J. Kittler (Eds.), Progress in Pattern Recognition, Image Analysis and Applications. XIX, 995 pages. 2006.

Vol. 4224: E. Corchado, H. Yin, V. Botti, C. Fyfe (Eds.), Intelligent Data Engineering and Automated Learning – IDEAL 2006. XXVII, 1447 pages. 2006.

Vol. 4223: L. Wang, L. Jiao, G. Shi, X. Li, J. Liu (Eds.), Fuzzy Systems and Knowledge Discovery. XXVIII, 1335 pages. 2006. (Sublibrary LNAI).

Vol. 4222: L. Jiao, L. Wang, X. Gao, J. Liu, F. Wu (Eds.), Advances in Natural Computation, Part II. XLII, 998 pages. 2006.

Vol. 4221: L. Jiao, L. Wang, X. Gao, J. Liu, F. Wu (Eds.), Advances in Natural Computation, Part I. XLI, 992 pages. 2006.

Vol. 4219: D. Zamboni, C. Kruegel (Eds.), Recent Advances in Intrusion Detection. XII, 331 pages. 2006.

Vol. 4218: S. Graf, W. Zhang (Eds.), Automated Technology for Verification and Analysis. XIV, 540 pages. 2006.

Vol. 4217: P. Cuenca, L. Orozco-Barbosa (Eds.), Personal Wireless Communications. XV, 532 pages. 2006.

Vol. 4216: M.R. Berthold, R. Glen, I. Fischer (Eds.), Computational Life Sciences II. XIII, 269 pages. 2006. (Sublibrary LNBI).

Vol. 4215: D.W. Embley, A. Olivé, S. Ram (Eds.), Conceptual Modeling - ER 2006. XVI, 590 pages. 2006.

Vol. 4213: J. Fürnkranz, T. Scheffer, M. Spiliopoulou (Eds.), Knowledge Discovery in Databases: PKDD 2006. XXII, 660 pages. 2006. (Sublibrary LNAI).

Vol. 4212: J. Fürnkranz, T. Scheffer, M. Spiliopoulou (Eds.), Machine Learning: ECML 2006. XXIII, 851 pages. 2006. (Sublibrary LNAI).

Vol. 4211: P. Vogt, Y. Sugita, E. Tuci, C. Nehaniv (Eds.), Symbol Grounding and Beyond. VIII, 237 pages. 2006. (Sublibrary LNAI).

Vol. 4210: C. Priami (Ed.), Computational Methods in Systems Biology. X, 323 pages. 2006. (Sublibrary LNBI).

Vol. 4209: F. Crestani, P. Ferragina, M. Sanderson (Eds.), String Processing and Information Retrieval. XIV, 367 pages. 2006.

Vol. 4208: M. Gerndt, D. Kranzlmüller (Eds.), High Performance Computing and Communications. XXII, 938 pages. 2006.

Vol. 4207: Z. Ésik (Ed.), Computer Science Logic. XII, 627 pages. 2006.

Vol. 4206: P. Dourish, A. Friday (Eds.), UbiComp 2006: Ubiquitous Computing. XIX, 526 pages. 2006.

Vol. 4205: G. Bourque, N. El-Mabrouk (Eds.), Comparative Genomics. X, 231 pages. 2006. (Sublibrary LNBI).

Vol. 4204: F. Benhamou (Ed.), Principles and Practice of Constraint Programming - CP 2006. XVIII, 774 pages. 2006.

Vol. 4203: F. Esposito, Z.W. Raś, D. Malerba, G. Semeraro (Eds.), Foundations of Intelligent Systems. XVIII, 767 pages. 2006. (Sublibrary LNAI).